Magill's Cinema Annual 1996

Magill's Cinema Annual 1996

15th Edition
A Survey of the Films of 1995

Beth A. Fhaner and Christopher P. Scanlon, Editors

Kelly M. Cross, Terri Kessler Schell, Devra M. Sladics, and Hilary Weber, Contributing Editors

Christine Tomassini and Michelle Banks, Associate Editors

A VideoHound® Reference

GALE
DETROIT • NEW YORK • TORONTO • LONDON

Beth A. Fhaner and Christopher P. Scanlon, *Editors*
James M. Craddock, Kelly M. Cross, Terri Kessler Schell, Devra M. Sladics, and Hilary Weber, *Contributing Editors*
Michelle Banks and Christine Tomassini, *Associate Editors*
David Kunath, *Assistant Editor*

Mary Beth Trimper, *Production Director*
Shanna Heilveil, *Production Assistant*

Cynthia Baldwin, *Product Design Manager*
Michelle S. DiMercurio, *Art Director*

Sherrell Hobbs, *Macintosh Artist*
Randy Bassett, *Image Database Supervisor*
Robert Duncan and Mikal Angari, *Imaging Specialists*
Pamela A. Hayes, *Photography Coordinator*

Jeffrey Muhr, *Editorial Technical Services Specialist*

∞™ The paper used in this publication meets the minimum requirements of American National Standard for Information Sciences--Permanence Paper for Printed Library Materials, ANSI Z39.48-1984.

A Cunning Canine™ Production

ISBN 0-7876-0762-2
ISSN 0739-2141

Printed in the United States of America

Table of Contents

Preface

Magill's Cinema Annual 1996 continues the fine film reference tradition that is part of the VideoHound series of entertainment industry products published by Gale Research. The fifteenth annual volume in a series that developed from the 21-volume core set, *Magill's Survey of Cinema,* the *Annual* was formerly published by Salem Press. Gale's second volume, as with the previous Salem volumes, contains essay-reviews of significant domestic and foreign films released in the United States during the preceding year.

The *Magill's* editorial staff at Gale, comprising the VideoHound team and a host of *Magill's* contributors, has continued with the enhancements that were presented with last year's volume. These features include:

- More essay-length reviews of significant films released during the year
- Photographs which accompany the reviews and illustrate the obituaries and Life Achievement Award sections
- Trivia and "fun facts" about the reviewed movies, their stars, the crew, and production
- Quotes and dialogue "soundbites" from reviewed movies, or from stars and crew about the film
- More complete awards and nominations listings, including the American Academy Awards, Chicago Film Festival, Golden Globe, New York Critics Awards, and others (see the User's Guide for more information on awards coverage)
- Box office grosses, including year-end and other significant totals
- Critics' and publicity taglines featured in film reviews and advertisements

In addition to these elements, the *Magill's Cinema Annual 1996* continues to feature:

- An essay reviewing the career and accomplishments of the recipient of the American Film Institute's Life Achievement Award presented each year to Hollywood luminaries. Actor/director/producer Clint Eastwood is the 1995 award recipient profiled in this volume.
- An obituaries section profiling major contributors to the film industry who died in 1995
- An annotated list of selected film books published in 1995
- Nine indexes: Title (now cumulative), Director, Screenwriter, Cinematographer, Editor, Art Director, Music, Performer, and Subject

Compilation Methods

A variety of entertainment industry publications, including trade magazines and newspapers, as well as online sources, are checked on a daily and weekly basis to select significant films for review in *Magill's Cinema Annual.* Reviews are written by the *Magill's* editorial staff and other contributing reviewers, including film scholars and university faculty.

Magill's Cinema Annual: A VideoHound Reference

Magill's Cinema Annual, part of the VideoHound family of movie and entertainment reference products, was acquired in 1995 from Salem Press Inc., an honored and highly respected publisher serving the library market. The *Magill's Survey of Cinema* series, now supplemented by the *Annual,* was honored with the Reference Book of the Year Award in Fine Arts by the American Library Association.

Gale Research, an award-winning publisher of reference products, is proud to offer *Magill's Cinema Annual* as part of our popular VideoHound product line, which includes *VideoHound's Golden Movie Retriever, VideoHound Multimedia, The Video Sourcebook, VideoHound's Family Video Retriever, The VideoHound & All-Movie Guide StarGazer, VideoHound's Complete Guide to Cult Flicks and Trash Pics, VideoHound's Sci-Fi Experience,* and many more. Other Gale film-related products include the *St. James Dictionary of Films and Filmmakers* and the *Contemporary Theatre, Film, and Television* series.

Electronic Formats Available

Data from the *Magill's* series is also available in the following alternate formats:

Knight Ridder (formerly Dialog): Includes nearly 4,000 entries from the *Magill's* core series as well as the

Annual, plus brief reviews not contained in the print series. These brief reviews offer credits information and a capsule description.

Prodigy: Includes nearly 4,000 reviews from the core series, nearly 7,360 brief entries, and approximately 1,750 full-length reviews.

Acknowledgments

Thank you, Judy Hartman, General Graphics Services, for your typesetting expertise, and Terri Dieckoff, Saztec Computer Services Corp., for your electronic processing assistance. Jeff Muhr, Gale Research, is thanked for his technical assistance, and Meghan O'Meara is most appreciated for her interest and goodwill. A special thank you to Jim Olenski of Thomas Video (Clawson, MI) for making videos available to our staff. The *VideoHound* staff is thanked for its contributions to this project, especially Michelle Banks, Christine Tomassini, Kelly Cross, Devra Sladics, Hilary Weber, Carol Schwartz, and Jim Craddock, for their hard work, patience, and understanding, as well as Marty Connors, Terri Kessler Schell, and Julia Furtaw for their continuous guidance and direction.

We most appreciate the following people for their assistance in obtaining photographs: Bob Cosenza, the Kobal Collection; Robyn Worthington, Miramax Films; Margarita Medina, Columbia Pictures; Larry McCallister, Paramount Pictures; Craig Skrzypecki, Castle Rock Entertainment; and Nancy Cushing-Jones, Universal Pictures.

Introduction

Considered by many critics to be a disappointing year for the film industry, 1995 was not so much mediocre as it was transitional. Changes in audience preferences resulted in an extremely diverse offering of films. Many of the year's most interesting and highly regarded (if lesser-seen) movies, such as *Leaving Las Vegas, Dead Man Walking, To Die For, Georgia,* and *Casino,* all explored the darker side of life and told tales of wrenching decline. Since the prevailing mood of many of the year's best films was so bleak, we turned to these charming films for a look at the lighter side: *The American President, Babe, Clueless, While You Were Sleeping, Sense and Sensibility,* and *Sabrina,* among others.

1995 was a dismal year for big-budget, Hollywood productions with *Cutthroat Island, Judge Dredd, Waterworld,* and *Assassins* all turning out to be flops. And who can forget the hype surrounding Demi Moore as Hester Prynne in the misguided retelling of *The Scarlet Letter,* and the laughable *Showgirls*? Screenwriter Joe Eszterhas earned millions for scripting not only *Showgirls,* but also *Jade*—both sexually graphic films and both box-office misfires. Audiences turned to more relationship-oriented movies with one-on-one performances, such as the delightful *Il Postino (The Postman)* and the dark, yet finely-executed *Leaving Las Vegas.* Perhaps corporate Hollywood should take note: American audiences *will* pay to see tasteful, well-scripted movies. For further proof that audiences don't need extreme violence and exploitation in their movie-going experiences, look at some of the year's biggest hits: *Toy Story, Babe, Apollo 13,* and *The Bridges of Madison County,* all beautifully done, and all significant box office players.

Independent cinema continued to thrive in 1995, especially with the Sundance Film Festival gaining in stature. The notable indies include the romantic comedy *The Brothers McMullen,* made by first-time filmmaker Ed Burns on a shoestring budget; the clever heist-gone-wrong film *The Usual Suspects;* the hilarious moviemaking comedy *Living in Oblivion;* Todd Haynes' hypnotic drama *Safe,* which explored the suffering of collective chemical poisons of the 20th century; and the riveting documentary *Crumb,* about underground-cartoonist Robert Crumb and his warped family. The indie film scene is already challenging the mainstream for both audience approval and dollars; in fact, *Crumb* made many critics' list as one of the best pictures of the year.

The prominence and success of family films was another promising trend of 1995. The animatronic barnyard of *Babe,* the computerized playthings of *Toy Story* and the digitized terrors haunting us in *Casper* matched impressive technological feats with all-ages comedy, while the trademark excellence of Disney's animation in *Pocahontas,* the well-written *An Indian in the Cupboard,* and the magical child's-eye view of *A Little Princess* provided solid family entertainment. As Hollywood targets the families of baby boomers, studio executives are trying to find a broader audience for family films. Movies must now appeal to all ages in a family, not just the 5- to 12-year-old set. Many parents, as well as older children, will certainly appreciate the broader look at the genre and the studios' approach to making movies that everyone in the family can enjoy together.

Film noir continued its recent revival, thanks partly to last year's tour-de-force, *Pulp Fiction.* Some of the new entries in the dark, fatalistic world of *noir* include *Bulletproof Heart, Kiss of Death,* Barry Sonnenfeld's adaptation of Elmore Leonard's novel *Get Shorty,* and director Carl Franklin's adaptation of Walter Mosley's popular detective novel *Devil in a Blue Dress.* Director-writer Steven Soderbergh also filmed a *noir* remake in 1995—*The Underneath* was based on the outstanding *noir* film, *Criss Cross* (1949). With contemporary directors like John Dahl and Soderbergh working, the *noir* canon will continue to make significant contributions to the look of American film.

In 1995, 19th century British novelist Jane Austen proved to be the hottest writer in Hollywood. It was Austen-mania as many film and TV adaptations were based on her work, with additional projects in the pipeline. Austen played a part in three feature films, each of which was well-received by critics and audiences alike. Art house hit *Persuasion* was a thoughtful, delicate, and well-acted telling of early 19th century English manners; director/writer Amy Heckerling's summer comedy smash *Clueless* was loosely based on *Emma;* and the witty, delightful costume drama *Sense and Sensibility* earned actress/writer Emma Thompson the Oscar for Best Adapted Screenplay. Although Jane Austen died almost two centuries ago, her work is all the rage in Tinseltown, further evidence that a good story, no matter how old, is crucial to successful filmmaking.

The Academy Award Best Picture nominees, *Apollo 13, Babe, Braveheart, Il Postino, (The Postman),* and *Sense and*

Sensibility, illustrated the diversity of filmmaking in 1995. The historical epic *Braveheart* won over the Academy, garnering Oscars for Best Picture, Best Director (Gibson), Best Cinematography, Best Makeup, and Best Sound Effects Editing. When Gibson nabbed his award for Best Director, he joined a select group of movie stars who have won Academy Awards for directing. Only four other stars have earned best director statuettes, including Robert Redford for *Ordinary People* (1980); Warren Beatty for *Reds* (1981); Kevin Costner for *Dances With Wolves* (1990); and Clint Eastwood for *Unforgiven* (1992). An important note: because *Braveheart* was originally budgeted at $60 million and no single studio was willing to take on a film that dealt with the 13th century Scottish movement for independence, two studios, Paramount and 20th Century Fox, ended up jointly producing the film.

Another Academy Award winner, Kevin Spacey, made a remarkable showing in 1995. Besides his Oscar-winning portrayal of the gimpy "Verbal" in *The Usual Suspects,* Spacey also appeared in *Swimming With Sharks, Outbreak,* and *Seven.* Spacey had always been the kind of actor who looked familiar, but was hard to place. With all of his recent recognition, he'll no longer be that anonymous character actor. In a breakthrough role, Nicolas Cage also won an Oscar for Best Actor for playing a drunk determined to kill himself in *Leaving Las Vegas.* Many in the industry thought that that role would be the kiss of death for his career, but, indeed, Cage proved otherwise as he copped every award the film world bestows upon great acting performances. Never one to play it safe, Cage took a huge risk that payed off nicely as his asking price rose dramatically and he was flooded with several offers after winning the Academy Award.

Two new genuine leading ladies graced us in 1995. Sandra Bullock secured her position atop Hollywood's list of bankable women with the romantic hit *While You Were Sleeping,* and Alicia Silverstone soared to stardom with the Beverly Hills High teen comedy *Clueless.* 1995 also marked the first time two of the world's finest film actors, Al Pacino and Robert De Niro, shared a scene together. Although the Oscar winners co-starred in *The Godfather Part II* (1974), they never appeared on screen at the same time. They finally met face to face for a few brief moments as a detective and professional thief, respectively, in Michael Mann's stunning crime drama *Heat.* Both newcomers and screen legends alike combined to make 1995 a most interesting and worthwhile year in cinema.

Sadly, the film industry also saw the loss of some beloved stars in 1995: the sultry Lana Turner, who was known as "The Sweater Girl"; easygoing actor and singer Dean Martin; highly acclaimed French director Louis Malle; trailblazing actress/director Ida Lupino; Ginger Rogers, the actress and dancer who was famous for her pairing with Fred Astaire; African-American actor Woody Strode; the Swedish actress Viveca Lindfors; and Academy Award-winning composer Miklos Rozsa. See the Obituaries section in the back of this book for profiles of these and other major contributors to the film industry who died in 1995.

As the silver screen fades out upon another year of moviemaking, the *Magill's* staff looks forward to preparing the 1997 *Annual,* for which additional changes and enhancements are planned. We invite your comments. Please direct all questions and suggestions to:

Editor, *Magill's Cinema Annual*
Gale Research
835 Penobscot Bldg.
Detroit, MI 48226-4094
Phone: (313)961-2242
Toll-free: 800-347-GALE
Fax: (313)961-6812

Contributing Reviewers

Michael Adams
City University of New York
Vivek Adarkar
Long Island University
Martin Bandyke
Freelance Reviewer
Michael Betzold
Freelance Reviewer
David L. Boxerbaum
Freelance Reviewer
Cynthia K. Breckenridge
Freelance Reviewer
Shawn Brennan
Freelance Reviewer
Beverley Bare Buehrer
Freelance Reviewer
Reni Celeste
Freelance Reviewer
Robert F. Chicatelli
Freelance Reviewer
Paul B. Cohen
Freelance Reviewer
Jarred Cooper
Freelance Reviewer
Cindy Cummings
Freelance Reviewer
Bill Delaney
Freelance Reviewer
Rick Garman
Freelance Reviewer
D. Douglas Grahame
University of Maryland
Roberta F. Green
Virginia Polytechnic Institute and State University
Diane Hatch-Avis
Freelance Reviewer
Glenn Hopp
Howard Payne
Patricia Kowal
Freelance Reviewer
Leon Lewis
Appalachian State University
Robert Mitchell
University of Arizona
Paul Mittelbach
Freelance Reviewer
Lisa Paddock
Freelance Reviewer
Carl Rollyson
Baruch College, City University of New York
Brenda Scott Royce
Freelance Reviewer
Kim Silarski
Freelance Reviewer
Kirby Tepper
Freelance Reviewer
Terry Theodore
University of North Carolina at Wilmington
James M. Welsh
Salisbury State University

User's Guide

Alphabetization

Film titles and reviews are arranged on a word-by-word basis, including articles and prepositions. English leading articles (A, An, The) are ignored as well as foreign leading articles (El, Il, La, Las, Le, Les, Los). Other considerations:

- Acronyms appear alphabetically as if regular words. For example, S.F.W. is alphabetized as "SFW."
- Common abbreviations in titles file as if they are spelled out, so *Mr. Holland's Opus* will be found as if it was spelled *"Mister Holland's Opus."*
- Proper names in titles are alphabetized beginning with the individual's first name, for instance, *Johnny Mnemonic* will be found under "J."
- Titles with numbers, for instance *12 Monkeys* are alphabetized as if the number was spelled out under the appropriate letter, in this case, "Twelve." When numeric titles gather in close proximity to each other, the titles will be arranged in a low to high numeric sequence.

Special Sections

List of Awards. An annual list of awards bestowed upon the year's films by ten international associations: Academy of Motion Picture Arts and Sciences, British Academy Awards, Directors Guild of America Award, Golden Globe Awards, Golden Palm Awards (Cannes International Film Festival), Los Angeles Film Critics Awards, National Board of Review Awards, National Society of Film Critics Awards, New York Film Critics Awards, and the Writers Guild Awards.

Life Achievement Award. An essay reviewing the career and accomplishments of the recipient of the American Film Institute's Life Achievement Award presented each year to Hollywood luminaries. Actor/director/producer Clint Eastwood is the 1995 award recipient profiled in this volume.

Obituaries. An obituaries section profiling major contributors to the film industry who died in 1995.

Selected Film Books of 1995. An annotated list of selected film books published in 1995.

Indexes

Film titles and artists are arranged into nine indexes, allowing the reader to effectively approach a film from any one of several directions, including not only its credits but its subject matter.

Title Index. A cumulative alphabetical list of nearly 4,570 films covered in the fifteen volumes of the *Magill's Cinema Annual,* including over 300 films covered in this volume. Films reviewed in past volumes are cited with a roman numeral indicating the volume number in which the film was originally reviewed; films reviewed in this volume are cited with the film title in bold with a bolded arabic number indicating the page number on which the review begins. Original and alternate titles are cross-referenced to the American release title in the Title Index. Titles of retrospective films are followed by the year, in brackets, of their original release. Also indexed are those films discussed at some length in the special sections.

Director, Screenwriter, Cinematographer, Editor, Music, Art Director, and *Performer Indexes* are arranged according to artists appearing in this volume, followed by a list of the films on which they worked and the titles of the special sections (such as "Life Achievement Award" or "Obituaries") in which they are mentioned at length.

Subject Index. Films may be categorized under several of the categories arranged alphabetically in this section.

Sample Review

Each *Magill's* review contains up to sixteen items of information. A fictionalized composite sample review containing all the elements of information which may be included in a full-length review follows the outline below. The circled number preceding each element in the sample review on page XV designates an item of information that is explained in the outline on the next page.

(1) **Title:** Film title as it was released in the United States.

(2) **Foreign or alternate title(s):** The film's original title or titles as released outside the United States, or alternate film title or titles. Foreign and alternate titles also appear in the Title Index to facilitate user access.

(3) **Taglines:** Up to ten publicity or critical taglines for the film from advertisements or reviews.

(4) **Box office information:** Year-end or other box office domestic revenues for the film.

(5) **Film review or abstract:** A one-paragraph abstract or 750-1500-word signed review of the film, including brief plot summary, and for full-length reviews, an analytic overview of the film and its critical reception.

(6) **Principal characters:** Up to 25 listings of the film's principal characters and the names of the actors who play them in the film. The names of actors who play themselves are cited twice (as character and actor).

(7) **Country of origin:** The film's country or countries of origin if other than the United States.

(8) **Release date:** The year of the film's first general release.

(9) **Production information:** This section typically includes the name(s) of the film's producer(s), production company, and distributor, director(s), screenwriter(s), author(s) or creator(s) and the novel, play, short story, television show, motion picture, or other work, or character(s), that the film was based upon; cinematographer(s) (if the film is animated, this will be replaced with Animation or Animation Direction); editor(s); art director(s), production designer(s), set decorator(s) or set designer(s); music composer(s); and other credits such as visual effects, sound, casting, costume design, and song(s) and songwriter(s).

(10) **MPAA rating:** The film's rating by the Motion Picture Association of America. If there is no rating given, the line will read, "no listing."

(11) **Running time:** The film's running time in minutes.

(12) **Reviewer byline:** The name of the reviewer who wrote the full-length review. A complete list of this volume's contributors appears in the "Contributing Reviewers" section which follows the Introduction.

(13) **Reviews:** A list of up to 25 brief citations of major newspaper and journal reviews of the film, including publication title, date of review, and page number.

(14) **Awards information:** Awards won by the film, followed by category and name of winning cast or crew member. Listings of the film's nominations follow the wins on a separate line for each award. Awards are arranged alphabetically. Information is listed for films which won or were nominated for the following awards: American Academy Awards, Australian Film Institute, Berlin Film Festival, Blockbuster Entertainment Awards, British Academy of Film and Television Arts, Canadian Genie, Cannes Film Festival, Chicago Film Festival, Directors Guild of America, Edgar Allan Poe Awards, French Cesar, Golden Globe, Independent Spirit, Los Angeles Film Critics Association Awards, Montreal Film Festival, MTV Movie Awards, National Board of Review Awards, National Society of Film Critics Awards, New York Critics Awards, Sundance Film Festival, Toronto-City Awards, Writers Guild of America, and others.

(15) **Film quotes:** Memorable dialogue directly from the film, attributed to the character who spoke it, or comment from cast or crew members or reviewers about the film.

(16) **Film trivia:** Interesting tidbits about the film, its cast, or production crew.

2

1 The Gump Diaries (Los Diarios del Gump)

3 "Love means never having to say you're stupid." —Movie tagline

"This was a really good movie. I liked it." —Joe Critic, *Daily News*

4 

Box Office Gross: $10 million (December 15, 1994)

CREDITS

6 **Jim Carroll:** Leonardo DiCaprio
Swifty: Bruno Kirby
Jim's Mother: Lorraine Bracco
Mickey: Mark Wahlberg

7 **Origin:** United Kingdom
8 **Released:** 1993
Production: Liz Heller, John Bard Manulis for New Line
9 Cinema; released by Island Pictures
Direction: Scott Kalvert
Author: Bryan Goluboff; based on the novel by Jim Carroll
Cinematographer: David Phillips
Editing: Dana Congdon
Production design: Christopher Nowak
Set decoration: Harriet Zucker
Sound: William Sarokin
Costume design: David C. Robinson
10 **Music:** Graeme Revell
MPAA rating: R
11 **Running time:** 102 minutes

5 In writer/director Robert Zemeckis' *Back to the Future* trilogy (1985, 1989, 1990), Marty McFly (Michael J. Fox) and his scientist sidekick Doc Brown (Christopher Lloyd) journey backward and forward in time, attempting to smooth over some rough spots in their personal histories in order to remain true to their individual destinies. Throughout their time-travel adventures, Doc Brown insists that neither he nor Marty influence any major historical events, believing that to do so would result in catastrophic changes in humankind's ultimate destiny. By the end of the trilogy, however, Doc Brown has revised his thinking and tells Marty that, "Your future hasn't been written yet. No one's has. Your future is whatever you make it. So make it a good one."

In *Forrest Gump*, Zemeckis once again explores the theme of personal destiny and how an individual's life affects and is affected by his historical time period. This time, however, Zemeckis and screenwriter Eric Roth chronicle the life of a character who does nothing but meddle in the historical events of his time without even trying to do so. By the film's conclusion, however, it has become apparent that Zemeckis' main concern is something more than merely having fun with four decades of American history. In the process of re-creating significant moments in time, he has captured on celluloid something eternal and timeless—the soul of humanity personified by a nondescript simpleton from the deep South.

15 "The state of existence may be likened unto a receptacle containing cocoa-based confections, in that one may never predict that which one may receive." —Forrest Gump, from *The Gump Diaries*

The film begins following the flight of a seemingly insignificant feather as it floats down from the sky and brushes against various objects and people before finally coming to rest at the feet of Forrest Gump (Tom Hanks). Forrest, who is sitting on a bus-stop bench, reaches down and picks up the feather, smooths it out, then opens his traveling case and carefully places the feather between the pages of his favorite book, *Curious George*.

In this simple but hauntingly beautiful opening scene, the filmmakers illustrate the film's principal concern: Is life a series of random events over which a person has no control, or is there an underlying order to things that leads to the fulfillment of an individual's destiny? The rest of the film is a humorous and moving attempt to prove that, underlying the random, chaotic events that make up a person's life, there exists a benign and simple order.

Forrest sits on the bench throughout most of the film, talking about various events of his life to others who happen to sit down next to him. It does not take long, however, for the audience to realize that Forrest's seemingly random chatter to a parade of strangers has a perfect chronological order to it. He tells his first story after looking down at the feet of his first bench partner and observing, "Mama always said that you can tell a lot about a person by the shoes they wear." Then, in a voice-over narration, Forrest begins the story of his life, first by telling about the first pair of shoes he can remember wearing.

16 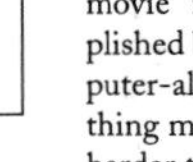

Hanks was the first actor since Spencer Tracy to win back-to-back Oscars for Best Actor. Hanks received the award in 1993 for his performance in *Philadelphia*. Tracy won Oscars in 1937 for *Captains Courageous* and in 1938 for *Boys Town*.

The action shifts to the mid-1950's with Forrest as a young boy (Michael Humphreys) being fitted with leg braces to correct a curvature in his spine. Despite this traumatic handicap, Forrest remains unaffected, thanks to his mother (Sally Field) who reminds him on more than one occasion that he is no different from anyone else. Although this and most of Mrs. Gump's other words of advice are in the form of hackneyed cliches, Forrest whose intelligence quotient is below normal, sincerely believes every one of them, namely because he instinctively knows they are sincere expressions of his mother's love and fierce devotion.

The action shifts to the mid-1950's with Forrest as a young boy (Michael Humphreys) being fitted with leg braces to correct a curvature in his spine. The action shifts to the mid-1950's to a in his spine. When the first U.S. Ping-Pong team to This of movie magic has not accomplished by special effects or computer-altered images, by something much more impressive and harder to achieve.

12 —*John Byline*

AWARDS AND NOMINATIONS

14 **Academy Awards 1994:** Best Film, Best Actor (Hanks), Best Special Effects, Best Cinematography
Nominations: Best Actress (Fields), Best Screenplay, Best Director (Zameckis)
Golden Globe Awards 1994: Best Film,
Nominations: Best Actor (Hanks), Best Supporting Actress (Wright), Best Music, Best Special Effects

REVIEWS

13 Entertainment Weekly. July 15, 1994, p. 42.
The Hollywood Reporter. June 29, 1994, p. 7.
Los Angeles Times. July 6, 1994, p. F1.

Magill's Cinema Annual
1996

Ace Ventura: When Nature Calls

"Jim Carrey's Best Yet!"—Ken Tucker, *Entertainment Weekly*

"Wackier than the original."—Jeff Craig, *Sixty Second Preview*

Box Office Gross: $104,194,497

The funniest thing in Ace Ventura: When Nature Calls—arguably the only funny thing in the entire awful movie—comes when a family of American tourists on an African safari think they are watching a baby rhinoceros being born, and instead out pops a naked Ace Ventura. Jim Carrey as an excretion—what could be more appropriate?

But even to get this genuine laugh, Carrey and writer/director pal Steve Oederkerk must contrive an ungainly situation. To spy on some sinister types meeting on the African plains, Ace puts himself inside a mechanical rhino, and sneaks up close. The fan breaks and it's sweltering inside, so Ace takes off his clothes. The lock breaks, so he's forced to exit through the rear of the rhino. And just then the family pulls up.

The joke is genuinely funny, but backtracking it, you can see that the punch line was thought up first, then the rest contrived to make it happen. Most of the other jokes in this excruciating film aren't nearly as belabored or elaborate, nor nearly as funny.

Carrey's debut as the cartoonish character in *Ace Ventura: Pet Detective* was annoying but extremely popular. Next he starred in *The Mask* (1994) and *Dumb and Dumber* (1994), and by the Ace sequel he had become a multi-millionaire. *When Nature Calls* shows him an extremely self-indulgent one.

Oederkerk, who directed his first film when Carrey booted Tom DeChercio, lets Carrey stay on camera for about 99 percent of the film, and he is in close-up at least half that time. This much camera time would tax the audience's tolerance even if the star were a real comic like Harpo Marx. Carrey not only isn't funny, he's dreadfully annoying. After two scenes one wishes he'd disappear from the film, but he goes on and on and on.

Carrey has one schtick. His hair is swept up to an impossible peak. He wears Hawaiian shirts and mismatched striped pants. When he walks, he twitches and swaggers exaggeratedly. And every word that comes out of his mouth is tortured. Overacting? Carrey is way beyond overacting. What he does can't justifiably be called over the top. That implies an actor with talent who is deliberately exaggerating. Carrey has no apparent talent and knows no other way of acting except speaking every syllable as if were written on the script in all capitals followed by ten exclamation points.

That Carrey has parlayed this character into a popular screen icon doesn't excuse his excess. In the original Ace movie there was at least a pretense at a story, albeit a dumb one, involving other actors and characters. This sequel is more grandiose—it wasted $44 million in the making—and it's just Carrey mugging, doing one awful bit after another.

The plot is inconsequential and insultingly stupid. For no apparent reason, the animal-loving pet detective is in the wilds of Africa. He has to rescue a sacred bat to stop two tribes from going to war. And it's no surprise that evil colonial types are behind the intrigue.

There is no other character of any consequence. British actor Ian McNeice is utterly wasted as a procurer of Ace's services; he is a straight man who has precious little to do, because Carrey's humor doesn't involve anyone but himself and his bodily functions. Sophie Okonedo has a small role as a love interest, but Carrey's so in love with himself that nothing happens with her either. The chief villain is played by Vincent Cadby, another British actor who deserves better. And that's it, except for some awfully embarrassing assemblages of African tribespeople who look and act as if they've come out of a racist 1930s safari adventure. They smile a lot, sing and dance, wear warpaint and fulfill every retrograde stereotype imaginable.

"Spank you—spank you very much."—Ace Ventura from *Ace Ventura: When Nature Calls*

Carrey and his fawning director obviously think Ace's every gesture and word are priceless. Few if any of them are. When a ten-year-old boy in the audience doesn't laugh more than a couple times in the film—at humor that's obviously directed straight at ten-year-old boys—there's the distinct possibility that Ace has worn out his welcome.

What's not funny in *When Nature Calls*? Ace and the natives spitting in each other's faces—as the tribe's equivalent of a handshake—is not funny. Ace talking with his rear end is not funny. Ace flipping over his jeep to get into a parking space is not funny. Ace spoofing meditation, Ace masturbating, Ace doing shadow play with his fingers over a filmstrip—now that's original! Ace trying to play Slinky on a thousand-step staircase. Ace dancing all over the sacred bat throne while the chief has his back turned. Ace regurgitating to feed a hungry baby bird. None of this is funny, not one bit.

At least there were three of the Three Stooges, and they were adept at pratfalls. There is only one of Jim Carrey, and he must be endured for 92 minutes. It's like going to the dentist and having the needle stuck in and never pulled out, the mouth never going numb and the drilling going on for an hour and a half. In one scene, trying to get information out of a possible villain, Ace conducts torture by skidding a knife and fork on an empty plate. It's a metaphor for the entire film.

What the $44 million was spent on, and why it was spent, is a mystery. The movie announces itself as being set in Nibia, but it was shot in South Carolina and the Canadian Rockies. There are no special effects to speak of. But there is some spectacularly tepid photography and editing. The money has bought a certain slickness and grandiosity that is totally incongruous for such a paltry story. Ventura semed to fit much better in Miami trying to save a football game from a silly plot, as in the original story. Here is he presented as some grand sort of animal liberator, which is ridiculous.

Once again, the notion that Ace Ventura is a friend to all species is hard to swallow. Carrey isn't as dignified as any animal, and his character never exhibits any heartfelt concern for the creatures he is supposedly defending. As in the original film, there is precious little interaction between Ventura and animals, and when it is, the animals come off the worse. One gets the distinct impression that Carrey really isn't all that fond of animals, or of other people for that matter. The strong impression left by *When Nature Calls* is that Carrey is fond only of himself.

CREDITS

Ace Ventura: Jim Carrey
Fulton Greenwall: Ian McNeice
Vincent Cadby: Simon Callow
Ouda: Maynard Eziashi
Burton Quinn: Bob Gunton
Princess: Sophie Okonedo
Wachootoo Warrior: Tommy Davidson

Origin: USA
Released: 1995
Production: James G. Robinson for a Morgan Creek production; released by Warner Brothers
Direction: Steve Oedekerk
Screenplay: Steve Oedekerk
Cinematography: Donald E. Thorin
Editing: Malcolm Campbell
Production design: Stephen J. Lineweaver
Art direction: Christopher Nowak
Costume design: Elas Zamparelli
Hair: Pauletta Lewis
Sound: Stacy F. Brownrigg
Animal training: Cathy Morrison
MPAA rating: PG-13
Running Time: 92 minutes

AWARDS AND NOMINATIONS

Blockbuster Entertainment Awards 1996: Comedy Actor-Theatrical (Carrey)

The marked lack of success of *When Nature Calls* in its Christmas 1995 theatrical release may mean that filmdom might possibly be spared more than a couple more Ace Ventura movies. Carrey's shallow comic well ran dry long ago. There is nothing funny left except his own excretion.

—*Michael Betzold*

REVIEWS

Chicago Tribune. Nov. 10, 1995, p. 5.
Entertainment Weekly. Nov. 24, 1995, p. 79.
The New York Times. Nov. 10, 1995, p. C8.
People. Nov. 27, 1995, p. 19.
USA Today. Nov. 10, 1995, p. D1.
Variety. Nov. 13, 1995, p. 53.
Wall Street Journal. Nov. 14, 1995, p. A12.

The Addiction

"The dark is their sunlight. Any stranger, their friend. What makes them different is what keeps them alive."—Movie tagline

Box Office Gross: $302,393

The philosophical and religious theme of man's struggle between light and darkness is taken to utterly intellectual extremes in Abel Ferrara's *The Addiction.* A heady black-and-white low budgeter about a young female vampire in contemporary New York, *The Addiction* follows closely in the wake of Michael Almereyda's similarly themed *Nadja* (1995). Less sensual than *Nadja*, Ferrara takes a much harsher stand with severe overtones of philosophical and religious theory that could be considered either quite pretentious by the less studied or a brilliant take on vampire lore by the Christian philosopher.

Kathleen Conklin (Lili Taylor) is a doctoral candidate in philosophy at the fictional University of New York, although the New York University Manhattan neighborhood is easy to recognize, who is pursued and attacked in a shadowy stairwell by a fiercely sensual woman billed only as Casanova (Annabella Sciorra). Casanova asks, "Why don't you tell me to leave you alone?" before sinking her fangs into Conklin's neck, thereby creating the theme that one has the power to choose between good or evil. Conklin's barely audible whimper doesn't offer enough resistance to stop the attack, which results in two bloody holes in her neck, followed by agonizing pain and an inability to eat. Unaware that her transformation is taking place, she is convinced that some kind of kinky attack has occurred. Eventually, the resulting blood addiction overcomes her and life becomes a twisted search for the next fix.

The film's urban soundtrack is a testimony to the parallel of vampirism with drug addiction. "I wanna get high, so high," resonates through scenes of Conklin desperately and pathetically commencing her nocturnal rounds. Unlike *Interview With The Vampire* (1994) where Brad Pitt launches into the netherworld feasting on animals, Con-

CREDITS

Kathleen Conklin: Lili Taylor
Peina: Christopher Walken
Casanova: Annabella Sciorra
Jean: Edie Falco
The Professor: Paul Calderon
Black: Fredro Star

Origin: USA
Released: 1995
Production: Denis Hann and Frenando Sulichin for a Russell Simmons production; released by October Films
Direction: Abel Ferrara
Screenplay: Nicholas St. John
Cinematography: Ken Kelsch
Editing: Mayin Lo
Production design: Charlie Lagola
Art direction: Beth Curtis
Costume design: Melinda Eschelman
Sound: Robert Taz
MPAA rating: R
Running Time: 82 minutes

AWARDS AND NOMINATIONS

Independent Spirit Awards Nominations 1996:
Best Film, Best Actress (Taylor)

klin uses a syringe to sheepishly draw the blood from a homeless man on the street and inject it into her veins as if it were heroin.

Conklin's lust for blood soon drives her to prowl the East Village for victims, eventually compelling her to prey on friends and associates for sustenance. Conklin, comically decked out in dark glasses, returns to society and school, a depressed, foreboding misfit, only to viciously attack her philosophy professor and school chum.

It becomes clear that Ferrara and screenwriter Nicholas St. John are taking the theme to an extreme level when glimpses of historical atrocities, including the Holocaust, the My Lai massacre, and other mass slaughters are connected to Conklin's struggle to oppose the dark side. Additionally, the philosophies of Nietzsche, Kirkegard, and Heidegger, among others, antagonize the Christian belief that humans have the innate ability to resist evil.

A fellow vampire (Christopher Walken) takes this theory to another level and lectures Conklin in the art of exercising will. Fond of quoting "Beyond Good and Evil," he describes his ability to control his lust for blood.

In an effort to control her own "addiction," Conklin experiences heavy withdrawal, but still manages to throw herself into her work and complete her degree. As she arrives at an elaborate reception to celebrate her success, Conklin approaches a street-corner preacher only to be nonchalantly rejected. Her first experience with rejection sparks a bloody massacre, with all of her previous victims relentlessly attacking the human guests.

The Addiction climaxes with Conklin in a hospital desperately trying to overcome the will of the vampire and ironically accepting the Christian version of eternal life from a priest. The ending is somewhat confusing, but a transcendence that seems to suggest triumph definitely occurs.

The film is extremely well-acted, especially by Lili Taylor who has been considered one of the most accomplished film actresses of her day. The extensive range of emotion, from ardent suffering to superlative power and resolve, are handled beautifully and hold the film together when the narrative gets choppy. Walken fits the vampire role to a tee, but his appearance is too brief.

The Addiction doesn't seem to follow the standard rule of vampire etiquette, which makes the film all the more intriguing. Walken's vampire feeds on another vampire, which contradicts traditional vampire lore. Also, victims always transform into vampires. Nobody dies in this horrendously violent and bloody film.

A horror show for the educated moviegoer, *The Addiction* is a dramatically inventive, stylish entry into the bloodsucker genre. It's intellectually appealing to an exclusive few and the lack of cohesion is sometimes hard to digest, but the impressive quality, moody style, and unique take on familiar themes is surprisingly captivating.

—Kelly M. Cross

REVIEWS

The New York Times. October 4, 1995, p. C16.
Rolling Stone. October 19, 1995, p. 159.
Variety. February 2, 1995, p. 29.
Village Voice. October 10, 1995, p. 69.
The Washington Post. October 27, 1995, p. 48.

Amateur

"The most spiritual action movie ever made."—Lisa Henricksson, *GQ*

"As close to perfect as any film you'll see this year."—Graham Fuller, *Interview*

"The nun, the amnesiac and the prostitute...deliciously droll, Hal Hartley's most ambitious view of the world yet."—Caryn James, *The New York Times*

"*Amateur* is Hartley heaven, a sharp-witted thriller. Huppert is delicious. Martin Donovan is in peak form. The extraordinary cast brings snap and surprising heart to Hartley's riffs on sex, lies and exploitation. *Amateur* marks another creative leap in the career of a fervently inventive original."—Peter Travers, *Rolling Stone*

Box Office Gross: $856,422

Like his other films—most notably *Simple Men* (1992), *Trust* (1991), and *The Unbelievalbe Truth* (1990)—director Hal Hartley's latest offering is another study in quirkiness. *Amateur*, Hartley's fifth film, begins, literally, in the gutter, with an image of a fallen man, unconscious on the cobblestones. His name is Thomas (Martin Donovan), but the audience knows nothing, really, about him. We later learn that he fell or was pushed from a second-story window above and that two men are seeking him with murderous intent, but Thomas can tell us nothing about his past. Falling to the street he struck his head on the pavement and has suffered a complete and total loss of memory. He defines himself through his words and instincts and seems decent enough. But he turns out to have been a criminal involved in pornography in the Netherlands. He seems to be innocent but is none the less a fallen man.

"I'm choosy."—Isabelle when asked how she can be both a nymphomaniac and a virgin in *Amateur*

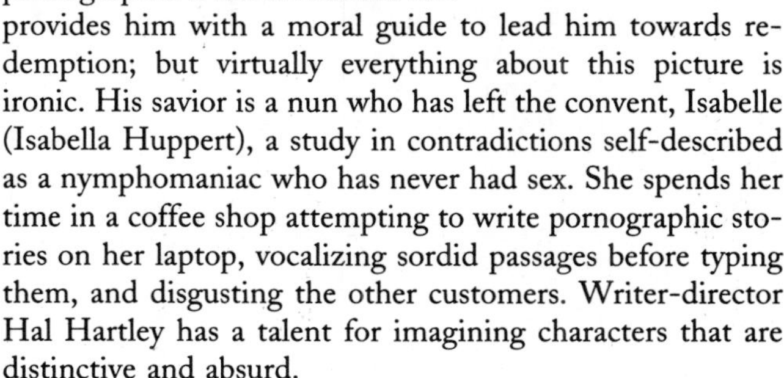

Even so, the film gives this doubting Thomas amnesiac pornographer a second chance and provides him with a moral guide to lead him towards redemption; but virtually everything about this picture is ironic. His savior is a nun who has left the convent, Isabelle (Isabella Huppert), a study in contradictions self-described as a nymphomaniac who has never had sex. She spends her time in a coffee shop attempting to write pornographic stories on her laptop, vocalizing sordid passages before typing them, and disgusting the other customers. Writer-director Hal Hartley has a talent for imagining characters that are distinctive and absurd.

Isabelle takes the confused Thomas in and is taken in by him. They soon discover that Thomas is married to a prostitute named Sofia (Elina Lowens"hn), who presumably pushed him out of the window and then ran away. Thomas the pornographer initiated her to drugs and prostitution when she was only twelve years old, then turned her into an international porn star.

Through Sofia the viewer learns about her husband's shady past. Thomas was on the lam because he had attempted to blackmail a Dutch kingpin named Jacques. Sofia tells a crooked accountant named Edward (Damian Young) that she has killed her husband. Then she telephones Jacques, who sends a pair of hitmen, Jan (Chuck Montgomery) and Kurt (David Simonds), after her. Looking for Sofia they find Edward, whom they torture. Thereafter, Edward is transformed into a psychotic killer —and a cop-killer at that.

Isabelle and Thomas are hiding at Sofia's apartment when Jan and Kurt arrive and then capture her. To keep Kurt from torturing Sofia, Isabelle, dressed in Sofia's leather and taking on her traits, forces Kurt back with an electric drill until he falls through the window to his death. Isabelle, Thomas, and Sofia then escape in Jan's car to upstate New York, headed for sanctuary at Isabelle's convent. Sofia holds the key to Thomas's identity but refuses to reveal his past.

The action comes to a bloody showdown when deranged Edward arrives to rescue Sofia, and gets in a confrontation with Thomas. Then Jan arrives, shoots Sofia, and is killed by Edward. They take Sofia to the convent, where she tells Isabelle who Thomas was. The police arrive seeking Edward the cop-killer and shoot Thomas by mistake in this black comedy of errors.

The plot of *Amateur* is one of convoluted intrigue and violent action but it distinguishes itself mainly as a study of eccentric characters blundering along at cross purposes. Ironically, the most violent and brutal characters are accountants. These bean-counters and number-crunchers are homicidal lunatics, closet sadists capable of inflicting torture. After Jan and Kurt torture Edward, the wild accountant who does not speak, he lumbers jerkily through the rest of the story (due to electroshock treatments inflicted on him) with a "deer in the headlight" expression on his face and his hair standing on end, an eccentric and unpredictable wild card who is desperate and dangerous.

Isabelle is another walking contradiction, a virgin nymphomaniac whose ambition to become a pornographic writer leads to a loopy dialogue exchange with her would-be editor and publisher, who reads her latest work at his office. As he finishes, he says the piece is very sad, like most of her work. "This is poetry, and don't you deny it," he says as he paces about the room and begins a lengthy, very funny monologue: "Come back to me when you've written something really perverse, really depraved." And then, as if to reassure her, he begins to tell her he didn't always want to publish a pornographic magazine; the porno editor explains he wanted to be a reporter for a tabloid magazine. There are numerous odd scenes such as this one played naturally in order to heighten the quirky realism of the characters. The action, dialogue and even the costuming seems to be utterly spontaneous, as when Isabelle is seen comically menacing as, dressed in leather and fishnets and toting her electric drill, she backs Kurt through the very window from which Thomas had previously fallen. She turns out to be more dangerous than she appears.

Thomas is another walking dichotomy. To Isabelle he is a gentle, lost soul; to his wife, he evokes such terror and disgust that she cannot bear to sit next to him. We never learn what or who Thomas really was, although we do learn

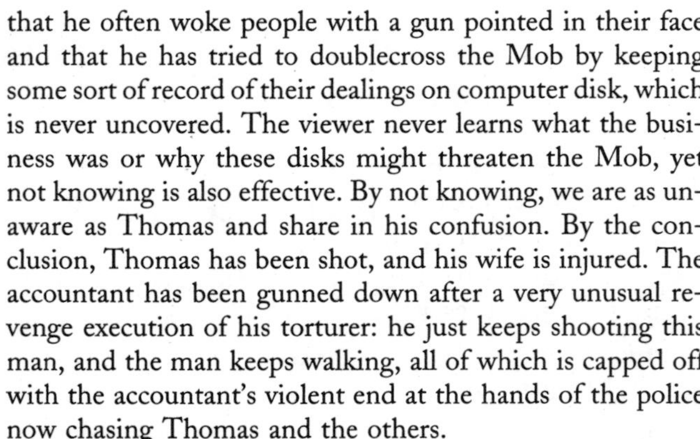

that he often woke people with a gun pointed in their face and that he has tried to doublecross the Mob by keeping some sort of record of their dealings on computer disk, which is never uncovered. The viewer never learns what the business was or why these disks might threaten the Mob, yet not knowing is also effective. By not knowing, we are as unaware as Thomas and share in his confusion. By the conclusion, Thomas has been shot, and his wife is injured. The accountant has been gunned down after a very unusual revenge execution of his torturer: he just keeps shooting this man, and the man keeps walking, all of which is capped off with the accountant's violent end at the hands of the police now chasing Thomas and the others.

Nothing has really been resolved by the conclusion as far as better understanding the characters; but, then, nothing in life is ever really resolved, either. In this sense, the film retains its air of realism, despite all the odd occurrences, the quirky turns of the plot, and the multi-faceted, mysterious characters. What saves the film is that those characters are so ingeniously designed that they become fascinating. The best of them are even charming. The old Thomas belongs to the plot that kills him, but the new Thomas is sweetly naive and seems to deserve a second chance, even if he is not able to escape his past.

The Sony Pictures Classics advertising set up the title of *Amateur* as an acronym standing for: Accountancy, Murder, Amnesia, Torture, Ecstasy, Understanding, and Redemption. Though most of these concepts are involved, the film is short on ecstasy and understanding. It might be seen as merely another neo-noir attempt at pulpier fiction, but the film is better than that and inventive rather than merely imitative. *Amateur* shows influences of film noir, but the style is probably closer to what André Breton called L'humour noir: "There is nothing that intelligent humor cannot resolve in bursts of laughter, not even nothingness," Breton wrote; laughter, which is "on the edge of nothingness, gives us nothingness as collateral security." The film courts absurdity with style and grace. The point has been made that Hal Hartley is beyond classification and a genre unto himself.

—James M. Welsh and Melissa Brabetz

CREDITS

Isabelle: Isabelle Huppert
Thomas: Martin Donovan
Sofia: Elina Lowensohn
Edward: Damion Young
Jan: Chuck Montgomery
Kurt: David Simonds
Officer Melville: Pamela Stewart

Origin: France/Great Britain/USA
Released: 1994 (1995 U.S.)
Production: Ted Hope and Hal Hartley; Jerome Brownstein, Lindsay Law, Scott Meek, Yves Marmion, for UGC, in association with American Playhouse, Theatrical Films, La Sept Cinema and Channel Four Films; A Zenith/True Fiction Pictures Production; released by Sony Pictures Classics
Direction: Hal Hartley
Screenplay: Hal Hartley
Cinematography: Michael Spiller
Editing: Steve Hamilton
Production design: Steve Rosenzweig
Art direction: Ginger Tougas
Set decoration: Jennifer Baime and Amy Tapper
Sound: Jeff Pullman
Costume Design: Alexandra Welker
Music: Ned Rifle and Jeffrey Taylor
MPAA rating: R
Running Time: 105 minutes

REVIEWS

The New York Times. April 7, 1995, C-21.
The New Yorker. April 17, 1995, pp. 109-110.
Rolling Stone, No.706, April 20, 1995, pp.88-89.
Sight and Sound. Vol.5, No.1 (January 1995), p.42.
The Times (London), January 5, 1995, p.33.
What's On (London), January 4, 1995, p.32.

The Amazing Panda Adventure

"In the sweeping highlands of China, a boy begins a magical journey to save the life of a natural wonder."—Movie tagline

"A great adventure filled with fun for the entire family. Don't miss it!"—Joanna Levenglick, *The Kids News Network*

Box Office Gross: $7,506,759

The Amazing Panda Adventure has some staples of good family fare: an exotic locale, kids in tight scrapes, a battle to win a parent's affection, and a cute animal. In this case, the cutest possible animal. Nothing is more cuddly and lovable than a panda and nothing more noble than trying to save it.

Unfortunately, *The Amazing Panda Adventure* is neither amazing nor particularly adventurous. The acting is unremarkable, the dialogue stilted, the plot forced and the action sequences unimaginative and clumsy. Only the scenery is compelling.

Like the *Free Willy* films and many others before, the story is about a young boy struggling for a parent's love who is redeemed by a friendship with an unlikely animal. It seems mandatory in 1990s films to script young protagonists with divorced, separated or widowed parents, and here is another one. Ryan Tyler (Ryan Slater) is a normal American boy who hasn't seen his father since his parents split up two years earlier. His dad, exact profession unclear, has gone to China to save giant pandas.

Michael Tyler (Stephen Lang) is so wrapped up in his work that Ryan feels abandoned, a feeling that intensifies when Michael sends him an airline ticket then fails to show up at the airport to meet him. That's only slightly more implausible than Ryan finding his way alone to the panda preserve deep in the Chinese interior, where his dad is boss.

"I'm an American. My life revolves around electronics."—Ryan to Ling in *The Amazing Panda Adventure*

As Ryan arrives, his father has to rush off because one of the preserve's few remaining pandas has been trapped by poachers. The scientists know this because they have attached a radio collar to the animal. The radio collar shows that the animal isn't moving. Why this indicates the panda is trapped and not merely sleeping isn't clear.

Insisting he won't be left behind again, Ryan guilt-trips his dad into taking him along. When Michael says "I promise I'll be back as soon as I can," Ryan shouts back: "That's what you said two years ago!" Dad makes a face like he's eaten a slug; he's been defeated. Ryan jumps aboard a tractor-drawn cart and meets the film's two other major characters, both indispensible to this genre: a smug pre-adolescent girl, Ling (Yi Ding), obviously scripted to pair off with Ryan, and her grandfather, Chu (Huang Fei), who speaks no English and is in tune with nature and his ancestors, just like the Native American in *Free Willy* (1993). Gramps is always sticking his finger in the wind, prompting Ryan to ask, "Is there, like, radar on his finger?" to which Ling replies, "Grandfather is very wise." Of course.

The two poachers, who resemble an Oriental Mutt and Jeff, come upon their prey. Throughout the movie, one shoots while the other inexplicably pulls up his partner's rifle in mid-shot. This makes no sense. That is how the poachers fail to shoot the mother panda while tipping off Michael Tyler as to their location. That is also how, when Tyler pursues, they shoot him in the leg rather than the heart, and how later they fail to shoot the pursuing youngsters at point-blank range.

An implausible series of events has the mother panda being rescued and taken back to the compound and the two youngsters recapturing the cub and getting lost in the outback while the buffoonish poachers haphazardly pursue. The action includes not one, but two, falls from a rickety bridge into a rushing river. These sequences feature some un-special effects as stunt actors tote what is obviously a panda doll down swollen torrents. Of course, the panda always emerges fluffy and dry.

The cub is unbearably cute. In a ridiculously scripted sequence in which Ryan tries to abandon the cub so that the preserve will be closed and his father will come back home, the cub rolls around like a helpless pet and emits lovable squeaks. That such a huggable furball is threatened with extinction and pursued by stupid and savage poachers should arouse great sympathy. It's a set-up that can't fail, yet it does, so unimaginative is the filmmaking. When the cub must dangle from a branch over the edge of a cliff, when it cries because it is starving from lack of mother's milk, the effect is merely cloying.

For many adults, this film will be spoiled by the price the producers paid to collaborate with the Chinese government. Part of that price is a long and distressing sequence, unnecessary to the plot, in which the kids and the panda stumble into a rural Tibetan village. In the real world, Chinese authorities have been repressing Tibetans and their culture. In this whitewash, happy Tibetans wear their colorful clothes and do their native dances, as if to show how tolerant a place China is.

Contrivance is key to *The Amazing Panda Adventure.* Authorities are threatening to close the panda preserve if a cub isn't produced, so the heroes must get the cub back before the officials' bus leaves and before the cub dies of starvation, which turn out to be the same time. How the limping Tyler and the stooped Chu manage to climb a rugged mountain for the film's ultimate rescue scene and then get the cub and the prickly poachers back down to their tractor-cart is nothing short of a miracle, so the filmmakers don't show how they do it.

How unimaginative is this film? When finally, near the end of the film, the two children decide to name the cub, they agree on the name of Ryan's best friend. They call the panda Johnny.

Slater is more annoying than endearing as Ryan. He is so boastful and whiny that his eventual heroism seems phony. He's like an apprentice Ugly American, smug and domineering. As his father, Lang is constantly scowling; if saving an endangered species is this disagreeable, who'd want to do it? As Ling, Yi Ding is the best of the cast, agreeable and sympathetic if a little stiff. Huang Fei is nothing more than a stereotype as her grandfather.

Fortunately, there is a lush background of wispy waterfalls, mossy forests, and golden meadows, pleasantly shot by Jack Green. *The Amazing Panda Adventure* might have made a great travelogue, but unfortunately someone attached a script to it.

—*Michael Betzold*

CREDITS

Michael: Stephen Lang
Ryan: Ryan Slater
Ling: Yi Ding
Chu: Huang Fei
Po: Zhou Jian Zhong
Shong: Yao Er Ga

Origin: USA
Released: 1995
Production: Lee Rich, John Wilcox, Gary Foster and Dylan Sellers; released by Warner Brothers
Direction: Christopher Cain
Screenplay: Jeff Rothberg, Laurice Elehwany, John Wilcox and Steven Alldredge
Cinematography: Jack N.Green
Editing: Jack Hofstra
Production design: John Willett
Art direction: Willie Heslup
Set decoration: Doug Carnegie
Costume design: Marjorie Chan
Sound: Andy Wiskes
Panda effects: Rick Baker
Casting: Marion Dougherty
Music: William Ross
MPAA rating: PG
Running Time: 84 minutes

REVIEWS

Variety. August 28, 1995, p. 66.

The American President

Box Office Gross: $50,305,552

As a variation on the romantic idealism of Frank Capra's *Mr. Smith Goes to Washington* (1939), *The American President* is a considerable improvement over *Dave* (1993), the last significant political comedy set in the nation's capital. With a mostly competent screenplay by Aaron Sorkin, movie-star charisma from the two leads, and good supporting performances, *The American President* is diverting light entertainment but hardly a return, as some reviewers claimed, to classic Hollywood filmmaking.

President Andrew Shepherd (Michael Douglas) heads into his reelection campaign with high approval ratings in public opinion polls, and his staff is delighted, looking forward to the forthcoming battle with his likely opponent, Senator Bob Rumson (Richard Dreyfuss). Then Shepherd, widowed just before his election, meets Sydney Ellen Wade (Annette Bening), a spunky lobbyist for an environmental organization. Taken with her almost immediately, he invites her to be his date at a state dinner, his first date since he has been in office. Romantic developments ensue.

Conflicts occur on two fronts. Shepherd has weakened an environmental bill in hopes it will more likely be passed by the House of Representatives. Wade wants him to restore the bill to its original strength (reducing automobile emissions by twenty instead of ten percent), and he promises to do so if she can convince sufficient members of Congress to support it. Meanwhile, the president's aides, led by A. J. MacInerney (Martin Sheen) and Lewis Rothschild (Michael J. Fox), convince him to sacrifice the environmental package in favor of a gun-control bill they consider more worthy of passage. In agreeing, Shepherd goes back on his word to Wade and loses his lover as well.

The other front consists of Rumson's innuendoes about the president's sex life and about Wade's trading passion for passage of a bill. Rumson also uncovers evidence of her being present years earlier when an American flag was burned at an anti-apartheid rally. Shepherd's approval rating plummets from sixty-three to forty-one percent, and his staff goes berserk over the effects of his public love affair.

"Sydney, this is just dinner. We won't be doing espionage or anything."—President Shepherd in *The American President*

While Lilly Kilvert and her production staff do an amazing job of creating a seemingly authentic White House setting, surpassing even the superb job J. Michael Riva did for the otherwise flawed *Dave*, *The American President* emphasizes romance and comedy over verisimilitude. Superficially resembling Bill Clinton and Michael Dukakis, Sorkin's Shepherd is vaguely liberal but is concerned only about these two bills. Not only is no information provided about Shepherd's previous presidential activities, but what he did before his election is also not revealed. (MacInerney says that if Shepherd had not gone into politics, his friend would be a history professor.) The screenwriter, who previously collaborated with director Rob Reiner on *A Few Good Men* (1992), adapted from Sorkin's play, allows Shepherd to be presidential primarily by having him make the tough decision to retaliate after an attack by Libya. The rest of the time, however, the president is a fraternity boy who refers to the Oval Office as the Rec Room.

Michael Douglas and Annette Bening star in *The American President.* Photo by Michael O'Neill.

The latter is typical of the film's humor. Shepherd tries to talk to his twelve-year-old daughter, Lucy (Shawna Waldron), about her schoolwork like he is a typical American father, but she cannot take him seriously because he is the president and has more important matters to worry about. Shepherd and Wade attempt to treat their public dates as ordinary events even though they are surrounded by Secret Service agents, the press, and curious onlookers. Two of the big comic moments occur when Shepherd tries to place a telephone order with a florist who will not believe she is speaking to the president and later when he impulsively goes into the florist shop only to have the salesclerk faint.

> Sydney Ellen Wade pronounces her first visit to the White House as Capraesque and the security guard begins discussing *Mr. Smith Goes to Washington* (1939) and *It's a Wonderful Life* (1946) with affection. Appropriately, the film's assistant director is Frank Capra III, grandson of the legendary director.

While Sorkin's dialogue is often amusing, *The American President* does not evoke memories of the banter between Jean Arthur and James Stewart or Katharine Hepburn and Cary Grant or Barbara Stanwyck and Henry Fonda or anyone else from the golden age of romantic comedies. It is more likely to recall Doris Day and Rock Hudson since Reiner's often plodding style resembles that of American screen comedies of the 1950's and early 1960's—Blake Edwards not Preston Sturges. Reiner uses too many closeups, directing the film almost like it was made for television. He uses the wonderful cinematographer John Seale, who shot *Witness* (1985), *Gorillas In The Mist* (1988), and *Rain Man* (1988), but has him light the film so that the results look cloudy and even ugly at times. Reiner's film may also set some kind of record for continuity errors with mismatched shots in almost every scene in which he cuts back and forth between actors. Even Reiner's inferior *When Harry Met Sally* (1989) was much more cinematic.

Reiner's greatest virtue as a director is his handling of actors, and *The American President* offers more good performances than any of his previous films. Dreyfuss, Fox, and Sheen have been foundering lately but redeem themselves here. Playing MacInerney as an amused bystander whose main function is to respond to the foolishness of the other characters, Sheen gives his best performance since *The Dead Zone* (1983). By playing Rothschild (meant to resemble George Stephanopoulos) as a temperamental prima dona who must have his way, Fox moves beyond the lovable near-adolescents he usually creates. Dreyfuss shows his considerable skills by portraying the mean-spirited senator as cold and calculating when conspiring with his cronies and nervously awkward when making charges against his opponent on television. David Paymer is amusing as the president's pollster with a quip for each crisis, and Waldron acts more naturally than most child performers.

Bening does easily her best work since *The Grifters* (1990). Though she comes close to making Wade a bit too perky and bouncy, she invigorates Sorkin's conception of this character with considerable energy, intelligence, and warmth. Bening can be bright, strong, and charmingly clumsy all in the same scene as when Shepherd telephones Wade to ask her for their first date and the lobbyist thinks the caller is a friend pretending to be the president. Why

CREDITS

President Andrew Shepherd: Michael Douglas
Sydney Ellen Wade: Annette Bening
A. J. MacInerney: Martin Sheen
Lewis Rothschild: Michael J. Fox
Leon Kodak: David Paymer
Robin McCall: Anna Deavere Smith
Janie Basdin: Samantha Mathis
Leo Solomon: John Mahoney
Susan Sloan: Wendie Malick
Lucy Shepherd: Shawana Waldron
Beth Wade: Nina Siemaszko
Senator Bob Rumson: Richard Dreyfuss

Origin: USA
Released: 1995
Production: Rob Reiner for Wildwood Enterprises, Castle Rock Entertainment, and Universal Pictures; released by Columbia
Direction: Rob Reiner
Screenplay: Aaron Sorkin
Cinematography: John Seale
Editing: Robert Leighton
Production design: Lilly Kilvert
Art direction: John Warnke
Set design: Nick Navarro, Louis Montejano, Eric Orbom and Alan S. Kaye
Set decoration: Karen O'Hara
Costume design: Gloria Gresham
Sound: Robert Eber
Music: Marc Shaiman
Casting: Jane Jenkins and Janet Hirshenson
MPAA rating: PG-13
Running Time: 113 minutes

AWARDS AND NOMINATIONS

Academy Awards Nominations 1995: Best Score (Shaiman)
Golden Globe Awards Nominations 1996: Best Film-Musical/Comedy, Actor-Musical/Comedy (Douglas), Actress-Musical/Comedy (Bening), Best Director (Reiner), Best Screenplay (Sorkin)
Writers Guild Awards Nominations 1995: Best Original Screenplay (Sorkin)

Sorkin burdens her with such an awkward name is another matter. If she has to be constantly referred to by her full name so that the audience will know the character is a woman, why name her Sydney to begin with?

Like Fox, Douglas has been in danger of falling into a stereotype, albeit the unusual one of weak philanderer victimized by a strong woman: *Fatal Attraction* (1987), *Basic Instinct* (1992), *Disclosure* (1994). In *The American President*, Shepherd and Wade are equals, though, ironically, he can be both stronger and weaker than her in certain circumstances. Douglas perfectly embodies the surface qualities many American voters apparently look for in their political figures while unveiling some depth, as with self-doubt, beneath this slick front. Douglas is at his best in the film's pivotal scene: Shepherd's impromptu press conference after his betrayal of Wade as he finds a way to a political solution of his either environmental protection or gun control dilemma while defending the woman he loves as a woman who does not need defending. While Sorkin's something-for-everyone solution to this situation is more than a tad pat, Douglas' performance in this hokey scene, patterned after Spencer Tracy's speech at the end of *State of The Union* (1948), is inspiring. The president's ability to think on his feet, to be fair and logical rather than peevish and impulsive, to communicate forcefully, and to stand up for his principles is obviously meant to make the film's audience wish that real-life politicians were exactly like this—and to think that this schmaltzy romance has more substance than it really does. Ironically, Robert Redford dropped out of the project after disagreeing with Reiner over the film's emphasis. Redford wanted it to be more of a romantic comedy, and the director wanted more political content. Is this what he thinks he has achieved?

—*Michael Adams*

REVIEWS

Entertainment Weekly. November 17, 1995, p. 56.
The New Republic. CCXIII, December 18, 1995, p. 28.
New York. XXVIII, November 20, 1995, p. 84.
The New York Times. November 17, 1995, p. B1.
The New Yorker. LXXI, November 20, 1995, p. 116.
Newsweek. CXXVI, November 20, 1995, p. 91.
Rolling Stone. November 30, 1995, p. 76.
Time. CXLVI, November 20, 1995, p. 117.
Variety. November 6, 1995, p. 71.
The Wall Street Journal. November 17, 1995, p. A1.

Angus

Box Office Gross: $4,821,759

In the tradition of Brian DePalma's 1976 thriller *Carrie, Angus* relates the story of a high school misfit, taunted by the never-ending throng of jocks, cheerleaders and other nearly perfect teens. And like the tormented Carrie White, Angus Bethune (Charlie Talbert) is elected king of the Freshman Winter Ball as a prank by the "in" crowd. Thankfully, *Angus* does not end in a fiery fit of bloodshed, but instead the bulky hero learns that being normal is not about being the most popular kid in school, but about being yourself.

So is the story of gawky Angus, the overweight, yet good-natured and intelligent teen, who just can't seem to fit in to the only place that matters to most teens—high school. To top things off, he has an ongoing riff with golden boy and star quarterback Rick Sanford (James Van Der Beek), who gets his self-esteem by humiliating Angus through heartless gags, like sending his boxers up the flagpole. Angus is a misfit in the land of cool kids. He's built like a wall and plays football like a champ, but he's an offensive lineman and, therefore, gets no credit when he makes the play which leads to the winning touchdown. Instead, Angus watches as Rick is carried away on the shoulders of his teammates and he is all but trampled in the celebration.

And the rivalry didn't stem from there. It dates back to their childhood, where Angus was picked on as a chubby tyke. And his reaction through the years was to use his one weapon—his strength—and pop Rick square in the nose. The rotund youth was constantly hearing his playmates echo, "Angus, I think you broke his nose!" Also, dating back to more tender years is Angus' unrequited love for Melissa LeFevre (Arianna Richards), a pretty, vivacious cheerleader, who Angus can't quite get the courage to speak to and who also happens to be Rick's girlfriend.

And of course, what story would be complete without a trusty sidekick? Angus has one of those, too, in the form of geeky, big-eared, gross-out master Troy (Chris Owen). The two spend their days being ruthlessly picked on by bad boy Rick and his jock cronies. But Angus has a plan to ditch the life of trying to fit the "normal" mold and applies to an advanced placement school, where with his knack for science, he would simply gel with the other students and not stick out anymore. Angus' doting mother Meg (Kathy Bates) cheers on this endeavor, picturing herself when she was her son's age and wishing him to be spared of the taunting of his peers. His cantankerous grandfather Ivan (George C. Scott) has other feelings on the subject. His motto is "screw 'em, it doesn't matter what other people think."

While Angus is working his way through the day-to-day tyranny of high school, Rick has noticed Angus' crush on his girlfriend and as an ultimate joke, rigs the votes to make Angus the unlikely king for Melissa's queen at the dance. Prank or not, Angus begins to prepare for the moment he's always dreamed of—to be close to Melissa LeFevre. Meanwhile, he is feverishly trying to complete his science project for admittance to the academic school. With some dancing lessons from Madame Rulenska (Rita Moreno) and coaching from grandpa Ivan, Angus counts down the days to the magical meeting. Troy joins in to lend a hand by trying to transform Angus from a "large, pathetic virgin, to a large, pathetic virgin with a new look." He supplies an inflatable doll for Angus to perfect his dance technique and videotapes the training as athletes do to review mistakes and improve.

Rick gets wind that Angus is going to go through with it and actually try to be a hit at the ball. He gets a little worried and needs some extra ammo against his nemesis. Rick and his friends force Troy to betray Angus by turning over the video of the dance lessons.

When the day of the dance finally arrives, it clashes with Angus' interview with the school admissions officer, who appears just as Angus is exiting in a plum-colored tuxedo (the only one that fit). Angus, determined to make a showing at the dance, hastily explains his science project—"The Bethune Theory." The theory holds that within every normal system there exists aberrations or differences and that if an aberration is strong enough to survive the forces against it, the system itself will be forced to change and adapt. Reflecting the theory on himself, he concludes there is no such thing as "normal" since differences change affect a system in such a way.

He arrives at the dance in time and finds that Melissa is just as nervous as he is. And when Rick breaks out his secret weapon, the videotape, Angus is given his own ammunition to fight back and give an inspiring speech rallying his classmates against Rick in *Revenge of The Nerds* (1984) style. In the end, Angus overcomes the taunting of the "in" crowd and finds that at least one of that crowd is not so different from himself.

The role of Angus was deftly managed by newcomer Talbert, who was discovered in line at a Wendy's restaurant. Though the movie is stacked high with cliches and concepts lifted from other films (mostly every other teen angst film out there), Talbert portrayed the hefty hero with the right balance of insecurity mixed with a will to fit in to pull the concept off yet again.

Playing out alongside the main plot is the side story of grandpa Ivan, a man pushing his early 70s who has managed to capture the heart of a woman 30 years younger between his frequent spells of napping. Though the subplot is hardly believable (the two are about to be joined in holy matrimony), it acts as an impetus for Angus to do whatever he can to get the girl of his dreams regardless of what others say, namely mother Meg, who doesn't want to see either her son or her father hurt.

Academy-Award winners Bates, Scott, and Moreno add warmth to the rather lukewarm story, functioning as a multi-generational support group for Angus, giving him the benefit of wisdom from those who have already experienced similar perils. Likewise, sidekick Troy, played by Chris Owen, gives his own warped, yet loyal support to his best

CREDITS

Ivan: George C. Scott
Madame Rulenska: Rita Moreno
Troy Wedberg: Chris Owen
Angus: Charlie Talbert
Principal Metcalf: Lawrence Pressman
Melissa Lefevre: Ariana Richards
Meg: Kathy Bates
April Thomas: Anna Thompson
Rick Sanford: James Van Der Beek

Origin: USA
Released: 1995
Production: Dawn Steel and Charles Roven for Turner Pictures and Atlas Entertainment; released by New Line Cinema
Direction: Patrick Read Johnson
Screenplay: Jill Gordon; based on a short story by Chris Crutcher
Cinematography: Alexander Grusynski
Editing: Janice Hampton
Production design: Larry Miller
Music: David Russo
MPAA rating: PG-13
Running Time: 91 minutes

friend and Arianna Richards from *Jurassic Park* (1993) plays a lovable teen queen with very typical teen flaws herself. (Melissa is bulimic.)

This movie will likely not appeal to most adults, but some who appreciate the sentimental view of youth may want to give it a look. Cinematographer Alexander Grusynski beautifully handles the photography, capturing the warm fall feel of the outdoor shots and the equally warm feel of the shots including the elder cast members, while keeping in line with the hipness of the high school scenery. Teens will be drawn to the ultra-cool soundtrack featuring music by groups like Green Day, Weezer, and the Goo Goo Dolls, as well as the typical funny teen scenes, which are a staple of most teen flicks.

However, good photography and music can not save *Angus*. The plot drags, the story is getting old, and the vulgar language of these teens takes away from the wholesomeness of the lesson to be learned. Though *Angus* doesn't shine and stand out as other teen angst films, and it may never have a cult following like John Hughes' popular films (*Sixteen Candles* (1984) and *Pretty in Pink* (1986)), it is a nice little movie with a nice little message about feeling happy with who you are.

—Devra Sladics

Apollo 13

"Houston, we have a problem."—Movie tagline

"Magnificent! A gripping, awesome journey that blasts you into an orbit of incredible adventure and suspense."—Bill Diehl, *ABC Radio Network*

"Riveting."—Roger Ebert, *Chicago Sun Times*

"Magnificent."—Susan Stark, *The Detroit News*

"Thrilling."—Michael Medved, *New York Post*

"Exhilarating."—Jack Mathews, *Newsday*

"A triumph."—Desmond Ryan, *Philadelphia Inquirer*

Box Office Gross: $172,071,312

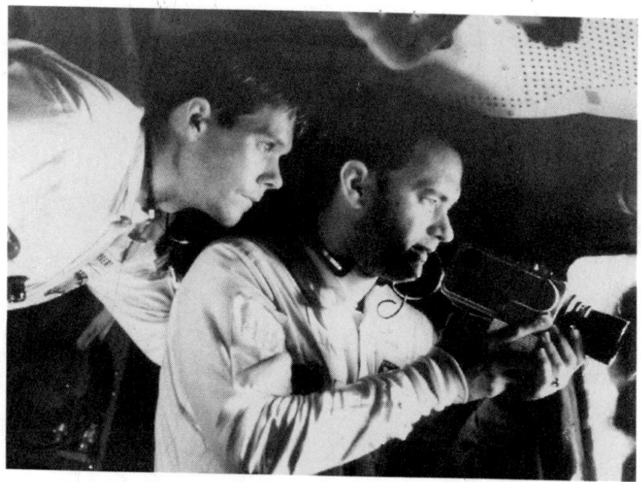

Kevin Bacon and Tom Hanks star as part of the crew of an ill-fated lunar mission in *Apollo 13*. © 1995 Universal City Studios, Inc. Courtesy of MCA Publishing Rights, a Division of MCA Inc. All rights reserved.

By 1970, spaceflight was old hat to Americans. Just the year before, Neil Armstrong became the first man to walk on the moon in Apollo 11, and Apollo 12 had repeated the feat. By Apollo 13, the third of seven attempts to land men on the moon, it had all been done before. Televised blast offs seemed like nothing more than summer reruns. So, when astronauts Jim Lovell (Tom Hanks), Fred Haise (Bill Paxton), and Jack Swigert (Kevin Bacon) put on a NASA PR broadcast from their spacecraft, regular prime-time programming was not preempted.

But, all of that would change when Lovell uttered five chilling words, "Houston, we have a problem." The routine procedure of stirring their oxygen tanks caused an explosion in the service module. As a result, their computer and guidance systems are off-line, they're losing electrical power and have lost their main engines, and their precious oxygen is venting into space. As Fred Haise succinctly states the problem, "the ship's bleeding to death." Now the term space race means quickly finding ways to bring these three men home alive.

For four days the world waited and watched as mission control in Houston tried to fix the myriad of problems facing the now aborted moon mission. Then it is learned that the astronauts have only fifteen minutes of oxygen left in the command module Odyssey; they must shut it down and move into the LEM (lunar exploration module), because, as flight director Gene Kranz notes, "the lunar module just became a lifeboat." With its separate engines and power, Aquarius, seems a logical choice, but there's one problem: it was designed to hold only two men for forty-five hours, not three men for the ninety it will take to get them back to earth.

If this story were made from whole-cloth fiction, audiences would never believe it. However, because it is all true, it becomes a riveting drama. And to director Ron Howard's credit, he doesn't try to improve on reality—because reality, here, is breathtakingly cinematic enough on its own.

"Houston, we have a problem."—Astronaut Jim Lovell to Mission Control from *Apollo 13*

With each locking click of the space helmets, each push of a space suit button, every clanging thud of the hatch lock, and the rumbling roar of the rocket engines, tension and claustrophobia build. In this triumph of film construction, our identification with the principle characters is so high that we really worry that they might suffocate to death from a lack of oxygen or from the buildup of their own carbon dioxide; that they might freeze to death from a lack of power to heat the capsule; or that they might be unable to correct their trajectory and skip off into space forever or burn up on re-entry.

Also in keeping with its commitment to the real event, unlike most Hollywood epics, *Apollo 13* does not bend the truth in order to make the story yet another one-man-saves-the-day star vehicle. This is the story of old-fashioned teamwork. And considering that one of the stars is Tom Hanks, who is coming off back-to-back best acting Oscars, (for *Philadelphia* and *Forrest Gump*) in less capable hands this easily could have become just another superstar film. Director Howard, however, wisely reflects the ensemble effort behind history in the making.

Although he is not the centerpiece of the film, Hanks once again turns in an impressive and solid performance proving himself to be a Mr. Everyman for this decade. But just as bringing the Apollo 13 home was a team effort, so is this movie. Despite his stardom, Hanks probably has no more closeups than do most of the other major stars.

And the cast Howard has assembled is a superior one. Gary Sinise's very human portrayal of Ken Mattingly shows a man who was snatched from the glory of the Apollo 13 mission because of exposure to the measles and sent into an alcoholic depression. But when his knowledge and perfectionist ways are desperately needed to simulate the activities on the spacecraft, he performs dependably as the intermediary on earth.

Kathleen Quinlan as Marilyn Lovell is also a standout in the cinematically difficult role of trying to show extreme

CREDITS

Jim Lovell: Tom Hanks
Fred Haise: Bill Paxton
Jack Swigert: Kevin Bacon
Gene Kranz: Ed Harris
Ken Mattingly: Gary Sinise
Marilyn Lovell: Kathleen Quinlan
NASA director: Joe Spano
Pete Conrad: David Andrews
Henry Hurt: Xander Berkeley
Dr. Chuck: Christian Clemenson
CAPCOM: Brett Cullen
John Arthur: Loren Dean
ECOM White: Clint Howard
John Young: Ben Marley
Glynn Lunney: Marc McClure
Mary Haise: Tracy Reiner

Origin: USA
Released: 1995
Production: Brian Grazer for an Imagine Entertainment production; released by Universal Pictures
Direction: Ron Howard
Screenplay: William Broyles Jr. and Al Reinert; based on the book *Lost Moon* by Jim Lovell
Cinematography: Dean Cundey
Editing: Mike Hill and Dan Hanley
Production design: Michael Corenblith
Art direction: David J. Bomba and Bruce Alan Miller
Set decoration: Merideth Boswell
Costume design: Rita Ryack
Music: James Horner
Casting: Jane Jenkins, Janet Hirshenson
Technical Consultants: Jim Lovell, Jeffrey Kluger, Dave Scott, Jerry Bostick, Gerald Griffin and Max L. Ary
MPAA rating: PG
Running Time: 140 minutes

AWARDS AND NOMINATIONS

Academy Awards 1995: Best Film Editing, Best Sound
Nominations: Best Picture, Best Supporting Actor (Harris), Best Supporting Actress (Quinlan), Best Score (Horner), Best Adapted Screenplay (Reinert/Broyles, Jr.), Best Art Direction
Blockbuster Entertainment Awards 1996: Drama Actor-Theatrical (Hanks)
Chicago Film Critics Awards 1995: Best Film
Directors Guild Award 1995: Best Director (Howard)
Screen Actors Guild Awards 1995: Best Cast
British Academy Awards Nominations 1995: Best Cinematography (Cundey)
Golden Globe Awards Nominations 1996: Best Film-Drama, Best Director (Howard), Best Supporting Actor (Harris), Best Supporting Actress (Quinlan)
Writers Guild Awards Nomination 1995: Best Adapted Screenplay (Reinert/Broyles, Jr.)

emotion while doing not much of anything but waiting and either staring at a television set or off into space. Our hearts break as she tells their son that "Something's broke on your Daddy's spaceship," and we cheer when she angrily addresses the media's role in this whole event with "If landing on the moon wasn't dramatic enough for them, why should not landing?"

(It is suspected that one part of the film's great authenticity is due to the fact that it is based on Jim Lovell's own book and that screenwriter Al Reinert was also the director of the acclaimed and Oscar-nominated space documentary *For All Mankind.* But the film's humanness probably comes from an uncredited rewrite by writer/director/actor John Sayles.)

To become acclimated to a space-life environment, Hanks, Paxton, Bacon, Sinise and Howard went to NASA's Space Camp in Huntsville, Alabama. After completing training exercises inside a simulated command module and lunar module, the group moved on to Houston, the home of Mission Control and the Johnson Space Center.

Another solid anchor in the drama is Ed Harris' chain-smoking Gene Kranz. He is stable, efficient, capable, and emits the unquestionable air of authority that is needed to keep Houston's mission control focused on solving the life-or-death predicament before them. "Let's work on the problem and not make things worse by guessing," says Harris' no-nonsense Kranz.

Through Harris' Kranz and others populating mission control (including Howard's brother Clint as ECOM White), director Howard makes the drama in Houston as effective as the drama in space. "We're improvising a new mission," Kranz says, "How do we get them home?" And when he says, "failure is not an option," we know it's not! Watching mission control solve difficult mathematical problems with nothing more than a slide rule, and discovering with them how to run the spaceship off sixteen amps (about what it takes to run the average vacuum cleaner), we are imbued with that old American "can-do" attitude that finds a way to fit a square CO2 filter into a round hole, with seemingly nothing more than a sock and a bit of duct tape. As a result of their efforts, the mission that everyone, including NASA, categorized as a failure is captured as a triumph of teamwork.

Just as a note, there are three other "actors" of interest to film buffs in *Apollo 13.* Ron Howard's own mother plays Jim Lovell's mother who innocently asks Neil Armstrong and Buzz Aldrin if they are in the space program, but then knowingly turns around and reassures her granddaughter with, "If they could get a washing machine to fly, my Jimmy could land it."

The second cameo belongs to director Roger Corman who plays the Congressman who hints that the space program could lose its funding. As the director who gave "Opie" his first chance at directing with 1977's *Grand Theft Auto,* he must be proud of how far yet another of his illustrious alumni has come. Finally, watch for the scene aboard the ship Iwo Jima which plucks the Apollo 13 crew from the Pacific Ocean. The briefly-viewed commander who greets the returning astronauts is played by Jim Lovell himself.

The fact that audiences are so willing to accept the suspense in a story to which they already know the ending is due not only to great acting and the fact that Ron Howard didn't replace the real heroism of the story with typical Hollywood bravado, but also to the many things he did to lend authenticity to the film.

For example, the actors went to NASA space camp in Huntsville, Alabama and filming was done in sequence as much as possible (which is harder for the director, but gives a heavy dose of realism to the actors' fatigue—especially after they went through more than three weeks filming at thirty-eight degrees in a cramped mock space capsule on Universal Studios Stage 34). But Howard didn't stop there. Knowing even special effects couldn't accurately depict weightlessness, he decided to shoot many of the space capsule scenes on a mockup aboard the NASA KC-135 jet known as the "Vomit Comet." Travelling on a parabolic trajectory, the plane's sudden dive earthward produces weightlessness...but only for twenty-three seconds at a time. Sometimes Howard had his cast and crew making as many as seventy-eight trips a day in order to capture the authenticity needed for a scene.

This is not to say Howard made the film with no special effects. In fact, what he did do without was any stock footage from NASA. Scenes like the incredible, visually-stunning liftoff are compliments of James Cameron's Digital Domain which provided the special effects, not NASA.

As if all this were not enough to make for a great film, there is the added element of James Horner's extraordinarily rousing music, the enhanced realism provided by Dean Cundey's cinematography, and some very sharp editing that creates tension in all the three main arenas of drama (the

REVIEWS

Chicago Sun Times. June 30, 1995, p. W17.
Chicago Tribune. June 30, 1995, p. 7B and 7C.
Entertainment Weekly. June 30, 1995, p. 78.
The New York Times. June 30, 1995, p. B1.
New Yorker. July 10, 1995, p. 79.
Newsweek. July 3, 1995, p. 55.
Rolling Stone. July 13-27, 1995, p. 116.
Time. July 3, 1995, p. 50.
USA Today. June 30, 1995, p. D1.
Variety. June 26, 1995, p. 78.
The Village Voice. July 4, 1995, p. 54.
The Wall Street Journal. June 30, 1995, p. A14.

crippled spaceship, mission control, and the waiting families). The result is a film that is emotionally satisfying and refreshingly honest, informative but not technically overwhelming, and thoroughly engrossing and exciting.

Apollo 13 may be the closest of all films to the real astronaut experience, and audiences were lining up to see it within its first week. "I believe this is going to be our finest hour," Kranz explains to the NASA director. Ron Howard's eloquent depiction of genuine heroes is a welcome reminder of an institution which has provided America with many of its finest hours.

—*Beverley Bare Buehrer*

Arabian Knight

"Nearly 30 years in the making, *Arabian Knight* dazzles."—Michael Wilmington, *Chicago Tribune*

"The liveliest, most satisfying animated film of the year."—Caryn James, *The New York Times*

Box Office Gross: $669,276

If crazed beatnik animators had attempted to satirize Disney's *Aladdin*, they might have made *Arabian Knight*, a mind-altering children's fable with visual and verbal treats for adults. *Arabian Knight* has more wild inventiveness and spectacular visual mosaics that any of the modern Disney mega-hits.

Unfortunately, *Arabian Knight* is a casualty of the commercial film business. It's been patched up, betrayed, pieced together and trotted out as what appears at first glance to be a minor *Aladdin* rip-off. But only at first glance. In fact, animator Richard Williams (who did *Who Killed Roger Rabbit?*) began this ambitious film about a princess, a cobbler, a villain and a thief in 1968, before *Aladdin* was even a gleam in Disney's eye. But Williams never found the wherewithal to complete it. It was supposed to premiere in 1993 under the title *The Thief and The Cobbler* but then was held hostage for financial reasons. Miramax rescued it and revamped it, adding some new sequences, several lamentably bad songs, new voices for some major characters (Matthew Broderick as the Cobbler, Jennifer Beals as the princes, and Jonathan Winters as the thief), and the unappealing new title.

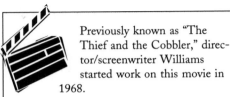

Previously known as "The Thief and the Cobbler," director/screenwriter Williams started work on this movie in 1968.

The bad news is that this reworking gives *Arabian Knight*, in many spots, the feel of a belated attempt at second-rate imitation of Disney. As an example, there's the de rigueur effort to make the impossibly thin, Barbie-like Princess Yum Yum into a frustrated feminist. In a sappy song, Yum Yum complains with these laughable lyrics: "She is more than this/ There's a mind in the body of this pretty miss . . . Outwardly, she's free/ Inwardly, she's bound/ Given half a chance/ She might prove profound." There are several such profoundly silly moments that clash miserably with the film's overall feel.

The good news is that the sprucing up still leaves intact enough of its antic, nearly subversive nature to make *Arabian Knight* a must-see for anyone interested in original animation. Though at first they seem flat and static, the visuals soon become disarming. Drawn without computer assistance, the cartoon sets for King Nod's realm (sometimes called the Golden City and sometimes Baghdad) are splendid labyrinths of mosaics, drawing for inspiration on the visual trickery of M.C. Escher. In a sequence where the cobbler is chasing the thief through the palace, there are two identical-looking tile patterns; one proves to be a flat surface and the other a well. These kind of surprises keep the visual landscape continually fascinating.

Opposing the Disney-led trend to give animation more depth and realism, the animators of *Arabian Knight* explore the outer limits of caricature and hyperbole. The characters move through a world of dramatically changing perspectives and the animators exploit all the possibilities of their craft. Much of this is more akin to the exaggerated Japanese style of animation than to what American audiences are used to seeing, and many viewers might not digest the images easily.

Unfortunately, the story line and the characters are somewhat stilted and shallow. Yum Yum, as noted, is an implausible mix of exaggerated femininity and assertiveness.

CREDITS

Zigzag: Vincent Price
Tack: Matthew Broderick
Princess Yum Yum: Jennifer Beals
Phido: Eric Bogosian
Nurse/Good Witch: Toni Collette
The Thief: Jonathan Winters
Singing voice of Princess Yum Yum: Bobbi Page
King Nod: Clive Revill
One-Eye: Kevin Dorsey

Origin: USA
Released: 1995
Production: Imogen Sutton and Richard Williams for an Allied Filmmakers presentation; released by Miramax Films
Direction: Richard Williams
Screenplay: Richard Williams, Margaret French, Parker Bennet, Terry Runte, Bette L. Smith, Tom Towler and Stephen Zito
Cinematography: John Leatherbarrow
Editing: Peter Bond
Master animation: Ken Harris
Music: Robert Folk
Songs: Robert Folk
MPAA rating: G
Running Time: 72 minutes

Tack, the cobbler hero, is portrayed as a rag doll and is nearly a cipher. Zigzag (the late Vincent Price) is an unctuous villain who speaks in rhyme but looks more silly than sinister. One-Eye (Kevin Dorsey) makes a rather clunky monster.

Winters' hapless thief carries the film with his implausible acrobatic feats. Flies buzz around his head and he narrates his exploits in a dry, self-deprecating way. Here the sly verbal and visual style converge into a comic gem of a character. Also wonderful is a sequence where Yum-Yum and Tack meet up with a band of desert brigands, great clumsy clods who sing a crazy ditty with the refrain: "We're what happens when you don't finish school." It's hilarious.

There is much that needs to be overlooked, but *Arabian Knight* could become a minor cult classic on video. There's so much going on in the dizzying animation and so many subtle throwaway lines that it merits repeated viewings. It's just too bad that Williams was never able to carry his original vision to completion. But even unfinished, touched-up masterpieces are worth a look.

—Michael Betzold

REVIEWS

The New York Times. August 26, 1995, p. 11.
Variety. August 28, 1995, p. 65.

A Reason to Believe

Charlotte Byrne (Allison Smith) attends a college party, gets drunk and passes out in a bedroom. Jim (Jay Underwood), a friend of Charlotte's boyfriend, sneaks into the room and takes advantage of defenseless Charlotte. When Charlotte finally realizes that she has been raped, she finds it very hard to convince her friends and boyfriend that she was a victim of date rape.

CREDITS

Charlotte Byrne: Allison Smith
Jim Current: Jay Underwood
Wesley Grant: Danny Quinn
Linda Berryman: Georgia Elmelin
Professor Thurman: Obba Babatunde

Origin: USA
Released: 1995
Production: Ged Dickersin and Douglas Tirola for a Pioneer Pictures; released by Castle Hill Productions;
Direction: Douglas Tirola
Screenplay: Douglas Tirola
Cinematography: Sarah Cawley
Editing: Sabine Hoffman
Production design: Carol O'Neil
Casting: Laura Adler
MPAA rating: R
Running Time: 109 minutes

Assassins

Box Office Gross: $29,339,122

In *Assassins* Sylvester Stallone does what Sylvester Stallone does best in the sort of film he helped to develop into a genre, only now he is playing a killer rather than a cop. Stallone again steps into the action-adventure arena, this time as a paid killer who decides it may be time to retire before someone "retires" him. Every time Robert Rath (Stallone) gets a contract, he finds another assassin beating him to the mark. The device that drives the plot is borrowed from the Western. Stallone's character is the best hired gun around, but there is a younger killer who wants to be "Number One." The challenger is Miguel Bain (Antonio Banderas), a hispanic hothead who is also a cold-blooded killer.

The film, written by Andy Wachowski, Larry Wachowski, and Brian Helgeland and directed by Richard Donner, begins with Rath marching a victim into a swamp. A mark of his compassion is that he allows the victim to commit suicide. But on his next assignment he is supposed to murder a mobster at a graveside funeral. Miguel, posing as a gravetender, hits the target first. He is apprehended, cuffed, and loaded into a police car. But, unlikely as this may seem, he somehow manages to escape, with Rath in hot pursuit.

Rath commandeers a taxi and just happens to be there to pick up Miguel after Miguel escapes from the wrecked police car. The two have a Mexican stand-off, since Miguel cannot shoot Rath through the cab's bulletproof shield, so Rath knows who the kid is. Miguel manages to escape from the taxi, proving that he is an adversary to be taken seriously.

The next assignment involves four Dutch hoodlums who are buying information on a stolen computer disk, the film's Macguffin. They meet at a hotel and are to buy the disk from a computer thief named Electra (Julianne Moore). Rath's instructions are to recover the disk and to take out the Dutchmen and the girl, but Miguel gets to the Dutch thugs first, and Rath decides to let the Electra live, not merely out of compassion but because he plans to use her disk to lure Miguel. Someone is willing to pay a lot of money for the information on that disk, information that is never quite explained or disclosed.

Rath, Electra, and Miguel finally end up in Puerto Rico for the exchange, which is to take place at a bank. Miguel sets up on the top story of a building opposite the bank to kill Rath as he comes out after the exchange. Rath anticipates the hit. He knows the territory, since he had begun his career as an assassin at that very same place, hitting a Russian assassin, Nicolai (Anatoly Davydov), who had been considered the best in the business and was Rath's friend. He also knows that Miguel knows his history. Miguel has researched the man whose reputation he intends to eclipse.

Rath knows what to expect from Miguel, and so does the audience, which has seen the black-and-white flashback memory of Rath's hit on Nicolai. He has patience on his side, and a lifetime of experience. He also has Electra as a sidekick, since her life is also in jeopardy, and she also wants her share of the money that is being exchanged. The problem is that Miguel is a wildcard, and the ending is not exactly predictable, despite the inevitability of a final showdown.

The framing device here is a high-tech computerized version of Murder, Incorporated, with a touch of "Mission Impossible." Rath takes his instructions by computer and fax, as does Miguel. It soon becomes apparent that Miguel and Rath are getting their instructions from the same source, and that source is playing one assassin against the other. The identity of this mystery criminal is revealed in the final

CREDITS

Robert Rath: Sylvester Stallone
Miguel Bain: Antonio Banderas
Electra: Julianne Moore
Nicolai: Anatoly Davydov

Origin: USA
Released: 1995
Production: Richard Donner, Joel Silver, Bruce Evans, Raynold Gideon, Andrew Lazar, and Jim Van Wyck for a Silver Pictures and Donner/Shuler-Donner production; released by Warner Brothers
Direction: Richard Donner
Screenplay: Andy Wachowski, Larry Wachowski and Brian Helgeland
Cinematography: Vilmos Zsigmond
Editing: Richard Marks
Production design: Tom Sanders
Art direction: Nathan Crowley
Set design: Alan Manzer, Gilbert Wong, Chad Griffin and Noelle King
Set decoration: Lisa Dean
Costume design: Elizabeth McBride
Sound: Petur Hliddal
Music: Mark Mancina
MPAA rating: R
Running Time: 132 minutes

shoot-out between Miguel and Rath. After two shootings and three chase sequences, the final shoot-out is inevitable.

As Nick James pointed out in *Sight and Sound*, the film begins with a noir flashback and ends up paying tribute to John Frankenheimer's *The Manchurian Candidate* (1962), but it never delivers "a genuine sense of noir fatalism," and the characters of this "nonsensical triangle" are oddly isolated from the world at large.

This film reunited award-winning cinematographer Vilmos Zsigmond with director Richard Donner, with whom he worked on *Maverick*.

The picture, of course, is ridiculously far-fetched, but Richard Donner keeps the pace moving so rapidly that no one is likely to notice. Donner proved his skills as an action- adventure director with *Lethal Weapon* (1987) and its sequels, both of which earned over $100 million. In typical Donner style, *Assassins* is paced like a thoroughbred running for the money.

Critics were quick to notice that the Antonio Banderas character shares some of the inspired manic looniness that defined the Mel Gibson character in the *Lethal Weapon* trilogy. The actor's sheer energy and unpredictable character make the film fun to watch.

Earlier in 1995 Banderas had also starred as a vengeful killer in *Desperado*, a film that took gunfighting over the edge of parody while imitating the ultra-violent style of John Woo. Though his performance here is toned down from his hyperactive gunslinger in *Desperado*, Banderas is a bundle of nerves in both films. In *Assassins* this is balanced against the subdued and almost listless performance of Stallone. Banderas is pushy and daring, unpredictable and dangerous, and his highly animated character is nicely balanced against the stoic and laconic Stallone, whose character is cautious and methodical to the point of being mechanical and robotic. Richard Donner's direction sets a rapid pace driven by the energy of Banderas.

Banderas made his American film debut in *The Mambo Kings* (1992), playing Cuban musician and composer Nestor Castillo. He played opposite Tom Hanks in *Philadelphia* (1993) and opposite Tom Cruise and Brad Pitt in *Interview With a Vampire* (1994). Before coming to America he had starred in five feature films directed by Pedro Almodovar, including *Woman on the Verge of a Nervous Breakdown* (1988). Banderas has appeared in over thirty Spanish films, and has made a total of 43 films.

Julianne Moore starred opposite Hugh Grant in *Nine Months* (1995) and opposite Wallace Shawn in Louis Malle's *Vanya on 42nd Street* (1994). Her role an eccentric hacker cyberthief in *Assassins* could not have been much of a stretch for this accomplished stage actress. She is as much a loner as Stallone's Rath, so at least they have something in common besides greed. But there is not much chance for romance here. Electra seems to prefer cats to people and seems also to avoid men.

Stallone's character is a survivor who is tired of his work. Rath is not especially sexy in this picture. He works with Electra, but no torrid romance develops, though one senses that she does grow fond of him. The two of them are governed more by greed than by lust. They are only lusting for a huge payoff. Stallone seems almost humane by the end of the picture, though he is still a pretty cold fish. There is not much of a soul in his hardbody this time around.

Even so, it is hard to forget that he is a cold-blooded killer and his profession has isolated him from ordinary humanity. If he really intends to retire, well, maybe that will change him. Stallone's acting, such as it is, does not preclude the possibility. In a way Stallone is doing a brave thing here: he is acting his age, with a certain amount of dignity, if not wit. How many more years the actor has left for this kind of role remains to be seen, but he is not yet over the hill, as this picture proves.

Assassins made under $10 million during its opening weekend, —about half of Stallone's salary—but his last two pictures, *Judge Dredd* and *The Specialist* also slumped at the box office. In general the critics were kinder to *Assassins*. But even without breaking records domestically, Stallone's pictures always do better in foreign markets. The star is still bankable, in other words.

Stallone, of course, is playing the sort of role with which he is most comfortable, but his character could be more appealing and less robotic. The one advantage of the character is that he is laconic, and the less the typical Stallone hero has to say, the better. The film offers maximum bodycount and minimum dialogue, and, for Stallone, that's the way it should be.

—James M. Welsh

REVIEWS

The Baltimore Sun. October 6, 1995, F5.
Entertainment Weekly. No.296. October 13, 1995, p.42.
The New York Times. October 6, 1995, C3.
Sight and Sound. Vol.5, No.12, NS. December 1995, p.39.
USA Today. October 6, 1995, D4.
Variety. October 2-8, 1995, p.39.
The Washington Post. October 6, 1995, B7.
The Washington Times Metropolitan Times. October 6, 1995, C17.

An Awfully Big Adventure

"A revealing comedy about what really goes on when the lights go down."—Movie tagline

"Hugh Grant is brilliant!"—Elizabeth Pincus, *Harper's Bazaar*

"This is Mike Newell's finest film!"—Graham Fuller, *Interview*

Box Office Gross: $258,195

Mike Newell's *An Awfully Big Adventure* paints a rich, dark portrait of Stella, an orphaned teenage girl, and her entry into the world of theater in post-World-War-II England. Newell shows how Stella's desperate need to believe in the magic of footlights and greasepaint at once saves her from the dreariness of post-War Liverpool, yet in the end keeps her a prisoner of illusion. *An Awfully Big Adventure* ambitiously attempts to show not only Stella's coming-of-age, but also the hereditary and environmental reasons for her being drawn into the world of fantasy the theater provides. The film flounders, however, in its failing to foreshadow Stella's parentage as the film's central issue. When the film takes a dark, incestuous turn seven-eighths of the way through, audiences are likely to be confused. As a result of this structural flaw, *An Awfully Big Adventure* falls short of its clearly lofty ambitions.

Based on the novel of the same name by Beryl Bainbridge, the film takes its title from J. M. Barrie's theatrical version of *Peter Pan*, performed by the acting troupe in the film and used as counterpoint to the story throughout. Peter, the eternal boy, remarks that death must be "an awfully big adventure." Although the film begins on that note of childlike whimsy, Newell ultimately pursues the line's underlying darkness to its full depths.

The film opens with a confusing montage of a ten-year-old girl shaking in an air-raid shelter in 1941 and a baby surrounded by candles. Although later it becomes clear that the baby is the same girl in infancy, it initially appears that the baby is frightened by the air raid.

The story proper begins shortly after the war. Stella (Georgina Cates) is 16 and stagestruck, obsessed with play-acting, theater, and fantasy. Her guardian, Uncle Vern (Alun Armstrong), cautions against her pipe-dreams and warns her that she will be "lucky to end up behind the counter in Woolworth's." Yet Stella's fantasy world is impregnable: Vern and her Aunt Lily (Rita Tushingham) overhear Stella spending hours at nights acting on the telephone—pretending to communicate with her long-lost mother, Renee. Stella also remains haunted by the memory of being left alone in the dark as a baby surrounded by candles.

Persistent, Stella wangles an interview with the director of a local repertory company, the foppish, monocled Meredith Potter (Hugh Grant), and gets a menial job as an assistant stage manager. In spite of Potter's obvious cruelty to his devoted stage manager, Bunny (Peter Firth), as well as his pining for an offscreen lover ambiguously named Hilary, Stella immediately falls in love with Potter.

Potter is a decidedly inappropriate target for Stella's burgeoning passions, but his very coldness and emotional inaccessibility attract her. A cruel, callous petty tyrant, Potter runs the company with sadistic glee. "You're all the very best people we could find," he tells the actors on the first day of rehearsals, blowing them a kiss. "The length and breadth of the profession. For the money." Stella, blindly infatuated and jealous of Potter's attachment to the absent

CREDITS

Stella: Georgina Cates
Meredith Potter: Hugh Grant
P.L. O'Hara: Alan Rickman
Uncle Vernon: Alun Armstrong
Bunny: Peter Firth
Rose: Prunella Scales
Aunt Lily: Rita Tushingham
Geoffrey: Alan Cox

Origin: England
Released: 1995
Production: Hilary Heath and Philip Hinchcliffe for Portman Productions with the participation of British Screen in association with BBC Films and Wolfhound Films; released by Fine Line Features and 20th Century Fox
Direction: Mike Newell
Screenplay: Charles Wood; based on a novel by Beryl Bainbridge
Cinematography: Dick Pope
Editing: Jon Gregory
Production design: Mark Geraghty
Costume design: Joan Bergin
Casting: Susie Figgis
Sound: Peter Sutton
Make-up/Hair design: Ann Buchanan
Stunt coordination: Martin Grace
Music: Richard Hartley
MPAA rating: R
Running Time: 112 minutes

Hilary, makes her first priority to alter an affectionate telegram Potter has sent to Hilary, in effect rejecting Potter's lover.

Stella likewise sees the rest of the company through rose-colored glasses, even though they are mostly actors so vain or emotionally stunted that none of them can stand up to Potter's bullying. Stella witnesses a drunk and pathetic former leading lady (Carol Drinkwater) raging against the dying of the limelight, and ultimately having a breakdown. Another actress (Nicola Pagett) nurses a hopeless passion for aging matinee idol Richard St. Ives (Edward Petherbridge). Stella is befriended by George (Gerard McSorley), the set designer, but resented by Geoffrey (Alan Cox), her fellow assistant stage manager, who makes a pass at her. She fails to realize that Geoffrey, briefly seduced by Meredith, has been rejected by Potter in favor of juvenile lead John Harbour (James Frain), and that Geoffrey's approaching her is a payback. A critic (Robbie Doolin) has her masturbate him in a dark theater in exchange for putting her picture in the paper and giving her a favorable mention in his review of the play. The kind, world-weary company manager, Rose (Prunella Scales), patches her up after this incident. But even this disgusting episode fails to remove the blinders from Stella's eyes.

Georgina Cates fooled the filmmakers into believing that she, like her character Stella, was an ambitious newcomer. Actually, she was a trained actress who already had a career under the name Clare Woodgate.

At home, her gruff but affectionate Uncle Vern views her starstruck awe with concern. "What do you know about life," he asks her, "how it can bowl you over, bowl you over?" Vern apologizes for his outburst, but afterwards he and Lily overhear Stella carrying on her ongoing imaginary telephone conversation with her mother. Pretending, they realize, is all she knows.

Potter's interpretations of plays reflect his own grim view of the world. When Stella tells him she thinks a play is about two people in love, Potter tells her he disagrees, and gives a convoluted interpretation of his own: instead, he says, it is about a funeral procession. Some of the mourners have fallen behind, so their relations with the loved one are "suspended." So, too, he says, are their relationships with those they think they love, who are behind corners, waiting to be caught up with. Potter's pseudo-intellectual pretensions intrigue her even further. Yet Stella remains oblivious to Potter's cruelty and his increasingly obvious homosexuality. Although each member of the company lives to see his own particular illusion shattered, Stella maintains a kind of denial that saves as well as imprisons her. Stella remains lost in a kind of blind aplomb, the aplomb she feigns in the upper-crust accent she uses in her breathless imaginary conversations with her mother. Even when Potter, slumped in a chair, drunk, and drooling vomit, greets the company with abuse as they arrive for morning rehearsals, Stella still sees him as brilliant and misunderstood. Meanwhile, Bunny, ever-protective of Potter, intercepts and burns a despairing, suicidal telegram for him from Hilary, sent in response to the telegram Stella has altered.

When Stella inadvertently causes St. Ives, playing Caesar, to trip and break his leg, however, the run of the company is jeopardized. Rose sends for her ex-lover, P.L. O'Hara (Alan Rickman), a legendary Richard II and Captain Hook and former member of the company, to save the day. Unbeknownst to Stella, this chance accident will represent an irrevocably dark turn for her and for the story.

O'Hara at first appears to be the company's salvation, a dashing, actorly figure who rides into town on his motorcycle. (His entrance seems an homage to and a parody of the opening shots of Peter O'Toole in *Lawrence of Arabia* (1962).) Hopes rise within the company that O'Hara will act as an antidote to Potter, an alternative father-figure who will stand up for the squabbling, childlike actors on whom Potter heaps abuse. But O'Hara is haunted by memories of his past in Liverpool: silently, he visits the docks, where his eye catches a glimpse of a woman carrying a baby, and visits an old, dank building that seems familiar to him—in which he decides to take a basement flat.

O'Hara proves to be a mesmerizing Hook, and opening night, with Stella manipulating a flashlight and mirror to represent Tinkerbell, is a triumph. O'Hara, charmed, asks Stella to dance at the cast party, then takes her back to his flat and seduces her. Stella, however, immensely practical, sees this merely as a way to gain experience for her inevitable union with Potter. O'Hara's manner combines actorly smarminess, genuine affection, and a mysterious inner yearning to recapture the past. Yet Stella will have none of it. "I'm beginning to get the hang of fucking," she says to O'Hara matter-of-factly. "Don't you love me just a little bit?" he asks. "No," responds Stella, "I love another."

Uncle Vern, sensing something is afoot, asks Potter, ironically, to act as Stella's protector. Within the company, this allows Potter to maneuver against O'Hara, and the film's story becomes a battle of father figures in Stella's life. Potter invites Vern to a soccer game between the company and a rival theatrical troupe, and here all the brewing tensions in the company come to a head. Meredith humiliates Geoffrey, who brutally punches him out, and the company asks the respected O'Hara to intercede. O'Hara confronts Potter about having seduced Geoffrey, and compares his treatment of Geoffrey to his treatment of Hilary—whom O'Hara reveals committed suicide. (Inadvertently, Stella's childish prank has caused Hilary's suicide—and Hilary, of course, turns out to have been a man.) O'Hara pleads with Potter to respect the company: "The play's about innocence,"

O'Hara tells Potter. "Not seduction. Not exploitation. Look at the play, man." But Potter turns the tables: he threatens to expose O'Hara's own liaison with Stella. Ironically, just as O'Hara stands up for something, he is crushed by his own profligacy.

At this point the film takes on an air of melodrama rather than tragic inevitability because the question of Stella's parentage was not initially set up as a major concern. O'Hara visits Vern and Lily. Attempting to find out more about Stella, he discovers that Vern and Lily had thrown her mother out when she returned from London unmarried and pregnant. Stella's mother then got a job recording the time for the local phone company, and took a basement flat with a group of actors, only to abandon Stella in the flat surrounded by candles. O'Hara realizes that his long-lost love is Stella's mother—and that he is Stella's father. Drunk and stricken with horror, O'Hara returns to the docks where he last saw Stella's mother, stumbles, and drowns.

The film ends on a strange, ironic note: only the audience knows the secret O'Hara took to the grave, and Stella will never know that the man to whom she lost her virginity was her real father. Mercifully spared this knowledge, Stella remains bereft of companionship—a mourner, in Potter's analogy, bending down in the midst of a funeral procession to tie her shoelace, only to discover that her loved ones have moved on. The film's final image is Stella, alone, in her usual telephone box, speaking to the phone clock that is her mother's voice, and telling it of Potter's story: that perhaps her loved ones are waiting, just around a corner. Potter's sad interpretation of life is her only balm, and her love for Potter, ironically, her only salvation. But it is a salvation at the cost of living any real life of connection with other human beings. As O'Hara dies, the film cuts back to *Peter Pan*, with Potter now in the role of Hook, forcing comparisons between Stella's life and the play's. In real life, children are not merely abandoned for the evening, but for life, and the sin of abandonment creates tragedy that cannot be foreseen. Apprenticing as a housekeeper to the Lost Boys—the actors—loses its charm, and Tinkerbell, in the form of O'Hara, does not come back to life.

An Awfully Big Adventure is Newell's darkest film since *Dance with a Stranger* (1985). The film shows Stella's primal need for fantasy in her life, and how the theater and its tawdry folk both save and mistreat her. In its ambitious scope, however, the film neglects to clarify some crucial plot points, and this sloppiness mars an otherwise brilliantly executed story of abandonment and initiation. The tragic dimensions of the story are insufficiently foreshadowed, and, in fact, too artfully hidden by the comic subplots involving the different actors.

The film nonetheless boasts a trio of superb performances from Hugh Grant, Alan Rickman, and newcomer Georgina Cates, as well as a seductive attention to period detail. Grant, in a role which is the polar opposite of his self-effacing romantic lead in Newell's *Four Weddings and a Funeral* (1994), endows the character part of Potter with bitchy verve and a deadness behind the quips. Rickman captures the essential child-like irresponsibility of O'Hara, and Cates turns in a finely tuned performance as a deeply disturbed young woman. The film's production design is vivid and accurate. (If its setting resembles the Dublin of Alan Parker's *The Commitments* (1991), that is because *An Awfully Big Adventure* was shot in Dublin. The filmmakers decided modern-day Liverpool had been too heavily modernized.)

An Awfully Big Adventure leaves its audience with a dark lesson: that denial of the truth is sometimes a child's only salvation, but comes at a price—an eternal waiting in limbo for love and affection, and an inability to engage life in any meaningful way. The eternal innocence of theater, in Newell's dark, melancholy film, may simply be purgatory in disguise.

—*Paul Mittelbach*

REVIEWS

The New York Times. CXLIV, July 21, 1995, p.B3 (N).
Rolling Stone. August 10, 1995, p.62.
Sight and Sound. V, April, 1995, p.38.
The New Republic. CCXIII, August 21, 1995, p.31.

Babe

"A little pig goes a long way."—Movie tagline

"Absolutely enchanting!"—Joel Siegel, *Good Morning America*

"Its gleeful antics define irresistible."—Kenneth Turan, *Los Angeles Times*

"*Babe* is in a league of its own when it comes to enchantment."—Susan Wloszczyna, *USA Today*

Box Office Gross: $56,737,040

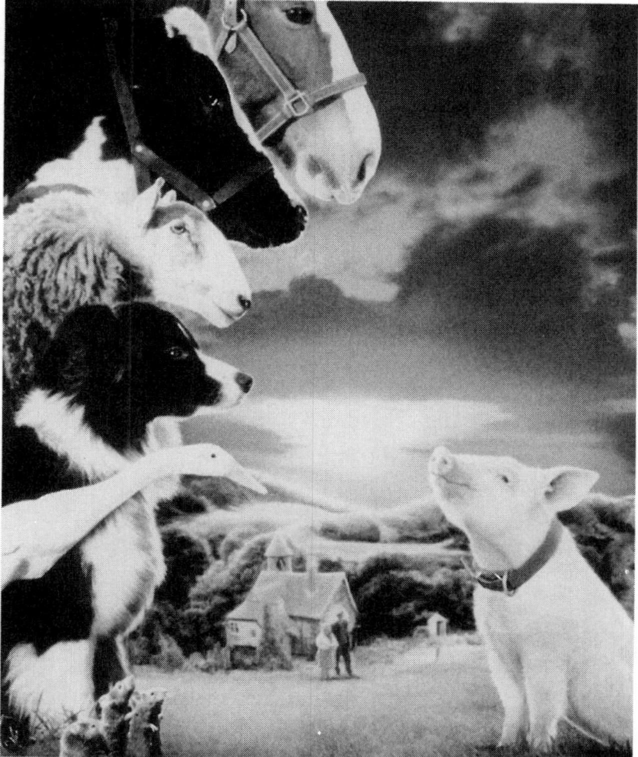

A pig who marches to a different drum touches hearts and lives at Hoggett farm in *Babe*. © 1995 Universal City Studios, Inc. Courtesy of MCA Publishing Rights, a Division of MCA Inc. All rights reserved.

"This is a tale of an unprejudiced heart that changed our valley forever..." So begins this allegorical tale of a little piglet who dreams of being a sheep-dog, an endearing film that is guaranteed to melt even the most cynical of hearts. Adapted from the children's book, "The Sheep-Pig" by British author Dick King-Smith, *Babe* weaves a tale about individuality and conformity, and teaches that no one need accept anyone else's limited vision of their own self-worth. Through computerized talking animals—and forty-eight of the cutest Large White Yorkshire piglets to ever grace the screen—*Babe* offers the "feel-good" movie of the century, *Rocky* (1976) in the barnyard.

As he watches his mother being taken away to "Pig Paradise"—a place so wonderful that no pig has ever wanted to return—Babe is snatched away from his siblings and taken to the fair. Used to raise money in a raffle, Babe meets the taciturn Farmer Hoggett (James Cromwell) for the first time when the farmer tries his hand at guessing the little pig's weight. If he is correct, the farmer wins the pig. "Ain't got no use for pigs. Only raise sheep," Hoggett replies. Nonetheless, the farmer enters a guess. "Just think of what a fine Christmas dinner he'd make," the farmer is told and even before the results are in, Mrs. Hoggett (Magda Szubanski) makes a mental list of all the fine meals to be had after she fattens up the little piggie.

Producer and co-writer George Miller, director/co-writer Chris Noonan, veteran animal trainer Karl Miller and the entire crew spent nearly three years in Australia bringing *Babe* to the screen.

Disoriented and missing his own family, Babe immediately befriends the maternal Fly, a Border collie who, along with her mate, the cantankerous Rex, herds the "stupid" sheep. The farm is an intricate social structure in which every animal knows his place, does his own job and follows the rules. But Babe is confused when he is ridiculed by the other farm animals because he "has no purpose in life"—other than being the master's dinner. When the Farmer sells off her litter of pups, the despondent Fly takes the sweet, non-judgmental Babe under her proverbial wing, despite Rex's objections. "Can I call you Mom?" the little pig asks. Soon both Fly and the Farmer notice that this sweet little pig has a peculiar rapport with the sheep and before long the dog is teaching Babe some new tricks—ones that just might save him from the main course at Christmas dinner. And before long, the Farmer's faith in this innocent little pig's abilities is so strong that he is willing to risk public humiliation in order to give Babe his shot at transcending others, expectations of what he should be. As the film's narrator tells us, "Those little ideas that tickle and nag should never be ignored...for in them are the seeds of destiny." Babe succeeds on his own terms, insisting on treating the sheep with respect, rather than insults and intimidation. And in a case of form mirroring content, *Babe*, the film, refuses to back away from its stance that all things are possible: the film remained in the top ten at the box office for nearly eight weeks, far surpassing industry expectations, particularly for a non- Disney family film.

It took George Miller nearly a decade before he was able to get *Babe* to the big screen. The director of such action-oriented films as the *Mad Max* (1979) series, along with the black comedy *The Witches of Eastwick* (1987), Miller seems a strange candidate to be so attracted to British author Dick King-Smith's children's book, *The Sheep-Pig.* Yet Miller believed that there was something epic in the story of the social order on a farm. Convinced that he wanted to use live action rather than animation to tell the pig's tale, Miller suspected that he lacked the patience required to direct the multitudes of live animals, and so chose documentary filmmaker Chris Noonan to helm the project. Having won accolades for his documentary about a theatrical group of mentally- challenged actors, *Stepping Out,* Noonan, who also co-wrote the screenplay with Miller, makes an extraordinary feature film debut with *Babe.* The Australian displays a deft hand at blending the story's comedic elements with the more serious issues of carnivorousness, ethical animal treatment and prejudice, never falling victim to preachiness nor heavy-handed dogma.

Babe is photographed like a storybook come to life, beautifully shot in golden tones, with even the farmhouse taking on a personality of its own. Interestingly, the animals do most of the talking in this film (although notably, never in front of the humans), while the human Farmer Hoggett, impressively portrayed by the six-feet seven inch tall actor, James Cromwell, is mostly monosyllabic. As Terrence Rafferty in his review in *The New Yorker* pointed out, one of the truly impressive things about the film is the filmmakers restraint in anthropomorphizing the feelings of the animals; they always remain in character as animals, maintaining their own respective views on their world, which do not necessarily coincide with the human take on things. One of the liberties that Miller and Noonan took with adapting King-Smith's book was to add the duck character, Ferdinand. While Babe is a total innocent, Ferdinand is savvy enough to know that he is also a candidate for the up-coming holiday feast. "Christmas is carnage," the duck moans. Ferdinand is intent on trying to convince the Hoggetts that he is a perfectly fine substitute for the morning rooster- -or any other alarm clock that comes along. In a hilarious sequence, Ferdinand enlists Babe's help in trying to steal Mrs. Hoggett's newly acquired mechanical clock, a folly that infuriates Rex, confirming to the dog that the rules cannot, and should not be broken.

The film utilizes conventions of the silent film to tell the story, such as iris closes and title cards which divide the individual segments. But the filmmakers update the feel by periodically interjecting some hilariously wacky elements, most notably the trio of field mice who read the title cards aloud, as well as singing the a capella classic, "Blue Moon," and the toreador aria from Bizet's opera, "Carmen." The result is a film that constantly catches its audience off-guard, traversing the gamut from tears to side-splitting laughter.

The state-of-the-art computer graphics and animatronics combine to give *Babe* a seamlessly natural look and feel, making it difficult to spot the technique. The film-

CREDITS

Farmer Hoggett: James Cromwell
Mrs. Hoggett: Magda Szubanski
Babe: Christine Cavanaugh
Fly: Miriam Margolyes
Ferdinand: Danny Mann
Rex: Hugo Weaving
Maa: Miriam Flynn
Cat: Russie Taylor
Narrator: Roscoe Lee Browne

Origin: Australia
Released: 1995
Production: George Miller, Doug Mitchell and Bill Miller for a Kennedy Miller production; released by Universal Pictures
Direction: Chris Noonan
Screenplay: George Miller and Chris Noonan; based on the children's book, "The Sheep-Pig" by Dick King-Smith
Cinematography: Andrew Lesnie
Editing: Marcus D'Arcy and Jay Friedkin
Production design: Roger Ford
Art direction: Colin Gibson
Music: Nigel Weslake
Animation/visual effects supervisor: Charles Gibson
Animatronic director: John Stephenson
Animal trainer: Karl Lewis Miller
MPAA rating: G
Running Time: 91 minutes

AWARDS AND NOMINATIONS

Academy Awards 1995: Best Visual Effects
Nominations: Best Picture, Best Director (Noonan), Best Supporting Actor (Cromwell), Best Adapted Screenplay (Noonan/Miller), Best Art Direction, Best Film Editing
Golden Globe Awards 1996: Best Film-Musical/Comedy
National Society of Film Critics Awards 1995: Best Film
British Academy Awards Nominations 1995: Best Film, Best Adapted Screenplay (Noonan/Miller)
Writers Guild Award Nominations 1995: Best Adapted Screenplay (Noonan/Miller)

makers succeed with the illusion of animal speech as a natural occurrence. Though used only sparingly, the animal puppets were painstakingly created by Jim Henson's Creature Shop in London, while the sheep were made by John Cox's Creature Workshop in Queensland. Once the key animals had been cast, Henson's sculptors then flew to Sydney to pose the animals. Never before did the animatronics have to be exact matches with other animals. The demands of creating carbon copies proved to be particularly trying when it came to the title character of Babe, since none of the forty-eight piglets had been born at the time. In the end, pre-production on *Babe* took some eighteen months, production six months and a year of post-production.

Actor James Cromwell may be familiar to audiences from his role as Stretch on the television situation comedy, *All in the Family*, as well as guest appearances on such diverse shows as *L.A. Law*, *Star Trek: The Next Generation*, and *M*A*S*H*. The California-born actor's film work includes *Pink Cadillac* (1989), *The Man With Two Brains* (1983) and all three *Revenge of the Nerds* (1984) films. Although one of Australia's top comediennes, Magda Szubanski (Mrs. Hoggett) makes her feature film debut with *Babe*. As for the vocal cast, American Christine Cavanaugh, providing the voice for Babe, was the title character in the television version of Cathy Guisewite's comic strip, "Cathy," as well as Gosalyn Mallard on Disney's *Darkwing Duck*. Academy Award nominee for Best Supporting Actress in Martin Scorsese's *The Age of Innocence* (1993), British stage and screen actress Miriam Margolyes is the voice of Fly, the Border Collie, while Rex's vocals come from Australian Hugo Weaving, who recently starred as Tick in *The Adventures of Priscilla, Queen of the Desert* (1994).

At a time in American cinema where the quotient of on-screen violence has reached an alarming high, *Babe* is refreshingly life-affirming. Producer Miller and director Noonan triumphantly succeed in transforming what could have been a mere kiddie picture into a charming film for all ages—one that marches, like its piggie protagonist, to the beat of its own drummer. Reviews for the film were resounding positive. To quote the poker-faced Farmer Hoggett, "That'll do, pig... that'll do."

—Patricia Kowal

REVIEWS

Entertainment Weekly. August 11, 1995, p.38.
Los Angeles Times. August 4, 1995, p.F1.
Newsweek. CXXVI, August 14, 1995, p.73.
The New York Times. August 4, 1995, p.B3.
The New Yorker. CXLIV, September 4, 1995, p.99.
People Weekly. XLIV, August 14, 1995, p.18.
San Francisco Chronicle. August 4, 1995, CLXXII, p.C1.
Time. CXLVI, August 21, 1995, p.69.
Wall St. Journal. August 11, 1995, p.A7.
Washington Post. August 4, 1995, p. 38 Weekend.

The Baby-Sitters Club

"A delightful, humorous, and refreshing film! Can be enjoyed by the whole family. I loved it!"—Elayne Blyth, *Film Advisory Board*

"Delightfully innocent...the cast couldn't be better. Entertaining and inspiring."—Elena Kellner, *L.A. Parent*

"A beautiful film that possesses the power to enchant all ages. Photographed gorgeously...all the young actresses, and a couple of the actors too, are impressive. An uncommonly promising feature directorial debut by Melanie Mayron."—Kevin Thomas, *The Los Angeles Times*

Box Office Gross: $9,685,976

With over 200 titles and 125 million copies sold in the last nine years, Ann M. Martin's "The Baby-Sitters Club" books are well-known stories of adolescent angst. Unlike other well-known teenaged literary heroines, such as Nancy Drew, the baby-sitters live lives not unlike those led by young people across the country, that is, lives punctuated more by puppy love and spats between friends than by abductions by murderous thugs and resolutions of major mysteries. "Being a kid is being a kid," says director Melanie Mayron in the production notes, "whether you're from Holland or Sweden or France or England or Stoneybrook, Connecticut [the fictional setting for the Baby-Sitters Club books and this film]. And crossing the bridge from being a kid to being a grownup is what this film's about, when you're not quite there but you sure aren't little anymore. It's a universal story about friendship and love that is powerful and emotional and never dated." Translated to the screen this summer, the members of the Baby-Sitters Club chart the elusive territories of right and wrong, of "want to" versus "have to," of forthrightness versus evasiveness, and of generosity versus selfishness.

With summer upon them, the members of the Baby-Sitters Club decide to start a summer camp for all of the families for whom the sitters work during the school year. While the camp is the biggest idea the Club members have had yet, running a business proves more of a burden than any of them expected, especially because their lives are filled with major dilemmas. For instance, Stacey (Bre Blair) has met an intriguing seventeen-year-old boy. Should she tell him she is only thirteen? And, more importantly, should she tell him that she is diabetic? Kristy (Schuyler Fisk) is enchanted by the return of her long-absent father, but can her friendships with Claudia (Tricia Joe) (whom she has promised to help with her science homework) and Mary Anne (Rachael Leigh Cook) (whom she has sworn to secrecy over the return of her father) survive? And what should be done about the grumpy neighbor (Ellen Burstyn) who dislikes the noise and intrusion of the camp? And what about the mean girls who try to steal Mary Anne's (Rachel Lee Cook) boyfriend? The Baby-Sitters successfully surf the rough tides of the 1990s, and, for better or worse entertainment, are learning valuable lessons in the process.

Tricia Joe, Stacey Linn Ramsower, Schuyler Fisk, Bre Blair, Zelda Harris, Larisa Oleynik, and Rachael Leigh Cook in *The Baby-Sitters Club*.

CREDITS

Kristy Brewer: Schuyler Fisk
Stacey: Bre Blair
Mary Anne Spier: Rachael Leigh Cook
Dawn: Larisa Oleynik
Claudia: Tricia Joe
Mallory: Stacey Linn Ramsower
Jessi: Zelda Harris
Luca: Christian Oliver
Elizabeth Thomas Brewer: Brooke Adams
Watson: Bruce Davison
Mrs. Haberman: Ellen Burstyn
Logan Bruno: Austin O'Brien
Patrick: Peter Horton

Origin: USA
Released: 1995
Production: Jane Startz and Peter O. Almond for a Scholastic Production; released by Columbia Pictures and Beacon Pictures
Direction: Melanie Mayron
Screenplay: Dalene Young; based on the book series by Ann M. Martin
Cinematography: Wally Kurant
Editing: Christopher Greenbury
Production design: Larry Fulton
Costume design: Susie DeSanto
Makeup: Kathryn Kelly
Set design: Daniel Bradford and Keith Cunningham
Choreography: Gui Andrisano
Casting: Mary Artz
Music: David Michael Frank
MPAA rating: PG
Running Time: 94 minutes

As *The Baby-Sitters Club* is an ensemble film, it necessarily succeeds or fails in large part on the appeal and skill of its actresses. The filmmakers auditioned 6,000 girls for the roles of the seven Baby-Sitters Club members, and all but the role of Christy (arguably the main character in the film) were filled with relative ease. However, production was ready to begin and still no Christy. Then director Mayron (perhaps best known for her role of photographer Melissa Steadman on television's *thirtysomething*) thought of filmmaker and performer Sissy Spacek's daughter Schuyler Fisk. Reports Mayron in *USA Today*, "I called Jack [Fisk, Sissy Spacek's husband and Schuyler Fisk's father] and Sissy and said, 'You have to put Sky on tape for me'. I faxed them the scenes and they sent me the tape of her reading them. I just started weeping in front of the TV and said, 'She's the part.'"

Like her performer mother, Fisk has strawberry blonde hair, which had to be dyed to a nutty brown for the role. While transforming her appearance for the role of Christy, Fisk nonetheless managed to bring a dose of teenage reality, a matter-of-factness to her role that makes her enjoyable to watch. For instance, when her out-of-touch dad arrives on the scene, Christy bounds back and forth between anger at his years of absence and pleasure at his arrival. Where initially she is petulant, eager for him to know how he has disappointed her, soon she is eager to please him, to be the daughter she thinks he wants. Therefore, in the first scene of his arrival, he waylays Christy on her way home from school. Christy gives her father a chilly reception, short answers and recriminations. However, by the time the father convinces her of his intention to stay, she is making every effort to please him: feigning interest in the shaped pancakes she once liked but has now outgrown; pretending to like the frilly dress he has chosen (while her wardrobe is more likely to include trousers and Converse All-Star tennis shoes). Whereas realistically father and daughter have little in common, goodwill stems the tide between them. Also, taking a bit of a risk, *The Baby-Sitters Club* dares to leave plot lines unresolved or unhappily resolved. Where it might have been reassuring to have everything work out between Christy and her father, the filmmakers opted for a more realistic approach to the difficulties of reconciling admiration and disappointment. Says director Mayron in the production notes, "The film is about the tests that we all have in relationships with our dearest friends....[T]he focus of the piece is about honesty and how when we start to lie and weave this web, it just keeps getting deeper and deeper."

The Baby-Sitter's Club was based on the best-selling book series with more than 125 million copies in print by Ann M. Martin.

The film also showcases the stereotypical battles between groups of girls. In such films as *Grease* (1978), *Anne of Green Gables* (1985), and *Heathers* (1989), filmmakers have focused on the battles that emerge between teen-aged girls, often over popularity, appearance and boys. In *The Baby-Sitters Club*, those battles are fought between the Club members and three of their snooty, wealthy classmates. For instance, in an effort to separate Mary Anne from her boyfriend Logan (Austin O'Brien), the rival group makes an overt attempt to woo him over with (what older audience members may find to be painful) outrageously flirtatious behavior: cooing, batting eyelashes, proximity. No doubt audience members will recognize or recollect such tactics, as in many ways they reflect the displacement and confusion that is life as a teenager.

While the teenagers have been drawn carefully, the adult characters ring less true. For instance, Kristy's mother, Elizabeth Thomas Brewer (Brooke Adams), is particularly one dimensional, questioning Kristy on her comings and goings, and inquiring into her eating habits and intentions. The mother is caught up in her new life and marriage, saving such enough attention (read: nagging) for Kristy to drive her to distraction. While Mrs. Brewer is ameliorated by film's end, throughout she is drawn with little more detail than the blaring-horn adults in Charlie Brown animations.

Equally stereotypical, at least early in the film, is Mrs. Haberman (Ellen Burstyn), the neighbor who objects to the sitters' noisy camp. Most of the film she spends sighing, grimacing, gardening: she is the typical older neighbor who has only an uneasy truce with young people, or so it would seem. Yet, as the film is nothing if not modern, it turns out Mrs. Haberman is a world-renowned photo-journalist, and from her, the club members learn about their world and their options as women in the modern world.

The Baby-Sitters Club series began in 1986, when Ann Martin, an editor at Scholastic Inc., came up with the idea of a book series about a group of friends, best friends, to be exact. Within two years, every book in the series had reached the rank of number one on the bestseller lists. Also in 1988, the fan clubs began, with over 60,000 members. Soon the fan clubs spawned a smaller sub-set of 1,000 baby-sitting cooperatives in 48 states, each of which has approximately 4-7 members, aged 11-13. In a short period of time, the popularity of the books and the clubs grew to phenomenal proportions.

While *The Baby-Sitters Club* is not for everyone, it is indeed the perfect film for a very select and recognizable audience: pre-teen and young-teen girls. Best yet, it is a film about how much girls can accomplish, particularly when they trust and work with their girl friends, it is hard not to be in favor of it, even if it is not particularly entertaining viewing for audience members over thirteen years of age.

—Roberta F. Green

REVIEWS

Chicago Tribune, August 18, 1995, p. 5.
New York Times, August 18, 1995, p. C6.
USA Today, August 18, 1995, p. 11D.
Variety, August 17, 1995, p. 55.
Washington Post, August 18,. 1995, p. 44.

Bad Boys

"Lawrence and Smith have the classic movie comedy team dynamic. At times they suggest Martin and Lewis, Crosby and Hope."—Michael Wilmington, *Chicago Tribune*

"A loud, fast action movie laced with comedy. *Bad Boys* is just high-energy entertainment which is what it delivers."—Caryn James, *The New York Times*

"For comedy and thrills, Lawrence and Smith are a dream team...these guys are primed to explode. They achieve an easy, natural rapport that makes you root for them."—Peter Travers, *Rolling Stone*

Box Office Gross: $65,807,024

Martin Lawrence as Marcus Burnett and Will Smith as Mike Lowrey star in *Bad Boys*. © 1995 Columbia Pictures Industries, Inc. All rights reserved.

Don Simpson and Jerry Bruckheimer, the producing wizards behind several box-office blockbusters, have reclaimed their crowns as kings of the high-speed, high-energy action genre with this engaging, if simplistic, cops-and-robbers film. Simpson and Bruckheimer were the producers of *Beverly Hills Cop* (1984) and *Beverly Hills Cop II* (1987) and *Top Gun* (1986). They found less success with the car-racing drama *Days of Thunder* (1990); this return to familiar territory has paid off handsomely for them.

It has also paid off handsomely for stars Martin Lawrence and Will Smith, both of whom have had extraordinary career boosts with the success of this film. It also provides the first big-screen starring role for talented and sexy Tea Leoni, who proves to be a perfect foil for Smith and Lawrence.

The story is a blend of predictable "buddy-cop" fare and the effervescent comedy of Smith and Lawrence. Mike (Will Smith, of TV's *The Fresh Prince of Bel-Air* and 1993's *Six Degrees of Separation*) and Marcus (Martin Lawrence of the popular TV show *Martin*) are two Miami cops who (surprise) don't play by the rules and (another surprise) are the thorn in the side of their commanding officer (Joe Pantoliano). They are assigned to protect the only witness to a brutal murder of a renegade cop who assisted in a $100 million heroin heist from the police department evidence vaults. The witness is Julie (Tea Leoni), who, in order to be protected from dangerous drug lord Fouchet (Tcheky Karyo), is forced to stay under the constant watch of Smith and Lawrence.

CREDITS

Marcus: Martin Lawrence
Mike: Will Smith
Julie: Tea Leoni
Fouchet: Tcheky Karyo

Origin: USA
Released: 1995
Production: Don Simpson and Jerry Bruckheimer; released by Columbia Pictures
Direction: Michael Bay
Screenplay: Michael Barrie, Jim Mulholland, and Dough Richardson; based on a story by George Gallo
Cinematography: Howard Atherton
Editing: Christian Wagner
Art direction: Peter Politanoff
Production design: John Vallone
Music: Mark Mancina
Music Supervisors: Michael Dibeck and Happy Walters
Casting: Francine Maisler and Lynn Kressel
MPAA rating: R
Running Time: 126 minutes

AWARDS AND NOMINATIONS

Blockbuster Entertainment Awards 1996: Male Newcomer-Theatrical (Smith)

Much of this plot is presented in a rather vague and by-the-numbers manner, as if the filmmakers know that the audience has seen this plot before in various forms, so they will dispense with the formalities and get right to the action. After a high-tech opening sequence depicting the drug heist, the film moves to an expository sequence intended to depict the relationship between Mike and Marcus, their relationships with their commanding officer, a vague plot point involving a tough Internal Affairs investigator (Marg Helgenburgher), and something about the DEA taking over the investigation in 72 hours. This mishmash of exposition and detail, much of it yelled by Pantoliano as the commanding officer, is a bit confusing and ultimately sounds like a mixture of many other films (including others produced by Simpson and Bruckheimer).

This is the first feature by 30-year-old director Michael Bay whose background is in music videos and commercials. Bay is the youngest director to have won just about every possible award given in the advertising industry.

However, the film is no worse for its predictability. The reason for this is that interwoven with the "get-the-bad-guys-before-the-clock-runs-out" story is a fun twist involving a role-reversal between Mike and Marcus. Family-man Marcus has to pretend to be smooth playboy Mike when protecting Julie: the reasons why are unclear, but it works anyway.

Lawrence is very funny as the confirmed family man, the more conservative of the two. But Lawrence doesn't allow his character to be completely nerdy: one of his problems is not getting enough "quality time" alone with his sexy wife (Theresa Randle). Wisely not straying too far from the randy clown he plays on "Martin," Lawrence mixes his proud father/good husband character with lines like "Come on, baby, you know I'm a better cop when I get it in the morning."

Meanwhile, Smith is a perfect counterpart with his rich playboy character. Complete with spotless Porsche and fancy bachelor apartment, Mike is the opposite of his married buddy. Evidence of Mike's glamorous life comes from Mike himself: "Everybody wants to be Mike Lowrey," he complains.

The fun begins when they switch roles, and the two comedians are given a chance to play off each other and to try and conceal their true identities from the skeptical Julie. Mike moves into Marcus' home and Marcus moves into Mike's bachelor pad, where they keep Julie in protective custody. Lawrence is particularly funny as he becomes convinced that sexy Mike is having an affair with his wife.

Smith and Lawrence are a wonderful comic team, nagging each other, trying not to blow their cover, wrestling each other to the ground as Lawrence tries to "save" his wife from Mike, or saving the day in the terrific action sequences.

Tea Leoni's sloe-eyed character provides much of the fun, as Julie's skepticism about the two apparently inept partners mounts. "You call this protective custody?" she complains.

First-time feature film director Michael Bay should be credited for his high-energy direction and his terrific (if loud) action sequences. A commercial and MTV director, Bay seems to know that in spite of all the action, the characters are the most important part of the film. Together with his stars, he keeps this film from being a predictable buddy flick, and makes it an entertaining film filled with crashes, explosions, a hip soundtrack, and some fun comic sequences.

—Kirby Tepper

Bad Company

"One Hot Thriller!"—*NBC-TV New York*
"Sexy!"—*New York Post*

Box Office Gross: $3,674,841

American cinema has always drawn a considerable amount of its material from real-life events. Whether it be political, socioeconomic, health, foreign policy, or military issues, eventually they will all end up on the silver screen. For example, audiences have been inundated with films concerning the Vietnam era, such as *Coming Home* (1978), *The Deer Hunter* (1978), *Apocalypse Now* (1979), and *Platoon* (1986), to mention a few. In addition, *The Walking Dead* (1995) deals specifically with the African American experience in the Vietnam War. These films were extremely topical and offered insight into the complexities of the entire decade. When the 1980s arrived, Oliver Stone's *Wall Street* (1987) reminded the nation of the widespread greed and corruption that reigned in modern society.

CREDITS

Margaret Wells: Ellen Barkin
Nelson Crowe: Laurence Fishburne
Vic Grimes: Frank Langella
Tod Stapp: Michael Beach
Julie Ames: Gia Carides
Judge Beach: David Odgen Stiers
Les Goodwin: Daniel Hugh Kelly
Walter Curl: Spalding Gray
Bobby Birdsong: James Hong

Origin: USA
Released: 1995
Production: Amedeo Ursini and Jeffrey Chernov for Touchstone Pictures; released by Buena Vista Pictures
Direction: Damian Harris
Screenplay: Ross Thomas
Cinematography: Jack N. Green
Editing: Stuart Pappe
Production design: Andrew McAlpine
Art direction: William Heslup
Set decoration: Elizabeth Wilcox
Casting: Deborah Aquila
Sound: Larry Sutton
Costume design: Richard Shissler, Charles DeCaro
Music: Carter Burwell
MPAA rating: R
Running Time: 108 minutes

Certainly, over the years, filmgoers have exhibited a certain fascination for the genre of espionage films. These films provide suspense, danger, and intrigue, along with an undercurrent of sex and glamour. Countries covertly spying on one another provide enough thrilling twists and turns to keep an audience keenly attentive for hours. Two major adversaries, Russia's KGB and the United States' Central Intelligence Agency (CIA), were the perfect opponents in many of these films. They provided the perfect breeding ground for cloak- and-dagger espionage. Following the end of the Cold War, the CIA explored new ways to exert its influence, and a prime target became the burgeoning business of industrial espionage. This field of endeavor became the theme of Touchstone Pictures' *Bad Company*, starring Ellen Barkin and Laurence Fishburne.

Ross Thomas, the award-winning mystery novelist, wrote the intricate screenplay for *Bad Company*. The film's production notes state that in an article Thomas wrote for the *Los Angeles Times*, he noted that "the new CIA director has claimed that economic espionage is 'the hottest current topic in the intelligence field.' And in April of 1993, according to one report, the FBI's industrial case load leaped from 10 to 500 in only nine months." This dramatic increase obviously illustrates that times have certainly changed, and films are changing along with them.

Films dealing with scandal and corruption have all invited their audiences into some inner sanctum of political intrigue and secrecy. As films such as *The Manchurian Candidate* (1962) show, many people are transfixed by covert conspiracy plots. It is to this genre that *Bad Company* aspires but ultimately misses the mark. Its visual style is reminiscent of television's *Miami Vice*, and as with many films, the narrative gets lost in the "style" or "look" of the piece.

In the opening, the camera moves in on the skyline of Seattle, where the story is set. It suggests that the viewer is being taken from the outskirts of town into the center of a private world—the "inner sanctum." The powerful score by musical composer Carter Burwell creates an ominous feeling, a heightened sense of impending calamity. Burwell's music successfully underscores the dramatic content of the material throughout the film. The talented composer has scored such films as *Blood Simple* (1985), *Raising Arizona* (1987) as well as the critically acclaimed HBO movie, *And The Band Played On*, and does a highly admirable job for *Bad Company*. It is unfortunate that the rest of the film does not equal the high standard set by Burwell.

Once inside the world of espionage, the complicated plot is steadily revealed to the audience. The film demands undivided attention from the viewer or one will become lost in a maze of confusion, which is a major drawback.

The main plot revolves around Nelson Crowe (Laurence Fishburne), a former CIA agent who is out of favor because of a controversial Iraqi gold deal. His latest and last assignment is to infiltrate the Grimes Organization. This company, also known as the Tool Shed, is a thoroughly unscrupulous, private industrial espionage company ruled by the villainous Victor Grimes (Frank Langella) and the equally wicked Margaret Wells (Ellen Barkin). Initially, Crowe's intentions are honorable, but slowly the lure of power and money wins out and his greed gets the best of him. He sells out with the aid of the formidable seductress Margaret Wells.

Bad Company is Edgar Award-winning mystery novelist Ross Thomas' first original screenplay. He is the author of 25 novels, five of them under the pseudonym Oliver Bleek.

Fishburne brings to the role the proper amount of focus and concentration that would be expected of an experienced CIA agent. Crowe is a man with a purpose and that purpose is to complete his last assignment and get on with his life. Fishburne is effective in certain aspects of the role; however, there is a key element that is missing in his characterization—mystery. There does not seem to be any mystery or shrouded past to Crowe. Based on the information that is given concerning the Iraqi gold deal, there should be a mystique to the performance. There should be some kind of inner turmoil and struggle going on when he switches his allegiance to the Tool Shed. There is no build, no arc to Fishburne's portrayal. It is too linear, with no surprises. To many, the fascination of Clint Eastwood's moody antiheroes is in the subtext—the events of the past that cause this man to behave this way. That is what makes a performance colorful and intriguing.

Ellen Barkin, who was so delightful as Robert Duvall's ill-fated daughter in *Tender Mercies* (1983), seems to be making a career of playing smoldering, steamy seductresses. Passion reigned supreme when she starred with Dennis Quaid in *The Big Easy* (1987), and sparks certainly were ignited when she paired up with Al Pacino in *Sea of Love* (1989). She is an alluring and intelligent actress and has given many outstanding performances in the past. Her Margaret Wells, however, is all sneering and stalking and indicating. Her conniving sexuality is so overblown that she comes across like a parody of Joan Collins' Alexis on the 1980s television soap *Dynasty*. Her wickedness is so blatant and apparent that no one with any reasonable amount of awareness would trust her as far as they could throw her. In one particular scene, she mounts Crowe as they plot to kill Grimes, who is the head of the agency. It is an important scene meant to show the audience the unbridled passion between these two people that leads them to murder. The scene is not only explicit but also comes across as awkward and choreographed, however, because of the lack of chemistry between the two actors.

It is interesting to note that director Damian Harris got his start in the industry by directing music videos. He made his debut as a feature-film director with his own adaptation of a Martin Amis novel, *The Rachel Papers* (1989). He also directed the psychological thriller *Deceived* (1991), starring Goldie Hawn and John Heard. It seems that the primary focus of *Bad Company* is the look and style of the film, giving it an exaggerated, almost surrealistic atmosphere. The characters appear extremely drawn; likewise, the sets, in some shots, look like something out of a *Star Trek* film. This may be an appropriate choice for some projects, but in *Bad Company* it becomes distracting, making the story difficult to follow.

Bad Company is not a "bad" film. It is simply not a very good one. It taxes the brain with a convoluted plot that never really pays off. It also never gives the audience the opportunity to look inside the psyches of the main characters. One only gets to see their somewhat stylized, one-dimensional personifications in the glossy veneer of their manufactured surroundings. Although the script and cast had potential, that potential was never realized.

—Jarred Cooper

REVIEWS

Daily Variety. January 20, 1995, p. 4.
Entertainment Weekly. February 3, 1995, p. 36.
The Hollywood Reporter. January 20-22, 1995, p. 10.
Los Angeles Times. January 20, 1995, p. F20.
The New York Times. January 21, 1995, p. 12.

Balto

"His story became a legend. His adventure is one you'll never forget."—Movie tagline

"*Balto* is a winner!"—Joanna Levenglick, *The Kids News Network*

"An inspiring adventure. With some of the best animation in years."—Chuck Rich, *Mutual Broadcasting System*

"One of the best family movies of the season. A thrilling adventure full of imagination and humor."—Michael Medved, PBS/*Sneak Previews*

Box Office Gross: $5,953,535

If Disney is the standard by which the public has come to judge all animated features, *Balto* doesn't have much of a chance to measure up. Plagued by weak writing, merely average animation and a few lackluster voice performances, this anthropomorphic fable of dog vs. dog, dog vs. man and dog vs. the elements seems to run far longer than its 74 minutes. Even so, its positive message and real-life inspiration combine to create a relatively adventurous tale of good and evil, determination and redemption. While it doesn't begin to approach the emotional highs and lows found in titles such as *The Lion King* (1994) or *Lady and the Tramp* (1955), *Balto* does borrow some elements from those films and certainly serves as a reasonable alternative to most Saturday morning cartoon fare. It's probably most appealing to children under the age of 10.

CREDITS

Balto: Kevin Bacon (voice)
Boris: Bob Hoskins (voice)
Jenna: Bridget Fonda (voice)
Steele: Jim Cummings (voice)
Muk and Luk: Phil Collins (voice)

Origin: USA
Released: 1995
Production: Steve Hickner for an Amblin Entertainment production; released by Universal
Direction: Simon Wells
Screenplay: Cliff Ruby, Elana Lesser, David Steven Cohen and Roger S.H.Schulman
Cinematography: not listed
Editing: Nick Fletcher and Sim Evan-Jones
Production design: Hans Bacher
Character design: Carlos Grangel, Nicolas Marlet and Patrick Mate
Animation production: Colin J. Alexander
Sound: Tom Paul
Music: James Horner
MPAA rating: G
Running Time: 77 minutes

A half-wolf, half-husky undertakes a daring mission to save the men, women, and children of Nome, Alaska in *Balto*. © 1995 Universal City Studios, Inc. Courtesy of MCA Inc. All rights reserved.

The film is loosely based on 1925 news reports of a diphtheria outbreak in Nome, Alaska which was quelled when a dogsled team braved a severe winter storm to deliver vital vaccine from a neighboring town. In fact, *Balto* opens and closes with live action segments of a fictional elderly woman and her granddaughter as they search New York City's Central Park for the actual bronze statue which commemorates the rescue. These segments lead viewers to believe the grandmother is Rosy, the little girl featured in the animated portion of the film who is saved, along with other children, by Balto, a stray wolf-dog crossbreed who is initially shunned by adults and other dogs in town.

The voice of Balto is supplied by actor Kevin Bacon, who lends a youthful energy and spirit to the outcast canine, making him by far the liveliest character in the pack. Balto's nemesis is the villain Steele, the town's purebred top dog, who is given a snarling, one-dimensional characterization by Jim Cummings. The selfish, unscrupulous sleddog champ takes great pride in his own achievements and the attention he's paid by the town's four-legged females, but he longs for the affections of only one, a rust-colored husky called Jenna (barely brought to life by Bridget Fonda) who belongs to the aforementioned Rosy. Balto also loves Jenna, and it's that affection, along with his desire to serve, which propel him to perform supercanine deeds. Comic relief, as in *The Lion King*, is supplied by a few supporting characters—Boris, a sarcastic Russian snow goose humorously portrayed by Bob Hoskins and a pair of charming twin polar bears, Muk and Luk, given cute Cockney voices by Phil Collins. The trio lend emotional support to Balto as he fends off the local bullies and makes the life-threatening decision to go in search of the serum.

Balto is loosely based on a true story about a courageous dog sled team who risked their lives bringing diphtheria medicine to dozens of storm-stranded children in Nome, Alaska, in 1925. A well-loved bronze statue still stands in New York's Central Park honoring the dogs' heroism.

As the animated portion of the film opens, a sled dog competition is about to begin. Rosy is delighted when her parents present her with her own dog sled and "a real musher's hat" as they prepare to watch the start of the race. Jenna is seen with other members of a female pack, who have clearly taken their cues from catty characters in Disney films. They drool over Steele, who, in an attempt to play to his audience, makes a careless move which endangers spectator Rosy. Jenna steps in to protect her mistress, and it's Balto, skulking in the background, who suddenly, daringly enters the racecourse and snatches the little girl's prized hat out from under the paws of the oncoming dog team.

Following the race, Steele and his mates seek out and harass Balto, chasing him out of town. Balto has an identity crisis of sorts when he comes nose to nose with a pack of wolves, who don't quite know what to make of the half-breed. Heading back to his shelter, an abandoned ship, Balto meets his three friends. Boris (a goose who has teeth!) tries using humor to lift Balto's spirits, while Muk and Luk show they, too, are shunned as polar bears who fear water.

Before long, youngsters begin to fall prey to the diphtheria epidemic, local supplies of antitoxins are exhausted and the town is put under quarantine. Balto and Jenna sneak into the makeshift hospital to check on Rosy, who's not doing well. Trying to lift Jenna's spirits, Balto creates his own version of the Northern Lights using pieces of broken glass. The beauty of the lights brings a small wellspring of optimism to the pair.

A frantic attempt to import serum is thwarted when a massive snowstorm hits the region, preventing travel by air, water or rail.

The town elders decide to hold another sled dog competition to choose a team to go after the serum overland. Balto is allowed to compete and wins, despite Steele's best efforts to knock him out of the running. Though Balto has proven himself, the men decide he cannot lead the potentially life-saving sled dog team, as his mixed blood renders him, in their opinion, undependable. Steele is selected and heads out with the team and its human driver. Balto, too, has decided to go out on his own to get the serum, joined later by his three pals.

Via the same doggy telegraph system seen in *101 Dalmations*, Balto learns the town carpenter is sadly building dozens of child-sized caskets, inspiring him to find and assist Steele, whose team, now carrying the serum, gets lost in the blinding swirls of snow, its human driver unconscious and injured. Steele and his team still show disdain for Balto, even as he ignores all odds, trying to fight off a massive, frighteningly-rendered bear by himself. Jenna now reappears to help the battling Balto, who almost drowns in an attempt to lead the bear onto a patch of thin ice. Muk and Luk manage to overcome their fear of water as they try to rescue Balto; Jenna is injured by the bear and returns to town with the goose and the polar bear twins, leaving Balto alone once again.

Returning to the stranded dogsled team, Balto is rebuffed when a weakened Steele refuses to give up possession of the antitoxin. There is a vicious battle between the two and Balto wins control of the team, with Steele trailing behind, unseen. All hope appears to be lost when Balto and the serum take a tumble over a cliff and Steele, returning to the town, lies about what happened. Jenna, in a last ditch attempt, creates her own Northern Lights display to attract Balto. It's that, and an encounter with a mystical white snow wolf, which give Balto the strength to scale the cliff and retrieve the serum. After escaping one more peril, a dramatic avalanche, Balto gets the serum through just in time to save Rosy and the other children.

His deception revealed, Steele finds he is now the outcast, while Balto is cheered by the townspeople and then adopted by Rosy's parents in your typical, patented happy ending.

Perhaps the most interesting part of *Balto* is the final live action sequence, in which the audience finally sees the Central Park statue, which bears the words "Endurance, Fidelity, Intelligence," all referring to the actual sled dogs who made the dangerous run in 1925. It's also revealed that the world-famous Iditarod dogsled race is run over the identical, 600-mile route taken initially by those courageous dogs. It's a satisfying payoff, but there isn't much to sustain viewers beforehand.

Balto was made under the aegis of Stephen Spielberg's Amblin Entertainment, but it doesn't have any of the magic of Spielberg himself. In terms of animation, much of it is simplistic; Balto is the only character given any sort of range of facial expressions, while the other dogs are just opening and closing their mouths. The animators do succeed occasionally, most notably during the latter portion of the film, when the snowstorm and other natural disasters befall the main characters. It's a world of grays, browns and blues that imparts a below-zero sense of danger to the audience.

In terms of script, the team of four writers present little comedic material to entertain children or adults. Perhaps the funniest line, uttered by the goose, is, "I was so scared. I've got 'people bumps'!" This is not a musical, so there are no amusing songs from packs of crooning dogs. Granted, the story revolves around turmoil and adventure, and the writers do an acceptable job of handling that type of material. The moral of the story is also made clear in a way children can understand. When Balto asks Steele, "Since when do you need a pedigree to help someone?" it's easy for youngsters to identify with the "underdog," to differentiate between discrimination and acceptance, to understand the benefit of providing assistance to those in need. In that sense, the lessons taught by *Balto* make it worthwhile viewing for young people, even though it lacks significant entertainment value for general audiences.

—Kim Silarski

REVIEWS

Boxoffice. February, 1996, p. R-17
Detroit Free Press. December 22, 1995, p. 4D
Detroit News. December 22, 1995, p. 3D
The New York Times. December 22, 1995, p. C16
USA Today. December 22, 1995, p. 3D
Variety. January 1, 1996, p. 83

Bandit Queen

"A rip-roaring action-adventure....The viscerally compelling portrayal of the title character lends the film a white-hot core of passion!"—Stephen Holden, *The New York Times*

"Compelling....A slice of life far fiercer than fiction."—Bruce Williamson, *Playboy*

"Vibrant....Moves with the feverish outrage of an Oliver Stone melodrama!"—Richard Corliss, *Time Magazine*

Box Office Gross: $399,748

In rural India, a young girl splashes in a river with her playmates. Her swim and her life are suddenly shattered by her father's call: "Phoolan." In her eyes is a terror that will never subside.

For a rusty bicycle and a starving cow, she has been sold at age 11 to a young man who needs a wife. Her father pushes her away, explaining: "A daughter is always a burden, and she is no beauty." Her husband forces sex upon her, the first of many degradations she will endure.

Poignantly photographed against an impassive Indian countryside, this horrifying series of events takes place before the opening credits of *Bandit Queen*, an unsparing and courageous depiction of one woman's brutalization and rebellion. Rarely has the screen seen such a searing depiction of violence against women.

Bandit Queen is the unauthorized biography of the notorious Phoolan Devi, a legendary lower-caste Robin Hood who has been a political nightmare for the Indian government. Based on Phoolan Devi's prison notes, the film follows her rise from an abused young girl to a populist outlaw.

Director Shekhar Kapur and screenwriter Mala Sen pull no punches. There is much more foul language in *Bandit Queen* than in *Pulp Fiction* (1994), and more brutal rapes than any film has ever depicted. Even Phoolan's bloody revenge is not whitewashed but displayed in all its horror.

Through it all, actress Seema Biswas retains Phoolan's dignity while depicting the most horrible effects of her brutalization. Biswas never mutes Phoolan's anger or softens her pain, yet a love for life shines through even her most hardened expressions. Biswas is magnificent. She has a fiery intensity that is mesmerizing.

The film has the sweep of an epic and the fine detail of a character study. Many scenes are delicately crafted and absolutely haunting, and Kapur has a fine eye for the most telling camera angle. At times, however, the techniques are overdone and overwhelm the plot and action, as when a slow-motion cinema-verite technique mutes a desert chase scene.

Bandit Queen succeeds completely in depicting the excesses of female subjugation. From the moment she is plucked from her playmates, Phoolan lives in a world of absolute terror. Almost every man she meets—the bandits, the police, her husband, her father—is a potential or actual rapist or an apologist for rape. As a lower-caste woman who has rebelled against the system, Phoolan is subject to random and relentless punishment from all corners.

As unsparing as they are in depicting what Phoolan must endure, Kapur and Biswas are equally blatant in depicting the horrible rage such treatment ignites in Phoolan. More convincingly than any other film, *Bandit Queen* demonstrates how violence begets violence.

Even more remarkable is how the director and actress refuse to make Phoolan a prisoner of her mistreatment. She has a wonderful, joking, comradely relationship with a playful uncle. She falls passionately in love with a dashing bandit leader, Vikram Mallah (Nirmal Pandey). She has an unquenchable thirst for life.

Achingly beautiful and heartrending is the scene depicting Vikram and Phoolan first caressing one another. There is no dialogue as the pair seem pinned in front of a stone wall. As the camera slowly pans, Phoolan alternately beats off Vikram's advances with her fists, shoves him away, then pulls him forward. Her loathing and distrust for men mingle with her passion and desire for Vikram. The struggling pair eventually embrace and disappear as the camera turns the corner of the wall. This is true-to-life filmmaking without any sugar-coating.

Violence on screen has become increasingly stylized, but Kapur's style is to bring us face to face with the reality of a society where women are systematically brutalized. He does not indulge in egregious explicitness nor titillation; there is no confusing rape with sex. Kapur knows when and how to use oblique camera angles to magnify reality. A scene in which Phoolan is gang-raped, the most wrenching episode of the film, is tellingly executed by means of swinging doors which usher her assailants in and out of her nightmare.

So intense was the depiction of the rape scenes that Seema Biswas reportedly experienced a nervous breakdown after the filming.

Unfortunately, *Bandit Queen* utterly fails in making clear to Western audiences, who are totally unfamiliar with the Phoolan Devi legend, exactly how she became a hero of the lower castes. Her rebellion is depicted as an outgrowth of her personal degradation and never does she make a coherent political statement about the caste system.

The film needs more explication. Passing references to the popular press making Phoolan into a heroine are hardly enough to explain how she quickly became such a political hot potato that the government was forced to negotiate her surrender. In fact, while *Bandit Queen* speaks volumes about the oppression of women in India, it says little about the caste system, how it works, what tensions are threatening it, and how Phoolan exploited those tensions. Kapur simply assumes his audience knows all this, a fatal mistake.

Unfortunately, the Indian masses who do know Phoolan Devi's tale won't see the film. Kapur's nude scenes, explicit language and graphic sexual violence ensured government censors in India would ban the film. If it had been able to do so, surely India's tourist board also would have prevented the film's release outside the country, given Kapur's unflattering depiction of a bleak, violent Indian society.

Instead of abject poverty and awesome wealth amidst majestic beauty, Ashok Mesra's cinematography portrays a barren, treeless landscape of dull towns amidst lifeless ravines. Gangsters in sunglasses swagger through parched villages with ancient wells. There is no safety; brutal violence may break out at any moment.

Even the film's best characters are deeply flawed. Phoolan's father is a fool, her mother a coward, her uncle ineffectual, the bandit leaders hypocritical. Phoolan herself is deeply compromised. She allows her own vengeful feelings against her attackers to explode into an awful massacre. Far from sanctifying Phoolan, Kapur lets us see the full human cost of her violence, focusing on the wailing women and children across the river from the massacred men's funeral pyre.

Throughout all the forms of brutality, Kapur deftly reminds us of how violence is transmitted from one generation to the next.

Despite having won over audiences at film festivals from Cannes to Toronto, India's censors have refused to release the film uncut. Officials claim it is too violent and vulgar, but the underlying trouble is that it offers a grim look at the fate of women in rural India and the injustice of the caste system.

CREDITS

Phoolan Devi: Seema Biswas
Vikram Mallah: Nirmal Pandey
Man Singh: Manjoj Bajpai
Mustaquim: Rajesh Vivek
Madho: Raghuvir Yadav
Sriram: Govind Namdeo
Kailash: Saurabh Shukla
Puttilal: Aditya Srivastava

Origin: India and the United Kingdom
Released: 1994 (1995)
Production: Sundeep Singh Bedi for a Kaleidoscope production; released by Mainline Pictures and Arrow Releasing
Direction: Shekhar Kapur
Screenplay: Mala Sen; based on the diaries of Phoolan Devi
Cinematography: Ashok Mehta
Editing: Renu Saluja
Art director: Ashok Bhagat
Costume design: Dolly Ahluwalia
Make-up: Edwin Williams and Mohd Iqbal Sheikh
Music: Nusrat Fateh Ali Khan
MPAA rating: no listing
Running Time: 119 minutes

Shots of children watching Phoolan's public humiliation, her vengeance and other sordid scenes serve to illuminate the horrible lessons being taught.

Bandit Queen is powerful but hard to follow. The gang rivalries and alliances are fuzzy. While Kapur has a deft and often beautiful way of framing scenes, he has difficulty with narrative flow and scene transitions. Action sequences are robbed of intrigue and tension by Kapur's grandstanding camera techniques and by the huge holes in the story. Minor characters pop in and out with little explanation of their role or purpose.

Perhaps unequalled in its no-holds-barred portrayal of a woman's victimization, *Bandit Queen* unfortunately leaves one with more questions than answers about the life of Phoolan Devi and her role in the class struggle in India. But the unflinching, even unnerving performance by Seema Biswas sustains the film. Her eyes never lose the terror and indignation of the little girl snatched from her play to become a plaything for a brutal system of domination. She has a raw grace and an unflagging dignity.

Bandit Queen is an eerie and unsettling experience, a one-way ticket to the hell that is the life of the low-caste women of India. The shocking journey is both terrifying and transforming.

—Michael Betzold

REVIEWS

Macleans. February 20, 1995, p. 77.
The New Republic. July 10, 1995, p. 24.
The New York Times. March 20, 1995, p. B4.
Village Voice. July 4, 1994, p. 59.

Bar Girls

"Finally...a romantic comedy without men."—
Movie tagline

Box Office Gross: $573,953

Bar Girls is a contemporary love story which takes a look at narcissism, coupling, monogamy, and intimacy among urban women, and does so with considerable intelligence. The film's low budget and first-time director and writer may account for some of its uneven qualities, but all in all it is a worthy companion to several recent films in the genre, such as *The Incredibly True Adventures of Two Girls in Love* (1995) and the more sophisticated *Go Fish* (1994).

Written by Lauran Hoffman, and based on her stage play by the same title, *Bar Girls* tells the story of Loretta (Nancy Allison Wolfe) and Rachael (Liza D'Agostino) as their relationship progresses from their first meeting in a bar called "Girl Bar" (taken from a real-life bar of the same name in West Hollywood, California). Loretta is one-half of a writing team of a cartoon on a cable channel. The cartoon written by her and her partner, Noah (Michael Harris) is "Heavy Myrtle," the adventures of a pudgy lesbian marriage counselor/superhero who flies around the city helping couples understand each other. While Loretta and Noah are able to create sane dialogue and clever solutions for Myrtle's clients, Loretta seems unable to find happiness in her own love life.

She meets beautiful actress Rachael at the bar, and, after finding her attractive immediately, she bets a friend that she can "get her in my car in 10 minutes." Her smooth talk does get Rachael into her car but not into her bed. They are both rather tentative about having sex with each other, opting to wait until they fall in love. Their hesitancy is exacerbated by the fact that Rachael is initially uncertain of her sexuality ("I'm married...to a man....well, I was married to a man") and Loretta has been involved with an emotionally unavailable woman whom she calls "the Psycho-athlete from Bakersfield."

A brief amount of time passes, and they re-meet in the Girl Bar, this time realizing that they are falling in love. After a courtship, they move in with each other. And then the troubles set in: Loretta's jealousy and hypocrisy rise to the surface while Rachael's fear of intimacy keeps Loretta at bay. Other encounters with different women from the bar cause them to reevaluate their relationship, and after several emotional events they learn how their fears have kept them from achieving the kind of comfort and intimacy they dream of.

A couple of subplots round out the action: Loretta's best friend Veronica (Justine Slater), a straight woman, decides that she wants to have an affair with a butch friend of Loretta's named Tracy (Paula Sorge); and a gorgeous soon-to-be policewoman name J.R. (Camilla Griggs) creates emotional havoc when she comes on the Girl Bar scene, particularly when she makes a play for Rachael.

Writer Hoffman produced this film with the director, Marita Giovanni. While Giovanni does a credible job with the material and with her actors, it is Hoffman whose work stands out. Hoffman has an excellent grasp of language, having created clever, contemporary dialogue for her characters. When another heterosexual friend of Loretta's named Destiny tells Loretta she wants to have sex with a lesbian and "you are the only lesbian I know," Loretta responds with "I need better wooing that 'You are the only lesbian I know'." After one character breaks a vow of monogamy, Veronica tells her, "If you are stupid enough to violate your fidelity, you have to be smart enough not to be honest about your stupidity." And Noah responds to the difficulties between Loretta and Rachael by wearily commenting that "living with someone has such a terrible misery/bliss ratio." A final example is an exchange between Loretta and her writing partner about her desire to mention Myrtle's menstrual cycle in the cartoon: "Women need to see themselves and their bodily functions positively portrayed in the media," says Loretta. Her partner responds, "All right, but no PMS...she'll destroy the city." It may not be Oscar Wilde, but the dialogue is always right on target, never sounds contrived, and is most definitely several notches more clever than many big-budget releases.

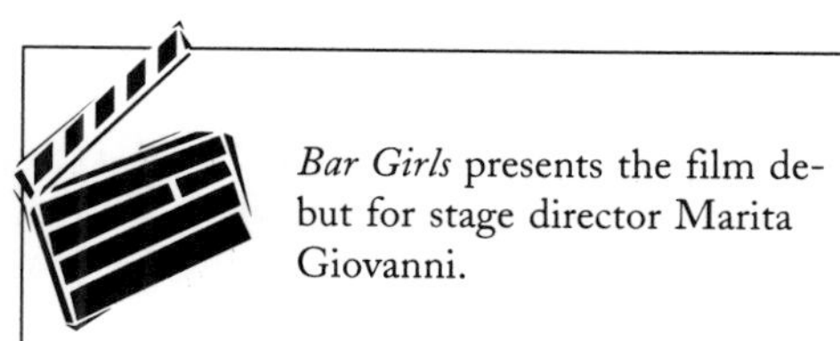

Bar Girls presents the film debut for stage director Marita Giovanni.

Hoffman also investigates and re-investigates her protagonist's motivations with sensitivity. Loretta's petulance and hypocrisy are discovered to be extensions of her fears of being alone, and she discovers these things after considerable personal anguish. It is in this area that Hoffman's script might be considered uneven: while Loretta is a rather fully fleshed-out character, Rachael is not. Her description of herself as being afraid to get "too close" sounds a bit like something out of a contemporary pop psychology book. Similarly, Veronica's instantaneous conversion to homosexuality after having been exclusively heterosexual seems too quick and rather contrived.

For the most part, the subplots are extensions of the complicated emotional contortions through which people (all people, not just lesbians) fall in love and break up. One subplot, however, teeters on the ridiculous, as Loretta and Noah steal a little troll doll from a vacuous television executive and hold it captive until the executive agrees to have a lesbian couple be counseled by "Heavy Myrtle". This sequence is underdeveloped and seems to come out of nowhere, and its broad style—Loretta inexplicably wears a Fedora and a black suit while anonymously calling the television executive with her demands—is out of sync with the film's otherwise subtle satire. As in last year's *Grief* (1994), the depiction of the inner workings of television is supposed to be "cutting edge," but in fact is depicted rather naively, and is to broad when compared to the rest of the film.

Hoffman does, however, use some fun devices to keep the action moving. For example, when Loretta and Rachael first meet (and return to Loretta's house), they tell each other about their old girlfriends in a most interesting way: they look straight ahead, as if looking at a projector, and flashback scenes portray the past relationships. Then, cutting back to Loretta and Rachael, they respond to what the audience has just seen as if they had seen it on a projector in a living room.

Of the performers, Nancy Allison Wolfe as Loretta has the meatiest role, and Wolfe jumps into it with gusto and intelligence. She occasionally becomes a bit self-conscious, as if she is aware she is a good actress—she sometimes hits the dark notes of the character with too much force. But all in all, she is an appealing and compelling heroine. In particular, her monologue toward the film's climax is touching. She also has a knowing smirk which helps her deliver her numerous zingers: "What are you guys doing?" asks one character of Loretta and Rachael, who are fighting in the bar. "Oh, we were just breaking up," smiles Wolfe, with a sneer just below the surface. She sets the right tone in the film's opening sequence, a silent montage of Loretta's attempts to find just the right outfit to wear to "Girl Bar." From motorcycle leather to whips to cowboy boots, Wolfe dons each outfit and applies the appropriate facial expression, only to decide it isn't right and go on to the next outfit.

As mentioned before, the role of Rachael is not as well-designed as Loretta, so Liza D'Agostino has less to work with in portraying her character. But D'Agostino does a credible job nonetheless, bringing a sweetness and a sense of innocence to her inherently confused character.

CREDITS

Loretta: Nancy Allison Wolfe
Rachael: Liza D'Agostino
Veronica: Justine Slater
Tracy: Paula Sorge

Origin: USA
Released: 1995
Production: Marita Giovanni and Lauran Hoffman; released by Orion Pictures
Direction: Marita Giovanni
Screenplay: Lauran Hoffman, based on a play by Lauran Hoffman
Cinematography: Michael Ferris
Editing: Carter DeHaven
MPAA rating: R
Running Time: 95 minutes

The film's smaller roles are filled by fine actresses who bring a wry sense of humor to the proceedings. The best is Justine Slater as Veronica. Slater's is actually the best performance in the film, perhaps because her ditsy character is the type of comic role that tends to steal a film from the more serious leading roles. But Slater's sexy smile, high-pitched voice, and excellent comic timing would make her a winner no matter the role.

For her directing debut, Marita Giovanni does a decent job, but there is a flatness to the lighting and camera blocking that keeps the film from being as sophisticated as it aspires to be. While all of the actresses are good, Giovanni is unable to maintain a continuity of style, so that some moments appear to be boldly satirical while others attempt to be thoroughly realistic. Giovanni's best moments are in the animated "Heavy Myrtle" sequences, which are execuated beautifully. However, the lack of subtlety in music and in the live-action cinematography add to the audience's awareness of the obvious: this is a first-time, low-budget film. When one considers that *Go Fish* (1994) or *The Brothers McMullen* (1995) were also first-time low-budget films, Giovanni's debut is not as impressive as one would hope.

The comparisons to *Go Fish* are inevitable, and though *Bar Girls* may come up a bit short, it is still an intelligent film with an earnest cast and several pithy things to say.

—*Kirby Tepper*

The Basketball Diaries

"The true story of the death of innocence and the birth of an artist."—Movie tagline

Box Office Gross: $2,424,439

The Basketball Diaries is the story of a tough urban kid whose life is devastated by crime and drugs. If it sounds familiar, it may be because drugs and/or "the streets" have been a favorite of filmmakers and actors for generations, from *Rebel Without a Cause* (1955) to *Bright Lights, Big City* (1988). However, this time around it is a true story: it is writer Jim Carroll's autobiographical story about his drug addiction, turned into a respectable film with a remarkable central performance by Leonardo DiCaprio.

DiCaprio plays Carroll, a high-school basketball player in New York City whose ambition is to play in the big leagues. He and his friends, Mickey (Mark Wahlberg), Pedro (James Madio), and Neutron (Patrick McGraw) play on the St. Vitus high school team. The early scenes of the film depict the fast-paced life of the boys, who seem to have a rapacious appetite for excitement. They dive off a dangerously high cliff; they "moon" the Circle Line (a New York tourist boat); they get high while riding the Staten Island Ferry, thrilled when they anger another passenger. The camera breathlessly follows them from one place to another, weaving in and out of crowds, sometimes running, sometimes walking, always appearing to race to the next exciting moment.

Soon enough, they become involved in selling and abusing drugs. Eventually they turn to robbery to support their habits, begin to have arguments with each other, and ultimately go their own ways. Jim (DiCaprio) is thrown out of his house by his mother (Lorraine Bracco), and spirals into life-threatening addiction and despair. He is briefly "saved" by a former drug-addict (Ernie Hudson) who tries to break through Jim's denial, but it doesn't work, and he goes back to the streets. Somehow, miraculously, he pulls himself out of addiction before the end of the film.

Carroll's original book, upon which the film is based, became something of a cult classic. Poet Jack Kerouac helped launch its fame when he praised its author for his poetic description of drug-addicted life. The film maintains the same kind of hip, grungy poetry of the book. Clearly, the "grunge factor" was an attraction to the filmmakers, given the current fascination of the public (particularly the "twentysomething" public) with grunge.

Screenwriter Bryan Goluboff retains the poetry of the book through DiCaprio's voice-over narration. Some of the images are quite evocative: after the funeral of a friend, Jim's voice is heard saying, "Rain remains on branches of a tree that will someday rule the earth...and it clears the streets of the silent armies so we can dance..." As he finishes this passage, the boys are seen playing basketball in the rain, a thin stream of bluish light barely illuminating them as the rain metaphorically washes them of the pain of their friends' untimely death. Sometimes Carroll's poetry shows the youth of its writer: one voice-over self-consciously states, "I tried makin' friends with God....He never showed." Perhaps aficionados of formal poetry will find Carroll's style to be self-conscious or raw, but it is undeniably filled with the kind of angst that makes for an involving film.

It is possible that the somber mood and melodramatic situations would have appeared artificial in the hands of a lesser actor than DiCaprio. It goes without saying that *The Basketball Diaries* is hardly about basketball. Experts may say that DiCaprio doesn't display the kind of basketball prowess that the young Carroll displayed. But no one can match DiCaprio's talent. DiCaprio is proving to be one the best young actors—or simply, best actors—in film today. This gut-wrenching performance follows his similarly visceral, Oscar-nominated performance in *What's Eating Gilbert Grape?* (1993) (which co-starred fellow grunge-meister, Johnny Depp). Hopefully, the lackluster reviews received by the film won't deter Academy Award voters to consider DiCaprio at award time. DiCaprio is an heir to the dynasty of actors, who, since James Dean, have perfected the art of understatement as a way of "chewing the scenery:" If the scenes in which Jim undergoes withdrawal are a bit over-the-top, they are balanced by DiCaprio's brooding realism in the scenes with his friends and co-addicts. In particular, his scenes with his selfish, macho best friend, played by Mark Wahlberg, are in the best tradition of film acting. Their dialogue overlaps, they halt and stammer—in short, they talk like real people talk.

Leonardo DiCaprio landed the role of the heroin-addicted poet that for years had been coveted by several young actors including Matt Dillon, Eric Stoltz, Anthony Michael Hall, Ethan Hawke and River Phoenix.

Mark Wahlberg is surprisingly effective, proving himself to be a real actor in this showy supporting role. Wahlberg is known to millions as the rapper "Marky Mark," and to many more millions as the Calvin Klein underwear model. He has slowly been building an acting career, wisely re-

CREDITS

Jim Carroll: Leonardo DiCaprio
Swifty: Bruno Kirby
Jim's Mother: Lorraine Bracco
Mickey: Mark Wahlberg

Origin: USA
Released: 1995
Production: Liz Heller, John Bard Manulis for New Line Cinema; released by Island Pictures
Direction: Scott Kalvert
Screenplay: Bryan Goluboff; based on the novel by Jim Carroll
Cinematography: David Phillips
Editing: Dana Congdon
Production design: Christopher Nowak
Set decoration: Harriet Zucker
Sound: William Sarokin
Costume design: David C. Robinson
Music: Graeme Revell
MPAA rating: R
Running Time: 102 minutes

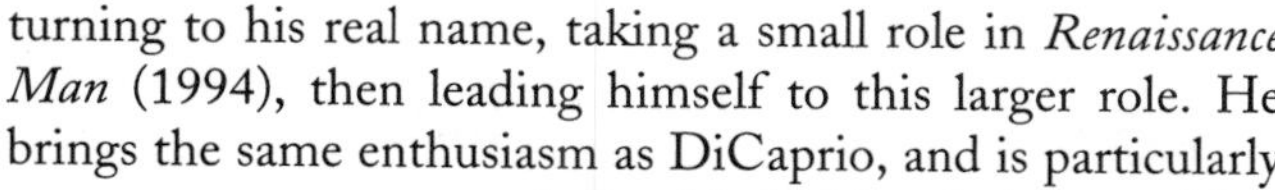

turning to his real name, taking a small role in *Renaissance Man* (1994), then leading himself to this larger role. He brings the same enthusiasm as DiCaprio, and is particularly believable in his spiral into a life a crime. He even makes credible dialogue such as, "His mother's a sneaker, his father's a loafer, somebody has to be the heel." Wahlberg deserves credit for turning himself into a real actor.

All of the performances have credibility and realism. Lorraine Bracco's painful turn as Jim's conflicted mother is right on target. The scene in which she blocks the door with her body rather than let him in is tragic. Bracco movingly portrays the mother's inner struggle between knowing that she mustn't enable her son's addiction and wanting desperately to help him. Bruno Kirby plays Swifty, the high-school basketball coach who makes sexual advances toward Jim. Kirby restrains himself from playing a stereotype, and it works. Swifty is a pathetic figure because of his own denial, not simply because he is homosexual.

First-time feature film director Scott Kalvert, whose credits include MTV videos for Marky Mark, has been criticized by some reviews for making a by-the-numbers tale of drug addiction and not truly evoking the powerful poetry and stinging verbiage of the novel. Without having read the book, however, audiences can appreciate Kalvert's visceral, visual approach to the material. His active camera work, particularly during the basketball sequences, serves the material well. A scene in which DiCaprio plays basketball with Ernie Hudson is filled with fast cuts and extreme close-ups that make the game more exciting on film than it probably was in person.

Kalvert does get a bit carried away with moody lighting, however, and in particular the bluish-black tones of the film threaten to make the audience sleepy. It is perfectly appropriate in the rain-soaked sequences in which the boys play basketball after their friend's funeral, but after a while, the overuse of such artsy, moody lighting, becomes taken for granted. Kalvert uses some effects rather self-consciously, as in an early scene in which the boys fight a rival team in slow motion, the use of distorted images during drug sequences, or in a scene in which DiCaprio scores some drugs while his mother prays for him, lit and posed like a Madonna.

One sequence is particularly cliche: DiCaprio goes to a hospital to take his dying friend (Steven Martini) on a wild wheelchair ride through Manhattan. Perhaps this happened in real life, but it is difficult to imagine that he was able to remove his terminally-ill buddy from the hospital without anyone knowing it.

Still, Kalvert shows a real ear for sound of truth from his actors, always maintaining a sense of realism. The scene in which Pedro steals a car and drives the others to sell it to his brother for drug money is excellent, as is a taut scene in which they are nearly caught by police while robbing a coffee shop: Pedro gets left behind, pinned by policemen, hand outstretched, pitifully calling "Jim!" as the other boys save themselves. In these scenes, as throughout the film, Kalvert avoids the choppy MTV style that one might expect from a successful director of videos, and allows the situations to unfold in more fluid sequence, aided by the crisp editing of Dana Congdon.

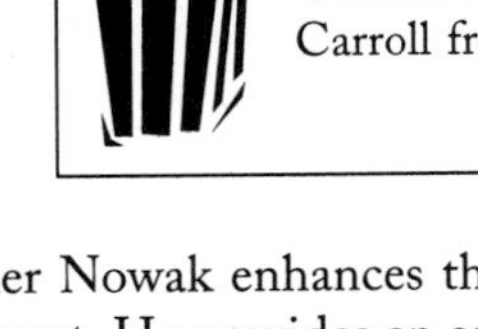

"I tried makin' friends with God....He never showed."—Jim Carroll from *The Basketball Diaries*

Production designer Christopher Nowak enhances the seediness of the character's environment. He provides an especially interesting set for the "headquarters," the decimated remains of several buildings where the junkies crash for the night. Old sofas, rubble, pieces of wood, and an ominous staircase create a metaphorical hell. The staircase in particular emphasizes the depths to which they've fallen even while it offers minuscule promise that they can climb out.

Eventually in the film (as in real life) Carroll does climb out, somehow getting himself recovered from his addiction and performing his poetry in front of audiences. This last scene, in which DiCaprio appears on stage, is rather abrupt. For the audience, it may appear to be an afterthought—an ending tacked-on to redeem the film from the unrelenting despair of the previous events. But in retrospect it seems that Carroll's own perception of his redemption might have seemed just as abrupt. Whatever its occasional limitations, Carroll's original material and DiCaprio's brilliant performance make this a worthwhile film.

—Kirby Tepper

Batman Forever

"A thrill-packed joy ride."—Peter Travers, *Rolling Stone*

"An enormous fun-house ride."—Brian Lowry, *Variety*

"*Batman Forever* is easily the most accessible and satisfying of the three movies based on the adventures of Bob Kane's Dark Knight."—Hal Hinson, *Washington Post*

Box Office Gross: $184,031,112

Holy cash cow! Batman is back with a new Bruce Wayne (Val Kilmer), a new sidekick, Robin (Chris O'Donnell), a new director (Joel Schumacher), and, therefore, a new look. It's more conventional, maybe, but no less extravagant in its villains, Harvey "Two-Face" Dent (Tommy Lee Jones) and Ed (E.) Nigma, a.k.a. The Riddler (Jim Carrey), who threatens to steal the show, then does. While Tommy Lee Jones gets decidedly tiresome as the ruthless, cackling schizophrenic criminal monster he plays, Carrey's Riddler is played to the hilt as a high-camp creature in a vivid and puzzling green suit and flaming red hair, strutting his stuff flamboyantly until he becomes too much of a bad thing.

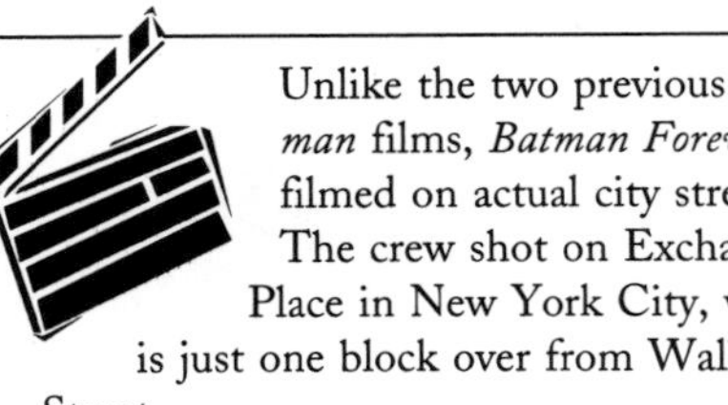

Unlike the two previous *Batman* films, *Batman Forever* filmed on actual city streets. The crew shot on Exchange Place in New York City, which is just one block over from Wall Street.

Ed Nigma is a techno-nerd inventor who works for Wayne Industries. He has designed an interactive-TV gizmo that somehow (don't ask how: this is fantasy, after all) allows him to enhance his own brainpower. After he markets the device which is boxed into television cables, he is able to soak up the accumulated brainpower of all his customers. When Bruce Wayne disapproves of this kind of mind manipulation, Ed Nigma goes ballistic, links up with Two-Face to fund his scheme, and becomes a major competitor to Wayne Industries in no time, leading a parallel kind of double-life (rather like Bruce Wayne)—by day a wealthy industrialist, by night, the riddling E. Nigma.

All the major players of this movie have a darkside. With Two-Face his dark side is his left side. Harvey Dent was once a district attorney who turned psychotic after a client disfigured half his face with acid. This guy is really from the 'toons, a D.C. Comics creation about as interesting as his bizarre Dick Tracy cousins.

Two-Face dominates the first half of the film, while E. Nigma undergoes his charismatic transformation into The Riddler. Two-Face likes to disturb the peace and blow things up. Each time he blows something up, most of his henchmen get blown up, too, but they are somehow replenished in cartoon-fashion.

Two-Face invades a charity circus with a bomb. Dick Grayson (later known as Robin) is performing there as part of a family of trapeze artists. The young man manages to get rid of the bomb, taking it through the roof before it explodes, but, meanwhile, his mother, father, and brother are all killed. His mission in life then becomes revenge. Bruce Wayne, seeing the young man going through what he himself once went through after his own parents were murdered, takes the boy in. Eventually Grayson discovers the Batcave and becomes Robin, in red and green tights (his trapeze costume), until a more appropriate rubberized costume can be fabricated.

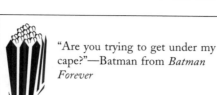

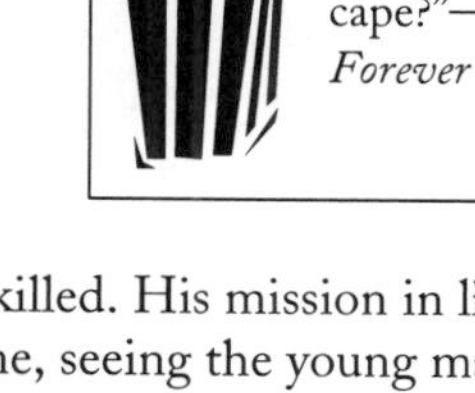

"Are you trying to get under my cape?"—Batman from *Batman Forever*

Together, Batman and Robin go after Two-Face and The Riddler. Robin destroys Two-Face (presumably), and Batman overcomes The Riddler. At the end The Riddler, after having gone over the top, goes around the bend and is incarcerated in an insane asylum under the care of a Dr. Burton, an apparent yet transparent homage to producer Tim Burton. Clearly, however, the door is left open for a Riddler sequel.

Since this man-boy crimefighting combo might seem a bit kinky, the script labors to work in a heterosexual love interest for the Caped Crusader, Dr. Chase Meridian (Nicole Kidman in a Veronica Lake wig), a criminal psychologist who is apparently into bats and hard-rubber suits. She is there when Batman makes his first public appearance ("Hot entrance," she tells him) and immediately starts flirting. She wants to write a paper to explain why a man would dress up as a "flying rodent." Batman corrects her, politely: "Bats aren't rodents, Dr. Meridian." Before long Chase is in his face, all a-pucker, but ultimately she falls for Bruce Wayne. "Are you trying to get under my cape?" Batman asks Dr. Meridian, as she behaves like a teenager in heat. Right there is the film's target audience—this movie is more tease than art. Writing "credit" goes to Lee Batchler, Janet Scott Batchler, and Avika Goldsman. The story is pretty empty after all is said and done. As Owen Gleiberman well and truly noted, "The plot is: The villains try to kill Batman."

One oddity about this movie is that everyone eventually seems to figure out who Batman really is—Dr. Meridian, Dick Grayson, and even The Riddler and Two-Face, who come calling at the Wayne Mansion and capture Dr. Meridian, whom they use as bait to lure Batman into an ambush. So what happened to the mystery of the Caped Crusader?

Some reviewers missed the "dark vision" of Tim Burton, who directed the first two Batman epics in his own eccentric way. Steven Rea of *The Philadelphia Enquirer* found this "a brighter, lighter Batman," but lighter is not necessarily brighter, in terms of the story. Bob Kane's Dark Knight becomes dark lite in Schumacher's sequel. Stephen Hunter of *The Baltimore Sun* and others seemed to agree that Val Kilmer makes a better Batman than Michael Keaton did in the first two outings. The problem is, as Owen Gleiberman remarked, "Kilmer doesn't get to show a lot of personality." He is dark; he is stark; he is stoic, and that's about it.

The film improvised new Bat designs and new Bat toys, a Batboat and a Batplane, both of which are useful after the Batmobile is destroyed by the villains. The new rubberized suits feature low-slung codpieces. Robin's rubberized costume has nipples and spiked sleeves on the forearms. He also gets a cape, though his is shorter and less stylized than the Caped Crusader's. The new costume is far more dramatic than the Boy Wonder's aerial tights, making him seem less an Ariel to Batman's Prospero. They both look great in

CREDITS

Batman: Val Kilmer
Two-Face: Tommy Lee Jones
Riddler: Jim Carrey
Robin: Chris O'Donnell

Origin: USA
Released: 1995
Production: Tim Burton and Peter Macgregor-Scott; released by Warner Brothers
Direction: Joel Schumacher
Screenplay: Lee Batcher, Janet Scott Batcher and Akiva Goldsman; based upon the *Batman* characters created by Bob Kane
Cinematography: Stephen Goldblatt
Editing: Dennis Virkler
Production design: Barbara Ling
Costume design: Bob Ringwood and Ingrid Ferrin
Special visual effects: John Dykstra
Music: Elliot Goldenthal
MPAA rating: PG-13
Running Time: 121 minutes

AWARDS AND NOMINATIONS

Blockbuster Entertainment Awards 1996: Action Actress-Theatrical (Kidman)
Academy Awards Nominations 1995: Best Cinematography (Goldblatt), Best Sound
Golden Globe Awards Nominations 1996: Best Song ("Hold Me, Thrill Me, Kiss Me, Kill Me")

costume. Chris O'Donnell is in the movie as the picture's teen heartthrob. Jim Carrey's Riddler is there to amuse the younger set with his incremental bad-boy act.

As the Riddler, Jim Carrey is over the top, and proud of it. Once he finds his image and his logo, it's easy to forget about the grotesque Two-Face. In fact, one almost forgets Batman and Robin. As Desson Howe noted in his review, after E. Nigma reinvents himself, the movie might be called "Riddler Forever." Many reviewers fell into line by praising Schumacher over Tim Burton, director of the earlier Batman films, for his strong storytelling ability—but that's baloney. The story is half-cocked, messy, improbable, and, well, cartoonish. What counts here is the peculiar and illogical action, the tilt-a-whirl camera techniques, and the even more peculiar, multi-personality, schizophrenic characters, who are really caricatures, designed to serve no purpose higher than commerce, to sell spin-off products and Happy Meals. Batman's first appearance in the Batcave with Albert (Michael Gough) and the Batmobile could be seen on McDonald's television commercials even before the film was released. The script was written to serve the Golden Arches, and the fast-food chain in turn hyped the movie with its television ad campaign.

Any fool should have noticed that, but many "sophisticated" big-city critics appeared not to notice in their rush to embrace the film. Only Janet Maslin of *The New York Times* protested the scam. Maslin appeared with two other critics, Stephen Schiff and David Denby, and Charlie Rose on his Public Television interview show (June 19, 1995) to puzzle over the tremendous success of the film, which opened on a precedent-setting 43,000 screens nationwide and set a box office record of $53.3 million for its opening weekend. They concluded, appropriately, that this was a disgraceful movie, a mess, because of its "shredded story." David Denby described the Riddler's spiteful psycho as "a ghastly, show-business wind-up toy." The "news" about *Batman Forever* was in the amount of money it made, not what was in the movie. But Warner Brothers should be credited for having produced a perfectly fabricated summer blockbuster, designed to make money. *Variety* described it as a "$200 million monster with not only wings but legs." One doubts that any summer film will eclipse its box office record this year.

—*James M. Welsh*

REVIEWS

The Baltimore Sun. June 16-22, 1995, Maryland Live, p. 4.
Entertainment Weekly. No. 280, June 23, 1995, pp. 34-35.
The Nation. Vol. CCLXI, No.2, July 10, 1995, pp. 68-69.
Newsweek. June 26, 1995, p. 54.
The New York Times. June 16, 1995, C1, C6.
The Philadelphia Inquirer. June 16, 1995, Weekend, P.3, p. 10.
Time. Vol. CXLV, No.26, June 26, 1995, p. 79.
The Washington Post. June 16, 1995, F1, F7.
Washington Post Weekend. June 16, 1995, p.45.
The Washington Times Metropolitan Times. June 16, 1995, C15.
Variety. June 19-25, 1995, p. 77, p. 81.

Before the Rain

"Four stars. Rugged, passionate, lyrical and wildly, improbably poetic. One of the most memorable motion pictures we're likely to see this year."—Michael Medved, *The New York Post*

"An overwhelming vision."—Janet Maslin, *The New York Times*

"Amazing. A film I may never forget. I was totally absorbed and thrown into another world."—Jeffrey Lyons, *Sneak Previews*

Box Office Gross: $763,847

Prior to *Before the Rain*, few would have suspected that the former Yugoslav republic of Macedonia even had a film industry. All that has changed. Screenwriter/director Milcho Manchevski's powerful debut film has assured his homeland a place in cinematic history. The first film made in Macedonia since it declared its independence from Yugoslavia, *Before the Rain* won the top prize—the Golden Lion—at the 1994 Venice Film Festival and earned an Academy Award nomination for Best Foreign-Language Film.

Before the Rain is told in three parts, each from the point of view of a different character. Part one, "Words," centers on Kiril (Gregoire Colin), a young monk who has taken a vow of silence in a mountain-top monastery in Macedonia. When he finds Zamira (Labina Mitevska), a terrified Albanian girl, hiding in his cell, Kiril does not turn her in. Kiril does not speak and he does not understand Zamira's language, yet the two communicate on a spiritual level. Kiril is drawn to the girl so much that he endangers the monastery by sheltering her when it is revealed that she is wanted for murder.

A band of gun-wielding Macedonian men storm the monastery looking for Zamira, who they claim killed their brother. She escapes with Kiril, who has disgraced himself to the order by his deception. Kiril is full of cheerful optimism for his future with Zamira as they run off together into the night. They do not get far, however, before Zamira's family intercepts them. They would rather see her dead than let her go off with a Christian. Zamira is gunned down by her own brother as Kiril looks on, horrified.

Making her film debut as Zamira, is eighteen-year-old Labina Mitevska. She was discovered by director Manchevski at an open casting call in Macedonia, which she attended only to accompany a friend. She researched her role by living with Albanian families both in Macedonia and Serbia.

Part two, "Faces," is set in London, where Anne (Katrin Cartlidge), a photo editor, faces a difficult choice. She is estranged from her husband, Nick (Jay Villiers), whom she still loves in a non- passionate way. Her affair with Aleksandar (Rade Serbedzija), an unpredictable Pulitzer Prize-winning war photographer, has resulted in her pregnancy. Aleksandar wants to return to his homeland of Macedonia, but that region's instability frightens Anne and she refuses to go with him. Moments after telling Nick that she wants a divorce, a psychotic patron opens fire on the restaurant where they are dining. Nick is one of several casualties of the bloody rampage.

Aleksandar returns to Macedonia for the first time in sixteen years in part three, "Pictures." The idyll of his childhood village has been replaced by violence, hatred, and war. His Moslem Albanian neighbors are now considered enemies. When Aleksandar visits his childhood love, Hana (Silvija Stojanovska), in the neighboring Moslem village, he is threatened by her family. Hana entreats Aleksandar to help when her daughter disappears. The daughter has been accused of killing Aleksandar's cousin with a pitchfork. As his kinsmen take up arms to seek revenge, Aleksandar helps the daughter—Zamira—escape. Aleksandar is shot and killed by his vengeful cousins, as Zamira flees toward a monastery nestled in the mountains.

Before the Rain breaks cinematic conventions by telling the story out of chronological order. Near the end of the third segment, events start taking on a familiarity. History seems to be repeating itself. That is when most viewers realize that part one is actually the conclusion of the story. Manchevski deliberately plants a hole in that theory, however, by showing Anne, in part two, looking at photographs of Kiril and Zamira. If parts two and three actually precede part one, Anne could not logically have those photographs. The story appears to have come full-circle at the end, but perhaps, as Father Marko (Josif Josifovski) cryptically tells Kiril in the opening and closing moments, "the circle is not round."

Though markedly different in tone and subject matter,

CREDITS

Anne: Katrin Cartlidge
Aleksandar: Rade Serbedzija
Kiril: Gregoire Colin
Zamira: Labina Mitevska
Father Marko: Josif Josifovski
Petre: Boris Delcevski
Mate: Dejan Velkov
Father Damjan: Kiril Ristoski
Trifun: Mladen Krstevski
Kuzman: Dzemail Maksut
Mitre: Ljupco Bresliski
Nick: Jay Villiers
Hana: Silvija Stojanovska

Origin: Great Britain, France, and Macedonia
Released: 1994
Production: Judy Counihan, Cedomir Kolar, Sam Taylor, and Cat Villiers for Aim Productions, Noe Productions, and Vardar Film, with the participation of British Screen and the European Coproduction Fund, in association with PolyGram Audiovisual and the Ministry of Culture for the Republic of Macedonia; released by Gramercy Pictures
Direction: Milcho Manchevski
Screenplay: Milcho Manchevski
Cinematography: Manuel Teran
Editing: Nicolas Gaster
Production design: Sharon Lamofsky and David Munns
Casting: Moni Damevski, Liora Reich
Sound: Aidan Hobbs
Costume design: Caroline Harris and Sue Yelland
Music: Anastasia
MPAA rating: no listing
Running Time: 115 minutes

AWARDS AND NOMINATIONS

Independent Spirit Awards 1996: Best Foreign Film
Venice Film Festival Awards 1994: Golden Lion
Academy Awards Nominations 1994: Best Foreign Language Film

Before the Rain drew frequent comparison to *Pulp Fiction* (1994), which also employed a nonlinear narrative form. While both films utilize an inventive plot device to challenge viewers to look at a story from a fresh perspective, the multiple time shifts in *Pulp Fiction* appear random and reckless in comparison to the purposeful circular motion of *Before the Rain*, which leaves viewers with a sense of fulfillment at its culmination.

"'Before the Rain' refers to the feeling of heavy expectation, when the skies are pregnant with the possibility of an outburst, when the people are silent, waiting for a tragedy or cleansing."—Writer/director Milcho Manchevski

The three leads are uniformly excellent in consummately convincing performances. Gregoire Colin speaks only a few lines of dialogue as his character maintains a vow of silence until he leaves the monastery, but his incredibly expressive eyes speak volumes. Serbian- born Rade Serbedzija is a powerful and commanding presence as the world-weary photographer. Katrin Cartlidge arouses audience understanding and sympathy for her plight as violence claims both of the men in her life.

Technical values are superlative, beginning with the breathtaking cinematography by Manuel Teran, which is enhanced by soulful music composed by Anastasia and exquisite production design by Sharon Lamofsky and David Munns. Teran's camera captures the timeless beauty of the Macedonian landscape, its majestic mountains and luminous skies. The unsullied Macedonian vistas give those segments a feel of belonging to a long-ago time, though rap music, Adidas sneakers, and a reference to "Ninja Turtles" serve as reminders that the setting is present-day.

In contrast, the London-set middle third of the film is unrelentingly contemporary. This episode also stands apart because it is primarily spoken in English, while the rest of the film's dialogue is Macedonian, with a small portion spoken in Albanian. Manchevski set part of his story in London to illustrate how a war in one region can alter the lives of people far removed from the action, as the Macedonian conflict affects Anne. Critics found this segment, which is strikingly different in tone from the other two, to be the film's weakest.

Before the Rain garnered wide acclaim in addition to its festival honors. *Variety* called it "a visually and narratively stunning tale," and *Boxoffice* lauded it as a "splendid and uniquely woven film ... the type of soul-stirring film that inspires late-night discussions about life and politics." Less enthusiastic about the film, *USA Today* accorded it only two and a half out of four stars, calling it a "slowly paced bilingual bummer whose separate stories do have collective power."

Rather than portray the political unrest in his homeland from a broad perspective, Manchevski chose to focus on three individuals whose lives become inextricably linked by the choices they make. By narrowing the scope in this way, he succeeds in showing that centuries-old recriminations can tear apart innocent lives in an instant, and taking sides can lead to disastrous consequences.

The solemn, somber mood of the piece is leavened by a few inspired moments of humor. As Anne and Aleksandar are in a passionate clinch in the back of a taxi, a woman interrupts them to ask if the cab is free. After an argument between a restaurant patron and a waiter escalates into a brawl, the manager calmly assures the crowd that the police will arrive any day now. These tension-breaking moments give only brief respite, however, from the brooding realism of the drama.

The film's title refers to the feeling of expectation before a rain, which Manchevski compares to the impression he got when he returned to his native Macedonia after an absence of several years and found the political climate exceedingly tense. "There was this sense of something heavy beginning to happen, something looming, something in the air," he said, according to the film's production notes. Since 1992, Macedonia's borders with Serbia and Albania have been patrolled by United Nations troops due to the volatile relations among the Balkan states. Within its own borders, Macedonia faces the threat of civil war due to the turmoil between the Orthodox Macedonians and the Albanian Moslem population. Yet Manchevski stressed that his film is not a documentary, because at the time of the film's release Macedonia remained the only republic in former Yugoslavia where not a single bullet had been fired in the war which followed the collapse of Yugoslavia.

Rather than delineate the region's current condition, Manchevski showed where it could be heading if tensions are not quelled. Without allying himself with either side, Manchevski provides a powerful warning of how petty rivalries can flare into war, destroying innocent lives in an instant. *Before the Rain* is a passionate outcry for peace which, in the words of Janet Maslin of *The New York Times*, leaves the audience "with a warning too strong to be ignored."

—Brenda Scott Royce

REVIEWS

Boxoffice. March, 1995, p. R-18.
Daily Variety. September 7, 1994, p. 6.
The Hollywood Reporter. January 24, 1995, p. 14.
Interview. March, 1995, p. 56.
Los Angeles Times. February 24, 1995, p. F1.
New York. March 13, 1995, p. 62.
The New York Times. February 24, 1995, p. B7.
The New Yorker. March 13, 1995, p. 109.
People Weekly. March 6, 1995, p. 19.
USA Today. February 24, 1995, p. 5D.
The Village Voice. February 28, 1995, p. 63.

Before Sunrise

"Can the greatest romance of your life last only one night?"—Movie tagline

"...an insatiably romantic and exuberantly witty film."—Rod Lurie, *Los Angeles Magazine*

"...a sharp, sexy funny romance with a radical core of intelligence that catches the fever and fleetingness of love."—Peter Travers, *Rolling Stone*

"Two thumbs up!"—*Siskel & Ebert*

Box Office Gross: $5,535,405

Julie Delpy as Celine and Ethan Hawke as Jesse embark upon a spontaneous expedition in Vienna in *Before Sunrise.* © 1995 Castle Rock Entertainment. All rights reserved. Photo by Gabriela Brandenstein.

Before Sunrise is a romance for Generation X, a traditional genre that has been given new life for a new generation. Dressed in the appropriate flannels and T-shirts, two twenty-something young people meet on a train somewhere in Austria. Celine (Julie Delpy), a beautiful Parisian student, and Jesse (Ethan Hawke), a sensitive young American, hit it off immediately, and it is easy to see why: It would be hard to find two more beautiful and hip young people on a train, or anywhere else, for that matter.

They strike up a conversation, joking about a German couple who are arguing on the train. With each espousing a twenty-year-old's wisdom about marriage, they impress each other and go to the dining car, where they discuss childhood, death, and even the afterlife. Just as Jesse and Celine are unabashedly enjoying each other's company, it is time for Jesse to disembark. Instead of parting, however, they leave together. Jesse persuades Celine to come with him, arguing that when she is old and dissatisfied with her marriage, she will always wonder what would have happened if she had gotten off the train with him. Charmed by his challenge, she agrees to roam the streets of Vienna with him until his plane leaves for home in the morning.

When they emerge from the railway station, they find themselves in the awkward position of having absolutely nothing to say to each other. To break the ice, Jesse starts a game of "truth or dare," in which they challenge each other to answer emotionally intimate questions. The dialogue is at first quite stilted as the screenwriters attempt to get the two to approach "deep" subjects quickly. That, afterall, is the challenge of the film itself: to take the viewer through the paces of how two people get from meeting to knowing to loving without leaving out any of the discomfort or the magic. In this case, the couple in question have only fourteen hours together.

The close camera angles are at first claustrophobic, making the viewer feel like the third wheel on a blind date. Yet as the two begin to be more at ease with each other, the viewer too becomes more comfortable. This is the beginning of the film's journey, exploring the sweet and sometimes moving evolution of the couple's relationship. Director Richard Linklater, of *Slacker* (1991) and *Dazed and Confused* (1993) fame, has successfully taken a love story and made it palatable for the twenty-something set. He carries it off with dialogue that is, at times, surprisingly tender and at other times youthfully callous and cynical.

In fact, the dialogue is the most important element of the film. As the two wander through the streets of Vienna, aimlessly traipsing through countless cafes, bars, parks, and alleyways, they bandy metaphysical one-liners and secondhand insights, letting slip the more interesting bits and pieces of their backgrounds in the process. Their honesty is disarming; they tell each other things they would not tell their best friends, and it is this candor that keeps the viewer intrigued.

> Director and co-writer Linklater aims for a lit-crit twist with references to Eric Rohmer, Antonioni, *The Third Man,* and Joyce's *Ulysses.*

If this were "real life," these two disparate personalities would very probably quickly tire of each other. In the film, however, their very different perspectives are tempered by their commonality. They both have just come from bad relationships a little battle-scarred, wary, and vulnerable.

They are both attracted to each other and the charm of their chance encounter. Further, they are both falling in love.

In one scene, Celine takes Jesse to a graveyard she had visited as a child, the "cemetery of those with no names." It is where the Viennese bury the bodies of those who wash up along the Danube, many of whom are suicides. Celine especially identifies with a fourteen- year-old girl whose grave she had first seen when Celine herself was fourteen. Now looking on the grave, she is struck by the fact that the girl will always be fourteen while she, twenty-three now, will continue to age. It is a sweet moment that underscores the idea that time is passing and their time together is coming to an end.

The substance of the film is basically the 101 minutes of dialogue between Jesse and Celine, interrupted only by a fortune-teller and a street poet, who add a touch of magic to the sometimes quasi-intellectualism of their conversation. The palm reader, played by Erni Mangold, reads Celine's palm and intimates what the viewer has already suspected, that Celine is an old soul in a young body.

Julie Delpy plays Celine with an intelligence and strength that give her character far more than just a pretty face. She also adds a sense of mystery to Celine and even, at times, a touch of passion. In contrast, Ethan Hawke as Jesse gives an excellent portrayal of the wary American "innocent abroad." Full of ideas, energy, and hormones, he wins Celine's heart with his boyish sensitivity and his beautiful liquid eyes.

When a street poet, played marvelously by Dominik Castell, approaches the couple and proposes to write a poem for them with any word they want, Celine sarcastically gives him the word "milkshake." The poet performs the impossible by writing a love poem that fits the couple, the night, and the word. They are both dazzled by the poem, but in an aside Jesse tries to convince Celine that the poet uses the same poem for everyone and simply plugs in the word.

As they enjoy many tiny adventures around Vienna, the night slowly passes away. The two have gotten to know and like each other more and more, when Celine reminds Jesse that in a few hours they will have to say good-bye forever. Jesse suggests that they say good-bye right then. That way, it would be out of the way, and they can continue to enjoy the remainder of their time together. Yet their real good-bye is still to come.

They decide to get a bottle of wine and wait out the sunrise in a park. There they debate whether to make love, the outcome of which, in a refreshingly ambiguous twist, is left to the viewer's imagination. Finally, daylight finds them at the railway station, where they must really say good-bye. The last traces of coyness slip away as they stand on the platform in love for all the world to see. Hastily promising to meet back there in exactly six months, they part, and the viewer is left to wonder if it is forever. In the final scene the camera revisits the places where Jesse and Celine have been the night before, which appear cold and empty without the lovers to warm them.

Before Sunrise, which premiered as the opening film of the 1995 Sundance Film Festival, is the third major feature film by director Richard Linklater. His first film, *Slacker*, had a cast of one hundred characters and took place over a twenty-four-hour period. It was while filming *Slacker* that the inspiration for *Before Sunrise* came to Linklater. He wanted to focus on two characters, "fleshing them out" over a short period of time. In the summer of 1993, he went to work on the script with his friend and cowriter, Kim Krizan.

Said Linklater, "We've all been in this type of 'holiday romance' situation. When you're travelling, you're much more open to experiences outside your usual realm. Aren't we all looking for interesting experiences with that 'no strings attached' aspect? Except here the entire relationship is compressed into one night. I think it's interesting how you can connect with someone the moment

CREDITS

Jesse: Ethan Hawke
Celine: Julie Delpy
Wife on train: Andrea Eckert
Husband on train: Hanno Poschl
Guy on bridge: Karl Bruckschwaiger
Guy on bridge: Tex Rubinowitz
Palm reader: Erni Mangold
Street poet: Dominik Castell

Origin: USA
Released: 1995
Production: Anne Walker-McBay for Castle Rock Entertainment and Detour Film, in association with F.I.L.M.H.A.U.S., Wien; released by Columbia Pictures
Direction: Richard Linklater
Screenplay: Richard Linklater and Kim Krizan
Cinematography: Lee Daniel
Editing: Sandra Adair
Production design: Florian Reichmann
Casting: Judy Henderson, Alycia Aumuller
Sound: Thomas Szabolcs
Costume design: Florentina Welley
MPAA rating: R
Running Time: 101 minutes

AWARDS AND NOMINATIONS

Berlin Film Festival Awards 1994: Best Director (Linklater)
MTV Movie Awards Nominations 1995: Best Kiss (Hawke/Delpy)

they open their mouth, how you can immediately sense a connection."

Director of photography Lee Daniel's filming of Vienna coincidentally incorporates many of the same set locations that were used in *The Third Man* (1949). Yet in *Before Sunrise*, the photography is fresh and romantic with tight angles alternating with wide views of the city.

> "If I turn out to be a psycho, you can bail out."—Jesse from *Before Sunrise*

Although *Before Sunrise* succeeds as a light romance, it has no depth. In fact, much of the intellectual posturing of the characters wastes good time that could have been used to flesh out their backgrounds a little more. It would have been more interesting to have put them in context with their generation in more ways than simply through their music, bars, or pop-philosophy. Linklater seems to be approaching this when Celine speaks of her revolutionary parents turned bourgeois. She says it is hard for her to fight for her ideals because she cannot recognize the enemy. Unfortunately, the remark is left to fall flat.

Linklater chose Vienna as the location for the film because "Vienna seemed like a European Austin. We found a *Slacker* connection in the cafe culture. The city was full of bright people at a loss what to do next. They were stifled and stuck here but there was still lots of mental activity going on." Yet a feeling for those "bright people at a loss what to do next" is not evoked in the characters of Jesse and Celine. The viewer never senses that sort of hopeless inertia from them. If anything, these two are irrepressively active, constantly moving from place to place.

The film does add a dimension, however, not often found in love stories. Ethan Hawke's boyish good looks and Julie Delpy's angelic beauty are realistically contrasted with their youthful cynicism and attempts at brilliance. In this, Linklater has achieved a far more realistic portrayal of how Generation X members really talk than can be found in most modern romantic comedies. This makes for dialogue that is not only realistic but also enlightening.

Ethan Hawke, although young, is a veteran of feature films. He has starred in such films as *Dead Poets Society* (1989), *White Fang* (1991), and *Reality Bites* (1994), beginning his film career at the age of fourteen with *Explorers* (1985).

His costar, Julie Delpy, also started her film career at fourteen in Jean-Luc Godard's *Detective* (1985). She has worked with some of Europe's finest directors: Carlos Saura in *The Dark Night* (1989), Agnieszka Holland in *Europa, Europa* (1990), Bertrand Tavernier in *Beatrice* (1988), and Volker Schlondorff in *Voyager* (1992). Delpy has also appeared in *The Three Musketeers* (1993), *White* (1993), and *Killing Zoe* (1994).

Before Sunrise explores the freedom, beauty, and sadness of a relationship that is not meant to last. The very brevity of their relationship is the doorway through which their love emerges— pristine and complete. Although two people endlessly talking to one another on screen for almost two hours sounds tedious, Linklater has made the audience privy to the delicate unfolding of a fragile love, as short-lived and beautiful as a butterfly.

—Diane Hatch-Avis

REVIEWS

Daily Variety. January 19, 1995, p. 2.
Entertainment Weekly. January 27, 1995, p. 30.
The Hollywood Reporter. January 19, 1995, p. 12.
Los Angeles Times. January 27, 1995, p. F6.
The New York Times. January 27, 1995, p. B9.

Beyond Rangoon

John Boorman's tight, gripping *Beyond Rangoon* finds the British director in total command of his craft. The film tells the fictional story of a young American woman vacationing in Burma in an effort to heal from the murder of her husband and young son in the States. Caught in the turmoil of the military coup of 1988, she is led through the chaos by a Burmese national whose grace, conviction, and courage in the face of death impel her to resume her life, until then suspended by grief.

In telling the story of an American changed by Third-World political turmoil, *Beyond Rangoon* becomes part of a small but distinguished genre of politico-historical films that includes Peter Weir's *The Year of Living Dangerously* (1982), Costa-Gavras's *Missing* (1982), Roger Spottiswoode's *Under Fire* (1983), Roland Joffe's *The Killing Fields* (1984), Oliver Stone's *Salvador* (1986), Richard Attenborough's *Cry Freedom* (1987), and Regis Wargnier's *Indochine* (1992). Most often directed by British or European filmmakers, the genre usually features, with some variation, an American "innocent abroad" whose illusions are shattered by genocide and upheaval in another country. As in *The Killing Fields* and *The Year of Living Dangerously*, the protagonist in *Beyond Rangoon*is exposed to the random nature of violence and terror in Southeast Asia, rendered comprehensible only by a spiritual guide who leads the hero through thickets of Eastern otherness.

Patricia Arquette stars as an American tourist visiting Burma who finds herself embroiled in the midst of a civil war in *Beyond Rangoon*. Photo by Bill Rubenstein.

Although the genre is designed first and foremost to appeal to the American box office, it also bears certain assumptions worth noting. First, the protagonist, whether American, British, Australian, or French, has illusions about civilized behavior, which must give way to a less rosy view of humanity. Second, the protagonist has a native spiritual guide, often with one foot in both East and West, who possesses an almost otherworldly ability to see and withstand suffering, and to communicate a holistic sense of purpose to the naive and linear-thinking foreigner. Third, the Western protagonist, innately good but ignorant, cynical, or disbelieving, must translate his new knowledge of human rights violations and the ways of the Third World, gleaned from his guide, into action by using his Western skills (medicine, journalism) to tell the world what he has seen. These films are, at bottom, pleas to American and European audiences to pay attention to the suffering their countries have left behind in the Third World, and to learn from natives of the Third World how to spiritually re-orient Western life. In these films, filmmakers combine the structure of a political thriller with elements of Herman Hesse's novels of Westerners transformed by Eastern spiritualism. Their goal is to sway Westerners, Americans in particular, into taking political action.

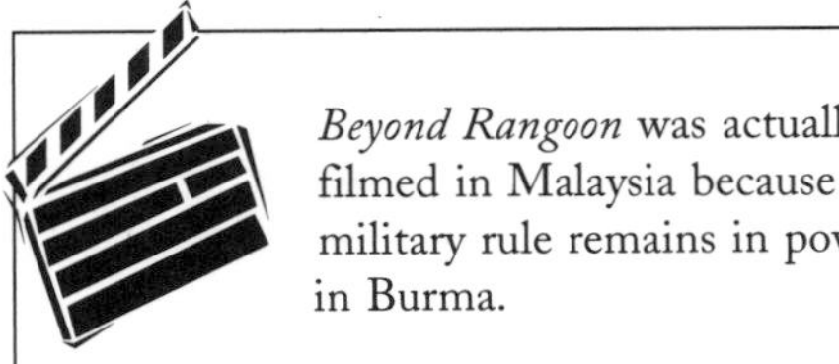

Beyond Rangoon was actually filmed in Malaysia because military rule remains in power in Burma.

The risks inherent in an artistic genre designed to sway public opinion are, first, that its films will play only to the already initiated, and, second, that they will become mere propaganda. (Stone's *Salvador* ran both these risks in 1986, yet succeeded in its goal of raising public consciousness about the dangers of U.S. military intervention in Central America.) In *Beyond Rangoon*, Boorman avoids these traps by telling a fictional story—albeit framed by real events—and by using as a backdrop the Burmese crisis in which Americans played little or no historical role. In so doing, Boorman is able to emphasize his protagonist's personal spiritual journey over political speechifying, and avoids placing the burden of American guilt for participation in an American-financed conflict on his protagonist. As in *The Emerald Forest* (1985), Boorman prefers the freedom of fiction to the strictures of docudrama.

Laura Bowman (Patricia Arquette), a doctor, has come to "exotic" Burma in an attempt to resolve her unfounded guilt at not having prevented the murder of her husband and young son in New York. The upbeat tour of serene Buddhist sites (led, with amusing irony, by Spalding Gray) provides little solace, however: Bowman remains spiritually and emotionally paralyzed. When a child falls at one of the tour's stops, only Laura's sister, Andy (Frances McDormand), also a physician, is able to intervene. Laura can no longer stand the sight of blood.

Waking in her hotel from a dream in which she re-experiences the loss of her son, Laura wanders onto the streets of Rangoon and witnesses pacifist leader Aun San Suu Kyi (Adelle Lutz) leading a peaceful pro-democracy demonstration. When soldiers aggressively block the route of the march, Laura gets a glimpse of Aung San Suu Kyi's grace in the face of an armed threat. Laura finds herself happy for the first moment since the murders—witnessing action, not nirvana. Back at the hotel, however, confronted by hotel police for breaking curfew, Laura foolishly begins yelling that Burma "doesn't seem to have a law against pointing guns at women." Her rage still has no proper outlet.

"The attainment of perfect detachment is the ultimate achievement."—An American guide from *Beyond Rangoon*

Laura almost willfully loses her passport and must remain in Burma while the rest of the tour group, including her sister, moves on. Now one of the few Western tourists left in the country, Laura affectlessly loses herself in the rhythms of Burma, unaware that a military crackdown is imminent. Rebuffing a blunt proposition from an American Embassy official, Laura instead chooses to drive into the Burmese interior with an "unofficial" English-speaking tourist guide, U Aung Ko (U Aung Ko). A purely sexual encounter with a cynical American has no appeal for her; rather, her friendship with this older Burmese man will become the basis for her spiritual renewal.

Laura feels comfortable in her anonymity with her new guide as they drive through the lush Burmese countryside. He tells her of his past as a monk and professor, and instructs her on the proper way to bribe the young soldiers who ominously man roadblocks. On a visit to a monastery, Laura senses that, like her, the monks seem to be "shutting life out."

As the result of car trouble, U Aung brings Laura to visit his former university students, leaders in the student democratic movement of the mid-1970s who were imprisoned and tortured for their activities. They reveal that U Aung was dismissed from his university professorship for helping the cause. With U Aung and his compatriots, Laura experiences a kind of group therapy. Rather than finding relief in mindless serenity or sex, Laura finds it in the company of others who have experienced loss—in their case, that of a nation. "That night," Laura says, "was the first night I was able to let go." She ends up sobbing in the rain and expressing to U Aung the grief about the murders she was never able to explain to her sister. She tells him that she was brought up with the Western notion that she had a right to happiness. U Aung Ko tells her that in Burma, by contrast, "we know that suffering is the only constant. So when happiness comes, we know it is only ours for a brief time." That night, Laura has another dream about her son and husband in which she feels at peace.

In the morning, however, the students reveal there has been a massacre of demonstrators in Rangoon, and the army has been tipped off about their presence in the countryside. U Aung is obligated to take Laura to the train station, where she will catch a train back to Rangoon and go directly to the American Embassy. Laura boards the train, but sees U Aung being beaten by soldiers on the platform. One of his students, Min Han (Johnny Cheah), tries to help him and is shot. Laura rescues U Aung, and the two flee by car through the jungle with the soldiers giving chase. In a harrowing scene, U Aung is shot and badly wounded, and Laura drives the car off a riverbank. Pursued by soldiers, Laura must drag U Aung through the water and dense riverbank foliage to safety— nearly losing the locket bearing a photo of her dead family.

Laura persuades an indolent and indifferent bamboo seller to take them downriver. On the journey, which goes from darkness to light, Laura becomes a doctor again, removing a bullet from U Aung's neck with a knife. At a brief stop, Laura eludes soldiers shooting and lynching villagers

CREDITS

Laura Bowman: Patricia Arquette
Andy Bowman: Frances McDormand
Jeremy Watt: Spalding Gray
U Aung Ko: U Aung Ko
Aung San Suu Kyi: Adelle Lutz
Johnny Cheah: Min Han

Origin: USA
Released: 1995
Production: Barry Spikings, Eric Pleskow and John Boorman for Castle Rock Entertainment; released by Columbia Pictures
Direction: John Boorman
Screenplay: Alex Lasker and Bill Rubenstein
Cinematography: John Seale
Editing: Ron Davis
Production design: Anthony Pratt
Art direction: Errol Kelly
Set decoration: Eddie Fowlie
Costume design: Deborah La Gorce Kramer
Sound: Gary Wilkins
Music: Hans Zimmer
MPAA rating: R
Running Time: 97 minutes

to obtain penicillin and morphine for U Aung, finding an ally in the boatman's young son, who prevents the boat from leaving without them. On shore, however, Laura must shoot a soldier who is about to rape and kill her.

U Aung recovers, but in Rangoon, the U.S. Embassy is surrounded by Burmese soldiers, who proceed to massacre unarmed monks, students, and nurses. U Aung and Laura flee by truck with other refugees toward camps along the Thai border. On the way, they meet a soldier disguised as a monk, who has defected because he could not stand to murder innocent people. In a camp at the Thai border, Laura has a third dream, in which she finally lets go of her son and husband. Laura reflects on the irony that when her family was killed, all she wanted to do was die to be with them, and that now she is fighting for her life. U Aung tells her that "the life in you is too strong. You are a healer. You healed me." Amid a hail of gunfire, Laura and U Aung cross a bridge into Thailand, where Laura immediately pitches in to help the Red Cross medical team.

Boorman skillfully shows how Laura's experience in the East allows her to let go of her guilt and to regain her sense of worth through work. What at first is a flight from from her past becomes a reconciliation with it, and an ability to rejoin the living. Using the framework of a political thriller, Boorman neatly introduces the theme that Americans seeking refuge from domestic violence will not find salvation in exoticism abroad, but rather in finding their own spiritual centers, and, in so doing, their connectedness with the world. Arquette, a second choice for the film after Meg Ryan dropped out of the project, brings an impressive physicality to the role, particularly in the scenes where she must drag the injured U Aung Ko along the river's edge to escape gunfire. Alex Lasker and Bill Rubenstein's tightly structured script, Australian documentary cinematographer John Seale's brilliant camerawork, and Ron Davis's economical editing help produce the tautest Boorman film since *Point Blank* (1967) and *Deliverance* (1972). The movie also uses visual and narrative shorthand to introduce several subthemes, such as the use of uneducated and unquestioning young men as the shock troops for military dictatorships.

Beyond Rangoon is a small masterpiece—an illustration of its own philosophy that wisdom can be acquired only through immersion in action.

—*Paul Mittelbach*

REVIEWS

The Nation. CCLXI, September 18, 1995, p.291.
The New Republic. CCXIII, September 18, 1995, p.38.
The New York Times. CXLIV, August 25, 1995, p.B1(N).
The New Yorker. LXXI, August 21, 1995, p.132.
Rolling Stone. September 7, 1995, p.77.
Sight and Sound. V, July, 1995, p.41.
Time. CXLVI, September 4, 1995, p.72.
Vogue. CLXXXV, September, 1995, p.336.
The Wall Street Journal. August 25, 1995, p.A6.

The Big Green

According to the United States Youth Soccer Association, team enrollments in youth soccer recently reached a record-breaking 2.3 million members. Therefore, it is no surprise that when Disney and Caravan Pictures asked Holly Goldberg Sloan (who wrote the successful *Angels in the Outfield*, 1994) what she would like to pursue for her next project, she said she'd like to do a soccer film. "Since my two sons and I love soccer, I said I'd like to do a soccer movie," Sloan is quoted as saying in the production notes. "As it turned out, both Joe [Roth, now the Walt Disney Studios' chairman] and Roger [Birnbaum, head of Caravan Pictures] played soccer in high school and love the game. So we shared a passion for the sport. And when I said I'd like a chance to direct the movie as well, they generously agreed."

Elma, Texas, is a town whose residents would no doubt agree that most of the good times ever to happen in Elma have already happened. The town is down on its luck. Whereas the adults relive golden moments from their past, embellished (as they are) by nostalgia, the children are mired, stuck in a town with no future, surrounded by people who have just given up. Then, Anna Montgomery (Olivia d'Abo), an exchange teacher, faces a room filled with bored, hostile students, and decides to make a difference. The difference is soccer.

Writer/director Sloan identifies her life as the source of many of her ideas. "Everything I write is sort of a big lexicon for my life," said Ms. Sloan. "There are a lot of things that have come from my life or my children's lives or some life that I've observed. I don't think I make up so much as I observe the world around me and try to incorporate it." For instance, in the opening scene of the film, several of the Elma boys ride their bicycles to the school yard, lie down, and throw Cheetos all over themselves. Soon an array of birds circles around, feasting on the snacks. A visually interesting scene (a little *ET*, 1982, with boys on bikes, and a little *The Birds*, 1963, with birds "feeding off" humans) and a novel entertainment, the idea originated with Ms. Sloan's sons, who feed the seagulls at Santa Monica beach.

Also drawn from Ms. Sloan's life is the idea of the outsider coming in with new perspectives and energies. Growing up as the daughter of a professor and Peace Corps consultant, Ms. Sloan lived in Holland and Turkey, and thereby experienced the "outsider" feeling first hand. "An outsider can change everything just by the force of their personality or the force of having a different cultural background. To me, that's really what *The Big Green* is about," she said.

Despite all the kids involved in the filming of *The Big Green*, production only had to stop once—and that was for adult injuries, when Guttenberg and D'Abo both pulled muscles in their legs during a routine workout.

The Big Green draws on several filmmaking traditions. The first involves teachers who come in and change the underachieving self-doubters into successful people who like themselves. Films such as *To Sir With Love* (1967) and *Dangerous Minds* (1995) place teachers into schools that are basically foreign to them, focus on the teachers' problems getting adjusted to the system, and then explore the extent of their success with their students. For instance, in *To Sir With Love*, Sidney Poitier's character inspires intellectual curiosity in his once-hostile, defeated students and encourages them to see beyond the drudgery and limits around them, beyond their parents' failure and ennui. His interest in them is the warmth of the sun to these otherwise forgotten, struggling students. Soon the students are interested in treating each other and their teacher with respect. Then they are interested in art. Soon they are grown up and ready to set about their lives.

In similar fashion, the school-aged children in Elma are largely forgotten. Without a dream of a future, mired in a town lost in the past, they are immobile. Anna works to motivate them about history, about world events, about math, but the surly students recline in their desks with blank stares. Finally, Anna can bear it no longer. She drags them out of the classroom and into the sun. She produces a soccer ball and virtually strong-arms them into playing. Initially hesitant, underskilled, the Elma team members (optimistically named The Big Green after the "glory" field in their town) barely push the ball along, exhausting themselves in the process. Soon the individual team members find something to work for or are inspired by their small successes. Even the assistant coach, the out-of-shape sheriff Tom Palmer (Steve Guttenberg) must become motivated, first by the beautiful new teacher and then, by his old rival who happens to coach the best team in the league that includes Elma. The outcome is no surprise.

Basically the format of the film is formula, just as in the countless *Bad News Bears* films (1976, 1977, 1978), or *Mighty Duck* films (1993, 1994) or countless other movies geared toward innocuous, "inspiring" family entertainment: uninspired children (who also happen to be out-of-shape in the formula's newest incarnation), who are good at heart but whose goodness and talent have yet to be tapped, are surrounded by self-absorbed grownups who have smothered or forgotten any creative ideas they ever had. However, salvation comes in the shape of an outsider, a misfit, sometimes even an unwilling subject. And together teacher and student, mentor and mentee, coach and player change their world view and achieve their goals. While the formula will probably not entertain the more grown-up persons in the audience, it should prove engaging to teens and preteens.

Other portions of the film are also pointedly geared to preteen and teen audiences. For instance, when Anna first arrives at the school, she sees the students reclining, engaged in feeding the birds (as discussed above). Filmmaker Sloan has chosen to speed Anna's approach by having her leap out of the car and "rescue" the boys all at double speed (i.e., fast forward). The result is a kind-of Keystone Cops flavor that

CREDITS

Tom Palmer: Steve Guttenberg
Anna Montgomery: Olivia d'Abo
Jay Huffer: Joy O. Sanders
Edwin V. Douglas: John Terry
Evan Schiff: Chauncey Leopardi
Larry Musgrove: Patrick Renna
Jeffery Luttrell: Billy L. Sullivan
Marbelly Morales: Yareli Arizmendi
Newt Shaw: Bug Hall

Origin: USA
Released: 1995
Production: Roger Birnbaum for a Caravan Pictures production; released by Walt Disney Pictures
Direction: Holly Goldberg Sloan
Screenplay: Holly Goldberg Sloan
Cinematography: Ralf Bode
Editing: John F. Link
Production design: Evelyn Sakash
Art direction: Harry Darrow
Set decoration: Helen Britton
Costume design: Rondi Hillstrom Davis
Sound: Robert Allan Wald
Music: Randy Edelman
MPAA rating: PG
Running Time: 100 minutes

is unsupported by what comes before or after. However, the young persons in the audience might find Anna's racing about to be funny. Ms. Sloan has also decided to present some of the Elma children's fears visually. That is, when Larry Musgrove (Patrick Renna) feels like he is defending a goal without weapons while a huge dragon or ninjas or pirates approach, Ms. Sloan depicts it just that way. While such a technique can be interesting when used sparingly, when used to the extent that it is during the "big game" in *The Big Green*, it detracts from the action and the acting. Grown audience members may find it a disappointment, while younger viewers may be entertained.

Nonetheless Ms. Sloan reports that she tried to make the film work for adults as well. "When family films work, they reach audiences from 6 to 96. In order to do that, you need a strong adult pull as well. It can't just be adolescent humor....[W]ell-grounded, realistic adult characters with a more sophisticated sense of humor...will specifically appeal to the older audience." However, it is important to note that the exchanges between d'Abo's and Guttenberg's characters are either clumsily flirtatious or angry. For instance, when Anna goes out jogging, Guttenberg's Tom Palmer backs his car alongside her so that he can continue to plead his romantic case. He pretends to be chasing a desperado in the hope that she will find him daring. Later in the film, d'Abo stands by as Guttenberg's character relives high-school aggression against the rival coach (Jay O. Sanders). Neither exchange would probably qualify as sophisticated.

Based in Austin, Texas, the production unit began principal photography in late 1994 and continued for nine weeks. According to the production notes, "Elma" is actually Dale, Texas, selected because of its "old school building in the midst of farmland and a collection of small houses that barely make up [the] town". Among the hazards of shooting a film in Texas in the winter, learned Ms. Sloan, are dry weather (which is especially problematic when a mud bowl sequence is needed), fire ants, snakes and a whole array of bugs.

The soccer sequences proved challenging as well. While 2.3 million children play soccer, they were not among those selected to appear in this film. Indeed, only a few of the leading actors had any soccer experience, and, as Ms. Sloan had made the decision not to use doubles, a soccer coach was hired: Robert Parr, head coach of the University of Texas' varsity soccer team and his staff of assistants. Both the teaching and the filming proved challenging. For instance, team tactics were not as important as how the game *looked*. Said Parr, "We emphasized keeping the ball on the ground because that's a nicer style of soccer to watch." Also emphasized, however, was the physical humor of these young, not-so-coordinated children, trying to learn to play soccer. Physical pranks abound, which may also entertain younger viewers.

The Big Green is not memorably bad, but it falls far short of entertaining family audiences. As a video rental for children on a rainy day without other possibilities, *The Big Green* would begin to look better. All in all, this film is one that most viewers will want to miss.

—Roberta F. Green

REVIEWS

Boxoffice, November 1995, p. R-98.
The New York Times, September 29, 1995, p. C6.
USA Today, September 29, 1995, p. 9D.
Variety, October 2, 1995, p. 40.
Washington Post, September 29, 1995, p. F8.

Billy Madison

"To inherit his family's fortune, Billy is going back to school...Way back."—Movie tagline

Box Office Gross: $25,588,734

Hollywood has always been fond of stupidity, but *Billy Madison* is one of the dumbest movies ever made. It's based on Adam Sandler's customary *Saturday Night Live* routine. Sandler wrote the script, perhaps in crayon.

Sandler can act like an idiot. For about a minute, his shtick is funny. He sits in a bathtub and has the shampoo bottle and conditioner arguing with each other as to who's the best. Little kids will laugh and adults will snicker. That's as good as it gets, and there are still 88 minutes left to endure.

Sandler mugs the part of Billy Madison, a spoiled, drunken and brainless young rich man set to inherit his father's hotel chain. His dad wants to retire and give Billy the company, but sniveling aide Eric (Bradley Whitford) objects that Billy's just too stupid. Since Dad bribed Billy's way through school, Billy vows to pass all 12 grades, on his own, two weeks at a time, to earn the chance to get the hotel chain.

It's an adequate premise for a 10-minute comedy skit, but not for a feature-length movie. Billy doesn't get out of the lower grades before his routine becomes insufferable, and it's not just the dumb stuff. What's really annoying is that, when challenged, Billy yells in people's faces, making him stupid and rude.

Adam Sandler first gained fame for his popular *Saturday Night Live* characters, "Opera Man" and "Cajun Man."

Naturally, a stupid, rude, dorky-looking overgrown kid is absolutely irresistible to a gorgeous young third-grade teacher named Veronica (Bridgette Wilson). It makes no sense, but there's got to be a love interest to sustain the film. But Wilson and Sandler fail the chemistry class.

Wilson's teasing sensuality is the film's sole attraction, and that's exploited in the most leering, adolescent way. Wilson tries hard, but who could believe an attractive, smart young woman like her would ever fall for a schmuck like Billy Madison? She has to recite lines like, "I believe you. And I believe in you. There are too many people in this world with no willpower, no brains, no vision. You have all those things. You're just afraid to use them." Right.

"But dad, I always thought we had this unspoken pact that you would go to work and build our future, and I would stay home and enjoy myself and one day, you'd hand over the business, and I'd really appreciate it."—Billy Madison from *Billy Madison*

Adam Sandler must repeat all 12 grades of school in less than six months in *Billy Madison*.

It gets worse, when the slimy Eric connives to sabotage Billy's matriculation. You can see the blackmail target coming about a half-hour before the clumsy plot gets around to revealing it.

It's hard to say which is dumber, the supposed romance or the supposed suspense. The comedy is no more than hit-and-miss, at best. There are a lot of potty jokes and very juvenile sex jokes. Target audience: high school boys. Very stupid high school boys.

Billy Madison clicks only a couple of times, once when Billy and Veronica satirize the film's own plot by breaking into a slapstick operatic musical number. The film could use a lot more of that kind of irreverence because in order to succeed as entertainment, it has to mock itself, and there is much to mock.

When Sandler tries to act serious and garner sympathy, he is unintentionally funnier than when he plays for laughs. He is a comic who can hit only one note, and it's a grating one. As a screen actor, he flunks.

Pity the others trapped in this mess. Director Tamra Davis lets Sandler run wild and brings no flair to the proceedings. Veteran Darren McGavin walks through the role of Billy's dad, Whitford is a rather lame villain, and poor Josh Mostel has to play a fat, gay principal who is the butt of too many of Billy's jokes. Dina Platias as first-grade teacher Miss Lippy is amusing in her small role.

On the comic genius scale, *Billy Madison* flunks kindergarten.

—*Michael Betzold*

AWARDS AND NOMINATIONS

MTV Movie Awards 1995: Best Comedic Performance (Sandler)

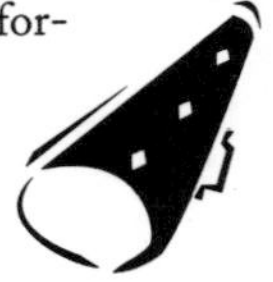

REVIEWS

Entertainment Weekly. Feb. 24, 1995, p. 90.
People Weekly. Feb. 27, 1995, p. 18.
Time. March 6, 1995, p. 100.
Variety. Feb. 13, 1995, p. 48.

CREDITS

Billy Madison: Adam Sandler
Brian Madison: Darren McGavin
Veronica: Bridgette Wilson
Eric Gordon: Bradley Whitford
Max Anderson: Josh Mostel
Frank: Norm MacDonald
Jack: Mark Beltzman
Carl Alphonse: Larry Hankin
Juanita: Theresa Merritt

Origin: USA
Released: 1995
Production: Robert Simonds; released by Universal Pictures
Direction: Tamra Davis
Screenplay: Tim Herlihy and Adam Sandler
Cinematography: Victor Hammer
Editing: Jeffrey Wolf
Production design: Perry Blake
Art direction: Gordon Barnes
Set decoration: Enrico Campana
Casting: Jaki Brown-Karman, Todd Thaler and Deidre Bowen
Sound: Allan Byer
Costume design: Marie-Bylvie Deveau
Music: Randy Edelman
MPAA rating: PG-13
Running Time: 89 minutes

Blue in the Face

"Just over the bridge, around the corner from reality is a place that's out of this world. Welcome to Planet Brooklyn."—Movie tagline

Box Office Gross: $1,275,999

An offbeat travelogue of Brooklyn that concentrates on the diverse human landscape of the borough, *Blue in the Face* is a moderately successful companion piece to *Smoke*, the Wayne Wang urban folk tale. Released only a few months after *Smoke*, *Blue in the Face* is not a sequel so much as a sidebar. Wang had some leftover footage and he and screenwriter Paul Auster had some unfinished ideas, as did some of his cast. The filmmakers convinced Miramax to give them an extra week to shoot, and the result is *Blue in the Face*.

Given the limits of five days, a low budget and no script, *Blue in the Face* isn't bad. Most critics will bleed it with inevitable comparisons to the far more complex and well-worked-out *Smoke*, but taken on its own, as it should be, *Blue in the Face* is a mildly entertaining curio. It's basically a series of improvisations by an unlikely conglomeration of talented actors, and it's interesting to watch them work. Viewing it is almost like being invited to a Hollywood rehearsal. It's the celluloid version of free-form jazz; some of the riffs sizzle, and some fall flat. But the films manages to retain its own strange sort of slice-of-life logic.

As in *Smoke*, the setting is Augie Wren's Brooklyn Cigar Company, a corner-store hangout in a quintessential Brooklyn neighborhood. Harvey Keitel is back as the bemused Augie who views the passing parade of life with equanimity and sympathy, except when it comes to purse-snatching kids. Getting larger roles this time are the store's owner Vinnie (Victor Argo) and Augie's feeble-minded broom-pusher Jimmy (Jared Harris). And there's a gaggle of celebrity walk-ons, including characterizations by Roseanne, Madonna, Lily Tomlin, Michael J. Fox, musician Lou Reed and filmmaker Jim Jarmusch.

Writer Paul Aster and director Wayne Wang had such a good time filming *Smoke*, they persuaded Miramax Films to let them make a second movie using the same setup and based almost entirely on improvisations. *Blue* was filmed in five days.

The paltry plot of *Blue in the Face* is mostly a distraction from the riffs. Vinnie threatens to close Brooklyn Cigar Company but changes his mind after a lecture from Augie and a visit from the ghost of Jackie Robinson (Keith David). That's stale stuff; nothing is more hackneyed than the old lament about the day the Dodgers moved to Los Angeles and Ebbets Field was torn down. There's also a bit of woman trouble for Augie, revolving around the sultry Violet (Mel Gorham) and Vinnie's unsatisfied wife Dot (Roseanne). That's mostly fluff, though Gorham has some sizzling moments in front of a vanity mirror.

Since it is a scriptless film, *Blue in the Face* rises and falls with its improv skits, and it has many peaks and valleys. There's a wonderful opener in which Augie catches a 12-year-old purse-snatcher and then flies into a rage when the victimized woman (Mira Sorvino) says she doesn't want to press charges. She flies into her own rage when Augie grabs the purse and gives it back to the kid. An entire debate about young people, crime, responsibility, justice and philosophy is condensed into a minute or so of shouting. It's well-done, and *Blue in the Face* would have been a remarkable film if it had sustained this kind of friction, but it doesn't.

Most of the best scenes in *Blue in the Face* are shouting matches. As a real Brooklyn resident explains in an interview early in the film, the "Brooklyn attitude" is "never stop following through on what you believe...not taking any crap from anyone." So when a female visitor to Augie's shop starts picking on a regular on behalf of his aggrieved girlfriend, the verbal fur flies; both parties are absolutely convinced of their righteousness. Dot and Vinnie have a hilarious verbal spat where Dot accuses Vinnie of not listening while Vinnie shouts that he is listening. And when a streetwise entrepreneur who flaunts his black pride (Malik Yoba) enters the story to sell watches and do some rapping, he rags on Tommy (Giancarlo Esposito), who is of mixed Italian/African heritage. All of these and a few other similar encounters work well because they seem like authentic exchanges.

Even better are some of the interviews, shot on videotape, with locals. A smart, engaging young woman on a boardwalk bench by the sea provides the film's most honest moments talking about her dope-smoking boyfriend and her 18th birthday. *Blue in the Face* could have used more of those snatches of realism.

What doesn't work, besides the Jackie Robinson bit, are the plentiful segments with Reed and Jarmusch. Reed rambles on about his attachment to Brooklyn, and most of what he says sounds either lame or stilted. "I live in New York because I know my way around New York. I don't know my way around Paris or Denver or Maui," he deadpans. Augie listens while Jarmusch smokes his last cigarette and talks about the meaning of smoking as related to growing up, sex, health and many other topics, and almost all of the discussion is precocious, self-indulgent and uninteresting. When

CREDITS

Auggie Wren: Harvey Keitel
Lou Reed: Lou Reed
Dot: Roseanne
Peter: Michael J. Fox
Jim Jarmusch: Jim Jarmusch
Derelict: Lily Tomlin
Violet: Mel Gorham
Jimmy Rose: Jared Harris
Tommy: Giancarlo Esposito
Vinne: Victor Argo
Singing Telegram Girl: Madonna
Jackie: Keith David
Blond woman: Mira Sorvino

Origin: USA
Released: 1995
Production: Greg Johnson, Peter Newman and Diana Philips for a Blue in the Face production; released by Miramax
Direction: Wayne Wang and Paul Auster
Screenplay: Wayne Wang and Paul Auster; in collaboration with cast
Cinematography: Adam Holender
Editing: Christopher Tellefsen
Production design: Kalina Ivanov
Costume design: Claudia Brown
Choreography: Linda Talcott
Sound: Drew Kunin, John Hurst
Casting: Heidi Levitt
Music: John Lurie
MPAA rating: R
Running Time: 89 minutes

Blue in the Face becomes focused on aging white male hippies rambling on about nothing in particular, the film seems flaccid. It's much better when it lets its more interesting ethnic characters take center stage, especially Gorham, who combines exaggerated Latin sexual energy with comic vamping.

Roseanne is less successful at heating up the proceedings when she comes on to Augie. Instead, she is mostly annoying as she complains about how Vinnie is a boring mate. Some of the other celebrity turns are simply strange. Tomlin is unrecognizable and gets little screen time as a straggle-haired male street person. Fox goes completely against his usual character, playing a researcher who has strange survey questions for Tommy; unfortunately, most of the questions are sophomoric. Madonna, playing a singing telegram girl, shows signs of age; she looks a little worn, though she's plenty sassy showing contempt for Augie's five-dollar tip.

At the center of things, Keitel has little to do except look amused; he's like the malt-shop owner in countless old TV sitcoms. His character needs more of the opinionated zing he put into the opening scene. And, overall, *Blue in the Face* would have benefited from more confrontations, controversy and surprises to fulfill Augie's opening pronouncement that it's a chronicle of a week where everyone he meets is acting crazy. Actually, they're not acting all that crazy.

"I think the only reason I live in New York is that I know my way around New York."—Lou Reed from *Blue in the Face*

Some David Byrne music helps inject life into a few dull spots, and there is just the right amount of subtle thematic continuity to tie together some of the disparate bits. But director Wang doesn't hit a home run with this material; he is too content to let the camera linger on skits that are not that compelling. It's always a mistake for directors to fawn on actors, and *Blue in the Face* has the unfortunate feel of a director and a cast showing off how good they are at ad-libbing. Most of the time, it's not nearly as cool as they want it to be.

Still, *Blue in the Face* is of passing interest for some of its keen observations of the human, urban condition, and it has its entertaining comic moments. All in all, it's not a bad week's work.

—*Michael Betzold*

The Blue Villa (Un Bruit Qui Rend Fou)

A quiet mediterranean island village suffers the return of a man believed to have been long dead in *The Blue Villa*, a film that takes as its subject the problematic nature of truth and narrative. Co-directed by Dimitri de Clercq and acclaimed French novelist and filmmaker Alain Robbes-Grillet, the film shares many of the theoretical themes and strategies of Robbes-Grillet's novels and previous films such as *L'Homme Qui Vevt* (1968) and *Trans-Euro-Express* (1966). An innovator in modernist debates, his films and novels focus on unreliable narrators, mistaken identity, unsolved riddles, and labyrinth point of views. Robbes-Grillet entered filmmaking with the screenplay *Last Year at Marienbad* (1961) and was heralded as an innovative director throughout the 60s, but *Blue Villa* is his first film since *La Belle Captive* (1983).

In the opening scene a travel weary and mysterious Chinese ship with torn red sails and sad eyes painted on its prow arrives empty into the harbor of a mediterranean island as a voice sings the tale from Wagner's opera "The Flying Dutchman." Despite the fact that the boat is empty, word begins to spread throughout the village that Frank (Fred Ward) is back. A narrator recounts a legend in which a pale mariner guilty of killing his lover, his sails soaked with her blood, is forced to return to port annually to repeat his crime. His soul can only be redeemed upon winning the heart of a virtuous prostitute and resting with her in a grave.

The narrator is the cynical and weary Edouard Nordmann, or Nord (Charles Tordjman), who is actually speaking the text of his screenplay into a tape recorder. He describes the island several times as a place where nothing ever happens and then embarks on his supposedly true account of the events that occurred. Constantly revising as he speaks, he describes how his beloved daughter, Santa (Sandrine Le Berre), was thrown from a cliff by her lover Frank, who then took his own life. Her piercing screams summon local fishermen, but she is only found later disfigured and unrecognizable. The graves of Frank and Santa rest side by side on the island.

Meanwhile Frank wanders around town like a haggard apparition terrifying the superstitious and remaining in a mysterious silence that leaves all possibilities open. His astonishing arrival drives the local investigator Thieu (Dimitri Poulikakos) to reopen the murder case and propose an interpretation in which Nord is the prime suspect. The investigator appears at Nord's home, confiscates the tape-recorded screenplay as evidence and reminds Nord that Santa was not his daughter but merely his despised step-daughter. Nord does not seem surprised, and even appears to have anticipated this move. It is now uncertain whether Nord's constant textual revision was creative editorial work or a hasty attempt to exonerate himself from a crime he has committed. The recorded text now appears to be testimonial, but in light of the accusation by Thieu, its veracity is as suspect as if it were a work of fiction. Nord's credibility is further diminished by his repeated drunken hallucinations of visits from both Frank and Santa. The viewer stands in the same relationship to these hallucinations as does Nord, uncertain of their actuality. A sordid suspicion of a history of sexual abuse between Nord and Santa gradually emerges from these images.

The movements of the town center around the local casino and whorehouse, the Blue Villa, where day and night the clattering of ivory chips in a perpetual game of Mah-Pong is known to drive men to madness. The sound of this constant negotiation of forces between players inspires the film's original French title, *Un Bruit Qui Rend Fou (A Noise Which Makes Mad)*, and serves as a central metaphor for the task of interpretation and power. The camera returns to this game repeatedly, focusing on the player's hands and the slamming of the chips against the table, and showing how the players perpetually change but the game never ceases. The final shot of the game consists of the key figures in the drama taking turns at the table.

CREDITS

Frank: Fred Ward
Edouard Nordmann: Charles Tordjman
Santa: Sandrine LeBerre
Thieu: Dimitri Poulikakos
The Father: Christian Maillet
Kim: Muriel Jacobs

Origin: Belgium
Released: 1995
Production: Jacques de Clercq for a Nomad Films, Euripide, La Sept Cinema, Canal Plus, Investimage 4 and CNC production; released by Nomad Films
Direction: Alain Robbe-Grillet and Dimitri de Clercq
Screenplay: Alain Robbe-Grillet and Dimitri de Clercq
Cinematography: Hans Meier
Editing: France Duez
Art direction: Alain Chennaux
Costume design: Bernadette Corstens
Sound: Francois Musy
Assistant direction: Denis Seurat
MPAA rating: not listed
Running Time: 100 minutes

In a secret room above the casino, under lock and key, is the waif-like Lotus Blossom, who besides receiving house patrons also receives caresses and opera lessons from the whorehouse madam Sarah-la-blonde (Arielle Dombasle). Beautiful, coy, and with a small girlish voice, Lotus tries unsuccessful to imitate the operatic sounds of the madam. Like a caged bird, she also tries to reach the decorative key that hangs outside her window. Her restless, naive, girlish gestures bear an uncanny resemblance to the Santa seen in flashbacks. It is only by using evidence gained from various unreliable sources including the theories of Thieu, the hallucinations of Frank, and the appearance of Santa's natural father, that we learn that Lotus Blossom is Santa in disguise. Her murder was staged in order to protect her from Nord, who was supposedly planning to kill her in order to acquire her lofty family inheritance.

Nord resists this interpretation, insisting that he was lured to the island from the mainland by the treacherous madam, Sarah-la-blonde, who sought to rob him of his daughter and his money. While Nord's resistance resembles paranoia, it is also justified by flashbacks of Sarah luring Nord to the island with promises of illicit sexual opportunities with young girls, as well as scenes of her negotiating and taking money from Santa's real father with whom she makes clandestine visits on the mainland. Her intentions remain under constant suspicion.

Just when a resolution seems impossible, Santa poses as a shrouded invalid and drags herself to her gravesite where she comes face to face with Frank and drops her disguise. The two supposed apparitions reclaim their existence and in the final scene are seen sailing past the island, the red sails of the ship now bright white and untarnished. The answers to the multitude of narrative strands and questions go unanswered and the viewer is left to create his or her own interpretation or story, assured only of its intrinsic incompleteness.

Though the film incorporates elements from every kind of traditional narrative, including the legend, fable, detective story, love story, and mystery, there is nothing traditional about this narrative. The viewer is never drawn into the story but instead remains a cool, outside observer, wandering from one image to the next, making associations which are later discarded in favor of new ones. *The Blue Villa* is thoughtful and visually striking, but it is also stifled by the dominance of its modernist theoretical agenda that makes events seem purely formal and lacking in necessity and visuals studied and merely aesthetic.

The film is supported by fine performances. Fred Ward, who barely utters a word, is exemplary as Frank, the questionable apparition haunting the roads of the village, without possessions and without speech, he retains the allure of an enigma from the sea. Arielle Dombasle, best known for her roles in several Eric Rohmer films, including *Pauline at the Beach*, is wonderful as the beautiful, soft, quietly strong madam Sarah-la-blonde, who maintains the economy of the island by luring men from the mainland to the remote island. And Sandrine Le Berre is excellent at creating the film's aura of illicit sex and obscenity with her exaggerated girlish voice and gestures.

Best known as the founder of Le Noveau Roman (The New Novel), Robbes-Grillet first challenged the traditional goal of the novel to convey the interior depths of the individual with the publication of *Les Gommes (The Erasers)* in 1953. He instead privileged a phenomenological account of the visual, surface appearances of objects, and in many respects created a novel resembling the visual logic of cinema. Robbes-Grillet's modernist conviction that meaning will emerge, not from psychological depth or symbols, but from the surface appearances of objects, is countered with the reality that the film never provokes more than a surface involvement. *The Blue Villa* is far more lyrical than his previous films, but in the end it remains a carefully studied lyricism.

—Reni Celeste

REVIEWS

Chicago Tribune, January 5, 1996.
The New York Times, Sept 14, 1995.

Bosnia!; Bosna!

A gut-wrenching look at the war in Sarajevo between the people of Bosnia and their aggressors, the Serbian soldiers. The narrator (Bernard-Henri Levy) presents graphic images of carnage and a reign of terror imposed on the Bosnians by the Serbs, conditions which Levy compares to the Holocaust under Hitler's rule.

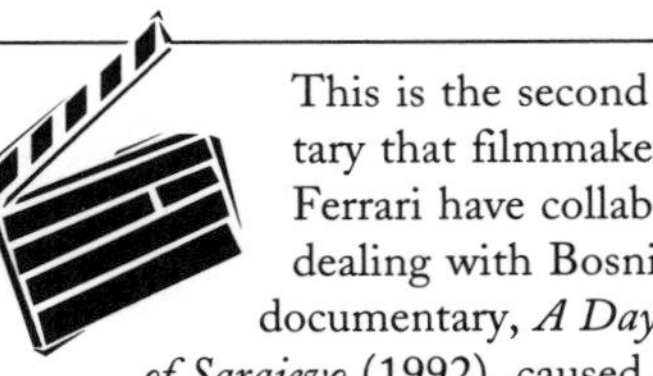

This is the second documentary that filmmakers Levy and Ferrari have collaborated on in dealing with Bosnia. The first documentary, *A Day in the Death of Sarajevo* (1992), caused a stir at the 1993 Berlin Int'l. Film Festival.

CREDITS

Narrator: Bernard-Henri Levy

Origin: France
Released: 1994 (1995)
Production: Les Films du Lendemain in collaboration with France 2 Cinema, Canal Plus, CNC and Radio Television of Bosnia-Hercegovina
Direction: Bernard-Henri Levy and Alain Ferrari
Screenplay: Bernard-Henri Levy and Gilles Hertzog
Cinematography: Pierre Boffety
Editing: Frederic Lossignol and Yann Kassile
Music: Denis Barbier
MPAA rating: not listed
Running Time: 118 minutes

Boys on the Side

"A motion picture that celebrates the art of survival, the gift of laughter and the miracle of friendship."—Movie tagline

"A comedy of wit and wisdom that can make you cry. *Thelma and Louise* plus one. Superbly directed. Award-worthy performances."—Susan Granger, *CRN & American Movie Classics*

"It soars! Wonderful performances and a rare loving spirit. It belongs at the top of your list."—Joanna Langfield, *The Movie Minute*

"An important film you can't forget. Whoopi Goldberg, Mary-Louise Parker and Drew Barrymore are brilliantly real."—Rex Reed, *New York Observer*

"Enjoyable! Three smashing all-stops-out performances."—Bob Campbell, *Newhouse News Service*

Box Office Gross: $23,440,188

The production notes for *Boys on the Side* proclaim that the film is "about life in the nineties and how three women bring strength, humor, hope and richness to one another's lives as, in the process, they create a family of their own." Certainly Hollywood has often speculated on and therefore showcased the relationships among women, such as in *The Women* (1939), *All about Eve* (1950), and *Where the Boys Are* (1960). *Boys on the Side*, however, filters the friendships among women through domestic violence, incurable illness, and dysfunctional families. If this is the 1990's, it offers little to recommend it.

Jane (Whoopi Goldberg) is a singer who begins the film on her way out of New York and on to California. Unfortunately, her fellow musician has decided not to make the trip, so Jane is searching for a way to reach Los Angeles. Enter Robin (Mary-Louise Parker), a perky, compulsive real-estate agent determined to reach San Diego and recapture her childhood memories of a family vacation there. She even has a mini-van in good enough shape to make the trip. Thus, the mismatched pair warily join forces and begin the road trip together.

Along the way, Jane and Robin stop in Philadelphia to visit Jane's friend Holly (Drew Barrymore), who is involved in an impossible, abusive relationship. Persuading Holly to go with them, Jane and Robin soon discover they got more than they bargained for: Holly is a fugitive from the law and pregnant. Throughout the course of the journey, each character learns to need and trust the other two, building a "family" as they go.

Perhaps it is unnecessary to begin by characterizing this film as maudlin; as filmgoers attending a Herbert Ross film, expect to cry. Among the director's best-known films are such famous tearjerkers as *Goodbye, Mr. Chips* (1969), *Funny Lady* (1975), *The Sunshine Boys* (1975), *The Turning Point* (1977), *The Goodbye Girl* (1977), and *Steel Magnolias* (1989). While the production notes characterize Ross's films as "explorations of friendship and other pivotal relationships," a truer description might be "explorations of the depressing, the despondent, and the morose, all told as high melodrama." They are the quintessential weepies, as is *Boys on the Side*, beleaguered as it is with health problems, money problems, men problems, women problems, family problems, strangers, death, and incarceration.

While arguably such could be the world of the 1990's, as proclaimed by the filmmakers, more realistically *Boys on the Side* presents the world a la Herbert Ross, which is a world filled with regret, loss, and people slogging through more ill-fated misfortune than reasonably believable. While the film avoids clichés such as having the women bond while singing girl-group hits, such as the Supremes' song "Stop in the Name of Love," it may not be a blessing that it takes the path less traveled—it is not pretty terrain: sickness among strangers, sickness in roadside bathrooms, unrequited love, obsessive love with law enforcement personnel. Audience members may find themselves overwhelmed by the "bad karma" amassed by these three women.

> The filmmakers spent three nights at the historic Tumacacori Mission, an ancient Spanish colonial cathedral located south of Tucson, Arizona, shooting the festival sequence amidst the ruins of a sacred Indian burial ground.

Nothing ever goes right, and perhaps worse yet, the camera never looks away, not when Robin becomes ill, not when the women fight, not when lovers fight, not when mother and daughter fight, never. In fact, the filmmakers create opportunities for making the audience unhappy, such as when Robin looks from her sickbed and sees her young brother, who died years before, beckoning her to the "world beyond." In another film, such a clumsy metaphor might be laughable; in this film, it just adds to the angst. Perhaps the best characterization of Herbert Ross comes from Barbara Shulgasser, staff critic at the *San Francisco Examiner* "He knows how to jerk a tear, and when you watch *Boys on the Side* you know that he can do it in his sleep."

The screenwriter of *Boys on the Side*, Don Roos, also wrote *Single White Female* (1992), which brings into question whether he writes these films out of an interest in and affection for women—or the opposite. In *Single White Female*, Jennifer Jason Leigh played a mentally disturbed young woman who became obsessed with her roommate, played by Bridget Fonda. Mayhem resulted. *Boys on the Side* features three women, each of whom has become an outcast from friends and family for one reason or another. The world has done a great job of beating them up. Depression awaits. Perhaps the clearest example of this is Robin, who spends the film dying, slowly.

"Yes, I am. And I'm sure you hear that from women all the time, but in my case it happens to be true."—Jane from *Boys on the Side* when asked if she is a lesbian

Whereas Robin brings her own brand of sanity to the domestic violence at Holly's house, interacting and reasoning with the lunatic boyfriend, it is not long before her AIDS (acquired immune deficiency syndrome) becomes debilitating. It feels as if Robin spends half the film sick or in bed or dying slowly, with tubes or in a wheelchair. She recounts how she contracted the disease: one night with a bartender in whom she was not really interested. Perhaps the encouraging portion of Robin's filmic life is that she builds a strong relationship with Jane and is able to rekindle something of a relationship with her mother. As it is clear that Robin will die, however, making such ties merely allows a respite before the final pitch of inescapable heartbreak. Reviewers described the film accurately with terms such as silly, melancholy, contrived, melodramatic, soggy, shameless, and indigestible.

While it may be unfair to question the ability of a male director and a male screenwriter to make a good film about women, it is inescapably true that nothing about the characters ties them to "women." That is, the same film could be made, with the same misadventures and losses, about three men. Ultimately, *Boys on the Side* is not a film about women, nor the friendships among and between women, nor the strengths of women; it is a film about how many bad things can happen in 117 minutes. The answer to that question is clear: more than anyone would like to watch.

The one bright spot in the film is its sound track, which received great critical praise. Among the artists appearing are The Indigo Girls, Melissa Etheridge, Annie Lennox, Bonnie Raitt, Sheryl Crow, and Stevie Nicks. Whoopi Goldberg also performs four songs, including the Janis Joplin classic "Piece of My Heart." Goldberg made her on-screen singing debut in *Sister Act* (1992), in which she also played a performer.

While the sound track was a hit, the songs fare less well on the screen, overwhelmed as they are with emotional baggage. For example, when Jane is performing in New York, a couple is talking, necking, and arguing loudly and lustfully at a nearby booth. Jane leaves the stage after her song and sets out to trick and humiliate the woman; Jane tells her that she has matter hanging from her nose. The woman, horrified by the revelation, hurries off to correct the damage. It is a pointless scene. It is never made clear why she picks on a couple lustfully engaged, nor why she preys on the woman's insecurities. Perhaps the message is that some women can not join the club and must remain outcasts and laughingstocks. Perhaps those to be excluded are those who engage in public displays of affection, or merely those who interrupt Jane's singing. At any rate, it is a mean-spirited and therefore disappointing scene. Women, it would appear, can be as unkind to each other as men to men, and men to women. Such a revelation hardly improves a film already capsizing under the weight of emotional bilge.

On a more technical note, this road film was indeed shot on the road, with filming beginning in New York dur-

CREDITS

Jane: Whoopi Goldberg
Robin: Mary-Louise Parker
Holly: Drew Barrymore
Abe: Matthew McConaughey
Alex: James Remar
Nick: Billy Wirth
Elaine: Anita Gillette
Massarelli: Dennis Boutsikaris
Anna: Amy Aquino
Louise: Estelle Parsons

Origin: USA
Released: 1995
Production: Arnon Milchan, Steven Reuther, and Herbert Ross for Le Studio Canal Plus, Regency Enterprises, Alcor Films, and New Regency/Hera; released by Warner Bros.
Direction: Herbert Ross
Screenplay: Don Roos
Cinematography: Donald E. Thorin
Editing: Michael R. Miller
Production design: Ken Adam
Art direction: William F. O'Brien
Set design: James Bayliss, Jann K. Engel and Stephen Berger
Set decoration: Rick Simpson
Casting: Hank McCann
Sound: Jim Webb
Costume design: Gloria Gresham
Music: David Newman
MPAA rating: R
Running Time: 117 minutes

ing what the production notes identify as "the worst winter weather recorded in the last decade." The New York portions of the film showcase Soho, Greenwich Village, and Battery City Park. The filmmakers drew other location shots from New Jersey, Pittsburgh, and Tucson, Arizona. The historic Tumacacori Mission, an ancient Spanish colonial cathedral near Tucson, served as the backdrop for the festival sequence, and local dancers and artisans added an authentic Southwestern flavor.

With three talented women in the lead roles, *Boys on the Side* should have been better, should have been a clearer picture of life, could have told a story audiences could bear to watch. As it stands, it is a great disappointment, "a shameless, indigestible lump of pathos," according to Lori Christofides of *The Cincinnati Post.*

—*Roberta F. Green*

REVIEWS

Atlanta Constitution. February 3, 1995, p. 9.
Baltimore Sun. February 3, 1995, p. 11.
Boston Globe. February 3, 1995, p. 54.
Daily Variety. January 23, 1995, p. 4.
Entertainment Weekly. February 10, 1995, p. 40.
The Hollywood Reporter. January 23, 1995, p. 10.
Houston Chronicle. February 3, 1995, Weekend Preview, p. 1.
Los Angeles Times. February 3, 1995, p. F1.
The New York Times. February 3, 1995, p. B1.
San Francisco Chronicle. February 3, 1995, p. C1.

The Brady Bunch Movie

"Wickedly funny - comic gold!"—Owen Gleiberman, *Entertainment Weekly*

"Nutty fun...well-cast."—Manohla Dargis, *LA Weekly*

"A laugh-a-second comedy. A romp for all ages."—Bonnie Churchill, *National News Syndicate*

"Riotous."—Jeff Craig, *Sixty Second Preview*

Box Office Gross: $46,576,136

Hollywood baby-boomer production executives, producers and writers have been feverishly re-creating icons of the 1960s and 1970s for 1990s audiences, producing such films as *The Flintstones*, *Dennis the Menace*, *The Beverly Hillbillies*, *Richie Rich*, and *Dragnet*, all with varying degrees of success. For the most part, reviews have been critical because the films have largely been second-class re-creations, heavy on production and special effects, and light on story, wit, and characterization—until *The Brady Bunch Movie* brought its vintage seventies charm to 1995 audiences.

Shag haircuts, macrame plant holders, astro-turf, platform shoes, banal pseudo-rock music—these wonderful memories of the 1970s are captured hilariously in the inventive and achingly funny film version of *The Brady Bunch*. The Bradys, to anyone who somehow escaped the 1970s, were the perfect suburban sitcom family whose biggest problems seemed to be which boy to take to the school dance or which sandwich to pack for the kids' lunch.

America's favorite TV family hits the big screen in *The Brady Bunch Movie*.

The original series, created by Sherwood Schwartz, starred Florence Henderson and Robert Reed as a newly married couple, he with three boys, and she with three girls, who face the difficulties of step-parenting. Schwartz, clearly recognizing the changing face of the American family, created one of the most successful television series to ever be syndicated. The show's reruns continue to play all over the country, and there is a whole generation of people who recite their favorite lines and remind each other of their favorite "bits" from the show.

The Brady Bunch phenomenon has spawned an animated series, several television films, two follow-up series—

The Bradys (1990), and *The Brady Brides* (1988), a successful stage production which featured re-creations of actual "Brady" scripts, and now this hit 1995 film.

This film version, produced by Schwartz and his son, Lloyd, wisely chooses to parody the relentless mediocrity and insipid virtuousness of the original Bradys. Director Betty Thomas and screenwriters Laurice Elehwany, Rick Copp, Bonnie Turner, and Terry Turner, know that the humor of the film lies in the Bradys' "do-gooder" demeanor, especially as it collides with the nasty world around them. The concept is extremely clever: The film takes place in the present day, but the Bradys remain trapped in the 1970s, oblivious to the fact that their plaid pants, "Have a nice day" stickers, and wholesome cheerfulness are completely out of place in the sophisticated and cynical nineties.

The story centers around several events familiar to knowledgeable "Brady" fans. These events include Marcia's (Christine Taylor) dilemma of having two dates for a dance, Greg's (Christopher Daniel Barnes) attempts to be a rock star, Jan's (Jennifer Elise Cox) jealousy of the beautiful Marcia, and housekeeper Alice's (Henriette Mantel) relationship with Sam the Butcher (David Graf). These events serve the film's central plot, which involves a campaign by the sinister Mr. Ditmeyer (Michael McKean) to sell the Bradys' house out from under them. The Bradys' discovery that they need $20,000 to keep the house from being taken from them is the driving force of the action.

The Bradys are played straight, with the actors all adopting a serious-as-a-stroke attitude which is the essence of good satire. These Bradys are the real thing. When father Mike Brady (Gary Cole) admonishes young Cindy (Olivia Hack) that "when you tattle-tale, you not only tattle on someone else, you tell a tattle on you, and you don't want to tattle on you, do you," his inane advice almost makes sense because of Cole's straightforward delivery. His stodgy expression and resonant voice sound exactly like Robert Reed, who played Mike on the sitcom.

Christine Taylor has generated much enthusiasm for her role as Marcia. The enthusiasm and good reviews are the result of her uncanny resemblance to the original Marcia, Maureen McCormick. With her perfectly straight hair and her double-knit polyester outfits, she is quite the seventies beauty. Taylor has mastered McCormick's bland expression, which was the height of sex appeal back in the 1970s. Her obliviousness to the sexually sophisticated world of the 1990s is a riot, especially since she is the apparent prey of everyone at school: In a bold twist, Marcia's best girlfriend (Alanna Ubach) even falls for her. In one very funny scene, Taylor keeps her naive cool when she and her friend are sharing a bed on a "sleepover," and Marcia wonders why her best girlfriend has to sleep so close. Taylor's obtuse naivete is hilarious.

As Jan, Jennifer Elise Cox provides many of the film's most memorable moments. Her constant complaint, "Marcia, Marcia, Marcia!" is done with a breathy whine that recalls Eve Plumb's nerdy performance in the original series, but adds a comic dimension that is hilarious. "Marcia, Marcia, Marcia!" has even begun to find its way into popular

CREDITS

Carol Brady: Shelley Long
Mike Brady: Gary Cole
Ditmeyer: Michael McKean
Mrs. Ditmeyer: Jean Smart
Alice Nelson: Henriette Mantel
Greg Brady: Christopher Daniel Barnes
Marcia Brady: Christine Taylor
Peter Brady: Paul Sutera
Jan Brady: Jennifer Elise Cox
Bobby Brady: Jesse Lee
Cindy Brady: Olivia Hack
Sam: David Graf
Eric Ditmeyer: Jack Noseworthy
Doug: Shane Conrad
Mrs. Cummings: RuPaul
Schultzy: Ann B. Davis
Grandma Brady: Florence Henderson

Origin: USA
Released: 1995
Production: Sherwood Schwartz, Lloyd J. Schwartz, and David Kirkpatrick; released by Paramount Pictures
Direction: Betty Thomas
Screenplay: Laurice Elehwany, Rick Copp, Bonnie Turner, and Terry Turner; based on characters created by Sherwood Schwartz
Cinematography: Mac Ahlberg
Editing: Peter Teschner
Production design: Steven Jordan
Art direction: William Durrell, Jr. and Nanci B. Roberts
Set decoration: Lynn Wolverton-Parker
Casting: Deborah Aquila and Jane Shannon
Sound: Russell Williams II
Costume design: Rosanna Norton
Music: Steve Tyrell, Guy Moon
MPAA rating: PG-13
Running Time: 88 minutes

AWARDS AND NOMINATIONS

MTV Movie Awards Nominations 1995: Best Dance Sequence (The Brady Kids)

lexicon as a way of showing exasperation. When Jan lapses momentarily into an almost hypnotic (nearly psychotic) trance, hearing her "good voice" and her "bad voice" argue about getting revenge on Marcia, Cox plays it as though this were the most serious, important moment ever to be filmed. When Cox puts on a huge Afro wig and tries to pass herself off as a "high-fashion model," she assures her place in the hearts of the audience.

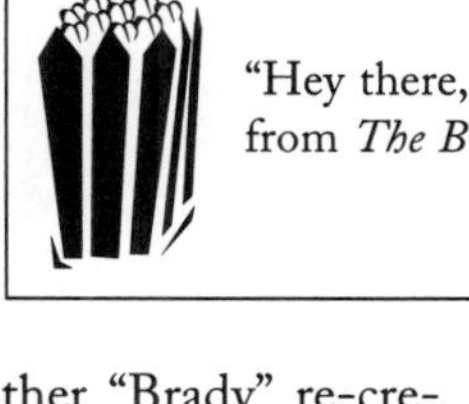

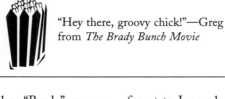

"Hey there, groovy chick!"—Greg from *The Brady Bunch Movie*

So much can be said of all the other "Brady" re-creations: Olivia Hack's obnoxious lisp as Cindy, Christopher Daniel Barnes' goofy attempts at cool as he sings a frightful song to the girl he has a crush on, and Henriette Mantel's imitation of Ann B. Davis's silly smirk as Alice are all winners. Two of the actors re-creating "Brady" kids appear to be shortchanged: Jesse Lee as Bobby and Paul Sutera as Peter have little to do, but acquit themselves nicely.

Michael McKean and Jean Smart play the Ditmeyers, the Brady's next-door neighbors who were mentioned in the old series but never shown. Here, Mr. Ditmeyer is a money-hungry swindler who snidely tells little Cindy to "beat it, Heidi," or to "jump back on the Swiss Miss Box." Jean Smart (from television's *Designing Women*) is a hoot as the boozy, sexy Mrs. Ditmeyer, who invites the two older Brady boys to come inside and "we can make ourselves a sandwich."

The original TV series first aired on ABC from 1969 through 1974 with a total of 116 episodes. Now in syndication, the series has inspired numerous trivia books, as well as a hit stage production, 'The Real Live Brady Bunch.' A Chicago theater troupe first performed the cult hit, which has since toured nationally and internationally.

One of the only disappointments of the film is Shelley Long's role as Carol. Long, the gifted comic actress from television's *Cheers* and from feature films such as *Outrageous Fortune*, has a curiously inactive role in this film. Perhaps this plot has not lent itself to a great role for Carol Brady, or perhaps it is in Long's performance. One reason for this could be that Long is actually the only actor playing a Brady whose persona is well-known outside of this film, and that could be working against her here, much as it did for Lily Tomlin as "Miss Jane" in *The Beverly Hillbillies*.

Director Betty Thomas, known to television audiences as Sgt. Lucy Bates on *Hill Street Blues*, keeps the pace moving rapidly with a bright, sitcom quality. She uses shots familiar to television viewers, such as simple two-shots and close-ups, and wisely stays away from bombastic special effects. Thomas has a subtle wit that keeps a nineties edge to the proceedings: For instance, a scene where the neighbors gather on the Bradys' front lawn subtly shows a gay couple in the background. Another funny scene is when the Bradys somehow bring sixties icon Davy Jones to sing at the school dance (the inclusion of yet another *Brady Bunch* episode plot). The kids seem to be indifferent to Jones, but the female teachers rush the stage, recalling the idol of their youth. Thomas' unerring eye for what will be true and funny at the same time helps make this film full of wonderful moments.

The architect of all of this is Sherwood Schwartz, who has shown remarkable tenaciousness over the years. When *The Brady Bunch* and his other famous series *Gilligan's Island* were dismissed by critics as silly dinosaurs, Schwartz continued to revive both series through television film follow-ups. As the audience grew, so did the characters; and the insipidity of the characterizations took a back seat to the audience's interest in what happened to its idols as the years passed by. The television film follow-ups for the *Bradys*, and for *Gilligan* received some of the highest ratings ever for television films. And Schwartz (and son Lloyd Schwartz) show no signs of stopping: *Gilligan's Island: the Musical* is being prepared for Broadway as of this writing.

For better or worse, Schwartz and *The Bradys* have carved themselves into the culture of America. That Schwartz would allow his Brady family to be laughed at is a testimonial to his ability to understand the current cultural climate and his canny ability to know what is going to sell in the marketplace. Ultimately, the juxtaposition of the do-good Bradys with the tough-talking people of the nineties becomes a comment on the current cultural debate on "family values." The Bradys' "family values" have for years seemed out-of-step with the march of time. But here they are again, and this time, they are leading the march.

—Kirby Tepper

Braveheart

"Every man dies, not every man really lives."—Movie tagline

"Wildly romantic. Powerful and confident."—Eleanor Ringel, *Atlanta Journal and Constitution*

"Entertaining and thrilling."—Roger Ebert, *Chicago Sun-Times*

"One of the best films I've ever seen!"—Rod Lurie, *Los Angeles Magazine*

"One of the most spectacular entertainments in years! An explosive action movie...an exhilarating new-fashioned epic."—Caryn James, *The New York Times*

"Action is nonstop. Full of passion."—Bruce Williamson, *Playboy Magazine*

"Rousing, romantic adventure...breathtaking."—Peter Travers, *Rolling Stone*

"Deliriously romantic. Director Gibson has delivered a real drum-banger."—Mike Clark, *USA Today*

Box Office Gross: $67,018,197

Mel Gibson, as William Wallace, leads his soldiers into battle in the Scottish epic *Braveheart.*

In 1994, Mel Gibson, an actor known for his good looks, as more usually showcased in action films (*Mad Max*, 1979, *The Bounty*, 1984, *Lethal Weapon*, 1987, *Tequila Sunrise*, 1988, *Air America*, 1990, *Hamlet*, 1990), made his directorial debut with the film *The Man Without a Face* (1994). Portions of his debut film were remarkable, including a scene in which Gibson, playing a deformed ex-teacher, recites Shylock's soliloquy from William Shakespeare's "The Merchant of Venice." Lighted with candles, actor/director Gibson captured true visual magic. However, other technical features were less reassuring. For instance, scenes ended abruptly, seconds after performers finished saying their lines. Further, camera placement often worked against the actors, cutting off a head here, catching the underside of the table there. With *Braveheart*, however, Gibson has attempted a full-scale, cast-of-thousands epic. While the film is weighed down by seemingly endless battle scenes, it is artfully constructed, smooth, technically a great step forward for this fledgling director.

Screenwriter Richard Wallace was on vacation in Edinburgh when he noticed a statue of William Wallace and learned some of the legends about him. He started writing *Braveheart* after reading a 1740 English translation of rhyming Scottish verse presenting legends about Wallace.

In the late 13th century, William Wallace (played as an adult by Mel Gibson) experiences loss, when his brother and father are killed, battling against the British for their freedom. At the funeral, a small child named Murron (played as an adult by Catherine McCormack) approaches the grieving William, and the two children exchange a glance. Then William's uncle takes him away. Decades later, the now grown William returns to Scotland an educated man to find his love and to rebuild his family's land. However, try as he might to avoid battling with England and the nobles of Scotland, it is inescapable. Soon he has dedicated himself to Scottish freedom and dedicates the rest of his life to it.

William Wallace may be Scotland's greatest hero. Born around 1267, Wallace refused the crown of Scotland when it was offered to him, fighting instead for Scotland's freedom. Very little is actually known about Wallace beyond his five-foot-long sword (currently displayed in Stirling Castle) and the 300 pages of rhyming verse recounting Wallace's life. Purportedly written by a blind poet, Blind Harry, the poem is allegedly drawn from the diary of Wallace's chaplain, who accompanied him everywhere. Therefore, while few of the details are verifiable, *Braveheart* effectively captures the mood and tone of the hero and his times. Certainly his impact on the Scottish people is accurate, as on June 24, 1861, 556 years after the death of Wallace, 100,000 people gathered for the opening of a monument to William Wallace in Stirling.

Braveheart has marketed itself as a romance as well as an action film. However, the majority of the film is dedicated to battles. Bloody, brutal, they will lose their charm for many viewers very early on. However, the epic scale of this film is nowhere more evident than in the battles; 1700 of the Irish Army's reserve forces acted as the Scottish and English armies. In order to begin shooting battle scenes at 8 a.m., the troops had to assemble at 4 a.m. and move in formation through makeup and costuming. Several of the "warriors" wear wode (face paint), which historically was worn to frighten enemies and to prepare soldiers mentally and emotionally for the upcoming battle. Ten thousand arrows with rubber tips were used in the battles scenes, and mechanical horses (moving 30 miles an hour on 20 feet of track) supplied realistic confrontations and falls. The fight scenes are remarkable in their brutality and gore, and the actors are burly and spirited. Peter Rainer, reviewing the film for *The Los Angeles Times*, has written about a scene in which one warrior "yanks arrows out of his chest with his bare hands and then laughs lustily." These guys aren't just medieval; they're practically Cro-Magnon.

"Men don't follow titles, they follow courage."—William Wallace from *Braveheart*

As for the romance in the film, it is virtually non-existent. Wallace's wife survives two scenes after the marriage, and his "romance" with Princess Isabelle (Sophie Marceau) takes moments of screentime. While Mel Gibson rose to box office fame at least in part due to his matinee idol looks and his romantic roles, his more recent films have worked against such an understanding. For instance, in *The Man Without a Face*, Mel Gibson has one side of his face radically deformed due to fire. In this film, he is often bloodied, painted, or in anguish. Courtship is virtually nil, confirming the film's status as a war picture á la *The Alamo* (1960), *The Green Berets* (1968), and *The Sands of Iwo Jima* (1949). Portions of *Braveheart* have been repeatedly compared to *Henry V*, particularly the scene in which Wallace cheers his troops with a speech not unlike Henry's St. Crispin's speech in Shakespeare's *Henry V*.

Messy and muddy, the film disguises the huge efforts made to make it realistic. For instance, production designer Tom Sanders created a village market complete with raw meat, dead fish, and piles of bones three feet high. Working with real castles, the crew worked to ensure that no damage befell the castles. "If anything was fixed to the real castle wall, we would first paint on a thin layer of latex rubber, which then peeled off when we came to strike the set. The old stone, underneath was left untouched," said Saunders in the production notes.

Costume designer Charles Knode designed more than 6,000 costumes for this film, working from designs on period carvings and tombstones. Knode based his plaid on a bit of cloth he had seen in a Scottish castle, also ensuring that the colors were neutral (historically kilts also served as camouflage for hunting). Scottish weaver Gordon Corvells on the Isle of Islay, wove 3,000 meters of plaid in eight different colors. The characters at court, however, were dressed in silk, damask, velvet and fine wool. Large gems were constructed out of fiberglass for belts, collars, and crowns.

Nearly three hours long, *Braveheart* appears to slow through endless battle scenes. Also prevalent are panoramic

CREDITS

William Wallace: Mel Gibson
Princess Isabelle: Sophie Marceau
King Edward I: Patrick McGoohan
Murron: Catherine McCormack

Origin: USA
Released: 1995
Production: Mel Gibson, Alan Ladd, Jr., and Bruce Davey for Icon Productions; released by Paramount Pictures
Direction: Mel Gibson
Screenplay: Randall Wallace
Cinematography: John Toll
Editing: Steven Rosenblum
Production Design: Tom Sanders
Costume Design: Charles Knode
Stunt Coordinator: Simon Crane
Music: James Horner
MPAA rating: R
Running Time: 170 minutes

AWARDS AND NOMINATIONS

Academy Awards 1995: Best Picture, Best Director (Gibson), Best Cinematography (Toll), Best Makeup, Best Sound Effects Editing
Nominations: Best Screenplay (Wallace), Best Score (Horner), Best Costumes, Best Film Editing, Best Sound
British Academy Awards 1995: Best Cinematography (Toll)
Nominations: Best Director (Gibson), Best Score (Horner)
Golden Globe Awards 1996: Best Director (Gibson)
Nominations: Best Film-Drama, Best Screenplay (Wallace), Best Score (Horner)
Writers Guild Awards 1995: Best Original Screenplay (Wallace)
Director Guild Award Nominations 1995: Best Director (Gibson)

vistas of an emerald green, cloudy Scotland. While the film is beautiful to see and Scotland so lovely it is almost otherworldly, the film loses momentum after multiple battles and scenery breaks. If *Man Without a Face* was choppy and abrupt, *Braveheart* may have slowed the pace a bit too much. For instance, near the film's end, Wallace is shown walking up a mountain path to the top of a rise from which he can see endlessly in every direction, a scene not unlike Maria (Julie Andrews) in *The Sound of Music* (1965) marching to an upper pasture and singing "The Hills Are Alive With the Sound of Music." This scene of Wallace's climb and his new perspective of his world would appear to be the end of the film, a good final resting place, yet the film picks up again and moves slowly into continuing battles and disappointments. While not painful, the scope and breadth of the film ask a great deal of audience members—perhaps too much.

Joan of Arc, Robin Hood, and William Wallace each rose to take the place that history provided them. Pushed to the fore when each sought solace and peace, nonetheless heroes' lives make exciting popular films, turning almost into hagiographies. What with its faults, *Braveheart* is finally a reasonably engaging story of a larger-than-life hero. However, some audience members may want to take a nap before attending.

—*Roberta F. Green*

REVIEWS

Atlanta Constitution, May 24, 1995, p. B10.
Baltimore Sun, May 24, 1995, p. 1D.
Boston Globe, May 24, 1995, p. 75.
Calgary Herald, May 25, 1995, p. D1.
Chicago Sun-Times, May 24, 1995, p. 55.
Denver Post, May 24, 1995, p. GO8.
Houston Chronicle, May 24, 1995, At the Movies, p. 1.
Los Angeles Times, May 24, 1995, p. F1.
Newsday, May 24, 1995, p. BO3
The New York Times, May 24, 1995, p. C3.
The Salt Lake Tribune, May 26, 1995, p. E3.
San Francisco Chronicle, May 24, 1995, p. D1.
The Washington Post, May 26, 1995, p. CO1.

Brian Wilson: I Just Wasn't Made for These Times

Beach Boys leader Brian Wilson is a living example of the thin line between genius and madness. This walking contradiction, the composer of some of the most enduring popular music of the century, is captured well in Don Was' documentary. Detroit-born Was co-founded the band Was (Not Was), and has since moved on to become one of the top music producers in the business. His skills have been utilized by the Rolling Stones, the B52's, Bonnie Raitt, Bob Dylan and a host of others. *Brian Wilson: I Just Wasn't Made For These Times* is his directorial debut, a loving, sympathetic glimpse of a musical visionary that clocks in at a skimpy 70 minutes and leaves the viewer wanting more.

Most compelling in this black and white film are Brian Wilson's on-camera recollections of his fruitful and turbulent life. Unlike his space cadet persona in the documentary *Theremin: A Musical Odyssey* (reviewed in this edition), Wilson comes across here as troubled, childlike, but always likeable and, what a relief, comprehensible. His father was horribly abusive, and the beatings Wilson suffered from his dad drove him to seek solace and transcendence in music. With no formal music training, Wilson spent countless hours mastering the piano himself, and soon was applying Four Freshmen-style harmonies to rock and roll rhythms.

The early days of the Beach Boys are glossed over too rapidly as director Was hastens to give screen time to their masterpiece "Pet Sounds." This album remains a landmark in the history of rock and roll. Such fiendishly complex arrangements, chord progressions and sophisticated harmonies had never been heard in pop music before. After hearing "Pet Sounds," the Beatles were inspired to create their landmark "Sgt. Pepper's" album. But the relative commercial failure of "Pet Sounds" coupled with drug excesses and emotional problems took its toll on Wilson, who has emerged from seclusion in recent years, becoming musically active once again.

The astutely chosen and eclectic bunch of musicians interviewed for this film include Tom Petty, Sonic Youth's Thurston Moore, Linda Ronstadt, Randy Newman, the Velvet Underground's John Cale, David Crosby, Graham Nash, and Wilson's longtime collaborator Van Dyke Parks.

Particularly appealing are Rondstadt's recollections of Wilson figuring out harmony lines for a song in his head while playing a totally different tune on the piano. Also compelling is the soft-spoken Parks, who worked with Wilson on the famous but unfinished 1960s "Smile" album. Their most recent collaboration was 1995's "Orange Crate Art," and Parks' affectionate recollections about his eccentric but gifted friend are delightful to watch.

Much of the film features performances by Wilson and a band done in a recording studio. The best musical moment happens last when Wilson and his cohorts perform "Do It Again" with back-up vocals provided by Wilson's daughters Carnie and Wendy. Only in the last few years has Wilson had anything resembling a normal relationship with his daughters, and the joy on all their faces as they sing together is a fine moment. As a whole, too many songs are included in the film, and more of Wilson's life and archival footage and less of the slick studio renditions would have been preferred.

Brian Wilson: I Just Wasn't Made For These Times does not delve into many of the darker aspects of Wilson's and the Beach Boys career. The death of Dennis Wilson, the Beach Boys drummer and the brother of Brian, is never touched upon. Brian Wilson's twisted relationship with psychiatrist Eugene Landy is also glossed over. To his credit, Landy helped to return Wilson to something approaching mental stability in the 1980s. But then Landy took control of Wilson's life around the clock, trying to dominate his career and take for himself a big chunk of Wilson's money. Lawsuit upon lawsuit ensued, and Wilson finally freed himself from Landy in the early 1990s. A more objective director could have portrayed Wilson as compassionately as Was while also including these unsavory details on the screen.

How strange it is that the man behind all of those lovely, innocent Beach Boys melodies is such a tortured soul, "always in turmoil," as he himself states. Was, so sensitive to the needs of the musicians he produces, is also sensitive as a filmmaker in the way he shows Brian Wilson. Resisting the tabloid tendency to amplify the bizarre side of Wilson, Was is full of understanding and love for his subject, a man-child who continues to escape harsh reality by making music of beauty.

—Martin Bandyke

CREDITS

Brian Wilson: Brian Wilson
Carl Wilson: Carl Wilson
Daniel Harrison: Daniel Harrison

Origin: USA
Released: 1995
Production: Don Was, Larry Shapiro, David Passick and Ken Kushnick for a Palomar Pictures and Cro-Magnon films production
Direction: Don Was
Cinematography: Wyatt Troll
Editing: Helen Lowe
Art direction: Justin Bailey
Sound: Bob Dreebin, Gary Gossett and Mike Fredirksz
Historian: David Leaf
MPAA rating: not listed
Running Time: 70 minutes

The Bridges of Madison County

"It's an affair to remember. The love story truly comes to life."—Susan Stark, *The Detroit News*

"Remarkable. A moving love story. Mr. Eastwood instills it with a soulful, reflective tone. Meryl Streep has her best role in years."—Janet Maslin, *The New York Times*

"Eastwood and Streep work together with real heat and power. The erotic tension that develops between them is a believable force."—Jack Kroll, *Newsweek*

"Two thumbs up."—*Siskel & Ebert*

"Intelligent movie passion. *The Bridges of Madison County* is Clint Eastwood's gift to women."—Richard Corliss, *Time*

"Irresistible. The most beautiful love story of recent memory. Meryl Streep's performance is beyond extraordinary. Eastwood's accomplishments are equally distinguished. His direction is flawless. A rapturous love story of life and renewal."—Gene Shalit, *Today, NBC-TV*

Box Office Gross: $70,112,709

"That's the problem in earning a living through an art form," murmurs supersensitive Robert Kincaid in Robert James Waller's *The Bridges of Madison County*, "you're always dealing with markets, and markets—mass markets—are designed to suit average tastes. That's where the numbers are." Ain't it the truth, Mr. Waller! Clearly, the novelist understands his "art" and his audience. The magical, otherworldly Kincaid thrills an Iowa hausfrau with his fancy talk about art and poetry and "bouncing light." Francesca Johnson has read William Butler Yeats and longs to suck "the golden apples of the sun," but she is stuck in rural Iowa, where she drinks iced tea seductively while her 16-year-old daughter Carolyn and her 17-year-old son Michael (played by Annie Corley and Victor Slezak as grown-ups), and her decent-but-dull husband Richard (Jim Haynie) have taken a bum steer to the Illinois State Fair.

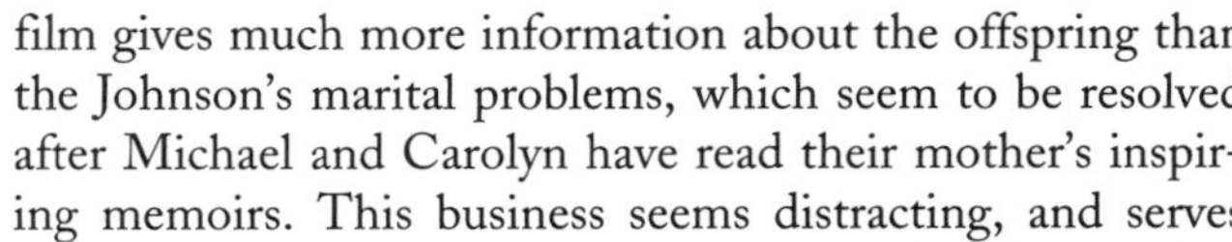

Bridges is not a film Eastwood even intended to direct. He signed on only after several other directors—including Sydney Pollack, Bruce Beresford, and Steven Spielberg—bailed out.

Then all of a sudden Robert Kincaid, this godlike apparition who "makes" pictures and moves "like the air," drives up her lane to ask directions, and she takes him to a quaint covered bridge, then cooks for him, then gets out an almost forgotten unopened bottle of brandy, and they drink, "to ancient evenings and distant music." What would the neighbors say? They would be wondering about more than the odd toast.

The story is told in flashback as Michael and Carolyn are given a letter from their mother at the reading of her will. They are disturbed first to learn that their mother wants to be cremated and have her ashes scattered by the covered bridge where she first met Kincaid. They are even more shocked to learn of their mother's affair, though Carolyn is more tolerant than her brother. Michael wonders, "do you suppose he had sex with her?" Carolyn responds, "For God's sake Michael, it must be nice living inside your head with Peter Pan and the Easter Bunny," but later she expresses surprise that "between bake sales my mother was Anaïs Nin!"

Francesca left a key in her safe-deposit box that would open a trunk containing Robert's possessions, including three journals Francesca wrote describing her affair. Michael and Carolyn take turns reading these aloud to one another, opening a window on the past for the viewers as well. The film gives much more information about the offspring than the Johnson's marital problems, which seem to be resolved after Michael and Carolyn have read their mother's inspiring memoirs. This business seems distracting, and serves only to make the film longer than it needs to be.

The novel is painfully and pretentiously sensitive. The screenplay plows through the purple patches and attempts to break new ground. Enough of the original story must remain to please the suckers who found the story beautiful and moving, but director Clint Eastwood also knows that he will have to win over skeptical reviewers who might have considered the novel unmitigated, hyper-romantic slush. The film therefore becomes an interesting balancing act.

Meryl Streep as Francesca Johnson is surely superior to the material. This is the actress who portrayed the unhinged Susan in the film adaptation of David Hare's *Plenty* (1985), the tortured Sophie of William Styron's *Sophie's Choice* (1982), the scandalous, soulful Sarah of *The French Lieutenant's Woman* (1981), and the pathetic Helen of William Kennedy's *Ironweed* (1987). This graduate of Vassar and the Yale Drama School is really too sophisticated to be a perfect fit for this role, yet she approaches it as a true professional, and leaves no visible traces of contempt. (The actress told Richard Schickel she considered the novel "a crime against literature.")

Long past being an ingenue, Streep is redefining her image. Last year she made quite a splash on the Kootenai River in *The River Wild* (1994), and she is obviously fighting to extend her horizons and her audience. The role of Francesca was one that some actresses would have killed for, even if taking it meant she had to ease herself into a story by a writer whose talent is so big he requires three names to describe himself.

Clint Eastwood told the *New York Times Magazine* (September 18, 1994) that Streep was the only actress offered the part of Francesca Johnson, "one of the most sought after female movie roles in years," according to Bernard Weinraub. "For some reason, everybody early in the game thought that we should find a European gal for the part," Eastwood told Weinraub. "I just didn't understand why. I felt they overlooked the importance of American actresses, and Meryl Streep is one of our most important." Though not

CREDITS

Robert: Clint Eastwood
Francesca: Meryl Streep
Caroline: Annie Corley
Michael: Victor Slezak

Origin: USA
Released: 1995
Production: Clint Eastwood and Kathleen Kennedy for Amblin/Malpaso Production; released by Warner Bros.
Direction: Clint Eastwood
Screenplay: Richard LaGravenese; based on the novel by Robert James Waller
Cinematography: Jack N. Green
Editing: Joel Cox
Production design: Jeannine Oppewall
Music: Lennie Niehaus
MPAA rating: PG-13
Running Time: 140 minutes

AWARDS AND NOMINATIONS

Academy Awards Nominations 1995: Best Actress (Streep)
Golden Globe Awards Nominations 1996: Best Film-Drama, Best Actress (Streep)
Screen Actors Guild Awards Nominations 1995: Best Actress (Streep)

an admirer of the Waller novel, Streep realized that Ron Bass and Richard LaGravenese had developed a first-rate screenplay and quickly accepted the offer.

As a result of this film and A *Little Princess*, which he also adapted this year, wonderfully, to the screen, Richard LaGravenese is sure to become 1995's hottest screenwriter. One wonders which of these adaptations will earn him an Academy Award nomination, for one of the two is sure to score with the Academy. Only time and taste will tell.

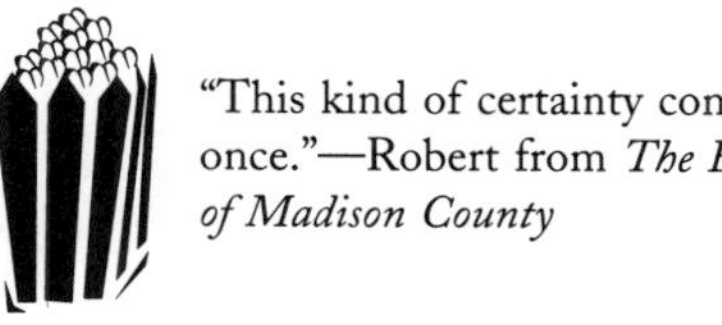

"This kind of certainty comes only once."—Robert from *The Bridges of Madison County*

The story of this life-embracing, life-fulfilling four-day fling is effectively told in flashback, as Francesca's grown-up children read about their mother's grand passion for the hypersensitive poet-philosopher who touched her Neopolitan soul, reminding her of art, beauty, and truth. Meryl Streep is about the right age for Francesca, and her slight accent is well nigh perfect. In his *Variety* review, Todd McCarthy wrote that she "has never been so warm, earthy, and spontaneous."

Born in 1930, Clint Eastwood is about thirteen years too old to play Robert Kincaid as Waller first imagined him. Casting himself against type, Eastwood told ABC's "Prime Time Live" (March 24, 1995) that the character he plays here is much closer to his own than the hard-bitten characters for which he is most famous. This is the film that reveals the softer side of Dirty Harry and opens up his soul. The surprise is that there is a very sensitive guy in there.

But this is still Eastwood, whose laconic style makes the ebullient Kincaid more tolerable, more down to earth, and less foolish, reducing the cringe factor of Waller's excessive style. For example, in the novel, Robert sends Francesca a "poetic" essay called "Falling from Dimension Z." In the film, Eastwood's Robert sends her a photo-book entitled "Four Days," dedicated to "F." and containing pictures of those nifty Iowa bridges, including the Roseman Bridge (built in 1883), where they fell madly in love.

"I've been that guy," Eastwood told Richard Schickel when the film was still in production. But if Eastwood looks good in long hair and suspenders, Streep looks even better as the hot-blooded Francesca, a university woman who came from Naples to rural Iowa to settle down and raise a family. In the film her background is slightly different. Though born in Italy, she is from Bari, not Naples, and a more simple, earthy, peasant woman. No mention is made of her university training, but she does tote around the collected works of W.B. Yeats once she gets to feeling amorous. (It is a pleasant surprise to see Meryl Streep driving a John Deere tractor and reading W. B. Yeats in the same movie.)

The screenplay certainly improves the novel in terms of dialogue and structure. It probably pays more attention than it needs to Francesca's annoying offspring. It adds a character, the adulterous Lucy, who helps Kincaid understand the kind of trouble he could be getting Francesca into. This encounter in the town of Winterset provides a motive for Robert to call Francesca and suggest that they cancel her second dinner invitation. In the film there is another significant change. The day before her husband is to return, Francesca packs her bags, intending to elope with Robert. But at the last minute, she thinks better of this out of consideration for her family. "They would never get around the talk," she tells Robert. "Some people search all their lives for this and never find it," Robert answers. "If I leave, we lose it," she remarks. It is as if she is well versed in the art of courtly love. But this is a wonderful touch and helps to explain her decision.

The screenplay reinvents the scene where Kincaid leaves town, with Francesca and her husband in their red pickup right behind him. In the novel, Francesca sees Robert's truck as he leaves town, but Robert is unaware that Francesca is near. Robert knows that Francesca is there in the film, and even begins to approach the truck on foot while it is parked, as Francesca waits for her husband Richard to return, but he stops, knowing that she should make the first move. The husband returns and pulls his truck out, following Robert's, without knowing, of course, who Robert is. As the two trucks are stopped at a stop light, Robert hangs up the first-communion medallion Francesca had given him in the film (not in the novel) on his rear-view mirror, a final visual invitation for her to join him and elope. Her hand is on the truck's door handle, but she delays too long. Robert finally drives off. This is what some theatergoers might call a three-handkerchief film.

The film should become a sentimental favorite and will no doubt be a boon for tourism in Madison County, Iowa, and Winterset (population 4,200), its county seat, which should become even more popular than Dyersville, Iowa, the setting for *Field of Dreams* (1989), some three hours distant. This time around Clint Eastwood is far too gentle to harbor thoughts of murder or mayhem, and the only shooting he does is with his camera. The film is good enough to strike the same responsive chords with moviegoers as the novella did with its readers.

—James M. Welsh

REVIEWS

Baltimore Sun Maryland Live. June 2—June 8, 1995, p. 12.
Newsweek. June 5, 1995, p.74.
The New York Times. June 2, 1995, C4.
Time. Vol.145, No.23, June 5, 1995, pp. 62-64.
USA Today. June 2, 1995, D1.
Variety. May 22—28, 1995, p.91, p.96.
The Washington Post. June 2, 1995, D1, D6.
Washington Post Weekend. June 2, 1995, p.57.
Washington Times Metropolitan Times. June 2, 1995, c13.

The Brothers McMullen

"Wonderfully funny! Captivating!"—Peter Travers, *Rolling Stone*

"Four stars! It's a joy!"—Peter Stack, *San Francisco Chronicle*

"Two thumbs up!"—*Siskel & Ebert*

Box Office Gross: $10,246,592

Even during a era when independent American films are in vogue, especially those made for extremely low budgets by first-time filmmakers, such as Robert Rodrigeuz with his $7,000 *El Mariachi* (1993), Edward Burns' *The Brothers McMullen* is an especially remarkable success story. After making two short student films at Hunter College and learning how to write a screenplay by completing seven feature - length scripts, Burns wrote *The Brothers McMullen* while working as a production assistant for *Entertainment Tonight* and shot it in sixteen millimeter after work and on weekends for $20,000 given to him by his father, a police sergeant.

Burns sent out a roughly edited, two-hours-plus version of his film to festivals and distributors in the summer of 1994, but none were impressed until it was seen by Tom Rothman, president of Fox Searchlight Pictures, a division of Twentieth Century Fox newly created to focus on non-mainstream films. Rothman put up $50,000 for post-production improvements in exchange for an option to distribute the film. After *The Brothers McMullen* became an unexpected hit at the Sundance Film Festival in January, 1995, winning the grand jury prize, Rothman exercised his option with Searchlight paying to transfer the film to thirty-five millimeter and to refine the film's sound. The result is the kind of engaging comedy-drama that might have been made by a young Woody Allen had he been an Irish-American from Long Island, New York.

The film focuses on the mostly comic travails of three Irish-American brothers. The middle brother, Barry (played by Burns himself), is a would-be screenwriter who would like to live in Greenwich Village but cannot find an apartment he can afford. He ends up living on Long Island with his older brother, Jack (Jack Mulcahy), a high school basketball coach, and Jack's wife, Molly (Connie Britton), a teacher. Joining them is the youngest brother, Patrick (Mike McGlone), a recent college graduate uncertain about what to do with his life.

The problems facing the brothers have varying degrees of seriousness. The cynical Barry, always hesitant about committing himself to a woman, is attracted to Audrey (Maxine Bahns), an actress he meets while looking for an apartment. The Barry-Audrey relationship is underdeveloped with Barry's primary role in the film being to comment on his brothers' predicaments. Jack's is the restlessness he begins to feel as he approaches middle age. Though Molly is a seemingly perfect wife, intelligent, attractive, and caring, Jack allows himself to be seduced by Ann (Elizabeth P. McKay), a girlfriend dropped by Barry at the beginning of the film. As Ann becomes bored by their being lovers, Jack becomes more aggressive. Molly discovers the affair, is hurt, but forgives him.

Patrick is the most fully realized and interesting of these characters. He resists going into the clothing business of his Jewish girlfriend's father. As he becomes unsure of his feelings for Leslie (Jennifer Jostyn), who wants him to convert to Judaism, she reveals she is pregnant and plans to have an abortion. As a devout Catholic, Patrick is appalled but cannot decide what to do, especially since he is becoming more interested in Susan (Shari Albert), an old friend from his neighborhood.

Hanging over the brothers is the revelation their mother made to Barry at their father's funeral five years earlier: that she married their father only because she was pregnant, re-

CREDITS

Patrick McMullen: Mike McGlone
Barry McMullen: Edward Burns
Jack McMullen: Jack Mulcahy
Molly McMullen: Connie Britton
Susan: Shari Albert
Leslie: Jennifer Jostyn
Ann: Elizabeth P. McKay
Audrey: Maxine Bahns
Released: 1995

Origin: USA
Production: Edward Burns and Dick Fisher; released by Fox Searchlight
Direction: Edward Burns
Screenplay: Edward Burns
Cinematography: Dick Fisher
Editing: Dick Fisher
Music: Seamus Egan
MPAA rating: R
Running Time: 97 minutes

AWARDS AND NOMINATIONS

Independent Spirit Awards 1996: Best First Film
Sundance Film Festival Awards 1995: Grand Jury Prize

jecting her true love, a musician named Finnbarr O'Shaughnessy. (Barry is named for him.) After she goes off to Ireland to be with O'Shaughnessy, Barry and Patrick worry about making the same mistake their mother made with their alcoholic, abusive father, and Jack wonders whether he has already erred, though Molly has considerably more to regret about him than he does about her. The film ends, following Leslie's going ahead with the abortion despite Patrick's protests, with Jack giving his youngest brother the money to go to California with Susan. Though *The Brothers McMullen* has a fondness for its principal setting, Burns makes clear that life on Long Island can be oppressive.

Much of *The Brothers McMullen* was shot in the home of Burns' parents with his mother providing food for the cast and crew. The film's credits describe her catering as Fine Irish Cooking.

Burns makes no attempt to treat such subjects as commitment and Catholic guilt seriously, exploiting them primarily for their comic potential. With Jack and Molly, however, he can find no light touch, and their uneasiness with each other and painful confrontations fail to mesh with the tone of the rest of the film.

"Hey, I like being a pessimist. It makes it easier to deal with my inevitable failure."—Barry from *The Brothers McMullen*

The Brothers McMullen is most knowing about the immaturity of the American male and his inability to understand women. Emotionally, all three brothers are the same age, although, ironically, Patrick may be the least immature since he at least acknowledges his fallibility. Half of the film is devoted to two or more brothers trying to explain the opposite sex to each other to no avail. All the women in the film seem to possess a knowledge of which the brothers are incapable. In one of the film's funniest scenes, Barry attempts to make Patrick understand the effect women have by peeling a banana, claiming that a woman gradually removes a man's protective layers until his sensitive, feminine side is exposed and he is done for.

Except for some graininess resulting from the film's being blown up from sixteen to thirty-five millimeter, *The Brothers McMullen* does look especially low-budget. Some of the limitations Burns worked under even turn out to be assets. Because much of the film had to be shot during late afternoons after Burns left his *Entertainment Tonight* job, many of the exterior scenes have an autumnal glow appropriate to the story of people on the verge of many changes. Some of the shots of Central Park, where many of the Barry-Audrey scenes are set, have a romantically rosy aura. The film's professionalism is somewhat undercut by Seamus Egan's insistently Celtic score. The spare earnestness of the music screams low-budget sincerity.

While the performances are uneven, they are serviceable. Burns cast himself to save money, but he performs with a raspy-voiced confidence and charm. Britton effectively portrays Molly's undeserved pain. While Molly is constrained by a collapsing marriage, Britton tries not to allow herself to be held back by an underwritten role. In contrast, Albert's Susan erupts in enthusiasm for life. The film's best performance by far is McGlone's. With the help of Burns' script, McGlone makes Patrick the most complex, most sympathetic, and funniest character. He exhibits expert comic timing as he displays Patrick's mixture of pain, confusion, and ineptness.

Though Burns may turn out to have a distinctive voice as a filmmaker, his first feature resembles the work of four other creators of small personal films. The leisurely pace of *The Brothers McMullen*, the attention to detail, and the empathy for family relationships recall the work of Wayne Wang—*Eat a Bowl of Tea* (1989), *The Joy Luck Club* (1993)—and Ang Lee—*The Wedding Banquet* (1993), *Eat Drink Man Woman* (1994). The Long Island setting and contrast of male and female perceptions of their relationships are reminiscent of such Hal Hartley films as *Trust* (1991) and *Simple Men* (1992). The major influence on Burns, however, seems to be Woody Allen. In interviews, the director has discussed his mother's making him watch *Annie Hall* (1977) and other Allen films numerous times. While Burns recalls Allen in his treatment of the battle between the sexes, his feel for New York, and his sometimes uneasy blend of comedy and drama, Burns owes his greatest debt to Allen in Patrick's bewilderment about sex and religion. Patrick's harangues over his guilt about abortion and his attempts to be a good Catholic carry echoes of the religious crisis experienced by the Allen character in *Hannah and her Sisters* (1986). Patrick is an Irish Catholic nebbish. That Burns' little film can be spoken of in this context indicates his potential as a filmmaker.

—*Michael Adams*

REVIEWS

Entertainment Weekly. August 18, 1995, p. 34.
The Los Angeles Times. August 9, 1995, p. F1.
The New York Times. August 9, 1995, p. B1.
Newsweek. CXXVI, August 14, 1995, p. 73.
People Weekly. XLIV, August 28, 1995, p. 17.
Rolling Stone. August 24, 1995, p. 110.
Time. CXLVI, August 28, 1995, p. 70.
USA Today. August 9, 1995, p D5.
Variety. January 30, 1995, p. 47.
The Village Voice. XL, August 15, 1995, p. 41.
The Wall Street Journal. August 18, 1995, p. A8.
The Washington Post. August 18, 1995, p. WW42.

Bulletproof Heart

"An endearingly wigged-out black comedy and a genuinely affecting love story."—Ella Taylor, *The Atlantic Monthly*

"An alluring, hardboiled sleeper that generates the same kind of excitement as *Red Rock West* and *The Last Seduction.*—Janet Maslin, *The New York Times*

"Mimi Rogers is terrific. She is an actress who belongs and seems to crave the edge. Her performance is among the best by an actress this year."—Mick LaSalle, *San Francisco Chronicle*

"Brooding, erotic and very funny. LaPaglia and Rogers are wonderful in the leads."—Glenn Lovell, *San Jose Mercury News*

"Thumbs up!"—Roger Ebert, *Siskel & Ebert*

Box Office Gross: $377,108

A dark, smart parable about vulnerability, *Bulletproof Heart* is another in a series of 1990s films in which soulless gangsters and heartless vamps plumb deep regions of the heart and soul. More restrained than *Pulp Fiction* (1994) and *The Last Seduction* (1995), this film is an original and fascinating concoction that lacks the rapid-fire dialogue and murderous pace of some of its contemporary noir cousins.

Bulletproof Heart is more an extended contemplation on human character and a meditation on various aspects of violence than an action-packed crimer. Eschewing egregious blood-spattering, it is a careful examination of various ways in which people wound each other and suggests that psychic wounds may pack more punch than physical hurt.

Debut director Mark Malone, who wrote the original story from which Gordon Melbourne fashioned a screenplay, weaves a simple but bizarre nihilistic tale about the varieties of human need and the uncharted borders of human emotions. He does it in a disarmingly neat, straightforward style that combines just the right measure of droll gangster wit and bleak landscapes.

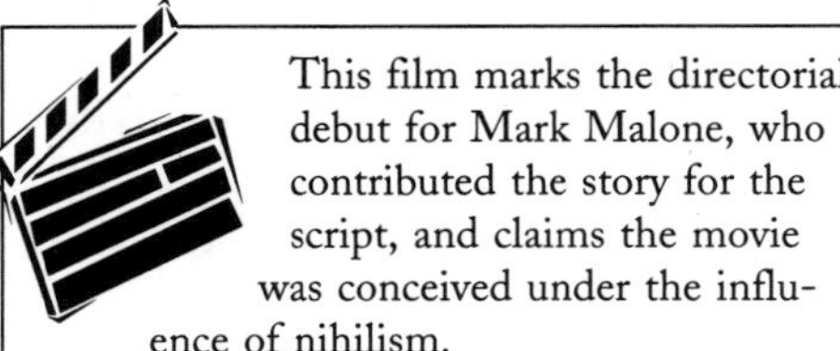

This film marks the directorial debut for Mark Malone, who contributed the story for the script, and claims the movie was conceived under the influence of nihilism.

On the surface, *Bulletproof Heart* is about a hit man hired to kill a disturbed woman who wants to die. When the woman seduces him and frees his heart from its glacial slumber, the hit man loses his nerve. The plot is uncomplicated, but the director adds some intriguing shadings to the material.

From the start, *Bulletproof Heart* has a deft, clean feel. Oozing evil, Mick (Anthony LaPaglia), the poker-faced assassin, rises up from behind a rack of suits in a closet like a vampire emerging from a casket. Dispassionately dispatching a snoring victim with baton and gloved hands, Mick sits on the edge of his mark's bed and forlornly watches a movie love scene on TV. He sighs. Though his work is rewarding, there is something missing in his life.

In the next scene, Mick is getting a reward for his work. A tantalizing high-class hooker (Monika Schnarre) is futilely trying to arouse a flicker of passion in him. It's like trying to use a blowtorch on rain-soaked wood to start a fire. When she offers Mick a scissors to cut off her bra, he considers stabbing her in the heart, but is interrupted by the entrance of his buffoonish sidekick, Archie (Matt Craven).

When mentor-client George (Peter Boyle) arrives, Mick confesses his near-crime and his total lack of feeling about it, saying that stabbing the hooker wouldn't have meant anything. In an evocative piece of directing, George's conversation flows seamlessly while Mick is shown basking under a heat lamp, taking a bath and shaving. When Mick talks about life's lack of meaning, the matter-of-fact George terms it "male menopause" and suggests Mick see a shrink. In fact, George says he'll arrange some sessions with a top-notch psychiatrist if Mick will dispatch a woman for him that night. When Mick balks, George gets down on his knees and begs.

This scene masterfully suggests Mick's boredom with his material success. Mick is a parody of a bourgeois businessman who, in a mid-life identity crisis, realizes his life has no center, though he's so estranged from his own emotions he can't even figure out what's missing.

Malone shoots the gangsters' transaction as a courtship, implying that Mick is a kind of prostitute and that his work, and its macho culture, is a substitute for sex. When Mick initially refuses to do the job, George asks: "Are you gonna break my heart?" and then begs "Please do this for me. Show me that you love me." When Mick agrees, George gushes: "If you had pants on, I'd kiss you."

George explains that the mark is a woman who owes a lot of money to a lot of important people, and that she must be dead before morning. He also says she knows what's coming and wants to be killed. Archie, a gabby weakling who has botched a previous job, begs Mick to give him a second chance and let him come along.

Arriving at his victim's apartment, Mick is flabbergasted to find the elegant Fiona (Mimi Rogers) hosting a party. "I was expecting something a little more impressive," she deadpans, eyeing the two hoods. She dismisses Archie ("I don't let assistants in") and the guests. Then she asks Mick to take a picture of her lounging provocatively on a couch while she quizzes him relentlessly about his work. "You like it?" she asks. "I like the money," Mick replies, adding "I'm good at what I do."

"I'm burnt out; there's something wrong with my brain."—Mick from *Bulletproof Heart*

So is Fiona, only what she does is turn strong men to putty. Seducing Mick, she ties him to a bed, alternately kisses and slaps him, then scratches his chest, pours wine over the wounds, and licks up the wine. The mild sadomasochism turns on Mick, but it also makes something new appear inside him.

Mick falls for Fiona, as have so many other men. At first it's hard to see why. Fiona is attractive, but no more so than the prostitute Mick rejected. Yet she has awakened a longing in him by demonstrating she can control him. Her domination has unearthed a vulnerability in Mick that no one, least of all Mick, suspected was there. Instead of just another victim whose death won't matter, Fiona is a woman

CREDITS

Mick: Anthony LaPaglia
Fiona: Mimi Rogers
Archie: Matt Craven
George: Peter Boyle
Laura: Monika Schnarre
Dr. Alstricht: Joseph Maler

Origin: USA
Released: 1995
Production: Robert Vince and William Vince for Keystone Films in association with Worldvision Enterprises; released by First Independent
Direction: Mark Malone
Screenplay: Gordon Melbourne; based on a story by Mark Malone
Cinematography: Tobias Schliessler
Editing: Robin Russell
Production design: Lynne Stopkewich
Art direction: Eric McNab
Set decoration: Elizabeth Patrick
Costume design: Maxyne Baker
Casting: Abra Edelman, Elisa Goodman, Marcia Shulman and Katie Eland
Music: Graeme Coleman
MPAA rating: R
Running Time: 98 minutes

who has made a victim of Mick, thereby opening in his soul a whole new window.

His own pain and need awakens him to a concern for Fiona's deep pain, which he cannot assuage. Fiona wants to die because she is mentally ill, haunted by unexplained demons. In one hilarious scene, a drug-crazed shrink, Dr. Alstricht (Joseph Maler), tells Mick that Fiona is incurable.

After a bizarre night that includes a picnic on Chinese carry-out food in a cemetery, Mick orders the annoying Archie to drive him and Fiona across the river to New Jersey (strangely, though the film is set in New York, it was shot in Vancouver). The place where Mick must shoot Fiona is a warehouse that opens up onto the river, suggesting a portal to another life; there are two chairs and an overhead light that look like a bare stage, suggesting the existential dilemma they are facing.

Malone uses an inventive mix of theatrical and cinematic techniques. Sections of the film are introduced with titles taken from the dialogue, giving the proceedings the primitive, experimental feel of a silent film and the episodic quality of a multi-act play. *Bulletproof Heart* builds to a Shakespearean climax, and a scene near the finale where the lovers lie down together, one dead and one alive, is evocative of "Romeo and Juliet."

Audiences who get up and leave as the final credits roll will miss a rather remarkable coda, a bleak and tragic epilogue that punctuates the movie with an almost unbearable sadness. Clearly Malone is a risk-taker; not only does he eschew a happy ending, he sends viewers home with a morose image of a man doomed to live with unbearable pain.

With her death, Fiona's anguish has become lodged in the heart of Mick, who cannot extract it. It is as if the hit man has finally taken a bullet he cannot remove. And he will spend the rest of his life suffering from it.

The choicest ironies in *Bulletproof Heart* revolve around the manipulation of aspects of masculinity and femininity, of duty and loyalty and friendship, of love and murder and life and death. It's not a neat psychological package and it doesn't all fit together, but it's provocative.

Each character is trapped in needs that cannot be fulfilled. Mick needs to become vulnerable in order to feel like life has any meaning, but killing the only person who can make him feel is not only his duty, but a loving act. Like Mick, Fiona easily dominates others but cannot heal her inner torments; she needs someone to love her enough to kill her, but can't find a man strong enough to do it. Archie needs to prove himself by overcoming his emotions and being manly enough to pull a trigger. George desperately needs Fiona to die to escape a tight spot.

The roles are challenging. For much of the movie, La-

Paglia seems to be doing a Robert DeNiro impersonation as the tough-guy gangster. As his character's persona is eroded, LaPaglia becomes a leaky furnace of emotions ready to explode, humanity oozing out between the hardened exterior just like the blood pours out of his victims.

Rogers is appropriately sultry but also turns disarmingly loony and heroic, even angelic, in confronting her turmoil. She has a slightly off-key manner that is intriguing. Rogers combines her physical allure with a quirky emotional appeal that is almost haunting.

Carrying much of the comic load in the picture are Craven and Boyle, and both are superb at that task. Like a lousy court jester, Craven is always saying things that shouldn't be said; he is an apprentice male who can't cut the mustard. Boyle, known for over-the-top performances, here delivers a nicely modulated one.

Bulletproof Heart is a promising debut for Malone. His grasp of his material is firm and the film is well-crafted, yet it has a natural and unpretentious feel. It's the kind of film which continues to be intriguing long after viewing.

—Michael Betzold

REVIEWS

Cosmopolitan. June 1995, p. 26.
Entertainment Weekly. April 7, 1995, p. 64.
Los Angeles Magazine. February 1995, p. 107.
New York Times. April 7, 1995.
Playboy. April 1995, p. 28.

Bushwhacked

"They wanted a great adventure. What they got was *Mad Max* Grabelski."—Movie tagline

"Silly fun, bouncy energy!"—Jami Bernard, *NY Daily News*

"A side-splitting comic adventure! Daniel Stern is at his wild and wacky best."—Jeanne Wolf, *Jeanne Wolf's Hollywood*

Box Office Gross: $7,450,990

In much the same vein as the Hayley Mills' films of yore—*The Parent Trap* (1961), *In Search of the Castaways* (1962), *The Trouble with Angels* (1966)—*Bushwhacked* takes a group of young people away from their parents and introduces a series of humorous and dangerous situations to test the youths' mettle. Whether featuring girls at camp, girls at school or boys/girls on a campout, the genre remains largely unchanged: the children must rely on each others' resourcefulness to succeed in the adventure, and on only the materials they have with them in this isolated location. They also must learn to judge people independently of what they have been told, and to appreciate their homes (albeit often broken or dysfunctional). And lastly, all loose ends must be resolved by film's (happy) end.

Bushwhacked clearly follows this model: Mrs. Patterson (Ann Dowd) is a single mother, raising her family, earning a living and filling in as her son's scout leader. Because she has helped the scouts earn cooking and sewing badges and little else, Mrs. Patterson's scouts are about to mutiny. Then she arranges for a real nature guide to take the scouts on an overnight camping trip. Across town, Max Grabelski (Daniel Stern), well meaning but clueless delivery man, is having a monumentally bad day. By arranging to deliver a customer's package at a certain time for an extra fee, Max has become an accessory to money laundering. He becomes a "wanted man," and in an effort to clear his name, he must reach Devil's Peak and find the man who hired him. Through a series of stock misadventures, Max is mistaken for the wilderness expert, and before he knows it, his choice becomes wilderness adventure or jail. Once it becomes apparent that Max is no wilderness expert, it is up to the scouts to determine whether Max is good or bad and whether he is to be helped or handed over to authorities.

As with any film intended for children, *Bushwhacked* has its share of simple humor, including physical comedy (e.g., a "scout leader" who continually chokes one camper by using the camper's binoculars while they are around his neck, along with countless prank falls), scatological jokes, and jokes in poor taste (e.g., "If you get the electric chair, you should put a light bulb in your mouth like Uncle Fester"). This film, however, branches out past such contrived tricks to include a few jokes which parents may enjoy more than their children. For instance, the film begins by parodying one of the most famous scenes of recent film history-the opening scene from *Saturday Night Fever* (1977), complete with jaunty walk (in this case, Daniel Stern rather than John Travolta), 1970s apparel (polyester fabric, exaggerated collar length, signature shoes) and the brothers Gibb singing the theme song. The scene has become an icon of the era of disco. In this case, however, it immediately characterizes Max Grabelski as a man behind the times and as a numskull (even if a well-meaning numskull). Where John Travolta's character in *Saturday Night Fever* walked the streets with a certain low-class, street-smart savoir faire, Daniel Stern's character looks not unlike the Disney character Goofy: slack-jawed, blankly good-humored, harmlessly and happily vague. Max Grabelski is stupid but happy. Indeed, the stupid-but-happy genre (i.e., the dumbing of America) appears to be the new vogue in films, and it is little surprise that two of the behind-the-scene writers on this film-Peter and Bobby Farrelly-have recently risen to prominence for having written the popular film *Dumb and Dumber* (1995).

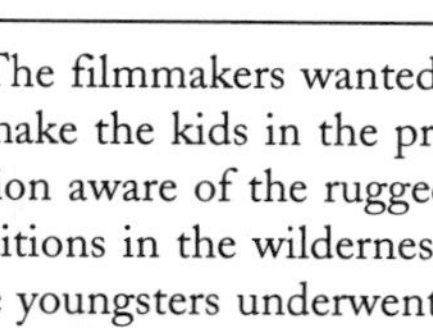

The filmmakers wanted to make the kids in the production aware of the rugged conditions in the wilderness, so the youngsters underwent extensive physical preparation. Stern, however, in keeping with the bumbling characteristics of his character, refrained from the training sessions.

CREDITS

Max Grabelski: Daniel Stern
Agent Palmer: Jon Polito
Jack Erickson: Brad Sullivan
Mrs. Patterson: Ann Dowd
Bragdon: Anthony Heald
Agent McMurrey: Tom Wood
Gordy: Blake Bashoff
Ralph: Corey Carrier
Dana: Michael Galeota
Barnhill: Max Goldblatt

Origin: USA
Released: 1995
Production: Charles B. Wessler and Paul Schiff; released by 20th Century Fox
Direction: Greg Beeman
Screenplay: John Jordan, Danny Byers, Tommy Swerdlow, and Michael Goldberg, from a story by Jordan and Byers
Cinematography: Theo Van deSande
Editing: Ross Albert
Production design: Mark Mansbridge and Sandy Veneziano
Art direction: Bruce Crone
Costume design: Mary Zophres
Sound: Tim Clooney
Music: Bill Conti
MPAA rating: PG-13
Running Time: 90 minutes

Visually, *Bushwhacked* offers very little that is original or interesting to watch. However, in all fairness to the film, it seems to aspire to little technical finesse beyond that of television fare. One scene (also featured prominently in the previews) has Daniel Stern extended across an abyss, while the scouts creep across his back, turning him into a human bridge. The scene makes mundane use of blue screen techniques, which will no doubt be particularly disappointing to sophisticated computer-age youngsters. Even more disappointingly, the scene is an example of the rather pointless vignettes that make up the film. It allows for the sight gag of Stern made into a bridge and Stern stuck as a bridge, but it fails to advance the plot in any way. Another such scene has Stern's Max Grabelski stereotypically approach a bear cub, cuddling and cooing, only to discover the mother bear close at hand. Each of these scenes demonstrates the patently obvious—Max is clueless in the wild—a fact that was evident from the first scenes of hiking mayhem. Indeed, reviews commented on how forgettable the film is, and how it is destined to end its days as a mediocre video rental. Such would seem to be the case, particularly in a summer filled with remarkably creative films such as *Babe* (a talking piglet raised with a litter of puppies).

Some of the characters in this film advance little beyond the stereotypical. While this is often the case in comedy (where characterization is often particularly shallow in order to make room for jokes and pranks), it is distressing here in some key areas. For example, when a young woman joins the scout troop, the "guys" groan. However, later in the film she earns their grudging acceptance, when she comes up with the idea of using her training bra as a slingshot to pelt the "bad guys" with rocks. First of all, little is gained by reinforcing the gender awkwardness and difference between preadolescent teens. Also, little is gained by having the girl's one contribution spring (as it were) from her training bra. At some point it would be reassuring to find filmmakers showing young people as just that, young people, without emphasizing gender differences for small (even if humorous) gains.

Perhaps most disappointing of all is finding Daniel Stern in this film at all. While he does an excellent job of portraying a bumbling fool, he has performed challenging roles well in films such as *Breaking Away* (1979), *Stardust Memories* (1980), *Diner* (1982), and *Hannah and her Sisters* (1986). Even in such comedies as *City Slickers* (1991) Stern manages to create a character that can bring a thinking person to laughter. Stern's Max Grabelski, however, falls far short of that mark. In one scene, Max stops at a road-side store, only to be discovered as a wanted man. When confronted by the nature guide (as luck would have it) and the shopkeeper, Max's eyes bulge to pickled egg proportions, his feet rotate in place like the cartoon character Roadrunner, before he is able to escape. Then he manages to take the nature guide's vehicle and glue the nature guide to the steering wheel of his (Max's) car. The scene is staged like a cartoon, which is a waste of Stern's acting abilities, and is an example of how, in this film, actions do not have repercussions and authority figures are portrayed as simpletons and/or crooks. Where once crime fighters were heroes, today filmmakers portray criminals sympathetically. For example, in *Bushwhacked*, one of the law-enforcement persons is crooked, greedy, and, as if to seal his fate, horribly out of shape. Viewers are invited to distrust and dislike his character, while Max Grabelski's character, would-be money launderer, is written in sympathetic terms.

Bushwhacked may indeed entertain youngsters of a certain age for a certain period of time. However, it is forgettable, unremarkable, and draws on the least creative shtick around. Families may want to wait to view this on video, as the large screen is made small by this film's nannering.

—Roberta F. Green

REVIEWS

Baltimore Sun, Aug. 5, 1995, p. 3D
Chicago Tribune, Tempo, p. 5
Washington Post Weekend, Aug. 4, 1995, p. 42
USA Today, Aug. 4, 1995, p. 4D
Variety, July 31, 1995, p. 36.

Bye Bye, Love

"Those laughs just keep coming!"—Robin Ward, *BBS (CFTO-TV, Canada)*

"*Parenthood* for the '90's!"—Scott Patrick, *Hollywood One on One*

"A winner! Non-stop fun. First-rate comedy, it's hilarious!"—Jim Ferguson, *Preview Channel*

"Paul Reiser is fabulous!"—Dawn Meadows, *WEWS-TV, Cleveland*

Box Office Gross: $12,096,673

In 1950s TV sitcoms, everybody lived in a happy nuclear family. In 1990s films, virtually nobody does. *Bye Bye, Love* is a nineties film with a sitcom flavor which features three pitiable but likeable dethroned dads navigating a universe of shattered dreams and broken families.

The upper-middle-class Southern California world of *Bye Bye, Love*—where marriages are measured in months, not years—is just as far removed from real America as the happy *Father Knows Best* world of fifties TV comedies. But exaggeration is a useful comic device, and since divorce in modern America is a fact of life, audiences will recognize the social landscape as somewhat familiar.

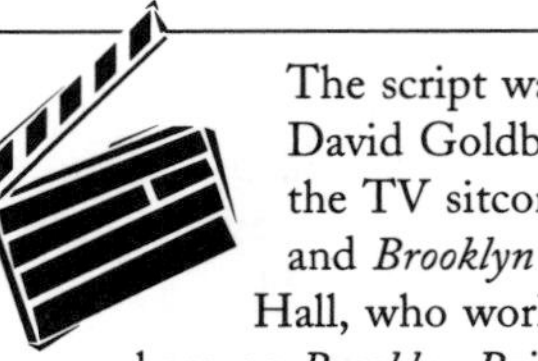

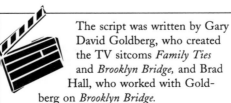

The script was written by Gary David Goldberg, who created the TV sitcoms *Family Ties* and *Brooklyn Bridge*, and Brad Hall, who worked with Goldberg on *Brooklyn Bridge.*

Since the film was written, produced and directed by men, it's no surprise that it's filled with sympathy for the dispossessed dads. Two of the three are cast as victims of heartless ex-wives. Donny (Paul Reiser) still pines for his ex, Claire (Jayne Brook), who is remarried, and feels rejected by his teenage daughter Emma (Eliza Dushku). Claire's new man refers to Donny as Emma's "birth father." Vic (Randy Quaid) still seethes with anger at Grace (Lindsay Crouse), who also has replaced him with a younger man.

Though the film wallows in self-pity and righteous indignation at the plight of Donny and Vic, some balance is provided by the character of Dave (Matthew Modine), who is a shallow, self- absorbed philanderer. Dave fooled around on his wife Susan (Amy Brenneman), and his pals protected him.

The script follows a weekend when all three dads take custody of their children. It's executed in the overused modern TV comedy/drama style of multiple short scenes, jumping from character to character. It's tied together with another familiar device, a radio talk-show host, Dr. Dave Townsend (Rob Reiner), doing a weekend call-in marathon on divorce.

The small-screen influences are many and obvious as the filmmakers and most of the cast have extensive TV backgrounds. Producers Gary David Goldberg, Brad Hall and Sam Weisman collaborated on the *Brooklyn Bridge* series. They concocted *Bye Bye, Love* after Goldberg learned of a McDonald's restaurant that was a popular spot for weekend exchanges of children among divorced families. Goldberg and Hall got script credit; Weisman directed.

Weisman directed the TV series *Family Ties* and also worked on *Moonlighting* and *L.A. Law.* Goldberg worked on *The Bob Newhart Show*, *Lou Grant* and *Family Ties.* Hall has written for *Frasier.*

"Basically, I'm just looking for a mammal."—Lucille from *Bye Bye, Love*

The script is filled with sitcom-like situations and jokes and the sappy, seriocomic poignant moments of modern TV drama. But there a lot of funny moments, crisp acting and editing, and plenty of wicked tugs at the heartstrings. The bits succeed more often than they fail, though there are some monumental clunkers.

A raft of fine actors, most of whom are TV veterans, carries the rather predictable proceedings with good spirit. The best is Reiser, the star and co-creator of the TV series *Mad About You.* In his first major film role, Reiser lifts a rather stereotyped hang-dog character to a figure tinged with tragedy and heroism. Quaid is almost as good, displaying a vast comic and dramatic range. Modine is suitably vacant and irritating while still managing to be likeable.

Two of the three actresses playing the wives, Crouse and Brook, are given little to work with. Crouse's spitting anger fires up the screen in her few moments and she and Quaid are lethal warriors.

CREDITS

Dave: Matthew Modine
Vic DiMico: Randy Quaid
Donny: Paul Reiser
Lucille: Janeane Garofalo

Origin: USA
Released: 1995
Production: Gary David Goldberg, Brad Hall, and Sam Weisman for UBU Productions; released by 20th Century Fox
Direction: Sam Weisman
Screenplay: Gary David Goldberg and Brad Hall
Cinematography: Kenneth Zunder
Editing: Roger Bondelli and Greg Papalia
Music: J.A.C. Redford
MPAA rating: PG-13
Running Time: 106 minutes

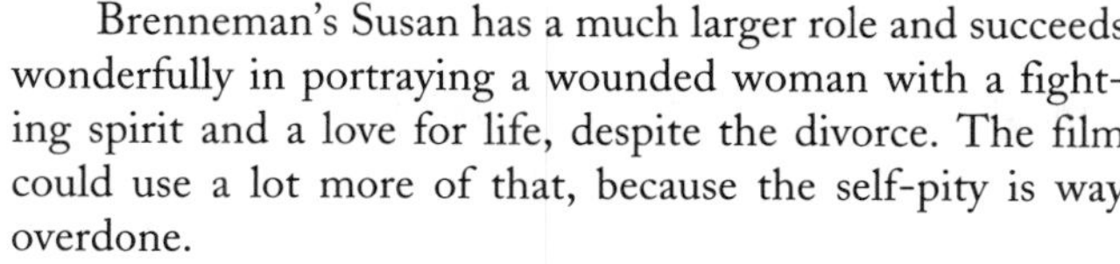

Brenneman's Susan has a much larger role and succeeds wonderfully in portraying a wounded woman with a fighting spirit and a love for life, despite the divorce. The film could use a lot more of that, because the self-pity is way overdone.

Dushku is very good as a teenager torn apart by her parents' divorce. Her sincere, modulated performance is one of the most quiet and effective things in the film, and provides a sort of moral linchpin for the far-flung, overwrought proceedings.

In the last half of the film, the very funny Janeane Garofalo (who debuted in 1994's *Reality Bites*) provides a tremendous comic uplift playing Lucille, Vic's prickly blind date. No screen date has ever been more wonderfully awful than this pair's doomed foray into an Italian restaurant.

Garofalo creates a toxic waste dump of post-feminist personality, unloading breezy emotional stink bombs with sunny, straightforward lethality. Staring at the menu, she kvetches: "Do you know how long veal stays in your colon?" Somehow, she manages to make Lucille appealingly loony.

Quaid's pores ooze indigestion as he endures an evening with this toad. He and Garofalo punch and jab verbally like Laurel and Hardy do physically. "Are you on medication?" Vic asks. "No, everybody asks me that," Lucille replies, smiling.

The minor characters sparkle as well. Reiner is infuriatingly funny as the hokey, hypocritical radio host who lectures listeners on divorce. Among Dave's many suitors, Dana Wheeler-Nicholson is choicest as Heidi, a soccer mom who's ready to do some kicking of her own.

Many of the child actors are effective, though some of the younger ones get the cutesy treatment. A sequence of tee-ball action will elicit knowing chuckles from any adults who have endured that quasi-sport.

While most of the characters are stepping through the mine fields of pre-existing families, two characters left bereft by their families are forming an unlikely friendship. It is unclear why ex-auto assembly worker and widower Walter (Ed Flanders) and his new boss at McDonald's, parentless young Max (Johnny Whitworth), hit it off. Their relationship obviously exists to make a point about human possibilities, but it feels forced and doesn't add much to the film.

Bye Bye, Love fits well on the small screen. Too bad it doesn't more fully exploit the possibilities of cinema. Like the TV fare that spawned these filmmakers, the movie predictably follows laughs with tears with more laughs, and no mood is left to linger for more than a few minutes.

All the characters speak snappy, clever lines, which makes the movie entertaining but distances the actors from the audience. With the possible exception of Reiser, no one's on screen long enough and no one's normal enough to evoke the kind of strong identification that would carry a film.

Fortunately, a surprisingly uplifting closing message saves the film from being nothing more than a visit to the town of Splitsville. Just as one longed in the 1950s to see a few non-nuclear families on TV, in *Bye Bye, Love* one would be glad to see just one happy, intact family. It might provide enough tension to spoil the trite formula.

—*Michael Betzold*

REVIEWS

Entertainment Weekly. March 17, 1995, p. 66.
Hollywood Reporter. March 13, 1995, p. 12.
Los Angeles Magazine. March 1995, p. 129.
Los Angeles Times. March 17, 1995, p. F6.
New York. March 27, 1995, p. 86.
People Weekly. March 20, 1995, p. 17.
Variety. March 13, 1995, p. 2.

Canadian Bacon

"A satire of American yahooism that aspires to be the 90's answer to *Dr. Strangelove*. It has enough comic asides to keep liberal funny bones tickled."—Stephen Holden, *The New York Times*

Known for his pranks on business leaders and his diatribes against corporate greed, Michael Moore puts his political bent in the form of a lunatic satire on the American public's gullibility for government propaganda in *Canadian Bacon*. Abandoning his quasi-documentary style entirely, Moore opts for laughs with an outrageous piece of fiction. Surprisingly, the outrageous shenanigans of this wacky film are thoroughly enjoyable. Moore's script fires off gags with the swiftness of a stand-up comedy routine.

A sort of latter-day *Dr. Strangelove*, though not nearly as good, *Canadian Bacon* is a delicious send-up of the military-industrial-government complex that created the Cold War. Moore makes his political points quite deftly, rarely letting them overshadow the broad, populist appeal of his humor. The best thing about Moore's satire is that he skewers both ruling-class arrogance and working-class stupidity with equal fervor.

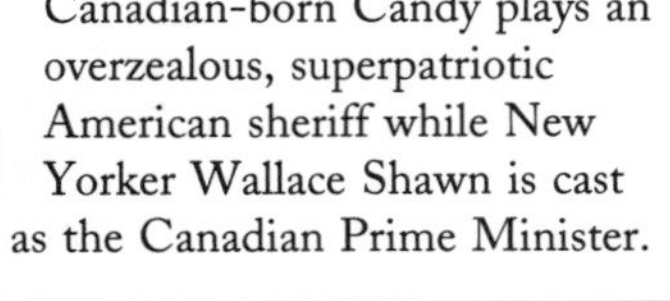

Canadian-born Candy plays an overzealous, superpatriotic American sheriff while New Yorker Wallace Shawn is cast as the Canadian Prime Minister.

With the Cold War over, a Clinton-style American president (Alan Alda) is floundering in the polls. Defense plants are closing, and there is no enemy to distract the American public from their dismal economic plight. Stu Smiley (Kevin Pollak), a weasely political operative who is head of the National Security Council, cooks up a plan with defense contractor R.J. Hacker (G.D. Spradlin) and an old-line Strangelove-type general, Dick Panzer (Rip Torn), to create a new enemy and a new Cold War to rebuild the president's popularity.

The target nation is chosen after news comes of a riot at a hockey game in Niagara Falls, Ontario. Sheriff Bud Boomer (John Candy), a laid-off Hacker plant worker who has a new job with the border patrol, casually remarks on how bad Canadian beer is, and players stop the game and attack him. Smiley decides Canada would be the perfect enemy, and begs the president to give him a week to convince the American public that their friendly neighbor is the new Evil Empire.

In hilarious fashion, the Smiley-propelled propaganda machine fills television airwaves. Newscasters note how Canadians, including William Shatner, Monte Hall and Alec Trebeck, have infiltrated the entertainment business; that 90 percent of the Canadian population is sinisterly situated within 100 miles of the U.S. border, threatening an invasion; and how the Canadians have a terrifying lead in Zamboni (ice-surfacing machine) technology. One show depicts a map oozing maple syrup southward across the border. An announcer mulls over what life would be like if the horribly bland Canadians took over American culture: "Mayonnaise on everything...and Anne Murray songs all day, every day."

Raised in Michigan, Moore lampoons everything that is possible to lampoon about Canadians, including their cleanliness and politeness. The jokes might not play so well with Americans who live further from the Canadian border, but they are consistently funny. A mountie, seeking to repel an invasion by Boomer and his laid-off buddies, who have been whipped into a patriotic frenzy, beckons, "Go back where you came from." His partner scolds, "You can't end a sentence with a preposition." In one of the film's most droll, Monty-Python-like sequences, Boomer and his crew are stopped by a Canadian patrolman who gestures disapprovingly toward anti-Canadian graffiti spray-painted on the side of their stolen truck. Rather than asking them to remove the slurs, he reminds them that Canadian law requires all signs to be bilingual and hands them a can of spray paint; they drive off with their profane slogans in English and French. In another bit, Boomer and friends get outraged when another mountie pronounces "about" as "a-boot." Pointing a gun at him, Boomer's sidekick says, "We got ways of making you pronounce the letter 'o'." Irony is added to the humor by the fact that Candy, who plays the anti-Canadian zealot, was born and raised in Toronto.

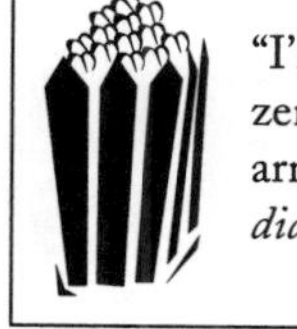

"I'm your worst nightmare: A citizen with the right to bear arms."—Bud Boomer from *Canadian Bacon*

Canadian Bacon mines most of its humor from its constant and mostly ingenious slams at Canadian culture. Given Moore's equally disparaging views of his working-class heroes' gullibility—the American public is depicted as a horde of mindless dupes—the tongue-in-cheek Canadian jokes come off as backhanded compliments. It's essentially a one-joke movie, but Moore keeps coming with so many variations on the theme that the laughs keep tumbling out. It helps that Moore has assembled a nice crew of comic actors, led by Candy and helped out in fine fashion by Rhea Perlman as Boomer's deputy, Honey, Pollak and Spradlin. There are a myriad of fine bits in small roles: by a Russian leader, a bumbling Mountie jailer (Steven Wright), and a paranoid CIA spook. The only false notes are struck by Alda, who is far too laid-back to be a poll-watching president, and by Torn, who makes his general a caricature but fails to go over the top.

Moore's direction is far from inspired, but the film's low-budget feel actually adds to its charm. The film falters in its final half-hour, never quite hitting the right tone with its ridiculous, hackneyed countdown to a nuclear Armageddon, but there's plenty of fun along the way with a bumbling, black-clad special tactics "Omega Force" chasing after Boomer to rub him out. Moore borrows liberally from *Strangelove*, Python, and *Airplane*-type humor but occasionally stumbles into contrivances. Still, in the best comic tradition, the wisecracks never stop coming, and the lunacy extends all the way to the end of the credits, where it's proclaimed: "No Canadians were harmed during the making of this movie."

If widely seen, *Canadian Bacon* may enhance Moore's appeal as a humorist, though it might disappoint some of his more serious politically minded fans. What's nice about Moore's version of propaganda, at least as presented here, is that it makes fun not only of the manufacturers of mass culture but also of its consumers. There is no escaping Moore's pointed suggestions that an indolent, ignorant public gets exactly the political exploitation and manipulation it deserves. In the best factory-rat tradition, this proletarian filmmaker pokes fun at working-class foibles and culpability while exposing the duplicity and venality of the ruling class.

Though many will consider it much more of a lightweight effort, in almost every respect *Canadian Bacon* is a much better film than *Roger and Me*, a one-dimensional prank film which won Moore amazing acclaim. It certainly is more entertaining. Political medicine goes down much easier with laughter, and most of the best subversive films are loony satires (Peter O'Toole's *The Ruling Class*, Richard Lester's *Oh What a Lovely War!* and Jules Pfeiffer's *Little Murders*, to name just a few). *Canadian Bacon* is no classic comedy, but it is a very funny movie, and Moore is much more tolerable in this scatter-shot, take-no-prisoners vein than he is in the more stuffy, self-righteous mode of *Roger and Me*.

But the prospects that *Canadian Bacon* will be widely seen are dim. The film has an unlucky history. First Candy died, aborting a planned ending in which Boomer invades Mexico. Then Spradlin suffered a heart attack on set. *Canadian Bacon* was then consigned to the scrapheap of the distribution pile, a victim of squabbles between PolyGram, the

CREDITS

President: Alan Alda
Bud B. Boomer: John Candy
Deputy Honey: Rhea Perlman
Stu Smiley: Kevin Pollack
Gen. Dick Panzer: Rip Torn
R.J. Hacker: G.D. Spradlin

Origin: USA
Released: 1995
Production: David Brown, Michael Moore and Ron Rotholz for a Polygram Filmed Entertainment; released by Gramercy Pictures
Direction: Michael Moore
Screenplay: Michael Moore
Cinematography: Haskell Wexler
Editing: Wendey Stanzler and Michael Berenbaum
Production design: Carol Spier
Sound: Douglas Gantor
Assistant director: Terry Miller
Music-Elmer Bernstein
MPAA rating: PG
Running Time: 110 minutes

film's backer, and MGM, its original distributor. It ended up two years on the shelf and its theatrical release was followed closely by video distribution. It deserves a better fate, and if word-of-mouth rescues it, it could have the makings of a cult hit.

—Michael Betzold

REVIEWS

Entertainment Weekly. Oct. 6, 1995, p. 44.
Maclean's. Sept. 25, 1995, p. 52.
New York Times. Sept. 22, 1995, p. C20.
USA Today. Sept. 22, 1995, p. 4D.
Variety. May 29, 1995, p. 54.
Village Voice. Sept. 26, 1995, p. 75.
Wall Street Journal. Sept. 22, 1995, p. A12 (E).
Washington Post. Sept. 22, 1995, p. D6.

Candyman II: Farewell to the Flesh

Box Office Gross: $13,940,383

It is virtually axiomatic in Hollywood that when a film does well, there should be a sequel. This theory seems to have particular influence in the genre of horror films, as proven by the success of *Nightmare on Elm Street* and *Halloween* series. *Candyman II: Farewell to the Flesh* tries to cash in on the success of *Candyman* (1992), perhaps trying to create a new series that might scare the living daylights out of horror fans. But alas, the only thing that this film does for the genre is provide yet another couple of hours of scary special effects, some fine cinematography (by Tobias Schliesser), and an evocative if overblown score by renowned composer Phillip Glass. Other than that, this film failed to generate any real heat at the box office, receiving tepid reviews and ho-hum audience response.

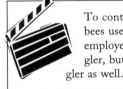

To control the large amount of bees used in shooting, the film employed not only a bee wrangler, but an assistant bee wrangler as well.

Horror master Clive Barker's story entitled *The Forbidden* was the basis for the first *Candyman* film. Barker's story was set in England, but the *Candyman* creators set that first film in the Cabrini Green housing project of Chicago, thereby setting the stage for some trenchant symbolism about the state of race relations in the United States. Candyman is the nickname of Daniel Robitaille (Tony Todd), an African-American man to whose right arm is attached a truly deadly hook instead of a hand. In the first film, considered a fine example of noirish, psychological horror, Candyman terrorized a fetching Ph.D., played by Virginia Madsen, who set out to learn about his origins.

"Sorrow and hate fill his mind; bees buzz about his lips."—A scholar from *Candyman II: Farewell to the Flesh*

This time around Candyman's "back story," as they say in Hollywood, becomes clearer. It seems Robitaille/Candyman was once a slave on a plantation whose artistic talent was so great that the owner of the plantation entrusted him to paint a portrait of his beautiful daughter, Caroline. But fate intervened when Robitaille and Caroline fell in love. As punishment for his "transgression," the slave's hand was cut off, and (this part is harder to explain) his head and chest were smeared with honey to attract bees, hence the nickname. Just before dying, Candyman is shown his face in a hand mirror by his beloved, thereby capturing his soul forever in the mirror.

Now, all anyone has to do is say "Candyman" five times into a mirror and he appears. In this film, Candyman turns up in New Orleans, just in time for Mardi Gras (which marks the beginning of Lent, also known as a "farewell to the flesh," hence the title.) He sets his sights on the Tarrant family, intending to destroy all of Caroline's (the beloved who held up the mirror) descendants.

Borrowing a storyline from the first film, Candyman gets involved with yet another lovely woman who is investigating his origins. This young woman happens to be Caroline's great-great-granddaughter, Annie (Kelly Rowan). She is part of the dysfunctional nuclear family headed by Octavia Tarrant (Veronica Cartwright), holder of a family secret and looking, as one review put it, suspiciously like the Southern matriarch played by Joan Crawford in *Queen Bee* (1955).

CREDITS

Daniel Robitalle/Candyman: Tony Todd
Annie Tarrant: Kelly Rowan
Paul McKeever: Timothy Carhart
Octavia: Veronica Cartwright

Origin: USA
Released: 1995
Production: Sigurjon Sighvatsson and Gregg D. Fienberg for Propaganda Films presentation; released by Gramercy Pictures
Direction: Bill Condon
Screenplay: Rand Ravich and Mark Kruger from a story by Clive Barker
Cinematography: Tobias Schlesser
Editing: Virginia Katz
Production designer: Barry Robison
Costumes: Bruce Finlayson
Special Visual Effects: Introvision International
Music: Philip Glass
MPAA rating: R
Running Time: 94 minutes

After killing much of the Tarrant family, Candyman tries to seduce the lovely Annie, played with brio by Kelly Rowan. The links between racism, violence, and sex, are somehow implied but not overtly explored, leaving the audience to assume that there is more here than meets the eye. Quite often it appears that the producers of "slasher" films, as this genre is often called, wish to appear as if there is a thematic raison d'etre for all of the violence. But here, the reason seems only to be to cash in on the previous *Candyman* film.

Director Bill Condon provides quite a bit of visual excitement, especially in a scene involving countless bees. ("Bee Wrangler...Norman Gary" has to be one of the oddest credits in recent film history.) Screenwriters Rand Ravich and Mark Kruger evoke a few more unintentional laughs than they may have intended with dialogue such as "swallow your horror and let it nourish you."

Tony Todd is once again a powerful presence as the Candyman. But unfortunately, the horror is a bit hard to swallow in this uneven follow-up to a decent film.

—*Kirby Tepper*

Carrington

"She had many lovers but only one love."—Movie tagline

Box Office Gross: $2,697,902

The Bloomsbury group of English writers and artists who flourished during the first half of the twentieth century have long fascinated intellectuals from all over the world. The group, named for the district where many had their London residences, included novelist Virginia Woolf; her husband, publisher Leonard Woolf; her sister, painter Vanessa Bell; Vanessa's husband, painter Clive Bell; economist Maynard Keynes; art critic Roger Fry; painter Duncan Grant; and Grant's cousin, writer Lytton Strachey. Only the latter and, briefly, the Bells appear in *Carrington*, writer-director Christopher Hampton's meditation on the doomed relationship between the homosexual Strachey and painter Dora Carrington, a member of the Bloomsbury circle only through her connection to Strachey. Hampton has wanted to film this story since the late 1960's, but what drew him to it, unfortunately, does not come across on the screen.

> Dora Carrington's paintings did not receive wide exposure until a 1970 retrospective exhibit in London.

Carrington opens as Strachey (Jonathan Pryce) and Carrington (Emma Thompson) meet at the Bells' country cottage in 1915 when he is still a minor literary figure. Strachey is attracted to Carrington, who insists upon being called by her last name, when he first sees her because he thinks she, with her bobbed hair, is a boy. She feels antagonism until, sneaking up on the sleeping writer to cut off his trademark, a long, unruly beard, she surprises herself by falling in love. What is a passionate young woman in love with a homosexual, who also loves her, though not physically, to do? Hampton spends two hours skipping along the surface of this question.

The first thing Carrington does is to yield, finally, her virginity to painter Mark Gertler (Rufus Sewell), who has been pursuing her for some time.

When she refuses to commit to him, however, he angrily attacks Strachey, who seems to enjoy the assault. She then marries the athletic but seemingly doltish Reginald Partridge (Steven Waddington) for no clear reason other than that Strachey, who rechristens his unrequited love Ralph, enjoys having the Great War veteran around to lust after.

The threesome live together for years with Ralph (pronounced Rafe) gradually drifting off into affairs until his mistress, Frances Marshall (Alex Kingston), becomes part of the equation. Carrington has affairs with writer Gerald Brenan (Samuel West) and yachtsman Beacus Penrose (Jeremy Northam). She treats Brenan badly, though he continues to cling to her, and feels she has finally captured the man she has been seeking until Penrose confesses that he is not that drawn to her.

Meanwhile Strachey becomes celebrated with the 1918 publication of his irreverent *Eminent Victorians*, credited by many with creating a new approach to biography. Carrington basks in his glory, jumps into bed with her lovers, and paints a little, now and then, until Strachey becomes fatally ill with cancer. The film ends with her suicide in 1932.

The first third of the film is entertaining as Strachey roams through English society tossing off witty epigrams in the manner of Oscar Wilde. But when the focus shifts to Carrington's inability to find true love with a heterosexual, *Carrington* quickly loses its focus and eventually begins crawling slowly, inevitably toward its sad, painful conclusion. Hampton, best known for his 1985 play *Les Liasions Dangereuses*, covers similar material much more effectively in his screenplay of the latter, *Dangerous Liasions* (1989), which presents well-delineated characters and clearly defined moral and ethical issues. *Carrington*, in contrast, is a muddle.

While Strachey is an attractive, sympathetic character, Carrington and her lovers remain ciphers. Except for the sex with Penrose, Hampton does not convey what draws her to these men nor what they see in her. The title character's vagueness extends to her art. All Hampton says is that she is not secure enough about her paintings to exhibit them. What her men and her many friends think is left unsaid. Carrington seems a dilettante until a series of her paintings are displayed during the film's closing credits and it becomes obvious that this woman should have been much more interesting than Hampton makes her. He employs only a tiny portion of the material, including her bisexuality, available in his source, Michael Holroyd's acclaimed biography of Strachey, first published in 1967-1968 and revised in 1994.

Hampton makes his debut as a director after a number of established directors, including Herbert Ross and Mike Newell, dropped out of the project. Many reviewers criticized Hampton for presenting his film as a series of disconnected snapshots of the protagonists, but this approach, typical in film biographies covering several years, could have worked if the vignettes had added up to anything. Hampton seems to have been attracted to the unusual quality of the Carrington-Strachey relationship without giving sufficient thought to ways of moving beyond its surface.

Hampton shows some cinematic skill when he has Carrington watches windows from a lawn while others (Ralph and Frances, Strachey and his latest boy, Penrose) prepare for bed. Her longing to be part of a vital love affair becomes quite apparent. More typical is the sluggish pacing with

CREDITS

Dora Carrington: Emma Thompson
Lytton Strachey: Jonathan Pryce
Ralph Partridge: Steven Waddington
Gerald Brenan: Samuel West
Mark Gertler: Rufus Sewell
Frances Marshall: Alex Kingston
Beacus Penrose: Jeremy Northam
Lady Ottoline Morrell: Penelope Wilton
Phillip Morrell: Peter Blythe
Roger Senhouse: Sebastian Harcome
Vanessa Bell: Janet McTeer
Clive Bell: Richard Clifford

Origin: Great Britain
Released: 1995
Production: Ronald Shedlo and John McGrath for Freeway/Shedlo and Polygram Filmed Entertainment, in association with Cinea, Orsans and Le Studio Canal Plus; released by Gramercy
Direction: Christopher Hampton
Screenplay: Christopher Hampton; based on the biography *Lytton Stratchey* by Michael Holroyd
Cinematography: Denis Lenoir
Editing: George Akers
Production design: Caroline Amies
Art direction: Frank Walsh
Costume design: Penny Rose
Music: Michael Nyman
Sound: Peter Lindsay
Casting: Fothergill and Lunn Casting
Makeup and hair design: Chrissie Beveridge
MPAA rating: R
Running Time: 123 minutes

AWARDS AND NOMINATIONS

Cannes Film Festival 1995: Special Jury Prize, Best Actor (Pryce)
National Board of Review Awards 1995: Best Actress (Thompson)
British Academy Awards Nominations 1995: Best Film, Best Actor (Pryce)

Strachey virtually disappearing for a half hour and such puzzling moments as Hampton's treatment of Carrington's suicide. As soon as she is about ready to kill herself, Hampton's camera drifts outside her house for a stroll through the garden before coming to rest on the lawn where it waits patiently for the gunshot. The emotional impact of her death is entirely dissipated.

"I can't stand the strain of worrying about you worrying about me."—Dora Carrington from *Carrington*

Thompson is a great actress with considerable range, able to play comic, tragic, vibrant, and ordinary characters with equal ease, as shown, in particular, by her work in *Dead Again* (1991), *Howard's End* (1992), and *Remains of the Day* (1993), but her Carrington is nervous and uncertain. (While the film's sexual content is relatively tame, it is strange to see someone of Thompson's stature doing nude sex scenes.) The fault is less hers than Hampton's. This woman should be seen striding through life embracing all its experiences, but he conceives her as without substance, merely a reflection of the men in her life.

Pryce, most acclaimed for his stage and television work, has never had such a substantial part in a film, and he makes the most of it. Strachey could easily have been a caricature of an effeminate aesthete in a funny beard, but Pryce infuses him with a goofy spirit that makes him larger than life. Named best actor at the 1995 Cannes Film Festival for this performance, Pryce is equally adept at the self-absorbed silliness of a man who easily makes others do his bidding and at the man's more serious side, especially at the end when he is both horrified and bored by the prospect of death. While Pryce avoids making Strachey either insufferable or sentimentalized, he does not make him believable as a writer since the character, as imagined by Hampton, seems too passive and uninterested in anyone but himself.

Cinematographer Denis Lenoir makes both the interiors and exteriors of the various residences beautiful, and production designer Caroline Aimes and art director Frank Walsh do a wonderful job in particular with the first cottage shared by Strachey and Carrington of which she decorates seemingly every surface, including a bathtub, with her art. After his popular but bland score for *The Piano* (1993), composer Michael Nyman returns to the much livelier type of music he has created for his many collaborations with director Peter Greenaway, especially *The Draughtsman's Contract* (1983). The repetitive quality of Nyman's music perfectly suits the characters' neuroticism. Unfortunately the film is not up to its technical expertise.

—*Michael Adams*

REVIEWS

Entertainment Weekly. November 17, 1995, p. 58.
The New York Times. October 13, 1995, p. B1.
The New Yorker. LXXI, November 27, 1995, p. 106.
Newsweek. CXXVI, November 20, 1995, p. 90.
Premiere. IX, December, 1995, p. 30.
Sight and Sound. V, September, 1995, p. 46.
Time. CXLVI, November 13, 1995, p. 118.
Variety. May 22, 1995, p. 95.
The Village Voice. XL, October 3, 1995, p. 76.
The Wall Street Journal. November 10, 1995, p. A10.

Casino

"No one stays at the top forever."—Movie tagline

Box Office Gross: $37,127,510

Casino is intended to be the completion of writer-director Martin Scorsese's Mafia trilogy which began with his first masterpiece, *Mean Streets* (1973), and continued with the highly acclaimed *Goodfellas* (1990). While Scorsese clearly intends to present a crime story with epic proportions and the early scenes have considerable style and energy, *Casino* soon degenerates into a squalid domestic drama.

Scorsese and co-screenwriter Nicholas Pileggi, who collaborated on *Goodfellas*, try to depict the corrupt Las Vegas of the 1970s as a paradise for hoodlums and hustlers whose greed and ego led to its decline into what the film characterizes as a Disneyized family resort. While crime, violence, power, and gambling have considerable dramatic allure and cinematic potential, the problem is that the inherent tackiness of Las Vegas considerably diminishes the filmmakers' efforts to attain tragedy. Even Barry Levinson's much-better *Bugsy* (1991) is limited by the triteness of the protagonist's endeavors to invent Las Vegas. The characters and events are inspired by Pileggi's non-fiction book, *Casino: Love and Honor in Las Vegas*, and the film's documentary style conflicts with the director's epic ambitions. Including elements simply because they really happened instead of because they work thematically and cinematically dooms the film.

Sam "Ace" Rothstein (Robert De Niro) is a professional gambler, an expert on the odds on sporting events. Because of this skill and his trustworthiness, Rothstein is placed in charge of the Tangiers hotel and casino by the mob who finance the venture with Teamster pension funds. (The real-life gambler ran four casinos.) He makes it prosper until two forces create conflict. His boyhood friend Nicky Santoro (Joe Pesci) arrives to provide muscle for the boys "back home." The hothead soon alienates almost everyone in Las Vegas, getting himself banned from every casino, so he and his gang turn to jewel robbery to keep themselves amused. The other force is prostitute-turned-hustler Ginger McKenna (Sharon Stone), with whom Rothstein falls in love at first sight. She agrees to marry him even though she does not love him and quickly begins to decline into drugs and alcohol. As his wife and friend deteriorate, Rothstein's carefully controlled empire begins to collapse.

> A billionaire Japanese business executive and expert gambler tricked into losing at Rothstein's casino is named Ichikawa. Japanese director Kon Ichikawa is known for grimly realistic dramas along the lines of *Casino*, two of his best being *Fires on the Plain* (1959), a graphic depiction of war, and *An Actor's Revenge* (1963), a stylized reprisal tale.

Sharon Stone as Ginger and Robert De Niro as gambler "Ace" Rothstein in *Casino*. © 1995 Universal City Studios, Inc. Courtesy of MCA Publishing Rights, a Division of MCA Inc. All rights reserved.

Casino opens with an excerpt from Johann Sebastian Bach's *St. Matthew Passion* (1727-1749) as Scorsese begins setting the stage for a lofty drama. The director explains in an insightful interview in *Sight and Sound* (January 1996) that his intention is to tell an Old Testament story of gaining and losing paradise. A Mafia-controlled casino that skims millions of dollars in profits to cheat the Internal Revenue Service is a paradise from the point of view of the person in charge, who lives for the action, the fast pace, the tawdriness of it all, but what if that person is a nonentity? Who cares if he loses his empire? The lack of sympathetic or even remotely interesting characters is the hollowness at the center of Scorsese's would-be epic. While many aesthetically successful films have been built around unsympathetic characters—*Aguirre, the Wrath of God* (1972), *A Clockwork Orange* (1971), *The Conformist* (1969), *Downhill Racer* (1969), *Natural Born Killers* (1994), *The Player* (1992), *The Sweet Smell of Success* (1958)—their protagonists had some depth, moral ambiguity, or satirical focus.

Scorsese and Pileggi give their characters no clearcut dimensions. Rothstein enjoys being a good gambler, loves being in control of a big-time operation like the Tangiers, falls for the wrong woman, and becomes distracted by her antics. His creating a seedy local television talk/variety show to use as a soapbox against the local politicians who refuse to grant him a gaming license is a sign of his desperation but is uncharacteristic of the cool, capable Rothstein at the beginning of the film. Since Ginger loves the excitement of being a hustler as much as the rewards, simply being given money and jewelry by her husband is not enough. Her sole complexity is her inability to sever her relationship with Lester Diamond (James Woods), the pimp who took her under his control when she was fourteen.

As Scorsese points out in the *Sight and Sound* interview, showing Santoro being brutally beaten to death at the film's end underscores that he is susceptible to the same chaos as anyone else. But that does not change the despicable nature of his character or the repugnance of the violent life he leads. (He squeezes a man's head in a vise until an eye pops out.)

Trust is a major theme of *Casino*, as Scorsese and Pileggi make clumsily clear by having Rothstein explain the necessity of trust and loyalty every half hour or so. Ginger betrays him by giving his money to Lester, by neglecting their daughter, Amy (Erika von Tagen), whom she ties to a bed when a babysitter is unavailable, and by having an affair with Santoro so that she can enlist his aid against her husband. Not only does Santoro embarrass his best friend all over Las Vegas and cuckold him, but he arranges for Rothstein's car to be blown up. This theme, as well as the religious overtones with which Scorsese embellishes it, works much better in some of his other films, *Mean Streets* in particular, because the characters and the settings are more original.

One of the more disastrous aspects of *Casino* is the music assembled by Robbie Robertson, whose rock group The Band is the subject of Scorsese's documentary *The Last Waltz* (1978). Almost constantly in the background are over fifty pop, rock, soul, blues, and country songs featuring such diverse artists as Dean Martin, Louis Prima, Brenda Lee, Little Richard, Otis Redding, Fleetwood Mac, Devo, and Roxy Music. Apparently Scorsese feels that the music indicates something about the times and values of the characters but exactly how is not clear. Presented in this context, the music seems cheap and desperate. One notable exception is employing "Can't You Hear Me Knocking?" by the Rolling Stones (several of whose songs are used) to create an energy and a sense of danger while Santoro assembles his jewel-robbery gang. Scorsese also alters the pace occasionally with music from the scores of other films, such as those of Georges Delerue for *Le Mepris* (*Contempt*; 1963) *and Elmer Bernstein for* Walk on the Wild Side *(1962)*. (Bernstein composed the score for Scorsese's 1993 film, *The Age of Innocence*.) The overall effect of the pop songs diminishes, rather than augments, the film's energy. During the final half hour, consisting mostly of the protagonists shouting, several tunes are even

"Pay attention. What I'm going to tell you is very important. All this stuff doesn't mean anything. Money doesn't mean anything without trust. I have to be able to trust you with my life."—Sam Rothstein from *Casino*

CREDITS

Sam "Ace" Rothstein: Robert De Niro
Ginger McKenna Rothstein: Sharon Stone
Nicky Santoro: Joe Pesci
Lester Diamond: James Woods
Billy Sherbert: Don Rickles
Frank Marino: Frank Vincent
Andy Stone: Alan King
Phillip Green: Kevin Pollack
Remo Gaggi: Pasquale Cajano
Pat Webb: L. Q. Jones
Don Ward: John Bloom
Senator: Dick Smothers
Jennifer Santoro: Melissa Prophet
Amy Rothstein: Erika von Tagen

Origin: USA
Released: 1995
Production: Barbara De Fina for De Fina/Cappa and Universal and Syalis D.A. & Legende Enterprises; released by Universal
Direction: Martin Scorsese
Screenplay: Nicholas Pileggi and Martin Scorsese; based on the book *Casino: Love and Honor in Las Vegas* by Pileggi
Cinematography: Robert Richardson
Editing: Thelma Schoonmaker
Production design: Dante Ferretti
Art direction: Jack G. Taylor, Jr.
Set design: Steven Schwartz and Daniel Ross
Set decoration: Rick Simpson
Costume design: Rita Ryack and John Dunn
Sound: Charles M. Wilborn
Casting: Ellen Lewis
MPAA rating: R
Running Time: 177 minutes

AWARDS AND NOMINATIONS

Golden Globe Awards 1996: Best Actress-Drama (Stone)
Academy Awards Nominations 1995: Best Actress (Stone)
Golden Globe Awards Nominations 1996: Best Director (Scorsese)

repeated for no obvious reason, adding to the ultimately depressing tone of *Casino*.

De Niro and Pesci give capable performances, though they have played these characters before. Pesci offers only a slight variation on his Academy Award-winning performance in *Goodfellas*. De Niro is effective in several early scenes, as when Rothstein registers shock, fear, disgust, and admiration all at once when Santoro brutalizes someone who has insulted his friend, but he seems at a loss when the gambler becomes desperate. Stone is likewise quite good as long as Ginger is using her brains and looks to make her way in a world of corrupt men. When she resorts to cliched histrionics when Ginger falls to pieces, the sight is not pleasant. The most notable performance comes in Woods' brief appearances as the slimy Lester. Woods has fun with this creep, particularly when he harasses Ace's daughter Amy.

While *Casino* is one of Scorsese's weaker films, the most acclaimed director of his generation, it is not without virtues. The documentary approach works well at the beginning as he explains how a gambling casino operates with all the bosses and employees spying on each other. The use of voiceover narration by Rothstein and Santoro succeeds too, providing a degree of ironic distance from the unpleasant goings-on.

One scene in particular is masterfully done. At the end of the Rothstein's wedding reception is a long shot of the emptying ballroom with Lester's voice in the background. Who is he talking to, where, and why? Scorsese cuts to a shot of Lester on the telephone and then to a teary Ginger talking to him from a small room off the reception area as if trapped in a new, claustrophobic world. Rothstein enters quietly, tentatively, with a noncommital expression. After a few moments, she hangs up and confesses that she had to say goodbye to the one who has been the most important person in her life. Rothstein calmly understands her gesture. The scene is full of longing and despair and is wonderfully performed by all three actors. It is an sad indication of what *Casino* could have been.

—*Michael Adams*

REVIEWS

Entertainment Weekly. December 1, 1995, p. 41.
The Nation. CCLXI, December 18, 1995, p. 803.
New York. XXVIII, November 27, 1995, p. 78.
The New York Times. November 22, 1995, p. B1.
The New Yorker. LXXI, December 4, 1995, p. 118.
Newsweek. CXXVI, November 27, 1995, p. 86.
Rolling Stone. December 14, 1995, p. 89.
Time. CXLVI, November 27, 1995, p. 93.
Variety. November 20, 1995, p. 47.
The Wall Street Journal. November 24, 1995, p. A6.

Casper

"*Casper* is hip, witty and original."—Scott Patrick, *Hollywood One-on-One/Starz*

"Magical! One of the summer's biggest crowd-pleasers."—Dave Kehr, *New York Daily News*

"Hilarious! Even in an age of escalating special-effects wizardry, *Casper* is astonishing."—Caryn James, *The New York Times*

"Two thumbs up!"—*Siskel & Ebert*

Box Office Gross: $100,328,194

Paranormal phenomena have been enduringly popular with filmmakers here and abroad. From the Topper films of the 1930s and 1940s (*Topper*, 1937, *Topper Takes a Trip, 1939, Topper Returns*, 1941) to *Blithe Spirit*

The friendly ghost befriends Christina Ricci as Kat Harvey in *Casper*. © 1995 Universal City Studios, Inc. Courtesy of MCA Publishing Rights, a Division of MCA Inc. All rights reserved.

(1945, British) and *The Ghost and Mrs. Muir* (1947) to the more recent *Ghost and Mr. Chicken* (1966), *Ghost Story* (1981), *Ghostbusters* (1984), *Ghost* (1990) and *Ghost Dad* (1990), moviegoers have fallen in love with, been charmed by, and basically have warmed up to the undead.

Casper begins with Carrigan (Cathy Moriarty), a modern-day Cruella DeVille, learning that, despite her last-minute ministrations, her newly deceased father has left her only Whipstaff Manor, a haunted mansion in Friendship, Maine. Always enterprising, Carrigan and her beleaguered sidekick Dibs (Eric Idle, of the famed 1970's British comedy troupe, Monty Python) find a treasure map concealed within the deed and travel to Maine to strike it rich. Upon their arrival, however, the couple finds the ghosts to be more pesky than they had imagined. With Casper's prompting, Carrigan decides to contact Dr. James Harvey (Bill Pullman), new widower and self-styled ghost therapist, who travels to Friendship with his teenaged daughter Kat (Christina Ricci). In Kat, Casper finds a kindred spirit.

Also popular in Hollywood have been films drawn from the comics and cartoons, for instance, *Dick Tracy* (1945, 1990), *The Flintstones* (1994), *Batman* (1989), *The Addams Family* (1991), *Superman* (1978), and *Mighty Morphin Power Rangers* (1995). However, in this season's cinematic rendition of *Casper*, the filmmakers made an effort to enhance the original. Indeed, the production notes report that, while still friendly and lonely, Casper is now "spunkier, more rambunctious," even after nearly a century of ill treatment by his three ghostly "uncles." For instance, Casper recognizes he has a problem and in this, the age of self-help, he ensures that Carrigan sees an interview with Dr. Harvey on television. He is sure that Dr. Harvey's credentials will appeal to the greedy owner, and Casper is also sure that he will be glad to have Kat Harvey as a friend. "We took the template of this character, and while not offending anybody's memories of what he was, we've made him more engaging for audiences today," muses director Brad Silberling in the production notes. "Casper, as we've created him, has a real sense of humor. I think audiences are going to be surprised at where the humor leads."

> Bringing transparent ghosts to life proved to be extremely challenging for the special effects wizards of Industrial Light & Magic. It took two years and 28 trillion bytes (equal to about 19 million floppy discs) to make Casper three-dimensional.

Cathy Moriarty and Eric Idle play their roles of villains with almost slapstick abandon. However, Bill Pullman (*While You Were Sleeping*, 1995) and Christina Ricci (*The Addams Family*, 1991) provide a strong center for the film. For instance, early in the film, Ricci's Kat is convinced her father is a hopeless misfit, dragging her from place to place, school to school, in search of an impossible dream. The father's attempts at humor and the teenager's sullen response both ring true. Later in the film, Kat grows to appreciate her father's knowledge and, better yet, wisdom. This film shows a variety of families, both normal and paranormal, and teaches a valuable lesson about each.

Christina Ricci received rave reviews in her role as Wednesday Addams in *The Addams Family*. Ricci's Wednesday was just the right combination of maudlin cynicism and teenage angst. Completely transformed for *Casper*, however,

CREDITS

Kat: Christina Ricci
Dr. Harvey: Bill Pullman
Casper: Malachi Pearson
Carrigan: Cathy Moriarty
Dibs: Eric Idle

Origin: USA
Released: 1995
Production: Colin Wilson
Direction: Brad Siberling
Screenplay: Sherri Stoner and Deanna Oliver; based on the character *Casper The Friendly Ghost* created by Joseph Oriolo and Seymour Reit
Cinematography: Dean Cundey
Editing: Michael Kahn
Production design: Leslie Dilley
Costumes: Rosanna Norton
Casting: Nancy Nayor
Animation directors: Eric Armstrong and Phil Nibberlink
Music: James Horner
MPAA rating: PG
Running Time: 95 minutes

REVIEWS

Baltimore Sun, May 26, 1995, Features, p. 8.
Boston Globe, May 26, 1995, p. 85.
Chicago Sun-Times, May 26, 1995, p. 37.
The Christian Science Monitor, May 26, 1995, p. 12.
The Houston Chronicle, May 26, 1995, Weekend Preview section, p. 1
Los Angeles Times, May 26, 1995, p. F1
Newsday, May 26, 1995, p. BO2
The New York Times, May 28, 1995, Section 2, p. 1
Rocky Mountain News, May 26, 1995, p. 6D
Salt Lake Tribune, May 26, 1995, p. E4
San Francisco Chronicle, May 26, 1995
The Seattle Times, May 26, 1995, p. G3
The Washington Times, May 25, 1995, p. M24

Ricci captures just the right combination of "Aw, shucks" and "Oh, Dad" that is a teenager. For instance, as the "new kid" at school, Ricci's Kat is shy, but definitely interested in the cute boy in her class. But when her dad treats her like a child, warning her of ghosts and other dangers, she is disgruntled to be treated like a child until the ghosts appear. A versatile actress, in her appearance and her demeanor, Ricci is engaging to watch.

Industrial Light & Magic created Casper and his uncles with the help of computers. Led by Dennis Muren (who created the dinosaurs for *Jurassic Park*, 1994), a team of technicians executed 350 shots. The film itself was shot on three of Universal's sound stages and on the studio's backlot.

Casper, for its rather thin plot, offers excellent performances and exciting special effects that the whole family can see and enjoy.

—Roberta F. Green

"I feel like Oprah on hiatus!"—Fatso from *Casper*

Circle of Friends

"A perfect date movie."—*American Movie Classics*

"This year's *Four Weddings and a Funeral*."—*Entertainment Weekly*

"A funny and touching romance. Minnie Driver is bewitching."—Peter Travers, *Rolling Stone*

"Two thumbs up! A marvelous romantic comedy."—*Siskel & Ebert*

Box Office Gross: $23,397,365

Set in Ireland in 1957, *Circle of Friends* is a good old-fashioned coming-of-age story about three friends who each confront their changing lives in their own distinct way. While the plot line and characters are fairly predictable, the actors consistently help to buoy this charming and nostalgic film above others in this genre. It is disappointing primarily in its failure to explore any new cinematic ground with regards to its subject matter, yet succeeds in demonstrating how the complex and confusing forces of church and Catholic morality, economics and social class structures, and sexual and societal pressures all combine to weigh heavily upon the choices made by each of these friends.

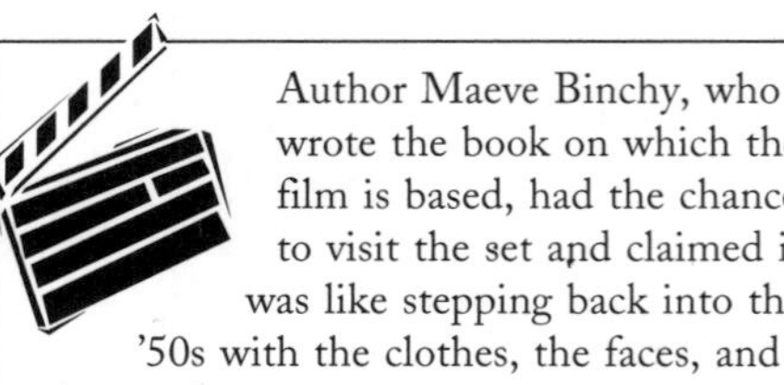

Author Maeve Binchy, who wrote the book on which the film is based, had the chance to visit the set and claimed it was like stepping back into the '50s with the clothes, the faces, and the music.

The story focuses on Bernadette "Benny" Hogan (Minnie Driver), a "big girl" whose non-traditional beauty comes shining through in a warm smile and sparkling eyes, and a confidence that radiates beyond other people's expectations and limiting views. Benny is one of those rare creatures who, for the most part, believes that all things are possible—even winning the heart of one of the most popular and handsome young men at the University of Dublin. Jack Foley (Chris O'Donnell) is the Captain of the rugby team, smart and charming, the son of a physician who clearly expects him to follow in his medical footsteps. The only problem is that Jack is more than a little squeamish when it comes to slicing people open. But what he is good at is succumbing to other people's expectations. So when he meets Benny, he is immediately attracted to her inherent independence and self-confidence. Here is a woman who may occasionally give into a self-effacing attitude about her looks, but never allows it to affect her self-worth. She believes, deep-down, that she can win Jack—or at least she is willing to risk all and to lay her desires on the line.

When Benny and her longtime friend Eve (Geraldine O'Rawe), an orphan raised by Catholic nuns, set out for what they view as their escape from what they regard as the religious and intellectual oppressiveness of rural life in the small town of Knockglen College in Dublin, the pair at long last reunite with the last third of their childhood trio, the beautiful and willowy Nan (Saffron Burrows). Along with their intellectual awakenings, the three soon are confronted with the blossoming of sexual desire. While Benny is immediately attracted to the handsome Jack, Nan sets her sights on Simon Westward (Colin Firth), a member of the town's faltering aristocracy and whose family serves as Eve's benefactor. Eve, meanwhile, enters into a relationship with fellow student, Aidan (Aidan Gillen). The writers do an excellent job of evoking both the time and the moral climate of Ireland in the 1950's. "Aidan says its his job to try and seduce me," says Eve to her friends, "and it's my job to try and stop him."

Circle of Friends takes an unfortunate melodramatic turn midway through with scenes of betrayal, broken hearts, unwanted pregnancy, familial death, corruption and attempted rape. Of the changes that occurred from converting the novel by author Maeve Binchy, whose latest work is the novel *The Glass Lake*, to the screen, the most obvious is the increase in the sexual content. It is interesting to note that once again we have a story about three women based on a novel written by a woman, yet the screenplay is ultimately written by a man.

"I know I may look like a rhinoceros, but I've got quite a thin skin about me."—Benny from *Circle of Friends*

To the film's credit, there is no scene in which the heroine transforms herself from the ugly duckling into a beautiful swan in order to win her prince charming. In fact, Benny never really has to change at all in order to get what she wants. She never compromises her ideals, and even though she does lose her father when he suffers a heart attack following a rare argument with his daughter over the calculating Sean, Benny never has to give up much, except temporarily, through the course of the story. This is more a story of holding firm to one's convictions rather than a story of self-discovery. While it is admirable and life-affirming to have a story showing that physical looks are not everything, in terms of dramatic structure, Benny is a fairly boring filmic protagonist, especially when contrasted with the character of Nan. Benny believes in herself from moment one, which is problematic because it allows her very little room for any kind of dramatic movement since she has no where to go in terms of self-realization. Benny is a character who already knows who she is. Nan is far more interesting because it is she who has the big life revelation, she's the one who must confront the realization that things don't always turn out the way one might hope and despite believing that things are possible, it is not always necessarily so. Sometimes one does not get what one wants, no matter how hard one tries, or how much one believes it is possible to change one's situation. While it is easy to dismiss Nan as the "bad girl," she is far more tragic, and consequently, far more interesting as a character because she wants the same things as Benny, yet goes about it all in the worst possible way, by trying to change in order to conform to others' standards and others' expectations. While outwardly Nan is the "perfect" looking one of the trio, it is really Benny who gets to be the least flawed. And sadly, it is Benny who learns nothing through the course of the story; she is right about Sean's involvement in her father's business, she's right about Jack's character. Minnie Driver possesses such a winning presence she almost obscures Benny's basic inactivity within the story.

The villain, the calculating assistant at Benny's father's clothiers, Sean (Alan Cummings)—and Benny's interaction with him—is also quite problematic. Sean is so creepy and so one-dimensional and the performance by Cummings so over-the-top that it is in jarring contrast to all of the other performers thereby undermining the intensity of the film. And as more than one reviewer has pointed out, Cummings plays Sean more like Pee-Wee Herman than Uriah Heep. But what is even more disturbing is the writer's missed opportunity to use Sean in a dramatic sense. There is never even an instant in which Benny is torn or tempted to go with Sean in order to "right" things with her parents. She knows from the beginning that Sean is not the man for her and we, the audience, are never afforded the moment of vicariously hoping that Benny will "see the light" and real-

CREDITS

Jack: Chris O'Donnell
Benny: Minnie Driver
Eve: Geraldine O'Rawe
Nan: Saffron Burrows
Sean: Alan Cummings
Simon Westward: Colin Firth
Aidan: Aidan Gillen

Origin: USA
Released: 1995
Production: Arlene Sellers, Alex Winitsky, and Frank Price for Price Entertainment/Lantana; released by Savoy Pictures in association with Rank Film Distributors.
Direction: Pat O'Connor
Screenplay: Andrew Davies; based on the novel by Maeve Binchy
Cinematography: Kenneth MacMillan
Editing: John Jympson
Art direction: Jim Clay
Music: Michael Kamen
MPAA rating: PG-13
Running Time: 96 minutes

AWARDS AND NOMINATIONS

Chicago Film Festival Awards 1995: Most Promising Actress (Driver)

ize that something she is about to do could ruin her life. It is a true disappointment, as well, that Jack never gets to interact with Sean and that we are denied any kind of cathartic "last minute rescue" at the altar, such as Benjamin's great race to the church in Mike Nichols's *The Graduate* (1967)—a technique that would have at least forced Benny to have to make a choice and therefore become more of an active character. In addition, it feels like yet another missed dramatic opportunity that the writer chose not to have any sort of confrontation scene between Benny and Nan following the revelation that Nan lied about Jack being the father of her baby. (What a potentially great scene it could have been, with Nan confronting her—and us—about the preconceived notions that people have about everything being easy for the pretty girl.) Once again, everyone else in the story resolves things for Benny and essentially makes things fairly easy for her.

Chris O'Donnell, perhaps best known for his role as the young prep school student who takes on the job of babysitting Al Pacino's blind Army officer in *Scent of a Woman* (1992)—for which he was awarded a Golden Globe nomination for Best Supporting Actor—as well as the swashbuckling D'Artagnan in the latest remake of *The Three Musketeers* (1993), was chosen over other authentic Irish actors for the pivotal role of Jack in *Circle of Friends*. His next filmic challenge was the summer of 1995's updating of Batman's crime-fighting sidekick, Robin, in Joel Schumacher's *Batman Forever*.

Reviews of *Circle of Friends* were generally positive, despite the predictability of the storyline, with its melodramatic third act, as well as the neatly defined characters. *Circle of Friends*, in large part due to the power and personal charisma of Minnie Driver's performance, is essentially a nice little film that missed out on the chance to be a truly powerful drama.

—Patricia Kowal

REVIEWS

Daily Variety. March 10, 1995, p. 4.
Entertainment Weekly. March 24, 1995, p. 43.
The Hollywood Reporter. March 13, 1995, p. 10
Los Angeles Times. March 15, 1995, CXIV, p. F5.
Macleans. March 27, 1995, CXIII, p. 62.
New Republic. CCXII, April 10, 1995, p. 30.
The New York Times. March 16, 1995, CXLIV, p. B3.
People Weekly. XLIII. March 27, 1995, p. 108.
San Francisco Chronicle. March 24, 1995, LVIII, p. C3.
Rolling Stone. March 23, 1995, p. 129.
Time. CXLV, March 27, 1995, p. 73.
The Village Voice. March 21, 1995, XL, p. 58.
Wall St. Journal. March 23, 1995, p. A12.

Clockers

"When there's murder on these streets, everyone's a suspect."—Movie tagline

"A riveting thriller!"—Jack Garner, *Gannett News Service*

"One of the year's most powerful films."—Jeffrey Lyons, *Sneak Previews*

Box Office Gross: $13,040,603

The title of this film is taken from a slang term for drug dealers who work around the clock. The key clocker is Strike (Mekhi Phifer). He deals drugs; he does not take them. He has his own crew of dealers who live in the Brooklyn projects and degrade the lives of their own people. Strike works for Rodney (Delroy Lindo), the drug czar of the neighborhood, a paternal but vicious criminal who precipitates the action of the film when he tells Strike that he can get off the benches and advance his "career" by killing a rival dealer. Rodney reminds Strike that he is a businessman who sells the world's best product—crack cocaine—and that Strike is like a son to him. When has he ever let Strike down? he asks Strike.

The benches are where Strike and his crew meet. Although Strike is their leader, he continually suffers challenges to his authority—not only from his subordinates but from a project mother who is furious at him for corrupting her twelve-year-old son. Just as Rodney mentors Strike, so Strike sees to make Tyrone (Pee Wee Love) his protege. When Tyrone's mother Iris (Regina Taylor) is not angrily denouncing him or slapping him around, there is Andre the Giant (Keith David), who has kept watch on Strike since he was a little boy. Andre is a cop, and he bullies Strike into doing good deeds—such as buying mattresses for a club of young boys Andre is mentoring. And when Andre is not hassling Strike, patrol cars show up and shake down Strike and his crew, looking for the drugs they are dealing.

Life seems to come at Strike from every angle, with his allies almost as threatening as his enemies. He is an extraordinarily isolated character. He no longer lives at home. His mother seems to have given up on him and placed her hopes on his brother Victor (Isaiah Washington), a happily married man with two young children. Victor holds down two jobs and is saintly in his dedication to his family and community.

Most characters in the film view Strike as a menace to society. He looks sullen and mean. But his face often registers convulsive pain and wrenching despair. When police interrogate him, he plays the tough guy, but as his final lines in the film demonstrate, he has a sense of wonder about his place in life. Why is it like this? He never actually asks the question, but his face is open to that existential query; it is not the shut-down, closed mug of a gangster. He does not have the requisite swagger for a life of crime. As most reviewers have said, his bleeding ulcer is his conscience. He doubles over with pain, spits up blood, and at one point is taken to the hospital in an ambulance. Strike is, in fact, an emergency case. He knows his life is out of control, but he does not know how to change it. That he dreams of another world is clear in his love of trains. He has a Lionel train set in his apartment, videos of trains, and other paraphernalia that transcend his place in the projects.

Mekhi Phifer as Strike Dunham is flanked by Harvey Keitel and John Turturro as homicide detectives Rocco Klein and Larry Mazilli in *Clockers*.

CREDITS

Rocco Klein: Harvey Keitel
Larry Mazilli: John Turturro
Rodney: Delroy Lindo
Strike: Mekhi Phifer
Victor: Isaiah Washington
Andre the Giant: Keith David
Tyrone: Pee Wee Love
Iris Jeeter: Regina Taylor

Origin: USA
Released: 1995
Production: Martin Scorsese, Spike Lee and Jon Kilik for a 40 Acres and a Mule Filmworks; released by Universal Pictures
Direction: Spike Lee
Screenplay: Spike Lee and Richard Price; based on the book *Clockers* by Richard Price
Cinematography: Malik Hassan Sayeed
Editing: Sam Pollard
Production design: Andrew Mcalpine
Art direction: Ina Mayhew
Set decoration: Debra Schutt
Costume design: Ruth Carter
Casting: Robi Reed-Humes
Sound: Skip Lievsay
Music: Terence Blanchard
MPAA rating: R
Running Time: 129 minutes

Strike is a tired young man, and Rodney is offering him a way out—just as party boss in Parliament might offer a backbencher a Cabinet position. But the price of success is murder. And Rodney knows he has to work on Strike in order to get him to do the bloody deed, and Strike's criminal life is already wresting the blood out of him.

Strike goes to see his brother Victor, telling him in a roundabout way that he needs a man murdered. Victor seems depressed, overworked, and angry because he sees so little of his family. He is vexed with Strike, but he also refers to "my man," someone who could do the killing. But Strike, apparently sensing he has pushed his brother too far, dismisses the suggestion and walks out to confront his victim, who laughs at and insults Strike, who stands stolidly in front of him, a gun concealed in a newspaper.

The next shot is the crime scene. It would seem that Strike has murdered his man—although he stands there with the crowd ogling the gruesome corpse while the police examine the body's wounds. Then in an amazing turnabout Victor confesses to the shooting, saying he shot the man in self-defense as he was walking in a parking lot.

Officer Rocco Klein (Harvey Keitel) cannot believe Victor, for nothing in Victor's background suggests he could possibly have killed a man. On the other hand, Rocco quickly turns to Strike as the likely culprit. Klein hypothesizes that the virtuous Victor is covering for Strike, thinking that he will get a light sentence for a self-defense plea whereas Strike would do hard time.

Rocco's partner Larry Mazilli (John Turturro) rejects Rocco's theory. "We have the shooter," Larry points out, as he argues that Rocco's interpretation is too complicated for the circumstances. Even if Victor wants to help his brother, does it makes sense for him to go to prison, even for a short time? Even if there is more to the case than the cops realize, can they really not pursue the case against Victor who has confessed and who has the gun?

But Rocco is relentless, dogging not only Strike but Strike's boss Rodney. Rocco is determined to nail Strike by further isolating him, making Rodney think that Strike is informing against him. A twenty-year veteran, Rocco knows that eventually Strike will have to turn to him as the only safe haven in a neighborhood that has rejected him. Rocco is both right and wrong about Strike—as the film's denouement makes clear. But exactly how things play out cannot be revealed without spoiling the intricate, thoughtful resolution of theme and plot.

"A clocker is a slang for the lowest level of drug dealer. He's called a clocker because he's out there around the clock."—Screenwriter Richard Price

Rocco and Strike only half see each other for what they truly are—not only because one is a white cop and other is a black suspect, but because both men cannot or refuse to articulate their complex natures. Rocco can sometimes seem like a racist, using epithets like "Nubians" to describe African-Americans or joking over the bodies of the dead black men he examines in the streets. In the office he uses thoughtless offensive language, although he apologizes to an African-American officer when he angrily objects to Rocco's crude words. Similarly, Strike can seem like the stereotyped black hood preying on his own people, willing to murder to please his drug lord and to advance in the drug hierarchy. Yet he lectures the twelve-year-old boy he mentors on violence and drug taking, telling him they are not the glamorous things portrayed in movies. Yet both Rocco and Strike find themselves in environments where it is dangerous to express their own humanity.

Universal had reportedly paid Richard Price $1.9 million to adapt his novel for the director-star duo of Martin Scorsese and Robert De Niro. When Scorsese and De Niro opted to make *Casino* instead, the studio offered it to Spike Lee with Scorsese staying on as producer.

Near the end of *Clockers* there is a moment between Rocco and Strike in which they seem about to share their plight. A puzzled Strike asks Rocco why he has taken the case so personally when most cops do not care about cases where blacks shoot each other. Rocco cannot bring himself to answer the question directly. He is dropping Strike off at Penn Station, where Strike will finally fulfill his dream of traveling cross country by train. Rocco, on the other hand, is stuck in his squad car. Perhaps this is why he answers Strike with a threat, saying that if he ever catches him in the projects again he will file charges that will insure Strike's imprisonment. Rocco cannot answer Strike without revealing more about himself than perhaps he understands or is willing to communicate.

But there is an earlier scene in the film that hints at Rocco's dilemma. When Rocco and his partner Larry bust Rodney and are taking him off to jail, Rodney asks Rocco about his name and comments that Rocco can't seem to decide if he is Jewish or Italian. Again Rocco does not respond. To do so, would be to acknowledge an inner conflict that isolates Rocco from everyone, including his partner Larry, who has done business with Rodney and who is much more complacent and tolerant of life in the projects than Rocco.

To say that Rocco identifies with Strike is patently false and simplistic. In many ways Rocco hates Strike, and yet he says more than once "Show me some respect" and "Haven't I shown you respect?" Rocco wants that acknowledgment of his humanity, and he wants to acknowledge the humanity of others—as hard as both things are to get in the world Rocco has to patrol. That he does not get a chance to show or to get that respect very often is what isolates him, and it is what binds him to Strike, for Strike wants exactly the same thing.

If there is a flaw in Spike Lee's version of Richard Price's script (the novelist adapted his own work for the screen, which was originally to be made by Martin Scorsese and Robert DeNiro), it is the way he subtly downplays Rocco and focuses on Strike. So much more is learned about Strike's background than Rocco's, and the result is that some viewers may be puzzled at Rocco's motivations. It is a tribute to Harvey Keitel's superb acting, however, that this flaw is minimized. His nuanced interpretation of the role shows Rocco's complexity, so that viewers do not have to be told what kind of character he is. Spike Lee has often been accused of being didactic, of shoving his films' messages to the fore, but here his choice of actors and shot selection fuse style and content into a nearly perfect performance.

—*Carl Rollyson*

Clueless

"Sex. Clothes. Popularity. Whatever."—Movie tagline

"Alicia Silverstone is a dream!"—Guy Flatley, *Cosmopolitan*

"a total winner!"—Jami Bernard, *New York Daily News*

"Alicia is the babe of the moment!"—Peter Travers, *Rolling Stone*

"Two thumbs up."—*Siskel & Ebert*

Box Office Gross: $56,436,496

Alicia Silverstone as Cher enjoys her Beverly Hills lifestyle in *Clueless*.

Clueless is a delightful coming-of-age comedy set in the sheltered, hot-house atmosphere of super-rich teenagers from Beverly Hills. Although the film's satire of Los Angeles wealth virtually replicates what has been seen in other films and television series—namely *Beverly Hills 90210* (1989-present), *Fresh Prince of Bel Air* (1990-1996), *Down and out in Beverly Hills* (1986), and *Beverly Hills Cop* (1985), writer-director Amy Heckerling keeps the satire fresh by several means. First, Heckerling daringly, and successfully, bases her story on Jane Austen's comedy-of-manners, *Emma* (1816). Second, taking a page from the sociological precision of her first film, *Fast Times at Ridgemont High* (1982), Heckerling peppers the script with a pungent Beverly Hills slang that is partly real Rodeo Drive idiom, partly Heckerling's own invention. Third, and most importantly, Heckerling lets the satire of Beverly Hills remain window-dressing for the real story: a sheltered, "clueless" girl's coming-of-age by growing to see how her coddled upbringing has protected her not merely from harm, but also from her own feelings. By concentrating on this transformation, Heckerling makes *Clueless* not merely amusing, but, in the end, actually touching.

Heckerling's master stroke in the film is the casting of newcomer Alicia Silverstone. As Heckerling's daffy protagonist and narrator, Cher, Silverstone turns in a star-making performance, a frothy blend of intelligence, naivete, and kookiness which perfectly serves Heckerling's tale of a ditzy Beverly Hills Barbie-doll who turns out to have more heart and spunk than she realizes.

> "You see how picky I am about my shoes, and *they* only go on my feet!"—Cher on why she's a virgin from *Clueless*

Wildly popular, stunningly beautiful, and filthy rich, Cher (Alicia Silverstone) remains, at 16, an innocent, fending off would-be suitors at Beverly Hills's Bronson Alcott High School with a scornful "As if!" Cher and her best friend, Dionne (Stacey Dash)—both, as Cher explains, "named after great singers of the past who now do infomercials"—are not so much spoiled as blissfully ignorant of anything outside their world of makeovers, massages, and exercise videos. When Cher's father, Mel (Dan Hedaya) asks her about her day, Cher's big news is that she "broke in a pair of purple clogs." Cher's fiercest ambition is to pass her driving test, and her greatest pleasure—in spite of her own self-imposed celibacy—is matchmaking. Indeed, Cher's matchmaking ability is the source of much of her popularity at school: when Cher's presentation for debate class nets her only a "C"—she compares the plight of the Haitian boat people to her father's fiftieth birthday party—Cher raises her grade and everyone else's by setting up her teacher, Mr. Hall (Wallace Shawn), with the school's frowzy English instructor, Miss Geist (Twink Caplan), putting him in a permanently giddy mood.

Unbeknownst to Cher, however, her focus on the needs of others allows her to hide from her own emotions. Heckerling deftly drops hints that Cher may have more depth than she knows. Cher's mother died when she was two, "during routine liposuction," and Cher's gruff, hard-driving lawyer father, twice divorced since her mother's death, needs her to look after him—even as he scolds her for having no direction in life except towards the mall. And Cher cannot fathom why her mildly pretentious ex-stepbrother, Josh (Paul Rudd), staying at the house during his college break, frustrates her so much when he tells her how shallow her interests are. Cher will discover that, even though she and her friends criticize fellow students as being "clueless," it is in fact she who is clueless in the world beyond the mall.

The catalyst for Cher's journey out of her sheltered life is the arrival of a new student, Tai (Brittany Murphy), an uncool East Coast stoner. Cher takes on Tai as her protege, giving her elocution, exercise, and fashion lessons. Tai, amazed and grateful that such a popular girl has taken her under her wing, tells Cher and Dionne with awe, "You guys talk like grownups!"

But suddenly Cher's project, and everything else, begins to go awry. Cher escorts Tai to a big party in order to fix her up with Elton (Jeremy Sisto), but Elton in fact has eyes for Cher. When Cher rejects him, he leaves her in a convenience-store parking lot in the San Fernando Valley, where she is robbed at gunpoint. Meanwhile, Tai has become fixated on Elton and cries every time she hears the one song they danced to, "Rollin' With the Homies."

Increasingly desperate to prove that she is in control not only of her circle of friends, but also of her own emotional life, Cher decides to lose her virginity (she no longer wants to be "hymenally challenged") and falls for the "brutally hot" Christian (Justin Walker), a boy in her Debate class. Cher fails, however, to correctly interpret Christian's love of fashion, of the film *Some like it Hot* (1959), and of the scene in *Spartacus* (1960) in which Laurence Olivier quizzes Tony Curtis about oysters. (Christian's cocky fashion attitude provokes some of the film's best exchanges. "What's with you, kid?" asks Cher's father when Christian arrives for a date. "You think the death of Sammy Davis left an opening in the Rat Pack?" As Christian accompanies a dressed-to-kill Cher to the door, Mel tells him that "anything happens to my daughter, I got a .45 and a shovel. I doubt anybody would miss you.") When Dionne breaks the news to her that Christian must be gay, Cher moans in disbelief. "Oh my God, I'm totally buggin'," she cries, "I feel like such a bonehead."

When rowdy teenagers nearly push Tai over a second-story rail at the mall, Tai turns an embellished version of her story into a newfound popularity at school—at Cher's expense. "What was happening?" Cher asks. "Dionne asking Tai for sex advice?

Tai being the most popular girl in school? It was like some kind of alternate universe." Cher's failing her driving test and Tai's ultimately turning against her provoke an "existential crisis" in Cher: she realizes she has totally insulated herself from the world and from her true desires, and that she is in fact "butt-crazy in love with Josh," the only person who, in spite of his criticism, accepts her for who she is.

Armed with this new knowledge about herself, Cher begins to find joy in life's simple pleasures: watching her friend Travis (Breckin Meyer) do his skateboard tricks in competition; watching Dionne's affectionate moments with her boyfriend, Murray (Donald Faison); and working for charity (Miss Geist's Pismo Beach hurricane relief fund)—and telling Josh how she feels. She also gets the acknowledgment from her father that she needs: her father, he says, hasn't "seen such good-doing since your mother." Cher turns over a new leaf, accepting who and where she is and the limitations of both.

The film's final scene finds Cher and Josh, Dionne and Murray, and Tai and her new boyfriend, Travis, attending the wedding of Mr. Hall and Miss Geist. As in Jane Austen's work, the romantic loose ends have been tidied up.

The film's settings, fashions, and jokes define the characters as precisely as Heckerling's Beverly Hills lingo. Befitting its tony setting, *Clueless* has a bright, glossy, candy-colored look — at one point Cher even says, "I bet you're,

CREDITS

Cher: Alicia Silverstone
Dionne: Stacey Dash
Tai: Brittany Murphy
Josh: Paul Rudd
Murray: Donald Faison
Travis: Breckin Meyer
Elton: Jeremy Sisto
Christian: Justin Walker
Mel: Dan Hedaya
Mr. Hall: Wallace Shawn
Miss Geist: Twink Caplan

Origin: USA
Released: 1995
Production: Scott Rudin and Robert Lawrence; released by Paramount Pictures
Direction: Amy Heckerling
Screenplay: Amy Heckerling; based on the novel *Emma* by Jane Austen
Cinematography: Bill Pope
Editing: Debbie Chiate
Production design: Steven Jordan
Art direction: William Hiney
Set decoration: Amy Wells
Casting: Marcia Ross
Costume design: Mona May
Music: Karen Rachtman
MPAA rating: PG-13
Running Time: 97 minutes

AWARDS AND NOMINATIONS

Blockbuster Entertainment Awards 1996: Female Newcomer-Theatrical (Silverstone)
National Society of Film Critics Awards 1995: Best Screenplay (Heckerling)
Writers Guild Awards Nominations 1995: Best Original Screenplay (Heckerling)

like, thinking, Is this a Noxzema commercial or what?" Heckerling's knack for gags remains sharp as well: among the best is a shot of Cher, Josh, and her father at the dinner table all talking on cellular phones.

But much of the film's success resides in the perfect match between the script and its star. Silverstone's Cher is beautiful, but never contemptuous of others; daffily opinionated, but never mean; sexy, but not really aware of her effect on boys. In short, Heckerling and Silverstone manage to keep Cher knowing yet innocent, and to make Cher's growth and acceptance of herself entertaining, appealing, and wholesome, even in the jaded environs of Beverly Hills. Cher, in the end, knows much less about the world than she thinks, and much more about herself than she realizes.

Clueless has occasional lapses; the teenagers' dialogue often seems too self-aware, even given the film's satiric bent. Also, little really seems at stake in the film: Heckerling makes it clear from the beginning that Cher is a nice, thoughtful, if ditzy, teenager, so little seems at risk in her fall from popularity other than her illusion that she is fully in control of her life and the lives of her friends. Still, if *Clueless* is a millimeter deep, its panache, its appealing, bright surfaces, and, most of all, its ideal match of role and star, make the film one of the most effortlessly enjoyable entertainments of 1995.

—*Paul Mittelbach*

REVIEWS

New York Times. CXLV, July 19, 1995, p.B1(N).
Rolling Stone. August 10, 1995, p.61.
Sight and Sound. V, October, 1995, p.46.
The Wall Street Journal. July 21, 1995, p.A8.

Coldblooded

Successful "black comedies" elicit laughter as their plots lurk through menacing shadows and generally unsettling territory. Establishing an agreeable blend of mirth and the macabre takes a deft touch, and a number of notable directors have tried their hand at it with varying degrees of success: Capra (1944's *Arsenic and Old Lace*), Chaplin (1947's *Monsieur Verdoux*), Hitchcock (1955's *The Trouble with Harry*), Kubrick (1964's *Dr. Strangelove*), Huston (1985's *Prizzi's Honor*), and, more recently, Tarantino (1995's *Pulp Fiction*). Wallace Wolodarsky, an Emmy-winning writer for *The Simpsons* and The *Tracey Ullman Show*, takes his shot at the genre in *Coldblooded*, his directorial debut. Unfortunately, unlike the main character here, a nerdy, expressionless bookie who comes into his own as a hit man with unerring aim, Wolodarsky (who also wrote the script) clearly misses his mark. Cosmo (Jason Priestley of *Beverly Hills 90210*), the aforementioned young schlep, has an exasperatingly monotone voice and only slightly more vibrancy than a corpse. He leads a solitary life, contentedly watching television and carefully recording bets on various sporting events that are phoned in to his bleak living quarters in the basement of a senior citizens' complex. Other than briefly checking with the elderly lady at the front desk to see if he has received any mail, the only person Cosmo sees on a regular basis is his prostitute, Honey (Janeane Garofalo). She not only supplies her undemanding client with sex, but also with compliments like "Of all the people who pay to have sex with me, I like you the best."

Cosmo's cloistered existence suddenly changes when Gordon (Robert Loggia), the head of the mob, informs him that a hit man has been killed and Cosmo is being promoted to take his place. Although Cosmo calmly states that he is "happy with things the way they are" and does not think that he has what it takes to kill, his boss insists that he be put under the immediate tutelage of the organizations No. 1 triggerman, Steve (Peter Riegert). Stating sagely that "Guns don't kill people. We kill people," Steve takes Cosmo to target practice, and is startled by the novice's proficiency. Cosmo shoots with amazing speed toward the silhouettes at the end of the range, hitting any and all body parts that his mentor calls out. Cosmo enjoys the experience so much that he tries firing two guns at once, and cannot stop pumping the triggers even after both weapons are empty. "I've never been good at anything in my life," he says with a smile and a hint of new-found confidence. "It's exciting."

When Steve and Cosmo go to deal with a man who owes the mob a fairly small amount of money, Cosmo wants to be reassured that the intended victim deserves to be roughed up. While the obese man kneels pleading before them, Steve orders Cosmo to smash the man's nose. After hesitating, Cosmo politely asks the man to hold still, apologizes after doing the deed, and expresses the hope the man can get it fixed. While Steve looks for the money, Cosmo suddenly realizes that his victim is Number 330, an amiable man who frequently calls in bets. The brief chat that follows is cut short by Steve's order to kill. With the relatively minor amount of money recovered and clear punishment doled out, Cosmo is startled by the command, and makes the man promise not to repeat his transgression. Steve soothingly says that he knows it is not easy, but insists that his order be followed. After the victim—and the audience—suffer through Cosmo trying to shoot the man with the safety still on, he fires three times into the man's corpulent gut. Cosmo's naivete, hesitancy, and politeness are clearly supposed to leaven the situation, but the fact that they don't heightens the impact of the scene's brutality to a sickening jolt. This scene is characteristic of the film's conspicuous impotency in generating any amusement amidst the shocking, repugnant circumstances.

Cosmo cannot handle the glint of unfamiliar emotions that his handiwork has triggered, and it is suggested that he enroll in yoga to relax. After he even has flashbacks during the yoga class, Cosmo cannot sleep, and he calls Steve for further reassurance. Unfortunately, the congenial killer who indulges in health food drinks during the day becomes a profane, weeping drunk at night. Cosmo talks of quitting the next morning, but Steve insists that the job may grow on him. Indeed, Cosmo soon starts fantasizing about holding a gun to the head of the yoga instructor's brutish boyfriend, and wants to be in the driver's seat, literally and figuratively, on the way to the twosomes encounter with Colombian drug dealers. The fact that Cosmo emerges unscathed while Steve is shot further bolsters his confidence. He draws upon that confidence when he pursues (romantically, that is) Jasmine (Kimberly Williams), his yoga instructor, who is dissolved in tears because her romantic history has consisted of a long parade of jerks. Cosmo thinks she deserves better treatment than that, but worries about the fact that he has never had a girlfriend before. (He tells Steve that he has been using the same hooker for awhile, but is told that that does not count.) On their first date, this latest odd choice for a beau lets her decide what the two will watch on television at her house. Unaccustomed to such chivalrous behavior, Jasmine is smitten.

Confident in homicide but still awkwardly stiff in love, Cosmo goes on his next job alone, paying a visit to Gordon's husband and wife accounting team (Michael J. Fox and Talia Balsam). Noting how ecstatically happy they are together, Cosmo begins asking the young couple for advice on romance and sex. After they cheerfully offer the secrets of their success, Cosmo kindly thanks them, and blows them away. Cosmo tells Steve that he did not mind killing them ("That's automatic."); he just cannot get over the fact that a couple could be so blissfully happy. Hoping to ensure that he will have the chance to develop that type of relationship with Jasmine, Cosmo takes care of her menacing ex-boyfriend by bashing in his nose. While blood seeps down his shaken victim's face, Cosmo decides to solicit relationship advice from him as well, finding out the kinds of flowers, gifts and sex that Jasmine might like. After extracting this useful information, Cosmo shakes hands with the man, and cheerfully waves goodbye.

Hailing Cosmo as an "overachiever" and a "prodigy," Gordon decides that Steve has become dispensable, and orders his gifted employee to make the hit. Cosmo is evidently distressed by this command to kill his mentor and friend (although, as usual, it is nearly impossible to tell what he is feeling), because he decides that he must find another line of work. Later, in the afterglow of his first sexual encounter with Jasmine, Cosmo feels that he must come completely clean, and announces with a laugh that he slaughters people for money but will never do it again. Jasmine throws him out, closing the door on his last pathetic "I love you" and, after considering the kind of man Cosmo is, locks it. He soon heads to Steve's house, and is told that the only way out of the organization is to kill both Gordon and his right-hand man, John. Cosmo reasons that he must kill Steve in order to remain close enough to the two men to accomplish that task. "You're too close" are the last instructions the teacher ever gives his talented pupil before being shot to death in perhaps the most startling of all the film's dreadful scenes. Cosmo then proceeds to Gordon's house and kills his two intended targets, only lingering long enough to snatch an expensive bottle of wine to ply Jasmine with. When she will not take him back, Cosmo threatens to kill himself, but then gives the gun to Jasmine to do the hon-

CREDITS

Cosmo Reif: Jason Priestley
Steve: Peter Riegert
Jasmine: Kimberly Williams
Gordon: Robert Loggia
John: Jay Kogen
Honey: Janeane Garofalo

Origin: USA
Released: 1995
Production: Brad Krevoy, Steve Stabler, Brad Jenkel and Michael J. Fox for a Snowback production; released by Polygram Filmed Entertainment/Propaganda Films/Motion Picture Corp. of America
Direction: Wallace Wolodarsky
Screenplay: Wallace Wolodarsky
Cinematography: Robert Yeoman
Editing: Craig Bassett
Production design: Rae Fox
Set decoration: Tim Colohan
Costume design: Matthew Jacobson
Sound: Giovanni DiSimone
Music: Steve Bartek
MPAA rating: R
Running Time: 92 minutes

ors. Next he suggests that he kill her first, because her death would make him sufficiently despondent to do himself in. "You love me that much?" she asks in amazement. After briefly considering their situation, Jasmine agrees to take back "the best boyfriend I ever had," because she figures that the people he killed probably deserved to die anyway, and, what is more, Cosmo has such unusually nice teeth.

Coldblooded was an entrant in the dramatic category at the Sundance Film Festival, but understandably failed to win. Critical reaction to the film was severely negative for the most part, with even the relatively positive reviews, like that in *The Hollywood Reporter,* admitting that *Coldblooded* possessed merely "intermittent charm." It earned an abysmal $8,423, never making it out of limited release. Among the film's five producers are Brad Krevoy and Steve Stabler, who enjoyed far more box-office success with *Dumb and Dumber* (1994). This latest offering finds Wolodarsky shooting blanks in his attempt at "droll black comedy," which leaves *Coldblooded* a distasteful, astoundingly flat presentation that is almost as muted as Priestley's intentionally-leaden Cosmo. Wolodarsky made a serious miscalculation when he thought that viewers would find themselves inexorably charmed by Cosmo because they come to the film with an unshakable affinity for Priestley's congenial *90210* character. "I like the idea of making a 'bad guy' likeable," the director enthuses. "In a way, it makes the audience guilty as well for rooting for him to win." Anyone who actually finds himself cheering for the grating gunman in this lightweight production must be cold-blooded indeed.

—David L. Boxerbaum

REVIEWS

Boston Globe. October 20, 1995, p. 24.
Chicago Tribune. October 27, 1995, p. K1.
Entertainment Weekly. November 3, 1995, p. 80.
The Hollywood Reporter. January 23, 1995, p. 41.
Los Angeles Times. September 15, 1995, p. F6.
San Francisco Chronicle. September 15, 1995, p. 3C.
Variety. January 23, 1995, p. 72.

Cold Comfort Farm

The credits roll, a small child dressed in turn-of-the-century togs runs through the woods, accompanied only by ominous music. She stops at a shed and slowly opens the door as the music crescendos and the screen fades to black. Now the camera pans a dusty ill-lit room, and we see the little girl, now an old woman thrashing about her unkempt bed, shouting feverishly, "I saw something nasty in the woodshed."

If you think *Cold Comfort Farm* is just another gloomy BBC period piece, then you're very much mistaken. In this opening scene, our legs are the first ones' pulled in this hilarious spoof.

Adapted from the 1932 novel by Stella Gibbons, *Cold Comfort Farm,* is a delightful comedy of manners. Set in the 30s, it nonetheless retains all of its freshness and wit. The British make fun of the British in this farcical portrayal of the overly sentimental and overly used literary conventions popularized in the novels of Thomas Hardy, Mary Webb, and D.H. Lawrence, among others.

The film spoofs such literary devices as the curse on the farm, the mad woman in the upstairs bedroom, the glorified farm laborer, and the wood nymph stereotypes. Parodying the Pollyanna theme, *Cold Comfort Farm* colors it with an eccentric wit and the British love of the absurd.

> Made for British TV, this film was based on Stella Gibbons' 1932 literary satire of the novels of D.H. Lawrence and Thomas Hardy.

This is the tale of a sophisticated but recently orphaned young woman, Flora Poste (Kate Beckinsale), who decides to live with and upon her rural relatives. Flora turns the farm upside down, but with such theatrical panache and "good common sense" that she is a delight to watch.

The whimsical atmosphere is set in the first scene, when we meet Flora's socialite friend, Mary Smiling (Joanna Lumley), busy with her hobby. She collects corsets. Dressmakers' mannequins clad only in corsets stand like headless soldiers in rows throughout her sitting room, and we meet Mary as she is pinning her newest brassiere on one of the dummies.

Flora has come to visit Mary after her parents' funeral to discuss her plans for her future. She has written to a number of her eccentric relatives, asking to come and live with them. When they return her letters, most sound dreadful, but the last is from Cousin Judith (Eileen Atkins) who invites Flora to come live with the Starkadder family on Cold Comfort Farm, so that they may be able to atone for the wrong done her father. Flora finds the idea interesting, which is just as well because our heroine needs material for the novel she intends to spring on the world when she is 53.

Flora arrives at Cold Comfort Farm to find a farming estate that has fallen into absolute disrepair and inhabitants who are practically medieval. The farm, the animals, and the Starkadders themselves appear to have been wallowing in mud for years, and if there is one thing that our Flora must have it is tidiness. As soon as she arrives she proceeds to tidy up Cold Comfort Farm and all of its inhabitants with a calm, no-nonsense manner that takes her rural relatives by surprise.

"I held a quivering audition for the local extras. They quivered and cried Hallelujah!"—Director John Schlesinger

Coming from the cocktails and dinner party set, Flora's sophisticated background stands in stark contrast to this grim group, and she meets an array of characters that could provoke anyone's sense of tidiness. On her first day on the farm, she is greeted by the wailing of the kitchen maid giving birth in the hay loft, and is soon after assailed by her oversexed cousin Seth's (Rufus Sewell) ribald diatribe. Her morning tea is spoilt by the sight of the manservant, Adam (Freddie Jones), washing the breakfast dishes with a twig, while Poor Daft Rennet dumbly watches on from the shadows. Luckily Flora's calm and absolute trust in her own good judgment sees her through these encounters with quiet resolution, and she soon has things tidied up quite neatly.

Gibbons' send up of the noble yet deathly serious characters of British rural novels is flawless. The disconsolate setting and ubiquitous filth are so perfectly spoofed and so maddeningly all-pervasive that when Flora sets about tidying up, you almost cheer.

Her first mysterious encounter with the matriarch, Ada Doom, is through the untouched dinner tray left waiting outside the locked bedroom door. The old woman lies within, alternately lamenting, "I saw something nasty in the woodshed," and "There have always been Starkadders on Cold Comfort Farm." Intrigued, Flora starts slipping travel brochures in on her food trays.

As Flora explores the nearby village, she stops for lunch at the local pub, "The Condemned Man," where a sign with a hanged man painted on it invites in the weary traveler. There she is re-introduced to a man she knew in London, Mr. Mybug, a novelist with Lawrentian tendencies. Flora discourages those tendencies, but her new-found beau is tenacious and she addresses his advances with candid common sense and hasty retreats.

Still struggling with her novel, Flora sets out to try to learn about writing from her Uncle Amos (Ian McKellen), who is the local preacher. She goes to hear his sermon, in an effort to understand how he gets his inspiration.

In a great scene and a wonderful farce on evangelism, Amos, with an almost incoherent accent, preaches to the townspeople his Sermon of the Quiver. He speaks the gospel of the Quivering Brethren and the townspeople listen to his fire and brimstone and respond with religiously correct and vigorous quivering.

Impressed with his parishioners' response, Flora convinces Amos that he needs to spread his word farther afield and, on her prompting, he decides to take it on the road, spreading the word of the Quivering Brethren to America.

Amos gone and happy, Flora turns her attention to Elfine (Maria Miles), her pretty young cousin who is in love with the local lord of the manor. Flora takes her to London and together with her friend Mary Smiling they give her a new look—very elegant, very glamorous, and very 1930s—a real change from the wood nymph look that Elfine had affected while leaping around the countryside spouting poetry. They teach her how to fashionably repress her volatile emotions and never—never let on that she writes poetry. Sneaking her into a ball at the manor, Elfine wins the lord's heart, who immediately announces his engagement before the assembled throng.

That taken care of, oversexed Cousin Seth is next. The worldly Flora sees beyond Seth's uncommon sexual prowess to uncover his star qualities. With her help, he is discovered

CREDITS

Flora Poste: Kate Beckinsale
Ada Doom: Sheila Burrell
Judith Starkadder: Eileen Atkins
Amos Starkadder: Ian McKellen
Reuben Starkadder: Ivan Kaye
Seth Starkadder: Rufus Sewell

Origin: Great Britain
Released: 1995
Production: Alison Gilby for a BBC/Thames Television production
Direction: John Schlesinger
Screenplay: Malcolm Bradbury; based on the novel by Stella Gibbons
Cinematography: Chris Seager
Editing: Mark Day
Production design: Malcolm Thornton
Art direction: Jim Holloway
Costume design: Amy Roberts
Sound: Jim Greenhorn
Casting: Noel Davis
Music: Robert Lockhart
MPAA rating: not listed
Running Time: 95 minutes

by a Hollywood mogul and, in a great parody of *Gone with the Wind*, Seth leaves Cold Comfort Farm for the silver screen.

With Cousin Judith's husband and son now both gone, she remains morosely sitting amid her Tarot cards unearthing even more doom and gloom to descend upon the cursed, barren land of Cold Comfort Farm.

All these changes occur against the wishes of the matriarch, Ada Doom (Sheila Burrell), who is still thrashing around in her bed, only coming downstairs to do the counting. Biannually, she emerges to count how many relatives are left, to make certain none have escaped from the farm, for "There have always been Starkadders on Cold Comfort Farm," as they all know too well.

But even Ada's wrath doesn't deter Flora, and she soon tidies up the lives of the few remaining residents of the farm. Brother Rubin takes over the farm and marries the heretofore too filthy to be appreciated Poor Daft Rennet, who cleans up tolerably well. Adam, the manservant, whose heart is torn between the bovine members of the farm and little Elfine, goes to live at the manor with her and brings his four cows. Ard, who had been promised to Elfine, marries the fecund kitchen maid, and morose Cousin Judith goes to live in a sanitarium with a psychiatrist who finds her case mesmerizing.

Now at the wedding feast of Elfine and her groom, with the country folk and the landed gentry in full regalia, Ada Doom makes her appearance. Flora has touched her life as well, and she emerges, dressed to the teeth, and announces that she is going to live in Paris.

Having completed her task and still none the wiser about the curse on the farm, what happened in the woodshed, or what wrong was done to her father, Flora flies off into the sunset in a biplane with her beloved Charles—to live happily and calmly ever after.

Although containing some changes from the original novel, director John Schlesinger's fast-paced comedy and non-stop nonsense will make you laugh out loud. *Cold Comfort Farm* was shot in Sussex, which is not only Schlesinger's home but also the milieu of the Hardy classic *Far from the Madding Crowd*, the 1967 film Schlesinger directed. It seems that in *Cold Comfort Farm*, Schlesinger is also parodying his own filming of Hardy, with its gloom-ridden atmosphere and lingeringly sentimental shots of livestock.

Schlesinger, known in Britain for both his film and his television work, is renown in the U.S. for his many films, which span almost thirty years, from his early work on *Midnight Cowboy* (1969), for which he won an Oscar for best director, to the more recent *Pacific Heights* (1990).

Cold Comfort Farm was adapted for the screen by Malcolm Bradbury. It was originally made for British television through the collaborative efforts of the BBC Screen One and Thames TV, who have come together for the first time on this film.

Kate Beckinsale, who plays Flora, is understated and intriguing as the waif with the alarming strength of character, and you'll watch on in delighted anticipation to see what she'll think up next.

Ian McKellen is fantastic as the preacher of Quiver, and the scene where he gives his sermon is unforgettably funny, as his brethren quiver uncontrollably to his scenes of hellfire.

Rufus Sewell is excellent as Seth, the oversexed yet starstruck cousin. His Rudolph Valentino entrance captures the mogul's heart and captures Hollywood at it's silliest.

It's difficult to praise one actor over another in this film, they all give such engaging performances. Each actor brings their own special talents and humor to their characters and you get the feeling that they are having a ripping good time in the process.

Cold Comfort Farm has made the rounds at film festivals in Montreal, Seattle, Los Angeles, and Telluride, where it has been one of the more popular films presented. It boasts fabulous performances and photography that belongs on the big screen.

For a taste of a more light-hearted fare than is usually encountered on the festival circuit, I would heartily recommend this entertaining spoof, replete with all the elegant trappings of a Woodhouse novel and plenty of Hardy mud.

—Diane Hatch-Avis

REVIEWS

Boxoffice, November 1995, p. 98.
Entertainment Today, October 27, 1995.
Hollywood Reporter, October 13, 1995, p. 1.
Hollywood Reporter, August 31, 1995, p. 5.
Variety, June 21, 1995, p. 10.

Congo

"Breathtaking action! Amazing special effects!"—Joel Siegel, *Good Morning America*

"Adventure at its best!"—Jim Ferguson, *Prevue Channel*

"You are in for a treat!"—Peter Travers, *Rolling Stone*

Box Office Gross: $81,022,333

Dylan Walsh, as primatologist Peter Elliot, is the guardian of Amy, a remarkable gorilla he decides must be returned to her jungle home in *Congo*.

The problem with having an older sibling is that people will always compare the two, usually to the detriment of the younger. He or she is never as smart or as talented or as pretty or as successful as his/her big brother or sister. Unfortunately, this is the case for poor *Congo*, which, like its several older and very successful siblings, was sired from a book by Michael Crichton. And also, unfortunately for *Congo*, it can't help being compared to its most recent sibling, the monster 1994 hit *Jurassic Park* which was brought into the world with world-class director Steven Spielberg as its midwife. It seems that most critics (and even worse, the film's distributor) are unable to grasp that *Congo* is NOT the same film as its older sibling. As a result, it is expected to be—and is being sold as—an edge-of-the-seat action/adventure film. However, in reality, this film is a lightweight and fun film entry in 1995's early glut of summer releases.

This is not to say that *Congo* is not an action-adventure film, for it is. However, one feels as though the screenwriter's and director's tongues were firmly planted in their cheeks as they lead the audience into the jungles of deepest and darkest Africa to the unexplored Virunga volcano range. Just look who is on the trip.

First there is Karen Ross (Laura Linney) an ex-CIA agent who is now a technologically-proficient project supervisor for the American communications company TraviCom. She needs to get into the Congo for two reasons: 1) the previous TraviCom expedition, which contained the boss's son and Ross's fiance, has mysteriously stopped communicating with the company, and its last transmitted video showed a scene of mass slaughter, and 2) Ross also needs to find what the original expedition was looking for, the type llb industrial diamonds that will give TraviCom a quantum leap to the forefront of the communications industry.

Production designer J. Michael Riva and his staff designed and constructed the Lost City and its fabled diamond mines on stages 15 and 30 at The Sony Studios. In erecting the mine set, over 700 blocks of industrial styrofoam were used, making the mine set for *Congo* the largest styrofoam set ever built.

The second adventurer is Peter Elliot (Dylan Walsh), a primatologist who has taught a young mountain gorilla, Amy, to speak via a data glove which gives voice to the American sign language she has learned.

But Amy has been having nightmares which she expresses to Peter not in words, but in finger-painted pictures. And these pictures show the jungle where she was born. Peter hopes that taking her back to her original jungle home will cure her nightmares.

Unfortunately, Peter does not have the money to undertake this trip, so enter the third traveller, self-styled Romanian philanthropist Herkermer Homolka (Tim Curry). It would seem that Herkermer is paying for the trip out of the goodness of his heart, but he has an ulterior motive. In Amy's pictures he detects the symbol of the "Open Eye," the sign of the lost city of Zinj, source of King Solomon's "lost" diamond mines.

The final major explorer on the trek is the prerequisite guide, the Great White Hunter...who just happens to be black. Monroe Kelly (Ernie Hudson) is a competent and cool jungle escort, and that is exactly what this crew is going to need. Through rockets and rebels, rain and snakes, rapids and hippos, restless natives and active volcanoes, and, most of all, an unknown species of killer gorillas who guard the diamonds, the voyagers will need all the help they can get. And Kelly's knowledge supplemented by Ross's technology just may help them to reach their quests...and get out alive!

So, obviously, there are exploits and action in *Congo* (most realized with outstanding special effects), it's just that they don't seem to be the center of the film. *Congo* isn't meant to scare one's socks off the way big brother *Jurassic Park* did, instead, it is more amiable and good-humored. Suspense is minimal, but that's all right; this is supposed to be more of a roller coaster ride than the trip in the space shuttle which characterized *Jurassic Park*.

"The Congo is a place that very few people have gone. It has been called the heart of darkest Africa—and you would need a very compelling reason to go there. Each of the characters in *Congo* has their own idiosyncratic reason for wanting to take this journey."—Screenwriter John Patrick Shanley

While the film's leads, Dylan Walsh and Laura Linney, offer little chance for over-the-top acting, they instead offer the solid motives for the film's basic storyline. But when it comes to the secondary characters, that's when the roller coaster crests the top of that first hill and goes into free fall. To see the accomplished African-American actor Ernie Hudson (best known for his role in the *Ghostbuster* movies) swaggering through an homage to the "heroes" in H. Rider Haggard's romanticized novels and their film incarnations (Stewart Granger and Richard Chamberlain) is truly amusing. And it's made all the better by the fact that Hudson really seems to be having fun in the incongruous role.

But when it comes to having fun with a character, no one can beat Tim Curry's Herkermer Homolka. With his rolling "r's" and his trade-mark eccentricity, Curry is riding this roller coaster with his hands high in the air and screaming with delight.

Interesting enough, one result of the fun most of the actors are having with their parts is that the character who was the heart of Crichton's book, Amy, is basically marginalized in the film. In the book she is strong and even sarcastic, in the film she is sweet and sheepish, characteristics emphasized all the more by the treacly sweet voice given her by the prosthetic arm. She is, however, still an appealing character, brought amazingly to life by Stan Winston's special effects wizardry.

Most of the humor and light-heartedness of *Congo* is due to one person, screenwriter John Patrick Shanley. Using just the bare bones of author Michael Crichton's 1980 best seller, Shanley (best known for his screenwriting Academy Award for *Moonstruck* in 1987) has replaced the book's original high-tech, cynical, cautionary tale with a breezier, funnier and lighter one. And by the time he is done, not only is the tone between the written and the filmed *Congo* completely different, so too is the story. The real suspense in the book is the competition between the American company TraviCom and its German-Japanese competitors (Amy was a ruse to throw them off), but since suspense is not the primary mover of the film, this element has been completely removed. And since amusement does seem to be the film's goal, Shanley has instead added characters, most notably Curry's Herkermer Homolka. Now, instead of Crichton's serious story and mechanical characters we are given scenes that verge on silly (when all the native porters join Peter in serenading Amy with the song "California Dreamin'") and characters whose dialogue verges on the goofy ("Don't be so John Wayne. You could get killed!" or "I don't have a price! I'm not a pound of sugar, I'm a primatologist!").

Another thing that is missing from the movie that was in the book is Crichton's original theme. The diamonds that TraviCom is seeking are to be used in lethal weaponry which Karen sarcastically calls "the latest thing in communica-

CREDITS

Peter Elliot: Dylan Walsh
Karen Ross: Laura Linney
Monroe Kelly: Ernie Hudson
Richard: Grant Heslov
R. B. Travis: Joe Don Baker
Herkermer Homolka: Tim Curry
Kahega: Adewale (Wale) Akinnuoye-Agbaje
Lead Porter: Willie Amakye
Charles Travis: Bruce Campbell
Jeffrey Weemes: C. Taylor Nichols

Origin: USA
Released: 1995
Production: Kathleen Kennedy and Sam Mercer for a Kennedy/Marshall production; released by Paramount Pictures
Direction: Frank Marshall
Screenplay: John Patrick Shanley from the novel by Michael Crichton
Cinematography: Allen Daviau
Editing: Anne V. Coates
Production design: J. Michael Riva
Visual effects: Michael Lantieri and Scott Farrar
Special visual effects: Industrial Light and Magic
Sound: Ronald Judkins
Makeup: Christina Smith
Costume design: Marilyn Matthew
Gorillas: Stan Winston
Gorilla choreography: Peter Elliott
Physical effects: Michael Lantieri
Music: Jerry Goldsmith
MPAA rating: PG-13
Running Time: 110 minutes

tions." Crichton makes a pointed comparison between this toxic use of technology in which nuclear weapons can go on killing long after those who created them are dead, and the tool-wielding killer gorillas who do the same thing in the city of Zinj. One can't help but wonder what Mr. Crichton thinks of this entertaining bastardization of his creation—and its missing theme.

Whether the original story would have made a better movie than this or whether the elements Shanley cast aside were cinematically better than those he added could make for very interesting discussions, but it seems only fair that one should discuss the movie that was made instead of the one that wasn't. We may never know whether audiences would have preferred to see Crichton's original, serious story instead of Shanley's more humorous adaptation, but this is certain, audiences are flocking to the *Congo* that was filmed.

Congo opened big in theaters on its first weekend, possibly from its being marketed as *Jurassic Park*'s little brother, but the critics were not very kind to it. Its second weekend it fell into second place only because of the overwhelming, but expected, big box office scores captured by the third installment of *Batman*. However, *Congo* continued to hold its own with audiences, and if viewed with no preconceptions except that of having a good time, *Congo* is perfect for an evening's escape in the summer, and will probably do very well when released on home video.

—Beverley Bare Buehrer

REVIEWS

Chicago Tribune. June 9, 1995, Section Friday, p. B and C.
Entertainment Weekly. June 11, 1995, p. 44.
Los Angeles Times. June 9, 1995, p. F1.
The New York Times. June 6, 1995, p. B1.
USA Today. June 9, 1995, p. C1.
Variety. June 12-18, 1995, p. 59.

The Convent (O Convento)

The use of a highly bankable film actor, John Malkovich, and a certified movie star, Catherine Deneuve, in his abstruse but amusing metaphysical mystery, is just one of the interesting oddities of veteran Portuguese director Manoel de Oliveira's latest work, *The Convent*. The premise of the film is itself offbeat: ambitious American professor Michael Padovic (Malkovich) and his gorgeous, bored wife, Helene (Deneuve), travel to Portugal so that he can research his theory that Shakespeare was a descendant of Sephardic Jews. Proof of his theory—which he is convinced will make his academic reputation—supposedly lies in the archives of a medieval Portuguese convent.

The Padovics first try out a convent that proves to be a dead end, although the reasons for this conclusion are left obscure. They turn next to the convent of Arrabida, which appears to house just the right combination of quirky characters, including: a devilish guardian named Baltar (Luis Miguel Cintra), his angelic archivist, Piedade (Leonor Silveira), his erratic assistant, Baltazar (Duarte D'Almeida), and his tarot-reading housekeeper, Berta (Heloisa Miranda). And Arrabida is also home to two icons that haunt the film: one a statute of Jesus to which the camera repeatedly returns, and the other a legendary statue of a blond Virgin said to have vanished from the convent centuries before.

Filmgoers might be tempted to make an equation between these statues and the Padovics, but Oliveira's mystery is not so schematic. Viewers would also be mistaken if they try to make too much of the names of the convent's inhabitants—even after Piedade makes a gift to Michael of a copy of Goethe's Faust. While it is true that Baltar (a version of Balthazar, one of Satan's pseudonyms)—he of the black clothing, piercing gaze, and demonic laugh—seems to be tempting Michael by leaving him much alone with the luminous archivist, Baltar does so because he is besotted with the equally beautiful Helene. Helene seems to have begun her flirtation with Baltar out of boredom, when it appears that her husband prefers his research in the convent's archives (or is it the archivist?) to her company. And just when we think Michael the only real victim here, we are thrown back on Oliveira's casting. Throughout his film career Malkovich has specialized in playing off-center, eccentric, even malevolent characters. His demeanor here—mild-mannered bourgeois American academic—does not disguise the qualities of fey irony and insincere knowingness that have led Malkovich to such parts. We recall, belatedly, that Michael has come to Arrabida in pursuit of a kind of immortality, which could make him either an apt subject for the temptations Baltar sends his way, or an arch manipulator—or both. And then there are those other weird denizens of the convent, the other Mephistopheles, Baltazar, and his fortune telling wife, Berta, who, as the Padovics enter the convent, ominously pronounces their arrival a dangerous development.

And what of Helene? Deneuve is as gorgeous as ever, making it difficult for viewers to believe that her husband would so ignore her. And yet, she is jealous of the attentions he pays to his books and to Piedade. Presumably she knew in advance that the nature of the trip to Arrabida would leave her at loose ends. Why, one wonders, did she come along? Indeed.

Baltar leaps eagerly into the breach, squiring Helene around the convent and its environs. And the two do seem to have a special bond. Although most of the dialogue in the film is conducted in English and Portuguese, when Helene and Baltar are alone together, they speak French. As they are thrown more together and their relationship becomes more intense, Baltar takes her to the edge of what he calls the enchanted forest, as whose center, he tells her, lies an abyss that beckons the pure of heart. At the crucial moment, Helene demurs, recommending that Baltar venture there not with herself, but with the conspicuously unblemished Piedade.

It is at this point that *The Convent* seems to be approaching its climax, but although something momentous does develop, it never appears on the screen. Instead, for the first time, the plot of *The Convent* is revealed through narrative. And the narrative voice belongs to an anonymous fisherman, a character who has played no part in the action. We never again see any of the other characters, and the mystery of what happened to them and how is left entirely unresolved. Oliveira leaves his audience to pursue its own interpretations of his intriguing retelling of the Faust legend.

—Lisa Paddock

CREDITS

Helene Padovic: Catherine Deneuve
Michael Padovic: John Malkovich
Baltar: Luis Miguel Cintra
Pedade: Leonor Silveira
Baltazar: Duarte D' Almeida
Berta: Heloisa Miranda

Origin: France
Released: 1995
Production: Paulo Branco for a Madragoa Filmes, Gemini Films, La Sept-Cinema, *Ipaca* Instituo Portugues da Arte Cinematografica e Audiovisual, Secretaria de Estado da Cultura and Canal Plus production; released by Strand
Direction: Manoel de Oliveria
Screenplay: Manoel de Oliveria
Cinematography: Mario Barroso
Editing: Manoel de Oliveria and Valerie Losieleux
Production design: Ze Branco
Sound: Jean, Paul Mugel
Running Time: 90 minutes

Copycat

"The suspense is high and the tension taunt. A powerful, impressive movie."—Susan Granger, *CRN & American Movie Classics*

"A chiller! It'll scare you every which way imaginable!"—Jeffrey Lyons, *Lyons Den Radio*

"A thrill a minute! Paralyzingly suspenseful."—Rex Reed, *New York Observer*

"The best suspense thriller of the year. Four stars."—Jeff Craig, *Sixty Second Preview*

"Shocking, exciting and highly entertaining. A wonderfully suspenseful thriller."—Paul Wunder, *WBAI Radio*

Box Office Gross: $31,203,644

Sigourney Weaver and Holly Hunter star in *Copycat*, the latest entry in a recent slew of serial-killer films that includes the box-office hit *Seven* (1995) with Morgan Freeman and Brad Pitt investigating a series of gruesome murders based on the Seven Deadly Sins. Both films are clever in their abiliy to find new twists in an old favorite, and feature smarter or perhaps just more creative psychopaths designed to push the envelope of terror and manipulation to new levels. Yet it is the more "feminist" *Copycat* that is the most disturbing. By employing two of Hollywood's most respected female actresses, the film gains not respect, but rather indignity. *Copycat* shows us that women can be not only victims, but also fully vested participants in their own exploitation.

Criminologist Helen Hudson (Sigourney Weaver) is an expert on serial killers, not only smart, but attractive, ironically referring to herself as "their damn pinup girl." During one of her lectures, a crazed admirer, a homicidal geek named Daryll Lee Cullum (balladeer Harry Connick, Jr. with bad skin and fake teeth) slips past security and terrorizes Hudson by stringing her up with cable in the women's restroom and threatening to murder her. Cullum is caught, but Hudson is so traumatized by the assault that she becomes an agoraphobic, a virtual prisoner in her own home who has withdrawn from both work and her life. The only contact she maintains with the outside is through her computer, via the Internet, and through her gay assistant, Andy (John Rothman). Hudson is so starved for human contact that she has three computers connected to several different services, communicating through e-mail messages and playing interactive chess.

To prepare for her role as a detective chasing serial killers, Holly Hunter accompanied two L.A. homicide detectives to court and on crime sprees.

When faced with an investigation of a possible new serial killer, San Fransicso Homicide Inspector M.J. Monahan (Holly Hunter) and her pretty boy partner, Ruben Goetz (Dermot Mulroney in a role traditionally assigned to the female) , go to Hudson for help. Despite her fears, the heavy-drinking, pill-popping Hudson finds her interest piqued by the details of the case, but is reluctant to become involved. When she once again becomes the victim of an increasing number of break-ins and visual harrassments, it is not long before Hudson figures out that the killer (William McNamara) is duplicating the murders of not just one, but several other prominent serial killers, ranging from the Boston Strangler and the Hillside Strangler to Son of Sam and Jeffrey Dahmer. Hudson is fascinated by the psychopath's attention to the most minute detail, each killing an homage to a murderer extraordinaire. Despite this revelation, Hudson and the police have no way of knowing who the next victim will be due to the random nature of the copycat murders. It is this twist that helps to elevate *Copycat* a notch above the confines of its formulaic conventions. The ending, however, is so cliched it is laughable. Audiences may applaud the revenge, but it is a hollow victory.

Both Ms. Hunter and Ms. Weaver give strong performances, as one would expect. However, one wonders what, aside from the potential for box office gold, was the appeal of these characters to attract such high-caliber actresses to a project that is merely a notch above a B-movie. (The same applies to Sally Field whose tv-movie-of-the-week quality film, *Eye for an Eye* (1996), is merely a role reversal variation of all those Charles Bronson *Death Wish* revenge films in the mid-seventies and eighties.) The casting of both actresses is problematic, given the differences in their heights and in their personal personas, as well as a definite lack of chemistry. It is distressing to see Sigourney Weaver, the tough heroine of all three *Alien* (1979-1992), be such a passive victim. The actress is anything but vulnerable and to see her dangling—not once, but twice—over a toilet and not even attempt to signal the police with her eyes or a slight nod of the head is both insulting and ludicrious. As for Hunter, the casting of the diminutive actress as a hardened homicide investigator asks that the audience totally suspend their disbelief. Hunter's size cannot be camouflaged by merely having the towering Sigourney Weaver always be seated, although to the filmmakers' credit, they do have Helen Hudson snidely refer to Monahan as "the wee inspector." It is difficult to imagine that Monahan could have made it through the screening process for acceptance to the police academy. Surely there were height requirements at the time Monahan was selected since she is not a new recruit and most probably has been on the force for some time to have attained her current status.

The distracting thing about the casting of William McNamara as the diabolical murderer in *Copycat* is not so much the attractiveness of the actor, as Janet Maslin of *The New York Times* complained, but rather his striking similarity to another, more famous actor, Tom Cruise. It was difficult to know whether this was accidental or if it was a further ex-

CREDITS

Helen Hudson: Sigourney Weaver
M.J. Monahan: Holly Hunter
Ruben Goetz: Dermot Mulroney
Peter Foley: William McNamara
Nicoletti: Will Patton
Andy: John Rothman
Quinn: J.E. Freeman
Daryll Lee Cullum: Harry Connick, Jr.

Origin: USA
Released: 1995
Production: Arnon Milchan and Mark Tarlov; Regency Enterprises presents an Amon Milchan production, released by Warner Bros.
Direction: Jon Amiel
Screenplay: Ann Biderman and David Madsen
Cinematography: Laszlo Kovacs
Editing: Alan Helm and Jim Clark
Production design: Jim Clay
Art direction: Chris Seagers
Costume design: Claudia Brown
Casting: Billy Hipkins, Suzanne Smith and Kerry Barden
Music: Christopher Young
MPAA rating: R
Running Time: 123 minutes

ploitation of the "copycat" theme. It is an unfortunate distraction, since McNamara turns in a controlled, yet eerily unstable performance as the murder groupie seduced by the fame brought on by media glorification—a topic explored at length in Oliver Stone's amusing and sensory-saturated satire, *Natural Born Killers* (1994). But the character is never developed and we never understand what it is that has pushed Foley to the point of such dastardly deeds. His relationship to women, particularly his mother, is sketchy, at best. If it is true that most serial killers are themselves victims of either physical or sexual abuse, then that seems an important issue to explore. Along the same lines, the filmmakers chose to set the story in San Francisco, home to another homicide investigator, the more forceful and certainly more contrasting in terms of height alone, Clint Eastwood's Inspector Harry Callahan, a.k.a. *Dirty Harry* (1971). Even the names of the two inspectors, Monahan and Callahan, are similar.

"These guys are like viruses. There's always some new mutation."—Helen Hudson from *Copycat*

The characters in *Copycat* are all thinly drawn, particularly Detective Monahan. Unlike the more complex and engaging thriller *The Silence of the Lambs* (1991), *Copycat* fails to explore any character issues for Monahan aside from the need she has to solve this newest case. In *The Silence of the Lambs*, Clarice Starling (played brilliantly by Jodie Foster in a role that won her an Oscar) was a complex and fascinating character, a woman caught in the proverbial patriarchal double-bind with two very different men who seemed to hold her success in their hands. The mentor issue in that film was as compelling, if not more so, than the more forthright solving of the serial-killer case. The writers of *Copycat* had the opportunity to present an equally interesting characterization in Monahan, yet chose to follow a more mundane route. We never understand what drives Monahan, what it is she needs to "prove." The relationship between Monahan and her ex-lover is confusing and certainly unnecessary. Monahan is not a character oozing sexuality, but rather is all business, cold and steely, and lacking in warmth, so this element, no doubt designed to provide a glimpse into the other side of the Inspector, does little except to muddle the already mirky plot waters.

Warner Brothers made a strange request during press junkets for *Copycat* that the identity of the murderer not be revealed. A similar ploy was used for Neil Jordan's *The Crying Game* (1992), understandable given that film's main conceit, but *Copycat* is a different type of film, one that does not depend on a surprise revelation—although the filmmakers begin to tease the audiences with only glimpses of the murderer, hoping to plant doubts about Monahan's ex-lover and fellow police investigator, Nicoletti (Will Patton). This line is quickly dropped about mid-way through the film, adding to its near-schizophrenic mood. The events tend not to stem from solid character development, but rather seem to be mere plot contrivances. It is confusing as to why Ruben is suddenly taken off the serial killer case and sent to work on some other case involving Chinatown drug gangs and his death seems totally unnecessary other than to render him absent from the final scenes.

One of the things that makes *Copycat* so much more disturbing than its contemporary serial killer thriller, *Seven*, lies in its vivid depiction of the violence. While the victims in *Seven* were almost totally "paper victims", that is, all were already dead by the time the audience meets up with them and their murders are described rather than shown, the murder victims in *Copycat* are all living, breathing human beings and as a result, the audience is asked to become active participants in their deaths. There is something very unsettling about watching the killer fill a syringe with glass cleaner as he gleefully announces to his helpless victim that "this is really going to hurt." Suddenly this is no longer a case to be solved, a puzzle to be unravelled; it is now gratuitous violence that serves no other purpose but to titillate its audience. The film becomes little more than an exercise in one-upmanship and if box office receipts are any indication, *Copycat* transcended the boundaries of how much gore audiences are willing to accept.

—*Patricia Kowal*

REVIEWS

Chicago Tribune. October 27, 1995, p. C1.
Entertainment Weekly. November 3, 1995, p. 45.
Los Angeles Times. October 27, 1995, p. F1
Macleans. CVIII, October 30, 1995, p. 58.
Newsweek. CXXVI, November 6, 1995, p. 86.
The New Yorker. LXXI, November 13, 1995, p. 130
The New York Times. October 27, 1995, p. B15.
Rolling Stone, November 16, 1995, p. 117.
Time. CXLVI, November 13, 1995, p. 120.
Variety. October 16, 1995, p. 93.
Village Voice. November 7, 1995, XL, p. 57.
Wall Street Journal. October 27, 1995, p. A12.

Country Life

"Four stars! *Country Life* is splendidly crafted and surprisingly entertaining."—Christopher Tookey, *Daily Mail*

"Let me say it right off: *Country Life* gave me enormous pleasure."—Alexander Walker, *The Evening Standard*

"A mixture of theatrical expertise and cinematic charisma."—Andrew Sarris, *New York Observer*

"Two thumbs up!"—*Siskel & Ebert*

"A gem!"—*Sixty Second Preview*

"*Country Life* is charming and boisterous...An engaging film!"—Geoff Brown, *The Times*

Box Office Gross: $350,354

A sly, wry transposition of Anton Chekhov's play "Uncle Vanya" into the Australian outback circa 1919, *Country Life* is a richly detailed, deftly presented and enchantingly acted surprise. It unfolds slowly and earns its laughs rather than milking the audience for them, and action-oriented audiences will find it a bore. But it's literate without being stuffy, wonderfully satiric without being cruel, and continually fascinating. It's much better than *Sirens*, another recent Aussie import set in the same time and place and dealing with the same themes of repression and liberation. Where *Sirens* teased with a lot of flesh and lightweight intellectual pretensions, *Country Life* delivers on its premises with admirable delicacy.

The film belongs to veteran British stage actor Michael Blakemore, an Australian emigre who has returned to his native land with a clever conceit. Blakemore wrote a finely layered and very arch script, directed with a gentle hand, and cast himself in the role of Alexander Voysey, an Australian emigre who became a London theater critic and is now returning for a visit to the family sheep farm. It's almost as if Blakemore is playing a huge joke on himself and satirizing his own situation.

The sheep farm offers plenty of literary allusions. It is called Canterbury and its houses the Dickens family. Its inhabitants are trying against all odds to keep an upper-class British culture alive despite wallowing in the crude outback, so much so that the matriarch takes pains to distance her family name from that Dickens fellow who writes all those popular novels. Alex fled to England 22 years previously after the death of his wife, leaving behind daughter Sally (Kerry Fox), brother Jack (John Hargreaves) and mother-in-law Maude (Patricia Kennedy).

When Alex returns, it's with a refined young wife, Deborah (Greta Scacchi). He finds Canterbury has lapsed into what he considers a terrible state of crudity, its beautiful English garden abandoned because the family's had to work so hard to keep the farm afloat through World War I. It's harboring a logder, Wally (Ron Blanchard), who is apparently a useless country bumpkin. Canterbury is frequently visited by the local doctor, Max Askey (Sam Neill), who is not only a pacifist but anti-British to boot. Jack has been beaten down by farm labors, transformed from a dashing young man with grand ambitions into a bitter middle-aged underachiever with paltry horizons. Jack believes he is cultured because he has a gramophone and a collection of third-rate opera.

Appalled at how far the locals have drifted away from proper British standards, Alex sets out to put things straight by way of pompous pronouncements delivered with irritating aplomb. "Could I suggest we have dinner at the more civilized hour of eight or even eight-thirty?" he huffs at his first seven o'clock supper, ignoring the fact that work must be done on the farm at sunrise. Blakemore is excruciatingly funny. He's very good at conveying Alex's insincerity and moral bankruptcy. Gradually throughout the film, Alex is unmasked as a shallow, insecure, lecherous fake and a hopeless hypochondriac, but he still wields great influence because he has spent two decades in Britain. By implication, Alex is a scathing satire of British civilization, an indictment of the empire's base motivations, and a mirror for displaying how foolish the colonizers are for wanting to import British culture down under.

Opposing everything Alex represents is Dr. Askey, considered a Bolshevik in the village for his relentless attacks on the British war machine. He is so radical that he treats aborigines. He's also an environmentalist, firmly opposing corporate attempts to turn the outback and its native animals and plants into pasture for agribusiness. He's tolerated because he's the only doctor in town, plus he's a sweet, generous sort.

"Could I put in a plea to have dinner at the more civilized hour of 8—or even 8:30?"—Alex from *Country Life*

One of the many appealing nuances of *Country Life* is that Alex and Max never clash about politics, only about medical treatment. They stand as polar opposites and everyone spins around them.

Jack soon comes to openly despise Alex, to whom he has sent his sister's share of the farm's monthly earnings for 22 years. When Jack discovers Alex is a charlatan whose career was a paltry excuse for hobnobbing with celebrities, Jack goes into a murderous rage. Like everything else in the film, it's defused into comic inconsequence.

A potent romantic quadrangle keeps things frothy. Deborah is revealed to be unhappy in her marriage. She's also not the snob she first appeared to be and is trying hard to break out of her constraints. This beautiful British flower is an irresistible attraction to both Jack and Max, but she is intrigued only by the doctor. To Deborah, Max is a man's man with radical views and a connection to the wild. He offers her a rush of fresh air after so many stifling years with the stuffy, silly Alex. Sally is Deborah's luckless rival, a plain, sincere country girl who loves animals and farm life and admires the doctor with an unrequited love hidden beneath an easygoing friendship.

While the principals are prevented by their circumstances from realizing their various loves and ambitions, a maid named Violet (Robyn Cruze) has a carefree romance with a returning soldier who has an amputated leg. Brief glimpses of their happiness serve to reinforce how tortured and trapped the others are.

CREDITS

Dr. Max Askey: Sam Neill
Deborah Voysey: Greta Scacchi
Jack Dickens: John Hargreaves
Sally Voysey: Kerry Fox
Alexander Voysey: Michael Blakemore
Hannah: Googie Withers
Maud Dickens: Patricia Kennedy
Wally Wells: Ron Blanchard

Origin: Australia
Released: 1995
Production: Robin Dalton for an Austrialian Film Finance Corp./Dalton Films; released by UIP and Miramax Films
Direction: Michael Blakemore; based on the novel *Uncle Vanya* by Anton Chekhov
Screenplay: Michael Blakemore
Cinematography: Stephen Windon
Editing: Nicholas Beauman
Production design: Laurence Eastwood
Assistant director: Colin Fletcher, James McTeigue and Guy Campbell
Set decoration: Donna Brown
Costume design: Wendy Chuck
Make-up: David Vawser
Sound: Ben Osmo
Music: Peter Best
MPAA rating: PG-13
Running Time: 107 minutes

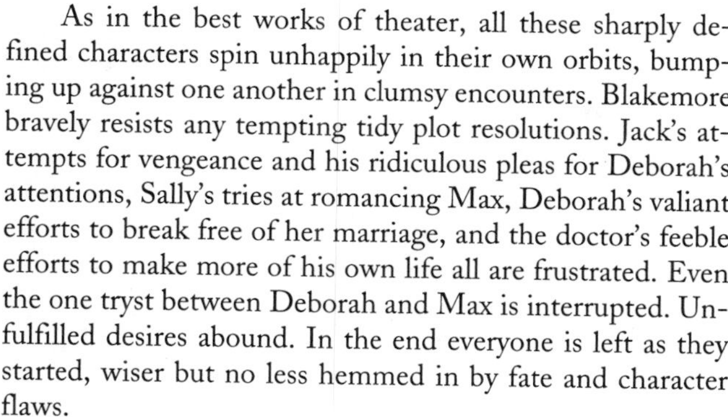

As in the best works of theater, all these sharply defined characters spin unhappily in their own orbits, bumping up against one another in clumsy encounters. Blakemore bravely resists any tempting tidy plot resolutions. Jack's attempts for vengeance and his ridiculous pleas for Deborah's attentions, Sally's tries at romancing Max, Deborah's valiant efforts to break free of her marriage, and the doctor's feeble efforts to make more of his own life all are frustrated. Even the one tryst between Deborah and Max is interrupted. Unfulfilled desires abound. In the end everyone is left as they started, wiser but no less hemmed in by fate and character flaws.

Country Life has a fine script and is masterfully directed, but it works largely because of fine ensemble acting. Blakemore makes a wonderfully despicable twit. Hargreaves, a veteran Australian actor rarely seen abroad, is splendid as a man sinking into the abyss of mundane everyday life. Neill, as usual, is charming and admirably understated. Refusing to look heroic, he deftly reveals his character's weaknesses. Scacchi is adept at presenting a portrait of a woman chafing against the restrictions of her place but not strong enough to break free. Best of all is Fox, who brings grace, dignity and heartful emotion to Sally, a role which could have sunk into stereotype. The minor characters are wonderful also, adding vibrant colors to the background of the film's rich landscape of personalities. Withers is a hoot as the stony cook who knows how to make mutton a million ways, Maurie Fields is hilarious as a drunken farmhand, and Cruze brings fine shadings to her small part.

The film's authenticity helps greatly. None of the characters transcends his or her time, place or upbringing. Whereas *Sirens* suggested that liberation is easily achieved through a little nudity, *Country Life* makes the more plausible point that repression planted by Victorian acculturation remains firmly rooted even in the wilds of Australia. Feminist awakenings or populist triumphs might have been crowd-pleasing for modern film audiences, but they wouldn't have been credible. Blakemore's observations on the foibles of British culture carry all the more punch for his refusal to give in to sappy resolutions.

Country Life is short on sentiment and emotion, and some might find it depressing. If so, they are missing a multi-layered comedy of manners and a subtle, trenchant commentary on imperialism. Blakemore has pulled off a coup and fashioned a real original. *Country Life* is a delicious treat.

—*Michael Betzold*

REVIEWS

The New York Times. July 26, 1995, p. C5.
Village Voice. August 1, 1995, p. 41.

Crimson Tide

"In the face of the ultimate nuclear showdown, one man has absolute power. And one man will do anything to stop him."—Movie tagline

"A powerhouse action thriller!"—*Rolling Stone*

"Two thumbs up."—*Siskel & Ebert*

Box Office Gross: $91,387,195

Political intrigue and international violence have been difficult cinematic concepts since the end of the Cold War. "The Enemy" now often includes greedy millionaires, depraved geniuses, or heartless fiends-regardless of political stance or ideology. Whereas films such as *From Russia with Love* (1963) and *The Spy Who Came in from the Cold* (1965) explored the glamorous and disillusioning lives of secret agents, films such as *Dr. Strangelove* (1964) and *Fail-Safe* (1964) reflected a nation's fear of living in a nuclear age. More recent films have also explored the lose-lose situation of nuclear war, such as *War Games* (1983), in which teenagers and computers learn that nuclear war can't help but end the world. In *Crimson Tide*, the World War II fighting soldier (whose orders-are-orders discipline arguably led to the bombing of Nagasaki and Hiroshima) comes face to face with the new philosophical soldier, a clash of the Titans not unlike Patton meets Grasshopper (star of television's "Kung Fu").

When Russian nationalists (read: Zhironovsky) seize control of a nuclear missile base, the U.S. military prepares for the worst. The USS Alabama, led by Captain Frank Ramsey (Gene Hackman) and Lieutenant Commander Ron Hunter (Denzel Washington), rushes to the Russian east to await further orders. World War III hangs in the balance. Quickly it becomes clear that the two men have very different management styles, and before any war is fought outside the ship, the battles for control within the ship will need to be resolved first.

During the mission, an emergency action message arrives, notifying the Alabama that the Russian rebels have gained access to the firing code of the Russian nuclear weapons. The crew of the Alabama prepares for battle. And then a second message is garbled. Have the orders been rescinded? Has the next world war begun?

Soon into the film, Ramsey selects Hunter to serve as his executive officer on the USS Alabama. Ramsey is of the old school: gruff, indeed, not unlike Captain Bly, he tests Hunter's fuse with jibes about Hunter's Harvard education. He leads through discipline, punishing misbehavior rather than rewarding achievement. Ramsey is a creature of habit: his ship, his dog, his cigars-it's enough. Hunter, on the other hand, has studied leadership at Annapolis, has studied the theory and philosophy of war, has discovered that in a war, the only winner is war. He comes to know the men in his charge; he leads not only by example but also through rewarding hard work. He speaks his men's language, citing everything from cartoon character Silver Surfer to the crew of television's "Star Trek"'s Enterprise. Increasing the torque in the film, screenwriter Michael Schiffer draws two complex, sympathetic, and often, appealing characters. One effective development technique is that the audience sees each character as a multifaceted person. Neither is a monster; neither is a saint. For instance, shortly after the Alabama begins its mission, a fire breaks out in the galley. As the ex-

CREDITS

Lieutenant Commander Ron Hunter: Denzel Washington
Captain Frank Ramsey: Gene Hackman
Zimmer: Matt Craven
Cob: George Dzundza
Weps: Viggo Mortensen

Origin: USA
Released: 1995
Production: Don Simpson and Jerry Bruckheimer for Hollywood Pictures; released by Buena Vista Pictures Distribution
Direction: Tony Scott
Screenplay: Michael Schiffer; based on a story by Michael Schiffer and Richard P. Henrick
Cinematography: Dariusz Wolski
Editing: Chris Lebenzon
Production design: Michael White
Visual Effects: Hoyt Yeatman
Costume Design: George L. Little
Sound: William B. Kaplan
Music: Hans Zimmer
MPAA rating: R
Running Time: 112 minutes

AWARDS AND NOMINATIONS

Academy Awards Nominations 1995: Best Film Editing, Best Sound

hausted firefighters are beginning to control the blaze, the captain announces a drill. Hunter finds Ramsey's actions foolhardy and disagrees publicly with Ramsey's decision. At this point the audience is willing to believe that Hunter is the thoughtful leader, while Ramsey is the proverbial "loose gun on deck." However, as the two men argue through their differences, Ramsey's argument begins to make sense: practice a drill during chaotic moments. The actual skirmish will not select a calm time and will not ensure that all are forewarned. No, according to Ramsey, readiness is only readiness if it can be achieved even out of chaos. It makes sense; Ramsey is humanized and earns the audience's respect. This balance is maintained throughout the film, even until the end, when each man wins and loses. Action and theory, the two men are more alike than they admit.

The Navy originally agreed to allow the crew of *Crimson Tide* to film inside one of their ports, but rescinded their offer after reading the first draft of the script. Upon discovering that a Navy submarine was scheduled to leave Pearl Harbor, director Tony Scott immediately flew to Hawaii with a camera crew and captured the submarine on film.

Filmmakers have given audiences a variety of submarine experiences, from the most hilarious (*Operation Petticoat*, 1959) to the most claustrophobic (*Das Boot*, 1981), among many others (*We Dive at Dawn*, 1943, *Run Silent, Run Deep*, 1958, *Up Periscope*, 1959). What it provides thematically is a barren, controlled landscape in which the tensions between the characters and the foibles of the characters themselves are in relief. With an unchanging background, with the same characters unremittingly locked in together, character development is all. For instance, throughout most of the film, the crew is at work, each man at his station. Also, throughout most of the film, the crew is on alert. Trouble abounds. The one evolving component becomes how the characters respond to the chaos, how they react when given a life and death choice. While the mechanics are state-of-the-art, the nature of the submarine itself provided the backdrop director Tony Scott (*Top Gun*, 1986) sought. "By its very nature, a nuclear submarine is a soulless, antiseptic environment,"says Scott in the film's production notes. "I want the audience to feel the anxiety that the characters feel. I wanted it to be very real and believable." Termed a "nuclear sub psychodrama," *Crimson Tide* is a psychology experiment, even as it is fast-paced entertainment.

The confined space of the submarine also helps build tension in the film. The audience, after being locked in with the crew for a significant time, is equally edgy. Tempers flare, disasters are succeeded by new disasters, and everything must be fixed, delivered, answered, handled NOW! If the crew ever strolls the hallways of the ship, *Crimson Tide* does not show it. Often the camera perches on stair landings, watching sailors half run, half jump down stairs, moving at break-neck speed to respond to the latest emergency. Only one character strolls in this film, and he, Ramsey, strolls to great effect each time. For instance, after a key skirmish, Ramsey strolls to his cabin, slowly, without sign of strain or anger. He is back in control, thinking, planning.

With the importance of the submarine thematically and stylistically, it is interesting and important to consider the set itself. *Crimson Tide* was shot mostly on two sound stages, one of which was rigged with the largest hydraulic gimbal ever created. The real USS Alabama is a Trident I C-4 configured Ohio class submarine, one of seven currently in existence. Standing six-stories high, and stretching 560 feet bow to stern (42 from port to starboard), the Alabama's purpose is to serve as a deterrent to war, although its warheads are more than 100 times more destructive than that dropped on Hiroshima.

Showcasing remains of the Cold War, conventional submarine mania and guys, guys and more guys, *Crimson Tide* charts little new territory. Nonetheless, its heart-pounding music, its endless perils, its high production values will provide great summer-time escapist fun.

—Roberta F. Green

REVIEWS

Atlanta Constitution, May 12, 1995, p. P4.
Baltimore Sun, May 12, 1995, Features, p. 4.
Boston Globe, May 12, 1995, p. 55.
Chicago Sun-Times, May 12, 1995, p. 35.
The Christian Science Monitor, May 18, 1995, p. 12.
Houston Chronicle, May 12, 1995, Weekend Preview, p. 1.
Los Angeles Times, May 12, 1995, p. F1.
Newsday, May 12, 1995, p. BO2.
The New Yorker, May 15, 1995, p. 94.
The New York Times, May 12, 1995, p. C1.
Rocky Mountain News, May 12, 1995, p. 4D.
The Salt Lake Tribune, May 12, 1995, p. E3.
The San Francisco Chronicle, May 12, 1995, p. C1.
San Francisco Examiner, May 12, 1995, p. C1.
The Wall Street Journal, May 18, 1995, p. A14.
The Washington Post, May 12, 1995, p. N48.

The Crossing Guard

"...some lives cross, others collide."—Movie tagline

Box Office Gross: $832,910

For someone so young, Sean Penn understands remorse very well. *The Crossing Guard*, which Penn wrote and directed, shows a disturbing maturity about matters of grief, loss and guilt. Whatever Penn's troubled personal life may have contributed to this film, he clearly has grown into a person who knows the territory of darker, sadder emotions.

As a character study and as a trip to the psychological underworld of humanity, *The Crossing Guard* is an accomplished and poignant effort. As pure entertainment, it is much less gripping, with long stretches where nothing much happens to advance the dramatic tension. In many respects, from its heavily atmospheric touches to its slow pace, it more resembles a European art film than a Hollywood movie with a big-name star and director. Its distributor seemed puzzled by how to market it, releasing it during the Christmas season where too many blockbusters pushed it off many multiplex screens and into more esoteric venues.

CREDITS

Freddy Gale: Jack Nicholson
John Booth: David Morse
Mary: Angelica Huston
JoJo: Robin Wright
Helen Booth: Piper Laurie
Stuart Booth: Richard Bradford
Roger: Robbie Robertson

Origin: USA
Released: 1995
Production: Sean Penn and David S. Hamburger; released by Miramax
Direction: Sean Penn
Screenplay: Sean Penn
Cinematography: Vilmos Zsigmond
Editing: Jay Cassidy
Production design: Michael Haller
Costume design: Jill Ohanneson
Sound: Per Hallberg
Casting: Don Phillips
Music: Jack Nitzsche
MPAA rating: R
Running Time: 114 minutes

The Crossing Guard explores the mental turmoil of Freddie (Jack Nicholson), a jeweler whose life has been unraveled by the tragic death of his eight-year-old daughter Emily. As the film opens, it's five years after Emily's death, and the man responsible, John Booth (David Morse) is being released from prison after serving a term for manslaughter. Possessed by a need to avenge his loss, Freddie has circled the date of Booth's release in red on his calendar. In a volcanic confrontation with his ex-wife Mary (Anjelica Huston), Freddie says he intends to kill Booth. Mary finds Freddie's plan abhorrent, but Freddie suggests that, if he carries it out, both he and Mary will feel pride and relief.

The name of Booth's character, which minus a middle name is identical to the man who assassinated Abraham Lincoln, suggests that Emily's death was just as cataclysmic among those it touched as Lincoln's was for the nation, and gradually the film reveals the scope and depth of the damage that was wrought. Not only did Emily die, but so did Freddie and Mary's marriage, which we find out, a little too late in the film, had been a joyous one. Freddie has lost not only a daughter, but a wife, a house, and all contact with two younger twin sons, who are being raised by Mary and her new husband Roger. Freddie is so damaged he cannot handle being a parent any more and he can hardly handle his business. Taking refuge in forays to a strip club (much as does the lead character in Atom Egoyan's *Exotica*), Freddie can't even handle a sexual relationship with one of the dancers. And what he can't handle at all is the swirling and confusing mix of emotions inside him: the rage, the grief and the loss of his own sense of worth.

Booth, too, Penn allows us to discover, has been irreparably damaged. For half the film, we don't know how Emily died or how culpable Booth was, which adds some needed mystery. In a quiet description of what happened, Booth tells a woman friend how he ran down Emily while driving drunk, then fled after she lay twitching on the pavement, apologizing to him for not looking both ways before she crossed the street. Booth's guilt and shame have left a huge hole in someone who quite obviously had been a very decent person.

AWARDS AND NOMINATIONS

Golden Globe Awards Nominations 1996: Best Supporting Actress (Huston)
Independent Spirit Awards Nominations 1996: Best Supporting Actor (Morse)
Screen Actors Guild Awards Nominations 1995: Best Supporting Actress (Huston)

The only person who's really grieved over Emily's death and who's had the courage to get on with her life is Mary. One of the best things about Penn's approach is that he resists the temptation to cast Mary as shallow or heartless. Huston, splendid as always in a fairly minor role, conveys a strong sense of how deeply she has been affected by Emily's death in her few scenes with Nicholson, which are among the best in the film. Mary isn't any less damaged than Freddie; she's only managed to do much better at putting the pieces of her life back together.

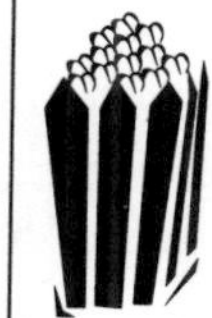

"I think freedom's overrated. If there's not something bigger than freedom, then freedom's just entertainment."—John Booth from *The Crossing Guard*

In fact, Penn casts no judgments on any of his characters. From his surface behavior, Booth appears to be a more decent man than Freddie, but that's only because Booth already has reached the depths of despair and self-abuse and Freddie is still plummeting downward. The film would be more palatable if Freddie were a more likeable character, if he didn't drink and hang out with low-lifes, if he didn't have a hair-trigger temper and a maniacal glint in his eye. It would be more palatable, but much less honest and rewarding.

Nicholson parlays some of his trademark touches—the crazed glare; the soft-spoken, barely controlled rage; the nervous twitches—into one of his best performances. Though as usual it's difficult for Nicholson to submerge his enormous presence as a very familiar actor into a new character, he downplays his usual sarcasm and substitutes much more heartfelt and troubling expressions of deep turmoil. Splendid in his scenes with Huston, Nicholson gives us a man with a deep sense of pride who has been betrayed by life and can't find the way out of his dungeon.

Though Booth is out of jail and Freddie never was confined, *The Crossing Guard* suggests that emotional prisons are much more impenetrable than the cement-block kind. Morse is fine if perhaps a little too understated, though Penn is much less successful at explicating Booth's emotional state than Freddie's; Morse must say some overly stilted lines such as "Freedom's overrated" and "What is guilt?" Penn wants to contrast Booth's friends' overly introspective encounters with Freddy's friends' drunken stupors, but Booth and his comrades come off sounding a little too much like refugees from a twelve-step meeting.

The film's main failing is that the plot is too simple and there is too much filler before the redeeming conclusion. It's inexplicable that Freddie agrees to Booth's request to give him three extra days to live, but it allows Penn to reveal more about the characters. Freddie's relationship with the stripper seems superfluous, and there are far too many scenes of the strip joint, causing one to wonder if Penn isn't using it as an excuse to put some female flesh into the film. Similarly, Booth's romantic fling seems a little far-fetched; it's not clear why a woman so classy would be so attracted to an ex-con, no matter how dreamy his eyes are. It's also implausible, near the film's end, when Booth undergoes a transformation from a gentle, guilt-wracked soul into a would-be vigilante.

Penn contributes some nice artistic touches, from an opening-scene grief encounter group to a raft of telling cinematic images. But he overuses slow motion and musical interludes so much that some sequences begin to look like music videos. Penn's techniques are a little too self-conscious and heavyhanded; if he had been a little more sparing with these flourishes, they would have been much more successful. *The Crossing Guard* would be a marvelous film if it had been more tightly edited.

Nonetheless, it's a remarkable second directorial effort for Penn, a sober and deeply affecting film. Penn is wise to resist the temptation to show any flashbacks or even still photos of Emily, so that the lost daughter is a hole in the film, just as she is a hole inside Freddie. It's much more effective for Booth to narrate how she died than for the film to show it; the loss thus becomes more gnawing and awful rather than being reduced to picture-postcard sentiment or nostalgia. *The Crossing Guard* is not about memory, but about deep black holes of emotion; it's not about trauma, but about the insufferable daily aftermath of unhealed trauma. It's only because Penn, Nicholson and Morse probe these depths so thoroughly and effectively that the reconciliation at film's end may seem a little too pat.

The Crossing Guard isn't easy to endure, but neither is life, as Penn well knows. In a rather brutally honest way, the film is remarkably uplifting. It's a genuine, earnest exploration of difficult territory, taking us down dim, twisted paths but suggesting there is light at the end of the journey.

—*Michael Betzold*

REVIEWS

New York Times. Nov. 15, 1995, p. B1 (N).
People. Nov. 27, 1995, p. 19.
Variety. Sept. 11, 1995, p. 104.
Wall Street Journal. Nov. 17, 1995, p. A16 (E).

The Crude Oasis

The Crude Oasis has the bare-bones look, sound and feel of an independent filmmaker's debut. It's not smooth, glitzy or high-powered, but it works reasonably well as a sort of sparse, moody Ingmar Bergman feminist western. It doesn't break new ground, but it shows promise.

The film is nearly a one-man show. Alex Graves wrote, directed, produced and edited it, and a small group of colleagues share multiple production roles. Its appealing star is a former television soap opera regular, Jennifer Taylor, who appeared on "The Edge of Night." In this film, she plays a woman whose life is so dim that it would be immeasurably enriched by watching soap operas.

Shot in two weeks for $25,000, *The Crude Oasis* is technically outstanding for such a low-budget effort. Graves has a knack for shooting ordinary scenes in haunting ways. The film's one love scene, shot outdoors in extreme close-up as the lovers are pelted with a torrential rainstorm, is memorable.

Most of what comes before that wondrous scene is as dry and bitter as a Kansas dust bowl. Taylor plays the emotionally parched Karen Webb, who lives a loveless, claustrophobic existence in a Wichita suburb. Her husband Jim (Robert Peterson) is a mean, crow-faced rail of a man who is an executive with a local oil company. Their marriage is like a waking nightmare for Karen. She wants desperately to have a baby, but Jim resists her advances and disappears in the middle of the night. When Karen confronts him, Jim admits to an affair, berates her for wanting a child, and tells her she's stuck with the way things are because she doesn't have it in her to cheat on him or make it on her own.

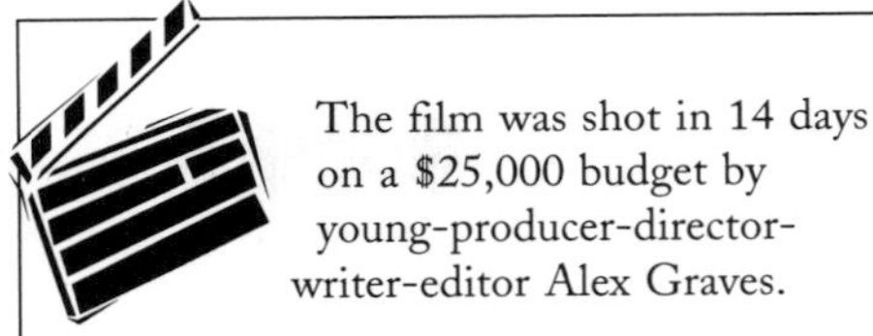

The film was shot in 14 days on a $25,000 budget by young-producer-director-writer-editor Alex Graves.

Sentenced to a life of meaningless isolation, Karen keeps house as a 1950's woman's magazine model: in high heels and modest, frilly dresses. Graves' shot of her standing stock-still, lost in a reverie, as she holds her vacuum is beautifully telling. Karen suffers from depression and is plagued by a recurrent nightmare involving a man who wears a crucifix coming towards her through a stump-infested swamp. Time weighs so heavily on her that the highlight of her day is taking her car to get gas, and she only buys $3 at a time so she'll have to visit gas stations more often.

After learning the score from her husband, Karen tries to kill herself by turning on the car in her garage, but she runs out of gas. Why she makes no other suicide attempts is never explained, but presumably it's because she's found the man of her nightmares pumping gas during one of her $3 stops.

Inexplicably, Karen stalks him. Taylor, whose performance is fascinatingly understated, gives the impression that Karen can't control her curiosity about this man, who seems incredibly ordinary. She follows him as he leaves work, stares at him as he gets coffee at a greasy spoon and pursues him to a remote, seedy bar, the Crude Oasis.

Ordinary life holds many terrors for Karen, and when trouble breaks out at the Crude Oasis, she hides herself in a bathroom stall. Graves expertly shoots her crouching on a toilet seat like a cornered deer. When the coast is clear, she follows the filling station attendant's truck to a bridge and confronts him as he is wading in the river pulling a rope. The man throttles her.

Graves has used a hackneyed plot device to stoke the tension behind these rather drab proceedings. A radio gives snippets of news reports about a missing local woman. You expect that Karen has met the woman's abductor and she is about to meet her own demise, especially when she wakes up in the man's trailer, bruised and beaten, and he begins shouting at her deliriously.

Later there are suggestions that Karen's husband is mixed up with the man in some nefarious business. Some of the company's oil is leaking into local rivers. With constant shots of a derrick pumping against a sunrise, Graves seems to be building a complicated plot about corporate terror or corruption, a la *Chinatown*, with Karen's husband and dream lover as the linchpins.

But *The Crude Oasis* turns out to be the kind of film that leads you on with perverse suggestions only to surprise you with the fact that there really is nothing much going on. Perhaps Graves' intent is to immerse his audience in Karen's insular, paranoid landscape only to liberate us and her, but that's an overly charitable explanation. More likely is that Graves wrote a start to an interesting script but couldn't figure out how to capitalize on his tantalizing foreshadowings.

The nightmare stalker turns out to be a very drab guy named Harley Underwood. As played by Aaron Shields, Harley has all the appeal of a dirty mop. His thin, straight hair hangs down in his whipped-dog face. He is beaten-down white trash. His only asset is that he has a remarkable ability to predict thunderstorms.

Karen is certainly a hard-up woman and Taylor does her best to make her look forlorn and unwanted. But even made plain and drab, Taylor is so attractive and intriguing that it's difficult to believe why she married such a dried-up, ugly man and why she's attracted to such a no-class, inarticulate and unsexy ne'er-do-well. It must be slim pickings indeed in Wichita.

The Crude Oasis boils down to an ordinary story about a ordinary woman's voyage of self-discovery, accomplished through a very ordinary means. A dejected housewife has an affair and awakens to life's possibilities. This is not very creative stuff.

But the way Graves takes us through the rather dull proceedings is inventive and shows the makings of a high-powered director. The little things are important in *The Crude Oasis*, and Graves has a way of exploiting them. The use of machine sound— the derrick, car engines, the ticking of a clock, the dull hum of appliances—is reminiscent of David Lynch's early work (in *Eraserhead* and *The Elephant Man*, especially). The sounds suggest that daily life in the featureless American landscape has a grating quality. Graves nicely contrasts Karen's penned-in home life with the limitless horizon of Harley's world, where a trailer sits amid a field that stretches endlessly and where the best entertainment is watching a thunderstorm roll in at night.

Then there's that scene: Karen and Harley embracing as the raindrops fall, kissing as torrents pound down on their faces. In a film rife with religious references, the scene is like a baptism into desire, a washing away of the oily, dirty, confined and limited life both have led. It is a masterful, oddly liberating moment.

Taylor, on screen for most of the film and in close-up for much of it, gives the film its wrenching emotional center. She is free of the movie-star aura that often ruins such a performance; she does not look like a prima donna deliberately playing against type. She is vulnerable and haunted but her eyes never lose a spark of dignity; she is an appealing real woman, not victimized or glamorized, and that makes her plight all the more immediate and unnerving.

The Crude Oasis is not going to be much-watched or much-adulated this time around, but if Graves makes it, it could end up being a debut film looked back upon for evidence of how a great director developed his techniques. It's raw, crude and ultimately unsatisfying, but it has touches of mastery that suggest possibilities as limitless as Karen's horizons at the film's exhilarating climax.

—Michael Betzold

CREDITS

Karen Webb: Jennifer Taylor
Harley Underwood: Aaron Shields
Jim Webb: Robert Peterson
Earp: Mussef Sibay
Stone: Lynn Bieler
Cheri: Roberta Eaton

Origin: USA
Released: 1995
Production: Alex Graves; released by Miramax Films
Direction: Alex Graves
Screenplay: Alex Graves
Cinematography: Steven Quale
Editing: Alex Graves
Art Direction: Tom Mittlestadt
Sound: Steven Rea
Music: Steven Bramson
Production manager/assistant director: Greg Tennant
MPAA rating: R
Running Time: 81 minutes

REVIEWS

The New York Times. July 7, 1995, p. C10.
Variety. July 10, 1995, p. 35.
Village Voice. July 11, 1995, p. 54.

Crumb

"A marvelous movie! An instant American classic!"—David Ansen, *Newsweek*

"A great and astonishing film."—Roger Ebert, *Siskel & Ebert*

"Amazing! *Crumb* is real: real funny, real creepy, really good....A spooky spellbinder!"—Richard Corliss, *Time Magazine*

Box Office Gross: $3,174,695

To say that Terry Zwigoff's documentary *Crumb* is unforgettable is to understate its impact. *Crumb*, the same film that won the Grand Jury Prize at Sundance, was unceremoniously halted by Oscar voters after only twenty-five minutes into its viewing. This gives you some idea of the unique and provocative nature of this documentary about R.(Robert) Crumb. In this fascinating yet disturbing film, filmmaker Terry Zwigoff has documented the life, the art, and the influences of the comic strip artist who created Fritz the Cat, Mr. Natural, and other early Zap Comix characters.

According to Zwigoff, "It's about what it's like to be an outsider, how sometimes that's an advantage, though not usually...And it has something to say about growing up in American families in the fifties.

Zwigoff has an extraordinary advantage when it comes to the topic of Robert Crumb; he has known him for more than twenty-five years. They met in the early seventies, when they worked together on an animal rights comic book. Thereafter Zwigoff published several of Crumb's comics, and even played in his band, The Cheap Suit Serenaders.

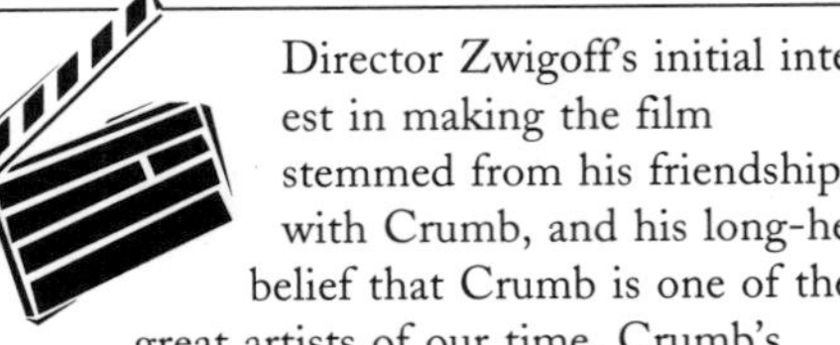

Director Zwigoff's initial interest in making the film stemmed from his friendship with Crumb, and his long-held belief that Crumb is one of the great artists of our time. Crumb's comic wcrk is more widely read today than ever.

The film combines interviews with Crumb's mother and two brothers, with comments from both his critics and his fans. Add to this samplings of Crumb's art, and a camera that unrelentingly follows this shy man—from public engagements to private moments at home, and even in quiet moments sketching—and what emerges is an unsettling gestalt of an artist.

The film, about the fifty-year-old cartoonist, reveals his humble beginnings in Philadelphia, his stint in Cleveland writing greeting cards, and finally his emergence as a major artist in the underground counterculture of the sixties. After the film's completion, which took six years to put together, it received the support of David Lynch, who has put his name to its "presentation."

In an interview with the *New York Times*, Lynch said that the film does three things. "One, it gives a full picture of the sixties, the whole ball of wax. Two, it shows one of the most unbelievable families I've ever seen. And three, better than any other film, it depicts the life and drives of an artist..."

Despite his renown, Crumb has not grown wealthy. In one scene where Crumb is speaking at the Philadelphia School of Art, he tells the audience that his famous record cover for Janis Joplin's Cheap Thrills album made someone else rich.

In 1970, when Ralph Bakshi acquired the rights to Crumb's cartoon character Fritz The Cat and made the first X-rated feature-length cartoon, Crumb again wasn't the financial winner. Crumb explains that he didn't have anything to do with the film and found the film such an embarrassment that he killed Fritz's character out of sheer anger.

Even the famous "Keep on Truckin'" poster caused Crumb financial grief when, in 1977, a judge ruled that Crumb didn't own the copyright.

If Crumb has neglected to receive financial recognition, he has certainly received critical recognition. *People*, *Newsweek*, and *BBC-TV* have all profiled Crumb and his work, and in 1990 the New York Museum of Modern Art featured Crumb's work in their show, "High and Low." This attention has widened Crumb's circle of admirers far beyond his comic book audience to include, among others, art collectors, critics, and other art experts, such as Robert Hughes, who praised Crumb as the "Brueghel of the 20th Century."

Crumb's artistic explorations are unbounded by the norms of so-called "good taste," exposing to the light of day the place where we may not necessarily live, but some of us have been known to visit now and then. Although many may find his comical journey into the anxieties and dark sexual fantasies of our tormented selves to be more frightening than enlightening, Crumb's popularity proves that he touches a chord in the souls of many of his fans.

Part of the humor of his art has always been its "political incorrectness," even before the term existed; he lampoons everyone, including his own fans. In the film, Dierdre English, former editor of *Mother Jones* magazine, and

Trina Robbins, a cartoonist, suggest that Crumb oversteps the boundaries of satire and enters the arena of racism, sexism, and pornography.

His images of women are disturbing in that many are dehumanized into pure sex objects. Crumb portrays women with large breasts, massive, muscular legs and buttocks, and fierce almost reptilian faces—that is, when he gives them faces. His sketches include nudes with buckets over their heads, and even one Amazonian woman who hasn't a head at all.

The hero is generally a skinny little guy whose small frame holds more anxiety than seems physically possible, and as his tension exudes from every pore, his eyes bug out in an alarming fashion.

Crumb's women are all larger than life, certainly larger than the comic's hero, who has a marked resemblance to Crumb himself. Crumb calls him, "the little guy who lives inside my brain."

In the film, we follow Crumb down a city street as he, in his trademark fedora and baggy pants, goofs among the people on the street, as detached as if he's watching TV, and just as critical. As he sketches the homeless people sitting on the sidewalk around him, his drawings reveal a dark humor and a detachment that are eerie. It is as though Crumb is not one of us, and frankly, doesn't care to be.

Crumb is a quiet, unassuming sort of guy, interested in the things of the past. He collects old jazz records, wears old clothes, has an old phonograph player, and watches an old black-and-white TV. You get the feeling that he's on his own private pilgrimage back to when things were good and wholesome. And yet...

Crumb was born in Philadelphia, the third of five children. When Crumb was a child, his ex-marine father, author of "How to Train People Effectively," broke his son's collarbone in anger. It appears from the other brothers' reminiscences that he was a brutal man, who had very specific expectations about his children. At one point his father told older brother Charles that if he didn't get a job he would make his life a living hell. Their father's manipulation extended to all the children, including Crumb. In the early seventies, his father cut off all communication with his son after he saw some of his work.

Their mother wasn't much more supportive. Addicted to diet pills when the children were young, she exposed the children to her violently erratic behavior, both toward them and her husband.

Although Crumb started drawing at a very young age, his brother Charles was the one who got him started in comics. Charles was the one who organized all five of the children into, what he named, the "Animal Town Comic Club." Each had an assignment, and, as Crumb says in the film, the experience taught him more about drawing comics than any art school could have.

Although Charles was a great inspiration, he had serious emotional problems. Obsessed with comics, Charles drew and drew, even at times dressing like one of his characters. But the fire that sparked this obsession grew out of control. In one of the last comics that Charles drew, the cartoons become overloaded with text, forcing the characters into the bottom of the comic frame. Finally it's all text, and even the text starts to become garbled. There follows page after page of unreadable text-like nonsense getting smaller and smaller, with more and more on the page until it becomes clear that Charles is slipping into the illness that will plague him all his life. At the time of the filming, Charles is living at home with his mother, under heavy medication for manic depression. His candor and wit in the film reveal an intelligent yet unhappy man who hasn't the will even to leave the house. Sadly, before Zwigoff finished the film, Charles had taken his own life.

Crumb's other brother, Maxon, is an artist who lives from begging Buddha-style on the streets of San Francisco. He is also emotionally troubled. Arrested for molesting a stranger, he was detained in a psychiatric ward. After that experience, he adopted the more innocuous lifestyle of self-mortification. Maxon lives in a run-down hotel, where we find him meditating on a bed of nails, and eating yards and yards of cotton tape to cleanse his bowels.

The film shows how Crumb's two brothers never escaped the emotional maelstrom of their childhood, and

CREDITS

R. (Robert) Crumb: R. (Robert) Crumb
Charles Crumb: Charles Crumb
Maxon Crumb: Maxon Crumb
Dierdre English: Dierdre English
Trina Robbins: Trina Robbins
Robert Hughes: Robert Hughes

Origin: USA
Released: 1995
Production: Lynn O'Donnell and Terry Zwigoff; released by Sony Classics
Direction: Terry Zwigoff
Cinematography: Maryse Allberti
Editing: Victor Livingston
Sound: Scott Breindel
MPAA rating: R
Running Time: 119 minutes

AWARDS AND NOMINATIONS

National Society of Film Critics Awards 1995: Best Documentary
Sundance Film Festival Awards 1995: Grand Jury Prize-Documentary, Best Cinematography (Alberti)

how precarious and fragile was R. Crumb's escape. Looking for the moment that Crumb found his freedom, you could say it was in 1965 when he took LSD for the first time. The visions he experienced at this time became the inspiration for his most famous characters, including Mr. Natural, Flakey Foont, and the Vulture Demonesses. He calls them stream of consciousness figures, and with their bug eyes, big pores, enormous breasts, and general ugliness, Crumb chronicles what he sees as the horror of life in America.

The film *Crumb* is insightful, almost unbearably so. It is the perfect no holds barred compliment to Crumb's own style of drawing. Like Crumb, Zwigoff has pushed the parameters of "good taste" and the result is an honest look at an elusive artist. And yet the light thrown on the artist and his life is like a strobe light: you think you are seeing everything, but really you only see half—but half is more than most filmmakers ever dare to reveal.

Zwigoff has made a courageous and startling documentary that honors and yet humanizes its subject. Crumb reveals his terrors through his art, Zwigoff simply gives them a context.

Martha Graham once said that, for the artist, to reveal oneself is his greatest privilege and his greatest terror. It could also be said of Crumb, that it is perhaps the artist's greatest salvation. Whatever you think of *Crumb*, one thing is certain. The images in this film will never leave you.

—Diane Hatch-Avis

REVIEWS

Detour Magazine, May 1995, p. 118.
Entertainment Today, May 4, 1995, p.15.
The Hollywood Reporter, September 27, 1994, p. 15.
L.A. Weekly, April 28, 1995, p.29.
The Los Angeles Times, April 23, 1995, p. 4 Calendar.
The New York Times, April 23, 1995, p.13.
The New Yorker, May 1, 1995, p.91.
Rolling Stone, May 4, 1995, p. 76.
Vogue, May 1995, p. 156.

Cry, the Beloved Country

Box Office Gross: $230,489

Cry, the Beloved Country is a faithful adaptation of Alan Paton's classic novel, published to great acclaim in 1946. The novel has sold more than fifteen million copies worldwide and is still regarded as the definitive, epic treatment of apartheid. Paton had a distinguished career as an activist against racial separation, founding the Liberal Party and continuing a writing career that emphasized the reconciliation of white and blacks. A recent biography by Peter F. Alexander, and now this film, carry on the efforts of South Africans to reassess the roots of racial conflict and harmony. An earlier adaption of the novel in 1952, starring Sidney Poitier and Canada Lee, stressed the divisions between people; this new adaptation brings out the novel's sense of hope for an interracial nation. It is the first feature film to be produced in South Africa since Nelson Mandela was elected president.

As reviewers have noted, the novel and film have a biblical tone. The characters seem to emerge from a parable, giving both the novel and film a mythic force, but also a sense of being a little to pat—even a little contrived. Father Stephen Kumalo (James Earl Jones) is a saintly, unworldly, Anglican Zulu minister. His whole life has been spent in the service of a small congregation in Natal, far away from city life and the political agitation over apartheid. He is drawn to Johannesburg in search of his missing son and sister. He is so naive and trusting that he is easily robbed by a black con man, and he has to rely on the help of Father Msimangu (Vusi Kunene), a younger man used to the city's corruption.

What Father Kumalo finds is not merely discrimination against blacks, but an underclass of young black men and women who have turned to crime as a means of survival. His sister has become a prostitute, and his son has killed a white man during a burglary. A bewildered Kumalo is angered and almost shattered by these revelations, yet he never loses his humanity, his desire to understand sin, or his belief in redemption.

It is difficult to see how James Earl Jones could have improved on his performance. Jones is a large man with a famous, resonant voice. He seems, in fact, just too big for the part of this humble man of the cloth. Yet Jones, now in his mid-sixties, adopts a slightly hunched-over posture in keeping with his character's modesty and sorrow. Jones cries easily and unaffectedly and has admitted in an interview that he began crying as soon as the filming began. At one point, his character is given a line referring to his constant tears, which distress Father Kumalo but which he does not try to conceal. The weeping reflects the film's and novel's a cry for a beloved country that has so aggrieved itself. Father Kumalo is lamenting not merely his family's misfortune but a nation's, for his son has killed a white man—not any white man but one who has worked wholeheartedly to abolish apartheid.

Absalom, Father Kumalo's son, has killed out of fear and panic. He is presented as a decent man who has made a grave mistake. But under apartheid he hangs—not only because he is black but because his accomplice, the son of Father Kumalo's brother John (Charles S. Dutton), has been able to shift all the blame onto Absalom. John has hired a good lawyer and has no compunctions about sacrificing Absalom, for John is as cynical as his brother is innocent. John is a political agitator, ruthlessly exploiting the system. When Absalom is convicted, John looks at his brother smugly, as if in vindication of his world view.

It would seem that there is no place for Father Kumalo's kind of Christianity. But a chance meeting between Father Kumalo and James Jarvis (Richard Harris), the father of the man Absalom killed, changes the dynamic of the story. The two men meet in Johannesburg while Father Kumalo is trying to find out what happened to his parishioner who left her home in Natal for the city. When Kumalo realizes that Jarvis is the father of the man his son killed, he turns away in fear and shame. Jarvis, impressed with Kumalo's gentleness and puzzled as to why Kumalo should express so much emotion, presses Kumalo to explain his feelings. Haltingly, Kumalo confesses that his son has killed Jarvis's son. This is the turning-point in the film. How will Jarvis react? He has been estranged from his son, angry over his son's anti-apartheid politics but also deeply hurt that his son has rejected him. The hardened but humiliated Jarvis is softened by Kumalo. He can hardly attack such a humble man. Rather he seems stunned that such a saintly figure could have a son who could commit such a heinous crime.

Father Kumalo brings out a gentleness in Jarvis. As the two men talk, Jarvis realizes that, in a sense, they know each other. In fact, Jarvis is a rich farmer whose land abuts Father Kumalo's church. Kumalo admits that he often saw Jarvis and his son traveling down the road, and Kumalo even comments on the boy's liveliness. That these two men should have been neighbors and had lives and experiences that approximate each other's is devastating to Jarvis. Until now, he has been able to keep the idea of apartheid sacrosanct and to see blacks as other than himself. Now he is united to Father Kumalo in the experience of losing a son.

The symmetry of the story is what makes it seem biblical and a parable of racial reconciliation. It verges on the sentimental and the contrived, but the performances of James Earl Jones and Richard Harris vivify the story and make is seem less schematic. Harris is magnificent. His craggy face seems at first stony with anger and hate. He is contemptuous of his son's politics and believes that his son's death vindicates his view that the blacks are not worth helping. When he is touched by Father Kumalo, his face retains its rigid veneer, but his eyes lose their fire and seem to absorb rather than reject what he sees of the black man. The turning-point scene is handled with incredible delicacy; it depends on Harris making the transition from enmity to compassion. The transition is credible because Father Kumalo's gentleness makes its impact on Jarvis before he learns that it is Kumalo's son who has killed his son. Jarvis is already speaking tenderly to Kumalo, and then the scene extends that emotion as Jarvis becomes involved in Kumalo's life.

Jarvis says little about his transformation. He remains hurt by what happened to his son, and he is not a man who would easily talk about his feelings. Instead, he makes gestures—visiting Kumalo's church, for example. Actually, he takes refuge in it during a storm, literally coming under Kumalo's roof, sharing his values, so to speak, and discovering

CREDITS

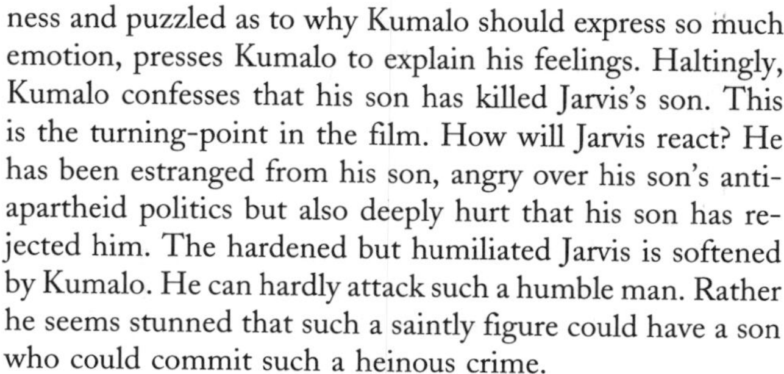

Father Stephen Kumalo: James Earl Jones
James Jarvis: Richard Harris
Father Msimangu: Vusi Kunene
Katie: Leteti Khumalo
John Kumalo: Charles S. Dutton
Absalom Kumalo: Eric Miyeni

Origin: USA
Released: 1995
Production: Anant Singh for a Distant Horizon, Alpine Films and Videovision Entertainment production; released by Miramax
Direction: Darrell James Roodt
Screenplay: Ronald Harwood; based on the novel by Alan Paton
Cinematography: Paul Gilpin
Editing: David Heitner
Production design: David Barkham
Costume design: Ray Filipo
Sound: Richard Sprawson
Casting: Marina Van Tonder
Assistant director: Graham Hickson
Music: John Barry
MPAA rating: PG
Running Time: 111 minutes

AWARDS AND NOMINATIONS

Screen Actors Guild Awards Nominations 1995:
Best Actor (Jones)

that the church's roof is so full of leaks it is hardly possible to find a dry spot in this sanctuary.

Near the end of the film, Jarvis tells Kumalo he will provide funds for a new church. The men meet outside and are set against a panoramic view of the South African countryside. Jarvis on his horse and Kumalo walking on the ground are still symbols of apartheid, of the distance that separates whites and blacks, but they are on common ground, the scene implies, and the beautiful, paradisal landscape seems to suggest there is room for all, and that sooner or later men like Jarvis will get off their high horses.

Cry, the Beloved Country remains faithful to the novel even as it is suffused with the spirit of a new South Africa. In 1952, the scene between Jarvis and Kumalo could not have seemed like anything more than wish fulfillment. Now, the scene seems prophetic and not at all improbable. Similarly, the scenes between blacks, in which the corruption of the apartheid system drives them to crime and cynicism, seem not merely a condemnation of whites for perpetuating social injustice but a challenge to blacks to rise above a system not of their own making. They are no longer merely victims but must redress evil and be active on behalf of their own salvation.

Father Kumalo cannot represent this aspect of the film, since he is plainly at a loss in an urban environment. But his nobility is complemented by the fierce, practical, and dedicated energy of Father Msimangu, played with great integrity by Vusi Kunene. There is nothing meek about Father Msimangu, whose toughness bodes well for the future. It is hard not to take him as a symbol of a new, resilient South Africa.

—*Carl Rollyson*

The Cure

"It is funny, sweet and marvelously acted."—John Corcoran, *KCAL-TV*

"A powerful tale of friendship. *The Cure* stands as a testament to friendship, loyalty, and love."—Garret Glaser, *KNBC-TV*

"One of those not-to-be-missed movies...smart, funny and poignant."—*WOR Radio*

Box Office Gross: $2,568,429

Joseph Mazello and Brad Renfro star as two 11-year-olds who form an unlikely friendship in *The Cure*. © 1995 Universal City Studios, Inc. Courtesy of MCA Publishing Rights, a Division of MCA Inc. All rights reserved.

It was only a matter of time before someone made a film about children with AIDS. It is good to report that *The Cure* deals with the subject with sensitivity and dignity. Its inherent melodrama does not keep the film from being humorous and entertaining, though it is assuredly a "three-hanky" film. Handled with grace and humanity at the hands of director Peter Horton, screenwriter Robert Kuhn, and actors Brad Renfro, Joseph Mazzello, and Annabella Sciorra, this film is a first-rate addition to two film genres: coming of age stories and weepy melodramas.

When the audience meets young Erik (Brad Renfro), he is being taunted by neighborhood boys because his new neighbor is a boy with AIDS. It is summer, and sullen Erik slowly drifts into a friendship with his new neighbor Dexter (Joseph Mazzello), if only out of boredom and loneli-

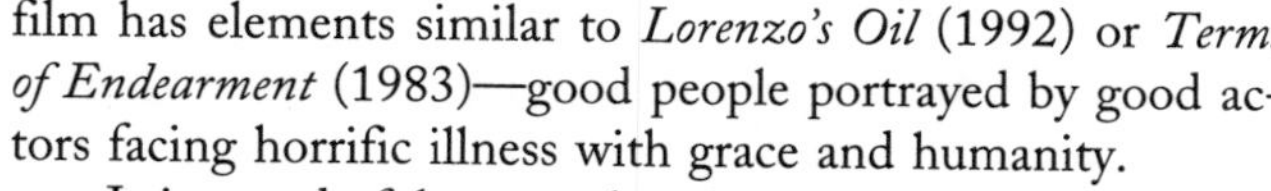

ness. Slowly and skeptically he becomes Dexter's best friend, protecting him from the ignorant neighborhood boys, playing elaborate war games, and "inner-tubing" down the river. They have much in common: both boys are fatherless, and both need companionship. Joseph, who received AIDS in a blood transfusion, lives with his mother (Annabella Sciorra) and Erik lives alone with his mother (Diana Scarwid). Their mothers could not be more different. Where Dexter's mom is loving and kind, Erik's is cool and distant.

This film marks Peter Horton's feature film directorial debut.

Some may find fault in this film in the lack of exposition regarding Dexter's family situation. The audience never knows what his mom does for a living, nor is it made clear what happened to Dexter's father. But this is a minor issue given that the film's focus is the relationship between the boys as it affects the progress of Dexter's illness. Eventually, Erik decides that he wants to find a cure for AIDS, and the boys embark on a journey to find the cure—and the search nearly ends up in disaster. As in *Philadelphia* (1993), *Longtime Companion* (1990), or other films dealing with this tragic illness, the characters fight on against formidable obstacles. The boys learn a great deal about themselves and the world, and the audience gets a truly cathartic experience.

There is no question that the film is manipulative; it pulls unabashedly at the heart strings, particularly in its last scenes where the characters display a nobility that Mother Teresa would find enviable. But Horton, in his debut as a feature film director, and company are so earnest in their telling of the tale of friendship and tragedy that the sense of manipulation (intended or unintended) is forgiven. This film has elements similar to *Lorenzo's Oil* (1992) or *Terms of Endearment* (1983)—good people portrayed by good actors facing horrific illness with grace and humanity.

It is wonderful to see that, in creating the story about the closeness of two boys struggling with AIDS, the filmmakers have made a film applicable to anyone dealing with AIDS, and indeed, to anyone fighting any terminal illness. Horton achieves an excellent verisimilitude in that he aims for a very real sense of boys at play, and he keeps the boys playing even in the face of death. Sometimes the tone is humorous, like when the boys try to hang some stuffed animals from Dexter's hospital bed, and sometimes the tone is more serious, as when they have a tender scene in a tent where Dexter expresses his fears. Perhaps they speak more eloquently and tenderly than boys of their age might, but the drama is served well by this scene, and it doesn't diminish the film's naturalism.

Horton always keeps the point-of-view interesting with creative camera work, aided by the excellent cinematography of Andrew Dintenfass. For example, he introduces the boys to the audience and to each other through a series of scenes where they each play on opposite sides of a picket fence, with Mazzello an invisible voice from the other side. As a symbol for the wall between them, the fence becomes an interesting visual element of the scenes, as Renfro begins to look through the fence and as Mazzello becomes occasionally (though incompletely) visible through the slats. (It is also a literary illusion to the fence painted by Tom Sawyer and Huck Finn, and the connection is reinforced later as the boys are rafting down a river in the deep south.) Horton mixes his sensitivity and creativity in the scene where Erik has dinner with Dexter and his mom. Unaccustomed to eating at a table with others present, Erik devours his ice cream sundae in a sequence of camera shots that accentuate his poor manners through loud sounds and extreme close- ups. Then, as Dexter is carried to bed by his mother in the foreground, the camera catches Erik in the background watching quietly through the dining room entrance, underscoring that he is an outsider to the close relationship between mother and son.

As Dexter, Mazzello brings the same efferevescence and polish that he brought to *Jurassic Park* (1994) and *The River Wild* (1995). He imbues Dexter with a sense of confidence and serenity which is an excellent counterpoint to Renfro's introverted petulance. In an early scene, before they become friends, Erik yells across the fence, "Do you want me to come over there and whoop your ass?" Mazzello's squeaky voice replies with a perky "How long will it take?" Later, when Erik comments on how short Dexter is, Dexter matter-of-factly explains that "If you look at the lower limit of what's normal for my age, I'm only 4 inches shorter."

CREDITS

Dexter: Joseph Mazzello
Erik: Brad Renfro
Gail: Diana Scarwid
Dr. Stevens-Bruce Davison
Linda: Annabella Sciorra

Origin: USA
Released: 1995
Production: Mark Burg and Eric Eisner for Island Pictures; released by Universal Pictures
Direction: Peter Horton
Screenplay: Robert Kuhn
Cinematography: Andrew Dintenfass
Editing: Anthony Sherin
Art direction: Armin Ganz
Music: Dave Grusin
MPAA rating: PG-13
Running Time: 95 minutes

Brad Renfro is perfectly cast as Erik. Renfro will be remembered for his title role in *The Client* (1994). As in that film, he plays a Southern boy on the brink of puberty who is forced to pretend he is more mature than his years because of a difficult home life. He captures the loneliness of this boy whose mom "works 20 to 22 hours a day," who cooks his own meals in a microwave oven, and who can create endless ways to torture his toy army men or teddy bears. Renfro, like Mazzello, is a natural. He has a naturalism that adult actors seem to work hard to achieve. Writer Kuhn has given him an active and very true-to-life character. Erik seems just like any boy his age: he attacks everything with the same kind of intensity, searching for a cure for AIDS as if it were of the same importance as playing army or inner-tubing down the river. He creates notebooks with descriptions of the different weeds and shrubs that he is sure will cure the AIDS virus, depicting a mixture of determination and cockiness that is humorous and poignant. The scene where Renfro presents Mazzello with "The Periodic Table of Candies," mixing Butterfingers and Mars bars as if they were Oxygen and Nitrogen, is funny—but it is poignant as well, since Renfro's earnestness and high expectations are clearly childhood delusions. Renfro's attempts at finding the cure for AIDS are emblematic of this young boy's inability to realize that in experimenting with the ingestion of huge amounts of candies, weeds, or shrubs, he might be endangering his sick friend's life. Nor does he know the danger of insisting that he and Dexter go on the journey to New Orleans to find the cure. Director Horton and Renfro wisely understand that to a boy this age (and in particular to this boy) every "project" is attacked with the same ferocity, because his world has not expanded enough to distinguish the difference between play and reality.

"These aren't moms, they're women!"—Erik looking at a copy of *Playboy* in *The Cure*

This lack of boundary between play and reality is the centerpiece of the film. It is the discovery of the difference that changes Erik forever, just as the discovery seems to have already changed Dexter and his mother. By the film's end, Renfro has gracefully (and subtly) changed, so that he is still a boy, but a boy sobered by facing reality.

As Linda, Dexter's mother, Annabella Sciorra turns in a restrained and touching performance. Her character seems nearly too good to be true: she seems to have virtually no conflict with her son in the beginning of the film, and maintains a stiff upper-lip throughout. However, her attempts to hold back tears make the situation seem even more painful, and one scene in which Erik discovers her crying on the stairs after putting Dexter to bed is very moving. She also has a terrific scene in which she confronts Erik's selfish mother, played by the excellent Diana Scarwid. It is a powerful and unusual scene, played by two excellent actresses.

Bruce Davison is excellent as Dexter's compassionate doctor: this makes the second AIDS-related film for Davison, having been Oscar-nominated for portraying an AIDS victim in *Longtime Companion*.

Dave Grusin, one of the best composers in film music today, provides another great score. And Marc Cohn wrote (and performs) a beautiful song for the film, "My Great Escape," which enhances the action and fits perfectly with Grusin's mixture of pop and folk sounds.

Though many may find its sentimatlity a bit heavy-handed and its characters a bit too noble, there is no denying that *The Cure* is a beautifully crafted and acted film. Its creators should be proud of their contribution.

—*Kirby Tepper*

Cutthroat Island

Box Office Gross: $6,554,449

From the time Karen Allen first punched Harrison Ford in *Raiders of the Lost Ark*, women of today have wanted hardy heroines with whom they could identify. No longer would they be willing to watch the leading female cower in a corner as the hero and villain duked it out. Nowadays, it is not unusual for women to want to partake in the heroic myths, to share in the "wild west," for example, as was offered in *Bad Girls* or to gain access to science fiction fantasy through Sigourney Weaver in the *Alien* trilogy. *Cutthroat Island* is their opportunity to share in the swashbuckler theme.

It's hard to believe, but after years of being a neglected genre, the best pirate story two screenwriters and four story writers could come up with is so familiar that it could have been made with Errol Flynn in the 1940s and no one would have known the difference. It seems the only innovation they could come up with was to give the Errol Flynn role to a woman. But even that doesn't help much. It's probably a shame that none of those six writers was a woman.

Cutthroat Island is the story of Morgan Adams (Geena Davis) whose father, Black Harry (Harris Yulin) is killed by her uncle, Dawg Brown (Frank Langella) because he refuses to relinquish his third of a map to her grandfather's treasure: the contents of a Spanish gold ship. Morgan, however, does have his portion of the map, but she can't read it because it seems to be written in Latin.

So, into town Morgan and a few trusty cohorts go to find someone who can. The result is the purchase of an educated con man and thief, William Shaw (Matthew Modine) who was arrested and is now being sold as a slave. The acquisition, however, does not go smoothly after someone matches Morgan to a wanted poster. Now she and Shaw must make a hasty getaway that virtually destroys the town of Port Royal, Jamaica.

The filmmakers combed the world in search of perfect locations for this story, and decided on Malta, a small island south of Sicily in the Mediterranean Sea. Malta is the home of the Mediterranean Film Studios, which houses the largest water tanks in the world that are perfect for filming controlled ocean scenes.

Next they're off to the town of Spittlefield where Morgan's other uncle, Mordachai Fingers (George Murcell), holds the last third of the map (the other third is in the hands of Dawg Brown). During a brawl which helps to destroy that town, Shaw suddenly finds himself in possession of Mordachai's part of the map.

Now they have a good indication of where the treasure lay—on the uncharted Cutthroat Island—and an idea of how to get there. But nipping at their heels, is Dawg Brown...and the governor of Jamaica. A chase and a storm at sea are followed by discovery of the island where our intrepid heroes steal Dawg's portion of the map, find the treasure, then are found by Dawg and his crew who promptly

CREDITS

Morgan Adams: Geena Davis
William Shaw: Matthew Modine
Dawg Brown: Frank Langella
John Reed: Maury Chaykin
Black Harry: Harris Yulin
Glasspoole: Stan Shaw
Mr. Blair: Rex Linn
Snelgrave: Paul Dillon
Bowen: Chris Masterson
Scully: Jimmie F. Skaggs
Bishop: Carl Chase
Captain Trotter: Angus Wright
Mordachai Fingers: George Murcell

Origin: USA
Released: 1995

Production: Mario Kassar and Renny Harlin for Carolco/Forge; distributed by MGM
Direction: Renny Harlin
Screenplay: Robert King and Marc Norman; from a story by Michael Frost Beckner, James Gorman, Bruce Evans, and Raynold Gideon
Cinematography: Peter Levy
Editing: Frank J. Urioste and Ralph E. Winters
Production design: Norman Garwood
Set decoration: Maggie Gray
Costume design: Enrico Sabbatini
Music: John Debney
Digital and Visual Effects: Jeffrey A. Okun
MPAA rating: PG-13
Running Time: 123 minutes

throw the heroes over a cliff. But of course they survive, and the result is a colossal battle on the high seas for control of the gold.

It is a plot with no surprises except for that of making the hero a woman. Davis can certainly swash a buckle with the best of them, and she is a credible but not quite on target Morgan Adams. She certainly earns her pay here climbing masts, fighting hand-to-hand with sabres, and falling off roofs onto racing carriages (one can't help but wonder if her husband who also happens to be the director, Renny Harlin, isn't a bit of a masochist to put his wife through it all), but one winces every time she has to deliver the story's stilted dialogue.

> "Historically, there were women pirates, famously ferocious ones. It was such a lawless time, and there weren't the kind of rules that one would expect in more 'polite society.'"—Geena Davis on her role as a woman pirate captain

Similarly, Matthew Modine, who replaced Michael Douglas when he dropped out of the film, is also passable as the scholarly rogue Shaw, but somehow the part seems beneath an actor who showed such promise earlier in his career (*Full Metal Jacket*, *Birdy)*. Together, the two create a typical Hollywood love-hate relationship, but there are no romantic sparks on the screen to let love win out in the end believably.

Director Harlin (*Cliffhanger*, *Nightmare on Elm Street IV*, *Die Hard 2*) is obviously a specialist in action films, but here he gives in so thoroughly to style that he abandons character development and story originality completely. In *Cutthroat Island*, Harlin has a mega-budget ($80 million), but the result is little more than just a inflated version of his earlier action films.

Oh, it looks great, with the island of Malta substituting for 17th century Jamaica, Thailand doubling as Cutthroat Island, and the talents of three-time Oscar nominated Norman Garwood (*Hook*, *Glory*, *Brazil*) providing the production's design, but its all a facade. *Cutthroat Island* fills the screen with beautiful scenery, evocative costumes and landscapes, and feverish and frequent action scenes, but what it really fills it with is ultimately empty. There's no wit, only strained humor, and action that is unrelenting and overblown (as is John Debney's over-the-top score).

Originally, *Cutthroat Island* was scheduled for release in the summer of 1996, but it was postponed until Christmas. This left MGM without a big summer movie (and *Cutthroat Island* would have made better summer than winter fare), but it also had another effect. In November, the film's production company, Carolco (whose coveted assets include such blockbusters as *Total Recall*, *Rambo*, and the *Terminator* series), declared Chapter 11 bankruptcy. It is doubted that the big-budgeted *Cutthroat Island* will do well enough at the box office to rescue it.

—Beverley Bare Buehrer

REVIEWS

Chicago Tribune. December 22, 1995, section Friday, p.
Entertainment Weekly. January 5, 1996
The New York Times. December 22, 1995
Variety. December 22, 1995

Dangerous Minds

"She broke the rules...and changed their lives."—Movie tagline

"Outstanding!"—Peter Travers, *Rolling Stone*

"Don't miss this film!"—*WBAI Radio*

Box Office Gross: $24,021,125

LouAnne Johnson (Michelle Pfeiffer) has a Bachelor's degree in English literature and a stint as a marine under her belt, but even that may not be enough to get her through her first teaching job. She has been assigned to teach in the "Academy" —a "sort of a school within a school made up of special kids," the assistant principal tells her enigmatically. But her friend Hal Griffith (George Dzunda) is a little more forthcoming. "These are bright kids, with little or no educational skills, and what we politely refer to as social problems." But after her first few out-of-control minutes, Johnson has her own analysis: they're "rebels from Hell."

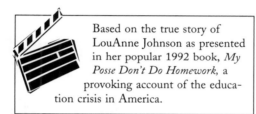

> Based on the true story of LouAnne Johnson as presented in her popular 1992 book, *My Posse Don't Do Homework,* a provoking account of the education crisis in America.

But no one messes with an ex-marine. So, refusing to admit defeat, Johnson trades in her Bobbie Brooks dress for a black leather jacket and blue jeans and goes back for a second day. Hal tells her to "get their attention or quit," and to get their attention she shows them a few karate moves. Karate leads to grammar, and with the help of a few "incentives," Johnson eventually wins over the hearts and minds of most of her students.

It is an uplifting story, but it's also simplistic, sanitized, predictable, and tries too hard to please.

> "My hope is that other kids will see themselves in the film's characters and realize they can be successful in spite of other people's prejudices. I want them to take energy they once expended on anger or on getting even, and focus on themselves."—Michelle Pfeiffer

Audiences have probably already seen movies about teachers using unorthodox approaches in order to reach seemingly unreachable students. *Up the Down Staircase*, *Conrack*, *Stand and Deliver*, *To Sir with Love*, *Blackboard Jungle* and *Dead Poet's Society* come to mind (which shows how often the topic has been treated). Unfortunately, *Dangerous Minds* offers nothing new. For LouAnne Johnson, the unorthodox method consists mostly of bribes: candy bars, a trip to an amusement park, a contest with the winners eating at the best restaurant in town. The expectation is that these bribes eventually will give way to the attitude that learning is its own reward. To get them interested in poetry, she has them study the lyrics of Bob Dylan's "Mr. Tambourine Man" and makes allusions to the drug culture they are familiar with. From here it is an easy glide into Dylan Thomas' "Do Not Go Gentle into That Good Night." However, although the story is based on the actual experiences of LouAnne Johnson (only she used rap music instead of Bob Dylan), as presented in the film, this methodology leads to cynicism, not believability. The educated audience may realize the "value" of reading and studying poetry, but what is its relevance to the lives of these students? Even when two of her students drop out for just this reason, no credible explanation is offered. It is easier to blindly accept than to explain.

Credibility is further strained by the casting of the delicate Michelle Pfeiffer as the ex-marine equal to any cast of delinquents. Here, her role consists of little more than scene after scene of LouAnne facing any problem and rising to the occasion with creativity and success (her inner unsureness only showing in the nervous hands-to-face mannerisms that Ms. Pfeiffer eventually overworks). The movie gives us little insight into her character. Andy Garcia's role as Johnson's love interest was cut from the film, and what is left of Johnson's character is one-dimensional with no life outside of her classroom to make her truly human, motivated, or interesting.

And Pfeiffer's Johnson is not the only overly-simplified character: so are her students. The film focuses on three of them; Raul Sanchero (Renoly Santiago), Emilio Ramirez (Wade Dominguez) and Callie Roberts (Bruklin Harris), and each of them represents a typical problem for troubled teens. Raul is reticent and wary, and burdened by his parents who are placing all their hopes on him to be the first in their family to graduate. Callie is the exceptionally smart student whose talents and intelligence may be wasted when she falls into the dead-end unwed mother trap which will send her off to another school to study motherhood instead of modifiers and metaphors. Emilio is the handsome natural leader (both in and out of the classroom) with a chip on his shoulder but whom LouAnne must win over if she wants to gain the respect of the class.

CREDITS

LouAnne Johnson: Michelle Pfeiffer
Hal Griffith: George Dzunda
Mr. George Grandey: Courtney B. Vance
Ms. Carla Nichols: Robin Bartlett
Mary Benton: Beatrice Winde
Waiter: John Neville
Irene Roberts: Lorraine Toussaint
Raul Sanchero: Renoly Santiago
Emilio Ramirez: Wade Dominguez
Callie Roberts: Bruklin Harris
Cornelius Bates: Marcello Thedford
Durrell Benton: Richard Grant
Gusmaro Rivera: Roberto Alvarez
Angela: Marisela Gonzales

Origin: USA
Released:- 1995
Production: Don Simpson and Jerry Bruckheimer for Via Rosa Productions and Hollywood Pictures. Released by Buena Vista
Direction: John N. Smith
Screenplay: Ronald Bass; based upon the book *My Posse Don't Do Homework* by Luanne Johnson
Cinematography: Pierre Letarte
Editing: Tom Rolf
Production design: Donald Graham Burt
Art direction: Nancy Patton
Set decoration: Philip Toolin
Costume design: Bobbie Read
Music: Kathy Nelson
MPAA rating: R
Running Time: 96 minutes

AWARDS AND NOMINATIONS

Blockbuster Entertainment Awards 1996: Drama Actress-Theatrical (Pfeiffer)

As familiar as these characters are (and as well acted as they are by a basically amateur cast), their fates are just about as easily guessed as is the story's conclusion. LouAnne will become their educational savior, but her courage will be tested by a tragedy, and in the end her students will become her professional saviors. Their minds, it turns out, are not all that dangerous after all.

On a simplistic level that's as "white bread" as LouAnne originally was to her students, *Dangerous Minds* is inspiring, but it is less than innovative. It trades any raw force or true instructiveness for a plot that is much more acceptable to mainstream audiences (just as Bob Dylan will entice them more than Snoop Doggy Dogg). *Dangerous Minds* is heartfelt (and has a great soundtrack), but it is too innocent for today's realities.

—Beverley Bare Buehrer

REVIEWS

Chicago Sun Times. August 11, 1995, p. W19
Chicago Tribune. August 11, 1995, Section Friday, p. H.
Entertainment Weekly. August 11, 1995
The New York Times. August 11, 1995, p. B3
USA Today. August 11, 1995, p. 4D
Variety. August 8, 1995

Dead Man Walking

"One of the year's best. *Dead Man Walking* is beyond comparison."—Roger Ebert, *Chicago Sun-Times*

"Beautifully directed and acted from first scene to last. Deeply compassionate."—Michael Wilmington, *Chicago Tribune*

"Sarandon and Penn do great work. A strange and powerful relationship."—Jack Mathews, *Newsday*

"An extraordinary film that takes viewers on an emotional journey."—Carrie Rickey, *Philadelphia Inquirer*

"Sarandon gives a glorious performance. Acting rarely gets better than this!"—Edward Guthmann, *San Francisco Chronicle*

"Sean Penn gives the most riveting, selfless performance of his career."—John Hartl, *Seattle Times*

"A great film! Astonishing performances."—Mike Clark, *USA Today*

Box Office Gross: $21,919,578

Make no mistake about it, *Dead Man Walking*—the title comes from the announcement that is made when a sentenced man walks those final thirteen steps to his execution—is not an easy film to sit through. Not because it is a terrible piece of filmmaking, just the opposite. Director-writer Tim Robbins has created a work of such intensity and depth that to be left untouched by this film one surely would have to be stone-cold dead, no matter what side of the death penalty issue one is on. What could have been turned into a piece of anti-capital punishment propaganda is instead gently molded by Robbins into a spiritual love story, unconventional and beautiful, one in which one nun and one convicted murderer must separate "the sinner from the sin" and find the man, and the love, within.

Based on her 1993 memoirs, Susan Sarandon plays the real-life Sister Helen Prejean, a Catholic nun who works, and lives, in a primarily black New Orleans housing project. Desperate to have his death sentence overturned, convicted murderer Matthew Poncelet (Sean Penn in a fictionalized composite of two real-life inmates) writes a letter to the parish where Sister Helen works, asking for help. Convicted of murdering and raping two teenagers on a deserted road one night, Poncelet insists that while he was at the scene, he is innocent of the crimes. He contends that it is poverty that landed him on Death Row, not truth, since it is he who awaits execution and not his co-conspirator who could afford better legal representation.

When she makes that first visit to the Louisiana State Penitentiary at Angola, Sister Helen finds a man who seems the very personification of evil. With his slicked up pompadour, long sideburns and devilish goatee, Poncelet looks like a strange cross between Elvis and Satan. He is wary, defiant, every inch the macho Southern white supremacist male, a working class loser. Sister Helen does not care much for his racist declarations, his macho posturings and sexual flirtations. And mostly she is shocked at the horrific nature of the crimes of which he is accused. Yet when Poncelet asks for her help, the nun, motivated by Christian charity, feels compelled to do what she can to help what she thinks is an innocent man. When the prison chaplin asks, "Do you know what you're getting into?" we know the answer is no.

Poncelet has built up a wall around himself, a facade of toughness long calculated to keep people, and his own feelings, at a distance. He has a daughter that he has not seen in years and eventually confesses to Sister Helen that he has never really loved nor been loved. Slowly, Sister Helen is allowed glimpses, often fleeting, of the human being behind the monster. Her friends and family are largely unsympathetic to her cause, but Sister Helen feels her only choice is to "follow the example of Jesus, who said every person is worth more than his worst act." Her tenets are severely tested, however, when she discovers the full extent of Poncelet's guilt and is faced with the bitterness and anger of the families of the victims. When attempts to gain a stay of execution are denied and death is eminent, Sister Helen must then help Poncelet to find a way to die with grace and in peace. She accepts the role of his spiritual adviser during his last seven days and attempts to lead the stubbornly proud Poncelet down the road to redemption. His only hope for salvation is to profess his guilt and to ask for forgiveness from both God and the victims' families, but Poncelet resists at every turn.

Robbins sent a rough cut of the film to musicians he admired, including Johnny Cash, Bruce Springsteen, Eddie Vedder, Patti Smith and others, who wrote and recorded songs that reflect various characters and scenes.

As Poncelet approaches the last half-hour of his life, Robbins daringly resorts to telling the story in what approaches real-time. The wait is unbearable and the tension so thick with dread as Sister Helen relentlessly pressures

Poncelet to confess his sins. In one of the most heartwrenching moments of any film, Poncelet's vulnerability in the face of death is so poignantly illustrated when he is denied a final ounce of dignity by keeping his boots on and is forced, instead, to walk to his death wearing a pair of prison slippers. "I want the last face you see to be one of love," Sister Helen tells him, and as Poncelet is about to receive the fatal injection that will end his life, the nun, seated behind the glass in the viewing chamber mouths the words, "I love you."

"I'm just trying to follow the example of Jesus, who said every person is worth more than his worst act."—Sister Helen from *Dead Man Walking*

Sean Penn's portrayal of convicted killer Matthew Poncelet is nothing short of acting genius. Penn, who made his filmic debut fourteen years earlier in *Taps* (1981), succeeds in building a character, only to deconstruct it through the course of the film by slowly peeling off the layers in order to find a man worthy of redemption. It is unfortunate that Penn's performance in *Dead Man Walking* was overshadowed by Nicolas Cage's flashier portrayal of a self-destructive alcoholic in *Leaving Las Vegas* (1995), for it is Penn who accomplishes the truly impressive feat of turning a sadistic, hardened killer into a man whose life is worth caring about. Not an actor that automatically elicits sympathy, like Tom Hanks, for example, Sean Penn often brings an aloofness that can at times be alienating. So it is not surprising that director Robbins sought the actor for the role of a Death Row convict. What is amazing, however, is the intensity and power that Penn brings to the role.

Susan Sarandon's characterization was, in many ways, more difficult to pull off than Penn's Poncelet, for her role is primarily one of listening. But no one listens better than Susan Sarandon. Her face registers a myriad of different emotions, changing with the slightest nuance. While Penn had the flashier change to accomplish, Sarandon had a narrower range of change in which to work. Sister Helen does not start out as a heroine; she is simply one of the many servants of God trying to do good where they can. But as events begin to pull her deeper and deeper into Poncelet's situation, she must decide her course, even if it alienates others close to her, and follow her convictions through to the end. Her Sister Helen moves quietly, but steadily from naivete through a sense of being overwhelmed to finally accepting her role as Poncelet's spiritual advisor. To her credit, Sarandon never resorts to sentimentality and there is never a moment of sanctimonious behavior on the part of Sister Helen. Finally, a filmic depiction of a nun that is grounded in human emotion.

The restraint, or perhaps it is balance, that director-writer Tim Robbins achieves in *Dead Man Walking* is the biggest surprise. Known for his political activism (along with off-screen partner Sarandon) and his outspokenness, Robbins, one first suspects, would never be able to contain his own views while dealing with such a volatile issue as the death penalty. His first film, the smart and very funny political satire, *Bob Roberts* (1992), was, after all, a scathing indictment of right-wing politics. Perhaps by virtue of being acutely aware of the potential criticism, Robbins succeeds in walking that fine line between emotion and intellect with

CREDITS

Sister Helen Prejean: Susan Sarandon
Matthew Poncelet: Sean Penn
Hilton Barber: Robert Prosky
Earl Delacroix: Raymond J. Barry
Clyde Percy: R. Lee Ermey
Mary Beth Percy: Celia Weston
Helen's mother: Lois Smith

Origin: USA
Released: 1995
Production: Jon Kilik, Tim Robbins and Rudd Simmons; a Working Title Films/Havoc production, released by Gramercy Pictures
Direction: Tim Robbins
Screenplay: Tim Robbins; based on the book "Dead Man Walking" by Sister Helen Prejean
Cinematography: Roger A. Deakins
Editing: Lisa Zeno Churgin
Production design: Richard Hoover
Art direction: Tom Warren
Costumes: Renee Ehrich Kalfus
Set decorator: Laurie Friedman
Casting: Douglas Aibel
Music: David Robbins
MPAA rating: R
Running Time: 120 minutes

AWARDS AND NOMINATIONS

Academy Awards 1995: Best Actress (Sarandon)
Nominations: Best Director (Robbins), Best Actor (Penn), Best Song ("Dead Man Walking")
Berlin Film Festival Awards 1995: Silver Bear (Penn)
Independent Spirit Awards 1996: Best Actor (Penn)
Nominations: Best Supporting Actress (Weston)
Screen Actors Guild Awards 1995: Best Actress (Sarandon)
Nominations: Best Actor (Penn)
Golden Globe Awards Nominations 1996: Best Actor-Drama (Penn), Best Actress-Drama (Sarandon), Best Screenplay (Robbins)

his latest film. He avoids every cliche and manages to transcend the limitations of the constricted settings —nearly all of the scenes between Sarandon and Penn are played out with a pane of bulletproof glass between them, yet the actors attain a level of intimacy rarely seen in American films. In *Dead Man Walking*, Robbins has found a way to take a highly charged issue and personalize it, to breathe life into it by giving it a face and a name. This is not a film about whether certain people deserve to die or not, or whether the government has the moral right to decide who should live and who should die, but rather it is a film about two specific souls who find love hidden in the hardest of hearts.

When Robbins intercuts the execution with scenes of the murder and rape, its exact meaning seems deliberately vague. As Terrence Rafferty suggests in his review in The New Yorker, these images could represent images of evilness dredged from a dying man's consciousness, an emotional justification for revenge on the part of the victims' families, or merely an attempt to draw a moral parallel between the killing of the victims and the killing of Poncelet. As is the case throughout the entire film, Robbins allows the viewer to draw his/her own conclusions.

Blessed with two of the year's strongest performances, *Dead Man Walking* is a compelling film that succeeds in presenting a balanced and human portrait of both sides of the capital punishment issue. It is not a story about conversion, about changing people's minds. It is far too complicated and volatile an issue. There is no melodrama nor preachiness and surprisingly, there are moments of dark humor. The film is unrelenting and is certain to stir up the rawest of emotions, be it sorrow or anger.

—Patricia Kowal

REVIEWS

Entertainment Weekly. January 19, 1996, p. 36.
Los Angeles Times. December 29, 1995, p. F1.
The New Yorker. LXXI, January 8,1996, p. 68.
The New York Times. December 29, 1995, p. C1.

Dead Presidents

"In this daring heist, the only color that counts is green!"—Movie tagline
"Wild action! Excellent!"—*Entertainment Weekly*
"Riveting!"—*The Hollywood Reporter*
"The best soundtrack of the year!"—*New York Daily News*
"The film never slows!"—*Newsday*
"Powerful!"—*USA Today*

Box Office Gross: $24,021,125

The twin-brother directing team of Albert and Allen Hughes co-directs this tale of a young African American man's turbulent life in the inner city in the 1960s. The Hughes brothers are the youthful but highly successful directors of *Menace II Society* (1993), which examined similar issues but looked at them through the lens of contemporary urban society. With this ambitious production, the brothers continue their intense examination of the moral and social dilemmas facing young African American men, and they do so with considerable power and talent.

It is 1968, and the Vietnam War is in full swing. Anthony Curtis (Larenz Tate), upon graduation from high school in the Bronx, decides to forgo college and enlist in the Marine Corps. He leaves behind is girlfriend Juanita (Rose Jackson) and his mentor Kirby (Keith David), a small-time numbers runner. Anthony's two best friends, Skip (Chris Tucker) and Jose (Freddy Rodriguez) decide to join the Marines as well. A sequence depicting their graduation night, which becomes (metaphorically) their last night as innocent youths, is excellent, establishing the close relationship of the three boys while demonstrating the relative simplicity of their lives prior to adulthood. In a funny and touching scene, Anthony and Juanita surreptitiously make love in her bedroom while her mother is gone. Anthony fumbles around for a condom, and them fumbles around Juanita, not quite the experienced lover he wants to appear to be. The entire "grad night" sequence culminates with Anthony running through backyards to escape Juanita's mother, and as he hurdles over fences, the scene melds into an image of Anthony running and jumping over bushes and foxholes in Vietnam. It is a beautifully executed transition, as if the film were switching from *American Graffiti* (1973) to *Platoon* (1986) before the audience's very eyes.

While in Vietnam, Anthony understandably and predictably becomes more cynical as he experiences the destruction and horror of war. His friends in Vietnam include the destructive and crazy Cleon (Bokeem Woodbine) and D'Ambrosio (Michael Imperioli), a good friend whose gruesome death poses a moral dilemma for Anthony. The events in Vietnam shape Anthony's character into a more pessimistic and unpredictable nature, which becomes evident when he returns home in 1972.

Upon returning to the Bronx, the images of the differences four years have made are startling: drugs have crept their way into the landscape, and as Anthony rides in a cab to his family home, the seediness that drug traffic has brought is on display. It is not the home he left. He finds a constantly degrading environment in which it becomes harder and harder to make money, becoming a greater problem after he rekindles his relationship to Juanita who has given birth to their baby.

Dead Presidents is the second feature film for the Hughes brothers, who have been making movies since the age of 12 and drew critical acclaim with their first feature, the highly praised *Menace to Society.*

Faced with no self-esteem, post-traumatic stress syndrome, and other burgeoning problems such as the lack of support for Vietnam veterans, racism, and money troubles, Anthony sees no alternative but to orchestrate an elaborate plot to rob an armored vehicle to get some "dead presidents" (cash). He enlists his old mentor Kirby and his friends Jose and Skippy (now drug addicts), Juanita's revolutionary, anti-war sister Delilah (N'Bushe Wright), and his former Vietnam buddy Cleon, now a pastor. Using his knowledge of combat techniques, Anthony sets up a plan that seems foolproof, but ends in disaster.

Dead Presidents is a difficult film to watch, due to its intensity, its grim picture of urban life, and its violence. Indeed, the violence is surprisingly graphic: several scenes involving a decapitation are particularly gruesome, and definitely not for the squeamish. Additionally, there is much bloodshed, none of which is shown off-screen, and virtually all of it is done in a manner befitting "slash and gore" films such as *Halloween* (1978). Perhaps, though, it is the Hughes brothers intention to present the violence of the inner city (and of the Vietnam war) as being as gruesome as the worst "slasher" film. The sad truth is that violence is an everyday, horrific fact of life in all of America's cities. It seems that the Hughes brothers want to say that if the violence is repulsive in a movie, their audiences should realize it is exponentially more repulsive in real life—and maybe the film is a "wake up call" to do more about it.

If this is true, then the moral lessons of this film make it above reproach, and make it a necessary film to see. Unfortunately, it is not as interesting a film as the much more naturalistic *Menace II Society.* Perhaps because Hughes and Hughes have graduated to a larger budget and fancier technical effects, the film seems the slightest bit more "show biz" than their earlier effort, and though the themes and the situations are just as intense and just as well-filmed, the slickness of the production makes the film seem more pretentious than *Menace II Society.*

Of course, that assessment does not apply to everyone who sees the two films. And it most likely will make not a bit of difference to audiences who view the film as an authentic representation of their own life experience. The scenes of street life in the 70s are authentic, and the difficulties Anthony faces are very real indeed.

As Anthony, Larenz Tate is excellent. His job is not an easy one, for he has to make Anthony's transition from earnest youth to hardened criminal believable, and he has to do so without losing sympathy from the audience. Happily, Tate is up to the task. He is very funny in the early scenes with Juanita, and then he begins to set up the arc of his character in the scenes immediately after his return from Vietnam. He displays his new found cynicism to his mother (Jennifer Lewis) after she asks if he picked up "any bad

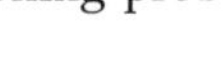

CREDITS

Anthony Curtis: Larenz Tate
Kirby: Keith David
Skip: Chris Tucker
Jose: Freddy Rodriguez
Juanita Benson: Rose Jackson
Delilah Benson: N'Bushe Wright
Mrs. Benson: Alvaletah Guess
Mr. Curtis: James Pickers, Jr.
Mrs. Curtis: Jenifer Lewis
Cutty: Clifton Powell

Origin: USA
Released: 1995
Production: Albert and Allen Hughes for an Underworld Entertainment production in association with Caravan Pictures; released by Hollywood Pictures
Direction: Albert and Allen Hughes
Screenplay: Michael Henry Brown, Albert and Allen Hughes
Cinematography: Lisa Rinzler
Editing: Dan Lebental
Production design: David Brisbin
Art direction: Kenneth A. Hardy
Set decoration: Karin Wiesel
Costume design: Paul A. Simmons
Sound: Frank Stettner
Casting: Risa Bramon Garcia, Mary Vernieu
Music: Danny Elfman
MPAA rating: R
Running Time: 121 minutes

habits" overseas. "No bad habits Mom, except a little killing for my country, of course." Anthony's transition from optimism to pessimism is reminiscent of the struggles of Ron Kovic, the real-life character on which *Born on the Fourth of July* (1991) was based, and Tate does a fine job making the audience realize that although his character is not based on a specific person in real-life, his is an accurate portrayal of real life nonetheless.

The other actors are fine in their roles, in particular Bokeem Woodbine as Cleon, who changes from wild Marine recruit to bookish pastor. Rose Jackson is a formidable presence as Juanita, questioning Anthony's manhood when he cannot provide for her and their daughter. Keith David is perfectly cast as Kirby, Anthony's mentor, and like the rest of the actors, David draws a fine delineation between the pre- and post-Vietnam scenes. David is particulalry adept at walking the line between drama and comedy, being both menacing and hilarious in an early scene in which he gets in a fight with a hoodlum and hits him with his artificial leg.

"I can't remember any other film that talks about Black men in leadership positions in the war where the characters don't come back simply as junkies or basket cases. This shows a very responsible kid going to fight, being decorated, but coming back with an expectation of receiving, not even a hand out, but just respect."—Actor Keith David on what attracted him to the story

The Hughes brothers have directed with great style. If some of the sequences do not seem naturalistic, they are still powerful: the Vietnam sequences seem obviously done on location somewhere in the United States. The actors wear grimy, bloody makeup, and the almost ritualistic scenes of killing in the Vietnam sequence are over-the-top. But, perhaps that is an effect Hughes and Hughes wanted to create.

The directors have stated in interviews that they are avid fans of Martin Scorsese and they prove it: Anthony accuses Juanita of cheating on him in a scene filmed with similar angles and dialogue to a scene in *Raging Bull* (1980). Several scenes at a pool table are reminiscent of shots from *The Color of Money* (1986).

Though the cinematography of Lisa Rinzler is lush and evocative, the lighting is dark throughout the film, to the point where it becomes hard to see some of the action. Sometimes the actors are in virtual silhouette in scenes which could be opened up to some more light without losing the intended intensity provided by shadows. It is likely, however, that the Hughes brothers intend for the darkness to be as disconcerting to the audience as it is to the characters, once again underscoring the intensity and futility of their protagonists' lives.

A final note must be made of the brilliant use of music in this film. Danny Elfman provides searing, eerie themes which augment a terrific series of period songs from the 60s and 70s. Lovers of that music (particularly of the Motown sound) will be carried away by the quality and the excellent utilization of the music. (The sound track album for this film was a huge success.)

Allen and Albert Hughes, all of 24 years old when they made this film, are at the beginnning of an illustrious career. Hopefully, as time passes, the themes of their films can have the social effect desired. It is admirable that these young men wish to contribute to change in American society while progressing as Hollywood film directors. Let's hope Hollywood doesn't make them as cynical as Vietnam made the protagonist of *Dead Presidents*.

—*Kirby Tepper*

Delta of Venus

Big screen newcomer Audie England joins Costas Mandylor to star in Zalman King's erotic epic. Based on the already emotionally over-charged writing of Anais Nin, the film is inundated with cliches and melodrama. Masquerading as an art film, *Delta of Venus* is merely soft-core porn without the strong characterizations by leads Mandylor and especially England necessary to redeem it, as Rourke and Basinger's performances did in another erotic King tale *9 1/2 Weeks* (1986). There is, however, some degree of watchability, stemming from Nin's fertile imagination and lush images. Boasting video rental revenue of $26 million, King's films obviously hit a nerve with some viewers.

An American in 1940's Paris, Elena (Audie England) is a would-be writer. Her agent Marcel (Eric Da Silva) warns her that work has dried up for even the most talented writers due to the war in Europe, but Elena prefers to remain where she is most inspired and where she has been following, daily, an oarsmen on the Seine with whom she fancies she is in love with from afar.

Cut to an elegant party hosted by Marcel where women are dressed as men, men wear make-up, Marlene Dietrich-types croon and artistes brood. Elena shows up and when Marcel asks her why she is not at home working as she planned, she gives an answer typical of the stilted dialogue heard throughout: "My muse must've gone to the beach. I haven't had a single coherent thought all day." The mysterious, and apparently well-loved, oarsmen enters the party, kissing every female he encounters. Elena locks her eyes onto him when an effeminate man sidles up to her with an ominous warning, "Watch out! Watch out!" Elena discovers the handsome hunk is another client of Marcel's and a very talented writer in his own right. Finally, Marcel's two prettiest clients meet. Of course, he immediately recognizes her as the woman watching him row every day from the bridge. Their ensuing banter is uninspiring, unerotic and stiff. They dance while Elena, narrating in an annoying voice-over throughout the film, observes, "Time stood still. We could've been on the dance floor for ten minutes or two hours. I don't know." Meanwhile, Lawrence is narrating a story of his own to the enthralled Elena, describing a party cum orgy he attended in St. Tropez. This seems to spark both their imaginations as evidenced in the numerous close-ups of the nubile couples' pouty lips. Just as the night gets going, Marcel's party turns into a political rally outside as communists and facists with snarling German Shepards invade the place.

Later that evening at Elena's, Lawrence explains he is going on tour with his book and leaves for New York soon. He too, takes his turn delivering the corny dialogue as he reveals to Elena, "I love whiskey. Whiskey and women on bridges in the early morning fog," as he doffs his coat to reveal the lumberjack build that most sensitive writers possess. This marks the brief moment of sexual tension as Elena tucks Lawrence into bed, while she stays up to write, "Until tonight I was growing sad with restlessness and hunger..."

The next day the couple roam the Paris streets as Lawrence opens her imagination even further, instructing her to describe their surrounding as a writer would describe them. Elena is sufficiently open enough now to consummate their two day relationship with a steamy love scene on the kitchen counter. Embarking on a post-coital trip to a local church, they visit a priest friend of Lawrence, John Luc (Marek Vasnt).

His departure imminent, Lawrence invites Elena to go with him. She again rejects the possibility of leaving her beloved Paree. She needs to work and apparently can only do so in the City of Light. More steamy love scenes of Elena

CREDITS

Elena Martin: Audie England
Lawrence Walters: Costas Mandylor
Marcel: Eric Da Silva
Leila: Raven Snow
Miguel: Rory Campbell
Ariel: Emma Louise Moore
Donald: Zette
Luc: Marek Vasnt
Bijou: Marketa Hrubesova
Pierre: Daniel Leza
Harry: Stephen Halbert
Millicent: Dale Wyatt
Priest: Jiri Ded

Origin: USA
Released: 1995
Production: Evzen Kolar for Alliance Communications; released by New Line Cinema
Direction: Zalman King
Screenplay: Elisa Rothstein and Patricia Louisianna Knop; based on an original story by Anais Nin
Cinematography: Eagle Egilsson
Editing: James Gavin Bedford
Music: George S. Clinton
Costume design: Jolie Anna Jimenez
Production design: Zdeneak Flemming
Set decoration: Miroslav Dvorak
Art direction: Milan Stary, Daniel Dvorak
MPAA rating: NC-17
Running Time: 101 minutes

and Lawrence solidify their relationship. As the newly carefree Elena frolics around Paris with her cosmopolitan friends, stopping only to reminisce on photos of her and Lawrence, Lawrence ends up with a red-haired prostitute Elena once observed from her window with a soldier. Elena is furious that Lawrence spent his last night with a stranger, while Lawrence defends his "passion for self-destruction" but also claiming she meant nothing to him. The scene is quietly observed by a blonde soldier who raided Marcel's party.

Although Lawrence leaves for America, Elena is still liberated and now even more open than before, getting work modeling nude for a friend's art class. Marcel calls her with a proposition from a mysterious, anonymous client who essentially wants porn stories on demand. When he mentions the pay, Elena is soon penning her first smutty story, which remarkably resembles the story of the orgy told to her by Lawrence.

Meanwhile, fascism abounds and the Germans are everywhere. The blond soldier makes a pass at the startled writer and Elena flees. Seeing the red-haired hooker Bijou (Marketa Hrubesova) Elena decides to approach her, curious about her night with Lawrence. Feeling sorry for the poor American girl, Bijou takes her to a clairvoyant from West Africa. Elena hides out as the two go through an intimate ritual. Elena writes about this, too, for her client. Her benefactor, liking it very much, continues to pay her but cautions her to "leave out the poetry and concentrate on sex." A good moral for the film as well. She resists but eventually tries to take her writing further.

Soon Elena is unstoppable. Everything is fodder for her stories as her male model partner, Pierre, becomes the subject of her now extremely fertile imagination. She concocts a story about a rich woman who's husband supplies her with anonymous strangers to have sex with while others watch. More carnal love scenes unfold as each story is "written." Elena is elated, feeling now she is finally writing the way she always knew she could.

With this new feeling of boldness and recklessness, Elena experiences her own version of "The Summer of My German Soldier," although hers is more akin to one minute. Meeting the blond German in an alley, Elena not only experiences animalistic, violent passion with him but generates new material for yet another story for her still satisfied patron.

Pandemonium breaks out in Paris as Hitler invades Belgium and Nazis march on France's borders. Elena remains but takes sanctuary in an opium den. Here, the film is at it's most racy, staging an all female orgy. Directly opposing her latest experience with the soldier, this loving, tender encounter leaves her discovering her "delta of Venus" and details the account for posterity and more money. Her last story and experience completed, her benefactor urges her to leave Paris. She again refuses. The military situation worsens, and things seem bad for artists in the community as Germans beat up a friend of Elena's and destroy his art studio. Marcel decides to leave Paris but still Elena remains.

Suddenly, Lawrence returns from abroad and confronts the still angry Elena. No longer the girl who watched him on the Seine, Elena argues she has changed and no longer wants him. He then (finally) reveals he is the anonymous patron she has written for all these months. Enraged at the ruse, Elena rushes through the streets with Lawrence trailing after her. Dramatically, the Nazis begin to chase them both as they take refuge in Luc's church. Here, they avoid the Nazi's, settle their differences, make love and Elena's transformation from innocent to thoroughly debauched artist is complete. Elena finally takes her cue and leaves Paris, leaving Lawrence behind, but content that she is now capable of many loves.

Recommended for rabid Nin fans only as few others will truly enjoy this film. Too arty to be strictly adult softcore and devoid of good acting or dialogue necessary for moderately entertaining erotica, *Delta of Venus* will be lucky to find a niche. The unintended humor derived from the wooden delivery of ridiculous lines may be the most appealing feature of this sub-par effort.

—Hilary Weber

Desperado

"Its sheer creative glee makes you glad to be alive."—Bob Strauss, *L.A. Daily News*

"Robert Rodriguez has a genuine hit on his hands. Antonio Banderas is headed for a big time career. He's a passionate, agile actor with wonderful comic timing. Seamless fun."—Jamie Bernard, *New York Daily News*

"Banderas is intense and electrifying, proving that not only can he carry a movie, he can walk away with it, leaving audiences breathless."
—Juliann Garey, *US Magazine*

Box Office Gross: $25,625,110

El Mariachi (Antonio Banderas) has given up his dream of becoming a legendary mariachi to become a man bent on avenging the death of his lady love. In order to carry out his dream of revenge, El Mariachi must kill the top Mexican drug lord, Bucho (Joaquim de Almeida), and all of his henchmen.

Salma Hayek and Antonio Banderas narrowly escape an explosion in *Desperado.*

CREDITS

El Mariachi: Antonio Banderas
Carolina: Salma Hayek
Bucho: Joaquim de Almeida
Short Bartender: Cheech Marin
Buscemi: Steve Buscemi
Right Hand: Carlos Gomez
Pick-up Guy: Quentin Tarantino

Origin: USA
Released: 1995
Production: Robert Rodriguez and Bill Borden for a Los Hooligans production; released by Columbia Pictures
Direction: Robert Rodriguez
Screenplay: Robert Rodriguez
Cinematography: Guillermo Navarro
Editing: Robert Rodriguez
Production design: Cecilia Montiel
Art direction: Felipe Fernandez del Paso
Casting: Reuben Cannon
Costume design: Graciela Mazon
Sound: Mark Ulano
Music: Los Lobos
MPAA rating: R
Running Time: 103 minutes

Associate producer Carlos Gallardo, who starred as the Mariachi in the first film, has a small role as Campa, a musician/gunslinger friend.

"Bless me, Father, for I have just killed quite a few men."—El Mariachi from *Desperado*

Destiny Turns on the Radio

"Hot Times, Cold Cash, Fast Cars, and a Slow Roll of the Dice."—Movie tagline

"Hipness to the Nth Degree."—*The New York Times*

Box Office Gross: $1,176,982

A film which boasts Jim Belushi singing an unaccompanied version of "Viva Las Vegas" as its funniest moment is surely not destined to become a cinema classic. *Destiny Turns on the Radio* aspires to the blend of hipness and weirdness that characterized David Lynch's 1990 television series "Twin Peaks;" it tries to create the aura of hip depravity that made *Pulp Fiction* (1994) a huge hit. Sadly, however, its weirdness is not hip, and it comes off more like a student film than the distinctive mind-bender it aspires to be.

The film begins with a series of shots of the desert, and director Jack Baran sets the mood well with arid, burnished images of the barren landscape accompanied by an interesting musical underscore (by Steve Soles) which sounds like an ersatz blend of cowboy movie music and 1960's pop-rock.

But rather quickly it seems Baran and company might be working a bit too hard to make their film interesting. Julian Goddard (Dylan McDermott) wakes up in the middle of the desert after getting out of prison. He stumbles on to the empty highway. With a terrific haircut and fashionable two-day stubble, McDermott looks every bit the young Hollywood stud ready for a movie premiere or Hollywood party—but his trendy hair and the stylish cut of his prison outfit are not in sync with the disheveled, weary ex-con he is supposed to be. He is picked up by a passing car driven by strange traveler Johnny Destiny (Quentin Tarantino). Destiny, having just turned on the radio (on which is heard the prophetic, "it's going to be a busy day for cops and robbers alike") is on his way to nearby Las Vegas. He says to Julian, "the name's Destiny...Johnny Destiny," and with some ominous foreshadowing ("Vegas...that's a town. Anything can happen there"), they are off.

Nancy Travis' singing voice is dubbed by Eleni Mandell.

Destiny drives Julian to the Marilyn motel, a wonderfully seedy creation of production designer Jean-Philippe Carp. It is a dilapidated one-story motel on the periphery of Las Vegas, with a gaudy neon sign of Marilyn Monroe resting atop its withered stucco exterior. In the middle of what was once a courtyard sits an empty swimming pool with a gash in the center, as if an eruption from beneath the surface created the hole. And it turns out that some sort of eruption did occur, for flashbacks show that Destiny is an otherworldly figure of indeterminate origin who emerged, naked, through the swimming pool. (Mercifully, Tarantino is fully clothed through the rest of the film). It seems that now Destiny has come into ownership of a car used by Julian and his buddy, Thoreau (James LeGros) in a robbery which ended with Julian's arrest three years ago. Destiny is also in control of the money they stole, and somehow Thoreau has come into ownership of the Marilyn motel. Julian is now returning to Las Vegas in order to claim his part of the loot and his girlfriend, Lucille (Nancy Travis.)

Thoreau explains Destiny's appearance thus: "this repeated act of gambling has conjured a deity...this pool's his path back to the spirit world." The rest of the film's plot concerns Julian's reconciliation with Lucille, Thoreau's search for understanding of Destiny's place in the world, and a subplot involving Lucille's potential recording deal. The pseudo-spiritual ending confuses matters well beyond repair.

On paper, it seems as if this could all work: the backdrop of Las Vegas is perfect for a story about the dreams of society's misfits, and the addition of the symbolic character of Destiny would make it seem that the film would have allegorical possibilities. But somehow, it never takes off.

Perhaps one of the film's problems is that the all-important role of Destiny is played by the impish Tarantino. The implication of having Tarantino playing the role is that he will imbue the film with some of the success and the "coolness" that have characterized his other films, such as *Reservoir Dogs* (1992), *True Romance* (1993), *Natural Born Killers* (1994), and *Pulp Fiction* (1994). The difference, though, is that he was the screenwriter and\or director of those films; he did not create this one. His Valley-guy speaking patterns undermine the devilishness inherent in his character, and his presence alone is not enough to make the film interesting.

The filmmakers have, in general, rested more on image than on great filmmaking—with the exception of the design elements. The production design of Jean-Phillippe Carp, as previously mentioned, is excellent: the Marilyn motel, the dusty, cracked exteriors, the sleazy restaurants and lounges that Carp creates make a statement about Las Vegas as an empty place where empty people have empty dreams. Beverly Klein's costumes also serve the same purpose, and are wonderfully evocative of Vegas (and perhaps America in the nineties) as a place where image takes a back seat to substance.

If only the other creative elements were as successful. In particular, the script by Robert Ramsey and Matthew Stone is an example of image over substance rather than a comment on it. The self-consciously quirky language, for example, tends to distance the audience from the characters, apparently trying to show how unique they are, but only emphasizing their banality. This happens because the language is quirky for the sake of being quirky, and ignores the real possibilities for communication between the characters. For example, Julian, when he hears Lucille has a new boyfriend (Jim Belushi), throws something against the wall and says "this is truly offensive." At another point, Thoreau tells Julian that "it's beyond one man's power to stem the tide of chaos." These kind of offbeat responses stop the flow of conversation between the characters merely for the sake of being unusual. And, unfortunately, the audience becomes removed from the emotional flow of the scene.

There is a feeling that some of the dialogue was either embellished during filming or was improvised altogether—it has a "free form" quality. For some actors and directors, the term "free form" becomes more like "free fall," and this film fits perfectly into that category. Its lack of focus and clarity only leave its otherwise talented actors twisting in the wind. A perfect example of the danger of improvisation is exemplified by the character of Ralph Dellapoza, played by David Cross. Actor Cross plays Lucille's fast-talking business manager; he speaks in endless tangential monologues which appear to be improvised. His rapid-fire sentences, punctuated by lots of "uhs" and stammering, apparently attempt to imitate the naturalism of Woody Allen or Robert Altman, but the lack of artifice is rather irritating. In one scene Cross ends a line by suggesting that Lucille go for a "snosh:" the actor appears to catch himself making a mistake, and tries to recover by saying "oh, that's a snack and a nosh." This kind of ill-advised improvisation has been the downfall of many films, such as *Inside Monkey Zetterland* (1993) or the films of Pauly Shore (yes, Shore's films make money, but they are not known as examples of brilliance).

Further, the flow of the plot seems to be stopped by Julian's interminable wanderings about Las Vegas: he says that he is trying to find the loot, but he stops to enter into meandering conversations with various characters which undermine the seriousness of his search. Consequently, it appears that if Julian is not particularly committed to his quest, the audience won't be, either.

Indeed, audiences have in general not found the film to their liking. In fact, they have not found the film at all, since largely negative reviews helped to close it early in its release. Reviewers have called the film, "smugly facetious," "hapless and hopeless," and a series of "thuddingly monochromatic readings of moviedom's most threadbare cliches."

The inclusion of these sharp criticisms is not meant to malign the film or its creative forces, but to underscore the fact that the inclusion of colorful locales, kooky characters, some New Age wisdom, and idiosyncratic dialogue are not enough to captivate an audience.

That having been said, it is important to note that there are actually a few captivating moments in this film. Nancy Travis, who may be making a career for herself out of offbeat fare (she starred in *So I Married an Axe Murderer* in 1993), makes a stunningly sexy and sweet chanteuse. Her two musical numbers are the highlight of the film. In particular, her rendition of "That Old Black Magic"is just plain terrific: while she is singing, the film is wonderful. Perhaps Director Baran should consider doing an old-style musical—and he should use the luscious and talented Travis. She is not the only member of the cast with talent—Dylan McDermott is a handsome and respectable actor, and Jim

CREDITS

Harry Thoreau: James LeGros
Julian Goddard: Dylan McDermott
Johnny Destiny: Quentin Tarantino
Lucille: Nancy Travis
Tuerto: James Belushi
Escabel: Janet Carroll
Ralph Dellaposa: David Cross
Gage: Richard Edson
Mr. Smith: Bobdcat Goldthwait
Dravec: Barry "Shabaka" Henley
Katrina: Lisa Jane Persky
Francine: Sarah Trigger
Pappy: Tracey Walter
Vinnie Vidivici: Allen Garfield

Origin: USA
Released: 1995
Production: Gloria Zimmerman for Rysher Entertainment; released by Savoy Pictures
Direction: Jack Baran
Screenplay: Robert Ramsey and Matthew Stone
Cinematography: James L. Carter
Editing: Raul Davalos
Production design: Jean-Phillippe Carp
Art direction: Easton Michael Smith, Dominic Wymark
Set decoration: Lisa R. Deutsch
Sound: Steuart P. Pierce
Costume design: Beverly Klein
Music: Steve Soles
MPAA rating: R
Running Time: 101 minutes

Belushi delivers a fun performance as a benign gangster—but Travis' musical numbers give the film the substance and the effervescence that it longs for.

Perhaps Destiny has something else in store for the people involved in this film. Until then, they are best advised not to use this film as an audition of their talents. Their intentions were good, but sometimes even the best laid plans go awry.

—*Kirby Tepper*

Devil in a Blue Dress

"In a world divided by black and white, Easy Rawlins is about to cross the line."—Movie tagline

"Four stars. A brutal, exhilarating ride through a Los Angeles we've all but forgotten. Carl Franklin handles all of it with a rare gift for mixing hard-hitting, realistic violence with tension-breaking humor and vulnerable, pathetic, endearing humanity."—Amy Dawes, *Los Angeles Times*

"Film Noir at its best! Slick, thrilling, tough and suspenseful."—Rex Reed, *New York Observer*

"The movie simmers with pungent suspense, humor and eroticism. Denzel Washington is flat-out perfection."—Peter Travers, *Rolling Stone*

Box Office Gross: $16,030,096

Some of the classic genres of American film—the Western, the musical comedy, the detective story—may seem to have been exhausted through continuous use, but in the hands of an inventive director, the vitality and pertinence that made them so compelling in earlier incarnations can be extended into contemporary times. Carl Franklin's handling of the film noir format designed to convey the angst and anomie of American life through the late forties and early fifties in *Devil in a Blue Dress* is an example of a filmmaker going beyond a skillful reproduction to demonstrate how traditional material can be energized by recognizing its applicability to a current conflict. Working with a screenplay of Walter Mosley's first novel in a series about an African-American detective living in Los Angeles after World War II, Franklin has taken some of the fundamental elements of the now-classic noir form to provide a distinctive vision of the flow of life in the black community, a subject still largely unexplored in American films. The craft evident in Franklin's first independent feature, the highly praised, riveting *One False Move* (1992), has been developed further so that some of the conventions of the noir film- - dark streets, confining locations, a nighttime narrative, a sorrowful, bluesy score—have been used to create a milieu which projects the nihilistic, dead-end world of shadows, menace and sin that can make noir films so enticing in their depiction of a forbidden zone.

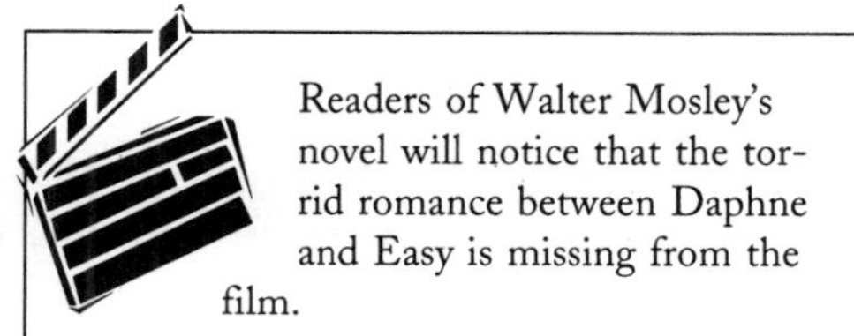

Readers of Walter Mosley's novel will notice that the torrid romance between Daphne and Easy is missing from the film.

What makes the film particularly relevant, however, is that Franklin has recognized that the psychological attitude of the noir era, which was built on a lingering hangover from the Depression, a post-war malaise, cold war anxiety and nuclear trauma, has its ongoing analogue in the black community throughout the twentieth century. The down-beat, discouraged, distrustful feeling of noir films with titles like *No Way Out* (1950) or *Kiss Me Deadly* (1955) informs the moods of *Devil in a Blue Dress* which offers an array of characters who have been caught in a web of corruption and criminality that the African-American community is especially vulnerable to due to the disinterest of the local government in law and justice. This makes it understandable that Mosley's main character, Ezekiel "Easy" Rawlins (Denzel Washington), a veteran from Texas working as a machinist who is laid off in a cavalier gesture of racist indifference, can be drawn into the intrigue of a complicated conspiracy where he is compelled to act with force and wit to avoid being crushed.

Rawlins is an ordinary, decent man who has come to Los Angeles, a city that "has always had a kind of racist thrust to it" as Franklin observes, in pursuit of the simplest side of the American Dream: to own a nice house in a pleasant, working-class neighborhood. The poignancy of his very modest quest is emphasized by his near-despair when he is fired by a callous supervisor for being unable to work a double-shift due to a short illness. His concern about paying the mortgage makes him disregard an instinctive uneasiness and he accepts an offer from a "friend" who puts him in touch with a man who can give him a "job." Rawlins immediately senses that he is dealing with unreliable people but he agrees to look for a mysterious woman involved with a mayoral candidate. She seems to have some affinity for black men which apparently qualifies Rawlins for the search. The idea of a regular guy drawn into the dark regions of the noir labyrinth instills a feeling of suspense and danger as Rawlins moves from the brightly lit, uncluttered surroundings of his home into the shadowy realm of the nightclub highlife. Washington is superbly suited to the part, since his ability to convey Rawlin's appealing affability is combined with a kind of determination that makes his decision to take action plausible and convincing. In the first of a chain of plot reversals common to the noir narrative, Rawlins appears surprisingly comfortable amidst the denizens of a smokey, sexually provocative club, a man who may have chosen a bland lifestyle but one who is also at ease with jazz, booze and adventurous women. The allure of the after-hours club is clear, since black people here can feel temporarily free from the dominance of the white world, a place where they are treated with respect as well as a source of escape from pressure. Franklin's careful reproduction of the Central Avenue club scene, highlighted by a soundtrack featuring some of the musicians (T-Bone Walker, Jimmy Witherspoon, Roy Milton) who figured prominently in the rhythm-and-blues revival, helps to ground a rather implausible story in an authentic milieu.

It is Washington's performance, however, that really holds the film together. The wry humor of his understated but forceful masculine style gives his voice-over commentary on the action an immediate appeal, leading the audience into his life and mind as he follows the twists, turns and complications of a characteristic noir plot. In many sequences, the camera moves with him into a shot, "taking the viewer into the movie" in Franklin's words, so that the tension Rawlins feels in a situation where he is threatened by racist assumptions and lethal adversaries is satisfyingly resolved by his wit and strength. Washington mutes some of the charismatic power he has displayed in previous performances, and the image of him sweating in a white undershirt, his body thicker and less trim than it appears in tailored suits, establishes his identity as a member of a beleaguered, hard-working community of regular guys, the African-American world rarely depicted on screen. When he begins to operate as the hip private eye he has become by the film's conclusion, the transformation is compelling because he is so unlike the cold killing machines of many recent films.

Franklin's interest in the social milieu of post-war Los Angeles and Washington's portrayal of "a hard-working American who fought for his country" as he describes Rawlins are crucial to the film's success since the details of a very convoluted plot don't ever quite coalesce into a coherent story. Both Rawlins and the audience remain uncertain about what is actually happening throughout but this aura of mystery is appropriate since Rawlins is being drawn into a world that isn't supposed to make sense anyway. Instead, he is constantly confronted by violent, ruthless people who are prepared to do anything to further their ends. Most prominent among these is Dewitt Albright who reeks of sleazy manipulation in Tom Sizemore's performance as a man who is murderously immoral and deceivingly amiable when it suits his purposes. Rawlins's inevitable shoot-out with Albright isn't as dramatically satisfying as it might be, though, and several other important figures in the story are underdeveloped and peripheral. As the almost archetypal

CREDITS

Easy Rawlins: Denzel Washington
Dewitt Albright: Tom Sizemore
Daphne Monet: Jennifer Beals
Mouse: Don Cheadle
Matthew Terell: Maury Chaykin
Todd Carter: Terry Kinney
Joppy: Mel Winkler
Odell: Albert Hall

Origin: USA
Released: 1995
Production: Gary Goetzman and Jesse Beaton for a Clinica Estetico/Mundy Lane Entertainment; released by TriStar Pictures
Direction: Carl Franklin
Screenplay: Carl Franklin; based on the book *Devil in a Blue Dress* by Walter Mosley
Cinematography: Tak Fujimoto
Editing: Carole Kravetz
Production design: Gary Frutkoff
Costume design: Sharen Davis
Casting: Victoria Thomas
Sound: Dan Yale, Steve Mann, Mark A. Lanza, Stu Bernstein
Music: Elmer Bernstein
MPAA rating: R
Running Time: 102 minutes

AWARDS AND NOMINATIONS

Los Angeles Film Critics Awards 1995: Best Supporting Actor (Cheadle)
National Society of Film Critics Awards 1995: Best Supporting Actor (Cheadle), Best Cinematography (Fujimoto)
Screen Actors Guild Awards Nominations 1995: Best Supporting Actor (Cheadle)

woman of mystery Daphne Monet, the "Devil" of the title, Jennifer Beals doesn't quite have the captivating magnetism of Kathleen Turner in *Body Heat* (1981) or Faye Dunaway in *Chinatown* (1974), and her nascent romance with Rawlins isn't as dangerously exciting as it might be. The interracial aspect of their relationship and the eventual disclosure that she is from a racially mixed family provides an element of intrigue and pathos but her character is underwritten and in spite of her attractive appearance, she is too fragile to exude the perilous attraction that might drive a man to his doom. As a kind of compensation for this flaw, Rawlins enlists the help of a homeboy from Houston, the ironically misnamed Mouse (Don Cheadle) who is a startling combination of sweetness, agreeable rustic humor and casual, affectless homicide. Mouse ricochets from moods of mildness to explosive, unrestrained will and Franklin uses him as a cautionary symbol of the unleashed anger that centuries of indignity and oppression can produce. During his slightly more reflective moments, he feels fully justified in using any means necessary to protect his friend and defend himself. Mouse offers macabre comedy and malice, a "brother" Rawlins both loves and fears recognizing parallel impulses in himself that are gratifying when indulged but unsettling and destructive.

"She likes jazz and pigs' feet and dark meat—you know what I mean?"—Hood Albright from *Devil in a Blue Dress*

Mouse's arrival signals a turning point in the film, the pivotal event when Rawlins, the abused protagonist, begins to strike back. The exhilaration inherent in this switch is fundamental, and carries a particular resonance due to the appeal of Washington's conception of Rawlins and the historical resonance of a black man resisting the depredations of racist cops, corrupt politicians, murderous thugs and false friends. Without exactly explaining anything fully, the mystery involving Monet and both mayoral candidates is revealed even if nothing is really resolved. Mouse heads back to Houston, Monet leaves before Rawlins can properly say good-bye, but the mood of bittersweet resignation is abruptly altered when Rawlins steps out of the noir realm and into a bright, warm light returning to a neighborhood presented as a community of friendly people connected by similar ambitions and a genuine respect for each other. This image of friendship and civility is clearly an optimistic comment by Franklin on the future of African-Americans, but as several reviewers have observed, the setting is the notorious Watts section, which exploded into riots during the 1960's. It is as if Franklin is hopeful but knows the history, his implied irony a cautionary note to the desire for a positive conclusion to an often dark vision of existence.

In spite of Franklin's direction, Washington's characteristically adept acting and the expert cinematography of Tak Fujimoto who has worked extensively with executive producer Jonathan Demme before, [notably *Something Wild* (1968) and *The Silence of the Lambs* (1991)] the film has not been particularly successful commercially even though influential critics for major magazines have written glowing notices. It may be that Franklin's interest in the black community, and his decision to avoid an audience-friendly white side-kick as Rawlin's buddy, has limited the box-office appeal of what is surely one of the most interesting films of the year.

—*Leon Lewis*

REVIEWS

The Nation. October 23, 1995, p. 480-481.
The New Republic. October 2, 1995, p. 87.
The New Republic. October 30, 1995, p. 34.
New York. October 2, 1995, p. 82.
The New York Times. September 29, 1995, p. C8.
Time. October 2, 1995, p. 72.
The Village Voice. October 3, 1995, p. 80.

Die Hard with a Vengeance

"Think fast. Look Alive. Die Hard."—Movie tagline

"*Die Hard* doesn't quit. Willis and Jackson are dynamite together."—Joel Siegel, *Good Morning America*

"tense, terrifically funny action dazzler"—*Rolling Stone*

"Fun with a vengeance!"—Gene Shalit, *The Today Show*

Box Office Gross: $100,012,499

When *Die Hard* (1988) appeared in theaters, it brought several new conventions to the screen. A new, bigger, better blockbuster in the age of blockbusters, *Die Hard* nonetheless took some of the currently popular conventions (such as black-white buddy films: *Lethal Weapon,* 1987, *White Nights,* 1985) and gave them a new twist, huge scale pyrotechnics, rapid-fire editing, and, at the center of the action, a loner, a misfit, maybe even a loser, who nonetheless is good at what he does. With the help of his sidekick, he will save many lives and stop the demented madman who has placed the world in peril. Now, after *Die Hard* was followed by *Die Hard II, Striking Distance* (1994) (same plot, water setting), *Speed* (1994) and a myriad other similar films, *Die Hard with a Vengeance* has a hard time bringing new life to what now has become a tired genre.

John McClane (Bruce Willis) is a jaded New York cop who has a knack for finding trouble. While audiences are familiar with his West Coast adventures in the first two *Die Hard* films, this time McClane is back in New York, fighting the "bad guys" on his own turf. Yet McClane is more than a little worse for wear, self destructive, hung-over, forgotten. Then a call comes in. A madman named Simon has blown up Bonwit Teller's department store and will continue to blow up more locations unless John McClane enters the "game." One of the first tests arises when Simon sends McClane into Harlem, wearing a sign sure to enrage each passerby. Zeus Carver (Samuel Jackson) rushes to McClane's side and is caught up in this dangerous game of cat and mouse.

Singer/songwriter Sam Phillips makes her film debut as a mute terrorist.

The cast of *Die Hard with a Vengeance* is nothing if not eclectic. Bruce Willis rose to stardom through a television detective show, *Moonlighting,* on which he played a well-known and loved character, David Addison. Jeremy Irons, who plays the villain in this film, has risen to prominence through a series of literature-to-film roles, such as playing the title role in the French film *Swann in Love* (1984), based on the first portion of Marcel Proust's epic novel *Remembrance of Things Past.* He has also appeared and been nominated and/or won prizes for his performances in *Brideshead Revisited, The French Lieutenant's Woman* (1981, British), *Dead Ringers* (1988), and *Reversal of Fortune* (1990). Samuel L. Jackson has played a variety of roles, from menacing law enforcer (*Kiss of Death,* 1995), to visionary assassin (*Pulp Fiction,* 1994), to techno-geek (*Jurassic Park,* 1994) to world-renowned intellectual (*Amos and Andrew,* 1993). Combined in this pressure cooker of a film, the three very different actors, from very different cinematic neighborhoods, create an interesting blend of acting methods and characterizations in what otherwise is the high-tech version of a western, complete with the bigger-than-life shoot-out on main street.

Zeus brings rationality and intelligence to the film. Given a word puzzle to solve by the madman, McClane jumps at the obvious answer. Zeus thinks a minute longer and finds the hidden, and correct, answer. McClane is an action character, jumping onto speeding, exploding subway trains, driving wildly in a huge tractor trailer. Zeus always introduces a note of caution, of sanity. Samuel Jackson describes the dynamics between McClane and Carver in the production notes: "McClane's kind of devil-may-care, and he can look at Zeus and realize here's somebody who really want to stay alive through all of this." Willis, on the other hand, sees McClane as a reluctant hero. "I've made the choice of playing him as a guy who doesn't want to be doing what he has to do in these films," says Willis in the production notes. "I think the interesting thing is that McClane's in situations where he has absolutely no other choice but to do the things he has to do: jump off a building, swing in the window on a hose, jump on the wing of an airplane, jump onto a train that he knows is about to explode."

Simon is the thinker, the worrier, the confused, business-like but distracted evil genius, plotting deadly but clever deeds. Says Jeremy Irons of Simon in the production notes, "He's also one of those men who is very highly intelligent, and who loves playing games. I think if you are a duelist in life, you like games, you like duels, and you're always looking for good opponents. Simon thinks McClane may be a good opponent." The set-up is intriguing, but the disappointment is that all this action and chaos fails to break new ground.

Additionally, New York police officers have become a genre of their own, with hit television programs such as *NYPD Blue* chronicling each moment of their lives at work and at home. Here, such fine actors as Graham Greene (*Dances with Wolves*, 1993) are wasted on small, meaningless roles, recreating roles already made tired by weekly television shows. Where in the era of *Serpico* (1973) it was a novel concept for police officers to pick on each other, today it is commonplace entertainment. This film is no different. For instance, it would appear that Greene's main role in the film is belittling McClane, confirming McClane's status as outsider to the force. It is a role that requires too little of this gifted actor and provides little (if any) entertainment for the audience.

"You don't like me because I'm white." "I don't like you because you're going to get me killed."—McClane and Zeus from *Die Hard With a Vengeance*

Earning its title as blockbuster, *Die Hard with a Vengeance* begins with what the filmmakers suppose is the largest stunt ever shot on the streets of New York. In portraying the exploding department store, the filmmakers chose a building on lower Sixth Avenue that was vacant except for a crystal shop on the ground floor. (The production notes reassure readers that none of the crystal was broken during the staging of this stunt.) Crowds gathered to watch the explosion which was powerful enough to shatter windows and overturn cars and vans. Seven cameras filmed the stunt for the production, but countless news reporters and amateur photographers captured the event on film. Other amazing stunts were staged around New York: an improbable car chase through Central Park, a heist filmed in part at the real Federal Reserve building, a mad dash across 90 rush hour blocks and death-defying stunts filmed on a real subway train, racing south from 42nd Street. Producer Michael Tadross found that filming in New York was unlike any place else on Earth. "New York is like one of the actors in the movie, and you don't get that in other towns."

What is perhaps most disappointing, however, is that even with all of the explosions, all of the danger and racing around, the small children in peril, the tidal wave of aqueduct flooding, *Die Hard with a Vengeance* is boring. Audiences who were once amazed by high-tech peril have been watching it in one form or another since *Towering Inferno* (1974) and the novelty has worn off. Nonetheless, some viewers remain hopeful. Earning $25 million its first weekend, the film did well at least initially at the box office, even if many reviewers are expressing their discontent and their disappointment. For instance, Peter Rainer, who reviews the film for the Los Angeles Times, writes, "The *Die Hard* series was never exactly big on nuance, but this new installment relentlessly zeros in on sensation. It's almost sadistically single-minded." David Sterritt of *The Christian Science Monitor* writes, "But where can the *Die Hard* series go from here? The answer: nowhere."

Die Hard with a Vengeance is a disappointment. New York in flames, actors racing the streets in worn, torn cars and suits, a madman interested in owning the world? Audiences have seen that, understand that, and are no doubt ready for a film with a story line. All but super pyro junkies should wait to view this film on television.

—*Roberta F. Green*

CREDITS

John McClane: Bruce Willis
Simon: Jeremy Irons
Zeus: Samuel L. Jackson
Joe Lambert: Graham Greene

Origin: USA
Released: 1995
Production: John McTiernan, Michael Tadross for Cinergi and Andrew G. Vajna production; released by 20th Century Fox
Direction: John McTiernan
Screenplay: Jonathan Hensleigh
Cinematography: Peter Menzies
Editing: John Wright
Production design: Jackson DeGovia
Casting: Pat McCorkle
Music: Michael Kamen
Visual Effects Supervisor: John E. Sullivan
Special Effects: Albert Griswold, Richard Cory, Paul Stewart, Gary Cruise
MPAA rating: R
Running Time: 125 minutes

REVIEWS

Atlanta Journal-Constitution, May 19, 1995, p. P3.
Baltimore Sun, May 19, 1995, Features, p. 4.
Boston Globe, May 19, 1995, p. 55.
Chicago Sun-Times, May 19, 1995, p. 33.
Christian Science Monitor, May 26, 1995, p. 12.
Houston Chronicle, May 19, 1995, Weekend Preview, p. 1.
Los Angeles Times, May 19, 1995, p. F1.
Newsday, May 19, 1995, p. BO2.
The New York Times, May 19, 1995, p. C1.
San Francisco Chronicle, May 19, 1995, p. C1.
San Francisco Examiner, May 19, 1995, p. C1.
Washington Post, May 19, 1995, p. N57.

Dolores Claiborne

"Sometimes an accident can be an unhappy woman's best friend."—Movie tagline

"A uniquely spellbinding piece of cinematic storytelling."—Michael Medved, *The New York Post*

"Two thumbs up!"—*Siskel & Ebert*

"An intense, superbly acted, extremely powerful drama."—Jeffrey Lyons, *Sneak Previews*

Box Office Gross: $24,361,867

Kathy Bates and Jennifer Jason Leigh star in *Dolores Claiborne*. © 1995 Castle Rock Entertainment. All rights reserved. Photo by John Clifford.

Dolores Claiborne, one of the first serious American films of the 1995 season, springs from an unlikely source, a psychological study of a battered, abused woman, written by Stephen King in 1992, but, then, *The Shawshank Redemption*, one of the best films of 1994, was also adapted from a Stephen King story, so maybe it is time to stop stereotyping King as merely a skilled writer of sensational horror fiction.

Stephen King dedicated *Dolores Claiborne* to his mother, and that's enough to make one wonder what kind of home life the novelist might have had; but this is fiction, set on Little Tall Island, sixteen miles off the Atlantic coast from Bar Harbor, population 527 in 1963, the year of the last total eclipse of the sun in northern New England in the twentieth century, and the year many people suspected Dolores killed her husband.

Dolores is a rough character in the novel, a woman who had had three children and a hard life (two more children than her counterpart in the film), and a woman who is far more colorfully colloquial than the movie version: "Oh, frig ya coffee! Take the whole pot and shove it up your kazoo." The novel rambles on in this idiom for nearly four hundred pages. At the end, Dolores is nearly sixty-six years old and ten million dollars richer.

Dolores Claiborne was directed by Taylor Hackford, who received five Academy Award nominations in 1982 for

The last time Kathy Bates was in a film based on a Stephen King novel, she won the Oscar (for *Misery*).

Everyone in her island village in Maine thinks Dolores is a "bitch" and a murderess. Eighteen years ago her husband got drunk, fell down a well, and was killed. Detective John Mackey (Christopher Plummer) did his best to convict Dolores for the murder of her husband; but convincing evidence was lacking, and she was acquitted. When Vera Donovan (Judy Parfitt), her employer, takes a tumble down a flight of stairs and dies, Mackey is certain Dolores has struck again. Dolores is so surly and ill-tempered that viewers might willingly share his suspicion.

Being a vengeful, spiteful person, Mackey sends a fax to Dolores's estranged daughter, Selena St. George (Jennifer Jason Leigh) of a story about Vera's death that appeared in the Bangor newspaper, with a note asking: "Isn't this your mother?" Selena is a successful investigative reporter for Esquire and has not seen her mother in fifteen years. They are not close. Selena holds her mother responsible for her father's death, but the story is more complicated than she remembers. Psychologically traumatized as a teenager, she has closed down all memories of her father, Joe St. George (David Strathairn), an alcoholic who sexually molested her. The buzzword here is "repressed memory."

The long-suffering Dolores remembers, however, what the daughter cannot bear to remember. Dolores became a servant to the wealthy and demanding Vera Donovan in order to save money to finance her daughter's education at Vassar. When Dolores figures out what Joe has been doing to Selena, she goes to the bank to withdraw her $3,000 savings in order to escape from the island with her daughter from a drunken, abusive husband, only to discover that he has taken the money without her knowledge.

That's the last straw. Dolores does not exactly murder Joe, but she sets up a string of circumstances that lead to his death, taking advice from her employer, Vera, who tells her:

"Sometimes being a bitch is all a woman has to hold on to." This sentence becomes a mantra for all of the women in this film. Vera understands Dolores and seems to have arranged her own unfaithful husband's death in an automobile accident as he was driving to see his mistress one night.

> "Sometimes being a bitch is all a woman has to hold on to."—Dolores from *Dolores Claiborne*

Vera's advice gives Dolores the strength to deal with her husband after Dolores breaks into tears one day at work and tells Vera what is bothering her. No one, except, finally, Selena, understands the bond between Dolores and Vera. After Joe dies, Dolores continues working for Vera for another eighteen years, despite low wages and treatment that often seems abusive. Finally, Vera, in terrible health after a stroke, decides she wants to die, wheels herself to the top of the stairs, and throws herself down the stairs after fighting off Dolores's attempts to stop her. When the fall does not kill her, she asks Dolores to finish her off. Dolores has kept house for Vera for twenty-two years and is probably Vera's only friend. The film begins with an incomplete rendering of this sequence, which leads viewers to believe that Dolores is probably guilty. It's all a matter of context.

Detective Mackey certainly believes Dolores is homicidal and discovers a motive after Vera's death, since Vera left over one million dollars to Dolores, who did not know that she had been named in Vera's will. After a desperately un-

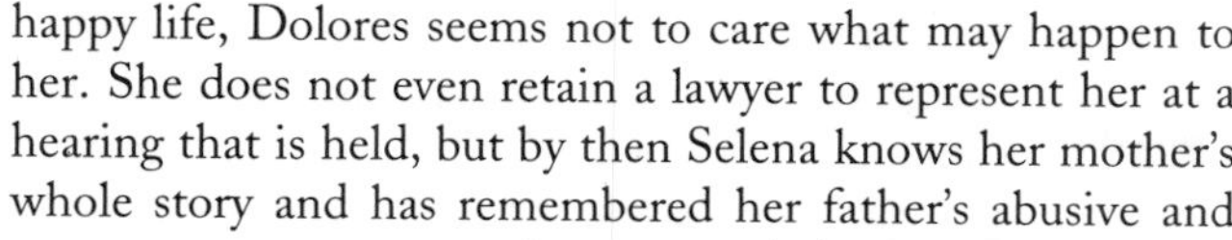

happy life, Dolores seems not to care what may happen to her. She does not even retain a lawyer to represent her at a hearing that is held, but by then Selena knows her mother's whole story and has remembered her father's abusive and incestuous behavior. Finally, she stands by her mother, who is ultimately the victim of all that has happened. The plot moves intelligently towards this moment of discovery and reconciliation.

The film, well-directed by Taylor Hackford, was skilfully adapted by Tony Gilroy from the Stephen King novel, written as an extended monologue. The challenge of the screenplay was to dramatize that monologue and to build up the other characters dramatically—Selena, her father, Vera, and the obsessed detective. The transformation appears to be flawless, building upon the conflict between mother and daughter.

Stephen King apparently has learned that his stories have been most successfully adapted to cinema by experienced directors and writers, such as Brian DePalma, Stanley Kubrick, Rob Reiner, Frank Darabond, and, now, Taylor Hackford, and the writer has judiciously distanced himself from the screen adaptations of his work. *Misery* was adapted in 1990 by William Goldman, one of Hollywood's most experienced and successful screenwriters. Tony Gilroy lacks Goldman's experience, but, as Desson Howe noted in his Washington Post Weekend review, Gillroy structured the story for "maximum watchability."

Kathy Bates owes her star status to Stephen King since her performance in *Misery* was a turning point in her screen career. The Bates character in *Misery* was a crazy, obsessed fan who tormented her favorite writer, holding him captive and forcing him to write to her specifications. In that film, Bates was an archetypal demented fan, a maniac incapable of growth. Dolores Claiborne has far more human potential, and for that reason her's is the more interesting story.

Bates earned an Academy Award for her mad performance in *Misery*, but her angry performance in *Dolores Claiborne* is even more worthy of an Oscar nomination. Jennifer Jason Leigh is also quite good as her daughter, a woman who has pushed herself too far to succeed and turned herself into a borderline neurotic who seeks solace from alcohol and drugs; but this tends to be a one-note performance that hardly ever goes beyond resentment and anger. At first she is morose and unforgiving and her feelings toward her mother are so ambiguous that one wonders why she has come to Maine after having entirely ignored her mother for fifteen years. Eventually she is tough enough to face the past as the screenplay dramatizes the conflict between mother and daughter and arrives at the disclosure of truth. At the conclusion, both women share a common toughness, understanding, and respect.

CREDITS

Dolores Claiborne: Kathy Bates
Selena St. George: Jennifer Jason Leigh
Joe St. George: David Strathairn
Vera Donovan: Judy Parfitt
Detective John Mackey: Christopher Plummer
Peter: Eric Bogosian

Origin: USA
Released: 1995
Production: Taylor Hackford and Charles Mulvehill for Castle Rock Entertainment; released by Columbia Pictures
Direction: Taylor Hackford
Screenplay: Tony Gilroy; based on the book by Stephen King
Cinematography: Gabriel Beristain
Editing: Mark Warner
Production design: Bruno Rubeo
Casting: Nancy Klopper
Music: Danny Elfman
MPAA rating: R
Running Time: 131 minutes

The cast is further strengthened by the presence of Judy Parfitt as Vera Donovan. Parfitt played an excellent Gertrude to Anthony Hopkins's Claudius in the Tony Richardson production of *Hamlet* in 1969 and has worked steadily in Britain; but this is her first major American screen role. Likewise Christopher Plummer has been imported from the London stage to play Inspector Mackey. Plummer was born in Montréal but soon moved to Broadway and London's West End, where he became a leading actor at the National Theatre and for the Royal Shakespeare Company. He has also been featured in over fifty motion pictures. David Strathairn, who plays the despicable husband to creepy perfection, has starred in six films by John Sayles and can also be seem playing opposite Jessica Lange in *Losing Isaiah*, also released in early 1995.

The setting for *Dolores Claiborne* is dark and gloomy in the present but more sunny and warm in the flashback sequences to 1975. Gabriel Beristain's cinematography effectively enhances the separation between present and past and between summer and winter as Dolores endures gloomy weather and gloomy circumstances. The film's transitions between present and past are nicely photographed and edited. After Vera's death, Dolores is forced to return to her family home with her sullen and hostile daughter. The rooms of that deserted house trigger memories that materialize into flashbacks of Joe and the teenaged Selena (Ellen Muth), and the lighting transforms the present into the past as the flashbacks seamlessly emerge.

Though some reviews were mixed, reviewers tended to praise Kathy Bates, Judy Parfitt (described by one reviewer as "awesome"), and David Strathairn ("brilliant loathsome"). Owen Gleiberman of *Entertainment Weekly* gave it a low grade (a D+ on his peculiar scale) and found it fully disagreeable. In his *New Yorker* review, Terrence Rafferty described Christopher Plummer as "hamming it up" (famous actors inspire such comments) and also had reservations about Jennifer Jason Leigh's "grim, dogged acting" because it introduced feelings of self-pity that King "scrupulously avoided in the novel."

Rafferty felt that King's point in the novel was that Dolores's suffering was heroic and that she was not turned into a victim by what she had gone through, an idea that is undercut by Leigh's "whining, petulant daughter," whose performance turns the film into a "warm mother-daughter soap opera." This warmth is fleeting, however, and only felt at the very end, when Selena defends her mother against Mackey's accusations before the judge. All in all, the film presents a psychological portrait that is both plausible and interesting, effectively adapted and dramatized from the novel.

—James M. Welsh

REVIEWS

Entertainment Weekly. March 3, 1995, p.44.
New York. Vol.28, No.14, April 3, 1995, pp.58-59.
The New Yorker. April 3, 1995, pp.93-95.
The New York Times. March 24, 1995, B6.
Rolling Stone. Issue 706, April 20, 1995, p.88.
USA Today. March 24, 1995. (Rated 3´ out of 4.)
Variety. March 20-26, 1995, p.48.
The Washington Post. March 24, 1995, C1, C4.
The Washington Post Weekend, March 24, 1995, p.42.

Don Juan DeMarco

"The best part of love is losing all sense of reality."—Movie tagline

"A great date movie. It really does work its magic."—*Siskel & Ebert*

Box Office Gross: $22,080,619

Although playing the title role in *Don Juan Demarco* is certainly not the type of dramatic part that shoots a Hollywood actor into the stratosphere of superstardom, the performance given confirms once more that Johnny Depp is a marvelously versatile—and appealing—performer. In director/writer Jeremy Leven's first feature, Depp is thoroughly engaging in this charming, escapist motion picture.

The opening sequence of the film aims to crystallize Don Juan DeMarco's devastating power over women—and it succeeds. Depp's unctuous, gorgeous Spanish accent narrates as a voiceover while his character applies scent, slips on black gloves, and assumes the dark mask he has sworn never to take off in company. After targeting a woman in a hotel to seduce, Don Juan reveals that after this conquest, he will commit suicide since the one woman who matters, Dona Ana, has rejected him. Sure enough, Don Juan bowls over the attractive woman—who is apparently waiting for her companion to join her for dinner—and swiftly he is dripping his love over her in a hotel room.

With a dashing bow to the woman, who is now back at her table, flushed with pleasure, Don Juan takes his leave. The next shot finds him perched atop a billboard, ready to jump. Dr. Jack Mickler (Marlon Brando) is hoisted up in a crane to talk him down. After hearing Don Juan's name, Mickler adopts the persona of Don Octavio—sounding rather like his Don Corleone in *The Godfather*—and persuades Don Juan to descend with him in the crane.

On a bright New York morning, Jack drives through the gate of the Woodhaven Mental Hospital in Queens for a morning meeting. Although he is only ten days from retirement, he asks to take on a new case: Don Juan's. After some resistance, his request is granted. Naturally, Jack is the best in the hospital or rather he was; as his boss, Dr. Showalter (Bob Dishy) points out, Jack is burnt out.

When Don Juan and Jack meet in the latter's office for their first session, the romancer's mask has been removed by the nurses, but despite his aggravation at this action, Don Juan's seductive power, his alluring personality, seem intact. As Jack talks in his normal American accent, Don Juan asserts that he will help the psychiatrist recover his "lost" identity of Don Octavio. He asks Jack for ten days without taking the prescribed medication to tell his story and prove who he is. If he fails to do so, he will take the pills. Jack agrees, and Don Juan commences his entrancing, fantastical story.

It was in Mexico, Don Juan relates, that he was born. In a tiny village, its flowers abloom despite the harsh sun that bakes the dusty square and the stucco walls of the houses that have been wonderfully painted, Don Juan's mother, Dona Inez (Rachel Ticotin), falls in love with a handsome Italian-American dancer moments after the visitor alights from a bus.

Don Juan's story is at once absorbing, so much so that a preoccupied Jack fails to pay attention to his wife's car troubles tale when he gets home. Their brief introductory scene is all that is shown to suggest a tepidness in the couple's marriage; the point is cursorily made, rather than shown.

Back in Jack's office the next morning, Don Juan's story continues, tracing the lover's first seduction at the tender age of sixteen. The woman in question is the lovely, but married, Dona Julia (Talisa Soto). Burning with virginal passion, Don Juan tries to resist temptation, all the while being taught the art of swordsmanship by his father.

Don Juan's heady tale is certainly affecting Jack, and once back home, wife Marilyn senses a change in his manner and spirit. The sight of Brando and Dunaway between the sheets in one scene is a moment to behold, even if it does break the film's spell by telegraphing the filmmaker's glee at having two such icons in bed together at this stage in their respective careers.

We learn that Don Juan at last succumbs to the charms of Dona Julia, and their affair rages until her husband catches them in fragrante delicto. The cuckolded man declares that he has been having an affair with Don Juan's mother, and so the boy's father—to avenge his honor—fights him in a duel. Don Juan's father is killed, and a furious Don Juan picks up the sword of his father and kills his lover's husband. In mourning for the death of his father, Don Juan assumes the black eye mask.

"You are a great lover like myself, even though you may have lost your way — and your accent."—Don Juan from *Don Juan DeMarco*

By now, Jack is clearly intoxicated by his patient, and eager to rekindle the fire in his own life, he lavishes Marilyn with a fancy dinner, diamond earrings, champagne, and even a Mariachi band. His boss at the hospital is less intoxicated, however, and pressures Jack to dispense the required medication to the young man in his care; Don Juan is affecting patients and health care providers alike with his powers. Jack refuses to hand out the mandated pills, but he does follow up a lead to his patient's grandmother.

She tells a very different story of her grandson's origin and family background. He grew up in Phoenix, she tells the psychiatrist. Yes, his father was killed—in a car accident. And as for Dona Julia, she is apparently just a "Playboy Pet of the Month," and a woman with whom the young man was infatuated. No close-up of the girl is given, but from a distance, the centerfold does indeed resemble Dona Julia.

At the hospital, Don Juan rejects his grandmother's version of his life, and resumes his story, recounting how he is dispatched by his mother—who goes into a convent—and put on a ship, from which he is sold into slavery into an Arabian Nights' type of kingdom. Dressed as a woman, he is seduced by the Sultan's main wife, and when he is not with her, he is allowed to sport with the 1499 other women of the harem. But all good things must pass, and once again Don Juan is sent off to sea when danger looms.

With Dr. Micklin still stalling his colleagues as to medication, he receives a visit from a nun who claims to be Dona Inez, but refuses fully to verify her son's tale. As for Don Juan, his epic concludes with his being shipwrecked on the island of Eros, where he falls in love with Dona Ana (Geraldine Pailhas). All is going beautifully until she hears of his 1,500 conquests, and she leaves him forever, apparently suspicious of his future fidelity to her.

CREDITS

Jack Mickler: Marlon Brando
Don Juan DeMarco: Johnny Depp
Marilyn Mickler: Faye Dunaway
Dona Ana: Geraldine Pailhas
Dr. Paul Showalter: Bob Dishy
Dona Inez: Rachel Ticotin
Dona Julia: Talisa Soto

Origin: USA
Released: 1995
Production: Francis Ford Coppola, Fred Fuchs, and Patrick Palmer for American Zoetrope; released by New Line Cinema
Direction: Jeremy Leven
Screenplay: Jeremy Leven
Cinematography: Ralph Bode
Editing: Tony Gibbs
Art direction: Jeff Knipp
Music: Michael Ramen
MPAA rating: PG-13
Running Time: 90 minutes

Back in the "real" world, a judge at Woodhaven rules on Don Juan's status. Although Jack believes in his identity, the young man speaks a few sentences in a normal American accent, even admitting to an obsession with the "Playboy" pet. The judge finds him sane, and has him released. We hear no more from Don Juan's lips as Jack takes over the narration. The good doctor and Marilyn take Don Juan with them to the sea shore of Eros, so that the lover can find his Dona Ana. Will she be there? "Why not?" says Jack in a voiceover. When she does appear and embraces Don Juan, the rejuvenated Micklins dance together in the sunshine.

Jeremy Leven's film self-consciously switches from the lushness of Don Juan's story to the sterilized surroundings of the hospital. Naturally, in the tall tale of our young lover, colors are vivid, costumes are plush, the Mexican and Arabian settings of Art Director Jeff Knipp impress, and Michael Ramen's music—reminiscent of *Carmen*—all help heighten the romantic mood.

The film's weak spots, although minor, fall into two areas: the length of the prosaic psychiatrists' meetings, and not enough investment in the depiction of the Micklins' marriage. As for the former, the discussions over Don Juan's treatment are necessary to the plot but a touch overlong. For the latter, and as noted above, writer/director Leven provides only one scene to illustrate the Micklins' stale relationship. Jack's inattention to his wife on this occasion is hardly a profound symptom of a worn-out marriage. It is a fact just thrust at the audience that their long relationship is tired, and one knows it will be revived. And, in fact, Don Juan's tale is just the tonic Jack Micklin needs for his own life.

Although it is a delight to see Dunaway on screen, her role is underwritten, and she is underused. She makes the most of her screen time, but apart from the bedroom scene when she catches popcorn in her mouth, her role is strictly a narrow one. As for Brando, his slur is evident, but he radiates a welcome confidence and energy as he responds to the charm of his patient. Seemingly aware of his huge bulk, Brando's character and Brando himself are the butt of several jokes, and in one scene, Jack is seen puffing away at weights as he tries to get in shape for his wife. A slow pan on the younger Brando in a black and white photograph in another scene reminds the audience—although a reminder is hardly needed—of how handsome Marlon Brando once was.

AWARDS AND NOMINATIONS

Academy Awards Nominations 1995: Best Song ("Have You Ever Really Loved a Woman?")
Golden Globe Awards Nominations 1996: Best Score, Best Song ("Have You Ever Really Loved a Woman?")

As Don Juan, Johnny Depp is superb. Without overplaying his role, Depp is enticing, larger-than-life and compelling. He brings an unexpected truthfulness to his fantasy role, enabling us to accept the reality of his Don Juan whilst wondering if in fact the young man is just a native of Phoenix, Arizona. Our preferences, naturally, are that he is who he claims to be.

Jeremy Leven's directorial debut is thus a success. Although *Variety* dismissed the film as not being "particularly well directed," Leven has written a sweet film and directed it at a fair pace. Lighter than a cream puff, *Don Juan Demarco* invites the audience to let down its guard and indulge in a flight of fancy. Don Juan's inventive tale, allied with the welcome appearances of Brando and Dunaway, make this film one to be warmly recommended.

—*Paul B. Cohen*

REVIEWS

The New York Times, April 7, 1995, p. C16.

The Doom Generation

"Sex. Mayhem. Whatever".—Movie tagline

"Lurid, funny. Araki is a dazzling and witty visual stylist."—Jay Carr, *The Boston Globe*

"A savagely funny ride fueled by director Araki's insight and blunt compassion. The dangerously seductive Johnathon Schaech is a star in the making. It's unsafe, unnerving and primed to explode."—Peter Travers, *Rolling Stone*

"Hilarious. Bound to be one of the most controversial films of the year."—Barry Walters, *The San Francisco Examiner*

Filmmaker Gregg Araki continues his quest of capturing raw teen angst with this follow-up to his shockingly titled *Totally F***ed Up* (1994), the second installment of his "Teenage Apocalypse" trilogy called *The Doom Generation*. Araki, a director not known for handling his subject matter with subtlety, as demonstrated by the previous film's title, holds nothing back in presenting this as a hellish excursion through eyes of three poster teens from the MTV generation. *The Doom Generation* is a road picture that certainly is a vulgar, tasteless, funny and graphically violent trip on the wild side of youth.

Foul-mouthed and bitter Amy Blue (Rose McGowan) and slightly dim boyfriend Jordan White (James Duval) feel trapped in their surrounding of nightclubs, traffic jams and drive-ins. Amy is convinced that the city is "sucking out her soul." But while sitting in Amy's car, and agreeing that the world is too confining for two free spirits, their lives take a 180 degree turn when mysterious drifter Xavier Red (Johnathon Schaech) literally drops in while running from a group of skinheads. Xavier forces himself inside the car and their dark and twisted odyssey begins.

The trio stops at a local Quickie-Mart operated by the stereotypical Oriental family. When Amy and Jordan are unable to pay for their items (they left their money in the car), the impatient clerk pulls a shotgun out demanding payment on their $6.66 bill. Xavier rushes in the store and tackles the clerk. In their struggle, Xavier blows the clerk's head off and it flies across the room and lands in the relish. In cartoon fashion only without the animation, the head spews vomit and continues to curse in Chinese. The horrified threesome jumps into the car with Jordan amazed at a talking severed head.

Their trek involves driving through America's wastelands, stopping to load up on junk food, beer and cigarettes, and their rest stops all seem to end with Xavier severing body parts from his victims. When an exasperated Amy yells at Xavier's for his penchant for murder, she exclaims "You murdered two people tonight. Doesn't that faze you at all?" "Yeah, I'm bummed," replies Xavier.

In his irreverent style, Araki has subtitled *The Doom Generation* "a heterosexual film" in the same fashion that he has done in the past. *The Living End* was "another Homo Movie by Gregg Araki" and *Totally F***ed Up* was "an irresponsible film by Gregg Araki." But to label *Doom* a heterosexual film would be callous since it contains the same homoerotic issues that Araki addresses in his previous films. With the commingling of the Amy, Jordan and Xavier, the inevitable menage a trois surfaces. But Xavier comes off as not so much as homosexual but omnisexual. Xavier is shown masturbating while watching Amy and Jordan have sex in a bath tub. He soon becomes an active participant with Amy, but has more of an attraction for weak and vulnerable Jordan than for Amy. Later in the film, Xavier evens admits to having sex with his golden retriever whom he called a "consenting adult." Therefore, *The Doom Generation* becomes a peep show into the lives of three kinky individuals.

Outside of Xavier's sex drive, he, Amy and Jordan are seemingly one dimensional characters. Araki does provide some background on each character as they crash for the night in a motel. This scene offers a brief and somewhat simplified logic to why Amy and Jordan are not in too much of a hurry to return home. Amy's mother is a drug addict and her father (now deceased) was an alcoholic whose fatherly love took on more than just hugs and kisses. Jordan, the only one with both parents, is alienated from his family and Xavier confesses as a child to witnessing his mother kill his father and then herself. Textbook explanations for an 18-year-old, chain-smoking young woman who compares sex with eating spaghetti, an innocent young man who is fascinated by childish things such as glow in the dark yo-yos and a sexually voracious serial killer. But, again subtlety or depth is not what you'll find with Araki. Despite the narrow range of characters, the three actors do rise to the occasion to offer the film just the right ambience of kitsch and B-movie feel. McGowan's Amy has the perfect rouge matte lips to create the universal pout of a Valley Girl turned angry young femme fatale. Duval has been compared to Keanu Reeves and he sways convincingly between idiocy and innocence with Jordan. But Schaech's performance is the one that will get the most attention and rightfully so. He is vile and sexy at the same time. His seductive good looks and wide smile are reason enough for women and men to make him an object of desire.

By naming his characters after the colors of the American flag, Amy (Blue), Jordan (White) and Xavier (Red), Araki is demonstrating biting imagination. Clearly these last names are both a badge defining these people and a slap in the face of American culture which Araki pokes fun at constantly in *The Doom Generation*. Amy is blue because of her temperament; Jordan is white because of his naivete and innocence and Xavier is red because of his violent and often volatile nature. In this regard, Jordan stands out from his companions. It's Araki's treatment of Jordan that he proclaims his most dark message. When violence surrounds him, Jordan still comes out sweet and innocent. But when a group on skinheads interrupt Jordan's and Xavier's first sexual encounter together (after repeated flirting from Xavier) a gruesome castration scene ends the film. The scene is very similar to Richard Brooke's *Looking for Mr. Goodbar* [1977], another movie that punishes sexual deviance), with a darkened room illuminated only by a blinking strobe light. According to Araki, Jordan's demise is symbolic to what happens to all that is innocent and good in American society.

The dark message aside, *The Doom Generation* is a film full of sight gags and running jokes. It is a true parody of road movies and pop culture. Jordan orders shrimp nuggets from a Quickie Mart that has a sign reading "we don't call 911." In every store the trio stops in, there is a big sign reading some apocalyptic message. The first Quickie Mart had huge sign over the chili dogs reading "Shoplifters will be executed." And every time they purchase something, there total always comes out to $6.66. The jokes are further installed by frequent cameo appearances by several celebrities. Christopher McKnight (Peter from *The Brady Bunch* series) and Lauren Tewes from *The Love Boat* series are newscasters. Amanda Bearse from *Married With Children* is a bartender and infamous madam Heidi Fleiss is a convenient store clerk.

Working with a $1 million dollar budget, *The Doom Generation* is the best looking of all Araki's films. He captures the basic colors that accentuate popular culture and kitsch, from the decor of the various seedy motels to photographing America's wastelands during their trip. The narrative is tightly strung along with an impressive soundtrack that includes such artists as Nine Inch Nails, Porno for Pyros and Jesus and Mary Chain. Combine all the colors, cameos, black humor and alternative music, watching *The Doom Generation* is more or less a psychedelic trip into perversity. It is true camp destined to become a staple of the midnight movie circuit where it will be truly appreciated.

Because of the violence and road trip scenario, the film can be compared to Oliver Stone's *Natural Born Killers*

CREDITS

Jordan White: James Duval
Amy Blue: Rose McGowan
Xavier Red: Johnathon Schaech

Origin: USA
Released: 1995
Production: Andrea Sperling and Gregg Araki for a UGC and Teen Angst Movie Co, Desperate Pictures, Blurco and Why Not production; released by TriMark
Direction: Gregg Araki
Screenplay: Gregg Araki
Editing: Gregg Araki
Cinematography: Jim Fealy
Production design: Therese Deprez
Costume design: Catherine Cooper-Thoman
Hair and make-up: Jason Rail
MPAA rating: R
Running Time: 90 minutes

AWARDS AND NOMINATIONS

Independent Spirit Awards Nominations 1996:
Debut Performance (McGowan)

(1994). But Araki obviously does not treat his material with Stone's heavy handed direction. *The Doom Generation* ends without any true resolution and is ultimately unfulfilling. It's similar to taking a long walk with no particular destination in mind, but sometimes life is like that, especially when you are young. Maybe that's why Araki's final teenage apocalypse film will be titled *Nowhere.*

—Michelle Banks

REVIEWS

Los Angeles Times. October 27, 1995. p.F6
The New York Times. October 25, 1995. p.C14
Rolling Stone. November 16, 1995. p.117
Variety. p.46.
The Village Voice. October 31, 1995. p. 80
The Washington Post. November 10, 1995. p.45

Double Happiness

"A delightfully absurd comedy."—Wolf Schneider, *Mademoiselle*

"Inspired, funny and endearing."—Christine Spines, *Premiere*

"Two thumbs up!"—*Siskel & Ebert*

"A delight! Witty, intelligent, savvy and heartfelt."—Jeffrey Lyons, *Sneak Previews*

Mina Shum knew she wanted to become a filmmaker when, as a freshman at the University of British Columbia, she watched *Gallipoli* (1981), which presents historical events by focusing on the individuals whose lives are shaped by those events. "I immediately thought, I should go into film[.]...This way.. .I can actually orchestrate an entire world." Unlike *Gallipoli*, however, which explores the sad history of two young idealists who enlist and meet their fates in World War I, Mina Shum's first feature-length film focuses on the cultural struggles still existing in her Chinese-Canadian family. Says Shum, "I'm not representing Chinese culture. I'm representing this one family. All I know is that the struggle [over whether and how much to assimilate] still exists in my family."

Double Happiness tells the story of the Li family, in particular the eldest daughter Jade Li (Sandra Oh), an aspiring actress. While Jade has begun to audition for small parts in her hometown Vancouver, her parents continue to look for the perfect husband for Jade: he must be Chinese and a doctor or lawyer. To placate her family, Jade goes on arranged dates, fixed up to look her family's version of presentable — a rather Asian Jackie Kennedy look or, as Jade laments, Connie Chung. However, try as the family might, Jade falls in love with a college student, a Caucasian college student at that. *Double Happiness* then addresses the question of whose happiness will take precedence or, to put it another way, whose life is it anyway?

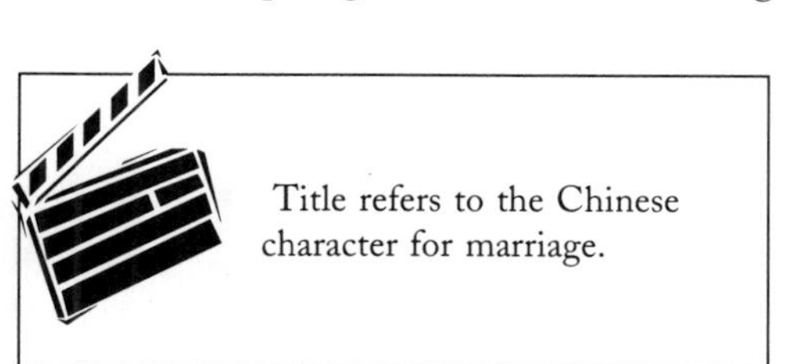

Title refers to the Chinese character for marriage.

Certainly the center of the film, and arguably its primary joy, is Korean-Canadian actress Sandra Oh, who received a 1994 Best Actress Genie (Canada's Oscar) for her performance. Throughout the range of emotions Oh is called upon by Shum's screenplay to produce, Oh successfully transports the audience with her. For instance, Oh's character Jade is eager for a role to play, not just the commercials for which she's auditioning, but a real part, "some really hard role, something I had to gain weight for." Before a big audition, the film includes a medium shot of Jade, working through Tennessee Williams-esque lines in a husky southern accent, her voice and far-away look filled with faded blossoms, summer turning into fall, smokey whiskey served in unclean glasses. It is a mesmerizing performance, full of loss and longing, and lighted in a chiaroscuro-esque manner, punctuated with rain drops that rest upon the glass through which she looks. Up to this point in the film, the audience has seen Jade as the petulant daughter, the teasing older sister, the sassy friend. Yet this brief scene teaches viewers a world of information about Jade's dreams and Sandra Oh's abilities.

Persons connected with the film find the above-referenced scene meaningful for other reasons as well. "You could see she had a clear vision of the film she wanted to make," said John Taylor, director of operations for Telefilm Vancouver. "Many of the interesting visual ideas come from Mina. There is a scene in the bathroom with rain on the window that is sort of silhouetted in shadows on characters' faces. It was Mina's idea, to give the scene a poignancy and a mood."

Beyond the staging of any one scene, the film acquires additional poignancy from the juxtaposition of scenes as well.

For instance, the audition that the audience attends with Jade is for a television commercial in which she will play a worker at a fast-food restaurant. When the persons conducting the audition ask Jade to try the lines with an accent, she asks, in a perfect Parisian accent, what type of accent would they like. The auditioners respond with stony stares, and Jade apologizes, responding instead with a stereotypical Chinese accent. The anger the audience feels and the humiliation it appears Jade feels at that moment would have been palpable in any case. However, after the audience has seen Jade's incredible range and ability, this gross racial stereotype is more than an unkindness, more than ignorance; it is an outrage, a slap, a crime. Much of the extraordinary power of this scene arises from its placement after the scene of Jade's private rehearsal.

The film has its lighter moments as well, some of which also rely on Jade's chameleon-like abilities. For instance, when Jade goes out with a couple of her friends to a night club, the bouncer stops Jade at the door and tells her that the fire code demands that not one more person enter the premises. After several folk march by Jade and are allowed to enter, it becomes clear that she has been found to be somehow unacceptable, or at least less acceptable than the other revelers. Soon she is joined in line by Mark (Callum Rennie), who attempts to strike up a conversation with her. Jade adopts a geisha-like demeanor, giggling girlishly behind her hand, looking only askance at Mark, shyly turning her body away from his as well. Mark, geekishly handsome in box-like glasses and a thatch of blonde hair, believes he has found a pearl in the rough, until Jade stops the pretense and amazes Mark with not only her "hip" American talk, but also her appetite: they adjourn to his place for sex.

In this scene, Jade has pulled a successful prank relying on a cultural stereotype. Where the geisha demeanor would have been an outrage if suggested by, for instance, the auditioners above, somehow when it is Jade's/Oh's/Shum's choice to do so, it becomes an effective cinematic device, emphasizing the difference between the Mark and Jade and their cultures.

Shum uses Asian culture effectively throughout the film in a variety of other, smaller ways as well. For instance, Jade's friend Lisa Chan (Claudette Carracedo) likes Asian men who have immersed themselves in the cultural ideal; Jade laughingly calls them "race kings". In another scene, Jade uses red-bean buns to placate her father (with little success). In another, Jade and her younger sister Pearl (Frances You) unearth a picture of their disowned brother Winston who has transgressed and dishonored the family in some unidentified way that remains a mystery. The film becomes a mosaic that invites the audience to create the family and its culture from the small, bright pieces before it.

That is not to say, however, that the film is without flaw. For instance, the idea of breaking away from home and family is hardly new, nor is the idea of breaking away from one's family and one's heritage. See, for example, *Long Day's Journey into Night* (1962), *Portnoy's Complaint* (1972), *The Godfather I, II* (1972, 1974), *Annie Hall* (1977) (in particular, Woody Allen's character's trip to visit Diane Keaton's character's family), and television's *American Girl.* Further, if certain scenes are eerily beautiful, it is also fair to say that certain scenes—labored as they are with cinematic (read: visual) jokes—fall flat. For instance, the film begins with the family at supper, speaking to each other in English and Chinese. The subject is whether it is true that if a woman is not married by the time she is twenty-two that she will never be married. As each family member comments on the subject (including some less-than-funny language jokes), the camera (seemingly placed in the center of the table) rotates between them, with the camera placed and rotating lazy-Susan style between them. It is a self-conscious scene altogether, the subject matter, the oddly twisting and turning camera, the unusual angle of the camera that accents everyone's jawline. It is a disappointment. Also, spaced throughout the film are mini-interviews with the characters, in which they address the audience and comment on the action afoot. These scenes destroy the flow of the film and

CREDITS

Jade Li: Sandra Oh
Mom Li: Stephen Chang
Pearl Li: Frances You
Andrew Chau: Johnny Mah
Mark: Callum Rennie

Origin: USA
Released: 1995
Production: Steven Hegyes and Rose Lam Waddell for a First Generation/New Views Films; released by Fine Line Features
Direction: Mina Shum
Screenplay: Mina Shum
Cinematography: Peter Wunstorf
Editing: Alison Grace
Production design: Michael Bjornson
Costume design: Cynthia Summers
Casting: Ann Anderson
Sound: Tim Richardson
Music: Shadowy Men on a Shadowy Planet
MPAA rating: No rating
Running Time: 96 minutes

AWARDS AND NOMINATIONS

Canadian Genie Awards 1994: Best Actress (Oh), Best Film Editing
Nominations: Best Film, Best Director (Shum)

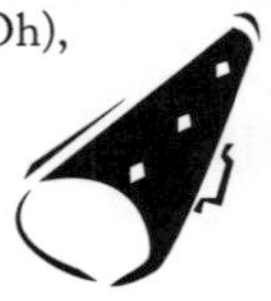

draw significant attention to themselves. If any part of the film can be said not to work, this is perhaps it.

Double Happiness, Mina Shum's directorial debut, was by all reports smooth sailing. One advantage was that the film was made under the joint auspices of New Views and Telefilm Canada BC Film and the National Film Board of Canada, which meant that while funds were not limitless, they were available without additional worry and fundraising. However, perhaps the greatest praise for this directorial debut comes from the actors who were led by Shum. Said Oh: "Stephen Chang, who plays my father, is a Rambo guy, a kung-fu guy. You can't speak to him with metaphors. [Mina] would talk to him very physically, literally block his every action in a very Hitchcockian way. 'Turn your head a little bit. Don't open your eyes too much. Just say the lines.' With me, she'd speak on a very, very broad emotional level, about memories, colors, feelings. Mina has an astute sensibility about how people respond to direction."

The title *Double Happiness* refers to the Chinese character for marriage, and it is true that a good bit of discussion about marriage ensues. However, the film offers much more than the stereotypical strain facing young women pulled between marriage and profession. *Double Happiness*, in the words of Jeff Brown of the *Village Voice*, is "small, occasionally coy, but mostly smart, resourceful, and peppy." It is a film about loving one's family, trusting one's self, and attempting to find romantic love in the process. It is a heart-felt and engaging film that any child of any parent will want to watch.

—Roberta F. Green

REVIEWS

The New York Times, July 28, 1995, C10.
Village Voice, August 1, 1995, p. 41.
The Washington Post, August 11, 1995, p. F6.

Dracula: Dead and Loving It

Box Office Gross: $7,564,936

Dracula: Dead and Loving It is a companion piece to Mel Brooks's classic spoof, Young Frankenstein (1974). Brooks virtually invented movie genre parodies in his brilliant *Blazing Saddles* (1973), which hilariously skewers the solemnities and absurdities of conventions such as good guy-bad guy shoot-outs. Brooks's burlesques work best when they are also a homage, in which he lovingly recreates the very scenes that have thrilled audiences, even when he exposes just how improbable those scenes actually are.

In *Dracula: Dead and Loving It*, Brooks revels in the Gothic atmosphere of Tod Browning's original screen version of *Dracula* (1931). For example, Dracula is accompanied by Renfield (Peter MacNicol), a young credulous English gentleman whom Dracula enslaves. MacNicol takes Browning's Renfield to a higher pitch of hysteria, making his obsession with eating insects ludicrous in a scene at the sanatorium where he breakfasts with his doctor, Seward (Harvey Korman). The setup evokes laughter because Korman plays Seward as stuffy and sententious while Renfield tries to swipe bugs out of the air and still maintain his dignity. What is even funnier is that Seward's only prescriptions are enemas. He is entirely at a loss as to what to do with Renfield or any of his other patients.

There is a good deal of satire on the medical profession in *Dracula: Dead and Loving It* just as there is a send-up of science in *Young Frankenstein*. Brooks plays Dracula's opponent, Dr. Van Helsing, so as to bring out the physician's pompous and power-mad personality. When listing Van Helsing's credits, Dr. Seward omits one field of specialization, which Brooks supplies with pretentious aplomb—gynecology. Ah, Dr. Seward murmurs in surprise, completely missing the humor apparent in Van Helsing's johnny-on-spot attendance on the women Dracula attacks.

Van Helsing, as Brooks plays him, is not only Dracula's nemesis, he is his double. When Dracula (Leslie Nielsen) and Van Helsing get into an argument, each struggle to get the last word, with Van Helsing continuing to reply to Dracula even after he leaves the room and is in the hallway. And like Dracula, Van Helsing has others do the dirty work—in this case, in the obligatory stake-in-the-heart scene when Van Helsing steps way back into the shadows as his assistant's stake thrust showers the assistant with volumes of blood. Like much of Brooks, the scene is silly but effective, diffusing the horror and mock-sincerity of genre pictures with therapeutic humor.

Reviewers have complained about the predictability of this movie, suggesting Brooks has not made a really fine parody since the late 1970's. It is true that in some Brooks pictures the predictability can be uninspiring and even dull, but in *Dracula: Dead and Loving It*, the repetition is done with such relish that it emphasizes why genre pictures are appealing.

CREDITS

Count Dracula: Leslie Nielsen
Renfield: Peter MacNicol
Van Helsing: Mel Brooks
Jonathan Harker: Steven Weber
Mina Seward: Amy Yasbeck
Lucy Weston: Lysette Anthony
Dr. Seward: Harvey Korman
Gypsy Woman: Anne Bancroft

Origin: USA
Released: 1995
Production: Mel Brooks for a Castle Rock Entertainment production; released by Columbia Pictures
Direction: Mel Brooks
Screenplay: Mel Brooks, Rudy DeLuca and Steve Haberman; based on the novel *Dracula* by Bram Stroker
Cinematography: Michael D. O'Shea
Editing: Adam Weiss
Production design: Roy Forge Smith
Costume design: Dodie Shepard
Choreography: Alan Johnson
Stunt Coordination: Gary Combs
Music: Hummie Mann
Casting: Lindsay D. Chang, Bill Shepard
MPAA rating: PG-13
Running Time: 89 minutes

Of course, what makes *Dracula: Dead and Loving It* so charming is Leslie Nielsen. He has perfected the persona of the sincere oaf in the *Naked Gun* series and uses it well here to embody the movie's subtitle. He is dead and feels no real connection with other human beings. He does not agonize over sucking people's blood; death has released him from considering the morality of what he does. And he loves it—parading in capes and cloaks as the suave Count Dracula even as he trips over himself, puts women into hypnotic states and then has to wake them up because he has not given them the proper directions.

Like his Frank Drebin character in *Police Squad* and the *Naked Gun* movies, Nielsen is a monomaniac. His tunnel vision prevents him from seeing the chaos he causes. He has no ability to scrutinize himself and takes himself so seriously that he is laughable. For Dracula, like Drebin, appearances are everything—a point Brooks shrewdly emphasizes by having Dracula show up at a party in the wigged headdress familiar to viewers of Francis Ford Coppola's vampire epic. When Nielsen takes off the wig like he would a hat, he is smugly confident and blind to his ridiculous appearance. Such moments remind viewers of what genre pictures are all about—conventions that seem to make sense in the context of the genre and yet are quickly deemed foolish if they are isolated for comic inspection.

Dracula: Dead and Loving It is a marvelous entertainment, especially for anyone not looking for some new brilliant twist on an old genre but rather for gags that so faithfully follow the traditional plot that the laughs seem a joint creation of Brooks and his audience.

—*Carl Rollyson*

Dr. Jekyll and Ms. Hyde

"Helen Hyde wants the doctor's body...She just doesn't want him in it at the same time."—Movie tagline

Robert Louis Stevenson's classic novel about a mad scientist and his monstrous alter-ego has served as a template for countless stories about experimentation gone awry. John Barrymore starred in *Dr. Jekyll and Mr. Hyde* (1920) in a classic silent film. Frederic March won an Oscar for the 1932 version directed by Rouben Mamoulian. Spencer Tracy essayed the role in a 1941 version which stressed Jekyll/Hyde's inner life rather than his gruesome exterior. In addition, the story was the basis for *The Incredible Hulk* comic and television series and two recent Broadway-style musicals. And now, it serves as the basis for a rather inept film comedy called *Dr. Jekyll and Ms. Hyde*.

The premise of this film is that a modern day scientist, Richard Jacks, (Tim Daly, of television's *Wings*) discovers that he is a direct descendant of Dr. Jekyll. He inherits Dr. Jekyll's notebooks, and tries to re-create Jekyll's experiments. Somehow, in investigating what went wrong with Dr. Jekyll's experiments, he decides that massive amounts of estrogen should be injected into the subject. He experiments on himself, and transforms into the evil seductress Helen Hyde (Sean Young). The premise of Dr. Jekyll turning into a woman has been used before, in the British film *Dr. Jekyll and Sister Hyde* (1972). It is safe to assume that '*Sister Hyde*' had considerably more style and substance than '*Ms. Hyde*.'

Richard, employed by a perfume manufacturer, is working on the formula for a new scent for the picky owner of the company, Mrs. Unterveldt (Polly Bergen, looking and sounding like Rosalind Russell). Having been unable to come up with a fragrance that Mrs. Unterveldt deems "feminine" enough, Richard retreats into his Jekyll experiments. He transforms into the voluptuous Helen, who says she is Richard's new assistant and that Richard is "out of town." Ecstatically discovering that she has Richard's brain and body, Helen improves Richard's perfume formula, bringing her into favor with Mrs. Unterveldt. She romances the goofy President of the company, Oliver Mintz (Stephen Tobolowsky) and the snippy fragrance expert, Yves DuBois (Harvey Fierstein) in order to get ahead. As Helen's star rises, Richard's life comes apart. His fiancee Sarah (Lysette Anthony) leaves him and moves in with his smarmy cousin Larry (Stephen Shellen), and he falls into disfavor with the company.

Helen eventually figures out a way to get rid of Richard forever, but not before Richard and Sarah re-team to destroy Helen and save their relationship. It is unnecessary to say everything comes out all right in the end because one could easily foresee that. The only losers are Helen and the audience. Anyone interested in a thoughtful and modern retooling of a classic tale will most likely be disappointed. It's a shame that Robert Louis Stevenson's classic would be reduced to something resembling a limp imitation of a *Bewitched* episode, complete with bumbling character actors, shallow lighting, cinematic cliches, and an ending worthy only of a 1960's sitcom.

This film attempts to enter the modern era with themes of workplace equality, sexual politics, sexual innuendo and technological references. But the action largely centers around Helen's attempts to torpedo Richard in his work through manipulation, coercion and seduction, thereby reinforcing the stereotype of strong-woman- as-emasculating-sexpot. The reinforcement of this stereotype could have sent the women's movement back a couple of years if the film had managed to fumble its way into success. Mercifully, audiences stayed away in droves.

After such a negative discussion of the film, it may seem contradictory to report that not everything is bad, but there are actually a few bright spots. In particular, Tim Daly acquits himself nicely in his role. He is a strong physical comedian as well as being an intelligent presence. Daly never overplays the already broad material, nor does he appear to be embarrassed by several moments which would cause another actor to squirm. In particular, he has a couple of scenes which depict Richard in a semi-transformed state, so that he is wearing men's clothing torn by the appearance of a bosom, or hair and fingernails suddenly grown long. In other scenes, the script requires him to be chained to a bed in his underwear, wear a skimpy nightgown, and stand near-naked in front of a room full of people with writing all over his body (don't ask.) But Daly is ever-professional, charming and engaging. His frenetic attempts to hide his transformations are played as well as any actor in a similar genre, from Tom Hanks in television's *Bosom Buddies*, to Robin Williams in *Mrs. Doubtfire* (1993).

Other good moments are provided by the performance of Stephen Tobolowsky as Oliver Mintz. Tobolowsky (who might be best known to audiences as the irritatingly friendly guy on the street in *Groundhog Day* [1993]) is funny and likable. His goofy face is perfectly suited to the over-the-top foolishness of this kind of character. He commits himself completely, especially in scenes in which he is seduced by Helen.

Another wonderful character actor, Harvey Fierstein, is ill-used in a subplot in which he falls in love with Helen. The ridiculous joke is that he is gay, and Helen is so sexy that even a gay man will find her attractive. That antiquated notion seems incongruent with Fierstein's previous work, and would certainly be forgivable if it were funny, but unfortunately, the talented Fierstein is not given much to work with. There is one funny scene in which Helen plays "footsies" under the table with both Oliver and Yves with music from "Carmen" underscoring. The ensuing argument about who has to get up from the table first is fun but in general, Fierstein's and Tobolowsky's talents are wasted here.

Sean Young, meanwhile, has a chance to play the femme fatale roles that have become her stock-in-trade. Young is best known for her off-screen behavior, having garnered a dubious reputation which is not ameliorated by this endeavor. Not quite as gorgeous as she used to be, but still a knockout, Young is certainly well-cast as the vixen Helen. However, she is not known for being a first-rate comic, something that the role could have used, and as a result her line readings seem rather one-note and her characterization is a bit one-dimensional. She does have fun with the seduction scenes with Tobolowsky and Fierstein, and seems to gain enthusiasm during the climactic scenes in which she fights off Richard and Sarah while chained to a bed.

The problem with the film largely rests in the script, which was penned by no less than four writers; Tim John, Oliver Butcher, William Davies, and William Osborne. It seems a significant amount of people spent valuable time to come up with the script. Interestingly, the trend in Hollywood toward writing scripts by committee seems to have a deleterious effect on the overall creativity of the script. Like Pauly Shore's *In the Army Now* (1994), the number of writers is in inverse proportion to the witlessness of the script. Specifically, there are three toilet jokes within the first ten minutes of film, and there are several other fecal references which are beneath the actors who are forced to utter them. Though there is a great demand for such humor, 1995's *Dumb and Dumber* being the best box-office example, it is unfortunate that writers turn to potty talk to get laughs.

The film's goofy humor would also be more welcome if presented in less cliche a manner. For example, when Richard is discovered in his office naked by the board of directors, the cliched reaction shot is not only sophomoric but worse, is unoriginal. Additionally, there is a running gag involving Helen's literal torture of a sexually predatory male co-worker which is overdrawn and ultimately revolting. His dialogue is offensive, and his makeup, after he is literally fried by Helen, is repulsive.

It would be hard to imagine a less auspicious calling card for director David Price, who directs his own story idea here. His inability to achieve a unified style from the actors (Daly plays it for real, Tobolowsky and Fierstein play it broad and shticky, and Young plays it like soft-core pornography) does not speak well for the integrity of Price's vision of the film. In addition, much of the settings and the camera angles are simplistic, with obvious stage settings for the interiors which detract from a foundation of believability that the film needs. If it wants to be a cartoon, then the settings might have been more stylized rather than appearing to be stand-ins for the real thing. Usually, blame for this kind of thing might go to the production designer, cinematographer, and other creative staff; but here, it might be assumed that Price was not able to preside over a well-planned comic vision, and that the film's flaws might have been reduced with some creative flair and conviction.

It is no fun to report that a film does not succeed at what it set out to do. But unfortunately, in this case, Price and company have taken a classic story and missed an opportunity to update it and make it interesting.

—Kirby Tepper

CREDITS

Helen Hyde: Sean Young
Richard Jacks: Tim Daly
Sarah Carver: Lysette Anthony
Oliver Mintz: Stephen Tobolowsky
Yves DuBois: Harvey Fierstein
Mrs. Unterveldt: Polly Bergen
Larry: Stephen Shellen
Valerie: Thea Vidale
Mrs. Mintz: Sheena Larkin

Origin: USA
Released: 1995
Production: Robert Shapiro and Jerry Leider for a Rastar/Leider-Shapiro production; released by Savoy Pictures in association with Rank Film Distributors
Direction: David Price
Screenplay: Tim John, Oliver Butcher, William Davies, and William Osborne; story by David Price based on the novel *The Strange Case of Dr. Jekyll and Mr. Hyde* by Robert Louis Stevenson
Cinematography: Tom Priestley
Editing: Tony Lombardo
Production design: Gregory Melton
Art direction: Guy Lalande
Casting: Mike Fenton, Allison Cowitt
Costume design: Molly Maginnis
Sound: Michel Charron, Patrick Rousseau
Visual effects supervision: Tim Landry
Make-up effects: Kevin Yagher
Music: Mark McKenzie
MPAA rating: PG-13
Running Time: 89 minutes

Empire Records

"They're selling music, but they're not selling out."—Movie tagline

Box Office Gross: $303,841

John Hughes was the undisputed king of the "teen movie" in the mid 80s, with such adolescent masterpieces as *The Breakfast Club* (1985), *Pretty in Pink* (1986), and *Sixteen Candles* (1987). No writer or director has since captured the essence of a generation, although many have tried. Hughes created entertaining, sometimes touching stories to which teenage boys and girls could easily relate. Everyone knew a jock, a geek, a princess, and a stoner in high school. A new brand of movie is trying to capture the essence of the younger generation of the '90s...the "Gen X-er." As Richard Linkater did in Slacker (1991) and *Before Sunrise* (1995), and Kevin Smith in *Clerks* (1994) and *Mallrats* (1995), Allan Moyle attempts to create a realistic story that teenagers and those in their early twenties can relate to. The problem is that these stories either take themselves too seriously or are simply too fantastic. Where Hughes' movies succeeded as fluffy entertainment, some of today's versions try to give wayward lives direction and shape a generation. Lofty goals for a 90 minute flick.

Empire Records (1995) attempts to deal with just about every dilemma a young person could face. Touching on the issues of personal identity, lifelong goals, responsibility, love, suicide, sex, and drugs is a lot to bite off, especially for a film that takes place almost entirely in a record store. (Not where I'd want my son or daughter learning major life skills.) The film also takes on staying true to oneself and not selling out to "The Man" as major lessons. ("The Man" is a slang term for the oppression slackers feel, also known as responsibility.) All of this is crammed into a day-in-the-life-of-a-record-store-clerk story which takes place in a funky, small-town, independent music store ironically named Empire Records.

Featuring a cast of little known and first-time Gen X actors, *Empire Records* is shallow and predictable from start to finish. Its attempts at comedy are bad, its attempts at drama cheesy and overwrought. No wonder it spent almost no time on the big screen before being relegated to the obscure shelves of the video store.

The story begins by introducing Lucas (Rory Cochrane), an employee of Empire Records who has just a few simple rules to follow: count the money twice, and keep his hands off Joe's (the manager) beer, cigars, and drumsticks. Within the first three minutes of the film, we see Lucas puffing on a stogie, drinking a beer, and playing drums on Joe's desk. While further demonstrating his slacker tendencies, Lucas starts digging through Joe's desk, where he finds information on a music store franchise, and in a display of utter brilliance, deduces that Joe is selling out. Oh, what's a slacker to do? How about jump on a motorcycle, drive to Atlantic City, bet the days profits on a single roll of the dice, and lose $9,000. The next day, Joe (Anthony LaPaglia) opens the store and immediately gets a phone call from the bank and the store's owner regarding the money that Lucas was supposed to deposit.

For someone who makes such bad decisions, Lucas sure seems wise, espousing such sage-like gems as, "Who knows where thoughts come from, they just appear," and in response to being asked if he's in trouble: "We're all in trouble Joe, you're in trouble, Corey's in trouble, Mark is in trouble...." This is representative of the pseudo-deep, McPhilosophizing spewed by these too- hip-for-their-own-good Gen X-ers.

As an example of the film's overwrought seriousness,

CREDITS

Joe: Anthony LaPaglia
Lucas: Rory Cochrane
A.J.: Johnny Whitworth
Corey: Liv Tyler
Gina: Renee Zellweger
Debra: Robin Tunney
Mark: Ethan Randall
Rex: Maxwell Caulfield
Jane: Debi Mazar

Origin: USA
Released: 1995
Production: Arnon Milchan, Michael Nathanson, Alan Riche and Tony Ludwig for a New Regency production; released by Warner Brothers
Direction: Allan Moyle
Screenplay: Carol Heikkinen
Cinematography: Walt Lloyd
Editing: Michael Chandler
Production design: Peter Jamison
Art direction: John Huke
Set decoration: Evelyne Barbier
Costume design: Susan Lyall
Sound: Douglass Axtell
Casting: Gail Levin
MPAA rating: PG-13
Running Time: 100 minutes

take the troubled young Deb (Robin Tunney) who storms into the store, ignores everyone's greetings, heads straight to the restroom and proceeds to shave her head, a la Sinead O'Connor. I guess we're supposed to feel her angst, her pain, without any explanation of why she's doing this. Wrong.

Liv Tyler, daughter of Aerosmith singer Steven Tyler, makes a less than impressive showing as Corey, the gorgeous, nearly perfect vestal virgin of the group. In a particularly unlikely dramatic scene, innocent Corey prepares an elegant lunch in a back room for visiting pop star Rex Manning (Maxwell Caufield). Stricken with accute puppy love for this plastic, '90s version of Barry Manilow or Tom Jones, she strips down to her undergarments and professes her love for him. Being the disgusting cheeseball that he is, Rex unzips his pants and offers himself to Corey. Utterly repulsed and humiliated, Corey grabs her clothes and runs off to the roof of the building and weeps. Why she would throw herself at someone who represents everything these kids seem to hate is a mystery, as is why she would be shocked by Rex's lecherous response to her offering (she's supposedly on her way to Harvard!).

Trouble in paradise continues when Gina (Renee Zellweger), the requisite slut and best friend of the ultra-pure Corey, not so covertly seduces Rex in another back room. Before long, all of the employees gather outside the office and when the two emerge, sweaty and disheveled, all hell breaks loose. Corey berates Gina, A.J. (Johnny Whitworth), who's in love with Corey, attacks Rex, Gina blows the cover on Corey's drug-problem secret, Joe kicks Rex out of the store, and Corey proceeds to go off the deep end and trash several displays in the store. Just a typical day in the tumultuous world of a record store employee.

Other requisite characters which seem to represent the not-so-broad range of this generation's personas include an angsty, spacey Eddie Vedder look-alike, not coincidently named Eddie, and Mark, the living incarnation of Beavis or Butthead. The frustrated artist and the wanna-be rock star are also represented thinly, as is a pubescent shoplifter who calls himself Warren Beatty. There just doesn't seem to be any well-adjusted, trauma-free employees at Empire Records. And it's the too-huge, opaque cast that further detracts from the already weak film.

The absurdity reaches a new height when the employees hold a mock funeral for Deb, the now bald, super angsty employee who recently tried to commit suicide. The eulogies turn into more vacant deep thoughts about personal problems like bed-wetting, wanting to sing in a band, and feeling "invisible." It's nothing more than a cheap platform for these twenty-something lost souls to offer siloloquies on their current dismal state of being.

Well, it's been quite a day at Empire Records. Sex, violence, rock & roll, drugs, and the problem with which this movie began, Lucas loosing $9,000 was almost forgotten. But Joe must now face the music and call Mitchell, the smarmy, suit-wearing owner. The tension mounts as everyone realizes that surely Joe will be fired and their beloved store will turn into a tacky franchise. But wait, here's Beavis with a solution: what does one do when "The Man's" got you down? Why throw a party, of course! A fund-raising party no less, complete with live music on the roof (hasn't that been done before?) and keg beer sold right in front of the store. Naturally, the employees raise enough money for Joe to buy the store from Mitchell, and alas, the System has been thwarted.

With its continuous musings about oppressive capitalism (by music store employees) and "The Man" being behind all that is wrong in the world, *Empire Records* seems like 90 minutes of whining. Beware of a movie whose soundtrack is more highly regarded and more of a selling point than the film itself.

—*Christopher Scanlon*

The Englishman Who Went Up a Hill But Came Down a Mountain

"A romantic comedy about a town that wouldn't give up. A man who couldn't get out. And the mountain that brought them together."—Movie tagline

"Two thumbs up!"—*Siskel & Ebert*

"Hugh Grant is irresistible."—Pia Lindstrom, *WNBC-NY*

Box Office Gross: $10,904,930

Hugh Grant stars in *The Englishman Who Went Up A Hill But Came Down A Mountain.* © Miramax Films.

Wales, located west of England, remains part of the United Kingdom. With a population of almost 3 million, it has approximately the same population as Ireland, half the population of Scotland and a twelfth the population of England. *The Englishman Who Went Up a Hill But Came Down a Mountain*, written and directed by a forty-four-year-old Welsh director, Christopher Monger, showcases an eccentric group of citizens in Ffynnon Garw, the cinematic equivalent of Monger's hometown.

While to the outsider, the village could appear to be Irish (a la *The Quiet Man*, 1952, or *The Playboys*, 1992), or British (a la *Room with a View*, 1985) or Scottish (a la *Local Hero*, 1983, or even *Brigadoon*, 1954), Director Monger has explained that it is important to understand the unique mindset of the Welsh: "Wales, the Celtic countries, have a different view of life from other places. They're more poetic, like Mexico, where pagan elements have crossed over into the Christian church. Strait-laced religion stands in contrast to the hedonistic propensity for poetry, drinking and melancholy."

Director Christopher Monger's screenplay is based on a family legend and is a remembrance of his Welsh childhood.

The film begins in 1917 with the arrival of two of Her Majesty's surveyors, Reginald Anson (Hugh Grant) and George Garrad (Ian McNeice). Only mountains will be listed by name on the map, and only rises of 1,000 feet or more qualify as mountains. Ffynnon Garw, the town, is particularly proud of what it terms the first mountain in Wales, the 984-foot-tall Ffynnon Garw, which to townspeople signals the end of English terrain and the beginning of Welsh terrain. Faced with the prospect of their mountain appearing on the map generally as a hilly region, the townspeople brainstorm to find a solution. The Rev. Robert Jones (Kenneth Griffith) suggests advocating a change in the criteria for mountains: 984 feet should be sufficient to qualify. Morgan the Goat (Colm Meaney) suggests adding twenty feet to the hill to build it into a mountain. With the help of such colorful characters as Johnny Shellshock (Ian Hart), Thomas Twp and Thomas Twp, Too (Tudor and Hugh Vaughn), and Betty of Cardiff (Tara FitzGerald), the townsfolk (and local recruits) work to put their mountain on the map.

Certainly one of the ways Wales is different is its language. The difficulty the two Englishman have trying to speak the language provides a running gag throughout this film. For instance, upon their arrival, the two surveyors wrestle with the name of the town (Ffynnon Garw), which is also the name of the erstwhile hill, now mountain. Quickly it becomes apparent that a rite of passage for English persons into Welsh acceptability is, first, a willingness to attempt the pronunciation of Welsh words and, second, an ability to do so. Like a huge number of male leads who "go native" during the course of the film (for instance, Mel Gibson's Mr. Christian in *The Bounty*, 1984), Hugh Grant's Reginald Anson masters the language and then learns to appreciate the people.

Certainly, the director's philosophy and philanthropy is reflected in the film: "I like people," said Director Christopher Monger in an interview with Howie Movshovitz of *The Denver Post.* "I'm bad at writing villains. In truth, this film is a love story between Morgan and the reverend. They come to respect each other." More literally, the film is also a love story between Anson and Betty of Cardiff. Played by Hugh Grant and Tara FitzGerald, the pair wobble toward romance with Betty coaxing Anson as if he were a shy animal, ready to bolt and run at the first sign of danger. Mr. Grant and Ms. FitzGerald also appeared in *Sirens* (1993), and while there they played husband and wife, once again she was more bold, he more shy. Indeed, it would appear that, not unlike Jimmy Stewart, Hugh Grant has made a career of reticence, of stumbling through a sentence, of indecision at each word or act. For example, in his courtship of Betty, Mr. Grant's Anson moves slowly, working scene after scene to a first kiss. This is not unlike his courtship in 1994's *Four Weddings and a Funeral*, in which a proclamation of love takes Hugh Grant's character perhaps ten minutes, which minutes are filled mostly with uncomfortable silence and stuttering, culminating in a reference to pop songster David Cassidy and his immortal lyric, "I think I love you."

Indeed, Hugh Grant has been heralded a "superstar" since his meteoric rise to fame through *Four Weddings and a Funeral.* While Mr. Grant had made no fewer than a dozen films, it was last year's hit that brought him to prominence. Critics have noted that he brings a sort of "elegant romanticism" to the screen that has been missing since the "Golden Era of Hollywood" and such greats as Cary Grant and Ralph Bellamy. "It's quite titillating to be recognized," admits Hugh Grant in an interview with Paul Freeman of *The Denver Post*. "On days when I'm not recognized, I mind bitterly. Having said that, there are moments when I have to summon up all my niceness, like when I've just arrived from a flight, I'm awaiting my bags and someone comes up and

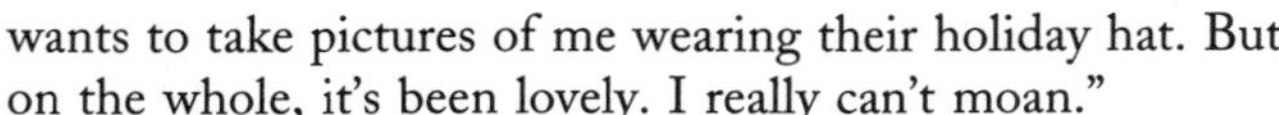

wants to take pictures of me wearing their holiday hat. But on the whole, it's been lovely. I really can't moan."

Beyond the intriguingly quirky villagers and the outsider Englishmen, another key character of this film is the Welsh countryside. Cinematographer Vernon Layton has captured the beauty and expanse of the countryside, even as he has captured the distance, darkness and worry of the World War I mindset and historical period. Over and over, Layton has captured the panoramic view from the hill, each time showing the audience the wonder the Welsh find in the perspective it gives them of their home. A patchwork quilt of greens and yellow, the Welsh countryside is all pastoral beauty, even while populated by persons such as Johnny Shellshock, who has seen the war and will not speak.

Most of the characters in this film are versions of stock characters, for instance, the elderly, confused twins, Thomas Twp and Thomas Twp, Too (in Welsh, "twp" means tetched); the fire-and-brimstone Rev. Robert Jones, who wars with the lascivious innkeeper Morgan the Goat (who fathers most of the children in town); Johnny Shellshock, the troubled lad with the pretty, strong, protective sister (a Welsh version of any character played by Maureen O'Hara), and Johnny Twostroke (Dafydd Wyn Roberts), the mechanic who can fix only two-stroke engines. However, what the characters lack in surprise, they more than make up for in precision. This little film is written and directed like clockwork, controlled action, language, plot, range. For instance, as the hill-to-mountain plan is hatched and as the villagers work to keep the Englishmen in town until the plan is completed, each character brings to bear the characteristic for which he or she is named. Specifically, the mechanic destroys the four-stroked engine car, the confused brothers supply confusing information, the shellshocked veteran brings the know-how of trench engineering. Even Betty of Cardiff, the "tart" from the neighboring village who enters the film at the beckoning of the prolific bartender, brings her wiles to the skirmish to help hold the Englishmen in place. While none of this is a surprise, it is nicely tuned and hums along enjoyably.

While *The Englishman Who Went Up a Hill But Came Down a Mountain* offers few surprises in plot or character-

CREDITS

Reginald Anson: Hugh Grant
Betty of Cardiff: Tara FitzGerald
Morgan the Goat: Colm Meaney
George Garrard: Ian McNeice
Johnny Shellshock: Ian Hart

Origin: GREAT BRITAIN
Released: 1995
Production: Sarah Curtis for Parallax Pictures; released by Miramax
Direction: Christopher Monger
Screenplay: Chirstopher Monger, based on his novel
Cinematography: Vernon Layton
Editing: David Martin
Production Design: Charles Garrard
Art Direction: Chris Lowe
Costume Design: Janty Yates
Casting: Michelle Guish
Music: Stephen Endelman

REVIEWS

Atlanta Journal-Constitution, May 12, 1995, p. P5
Boston Globe, May 12, 1995, p. 59
Chicago Sun-Times, May 12, 1995
The Christian Science Monitor, May 18, 1995, p. 12
The Denver Post, May 12, 1995, Weekend, p. 6
Houston Chronicle, May 12, 1995, Weekend Preview, p. 6
Los Angeles Times, May 12, 1995, p. F1
Newsday, May 12, 1995, p. BO2
Salt Lake City Tribune, May 12, 1995, p. E3
San Francisco Chronicle, May 12, 1995, p. C3
San Francisco Examiner, May 12, 1995, p. C3
Washington Times, May 11, 1995, p. M21

ization, it is enjoyable and entertaining to watch. It is a "little film" in the best understanding of that term and needs little of the Hollywood-style glamour or glitz to make it work. However, for those less drawn to the countryside and quirky villagers, the film also offers Hugh Grant in a variety of entertaining situations and attractive period outfits. Viewers of all tastes should find something to their liking in this small but wonderful film.

—Roberta F. Green

Ermo

In the pitch-black night in rural China, the low houses of a backwater village huddle together. From a few of the houses a luminous, eerie light flickers. It's an otherworldly glow... television.

Ermo, a spunky villager, just has to have one. Her son, Tiger, is always jumping up from his rice bowl to go next door to watch a cartoon. It infuriates Ermo (played by the Chinese actress known only as Alia) that her snotty neighbor, Fat Woman (Zhang Haiyan), has the village's latest and most powerful status symbol.

Ermo's husband, Chief (Ge Zhijun), disagrees. He says televisions are useless, and would rather spend their money building a bigger house. "A TV is just an egg. A house, now that's the chicken," Chief says. But Ermo, who does the work that earns the money while the older Chief nurses various ailments, calls the shots in the family, and she embarks on a hell-bent quest to get a bigger set than Fat Woman's.

This is the simple plot of the hilarious *Ermo*, an unheralded but delightful Chinese film which has all manner of fun with envy, jealousy, status-seeking, modern pretentions and even gender roles. With deadly comic aim, it blasts consumerism by laying bare its most primitive elements. It's all about keeping up with the Joneses. But *Ermo*'s skewering is done delightfully, and the message goes down easily.

CREDITS

Ermo: Alia
Blindman: Liu Peiqi
Chief Ge: Zhijun
Fat Woman: Zhang Haiyan

Origin: China
Production: Chen Kunming and Jimmy Tan; released by Arrow Releasing
Direction: Zhou Xiaowen
Screenplay: Lang Yun
Cinematography: Lu Gengxin
Editing: Zhong Furong
Music: Zhou Xiaowen
Running Time: 93 minutes

In stark contrast to the Chinese films of the Cultural Revolution that denounced bourgeois modernism and glorified the noble peasantry, director Zhou Xiaowen, working from a script by Lang Yun, gives us a foursome of ignoble rubes. Chief and Ermo and their neighbors Fat Woman and Blindman are at least as crude and ridiculous as the Flintstones.

Ermo's husband is a former village chief who declares "I'm not the Chief anymore" every time anyone calls him Chief. He is a clumsy, useless hypochrondriac trying vainly to hang on to the last vestiges of patriarchal prestige. His neighbor Blindman, who is not blind, is a henpecked, socially inept entrepreneur who owns a dilapidated truck that can make the long trek through the barren countryside to the nearest city, where Blindman has connections. The truck also allows him to escape his wife, Fat Woman, who really is fat. She's a lazy, gossiping slob who teases and taunts Ermo. Fat Woman and Blindman are jealous of their neighbors because they've produced only a daughter, while their neighbors have a son, and in their culture a boy is still much more prestigious than a girl.

While Chief moans about his backaches, Ermo slaves to eke out a living for the family. She makes and sells baskets and noodles. To make the noodles, she must knead dough with her feet, and then lean on a wooden lever to push the flour through a sieve. It is brutally hard work. But once she gets to town and sees the 29-inch color TV that's on sale at the local department store, she starts working all night long making noodles. Her determination to triumph over her neighbor and to get the biggest television in the county is boundless.

Both marriages are bankrupt, held together by duty and habit. When Chief berates Ermo for not being sufficiently feminine and deferential, Ermo blasts him for not being much of a man. They jostle around a fragile balance of power: Chief can ask Ermo to sweeten his tea once, but dares not ask twice. Blindman is disgusted at what's become of his wife. About the only thing he says to her is "Shut up." To Ermo, Blindman describes his wife thus: "If she had maggots in her ass, she'd be too lazy to pick them out."

Ermo is no saint herself. She's a conniving, selfish hustler with a fierce sense of pride. After being humiliated by Fat Woman, she poisons her neighbors' pig. When she later confesses over dinner to Blindman, he sluffs it off, adding, "Anyway, you won't do it again." Stuffing her face, she replies, "Don't be too sure." To sell her noodles at the market, Ermo sits down right next to a competitor and tries to outscream her. She takes a job in a restaurant that Blindman helps her get, but later rebuffs his offers for financial help.

Ermo's all-out assault on the money needed to get the television is merciless. Without nary a word of farewell, she walks out on Chief and Tiger to take the restaurant job, moving into slum lodgings in town. At the restaurant, there is an accident as the staff prepares a meal for a wedding reception. Ermo's co-worker has cut off his hand. Blindman's truck is the quickest route to the hospital, so the restaurant owner urges guests at the reception to hop on and go there to donate blood. They clamber aboard a pile of coal in the dirty pick-up; of course, the heap won't start. It's one of the film's funniest scenes.

When Ermo finds out she can get paid to donate blood, she starts donating every day. "Women lose blood anyway," is her excuse. As played to perfection by Alia, Ermo is a fascinating comic lead. Director Zhou resists all attempts to glamorize her. The closest she comes to looking sultry is not in the film's silly sexual encounters, which are played for laughs, but when she's sweating at the noodle-making machine. Otherwise, she's clad in bulky, mismatched sweaters and bandanas. In the city, she's a hopeless rube, too dumb to get out of the way of traffic. She eats like a pig and talks like one too. She drives herself nearly insane with the jealousy which stokes her quest for the television.

The three other main actors also are excellent. Ge as the Chief wears a befuddled, hangdog look. Liu as Blindman, wearing an ill-fitting leather jacket, is a wonderful buffoon, and Zhang as his wife is a comic masterpiece of fearsome proportions.

Ermo is comic in a unique way. It pokes fun both at the cultural change which is enthroning television in rural China and at the easily manipulated people who are slaves to that change. Its best scenes are in the department store, when crowds of Chinese shoppers crowd around the television screens, gaping open-mouthed at ludicrous scenes of Westerners in soap-opera bedroom scenes speaking dubbed Chinese. When Ermo finally gets her set and the villagers crowd around for a look, they stare blankly at a football game. "The Westerners are fighting," observes one viewer. "It's a gang fight." A more savvy member of the audience replies, "No, it's a game. Don't you know? It's called basketball."

Zhou's biggest accomplishment is that he keeps his characters sympathetic even as he lampoons them. When Ermo tries to please Blindman by displaying the fringed brassiere she's bought, saying "Do I look like a city girl now?" she reveals her own insecurity. When she's afraid, as when she's giving blood for the first time, she cries like a child. All the characters, especially Ermo, display a childlike vulnerability, and the film suggests that this very innocence is what makes them most susceptible to the corrupting power of television and all it represents. But Zhou allows himself one last laugh at this mighty invader's expense, in a deft, understated climax that reveals how foolish our most ardent materialistic strivings can become.

When Shakespeare wrote, "What fools we mortals be," he must have had Ermo's villagers in mind. Laughing at human foibles is one of the best ways of examining our values. Though there are some lackluster stretches, *Ermo* is wonderful entertainment of the top order. The greed and envy which drive modern society are all apparent in *Ermo*, and it's easy to see by looking at the behavior of these hapless provincials how ridiculous the world is becoming. All consumers are as hapless as Ermo and her friends. Most of us just hide it better.

—Michael Betzold

REVIEWS

New Republic. June 12, 1995, p. 32.
The New York Times. May 12, 1995,p. C10.

Erotique

"Sexy, steamy, audacious, stylishly outrageous..."—Kevin Thomas, *Los Angeles Times*

Box Office Gross: $1,109,822

Movies are wonderful at foreplay. But they are not usually so great in the sack. There's a good reason for this. Films can come on deliciously with luxurious shots of seductive glances, luscious lips and bulging biceps. Handsome actors and attractive actresses can make magical visual moments together.

But sex isn't about appearances. It has more to do with passion. And while truly great acting can explore passion, it cannot substitute for it. So substitutes must be found. Sex in cinema most often is depicted symbolically, or by facial expression, sounds and gestures. If it gets too explicit, it often looks clinical, even in the raciest films.

Most efforts to explore sexuality on legitimate film have been resounding failures. The attempt to extend cinema's romantic power into authentic depictions of sexuality most often produces dismal failures. Short of hard-core pornography, which is another matter altogether, real sexuality has remained largely unconquered territory, one of cinema's last frontiers.

The three films that comprise *Erotique* are efforts to explore this territory. All have women as directors, each from a different country, offering the hope of a perspective markedly different from male-dominated sex scenes.

As expected, *Erotique* has been marketed exploitively, but it is not necessarily exploitive. However, the film is in many ways disappointing. Its female viewpoint, and language and situations which clearly merit an NC-17 rating, but fall far short of hard-core pornography, are not enough by themselves to overcome cinema's sexual shortcomings.

Ironically enough, the most successful of the trio at probing the deep psychological and emotional territory of sexual interaction is the one that is the most visually oblique. Offbeat American director Lizzie Borden's segment, "Let's Talk About Love," uses words, not pictures, as its main instruments. Kamala Lopez-Dawson plays Rosie, a Latin phone-sex operator and frustrated actress who is fed up with catering to men's fantasies. She feels controlled economically and emotionally but also is well aware of her sexual power. When she hooks up on the phone with a caller named Robert Stern (Bryan Cranston) who is willing to listen to her fantasies, she is intrigued, and they begin an elaborate game of cat-and-mouse. In these calls Rosie gets to play out her desires for more power and domination and uses rough and direct language to exact her price.

When Stern turns out to be a sex therapist with his own unmet needs, Rosie is enraged to discover she has been used as well in a sort of experiment. She hatches a plot to meet Stern and exact the ultimate humiliation, but this climactic encounter turns into a strange verbal charade. The ending of the segment forces the viewer to reinterpret most of what's transpired before. Unfortunately, it's a clumsy way out of a highly-charged situation. Far from giving Rosie her triumph, it reveals the inadequacies of both participants in the phone-sex game. Borden's effort is nonetheless creative and admirably risky, and Lopez-Dawson and her volatile words are definitely the hottest thing in *Erotique.*

German director Monika Treut's middle segment, "Taboo Parlor," is the segment of the film that is closest to standard soft-core pornography. It uses that old staple of

CREDITS

Rosie: Kamala Lopez-Dawson
Dr. Robert Stern: Bryan Cranston
Claire: Priscilla Barnes
Julia: Camilla Soeberg
Victor: Michael Carr
Adrian: Tim Lounibos
Ann: Hayley Man

Origin: USA, Germany
Released: 1994
Production: Christopher Wood, Vicky Herman, Marianne Chase, Monika Treut, Michael Sombetzki, Teddy Robin Kwan, Eddie Ling-Ching Fong for a Brandon Chase production; released by Beyond Films in association with Group 1/Trigon/Tedpoly Films
Direction: Lizzie Borden, Monika Treut and Clara Law
Screenplay: Lizzie Borden, Susie Bright, Monika Treut and Eddie Ling-Ching Fong
Cinematography: Larry Banks, Elfi Mikesch and Arthur Wong
Editing: Richard Fields, Steve Brown and Jill Bilcock
Production design: Jane Ann Stewart, Petra Korink and Eddie Mok
Casting: Jerold Franks
Costume design: Jolie Jimenez and Susann Klindtwordt
Music: Andrew Belling and Tats Lau
Sound: James Thornton, Wolfgang Schulkrafft and Gary Wilkins
MPAA rating: NC-17
Running Time: 93 minutes

male fantasy, two lesbian women who decide to prowl for a man they can toy with. They go to an s/m club and find an object for their enjoyment. He is an excellent dupe who believes he'll get both women in the sack. There is a steamy sequence on the bus ride home, where the women start fondling each other while squeezed among leering passengers. It is the most erotically charged visual in *Erotique.* But the conclusion to Treut's sequence is off-putting and out of keeping with the coy tone of the rest of the segment. Ultimately, there is little to distinguish this short film from more standard sexploitation fare.

The final episode, "Wonton Soup," by Hong Kong's Clara Law, seems out of place. It is a visually experimental, plodding film about alienation and cultural conflict. Much of it is shot in an empty apartment and there are too many scenes of downtown buildings and brooding skies. Its two lovers engage in by-the-book, clinical sex, and there is little humanity in their lovemaking. It's overlong, boring and ultimately inconsequential. It's like a sex film made by a philosophy teacher who forces her audience to sit through a pallid half-hour intellectual dissertation for the sake of a few seconds of meaningless humping.

Erotique was originally conceived as a foursome, but an episode shot in Brazil was excised before the film's release. It suffers greatly from the sampler feel that is common to most multi-director montages. Apart from the fact that these are three films by women that have sexuality as a main theme, there is nothing to tie them together. Stylistically, they are as different as three films could be. There does not emerge any coherent new perspective nor do they collectively make much headway against cinema's difficulties in depicting sexuality.

Borden's segment shows it is possible to talk about sex on camera explicitly and to do so in a way that explores the power relationships between men and women, but her characters don't go beyond play-acting. In fact, the point is that these are people skilled in the deceits of language but hopelessly incapable of translating words into actions. Treut's segment suffers from hackneyed sexual plotting. And Law's film really belongs in a cinema class, not on commercial screens.

Those intrigued by *Erotique* for different reasons may all come away disappointed. Feminists expecting to find, at long last, a film which honestly combines a woman's perspective with audacious sexuality may end up being frustrated by the limited new insights provided. Any of these films probably could have been made by men. Those lured to *Erotique* for prurient reasons will be teased and let down; it's not much sexier than a lot of commercial films, and it gets decidedly less so as the film progresses. Those seeing in *Erotique* the possibility that filmmakers may finally find a way to overcome cinema's sexual handicaps and conquer new territory will find only small amounts of progress and huge gaps remaining.

Ultimately, *Erotique* is just a baby step away from convention. It is not audacious enough, not inventive enough, not honest enough, not sexy enough. It is still, essentially, foreplay.

—Michael Betzold

REVIEWS

Los Angeles Times. Jan. 20, 1995, p. F12.
Variety. June 6, 1994, p. 38.

Exotica

"Powerfully seductive."—*The New York Times*
"Two enthusiastic thumbs up!"—*Siskel & Ebert*

Box Office Gross: $4,428,978

Mira Kirshner stars in *Exotica*. © Miramax Films.

Exotica is a refreshingly unique, creative, intriguing and almost perfectly executed parable about the clash between appearances and purposes. By all rights, it ought to propel Canadian filmmaker Atom Egoyan into the front ranks of young directors.

It ought to, but probably won't because it is too delicate and subtle to be lionized by the critics and audiences that made *Pulp Fiction* the height of hip mid-1990s filmmaking. Egoyan clearly doesn't care whether he is hip. He breaks all the rules, old and new. Though *Exotica* is about the effects of a violent society, there is scarcely any violence in it. Though *Exotica* appears to be about sleazy sex, there is no sex in it. Its characters don't indulge in profanity for its own sake, they don't swagger or grandstand. They are all too disappointingly human.

The dictionary defines "exotica" as "things excitingly different and unusual." There are at least two aspects of this film that are rare and remarkable. First, its characters don't talk in movie dialogue, but in real voices; they aren't histrionic, but act like ordinary people. Second, nothing is quite what it seems in *Exotica*—it's a meditation on the clash between surface appearance and deeper meaning, between form and function.

The primary setting for the film is a Toronto strip club. Francis (Bruce Greenwood) goes there regularly for one purpose: to pay extra for the tantalizing Christina (Mia Kirschner) to do a table-dance for him. This is a setting and story line that, if recounted without further explanation, is guaranteed to win writer-director Egoyan enmity from some quarters. But Egoyan has disdain for superficialists, and in fact the entire film is a prank on people who jump to conclusions.

Director/writer Atom Egoyan got the idea for this film when he was audited back in the winter of 1993. Arsinee Khanjian, who portrays Zoe, is Egoyan's wife and was pregnant with their first child, a son, during filming.

One assumption Egoyan unmasks is that the sex industry peddles and delivers sex, when in fact its main commodity is solace. It is a poor and addictive substitute for real understanding and affection, but desperate customers pay for it. Strip clubs sell only the appearance of sexual availability. Touching the performers is strictly prohibited. Men who go there to watch often are trying to quench a deeper, unspoken need.

If one buys that premise, one may understand what Francis is doing at the strip club, which looks like a tropical jungle but is more uptight than steamy. It's the only way he seems to know of to get out of the mental mess he's in. It's important to note that Egoyan isn't praising his characters and their actions, just depicting them.

Egoyan also teases moralists with scenes of Francis repeatedly dropping off a young babysitter and thanking her warmly. It's natural to think there's something immoral going on between the two. But later Egoyan reveals that the babysitting is also a kind of mutual charade that is part of Francis's self-therapy.

All the characters, in fact, have hidden, loftier reasons for engaging in actions that appear to be immoral or degrading. They are driven by their sense of obligation to themselves and others to engage in and repeat behavior that seems senseless but has its own inner logic.

Christina displays a cool detachment while doing a hot routine in a schoolgirl outfit. Her dance is purposeful and ritualistic but not jaded. It is innocence lifting up a skirt.

Kirshner, who shows tremendous promise, is masterful at conveying a likeable, sensible person behind the exotic performer. In other films, such a character would be scripted as having a few screws loose, but Christina is straightforward and matter-of-fact. Like the other characters, she is an ordinary person caught in an extraordinary situation. Just why she's doing what she's doing is part of the puzzle.

Eric (Elias Koteas), the macho announcer at the strip club who tries to put patrons in the mood to buy, clearly is agitated by Christina's performance. He spies on her while she dances for Francis. He is enraged, but is it merely with jealousy? All we know at first, through flashbacks, is that Eric and Christina first met on a walk through fields, which turns out to be a search for a missing child.

Other characters are equally puzzling. Thomas (Don McKellar), a timid-looking pet shop proprietor, has strange liaisons and unlikely criminal ties. Zoe (Arsinee Khanjian), the owner of the strip club, is carrying on a family tradition and using an unlikely method to start a new one, having contracted Eric to make her pregnant. Tracey (Sarah Polley), the babysitter, is learning about the uncomfortable relationship between her father and Francis, who turns out to be her uncle.

Many of the characters, one eventually realizes, are in various kinds of trances. Christina is in a trance when she dances, Francis when he watches her, Eric when he announces, Thomas the petshop owner when he goes to a concert looking to pick up a date. Eventually, the characters become enmeshed in a tangle of love, blackmail and murderous intent. And they are redeemed only when all assumptions are exploded.

> "Let me ask you something gentlemen. What is it about a schoolgirl that gives her her special innocence? Is it the way that they gaze at you? Waiting for you to say something with so much expectation and hope that you're paralyzed into — into silence."—Emcee Eric from *Exotica*

Watching the film is like working a jigsaw puzzle. One keeps picking up the same pieces, finding new ones, trying out combinations until the scenes gradually take larger shape and begin to make sense. It's demanding and often frustrating work. Egoyan doesn't let the picture emerge easily, and there's plenty of opportunity for mistaken interpretations. Don't judge people and their actions until you know them completely, he seems to be saying. And even the final picture has plenty of gaps—like real life.

Other directors have attempted this sort of story, where a web between characters gradually emerges. Robert Altman comes to mind, in films such as *Nashville* (1975) and *Short Cuts* (1993), but his characters are always talky and outgoing. Except for their circumstances, Egoyan's characters are utterly unremarkable and rather quiet. Their dialogue is disarmingly ordinary. They don't engage in movie actions, and they don't talk movie talk. Surprisingly, this makes them both more appealing and more unsettling.

Egoyan is masterful at creating a mood and getting all his actors to conform to it. The acting is so good that one never thinks one is watching anyone other than real people. Greenwood's portrayal of Francis is eerie and disarming. Koteas as Eric always appears to be on the brink of erupting, but that behavior is a mask for his real motivations. Kirshner blends titillation, innocence and honesty in a compelling performance. As the petshop owner, McKellar brings incredible restraint and authenticity to what starts out as a minor role and grows into a crucial one. Polley is perfect in her part as a kind-hearted teenager learning things about life she'd rather not know.

Clearly, *Exotica* isn't everyone's cup of tea. It isn't meant to be. Some will find it unbearably dull; others frustrating.

CREDITS

Francis: Bruce Greenwood
Christina: Mia Kirshner
Thomas: Don McKellar
Zoe: Arsinee Khanjian
Eric: Elias Koteas
Tracey: Sarah Polley
Harold: Victor Garber
Customs officer: Calvin Green

Origin: Canada
Released: 1994
Production: Atom Egoyan and Camelia Frieberg for Alliance Communications Corporation and Ego Film Arts, with the participation of Telefilm Canada and the Ontario Film Development Corporation; released by Miramax Films
Direction: Atom Egoyan
Screenplay: Atom Egoyan
Cinematography: Paul Sarossy
Editing: Susan Shipton
Production design: Linda del Rosario and Richard Paris
Sound: Ross Redfern
Costume design: Linda Muir
Music: Mychael Danna
MPAA rating: R
Running Time: 104 minutes

Canadian Genie Awards 1994: Best Film, Best Director (Egoyan), Best Supporting Actor (McKellar), Best Cinematography (Sarossy), Best Screenplay (Egoyan), Best Score (Danna), Best Art Direction, Best Costumes
Nominations: Best Actor (Greenwood), Best Actor (Koteas)
Toronto City Award 1994: Best Canadian Feature Film
Independent Spirit Awards Nominations 1996: Best Foreign Film

Many will miss the point. Critics were sharply divided on it, and to no one's surprise, it didn't become a box-office hit.

It is risky business to construct a film story around events that are never depicted. The violence that has set the main characters into their ritualized motion is alluded too late in the film and never shown. Egoyan's tack is the exact opposite of filmmakers who try to shock with graphic depictions of brutality and profanity. Egoyan keeps the turmoil that lurks beneath our civilized society quiet and hidden.

That's why *Exotica* is unsettling—because it is closer to the truth. Random violence does erupt in the most ordinary settings while the rest of life goes on seemingly undisturbed. The violence carries with it an air of unreality and everyone shares a sense that it couldn't really be happening. That only adds to its power over us.

Egoyan's characters are gentle people trying to construct and reconstruct their lives, struggling imperfectly to make sense out of a nonsensical society. When violence happens to people like them, they aren't necessarily good at handling it or processing it, especially in the middle of a placid society. So their healing can take on exotic forms.

With exhilarating acuity, *Exotica* debunks the rumors and assumptions that societal prejudices feed on. In a disarming way, it explodes preconceptions. At its heart it is full of genuine humanity.

The flaws in *Exotica* are that the story is somewhat contrived and forced; some of the connections between characters are strained; some characters are not as well developed as they could be; and the film could be tighter and more suspenseful. But these flaws only show what a short distance Egoyan has to go to bridge the gap between virtuosity and a masterpiece. Egoyan is in total control of a very unique approach to moviemaking. His style—though harkening on occasion to that master of deception and irony, Bunuel—is fresh and uncompromising.

Exotica is not a masterpiece, but it is masterful. It is excitingly different and unusual. It holds many marvels for those with the patience to stick with it.

Egoyan's vision has the scope and depth to transcend cult film status. He has the talent and integrity to be one of those rare directors who force the business of film to conform to his artistic vision, rather than the other way around.

—*Michael Betzold*

REVIEWS

Detroit Free Press, March 19, 1995, p. 4C.
Entertainmently Weekly, March 24, 1995, p. 46.
Los Angeles Times, March 3, 1995., p. F10.
New York, March 13, 1995, p. 63.
The New York Times, September 24, 1994, p. 13.
Variety, May 16-22, 1994, p. 40.
Wall Street Journal, March 16, 1995, p. 20.

Fair Game

"Sexy, exciting and fun."—Chris Hewitt, *Knight-Ridder Tribune News Wire*

Box Office Gross: $11,190,582

Producer Joel Silver is known for his over-the-top action films such as the *Die Hard* and *Lethal Weapon* series. If one were to take out any interesting dialogue or any meaningful plot from those films, what would be left is *Fair Game.*

Kate McQuean (Cindy Crawford) is a civil lawyer who handles, among other things, divorce cases. But when she is shot at and wounded while jogging, Dade County homicide detective Max Kirkpatrick (William Baldwin) can't help but wonder if she has a very angry client somewhere. When her home blows up, he's sure of it.

So Max and his crew hide Kate in a safehouse that isn't so safe because Kate's pursuers are more than just your run-of-the-mill murderers. Kate has run afoul of some ex-KGB agents with access to the most sophisticated high-tech surveillance and extermination equipment ever to sail across the Caribbean from Cuba. As a result, Max and Kate barely manage to stay one step ahead of these ex-Commie killers.

The reason they are harboring a hatred for Kate is that they are using a ship, the Tortuga, to tap into a phone cable under the ocean. Head villain Colonel Ilya Kazak (Steven Berkoff) plans on using this illegal link to transfer into his own Swiss account money from the secret bank accounts of corrupt officials which he helped to set up throughout the free world. But the Tortuga was one of several hidden assets in a divorce case Kate was handling, and in an attempt to get the husband to fork over more money, and not realizing what the ship was being used for, she has threatened to send U.S. Marshalls to seize the ship.

That is the essence of what passes for a plot in *Fair Game*. However, it is so illogical that one can't help but feel that it is nothing more than the feeblest of frameworks on which to hang some spectacular explosions and chases. *Fair Game* is long on action and very short on brains.

For example, with all their incredible computer sophistication and handy high-tech gadgets, why must the villains tap into a junction box on transoceanic cable? Why don't they just use a pay phone? And why does the first hit attempt on Kate's life happen before she threatens the husband's divorce lawyer with the U.S. marshalls? And why is it that no matter how spent or destitute Max's condition becomes, he never runs out of bullets? And why, in the depths of her troubles, would Kate run away from Max and jump a train?

However, most glaring of all, why is it that these assassins who are so quick to come up with perfect FBI credentials, and so fast at tracing Kate's credit cards or Max's auto, seem to be so incompetent when it comes to actually hitting their prey?

In fact, since the plot requires no intellectual involvement, one could say that the most entertaining aspect of the film is to count the number of failed assassination attempts. I counted five, several of which were multiple attempts. Lastly, why, after spending the entire film trying to kill Kate, do the villains suddenly decide they want her alive? (Obviously it's so they can lure Max to the ship for the film's explosive finale!)

At one point in *Fair Game*, Max tells Kate that obviously those who are trying to kill her are professionals. Kate sarcastically replies, "I'd hate to be killed by amateurs." Well, it may be amateurs who killed *Fair Game*. Andrew Sipes, whose career includes writing virtually unknown scripts, here is making his directorial debut. And similarly, scriptwriter Charlie Fletcher also has no major credits to his name. It would appear that this film is providing on-the-job training for more than a few people.

CREDITS

Max Kirkpatrick: William Baldwin
Kate McQuean: Cindy Crawford
Ilya Kazak: Steven Berkoff
Meyerson: Christopher McDonald
Juantorena: Miguel Sandoval
Jodi: Johann Carlo
Rita: Salma Hayek
Louis: John Bedford Lloyd
Zhukov: Olek Krupa
Rosa: Jenette Goldstein

Origin: USA
Released: 1995
Production: Joel Silver; released by Warner Bros
Direction: Andrew Sipes
Screenplay: Charlie Fletcher; based on the novel by Paula Gosling
Cinematography: Richard Bowen
Editing: David Finfer, Christian Wagner and Steven Kemper
Production design: James Spencer
Music: Mark Mancina
MPAA rating: R
Running Time: 110 minutes

The most famous amateur in the film, however, is probably supermodel Cindy Crawford who makes her film debut here. Unfortunately, it's hard to tell if she contributes to the problems of the film or if she suffers from them? Her role seems to be nothing more than that of the lovely damsel in distress. But for some reason, Crawford comes across as basically miscast in her role and bland in her beauty. Her character is as hollow as the plot. And when at one point in the film Max gratuitously tells Kate it is her last chance to change T-shirts, we know exactly why she's in the film—to show her breasts.

It may be that blandness which contributes to the fact that there is also no chemistry between Baldwin and Crawford. They spend most of the film fighting and fleeing for survival and verbally sniping at each other, but then, when their fighting actually turns into a boxing match, suddenly the kissing starts. It is an eye-rolling, groaningly annoying lead in to a love scene whose purpose is probably nothing more than to provide shots of Baldwin's naked butt (...and failed assassination attempt number five).

Another problem with this film is that Cindy may always look good, no matter how many canals she falls into, but Florida looks flat. All of Miami's striking architecture and scenic landscapes are obliterated by the murky, dull filming. And speaking of dull, dialogue doesn't come much duller than in *Fair Game*.

If there is a bright spot in this film, it might be the evil villainess Rosa (Jenette Goldstein). Goldstein, who also provided a strong female presence in *Aliens*, rivals and updates the legendary James Bond villainess Lotte Lenya in *From Russia with Love*. It's just a shame that when she does her best handiwork beating Baldwin's face to a pulp at the end of the film, her work is underappreciated by the make-up people so he can still keep his matinee idol good looks for the finale.

If there were ever an indication that *Fair Game* was in trouble—besides the fact that its release date was pushed back several times, even after Crawford made the publicity rounds for it — it might be that the film actually lists three editors in its technical credits. This is very unusual. But it also might account for the fact that the film is often listed with several different running times. I don't know how long the movie actually was, but it seemed like an eternity.

—Beverley Bare Buehrer

REVIEWS

Entertainment Weekly. November 10, 1995.
New York Times. November 3, 1995.
Variety. November 3, 1995.

Far From Home—The Adventures of Yellow Dog

Box Office Gross: $11,642,946

When teenager Angus McCormick first lays eyes on a rangy tan dog in a field behind his family's farmhouse, the camera lingers on both the boy's enraptured face and the dog's sincere stare. It's love at first sight, and all that's missing is a romantic crescendo.

Countless family movies have been based on boy-meets-dog, boy-loves-dog, dog-saves-boy, boy-loses-dog, boy-regains-dog. *Far From Home—The Adventures of Yellow Dog* breaks no new ground in plot lines, characters or its reverential attitude toward teen and canine and their undying friendship. The only difference is that the Old Yeller of bygone days has now become Yellow Dog, a much less appealing moniker.

Far From Home is a solid but unremarkable effort. As played deftly and sincerely by Jesse Bradford, Angus is a handy, humble kid who doesn't have movie-star looks or attitude. He lives on a farm in the Pacific Northwest with parents Katherine (Mimi Rogers) and John (Bruce Davison) and with younger brother Silas (Joel Palmer) who for unexplained reasons is almost always in a Halloween costume. It's also unclear why Katherine always refers to her husband as "McCormick."

Writer-director Phillip Borsos' film moves through its idyllic surroundings as if by rote. The dog appears, there's the obligatory "gee-mom-can't-we-keep-him?" sequences and a few cute-dog tricks. Dad's some sort of freelance shipper and they're preparing for a voyage, and it's not hard to guess what will happen next, especially after father presents son with a new pocket knife. There's even a discussion with a friend who specializes in rescues. On the dock, a girl who's after Angus presents him with a tin of burned cookies; the girl tells him they'll heat him up if he gets cold and damp. Borsos obviously was paying attention in the scriptwriting seminar the day foreshadowing was taught.

The storm at sea, shipwreck, rescue of dad, and tearful search for Angus all are handled perfunctorily. Angus and Yellow are as masterful at surviving their ordeal as the rescuers are inept. As the days pass, Angus proves resourceful and wise beyond his years and beyond all credibility, and helicopters keep buzzing overhead without spotting them. There are an annoying number of scenes where the rescue boss keeps hinting it's time to abandon hope and the parents insist on keeping up the hunt.

Most of the focus is, as it should be, on the boy and his dog and their struggle for survival. Angus has managed to hold onto an impressive number of useful things including cooking pots, a rope, and of course the leaden cookies. He also seems to have an encyclopedic knowledge of nutrition and woodsmanship and nearly infinite patience. Yellow mostly tags along, saving him from a few predators along the way. For a movie about a dog, Yellow (played by a labrador named Dakotah) has too few feats to perform.

There are no surprises in *Far From Home*. The film is dignified and well-edited, with a minimum of schmaltz and filler. Bradford's fine performance and the British Columbia scenery keep things interesting. But the directing is flat, and there is no zing. Even the most dramatic sequences seem blase; suspense and tension are constantly deflated by the matter-of-fact style.

The parents are the usual cardboard characters. Davison looks mostly bewildered, Rogers looks eager to break through the restraints of her underwritten, predictable role.

Things fall apart completely in the final 15 minutes, after the boy is rescued and the dog is lost. You can almost hear the clock ticking until Yellow's triumphant return. It's

CREDITS

Katherine McCormick: Mimi Rogers
John McCormick: Bruce Davison
Angus McCormick: Jesse Bradford
John Gale: Tom Bower
Silas McCormick: Joel Palmer
David Finlay: Josh Wannamaker
Sara: Margot Finley
Yellow Dog: Dakotah

Origin: USA
Released: 1995
Production: Peter O'Brian; released by Twentieth Century-Fox
Direction: Phillip Borsos
Screenplay: Phillip Borsos
Cinematography: James Gardner
Editing: Sidney Wolinsky
Production design: Mark S. Freeborn
Art direction: Yvonne J. Hurst
Casting: Linda Phillips Palo
Sound: Michael McGee
Costume design: Antonia Bardon
Technical advise: Major Denis Lajeunesse
Animal training: Dawn Martin
Music: John Scott
MPAA rating: PG
Running Time: 80 minutes

as if Borsos insists we must endure a certain amount of time of Angus being melancholy (even a kiss from his young admirer doesn't soothe his broken heart). But Borsos doesn't much know what to do with that time. The ending comes as a relief.

In every respect, *Far From Home* is a professional production and it's passable entertainment for children. But there's absolutely nothing new or exciting in the film. Marketers probably like that, but most of the rest of us probably will find the film instantly forgettable.

—Michael Betzold

REVIEWS

Entertainment Weekly. June 9, 1995, p. 72.
The Hollywood Reporter. Jan. 9, 1995, p. 10.
Maclean's. Jan. 16, 1995, p. 60.
The New York Times. Jan. 13, 1995, p. D20.
People Weekly. Jan. 30, 1995, p. 17.
Variety. Jan. 9, 1995, p. 71.

Farinelli

"Amazing! A sensual delight, erotic love-making, opulent costumes and sets, and breathtaking music!"—Jack Garner, *Gannett News Service*

"A triumph! Dazzling! *Farinelli* sounds like nothing you've heard before—eerie, androgynous and electrifying!"—Kevin Thomas, *Los Angeles Times*

"Overflowing with high passion and reckless emotion. Exuberantly sexual!"—Bob Campbell, *Newhouse News Service*

Box Office Gross: $2,122,948

A tall, dark and handsome leading man gives any film a good shot at success. But when your leading man is tall, dark, handsome and castrated, you're looking at a tough sell.

That *Farinelli* conquered its unusual handicap and won a Golden Globe for Best Foreign Film of 1994 says much for the sumptuous cinematography of Walther Vanden Ende. It also may speak to the Globe voters' penchant for the offbeat, for *Farinelli* is clearly a matter of taste.

If your taste runs to the operatic, morose and introspective, *Farinelli* is a feast. But if you like the meat and potatoes of wit, action and character development, *Farinelli* is little more than a good-looking snack.

Farinelli is based loosely on the careers of the Broschi brothers, big stars on the European operatic circuit in the early 18th century. Singer Carlo Broschi is a castrato—a singer castrated in his youth to preserve his boyish soprano. His brother Riccardo writes popular but shallow operas to suit the voice of his brother, whose stage name is Farinelli.

Farinelli sends audiences swooning all over Europe. The film never makes it clear why Carlo's high-pitched, canary-like trilling excites women to fits of ardor. But it does. And the brothers have a bizarre pact. In after-show liaisons with female fans, Carlo the castrato gets things rolling and Riccardo finishes up.

As in most movies about music superstars, there's trouble inside the singer's head. Carlo is afraid he's losing his voice, he's addicted to opium and he's plagued by flashbacks about the horse-riding accident that Riccardo tells him caused his castration. It is easy to suspect the real story, and so the movie's revelations about Riccardo's responsibility for the castration do not provide the shock value intended.

The cult of the castrato is such an outdated and foreign cultural phenomenon that it inspires curiosity. But that is not enough to sustain our interest, so director Gerard Corbiau has added a lot of emotional baggage.

Beneath a heavy glaze of psychological hokum *Farinelli* trafficks in the staples of the star biography genre. Just as if it were a film about Elvis Presley, the sum and substance of *Farinelli* is the immense and fragile ego of its pampered star.

That can be enough to make a fascinating film if the lead character is compelling or if the adulation of the star reveals larger truths about society. *Farinelli* makes labored efforts to fulfill both criteria but falters on each. Besides the predictable disintegration of the star and the unsurprising conflict with his starmaker brother, the tension is supposed to come from Carlo's self-torture about the integrity of his artistry. But this is the most contrived aspect of the movie.

The catalyst for Carlo's doubts is legendary composer Friedrich Handel. Handel challenges Carlo to go beyond his brother's crowd-pleasing trifles and sing music that speaks to the soul, not just the heart. That challenge completely

CREDITS

Farinelli/Carlo Broschi: Stefano Dionisi
Riccardo Broschi: Enrico Lo Verso
Alexandra: Elsa Zylberstein
Handel: Jeroen Krabbe

Origin: Italy
Released: 1994 (1995)
Production: Vera Belmont of a Stephens Films, Alina Films, UGC Images, Studio Canal Plus, RTL, TVI production; released by Bac Films
Direction: Gerard Corbiau
Screenplay: Andree Corbiau and Gerard Corbiau; adapted to the screen by Marcel Beaulieu
Cinematography: Walther Vanden Ende
Editing: Joelle Hache
Production design: Gianni Quaranta
Costume design: Olga Berluti
Special make-up and hair: Kuno Schlegelmilch
Music: Christopher Rousset
MPAA rating: R
Running Time: 110 minutes

AWARDS AND NOMINATIONS

Cesar Awards 1995: Best Art Direction, Best Sound
Golden Globe Awards 1995: Best Foreign Film
Academy Awards Nominations 1994: Best Foreign Language Film

unnerves the castrato, who has been spoon-fed nothing but adulation and is unused to criticism. The flappable Carlo—whom the filmmakers repeatedly and rather ridiculously suggest lacks courage because he lacks testerone—faints at the very sight of Handel in the audience.

> The castrato voice of Farinelli is a digitally enhanced combination of counter-tenor Derek Lee Ragin and soprano Ewa Mallas Godlewska.

Handel is the main force behind the King of England's theater at Coventry Gardens. The Broschi brothers embrace a rival theater and lure crowds from Handel, who becomes a genius without an audience. It is easy to grasp the point that popularity and authentic artistry are at odds, but the film hammers home the theme ad nauseum. Subsequent developments are not hard to guess.

Director Corbiau, who wrote the screenplay with his wife Andree, takes some liberties with the historical record. Farinelli was the most popular of all the castrato singers, and his voice reportedly covered three and a half octaves. After retiring from public singing at 32, he became the court singer for King Philip V of Spain and was credited with curing the king's depression.

> "A castrato's voice is an example of nature abused...rerouted from its goal, in order to deceive. You've subverted your voice to virtuosity without soul...devoted only to artifice!"—Handel from *Farinelli*

Corbiau trumps up the conflict with Handel to provide Farinelli's story with some dramatic tension. He contrives Riccardo's culpability to create psychological complexities. He adds the bizarre sexual pact to create some erotic interest for modern audiences. But none of these embellishments succeed to add passion to a rather bloodless story.

Sweeping, operatic gestures define the film's power and its shortcomings. Vanden Ende's cinematography is achingly gorgeous though unfortunately often superfluous. At its best moments, when Carlo's voice soars over a painterly cinematic canvas, the effect is stunning. But the thrill is that of looking at well-executed but uninvolving art because the film is as dry as a thesis.

The performers are hampered by a script which has no wit, levity or intrigue. *Farinelli* is terribly earnest. Watching the film at times is like attending a compulsory lecture on a subject of great academic import but no personal interest. The filmmakers seem to be constantly reminding the audience that this is supposed to be serious stuff about art and truth and the human soul. But too often the proceedings just seem silly, as when Handel tells Carlo he will never compose again because "you have castrated my imagination."

It is a Herculean task to make Carlo a compelling figure, and Stefano Dionisi fails to move the mountain. His portrayal of an unraveling prima donna is pretty standard fare. Dionisi is handsome but hardly heroic. He is too aloof to evoke much sympathy.

The question *Farinelli* poses is whether it was justified to castrate Carlo to serve the higher purpose of art. The answer it supplies is no. But Farinelli is so unappealing in the film that one is left wondering whether the answer should be yes. Carlo the character is not involving enough; he is simply a tortured superstar from another era.

As Riccardo, Enrico Lo Verso wears a permanent hang-dog expression that deepens into anguish. Clearly, he is deeply burdened. He is not modulated or interesting. Neither is Jeroen Krabbe, who plays Handel as a pompous ass.

The filmmakers have a decidedly retrograde take on sexual roles. All the women are spilling out of their tightly corsetted costumes, and have little part to play other than to lust after the Broschis.

While the Farinelli of history was known for his humility and generosity, Corbiau has made him into a spoiled and deficient eunuch who is doomed to spells of fainting and hysteria. Carlo is scripted just as a woman would be scripted by a misogynist. The movie's bizarre ending cements the interpretation that Carlo needs his brother to complete him. Carlo's rage at Enrico is forever soothed by the gift of a child, just as a traditional woman is supposed to find fulfillment in maternity.

As a study of androgyny, *Farinelli* fails to comprehend the power of the concept. Modern musical superstars like Michael Jackson, David Bowie and the formerly named Prince have mass appeal because they combine powerful aspects of masculinity and femininity. Corbiau's view of Farinelli's androgyny is that he was deficient in both masculinity and femininity. That makes for a pretty pathetic protagonist.

It is difficult to construct a film of heroic proportions upon a central character who is weak and often despicable. Because Farinelli himself is so unappealing, this film is like the music Riccardo Broschi composes: heavy on style and flourish but short on substance. One reviewer likened it to "a James Dean movie directed by Lina Wertmuller at her most threadbare hysterical." It is hard to argue with that assessment.

REVIEWS

Entertainment Weekly. March 17, 1995, p. 68.
The Hollywood Reporter. Feb. 24-26, 1995, p. 11.
New York Times. March 17, 1997, p. B10.
Opera News, March 4, 1995, p. 47.
Variety, Dec. 19, 1994 - Jan. 1, 1995, p. 74.

Father of the Bride II

"Absolutely hilarious!"—Ron Brewington, *American Urban Radio Networks*

"Completely irresistible!"—Joanna Langfield, *Movie Minute*

"It doesn't get any better than this!"—Bonnie Churchill, *National News Syndicate*

"More fun the second time around!"—Dixie Whatley, *WCVB-TV*

Box Office Gross: $49,881,012

Father of the Bride II is unique in that it is a sequel to a remake that is also a remake. *Father of the Bride* (1991) starring Steve Martin was a remake of *Father of the Bride* (1950) starring Spencer Tracy. The 1991 version was so successful that it spawned a sequel, just as the original did. The sequel to the original film was titled *Father's Little Dividend* (1951). The 1995 sequel uses the far less original numeric after its name—*Father of the Bride II.*

This film stars all of the cast from the 1991 version, and is based on *Father's Little Dividend.* Steve Martin, Martin Short, Diane Keaton, and director Charles Shyer have duplicated the success of their first film, creating a charming, middle-of-the-road comedy that has something for everyone. It is an amiable film with characters and situations that will resonate for anyone who has been pregnant, or has been a father, family member, or friend of anyone who has been pregnant. That about covers everyone, and insures the film's success.

Steve Martin stars as George Banks, the father of the bride, who tells the audience in a friendly narration about how "they lowered the boom on me" just as he began to recover from his daughter's wedding. The "boom that got lowered" is that his daughter, Annie (Kimberly Williams) and her husband Bryan (George Newbern) are going to have a baby. This immediately sends still-youthful George into a tailspin, horrified that he is going to be called "grandpa." "Grandfathers wear cardigans and hearing aids," he complains. Intent on keeping his youth, he dyes away his grey hair and considers doing some crazy things: "I can get that Harley I always wanted," he tells himself. Among other things, he decides that he and his wife Nina (Diane Keaton) must sell their beautiful suburban home and move to a condo at the beach. They sell it to a wealthy man named Mr. Habib (Eugene Levy, in a funny but stereotypical role), who plans to demolish the enormous home and build two smaller ones.

But just before the house is sold, George and Nina recapture their youth with some spontaneous lovemaking, and immediately after they move out of their beloved home they discover that Nina is pregnant. Through various machinations George buys back their home, and is forced to watch over the final months of pregnancy of both his wife and daughter (whose husband is called out of the country on business.) Meanwhile, Franck Eggelhoffer, the effete decorator who planned Annie's wedding, is overseeing construction on the new baby's room. Franck's presence, combined with the two pregnant women, provides a lot of comic fodder for Steve Martin, who makes the most of all the situations.

One of the joys of this movie is that there is no purpose other than to entertain, and that is exactly what it does. Director Charles Shyer keeps a brisk pace that is farcical when it needs to be (such as in the hospital sequence) and very touching at other times, such as in the scenes between George and the kind young doctor (Jane Adams) who is delivering his wife's baby.

Shyer and screenwriter Nancy Meyers wisely stay with the elements that worked in the first film. The cast remains the same, as does the gently comic tone. The focus, as before, is on the mixture of sweetness and crankiness that is intrinsic to George's character. The humor comes from the character's overprotectiveness about his daughter, his internal fears about aging, and his desire to have a perfect, easy life. It is a given that any character who wants to have an easy life in a comedy cannot have one. And when things go wrong for George, they go wrong in a big way. Meyers and Shyer make the situations just odd enough to be interesting for the screen but still human enough for audiences to relate. It is hardly realistic that a mother and daughter would become pregnant within four weeks of each other and then deliver on the same night. Yet Shyer and Meyers make the ridiculous situation believable and funny.

"After all, we will be in our fifties when he's in pre-school. In our seventies when he graduates college. But really, that'll be a great day...to see another kid in a cap and gown...if we can still see by then....He certainly won't have to worry about us hearing him come in late..."—George Banks from *Father of the Bride II*

The comedy always comes from real situations and from their character's reactions to those situations. When George has not had enough sleep after caring for his pregnant daughter and wife, Franck gives him some sleeping pills. The pills are a bizarre drug from Franck's country, and they cause George to fall asleep at the dinner table. Of course, as soon as he falls asleep his daughter goes into labor, and Franck must try and rouse him while getting the women ready to go to the hospital. Short is hilarious as he drags Martin across the room, trying to get him to the car. Like *I Love Lucy* or any classic comedy, these situations are based in the reality set up by the writers and actors.

As in the first film, Martin is excellent as George Banks. Though he is not an actor of the same caliber as Spencer Tracy (the original George Banks), Martin has a charisma that transcends his acting ability. He commits himself completely to whatever he does, and is just plain funny driving around in his convertible trying to look twenty years younger, or running back and forth between his wife and his daughter's hospital rooms. When called to do so, Martin is appropriately dewy-eyed and sincere, especially when he is holding his baby daughter and his grandson after their delivery.

Since physical comedy is Martin's forte, much screen time is devoted to highly visual situations, such as when he confronts the two Doberman's at his in-laws house, or when he is mistakenly wheeled into a doctor's office for a prostate exam while he is asleep. Some audiences may think his best moments come in the scenes where he is asleep: Martin is even funny when he is out cold.

Diane Keaton provides a perfect balance to Martin's rather chaotic character. In this film, Keaton has more to do than in the last film. Her brilliance is never quite used fully in the role, but the film is better for having her steady, sweet presence. One of her best moments comes when she demands that George stop thinking about himself and about how they are too old to be parents again: "I know how old I am, George; I'm nervous, and very much alone," she tells him, with great feeling.

The film's extreme moments come (as they did in the first film) from Martin Short's way-out character of Franck. At first it feels as if Franck's bizarre accent, wild clothing, and outlandish behavior will seem out-of-place when juxtaposed with the more sedate other characters. But Short seems to make the character grow as the film progresses, and Franck never wears out his welcome. He takes on a more naturalistic style than he did in the first film: Short seems to know that audiences can tolerate only so much of a ridiculous character in the middle of not-so-ridiculous ones. When Franck shows the completed nursery to George, Short infuses his character with a great deal of humanity. He is proud of his beautiful work. Later, when called on to help with Nina and Annie during labor, Franck turns to George and says, "we're bonding, aren't we?" with a mixture of absurdity and tenderness that few actors could pull off.

This film is truly a "feel-good" movie, due to its sweet script, its mainstream values, and its fine performances. It is aided by a wonderful musical score by Alan Silvestri, who provides excellent original music that enhances the action perfectly. Silvestri also oversaw the arrangement of two songs which are integral to the feel of the film: "Give Me the Simple Life" and "On the Sunny Side of the Street," both performed by Steve Tyrell. These recordings are important elements of the success of the film.

Finally, the "simple life" alluded to by the songs and by George's character is beautifully realized by Production designer Linda DeScenna and by Cinematographer William Fraker. Fraker captures DeScenna's design with lush depth and texture. DeScenna and her designers and crew have created a suburban fantasy home that Martha Stewart would envy.

It is not surprising that in this turbulent era, where so much gritty realism is present on film and television screens, that *Father of the Bride I* and *II* would be successes. For some, the film will depict a life that they can never have. Some may not want it—after all, it is a little "white bread." But it is hard to imagine audiences not responding on some level to George and Nina's experience of trying to be happy in a fast-paced world. Sure it is escapist fare, but it's based in very real human concerns.

—Kirby Tepper

CREDITS

George Banks: Steve Martin
Nina Banks: Diane Keaton
Franck Eggelhoffer: Martin Short
Annie Banks-MacKenzie: Kimberly Williams
Bryan MacKenzie: George Newbern
Matty Banks: Kieran Culkin
Howard Weinstein: B.D. Wong
Mr. Habib: Eugene Levy

Origin: USA
Released: 1995
Production: Sandy Gallin and Nancy Meyers for a Touchstone Pictures production; released by Buena Vista
Direction: Charles Shyer
Screenplay: Nancy Meyers and Charles Shyer; based on the screenplay *Father's Little Dividend* (1951) by Albert Hackett and Frances Goodrich; based on the characters created by Edward Streeter
Cinematography: William A. Fraker
Editing: Stephen A. Rotter
Production design: Linda DeScenna
Art direction: Greg Papalia
Costume design: Enid Harris
Sound: Richard B. Goodman
Casting: Jeff Greenberg
Music: Alan Silvestri
MPAA rating: PG
Running Time: 106 minutes

AWARDS AND NOMINATIONS

Golden Globe Awards Nominations 1996: Best Actor-Musical/Comedy (Martin)

Feast of July

"A feast for the eyes, ears & heart."—Michael Medved, *New York Post*

"One of the best films of the year."—Jeffrey Lyons, *Sneak Previews*

"Spellbinding!"—Paul Wunder, *WBAI Radio*

Box Office Gross: $293,274

The striking panorama of the English countryside in the opening scene of *Feast of July* immediately brings to mind the late David Lean and, in particular, the beginning of his *Oliver Twist* (1948). In Lean's work, a pregnant woman stumbles in agony as she crosses forbidding English terrain, whipped by the wind and with lightning flashing and thunder booming ominously overhead. In *Feast of July*, harsh winds lash at another pregnant Englishwoman in distress, this one as she makes an arduous cross-country journey on foot to find the wayward rascal who loved and left her. This similarity may be attributable to the fact that Christopher Neame, the screenwriter and a producer for the newer film, is the grandson of Ronald Neame, producer of the earlier one. The young woman in *Feast* is Bella Ford (Embeth Davidtz of *Schindler's List*), utterly exhausted and still far from Nenweald, the small town where her lover had told her he resides. The dark, threatening sky and formidable, looming hills appear ready to engulf her and finish her off. In a deserted barn, Bella is able to find refuge from the elements but not from her heartache, as a miscarriage leaves her crumpled on the dirt floor. Finally, seemingly more dead than alive, she stumbles into the mist-enshrouded village and is taken in by Ben Wainwright (Tom Bell), a kindly lamplighter and head of a family of shoemakers. She is nursed back to health by Mrs. Wainwright (superbly portrayed by Gemma Jones, whose face here looks like a wonderful portrait by John Singleton Copley.) While fighting to regain her strength, Bella also does battle with the memories that haunt her of her brief affair with Arch Wilson (Greg Wise). She recalls, in flashback, his tender and seemingly sincere expressions of love for her (both verbal and physical), as well as his assurances that he would not desert her. Mrs. Wainwright guesses what has happened to Bella, and she seems unsettled by the beauty that her ministrations have returned to the young woman's face. Her trepidation seems to be well-founded, as all three of her handsome grown sons begin competing for the affections of this mysterious, alluring creature whose sudden materialization adds interest to their prosaic lives. The rivals involved in all this pastoral preening are Matty (Kenneth Anderson), a quiet, level-headed cobbler, Jedd (James Purefoy), a dashing, flirtatious soldier brimming with cockiness, and Con (Ben Chaplin), a dark, brooding loner who veers between childlike gentleness and explosions of rage and jealousy. Curiously, despite the fact that he is obviously a pressure-cooker, crammed to bursting with frustrations, Con is the brother that Bella finds herself drawn to the most. (Perhaps it is empathy for a fellow sufferer.) When Jedd playfully asks Bella for a kiss while working in the fields, it is not particularly surprising that Con erupts and charges at his brother with a razor-sharp scythe. Mrs. Wainwright briefly surveys this inevitable battle before sternly ordering everyone back to work. She adopts a noticeably more scornful tone when she turns to give the same order to Bella. It is clear that the family's matriarch angrily resents what Bella's mere presence has wrought upon her household. Feeling the heat and honestly not wanting to cause trouble within the family, Bella packs her bags and heads for the train station. Con chases after her, and after earnestly expressing his love, he triumphantly returns home with Bella proudly on his arm. "Well, you always do what you want," a disapproving Mrs. Wainwright frostily tells her son, "so I won't waste my breath." Con proceeds to blurt out a marriage proposal in the middle of a meal, and his mother's expression freezes when Bella accepts. In contrast to his wife, Mr. Wainwright immediately reacts with hearty good wishes, apparently—and oddly—oblivious to all the tensions in his own home.

It is of course at this point, when Bella thinks she has finally secured lasting happiness, that Arch resurfaces. Bella is shocked when she sees that he has a wife, not to mention a child, in another town, and she disgustedly tells the cad off. Unfortunately, it is not their last meeting. The day of the Feast of July, a festive harvest celebration, Con and Bella are enjoying a lazy boat ride down the river when they are spotted by Arch, who is fishing on the bank. While Bella sloughs off the boor's teasing and taunting, Con cannot, and he bashes Arch's head to a bloody pulp. On the run, the two make it to the coast, and while Bella arranges for their passage on a departing vessel, Con's burning jealousy makes him fantasize about killing the man she is dealing with. The super-sensitive, tortured soul finally decides that he cannot live with what he has done, and he turns himself in. After visiting Con in prison, Bella boards the ship alone. She rubs her abdomen, suggesting that she is once again pregnant. The last shot of Bella staring blankly out from the bow is too reminiscent of the indelible final image of Greta Garbo in Mamoulian's excellent *Queen Christina* (1933). That shot of Garbo was overwhelmingly powerful, while the shot here of Davidtz is far less potent and meaningful.

Like *A Month by the Lake* (also 1995), *Feast of July* is based on a work by British author H.E. Bates (1905-1974). In the perceptive 1983 study of the author and his works, Dennis Vannatta notes that Bates' novel "is rather predictable...and the characters are all people we have seen before." What makes it a book worth reading, he goes on to say, is the author's vivid depiction of life in the red-brick English shoemaking village towards the end of the 19th Century. Anyone who has enjoyed other Merchant Ivory productions, such as *Howard's End* (1992) or *The Remains of the Day* (1993), will not be surprised that this latest period piece has been brought to the screen with a fair degree of Bates' attention to detail still intact. It is often a decidedly lovely film to look at: Peter Sova's cinematography, Phoebe De Gaye's costumes, Jill Quertier's sets, and Christopher Robilliard's overall production design all display Merchant Ivory's characteristically high production values. Still, all this finery cannot totally obscure the fact that the book's weaknesses have been transferred to the screen along with its strengths. It is not hard to see where this production is going, and, to make matters worse, the tone and pace that the film adopts along the way are too static and lifeless. The characters and script are never especially captivating or intriguing, and what happens to Bella and Con is able to be viewed with too much detachment. The film seems to skim over surfaces, failing to explore, or sometimes reveal at all, a necessary complexity or depth of character. Furthermore, the reasons behind the actions of various characters are not sufficiently clear. This lack of illumination leads to puzzlement and questions, the most obvious one being why Bella chooses Con, whose behavior is rather conspicuously and unsettlingly creepy. In his first feature film, director Christopher Menaul, who earned accolades for his work on British TV's *Prime Suspect,* delivers a story that never gets up much steam until the very end, which may be too late for many viewers. Still, while *Feast of July* takes a rather flat, predictable course, at least it's the scenic route.

—*David L. Boxerbaum*

CREDITS

Bella Ford: Embeth Davidtz
Ben Wainwright: Tom Bell
Mrs. Wainwright: Gemma Jones
Jedd Wainwright: James Purefoy
Con Wainwright: Ben Chaplin
Matty Wainwright: Kenneth Anderson

Origin: Great Britain
Released: 1995
Production: Henry Herbert and Christopher Neame for a Merchant Ivory production; released by Touchstone Pictures
Direction: Christopher Menaul
Screenplay: Christopher Neame; based on the novel *Feast of July* by H.E. Bates
Cinematography: Peter Sova
Editing: Chris Wimble
Production design: Christopher Robilliard
Art direction: Roy Stannard and Caroline Smith
Costume design: Phoebe de Gaye
Sound: Paul Bradley
Assistant direction: Gary White and Waldo Roeg
Casting: Kathleen Mackie
MPAA rating: R
Running Time: 116 minutes

REVIEWS

Atlanta Constitution. October 20, 1995, p. P6.
Boxoffice, November 1995, p. R91.
Chicago Sun-Times. October 27, 1995, p. 3D.
Entertainment Weekly. October 27, 1995, p. 73.
Los Angeles Times. October 13, 1995, p. F18.
New York Times. October 13, 1995, p. C12.
St. Louis Post Dispatch. October 27, 1995, p. E3.
San Francisco Chronicle. October 20, 1995, p. C3.
Wall Street Journal. October 17, 1995, p. A18.
Washington Post. October 21, 1995, p. H5.
Variety. August 28, 1995, p. 67.

Federal Hill

"A winner! Invested with detail and freshness recalling Fellini and Scorsese."—Jay Carr, *Boston Globe*

"An expert director's touch...swift action, clever dialogue and clear-cut characters...Michael Corrente really does know how to make a movie."—Caryn James, *The New York Times*

"Robustly entertaining...with fresh humor, insight and a dynamite cast!"—Peter Travers, *Rolling Stone*

Box Office Gross: $322,075

Five testy young Italian-American buddies take joyrides, ogle women, play poker, eat pasta, trade insults and get in hot water in a working-class neighborhood of Providence, R.I. in *Federal Hill*, a film that looks all too familiar. First-time writer-director-producer Michael Corrente isn't treading any new territory with yet another evocation of the ethnic culture celebrated in Martin Scorcese's *Mean Streets* (1973). Corrente has familiar wise guys getting in predictable scrapes. What he lacks is enough heroism, villainy and vitality to make *Federal Hill* exciting. It's a clunker with very uninspired directing and only occasional interesting moments.

Corrente has little sense of how to introduce characters or move a story along. His timing is awful and his transitions are awkward. The film was shot in black-and-white for $80,000, but it has none of the visual innovation or daring technique one might expect from a low-budget film by a new auteur. Distributor Trimark Pictures, hoping to give *Federal Hill* some commercial appeal, colorized it without Corrente's consent. The colorized video version looks wan and washed-out; it probably should have been left alone. What it really needed was not color, but more intrigue.

In slice-of-life fashion, Corrente plunks us down, almost in mid-conversation, in the midst of the five pals as they hang out in a parking lot. It takes nearly a half-hour of seemingly aimless and disconnected scenes to sort out the characters and their relationships.

The only action in the first half of the film comes near the beginning. Out for a ride, the five buddies are incensed when a driver ahead of them won't let them pass; the volatile Ralph (Nicholas Turturro) smashes the guy's windshield with a tire iron. This is the same Ralph who likes to burglarize houses, and this is the character for which Corrente strives to evoke sympathy.

We're supposed to like Ralph, even though he's a thief and a hothead, because he's devoted to his father, a mason who suffers from a mysterious depression. Family loyalty absolves all sins in this genre. We're also supposed to care about Nicky (Anthony DeSando), even though he sells cocaine. Nicky turns into a sap when he falls for the beguiling Wendy, a Brown University coed. We're supposed to feel sorry for Nicky because Wendy and her family and college chums are snobs and Nicky, a low-life ethnic, can't cut it in the big, cruel world. His plight is overplayed hokum; there's even a scene where Nicky looks longingly through a closed fence at the campus and a guy wearing Docksiders.

We're also supposed to feel sorry for Joey (Robert Turano) when he gets in trouble for going too far with a counterfeiting scheme and a hood gives him one week to repay

CREDITS

Ralph: Nicholas Turturro
Nicky: Anthony DeSando
Frank: Michael Raynor
Joey: Robert Turano
Bobby: Jason Andrews
Wendy: Libby Langdon
Sal: Frank Vincent
Fredo: Michael Corrente

Origin: USA
Released: 1994
Production: Michael Corrente, Libby Corrente, and Richard Crudo for Eagle Beach Productions; released by Trimark Pictures
Direction: Michael Corrente
Screenplay: Michael Corrente
Cinematography: Richard Crudo
Editing: Kate Sanford
Production design: Robert Schleinig
Sound: Matt Sigal
Costume design: Sara Slotnick
Music: David Bravo, Bob Held
MPAA rating: R
Running Time: 100 minutes

AWARDS AND NOMINATIONS

Independent Spirit Awards Nominations 1995: Best Supporting Actor (Turturro)

$30,000. And we're supposed to feel elation when Ralph hatches a scheme to steal back the money. We're supposed to pity Frankie (Michael Raynor) when his gangster father orders him to get back at Ralph for stealing from gang members, and Frankie makes a fatal mistake. We're supposed to feel bad for Bobby (Jason Andrews), who treats his wife like dirt, because he gets pushed around by the rest of the gang.

Director Corrente does a cameo as a foreman on a building site.

But it's difficult to feel much sympathy for these characters. Corrente seeks to excuse their behavior because they are only small-time wrongdoers, not real gangsters. They're portrayed as victims of their own culture and of the world's lack of acceptance of Italian-Americans. But these guys don't live a life of victims; they move with impunity in their own world and seem to escape punishment for any transgressions.

If they were big-time criminals, their characters could be assessed in light of their villainy, and they might even be capable of acts of heroism. But these guys, no matter how witty and authentic, don't rise above their milieu and don't rate any special consideration. Corrente, a native of the Federal Hill neighborhood, knows the turf but fails to give his characters any resonance beyond their insular world.

"That broad comes from somewhere in the middle of the West, and you're Johnny wanna-buy-a-kilo from Federal Hill."—Ralph to best friend Nicky from *Federal Hill*

Plot developments, when they finally arise in the film's second half, come out of the blue. All of a sudden Joey's in trouble, and he has to explain why because we've been given no inkling of what he's been up to. When Ralph goes on a crime spree, heat comes down because, as Frankie's father explains, he has burglared the homes of some "made men"—a translation is not provided. Tensions don't build into confrontations; the tragic events at film's end just explode out of nowhere.

The way Corrente shoots many scenes is ridiculously amateurish. His camera is static and he often employs long, unmoving shots. One scene where a tailor talks to Frankie is horribly framed, with the tailor leaning back in a recliner so that his face is small and distant. When the camera finally moves in on such scenes, it's almost a relief.

Fortunately, there are some bright comic moments, though they are few and far between. The best is a scene where a coed at a fraternity party brushes off Ralph's brash come-on with a zinger of her own.

Nicky's affair with Wendy starts out sweet but turns silly. He cooks her an Italian dinner and they jump into bed, and roommate Ralph interrupts their lovemaking. From there on, it's a triangle, with Ralph jealous of Nicky's attentions to Wendy. What could be more trite in a buddy movie than a girl who gets in the way of the weekly poker game? But there are puzzling overtones. Ralph's vicious trick on a gay pedestrian suggests Ralph is repressing his love for Nicky; they share the same bed, which seems odd for adult, heterosexual roommates. If that's not what the gay-assault scene suggests, then it's merely gratuitous violence.

Ralph keeps telling Nicky that Wendy is too good for him — "she shits vanilla ice cream" is how Ralph delicately puts it. The gap between Ralph's ethnic background and Wendy's upper-class upbringing is milked for much more than it's worth. Wendy's father explains to her mother, "His last name is Russo, dear," as if he were exposing Nicky as an axe-murderer.

As played by Langdon, Wendy is a classy, saucy and smug young woman who seems much too sophisticated to be a coed. Predictably, Corrente puts her in librarian's glasses when she is studying. DeSando plays Nicky with more aplomb than the script suggests, turning his macho character into jelly at the very sight of Wendy.

Turturro, whose older brother John's career is much farther along, almost saves the film. Asked to make a character whose actions are despicable into a likeable hero, Turturro nearly pulls it off. He is fresh, energetic and unique—everything the rest of *Federal Hill* is not.

The other performances are uniformly good, but not good enough to lift *Federal Hill* out of the low-rent district and into the neighborhood of original, mesmerizing and resonating films about the Italian-American culture. Scorsese and Coppola have nothing to fear from Corrente.

—*Michael Betzold*

REVIEWS

Entertainment Weekly. Jan. 20, 1995, p. 38.
Hollywood Reporter. Oct. 13, 1994, p. 6.
Los Angeles Times. Feb. 24, 1995, p. F6.
New York Times. Dec. 10, 1994, p. 13.
Playboy. December 1994, p. 30.
Rolling Stone. Dec. 1, 1994, p. 134.
Variety. Feb. 15, 1994, p. 21.

First Knight

"Their greatest battle would be for her love."—Movie tagline

"You couldn't ask for a better King Arthur or Lady Guinevere."—Leonard Maltin, *Entertainment Tonight*

"A magnificent epic full of spectacular battles, blazing passion and grand performances."—Jeanne Wolf, *Jeanne Wolf's Hollywood*

"Rousing and spirited, brimming with action and filled with romance."—Neil Rosen, *NY1 News*

"A medieval festival for the eye and ear."—Susan Wloszczyna, *USA Today*

Box Office Gross: $37,600,435

Sean Connery stars as King Arthur and Julia Ormond as Guinevere in *First Knight*. © 1995 Columbia Pictures Industries, Inc. All rights reserved.

Based on scraps of history and legend, tales of King Arthur abound both in literature and in film. From Malory's "Le Morte d'Arthur" to John Boorman's *Excalibur* (1981), from *Connecticut Yankee in King Arthur's Court* (1949) to *Camelot* (1967), the failed dream of idyllic happiness has wooed audiences and readers over and over again. In Jerry Zucker's version of the dream, action is all, and love requires less explanation and is much more transitory than warfare. It is a life where people fight endlessly, even for the chance to love. Says Arthur (Sean Connery), "For the first time in my life, I wanted what all wise men say doesn't last. What can't be promised or made to linger any more than sunlight. I don't want to die without having felt its warmth on my face."

Unlike *Camelot*, which focused on Arthur and Guinevere, *First Knight* begins with Lancelot (Richard Gere), master swordsman, a fighter without peer. Living in the harsh, brutal conditions of the Middle Ages, Lancelot is without a home or a family, and wanders without a destination. Next the film focuses on Guinevere (Julia Ormond), prccariously perched at the helm of a land caught in a maelstrom, Leonesse, she is working to save her people from the evil deeds of Malagant (Ben Cross). Finally, the film turns to Arthur, beloved king, who leads his kingdom with an even hand, shares the power with the knights of the round table, and brings to life the maxim "In serving each other we become free." Once the three strands of the story are revealed, the braiding begins: Guinevere is caught between the passion of Lancelot and the fatherly wisdom of Arthur.

Lancelot is a character steered by his passions. Not unlike *The Outlaw Josey Wales* (1976), Lancelot fights his way across county, driven by the horrible memories of his family's death and by his hate for the knight-turned-murderous-thug who slayed them. In flashback, a young Lancelot watches his family killed and his village burned to the ground. When as an adult he fights, he fights with complete abandon, feeling he has nothing more to lose. For instance, early in the film, Lancelot is fighting a villager in Leonesse. Bested in the fight, the villager asks the tricks, the moves, behind the winning style. Lancelot explains some very workable steps, such as study your opponent. However, when he reaches the truly indispensable ingredient—don't care whether you live or die—the villager is dissuaded, and Zucker's Lancelot is identified as a nihilist for the Dark Ages, a rebel without a cause. He is also highly skilled: he is the one person to survive the obstacle course of swinging swords and sandbags intended to entertain the residents of Camelot. Richard Gere built his career by playing a series of disenfranchised, angry, marginal characters in such films as *Looking for Mr. Goodbar* (1977) and *Breathless* (1983), and here he combines that persona with his more romantic leads (e.g., *Pretty Woman*, 1990). In sum, Lancelot's balm is Guinevere's love and Arthur's respect—an inescapably tragic combination.

Guinevere has more traditionally been portrayed creating flower wreaths, feasting and picnicking, dancing. For instance, in *Camelot*, Guinevere (Vanessa Redgrave) picnics, weaves flower crowns and sings lustily about the joys of the month of May when everyone goes happily astray. In *First Knight*, Guinevere is seen playing an early version of soccer, happily laughing and running even as Leonesse is in great need. She rides and plays soccer exceedingly well, and fights off kidnappers with wile and ease. In her short film career,

Julia Ormond has had a series of thankless roles as a trophy. In *Legends of the Fall* (1995) she portrays a woman who becomes a prize fought for not only by three brothers but also by their father. Soon, she will appear in the remake of Billy Wilder's *Sabrina* (1955), playing Audrey Hepburn's role of a young beauty bounced back and forth between two older brothers. In *First Knight* as well, Julia Ormond plays the role of beauteous bounty, a prize most valued. Indeed, Julia Ormond can be seen as the latest in a series of young actresses, cast it would appear (at least in part) for their ripe good looks. Just as Olivia Hussey radiated beauty and youth in *Romeo and Juliet* (1966), as did Helena Bonham Carter in *Room with a View* (1985), so too Julia Ormond is cast as the beautiful and fresh prize, unlike actresses such as Madeline Stowe (*Last of the Mohicans*, 1993, *Unlawful Entry*, 1994) who is tougher, more sinewy and plays roles in which she fights for what she wants rather than allowing herself to be awarded to the person who wants her. For instance, in *First Knight*, Arthur agrees that he will allow any man who can successfully navigate the obstacle course to kiss Guinevere. She is literally the prize, and her affection is literally Arthur's to distribute.

"What's very different about this telling is that Lancelot doesn't come to serve Arthur. Lancelot comes to Camelot because he's in love with Guinevere, but during the course of the movie, he learns the meaning of knighthood."—Director Jerry Zucker on his movie's revisionist take on Camelot

Sean Connery's Arthur is engagingly familiar, a man whose dreams of a democratic kingdom blossom, even as his dreams of love die upon the vine. However, for what may be the first time, Connery is playing a character whose age is a defining characteristic. With the possible exception of his role in *The Untouchables* (1987), Connery has continued to play romantic leads without reference to his age (even when paired with significantly younger co-stars). For instance, in the otherwise unnoteworthy film *Medicine Man* (1992), Connery plays opposite a much younger Lorraine Bracco without any reference to his age or younger men, and in *Rising Sun* (1994), Connery plays teacher to Wesley Snipes and also manages to surprise Snipes through his passionate liaison with a comely computer expert (Tia Carrere) who has made it clear that she is impervious to Snipes' advances.

Perhaps part of the problem with the film *First Knight* is that the action scenes ring particularly true, while the romantic scenes arrive without precedent and fall flat. Part of this problem might arise from the filmmaker's emphasis on battles. For instance, when Lancelot, Arthur and Guinevere travel to rescue Leonesse, their strategy and the battle are considered and shown in great detail. So too, Malagant's initial attempt to kidnap Guinevere goes on and on, each fall, each slug, each thundering hoof, each scream. Compare this to the mooning that goes on between Lancelot and Guinevere throughout the film. For instance, after Lancelot rescues Guinevere from Malagant's men, he tries to persuade her to give herself to him. He appears to have no realization of the absurdity of rescuing her only to try to violate her himself. Additionally, his advances are so clearly motivated by her beauty that it is hard to believe that romantic love, i.e., sentiment, ever enters the picture. It would appear that near-miss kisses, escapes via horseback and endless battles serve prelude to the love. And, as such an absurd statement would suggest, the love between Guinevere and Lancelot is not believable. The filmmakers have missed a key factor here, for if a kingdom and a king are lost for love, the audience had better believe that love exists, or the whole exercise becomes futile.

The production notes report that the principal locations were the grounds of Pinewood Studios. The towers of Camelot (a city on a hill, glowing in the distance) rose six stories about the trees of the studio's backlot. It appears that the filmmakers attempted to make some sites appear feminine and others masculine. For instance, in an attempt to make Lionese a "feminine" village: a gentle windmill window sail, warm terra cotta hues. Conversely, Camelot fea-

CREDITS

Arthur: Sean Connery
Lancelot: Richard Gere
Guinevere: Julia Ormond
Malagant: Ben Cross
Air Agravaine: Liam Cunningham
Sir Kay: Christopher Villiers

Origin: USA
Released: 1995
Production: Jerry Zucker and Hunt Lowry for a Zucker Brothers production; released by Columbia Pictures
Direction: Jerry Zucker
Screenplay: William Nicholson; based on the story by Nicholson, Lorner Cameron and David Hoselton
Cinematography: Adam Greenberg
Editing: Walter Murch
Production design: John Box
Art direction: Bob Laing, Michael White, Stephen Scott and Giles Masters
Set direction: Malcolm Stone
Special effects: George Gibbs
Costume design: Nana Cecchi
Music: Jerry Goldsmith
MPAA rating: PG-13
Running Time: 132 minutes

tures simple lines and cool blues, grays and whites. Indeed, the exterior of Camelot is in fact a deserted nuclear power plant in North Wales. Additionally, special credit is given in the production notes to a medieval weapons expert who served as technical advisor, 200 horses and 250 stuntmen, and armorer Terry English who made almost 300 suits of full body armor and over 200 sets of horse armor (the most armor ever made for a film).

Clearly *First Knight* is an action film that opens by promising a kiss not delivered until the end. Far from compelling, the film falls flats and sinks in a mire of dialogue. Nonetheless, as summer films fare, a trip to the theater to see *First Knight* may offer a respite from otherwise unbearable, sweltering heat, especially for those audience members who love a good sword fight, whoever you may be.

—Roberta F. Green

REVIEWS

Baltimore Sun, Maryland Live, July 7-13, 1995, p 5.
Boston Globe, July 7, 1995, p. 27.
Chicago Tribune, Tempo, July 7, 1995, p. 4.
The New Yorker, July 17, 1995, p. 84.
USA Today, July 7-9, 1995, D1.
Washington Post, Weekend, July 7, 1995, p. 36.

Fluke

"The magical story of a love that spans lifetimes."—Movie tagline

"very entertaining and deeply moving tale"—Jeanne Wolf, *Jeanne Wolf's Hollywood*

"Two thumbs up!"—*Siskel & Ebert*

Box Office Gross: $3,987, 649

Fluke is a pleasant fluke—a shaggy dog story with more bite than bark. Unlike most animal movies, *Fluke* aims at more serious targets than the cute button.

The story line sounds weak: a man is killed in a car crash and reincarnated as a dog; the dog is aware of its previous life and tries to return to its former wife and son. The screenplay is based on a popular James Herbert novel.

Despite the bizarre premise and a few unappealing plot developments, director Carlo Carlei passionately believes in the simple story. The passion shows through in every frame of the film, with mixed results. It lifts what might have been banal sequences to nearly inspiring heights. But, especially toward the film's end, the directing becomes tedious and heavy-handed. These are errors of enthusiasm as Carlei is overly eager to make his points.

Comet, who starred for six seasons on television's *Full House*, is a golden retriever. To perform as Fluke, a mixed-breed dog, his coat was dyed brown with vegetable oil.

Fluke dares to suggest how reincarnation actually might happen. By giving an animal a prior human life, it turns the idea of interspecies connectedness into something palpable, dangerous and exhilarating. This is the kind of risky business that most modern filmmakers shun, looking for the safest roads to box-office success.

Fluke walks its own dangerous path. It may offend some parents and frighten some children who thought they were going to see another cuddly animal movie. It may lack the sophistication and cynicism needed to capture a large adult audience. To appreciate *Fluke*, you have to admire Carlei's reach and excuse his excesses.

The film opens with tragedy. Tom (Matthew Modine) and business partner Jeff (Eric Stoltz) are having a high-speed argument while driving side-by-side down a two-lane country road. Tom head-ons a truck and crashes into a tree. We are taken with him through a golden tunnel of light that symbolizes death. He emerges as one among a litter of homeless puppies scrapping for food in the back of a Chinese restaurant in downtown Atlanta.

Barely escaping the clutches of the city dog catcher, Fluke is adopted by Bella (Collin Wilcox Patton), a homeless woman. Fluke helps Bella earn money by playing a shell game with walnuts for street crowds. But soon another tragedy occurs: Bella dies.

The film shifts gears when a street-wise dog named Rumbo befriends Fluke. Rumbo and Fluke talk in human language, with Samuel L. Jackson supplying Rumbo's sassy voice. In the film's most amusing sequences, Rumbo teaches Fluke the proper way to urinate on the street and beg for food at local restaurants. Rumbo brings Fluke to his junkyard home, the only place, Rumbo says, where "you can chase car tires and not worry about getting run over." Jackson does the Rumbo thing to heartwarming perfection.

Though these sequences are fetching, *Fluke* doesn't turn into a cute talking-dog movie. Many things remind Fluke of his former life and when he tells Rumbo about a flashback, Rumbo advises: "Pictures got no business being inside your head... just growl and chase them away."

Carlei never lets us get comfortable with the dogs as mere funny, talking pets, always keeping us aware that Fluke once was a man. There's a continual edge of discomfort in the film that makes for some surprisingly heart-wrenching moments.

There are also many heavy-handed touches, especially with minor characters. An ape-faced villain catches Fluke and delivers him to an cosmetics laboratory where an evil-looking scientist does medical experiments on him. Rumbo helps Fluke escape in a sequence that is sure to exhilarate animal lovers. It would be even more effective if the villains were not such caricatures.

Fluke suffers yet another tragedy when Rumbo is fatally wounded rescuing him from the laboratory, but Fluke makes the long journey back to his human family. The film then turns to Fluke's efforts to make his former wife Carol (Nancy Travis) and son Brian (Max Pomeranc) understand who he is. There are many strangely poignant scenes, as the dog plays games with Brian and climbs into bed with Carol.

Pomeranc, who excelled as the chess prodigy in *Searching for Bobby Fischer* (1994), is wonderful again: straightforward and believable. Travis is beautiful but a bit wooden. As the warring business partners, Modine and Stoltz are fine but given little to work with.

The real star of the film is Comet, the transformed golden retriever who is a veteran television performer. Comet's soulful eyes and expressive face allow audiences to make the human identification necessary for the film's success. A dog named Barney is also effective as Rumbo, with Jackson helping greatly to give Rumbo an endearing personality. Children will love Rumbo even more than Fluke.

The last half-hour of the film, which concerns Fluke's efforts to straighten out Tom's squabbles with his partner Jeff, will frustrate children and many adults who might wish for a simple happy ending. Instead, there are histrionics, character reversals and a few heroic moments.

The film becomes very somber, straining toward a moral that has to do with the importance of appreciating life's simple pleasures. Tom/Fluke becomes a tragic figure who wasted his chances for happiness as a man and only realizes his mistakes in his next life as a dog, where he cannot regain what he has lost. A sunny ending will help kids get over the disappointment they will feel at Fluke's inability to reconcile with his family.

Fluke is a remarkable film, unlike any other. Carlei is uncomprising, plunging into unabashed sentimentality but never yielding to it. He is masterful at telling a story without dialogue.

From a unique perspective, *Fluke* is a meditation on the wonders of existence. It will annoy those looking for an unchallenging family film, but it offers plenty of entertainment along with its moral lessons.

Many critics unfairly panned *Fluke* for not being innocuous enough for children, but Carlei is trying for much more than that. Many children, especially older ones, will grasp some of *Fluke*'s deeper lessons. Adults willing to suspend their disbelief and indulge in some speculative metaphysics may also find the film rewarding.

Fluke is not kids' stuff. Its whole point is that adults would do better approaching life with the wonder and perspective of children and even animals. It expands the definition of what is means to be human, and isn't that what films are supposed to do?

—Michael Betzold

CREDITS

Fluke/Thomas Johnson: Mattew Modine
Carol Johnson: Nancy Travis
Jeff Newman: Eric Stoltz
Brian Johnson: Max Pomeranc

Origin: USA
Released: 1995
Production: Paul Maslansky and Lata Ryan for a Rocket Pictures production; released by Metro-Goldwyn-Mayer
Direction: Carlo Carlei
Screenplay: Carlo Carlei and James Carrington; based on novel by James Herbert
Cinematography: Raffaele Mertes
Editing: Mark Conte
Production design: Hilda Stark
Costume designer: Elisabetta Beraldo
Visual Effects supervisor: Paolo Zeccara
Music: Carlo Siliotto
MPAA rating: PG
Running Time: 96 minutes

REVIEWS

Entertainment Weekly. June 9, 1995, p. 36.
The New York Times. June 2, 1995, p. B8.
People Weekly. June 12, 1995, p. 18.
Variety. June 5, 1995, p. 36.

The Flying Dutchman (De Vliegende Hollander)

The Flying Dutchman (De Vliegende Hollander), despite its mythical allusions, is an adult fantasy of a man's struggle for a decent life in an imperfect world. Director Jos Stelling has said that the film "deals with man's longing to come to terms with the struggle for life through death." In order to bring this message across, Stelling has nearly killed his hero at least three times in the film, only to revive him at the last moment so that he can continue on with his wretched life.

The Flying Dutchman is a new version of the old myth of the ship's captain who is doomed to sail the seas for eternity. In this story, a traveling troubadour tells a young orphaned Dutch boy that his father is a sailor who can fly.

The film opens in 16th century Holland, a time when Dutch iconoclasts, rebelling against Spanish rule, smashed images of the saints and robbed Catholic churches. In the opening scene, one such group carrying the head of a huge statue is attacked by Spanish soldiers while passing through a field owned by a Dutch farmer named Nettleneck (Willy Vandermeulen). They are slaughtered by the soldiers, but one man, hiding within the head of the statue, escapes. Nettleneck's wife finds him and they make love in the field.

An Italian troubadour, Campanelli (Nino Manfredi), witnesses this event, which turns out to be the conception of the couple's son. Years later when the minstrel returns to the farm, he tells the boy, now an orphan, that his father is alive and sails the seas with his own ship. But most important, he tells him his father has the gift of flight. This fantasy helps the boy endure his miserable life on the farm, where he is treated like an outsider. When the boy (Rene Groothof) grows up, he leaves the farm and his sweetheart, Lotte (Veerle Dobbelaere), to find his father and his destiny.

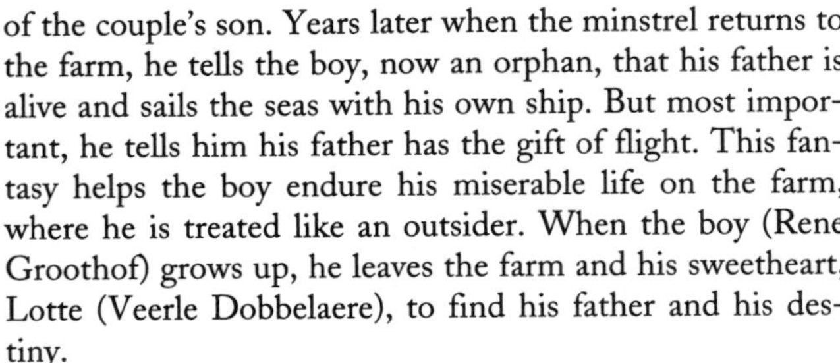

In his search, this innocent encounters many dangerous misadventures, and often appears to have died when, as astounding as it seems, he somehow survives. But each time he revives from a near death experience, it is as if he is reborn, and we begin to believe that he has a destiny that he must live to realize—some reason for his life.

On his journey he meets a cunning and greedy dwarf (Rene van't Hof) who is living in an old dilapidated ship that has washed up into a marsh. The Dutchman is certain that fate has led him to his father's ship. He buys it from the dwarf and tries to ready it for sailing. But in the process, he unwittingly tips off Spanish soldiers who raid the abandoned ship and take him and the dwarf off to prison.

Undaunted by the horrors of prison life, the Dutchman retains his unsuspicious nature. He gathers a group of prisoners around him who believe in him and his stories. But he also attracts some prisoners who betray him and land him in a dark hole in the dungeon where he struggles to remain alive.

One day his old sweetheart Lotte, now married to Nettleman's son, visits the prison and discovers that her lover is incarcerated there. Bribing the dwarf, who has insinuated himself into the warden's good graces, she visits the Dutchman in the dungeon and tells him that he has a son.

She returns with the key to his cell and brings his son to meet him. When he leaves his cell we realize that he has again defied death, but this time he is changed. This time he appears to have reached a transcending level of consciousness, and the film's first intimations of light emerge from this dark film as the Dutchman passes onto his son the legend of his father—the Flying Dutchman.

That night he makes his escape from prison, and as the camera pans up the impossibly high prison wall to the sky, we are left imagining the Dutchman soaring over it like a bird. But this final hint of meaning comes far too late in the film, and after trudging through cesspools, murky marshes, and filthy prisons, this ray of hope is too faint to enlighten the profoundly dismal images of the preceding 130 minutes.

This is filmmaker Jos Stelling's first film since *The Pointsman* in 1986, and bears his trademark impressionistic visual style. It is a Dutch/Belgian/German co-production,

CREDITS

The Dutchman: Rene Groothof
Lotte: Veerle Dobbelaere
Campanelli: Nino Manfredi
Dwarf: Rene van't Hof
Nettelneck: Willy Vandermeulen

Origin: Belgium and Germany
Released: 1995
Production: Jos Stelling, Alain Keytsman and Christoph Meyer-Wiel for a De Vliegende Hollander BV and Mikado Films production; released by UGC D.A.
Direction: Jos Stelling
Screenplay: Jos Stelling and Hans Heesen
Cinematography: Goert Giltaij
Editing: August Verschueren
Production design: Gert Brinkers
Art direction: Andre Fontaine and Peter van Laar
Costume design: Anne Verhoeven
Sound: Robi Guver
Special effects: Harry Wiessenhahn and Rik Wiessenhahn
Music: Nicola Piovani
MPAA rating: not listed
Running Time: 128 minutes

and cost $5.5 million to produce—a very expensive film by European standards. The hope is that the film will attract an audience larger than the usual art house clientele. But for U.S. audiences the film lacks a main character with whom the audience can empathize. Groothof's Keatonesque character, for all his innocence and buffoonery, never connects with the viewer, and we are left scratching our heads in wonder at his incomprehensible stupidity. The Dutchman comes across as intolerably simple in his saintly trust and even though the Dutchman never gives up hope, Stelling's heavy pessimism wrings the last drops of hope out of his audience, making the ending almost unbelievable.

Another difficulty is Stelling's unrelentingly depressing vision of the Middle Ages, remorselessly somber and perpetually muddy. His drab characters inhabit backdrops of frozen barren fields, with egg-shell colored skies, clad in dirty mud-spattered brown rags, until you almost yearn for some cheery urban squalor. It is almost as if Stelling has forgotten the Dutch saying, "The eye also wants something," denying us even the comfort of a simple clear blue sky.

Stelling had hoped that this big-budget epic would attract mainstream moviegoers, and was counting on courting an audience through Nino Manfredi's appearance in the film. Although Manfredi is a familiar face—he has appeared in more than 60 films and is a famous name in Southern Europe—he is relatively unknown in the U.S., which doesn't in any way discredit his wonderful performance in *The Flying Dutchman.* His portrayal of the minstrel is as campy as a court jester, and he is flamboyantly captivating in the part. His character brings color and passion to *The Flying Dutchman*, standing in delightful contrast to Rene Groothof, whose acting is perfectly understated. After each rebirth, we search in vain on Groothof's deadpan face for a hint of illumination—only finding it at the very end when he seems totally transformed, having transcended naivete to enlightenment in one fell swoop.

Rene van't Hof, in his magnificent portrayal of the sly dwarf, is easy to hate, embodying the spirit of avarice and deceit, while bringing a certain comic relief to the unabated misery of the Dutchman's life.

Credit also goes to cinematographer Goert Giltaij, who has successfully created an ambience that is both visually captivating and mystical. Beginning with the mud-soaked farm where misery reigns to a forlorn yet magical galleon mired in a foggy swamp and leaving us in a horror of a dungeon, all of the film's images evoke a feeling of fantasy edged with an ugly reality.

During the filming of *The Flying Dutchman*, the producers of the film told the press that their intention was to produce a box-office hit that could vie for an Oscar. Using a big name star, a strong story line, a big budget, and plenty of marketing seemed to be the formula to reach this goal. But it doesn't work. It is as if Stelling wants to go mainstream, but the better angels of his nature won't let him.

What he has achieved is an expensive art film that won't satisfy the visceral needs of the mainstream U.S. audience or even compensate for that omission by leaving them with a warm fuzzy feeling. In the end, it is a visually interesting, yet pessimistic art film.

—Diane Hatch-Avis

REVIEWS

Screen International, January 7, 1994, p. 14.
Variety, October 1, 1995.
The Wall Street Journal, March 28, 1994, p. A9C.

Forget Paris

"Touching, funny, unforgettable."—Bill Diehl, *ABC Radio Network*

"A wonderful film...filled with romantic moments and great big laughs."—Roger Ebert, *Chicago Sun-Times*

"...so warm, witty and delightfully romantic that you won't forget it."—Jeanne Wolf, *Jeanne Wolf's Hollywood*

"...breezily charming and funny."—Caryn James, *The New York Times*

"Hilarious! Laugh out loud funny."—Bruce Williamson, *Playboy*

"Two thumbs up!"—*Siskel & Ebert*

Box Office Gross: $33,194,512

Debra Winger as Ellen Andrews, an American living in Paris, captures the heart of an American professional basketball referee played by Billy Crystal in *Forget Paris*. Photo by Bruce McBroom.

As this year's second entry in the "I Love Paris" film series, Billy Crystal's *Forget Paris* joins the Meg Ryan/Lawrence Kasdan romantic comedy, *French Kiss* (1995) in providing Francophiles with at least a fleeting glimpse of the city most noted for bringing couples together. While the Kasdan film chose the more traditional storytelling route of featuring two disparate characters who fight their way through the film only to be united by the end, *Forget Paris* is an entertaining film that attempts to take an adult look at what happens when the honeymoon is over and the marriage begins. It is a movie about love, but not about falling in love. While an engaging premise, there is one sizable problem with the film: Billy Crystal. And considering he is the film's producer, co-writer, director and star, this could be the major determinant of how much one enjoys *Forget Paris*.

While waiting for his friends to arrive at a restaurant, sportswriter and inveterate bachelor Andy (Joe Mantegna) begins to tell his fiancee, Liz (Cynthia Stevenson), the story of how his best friend, Mickey Gordon (Billy Crystal), a professional basketball referee, met the love of his life, Ellen Andrews (Debra Winger), an airline customer service representative, when the casket bearing his father's dead body ends up missing en route to its final resting place with the remainder of his World War II regiment in a small town outside of Paris. As the tale unfolds, other members of the celebratory dinner party arrive, including car salesman Craig (Richard Masur) and his wife, Lucy (Julie Kavner), who continue to provide details about the couple's descent from romance to reality. As Lucy points out, "Nobody should tell this story to someone who's about to be married."

After a quick and seemingly unlikely romance, Mickey returns home for the start of the new basketball season. But he misses Paris, with its art galleries and tourist attractions. And surprisingly, he finds he misses Ellen. For the first time in his life Mickey has found something that he cares about almost as much as his work. Eventually Ellen gives up her life in Paris to follow Mickey to Los Angeles. They marry, but it is not long before Ellen grows discontent with her life and with Mickey's long absences from home. She pressures Mickey into giving up his job as a referee and taking a more stationary one as a car salesman with Craig, while she finally begins to flourish when she is promoted to an airline job more worthy of her experience. Pressures mount when Ellen's senile father, replete with a fondness for commercial jingles, moves in and eventually the couple separates. But as Mickey tells Ellen later, "We're better together than we are apart," and by film's end, the couple has found their way, at long last, to matrimonial compromise.

Crystal turns up his questionable charm, using every situation as a set-up for his patented one-liners and verbal zingers. The trouble is we have seen it all before. Crystal offers up no new surprises, just predictable schtick. What is painfully missing, particularly for a love story, is heart. Crystal hits all the right moves and yet the film falls embarrassingly flat. It lacks any real emotion and as a result, it becomes increasingly difficult to care about the main characters. Even the story structure which utilizes a storytelling technique in which five long-time friends share anecdotes about the couple's tempestuous relationship tends to distance the audience from the couple.

More than one film critic commented on the level of self-involvement on the part of Billy Crystal. Most felt that as co-writer/producer/director/actor, the comedian had once again taken on too much responsibility for the project, as he had with his directorial debut, the box-office flop, *Mr. Saturday Night* (1992). There is no denying that Billy Crystal is a talented performer. As the host of the annual Academy Awards ceremony, Crystal wooed audiences with his quick wit and relentless verbal acerbity. What is in question here is his ability to direct a feature film. The comic timing he displays during his stand-up routines is all but absent from his directing; he misses beats and allows his fascination with "Billy Crystal the star" to get in the way of both the film's pacing and the storytelling.

Crystal reportedly had a very strained relationship with actress Debra Winger while filming *Forget Paris* and it is easy to speculate that the talented Ms. Winger was more than a little frustrated by her role in the film. Often her character has very little to do on-screen except smile and be an audience for Crystal's endless one-liners. Winger tries desperately to find something to work with in Ellen, but at times the actress' facial expressions are so pained and forced that it is difficult to not empathize with her, despite the skewed writing that has a tendency to place the burden of guilt for the couple's unhappiness most squarely on Ellen. And as with Glenn Close's character in *Fatal Attraction*, Ellen must succumb to the ultimate cliched indicator of yuppie angst: consuming pints of trendy up-scale ice cream as she agonizes over the emptiness of her life and the absence of the man. Winger, however, does display a knack for slapstick in the scenes of her dealing with a hapless pigeon who manages to end up glued to her head while driving to the veterinarian. Sadly, Winger and Crystal not only lack chemistry, they never even seem to be in the same movie. As Stanley Kaufmann from *The New Republic* pointed out in his review of *Forget Paris*, Debra Winger is an actress, Billy Crystal is a performer.

The supporting cast is uniformly entertaining while amusing themselves with the Woody Allen-esque repartee around the restaurant table. Most notable are character actors Richard Masur—one of the most recognizable faces in Hollywood, ranging from one of his few turns as a sadistic villian in Karl Reiss's *Who'll Stop the Rain* (1976) to the more recent HBO drama, *And the Band Played On* (1994)—and Julie Kavner, always funny and one of Woody Allen's favorites, appearing in *Hannah and Her Sisters* (1986), *Radio Days* (1987), *Oedipus Wrecks* from *New York Stories* (1988), *Shadows and Fog* (1992), and the voice of Marge Simpson on tv's *The Simpsons*. It was particularly satisfying to see that the pair has not lost the rapport they had established during their early days on the television sitcom, *Rhonda*.

Of the most glaring omissions from the story is the failure to capitalize on the potential for Mickey's infidelities while on the road as an NBA referee. It is not at all unthinkable for this character to at least be tempted by other attractive females, especially since the writers had set up Mickey as a man with a history of dating comely professional cheerleaders. It is unfortunate that the writers chose not to pursue this line because that element could have added some concrete conflict into an otherwise whiny, self-involved relationship. And the whole joke about the couple moving to the San Fernando Valley when Ellen joins up with Mickey in the United States is most likely only funny to those viewers who are familiar with the Los Angeles area. While the scenes of Mickey refereeing NBA games, com-

CREDITS

Mikey: Billy Crystal
Ellen: Debra Winger
Andy: Joe Mantegna
Liz: Cynthia Stevenson
Craig: Richard Masur
Lucy: Julie Kavner
Arthur: William Hickey
Jack: John Spencer
Lois: Cathy Moriarty

Origin: USA
Released: 1995
Production: Billy Crystal and Kelly Van Horn for a Castle Rock Entertainment presentation of a Face Production; released by Columbia Pictures
Direction: Billy Crystal
Screenplay: Billy Crystal, Lowell Ganz and Babaloo Mandel
Cinematography: Don Burgess
Editing: Kent Beyda
Production design: Terence Marsh
Costume design: Judy Ruskin
Casting: Pam Dixon Mickelson
Music: Marc Shaiman
MPAA rating: PG-13
Running Time: 101 minutes

REVIEWS

The Christian Science Monitor. LXXXVII, May 19, 1995, p. 12.
Entertainment Weekly. May 26, 1995, p. 61.
Los Angeles Times. CXIV, May 19, 1995, p. F12.
The National Review. June 26, 1995, XLVII, p. 63.
The New Republic. June 12, 1995, CCXII, p. 32.
New York. May 29, 1995, XXVIII, p. 53.
The New York Times. CXLIV, May 19, 1995, p. B2.
The New Yorker. May 22, 1995, LXXI, p. 98.
People Weekly. May 29, 1995, XLIII, p. 20.
Variety. CCCLIX, May 15, 1995, p. 95.
The Village Voice. LX, May 30, 1995, p. 62.

plete with cameo appearances by several top basketball players, are amusing and help to illustrate Mickey's gutsiness, particularly when Mickey suffers a breakdown on court, some scenes go on far too long and tend to interrupt the flow of the story, ending up as more of a short man's adolescent jock fantasy.

While not without its laughs, *Forget Paris* is, overall, a disappointment. Despite a promising premise, the film is hampered by Billy Crystal's failure to act with anyone other than himself. Reviews for the film were generally negative.

—*Patricia Kowal*

Four Rooms

"Antonio Banderas is hilarious! Robert Rodriguez's segment is very funny!"—Roger Ebert, *Chicago Sun-Times*

"Quentin Tarantino wins us over! Tim Roth out-Aces Jim Carrey!"—Michael Wilmington, *Chicago Tribune*

"A wildly outrageous comedy!
"—Jeanne Wolf, *Jeanne Wolf's Hollywood*

Box Office Gross: $2,155,523

Directorial samplers are dangerous notions. Too often, the concept of several directors' short films cobbled together into a feature produces an incoherent mess. At its worst, the idea promotes self-indulgent excesses excused in the name of auteurism. That's exactly the case with *Four Rooms*, a wretched, mismatched four-piece set of cinematic baggage.

The setting is New Year's Eve at a somewhat faded Los Angeles luxury hotel. Nervous novice bellhop Ted (Tim Roth) is alone on duty and faces various terrors from manic guests in four rooms. The story of each room is separately scripted and directed by each of four hip independent directors—Allison Anders, Alexandre Rockwell, Robert Rodriguez and Quentin Tarantino, in that order.

The only room worth the price of admission is that directed by Rodriguez, who alone fashions the right tone of edgy comic mayhem that the others fail to achieve. Rockwell's room is passably intriguing but ultimately unsatisfying. Anders' segment is incredibly silly. And Tarantino cements a growing reputation as an unbearably self-absorbed, vastly overrated director with a huge ego and an even bigger disdain for the intelligence of his audience.

As is sadly the case with sampler films, the sum of *Four Rooms* is less than the parts. The only thing holding together the concept is the bellhop character, and Roth is not equal to the task. His twitchy, taut, frenetic portrayal is rarely funny and often annoying. He seems to be trying for an amalgam of Jim Carrey and Jerry Lewis but falls far short of comic genius. Roth goes in and out of a British accent, in and out of fear and braggadocio, in and out of insight and inanity. His Ted the bellhop isn't consistent, doesn't make sense, and is grating rather than ingratiating. For the film to work, the audience must develop some sort of affection or sympathy for Ted, but Roth's performance is so off-putting that there is little chance of that.

Most of the rest of the large cast is trying to have some fun with over-the-top characters, and only Antonio Banderas, as a fearsome patriarch in the Rodriguez segment, rings the bell. Jennifer Beals also gets a lot of mileage out of her sultry, soft-spoken, foul-mouthed spoiled dame, a variation of her excellent portrayal in *Devil in a Blue Dress* (1995). Beals, the only actor besides Roth to appear in more than one segment, is deliciously wicked and genuinely funny, an island of true mirth in a sea of very strained and forced humor.

Originally titled *Five Rooms*, it was filmmaker Alexandre Rockwell's idea to bring together five young directors to make an anthology comedy. After meeting on the film festival circuit, Rockwell convinced Quentin Tarantino, Allison Anders, and Robert Rodriguez to join in. The fifth, Richard Linklater, bowed out.

With Anders' vastly disappointing segment, *Four Rooms* starts off on a very flat foot. Her "The Missing Ingredient" is a paltry tale of a coven of comely witches who gather in the hotel's Honeymoon Suite to stir up a potion in the jacuzzi that will revive their goddess, a 1950s porn star frozen into stone on her wedding night. From the moment Madonna vamps into view, Anders launches into the silliest of soft-core put-ons.

It's like some frothy concoction you might see on late-night cable, an insultingly stupid excuse for a few bared breasts and dirty talk. The segment is not titillating, not funny and not memorable, and should be just as roundly condemned for its Penthouse-magazine-type parading as if it were directed by a man rather than Anders.

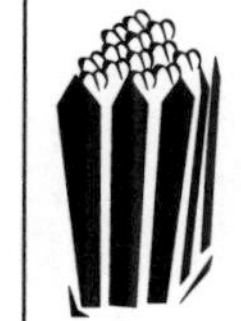

"Stay away from night clerks, kids, hookers, and marital disputes. Never have sex with the clientele. Always get a tip."—Sam to Ted the Bellhop from *Four Rooms*

In fact, the rest of *Four Rooms* bogs down in a vein that can only be described as disturbingly misanthropic, with generous dollops of gratuitous sex and violence. In Rockwell's "The Wrong Man," Roth lands in the middle of a strange marital game between a gun-toting maniac (Dave Proval) and his bound-and-gagged wife (Beals, Rockwell's real-life wife). What goes on is at first frightening, then laughable and finally nonsensical. The segment is occasionally funny, particularly when Beals blurts out some funny foul-mouthed dialogue and proves much more lethal than her apparent torturer. The twist on sado-masochism is that the dominant partner, the wife, is only playing at being dominated. This is mostly harmless fun but it certainly doesn't live up to its initial promise of electrifying sexual tension; it succumbs to being merely a clever joke.

Batting third, Rodriguez hits the film's only home run with "The Misbehavers," his twisted tale of Banderas' red-hot Hispanic lover who wants to have fun on New Year's Eve with his gorgeous hot-to-trot wife. But to do so, they must dispose of their two kids. So the overbearingly macho father decides to leave them in the room watching TV, with the bellhop paid a handsome sum to check up on them. The children, of course, make life miserable for Ted, but hardly in predictable ways. Ted has his own child care tricks learned from the days he was sat for, but the two youngsters have no trouble outsmarting him. Rodriguez manages to make his room terrifyingly funny, and if the rest of the film came close to matching his wit and execution, it would be fine entertainment. The only things that spoil this segment are Roth's overdone mugging and disturbing hints of barely concealed abusive behavior toward the children. And while there's a boffo ending, Ted inexplicably escapes the punishment threatened him, like a cartoon character who is flattened in one scene and then becomes whole again in the next.

Unfortunately, the longest and the dullest segment comes last, and it's the latest showcase for Tarantino's boundless narcissism. In "The Man From Hollywood," the hot-shot director unabashedly casts himself as an drunken, egotistical film star out to have a little sick fun with two buddies while Beals, imported from one of the other rooms, looks on in sarcastic amusement. Tarantino obviously thinks his thin little joke is extraordinarily precious and his own portrayal mesmerizing. He allows himself to ramble on in long, pointless monologues that he seems to believe are unbearably clever. In fact, there is nothing in the segment except a paltry adolescent dare involving a cigarette lighter, a hatchet and a finger, a bit stolen from an Alfred Hitchcock television show and raised to the level of some sort of faux-macho showdown. Not even a cameo from Bruce Willis can salvage this segment. This is what all the adulation for *Pulp Fiction* has wrought: a director who thinks the slightest twitch of his mind will make film audiences swoon in admiration. "The Man From Hollywood" is a terribly self-indulgent piece of filmmaking, replete with senseless, over-

CREDITS

Ted, the bellboy: Tim Roth
Athena: Valeria Golino
Elspeth: Madonna
Elspeth's Girl: Alicia Witt
Raven: Lili Taylor
Eva: Ione Skye
Jezebel: Sammi Davis
Diana: Amanda DeCadenet
Angela: Jennifer Beals
Sigfried: David Proval
Father: Antonio Banderas
Mother: Tamlyn Tomita
Chester Rush: Quentin Tarantino
Leo: Bruce Willis
Norman: Paul Calderon
Margaret: Marisa Tomei
Betty: Kathy Griffin

Origin: USA
Released: 1995
Production: Lawrence Bender for A Band Apart production; released by Miramax Films
Direction: Allison Anders, Alexandre Rockwell, Robert Rodriguez and Quentin Tarantino
Screenplay: Allison Anders, Alexandre Rockwell, Robert Rodriguez and Quentin Tarantino
Cinematography: Rodrigo Garcia, Phil Parmet, Guillermo Navarro and Andrezej Sekula
Editing: Margie Goodspeed, Elena Maganini, Robert Rodriguez and Sally Menke
Production design: Gary Frutkoff
Art direction: Mayne Schuyler
Costume design: Susan Bertram and Mary Claire Hannan
Music: Combustible Edison and Esquivel
MPAA rating: R
Running Time: 102 minutes

wrought stylistic long shots that almost cry out for attention. It's a gee-whiz-look-how-clever-I-am piece of garbage, and attentive audiences will see that Tarantino is basically just another good old boy in hip disguise. It's further evidence that behind the clever facades, Tarantino is a misogynist who dresses up the same old brainless machismo in post-modern drag. And his room is definitely a drag.

With Tarantino providing the unfortunate coda, *Four Rooms* leaves the bitter aftertaste of a senseless, almost masturbatory filmmaking exercise. To intelligent movie audiences, nothing is more insulting that the conceit that any contrivances by notable directors are worth cobbling together, that a film can be made just because a few auteurs have gotten together on a concept, gathered up a few hip actors, and decided whatever they produce is worth a few million in expense. In fact, it's not much more than a celebrity round-up, and if it were a cavalcade of over-the-hill stars and directors it wouldn't make it to a single screen.

—Michael Betzold

REVIEWS

Variety. Sept. 25, 1995, p.93.

Francois Truffaut – Stolen Portraits

The checkered life of filmmaker Francois Truffaut is the subject of this documentary, which includes interviews with such friends and colleagues as Claude Chabrol, Eric Rohmer, and Bertrand Tavernier.

CREDITS

Gerard Depardieu: Gerard Depardieu
Ewa Truffaut: Ewa Truffaut
Claude Chabrol: Claude Chabrol
Jean-Louis Richard: Jean-Louis Richard
Jean Gruault: Jean Gruault
Alexandre Astruc: Alexandre Astruc
Claude de Givray: Claude de Givray
Jean Aurel: Jean Aurel
Annette Insdorf: Annette Insdorf
Olivier Assayas: Olivier Assayas
Marcel Berbert: Marcel Berbert
Madeleine Morgenstern: Madeleine Morgenstern
Eric Rohmer: Eric Rohmer
Robert Lachenay: Robert Lachenay
Janine Bazin: Janine Bazin
Bertrand Tavernier: Bertrand Tavernier
Marcel Ophuls: Marcel Ophuls
Monique Lucas: Monique Lucas
Albert Duchesne: Albert Duchesne
Liliane Siegel: Liliane Siegel
Laura Truffaut: Laura Truffaut
Marie-France Pisier: Marie-France Pisier
Yann Dedet: Yann Dedet
Claude Miller: Claude Miller
Nathalie Baye: Nathalie Baye
Fanny Ardant: Fanny Ardant

Origin: France
Released: 1993
Production: Monique Annaud for Chrysalide Films, co-produced by France 2 Cinema/INA Entreprisemaecenas Films/Premiere, with the participation of Canal Plus; released by Myriad Pictures
Direction: Serge Toubiana and Michel Pascal
Cinematography: Maurice Fellous, Jean-Yves Le Mener and Michel Sourioux
Editing: Dominique B. Martin
MPAA rating: no listing
Running Time: 93 minutes

Frank and Ollie

Walt Disney has been responsible for creating some of animation's most beloved characters. Two animators, Frank Thomas and Ollie Johnston, played an integral part in creating these characters and setting the high standard of entertainment for the Disney company. This portrait shows how Frank and Ollie came to Disney 40 years ago and created their pioneering partnership and friendship.

CREDITS

Frank Thomas: Frank Thomas
Ollie Johnston: Ollie Johnston
Sylvia Roemer: Sylvia Roemer
John Canemaker: John Canemaker
John Culhane: John Culhane
Marie E. Johnston: Marie E. Johnston

Origin: USA
Released: 1995
Production: Kuniko Okubo and Theodore Thomas for a Walt Disney production; released by Buena Vista Pictures
Direction: Theodore Thomas
Screenplay: Theodore Thomas
Cinematography: Erik Daarstad
Editing: Kathryn Camp
Music: John Reynolds
Sound: Marc Fishman
Sound effects: Ann Scibelli and Tim Gedemer
MPAA rating: PG
Running Time: 89 minutes

Frankie Starlight

"*Frankie Starlight* plays like a kid brother to *My Left Foot*, but with a gentle, fanciful flavor of its own."—Jay Carr, *The Boston Globe*

"It touches the heart in a genuine way about the search for beauty and love."—Howie Movshovitz, *Denver Post*

"It captures your heart. If you're looking for something a bit different than typical Hollywood fare...*Frankie Starlight* is a good bet."—Jeff Craig, *Sixty Second Preview*

Touted as similar to *My Left Foot* (1989), *Frankie Starlight* was celebrated as part of the new genre exploring loneliness and love in Ireland. A gentle and charming movie, it affirms that each individual experiences his private pain and that we are all united in our search for love. Based on Chet Raymo's best-selling book, *The Dork of Cork*, *Frankie Starlight* portrays a young dwarf's search for love and beauty in a world of cruel and confusing people.

Bernadette (Anne Parillaud), a young French girl, flees from France following her father's death at the hands of the Nazis and her mother's subsequent suicide. Stowing away on an American war ship, Bernadette earns her passage by selling sexual favors to the servicemen. Discovered, she is put ashore in Ireland, and is befriended by immigration official Jack Kelly (Gabriel Byrne). Kelly shelters her during her pregnancy and the birth of her child, Frankie (Alan Pentony), a dwarf. Kelly's adultery is witnessed by his daughter Emma (Georgina Cates), leading to a long and painful battle with mental illness. Kelly's betrayed wife, Effa (Dearbhla Molloy), determines that the entire family will care for Bernadette and Frankie, and for a while, Frank blossoms under the kind and generous care of Kelly, who teaches him about the wonders of the universe.

When Emma's health deteriorates, the Kellys move away, leaving Bernadette and Frankie alone. Soon wooed by a former U.S. navy serviceman, Terry Klout (Matt Dillon), Bernadette and Frankie move to Texas with him. Immediately recognizing that it was a mistake to leave Dublin, Bernadette works to earn their passage home. As she walks the fine line between indepedence and insanity, Bernadette teaches Frankie about pain and strength.

All this is told in a series of flashbacks, as the adult Frank (Corban Walker) pursues the publication of his first book, an amalgam of his mother's biography, his autobiography and astronomy. As he pushes his way passed his old pain, he is reunited with an adult Emma (Rudi Davies), finally finding love and acceptance.

While frequently compared to *My Left Foot* (by the same producer, Noel Pearson), Frankie does not experience the same cruelty and abandonment as Christy Brown.

Blessed with a loving, if ultimately profoundly unhappy, mother, and the attentiveness and care of the two men in her life, Kelly and Klout, Frankie lives a life of starlight and music, books and baseball. Confronted by the occasional hatred or fear, Frankie's pain and alienation never reaches the same depth as Christy Brown's (though the horror of Brown's life may be an unfair yardstick by which to measure alienation). *Frankie Starlight* does, however, a solid job of furthering the genre of showing that everyone is more similar than they are different, and that love is available to all who will love. It does well as part of the slice-of-a-weird-(but, then again, normal-) life genre.

While Michael Wilmington admitted that the movie "does have virtues: tenderness, compassion, a sense of life's often irresolvable mysteries," he, as most other critics, concluded that it does not, somehow, reach us ("the sadness never pierces us; the joy doesn't exalt"). Kim Williamson agrees that "the material seems to want to tug deeper." These problems with the movie, however, do not detract from its charming and compassionate portrayal of strong individuals searching for love and respect.

CREDITS

Bernadette: Anne Parillaud
Terry Klout: Matt Dillion
Jack Kelly: Gabriel Byrne
Emma: Rudi Davis
Young Emma: Georgina Cates
Young Frank: Alan Pentony

Origin: USA
Released: 1995
Production: Noel Pearson; released by Fine Line Pictures
Direction: Michael Lindsay-Hogg
Screenplay: Chet Raymo and Ronan O'Lear; based on the novel *The Dork of Cork* by Chet Raymo
Cinematography: Paul Laufer
Editing: Ruth Foster
Production design: Frank Conway
Costume design: Joan Bergin
Music: Elmer Bernstein
MPAA rating: R
Running Time: 101 minutes

Frankie Starlight is, moreover, rewarded with superb performances by newcomers' Corban and Pentony. Demonstrating at once the astonishment and hurt, the tentativeness of love and the definitiveness of rejection, and the million unintentional slights of an uncaring world, Corban and Pentony also show the strength of the soul in Frankie. As adult Frank wrestles with the demons of his past, he is mesmerizing in is portrayal of an adult hurt by the adults around him but unwilling to blame them for their weakness.

Parillaud is wonderful as the resourceful—and psychic—Bernadette quietly protecting her son. Her joy and loss are conveyed with the same subtleness and certainty as in *Map of the Human Heart* (1993) and her energy is equal to that which she displayed in *La Femme Nikita* (1991). As she descends into despair and ultimately commits suicide, we almost understand, with Frankie, that this was not a selfish abandonment of her child, but the only way to relieve her pain.

Byrne and Dillon both deliver solid performances, but it is Emma— both young and adult (Georgina Cates and Rudi Davies)—that is breathtaking. Cates' portrayal of the horror of witnessing her father's adultery, and her gradual withdrawal from the family and descent into madness (dog lovers be forewarned—Frankie's puppy doesn't last long) is beautifully done and painful to watch. Davies, as adult Emma, shows Emma's wish— and fear—of reaching out to Frank. Adult Emma is shown as a gentle and timid soul, removed from a painful past, and determined not to hurt anyone anymore.

Frankie Starlight perhaps suffers by comparison to *My Left Foot*; the intensity of *My Left Foot* may make *Frankie Starlight* seem tepid by comparison. However, *Frankie Starlight* is a quiet, gentle movie, full of compassion and hope. It is beautiful, and, as the first line in the movie goes: "Let us begin with beauty."

—*Meghan Appel O'Meara*

REVIEWS

Boxoffice, November 1995, R-93.
Chicago Tribune. January 19, 1996.
Entertainment Weekly. December 8, 1995, p. 49.
Los Angeles Times. November 22, 1995, p. F18.
The New York Times. November 22, 1995, p. C18.

Free Willy II: The Adventure Home

"Smarter and more endearing than the original."—Caryn James, *The New York Times*

Box Office Gross: $30,077,111

Free Willy (1993) was a sleeper hit family film, silly at times but with a pleasing dollop of quirky charm. Unfortunately, hits spawn sequels, and so there is *Free Willy 2*, which flounders and flops like a fish out of water. It is pretentious, contrived and consistently weak.

Keiko, who single-handedly turned the image of killer whales from menaces to cuddly pals, is back to play Willy. Like Flipper, the hit TV dolphin of the 1960s, Willy is a kid magnet. On the animal cute meter, playful mammals that jump in the water and respond to human instructions rate high, and nothing works better on young crowds than water tricks.

Between his first screen spawning and this second coming, Willy attained instant star status, with his own TV cartoon spinoff. So it's enough for Willy to be his cute self again to assure box office bang with the pre-school and early-graders.

Sadly, the studios wanted more bite, so they've tried to expand into older age brackets. Something terrible has happened to Jason James Richter, who plays Willy's pal Jesse: puberty. So instead of a cute boy and his whale, we get a teenager with raging hormones and a girl to impress. Making this a sort of coming-of-age film is a calculated way to lure the teenage market, but it clashes badly.

Playing this sort of role, Richter is in way over his head. His attempts to be a wolfish young man seem forced, because the rest of the time he has to portray an impressionable boy.

So we don't lose the sub-teen boys, who would be turned off by too much mushy stuff, we get a new character, eight-year-old Elvis (Francis Capra). For the New Age crowd, we still have the all- knowing Native American, Randolph (M. Emmet Walsh), who is hooked into the spirit world and knows where to get herbal whale medicine. For environmentalists, there is an oil spill and evil corporate connivers to loathe. Yes, the film fancies itself a message movie, though all the messages are the most hackneyed imaginable.

This is a mighty awkward stew with ridiculous aspirations. The first hint of trouble comes during the opening credits when we learn the sequel has become "A Film by Dwight Little." Camera pans of the rugged Puget Sound setting promise a sweeping, meaningful commentary on nature and humans, which never materializes.

Woodenly, Little introduces all the characters from the first film and brings them back together with hugs all around. A cheerless start has Jesse learning the news that the mom who abandoned him is dead but has left him a step-brother. The addition of Elvis gives us two boys abandoned by their mother, which is two too many. That Willy has found his mother, sister and little brother only adds salt to the proverbial wounds.

Free Willy had a strange, off-putting psychological subtext about maternal abandonment; in the sequel it's even more pronounced and unpalatable. Why a boy searching for motherly love would find solace in a young male whale didn't make sense the first time around; it makes even less sense here.

Jesse's foster parents, who might be expected to fill in the gaps, are sincere and well-intentioned ciphers. As Anne, Jayne Atkinson is dull and unappealing. As substitute dad Glen, Michael Madsen reprises his loopy Elvis imitation, playing Glen as a slow, helpless dolt who looks and acts like he should own a '56 Chevy but is married to Annie, who looks and acts like she should be in a *Better Homes & Gardens* spread.

Little provides absolutely no plot tension during the first half of the film. We get Jesse showing off for Randolph's goddaughter Nadine (Mary Kate Schellhardt), and Elvis and Jesse getting on each other's nerves. A few rides on Willy for Jesse and Nadine are the only action in the pointless first half.

When a bad captain (you know he's evil because he's piloting a ship with a black hull) runs an oil tanker aground, everything is set up for the kids, led by Jesse, to be heroes again, with the spiritual assistance of Randolph, the only admirable adult.

The heroics are played and filmed like a sporting event. As Jesse keeps Willie happy in the water while a whale doctor gives a huge hypodermic injection to his oil-slicked sister, the rest of the cast stands and cheers on the docks.

The same thing happens whenever the whales twist and spout. Observers stand on shore and say things like "Oh, wow" and "cool." The whales are wonderful, of course, but it's like going to a ball game where the public address system orchestrates all the cheering. No seconds of frolicking whales footage passes without an "Oh, wow" reaction. If you care to count, I'd bet *Free Willy 2* has more utterances of "Oh, wow" and "cool" than any film since *Woodstock*, 1969.

The plot lurches along with disjointed sequences, awkward transitions and flagrant inconsistencies. The oil spill threatens to trap the whales in a cove, but at least three nights pass without anything happening. Elvis suddenly runs

CREDITS

Jessie: Jason James Richter
Glen Greenwood: Michael Madsen
Randolph Johnson: August Schellenberg
Anne Greenwood: Jayne Atkinson
John Milner: Jon Tenney
Kate Haley: Elizabeth Peña
Elvis: Francis Capra
Nadine: Mary Kate Schellhardt
Dwight Mercer: Mykelti Williamson
Wilcox: M. Emmet Walsh

Origin: USA
Released: 1995
Production: Jennie Lew Tugend and Lauren Shuler-Donner for a Shuler-Donner/Donner production in association with Le Studio Canal+, Regency Enterprises and Alcor Films; released by Warner Brothers
Direction: Dwight Little
Screenplay: Corey Blechman, Karen Janszen and John Mattson
Cinematography: Laszlo Kovacs
Editing: Robert Brown
Production design: Paul Sylbert
Art direction: Greg Bolton
Set decoration: Casey Hallenbeck
Costume design: Erica Philips
Special effects: Walt Conti, Michael McAlister and Jon Belyau
Sound: Robert Janiger
Casting: Judy Taylor and Lynda Gordon
Music: Basil Poledouris
Song: Michael Jackson, "Childhood (Theme for *Free Willy II*)"
MPAA rating: PG
Running Time: 98 minutes

away and a maudlin, inane Michael Jackson song jumps rudely into the film. Scenes are slapped together willy-nilly. All the themes, plot lines and styles go on and off like blinking Christmas lights.

Randolph is scripted with exacting political correctedness as a sage in tune with ancestral medicines and the spirit world and a computer-wise ship captain capable of picking out Willy's tone on Sonar. The reverential depiction is almost as insulting to real Native Americans as the old stereotypes. In an unintentionally hilarious sequence, Randolph and Jesse go into the woods to find sacred roots, pound them into a paste that looks like pesto, and slap it into a sick whale's mouth. Good medicine, perhaps, but exceedingly strained filmmaking.

Little has no flair for exploiting the obvious possibilities. He seems to think assembling the former cast and having them run through set pieces is enough to make this sequel a winner. A fairly effective, action-packed ending involving flaming water and daring rescues isn't enough to save the film. Even young audiences will find the action highly predictable.

The first film at least had the punch that came from the exhilaration of freeing a whale that had been turned into an amusement park attraction. *Free Willy 2* must invent circumstances that would once again make the whale an object of an entertainment predator. It's extremely forced.

Almost alone in giving life to his character is Capra as the boastful, fibbing Elvis, the vulnerable kid beneath the worldly, wise-guy, grown-up front. If there is, God forbid, a *Free Willy 3*, the scripters would do well to put Capra front and center and retire Richter to a mall where he can ogle babes to his heart's content.

Apart from the whales, there is no magic and no charm in *Free Willy 2*. Its only mark of distinction is that it ends with an 800 number in case you want to help save the whales. Save the whales, yes, but spare us the Willies.

—Michael Betzold

French Kiss

"a delightful cinematic bonbon...the stuff of classic moviemaking."—*The Hollywood Reporter*

"the perfect croissant: light, buttery and... sweet."—*People Magazine*

"Sweet, smart and sexy...if there is such a thing as chemistry, Kline and Ryan have it!"—Peter Travers, *Rolling Stone*

"Kevin Kline is hilarious and Meg Ryan is the most adorable comedienne in movies."—Jeffrey Lyons, *Sneak Previews*

Box Office Gross: $38,896,854

The degree to which one might enjoy the latest Meg Ryan romantic comedy, *French Kiss*, most likely will depend on how much one enjoys Meg Ryan. Depending on the level of tolerance one has for her patented mannerisms and wide-eyed expression, the perky actress will either beguile or irritate, particularly since she is on screen for the greater part of the film. Ryan is, if one is to believe the film's press kit promoting the film, "one of the most skilled and beloved practitioners of the fine art of romantic comedy." Following on the heels of *Sleepless in Seattle* (1993) and *When Harry Met Sally...* (1989), Ms. Ryan tries her luck one more time by not only starring in, but producing this Lawrence Kasdan directed/Adam Brooks scripted romp through scenic France.

Struggling hard to have the perfect life in Toronto, American ex-patriate, Kate (Meg Ryan), tries to overcome her fear of flying in order to accompany her Canadian doctor fiancee, Charlie (Timothy Hutton), to a medical conference in Paris. Kate is a big Francophobe anyway, so perhaps her motivation is a little thin. The French, she explains, "smoke and have a whole relationship with dairy products that I just don't understand." Despite her desire to see the Eiffel Tower and, more importantly, to be with Charlie in the City of Lights, Kate simply cannot get herself on that plane—that is until she receives a call from Charlie shattering her dreams. It seems Charlie has fallen in love with a French "Goddess" (Susan Anbeh) and intends to marry her.

This is Kevin Kline's 5th film for director Kasdan.

When Kate does finally strap herself into that airplane seat, her second worst nightmare comes true: not only must she fly, but she must do it seated next to her image of the quintessential French male, Luc (Kevin Kline), an unkempt, uninhibited jewel thief who wastes no time in sizing her up. "I know your type," he tells her, "you're afraid to live," egging her into an argument in a sweetly compassionate attempt to get her past the plane's take-off. When Kate confesses her plan to win back Charlie, Luc is appalled at her puritanical outlook. He snarls in disgust, "One love would be like eating in the same restaurant for the rest of your life." But after more than a few drinks, Luc begins to open up and shares the story of his first sexual encounter, with a prostitute. With just a hint of regret he explains that he could not kiss the woman because he did not have enough money. In a moment of foreshadowing, Kate sighs, "Of course...a kiss is where the romance is."

When the two finally land in France, Luc slips a stolen diamond necklace and a plant cutting into Kate's bag in order to get past customs. When he is separated from Kate and her bags are stolen, the two are inevitably linked together for an adventure that will take them through the lush vineyards of Provence to the beaches of Cannes. "I'll get him back," she cries after seeing Charlie with his new love, "I'm going to make him love me." Disgusted by her willingness to humiliate herself in front of Charlie, Luc goads Kate, "Goddess in a negligee next to Charlie, you on your knees begging...poor Charlie, tough decision." But Luc agrees to help Kate win back Charlie by schooling her in the ways of love. "I admire your persistence..." Luc tells her, "it's so American."

The filmmakers cleverly use the Eiffel Tower as a metaphor for Kate's inability to notice the joy and beauty surrounding her by having her on several occasions turn her head at just the precise moment to miss seeing the famous landmark. The story gets side-tracked by the writer's desire to make Luc a truly redeemable character, not at all a cad, but merely the wayward son of a wine grower from Provence and an all-around sensitive nineties kind of guy, resulting in a drag to the film's pacing and momentum. The ending, albeit extremely manipulative, helps to redeem this unfortunate turn of events by providing the woman with the opportunity to save the man for a change.

Romantic comedy is perhaps one of the trickiest of all film genres to execute, but that does not stop Hollywood filmmakers from trying, for when the elements click, it can spell box office gold. What makes romantic comedy so slippery is its very oxymoronic nature. Comedies tend to distance us from the main characters, while love stories need to draw us closer in order to hook us into caring that the couple ends up together. Comedy asks the viewer to laugh at the character's shortcomings, while love stories require that the viewer empathize with the plight of the characters. It requires a very deft hand at maintaining this push/pull—and unfortunately, neither Mr. Kasdan nor Ms. Ryan have the depth to fully succeed. This is not to say that *French Kiss* isn't entertaining. It has some very funny moments, it is beautifully photographed by Owen Roizman and offers a winning soundtrack that includes an amusing rendition of "La Mer" (made popular in the sixties by Bobby Darrin's english version "Beyond The Sea") sung in French by Kevin Kline. But one of the most serious problems with the film comes from a lack of sexual chemistry between the two leads. Kline and Ryan are fun to watch together —they are such opposites, not only physically, but in their acting styles—but there is not an inkling of sexual tension between them. This is an absolute necessity, particularly in order to overcome the predictability of the plotline, and for a story about two completely different people overcoming obstacle after obstacle to end up together, this proves to be the film's downfall.

"You are afraid of life, you are afraid of love, you are afraid of sex." "Do I look like the kind of person that doesn't like to have a good time?"—Luc and Kate from *French Kiss*

Kevin Kline has the most fun in his role as the roguish Luc, not pretending to be French, but rather just accepting that he is merely playing a French character. His accent is so curious, nearly as fake as Peter Seller's Inspector Clouseau in Blake Edwards' *The Pink Panther* (1964), that one expects to discover by film's end that Luc is not really a Frenchman at all, but is merely masquerading as French. Alas, that is not the case and so we are left to speculate that Mr. Kline was merely having fun amusing himself, and us, along the way, much in the same vein as his flamboyant Oscar-winning turn in *A Fish Called Wanda* (1988). The actor easily negotiates the change in Luc from obnoxious loner to lover. And when the long awaited moment comes when the couple finally kiss, the look of realization that passes over Luc's face is one of the film's highlights, thanks primarily to Kline's ability to convey the moment's importance.

Unfortunately, Meg Ryan does not fare as well in her role as the control freak Kate, venturing precariously close to Goldie Hawn territory with her foray into slapstick comedy as she does a pratfall into a dessert cart. The actress has difficulty imbuing her character with anything other than quirky mannerisms. She even resorts to a variation on her famous orgasm-in-a-deli scene from *When Harry Met Sally...* (1989); this time it is a case of lactose intolerance. There is nothing new in Ryan's performance. That does not mean there is nothing to like; it simply means we have seen it all before.

Lawrence Kasdan's direction is clean and relaxed for the most part, though he seems a bit too smitten with his leading lady. But then again, apparently so is most of America. *French Kiss* may not be the most memorable romantic comedy, but it offers a pleasant enough diversion for two hours. Critics were unimpressed, for the most part, by the film.

—Patricia Kowal

CREDITS

Kate: Meg Ryan
Luc: Kevin Kline
Charlie: Timothy Hutton
Jean-Paul: Jean Reno
Juliette: Susan Anbeh

Origin: USA
Released: 1995
Production: Tim Bevan, Eric Fellner, Meg Ryan and Kathryn F. Galan for A Working Title Production, in association with Prufrock Pictures; released by 20th Century Fox
Direction: Lawrence Kasdan
Screenplay: Adam Brooks
Cinematography: Owen Roizman
Editing: Joe Hutshing
Production design: Jon Hutman
Costume design: Joanna Johnston
US Casting: Jennifer Schull
Music: James Newton Howard
MPAA rating: PG-13
Running Time: 111 minutes

REVIEWS

Christian Science Monitor. LXXXVII, May 5, 1995, p. 13.
Entertainment Weekly. May 5, 1995, p. 46.
Los Angeles Times. CXIV, May 5, 1995, p. F1.
Macleans. May 15, 1995, CVIII, p. 73.
The New York Times. CXLIV, May 5, 1995, p. B11.
New York. May 15, 1995, XXVIII, p. 62.
The New Yorker. May 22, 1995, LXXI, p. 97.
The New Republic. May 22, 1995, CCXII, p. 28.
Time. May 22, 1995, CXLV, p. 79.
Rolling Stone. May 18, 1995, p. 96.
Variety. CCCLIX, May 1, 1995, p. 36.
The Village Voice. XL, May 16, 1995, p. 52.
The Wall Street Journal. May 11, 1995, p. A14.
The Washington Post. May 5, 1995, Weekend P.49.

Friday

"a lot can go down between thursday and saturday..."—Movie tagline

"*Friday* is a high energy comedy."—Caryn James, *The New York Times*

"This is one funky, raw, rambling jokefest!"—Susan Wloszczyna, *USA Today*

"*Friday* is incredibly funny."—Desson Howe, *The Washington Post*

Box Office Gross: $27,467,564

There have been an increasing number of powerful films dealing with the serious side of life in the "hood." They have examined the social problems of drugs, guns, unemployment, gangs and drive-by shootings. These issues warrant consideration and have serious dramatic value. But, as rapper/actor Ice Cube explained in USA *Today*, "All the movies coming out about where I live were all dark and hardcore. I was like, man, we had a lot of fun growing up in South Central L.A. I wanted to show that." Audiences were already familiar with his dramatic performances in John Singleton's *Boyz n the Hood* (1991) and *Higher Learning* (1995). Therefore, there was some genuine anticipation and interest when New Line Cinema's release of *Friday*, starring Ice Cube, opened in late April of 1995.

The film, which was co-written with Ice Cube's longtime partner D.J. Pooh, was directed by first timer Gary Gray, who directed videos for Ice Cube and fellow rap artists Queen Latifah and Cypress Hill. The action of this uninspired and witless comedy takes place on an ordinary Friday in the lives of Craig (Ice Cube) and his manic friend, Smoky (comedian Chris Tucker). It seems that Craig has lost his job and is instructed by his nagging father (John Witherspoon) to look for a new one. Dad counsels his son while sitting on a toilet, spraying room deodorizer in the air. Smoky, on the other hand, encourages Craig to simply hang out with him and smoke dope. This idea apparently appeals to Craig much more so than Dad's, and the two pals head for the front porch. They are surrounded by a menagerie of cartoonish characters, such as a buxom vamp who lives with a midget, a nasty sissy neighbor, a kleptomaniac crackhead, a braying jealous girlfriend, a cross-eyed bully and a drug dealer named Big Storm, adorned with a headful of light blue hair curlers. The thin plot line revolves around Smoky owing $200 to Big Storm. It seems Smoky (whose nickname seems relevant) smoked the dope he was supposed to sell. Most of the film deals with this dilemma, as the colorful neighbors parade past the porch.

Friday, which was targeted to young black audiences, was supposed to take a light-hearted look at "hanging out in the 'hood." It attempts to poke fun at drug abuse, violence against women, religion, constipation and unemployment. Unfortunately Ice Cube's "fun times" do not translate onto the screen in this amateurish excursion into bad taste. It assumes that mindless scripts and vulgar dialogue provide an amusing insight into real human beings. Granted, people can be crude at times, but humor does not spring from degradation, nor does social awareness grow from insult. *Friday*, unfortunately, insults and degrades without providing the smallest amount of originality or creativity. It relies on an over-abundance of stupid jokes, dumb sight gags, ceaseless obscenities and an inordinate fascination with bodily functions. The only enlivening aspect of this film is the soundtrack, featuring Dr. Dre and Cypress Hill among others. It's too bad that director Gray could not have brought the same street-smart energy and vitality of his music videos to this film. Instead it appears that he gave his actors full rein to over-indulge in exaggerated expressions, annoying line readings and over-used gimmicks.

In a recent *Playboy* interview, respected actor Samuel L. Jackson (who was nominated for an Oscar for his performance in last year's *Pulp Fiction*), when asked whether rappers should stick to their own turf, responded, "You can get people into the theater the first weekend because you have Ice Box, Ice Tray, and Ice Pick in your movie. But by the second week, word is going to be out that the movie ain't shit, and it'll be relegated to video. Acting deserves a lot more respect than it gets." And so do audiences!

—Rob Chicatelli

CREDITS

Craig: Ice Cube
Smoky: Chris Tucker
Debbie: Nia Long
Mr. Jones: John Witherspoon

Origin: USA
Released: 1995
Production: Pat Charbonnet and Ice Cube for Priority Films; released by New Line Cinema
Direction: F. Gary Gray
Screenplay: Ice Cube and DJ Pooh
Cinematography: Gerry Lively
Editing: John Carter
Production Design: Bruce Bellamy
Casting: Jaki Brown and Kimberly Hardin
Costume design: Shawn Barton
Music Supervisor: Frank Fitzpatrick
MPAA rating: R
Running Time: 89 minutes

From Dusk Till Dawn

Criminal Gecko brothers Seth and Richard (George Clooney and Quentin Tarantino) are on there way to the Mexican border, but with cops on their trail they take ex-preacher Jacob Fuller (Harvey Keitel) and his children hostage. The brothers and their captives seek temproary refuge at a mysterious bar that turns out to be a secret haven of vampires. The brothers and the Fuller family must fight an evil army of vampires if they want to stay alive.

CREDITS

Jacob Fuller: Harvey Keitel
Seth Gecko: George Clooney
Richard Gecko: Quentin Tarantino
Kate Fuller: Juliette Lewis
Border Guard/Chet Pussy/Carlos: Cheech Marin
Frost: Fred Williamson
Santanico Pandemonium: Salma Hayek

Origin: USA
Released: 1995
Production: Gianni Nunnari and Meir Teper for A Band Apart and Los Hooligans production; released by Dimension Films
Direction: Robert Rodriguez
Screenplay: Quentin Tarantino
Cinematography: Guillermo Navarro
Editing: Robert Rodriguez
Production design: Cecilia Montiel
Art direction: Mayne Schuyler Berke
Set design: Colin de Rouin
Set decoration: Felipe Fernandez del Paso
Costume design: Graciela Mazon
Sound: Mark Ulano
Visual effects supervision: Daniel A. Fort and Diana Dru Botsford
Music: Graeme Revell
MPAA rating: R
Running Time: 107 minutes

Funny Bones

A struggling comic looks in the dressing room mirror. It's his big night in Vegas, first time as headliner. "I'm gonna die," he wails. And then he walks out on stage and does just that.

Peter Chelsom's *Funny Bones* sticks a needle into the gut and pulls out plenty of fear and loathing. To Chelsom, life might be an extended comedy routine: you rehearse, you perform and then you die. His movie is a slapstick meditation on the horrors of mortality. It's also one breathtaking carnival ride.

"Offbeat" is too ordinary a word to describe Chelsom's dazzling mixture of silliness, tragedy, mystery, and mayhem. Fellini's absurdist excursions seem tame in comparison with *Funny Bones*. This is filmmaking at its most adventurous.

Tommy Fawkes (Oliver Platt) tells his gag writer before his make-or-break Vegas opening: "I'm going to take it to the edge and do pirouettes." That's exactly what Chelsom does. As in any comedy routine, there are jokes that fall flat and things that don't make sense. But Chelsom has far more hits than misses in this excursion into the darker and weirder side of comedy.

As in his 1993 film *Hear My Song*, Chelsom explores the world of show business on both sides of the Atlantic. Tommy Fawkes is the hapless son of comedy legend George Fawkes (Jerry Lewis). George is everything Tommy wants to be: smooth, funny, famous, and most of all, at ease with himself.

After bombing in Las Vegas, Tommy flees to England, returning to Blackpool where he lived the first six years of his life. Blackpool is a resort town with a rich but fading show-biz tradition, and Tommy embarks on a search for an act that can make him laugh. He auditions an endless parade of hilariously bad comic acts, including a man who sings with a condom over his head and another who tap-dances with his feet in biscuit tins.

Blackpool's tourist industry is in trouble because a dead man's foot has washed ashore and a lunatic is threatening to jump from the town tower. Jack Parker (Lee Evans) is the jumper. He is mixed up with smugglers who are trying to get a complete set of strange eggs that contain some sort of life-extending powder. They are working in the service of the mysterious Dolly Hopkins (Oliver Reed).

Jack is exactly what Tommy has been looking for: a physical, rubber-faced comic with a fresh act and tremendous talent. After Jack is lured down from the tower, he befuddles a psychiatrist in one of the funniest psychological tests ever filmed: "Have you lived here all your life?" asks the shrink. "Not yet," deadpans Jack. Jack's father and uncle are a venerable comedy duo, now out of work, who live in a crazy shack under a roller-coaster. The Parkers make ends meet by working at the local carnival.

The only voice of sanity is Jack's mother Katie (Leslie Caron). She objects when Tommy tries to buy the rights to the Parkers' act. Eventually she confirms Tommy's childhood memories of a deeper connection between her family and his.

Tommy approaches comedy as a commercial enterprise. Tommy's desperate attempts to hire people to make him as funny as his father fail because Tommy lacks "funny bones." Jack's brutal education in comedy has created a maniac. So it is left to Jack, in his own crazy way, to teach Tommy that plumbing the depths of mortality is the only way to conquer the stage fright.

In larger terms, Chelsom has fashioned a relentlessly entertaining lesson about the importance of coming to grips with one's demons and heritage. It's a sort of shock therapy, and not for the faint-hearted. Unfortunately, Chelsom undermines his effectiveness by getting too serious and even maudlin at times in the last half of the film. There are also sizeable holes in the plot and characters. Hopkins, the villain who is trying to get the mysterious powder, is completely unexplained, and so is the powder.

Nevertheless, Chelsom and his cohorts manage to make this film work. In firm command of the material, Chelsom builds his story from a brilliant and prolonged opening sequence through a dizzying ending. The frantic tone helps audiences get through the rough spots and keeps the tragic material from becoming too somber.

"I never saw anything funny that wasn't terrible," one of the Parker brothers observes toward the film's end. Tragic, brutal stuff is what really gets audiences laughing, Chelsom tells us. But he does it in such a bizarre and fascinating way that we appreciate the lesson.

The look of the characters and the two settings emphasize the divide between comedy as an American institution—where everyone has the glad-handing glitz and schmoozing phoniness of a Las Vegas club—and the raw roots of British vaudeville and carnival routines. The Parkers and their ilk have funny faces and rubbery bodies; they are wan and pale and close to death; their humor is, like much circus fare, tinged with ghoulishness and violence. The Fawkes and their entourage are tanned, slick, sophisticated.

The Blackpool of the film is a run-down carnival of a town, complete with sleazy sideshows and underground clubs where remarkable talents emerge. Vegas is pat and fat. One of the sub-texts of *Funny Bones* is how upper class Americans have stolen their entertainment from the European working classes and then wrung the soul out of it.

The ensemble cast is loaded with remarkable performances. Lewis is wonderful as the aging smooth talker who has obliterated his humble origins and lost track of his comic soul. George Fawkes could have been a villain except that Lewis insists on portraying him as a human being who made the sort of moral compromises most people do. Platt, as his son, has that square face and jaded expression prototypical of the modern American comic and deftly displays Tommy's anguish and fears. Caron is warm, dignified and beautiful in a soulful portrayal of a show- biz mother with a heart.

As the Parker Brothers, veteran British comics George Carl and Freddie Davies combine the deadpanned expressions of the Marx Brothers with the antic moves of a vaudeville team. They perfectly embody the comic sub-culture—springing from circuses, carnivals and vaudeville—that spawned George Fawkes.

As Jack, British cabaret wunderkind Lee Evans steals the show. His face is enormously pliable and expressive, and he is always on the edge of insanity. It is Evans' amazing performance more than anything else that drives home

CREDITS

Tommy Fawkes: Oliver Platt
George Fawkes: Jerry Lewis
Thomas Parker: George Carl
Katie: Leslie Caron
Bruno Parker: Freddie Davies
Jack Parker: Lee Evans
Dolly Hopkins: Oliver Reed
Laura Fawkes: Ruta Lee

Origin: USA
Released: 1995
Production: Simon Fields and Peter Chelsom for Hollywood Pictures Company; released by Buena Vista Pictures Distributions, Inc.
Direction: Peter Chelsom
Screenplay: Peter Chelsom and Peter Flannery
Cinematography: Eduardo Serra
Editing: Martin Walsh
Production design: Caroline Hanania
Art direction: Andrew Munro
Casting: Janey Fothergill, Maggie Lunn, Mary Gail Artz and Barbara Cohen
Sound: Peter Lindsay
Costume Design: Lindy Hemming
Music: John Altman
MPAA rating: R
Running Time: 118 minutes

Chelsom's point that effective comedy involves terrifying risk-taking and dangerous pirouettes on the edge of sanity. Jack's act cannot be bought and sold, cannot be copied, because it is the authentic expression of a tortured soul. You can't fake being on the edge.

Funny Bones is deadly stuff. You won't die laughing, but you might get close to the edge and pirouette.

—*Michael Betzold*

REVIEWS

Entertainment Weekly. March 3, 1995, p. 45.
The New York Times. March 24, 1995, p. B1.
Newsweek. April 17, 1995, p. 66.
People Weekly. April 3, 1995, p. 17.
Rolling Stone. April 20, 1995, p. 86.
Variety. January 30, 1995, p. 48.

Georgia

"Marvelous! Mare Winningham gives a stunning performance!"—Michael Wilmington, *Chicago Tribune*

"A nearly perfect movie!"—Ken Tucker, *Entertainment Weekly*

"Different from anything else you'll see this year: fearless, and ambitious."—Thelma Adams, *New York Post*

"Jennifer Jason Leigh stunningly gives a piece of her heart to the main role. ...Directed with intuitive brilliance by Ulu Grosbard."—Janet Maslin, *The New York Times*

"...Barbara Turner's keenly perceptive screenplay refuses to nudge characters into the usual cliched corners."—Peter Travers, *Rolling Stone*

Georgia is one of those films that should be called "outstanding," but is best described as "very good." Fine performances, particularly by Jennifer Jason Leigh and Mare Winningham as dysfunctional sisters, sensitive direction by Ulu Grosbard, and realistic production values certainly make this a film worth seeing. But ultimately, Barbara Turner's script does not deliver on its early promise, and somehow all the fine elements seem underused. In retrospect, it is a film that is best described as having a showy central performance by Jennifer Jason Leigh, a sensitive supporting performance by Winningham, and a disappointing climax. Of course, disappointment is a central theme of the film, and perhaps screenwriter/co-producer Barbara Turner, director Ulu Grosbard, and co-producer/star Leigh are so adept at portraying disappointment that the audience merely walks out of the theater feeling that way.

Both Mare Willingham and Jennifer Jason Leigh do their own singing in the movie. Screenwriter Barbara Turner is Leigh's mother.

Georgia is the story of Georgia (Winningham) and Sadie (Leigh) Flood, two sisters from Seattle, both of whom are singers. But there is a disparity: Georgia has talent and a great deal of success; Sadie's lack of success is only surpassed by her astounding lack of talent. Where Georgia is graceful and unassuming, Sadie is loud and narcissistic. Georgia has a glorious home life straight out of a magazine; Sadie goes from one squalid flophouse to another, constantly drunk or high. And where Georgia has a seemingly perfect husband, Jake (Ted Levine), Sadie has taken up with a series of losers.

As the film opens, Sadie is returning to Seattle after a presumably wasteful period in San Francisco. She meets Axel (Max Perlich), a twenty-four-year-old grocery delivery boy who idolizes her. Axel doesn't drink or smoke, is extremely polite ("I don't like to disturb...it's not my nature"), and worships Sadie. The bulk of the film revolves around Sadie's attempts to break into the music scene in Seattle ("Things are gonna break for me; there isn't a doubt in my mind") and her relationship with Georgia. All of Sadie's actions are affected by her heavy drug use and drinking, and eventually Sadie's self-destructive nature causes virtually everyone around her to run away or shut her out.

Though Sadie marries Axel and her behavior eventually drives him away, the focus of this film is on her feelings about Georgia. It becomes clear that Sadie's entire life has been aimed at proving herself to Georgia—and in spite of Georgia. Sadie retains an outwardly optimistic stance, always saying that life is "great," and that Georgia is "the one person I will miss when I leave this earth," but the strain of their relationship is palpable.

Screenwriter Turner has chosen to hang the story on Sadie's aimlessness and addiction. Sometimes there seems to be a point to the action; other times, it seems as if plot points are haphazardly thrown in. Turner has written a character-driven vehicle, supported by a character who is mercurial and dysfunctional. The film's meandering quality seems appropriate, given that it follows Sadie's unstable life. But it is precisely their ability to capture Sadie's waywardness that ultimately undermines their film. Sometimes the action seems to be directed toward a climax (such as a sequence involving Sadie's drug rehabilitation): It seems for a moment that Sadie's short period of clarity will allow her to have a meaningful confrontation with Georgia about the effects of their relationship on their lives. But just at that point in the film, Georgia seems to clam up, telling Sadie she is fed up with her. The film concludes without showing how they ended up being so different, where Sadie's life took such a disastrous turn, and how Georgia ended up being so apparently perfect.

It is certainly not essential to show every motivation and "back story" for each character. But since this film aims to be a story about the sibling relationship—its opening credits show Sadie and Georgia as young children, happily performing together for family—it would be reasonable for the audience to expect more information about their past relationship. A little more information might have fueled a richer conflict for the film's climax, and might have provided a stronger sense of an arc to the story.

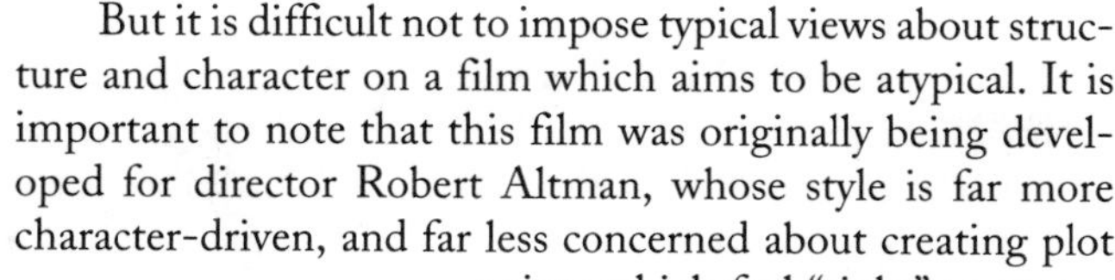

"How did it feel to be able to pull me out?" "It felt like a thousand pounds of dead weight, Sadie."—Georgia and Sadie from *Georgia*

But it is difficult not to impose typical views about structure and character on a film which aims to be atypical. It is important to note that this film was originally being developed for director Robert Altman, whose style is far more character-driven, and far less concerned about creating plot points which feel "right" to an audience used to having a conflict happen approximately 20 minutes after the film begins and a climax 20 minutes before it ends.

Director Grosbard is adept at driving character-driven vehicles, and does a fine job here. If the final conflict seems to fall flat, it is ameliorated by Grosbard's simplicity and eloquence with his camera. Some critics complained that Grosbard allowed Leigh to sing too many songs in this film. But Grosbard wants to portray both Sadie's lack of talent and her utter inability to know when to quit. A scene in which she embarrasses herself and Georgia by staying onstage too long is excellent. Not only is Leigh terrific at showing Sadie's lack of talent, but Grosbard's camera slowly closes in on Sadie, capturing every moment of her endless, shallow song. The fact that she goes on as long as she does is actually a rather bold move on Grosbard's part: Sadie is awful, and after this scene, her narcissism and absolute lack of ability are certain.

With *Georgia*, actress Jennifer Jason Leigh has dug far into her soul to find a character full of raw desperation and intensity. Like her performances in *Last Exit to Brooklyn* (1989) and *Mrs. Parker and the Vicious Circle* (1994), Leigh plays a self-destructive character with astonishing commitment and depth. She wears jewelry all over her body and has spider web tattoos on her hands. Leigh has chosen to virtually cover her character's eyes with slabs of mascara and eyeliner, to the point that she looks like a raccoon. Leigh manages to make Sadie look a little like a prostitute, a lot like a rock-star wanna-be, and a lot more like a little girl playing dress up. Her understanding of Sadie's lack of control overflows from everywhere—from clothes to sex to drugs to singing, Leigh's Sadie doesn't know when to quit. The

CREDITS

Sadie: Jennifer Jason Leigh
Georgia: Mare Winningham
Jake: Ted Levine
Axel: Max Perlich
Bobby: John Doe

Origin: USA and France
Released: 1995
Production: Ulu Grosbard, Barbara Turner and Jennifer Jason Leigh for a Ciby 200 production; released by Miramax
Direction: Ulu Grosbard
Screenplay: Barbara Turner
Cinematography: Jan Kiesser
Editing: Elizabeth Kling
Production design: Lester Cohen
Costume design: Carol Oditz
Sound: Mark Weingarten
Assistant direction: Craig Huston
Casting: Renee Rouselot
Music: Steven Soles
MPAA rating: R
Running Time: 117 minutes

AWARDS AND NOMINATIONS

Independent Spirit Awards 1996: Best Supporting Actress (Winningham)
Nominations: Best Director (Grosbard), Best Actress (Leigh), Best Supporting Actor (Perlich)
Montreal Film Festival Awards 1995: Best Film, Best Actress (Leigh)
New York Film Critics Awards 1995: Best Actress (Leigh)
Academy Awards Nominations 1995: Best Supporting Actress (Winningham)
Screen Actors Guild Awards Nominations 1995: Best Supporting Actress (Winningham)

aforementioned scene where she sings too long is brilliant: with her raspy voice, and her over-commitment to emotion, Sadie thinks she is Janis Joplin. This performance has deservedly won acclaim for Leigh, whose extraordinary attention to detail might seem like overkill to some but seems like genius to others. Either way, Leigh's performance is fascinating.

Mare Winningham finds one of her best roles as the perfect Georgia. A singer/composer in her own right, Winningham provides the perfect balance to Sadie's overly dramatic persona. (She also provides one of the film's best songs, called "If I Wanted.") Cooking in her perfect kitchen with her perfect family, Winningham's Georgia is unnervingly "together," but hints at something going on beneath the surface. Winningham knows when to show bits of what lies underneath: a scene in which she loses her cool while driving a drunk Sadie home is excellent. Other scenes bring further suspicions: she practically cringes when having to take the stage with Sadie at a benefit, but still maintains her stoic reserve; she tells Sadie one day that "you were the one with the ambition; I never gave a damn" with an almost patronizing tone that suggests that the statement is not as casual as it sounds. Unfortunately, Winningham is hamstrung by the script. As mentioned before, just at the moment when the two sisters could have a truly cathartic experience, Turner and Grosbard have Georgia sputter some brief emotional dialogue and leave it at that. "Sadie's pain has to be fed; and we're all here, ready to serve," says Georgia. Winningham is excellent in the scene, but by this point it seems redundant. The actress and the audience deserve more.

In the end, it is Sadie's pain that gets served in this film. And the problem is that audiences want to see more than a portrait of pain. The problem may be that mainstream audiences expect either a resolution or a return to the status quo. In *Georgia*, it is hard to discern whether there is resolution: if so, the film might be making a statement about how the only way to overcome disappointment is to confront it, admit defeat, and start over. It is just as hard to tell if Sadie and Georgia will return to the status quo: if so, then at least the film would be making a comment on the difficulty of overcoming one's inner demons. Sometimes, as in life, films do not need to resolve their problems. But a film which only "feeds Sadie's pain" will ultimately be only about "Sadie's pain," and it may not reach past the screen to live in the memory of its audience.

—*Kirby Tepper*

Get Shorty

"Attitude plays a part."—Movie tagline

"One of the best movies of the year and by far the most entertaining."—Peter Travers, *Rolling Stone*

"Two hours of hilarious, beautifully acted screen time."—*Time Magazine*

Box Office Gross: $68,645,723

With *Get Shorty*, the latest adaptation of an Elmore "Dutch" Leonard novel, John Travolta continues to resusitate his once-floundering film career with a winning performance as a shylock with Hollywood stars in his eyes. Filled with tough guy badinage and a smartly complex plot, *Get Shorty* is an amusing, yet superficial film about the superficiality of Hollywood. While Angelenos, particularly those in the film industry will undoubtedly be quick to identify the prototypes for each of Leonard's characters, it is questionable as to whether audiences outside of Los Angeles will find the scenario quite as amusing. It is Travolta, along with witty dialogue, most of which screenwriter Scott Frank reproduced directly from Leonard, that lifts this film above average.

Chili Palmer (John Travolta) is a loan shark, or as he prefers, a shylock, who reluctantly agrees to go to Las Vegas in order to track down a man who faked his own death in order to escape his debts. The trouble is, the dry cleaner (David Paymer) is stupid, spending far too much of the $300,000 he scammed from the insurance company and the trail leads straight to Los Angeles. As a favor to the casino owner who gives him the tip, Chili agrees to collect on a debt owed by schlock filmmaker, Harry Zimm (Gene Hackman), whose cinematic masterpieces include such classics as "Grotesque" and several "Slime Creatures," all starring Harry's latest romantic interest, scream queen actress Karen Flores (Rene Russo). As one of the characters tells Harry, "I've seen better film on teeth."

It does not take the charismatic Chili long to size up this new game and when he breaks into Karen's house to put the squeeze on Harry, he seizes the opportunity, in true Hollywood form, to pitch his idea for a movie. The story piques Harry's interest, but Karen is savvy enough to understand the subtext of the moment: this is not fiction, it is real-life, which is why Chili has no ending for his movie.

He has to wait to play out the drama with the dry cleaner and the mob, but in the meantime, Chili moves into producing with all the ease of a major Hollywood player. When Chili is asked who he thinks he is, the answer is simple: "I'm the one telling you how it is."

Underneath that tough guy exterior, Chili is a man unimpressed by others, as well as by himself. When a mob associate questions Chili's lack of experience, he replies, "I don't think the producer has to know much." One of the film's most compelling moments comes unexpectedly in a scene where Chili sits in a darkened theatre watching Orson Welles' *Touch of Evil* (1958), quoting dialogue. When the lights come up, Chili reaches out to touch a stranger on the shoulder. "Wow, huh?" he asks in a near desperate attempt to share the experience.

> Travolta turned down the role of Chili Palmer twice, before Quentin Tarantino called him and convinced him to do it.

No stranger to the perils of Hollywood, Leonard himself suffered numerous failed attempts by other filmmakers at adapting his work to the screen. For nearly three decades, Hollywood has been romancing the crime novelist, but to no avail. Director John Frankenheimer tried his hand with *52 Pick Up* (1986)—the same novel had been the source of *The Ambassador* (1984) with Robert Mitchum and Rock Hudson in his final theatrical fim. Then came *The Big Bounce* (1969) with Ryan O'Neal, *Mr. Majestyk* (1974) with Charles Bronson as a watermelon farmer—which curiously was scripted by Leonard himself—and *Stick* (1985) with Burt Reynolds as both director and star. Perhaps all Hollywood really needed when it came to Elmore Leonard was...Hollywood.

Get Shorty is a good film that could have been an even better film with a different director. While there is no denying that Barry Sonnenfeld is talented, both as the director of *The Addams Family* (1991) and *Addams Family Values* (1993) and as a cinematographer, most notably on Danny DeVito's *Throw Momma from the Train* (1987) and the Coen Brothers' *Raising Arizona* (1987), his broad comedic style, a kind of visual slapstick, is ill-suited to the dark and verbally menacing style of writer Elmore Leonard. Sonnenfeld lingers far too long at the end of scenes and over-all the pacing is sluggish, throwing the timing into a tailspin and undercutting the element of danger, particularly with regards to the character of Chili Palmer. One cannot help but wonder what *Get Shorty* would have been like under the strong arm of director Danny DeVito, whose odd point of view on life and his favored cockeyed camera angles that were used so effectively in both *Throw Momma from the Train* (1987) and the less successful *The War of the Roses* (1989) might have given this film the bite that it is missing.

It is a pleasure to see John Tavolta having such fun onscreen. While he has lost some of that sweet cockiness that marked his earlier work in *Saturday Night Fever* (1977), he still retains the swagger in his walk, perhaps more confident, more secure in his personal power. Travolta, after a long string of disappointing films, resurrected his career with the role of the heroin-shooting hitman in Quentin Tarantino's smash hit, *Pulp Fiction* (1994). According to Travolta, it was his friend Tarantino, the epitome of Mondo Hollywood, who convinced him to finally take the role of Chili Palmer after the actor had twice turned it down.

Fortunately, the talented cast helps to elevate *Get Shorty* to a higher plane than it probably deserves to be. The always engaging Gene Hackman gives a dead-on interpreta-

CREDITS

Chili Palmer: John Travolta
Harry Zimm: Gene Hackman
Karen Flores: Rene Russo
Martin Weir: Danny DeVito
Ray "Bones" Barboni: Dennis Farina
Bo Catlett: Delroy Lindo
Bear: James Gandolfini

Origin: USA
Released: 1995
Production: Danny DeVito, Michael Shamberg and Stacey Sher for a Jersey Films production, released by MGM/UA
Direction: Barry Sonnenfeld
Screenplay: Scott Frank; based on the novel *Get Shorty* by Elmore Leonard
Cinematography: Don Peterman
Editing: Jim Miller
Production design: Peter Larkin
Art direction: Steve Arnold
Costume design: Betsy Helmann
Sound: Jeff Wesler, Don Coufal and Gary Holland
Casting: David Rubin and Debra Zane
Music: John Lurie
MPAA rating: R
Running Time: 105 minutes

AWARDS AND NOMINATIONS

Golden Globe Awards 1996: Best Actor-Musical/Comedy (Travolta)
Nominations: Best Film-Musical/Comedy, Best Screenplay (Frank)
Screen Actors Guild Awards Nominations 1995: Best Cast
Writers Guild Awards Nominations 1995: Best Adapted Screenplay (Frank)

tion of a slimy film producer hoping to crack the Big Time, while Rene Russo brings a sexy cynicism to the role of "Scream Queen" Karen Flores. The perfectly cast Danny DeVito as the egomaniacal Shorty of the film's title provides the proper counterbalance between his untraditional looks and his leading man ego and self-confidence. The role reportedly was first offered to actor Dustin Hoffman who, like Martin Weir, backed out of the project at the last minute. Interestingly, DeVito, whose company Jersey Films produced the film, initially envisioned himself in the role of Chili Palmer. Both Dennis Farina, who gives an amusing turn as the Mafioso boss prone to temper tantrums and Delroy Lindo as the drug dealer who also longs to produce, provide the perfect counterpoint to Chili's cool, low-key approach to a life of crime. While Chili can emasculate with one stare, one "Look at me," both Barboni and Bo demand respect but walk away with none. The curious thing about the characters in *Get Shorty* is how one-dimensional they all are. It is simplistic to dismiss this serious shortcoming as representing Leonard's point since all of the characters, including the petty criminals and their families, equally lack complexity and development. If this is Leonard's view of people in general, why should the audience be the least interested in what happens to these characters?

"Rough business, this movie business. I may have to go back to loan sharking just to take a rest."—Chili Palmer from *Get Shorty*

There is something a bit tiring about films that focus on the art and business of making movies. Robert Altman's *The Player* (1992), which showed us how the film industry gets away with murder, literally and figuratively, was a far more scathing indictment of power and greed in Hollywood than this latest offering. While *Get Shorty* is amusing in its allusion that a life of crime and one of film are more like flip sides to the same coin, it never seems to go far enough.

Dubbed snidely by some critics as "Tarantino lite," *Get Shorty* resembles a shark without teeth, circling its prey, but not possessing the strength to inflict any lasting damage. Reviews for the film were consistently favorable and compared to many of the other films released at the time, *Get Shorty* provides amusing entertainment without requiring any deep analysis.

—Patricia Kowal

REVIEWS

Christian Science Monitor. LXXXVII, October 27, 1995, p. 12.
Entertainment Weekly. October 27, 1995, p. 64.
Los Angeles Magazine. XL, November 1995, p. 152.
Los Angeles Times. October 20, 1995, p. F1.
Macleans. CVIII, October 23, 1995, p. 68.
Newsweek. CXXVI, October 23, 1995, p. 75.
New York Magazine. XXVIII, October 23, 1995, p. 54.
The New Yorker. LXXI, Octber 23, 1995, p. 96.
The New York Times. October 20, 1995, CXLV, p. B1.
Rolling Stone. November 2, 1995, p. 73.
Variety. October 9, 1995, CCCLX, p. 61.
The Village Voice. October 24, 1995, XL, p. 71.
The Wall Street Journal. October 20, 1995, p. A12.

The Girl with the Hungry Eyes

Talking dogs, talking horses, talking ghosts, talking babies, talking Leprechauns, talking willow trees—they've all tested film audiences' credulity at various times. But the enigmatic *The Girl with the Hungry Eyes* must be the first film to feature a talking building in a prominent role. The effect is as uninspiring as the concept.

The oddest of vampire movies, *The Girl with the Hungry Eyes* stars The Tides, a dilapidated South Beach, Miami, hotel, fighting to save itself from condemnation. Its instrument is the undead former fashion model Louise (Christina Fulton), who committed suicide in the 1930s after learning her husband was cheating on her. Louise was the hotel's co-owner, and her mission is to find the key to a bank deposit box wherein the building's deed is kept.

This much is clear only if you can decipher more than half the garbled words that the hotel speaks to Louise after she is let down off her hanging rope in the film's opening sequences. Understanding the hotel's messages is a difficult task, since the voiceovers are spoken in what sounds like a computer-synthesized growl. Imagine a hoarse Vincent Price played at the wrong speed. And The Tides' barking, husky commands are ludicrously stilted: "Love is our only enemy," it tells its vamping alter ego.

What's not clear is who or what is controlling Louise, whether she's become half-building during her sixty years of death, or exactly why finding the deed will save the building or Louise. The concept is so ridiculous it hardly matters. And it gets worse. Somehow the key has fallen into the hands of Carlos (Isaac Turner), a budding fashion photographer, and Louise, against the hotel's thunderous advise, is smitten and reluctant to bite Carlos' neck even to save her own.

Carlos owes money to a group of thugs, and Louise, who walks unbidden off the street into his apartment, is his ticket to fame and fortune. But she demands he hide her identity from his boss Bud (Bret Carr), a licentious powerbroker who is foaming at the mouth to meet the mystery babe.

How this all plays out is fairly predictable and inconsequential. Suffice it to say that *The Girl with the Hungry Eyes* adds precious few new insights or twists into the vampire story, apart from a sort of subversive feminist slant to the script by Jon Jacobs, based on a short story by Fritz Leiber. Seducing a few bad men, Louise throws back at them their worst secrets, recounting their role in long-forgotten rapes, just before she bites into their necks. "I'm gonna take some weight off your shoulders," she growls to one victim before twisting his head. Apparently this is her way of raping them. And posing for Carlos also apparently lets Louise get a one-up on the men who have betrayed and tormented her through at least a couple of lives.

Yet she tells Carlos, "I want to be the perfect object." She seems more like a caricature of a sex object. With a powder-white face and ridiculously swollen red lips, heavy eye makeup and stringy blond hair hanging in her face, Fulton's vampiress goes beyond sultry and trashy into just plain funny. Fulton plays the part ferociously and with no trace of subtlety; she's singularly unappealing, which might be director Jacobs' purpose. It's hard to say.

It also could be that Louise's willingness to engage in raw, bloody sex and to pose bare-breasted for Carlos' fashion shoots are attempts to add prurient interest and perhaps some excitement to a turgid film. *The Girl with the Hungry Eyes* might have been entertaining if played as camp, which is apparently how the story was meant, but Jacobs does everything darkly and deadly seriously. There are no light touches and no needed humor to break out of the low-budget, faux-artsy mood.

The affection between Carlos and Louise, an element that is crucial to developing any interest in the film, is inexplicable. Louise simply appears in his apartment and starts reading Byron; she's a poetic bloodsucker, it seems. Turner

CREDITS

Louise: Christina Fulton
Carlos: Isaac Turner
Johnny: Leon Herbert
Bud: Bret Carr
Mandy: Susan Rhodes
Zippo: Leroy Jones

Origin: USA
Released: 1995
Production: Michael Kastenbaum and Seth Kastenbaum for Kastenbaum Films/Smoking Gun; released by Merton Shapiro and Cassian Elwes
Direction: Jon Jacobs
Screenplay: Jon Jacobs; based on the short story by Fritz Leiber
Cinematography: Gary Tieche
Editing: Jason Rosenfeld
Production design: Clare Brown
Art direction: Tony Parras
Casting: Jeffrey Passero
Makeup: Susan Dextersound and George Lockwood
Costume design: Evelina Diaz
Music: Paul Inder, Oscar O'Lochlainn
MPAA rating: no listing
Running Time: 100 minutes

brings a vacant, clueless expression to his role as Carlos, but to be fair to the actor, there's nothing much with which to work. The minor characters are even more heavyhanded, especially Carr as the drooling Bud and Leon Herbert as the hood Johnny.

The script is unrelentingly stupid. When Louise gets sexy with a potential victim, the hotel lights start flickering on; when she bites a neck, the voltage soars. But making blood and electricity analogous isn't a recipe for excitement.

At times, it appears as if Jacobs is going for B-movie cult-film appeal, but those attempts are weighted down by the film taking itself so seriously. If this is a spoof, there should have been more spoofing. But *The Girl with the Hungry Eyes* can't be taken seriously either. As feminist revenge motif, it's exceedingly dim-witted. As a message film about the power of love to transcend death, it's incredibly ill-formed. What it lacks most is suspense or thrills, indispensable staples of the genre.

The fangs behind the fashion model are supposed to represent a turning of the tables of sexual dynamics, but *The Girl with the Hungry Eyes* is dragged down by its own heavy-handed symbolism. Louise is menacing, but not seductive enough to ensnare audiences. Watching her makes one want to laugh out loud, which is hardly the response Jacobs is aiming for.

—Michael Betzold

The Glass Shield

"A no-holds-barred thriller!"—Jeanne Wolf, *Jeanne Wolf's Hollywood*

"Riveting, volatile and engaging! Ice Cube gives a powerful performance!"—Dwight Brown, *Upscale Magazine*

Box Office Gross: $3,313,633

Charles Burnett remains one of America's least-seen great filmmakers. The recipient of a MacArthur Fellowship "genius" award in 1988, as well as Guggenheim and Ford Foundation grants, the African-American, Los Angeles-based writer-director has made only four feature films since his completion of UCLA's graduate film program in 1973. Of these four, only two have been commercially released. In 1990, the Library of Congress awarded Burnett's first unreleased film, *Killer of Sheep* (produced 1973, first seen 1977), a place on its National Film Registry of American cinematic treasures to be preserved, but *Killer of Sheep* is rarely screened and remains unavailable on video. *To Sleep with Anger* (1991), Burnett's rich, folkloric tale of a Los Angeles family haunted by a mysterious, visiting relative from the South, played by Danny Glover, received critical acclaim, but performed poorly at the box office. Even when re-released and marketed specifically to black middle-class and art-house filmgoers, *To Sleep with Anger* failed to find an audience.

Burnett's *The Glass Shield* unfortunately seems destined, if not for the total oblivion of *Killer of Sheep*, then for the obscurity of *To Sleep with Anger*. Funded by CIBA 2000, the French consortium that now funds David Lynch's films, and released by Miramax, *The Glass Shield* disappeared from theaters within three weeks of its release, having grossed just under three million dollars. Yet *The Glass Shield* is among the handful of classic American films of the last decade, at once a taut tale of the downfall of a truly tragic protagonist and a sprawling, relentless study of power, corruption, and institutional racism and sexism in the United States. Thematically and stylistically, *The Glass Shield* most resembles Sidney Lumet's *Prince of the City* (1981), in which the protagonist was also a flawed cop unable to escape from the muck of big-city corruption. But *The Glass Shield* also addresses a theme that *Prince of the City* could not: the central question of race in American society. *The Glass Shield* portrays contemporary American institutions as historical battlegrounds, in which the remaining bastions of white, male power like police and sheriff's departments are circling the wagons. Given *The Glass Shield*'s relatively small budget, Burnett's ability to make a film of such depth and breadth is extraordinary.

Based loosely on a true story and on a screenplay by Ned Walsh entitled *One of Us*, *The Glass Shield* traces the moral education of J.J. Johnson (Michael Boatman), the first black deputy at a substation of the Los Angeles County Sheriff's Department. J.J.'s discovery of corruption, negligence, even murder within the department leads to the unfolding of a massive scandal, but his story is neither a revenge fantasy nor an uplifting tale of moral rectitude in the face of evil. Instead, Burnett focuses on J.J.'s wrenching transformation from idealistic rookie to fully conscious moral adult: from the first shot of the film, Burnett systematically undermines J.J.'s naive belief in the American

Dream, and shows how only when one truly sees his environment, in all its injustice and complexity, can one understand oneself. J.J.'s coming of age in that environment is one of the most emotionally brutal in American cinema—a remarkable achievement in a film which virtually eschews images of physical violence and the utterance of racial slurs.

Burnett begins the film with J.J.'s comic-book reveries of becoming a black superhero. Wounded in the course of saving a girl from drug-dealing thugs, J.J.'s cartoon self is lauded by his fellow deputies. "You proved yourself," the dialogue bubbles say. "Your badge is made of gold." J.J. believes that he is "about to make history," as someone says to him at his graduation from the sheriff's academy, but *The Glass Shield* is about how the history of black-white relations in America clashes head-on with J.J.'s comic-book visions of the American Dream.

From his first days on the job, J.J.'s fellow deputies treat him as an outsider, and subject him, along with a fellow Jewish, female rookie, Fields (Lori Petty), to humiliating oversight and reprimands. In one scene, J.J. stops an attractive black woman for speeding and lets her go with a warning. His motive for doing so is sexual attraction rather than racial preference, but his partner makes a point of chasing the woman down and telling J.J. to remember that "you're not a brother, you're one of us. You learn how to surf, okay?" Back at the station, J.J.'s commanding officer, Massey (Richard Anderson) pointedly rides him for misspelling "Sepulveda," a Westside street, on an arrest report.

Yet J.J. himself is no prize, no superhero either. He's careless, self-serving, and sexist—and this is what makes *The Glass Shield* a great film. It is J.J.'s absurdly romantic conception of himself, in a world rotten with corruption, including his own, that leads to his tragic fall. J.J. truly believes that a sheriff's badge automatically confers moral supremacy on its wearer, and that the shield makes him part of an elite corps that can do no wrong. Accordingly, J.J. goes along to get along, justifying to himself the corruption and mutual back-scratching he sees in the department because it is all in the name of a higher good. Most naively, J.J. considers himself a part of the white male power structure. Although the white deputies clearly treat him with disrespect, he joins in their sexist mistreatment of Fields because he really believes himself an insider, one of them. Fields eventually becomes J.J.'s only ally as he uncovers the scandal in the department, but for the first half of the film, J.J.'s hubris prevents him from seeing that they are in fact in the same boat. J.J. treats his girlfriend with similar condescension — as a would-be superhero of the streets, he refuses to be tied down to the mundane details of a relationship. Without knowing it, he is isolating himself from people who care, even as the colleagues whom he feels understand him are ostracizing him.

The film's turning point comes when J.J. makes a fatal moral mistake: he lies on the stand about the details of the arrest of a young black man, Teddy Woods (Ice Cube), charged with a murder he clearly did not commit. In fact, deputies in J.J.'s station are framing Teddy as part of a payback scheme in an elaborate cover-up of other corruption. But J.J. is oblivious to the cover-up, and happily shaves the truth in his testimony. Again, *The Glass Shield* refuses simplistic storytelling: Teddy is just as clearly guilty as he is innocent, and J.J. justifies his lying as putting away "lowlife scum." As J.J. realizes what he has done, the repercussions from this moral lapse force him to re-examine everything he holds dear: his commitment to public service; his desire for upward mobility; his cavalier treatment of his girlfriend; and, most of all, his idealistic conception of himself within the American system. The corruption J.J. discovers is like a cancer (an analogy Burnett makes in the film), and J.J. painfully learns not only the impossibility of rooting it out in one fell swoop, but the peril to one's own conscience of ignoring it. Even more painfully, J.J. must face his own role in the nastiness. The shield has failed him.

The film barrels along with subplots involving lawyers, ministers, insurance agents, city councilmen, child molesters —the whole array of big city life, but Burnett never loses sight that each step of the plot alters J.J.'s conception of the world, and of himself. The number of American films that have a truly tragic protagonist, in the Greek and Shakespearean sense, is miniscule; *Citizen Kane* (1941) is one, and *The Glass Shield* is another. That *The Glass Shield* refuses to romanticize its flawed protagonist, whose hubris as much as the system brings him down, makes *The Glass Shield* that rarest of great American films—one with a truly tragic cen-

CREDITS

J.J. Johnson: Michael Boatman
Deborah Fields: Lori Petty
Teddy Woods: Ice Cube
Massey: Richard Anderson
Luckett: Bernie Casey
Baker: Michael Ironside
Mr. Greenwall: Elliott Gould

Origin: USA
Released: 1995
Production: Thomas Byrnes and Carolyn Schroeder; released by Miramax
Direction: Charles Burnett
Screenplay: Charles Burnett; based in part on the screenplay *One of Us* by Ned Walsh
Cinematography: Elliot Davis
Editing: Curtiss Clayton
Production design: Penny Barrett
Music: Stephen James Taylor
MPAA rating: R
Running Time: 109 minutes

tral character. But if Burnett refuses to make J.J. a conventional hero, he also declines to judge him. J.J. must see the world as it is before he can see who he really is, and while Burnett spares him nothing, he never condescends to branding him a traitor. J.J. is, in Burnett's world, a man caught between American history and the naive hopes with which his generation grew up. Burnett tells J.J.'s story methodically, almost quietly; the violence he shows is moral and emotional, never merely to satisfy an audience.

Burnett's final scene is shocking. His visual concept for the film until then has been deceptively simple: at the beginning of the film, during J.J.'s first days on the force, Burnett shoots Los Angeles as it is rarely seen in films, in completely naturalistic light. It may be flat, dry, and boring, but J.J. is in harmony with it. As J.J.'s role in the corruption haunts his conscience, and as he begins to see himself as outside the power structure yet also part of its evilness, Burnett's lighting turns more garish, menacing, and isolating, so that at the film's end, when J.J. smashes his car window and threatens his girlfriend in broad, natural daylight, he is totally alienated from himself and from the sunny Los Angeles he thought he knew. The final scene, like everything in the movie, is completely unexpected yet completely right: his girlfriend doesn't leave him, but gives him the brutal truth. "Look," she says, "I'm not going to say you were right just because I love you. I can see through that badge. It doesn't hide the evilness." "I thought I did the right thing," says J.J., falling into his girlfriend's arms, and his understanding that he did not is his first step toward becoming an adult. (Burnett re-shot this scene for American distribution. In the original version, screened at Cannes, J.J. begins sobbing uncontrollably.) The scene also neatly explains the meaning of "the glass shield": not only has the badge not protected him or hidden his flaws, but it has also isolated him from the rest of the world. J.J. has entered the world of cops which no one on the outside can understand, yet he is a pariah among his colleagues. It is a shatteringly lonely conclusion, but not one without hope. J.J. has been educated, painfully, but not destroyed.

The Glass Shield, in spite of its small budget, is one of the most ambitious American films in recent memory, in no small part because it is in the rarely used tragic form. Burnett has had the courage to tell what he sees as the unvarnished truth about this moment in American history and in black-white relations, and it is indeed bad news: a racist, sexist power structure is not only firmly entrenched in 1995 in parts of the United States, but is also winning, with soldiers like J.J. Johnson as its casualties. It may be that Burnett's refusal to romanticize his flawed central character, to indulge in black revenge fantasies, or to find simple solutions to the race problem in America makes him a filmmaker-without-portfolio in the United States. As a study of power, corruption, and isolation, his tightly told, brilliantly written film ranks with Kubrick's *Paths of Glory* (1957) and *The Godfather* (1972). In spite of its failure at the box office, *The Glass Shield* is an American classic, a true film maudit, and a masterwork of the highest order.

Paul Mittelbach

REVIEWS

The Nation. CCLXI, July 10, 1995, p.68.
The New York Times. June 2, 1995, p.B3(N).
The New York Times. June 25, 1995, p.H25(N).
The New Yorker. LXXI, June 12, 1995, p.109.
Variety. CCCLV, May 30, 1994, p.44.

Gold Diggers: The Secret of Bear Mountain

"Some friendships are worth a fortune."—Movie tagline

Gold Diggers: The Secret of Bear Mountain is one of those rare youth-oriented films that does not portray teenage girls as boycrazy, sullen, or psychotic. Indeed, by endowing its adolescent heroines with spunk, bravery, and brains, *Gold Diggers* treads into normally male-dominated territory: the adventure story. For risk-taking alone, the film gains its merit.

Thirteen-year-old Beth Easton (Christina Ricci) moves with her widowed mother Kate (Polly Draper) from Los Angeles to sleepy Wheaton, Washington. As she reluctantly settles into small town life, bored Beth has a few chance meetings with tough, troubled tomboy Jody Salerno (Anna Chlumsky). Jody lives with her alcoholic mother Lynette (Diana Scarwid) and Lynette's boyfriend Ray (David Keith), and has a reputation as a liar and a thief. Despite Jody's alleged faults and her general unpleasantness, Beth is intrigued by Jody; she's without question the most interesting person Beth's met since leaving Los Angeles, and, after discovering a common affinity for Winnie the Pooh, the two girls become quick if unlikely pals.

CREDITS

Beth Easton: Christina Ricci
Jody Salerno: Anna Chlumsky
Kate Easton: Polly Draper
Sheriff Matt Hollinger: Brian Kerwin
Lynette Salerno: Diana Scarwid
Ray Karnisak: David Keith
Molly Morgan: Amy Kirk
Mystery Woman: Betty Phillips
Everett Graham: Jay Brazeau

Origin: USA
Released: 1995
Production: Martin Bregman, Rolf Deyhle, Michael S. Bregman
Direction: Kevin James Dobson
Screenplay: Barry Glasser
Cinematography: Ross Berryman
Editing: Stephen W. Butler
Production design: Michael Bolton
Art direction: Eric A. Fraser
Set decoration: Elizabeth Wilcox
Costume design: Mary McLeod
Sound: Ralph Parker
Music: Joel McNeely
MPAA rating: PG
Running Time: 94 minutes

Christina Ricci and Anna Chlumsky follow the trail of a legendary treasure in *Gold Diggers*. © 1995 Universal City Studios, Inc. Courtesy of MCA Publishing Rights, a Division of MCA Inc. All rights reserved.

The girls spend their days exploring the woods, getting to know each other, and swapping family stories. Jody tells Beth the story of Molly Morgan, a young Scottish woman who at the turn of the century escaped from prison in her own country, stowed away to America, and, disguised as a man, mined for gold in the Pacific Northwest until she was left for dead in a mine collapse. According to local legend, Molly indeed escaped death and remains with her treasure inside Bear Mountain, and Jody invites Beth on her quest to find Molly's gold. Beth reluctantly agrees to help, and the pair cruise down the river on Jody's makeshift boat to Bear Mountain, where the reflection of the noon sun marks the alleged spot of Molly's gold. The girls explore the caves inside the mountain, where Jody has set up a primitive "condo", as she calls it. After Beth discovers a bruise on Jody's back, Jody reveals to Beth that the night before she accidentally killed Ray when he came after her in a drunken rage, and that she plans to hide out in the mountain, just like Molly. When Beth slips on some rocks and nearly drowns, however, Jody leaves her hideout and runs several miles through the woods to the highway for help, and Beth is rescued and taken to a hospital. Both girls are surprised when Ray shows up at the hospital to take Jody home—he's alive after all. Beth tries to warn Kate and Matt (Kerwin), the local sheriff, that Jody is in danger with Ray, but they dismiss her concerns.

After the accident, Kate tells Beth she thinks Jody is a bad influence and refuses to let the girls see each other; Beth adamantly defends her friend, but obeys to her mother's rule. Two weeks pass before Kate agrees to let Beth visit Jody. When they get to Jody's home, however, they find the place ransacked and Lynette slumped on the floor; Ray and Jody are nowhere to be found. Beth is certain that Ray has kidnaped Jody to Bear Mountain so she can show him where the gold is hidden, and she convinces Matt to look for them their. A hunt for Jody and Ray ensues inside the mountain, with Beth leading the way. Beth finds Jody, who managed to escape from a drunken Ray, but he finds the girls again and chases them. An old woman mysteriously appears and whacks Ray in the head with a shovel, then seemingly vanishes; Jody is convinced it was Molly who saved her. Later that summer, after Ray has been jailed and Lynette has recovered, an anonymous benefactor presents each girl a sack of gold; perhaps the girls finally have Molly's fortune after all.

Gold Diggers gets points for good intentions, but its noble themes—friendship, trust, loyalty, and bravery—are less than subtle and are mucked by flat performances and a surprisingly somber plot. Chlumsky and Ricci, lauded for their charming, natural performances as little girls (Ricci in *Mermaids* [1990], Chlumsky in *My Girl* [1991]), seem bored and stilted. The relationship of Beth and Jody is never quite plausible, making their intense and oft-repeated pledges of trust and friendship seem trite. The adult roles are thankless as well; as usual in youth-oriented films, the grown-ups are either dense or evil. And by saddling its young heroines with some heavy problems (alcoholic parents, domestic abuse) that neatly disappear at the end, the film looses much of its charm; unlike the complex issues that drove Huck Finn's river adventure, for example, this story is not strong enough to sustain the weight. A good idea gone unfortunately awry, *Gold Diggers* is ultimately bland and contrived, and save a few fun moments, fails to establish itself as more than a novelty.

—Terri Schell

Goldeneye

"*Goldeneye* is the best Bond film ever!"—Ron Brewington, *American Urban Radio Network*

"A celebration of the art of action filmmaking."—James Verniere, *The Boston Herald*

"On a scale of one to four, *Goldeneye* gets seven stars!"—Bonnie Churchill, *National News Syndicate*

Box Office Gross: $92,436,092

Everything about *Goldeneye*, the seventeenth installment in the James Bond franchise that began with *Dr. No* in 1962, reeks of Political Correctness. M, head of MI6, is now a woman (played by the formidable Dame Judi Dench), who quickly informs Bond that she views him as a "sexist, misogynist dinosaur" and threatens to dismantle the entire branch of Her Majesty's Secret Service. The Bad Bond Girl smokes the oh-so-Nineties de rigueur cigar and drives "like a man," while even the ever-hopeful Ms. Moneypenny (Samantha Bond) threatens James with sexual harassment. But in the end, it is all merely window-dressing, a desperate attempt to bring 007 into the Nineties. Despite all its attempts to follow the tried-and-true formula of previous Bond adventures, there is something missing from the film: a sense of danger, a really nefarious villain and yes, even a compelling soundtrack. *Goldeneye,* which takes its title not from an Ian Fleming book, but rather his Jamaican beachhouse, is very much "Bond Lite" and to quote the tongue-in-cheek headline from Richard Schickel's review in Time Magazine, this Bond is very much "shaky, not stirring."

When Timothy Dalton abdicated the 007 throne after legal problems for MGM/UA caused a six year hiatus in filming the next installment and his contract expired, the producers mounted a bogus publicity campaign as they searched for the new James Bond. Mel Gibson and Liam Neeson were both mentioned, as well as the foppish Hugh Grant; but few doubted that it would be Pierce Brosnan who would be chosen. After all, the actor has admitted to feeling a deep connection to the character. His now deceased wife, actress Cassandra Harris had appeared in *For Your Eyes Only* (1991) and Brosnan had been offered the role eight years earlier, but was forced to turn it down when NBC refused to release the actor from his contract on television's *Remington Steele*. Brosnan was finally granted his license to kill, accepting the part reportedly at a mere $1.2 million, compared to the reported $15 million offered to Gibson.

Brosnan, the fifth actor to portray Agent 007, with his suave good looks and self-confident swagger, looks more like he stepped straight out of the pages of GQ rather than the Cold War. Brosnan's build is so slight, his acting style rather "lightweight" and while practiced at the art of wry line delivery, the actor seems too coiffed, too prissy and well, too darn pretty to be a world-weary secret agent. Unlike his predecessor Timothy Dalton, Brosnan lacks that danger element, that hint that there is very little different about this man than the hundreds he has killed, except perhaps for some remaining morality, or merely a sheer blind duty to his Queen and country. Brosnan's photogenic good looks are intensified by the actor's tendency to pose in scenes, whipping around so the camera is sure to capture his best side. (He's ready for his close-up, Mr. Broccoli.)

The 750-foot bungee jump (performed by stuntman Wayne Michaels) that starts off the action was shot at the Contra Dam near Lugano, Switzerland.

The prologue is set in the old Soviet Union where Bond and Agent 006, Alec Trevelyan (Sean Bean) penetrate a chemical weapons facility. The mission goes awry, 006 is killed and Bond escapes, filled with remorse over the death of his friend. Nine years later, Bond encounters the ferocious Russian operative, Xenia Onatopp (Dutch beauty Famke Janssen in a laughable portrayal that inadvertantly makes a joke of female empowerment), a cold-blooded killer who derives sexual pleasure from killing men with her vise-like thighs. (Remember Thumper and Bambi in Sean Connery's *Diamonds Are Forever*, 1971?) Working not for the old foes *Spectre* or *Smersh*, but rather a Post-Communist mafia crime syndicate bent on world domination, Onatopp and General Ouromov (R.W. Fassbinder regular Gottfried John) steal a Stealth helicopter, wipe out the entire staff of a Space Weapons Control station while activating the nefarious plan to cripple the world economy by neutralizing computer networks with an electromagnetic pulse from a satellite system known as "Goldeneye". (Look to Connery's *Thunderball*, 1965, for inspiration here.) Unbeknownst to the villains, only one person survives, the fetching computer programmer Natalya Simonva (Izabella Scorupco). Later Natalya will discover that her co-worker, computer nerd Boris Grishenko (a particularly hammy Alan Cummings), also escaped the blast and is actually an accomplice to Onatopp and Ouromov.

Tracking Onatopp to St. Petersburg, Bond discovers that Trevelyan is still alive and he is the mastermind behind the plot. Among the ruins of an old Soviet industrial junkyard littered with statues of old Communist leaders, Trevelyan shares his ludicrous backstory that supposedly explains his current actions. (A Bond villain with motivation—what next, therapy for Bond? Whatever happened to good old pathos?) From Monte Carlo to St. Petersburg to Puerto Rico, the film has the look of a travelogue. Most curious, and symptomatic of the film's pacing problems, Bond, supposedly in a rush to save the world from ruin, still has the time to linger on the beach with Natalya before finally going off to Cuba to do battle with Trevelyan at his island hideaway beneath the sea. (Not to be confused with the volcano in Connery's *You Only Live Twice*, 1967.)

CREDITS

James Bond: Pierce Brosnan
Alec Trevelyan: Sean Bean
Natalya Simonova: Izabella Scorupco
Xenia Onatopp: Famke Janssen
Jack Wade: Joe Don Baker
M: Dame Judi Dench
Boris Grishenko: Alan Cumming
Q: Desmond Llewelyn
Moneypenny: Samantha Bond

Origin: USA
Released: 1995
Production: Michael G. Wilson and Barbara Broccoli; released by MGM/United Artists
Direction: Martin Campbell
Screenplay: Bruce Fierstein and Jeffrey Caine; story by Michael France; based on characters created by Ian Fleming
Cinematography: Phil Meheux
Editing: Terry Rawlings
Production design: Peter Lamont
Art direction: Andrew Ackland-Snow, Charles Les and Katherin Brunner
Set decoration: Michael Ford
Costume design: Lindy Hemming
Special effects: Chris Corbould
Stunt coordination: Simon Crane
Casting: Debbine McWilliams
Music: Eric Serra
MPAA rating: PG-13
Running Time: 130 minutes

AWARDS AND NOMINATIONS

Blockbuster Entertainment Awards Nominations
1996: Action Actor-Theatrical (Brosnan)

Most of the principals on *Goldeneye* are new to the series—with the exception of Desmond Llewelyn as the cranky gadgetmeister, Q. This is the first script that was not penned by American screenwriter Richard Maibaum, who died sometime after *License To Kill* (1989). Written instead by newcomers Jeffrey Caine and Bruce Feirstein and based on a story by *Cliffhanger's* (1993) Michael France, the script delivers lines that are seldom witty or wry and the story never fully jells. At two hours and ten minutes, *Goldeneye* goes on far too long with more than one false ending and is never able to outdo the pre-credit teaser that contains a spectacular 750-foot bungee jump by stuntman Wayne Michaels over the side of a dam. Unfortunately, even the opening is undone by a ridiculous stunt in which Bond, or in this case a reasonable facsimile stuntman, falls through the air in an attempt to board a pilotless airplane. Even this stunt is nothing new, a variation using a falling automobile having appeared in the Charlie Sheen-Nastassja Kinski skydiving action film, *Terminal Velocity* (1994).

"I think you're a sexist, misogynist, dinosaur..."—M from *Goldeneye*

Sean Connery reportedly suggested Quentin Tarantino for the directing job, but the producers instead chose New Zealander Martin Campbell, perhaps best known for his episodes of television's *Homocide*, as well as the Ray Liotta sci-fi prison film, *No Escape* (1994). Campbell relies primarily on keeping the car chases and explosions coming at a feverish pace, but fails to build the tension; as a result, the ending is fairly anti-climactic. To the film's credit, *Goldeneye* is perhaps the most beautifully photographed of all Bond films. One of the film's weakest elements, sadly, is the score by Luc Besson favorite, Eric Serra, best known for *La Femme Nikta* (1990) and *The Professional* (1995). Longtime composer John Barry apparently refused to score this latest Bond after having read an early draft of the screenplay. In one of the cruelest moves, Serra denies viewers the comfort and pleasure of hearing that famous Bond theme. As for the credit sequence, Daniel Kleinman creates a pretentious music video that employs the same basic silhouetted-women approach favoured by the late Maurice Binder, yet injects its own brand of Freudian imagery as guns appear and disappear from the mouths of women as they destroy Communist iconography.

Goldeneye is not an unwatchable film nor is Pierce Brosnan an unlikable James Bond. Both have sparks of excitement, but sadly, neither ever catches fire. Perhaps there was too big of a burden of expectation and anticipation after six years of screen absence, but it remains a disappointment when a non-007 adventure such as *True Lies* (1994) feels more like a Bond film than a true Bond film. Perhaps M was right, Bond is a dinosaur whose time has come and gone. Or it would be best, as Anthony Lane of *The New Yorker* suggests, to return Bond to the 1950's and his real home in the Cold War.

While critics for the most part were split in their opinions of *Goldeneye*, the film redeemed itself at the box office, making it the highest grossing film of the franchise, bringing in more than both *The Living Daylights* (1987) and *License To Kill* combined.

—Patricia Kowal

REVIEWS

Entertainment Weekly. November 24, 1995, p. 76.
Los Angeles Times. November 17, 1995, p. F1.
The New Yorker. LXXI, November 27, 1995, p. 105.
The New York Times. November 17, 1995, p. B3.
Time. November 27, 1995, p.92.
Variety. November 20-26, 1995, p. 47.
Village Voice. November 28, 1995, XL, p. 64.
The Wall St. Journal. November 17, 1995, p. A12.
The Washington Post. November 17, 1995, p. F1.

A Goofy Movie

"*A Goofy Movie* is bright and big-hearted. It's more quality goods from Disney, and a real comeback for one of Hollywood's true pen-and-ink superstars."—Hal Hinson, *The Washington Post*

Box Office Gross: $35,348,597

A *Goofy Movie* crept into theaters this spring without fanfare, obscured by the vast media attention surrounding the 1995 release of *Pocahontas.* While it is not as grand nor as opulent as recent Disney releases such as *Beauty and the Beast* (1991), *Aladdin* (1992), or *The Lion King* (1994), it deserves the same attention and praise as any of the Disney fables of recent years. *The Goofy Movie* is simply terrific entertainment—and not just for children, though children are its target audience.

This is the first "starring" role for Goofy in the six decades since the character's inception. It tells the story of Goofy's (Bill Farmer) relationship with son, Max (Jason Marsden). Max, trying to shed the goofy image of his family, is a typical teenager whose obsessions include a rock band named Powerline and a girl named Roxanne (Kellie Martin). When he tries to impress Roxanne by impersonating the lead singer of Powerline at a school assembly, he winds up in the principal's office for his behavior. Father Goofy is warned by the principal (Wallace Shawn, in a witty vocal performance), that his son caused the "student body to go into a riotous frenzy" and is on his way to a life of crime. So Goofy decides to "bond" with Max, insisting they take a trip together to Lake Destiny for some fishing and father-son bonding. Max tells Roxanne that he is going to Los Angeles to perform with Powerline, setting in motion a whole series of misadventures which ultimately lead to a better relationship between father and son.

Along the way, they encounter BigFoot, white-water rapids, monster truck rallies, jet skiing, and a variety of hilarious characters. Their adventures, while very funny, are just dangerous enough to make the father-son bonding appear real. For instance, when their car, decimated from a series of accidents, ends up floating down the rapids and headed toward a waterfall, Max is forced to use a fishing pole the way Goofy taught him in order to save his Dad—and the suspense is real.

From the first moments, where bright fields of gold yield to a blue sky, production values are spectacular. Animated in France by an international team (a departure for a Disney film), the typical Disney standards are upheld and even exceeded. From Max's pyrotechnic performance at the school assembly, where he swings from a rope and then dances onstage in silhouette, to the hilarious parody of a recreation vehicle complete with bowling alley, spa, billiard tables, and wide-screen TV, the animators have let their imaginations run wild.

The film's creators even allowed themselves to spoof Disneyland: Goofy drags Max to a dilapidated amusement park called "Possum Park," where they watch threadbare fake possums performing songs in an on-target parody of Disneyland's "Country Bear Jamboree" called "Possum Posse Jamboree." Then, the head Possum, Lester (voice of the late, great Pat Buttrum) insists they buy Possum hats. Max, finally sick of the whole thing, hauls off and hits Lester, saying "beat it, doofus."

CREDITS

Goofy: Bill Farmer
Max: Jason Marsden
Pete: Jim Cummings
Roxanne: Kellie Martin
PJ: Rob Paulsen
Principal Mazur: Wallace Shawn
Stacey: Jenna Von Oy
Bigfoot: Frank Welker
Lester: Kevin Lima
Waitress: Florence Stanley
Miss Maples: Jo Anne Worley
Photo Studio Girl: Brittany Alyse Smith
Lester's Grinning Girl: Robyn Richards
Lisa: Julie Brown
Tourist Kid: Klee Bragger
Chad: Joey Lawrence
Possum Park Emcee: Pat Buttrum
Mickey Mouse: Wayne Allwine
Security Guard: Herschel Sparber

Origin: USA
Released: 1995
Production: Dan Rounds for Walt Disney Pictures; released by Buena Vista Pictures Distribution
Direction: Kevin Lima
Screenplay: Jymn Magon, Chris Matheson, and Brian Pimental
Editing: Gregory Perler
Art direction: Wendell Luebbe
Music: Carter Burwell
MPAA rating: G
Running Time: 78 minutes

The dialogue is crisp and witty and the vocal performances, while truly silly at times (Bill Farmer's singing as Goofy is...well...goofy), are a perfect Disney blend between fantasy and reality. Goofy and Max share an intimate moment toward the end when Max simply says that "I've got my own life, now, Dad," and Goofy replies "I know...I just wanted to be a part of it."

But the tenderness never appears heavy-handed, nor does the message of father and son tolerance ever appear preachy. The tenderness is well-tempered by amusing sequences led by director Kevin Lima, who keeps the pace moving at all times in classic Disney tradition. It appears basic to Disney films that all action is punctuated and exaggerated. For example, when Max is startled by Roxanne, he knocks over her books, setting in motion a shock wave of consequences, punctuated by funny sounds and noises.

The first full-length animated feature for the character of Goofy, who began appearing in Disney shorts in the early '30s.

This constant activity occurs in the "staging" of the six delightful songs as well. Particularly funny is the song "Open Road," by Tom Snow and Jack Feldman, in which Goofy and Max sing about their upcoming vacation, accompanied by an abundance of funny characters who are also driving the highway. The characters include a group of singing nuns, a grandma who burns up the road, a guy in a coffin, several people singing from planes overhead, and others. By the end of the song, they are all joyously singing, balancing each other on top of their vehicles, and happily riding along.

Audiences cannot help but be caught up in the infectious charm of this wonderful film. The fact that it is not a fairy tale shouldn't detract audiences from savoring this film just as much as any other Disney musical.

—*Kirby Tepper*

Gordy

"Capital G-rated Gem! The "G" stands for good clean fun!"—*Chicago Daily Herald*

"Kids will squeal over *Gordy!*"—Roger Ebert, *Chicago Sun Times*

"Piglet Gordy warms its way into hearts!"—*Los Angeles Times*

"*Gordy* is the *Forrest Gump* of the barnyard set!"—*The Seattle Herald*

Box Office Gross: $3,992,809

Twenty-five pigs spent a lot of energy playing Gordy, the adorable pig whose name provides the title of this film. Directed by Mark Lewis, *Gordy* is a kind of Saturday matinee movie whose family values politicians might extol. But not even a politician could say that he or she thinks this well-intentioned film is anything but an awkwardly made children's story. It has questionable appeal even for the most undiscerning of children, much less their parents.

Gordy tells the tale of Gordy the pig, whose family is taken away to the slaughterhouse when the farm they live on goes bankrupt. Gordy seems to have missed the truck on which they are taken, and, in a tearful goodbye to his father (a large brown hog), he promises to help save his mother and siblings. His journey north (to find the whereabouts of his family) lead him to be taken in first by pleasant country singer Jinny Sue (Kristy Young) and her father (Doug Stone), and

CREDITS

Luke MacAllister: Doug Stone
Hanky Royce: Michael Roescher
Gilbert Sipes: James Donadio
Jessica Royce: Deborah Hobart

Origin: USA
Released: 1995
Production: Sybil Robson for Robson Entertainment; released by Miramax
Direction: Mark Lewis
Screenplay: Leslie Stevens
Cinematography: Richard Michalak
Editing: Lindsey Frazer
Production design: Philip Messina
Costumes: Barcie Waite
Casting: Shari Rhodes
Music: Tom Bahler
MPAA rating: G
Running Time: 90 minutes

then by young Hanky Royce (Michael Roescher). Jinny Sue gives Gordy to Hanky when Gordy saves his life. These children, because they are "pure in heart" are able to talk with and understand Gordy. It turns out that Hanky is the heir to a multi-million-dollar industrial conglomerate, and when his grandfather dies, Hanky becomes chairman of the board. Meanwhile, the nefarious Gilbert Sipes (James Donadio) and Hanky's bubble-headed mom (Deborah Hobart) wring their hands (and chew the scenery) over Gordy's rise to fame as the "hero pig." Gordy's extraordinary fame allows him to find his way back to save his family just in the nick of time, and everyone lives happily ever after.

Gordy features popular country music star, Doug Stone, in his acting debut, as well as appearances by many of country's biggest talents, including Roy Clark, Moe Brandy, Mickey Gilley, Jim Stafford, Box Car Willie, Cristy Lane, and Buck Trent.

The temptation with this film is to make fun of it. After all, it is not often that a film starring a pig makes it to wide commercial release. The last time was *A Private Function* (1985) starring Maggie Smith. Pigs have not been renowned for their acting ability, with the possible exception of Arnold the Pig from the 1960's television series *Green Acres.* And interestingly enough, the man who played Arnold's owner (Eb) on *Green Acres* is in *Gordy* as well (Tom Lester). Coincidence? You be the judge.

In any case, *Gordy* is probably as dreadfully dull for adults as it is fun for only the youngest of children. Its appeal might have been wider were it not for the rudimentary acting ability of virtually all of its actors, especially young Michael Roescher in the pivotal role of Hanky, and Michael Donadio as the villainous Gilbert Sipes. Donadio's constant arched eyebrows and overacting are not campy enough to make him a fun villain. Deborah Hobart struggles in a difficult role in which she is supposed to be a loving mom (and potential love interest for Doug Stone) and accomplice to the bad guy Gilbert. She is rather funny in a sequence where she loses a modeling job to Gordy, but the lack of clarity of her character combined with her unrefined acting technique do not help her to shine in this film.

Virtually all of the acting is very simple and declamatory. It would be difficult for any of the actors to overcome such dialogue as "Hanky keeps asking for the pig" and "ceremonies to honor the pig are planned for this afternoon," or "why doesn't this company make natural foods; they're better for people's health, and are full of natural vitamins." Unpretentious Doug Stone as the country-singing father of Jinny Sue fares the best of all the actors. Stone's simplicity and naturalism are a welcome relief from the stiff overacting of the other characters. He gets a chance to shine in a brief singing sequence, showing off his musical ability to great advantage and raising the level of the film's quality for a brief time.

Given that the film seems targeted for young children, there are a couple of areas which seem to be out of place. First, the "Stock Fattening Yards" scenes, with their ominous music, shadowy cinematography, and images of sharp knives and motorized sausage grinders might be too intense for young children. Additionally, the corporate-intrigue subplot, in which Gordy and Hanky are kidnapped and presumed to be thrown off a bridge, are a bit sophisticated. Otherwise, the theme ("Gordy gives people hope") and the sweet vocal character of the pig (provided by Justin Garms) might intrigue very young children. Beyond the two country songs by Doug Stone and some guest appearances by Roy Clark, Ray Stephens, and a few more country stars, parents might want to use the time to reminisce about Arnold on *Green Acres.*

—*Kirby Tepper*

Grosse Fatigue

Grosse Fatigue is a darkly comic tale of mistaken identity which illustrates the privileges and pitfalls of fame, utilizing a number of noted French comedians all playing themselves. A famous French comic actor and director himself, Michel Blanc (playing a morose rendition of himself) is an overwrought mess when a series of events lead him to believe that serious over-work has brought on some kind of memory lapses. It seems that suddenly the reclusive writer Blanc, who has been struggling with penning a screenplay for the last seven years, is turning up at a variety of suspicious events he has no memory of and seems to be acting strangely. Blanc and his friends write it off as stress until close friend Josiane Balasko (Josiane Balasko) accuses him of chaining her to a radiator and raping her. Questioned by the police who obviously delight in harassing the suddenly down-on-his-luck star, he is subsequently thrown into jail where his movie star status only makes him a target for further harassment and threats from the inmates. Fame turned to infamy, Blanc wonders if he is going out of his mind.

Apparently, because of their past relationship, Balasko drops the charges and Blanc is set free. Blanc's sympathetic and equally famous friend, actress Carole Bouquet (famous French actress and face of Chanel) attends a therapy session with him and offers to house Blanc at her retreat in Provence, where he can relax. Here, the duo discover the reason for all the unlikely events that have been driving Blanc mad. A Blanc look-a-like, local churl Patrick Olivier, has been impersonating him, perpetrating the ruse to cash in on Blanc's fame. Olivier has managed to ruin Blanc's reputation, stealing from his famous friends and even commiting rape. An engraged Blanc and Bouquet confront the clone in a dunk tank at a nearby supermarket event he was promoting, causing the imposter to flee, but not without leaving behind some clues.

Carole Bouquet stars in *Grosse Fatigue*. © Miramax Films.

CREDITS

Michel Blanc/Patrick Olivier: Michel Blanc
Carole Bouquet: Carole Bouquet
Philippe Noiret: Philippe Noiret
Josiane Balasko: Josiane Balasko
Mathilda May: Mathilda May
Thierry Lhermite: Thierry Lhermite
Roman Polanski: Roman Polanski
Gilles Jacob: Gilles Jacob

Origin: France
Released: 1994
Production: Patrice Ledoux for a Gaumont/TF1 Films production; released by Miramax Films
Direction: Michel Blanc
Screenplay: Michel Blanc
Cinematography: Eduardo Serra
Editing: Maryline Monthieux
Production design: Carlos Conti
Costume Design: Elisabeth Tavernier
Sound: not listed
Music: Rene Marc Bini
MPAA rating: R
Running Time: 84 minutes

Eventually, the two track Olivier to his mother's home, who believes her son is the comedian under a pseudonym. She welcomes the man she believes is her son and is impressed with the gorgeous movie star friend whom he has brought. Here, the power and impact of fame and the famous is almost hilariously drawn, as Bouquet visits a star-struck neighbor's crippled son who, upon seeing Bouquet in person, is miraculously healed and able to walk. Bouquet is awed by her own stardom, while Blanc poo-poos the ridiculous, egotistical notion, in essence, telling her to get over herself.

Blanc eventually meets up with his inept understudy who convinces the star that life would be a lot easier if he had a stand-in for the less enticing aspects of fame—appearing on talk shows, attending press events, doing television—and save his time and energy for writing, doing film, and taking more vacations. Director Blanc jokingly comments on the over exposure of certain stars, as Olivier uses the argument that many actors already use doubles to do more work than one person possibly could, citing Gerard Depardieu as an example. The duped actor agrees and while Blanc is off scuba diving, Olivier is busy convincing friends that he is the real Blanc. Blanc returns to find his locks changed and friends sure that he is the poseur. The desperate Blanc turns to crime and soon lands himself back in jail, only this time, there is no bail and no Bouquet to save him.

The rest of the film deals with Blanc's life after he has served his sentence and he is no longer rich nor famous. More famous film figures turn up in cameos here, such as Phillipe Noiret and Roman Polanski delivering ironic commentary on the future of film. Here, the state of modern cinema, both French and American is overtly criticized. The message is that real talent is being usurped by imposters and formerly great French cinema replaced by American action pictures. Nowhere is this more apparent than when the now unemployable Blanc and Noiret both seek jobs as celebrity look-alikes (their own) and both fail to get the part.

Facets of identity and the search for identity through fame are thoroughly explored. As Blanc and Bouquet drive through the countryside, Bouquet remarks that Blanc should accept his current state of confusion and memory lapses as a wonderful mystery of life. Blanc, of course, thinks that a ridiculous notion and sarcastically suggests that Luis Brunel (who directed Bouquet in her film debut, *That Obsicre Object of Desire* (1977), another comic nightmare of identities) turned her into a mystic. Bouquet replies that some of Brunel's philosophy could do him good.

The persona of Blanc in the film begs the inevitable comparisons to Woody Allen: the neurotic, yet sympathetic victim. Bouquet is also reminicient of Allen's strong-willed heroines with good intentions. However, unlike Allen, Blanc's broad farce is far from believable, distancing the audience from characters who are only around to illustrate the grander themes: search for the self and fame vs. the quest for art. The curse of celebrity and all it's accompanying trappings are summed up in the Blanc doppleganger. He actually becomes a more successful celebrity, doing "typical Blanc" in his films, than the real Blanc who has burned out somewhat. Talent is less important, Blanc seems to observe, than persona and attitude.

While most of biting wit and comedic situations are readily graspable, some relatively obscure French references may not be to non-French or non-European viewers and less avid film fans. Similar to Altman's *The Player* (1992) satirizing American movie business by exposing shallow values by questionable talent, Blanc also references famous films and filmmakers of the past and contrasts them with today's films and stars of cinema. Because the French film in-jokes and star cameos add to the understanding and appeal of the humor, the unquestionably funny and thoughtful *Grosse Fatigue* may do better with European audiences.

—Hilary Weber

REVIEWS

Chicago Tribune. July 21, 1995.
The Village Voice. Jly 18, 1995.
Variety. May 18, 1994.

Grumpier Old Men

"Pure delight...a wonderfully warmhearted comedy that bridges the generation gap. Lemmon and Matthau take their older odd couple comic crankiness to new heights of humor."—David Sheehan, *CBS-TV*

"Hollywood's happiest holiday gift delivers a big smile that will last for days."—Joanna Langfield, *The Movie Minute*

"A holiday heart-warmer! Sophia Loren is stunning!"—Garrett Glaser, *NBC 4*

"Riotously funny. Sophia Loren will enchant me forever."—Jeffrey Lyons, *Sneak Previews/Lyons Den Radio*

Box Office Gross: $28,004,723

Grumpier Old Men reteams one of Hollywood's most enduring and endearing comedy twosomes—Jack Lemmon and Walter Matthau—in the sequel to their 1993 hit, *Grumpy Old Men.* The first film, also released during the Christmas holidays, became a sleeper success, grossing over $70 million in domestic receipts and over $140 million in worldwide grosses combined with video rentals and sales.

The original film is set in the town of Wabasha, Minnesota, during the winter season. John Gustafson (Jack Lemmon) and Max Goldman (Walter Matthau) play a pair of cantankerous, long-time feuding neighbors—retired widowers who have been on-and-off-again friends and enemies for more than five decades. The original rift between both men is never fully explained. Their lives revolve around eating and boozing, watching television, and ice fishing which they pursue with religious intensity. At the frozen lake called Indian Slough, they pal around with Chuck (Ossie Davis), who runs a popular bait store, but dies during the movie, and Grandpa Gustafson (Burgess Meredith), John's foul-mouthed father.

Both Max and John are combative by nature and openly contemptuous of one another. They play adolescent tricks on each other, both at home and on the lake. Their mutual hostility rises to a new level, however, when an attractive woman moves in across the street. Ariel (Ann-Margaret) is divorced, flirtatious by nature, and available. She immediately scales off years of romantic rustiness in the two men who pursue her with the same single-minded determination given to fishing.

Mutual jealousy and frustration over Ariel's affections flame up their rivalry. Soon, John and Max are at each others' throats, destroying personal possessions. Sanity and friendship return when John succumbs to a life-threatening illness, and Max realizes what this loss would mean. Reinforcing and bonding both men's relationship is a parallel subplot involving their grown children, Melanie Gustafson and Jacob Goldman (Darryl Hannah and Kevin Pollack, respectively) who fall in love with each other.

Grumpy Old Men builds slowly to an interesting and convincingly satisfying conclusion. John weds the lovely Ariel with a beaming Max by his side. The film ends with a series of spontaneous and outrageous outtakes during the end credits showing the principals flubbing lines. Particularly hilarious is Meredith's contribution of off-color one-liners. Artistically, the film is a modest, charming, good-natured effort that underscores the enduring values of mature friendship, loyalties, and love. These virtues overshadow the defects of a stilted script and dialogue, uninspired direction, wooden characters, and scatological humor.

Grumpier Old Men picks up where the first left off—two colorful codgers still battling each other. The sequel builds directly on the first, with all the principals (and same cast) back to reprise their roles. The setting is still Wabasha. Six months have elapsed, so now the season is late summer. John and Ariel have slipped into a peaceful wedded state that neighbor Max will soon shatter.

At film's opening, Max and John have two things on their minds—planning for the forthcoming wedding nuptials between Melanie and Jacob and trying to prove who is the better fisherman by landing the unhookable "Catfish Hunter" swimming in Indian Slough. Into their lives steps the attractive Maria Ragetti (Sophia Loren) and her mother, Francesca Ragetti (Ann Guilbert), both newly arrived from Italy. They have purchased the deceased Chuck's beloved bait shop and plan to turn it into a romantic Italian restaurant. A visibly attracted, but disbelieving, Max rallies the help of John to thwart their plans.

John and Max carry out a campaign of gossip, innuendo, and aggressive maneuvers to either close the restaurant (passing off a guinea pig as a rat during a health inspector's visit) or drive customers away (putting crime scene barriers around the place). They succeed. The new eatery, elegantly decorated with a charming

Italian superstar Sophia Loren was seriously considered for the role of Ariel (played in both films by Ann-Margaret), after the producers' first choice Audrey Hepburn, died before production began. Loren was the overwhelming first choice for Maria in *Grumpier Old Men.*

atmosphere and beautiful view of the lake, attracts no customers. An enraged Maria, realizing two can play at this game, decides to bait the two buddies in their own haunts. She seeks them out at their favorite bar. Provocatively dressed, she deliberately taunts Max whose libido kicks into overdrive. Max, however, is not the only one smitten by the Italian newcomers. Grandpa Gustafson also gets involved, as well, by wooing and winning over Mama Ragetti. During the ritual of courtship, Max and John continue to bedevil each other through a series of pranks increasing in destructive tendencies.

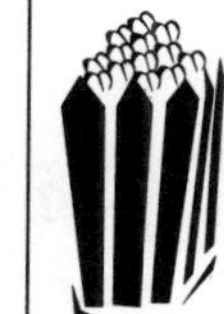

"People ain't going to come down here for Italian when we got a Chuck E. Cheese in town."—Max from *Grumpier Old Men*

Grumpier Old Men, like its predecessor, also has the same subplot involving the children—Melanie and Max—who are now engaged to be married. Their problem remains fathers who will not leave them alone. Both John and Max insist on running the whole show, driving Melanie to break off the engagement while a frustrated Jacob watches helplessly. Also, complicating their romantic relationship is Melanie's daughter, Allie Gustafson (Katie Sagona), who dislikes Jacob. Melanie is soon joined by Ariel who has left John both because of his silly escapades with Max and her discovery that John spent all night (innocently) with Maria at her place.

Everything falls back into perspective again with the unexpected death of Grandpa Gustafson. John discovers his father's body at Indian Slough. All the principals gather at the lakeside funeral service and the healing process begins. Soon, all the romantic couples are paired up again. Time passes and summer slips into fall. Max and John even catch the legendary Catfish Hunter, but allow the fish to slip overboard to plague other fishermen.

The film ends happily with the expected wedding between Max and Maria, John standing in as best man. Jacob and Melanie announce they will elope, and so all is well in Wabasha. The film closes with Max and Maria departing and the outtakes flashing over the end credits. Silly, spontaneous and funny, the clips—most of them with Burgess Meredith—are as much fun to watch as the preceding movie.

Grumpier Old Men is released at a of time when sequels and remakes are a Hollywood staple. The film actually has the features of both. It is billed as a sequel, but structured more like a remake of the original. Therefore, *Grumpier Old Men* has all the virtues, as well as, all the defects of the original. Its greatest asset is bringing Walter Matthau and Jack Lemmon back together again. In an almost thirty-year collaboration, beginning with *The Fortune Cookie* (1966) and *The Odd Couple* (1968) to the present, they have starred or worked together in seven pictures. Interestingly, the two Oscar-winners have successfully created separate movie careers, but it is their teaming together that showcases some of their finest work. Lemmon and Matthau have aged well on the big screen as they have seamlessly segued from "The Odd Couple" to "The Old Couple." Watching them act together is a joy as they zip through their stinging resumes of each other.

Supporting both comic actors is a very strong supporting cast featuring veterans Burgess Meredith, Sophia Loren, Ann-Margaret, and not-so-young Darryl Hannah and Kevin Pollack. (The statistics on Matthau, Lemmon, Ann-Margaret, Loren, and Meredith are very impressive: combined age of 347; over 300 films; 4 Oscars; and 17 Oscar nominations.) The crusty Meredith, sixty-year veteran of the screen and years of Broadway experience before that, is a marvelous scene stealer. His inspired one-liners during the end credits, as in the original, are worth the price of admission. (Killing him off may prove to be a big mistake if a second sequel is planned.) Actresses Sophia Loren and Ann-Margaret also hold their own against the dynamic duo and they make for strong feminine counterparts. Only Darryl Hannah and Kevin Pollack, here, as in the original, seem ill-suited and wooden, but the fault lies not with their talents, but with the script, which treats them as plot points or symbols rather than believable characters.

CREDITS

Max: Walter Matthau
John: Jack Lemmon
Ariel: Ann-Margret
Maria: Sophia Loren
Grandpa: Burgess Meredith
Melanie: Daryl Hannah
Jacob: Kevin Pollak

Origin: USA
Released: 1995
Production: John Davis and Richard C. Berman for a John Davis/ Lancaster Gate production; released by Warner Brothers
Direction: Howard Deutch
Screenplay: Mark Steven Johnson
Cinematography: Tak Fujimoto
Editing: Billy Weber, Seth Flaum and Maryann Brandon
Production design: Gary Frutkoff
Costume design: Lisa Jensen
Art direction: Bill Rea
Set decoration: Peg Cummings
Music: Alan Silvestri
MPAA rating: PG-13
Running Time: 105 minutes

What also fails in *Grumpier Old Men* is its carbon copy replica of the original story, from feuding neighbors to mischievous antics, to untimely death, to romantic rivalry, to close-out wedding. There is really nothing new or original here. The plot, what there is of it, is creaky, the dialogue is often banal, lesser characters remain lifeless, and many of the jokes, gestures, and behavior patterns are shamelessly crude. Director Howard Deutch brings little creativity to the sequel; his approach is workmanlike at best.

Grumpier Old Men, even with its strong cast, works because of its timeless appeal to friendship and loyalty. Watching the two Geritol-swigging old coots fighting nonstop, whether over a fish or frolicking feline, underscores the spirited view of old age friendship and romance among the AARP generation. Do not be surprised if a second sequel appears within two years. Possible title could be *Grumpiest Old Men*, of course.

—*Terry Theodore*

REVIEWS

Variety. December 18, 1995. p. 66.

Hackers

"Information is the most dangerous weapon of all."—Movie tagline

"A must-see of stupendous thrills!"—Ron Brewington, *American Urban Radio Networks*

"Smart and entertaining."—Roger Ebert, *Chicago Sun-Times*

"*Hackers* has high-tech speed and a splashy style of its own."—Bob Ross, *Tampa Tribune*

Box Office Gross: $7,555,834

Relying on a rationale not unlike that behind the Aristotelian notion of catharsis through tragic drama, film scholars have posited that "teen films" often fall under the general category of Bildungsroman, that is, an exploration of psychological development and moral education. Films thereby allow young people to "act out" within the confines of art, while becoming initiated into the adult world and learning to identify and deal with the realities and failures of the adult world that surrounds them. From *Rebel Without a Cause* (1955) and *The Blob* (1958) to *War Games* (1983), from *Peyton Place* (1957) and *Summer Place* (1959) to *Last Picture Show* (1971) and *Buffy the Vampire Slayer* (1993), "teen films" ease the passage to adulthood by showing how other teens have dealt with it. *Hackers*, while derivative in many senses, fits the mold by pitting young people against corporate giants and middle-aged "bad guys." Also, visually it is a product of its time: in the words of Chicago Tribune critic Michael Wilmington, *Hackers* "is loud, fast, visually zingy and imaginative...empty and dehumanized[.]...[It] zap[s] you with techno-cliches and trap[s] you in constant visual crash and burn."

Actress Angelina Jolie is the daughter of actor Jon Voight.

Dade Murphy (Jonny Lee Miller—a British actor, hiding his accent), a.k.a. Zero Cool, is a legend. As a pre-teen, he had crashed computers on Wall Street, creating chaos in financial markets and sending him into an FBI-enforced computer exile. Years later, however, he is ready and willing to hack again. Surrounded by other enthusiasts—including his love interest Kate Libby (Angelina Jolie, daughter of Academy Award winner Jon Voight), a.k.a. Acid Burn—Zero Cool is drawn into the world of computer spelunking when he is wrongfully accused of holding the world for ransom by orchestrating a computer-initiated environmental disaster. The group of renegade hackers sets out to recruit the best of the cybernet underground to capture the real villains and clear their names.

The structure of the film is reminiscent of a variety of suspenseful intrigues. For instance, not unlike television's "Mission Impossible" or the large screen's *Fright Night* (1985) and *Sneakers* (1993)—or even *St. Elmo's Fire*, *Singles* (1993) and *Big Chill* (1983), *Hackers* is an ensemble film, showcasing the idiosyncracies of a group of friends even as it works to solve a larger mystery. For instance, the film begins with Kate, the ultimate cyberpunk New Yorker giving a tour of the high school to new student Dade, who has moved from the Pacific Northwest. Unwittingly Dade becomes the victim of a prank, and to save face and seek revenge, he enters the computer system and rigs his own surprise for his classmates, in the process impressing the other hackers with his ability to "surf the net." From this series of scenes, the audience learns that Kate is nice enough but never gentle, that Dade is a computer wizard with an eye for an attractive classmate, and that the school is filled with a group of Generation X-style misfits.

Hackers may also remind audience members of films such as F/X (1986) or *Jumpin' Jack Flash* (1986), in which persons with specialized abilities become caught up in intrigues that test their abilities and put them at great risk. In this film, Dade is confronted by the FBI and must decide whether to stay in the "game" to rescue his friends or remain uninvolved in order to protect himself, please his mother and play it safe.

Director Iain Softley, who also directed the stylish biopic *Backbeat* (1994), worked to create a visually interesting world that also was true to life. Said director Softley, who worked from a budget approximately triple the $5 million he spent

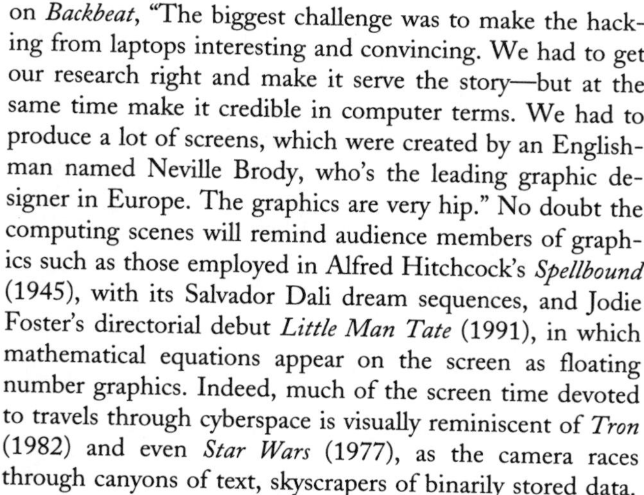

on *Backbeat*, "The biggest challenge was to make the hacking from laptops interesting and convincing. We had to get our research right and make it serve the story—but at the same time make it credible in computer terms. We had to produce a lot of screens, which were created by an Englishman named Neville Brody, who's the leading graphic designer in Europe. The graphics are very hip." No doubt the computing scenes will remind audience members of graphics such as those employed in Alfred Hitchcock's *Spellbound* (1945), with its Salvador Dali dream sequences, and Jodie Foster's directorial debut *Little Man Tate* (1991), in which mathematical equations appear on the screen as floating number graphics. Indeed, much of the screen time devoted to travels through cyberspace is visually reminiscent of *Tron* (1982) and even *Star Wars* (1977), as the camera races through canyons of text, skyscrapers of binarily stored data.

Also visually interesting are the youthful characters themselves. Traveling largely by rollerblade (cast members attended rollerblading workshops), they also break down tradition by wearing their hair too short or too long, and by wearing wildly colored apparel in unusual combinations. A running competition is sustained throughout between Dade and Kate, with a date—loser wears a dress—as the prize. According to director Softley, "They're living slightly on the edge of what's considered acceptable behavior. They are at the forefront of a phenomenon that's just breaking—a phenomenon that in many ways expresses the aspirations, frustrations and desires of young people to create a world in their own image."

In similar fashion to the various teen films above, such as *Summer Place*, in which the teens—young lovers—rendezvous in the same spot each evening, so too in *Hackers*, the "keyboard punks" gather at a club named Cyberdelia, filled with state of the art video games and techno/industrial music. Whereas in a simpler time, young people gathered for romance, here they gather for conversation and competition. In fact, so modern is the world of this film that it comments on the generation's disgust with 1960's-style free love in an era of AIDS. That is, the young hackers, attracted though they are, experience love without sex and are defined by their abilities, their creativity and their loyalty to each other. The devilish "bad guys," who also are members of the older generation (read: middle-aged, parent-aged) have sex without love and are defined by their lust, whether for money or for flesh. Particularly unpleasant is Margo (Lorraine Bracco), who positively shrieks her fear, greed, and ignorance. While Lorraine Bracco has had a variety of roles in which she plays characters whose features include intelligence, beauty and desirability (for example, *Medicine Man*, 1992), in this film, next to the young, beautiful, artfully subversive cyberpunks, she looks tired, puffy, overripe. No doubt audience members will be disappointed with her role in this film, as she is a fine performer, showcased much more ably in other films.

CREDITS

Dade: Jonny Lee Miller
Kate: Angelina Jolie
Plague: Fisher Stevens
Joey: Laurence Mason
Phantom Phreak: Renoly Santiago
Agent Gill: Wendell Pierce
Lauren: Alberta Watson
Cereal Killer: Matthew Lillard
Hal: Penn Jilliette
Margo: Lorraine Bracco

Origin: USA
Released: 1995
Production: Michael Peyser and Ralph Winter; released by United Artists
Direction: Iain Softley
Screenplay: Rafael Moreu
Cinematography: Andrezej Sekula
Editing: Christopher Blunden and Martin Walsh
Production design: John Beard
Art direction: John Frankish
Set decoration: Joann Woolard
Costume design: Roger Burton
Sound: Roger Burton and Peter Lindsay
Music: Simon Boswell
MPAA rating: PG-13
Running Time: 109 minutes

As is the case in other teen pictures (such as *Fright Night*, in which most parents are totally missing, except for one mother who is largely clueless, and *Buffy, the Vampire Slayer*, 1993, in which clueless mom is matched by materialistic dad), *Hackers* presents a couple of mothers who urge their children to communicate, to behave, to enter the mainstream. For instance, Dade's mother urges him to apply to colleges and to stay out of trouble with the FBI, even as she dashes off to work, leaving Dade home alone. Kate's parents are completely absent, represented instead by the empty house, in which she throws a party. Clearly adults are outside the loop in this film.

Hackers is visually appealing, fast-paced and a new wave of teen cinema. Even where implausibility and style threaten to swamp the production, it is a memorably viewing experience. Students of film —and of youth and cyberculture— will not want to miss this one. —*Roberta F. Green*

REVIEWS

The Chicago Tribune, September 15, 1995, p. 4.
Detroit Free Press, September 15, 1995, p. 3G.
USA Today, September 15, 1995, p. 4D.

La Haine (Hate)

Set in the poverty-stricken neighborhood of Paris where riots are commonplace due to police brutality, three friends from different ethnic backgrounds, Vinz (Vincent Cassel), Said (Said Taghmaoui), and Hubert (Hubert Kounde) become embroiled in violence as Vinz recovers a gun lost by police and is bent on revenge for the brutal beating of his Arab friend at the hands of Parisian police.

CREDITS

Vinz: Vincent Cassel
Hubert: Hubert Kounde
Said: Said Taghmaoui
Asterix: Fancois Levantal
Samir: Karim Belkhadra
Darty: Edouard Montoute

Origin: France
Released: 1995
Production: Christopher Rossignon for a Les Productions, Lazennec, Le Studio Canal, La Sept Cinema, Kaso Inc.,Canal Plus, Cofimage 6 and Studio Images production; released by Metro Tartan
Direction: Mathieu Kassovitz
Screenplay: Mathieu Kassovitz
Cinematography: Perre Aim and Georges Diane
Editing: Mathieu Kassovitz and Scott Stevenson
Production design: Guiseppe Ponturo
Sound design: Vincent Tulli
Set decoration: Sophie Quiedeveille
Casting: Jean-Claude Flamand
Costume design: Virginie Montel
Make-up: Sophie Benaiche
MPAA rating: R
Running Time: 97 minutes

Halloween: The Curse of Michael Myers

"The scariest *Halloween* of them all!"—Dr. Donald Reed, *Academy of Science Fiction, Fantasy and Horror*

Box Office Gross: $15,126,948

The unstoppable Michael Meyers (George P. Wilbur) returns to Haddonfield to finish what he started, but his archnemesis, Dr. Loomis (Donald Pleasance), tries to foil Michael's plans of wiping out an entire family.

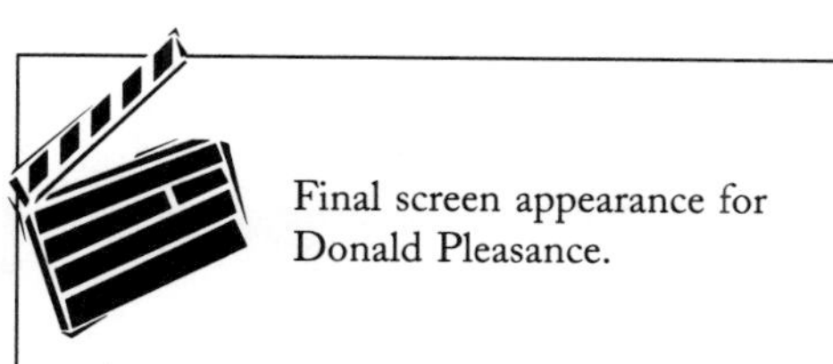

Final screen appearance for Donald Pleasance.

CREDITS

Dr. Loomis: Donald Pleasance
Dr. Wynn: Mitch Ryan
Kara Strode: Marianne Hagan
Tommy Doyle: Paul Rudd
Barry Simms: Leo Geter
Michael Meyers: George P. Wilbur
Danny Strode: Devin Gardner

Origin: USA
Released: 1995
Production: Paul Freeman for a Nightfall production; released by Dimension Films
Direction: Joe Chappelle
Screenplay: Daniel Farrands
Cinematography: Billy Dickson
Editing: Randy Bricker
Production design: Bryan Ryman
Art direction: T.K. Kirkpatrick
Costume design: Ann Cray Lambert
Sound: Mark Hopkins McNabb
Special makeup effects: John Carl Buechler
Casting: Ross Brown, Mary West
Music: Alan Howarth
MPAA rating: R
Running Time: 88 minutes

Heat

"A stunning crime drama. Mann's sprawling saga has the most impressive collection of actors in one movie this year. Pacino and De Niro are great. This one sticks to your gut."—David Ansen, *Newsweek*

"Awesome. Truly epic. A masterpiece. Wholly original."—Richard Schickel, *Time*

Box Office Gross: $34,493,095

Writer-director Michael Mann, best known as the creator-executive producer of *Miami Vice*, brings a great deal of style and masculine posturing to his films. He has made a stylish crime drama, *Thief* (1981), a flawed horror tale, *The Keep* (1983), a suspenseful serial-killer drama, *Manhunter* (1986), and one of the best screen adaptations of classical American literature, *The Last of the Mohicans* (1992). *Heat* is even more accomplished than Mann's previous films, combining film noir with traditional elements of heist films and police procedurals while throwing in some existentialism and a masculine code of honor borrowed from American literature and films. Having two true icons together on screen for the first time heightens the quality of this immensely entertaining film.

The film opens with the gang of thieves led by the coolly professional Neil McCauley (Robert De Niro) staging a minutely orchestrated robbery of an armored car. Everything goes smoothly until one of McCauley's men, Waingro (Kevin Gage), panics and begins shooting the three guards. Robbery and homicide detective Vincent Hanna (Al Pacino) admires the craftsmanship that went into the robbery and sees tracking down the thieves as a challenge worthy of his skills. McCauley, who resorts to violence only when absolutely necessary, tries to kill Waingro for bungling the job, but his victim escapes.

Mann then fleshes out his characters by delving into their personal lives. Hanna is on his third marriage, and his wife, Justine (Diane Venora), is beginning to strongly resent the fact that his work comes before her. Hanna is devoted to his adolescent stepdaughter, Lauren (Natalie Portman), but she suffers psychologically because her real father neglects her. McCauley's closest comrade, Chris Shiherlis (Val Kilmer), blows most of his money through gambling, leading to conflicts with his wife, Charlene (Ashley Judd), who begins an affair with Marciano (Hank Azaria) to get back at her husband. Breedan (Dennis Haysbert), a former fellow convict of McCauley and Shiherlis, is trying, with the support of his girlfriend, Lillian (Kim Staunton), to lead a normal life, but he is constantly humiliated by his surly coffee-shop boss (Bud Cort).

McCauley's code of conduct leads him to develop no attachments to anything he cannot walk away from in thirty seconds. As a result, his expensive beachfront house is nearly empty. Despite his air of controlled professionalism, however, McCauley is human, and he finds himself falling in love with Eady (Amy Brenneman), a graphic designer he meets in a restaurant.

Because Michael Cheritto (Tom Sizemore), is overheard calling Waingro "Slick" by a homeless man at the robbery site, Hanna is able to identify McCauley and his men and follow them. Hanna's crew plans to arrest them after their next heist, but a noisy policeman scares them off. McCauley's fence, Nate (Jon Voight), wants to sell back the bonds stolen in the armored-car operation, and the sleazy money launderer Van Zant (William Fichtner) agrees but instead has his thugs attack McCauley and Shiherlis at a deserted drive-in movie theater. Because McCauley promises to kill Van Zant, the latter brings in Waingro to help him get to the thief first.

> Michael Mann wrote his first version of *Heat* in 1980, inspired by a thief killed by an admiring detective in Chicago in 1963. In 1989, Mann used some of the same material, including naming the detective Vincent Hanna, for a failed NBC pilot entitled 'L.A. Takedown.'

One of McCauley's men sells him out to Van Zant who alerts Hanna to a bank robbery in progress, leading to the film's centerpiece, a lengthy, brilliantly choreographed gunfight on the streets of Los Angeles that leaves Shiherlis badly wounded and Cheritto, as well as numerous policemen, dead. After killing Van Zant, McCauley must decide between escaping to New Zealand with Eady or exacting revenge on Waingro. He suffers the consequences of his choice.

At first, dragging in the characters' private lives seems an attempt at providing a respite from the action. Eventually, however, Mann makes clear, at least with McCauley and Hanna, that these relationships are central to his larger theme, and that he is trying to make more than just a stylish action film. The master thief and the obsessive cop are not opposites or incomplete men whose halves would make one whole person. They are the same person, as they acknowledge in their two brief encounters.

As Mann illustrates in his prior film and television work, he is compulsively drawn to men who live on the edge.

This compulsion explains Shiherlis' gambling addiction and leads Breedan to throw away his honest life when McCauley needs him to drive a getaway car. When McCauley offers Cheritto the chance to leave the gang before the bank robbery, his friend refuses because the action is too vital to his existence.

> "I gotta hold on to my angst. I preserve it because I need it. It keeps me sharp, on the edge, where I gotta be."—Vincent Hanna from *Heat*

McCauley and Hanna are also motivated by a code of conduct that compels the policeman to pursue his prey at all costs and the thief to jeopardize a certain escape to seek revenge. This code, a combination of duty and macho ego with an overlay of an existential sense of fatalism, was created by Ernest Hemingway, Dashiell Hammett, and Raymond Chandler and modified for the screen in the films of John Ford and, especially, Howard Hawks. Hanna's pursuit of McCauley recalls Ford's enormously influential *The Searchers* (1956), and the masculine bonding and attempted exclusion of women are reminiscent of Hawks' *Only Angels Have Wings* (1939). *Heat* ends with Hanna and the dying McCauley tenderly grasping hands as the detective sees some essence of himself being lost. Like *Reservoir Dogs* (1992) and *The Usual Suspects* (1995), *Heat* is self-conscious about the inescapable homoerotic content of such films.

Women are a strong presence in Hawks' films and are increasingly so in Mann's. Mere appendages before *The Last of the Mohicans*, Mann's women began to become more assertive with Madeleine Stowe's strong portrayal of Cora Munro in his version of James Fennimore Cooper's novel. The three main women in *Heat* have varying degrees of complexity. Charlene both loves and resents her husband. Judd ably conveys her affection and weariness when she warns Shiherlis of a police trap near the film's end. Eady is a relative innocent who struggles against McCauley when she discovers who he really is before giving in to her love for the outsider. Brenneman is especially moving as Eady waits outside a hotel while McCauley is inside killing Waingro and she quietly conveys concern, fear, horror, and despair. (Throughout the film, Mann explores his actors' often-flawed faces, giving each opportunities to display a wide range of emotions silently.) The world-weary Justine is Hanna's equal in coolness and anger, and, likewise, Venora, a wonderful actress who has never had the film roles she deserves, matches Pacino in all their confrontations.

Having Pacino and De Niro, the most acclaimed actors of their generation, together on screen for the first time is obviously one of the main attractions of *Heat*. (Since De Niro plays Pacino's father in flashbacks in the 1974 film *The Godfather, Part II*, they share no scenes.) Pacino loves to overact, as he has shown in *Dick Tracy* (1990) and *Scent of a Woman* (1992), and Hanna shouts several times, shrieking, "By the time I get to Phoenix," to intimidate a reluctant informant. However, such outbursts are in character since the detective often seems on the verge of losing control. Mann allows this excess to create contrast elsewhere as when a noisy policeman spoils a stakeout and Hanna boils but does not explode, destroying the culprit with a venomous glance. Similarly, De Niro has balanced his brilliant career between flamboyance, as with the boxer Jake La Motta in *Raging Bull* (1980), and much subtler portrayals, as with the priest in *True Confessions* (1981). His McCauley belongs with the latter, displaying all his emotions with economic gestures. At the end, McCauley approaches Eady with happy relief that his ordeal is over only to see her anxiety and the approaching Hanna. He has violated his code by allowing himself to fall in love, and De Niro quickly displays McCauley's intense regret and acceptance of his fate.

These two great actors have their showdown when Hanna pulls over McCauley's car and invites the thief for coffee. During their conversation in the restaurant, the two

CREDITS

Vincent Hanna: Al Pacino
Neil McCauley: Robert DeNiro
Chirs Shiherlis: Val Kilmer
Nate: Jon Voight
Michael Cheritto: Tom Sizemore
Justine: Diane Venora
Eady: Amy Brenneman
Charlene: Ashley Judd
Drucker: Mykelti Williamson

Origin: USA
Released: 1995
Production: Michael Mann and Art Linson for a Forward Pass and New Regency production; released by Warner Brothers
Direction: Michael Mann
Screenplay: Michael Mann
Cinematography: Dante Spinotti
Editing: Dov Hoenig, Pasquale Buba, William Goldenberg and Tom Rolf
Production design: Neil Spisak
Art direction: Majorie Stone McShirley
Set design: Robert Fectman, Steven Schwartz and Paul Sonski
Costume design: Deborah L. Scott
Sound: Lee Orloff
Stunt coordination: Joel Kramer
Casting: Bonnie Timmermann
Music: Elliot Goldenthal
MPAA rating: R
Running Time: 172 minutes

feel each other out expertly as they tentatively discuss their personal lives, at first trying not to reveal anything that would give the other an edge. Finally, becoming more at ease as the conversation begins taking on more philosophical overtones, they discover they share a similar way of looking at their violent world. Mann masterfully ends the scene with quick shots of each as both smile ironically, revealing their awareness of their kinship and of its inevitable doom. This is a mythic meeting created by a filmmaker who thoroughly grasps how to take genre cliches and explode them to epic proportions.

—Michael Adams

REVIEWS

Entertainment Weekly. December 22, 1995, p. 46.
New York. XXVIII, December 18, 1995, p. 50.
The New York Times. December 15, 1995, p. C18.
The New Yorker. LXXI, December 25, 1995, p. 145.
Newsweek. CXXVI, December 18, 1995, p. 68.
Rolling Stone. December 26, 1995, p. 138.
Time. CXLVI, December 11, 1995, p. 81.
USA Today. December 15, 1995, p. D1.
Variety. December 11, 1995, p. 82.

Heavyweights

"Hilarious! Filled with nonstop laughs!"—*New York Newsday*

Box Office Gross: $17,689,177

Making fun of fat people has been a film staple since the earliest reels of the silent comedies. In an industry where looks count for almost everything, overweight actors don't get taken seriously. But the 1990s are the days of political correctness and overweight people want sensitive portrayals in film.

Filmed at Camp Pinnacle, a 150-acre summer camp in the Blue Ridge Mountains near Hendersonville, North Carolina.

In a movie about overweight kids who go to a summer "fat camp," how does a director signal sensitivity to the obese and still milk laughs from the usual fat jokes? Simple: Make the chubby cherubs into victims. The result is *Heavyweights*, a passably entertaining but terribly wrong-headed family comedy which panders to fat folks while making fun of them.

The plot is a no-brainer: Budding adolescent Gerry Garner (Aaron Schwartz) gets sent to Camp Hope by parents who want him to lose weight. Camp Hope is a fun, feel-good place and Gerry lands with a cool group of guys and a kind, witty veteran counselor, Pat (Tom McGowan). But the camp's taken over by a crazed fitness guru, Tony Perkis (Ben Stiller), who wants the kids to be guinea pigs for the weight-loss video he wants to market. That sets up the film to be a variation of the usual summer-camp plot: loveable campers against their authoritarian keepers.

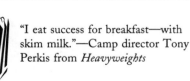

"I eat success for breakfast—with skim milk."—Camp director Tony Perkis from *Heavyweights*

Logic takes a vacation too. How has the old Camp Hope marketed itself as a fat camp when its counselors don't even try to help the campers lose weight? And how is that any less dishonest than the Perkis regime? The campers are outraged at Perkis' brutal ways, but rally behind Pat's kinder, gentler version of the same program. The film's message changes more often than the weight of a binge-and-purge dieter: First it's not OK to be fat, then it is, then it isn't, then it is, but only if you want to change.

Director and co-writer Stephen Brill wants to have it both ways: He wants us to root for Gerry, Pat and his pals, and he wants us to laugh at them. The jokes about the fat kids are gratuitous and insulting. Gerry is so uncoordinated he can't throw a ball over a fence. At a lemonade stand, he picks up the whole pitcher and guzzles it. The fat kids and Pat are shy around girls. They are athletically inept. They are jolly and laugh a lot. They are all addicted to food, so much so that after Perkis is overthrown, they have a food orgy. They spew food all over and wake up the next morning stupefied and covered with sweets and junk. It's one of the most brutally offensive scenes imaginable. It's followed by an equally implausible and patronizing sequence where Pat tells the campers it's time for them to start respecting themselves, and they all agree and begin a more sensible exercise program.

The message *Heavyweights* sends is that all fat kids are victims of uncontrollable impulses for food but can be instantly transformed if only they accept themselves. That's the same philosophy that Brill spends most of the movie satirizing by casting Stiller as the ridiculous villain.

CREDITS

Pat: Tom McGowan
Gerry: Aaron Schwartz
Tony Perkis: Ben Stiller
Josh: Shaun Weiss
Lars: Tom Hodges
Julie: Leah Lail
Tim: Paul Feig
Roy: Kenan Thompson
Phillip: Max Goldblatt
Maury Garner: Jeffrey Tambor

Origin: USA
Released: 1995
Production: Joe Roth and Roger Birnbaum for Walt Disney Pictures, in association with Caravan Pictures; released by Buena Vista Pictures
Direction: Steven Brill
Screenplay: Judd Apatow and Steven Brill
Cinematography: Victor Hammer
Editing: C. Timothy O'Meara
Production design: Stephen Storer
Art direction: Harry Darrow and Jack Ballance
Set decoration: Chris Spellman
Casting: Judy Taylor and Lynda Gordon
Sound: Mary H. Ellis
Costume design: Kimberly A. Tillman
Music: J. A. C. Redford
MPAA rating: PG
Running Time: 98 minutes

The rest is all padding and formulaic camp-movie fare. A raid by the campers on Perkis' cabin is long and overwrought, and what they're after is never explained. When the campers figure out a system for sneaking food into the camp, it's not clear who's the outside source. A subplot that has Pat getting the girl, the camp nurse named Julie (Leah Lail), is sappy.

Stiller directed and starred in *Reality Bites* (1994), but he is so physically different, he's hardly recognizable as the same actor. Stiller single-handedly saves the film with an over-the-top performance that is wickedly satirical and mostly on target. When he tells the kids to take a one-hour meditation break and "feel the chi" before climbing a rock face, it's a devastating send-up of New Age fitness gurus. Stiller conveys the phoniness and hypocrisy of an entire class of entrepreneurs, and it's a great put-down. Stiller's comedy-team parents, Jerry Stiller and Anne Meara, appear briefly as the camp's old owners.

Brill, co-author Judd Apatow, Schwartz, two other campers (Shaun Weiss and Kenan Thompson) and Lail are all alumni of the "Mighty Ducks" films. A predictable ending tacked on to *Heavyweights* pits the campers in a competition against a rival camp of studs. It's a Ducks-type situation, with the underdogs against the overbearing. In fact, *Heavyweights* is little more than the Ducks transformed from inner-city victims who triumph against all odds to fat-kid victims who triumph against all odds. And it's just as insulting to real kids, who don't need to be cast as victims to win self-respect.

—Michael Betzold

REVIEWS

Hollywood Reporter. Feb. 17, 1995, p. 10.
Los Angeles Times. Feb. 17, 1995, p. F4.
New York Times. Feb. 17, 1995, p. C16.
People Weekly. Feb. 27, 1995, p. 18.
Variety. Feb. 20, 1995, p. 74.

Hideaway

"Extravagant special effects. It takes no hostages and makes no compromises. A berserk and extravagant entertainment."—Roger Ebert, *Siskel & Ebert*

"Gripping and intense. It scared the bejeezus out of me."—Jeff Craig, *Sixty Second Preview*

"This is not a film you'll easily forget."—Tom Kertes, *Village Voice*

Box Office Gross: $12,201,255

Horror is a relative concept. For some audiences, "horror" is a word saved for stories about epic battles between good samaritans and emissaries from hell; the struggle between Satanic evil and middle-class American goodness is the stuff of countless films in the genre.

But there is another type of horror. Novelist Dean Koontz experienced it during the making of *Hideaway*. He discovered that the film did not resemble the story he originally wrote. And he apparently hated it. Koontz went to great lengths to remove his name from the credits of this film, saying that the script "seems to have been written by someone who is no more a writer than Jeffrey Dahmer is a gourmet chef." In letters to the executives at Tri-Star, where this film was made, the horrified Koontz called the script "astonishingly incoherent" and "filled with contradictions and moronic logic." And Koontz's nightmare will never end, for he lost his battle to remove his name, and the credits now read "Based on the novel by Dean R. Koontz."

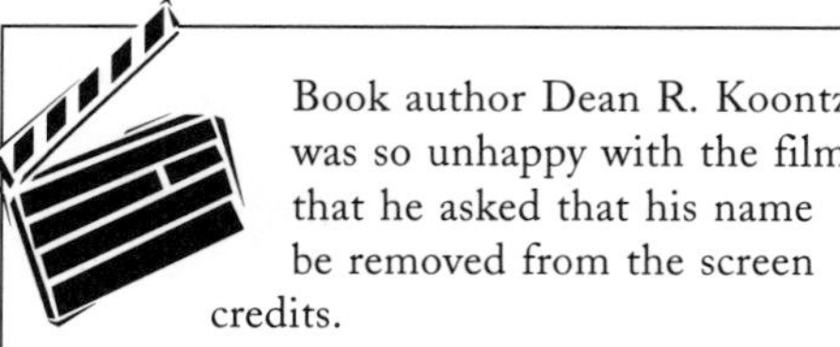

Book author Dean R. Koontz was so unhappy with the film that he asked that his name be removed from the screen credits.

The truth is that as films go, this one is not half bad. It is only half good, mind you, but in a genre which has spawned such cinematic gems as *The Prophecy* (1995) or *Children of the Corn II, The Final Sacrifice* (1993), the adjective "not half bad" is quite a compliment. Like many horror films, *Hideaway* tells a story of some innocent and generally likeable humans who unwittingly fall into a struggle between good and evil. Usually, such films deal with the battle for a soul, as in *The Exorcist* (1973), the coming of the devil *The Omen* (1986), or a variation thereof. The recent (and truly dreadful) *Prophecy* told the story of humans caught in a battle between Lucifer and Gabriel.

In this case, the struggle is a little less allegorical. Hatch Harrison (Jeff Goldblum) and his wife Lindsay (Christine Lahti) and daughter Regina (Alicia Silverstone) are a loving and incredibly sane family recuperating from the tragic death of their youngest daughter. Within the first few minutes of the film, while driving their car on an icy, winding mountain road (is there any other kind in a horror movie?) Hatch swerves away from an oncoming truck only to land in a frozen lake. Regina and Lindsay escape, but Hatch dies.

Cut to Hatch being revived by a strange doctor, Dr. Nyebern (Alfred Molina), who happens to specialize in resuscitating people from the dead. In an ominous (and unintentionally funny) portent of things to come, Dr. Nyebern's nurse warns him, "are you sure you want to revive him after 120 minutes down? We both remember what happened last time...."

The audience does not discover precisely what happened "the last time" until the end of the film. But until then, Hatch and his family undergo an ordeal that, in the hands of a different screenwriter and director, may have been truly terrifying instead of mildly scary. In any case, Hatch begins to have visions of the murder of several young girls. He discovers that in his "death," he became connected somehow to a deranged killer named Vassago (Jeremy Sisto) who preys on young virgins and is stalking Hatch's daughter (what a surprise!). The catch for Hatch is that he sees through Vassago's eyes, and vice-versa. Though it is never adequately explained, Hatch and Vassago have gotten their cosmic signals crossed, and they are able to follow each other's every move. Hatch tries to protect his daughter even while he knows that he is partially responsible for the mortal danger in which she finds herself.

It is all rather Freudian, and if anyone wanted to, they could do a term paper on the symbolism of an attractive middle-aged man trying to stop his youthful alter-ego from raping and killing his nubile fifteen-year-old daughter. This theme is underplayed by writers Andrew Kevin Walker and Neil Jimenez and director Brett Leonard. It is probably for the best: these are not the most subtle or intellectual of filmmakers, and perhaps they knew their limitations. They choose to allow the symbolism to stand on its own without trying to investigate it. The filmmakers instead opt for a simple horror-film formula. Hatch is racing against the clock to battle the evil Vassago, and the film's symbolism takes a back seat to some energetic if uninspired suspense.

For the most part, Leonard directs with a technically assured style, and with a sense of urgency that is appropriately suspenseful. Leonard has the dubious distinction of directing another horror film in which the author tried to remove his name: *The Lawnmower Man* (1992). Similar to Koontz, Stephen King asked to have his name disassociated from that film, but it was not reported to have been because of Brett Leonard's direction.

"One man with a very bad soul returns from death and brings back something dark, and a good man brings back something very light, and they battle between light and dark—it was a very interesting concept to me."—Director Brett Leonard on what intrigued him about *Hideaway*

Leonard certainly does an excellent job with pace (he keeps it brisk) and with new computer technology (his computer-enhanced vision of the afterlife is visually impressive). Leonard creates a fine blend of dramatic tension and cinematic technique in the early traffic-accident sequence. He develops a harrowing feeling of tension as the family's car is perched precariously on the edge of a cliff: sure, the "edge of the cliff" routine is cliche, but it is done with style. He then does some masterful work when the car falls down the cliff into the river. Leonard and cinematographer Gale Tattersall wisely never stray too far from the reactions of their actors during this sequence. They also do some fine shots of the car's plunge into the water: the camera is at water level, simultaneously recording the events above and below the water surface.

The film's pace is taut and absorbing until the last several minutes. Vassago's underworld lair (beneath an amusement park) and his climactic battle with Hatch and Lindsay is interrupted by some special effects that are visually engaging but seem a bit overly stylized at this point in the film. Additionally, the film ends abruptly and rather predictably; it generally loses steam once Hatch and Vassago get closer to their final battle.

It is a shame, too, for *Hideaway* has many fine elements. In particular, Jeff Goldblum makes a strong and unusual hero. Goldblum made his mark in *The Fly* (1986), in which he played another character who unwittingly brings horror and tragedy into his life. He is a unique actor, bringing his self-conscious quirkiness to this film as he has to all others. His initial scenes with Christine Lahti are badly written and rather unbelievable, but he (along with Lahti) commits so strongly to his role that he gets the audience past the foolishness. For example, there are not one but two scenes in which he and Lahti sing old standards and dance while preparing an impeccable meal and sipping wine. Another area in which Goldblum successfully manages to bypass the inanity of the script is in a series of scenes in which he calls the police to report Vassago's crimes (or to warn police about upcoming ones.) It would seem that Hatch himself would be a likely suspect, but the police are too dense to consider such a thing, and somehow Goldblum's quasi-naturalistic performance keeps the audience interested enough to ignore (but not forgive) the glaring script problems.

Christine Lahti is one of the best actresses around. Every now and then she is given a good role (*Housekeeping* [1987], *Running Scared* [1988]), but is rarely used to advantage on the big screen. In this film she is primarily required to be skeptical of Hatch's growing paranoia, and then fearful for her daughter's life. Lahti fills in the blanks of her rather sketchily drawn character with grace and intelligence.

This film might become known as one of the early films of Alicia Silverstone, who went on to great acclaim for her leading role in *Clueless* (1995). The young Silverstone mixes innocence with sophisticated sexiness. Silverstone has an excellent sense of truth, which particularly aids her scenes with her parents: about her father she says, sarcastically, "I mean, he's really on edge...dying and all" with perfect sarcasm and believable disdain for the older generation.

Other performances are satisfying if not brilliant: Alfred Molina is serviceable in a difficult role full of unintentionally humorous lines, such as "Your husband may seem a bit different to you"; Jeremy Sisto (who also appears in

CREDITS

Hatch Harrison: Jeff Goldblum
Lindsey Harrison: Christine Lahti
Regina Harrison: Alicia Silverstone
Vassago: Jeremy Sisto
Dr. Jonas Nyebern: Alfred Molina
Rose Orwetto: Rae Dawn Chong
Detective Breech: Kenneth Welsh
Zoe: Mara Duronslet

Origin: USA
Released: 1995
Production: Jerry Baerwitz, Agatha Hanczakowski, and Gimel Everett for S/Q; released by TriStar Pictures
Direction: Brett Leonard
Screenplay: Andrew Kevin Walker and Neil Jimenez; based on the novel by Dean R. Koontz
Cinematography: Gale Tattersall
Editing: B. J. Sears
Production design: Michael Bolton
Art direction: Sandy Cochrane
Set decoration: Elizabeth Wilcox
Casting: Amanda Mackey and Cathy Sandrich
Visual effects supervision: Tim McGovern
Sound: Rob Young
Costume design: Monique Prudhomme
Music: Trevor Jones
MPAA rating: R
Running Time: 112 minutes

Clueless), plays Vassago with a pretty-boy sneer and a valiant attempt at being frightening. If Sisto is a bit less than believable as a serial killer, it may only be because his physical appearance and stature are not immediately threatening. Finally, Rae Dawn Chong appears in a small cameo as a psychic. Chong has grown up gracefully since her early film roles, and plays her role in such a way that she avoids stereotypical New Age affectations and is still believable as a psychic.

This film is not great, but it is not bad, either. If it is a little less than horrifying, then audiences can scare themselves by thinking how Koontz as the author of the original book must feel.

—Kirby Tepper

Higher Learning

"Singleton sees with a clear eye and a strong will. His movies are thought provoking."—Roger Ebert, *Chicago Sun-Times*

"*Higher Learning* takes a lot of risks and shows a lot of cinematic skill."—Michael Wilmington, *Chicago Tribune*

"Bold and provocative."—Arthur Salm, *San Diego Union-Tribune*

Box Office Gross: $38,290,723

Michael Rapaport stars as a lonely student corrupted by a group of skinheads in *Higher Learning*. © 1995 Columbia Pictures Industries, Inc. All rights reserved.

For some people, an excellent film is a film that diverts its viewers from their daily life. For some, it requires action, great performances, or extravagant special effects. For others, it has to resonate with a message—to explore a theme in an intelligent way, examine it from all sides, and draw conclusions. *Higher Learning* is the latter—an intelligent film with a message. Its story and theme reflect cultural and political imperatives of the 1990's. For many, *Higher Learning* may be polemic or even corny, but it is undeniably germane to the American cultural context, of its time and it is unquestionably a film made with authority and insight.

John Singleton, the twenty-something wunderkind of American popular cinema, has made another socially relevant and engrossing film to add to his oeuvre. Singleton first came to the attention of the filmgoing public with *Boyz 'n the Hood* (1991); he was nominated for an Academy Award for that film's screenplay, and some critics believed that the film itself should have been nominated for best picture. *Boyz 'n the Hood* was followed by *Poetic Justice* (1993), which was not well received at the box office or by critics, and became notable mostly for the film debuts of its stars, Janet Jackson and Tupac Shakur.

College exteriors were filmed at USC and UCLA.

Yet Singleton seems to have touched a nerve again in *Higher Learning*. This film is powerful in large part because of its depiction of the current state of "multiculturalism" in America (as represented by its young people). The tragedies depicted in *Higher Learning* reflect the intensity of racial, ethnic, and sexual tensions that pervaded life in the United States at the time of its release. Most especially, this film is a polemic about the dangers of the "angry white male," a stereotype which could be tossed off as merely cinematic excess if it had not foreshadowed real-life events.

Singleton's prescience is remarkable: After this film was made, the United States' general elections of November, 1994, were swept by a conservative tide led by what media and political pundits termed "the angry white male." Racial issues dominated the new Congress: Funding for the Congressional Black Caucus was stopped, and nationwide affirmative action programs were on alert. Into this cultural context came Singleton's polemic about the dangers of angry white youth.

"You must rid yourself of the attitude that the world owes you something."—Professor Phipps to a student from *Higher Learning*

The story follows several students in their first year at fictional Columbus University. It emphasizes their growing awareness of, and varying degrees of difficulty with, the diversity on their campus. Malik (Omar Epps) is an urban African American on a track scholarship; Kristen (Kristy Swanson) is a debutante-type from conservative Orange County, California; and Remy (Michael Rapaport) is a disaffected youth from rural Idaho. Their stories are intermingled with those of several other students, most notably Fudge (Ice Cube), a student in his sixth year at Columbus who has much angry wisdom to impart. The students also come under the spell of the autocratic Professor Maurice Phipps (Laurence Fishburne).

The three main characters' stories are intertwined in a mosaic reminiscent of the style of Robert Altman's *Nashville* (1975) or *Short Cuts* (1993), in that the stories appear unrelated, but intertwine as they hurtle toward a melodramatic climax. Malik grows from a callow youth to seasoned adult. At first, he assumes that all he is good for is to run track, and that any learning is incidental to his experience at college. Encounters with Fudge—who says Malik should learn "just to learn," not to be a "trained Negro...a bell goes off and you run"—teach him that learning is found in other places than books. Dr. Phipps tells Malik that learning is more than memorization, that the purpose of the university is to teach him how to think.

Meanwhile, Kristen, a sheltered young woman, is introduced in a scene in an elevator that illustrates American racial tension perfectly: She holds her purse when Malik enters, afraid when she is alone in an elevator with a black youth. Yet the African Americans are not the ones she needs to fear: She is raped by a white youth. She then begins an inner journey, during which she becomes involved in a lesbian relationship and in political activism. She organizes the campus-wide "multicultural rally" that is the backdrop for the film's climax.

Remy, the disaffected white youth from Idaho, joins a group of skinheads led by the sinister Scott (Cole Hauser). Eventually, Remy's rage at his imagined loss of power—as a white male in a culturally and ethnically diverse school—sets off the tragic climax of the film. Though each one of the characters is a stereotype—the black athlete, the conservative-turned-liberal, and the angry-white-male—they are important to Singleton's theme that America in the 1990's had become a dangerous cauldron of seething enmity.

The performances are all first-rate. If anyone stands out, however, it is Michael Rapaport as Remy, perhaps because of the juiciness of his role. He appears to be the quintessential "nerd" whose powerlessness turns dangerous. His eruption in the dorm room with his Jewish roommate is powerful, and his scenes with the other skinheads are sinister.

Singleton's direction is stylish and perceptive. He uses some interesting devices in his storytelling: For example, when the youth who rapes Kristen calls her dorm room afterward to talk to her, Kristen's roommate, Monet (Regina King), answers, telling him he cannot talk to Kristen. This is done on a split screen; when he calls Monet a "black bitch,"

CREDITS

Malik Williams: Omar Epps
Kristen Connor: Kristy Swanson
Remy: Michael Rapaport
Taryn: Jennifer Connelly
Fudge: Ice Cube
Wayne: Jason Wiles
Deja: Tyra Banks
Scott Moss: Cole Hauser
Professor Maurice Phipps: Laurence Fishburne
Officer Bradley: Bradford English
Monet: Regina King
Dreads: Busta Rhymez
Billy: Jay Ferguson
Knocko: Andrew Bryniarski

Origin: USA
Released: 1995
Production: John Singleton and Paul Hall for New Deal; released by Columbia Pictures
Direction: John Singleton
Screenplay: John Singleton
Cinematography: Peter Lyons Collister
Editing: Bruce Cannon
Production design: Keith Brian Burns
Art direction: Richard Holland
Set design: Charles Daboub, Jr.
Set decoration: Michael C. Claypool
Casting: Jaki Brown-Karman and Kimberly Hardin
Sound: Veda Campbell
Costume design: Carol Oditz
Music supervision: Danny Bramson
Music: Stanley Clarke
MPAA rating: R
Running Time: 127 minutes

a "boing" sound highlights the stupidity of his statement, and her image on the screen appears to become larger.

The next scene shows African American youths going to the villain's fraternity house, pulling him outside, and demanding that he look Monet in the eye and tell her that she is a "beautiful black goddess, mother of the earth, queen of the universe." This unexpectedly poetic, and humorous, moment runs counter to racial stereotypes of the time: One would have expected the African Americans to beat up the white youth for revenge. It is an interesting sequence that speaks volumes about the insidiousness of racial prejudice.

Another interesting sequence occurs when Kristen makes love for the first time to Taryn (Jennifer Connelly). Singleton manipulates the screen, and the audience, to make it unclear whether Kristen is in bed with Taryn or nice-guy Wayne (Jason Wiles). The camera alternates between Kristen and her partner, and each time it returns to her partner, the partner alternates between Taryn and Wayne. All of this appears to be done in one "take," which makes it all the more interesting and better helps to underscore Kristen's ambivalence.

Singleton uses symbolism to great advantage; in particular, the statue of Columbus figures prominently. For example, when Remy meets the other skinheads for the first time, they are hovering around the statue of Columbus; their impending "takeover" of the university parallels Columbus' "takeover" of the indigenous people of this country. Later, the statue becomes the site of the death of an important character during the climactic melee. This strong imagery provokes comparison with Columbus' "discovery" of America, which many would say started the racial divisions in this country even before the country was formed. The death is the symbolic legacy of the white-male aggression.

Some critics said that the simplicity of Singleton's stereotypes belies his youth. In addition, the crowd scenes, such as the chaotic climax, are far from nuanced: At times, all the African Americans are in one group, all the Asians in another, the Latinos in another, and so on. Though the thematic importance of the balkanization of these disparate groups is evident, the visual images may be too simplistically drawn for some.

Whether this film is described as heavy-handed or brilliant, however, Singleton's commitment to his material and his ability to make interesting cinematic choices, derive good performances from young actors, and tell a story that makes its audience think are representative of the best in American filmmaking. Singleton holds great promise as both a fillmaker and a social critic.

—Kirby Tepper

REVIEWS

Daily Variety. January 9, 1995, p. 4.
Entertainment Weekly. January 13, 1995, p. 32.
The Hollywood Reporter. January 9, 1995, p. 10.
Los Angeles Times. January 11, 1995, p. F1.
The New York Times. January 11, 1995, p. B1.

Highlander: The Final Dimension

Box Office Gross: $13,829,734

Mario Van Peebles and Christopher Lambert star in *Highlander: The Final Dimension*. © Miramax Films.

Highlander: The Final Dimension is a sequel to *Highlander* (1986) and *Highlander II: The Quickening* (1991). The original *Highlander* began as a senior thesis by a film student at the University of California, Los Angeles and was produced on a modest budget. In that version, Connor MacLeod (Christopher Lambert), a 16th-century Scottish warrior, was grievously wounded in battle but discovered that he was immortal and would survive for many centuries until the "last gathering." Evidently the last gathering is something like the playoffs in professional basketball; most of the immortals who have died in combat over the centuries will manage to come back to life in order to participate in the climactic free-for-all.

The first two episodes of *Highlander* featured Sean Connery in a supporting role. His strong screen presence lent those films a certain gravity which is missing in the third and last "dimension." As Ramirez, a warrior who had lived for some 2,600 years and became a dashing Spanish caballero in his most recent incarnation, Connery provided a sorely needed explication of what had taken place in the past and what could be expected to take place in the future. In *Highlander: The Final Dimension* the viewers are evidently expected to be cultists who need no further guidance through the labyrinthine and seemingly endless story. It is difficult for a newcomer to understand the sequel without having seen the original.

The producers of *Highlander: The Final Dimension* reportedly spent $34-million, much of it on location shooting and elaborate special effects, and gave the production a big advertising and publicity sendoff in print and electronic media. The box-office results, however, were disappointing, proving once again that legendary director John Huston was right when he said that the three most important ingredients of a film were story, story and story. By the ninth week the film had faded from Variety's Domestic Box Office chart after grossing about $14-million on the reputed $34-million investment.

"After 400 years, patience is a virtue."—Kane from *Highlander: The Final Dimension*

Highlander: The Final Dimension is full of spectacular, state-of-the art special effects, including the recently developed trick of turning one person into someone else without any cutting-room hocus-pocus being detectable, as used to be the case in the days of *The Wolf Man* (1940) and *Dr. Jekyll and Mr. Hyde* (1941). In describing these computer-aided transformations, most of the reviewers have relied heavily on the neologism "morphing," short for "metamorphosizing," and sure to become an indispensable part of the language because so much morphing is being seen in films and on television commercials. The story, however, is weak, confusing, and buried under technical effects. The principals move back and forth in time, leapfrog from country to country, change identities, and come back to life after they have been decapitated or disemboweled. The protagonist and antagonist seem to be motivated by nothing but the most inflated macho egotism, as was the case in both *Highlander* and *Highlander II: The Quickening*. They keep repeating the phrase, "There can be only one," as if to assure the audience that all the chasing, fighting, shouting, and posturing has some serious purpose.

The film opens with a long prelude in which the wicked immortal warrior Kane (Mario Van Peebles) attacks Connor MacLeod (Christopher Lambert) and his teacher Nakano (Mako) in Nakano's secret hideaway in Japan. Mako prepares the viewers for all the morphing that is to follow by telling his devoted pupil, "Nothing is what it seems. First you must be aware and respect the power of illusion." Kane decapitates Nakano in a sword fight but is then buried under an enormous landslide. Some four hundred years later, Kane has escaped and is once again in pursuit of MacLeod because there can be only one immortal with power to rule the world. The chase takes the hero to many different parts of the world, including Japan, Morocco, Scotland, France, New York City and nearby New

Jersey. Along the way MacLeod meets beautiful archaeologist Alex Johnson (Deborah Unger), who has enough background knowledge to believe he is telling the truth about being an immortal. It turns out that Alex is actually the reincarnation of MacLeod's second wife Sarah, whom he has not seen since the French Revolution. They quickly make up for lost time in a nude love scene.

There is nothing tangible at stake until late in the film when Kane gets the idea of kidnapping Macleod's young adopted son. The viewer wonders why the villain, with his centuries-old store of villainous experience, did not come up with that inspiration sooner. Suddenly the story takes focus, whereas it has previously seemed like one of the many video games in which two duelists in exotic costumes are clashing just to provide entertainment for the player. Kane gets hold of the boy by morphing into the spitting image of MacLeod and going to pick him up at the airport. For some reason the supposedly crafty villain morphs back into his own terrifying persona as soon as he gets the boy into his car. Naturally the boy flees for his life. It would seem that morphing is only a short-term phenomenon because it uses up a lot of supernatural battery power. This is fortunate because otherwise nobody, either in the cast or in the audience, could be sure who anybody was. Anita Gates, a New York Times reviewer pointed out that after seeing this latest *Highlander* offering, "small children may be afraid to accept a ride home from adults they do know. ('How can I be sure you're really Aunt Sharon?')."

CREDITS

Connor MacLeod (Russell Nash): Christopher Lambert
Kane: Mario Van Peebles
Alex Johnson: Deborah Unger
Nokono: Mako
Sarah: Deborah Unger

Origin: USA
Released: 1995
Production: Claude Leger for Transfilm, Lumiere, and Fallingcloud; released by Dimension Films
Direction: Andy Morahan
Screenplay: Paul Ohl; based on a story by William Panzer and Brad Mirman, and on characters created by Gregory Widen
Cinematography: `Steven Chivers
Editing: Yves Langlois
Production design: Gilles Aird and Ben Morahan
Casting: Nadja Rona, Vera Miller
Costume design: Jackie Budin and Mario Davignon
Music: J. Peter Robinson
MPAA rating: PG-13
Running Time: 99 minutes

The film culminates in the long-expected final showdown between Kane and MacLeod. As in the first two episodes, both opponents are bathed in spectacular electrical effects which have something to do with the fact that they are immortal and hence are charged with neon-blue supernatural energy. MacLeod and Kane seem to be in greater danger of being electrocuted than of receiving a fatal blow from one of the unwieldy, old-fashioned broadswords. This combination of state-of-the-art special effects with old-fashioned weaponry has been the distinguishing feature of the entire series.

Christopher Lambert has played Connor MacLeod in all three *Highlander* films. The villains, heroines, and minor characters have been played by new actors and actresses in each sequel. Lambert does a creditable job in a difficult role. It has been pointed out, however, that there is a discrepancy between his rather weak voice and the macho character he portrays. Mario Van Peebles is effective as the villainous Kane and steals every scene in which he appears with the taciturn and world-weary MacLeod.

The reviews of *Highlander: The Final Dimension* were uniformly unfavorable. Film critics inured to horror, fantasy, and comic book characters seemed to be trying hard to evaluate this film on its own terms and searching for something good about it. The best they could come up with was a few kind words about the performance of Mario Van Peebles.

A film with such a jumbled story seems to bring out the sardonic wit in critics. The consensus was that the spectacular special effects and gratuitous springboarding from continent to continent were designed to cover up an empty story. Susan Wloszczyna of *U.S.A. Today* called it "Time-traveling tripe." Stephen Holden, reviewing the film for *The New York Times*, expressed the general sentiment when he wrote: "morphing is no substitute for acting." He also noted that Lambert's voice "sounds like a meek hybrid of Vincent Price and Peter Lorre." Derek Elley, reviewing the film for *Variety*, started off by calling it "an unbelievably trashy melt-down of the tartan warrior franchise" that provides "brainless fodder for undiscriminating auds." Johanna Steinmetz probably made the most accurate assessment when she wrote in the *Chicago Tribune:* "It's a movie best suited to audiences who greet flashy effects (such as talking severed heads), visible electric currents and the occasional morph with appreciative sighs of 'Cool!'"

Another critic used the compound adjective "straight-to-video" to describe the film and predict its probable fate at the same time. Producers of the many action-adventure and horror films flooding the market seem unperturbed by poor box-office receipts. The real prize seems to be the video market. Films that fail miserably at the box office and go more or less "straight to video" can still earn substantial profits after the stigmata of bad reviews and bad word-of-mouth reporting have worn off.

The first-run theaters cannot be ignored, however, because home viewers want to feel they are watching a feature film and not one that was "made for cable" or "made for video," although, in a sense, many of horror and science-fiction films were. It has been predicted by industry futurists that the major market for motion pictures will be in viewers' homes around the world and that movie theaters will serve primarily to validate productions as authentic feature films for which theater audiences paid top admission prices. This may explain why suburban multiplexes are often so empty on weeknights that the auditoriums are scarier than some of the features.

—Bill Delaney

REVIEWS

Daily Variety. December 28, 1994, p. 5.
The Hollywood Reporter. January 30, 1995, p. 12.
Los Angeles Times. January 30, 1995, p. F8.
New York Times. January 28, 1995, p. 11.
New York Times. February 5, 1995, p. H26.
Variety. December 5-11, 1994, p. 75.

High Risk

The cartoonish world of kung-fu and high-tech action movies is relentlessly spoofed in the remarkable *High Risk*, a dead-on parody of macho thrillers. Chinese director Wong Jing is so skilled at concocting characters, situations and dialogue that his film transcends the very cliches it mocks. The action and dramatic sequences are better executed than many of the films it satirizes, but rarely does a minute go by without a priceless comic punch. Devastatingly funny, often silly and sublimely over- the-top, *High Risk* is hampered only by the broken English of its subtitles, though at times the inept translation only adds to the effect.

High Risk is a send-up of everything brash and bold and bloody that Hong Kong or Hollywood has ever foisted on the world marketplace, from James Bond through *Die Hard*. It makes mincemeat out of the martial arts genre. At times Wong Jing may strain too hard to milk a laugh and he won't hesitate to get goofy, but the film doesn't rely on the inanity of the *Airplane*! or *Hot Shots!* school of parody. In fact, in its fight sequences and hardware wars *High Risk* is so well-done that it may confuse audiences into thinking it's serious.

The film is a relentless parody of Hong Kong film superstar Jackie Chan. As played by the rubber-faced Jacky Cheung Hok-Yau, the martial arts matinee idol Frankie Lane is a shallow, adolescent womanizer and boozer. He's become flabby with fame, chasing babes in bikinis around his mansion, drinking with abandon and relying more and more on stand-ins to execute his stunts, though his publicists still tell the lie that he never uses doubles.

His main double is his bodyguard, Kit Li, a loyal stand-in who is much more trim, fit and skilled than his famous boss. Kit Li is played by Jackie Chan's up-and-coming action-film rival, Jet Li. In a startling prologue to the film, we learn how two years earlier Kit Li, a counter-terrorist special agent, was foiled by a mysterious criminal known as the Doctor, who had taken a schoolyard full of children and teachers hostage on a bus. The quarry includes Kit Li's wife and young son. When Kit Li cuts the wrong wire on the bomb, the bus explodes, leaving him alone and bitter.

Naturally, the Doctor resurfaces as the mastermind behind a plot to steal a Russian Czar's priceless crown jewels during a glamorous exhibition at a Hong Kong hotel. Naturally, Frankie is invited and he brings along his father, a martial arts-wise elder who looks remarkably like Pat Morita of *The Karate Kid* flicks. Frankie doesn't think it's necessary to call on Kit Li. But Kit Li by chance overhears the Doctor speaking on a car phone when he pulls alongside him at a stoplight, and follows him to the hotel.

The Doctor's army of thugs includes a long-haired badass named simply Bond, whose lifelong ambition is to fight the megastar Frankie, and a spike-heeled black-haired heartless vixen. When the Doctor fingers an informant in his ranks and the guy takes the vixen hostage, the Doctor is unfazed: "She is always ready to die for me," he smirks. The Doctor's minions gain entry to the hotel and his troops eventually storm the place and shoot up the lobby. Filming the thievery through her handbag is a tough TV re-

CREDITS

Frankie Lane: Jacky Cheung Hok-Yau
Jet Li: Kit Li

Origin: Hong Kong
Released: 1995
Direction: Wong Jing
Running Time: 100 minutes

porter (Chingmy Yau) who is trying to get the goods on Frankie.

The mayhem that ensues allows Kit Li to hook up with a mild- mannered undercover cop and storm the hotel to take it back from the gangsters. They make the obligatory buddy duo, dodging the hail of bullets and crashing into the lobby in a small car that spins around in an hilarious gun battle. The car eventually rides up an elevator to the penthouse, where the gangsters are holding the guests hostage while their computer expert tries to crack the code that keeps the jewels encased in glass.

And that's only half the story. *High Risk* loads up on familiar action characters and plot devices, and all are dead on target. The humor plays off all the macho stereotypes of the genre. In a cleverly silly scene at a urinal, Frankie's output sound likes a trickle, then Bond steps up and you hear a river flowing. Kit Li, nicknamed simply Bold, is so courageous that when Frankie steps on an exploding mine, Kit Li grabs a baseball bat and hits the bomb away after Frankie removes his foot and it shoots into the air. When the TV reporter takes refuge in a bathroom, the gangsters discover her and start throwing in snakes—by the dozens—so she can portray the ultimate woman in peril.

The action is as relentless as the gags. As the police surround the hotel, the Doctor threatens to throw guests from the penthouse window every five minutes until his demands are met. Kit Li commandeers a police helicopter for a fiery rescue. There are extended showdown fight sequences between Kit Li and the Rabbit, the Doctor's right-hand man, and of course between Bond and Frankie, where Frankie finally sheds him wimp image and returns to razzle-dazzle kicking, leaping and karate-chopping. It's rare that a spoof does a better job at the essentials of the genre than the films it's spoofing, but that's one of the most amazing things about *High Risk*.

Wong Jing is so determined to exploit every opportunity to mimic standard action-film situations and characters that the film is a bit overlong, but it's not a big problem because it rarely slows down. There are plenty of plot twists and turns, but it's the over-the-top characters and the frenzied battles that carry the film. Down to the smallest part, the characters are perfect at their charade of mimicking familiar thrill-film roles. You've seen all these people before, but you haven't seem them quite this outrageous.

The only glaring problem with the English-language version of the film is that the subtitles are only passably English. But this almost adds to the hilarity. Since *High Risk* mocks just about everything that Hollywood has exported, it's only fitting that American audiences should read the dialogue in fractured form. The essential points come across unmistakably well.

If the Marx Brothers were still around and took a sabbatical in Hong Kong, they might have come up with something akin to *High Risk*. Mop-topped Jacky Cheung is a broad comic who is funny at being a ridiculous clown. But everyone else plays it straight, with tongues firmly in cheek.

High Risk is too low-brow and cheesy to be hailed as brilliant by critics, but it's the kind of film that could garner worldwide appeal through word of mouth. For fans of the action genre as well as for those who jeer at the stupidity of many action films, *High Risk* has the makings of a cult classic. It is thoroughly satisfying entertainment. And while it amuses, it reveals how absurd our global video amusement park has become.

—*Michael Betzold*

REVIEWS

Los Angeles Reader. July 14, 1995.
San Francisco Chronicle. Dec. 15, 1995, p. C3.

Home for the Holidays

"On the fourth Thursday in November, 84 million American families will gather together...And wonder why."—Movie tagline

"A lastingly enjoyable comedy. Filled with juicy performances."—Jay Carr, *The Boston Globe*

"A rambunctious comedy! A spirited cast! Foster keeps the party hopping!"—Peter Travers, *Rolling Stone*

"Foster piles on plenty for her terrific cast to chew on and for us to savor."—Susan Wloszczyna, *USA Today*

Box Office Gross: $17,237,852

For any adult who has ever been faced with a visit back to his or her childhood home, *Home for the Holidays*, the second film from actress-turned-director Jodie Foster, offers up a celebration of dysfunctionalism in an amusing collection of cinematic recollections about one family's attempts to make it through yet another Thanksgiving holiday. For a filmmaker so character-driven in her own work, Ms. Foster's choice of material here is puzzling. Rather than presenting a small, intimate portrait of a family, Ms. Foster chooses instead to resort to farcical vignettes with such cloying inter-titles as "Relatives" and "The Point."

For the first time in her career as an art restorer, Claudia Larsen (Holly Hunter) discovers passion in her work. Too bad it happens on her last day on the job. Budget cutbacks cause her to be fired right before she is to fly home to Baltimore to spend Thanksgiving with her family, leaving behind her teenaged daughter, Kitt (Claire Daines), who intends to lose her viginity while her single mother is away. The family reunion soon degenerates into maliciousness and familial loathing.

Ms. Foster succeeds in presenting a family that is simultaneously worse and better than most realistic families, one with more than its fair share of quirky characters, but also more accepting and compassionate than most. The Larsons are a collection of crackpots who are supposed to be lovable in their eccentricities: the father (Charles Durning) who frustrates his bitter, chain-smoking wife (Anne Bancroft) with his senile ineffecutality, the gay son (Robert Downey, Jr.) with a secret alternative lifestyle who tortures his sisters with his juvenile pranks, the flatulent aunt (Geraldine Chaplin) with a fondness for lamps and inappropriately timed confessions who still harbours an unrequited love for her sister's husband. The problem is Ms. Foster, in true Hollywood form, has embraced these quirky—and often selfish—characters at the cost of those who have done little wrong except to have accepted their "normalcy." Claudia's sister Joanne (Cynthia Stevenson) and her hard-working banker husband Walter (a perfectly cast Steve Guttenberg) are the butt of the family's jokes and contempt, despite the fact that it is Joanne who performs her daughterly duties as caretaker to her aging parents, thus allowing Claudia and Tommy the freedom to live more independent lives, far removed from the family's controlling grasp. One of the film's few truly revealing—and human—moments occurs when Joanne confesses to Claudia that one of the only times she relishes in her life is when she is exercising on her Stairmaster. As Joe Morgenstern writes in his *Wall Street Journal* review, "...she's a picture of antisocial climbing in the age of aerobic isolation."

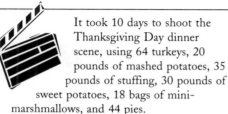

It took 10 days to shoot the Thanksgiving Day dinner scene, using 64 turkeys, 20 pounds of mashed potatoes, 35 pounds of stuffing, 30 pounds of sweet potatoes, 18 bags of mini-marshmallows, and 44 pies.

Lacking any deep insights into family dynamics, the script by W.D. Richter, best known for his directorial work on the sci-fi cult favourite *The Adventures of Buckaroo Banzai Across the Eighth Dimension* (1984), was based on a short story that appeared in the *Boston Phoenix* newspaper and offers little more than stereotypical characters who stubbonly refuse to change through the course of the story. Or perhaps it is Ms. Foster's direction that is more to blame, serving up broad-stroked farce in lieu of storytelling, for there are traces of a deeper, painful need and longing within Claudia that periodically force their way to the surface.

The basic premise of *Home for the Holidays* is a good one, one that most Americans in their thirties and forties can probably relate to: being subjected to the scrutiny of well-meaning relatives who can quickly reduce the less-than-complete confidence of adults into dependent children longing for acceptance. It appears that even the most self-sufficient, successful adult can be left feeling like a failure after one trip back to their childhood home. But Ms. Foster and Mr. Richter seem reluctant to explore the pathos of dysfunctional families; it is as though they are afraid of offending the viewer, lest they not be liked (a sign of true codependency!) and as a result, the film never cuts to the emotional bone. It takes a swipe at its victims, but immediately backs away from any kind of real confrontation. The result is all surface meanness without any deeper understanding of the underlying dynamics at work. Ms. Foster seems reluctant to incorporate her own personal experiences into the work. (The actress/director reportedly was alienated for a time from her real-life mother.) The writer and director miss golden opportunities to "go for the jugular," which is what many family members might do, in part because emotions at this time of the year are so raw. The family in the film is quirky and annoying, but there are only fleeting glimpses of the anger and the fear that obviously formed the dynamics of their relationships. Why, for example, is Tommy so reluctant to reveal that he is gay? His parents may not wish to discuss the issue, but in the end they seem to accept things without much resistance. In this film, things are uncomfortable, but rarely painful. In the film's most painfully touching scenes, sister Joanne confesses her dislike for Claudia. "If we met on the street and you gave me your phone number," Joanne tells her sister, "I'd throw it away." "We don't have to like each other, Joanne," Claudia replies, "we're family." Unfortunately, this relationship is abandonned in lieu of the more unbelievable Prince Charming episode where Claudia finds her apparent soulmate in the form of Leo Fish (Dylan McDermott at his most charming), brother Tommy's mysterious friend whom Claudia assumes is also his latest lover. At a time when Claudia seems to be fighting for her independence, she is forced (through story conventions) to find her true salvation in the arms of a dashing knight sent to rescue her. This whole sequence is jarring and disturbing in its old-fashionned sentimentality and insulting in its insinuation that all Claudia really needs is a man to make it all better. The cameo appearance of David Strathairn as an old lovelorn schoolmate succeeds in succinctly painting a far more revealing, albeit painful, portrait of a man afraid to take chances in life.

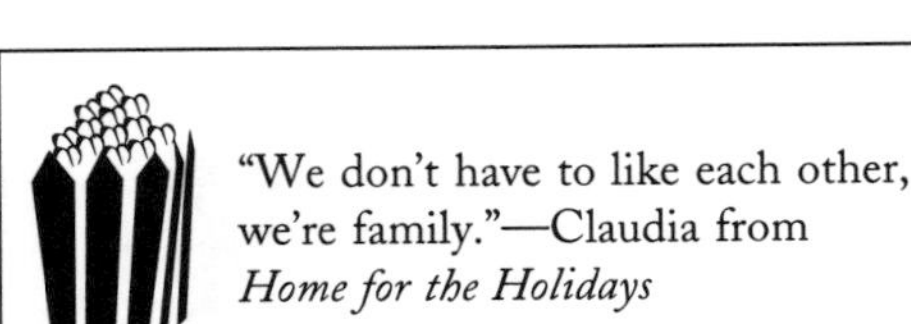

"We don't have to like each other, we're family."—Claudia from *Home for the Holidays*

As a director, Jodie Foster lacks a definite vision. Perhaps it is her youth and over time she may find a visual style with which she is comfortable. Unlike fellow directors Diane Keaton (*Unstrung Heroes*, 1995) and Quentin Tarantino (*Reservoir Dogs*, 1992 and *Pulp Fiction*, 1994), both of whom possess a strong sense of connectedness to their choice of material, Ms. Foster's work remains competent, but uninspired. She may connect to her material on some emotional level, thus explaining her first film, *Little Man Tate* (1991), yet she never fully succeeds in the visual translation of that passion. She remains detached and risks little by playing it safe in most of her choices.

Holly Hunter's presence helps to hold this film together, with her girlish yet aging looks and her forced smile, but the role of Claudia offers her little chance to extend her character repertoire. Essentially a reprise of her character from *Broadcast News* (1985), Hunter brings no surprises to her work here, which is not to say that she is in any way unwatchable. The actress imbues Claudia with an undercurrent of sadness and longing that could easily have been missed. It is a pity that she has very little to work against in the other characters. The other actors are all competent, but

CREDITS

Claudia Larson: Holly Hunter
Adele Larson: Anne Bancroft
Henry Larson: Charles Durning
Tommy Larson: Robert Downey, Jr.
Leo Fish: Dylan McDermott
Aunt Glady: Geraldine Chaplin
Joanne Wedman: Cynthia Stevenson
Walter Wedman: Steve Guttenberg
Kitt: Claire Daines
Russell Terziak: David Strathairn

Origin: USA
Released: 1995
Production: Peggy Rajski and Jodie Foster for an Egg Pictures production; released by Paramount Pictures
Direction: Jodie Foster
Screenplay: W.D. Richter; based on a short story by Chris Radant
Cinematography: Lajos Koltai
Editing: Lynzee Klingman
Production design: Andrew McAlpine
Art direction: Jim Tocci
Set decoration: Barbara Drake
Costume design: Susan Lyall
Music: Mark Isham
Casting: Avi Kaufman
MPAA rating: PG-13
Running Time: 103 minutes

REVIEWS

Boxoffice. December 1995, p. R-104.
Entertainment Weekly. November 10, 1995, p. 35.
Los Angeles Times. November 3, 1995, p. F1.
Macleans. November 13, 1995, CVIII, p. 78.
The New Yorker. LXXI, November 13, 1995, p.128.
The New York Times. November 3, 1995, CXLV, p. C8.
Rolling Stone. November 16, 1995, p. 116.
Variety. October 30, 1995, CCCLX, p. 70.
Village Voice. November 14, 1995, XL, p. 90.
Wall Street Journal. November 3, 1995, p. A12.

their characters are for the most part too thinnly drawn to have much impact. In fact, when Claudia queries, "Who are these people? Where did I come from?" one tends to have a greater sense of empathy than the filmmakers might have intended.

Reviews for *Home for the Holidays* were decidedly mixed. Some critics, including *Entertainment Weekly*'s Owen Gleiberman, went so far as to call the film a "turkey," pun intended.

—*Patricia Kowal*

Houseguest

"an enjoyable romp!"—*New York Post*
"Hilarious!"—*Sneak Previews*

Box Office Gross: $26,325,256

What do *My Blue Heaven* (1990), *Milk Money* (1994), *Trapped in Paradise* (1994) and *Groundhog Day* (1993) have in common? They are all recent fish-out-of-water stories whose urban protagonists somehow find their way into suburban America, with varying levels of success in their resultant humor.

Houseguest (1995), starring *Saturday Night Live* star Phil Hartman and television comic Sinbad, similarly takes an urban fish out of the city and puts him in suburban paradise, also with varying results. Of those films mentioned, only *Groundhog Day* seemed to fully catch on with audiences, perhaps because of its clever script and Bill Murray's deadpan performance. *Houseguest* succumbs to some of the same over-the-top antics that submerged *My Blue Heaven*, yet it gives some decent screen time to the charismatic Sinbad and the brilliantly funny Hartman.

Besides being a fish-out-of-water film about the collision of urban life and suburbia (with racial overtones), this is also a buddy film. And like all buddy films (and more sitcoms than anyone would care to count), this one teams two personalities which are polar opposites, predictably having each of them learn from the other. This premise is as old as the hills, but continues to be used frequently. It has become axiomatic (and cliche) that if there are two lead males in a film or television comedy, the free-wheeling and mischievous nature of one will be in direct, inverse proportion to the uptight and conservative other. *Houseguest*, while having some very funny moments, nevertheless reminds its audience that these buddy/polar opposite films have become too formulaic. There is little left to surprise an audience, and as good as its two leads are, a weak script and some tired cliches put its stars at a disadvantage as they try to invoke the memory of great comic duos like Abbott and Costello, Laurel and Hardy, and even Eddie Murphy and Nick Nolte.

The story is simple. Kevin Franklin (Sinbad) is a destitute pie-in-the-sky optimist who owes $50,000 to a gangster named Happy Marcelli (Don Brockett). His two henchmen, the Gasperini brothers (Paul Ben-Victor and Tony Longo), threaten to kill Kevin if he doesn't pay off his loan. Trying to save his skin, Kevin attempts to leave town, but is chased around the airport by the inept Gasperinis. He finds a safe escape amidst the dysfunctional but friendly family headed by Gary Young (Phil Hartman), a man who mistakes Kevin for a college buddy he is supposed to pick up at the airport. Kevin pretends to be Gary's old college friend so he can hide out with Gary's family. During his stay at the chaotic Young household, he learns the value of friendship and selflessness, and Gary learns the importance of enjoying the wonderful gift of his family, and the importance of enjoying each day. The lessons they learn aren't exactly complicated discoveries, but they are certainly in keeping with the values portrayed in most contemporary film comedies.

Along the way to these discoveries are some fun episodes in which Kevin is forced to pretend he is the college friend (whose name is Derek Bond), a world-renowned dentist, wine connoisseur, and all-around bon vivant. Some of the situations are inane (such as most of the scenes with the Gasperini brothers), but many sequences are downright hilarious. The best comedy comes from Kevin's initial attempts to discover information about the man he is impersonating so he can remain safely undercover. From the beginning, Gary's ingenuousness helps Kevin lie about his identity: Gary doesn't seem to no-

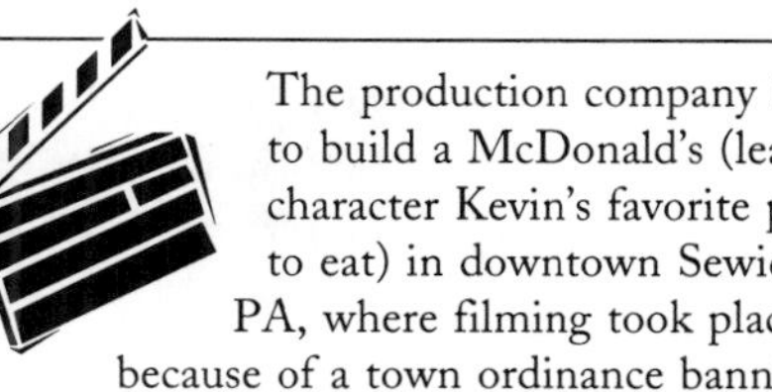

The production company had to build a McDonald's (lead character Kevin's favorite place to eat) in downtown Sewickly, PA, where filming took place, because of a town ordinance banning fast-food restaurants in the historic village.

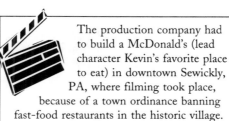

tice that his old college buddy has trouble remembering the lyrics to their old college song, or that Kevin doesn't seem to know anything about "the thing" that he has come to town to do. His willingness to do "the thing" becomes very funny, as Kevin simply nods knowingly whenever it is mentioned. "The thing" turns out to be a career day for the local school, but until he is pushed out on stage in front of a school assembly, he has absolutely no clue what he does for a living. Compounded by the fact that the hostess of the event has "lost your card, but you can introduce yourself," Kevin's dilemma seems to have gotten as bad as it can when the hostess reminds him that the slide show he sent in advance is ready to go. He starts the slide show, discovering that Derek Bond is a dentist when huge slides of decaying teeth appear on an enormous screen.

This sequence is emblematic of what director Randall Miller is capable of: he stacks the deck against his protagonist and lets him squirm—with hilarious results. Unfortunately, the rest of the film lacks the wit demonstrated in the aforementioned scene. But Kevin is confronted with a few of these situations before the film's end, and Sinbad's rapid fire talk and charming delivery are what keeps the film buoyant.

CREDITS

Kevin Franklin: Sinbad
Gary Young: Phil Hartman
Ron Timmerman: Jeffrey Jones
Emily Young: Kim Greist
Larry the tattoo artist: Stan Shaw
Joey Gasperini: Tony Longo
Pauly Gasperini: Paul Ben-Victor
Mr. Pike: Mason Adams
Jason Young: Chauncey Leopardi
Sarah Young: Talia Seider
Brooke Young: Kim Murphy
Dr. Derek Bond: Ron Glass
Vincent Montgomery: Kevin West
Steve: Kevin Jordan

Origin: USA
Released: 1995
Production: Joe Roth and Roger Birnbaum for Hollywood Pictures, in association with Caravan Pictures; released by Buena Vista Pictures
Direction: Randall Miller
Screenplay: Michael J. Di Gaetano and Lawrence Gay
Cinematography: Jerzy Zielinski
Editing: Eric Sears
Production design: Paul Peters
Art direction: Gary Kosko
Set decoration: Amy Wells
Casting: Rick Montgomery and Dan Parada
Sound: David MacMillan
Costume design: Jyl Moder
Music: John Debney
MPAA rating: PG
Running Time: 109 minutes

Sinbad is particularly adept at being charming and sharp-witted without crossing the boundary into the world of the obnoxious. His rapid-fire, improvisational style is sure to remind filmgoers of Robin Williams: both have a loose-cannon quality mixing cutting-edge humor and screen charisma, and though Sinbad is not as well-rounded an actor as Williams, his ad-lib style is far less chaotic.

He falters a bit in the climatic (and more serious) scenes, in which Kevin is called upon to make the obligatory eleventh-hour switch from being a selfish oaf to being an enlightened do-gooder. But the scenes in which he tries to figure out how to behave are fun, as are his funny put-downs of an irritating would-be rapper (Kevin Jordan) and his sweet interactions with the youngest of Gary's children (Kim Murphy). (Like *ET* [1982] and numerous other films, it is the youngest daughter who is able to see the truth.)

Phil Hartman gets a chance at a big-screen role after years of work on television's *Saturday Night Live* and years of second-banana work in television and films, and does a characteristically wonderful job. He is among the most sophisticated of comic actors working today, texturing his broad character with subtle looks and gestures that make him believable. Hartman plays Gary as a stressed-out Dad who is bright at work but oblivious to the dysfunction going on at home. His obsequious attention to his bigoted boss (Mason Adams) mixed with his inattention to the problems with his children (one has problems at school, one wears all black and reads Sylvia Plath poetry all day), make him a character who would be otherwise unlikable. But Hartman's good-natured acceptance of the imposter in his home make him a sort of a suburban Mr. Magoo: he's so myopic about life that his is somehow lovable. He can make a non-funny line like "You're gonna have to work harder, son, if you wanna make the big leagues" hilarious just by adding a satirical edge that is impossible to describe.

Director Miller has an unusual style that might serve other vehicles quite well. A young director (and former actor) of such television as *Northern Exposure*, Miller brings a fast pace to the film adding some visual spice by utilizing occasional slow-motion or high-speed film to enhance the comic effect. Often Miller and editor Eric Sears create an occasionally breakneck pace characterized by extremely fast edits. These quick cuts seem to be designed to enhance the dialogue by writers Michael J. Di Gaetano and Lawrence Gay. At times the pace becomes dizzying, especially in more than one sequence featuring the Gasperinis and their boss. These fast sequences, besides being visually a bit irritating, can make it hard to follow just who is saying what to whom. Where the film truly misses is in its cliche moments (such as Kevin's insipid speech about friendship at the end of the film), its over-the-top comic villains, its overly fast pace, and its occasional lapses into crudeness.

Like a lot of films these days, the director and writers have been trained in the fast-paced medium of television, where jump cuts are de rigueur and humor doesn't always have to be truly clever since it can be "sweetened" by a laugh track. Without the safety net of a laugh track, the film's unfunny moments stand out when compared to its numerous funny ones. Perhaps these creators will fully reach their potential next time out.

—*Kirby Tepper*

How to Make an American Quilt

"There's beauty in the patterns of life."—Movie tagline

"A world-class ensemble performance piece."—Garrett Glaser, *KNBC*

"Absolute perfection."—Rex Reed, *New York Observer*

"Wonderful and joyous. Do yourself a favor and go."—Jeffrey Lyons, *Sneak Previews*

Box Office Gross: $23,574,130

Anne Bancroft, Ellen Burstyn, Winona Ryder, Alfre Woodard, and Kate Nelligan in *How To Make An American Quilt.* © 1995 Universal City Studios, Inc. Courtesy of MCA Publishing Rights, a Division of MCA Inc. All rights reserved.

An impressive cast of female actresses is spread far too thin in Jocelyn Moorhouse's *How to Make an American Quilt,* a feeble attempt to recreate the multi-generational, episodic "chick's flick," *The Joy Luck Club* (1994). Based on the best-selling novel of the same name by Whitney Otto, this film adaptation suffers from too many characters too thinly drawn. The stories, told through flashbacks, tend to be repetitive, all centering around the core belief that while men are basically adulterous liars incapable of monogamy, any man, apparently, is better than no man at all. If the viewer is searching for a "thinking woman's film" about relationships, both male/female and female/female, one would do better to keep looking. Given the countless stories of smart women making foolish choices, *American Quilt* could more easily have been renamed after the pop-psychology self-help bestseller by Dr. Laura Schlessinger, *Ten Stupid Things That Women Do to Mess up Their Lives.* While no one expects perfection—it would not make for very compelling story-telling, even if it existed—the only healthy relationship to be found in this film involves a man who is already dead.

Winona Ryder stars as the 26-year-old Finn Dodd, a graduate student who suffers a serious fear of commitment, both in her reluctance to settle on a thesis topic and in her personal relationship with Sam (Dermot Mulroney), a carpenter who has just asked Finn to marry him. "The more I know about something, the less I want to know," Finn reveals in her narration. When Finn panics and decides to spend the summer at her grandmother Hy's house in northern California, Sam reluctantly drives her, intending to renovate the house that they share while she goes off for her third attempt at finishing her thesis, this time on handicrafts and culture. Despite their share of marital mishaps that threatened to destroy their relationship, Hy (a subtle performance from Ellen Burstyn) shares her house with her peppery sister Glady Joe (an over-the-top Anne Bancroft). The two are members of a quilting bee, headed by master quilter, Anna (poet Maya Angelou). As the group, which includes Anna's illegitimate daughter Marianna (Alfre Woodard), the critical Em (Jean Simmons), and the frustrated and bitter Sophia (Lois Smith), gathers to make a wedding quilt for Finn, they each reveal their own, mostly tragic, significant relationships through the use of flashbacks. While the stories are intended, one suspects, to help Finn overcome her rampant anxiety, it is surprising that the young woman stays around as long as she does. The quilt is "where love resides," we are told, and is meant as a metaphor for life and love, made with a variety of experiences and emotions—a metaphor that tires after only two stories.

Taking on a strange mystical bent that attempts to parallel Anna's story of the black raven that led her great grandmother to the man of her destiny, the hokey ending finishes off the film, which throughout has been less than favorable in its depiction of men's ability, or rather inability to sustain a relationship, with a touch of the proverbial toss of the dice. Forget about following your heart, follow that crow instead. Nowhere are women held responsible for the choices they make in their lives: it is all held up to fate. None of the women in the film acknowledge, however, that Finn's anxiety about marrying Sam might indeed be justified. These characters all seem so cosmic, yet no one is willing to grant Finn her moment of "woman's intuition" that seems to be telling her to flee from marriage. Instead, it is all written off as some sort of fear of commitment on Finn's part. One wonders how none of these "wise" women could question whether Sam is indeed the right man for Finn. It doesn't matter, they all seem to be saying to Finn, if the idea of marriage is causing you such torment, do it anyway. In di-

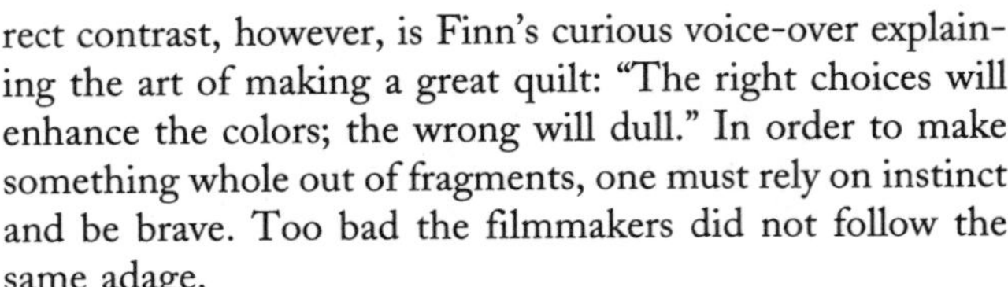

rect contrast, however, is Finn's curious voice-over explaining the art of making a great quilt: "The right choices will enhance the colors; the wrong will dull." In order to make something whole out of fragments, one must rely on instinct and be brave. Too bad the filmmakers did not follow the same adage.

In order to transform Otto's novel into film, several significant changes had to be made, most of which resulted in a severe weakening of the very elements that made the book such a resounding critical success. Screenwriter Jane Anderson, who scripted the hilarious HBO film, *The Positively True Adventures of the Texas Cheerleader Murdering Mom* (1993), chose to restructure the *Quilt* story by grafting on the narrative of Finn's rocky relationship with Sam and by concocting the inane rival for Finn's affections, Leon (Johnathon Schaech), as if there is ever a moment that the audience doubts who Finn will end up with. Otto's novel was cinematically problematic from the beginning since it lacked a strong character presence throughout the course of the book, as well as a definite narrative line. In many ways it is more of a short story collection than a novel. Nonetheless, the filmmakers would not be deterred in their search for box office gold and so they plunged ahead with their plans to bring *How to Make an American Quilt* to the screen. (Even the title was confusing: many people thought the story was about the making of the Aids Memorial quilt, rather than an exploration of relationships.)

Australian director Jocelyn Moorhouse, whose edgy story of a blind photographer, *Proof* (1991), was a memorable debut, fails to give *American Quilt* a definitive voice of its own. The film meanders, metaphorically searching for an answer to any question. The film has its moments—most notably when Ms. Nelligan movingly conveys the significance of her quilting square, which Anna objects to because it throws off the color scheme of Finn's quilt—but overall the film suffers from stodgy pacing and simply too many stories that are not imaginatively sequed to and from, as in the far more effective *The Joy Luck Club*.

Winona Ryder is by far the film's weakest link. Her voice drones through the voice-over narration with a pervasive ennui that mirrors the actress's on-screen performance. The actress is so bland and boring that it becomes increasingly difficult to care much about her character's dilemma. "How do you merge into a couple and still keep a piece of your own identity?" Finn asks. It is helpful if you have an identity to begin with. The talented Ryder is so stifled in this role that

CREDITS

Finn Dodd: Winona Ryder
Anna: Maya Angelou
Glady Joe: Anne Bancroft
Hy: Ellen Burstyn
Constance: Kate Nelligan
Em: Jean Simmons
Sophia: Lois Smith
Marianna: Alfre Woodard
Sally: Kate Capshaw
Sam: Dermott Mulrooney
Dean: Derrick O'Connor
Arthur: Rip Torn

Origin: USA
Released: 1995
Production: Sarah Pillsbury and Midge Sandford; A Univeral release of an Amblin Entertainment production
Direction: Jocelyn Moorhouse
Screenplay: Jane Anderson, based on the novel by Whitney Otto
Cinematography: Janusz Kaminski
Editing: Jill Bilock
Production design: Leslie Dilley
Art direction: Ed Verreaux
Costume design: Ruth Myers
Music: Thomas Newman
MPAA rating: PG-13
Running Time: 116 minutes

AWARDS AND NOMINATIONS

Screen Actors Guild Awards Nominations 1995:
Best Cast

one wonders if she was merely overwhelmed by the sheer star power of her legendary co-stars. Ellen Burstyn, of Martin Scorsese's *Alice Doesn't Live Here Anymore* (1974) and the beautiful and highly underrated *Resurrection* (1980), has aged beautifully and elegantly and still captivates the screen, while her counterpart, the formidable Mrs. Robinson to Dustin Hoffman's *The Graduate* (1968), Anne Bancroft has the most fun with the more flamboyant Glady Joe, a woman nearly destroyed by the revelation that her husband (Rip Torn) has a brief liaison with her own sister. Alfre Woodard, a consistently exceptional actress, is wasted here in a thinly conceived part. It is never clear how her character ended up in Paris nor why she chose to return to her hometown. Instead we are treated to the occasional French phrase and a cup of cafe au lait. So much for character development. Most notable among the younger cast members is Samantha Mathis as the young Sophia.

"I've never liked full moons; it gives people an excuse to act foolish."—Anna from *How to Make an American Quilt*

One of the film's more obvious problems is the audience is only told of the touching qualities of men, but they are never dramatized, merely drawn in overblown sentimental ways. For example, the philandering artist, Dean, is to be forgiven for his consistent adulterous ways merely because he has several paintings of his wife on display in his studio? Seems like a very pathetic trade-off. In fact, all of the women's stories, with the exception of Constance (Kate Nelligan), the outsider who moved to town with her now deceased husband, leave one feeling as though the single greatest thing that women do in life is take abuse—and they are proud of it. It is one thing to praise women's ability to survive, to endure hardship; it is another to celebrate their willingness to be treated poorly and their apparent need to be in a relationship at all costs. Not being able to walk away from a dysfunctional relationship when it is inflicting pain is not love, it is co-dependency with a capital C. The fact that this film was written, directed and produced by women and stars some of the most talented actresses in the business is sad. There is very little uplifting and encouraging about *How to Make an American Quilt*; it is refreshing, however, to finally have a story that acknowledges that there are strong women alive and well and living outside of the South. Reviews for the film were decidedly mixed—depending, perhaps, on the respective critic's vulnerability with regards to his/her own relationship at the time of viewing.

—*Patricia Kowal*

REVIEWS

Chicago Tribune. October 6, 1995, p 5.
Detroit Free Press. October 6, 1995, p. D1.
Entertainment Weekly. October 13, 1995, p. 56.
Los Angeles Times. October 6, 1995, p. F6.
New Republic. October 30, 1995, p. 34.
The New York Times. October 6, 1995, C12.
USA Today. October 6, 1995, 2D.
Variety. October 2, 1995, p. 61.
Village Voice. October 24, 1995, XL, p. 76.

How to Top My Wife

When a philandering film executive (Joong-Hoon Park) decides to have his shrewish wife (Jin-Sil Choi) killed, he makes the mistake of hiring an extremely inept professional assassin (Chong-Won Choi) to do the job.

CREDITS

Bong-Soo Park: Joong-Hoon Park
So-Young Chang: Jin-Sil Choi
Heri: Joung-Hwa Eum
Killer: Chong-Won Choi
Director: Hyoung-Gi Cho

Origin: Korea
Released: 1995
Production: Woo-Suk Kang for Kang Woo Suk Production Company Ltd.; released by Morning Calm Cinema
Direction: Woo-Suk Kang
Screenplay: Sang-Jin Kim and See-Uk Oh
Cinematography: Kwang-Suk Chong
Editing: Hyun Kim
Music: Kyung-Shik Choi
MPAA rating: no listing
Running Time: 100 minutes

The Hunted

"He's trapped in a world where killing is an art and revenge is an obsession."—Movie tagline

Box Office Gross: $6,607,652

Among the sharp, rather negative reviews that were written about *The Hunted* was a review titled "Ninja Nonsense" in the *Chicago Tribune*, by Michael Wilmington who was right on target. This is a rather ridiculous, violent film with a silly plot about a New York businessman (Christopher Lambert) who stumbles into an ancient Ninja warrior battle while in Nagoya on business. Talk about your nightmare business weekends! And it is hard to tell which is more nightmarish, the mayhem witnessed by Lambert's character, or the excruciatingly foolish film witnessed by audiences. (Anyone who intentionally rents the video deserves what s/he gets.)

Written and directed by J.F. Lawton, whose previous writing credits include *Under Siege* (1992) and *Pretty Woman* (1990), neither of which are remembered for the brilliance of their screenplays, this story seems intended to be an action thriller with occasionally dry wit. Instead, there are periodic moments of wit, and occasionally strong visual images, but Lawton outdoes even *Pretty Woman* in laying on the cliches. It is the story of Paul Racine (Lambert), who has one night of passion with a exotic temptress played by Joan Chen. Having met in the bar of his hotel, and sharing a romantic exchange about his boxer shorts ("Piggies?" squeals Chen. "I love piggies," Lambert revealingly responds). Chen's character is stalked and killed by a legendary Ninja warrior (who happens to be her old boyfriend) named Kinjo (John Lone). But unfortunately for Lambert (and for the audience, for this is what propels the rest of the film's plot), Lambert has returned to the room long enough to glimpse—in slow motion—the entire murder. And more importantly, he sees Kinjo's face. Ancient Ninja custom being what it is, Lambert must die now that he can identify Kinjo.

Christopher Lambert is a Western businessman fighting for his life in *The Hunted*. © 1995 Universal City Studios, Inc. Courtesy of MCA Publishing Rights, a Division of MCA Inc. All rights reserved.

The rest of the film concerns itself with Lambert's flight from Kinjo under the protection of yet another legendary

Ninja warrior named Takeda (Yoshio Harada). Takeda, out to revenge some vaguely explained wrongs done in the past, is the greatest swordfighter this side of...well...everywhere. So, Lambert's character must learn to use a samurai sword as well, if only to show that he learned something during the production of his previous swordfight epics, *Highlander* I (1986) and *Highlander II* (1991).

Takeda is aided in his protection of Racine by a devoted woman named Mieko (Yoko Shimada). They wisk Racine off to an island which seems to be a training ground for Ninja warriors, and is highly reminiscent of the mysterious-island-samurai-training-grounds found in *Enter the Dragon* (1973) and countless other martial-arts films. The reader can predict the ending, so it is unnecessary to point out that Racine proves to be a man of great character—not to mention that he learns how to be a samurai in a matter of days. It never seems to occur to him that he should hop on a plane and get away from all these dueling samurai, but then, that would ruin the plot.

Jonathon F. Lawton (whose screenplays include *Pretty Woman* and *Under Siege*) makes his feature directorial debut based on his original screenplay.

CREDITS

Paul Racine: Christopher Lambert
Kinjo: John Lone
Kirina: Joan Chen
Takeda: Yoshio Harada
Mieko: Yoko Shimada
Junko: Mari Natsuki
Oshima: Tak Kubota

Origin: USA
Released: 1995
Production: John Davis and Gary W. Goldstein for Bregman/Baer Productions and Davis Entertainment Company; released by Universal Pictures
Direction: J. F. Lawton
Screenplay: J. F. Lawton
Cinematography: Jack Conroy
Editing: Robert A. Ferretti and Eric Strand
Production design: Phil Dagort
Art direction: Sheila Haley
Set decoration: Lin MacDonald
Casting: Karen Rea and Doreen Lane
Sound: Larry Sutton
Costume design: Rita Riggs
Stunt coordination: Buddy Joe Hooker and John Wardlow
Music: Motofumi Yamaguchi
MPAA rating: R
Running Time: 110 minutes

Lawton's script seems to have some subtextual undercurrents about the strength of the soul and the nobility of fighting to the death. It is hard to discern whether Lawton, who once penned a film called *Cannibal Women in the Avocado Jungle of Death* (date unknown), is serious. Sometimes it is obvious that he is kidding, and he hits the mark. When a skeptical police detective (Tak Kubota) is issuing orders to his underlings, they respond to nearly every one of his phrases with "hai" (yes), nodding each time. At the end of their exchange, he tells them, "just one 'hai' at the end is sufficient." There are also a couple of fun moments as Racine flips channels on a television set and encounters *Magnum P.I.*, starring Tom Selleck, dubbed into Japanese; and another scene where the detective says "this isn't ancient Japan; we don't have Ninjas running around with swords"—and just then, a Ninja shoots a dart into his back, killing him. Lastly, when Mieko tells Racine about a particular type of poison, saying "in small doses it helps you see into the world of the spirits," to which he responds, "I'll use it next time I go to a Grateful Dead concert." For those brief—very brief—moments, the film feels like it wants to have the fizz of and old *Get Smart* episode, where the characters played it straight but the satire was unmistakable.

But unfortunately, it seems that satire was not Lawton's priority. In trying to make an exciting action film, he has reverted to numerous tired cliches, and the result is an unintentionally funny film. One of *The Hunted*'s most wonderfully tacky dialogue exchanges goes as follows: "Was it not your plan to have my soul weakened so you could betray me?" says one character. The other responds, "The foreigner has stolen a piece of my soul...test me...see if I have lost my powers." Another comic moment is when John Lone, a fine actor whose credits include *The Last Emperor* (1987) and *M. Butterfly* (1993), waxes eloquent about Joan Chen's character: "Kirina...the whore with the face of a goddess and the spirit of a tiger. I can't believe that the Gods wanted such a woman to die."

Another endless sequence is as unintentionally campy as it is violent. When Takeda and Mieko first try to protect Racine, they rather callously use him as bait to get the bad-guy Ninjas to follow them on to a commuter train. The two move from car to car, politely telling the passengers, "ladies and gentlemen, dangerous men are coming from the front of the train...please move to the rear..hurry." The passengers comply wordlessly, which seems impossible, even if director Lawton were playing this for laughs. Takeda, Mieko, and Racine (who tries to use a gun only to have it tossed out the window by Takeda) hold back the army of bad guys, and somehow end up in the lounge car, fighting Kinjo's henchmen to the end. Besides the attempted humor in that

they end up in the lounge car, the purpose of this sequence is unclear. But the effect is certain: it further anesthetizes its audience.

With all of the intentional and unintentional humor described above, it would seem that this film might have some campy appeal to audiences who enjoy movies that are "so bad they're good." But this one is hard to fit into that category. It lacks that "certain something" found in camp classics such as *Plan Nine from Outer Space* (1959). Perhaps that "certain something" is naivete. Lawton's insistence on real gore, and on the constant use of dramatic and insipid references to the spirits and to the soul, indicate that the film aspires to more than laughs. A film this violent could hardly be considered a spoof, intentional or not.

"How much blood must I bathe in to get clean?"—Assassin Kinjo from *The Hunted*

Additionally, Lambert's sleepy performance as the Hitchcock-style hero who falls into trouble quite accidentally is no help to the film. Lambert is rather droll at times, but is too dry to make the film a cartoon, and too laconic to infuse it with some badly needed energy. As Takeda, Yoshio Harada has some strong moments as a man who has an ancient score to settle. Harada is reminiscent of Charles Bronson, only he seems to be an actor of wider range and more depth. His is the best performance in the film. Joan Chen's brief turn is fine—she is luminous, as always, but the role is small. And John Lone is only a disappointment because of the silliness of his role and because his commitment to the truth of the character seems ludicrous in the face of the insipid dialogue he must utter.

Oddly enough, one of this film's worst enemies is its lighting. It seems to be lit as if all of the action were taking place on a stage: overly theatrical lighting takes away a much-needed illusion of reality, not to mention that the daylight and indoor scenes seem simply too bright. Lawton does find some nice visual images, however, most strikingly in dreamlike sequences where Kirina returns to Racine to foretell the future or to just merely look lovely. One of the best of these scenes is shot entirely in black and white, except for the red of Kirina's dress and lips. It is quite beautiful, and seems an anomaly among the other rudimentary visual images in the film.

It is difficult to discern whether writer/director J.F. Lawton started to write a spoof and lost his way, or merely wrote and directed a cheesy martial arts action picture which coincidentally had some funny lines. Perhaps the fairest thing to be said is that *The Hunted* aims high and misses the mark.

—*Kirby Tepper*

I Can't Sleep

"Daring and original! With its rough-edged chic, this is the most pungent vision yet of the new multiculti Paris."—J. Hoberman, *Premiere*

"Sensational! Definitely one of the year's best films."—Georgia Brown, *Village Voice*

The appeal of film genres, in particular that of the thriller, could be said to lie in playing upon our expectations, as much as rising above them. In other words, the familiar plot elements in a successful thriller form a kind of inviolable substratum. Only Hitchcock could risk killing off his heroine in the first reel in Psycho (1960).

French director Claire Denis, known here for her first feature *Chocolat* (1988), takes a Hitchcockian gamble in *I Can't Sleep*, by playing up the socio-political dimensions of her thriller plot, and keeping its customary elements at a cold distance. Given her trans-cultural background, having grown up in Africa and now working in France, it would appear natural for her to be concerned with the present cultural remapping of Europe, after the lifting of the Iron Curtain.

While a true case, comprising twenty serial murders of elderly Parisian women, seems to have provided the film with its inspiration, its real concern would appear to be not that well-publicized case, which has been solved, but similar cases that remain unsolved beneath the city's veneer of normalcy, creating an existential dislocation from which there is seemingly no recourse.

"Security is very subjective," a local radio talk-show host muses, as the hysteria mounts. "Who can be safe from death?" Irony thus functions as the film's predominant tone. The film opens inside a police helicopter over Paris. The two police officers who should be surveying the city are instead laughing hysterically, at what we do not know. As the camera looks down at the traffic, through the morning fog, it becomes clear that the film's omniscient viewpoint is going to provide us the thrill of watching human lives intersect. Amongst them, we first come to know Daiga (Katerina Golubeva), who is driving into the city from Lithuania. As an aspiring actress, who also happens to resemble Michelle Pfeiffer, her hopes of acting on the Parisian stage have to be put on hold, while she ekes out a living as a maid in a hotel that caters mostly to foreign tourists.

In turn, we come to know Theo (Alex Descas), a black violinist, who is living with his little son, whom he intends to keep from the clutches of his estranged French wife, Mona (Beatrice Dalle). Theo dreams of returning to Martinique and living an idyllic existence. Meanwhile, he supports himself doing odd jobs as a carpenter. Theo's brother, Camille (Richard Courcet), is a homosexual druggie who, with his male lover, Raphael (Vincent Dupont), lives in the hotel where Daiga works. From all appearances, Camille is a harmless gender bender, who gets his kicks by performing as a transvestite singer. It is only in the second half of the film that we come to know that it is he and Raphael who are the serial killers.

The film's mosaic of nonconformist lifestyles brings into relief two sets of interrelationships: one, between Theo, his son and Mona; and two, between Camille, Raphael and their rich, elderly victims. Daiga, in their midst, functions as the rootless outsider, at the bottom of the economic heap, but whose faculties as a detached observer allow her to get the better of them all. It is only when one of their victims pretends to be dead, and subsequently describes them to the police, that sketches are circulated that closely resemble Camille and Raphael. When Daiga is brought into a police station for a traffic violation, she notices the sketches, but says nothing. Instead, Daiga follows Camille to make sure of his whereabouts. She then sneaks into his room and ransacks his belongings until she finds what he has stolen. That night, Camille is nabbed by the police. In the morning, he calmly confesses to each of the murders. Only Daiga seems to have won out, as she slips back into anonymity, no longer excluded from what the free world has to offer.

> Based on the true story of the 1987 French murders of more than 20 elderly women. "Granny Killer" Thierry Paulin died of AIDS before his trial, while partner Jean-Thierry Mathurin is serving a 20-year sentence.

Georgia Brown, in *The Village Voice*, calls *I Can't Sleep* "one of the best films" to be released in 1995. She notes that "the film is not scary or suspenseful," nor is it a portrait of a serial killer. She finds the murders "are so distanced, you don't experience them as real and Camille never really becomes a murderer in the viewer's eyes. The killer, this sort of movie says, can be any one of us." Caryn James in *The New York Times* also notes the film's deviation from the norms of its genre: "This work is nothing like *Henry: Portrait of a Serial Killer* (1990) and other films infused with a sense of psychosis. Instead, its eerie, ominous tone comes from the sense that evil is subtle and inconspicuous, not worn like a sign around a killer's neck." Dave Kehr, in *The New York Daily News*, remains unconvinced that the killer could be a product of social alienation. "Surely," he argues, "it takes more than a sense of difference to turn a person into a cold-blooded destroyer of human life. Denis leaves too great a gap between the character she portrays and the acts she depicts."

No doubt the film's uncompromising stance towards its subject matter could well explain the nearly two year wait for an American distributor.

—*Vivek Adarkar*

CREDITS

Daiga: Katerina Golubeva
Camille: Richard Courcet
Raphael: Vincent Dupont
Doctor: Laurent Grevill
Mona: Beatrice Dalle
Theo: Alex Descas

Origin: France
Released: 1995
Production: Bruno Pesery; released by New Yorker Films
Direction: Claire Denis
Screenplay: Claire Denis and Jean-Pol Fargeau
Cinematography: Agnes Godard
Editing: Nelly Quettier
Running Time: 110 minutes

REVIEWS

Entertainment Weekly, September 8, 1995.
New York Times, August 11, 1995.
The New York Daily News, August 11, 1995.
Village Voice, August 15, 1995.

In the Land of the Deaf

In the Land of the Deaf is a documentary about French people born deaf and taught to communicate in sign language. Although some are adults, it is the children who make the film appealing. Their natural charm, their unawareness of the future consequences of their affliction, and their very normal playfulness make the viewer identify with their teachers, who display admirable concern and tolerant affection. Viewers may be reminded of Francois Truffaut's *Argent De Poche* (1976, *Small Change*), although the low-budgeted *In the Land of the Deaf* lacks Truffaut's storytelling skill and professionalism.

Adults describe their past lives in sign language translated in English subtitles. Each story is one of rejection and suffering. Often as children they were thought to be retarded and not worth teaching. Some were so mistreated by parents and siblings it was a miracle they survived.

During much of the running time there is no sound. The effect of silence is to transport the viewer into "the land of the deaf." The viewer begins to realize that this land is not altogether inferior to the land of honking horns, blasting stereos, and strident commercials.

Jean-Claude Poulain, the head sign-language teacher, explains in sign language so eloquent it hardly needs subtitles that the deaf compensate with heightened visual awareness which helps them appreciate things "hearing" people overlook. It is one of the advantages of being born deaf. They are also more sensitive to figures of speech in language (e.g. having "one's head in the clouds" or being "all tied up").

The charming Poulain—who has the same gift for communicating with facial expressions and body language as his celebrated countryman Marcel Marceau—explains that sign language is not an international language. There is French sign language, English sign language, and so forth. The various sign languages have so much in common, however, that a French visitor to China can converse with a deaf Chinese within a matter of days. This is another advantage of being born deaf, provided that one has the kind of instruction demonstrated in the film.

There is hardly any plot. The film is a pastiche of intercuts. A little boy named Florent co-stars with Poulain. This mischievous child, who has yet to realize the gravity of his affliction, tries his teacher's patience to the limit. The viewer is made to appreciate the Herculean work involved in teaching deaf children, not only to communicate in sign language, but to enunciate well enough to communicate with the dominant majority who can hear.

The film intermittently follows a young deaf couple for a period of about a year. They are married in a ceremony conducted in sign language. Later they go to rent an apartment and have to bring along a translator to negotiate with the landlord. Although they will be living among hearing people, they will still be living in the land of the deaf. Nevertheless, their relative success in leading normal lives is used to dramatize the hope now held out.

The viewer feels some degree of envy for these deaf people who, like artists, can see more in the world around them. In addition, those who have had good training in sign language can communicate with one another more poetically, more metaphorically, than most hearing people would dream of trying. In one scene six people carry on three separate conversations at a table without any of the confusion that would result if three hearing couples tried to talk at once. It seems as if these deaf people enjoy their conversations more than others. They communicate with faces as well as hands, making them look more animated, more vivacious, more intelligent, and more attentive. They also belong to a sort of international fraternity and find friends everywhere.

The viewer leaves the theater with mixed emotions. One is enhanced appreciation of human intelligence, resilience, and adaptability. Another is compassion for the people—and especially for the children—born with this handicap. Still another is respect for those dedicating their lives to helping people who in earlier times could have ended up as beggars or village idiots.

CREDITS

Jean-Claude Poulain: Jean-Claude Poulain

Origin: France
Released: 1994
Production: Serge LaLou for Les Films d'Ici, La Sept-cinema, Centre Europeen, and Cinematographique Rhone-Alpes; released by the International Film Circuit
Direction: Nicolas Philibert
Screenplay: Nicolas Philibert
Cinematography: Frederic Labourasse
Editing: Guy Lecorne
Sound: Henri Maikoff
MPAA rating: no listing
Running Time: 99 minutes

REVIEWS

The New York Times. September 14, 1994, p. B3.

The title *In the Land of the Deaf* encapsulates the thesis of this touching documentary. Those who are born deaf live in a world within a world—a world of deprivation and pain but sometimes surprising beauty. Implicit throughout is the message that the deaf are worth helping, both for humanitarian and pragmatic reasons. It is wrong to consider them retarded or otherwise inferior. They can become successful members of society. They have no need of pity or charity, only understanding.

—*Bill Delaney*

In the Mouth of Madness

"The best film in John Carpenter's career."—Paul Wunder, *WBAI Radio*

Box Office Gross: $8,946,580

Director John Carpenter returns to his horror-film roots with *In the Mouth of Madness*, a confused and confusing jumble of high-minded fear and low-brow cheap thrills. Ultimately it fails on both levels.

As the film opens, insurance investigator John Trent (Sam Neill) is being dragged kicking and screaming into an asylum. It is intimated, through cryptic whispers, that the world outside the institution has gone crazy—perhaps murderously so—and that John is just one of many more to come. Despite his protestations of sanity, John is thrown into the proverbial padded cell and has to tell his story to a psychiatrist. Much of the rest of the film is told in flashback, an odd choice considering the ultimate theme.

At first, John was leery when he was told of the disappearance of horror novelist Sutter Cane (Jurgen Prochnow), thinking it to be a publicity stunt. Charlton Heston plays the novelist's publisher who persuades John to try to find Sutter Cane. Without warning, John is plunged into the horrific world of the writer as he is attacked, quite without provocation, by an ax-wielding maniac. Apparently, Sutter Cane's readers are fanatics who anticipate his new novel, entitled *In the Mouth of Madness*, with a frenzied glee. Rumor has it that simply reading the book will drive the reader insane.

Screenwriter Michael De Luce says his work was inspired by American macabre novelist H.P. Lovecraft, whose work frequently appeared in *Weird Tales Magazine*.

John gleans an idea from Cane's novels as to where he may be hiding. He teams up with Cane's editor, Linda Styles (Julie Carmen). John and Linda develop an immediate love-hate relationship: He is the sarcastic cynic, and she the hardened New Yorker with an attitude as tight as her hair bun and a temper as short as the skirts she wears. They travel through New England and wind up in Hobb's End, a picture- postcard little town that cannot be found on any map. It is the setting of Sutter Cane's novels.

Once there, Linda slowly begins to believe that they have somehow been transported inside of Cane's new novel. It is a fascinating concept: Are they real or merely characters at the whim of an obviously mad author? Or are they simply being set up as John believes? It is a shame that the filmmakers could not do more with such a great premise.

Although the device of telling the story in flashback does not mesh well with the concept, it is the first few minutes of the film that are the most interesting. Armed with a deliciously macabre humor, the opening scenes in the insane asylum are a great hook. Look for a great cameo appearance by John Glover—it will be difficult to listen to The Carpenters' music in quite the same way.

As soon as it delves into the meat of the story, *In the Mouth of Madness* sinks under its own pretensions, trying for a cerebral scare that is not very scary. In fact, the story's villain, the murderous and insane Sutter Cane, simply is not frightening. He is more odd than evil, engendering a good chuckle rather than a good scare.

The film labors along with characters that are not developed enough for the audience to understand what is happening to them, much less care. With considerations to the reality vs. fiction premise aside, it would have been interesting, for example, to examine the roots of John's cynicism. Armed with this knowledge, the viewer may have been more inclined to accept the plot developments that otherwise leave nothing more than a bewildered look of amusement. All of this finally leads to an ending so confusing that the viewer is left expecting another twenty minutes of film.

Sam Neill acquits himself well with what he has to work with. His portrayal of John Trent is the most interesting aspect of the film. Having developed his skills at acting against special effects in *Jurassic Park* (1993), Neill does well up against the various gremlins and goblins that inhabit Hobb's End. When he has to have a conversation with another person, however, the poorly written dialogue tends to weigh him down. Ultimately it is difficult to fault the choices or acting style of anyone in this film; they may have been a group of talented people looking for a way out of a bad script.

"Yeah, well, you'd think a guy that outsells Stephen King would find better representation."—John Trent from *In the Mouth of Madness*

Having stated that, Julie Carmen seems utterly bewildered in her role as the tough yet sensitive New York editor Linda Styles. Again, it is difficult to differentiate which was the culprit, the actor or the part, but some of her lines will inspire unintentional laughter. Carmen has had a long and varied career on stage, television, and screen, so one has to give her the benefit of the doubt.

Distinguished German actor Jurgen Prochnow plays the horror novelist Sutter Cane. As stated earlier, he is supposed to be the villain of the piece, the man responsible for madness, murder, and the return of Satan himself. Yet he is not particularly frightening. Prochnow plays the man who is evil incarnate as a grandiose version of a tent- revival preacher. If he is not saying something "important" (which the audience is cued into by the low-angle close-up and swelling underscore), he is looming in the background or laughing maniacally.

Charlton Heston is, quite simply, wasted in this film. His part is small, almost inconsequential to the plot, and poorly written. This is the man who played Moses in Cecil B. DeMille's *The Ten Commandments* (1956) and now he gets three scenes where he sits behind a desk and does nothing but grin knowingly. This is yet another example of wasted resources, which plagued this film.

Director John Carpenter practically reinvented this genre. His *Halloween* (1978) moved horror films into modern times and inspired countless imitators. Whether this is a compliment or an indictment depends upon one's point of view. Perhaps this is why *In the Mouth of Madness* is so disappointing. Carpenter seems to have been undecided as to what this film should have been. It could have been a great dark comedy, as the first fifteen minutes of the film suggest, but then the humor is all but abandoned. It could have succeeded as a cerebral and psychological mind-bender, but a lack of logic reduces it to a mishmash of half-thought ideas and boring cliches. It could have been a visceral thrill ride, but even the simple (some would say cheap) scares do not work.

An example of this last point is how, at a quiet moment, something slams into the door near the hero and the door practically cracks down the middle from the sheer force. This is a standard setup: Lull the audience into a false sense of security, make them think that everything is going to be all right, and then scare the hell out of them. In *Halloween* it was the moment when Laurie, having just done in Michael Myers with a well-placed coat hanger to the eye, practically collapses in the doorway—with her back to the supposedly dead killer. The happy music plays and the audience thinks the credits are about to roll when he sits up suddenly!!! The audience screams, popcorn is spilled, and the arms of chairs are gripped tightly.

These kind of scares, of which there are many, do not work in *In the Mouth of Madness*. It could be the direction, the editing, the script, or even that this device has simply become cliche. Whatever the reason, the result is a horror film that does not horrify.

The script, by a former film-company executive, is full of half- realized ideas and underdeveloped characterizations. Some of the dialogue is so corny as to be laughable, and certain entire scenes inspired the same reaction. For example, John Trent hears muffled screams and a gruesome, wet

CREDITS

John Trent: Sam Neill
Linda Styles: Julie Carmen
Sutter Cane: Jurgen Prochnow
Jackson Harglow: Charlton Heston
Dr. Wrenn: David Warner
Saperstein: John Glover
Robinson: Bernie Casey
Paul: Peter Jason
Mrs. Pickman: Frances Bay

Origin: USA
Released: 1995
Production: Sandy King; released by New Line Cinema
Direction: John Carpenter
Screenplay: Michael De Luca
Cinematography: Gary B. Kibbe
Editing: Edward A. Warschilka
Production design: Jeff Steven Ginn
Art direction: Peter Grundy
Set decoration: Elinor Rose Galbraith
Casting: Back Seat Casting, Ross Clydesdale
Visual effects supervision: Bruce Nicholson
Special visual effects: Industrial Light and Magic
Sound: Owen A. Langevin
Special makeup effects: Robert Kurtzman, Gregory Nicotero and Howard Berger
Costume design: Robert Bush and Robin Michel Bush
Music: John Carpenter and Jim Lang
MPAA rating: R
Running Time: 94 minutes

chopping noise coming from the basement of an inn. Now the average person would have called the police, run from the inn, moved to Bolivia, anything except go into that dark basement. This being cinema, however, this otherwise intelligent man descends into the murky cellar calling out someone's name merely to draw a little more attention to himself.

It all comes back to the premise of the film—reality vs. fiction: Are these real people or characters within a novel? If they were real people (within the film) then there may have been a chance for the audience to get involved with their story. This is the foundation for any film, be it comedy, drama, romance, or horror. If they are fictional characters within a fictional story making choices that only occur in fiction, it is nearly impossible to "hook" the audience and get them to come aboard for the ride. *In the Mouth of Madness* suffers from a weak script and fails to deliver the anticipated chills and thrills.

—Rick Garman

REVIEWS

Boston Globe. February 3, 1995, p. 55.
Daily Variety. January 31, 1995, p. 10.
Denver Post. Feburary 3, 1995, Weekend Section, p. 6.
The Hollywood Reporter. January 30, 1995, p. 6.
Houston Post. February 3, 1995, Section F, p. 1.
Los Angeles Reader. February 10, 1995, p. 30.
Los Angeles Times. February 3, 1995, p. F6.
Los Angeles Weekly. February 10-16, 1995, p. 58.
The New York Times. February 3, 1995, p. 17.
The Village Voice. February 7, 1995, p. 51.

The Incredibly True Adventures of Two Girls in Love

"A dazzling debut that brims over with humor and heartbreak."—Peter Travers, *Rolling Stone*

"Tender, witty, and unabashedly romantic."—Amy Taubin, *Village Voice*

"It's *Pretty in Pink* with lesbians."—Rita Kempley, *Washington Post*

Box Office Gross: $1,977,544

The Incredibly True Adventures of Two Girls in Love is an incredibly delightful find. This romantic and charming film is the sort of independent film, like *Ruby in Paradise* (1994) or *Spanking the Monkey* (1994), that audiences love to discover. Its subject matter—a love story about two high-school-aged lesbians—may cause potential audiences to stay away, thinking that it has nothing to do with them.

Audiences who miss this film will miss a delightfully told story about two very sweet people who meet and fall in love. *Two Girls* has the sense of truth found in other excellent films about high school love, such as *Say Anything* (1989). It is a thoroughly charming film whose central relationship is sweetly performed by two unknown but gifted actresses. Its effervescent direction by Maria Maggenti (who wrote the script) represents the best in independent filmmaking.

"I didn't say I was gay. I said I was in love. I'm the same Evie."—Evie explaining her homosexual relationship to old friends in *The Incredibly True Adventures of Two Girls in Love*

The story behind the film is that director Maggenti pretended she was a lesbian in order to circumvent fears from potential investors that she would not be able to accurately or respectfully portray the subject matter. This is the kind of rumor that swirls around the making of a successful independent film, especially ever since the inspiring true stories of the making of *Hollywood Shuffle* (1987) and *El Mariachi* (1992), both of which have achieved legendary status for the ingenuity of the directors in getting their films made. Whether or not this rumor is apocryphal, in an increasingly political world it is likely that a heterosexual director might feel that gay or lesbian investors would feel uncertain that this material would be handled without bias or stereotype. (In any case, the story goes that after the filming, she "came out" as a heterosexual.)

Rumors aside, the important issue is that Maggenti is a talented writer and director, not whether she is heterosexual. She presents the film in a loving and matter-of-fact way. Never are the characters portrayed as curiosities because they are lesbian. Unlike the tragic lesbian characters of other films, such as *Sister, My Sister* (1995) or *Heavenly Creatures* (1994), these characters are not pathological or bizarre. They are a family of people who have the same struggles as anyone else. "Let's sit down and eat dinner like the normal family that we are," says one character.

And they are a normal family. They just aren't typical. Randy (Laurel Holloman) is a free-spirited ("I'm a strong believer in impulsive behavior") teenager who lives with her aunt Rebecca (Kate Stafford) and her aunt's girlfriend (Sabrina Artel). They are also playing host to her aunt's former girlfriend (Toby Poser) who is now a friend of the family. Just like any family, they are concerned about their jobs ("yesterday at work a man called me 'sir'") and about Randy's education ("that's the tenth time in two weeks that you've been late [to school].") While struggling to get good enough grades to graduate, Randy works at her aunt's gas station and is involved in a relationship with a married older woman, Wendy (Maggie Moore).

She breaks the relationship with Wendy when she meets beautiful Evie (Nicole Parker), a straight girl from school who is breaking up with her boyfriend. Discovering a mutual bond that transcends their cultures (Evie is African-American) and their socio-economic status (Evie is rich, Randy is poor), they form a relationship that is tender and loving. Unfortunately, their families and friends don't seem to think it is such a good idea for them to be together, and the latter part of the film is centered on their efforts to remain with each other in spite of the injunctions of their families.

The *Romeo and Juliet/West Side Story* angle to the film works to provide conflict where none otherwise exists, and might seem a bit contrived to some audiences. It is hard to discern the reason for the urgency with which their families and friends descend upon them in the final scenes, all of them hell-bent on destroying the girls' relationship. However, it does provide a fine backdrop for the romance, and it is fun to watch all the characters descend upon the hotel where the girls are fugitives, ready to duke it out for the final scene.

Writer-Director Maggenti, without spending a great deal of money (the simple lighting, the lack of special effects, and the use of unknown actors keeps the budget way down), has imprinted the film with her own sense of style. For example, after Evie and Randy first meet, a series of scenes showing them at home listening to very different types of music is an interesting way to illustrate the differences between them. Maggenti also handles the love scenes with great delicacy: a scene in which they silently hold each other's hands over the table in a restaurant is erotically charged. The lovemaking scenes are handled with a restraint and intelligence that would have been welcome in "mainstream" films (the overexaggerated and overplayed love scenes in *Basic Instinct* [1992] come to mind).

That is not to say that this is a wildly original film: there are still the ubiquitous scenes of the girls getting to know each other amidst lush pastures and tall grasses, the kind of scenes found in *When Harry Met Sally* (1989) and countless other films about romance. But Cinematographer Jack N. Green's camera occasionally catches its protagonists from a different angle, such as high overhead looking down over a high school locker; these moments add up to illustrate Maggenti's ability to inject her own visual style. It will be interesting to see what she does with a bigger budget.

As Randy, Holloman is funny and vulnerable. This actress is quite a find, able to provide a balance between intelligence and sexiness. She wears her character's free-spirited nature like a comfortable old shoe (in fact, her character's free-spirit is represented in part by her old Converse high-top sneakers.) It is hard to see why anyone as "cool" as Randy would have trouble making friends, but a scene in which other kids make fun of her points out how hard it is to be in high school and to be "different." Holloman is a perfect protagonist, always engaging and touching.

Parker is a fine counterpart to Holloman's easygoing goofiness. She confronts her mother with grown-up psychobabble ("Why, when I try to separate from you, which is a natural adolescent impulse, and in fact, crucial to my development....") and is very mature, indeed. But Parker has an underlying naivete that is valuable to her character: she is very much the "poor little rich girl" whose life is enriched by her relationship to Randy. She is also a perfect foil to three selfish friends who respond to her disclosure that she is a lesbian with "who can we tell...why do we have to be the only people with this information?" The scenes between the four friends are very funny, especially when one friend tells her that she is "under some sort of spell." Parker is adept at showing the hurt underlying her beautiful exterior, and when her friends decide to end the friendship rather than condone her relationship with Randy, Parker's sense of loss is palpable.

CREDITS

Randy Dean: Laurel Holloman
Evie Roy: Nicole Parker
Wendy: Maggie Moore
Rebecca Dean: Kate Stafford
Vicky: Sabrina Artel
Lena: Toby Poser
Frank: Nelson Rodriguez

Origin: USA
Released: 1995
Production: Dolly Hall; released by Fine Line Features
Direction: Maria Maggenti
Screenplay: Maria Maggenti
Cinematography: Tami Reiker
Editing: Susan Graef
Production design: Ginger Tougas
Art direction: Betsy Alton
Costume design: Cheryl Hurwitz
Sound: Steven Borne
Music: Terry Dame
MPAA rating: R
Running Time: 90 minutes

The other actresses are not quite as sophisticated in their performances as the two leads. In particular, Maggie Moore seems to try a bit harder than is necessary in order to portray the slatternly Wendy. Perhaps Maggenti allows Moore a bit much latitude in playing the comedy of her character, but the character's broadness does not match the realism of the other actresses. She is aided in broadly sketching her character by costumer Cheryl Hurwitz, who has dressed her in clothes that are a bit over-stylized.

Though there are some rudimentary shooting techniques (Randy and her "normal, typical lesbo household" share a meal crowded around one side of a table in order to fit into the camera frame) and a couple of missteps in the acting (long pauses in an important argument between Evie and Randy take away from the momentum and the realism), this is an entertaining and well -played film. Maggenti has a way with dialogue: when someone says that girls mature faster than boys, the response is "don't you think they would even out by the age of 17?" And occasionally, Maggenti's overhead shots and unusual angles suggest an artistic and clever visual eye. With a bigger budget, Maggenti could make better films than the over-praised king of the high-school genre, John Hughes (*Ferris Bueller's Day Off* [1986], *Pretty in Pink* [1986]).

Whether or not audiences find this to be a brilliant film, they are sure to be entertained. Beyond that, this film is atypical enough to show a slice of American family life not covered under the traditional and hackneyed "family values" structures, and simple enough to be classified as "not too threatening" for those who would dare to venture beyond conventional, big-budget filmmaking.

—Kirby Tepper

REVIEWS

Philadelphia Inquirer. June 30, 1995. p. 6
Detroit Free Press. July 2, 1995. p. 6G
New York Times. June 16, 1995. p. C3
Village Voice. June 20, 1995. p. 48.

The Indian in the Cupboard

"Enchanting...Classic..."—Michael Medved, *New York Post*

"Unlock the secret of the best family entertainment choice of the year."—Michael H. Price, *New York Times News Service*

"Thumbs up! A wonderful new movie. Cutting edge special effects."—Gene Siskel, *Siskel & Ebert*

Box Office Gross: $35,617,599

The only mystery in *The Indian in the Cupboard*, a remarkably restrained family film, is why it took fifteen years for Lynne Reid Banks' wonderful 1980 novel to get to the big screen. Banks' smartly conceived and perfectly executed fantasy about a nine-year-old boy with a magical cupboard that brings toys to life is a natural for film.

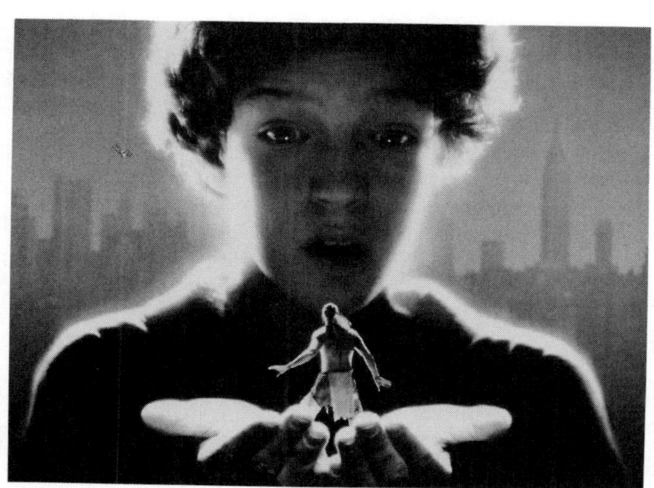

Hal Scardino as Omri and Litefoot as Little Bear, a three-inch tall, living Indian, in *The Indian In the Cupboard*. © 1995 Columbia Pictures Industries, Inc. All rights reserved.

Director Frank Oz (best known for his Muppet movies), young newcomer Hal Scardino, a native American rap singer named Litefoot, character actor David Keith and a large crew of technological wizards prove a winning combination. They and screenwriter Melissa Mathison give *The Indian in the Cupboard* almost reverential treatment. Despite a huge budget, the filmmakers do not overwhelm the story with bells and whistles.

In fact, the effort is a bit underwhelming. Mathison, who wrote *E.T.* (1982) and co-authored *The Black Stallion*

(1979), excluded a few plot twists from what was already a simple story. Instead of London, she has moved the setting to New York. But otherwise Mathison hasn't modernized or jazzed things up much, and the film is still a powerful lesson about growing up.

Omri (Scardino) gets a strange present for his ninth birthday: an old cupboard his older brother has found. Omri's mother Jane (Lindsay Crouse) has a collection of keys, one of which fits the cupboard. Omri puts a toy Indian in the cupboard, then hears a stirring; he opens it to find the Indian is real and alive. He is Little Bear, an Iroquois from the eighteenth Century.

Rap singer Litefoot makes his feature film debut as an Indian who calls himself Little Bear.

At first, Omri treats the miniature man as if he's just a really cool toy and Little Bear treats Omri as if he is the Great Spirit. But Omri soon realizes he's been saddled with the heavy responsibility of guarding the life and welfare of a grown man from another time. And Little Bear realizes the little magician is a mere child who does not understand his own powers.

Omri can't resist sharing his secret with his best friend, Patrick (Rishi Bhat), who is even less mature than Omri. Despite Omri's warnings, the willful Patrick brings to life a toy cowboy, Boone. Boone is a drunkard with a built-in enmity toward "redskins," but he turns out to be a soft-hearted cowpoke given to crying fits. Keith's wacky, over-the-top performance gives the film some needed humor.

The Indian in the Cupboard works its technical magic with seamless perfection. The special effects crew used a variety of methods to shoot scenes involving real actors who appear on screen in vastly different scales.

Scardino and Litefoot shot almost all of their scenes separately, hearing each other's lines spoken by other actors through earphones. Given such a handicap, the connection the boy and the Indian make is all the more remarkable.

Both were virtual newcomers to acting. Scardino in particular bears a heavy load; Oz labors hard to illustrate that the real action of the story is taking place inside Omri as he is transformed from an innocent boy to someone wise beyond his years. The film's climax is a slow pan of Scardino's face, a scrutiny many veterans might not be able to withstand. Scardino is equal to the task.

Unlike many child actors, Scardino is neither overly-cute, precocious, or hip; he is a very authentic boy. He doesn't look or behave like a trained actor; he's just like your own son, brother, or the kid next door. His eyes and face convey wonder, fear, concern and enlightment with the clarity only a child can show. And his voice goes in and out of a little-kid squeak just like real nine-year-olds who still have one foot in innocent childhood while pointing toward the self-critical shoals of pre-adolescence.

Scardino has the crucial quality many actors labor a lifetime for but often fail to achieve: he is very easy for audiences to bear. And so, thanks to Scardino, there is a crucial bond of identification with the protagonist.

Litefoot also gives a fine performance. A writer and singer of Native American rap songs, Litefoot exudes pride, bearing and intelligence but is not afraid to show fear, remorse, or anger. He is representative of a well-balanced man.

Unfortunately, the filmmakers strain to sanitize any rough edges to Little Bear. In the book, Banks has the Indian and cowboy gradually emerge from the rigid stereotypes their toy forms portrayed. Banks casts no judgments on history but is firm and fair in her insistence that Little Bear and Boone share some qualities with the historical stereotypes that made them into toys but are also real human beings with integrity and quirks.

In the film, Little Bear is made into a hero and great care is taken to not offend by using Indian stereotypes. (Of course, there is not equal care to rescue Boone from the cowboy stereotype.) In the book, Litefoot and Boone squabble much more, with both at fault for being temperamental. In

CREDITS

Omri: Hal Scardino
Little Bear: Litefoot
Boone: David Keith
Jane: Lindsay Crouse
Victor: Richard Jenkins
Patrick: Rishi Bhat

Origin: USA
Released: 1995
Production: Kathleen Kennedy, Frank Marshall and Jane Startz for Kennedy/Marshall Company in association with Harris & Co. and Scholastic Pictures; released by Columbia Pictures and Paramount Pictures
Direction: Frank Oz
Screenplay: Melissa Mathison; based on the novel by Lynne Reid Banks
Cinematography: Russell Carpenter
Editing: Ian Crafford
Production design: Leslie McDonald
Art director: Tony Fanning
Set decorator: Chris Spellman
Costume design: Deborah Scott
Special effects: Michael Lanteri
Sound: Art Rochester
Casting: Margery Simkin
MPAA rating: PG
Running Time: 96 minutes

the film, the fight that leads to Boone's wounding is caused by the boys and their charges watching an old TV movie of cowboys slaughtering Indians.

The film's one glaring false step comes just before that, when the boys are seen watching a sexually suggestive music video. What this is doing in the middle of an old-fashioned story about innocence is perplexing. It appears Mathison and Oz want to preach about too much sex and violence on television; but this is an intrusion upon a strongly moral story which doesn't need an ancillary message.

Mathison scripts Crouse as an all-patient, ever-smiling, extremely tolerant and uninquisitive wonder-mom. The father, Victor (Richard Jenkins) plays almost no role. That's fine, because the adults should be background in this tale.

Unfortunately, a tense confrontation in school that is one of the book's fine moments has been reduced to a rather tame scare involving Omri's teacher. The script needs a little more, not less, of such tension. There is one magnificent moment of fright but otherwise the proceedings verge on the dull side. One leaves the film feeling a little puzzled that there was not more action in a story that was so lavishly filmed.

The Indian in the Cupboard may be too tame to be a blockbuster, but if it is a success, there are three Banks sequels which are sure to tempt Hollywood. The story gets richer and more complex in the other books while keeping its fresh and straightforward appeal.

Erring on the side of modesty is better than the more customary Hollywood excesses, so Oz and associates should be commended for producing such a finely modulated film. Most remarkably, the special effects never distract from the story—a rare feat when so much money has been spent on the gizmos. The focus is always on Omri and Little Bear, as it should be. It is their friendship which makes *The Indian in the Cupboard* magical.

—*Michael Betzold*

REVIEWS

Cleveland Plain Dealer. July 14, 1995, p. 6.
Newsweek. July 17, 1995, p. 60.
USA Today. July 14, 1995, p. 2.

The Innocent

"Caught between deadly secrets...and forbidden passions!"—Movie tagline

"Intriguing!"—Roger Ebert, *Chicago Sun-Times*

"Suspenseful!"—Caryn James, *The New York Times*

Adapted by Ian McEwan from his successful novel, *The Innocent* combines the John Le Carre spy tradition with a touch of Edgar Allan Poe. The story of a spy whose double identity inadvertently turns a simple act of self-defense into horror, guilt, and treason, *The Innocent* is in the end a tale of personal lives shattered by the Cold War. For McEwan, spying and the Cold War pitted not only the Soviet Union against the West, but British against Americans, Germans against Germans, and, ultimately, lovers and friends against each other.

McEwan based his novel and screenplay on the real Operation Gold, a joint American-British espionage mission in Berlin between 1954 and 1956, in which the Americans and British tunneled under East Berlin to tap East German telephone lines into the Soviet Union. The operation and its consequences act as a metaphor for the futility of the Cold War and the corrosive effects of the mutual suspicion it engendered. Unfortunately, *The Innocent*'s obvious ambition does not match its execution. Directed by John Schlesinger in his usual high style, *The Innocent* suffers from a sluggish adaptation, odd casting choices, an overly upbeat framing story, and a climactic scene that shamelessly imitates the airport scene in *Casablanca* (1942). The film does boast, however, an astonishingly gruesome and suspenseful dismemberment scene—which in fact ranks among Schlesinger's finest work.

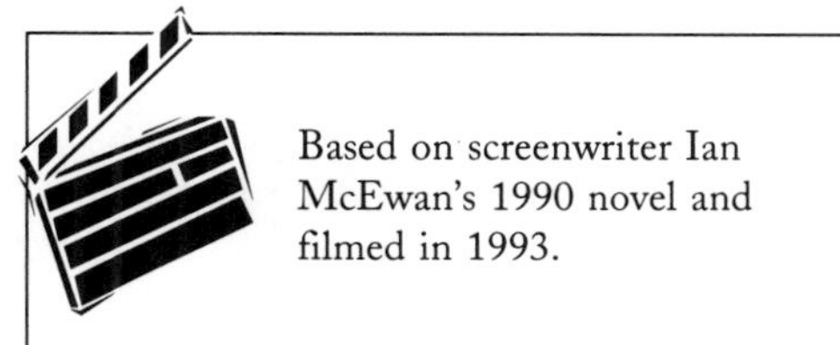

Based on screenwriter Ian McEwan's 1990 novel and filmed in 1993.

The film begins with a framing story at the time of the fall of the Berlin Wall in 1989, 34 years after the film's main action takes place. A somber, late middle-aged Leonard Markham (Campbell Scott) checks into a Berlin hotel during the joyful mayhem surrounding the dismantling of the wall. In his room he reads a letter from Maria (Isabella Rossellini), which asks him to meet her in Berlin, even though she is not sure the letter will reach him, or if he is even alive. In the letter she pleads with him to remember their young, innocent selves of an earlier time, and asks for forgiveness for "our terrible deed." Leonard's memories flash back to 34 years earlier.

Leonard, a British postal-service employee with an expertise in electronic circuitry, enters 1955 Berlin truly innocent of the atmosphere of suspicion that pervades any human transaction or intercourse in the city. Believing himself purely on a technical mission to assist in electronic eavesdropping on the East Germans by the British and Americans, Leonard in short order enters into a secret affair with Maria, a German national, against the express orders of his American CIA boss, Bob Glass (Anthony Hopkins). "Secrecy is individuality, Leonard," Glass tells him. Glass, a man of apparently few human contacts, discourages Leonard from any fraternization with German civilians—or with any other human beings. Other characters intimate that Maria may have a shady background, and that Glass may even be homosexual, but things are not what they seem.

"Everybody cheats a little."—American security expert/spy Bob Glass from *The Innocent*

CREDITS

Leonard Markham: Campbell Scott
Maria: Isabella Rossellini
Bob Glass: Anthony Hopkins
Russell: Hart Bochner
Otto: Ronald Nitschke
MacNamee: James Grant
Cpt. Lofting: Jeremy Sinden
Black: Richard Durden
Lou: Corey Johnson
Piper: Richard Good

Origin: Germany and Great Britain
Released: 1995
Production: Norma Heyman, Chris Sievernich and Wieland Schulz-Keil for Lakehart/Sievernich-Film/Defa Studios Babelsberg production, in association with Film Kredit Treuhand, Filmstiftung Nordrhein-Westfalen; released by Jugendfilm.
Direction: John Schlesinger
Screenplay: Ian McEwan; based on his novel *The Innocent*
Cinematography: Dietrich Lohmann
Editing: Richard Marden
Production design: Luciana Arrighi
Casting: Noel Davis and Jeremy Zimmerman
Assistant director: David Tringham
Costume design: Ingrid Zore
Sound: Axel Arift
Music: Gerald Gouriet
MPAA rating: R
Running Time: 118 minutes

Not only are things not what they seem in Berlin, but all things must also be seen from the reductive perspective of East vs. West. With Operation Gold at stake, all human foibles and motives— Leonard's, Maria's, Glass's—will ultimately be deformed and twisted by the Cold War's Manichean logic. Maria's past, her and Leonard's innocent love, Glass's sense of duty, will, by film's end, be warped beyond recognition.

As Leonard's involvement with Operation Gold intensifies, relationships are poisoned, trust becomes impossible. In bed, Leonard and Maria begin asking questions about each other, trying to find out for whom the other works. Maria becomes frightened when she sees someone tailing Leonard, and becomes suspicious of his big apartment on a telephone company salary. Leonard begins to believe Glass's intimations that any German who befriends him may be a Soviet spy.

Glass, discovering the affair, has Maria's apartment ransacked, and brings her in for questioning. Although Glass officially clears Maria of any wrongdoing, Leonard returns home to find Maria beaten up by her estranged husband, Otto (Ronald Nitschke). They realize they have both been lying to each other, Maria by not telling him about Otto, Leonard by remaining mum about his espionage activities. Leonard assures Maria he loves her, but each now has reason to suspect the other of lying. A mysterious British neighbor, Geoffrey Black (Richard Durden), exacerbates the mutual suspicion.

Returning to Maria's from a party at which Glass has toasted them and given them his blessing, Leonard and Maria find Otto passed out in her bed. Leonard calls Maria a "lying bitch." Otto demands 10,000 marks and information about Leonard's activities in exchange for signing divorce papers. Maria threatens to have him arrested, and Otto fires back that he has gotten her to do his spying for him. A brilliantly staged fight ensues. In self-defense, Maria jams a butcher knife into Otto's head; he convulses and bleeds to death on the floor. Crazed with fear and adrenaline, Leonard and Maria have sex while the body lies on the floor beside them.

Leonard proposes that they tell Glass, rather than any authorities, of Otto's attempt at blackmail and his death. In the meantime, they must dispose of the body. In a tribute to both *Rear Window* (1954) and the stories of Edgar Allan Poe, Leonard returns with two suitcases and a saw, and he and Maria prepare to dismember the body. Schlesinger's camera pans down from the window of Maria's apartment to the courtyard below, where children play ball and chalk the sidewalk, and elderly folks beat rugs and play chess; he

cuts back only once to Maria soaked in blood. Schlesinger finally pans back up to the window, which Maria opens, gasping, in a towel having come from the shower.

Leonard tries to put the suitcases in a locker at the train station, but the suitcases do not fit, and attract the attention of a porter. Trying to dispose of the body on no sleep, Leonard inadvertently lets slip to Black information about Operation Gold, and Black is revealed to be a spy. Hoping to dispose of the suitcases in the tunnel, Leonard nearly blows his cover when American G.I.'s demand to search his baggage. Leonard's panic arouses Glass's suspicions as well. But just as Glass is about to inspect the suitcases, the whole operation is put on alert: Leonard's slip to Black has blown the entire operation.

Glass refuses to cooperate with Maria to save Leonard from prosecution. She lies, telling Glass that it is all over between her and Leonard, and that she knows Glass, in fact, has feelings for her. Glass agrees to remand Leonard back to British authority and secures him a plane out of Berlin. Leonard demands to see Maria on the runway, but Maria, again betraying herself to save Leonard, tells him she hates him. Leonard yells that he doesn't believe her, and yells her name over and over as he watches her disappear arm in arm with Glass.

In 1989, Leonard and Maria finally meet again. Maria is accompanied by her daughter by Glass, now dead. Maria tells Leonard that Glass was a good father, but that he drank, tortured by the knowledge of what Maria did to save Leonard. As they stand among the celebrating crowds and watch Maria's daughter atop the Berlin Wall as it is dismantled, Leonard and Maria look at each other, finally acknowledging their shared past and shared loss of innocence. Schlesinger freezes the frame; perhaps a new life can begin.

The Innocent spends too much time setting up Leonard's mission, Operation Gold. Although the detail and exposition about the tunnel are fascinating, they come at the expense of suspense in the film's first half. Most odd is the film's strange miscasting of the American Scott as a young Englishman and the English Hopkins as a no-nonsense American. Both are among the finest actors working in their respective countries, but their accents here are so disconcerting that their performances come to seem stilted and mannered. (Hopkins acquits himself better than Scott.) The film also borrows a number of touches from Hitchcock's *Rear Window* and *Notorious* (1946) and from Carol Reed's classic *The Third Man* (1949), to distracting effect. Its most egregious homage is the airport scene, lifted poorly from *Casablanca* and made all the more strange by the presence of Rossellini, Ingrid Bergman's daughter. These stylistic homages stand out and detract from the film's careful attempts at verisimilitude, particularly in the tunnel sequences. Finally, the framing story lends a falsely sentimental note to an otherwise dark and downbeat tale.

Lucianna Arrighi's sets, including the tunnel and underground spying installation which actually existed, provide a fascinating backdrop for the story, and Dietrich Lohmann's dark-toned camerawork skillfully evokes the real and moral shadows of divided 1950's Berlin. The central scene of murder, blood and guilt is as finely suggestive a sequence as any Schlesinger has ever directed.

But like many of the greatest directors of the Sixties and Seventies, Schlesinger has worked with material mostly beneath his abilities over the last 15 years. The director of *Darling* (1965), *Midnight Cowboy* (1969), and *Sunday Bloody Sunday* (1971) is here saddled with an over-literary project that never quite makes the transition to suspenseful film, much as he tries to make it happen. *The Innocent* in the end suffers in comparison to Schlesinger's adaptation of Alan Bennett's *An Englishman Abroad* (1983), another British spy tale that builds, unlike *The Innocent*, with the intimacy of a perfect chamber piece.

—Paul Mittelbach

REVIEWS

The New York Times. CXLIV, September 2, 1995, p.8(N).
Sight and Sound. IV, August, 1994, p.42.

It Takes Two

"Two identical strangers. Two different worlds. One perfect match."—Movie tagline

"A double dose of fun and magic."—Joanna Evenglick, *The Kids News Network*

"The Olsen Twins are natural charmers. Irresistible."—Michael Medved, *Sneak Previews*

"Utterly charming romantic comedy."—Paul Wunder, *WBAI Radio*

Box Office Gross: $17,447,907

Once upon a time there were two little twins named Mary-Kate and Ashley Olsen. They had beautiful blond hair and cute faces, and were fortunate enough to land a sitcom which netted them a great deal of money and a movie deal. The movie was called *It Takes Two*, and it was surprisingly not half bad. They were directed by Andy Tennant, a situation comedy veteran making his screen debut. The movie was hardly a classic; it was hardly even anything more than an excuse for putting the twins' adorable-ness on display. But somehow the film managed to be pleasant.

The Olsen twins stint on television's *Full House* made them famous; their cuteness was enhanced by the insipid writing of that program and landed them on the big screen.

Amanda Lemmon (Mary-Kate...or Ashley...no, Mary-Kate) is a cheerful eight-year-old tomboy who lives in the middle of Manhattan in an orphanage. She is the star baseball player for the orphanage and is adored by everyone, especially her supervisor, Diane Barrows (Kirstie Alley). Unmarried Diane would like to adopt Amanda but doesn't have the husband or the income to do it just yet.

Meanwhile, in another part of town, Alyssa Callaway (Ashley Olsen) and her billionaire father, Roger (Steve Guttenberg) are getting ready for his impending marriage to a beautiful, scheming, nasty socialite named Clarice Kensington (Jane Sibbett). Rarely seeing her busy dad, Alyssa is lonesome for her beloved, deceased mother, and immediately sees her future stepmother for the gold-digging meanie that she is.

A series of coincidences land Amanda and Alyssa in the middle of a forest in-between Alyssa's mansion and Amanda's summer camp. They bump into each other, while looking the other way. "Do you see what I see?" says Amanda. "I see two of me," says the other one. "Does that mean there's two of you or two of me?" she asks. The scene is surprisingly devoid of fakery: director Tennant seems to want to keep things moving forward, and doesn't force the twins into a long sequence of wide-eyed wonder about finding a person who looks exactly like them. This is to the film's credit, for audiences will either suspend disbelief or not, and no amount of drubbing from the script, actors and directors would cause them to see this as anything but a frothy fairytale.

Predictably, the twins join forces to bring together Alyssa's dad (Guttenberg) and Amanda's would-be mom (Alley), and the rest of the film is spent showing their plan in action. Their scheme is nearly foiled by the nefarious Clarice, who catches on that she might lose her meal-ticket to the supervisor of an orphanage. Of course, it all ends up as expected in the end. The story is suggestive of *The Parent Trap* (1961), which was based on a British film called *Twice upon a Time* (1954). There are also elements of Mark Twain's *The Prince and the Pauper* which was made into a film in 1937.

Tennant keeps a brisk pace, and seems to understand that this film is not going to win any awards for being a work of art. The humor is, for the most part, sophomoric: a food-fight in the camp dining hall is a center piece of the action, and a scene where Alley and Guttenberg push each other into the lake constitutes the big love scene. At times Tennant allows the twins to lapse into too much cuteness. One example is toward the end, when they yell "kiss her, already!" at the same moment to Alley and Guttenberg. But these silly moments seem appropriate to the subject matter and to the audience; after all, the film is clearly meant to be for kids under 10 years of age. Of course, not all children will take to the film. Sometimes the action is a bit predictable, particularly in the food-fight scene. And there are moments that will be hard even for children to swallow: Clarice decides that she and Roger should get married "tomorrow," and presto! The next day there is a complete wedding with flowers, tuxes, caterers, and hundreds of guests. Hard to believe, but fun anyway.

The script, by Deborah Dean Davis, is like a story told to children: the jokes stay at their level, and the story is unencumbered by adult rules about reality. There is no explanation why the twins look alike, and no explanation of why such a nice man as Callaway would end up with a witch like Clarice Kensington. Good and bad are simple and well-defined, and the story is basic and easy for kids to follow.

The performances are winning without being exceptional. Guttenberg gets a chance to redeem himself a little after his dreadful (though mercifully brief) performance in *Home for the Holidays* (1995). He is handsome and sweet, and does a credible job with the gently comic scenes with Kirstie Alley.

Alley has not had much luck in films portraying characters as well-written as was Rebecca on *Cheers*. And she somehow seems wrong for Guttenberg, as if she should play his big sister instead of his love interest. But that is the bad news: the good news is that Alley is always likable and is certainly believable enough as a woman who works with children. She gets a chance to be funny only a couple of times: she is quite winning in the brief scene where she crashes Callaway's wedding.

The highly respected Philip Bosco makes a dignified appearance as Vincenzo, Callaway's butler. Bosco plays well with the twins without losing a shred of dignity after being called "Lurch" by one of them. As Clarice, Jane Sibbett is a bit overdone, even by her character's standards. She seems to try too hard to show how vicious a character she is. Perhaps director Tennant could have helped to control her; after all, as the villainess of the film, she is the butt of several pranks caused by the twins, and is required to react angrily much of the time. Perhaps a little restraint might have helped her appear less shrill.

The production values are reminiscent of the recent *Richie Rich* (1994). The big, colorful mansion and its lavish interiors are beautiful. There are also some fun set pieces, such as a junkyard where Alyssa becomes entrapped by the "Buttkiss" family. Vivid cinematography by Kenneth Zunder and appropriately youthful music by Sherman Foote and Ray Foote make the film highly professional in spite of its childish appeal. One note is that the use of such songs as "Tutti Frutti" (during the food fight scene) and "I Got You (I Feel Good)" (when the grown-ups go away) are a little cliche. These songs have been around forever, and perhaps the music supervisors wanted to evoke Pavlovian responses from their youthful audience, but somehow the songs just seem redundant.

And then there are those adorable Olsen twins. They are sweet and well-intentioned, with (okay, the truth is out) Mary-Kate stealing the show as the tomboyish Amanda. One of the funniest scenes come after the two girls switch identities. Trying to be like the more cultivated Alyssa, Amanda apologizes to Vincenzo by saying "I'm terribly relived that you aren't pissed" in her most ladylike voice. She also has the better entrance of the two, being introduced as the slugger of the baseball team. Ashley doesn't fare as well, perhaps because she is required to stress every "t" and to sound very proper. It just doesn't seem real. These two actresses are not half as bad as many curmudgeons would expect. In fact, they are rather ingratiating. And make no mistake about it. They are darn cute.

—Kirby Tepper

CREDITS

Diane Barrows: Kirstie Alley
Roger Callaway: Steve Guttenberg
Amanda Lemmon: Mary-Kate Olsen
Alyssa Callaway: Ashley Olsen
Vincenzo: Philip Bosco
Clarice Kensington: Jane Sibbett

Origin: USA
Released: 1995
Production: James Orr and Jim Cruickshank for an Orr & Cruickshank production; presented by Rysher Entertainment; released by Warner Brothers
Direction: Andy Tennant
Screenplay: Deborah Dean Davis
Cinematography: Kenneth Zunder
Editing: Roger Bondelli
Production design: Edward Pisoni
Art direction: Vlasta Svoboda
Costume design: Molly McGuiness
Sound: David Lee
Casting: Amy Lippens
MPAA rating: PG
Running Time: 101 minutes

Jade

"Packed with talent, polished and technically dazzling."—Michael Wilmington, *Chicago Tribune*

"Fiorentino heats up the screen."—Neil Rosen, *NY1 News*

"The most hypnotic sensual thriller this year."—Veronica Mixen, *Philadelphia Inquirer*

Box Office Gross: $9,795,017

It has long been customary to refer to a film as the creative result of the director's efforts; the writer is usually relegated to second banana status. Not so with Joe Eszterhas, the highest paid screenwriter in America: the scripts he works upon almost always become Eszterhas movies. At one time, the epithet of "a Joe Eszterhas script" had cachet, but sadly, one's expectation of quality and originality from this writer has all but dissipated. After a viewing of *Jade*, there is no reason to raise one's expectations for the future.

Although predicated on the question of whether well-heeled career woman Trina Gavin (Linda Fiorentino) is a murderer or not, the plot's engine is David Corelli (David Caruso). Corelli is a high-flying assistant D.A. and an old friend not only of Trina, but her even higher-flying lawyer husband Matt (Chazz Palminteri). Corelli and Trina dated at Stanford; Matt and Corelli play racketball regularly, and Matt even offers his friend a partnership in his law firm.

Corelli is called in after the murder of a man called Medford, a very rich San Francisco businessman and art collector. Investigating in Medford's mansion, Corelli is intrigued by the dead man's multi-faceted collections, including a number of locket cases, one of which has an unknown symbol on it. With the help of a member of the Chinese community, Corelli discovers that the symbol means jade. But he keeps to himself an unusual cufflink that he found at Medford's bedside, unsure where this clue might fit into the puzzle.

"There's only three things in life—money, sex, and power."—Matt Gavin from *Jade*

A more alarming discovery from the murder scene is of photos of California's Governor Edwards (Richard Crenna) in bed with an unknown young woman. Not surprisingly, the Governor is anxious about others discovering the photos, and tries to enforce Corelli's silence when the assistant D.A. travels to Sacramento. Soon Corelli is on the track of the girl in the photos, and after a brief chase, the young woman (Angie Everhart) is caught and interrogated.

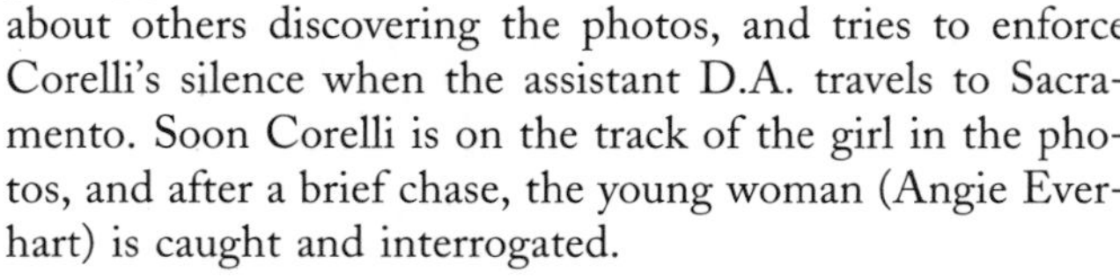

From her revelations, it is learned that Medford and the Governor took a series of women to a house on the ocean in Marin County, and various sexual acts in various combinations would take place there. As the police search the house, they retrieve from the ashes of a fire a half-burnt video cassette tape. A computer-aided reconstruction of the images provides a glimpse of a woman who looks like Trina having rough sex with Medford. She is identified by the millionaire's mistress as 'Jade.' By this time, the audience knows that Matt is having an extra-marital affair.

At first Trina denies having more than social contact with Medford. Meanwhile, Corelli's life is endangered by his brakes being cut as he travels the hills of San Francisco. Although his car eventually rolls over and over engulfed in flames, our hero survives without major injury—except to his psyche. Shrugging off his supervisor's request that he drop the case, Corelli relentlessly pursue his investigation. The tepidness of Matt and Trina's marriage is depicted, and especially, the sexual inadequacy of Matt with his wife. Corelli arranges to talk once more to Medford's mistress, but as he waits for her, nursing his coffee, she is run down at North Beach in front of him. What follows is a thrilling chase sequence—partly through Chinatown— when Corelli maniacally follows the killer, until he finally loses his man and ends up in the waters of the bay, gasping for air.

Trina and Matt Gavin are shown the sex tape, at which point, Trina admits to having been at the Pacific house. Later, she pays a desperate visit to her old flame Corelli. After she admits there have been lots of men as sexual partners, she tries to seduce him. Corelli, with difficulty, resists. At the same time, another witness is being murdered, thus proving before the climax that Trina is not the killer.

As matters reach their crescendo, Trina and Corelli are trapped as two men rampage through the Gavins' house, looking for documents and killing anyone (such as the Gavins' maid) who gets in their way. Ultimately, Matt and Corelli take out the hitmen in a scene that is hard to follow and unnecessarily confusing.

In a coda to the film, Corelli pays a second visit to the Governor—the man truly behind the killings. Corelli, however, is powerless to prosecute his man, given the entrenched power of the Governor's office and his connections. And in a characteristic Eszterhas touch, the last scene reveals that it was Matt who initiated the killing spree after learning of Medford's involvement with his wife.

Critical reaction to *Jade* has not been favorable. For example, *Variety* correctly pinpointed that the film's "climactic sequence proves so murkily shot there's scant suspense, as it's difficult to keep track of who's doing what to whom." Bruce Diones in *The New Yorker* was less subtle, calling the picture "hopeless," the story "ridiculous," and concluding that "Ezsterhas may be fixated on money, power, and sex, but his scripts are cheap, humorless, and limp." And Kenneth Turan in *The Los Angeles Times* called *Jade* a "movie where the car chases have more personality than the people."

Joe Ezsterhas might be the highest paid writer in Hollywood, but he has no gift at all for characterization. His characters are usually ambitious, power-hungry, and sexually rapacious, but they do not come to life. They are puppets of the plot. Consequently, the trio of actors at the heart of the film have little to fasten onto in their roles—despite the enthusiasm they profess for their characters in the film's press notes.

David Caruso is the driving force of the action, and although he could easily be back in an episode of *NYPD Blue,* his commitment to his part cannot be faulted. As Corelli, Caruso is intense and reckless, a man haunted by his past—especially Trina—and although his work in *Jade* will not propel his career forward, it should not damage it either.

As Trina, Linda Fiorentino has little with which to work. In *Jade,* she is generally depicted as no more than a rich man's sexual object. Her sex scenes bring to mind *The Last Seduction,* but in *Jade* she is not allowed the power of her character in that film. Ezsterhas gives her a scene in which she lectures to an audience of businesspeople, but her supposedly sophisticated mind is hardly an issue in the film. She is a woman who looks for kinky sex, and that predilection underpins her role, especially as several times it is stated that she agrees to do anything for sexual kicks.

As for Chazz Palminteri, his role as a high-powered lawyer is only marginally more fleshed out than Fiorentino's because his job has an impact on the plot. When Trina is threatened, he can threaten back with his prowess in the courtroom. But Palminteri also only services the plot, and one gets little insight into the man. In an even more limited role, however, is Richard Crenna as the creepy and menacing Governor Edwards.

The technical aspects of *Jade* are more satisfying. The car chase through Chinatown is an exciting, original one, and credit for its twists and turns goes to stunt co-ordinator Buddy Jo Hooker. Cinematographer Andrzej Bartowiak does good work until the obscure climax in the Gavins' house. Trina and Matt's upper-class lifestyle is clothed by costume designer Marilyn Vance and there are the interiors are splendid thanks to production designer Alex Tavoularis, and the beauty of the buildings themselves.

Jade is by no means a disaster. Indeed, had one not seen *Basic Instinct* (1992), not to mention the superior *Jagged Edge* (1985) and *Music Box* (1989), some pleasure might be derived from the movie. But if one is familiar with these previous scripts, *Jade* comes across mainly as a tired rehash. It is infuriating to find Ezsterhas using exactly the twists he has utilized in his previous scripts, no more so when the cufflink found by Corelli at the beginning is identified as being Matt Gavin's in the final scene, thus proving that the lawyer was the original killer in the murdering sequence later set in motion by the Governor. The use of such a prop is a facsimile of the twist at the end of *Jagged Edge.*

As for William Friedkin's work, he brings a more sober hand to proceedings than director Paul Verhoeven did to Ezsterhas's *Basic Instict.* Unlike Verhoeven, he does seek to exploit the female lead's sexuality, and he avoids melodrama in what is already a convoluted skein of impulses and desires. But *Jade* will not stand as a notable effort in Friedkin's career. All that one truly takes away from *Jade* is a memory of the superior car chases, and that is precious little given the films' high-priced talents.

—*Paul B. Cohen*

CREDITS

David Corelli: David Caruso
Trina Gavin: Linda Fiorentino
Matt Gavin: Chazz Palminteri
Bob Hargrove: Michael Biehn
Gov. Edwards: Richard Crenna
Karen Heller: Donna Murphy
Petey Vasko: Ken King

Origin: USA
Released: 1995
Production: Robert Evans, Craig Baumgarten and Gary Adelson; released by Paramount Pictures
Direction: William Friedkin
Screenplay: Joe Eszterhas
Cinematography: Andrzej Bartkowiak
Editing: Augie Hess
Production design: Alex Tavoularis
Art direction: Charles Breen
Set design: Robert Goldstein and John Chichester
Set decoration: Gary Fettis
Costume design: Marilyn Vance
Sound: Kirk Francis
Casting: Ronnie Yeskel
Music: James Horner
MPAA rating: R
Running Time: 95 minutes

Jefferson in Paris

"Passionate!"—Rex Reed, *New York Observer*
"Extraordinary!"—Janet Maslin, *New York Times*

Box Office Gross: $2,473,668

Thomas Jefferson, our first Secretary of State, our third President, an elegant, sophisticated intellectual, is no longer unassailable. "Now some scholars detect a whiff of hypocrisy behind his republican values," tooted the Table of Contents of the premiere issue of *Civilization* (The Magazine of the Library of Congress) to draw attention to the cover story by Joseph J. Ellis entitled "American Sphinx." Ellis raised the issue of Jefferson's hypocritical attitude toward slavery and his alleged affair with Sally Hemings, his mulatto slave. So does the Merchant-Ivory film *Jefferson in Paris*.

Culturally, the first few months of 1995 were dominated by the memory of Thomas Jefferson, since the film comes on the heels of the 250th anniversary of Jefferson's birth. In April, George Green Shackelford's scholarly treatment of *Thomas Jefferson's Travels in Europe*, 1784-1789, was published by the Johns Hopkins University Press, a scholarly but readable account of Jefferson's diplomatic mission to Paris; but the popular image was set by a documentary on Public Television and the Merchant-Ivory feature film *Jefferson in Paris*, which was visually splendid, but oddly imagined within a chastizing, politically correct framework. With its odd romantic diversions in Paris, the film cannot do justice to the idea of Jefferson as an "Apostle of European Culture."

The film begins in 1823 in Pike County, Ohio, long after the death of Thomas Jefferson, as a reporter (Tim Choate) traces down Madison Hemings (James Earl Jones), who claims to be the son of the man who framed the Declaration of Independence then went on to become Secretary of State and President of the United States. He tells the reporter the story of *Jefferson in Paris*, a story handed down to him by his mother, Sally Hemings (Thandie Newton), though she arrived late in Paris after Jefferson had been serving as ambassador for some time, and she could not have known the whole story. Hence the plot is set in motion by an unreliable narrator—not a promising start.

Screenwriter Ruth Prawer Jabhvala was inspired by Fawn M. Brodie's 1974 book *Thomas Jefferson: An Intimate History.*

In 1784, at the age of forty-one, Thomas Jefferson (Nick Nolte) went to Paris with his elder daughter Patsy (Gwyneth Paltrow) as Ambassador to the Royal Court at Versailles during the last years of the reign of Louis XVI (Michael Lonsdale, a very famous actor in a very limited role here) and Marie Antoinette (Charlotte de Turckheim). Jefferson remained in France until after the fall of the Bastille on July 14, 1789. At first, Jefferson had with him only his elder daughter, whom he enrolled in a convent school, and a servant, James Hemings (Seth Gilliam), a slave who gets a longing for freedom in Revolutionary France, though on the issue of slavery his master is something of a reactionary.

Jefferson is later joined by his younger daughter Polly (Estelle Eonnet), who arrives in the company of her nurse, the fifteen-year-old mulatto slave Sally Hemings, said to be the illegitimate half-sister of Jefferson's departed wife. By this time she arrives, but by that time Jefferson has become deeply involved in a platonic relationship with the beautiful Anglo-Italian painter and musician, Maria Cosway (Greta Scacchi), locked into a marriage of convenience with the apparently homosexual British painter Richard Cosway (played to mannered aristocratic perfection by the incomparable Simon Callow). The details of this ill-fated romance between Jefferson and Maria are central to the film, but the romance is far advanced before Sally comes upon the scene.

The film takes an unexpected and unexplained turn when Jefferson indulges himself carnally with this child-nurse and gets her pregnant, a common course of events, the film seems to suggest, for Virginia gentlemen. Daughter Patsy knows what has transpired and is so repulsed by her father's behavior that she decides to become a nun and remain in France, but her father will have none of that. He has very strong opinions indeed against granting freedom of choice to women and slaves. The man seems to be a perfect hypocrite when he is questioned about the meaning of freedom of religion by his daughter's Mother Superior, but he does not flinch or falter when confronted about his hypocritical decisions. Problem is, he also seems to be something of a fool.

Nolte's Jefferson argues American slavery as a special case for which exceptions must be made, and he manages to alienate himself from an attractive and cultivated woman of taste by his sexual dalliance with Sally, who barely speaks literate English and has little to recommend beyond her girlish high spirits. Why a cosmopolitan man over forty who is an inventor, a diplomat, a musician, an architect—in many ways a Renaissance man—would be so taken by an ignorant teenager is not successfully explained by either the screenplay or the acting.

When Patsy tells Maria that her father has made his slave pregnant, Maria breaks off her relationship with Jefferson and returns to England and her husband. As the French monarchy begins to collapse and the King is taken prisoner, the story ends, and viewers are transported back to that humble farm house in Pike County, Ohio, for a few final sonorous words by James Earl Jones, who is given heavy competition here from Simon Callow and Michael Lonsdale, as well as Lambert Wilson as the Marquis De Lafayette, Daniel Mesguich as Dr. Mesmer, whose hypnotic tricks make him an important person at the French court, allowing tactile privileges with Marie Antoinette, and Steve Kalfa as Dr. Guillotin, who invents his device for "humane execution" at exactly the "right historical moment." The international cast is so brilliantly assembled that Nick Nolte has to work very hard to hold his own in the lead role. He certainly looks the part, but his Virginia accent makes him sound a bit like a colonial rube. His "natural behavior" is contrasted with that of the mannered, decadent aristocracy, whose days are sadly (though perhaps justly) numbered. Dr. Guillotin's invention will not be a laughing matter for them after Jefferson leaves Paris and the whole enterprise turns bloody and chaotic.

"The earth belongs to the living, not to the dead."—Thomas Jefferson from *Jefferson in Paris*

Jefferson in Paris is the first of a multi-picture deal producer Ismail Merchant and director James Ivory signed with Touchstone Pictures. They have collaborated once again with their favorite screenwriter, Ruth Prawer Jhabvala, the novelist with whom they have worked successfully through fourteen pictures, of which two have earned Academy Awards for Best Adapted Screenplay: A *Room with a View* (1986) and *Howard's End* (1992). Her work on *The Remains of the Day* (1993), adapted from the novel by Kazuo Ishiguro, also received an Oscar nomination, but on *Jefferson in Paris* her task was to formulate an original screenplay derived from history, even though her best work has involved literary adaptations. Here there are rather too many loose ends.

Nonetheless, the picture is stunning as an historical reconstruction and praise of the highest order should go to Production Designer Guy-Claude François, whose high-concept rendering of royal decadence is magnificently photographed by cinematographer Pierre Lhomme, who also shot the E. M. Forster adaptation *Maurice* in 1986. An army of Art Directors (led by Thierry François), Costume Designers (Jenny Beavan and John Bright) and Hairdressers, Wig-makers, and Make-up Artists (led by Carol Hemming) have labored mightily to create a visual miracle here, right down to the staging of scenes from Antonio Sacchini's opera *Dardanus*. According to Costume Designer John Bright, there were "83 speaking parts—twice the number of a normal Merchant-Ivory film, and the whole cast required over 400 costumes. The film sets exacting standards that any other films competiting for the Academy Award nominations will find difficult to match."

CREDITS

Thomas Jefferson: Nick Nolte
Patsy Jefferson: Gwyneth Paltrow
Polly Jefferson: Estelle Eonnet
Sally Hemings: Thandie Newton
James Hemings: Seth Gilliam
William Short: Todd Boyce
John Trumbull: Nigel Whitmey
Monsier Petit: Nicolas Silberg

Origin: Great Britain
Released: 1995
Production: Ismail Merchant for Merchant Ivory Productions, Ltd.; released by Buena Vista Pictures Distribution Inc.; Touchstone Pictures
Direction: James Ivory
Screenplay: Ruth Prawer Jhabvala
Cinematography: Pierre Lhomme
Editing: Andrew Marcus and Isabel Lorente
Production design: Guy-Claude Francois
Casting: Sylvie Brochere, Joanna Merlin and Celestia Fox
Sound: Mike Shoring, David Motta, Francois Groult and Bruno Tarriere
Costume Design: Jenny Beavan and John Bright
Music: Richard Robbins
Hairdressing and Make Up: Carol Hemming
MPAA rating: PG-13
Running Time: 142 minutes

REVIEWS

Civilization. Vol.1, No.1 (November-December 1994), pp.35-45.
Entertainment Weekly, April 7, 1995, pp.61-62.
Newsweek. April 3, 1995, pp.69-70.
New York. Vol.28, No.16, April 17, 1995, p.106, p.107.
The New York Times, March 31, 1995, C1, C12.
Rolling Stone. Issue 706, April 20, 1995, p.89.
Sight and Sound. Vol.5, No.6 (NS), June 1995, pp.46-47.
Time. Vol.145, No.15, April 10, 1995, p.82.
Variety. March 27-April 2, 1995, p.74, p.77.
The Washington Post, April 7, 1995, D7.
The Washington Post, April 9, 1995, G4.
Washington Post Weekend, April 7, 1995, p.45.
The Washington Times Metropolitan Times, April 7, 1995, C17.

But for some reviewers there was too much background and not enough foreground, too much history and too little drama, in this Jefferson story. Ken Ringle of *The Washington Post* (April 9, 1995) stated his preference for the PBS television documentary *Thomas Jefferson: a View from the Mountain*, produced on a budget of $400,000 in comparison to the $14 million that went into the Merchant-Ivory film, and especially ridiculed Thandie Newton's "fiddle-dee-dee" portrait of Jefferson's purported slave mistress, who was, he asserts, "almost certainly a woman of substance." One cannot believe that the film does justice to either her or Mr. Jefferson, as the screenplay opts for rumor over what can be proved by historical evidence. Even though this dramatic license is not justified by the dramatic movement of the story, the film is well worth viewing as an historic spectacle set against the turmoil of pre-Revolutionary France.

—James M. Welsh

Jeffrey

"What do you do when you meet Mr. Right but the timing is all wrong?"—Movie tagline

"I can't remember when I've laughed so much. *Jeffrey* is a hilariously touching gem."—Bill Diehl, *ABC Radio*

"Laugh-out-loud funny."—Scott Siegel, *WNEW-FM*

Box Office Gross: $3,487,767

It has a Busby Berkeley-style dance number; it has comedy, parody, satire, and tragedy; it has *Star Trek's* Patrick Stewart; and it even has Mother Teresa in a recurring role. Paul Rudnick's *Jeffrey* leaves no stone unturned in its drive to touch and entertain audiences. Adapted by Rudnick from his own successful Off-Broadway play, the film is less delectable than it was on stage, but is still a great deal of fun. (The stage success helped Paul Rudnick to become the screenwriter of *Addams Family Values* [1994], the sequel to the *Addams Family* [1993].)

It is the story of Jeffrey (Steven Weber), an attractive gay man who works as a waiter but wants to be an actor (sort of) and lives in New York. At the beginning of the film, Jeffrey has discovered that sex isn't what it used to be. With the fear of AIDS, and with his own maturation, Jeffrey seems to need more than the one night stands to which he has become accustomed. The initial sequence, which depicts him in varying sexual situations, is very funny. Addressing the audience directly, he tells the audience that he is giving up sex.

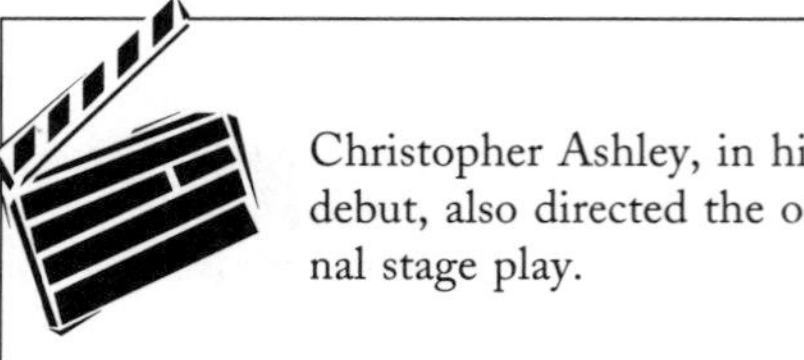

Christopher Ashley, in his film debut, also directed the original stage play.

Enter Steven (Michael T. Weiss), a sexy, gym-built guy who comes on strong to Jeffrey when they meet at (surprise) the gym. Steven asks Jeffrey if he needs help at the bench press, and, prone on the bench, Jeffrey is very vulnerable to Steven's suggestive (though not lascivious) come-on. Having told himself that he was not going to have any more sex, Jeffrey rebuffs Steven.

But Steven turns up a few more times, enough for Jeffrey to realize that he is highly attracted to Steven. They meet a second time while they are both working as caterers. (Actually, Steven is a bartender, which is higher up on the food chain than Steven's mere waiter position.) The affair at which they are working is called "A Hoedown for AIDS", hosted by an affected New York socialite (Christine Baranski). It is an hilarious satire on the overblown AIDS charity events which have proliferated in recent years. (And it is based in fact: "Two-Steppin' for a Cure" is an annual benefit which has raised a lot of money for AIDS research.)

They meet again, at the apartment of Sterling (Patrick Stewart), and his lover Darius (Bryan Batt). Even after several meetings, even after having kissed each other, Jeffrey decides he can't go out with Steven. Then, even after being turned down a few times, and even after having been brushed off by Jeffrey, Steven still makes himself available. It is a bit hard to figure out why this very handsome and incredibly nice man would go after the somewhat nerdy and stand-offish Jeffrey, but it is, after all, a movie.

A scene in which Steven, Darius, Sterling, and several New York City pedestrians pester Jeffrey into consenting to go out with Steven is very funny. "You're gay, you're single...it isn't pretty," says Darius. And it serves as a turning point. The romance is on. Or is it? Jeffrey waffles once again when Steven reveals that he is HIV positive. The rest of the film involves Jeffrey's search for answers about what to do about himself, about sex in general, and about Steven in particular.

Eventually he decides to run away, back to his Midwestern home. But not before a tragedy strikes that makes him search even deeper within. Eventually, he learns that he lives life less fully than those who are dying around him. As deep as Jeffrey the character searches, *Jeffrey* the film never becomes dramatic. Rudnick's style is to maintain a gently satirical and lighthearted tone, even though the characters face life and death issues.

> "Enough! Sex was never meant to be safe or negotiated or fatal."—Jeffrey from *Jeffrey*

The film's strength is in its numerous satirical sequences. The only sequence that does not hit its mark is a fantasy gameshow sequence, with Robert Klein as an unctuous emcee. But others are hilarious. At one point, Jeffrey calls his stodgy midwestern parents. In split-screen, his dowdy mom (who is baking while on the phone) and bespectacled dad express their dismay that Jeffrey is giving up sex. "Have you tried phone sex, dear?" says his mother. And then she tries to help Jeffrey by practicing phone sex: "What are you wearing, dear?" she says, as if she were talking to a Sunday school class.

One sequence lampoons New Age guru Marianne Williamson, whose books (*Return to Love*, etc.) have made her a favorite of such spiritual people as Elizabeth Taylor. In this film, she is known as Debra Morehouse (Sigourney Weaver), and Jeffrey attends one of her lectures while on his search for answers about life. "I'm a waiter, so I can't afford your cassettes and calendars", Jeffrey shyly explains before asking her a question. And when he does ask her to help with his dilemma, her stock New Age answers ("find that source of unconditional love") are a hoot. "You!" barks Weaver, calling on a spacey audience member (Kathy Najimy) during the question/answer period, "You, with the bad perm!" Najimy and Weaver make the most of their cameos, and it is a terrific scene.

There are several fun cameos, the most on-target of which is Christine Baranski's overdressed society matron, Ann Marwood Bartle, at the "Hoedown for AIDS." With a tiny, jeweled cowboy hat pinned to her huge hair-do, Baranski (Emmy winner for television's *Cybill*) is wonderful. Mother Teresa makes a cameo as well. (She is played by Irma St. Paule, who looks strikingly like the real thing.) Perhaps the funniest moment is when Mother Teresa plays romantic background music on a grand piano to underscore a love scene between Jeffrey and Steven. One of the best scenes is reserved for Tony award-winning Nathan Lane, whose film career is only beginning with *Jeffrey*. (After making this film, Lane went on to star in the Mike Nichols remake of *La Cage Aux Folles* [1978], called *The Bird Cage* [1996]). Lane plays a lecherous priest to whom Jeffrey tries to make confession, but who instead offers some melancholy wisdom, saying that the proof that God exists is simply in "the very best in all of us".

Jeffrey's journey takes him around the confines of Manhattan, and though it is hardly an epic journey, Rudnick manages to get Jeffrey through a lot of experiences. With the various cameos and the episodic nature of its story, it resembles a gay *Alice in Wonderland*, set in the bizarre world of New York in the 1990's.

Bryan Batt, as Darius, is perfectly cast as an aging chorus boy who knows a good thing when he sees it: "People say I'm dumb...but I'm living rent free in a penthouse..." And though he and Sterling seem mismatched, they are genuinely kind to each other. Batt is the only leading actor recreating his original role. It would be hard to imagine the film without the sweetness and simplicity he brings to the role. Stewart is, as usual, excellent, having a wonderful time with the flamboyance, but bringing a welcome depth during the tragic scenes. These two characters, while stereotypes, are well-written, and avoid being one-dimensional through the excellent performances of Batt and Stewart, and through Rudnick's loving and careful determination to walk the line between drama and comedy.

Michael T. Weiss, though lesser-known than his costar, fares better than Weber. Weiss seems more comfort-

CREDITS

Jeffrey: Steven Weber
Steve: Michael T. Weiss
Mother Teresa: Irma St. Paule
Sterling: Patrick Stewart
Skip Winkley: Robert Klein
Ann Marwood Bartle: Christine Baranaski
Darius: Bryan Batt
Debra Moorehouse: Sigourney Weaver
Mrs. Marcangelo: Olympia Dukakis

Origin: USA
Released: 1995
Production: Mark Balsam, Mitchell Maxwell and Victoria Maxwell for A Workin' Man Films Production; released by Orion Classics
Direction: Christopher Ashley
Screenplay: Paul Rudnick; based on his play *Jeffrey*
Cinematography: Jeffrey Tufano
Editing: Cara Silverman
Production design: Michael Johnston
Choreography: Jerry Mitchell
Set decoration: Andrew Baseman
Costume design: David C. Woolard
Sound: Matthew Price
Casting: Marcia Shulman
Music: Stephen Endelman
MPAA rating: R
Running Time: 92 minutes

able and more suitably cast than does Weber, and Weiss' mixture of humility and sexiness is appealing. Weiss is known to soap opera fans from several seasons on *Days of Our Lives*, and it is good to see this fine actor get a big-screen opportunity.

Perhaps it is Weber who is most disappointing—and that is not to say he is bad in the role. He is a fine actor; emotionally present for Jeffrey's ups and downs, and comfortable enough with the comic scenes to be charming. Maybe it is because Jeffrey is inherently rather selfish, maybe because he is so confused that he is almost irritating, but more than anything, Weber's character is actually one of the film's biggest flaws. Even a good actor such as Weber cannot overcome some inherently problematic aspects of his character. He may simply be miscast.

Still, it seems as if Rudnick and director Ashley accomplished what they set out to do. It is a bright and funny film, full of fun visuals, such as Jerry Mitchell's choreography in the "Hoedown", the excellent costumes by David C. Woolard, and the playful production design of Michael Johnston.

Certainly director Christopher Ashley does a credible job bringing all these elements together. And he achieves some fine and funny performances. But perhaps another more experienced director might have been able to blend the play's theatricality with a film's need for verisimilitude.

Ultimately, *Jeffrey* rises and falls on its clever dialogue and simple plot. Even with its flaws *Jeffrey* is a winning film, and one that Rudnick and company should be proud of.

—Kirby Tepper

The Jerky Boys

"Comic dynamos!"—Kevin Thomas, *Los Angeles Times*

Box Office Gross: $7,557,877

Johnny Brennan and Kamal Ahmed are two self-described "low-lifes from Queens" who have turned the old standby teenage prank of making crank phone calls into a lucrative entertainment career. Two tapes of their foul-mouthed phone routines became Billboard chart-toppers, they became regulars on MTV, they got their own 900 number, and that was enough to land them their own film, *The Jerky Boys*.

The Jerky Boys isn't really a movie, it's just a few of the stars' phone calls cobbled together into what passes for a script about mobsters. Few of the prank calls are funny, and what occurs between the prank calls is boring. The two comics have a very limited repertoire, which consists of using profanity and calling people unimaginative names such as "fruityass," "rubberneck," and "liver lips."

It's sophomoric humor at its best. The Jerky Boys, apparently so named because people they called considered them jerks, can't act. Their routines don't translate from audio to video. The humor in doing funny voices over the phone depends greatly on the disembodied voice; when you put a face with the voice, especially an unexpressive face, the mirth evaporates quickly.

Based on Brennan and Kamal's, two self-described 'lowlifes from Queens,' two gold-record albums of prank phone calls.

Johnny B and Kamal, as they bill themselves, trade on a mild form of working-class anger. In the film, they engage in plenty of gay-bashing and a mild bit of misogyny. Rarely do more than a few seconds pass without an anal reference. Other than that obsession, their humor has no particular focus or target; it lands on whomever picks up the phone. Their pranks aren't nearly as inventive or involved as the average teenager's.

It is obvious that the telephone has become a favorite instrument for people to use to vent their frustrations and desires while hiding behind their anonymity. A billion-dollar industry is predicated on the fact that people lose their inhibitions over the phone. The Jerky Boys are breaking no new ground here. Uninhibited put-downs can be a funny comic form; Groucho Marx was its original master. But Johnny B and Kamal aren't funny actors. Their vocal routines are passable but they have no screen presence. Their facial expressions are extremely limited: Kamal depends heavily on a shrug and a vacant look, while Johnny B (who looks like a downsized version of baseball's John Kruk) has nothing but a catatonic stare. Picture two of the Three Stooges, but without any physical slapstick, and you'd be close to the Jerky Boys' repertoire. Compared to these two, Cheech and Chong were geniuses.

Many have noted the dumbing-down of the motion picture industry, and it's hard to imagine getting any dumber than *The Jerky Boys*. That the film's co-producer Joe Roth is the chairman of the Walt Disney Motion Pictures Group speaks volumes about how low Disney has fallen. Walt himself would be shocked at this film, probably not so much at the constant anal humor as at the total lack of production values.

Mercifully, *The Jerky Boys* is only 81 minutes long, but despite its length it seems to drag on forever. There's so little of interest in the plot that the film seems padded. The Jerky Boys are, true to life, just a couple of friends from Queens who would rather sit around the house and make phone calls all day than go out and work. Johnny B is apparently the brains and brawn of the operation; Kamal is something of a foil who occasionally gets slapped around and constantly smiles.

Since their antics have never landed them in serious trouble before, it's preposterous to buy the script's idea that the Jerky Boys would make prank calls to mobsters and concoct a story about being big-shot hit-men from Chicago. Viewers who aren't Jerky Boys fans will miss the fact that the fictional mob boss Frank Rizzo is a Jerky Boys staple. Viewers who are Jerky Boys fans probably don't know that Frank Rizzo was a former mayor of Philadelphia with mob connections.

The plot, such as it is, has the two boys currying favors from the mobsters, getting ratted on, getting in hot water and defending their favorite bar owner from the mob. As Johnny explains, "There's some things in this world we're fighting for," —a statement which rings completely hollow, because the boys don't stand for anything except loafing and amusing themselves at everyone else's expense.

Johnny B does most of the talking on the phone, using a rapid-fire, caustic insult style that depends almost entirely on toilet humor. It's Howard Stern without the political or social content. Kamal gets only a few bits—one as a turbaned taxi-cab driver and one as a stand-in Egyptian magician (another bit from the boys' album). He fails to generate many laughs in either.

The mob boss is played by Alan Arkin, a veteran actor who is totally miscast; he looks befuddled and tired. Brad Sullivan plays a cop who's excited about tracking down Rizzo; his role is a throwaway. Suzanne Shepherd is Johnny's beehive-haired mother who has a mildly funny bit when she must walk around with feet encased in cement-filled detergent boxes. Rock star Ozzy Osbourne has an awful cameo as a band manager.

Director James Melkonian, who wrote the script in a few weeks with the Jerky Boys and filmed it in a few months, has absolutely no concept and no style. The idiotic plot and lackluster characters are played straight, when they should have been camped up to milk some needed laughs. There is no dramatic tension despite the concoction of mob peril; there is no action; there is no slapstick; there is plenty of dead space.

The film is so paltry that a nightclub song from Tom Jones is one of the high points. The band "Helmet" also does a heavy-metal ditty. Even the music is uninspired, a limp collection of various genres.

There must have been a better way to capitalize on the Jerky Boys' aggressive, insulting style and skewer a few societal pretensions along the way, but whatever comic flair the duo possesses is dragged down by the leaden script. The trouble with the modern world of entertainment is that talent gets leveraged into new venues; the Jerky Boys found

CREDITS

Johnny Brennan: Johnny Brennan
Kamal: Kamal Ahmed
Lazarro: Alan Arkin
Uncle Freddy: William Hickey
Mickey: Alan North
Worzic: Brad Sullivan
Brett Weir: James Lorinz
Mrs. B.: Suzanne Shepherd
Tony Scarboni: Vincent Pastore
Geno: Brian Tarantina
Sonny: Peter Appel
Band manager: Ozzy Osbourne
Host: Paul Bartel
Tom Jones: Tom Jones

Origin: USA
Released: 1995
Production: Joe Roth and Roger Birnbaum for Caravan Pictures and Touchstone Pictures; released by Buena Vista Pictures
Direction: James Melkonian
Screenplay: James Melkonian, Rich Wilkes, John G. Brennan, and Kamal Ahmed
Cinematography: Ueli Steiger
Editing: Dennis M. Hill
Production design: Dan Leigh
Set decoration: Ronnie von Blomberg
Casting: Douglas Aibel
Sound: Michael Barosky
Costume design: John Dunn
Music: Ira Newborn
MPAA rating: R
Running Time: 81 minutes

REVIEWS

Entertainment Weekly. Feb. 17, 1995, p. 44.
The Hollywood Reporter. Feb. 6, 1995, p. 5.
New York Times. Feb. 4, 1995, p. 10.
Variety. Feb. 6, 1995, p. 77.

their niche as low-life audio successes and should have stopped there.

The Jerky Boys is obviously just a trip to the bank for all concerned. Little effort and enthusiasm and creativity went into it. The movie leaves you feeling like making a prank phone call yourself, to Disney Pictures. How about a call from Mickey Mouse, complaining that Roth, Melkonian and colleagues have given him a bad name?

—*Michael Betzold*

Johnny Mnemonic

"A riff on *Blade Runner*...a snappy chase thriller with often unexpected turns from its oddball cast. This chase thriller boasts sharp cyber effects...that generate a real kick. Johnny's 98 minutes rate as a big plus."—Stephen Schaefer, *Boston Herald*

"*Johnny Mnemonic* is a movie bursting at the seams with energy, with ideas and images."—Tom Maurstad, *Dallas Morning News*

"Science fiction at its best. It's a must see."—Jim Ferguson, *Prevue Networks*

Box Office Gross: $19,075,720

The future looks bleak for Johnny (Keanu Reeves). The year is 2021, and the premium commodity is information. This means that stealing data is the ultimate big heist, but it seems that transferring that information cannot be done on any one of the high-tech information highways but must be carried by very low-tech, human, mnemonic couriers. But these humans don't really have to use mnemonic devices. Instead, they are "wet-wired" with a brain-implanted computer chip to help them do their job. (For those who are not familiar with the word, mnemonic devices are mental tricks used to remember things. For example, using the word *Homes* to remember the five great lakes of Huron, Ontario, Michigan, Erie, and Superior.)

For some reason, though, to make room for this memory-enhancing chip, Johnny has had to dump all his childhood memories. But now he wants the chip out and his memories back. His agent Ralfi (Udo Kier) tells him it will be an expensive operation, but if he undertakes one last job he should have enough money to afford it.

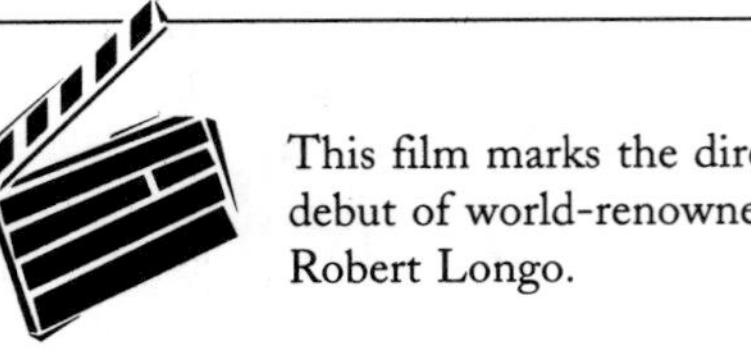

This film marks the directorial debut of world-renowned artist Robert Longo.

The job involves smuggling data stolen from a large pharmaceutical corporation, Pharmakom. Unfortunately, Johnny is wet-wired to carry only 160 gigabytes while the data is 320, but that doesn't stop him. When the procedure is completed, the informationally taxed Johnny says, "It feels like my brain's going to explode. What did they upload, the Library of Congress?" This is information overload of a lethal sort, because this information really can make his brain explode.

But it's not the Library of Congress Johnny is carrying. It's the cure for the world-wide epidemic of Nerve Attenuation Syndrome which makes those it attacks shake as if their own circuits were overloaded —a disease whose symptoms Pharmakom makes a tidy profit from treating, and whose cure would make the company's profit and loss ledger go from black to red.

Johnny has to take the information to Newark, New Jersey, but there are a few problems. For one thing, because the transfer of information was interrupted by Pharmakom's Yakuza gangsters, Johnny only has a part of the code needed to retrieve the information from his brain. Secondly, the enormous amount of data is a lethal load for Johnny who must now download it or die within twenty-four hours. Finally, as a street doctor tells him, "You got a head full of Pharmakom data and they hired the Yakuza to get it out." And Pharmakom is only interested in Johnny's cryogenically frozen head. To make matters worse, after several failed attempts by the Yakuza, Pharmakom brings in a ringer, the Street Preacher (Dolph Lundgren), a futuristic televangelist with a mean streak.

Working on Johnny's side is his technologically enhanced bodyguard Jane (Dina Meyer) and her friends the LoTeks, a counter culture living in a "city" named Heaven which is suspended under a bridge. Led by J-Bone (Ice-T), the LoTeks' goal is to wage guerilla warfare on the high- tech society whenever possible by doing things like scrambling television broadcasts.

When they find out what Johnny is carrying, they bring out their secret weapon, Jones, an armor-plated, technologically enhanced, code-breaking dolphin once employed by the Navy.

The question is, will Jones be able to retrieve the information without the full code before the Yakuza or the Street Preacher find them or before Johnny's head "explodes?"

Well, maybe the real question is whether *Johnny Mnemonic* will be able to capture more than a core cyberspace-Keanu Reeves audience, because basically, it is only a minimally appealing film.

This first realization of the writings of popular punk cyberspace writer, William Gibson, author of the multi-award winning novel *Neuromancer* (1984), was eagerly awaited by his fans, but they'll find it was better as a short story than as a screenplay. What plot there is seems to be nothing more than an excuse to demonstrate computer special effects. And while they may be interesting, they are not dramatic or thrilling.

The film is also hampered by a few questionable premises: Just why can't data be encrypted and electronically transmitted in the future? Why are physical couriers any more safe than a high-tech method of information transfer? Why does Johnny's childhood have to be purged to make way for a computer chip?

When Gibson adapted his own story for the screen, he seems to have forgotten how to pace a story to create suspense or excitement. Consequently, *Johnny Mnemonic* is not well told, has little tension, and even less human interest.

This last point may, in part, be due to the flat line delivery which Reeves's character gives. We know Johnny had his childhood memories removed in order to be a mnemonic courier, but did he have to have his personality removed also? His dialogue is stilted and his character unlikable, selfish and one-dimensional. (Is this really the follow-up Reeves wanted after last year's successful *Speed*?) Furthermore, most people will have difficulty swallowing Reeves as the brainy 007ish courier when he is better known as the air-guitar playing Ted of *Bill & Ted's Excellent Adventure* (1989)? (The film originally starred the new Batman, Val Kilmer, but he walked out on the project.)

Added to these problems is the fact that this is the very first feature film from Robert Longo, who is much better known as a conceptual artist. This might lead one to think that at least the film would be visually stunning, but it's not. This is a very dark, gloomy, bleak future in which there appear to be absolutely no daylight hours. While one assumes this was meant to try and create an appropriate atmosphere for the film, it instead helps to make it flatter than Reeve's dialogue delivery.

However, there are a few nice touches to the film. The LoTek's Heaven is engrossing. Suspended high above Newark (really Toronto) and under a bridge, it is concocted from cast off buses, campers, airplanes and railway cars connected by catwalks and protected by trashed VWs which act as firebombs when dropped from the bridge. Also, Dolph Lundgren's Jesus-like Street Preacher is an evangelical extremist with an amusingly merciless hit-man mentality and more lives than Arnold Schwarzenneger's Terminator.

The rest of the cast, unfortunately, is basically wasted. The popular Japanese star Takeshi, better known to American audiences as the sadistic Sgt. Hara in 1983's *Merry Christmas, Mr. Lawrence* is rarely on the screen (although the Japanese version of the film has an extra 15 minutes starring him). The accomplished Barbara Sukowa (*Berlin*

CREDITS

Johnny Mnemonic: Keanu Reeves
Street preacher: Dolph Lundgren
Takahashi: Takeshi
J-Bone: Ice-T
Jane: Dina Meyer
Shinji: Denis Akiyama
Spider: Henry Rollins
Anna K: Barbara Sukowa
Ralfi: Udo Kier
Pretty: Tract Tweed

Origin: USA
Released: 1995
Production: Don Carmody for an Alliance production; released by Tri Star Pictures
Direction: Robert Longo
Screenplay: William Gibson based on his short story
Cinematography: Francis Protat
Editing: Ronald Sanders
Executive producers: Steffan Ahrenberg, B.J. Rack, Victoria Hamburg and Robert Lantos
Production design: Nilo Rodis Jamero
Art direction: Dennis Davenport
Set decoration: Enrico Campana
Costume design: Olga Dimitrov
Music: Brad Fiedel
Special Effects supervisor: Rory Cutler
Visual Effects supervisor: Gene Warren, Jr.
MPAA rating: R
Running Time: 98 minutes

REVIEWS

Chicago Tribune. May 26, 1995, section Friday, p. J.
Entertainment Weekly. June 9, 1995. p. 36.
Los Angeles Times. May 26, 1995, p. F1.
New York Times. May 26, 1995, p. B3.
USA Today. May 26, 1995, p. 3D.
Variety. May 22-28, 1995, p. 92.

Alexanderplatz, 1980, and *Rosa Luxzemburg*, 1986) as Anna K also has little to do beyond being a computer presence and the conscience of Pharmakom's founder. And the usually scene-stealing Udo Kier, from Andy Warhol's stable of actors, is killed much too early in the film to be much fun.

Comparisons to other sci-fi films are inevitable. *Blade Runner*'s (1982) bleak Japanese oriented future is here, but it is never as atmospheric or interesting. The visual graphics certainly outperform those of its predecessor, *Tron* (1982), and even the more recent *Ghost in the Machine* (1993). But when it comes to heroes with brain chips, *Total Recall*'s (1990) hero was a lot less stiff than Johnny—and we cared more about him.

Johnny Mnemonic may be an indication that cyberspace could be more interesting on the printed page or the computer monitor (or in our own minds) than it is on the silver screen. It will be fascinating to see if anyone will eventually be able to pull it off with enough style, wit, and excitement to carry its weight in the movies.

—*Beverley Bare Buehrer*

The Journey of August King

"Director John Duigan demonstrates intelligence and cinematic skill, as well as a rare, always welcome gift for eroticism on-screen."—Stephen Farber, *Movieline*

"Strikingly suspenseful. A humane and intelligent film."—Bruce Williamson, *Playboy*

The Journey of August King is one of those films that did not make a great deal of money at the box office, but may be a nice discovery at the video store. It is a simple, well-crafted, intelligent film. With good lead performances from Thandie Newton, Jason Patric, and Larry Drake, and fine direction by John Duigan, this film rises above much of the simplistic storytelling found in contemporary mainstream films. As well-crafted a film as it is, however, it is curiously uninvolving.

To call this film unexciting is probably to miss the point: it is hardly a blockbuster, and doesn't intend to be. It is a simply story about the price of moral behavior and about the nature of freedom. It follows classic storytelling technique by telling its story through its protagonist's journey. It has only a few moments of violence, and has no sex—it clearly does not intend to appeal to the widest audience possible. It is a piece for followers of "art-house" films in general, and period films in particular.

The Journey of August King takes place in 1815. It is the story of a young widower, August King (Jason Patric), living in the Appalachian mountains, who has just come into town to sign the deed on his property and go to market. Upon arrival, he hears about the escape of two slaves belonging to Olaf Singletary (Larry Drake). He encounters one of the slaves, a woman named Annalees (Thandie Newton), and offers her assistance in the form of food and shelter for the night.

First American feature for Australian director John Duigan.

Aware that he is risking everything—even his life—August decides to help Annalees by allowing her to ride with him on his return trip home. He hides her in his wagon, covering her up with blankets and dry goods, and sets out for his property. As they travel, it becomes known that one of the slaves is traveling with a man who has a wagon, making their journey extremely dangerous. They are pursued by Olaf, who is emotionally distraught over the escape of his favorite slave.

As they travel, August and Annalees learn about each other and develop a close bond which turns perilously close to love. Knowing that love is out of the question, August sends Annalees walking over the mountains to the North (and to safety) upon their return to his home. But not before Olaf's discovery that August was the man with the wagon who took in his slave. The punishment is to lose his property. The author shows that material possessions mean nothing when compared with a human soul, and that one human soul cannot truly possess another.

John Ehle is the screenwriter, adapting his own novel of the same title. Ehle has been compared to William Faulkner, perhaps because he writes about uneducated Southern people with a deep respect of the inherent poetry in their speech. He provides a literate and verbally intelligent script which serves its theme well. There are lyrical moments seemingly lifted from the novel, such as when Annalees says of August's deceased wife, "God must have caught her, August...caught her in his hand." Another moment comes when

Annalees asks August about love. "A preacher told me love is a feeling that overflows," says August. "Where does it overflow to?" asks Annalees. "I don't know; I never have overflowed," he responds.

Occasionally, Ehle's poetic style seems only to exist in order to sound poetic. When August asks Annalees why she ran away from Olaf, she responds, "to keep him from taking my soul." Another moment comes when a traveler tells August, "You had a woman here last night, I allow....You had a woman last night, you did." Though the addition of the "I allow" and the "you did" are probably historically accurate, they seem a bit out of place, given that the language is only peppered with such phrases. If Ehle had chosen to have his characters always speak with this historical accuracy, perhaps these moments would not stand out. (But then again, perhaps the entire script would have been as difficult to decipher as Shakespeare.) But more than the addition of the vernacular, Ehle's theatrical dialogue seems a bit out of place in the naturalistic setting of the film.

> "I demand her back unsullied."—Slave owner Olaf from *The Journey of August King*

In particular, it is the naturalism of the direction and the production design which work against the poetic, rather lofty dialogue. Director Duigan, an Australian native known for directing *Flirting* (1990), does an excellent job of overseeing the recreation of Appalachia, circa 1815. He gets wonderful assistance from his production team, presenting a thoroughly believable physical environment. From the authentic wagons, to a maypole dance, to the extraordinary detail in the set decoration and costuming, this film is a visual winner. It is lovingly filmed by cinematographer Slawomir Idziak, known for his sensitive work on the Polish film *Blue* (1993). Duigan and Idziak are careful to make beautiful images wherever possible. The very first image of the film, for example, is of a drop of blood on a thorn, followed by a bear in a tree, and then a spider crawling across a foot. These interesting images command the audience's attention even as they foreshadow the story.

On occasion Duigan allows himself to get fancy with some shots, that, like some of the dialogue, seem to have been created simply for effect. One shot of August and Annalees, is just such a moment: the two share dialogue posed in front of trees in a rather unrealistic fashion.

The pace of the film may seem slow to many audience members. Only in an excellent river-crossing sequence, or in one or two moments of the near-discovery of Annalees does this film cause pulses to increase. Duigan was so intent on creating a simple film that he seems to have diluted some of the suspense of the story.

Of course, some of the lack of suspense may be due to the lead characters and the actors portraying them. August King is the kind of character that Gary Cooper might have played: stoic, strong, moral, and rarely excitable. Patric captures his sense of morality, but lacks a certain something that Cooper brought to this type of role. It is hard to know what is going on inside Patric's head and heart: perhaps in trying to capture August's simplicity, Patric missed some of the complex emotions which must be going on inside him. When he says, "I always breathe easier when I'm near home," it is hard to remember if he was not breathing easier before. Additionally, Patric's contemporary, pretty-boy good looks belie the hard life of a man who lives alone in the wilds of the Appalachian mountains. Like Robert Redford in *Jeremiah Johnson* (1972), Patric's attractiveness works against credibility.

Thandie Newton turns in a fine, if by-the-numbers, performance. She is required to be very wide-eyed much of the time, and the character's innocence cause her to appear passive once she joins August on his journey home. But Newton provides a touching and beautiful moment at the end of the film, gracefully saying goodbye to August, and making her way purposefully across the top of the mountain. It is an achingly beautiful moment, and though most of the success of the image rests in the camera work of

CREDITS

August King: Jason Patric
Annalees Williamsburg: Thandie Newton
Olaf Singletary: Larry Drake
Mooney Wright: Sam Waterson
Mr. Cole: Nesbitt Blaisdell
Bolton: John Doman

Origin: USA
Released: 1995
Production: Nick Wechsler, Sam Waterston and Keith Addis; released by Miramax
Direction: John Duigan
Screenplay: John Ehle; based on the novel *The Journey of August King* by John Ehle
Cinematography: Slawomir Idziak
Editing: Humphrey Dixon
Production design: Patricia Norris
Costume design: Patricia Norris
Sound: Paul Ledford
Casting: Billy Hopkins, Suzanne Smith and Kerry Barden
Assistant direction: Skip Cosper
Music: Stephen Endelman
MPAA rating: PG-13
Running Time: 91 minutes

Duigan and Idziak, Newton's gentility and strength shine in her close-ups.

The film's best performance belongs to Larry Drake. Drake, known to audiences for his fine portrayal of a mentally retarded man on T.V.'s *L.A. Law*, will surprise everyone with the power and strength of his performance here. He plays Olaf as a dangerous man with no sense of morality, and is quite frightening in several scenes in which he displays his frustration at not finding Annalees. Drake is able to transcend Duigan's laid-back direction to provide the only sense of real danger in the film.

It should be noted that this film was co-produced by Sam Waterston, who plays a small but pivotal role. Waterston brings his usual strength and stature to this film, in the role of the lawmaker who must enforce the destruction of August's property.

Ultimately, the success or failure of this film rests on its ability to touch the hearts of its audience. When August loses his home, he realizes that the only possessions he needs are his soul, which no one can take away. August arrives at his spiritual destination after an arduous and dangerous journey, but curiously, it doesn't feel like we went on the trip with him. The film is good, and its theme is clear. But it feels as if the journey happened in a very good, very historically accurate book. It would be great to feel as if we went on the journey with August instead of reading about it.

—*Kirby Tepper*

Judge Dredd

"Non-stop action!"—Todd McCarthy, *Variety*

Box Office Gross: $34,693,581

In recent years, computer graphics have allowed films to be increasingly larger in scope and more interesting with their visual images. The grandaddy of them all has become *Jurassic Park* (1993), with computer-enhanced graphics of dinosaurs so real, one would swear that the dinosaurs were filmed in their own habitats. The extraordinary surge in film special effects has, however, tended to surpass the writing of the films. There are a lot of wonderful-looking films out there which have dreadful stories and even worse dialogue. *Terminator* II (1991) is an example of a film that made bags of money in spite of its weak script and inattention to character development.

Now comes *Judge Dredd.* And happily, this film has substance and style beyond its extraordinary special effects. Unlike other wonderful special effects-heavy films, such as *Total Recall* (1990) or *Running Man* (1987), this is a film that actually has a theme. Granted, it isn't *Hamlet* or even *Forrest Gump* (1994), but its themes about justice vs. humanity have enough depth to be interesting to viewers who like a little intelligence with their special effects.

Judge Dredd was created by John Wagner and Carlos Ezquerra 18 years ago for the British comic magazine *2000 A.D.*

Taken from the popular British comic hero, *Judge Dredd* takes place during the twentysecond-century in the United States. The country is now divided into three "MegaCities" with "The Cursed Earth" and the foreboding penal colony of Aspen between them. Sharing the same hellish vision of the future presented in films including *Metropolis* (1926), *Blade Runner* (1982), and *The Terminator* (1984), the United States is presented as a violent place where cities have grown vertically instead of horizontally, so that sixty-five million people are crammed into what was once known as New York. A scrolling prologue, similar to that of *Flash Gordon* (1930's) or *Star Wars* series (1980's), describes how MegaCity was overrun with "roving bands of street savages [who] created violence the justice system could not control," and how the system was changed to create "street judges" who would be judge, jury, and executioner on the spot.

And in this perilous place, Judge Dredd (Sylvester Stallone) is the most feared among street judges. Having no emotions ("there ought to be a law against them") and no personal relationships ("I had a friend once...but I judged him,") Dredd believes only in the law and metes it out with cruel certainty. He comes up against the evil Griffin (Jurgen Prochnow), who, with the aid of bloodthirsty Rico (Armand Assante), is involved in eliminating the justice system and taking over MegaCity. Dredd is framed for murder, and his mentor, the kindly Chief Justice Fargo (Max Von Sydow), is forced to roam The Cursed Earth. Aided by petty criminal Herman Ferguson (Rob Schneider) and the earnest Judge Hershey (Diane Lane), Dredd uncovers Griffin's plot and restores justice to MegaCity. But not without a lot of mayhem.

"I never broke the law! I am the law!"—Judge Dredd from *Judge Dredd*

This is a very violent film. The violence, as intense as Stallone's *Rambo* series (1980s) or in any Arnold Schwarzenegger film, may put some audiences off. There are graphic images of knifings and amputations and countless deaths by firearms. Most action films seem to require assault weapons nowadays, as if any other murder is just too tame. It is interesting to note that a scene which shows numerous genetically-cloned males standing upright does not depict their sexual organs. Presumably, the Motion Picture Association of America still feels that the depiction of anatomically correct sexual organs is pornographic, while the graphic depiction of 100 or more murders is not. This point will go unnoticed by audience members who are inured to violence. But it is paradoxical that for a film whose central theme deals with the humanization of the justice system, the motion picture "justice system" requires it to view human sexuality as more dangerous than human savagery.

Polemics aside, this is a film that can be enjoyed by anyone willing to succumb to the mile-a-minute action helmed by director Danny Cannon. Surely one of Stallone's best films, *Judge Dredd* offers some of the most eye-popping visuals in a long time. From the beginning, production designer Nigel Phelps, director of photography Adrian Biddle, visual effects supervisor Joel Hynek, and art director Les Tomkins provide an extraordinary vision of the twentysecond century. (It is hard to tell whom to credit for the film's extraordinary look—countless individuals contributed their expertise). The "exteriors" of MegaCity provoke audible responses from the audience. As the camera rolls through the city, layers and layers of strangely shaped towers mix with familiar images of the present day to imply just what might happen to our world if unchecked growth continues. The Statue of Liberty is buried deep within the labyrinth of the mile-high city, and everywhere there are signs selling Coors and other familiar twentieth-century brand names. Though these are surely "product placements" (companies pay a premium to prominently display their names in motion pictures), the familiar names offer a way for the audience to identify with the environment.

Several effects are mesmerizing. One of the best is a airborne motorbike chase through the byzantine towers of MegaCity, where Dredd and sidekick Fergie, with the aid of computer graphics, take a ride that is as exciting as anything offered by Disneyland (and reminiscent of the magic carpet ride in Disney's *Aladdin*, 1992). Another wonderful effect happens when Dredd and Fergie, escaping a huge fireball, jump into a chute, out of which they free fall off the side of a building. Finally, a climactic fight taking place inside the destroyed head of the Statue of Liberty is awesome, with the camera appearing to view the action from far above the Statue, dwarfed by huge buildings, and surrounded by flying vehicles and countless lights.

Director Danny Cannon, who has only one other commercial film to his credit (*The Young Americans*, 1995) does a simply wonderful job with this material. Though he never misses a chance to keep the action moving, he also knows when to slow it down. A fine scene between Stallone and Von Sydow brings some humanity to the action, and several scenes in which Judge Hershey (Lane) tries to learn more about Dredd's past are excellent.

In addition, Cannon and screenwriters William Wisher and Steven E. deSouza provide a good deal of humor. It is less leaden than the famous "I'll be back"-style witticisms of the *Terminator* films, and very much in keeping with the comicbook-style of this film. Dredd has his own signature saying because ever since *Dirty Harry*'s (1971) "go ahead, make my day," action stars have been provided with such signature sayings. Whenever a criminal pleads his innocence, Dredd replies, "I knew you'd say that," with an impassive sneer. Stallone uses the saying to comic advantage, and he

CREDITS

Judge Dredd: Sylvester Stallone
Rico: Armand Assante
Fergie: Rob Schnieder
Judge Griffin: Jurgen Prochnow

Origin: USA
Released: 1995
Production: Charles M. Lippincott, Beau E.L. Marks for a Cinergi production; released by Hollywood Pictures
Direction: Danny Cannon
Screenplay: William Wisher and Steven deSouza; based on the *Judge Dredd* comic book series by John Wagner and Carlos Ezqerra
Cinematography: Adrian Biddle
Editing: Alex Mackie and Harry Keramidas
Production design: Nigel Phelps
Art direction: Les Tomkins
Special Effects and ABC Robot Supervisor: Joss Wiiliams
Sound: Leslie Shatz
Costume Design: Emma Porteous
Music: Alan Silvestri
MPAA rating: R
Running Time: 91 minutes

somehow manages to imply a wink when saying the line. Other funny moments come in the form of technology (a transportation vehicle radio says, "take caution in this sector, there is a citizen riot in progress; have a nice day,") and from sidekick Fergie (referring to Dredd, he tries to save his skin from some ruthless killers by saying, "excuse me...we're not together"). Fergie and Dredd develop a classic hero/sidekick relationship, and the constant asides from Fergie help reduce the intensity of the violence.

Stallone is excellent in this film. It is ironic that he is funnier here than when he tried to be funny in the dreadful *Rhinestone* (1984) with Dolly Parton. It is also ironic that in this stoic, almost inhuman character, Stallone displays more humanity and is more real than in most of his past films. Perhaps he is older and wiser, perhaps he is working with better material, but he is just plain better than ever. When he tells Hershey (who defends him in the framed murder charge) "you did your best" after he is convicted, his brief words speak volumes. He is excellent in a scene where he has trouble reconciling that "the law" that he so reveres is inaccurate and corrupt. Stallone isn't Anthony Hopkins or John Gielgud, but he is at his best as this well-developed action character.

Armand Assante provides a wonderful villain as Rico. He is pure evil and is a worthy and dangerous foil for Stallone. "You want chaos," he says, "I am chaos. You want fear, I am fear." And he is. Assante appeared once before with Stallone, playing his brother in *Paradise Alley* (1978); he is a consistently excellent screen villain whose most recent outing was as a sinister mob killer in 1994's *Trial by Jury*.

Diane Lane is a strong presence as thoughtful Judge Hershey; she does not allow herself to be a winsome, hyper-feminine woman, nor does she allow the toughness of her character to reduce her own sense of what it means to be feminine. The venerable Max Von Sydow lends dignity to his role as the compassionate Judge Fargo.

For visual thrills, for auditory stimulation (this is a loud film), and for a lightning-fast hour-and-a-half of sheer escapist entertainment, this film can't be beat.

—*Kirby Tepper*

Jumanji

"An extraordinary movie, like nothing you have seen before!"—Sam Rubin, *KTLA Morning News*

"The greatest movie adventure you will ever take!"—Nancy Jay, *KTVT-CBS, Dallas*

"*Jumanji* is a fabulous adventure full of suspense and surprise! Robin Williams is hilarious!"—Alan Silverman, *Voice of America*

Box Office Gross: $53,745,261

In the deepest dark of night in 1869 New Hampshire, two boys bury a chained and locked chest deep into the ground. One hundred years later, drawn by the sound of mysterious, beating drums, it is found by young Alan Parrish (Adam Hann-Byrd) as he wanders about the construction site of the annex for his wealthy father's shoe factory. Inside the box Alan finds not a cache of gold coins, but what appears to be a better treasure for one so young, a game, Jumanji. But this is no ordinary "children's" game. Once one has started to play it, and unleashes its hidden forces, one must finish the game in order to restore things back to the way they were.

That night, after fighting his way home against a band of bullies and following an argument with his father (Jonathan Hyde), Alan and his friend Sarah (Laura Bell Bundy) begin to play the game. A role of the dice by Sarah causes the game pieces to move themselves, a mysterious message unveils itself in the center of the board, African bats are turned loose in the house. Terrified, Alan drops the dice, but the game "thinks" he has rolled. His playing piece also automatically moves itself and the message reveals Alan's fate: "In the jungle you must wait, until someone roles a 5 or 8." With that Alan magically disappears into the board, and Sarah runs screaming out of the house.

Twenty six years later, the once opulent and now derelict Parrish mansion has just been bought by Nora (Bebe Neuwirth). She plans on turning it into a bed and breakfast where she can raise her newly orphaned niece Judy (Kirsten Dunst) and nephew Peter (Bradley Pierce). But just as before, one day the children follow the mesmerizing sounds of beating drums right up into the attic where they, too, find the game and begin to play it. The first turn releases giant mosquitoes on the unsuspecting town of Brantford and the next mischievously malevolent monkeys. But when one of the children roles the magic number, Alan is suddenly liberated from the jungle in which he has been trapped for all those years.

It doesn't take long for the now grown up Alan to find out that the world he left in 1969 has changed dramatically. The shoe factory, like the house, is in ruins, and, after spending all they had looking for the vanished Alan, his parents have died. Judy and Peter, however, have a more pressing problem. The mosquitoes and monkeys are terrorizing the town and how will they ever explain the lion trapped in Aunt Nora's bedroom?

The animals are a combination of computer animation from Industrial Light & Magic and animatronics by Amalgamated Dynamics.

At this point they find the game's caveat about once it has been started it must be finished. They try to enlist Alan's help, but as he tells them, "I've seen things you've only seen in your nightmares." He has no desire to replay this pernicious boardgame. However, he does eventually offer to stand by and help as Peter and Judy try to play out the game. Unfortunately, when one of them roles the die, no game piece moves. It is not their turn. Instead, they are just players three and four of the game Alan and Sarah started in 1969. Alan not only has to play, he has to find Sarah (Bonnie Hunt) so she too can play.

What the game has unleashed so far is nothing compared to what it has in store for the quartet. The house's floor suddenly turns into quicksand and just as quickly solidifies, trapping Alan and Sarah in the boards. Giant spiders menace them, the Great White Hunter Van Pelt stalks Alan, vines with deadly purple flowers consume the house, a stampede of elephants, zebras, rhinos and pelicans tear through the walls and out into the streets of Brantford, and the coups de gras is delivered by a monsoon and flood complete with alligators . Will the four ever finish the game in time? And if they do, will the world be restored to the 1969 when the game was begun or to 1995 when Judy and Peter joined?

Jumanji began its life as a very sparse 1981 children's book written by award-winning author Chris Van Allsburg. But the story was so meager that in order to bring it to the screen something had to be added. What was added were several characters including Alan, Sarah, and officer Bentley (David Alan Grier); three time frames; several additional hazards; and incredible special effects. In fact, one can easily say that the special effects steal *Jumanji* as easily as the game stole Alan back in 1969. Created by George Lucas' Industrial Light and Magic, and combining computer animation and animaltronics, the hazards that menace the game players are brought not only to life, but realistically into the life of the movie. But as created by special effects, these threats weren't meant to look like the real thing, they are larger than life. The lion is more menacing, the vines more insidious, the monkeys funny, but positively evil.

Director Joe Johnston (*Honey, I Shrunk the Kids*; *The Rocketeer*) who started his cinematic career as a visual effects co-ordinator at Industrial Light and Magic, easily has carried his facility with special effects over to this film. In fact, some have complained that with all these effects, Johnston has sacrificed the story's message and the characters have been overwhelmed. I don't agree. Alan has to learn several valuable life lessons through the game: finish what you start, face your fears, and most of all, the value of one's parents. These themes should be obvious to all but the youngest viewers.

And it is with the youngest viewers that one might have a qualm with *Jumanji*. It is not for the young or faint of heart because this is essentially a horror story dressed as fantasy. Most of the humor is that nervous laughter one expresses after the monster is no longer on screen. And the dangers are probably too intense for young children.

For older audiences, however, this roller coaster of a film is as enjoyable as a lesser quality *Indiana Jones*. And it

CREDITS

Alan Parrish: Robin Williams
Van Pelt/Sam Parrish: Jonathan Hyde
Judy Shepherd: Kirsten Dunst
Peter Shepherd: Bradley Pierce
Sarah Whittle: Bonnie Hunt
Nora: Bebe Neuwirth
Carl Bentley: David Alan Grier
Carol Parrish: Patricia Clarkson
Young Sarah: Laura Bell Bundy
Young Alan: Adam Hann-Byrd
Exterminator: James Handy

Origin: USA
Released: 1995
Production: Scott Kroopf and William Teitler for Interscope Communications/Teitler Film Production; distributed by Tristar Pictures
Direction: Joe Johnston
Screenplay: Greg Taylor, Jim Strain and Chris Van Allsburg; based on the book by Chris Van Allsburg
Cinematography: Thomas Ackerman
Editing: Robert Dalva
Production design: James Bissell
Art direction: David Willson and Glen Pearson
Set decoration: Tedd Kuchera and Cynthia T. Lewis
Costume design: Martha Wynne Snetsinger
Music: James Horner
Special Visual Effects and Animation: Industrial Light and Magic
Animaltronics Effects and Special Make-up designer and creator: Tom Woodruff, Jr, and Alec Gillis
MPAA rating: PG
Running Time: 100 minutes

is made more watchable by a winning cast. Bonnie Hunt plays Sarah as someone on the edge but still capable. She brings warmth, humor and empathy to a character whose world fell apart when she was young but must now transcend her own limitations. Kirsten Dunst, the young star of *Interview with a Vampire*, once again brings maturity to her role, and along with young Bradley Pierce, manages to avoid being they type of child characters who are too cloying and syrupy. Of the supporting players, David Alan Grier probably has the most thankless, yet funniest role. As a caricature of a cop for whom everything goes wrong, Grier is not only hilarious, but also sympathetic.

"Everybody in this town has been calling me crazy ever since I saw you sucked into a board game."—Sarah Whittle from *Jumanji*

But everyone knows that if anyone can steal a film, it is Robin Williams. To play Alan, a boy who is trapped in a man's body, a wild child brought up on his own in the jungle, no one can beat Williams. It is an enthusiastic and genuine performance by an actor who, as Gene Siskel has said, is "a special effect all by himself." Consequently, as incredible as it may seem, he does compete on equal ground with the vines, hunters, and alligators.

Jumanji, which was the top box office grosser for the weekend it opened, is a perfect film for the time in which is was released. Everyone complains that during the holidays they want a good family film, and while this one may scare some younger viewers, it is still good family fun. It's not a great film; it's not a classic, but it is good entertainment.

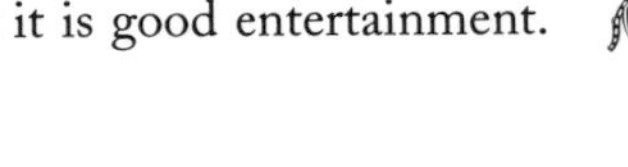

—Beverley Bare Buehrer

REVIEWS

Chicago Tribune. December 16, 1995
Entertainment Weekly. December 15, 1995
Time. December 18, 1995, p. 75
New York Times. December 15, 1995
Variety. December 7, 1995.

Jury Duty

Box Office Gross: $17,014,653

Pauly Shore has made a lucrative career out of being a "slacker," and here he turns his irresponsible nitwit character loose on the American justice system. Some will find this film amusing. Many will find *Jury Duty* guilty of not even being one of those films that is "so bad it's good."

It is the story of Tom Collins (Pauly Shorc), a lazy young man who is pampered by his trailer-park-trash Mom (Shelley Winters). Tommy's Mom and her boyfriend Jed (Charles Napier) head off to Las Vegas to get married, taking their trailer with them. But coincidentally, two minutes before they leave, Mom discovers a jury duty notice, and Tommy instantly gets the idea to let the American taxpayer pay for his room and board, thinking that jury duty will be an easy way to get free meals and five bucks a day.

Predictably, Tommy offends everyone on the jury with his antics, until he somehow discovers a sense of civic pride, wins over his fellow jurors (including beautiful Tia Carrere), and saves the day.

It is a turn on *Twelve Angry Men* (1957), the Henry Fonda film of days gone by, only this time there are eleven angry people and one rather irritating comedian. The other eleven jurors are stock characters and each appears to be given one identifying characteristic intended to be humorous, like the redneck military man who misses his girlfriend and shows pictures of her at every turn. Their only truly funny moment is when, after Tommy has been the lone hold-out on what seems to be an open-and-shut case, the jurors literally try to torture him in order to end their deliberations. It is the culmination of a montage which is actually brisk and funny, and it is surprising that the rest of the film lacks the wit of this sequence.

But perhaps the reason wit is lacking is that Shore appears disinterested in being witty. Shore's comedy is based more in sophomoric jokes such as being overheard in the bathroom, or pouring milk all over himself in a questionable sequence depicting Shore as a male stripper in a dairy outfit. On paper, these may sound like they have comic possibilities, but Shore does not do them justice. Unlike Jim Carrey, whose *Dumb and Dumber* (1994) struck box-office gold, Shore does not appear to back up his antics with any technique or talent.

In addition, the script, by Neil Tolkin, Barbara Williams, and Samantha Adams, relies on Tommy's selfishness for its story. The selfish laziness of the character seems so intrinsic, so fundamental to Shore's character, that he is ultimately very hard to like. When his mother leaves to get married, his only response is "where will I eat, sleep, and watch TV?" While the other jurors are stuck in a dilapidated wing of the hotel, Tommy connives his way into a beautiful suite—and he breaks the law in order to do so. He breaks another law when he speaks alone to the accused killer.

The writers and director John Fortenberry might correctly counter that this is a only a comedy, and more specifically a satire, commenting on the ways people like to rip off the system. It is also a spoof of the media circus surrounding the O.J. Simpson trial. And they might also say, correctly, that it is unfair to harshly judge a comedy that is simply a vehicle for the antics of an improvisational comedian. All of that is fine, but this particular comedy commits the crime of not being particularly clever or funny.

Perhaps, though, fans of Pauly Shore will enjoy the ways he finds of disrupting the trial. And the film does have a few good things going for it, such as the facial contortions of accused killer Murphy (Jack McGee) and the parody of the Simpson trial media circus (a rip-off of *Court TV* is right on target). In addition, the production design of Deborah Raymond and Dorian Vernacchio shows wit and style. Shelley Winters provides a brief glimpse into Tommy's homelife with gusto, though it may be hard for cineastes to see Winters in this film. Her fans should note that she is a friend of Shore's family, and has an off-screen friendship with Pauly Shore, perhaps explaining why she is in this film.

On the whole, *Jury Duty* can best be described as being targeted for those who felt *Dumb and Dumber* was too artsy. Some stars can be wildly successful while being widely detested at the same time. It is futile and rather rude to say that *Jury Duty* is a bad film—but it is wise to warn those who dislike Shore that they should stay at home and rent *Twelve Angry Men* instead.

—*Kirby Tepper*

CREDITS

Tommy: Pauly Shore
Monica: Tia Carrere
Frank: Stanley Tucci
Harry: Brian Doyle-Murray
Judge Powell: Abe Vigoda
Jed: Charles Napier
Principal Beasely: Richard Riehle
Sarah: Alex Datcher
Nathan: Richard T. Jones
Libby Starling: Sharon Barr
Murphy: Jack McGee
Richard Hertz: Nick Bakay
Ray: Ernie Lee Banks
Mom: Shelley Winters

Origin: USA
Released: 1995
Production: Yoram Ben-Ami and Peter M. Lenkov in association with Weasel Productions; released by TriStar Pictures and Triumph Films
Direction: John Fortenberry
Screenplay: Neil Tolkin, Barbara Williams, and Samantha Adams
Cinematography: Avi Karpick
Editing: Stephen Semel
Art direction Deborah Raymond and Dorian Vernacchio
MPAA rating: PG-13
Running Time: 86 minutes

Just Cause

"A classic thriller with a knockout finish."—Bill Diehl, *ABC Radio Network*

"An edge-of-the-seat psychological thriller that keeps you guessing until the final scenes."—Bobbie Wygant, *KXAS-TV*

"A riveting, action-packed thriller! Brimming with suspense."—Neil Rosen, *NY1 News*

Box Office Gross: $36,853,222

Just Cause begins with Sean Connery playing Harvard law professor Paul Armstrong, arguing against the death penalty in a public forum, indicating that the film is going to be "about" criminal justice and capital punishment. In fact, the film offers an extended argument concerning the death penalty, but its position on the issue is ambiguous and shifting. If Connery's lawyer is a spokesman for the whole film, then the thrust of the argument will be liberal and compassionate, but ultimately this is not a compassionate film. The film's debate is loaded, subversive, reactionary, and mean-spirited.

After arguing against the death penalty, Armstrong is approached by a grandmother (Ruby Dee) who has taken a bus to Massachusetts all the way from Florida to see if he will represent her grandson, Bobby Earl Ferguson (Blair Underwood), who is on death row awaiting execution for the brutal murder in the Everglades of an eleven-year-old girl. Bobby Earl later claims that another convict on death row, a psychopathic serial killer named Blair Sullivan (Ed Harris) in fact killed the girl.

Armstrong has not practiced law for twenty-five years and refuses the case; but he later shows the grandson's letter to his wife (Kate Capshaw), who was also once a lawyer and had practiced in Florida. She persuades him to reconsider, and the viewer later discovers she has her reasons. She had once represented Bobby Earl on an earlier charge of rape, after he had been railroaded into jail by the white victim's former boyfriend, who also happened to be the arresting officer. She handled this case badly and still feels guilty about it. Her black client got a record and lost his full scholarship to Cornell University.

"Every once in awhile you gotta get a little bloody—it's good for the soul."—Laurie Armstrong from *Just Cause*

This former conviction also made Bobby Earl a prime suspect after the eleven-year-old girl was found raped and murdered in 1986. A redneck cop first came after him, but Bobby Earl's worst nightmare turned out to be a black officer, detective Tanny Brown (Laurence Fishburne), who brutally coerced Bobby Earl into signing a confession. There is no question that the confession was illegally obtained, and, although the Harvard professor is roughed-up and intimidated by Tanny Brown and his redneck deputy, who do not want the prisoner released, Armstrong is smart enough to get an acquittal. One expects the film to end there, but it is not yet over; in fact, as far as understanding the plot and the characters, it's just getting started.

Bobby Earl had told Armstrong that the real murderer, Blair Sullivan, played to creepy perfection by Ed Harris, was also on death row, and there is no reason to doubt his word, since the lawyer takes it as truth, and the viewer is likely to trust his judgment. The psychopath Sullivan, who is soon to be executed, plays mind games with the lawyer, giving him obscure biblical clues that lead him to the murder weapon. As a psychodrama, the film succeeds, but after it moves effectively in the direction of *The Silence of the Lambs* (1991), it then changes course quite unexpectedly and begins to resemble *Cape Fear* (1991). The viewer is likely to feel exploited, misled, and manipulated as a result; but the plot moves so rapidly that there is hardly time to resent the manipulation as it occurs.

During the opening academic argument over the death penalty, the man who debates Connery's humane lawyer on the issue asks him how he would "feel" if the case involved a man who had murdered Armstrong's own wife. This emotional ploy brings about an abstract liberal response, but one wonders if Armstrong feels the same way at the end of the final reel, after he has had to fight like hell to protect his wife and daughter from a raging, revengeful psychopath. The same Tanny Brown who was set up as a villain in the first reel becomes the hero in the last one as the film reverses its stand on justice in America. *Just Cause* seems intended to demonstrate an extreme example where, the film seems to suggest, one's Constitutional rights should be aborted.

Writing for *Sight and Sound*, Claire Monk concluded that because everything the audience is "shown or told is in danger of not ringing true," the film is both "narratively and morally perverse." The message panders to the popular notion that the legal system is corrupt because of loopholes that allow dangerous and devious killers to be set loose on society. The only way to achieve justice, in other words, is to subvert due process and trick a legal system that offers too much protection for the guilty. It's as though the presumption of innocence is somehow passé, and that is what makes the film subversive. Writing from a British perspective, Claire Monk cannot understand how "perverse" and subversive this film may be.

Just Cause, then, is finally about revenge, not justice, and it presents, finally a brutal and frightening argument in favor of the death penalty imposed by corrupted means. Although Connery's lawyer is hardly a liberal wimp, the film sides firmly with Fishburne's cynical cop who is willing to bend the law in order to get revenge. It's a mean world that *Just Cause* presents as an evil spectacle. The deviousness of the film is that it is designed to placate people on both sides of a really complex issue, but emotionally it sides with mean justice riding roughshod over the legally protected rights of the accused.

Connery's Paul Armstrong is more sedate than characters he has been playing recently. As in *Rising Sun* (1993), Connery plays an expert who is brought in on a case to resolve a question of guilt, and, as in *Rising Sun*, his main competition comes fron an African-American who ends up being a kind of partner, but in *Just Cause* he is challenged by a stronger actor. Laurence Fishburne's Tanny Brown is a piece of work, a man driven by strong family values and a sense of righteousness.

Because of the plot reversal that is manipulative but still logical, neither Tanny Brown nor Bobby Earl are what they first seem to be. The film depends upon strong, highly-defined characters well enough acted to overcome the contrivances and turnings of the plot. The psychopath played by Ed Harris recalls Anthony Hopkins in *The Silence of the Lambs* in the actor's mad and manacing stare and in the way he is framed in close-up and lighted from below; but the most that can be said of Harris's acting is that it is a passable imitation.

Reviewers were quick to notice also that the final hunt and confrontation in a Florida swamp seems to imitate the Martin Scorsese remake of *Cape Fear*, but if the competition here is between Blair Underwood and Robert De Niro, it's no contest in terms of menace, though Underwood gives a good journeyman performance. As far as the directing goes, moreover, Arne Glimcher is no Martin Scorsese. The best this film can do in its better moments is to imitate better films.

Arne Glimcher directs the film with flashy pyrotechnics equally applied to a car chase in Miami, Armstrong's discovery of two decomposing corpses, and a splashy confrontation in a swamp decorated by designer alligators with day-glo eyes. The director seems to care more about how the film looks than about what it means. *Just Cause* is a law-and-order nightmare, a slick exercise in designer justice offering a repulsive spectacle of revenge. It should be troublesome to anyone who cares deeply about Constitutional rights.

—James M. Welsh

CREDITS

Paul Armstrong: Sean Connery
Tanny Brown: Laurence Fishburne
Laurie Armstrong: Kate Capshaw
Bobby Earl: Blair Underwood
Blair Sullivan: Ed Harris
Wilcox: Christopher Murray
Evangeline: Ruby Dee
Kate: Scarlett Johansson
Warden: Daniel J. Travanti
McNair: Ned Beatty
Delores: Liz Torres
Ida Conklin: Lynne Thigpen
Lena: Taral Hicks
Sergeant Rogers: Victor Slezak
Phil Prestiss: Kevin McCarthy
Libby Prentiss: Hope Lange
Lyle Morgan: Chris Sarandon
Elder Phillips: George Plimpton

Origin: USA
Released: 1995
Production: Lee Rich, Arne Glimcher, and Steve Perry, in association with Fountainbridge Films; released by Warner Bros.
Direction: Arne Glimcher
Screenplay: Jeb Stuart and Peter Stone; based on the novel by John Katzenbach
Cinematography: Lajos Koltai
Editing: William Anderson
Production design: Patrizia von Brandenstein
Art direction: Dennis Bradford
Set design: Mark Garner
Set decoration: Cloudia and Maria Nay
Casting: Billy Hopkins, Suzanne Smith and Kerry Barden
Sound: James Sabat
Costume design: Ann Roth and Gary Jones
Music: James Newton Howard
MPAA rating: R
Running Time: 102 minutes

REVIEWS

The Detroit Free Press. February 17, 1995, F-4.
Entertainment Weekly. No.262, February 17, 1995, pp.18-24.
The Los Angeles Times. February 17, 1995, F-4.
The New York Times. February 17, 1995, C-18.
Sight and Sound. Vol.5, No.5 (NS), May 1995, pp.47-48.
Variety. February 13-19, 1995, p.47, p.49.

Kicking and Screaming

"*Kicking and Screaming* benefits from an appealing cast and Mr. Baumbach's keen recollection of what it's like to be smart, promising and temporarily adrift."—Janet Maslin, *The New York Times*

Box Office Gross: $510,903

Well, it's about time someone did it right. With *Kicking and Screaming*, writer/director Noah Baumbach has finally made a film about the twentysomething generation that is accessible to someone older than 24. Granted, the makers of the television comedy *Friends* have been doing it for a couple of years now. But recent films dealing with the aimlessness and perpetual self-analysis of "Generation X" members have been generally bloated and dull. Parting from the overly hip style of *Reality Bites* (1994), the pompousness of *Metropolitan* (1990) and the over-indulgent philosophizing of *Bodies, Rest, & Motion* (1993), Noah Baumbach (in his debut film) creates a delightful and witty film.

As the film opens, Grover (Josh Hamilton), Skippy (Jason Wiles), Max (Chris Eigeman), and Otis (Carlos Jacott) have just graduated college. The four best friends are about to be dragged kicking and screaming into real life. During their graduation night party, Grover and Jane break up because she has decided to go to Prague to continue her studies. Subsequently, the four men wander aimlessly into the summer wondering what to do with their apparently useless English literature degrees. Most of the film deals with their escalating conflicts with each other, as they have nothing to do but sit around and play trivia games, drink beer, and complain. As unpleasant as they sound, Baumbach and his actors manage to make the characters sympathetic: they are victims of their own narcissism, and the trouble they have overcoming the disparity between their expectations and the reality of the world makes them ultimately sympathetic.

Max is the worst of the bunch, a dyed-in-the wool cynic whose inner dissatisfaction is projected onto the others, catalyzing a climactic conflict between the inseparable friends. As played by Eigeman (a veteran of Whit Stillman's *Metropolitan* as well as *Barcelona* [1994]), Max is a curmudgeon with a ready quip and an underlying sadness. Eigeman has honed his act well in past films, and his razor-sharp delivery renders insipid the word "snide." One of his funniest and most revealing moments comes with the earthy Kate (Cara Buouno): against his better judgment, he is dating Kate, a young "townie", an uneducated Brooklynite. When she tells him "today is my seventeenth birthday," he tells her, "good, now you'll be able to read *Seventeen* magazine and get all the references." Eigeman's delivery suggests more than a snide swipe at her age and I.Q., however; the smirk on his face suggests he is a bit embarrassed that he is dating her, and reinforces his own inner dissatisfaction.

Debut of 25-year-old writer/director Noah Baumbach.

As important as Max's quips (and Eigeman's performance) are to the film, Grover is essentially the protagonist. Having lost his girlfriend Jane (Olivia D'Abo) to Prague, Grover is sent into a tailspin which fuels much of the film. Sensitive, well-filmed and well-written flashbacks show the evolution of Grover and Jane's relationship, making it increasingly clear what a fool Grover was to choose not to join Jane in Prague. As Grover, Josh Hamilton is a stalwart hero, and he does a fine job portraying Grover's weakness without appearing weak as an actor. Hamilton has some fine scenes with Elliott Gould, who plays his overly earnest (and somewhat childish) father. Like the others, Grover is clever with words, and has some choice responses to situations. One of his best is "what I was thinking might only be a bad summer may actually turn out to be a bad life." Hamilton plays him as a young man to whom it never occurred that life would require some decision-making. Hamilton creates Grover as a twentysomething everyman who is powerless against the forces of reality, but who finally learns (toward the end of the film) that action is preferable to inaction. Certainly it is clear that Baumbach wants Grover and the others to represent that part of us which would rather hide away than face the exigencies of life. But through Hamilton's performance and Baumbach's writing, it becomes clear that Grover's inaction is seen as cowardice.

Additionally, Baumbach almost explains the cowardice of Max, Grover, and their friends by making them victims of their culture. The priorities of trivia over true knowledge, or image over depth have created a whole generation of people who, like the heroes of this film, think they are deep because they can name "six empirical philosophers" and still know "the name of the puffy guy who flew" on television's animated *Josie and the Pussycats*. Baumbach suggests that the difficulty of finding a job in today's world makes it doubly confusing to young white men who believe that a good education will make them effortlessly rich and happy. He emphasizes his point by making the men in this film completely ineffectual while the women have a sense of purpose. For example, Jane decides to go to Prague in order to progress in her career and to expand herself as a person. Skippy's girlfriend Miami (Parker Posey) is as self-possessed as Skippy is foolish—Baumbach reverses traditional roles to have Miami conducting an affair behind Skippy's back. And when Kate and Max go out on their first date, Max waits for Kate to open the car door for him; then, it is Kate who gets into an argument with someone over a parking space, threatening to beat him up while Max sits quietly in the car. The women are going somewhere; the men are staying right where they are. With this dichotomy, Baumbach makes a strong case for the selfishness of the current "angry white man" syndrome. These men could have more, but they feel such a sense of entitlement that they are unwilling to do any real work to get more out of life.

One of them, however, does try to get a job, and it is hilarious. Otis applies at a video store, and his interview scenes are hilarious. "What are your influences?" is one of the questions he is asked at the interview. Otis does land the job, and the scenes in the video store are a hoot, as he is trained to learn the various categories of films, from "dog films" to "terminal illness." These sequences are more than just funny, though, as they amplify Baumbach's assertion of the intellectual dangers of pop culture's dominance. A vague reference to the video store owner wishing to sell a screenplay is a fun allusion to overblown pop culture star Quentin Tarantino.

Eric Stoltz plays a role in the film, as an older (28 years old) guy who has been in school for ten years and works in a bar. Having taken every class several times, and having seen it all by now, Stoltz' character (named Chet) is a kind of granddad to the "younger" men. Max sees Chet for the insufferably pompous pseudo-intellectual that he is, but Otis thinks of Chet as a guru. (Several scenes involving a book club started by Chet and Otis are hilarious, particularly when Otis tries to discuss a book he didn't read, only to discover that it is written in Spanish.) Stoltz has great fun with this droll character, but it is hard to tell if Stoltz thinks of himself as a grand old character actor compared to these young upstarts; after all, Stoltz has been the self-consciously "cool" star of such vacuous films as *Bodies, Rest, & Motion* and *The Prophecy* (1995). It seems that this time around, Stoltz knows that his character is meant to be amusing: he has fun with Chet's constant use of the pompous phrase, "maybe I'm paraphrasing myself here..." before he begins to philosophize.

Baumbach constantly creates clever new ways to verbalize the feelings of his characters. Max's boredom is perfectly expressed when he says, " I caught myself writing 'go to bed' and 'wake up' in my date book as if they were two separate events." Besides the cleverness of the lines, they are somehow revealing of the characters' inner feelings, no small feat given the inability of the characters to display much beyond peevishness. Occasionally, Baumbach throws in a sly reference or quiet little joke, such as the name of one of the college campus buildings—"Wilkes Booth Hall," or a passing line where one student tells another that "there's an 80's party in the dorms."

But Baumbach doesn't reserve his cleverness for little jokes or clever quips alone. The scenes between Grover and Jane are very simple and quite touching (and D'Abo makes an offbeat, gently comic heroine.) Grover's speech where he tries to convince an airline reservations person to get him on a plane to Prague is quite poetic, if a bit unrealistic (given that he is talking to a total stranger.) One line, delivered by Eric Stoltz toward the end of the film, may sound a little too clever to some but is emblematic of the theme and tenor of the film: "How do you make God laugh?" asks Stoltz. "Make a plan," he says. Baumbach's plan worked: he made an excellent film.

—*Kirby Tepper*

CREDITS

Grover: Josh Hamilton
Jane: Olivia d'Abo
Otis: Carlos Jacott
Max: Chris Eigeman
Chet: Eric Stoltz
Skippy: Jason Wiles
Miami: Parker Posey
Kate: Cara Buono
Grover's Dad: Elliot Gould

Origin: USA
Released: 1995
Production: Joel Castleberg; released by Trimark Pictures
Direction: Noah Baumbach
Screenplay: Noah Baumbach and Oliver Berkman
Cinematography: Steven Bernstein
Editing: J. Kathleen Gibson
Production design: Dan Whifler
Assistant direction: Michael J. Allowitz
Casting: Ellie Kanner
Costume design: Mary Jane Fort
Music: Phil Marshall
MPAA rating: R
Running Time: 96 minutes

A Kid in King Arthur's Court

Box Office Gross: $13,406,717

The legend of King Arthur and Camelot has inspired countless films. Even the fantasy of a modern American being placed at the Round Table is a timeworn one. No fewer than four Hollywood films have been made based on Mark Twain's novel, *A Connecticut Yankee in King Arthur's Court*—in 1921, 1931, 1948 and 1949.

From the Disney stable now comes an attempt to update Twain's Camelot yarn for the 1990s. It's a real stretch. Few Camelot fantasies are as bizarre as A *Kid in King Arthur's Court,* a movie that is a two-headed dragon at war with itself.

Hapless young Calvin Fuller (Thomas Ian Nicholas), who belongs to a youth league baseball team nicknamed the Knights, has just struck out again when the earth opens up and swallows him. He lands in the Middle Ages, atop a black knight who is stealing something from King Arthur.

CREDITS

Calvin Fuller: Thomas Ian Nicholas
King Arthur: Joss Ackland
Lord Belasco: Art Malik
Princess Katey: Paloma Baeza
Princess Sarah: Kate Winslet
Merlin: Ron Moody
Master Kane: Daniel Craig
Ratan: David Tysall

Origin: USA
Released: 1995
Production: Robert L. Levy, Peter Abrams and J.P. Guerin for a Trimark Pictures and Tapestry Films; released by Buena Vista
Direction: Michael Gottlieb
Screenplay: Michael Part and Robert L. Levy
Cinematography: Elemer Ragalyi
Editing: Michael Ripps
Production design: Laszlo Gardonyi
Art direction: Beata Vaurinecz
Costume design: Maria Hruby
Sound: Otto Olah
Stunt coordination: Bela Unger
Casting: Allison Gordon-Kohler
MPAA rating: PG
Running Time: 89 minutes

All is not right in Camelot. Arthur (Joss Ackland) is old, weak, half-corrupted and full of self-doubt. Guinevere is dead, and Merlin (Ron Moody) is nothing more than an apparition that appears in a cistern in the bowels of the castle. The mighty sword Excalibur is covered with cobwebs. Merlin apparently has lost his touch too, for it seems he has bungled in bringing Calvin to Camelot to be the brave knight who will save Arthur from his demise.

Instead of chivalrous knights fighting for noble ideals, Arthur is surrounded by treacherous cowards whose thievery has turned the peasants against his rule. The chief conniver is the oily Lord Belasco (Art Malik), who is plotting to overthrow Arthur while feigning to be his most loyal servant. Belasco wants the hand of Arthur's eldest daughter Sarah (Kate Winslet) so that he can inherit Camelot. Also apparently working against Arthur is a mysterious, dangerous Black Knight.

This fantasy has the makings of an absorbingly dark twist on the Camelot legend. It's about how lofty ideals can dissipate into selfishness. Played straight, it would have a chance of holding an audience's interest.

But the other head of the dragon is that A *Kid in King Arthur's Court* is an adolescent comedy featuring Nicholas in a weak, pubescent imitation of a Monty Python parody. Wearing his baseball uniform and toting a backpack, Calvin Fuller is a crude colonizer from the planet of Beavis 'n' Butthead. Arriving at a royal feast, he asks where the rest room is "because I've been holding it since the third inning." He uses a boom box as a weapon in a duel against Belasco, gets the local smithy to fashion him Medieval versions of roller blades and a mountain bike, and fixes homemade Big Mac cheeseburgers after tiring of boar's snout. He also cooks up a romance with the king's younger daughter, Princess Katey (Paloma Baeza).

Almost all these bits fall flat. They are plunked into the middle of a rapidly unfolding and offbeat drama that is played to an unending, swelling musical score that speaks of import and purpose, not throwaway comedy. It is a jarring juxtaposition that continues throughout the film: a wisecracking adolescent skit in the middle of a somewhat compelling and very earnest reworking of the Camelot legend.

If comedy is their purpose, the filmmakers continually thwart it with their racing, unconventional drama. But whenever the drama starts to get interesting, it is spoiled with a knockoff mini-skit exploiting the modern/medieval rift.

One minute Calvin is being threatened by Lord Belasco within an inch of his life, the next he is teaching King Arthur how to chew bubble gum. One minute the sisters are discussing love and the demise of their family honor in noble British accents, the next Princess Katey is learning 1990s

American slang. This is meant to be charming, but it's rarely more than annoying.

Director Michael Gottlieb never achieves a consistent tone. It doesn't appear he's trying for one. The medieval characters all slip into and out of the "thou" and "ye" forms of old English. Sometimes they are bewildered by Calvin's slang, other times they inexplicably understand it.

Screenwriter Robert L. Levy conceived the film after reading Twain's *A Connecticut Yankee in King Arthur's Court* with his son and then imagining his son as the protagonist in a new version of Twain's story.

With a rubber face and a shock of thick black springy hair, the young Nicholas (who starred in *Rookie of the Year*) is a deadpan comedian with a bright future. His performance often rescues the film from being exposed as downright silly. But Nicholas never makes us believe in him as much more than a wisecracking underdog.

Baeza has a smart, winning presence as Princess Katey, and Winslet is intriguing as the enigmatic Sarah. Ackland plays Arthur in the typical knockoff British fashion of a bumbling, senile dolt. Moody is silly as Merlin.

The film bogs down in rather obvious and contrived proceedings that concern Calvin's rescue of Arthur from his moral doldrums. Calvin learns he has some gumption and that heart is more important than knights' armor. Arthur is redeemed by the visitor's refusal to give into evil.

This very serious segment gives way to a wacky and highly unusual series of climactic scenes that topple plenty of preconceptions. The ending makes audiences reconsider the film in a new light. Just what what is going on here? Parody? Social commentary? It's not clear, but it is intriguing.

The film's remarkable ending, one that comes literally out of left field, makes it impossible to dismiss *A Kid in King Arthur's Court* entirely. It is a mess, but an unconventional stew is tastier than the same old formulas. This film follows formulas only to blast them apart in the end.

With a lot more attention to script, plot and direction, *A Kid in King Arthur's Court* might have succeeded as a cult film. The makings are there, but the recipe doesn't work. Part of the problem is a badly underwritten role for the male hero of the film, Master Kane (Daniel Craig).

Marketers must have been puzzled about how to sell this film. Trailers picked out slapstick sequences and tried to sell it as a kids' comedy. But those expecting light comedy will find a film that is surprisingly frightening at times, corny at others, and ultimately quite pointed.

—Michael Betzold

REVIEWS

New York Times. August 11, 1995, p. C16.
USA Today. August 11, 1995, p. 40.
Variety. August 14, 1995, p. 55.

Kids

"A wake up call to the world."—Janet Maslin, *New York Times*

"An astonishment of a movie. Daringly original, touching and alive with unsettling erotic power."—Peter Travers, *Rolling Stone*

"A masterpiece. It pulls the ground out from under you."—Amy Taubin, *Village Voice*

Box Office Gross: $7,417,210

"Kids, what's the matter with kids today?" lamented Paul Lynn in the film version of the sixties musical "Bye Bye Birdie." Little did he know what lay ahead for troubled youths. The problems facing America's teenagers has been great fodder for film-makers for decades. These films have usually stirred up great interest and also considerable controversy. This subject is the focus of former photographer Larry Clark's debut film *Kids*, released by Miramax Pictures. It is a bold and explosive story of teen-sexuality and drug abuse in the turbulent climate of urban life in New York City. *Kids* made it's debut one evening at the Sundance Film Festival held by Robert Redford, and people and critics have been talking ever since. *Rolling Stone Magazine* called it "the real movie event of the summer." *Siskel and Ebert* gave it "two thumbs up" and Amy Taubin of *Village Voice* called it "a masterpiece." What it is, is a fine piece of American film-making that deals with a compelling and disturbing problem that faces the core of a nation and threatens its very existence.

Teenagers have always been perceived as a hormonally confused group of individuals and films have consistently reflected this conflict. In the 1950s, James Dean and Natalie Wood in the classic teen movie *Rebel Without a Cause* flirted with death in a dangerous pastime called drag racing. Carole Lynley and Brandon de Wilde in *Blue Denim* made filmgoers examine teenage pregnancy, which was certainly a bold move for the 1950s. Marlon Brando in *The Wild One* helped a nation coin the phrase "juvenile delinquent" and brought leather jackets into fashion. The film version of *Hair* brought to the screen a new breed of teenager called "hippies." They blasted middle America with the concept of free love, drugs and war protests. From *Blackboard Jungle* to *Menace II Society* film audiences have been exposed to gritty, realistic and disturbing insights into the world of the modern teenager. *Kids* is perhaps the most explosive look at this phenomena to date. It pulls no punches in honestly depicting the rage, the erosion of morals and the reckless behavior of todays urban teen.

Larry Clark, a 52-year-old photographer turned film-maker, got the idea for *Kids* during the summer of 1992 when he was photographing skateboarders in New York's Washington Square Park. It was here that he met Harmony Korine, a teenager himself, and asked him if he wanted to write a movie about skaters and drugs and sex. He also asked him to include something about AIDS. It took the young skater only three weeks to finish the script and director Clark never asked him to change a thing. The script that went into pre-production is exactly the script that's on the screen, minus a few lines here and there. It is a relentlessly raw and compelling story that is meant to shock, inform and confront audiences with its explosive and riveting realism.

The story follows a group of teens through one sweltering summer day in frenetic New York City. There are three main characters: Telly (Leo Fitzpatrick), who calls himself the "virgin surgeon;" Jennie (Chloe Serigny) who lost her virginity to Telly and has discovered that she has been infected with the AIDS virus from him; and Casper (Justin Pierce) a skateboard ace whose main ambition in life is to do drugs and have sex as often as possible. These three characters are the main players in a thinly structured story line that revolves around Chloe trying to find Telly to inform him that he has infected her with the deadly virus. The action of the teens throughout a "typical" day is shot in a documentary style by director of photography, Eric Edwards. It has the look and feel of an X-rated segment of *Dateline* NBC. This "cinema verite" form works in effectively drawing the viewer into the reckless and volatile world that many teenagers inhabit in today's society.

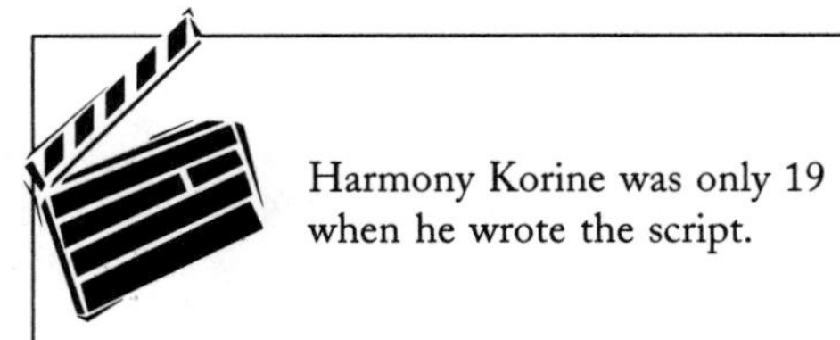

Harmony Korine was only 19 when he wrote the script.

Kids does not pull any punches. It opens with a rather explicit scene of seventeen-year-old Telly attempting to seduce an angelic-looking teenager who looks to be around fourteen years old. The camera pans through the bedroom showing an array of stuffed animals, making the girl appear even more like a child. Telly pants "Boy, do you know what I wanna do?" and proceeds to deeply kiss the girl in extreme closeup. She appears to be apprehensive and somewhat reluctant, but through Telly's persistence she gives in to his lust. As the couple have intercourse it becomes evident that Telly has no intention of making the experience pleasurable. The young girl whimpers "It hurts, it hurts" but nothing stops Telly from agressively continuing. At this point in this already unsettling scene, a blaring soundtrack begins and the viewer is made aware from the start that they are about to witness some harsh and disturbing images.

"That bitch was so clean," Telly says to Casper as he boasts about his latest conquest. The two pals carry on a vulgar conversation about the experience as they walk through the urban jungle. They seem oblivious to the city's chaotic atmosphere surrounding them. They jive and strut and urinate on the street. They rob a convenience store of a quart of beer while swearing racist remarks at the owner. The moving camera tracks their every move as they reach their destination, a crash pad that serves as a drug haven for more exiled kids. The scene is riveting because of the immediacy and honesty of the actors. The camera disappears and its like being on the street with these hardcore teens. All illusion is stripped away and the fierceness of their lifestyle is on display.

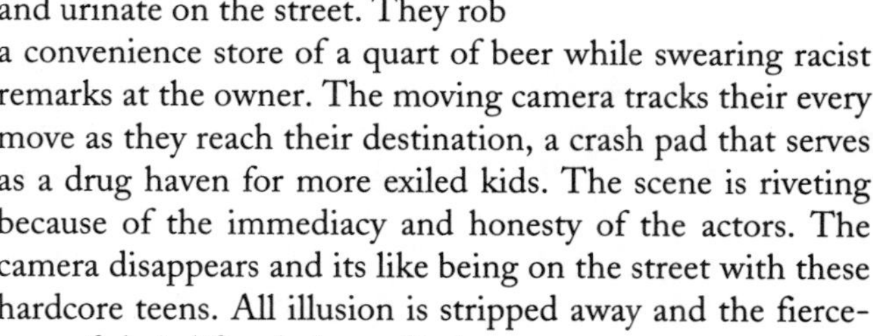
"But I only had sex one time with one boy."—Jennie on finding out she's HIV-positive from *Kids*

As the days events unfold, Jennie discovers she has tested positive for the HIV virus and has only slept with Telly. Suddenly the sexual escapades of the young Lothario take on new meaning. Not only is he seducing these young girls, he may, in fact, be killing them. Oblivious to these events, Telly and Casper continue their prowl through the "asphalt jungle" and wind up in Washington Square where they connect with the skateboarders. The power in this scene again is that everyone seems absolutely real. There are no visible signs of the mechanics of acting. The scene initially has a festive quality to it; everyone's having a good time and getting high. However, it soon turns into a ghastly display of racism and violence. Casper gets into an altercation with a black skater and it turns into a fight. Soon everyone jumps in and gangs up on the lone skater, like a pack of rabid wolves. It ends with Casper smashing the man's head with his skateboard. The bloodied, half-dead man lies crumpled on the ground while Telly spits on his face, making racist remarks. As disturbing as this scene is, it is extremely relevant to what this movie is saying. These kids are angry, very angry. They are time-bombs ready to explode, to lash out at anyone who threatens them. Whose to blame for this tragic state of affairs? The parents, society, politicians, the educators, the media, the kids themselves? These are some of the serious questions that *Kids* raises and asks the viewer to ponder.

"I always wanted to make the great American teenage movie," said Larry Clark in an interview in *Harpers Bazaar* in August 1995. "The kind of film that's immediate, like John Cassavetes' *Shadows*, but in 1994. I didn't want to make a documentary. I wanted a film that would play in malls across America." Whether Clark has made a masterpiece is debatable, but he has succeeded in bringing to the screen a vivid, honest and sometimes brutal portrait of some of America's troubled teens. The one important element that saves the film from the category of exploitation is the seriousness of the questions it raises about responsibility. Not only the responsibility of the teens themselves, but of everyone. These disillusioned youths did not suddenly appear out of nowhere. They are the byproduct of a breakdown in the family unit, economic hardship, ecological predictions of doom, drugs "atomic" viruses and leaderless government. They symbolize the woes of a nation. Therefore they represent an important segment of the population, worthy of examination. *Kids* does this with intense scrutiny and honesty. The expression "tell it like it is" aptly applies to this brave film. If there is to be a future, there needs to be a frank evaluation of the present, shocking though it may be.

—Rob Chicatelli

CREDITS

Telly: Leo Fitzpatrick
Casper: Justin Pierce
Jennie: Chloe Sevigny
Girl No.1: Sara Henderson
Ruby: Rosario Dawson
Harold: Harold Hunter
Darcy: Yakira Peguero
Taxi Driver: Joseph Knofelmacher

Origin: USA
Released: 1995
Production: Cary Woods for an Independent Pictures & The Guys Upstairs presentation; released by Miramax.
Direction: Larry Clark
Screenplay: Harmony Korine; based on a story treatment by Larry Clark, Jim Lewis, Leo Fitzpatrick and Justin Pierce.
Cinematography: Eric Edwards
Editing: Chris Tellefson
Production design: Kevin Thompson
Set decoration: Ford Wheeler
Costume design: Kim Druce
Sound: Charles R. Hunt, Jan McLoughlin
Music: Randall Poster
MPAA rating: R
Running Time: 90 minutes

AWARDS AND NOMINATIONS

Independent Spirit Awards 1996: Debut Performance (Pierce)
Nominations: Best First Feature, Best Supporting Actress (Sevigny)

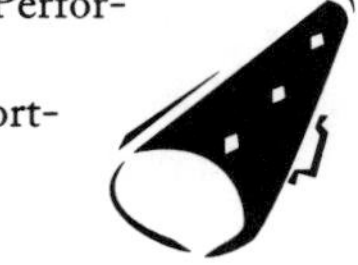

The Kingdom

"An acidly funny gothic soap. You'll laugh, you'll cry, you'll realize *ER* is for wimps."—Graham Fuller, *Interview*

"A giddy, pull-out-the-stops, house-a-fire, loop-the-loop ride."—Jan Stuart, *New York Newsday*

"Undeniable brilliance! Unlike anything you have witnessed or are likely to again."—Larry Worth, *New York Post*

The Kingdom is an extraordinary film made for Danish television. One critic has called it a "comedy of the supernatural," and many others have likened it to Twin Peaks. The setting is an enormous hospital precariously perched on boggy ground. This modern steel and concrete edifice is a tribute to human engineering gone awry. This scientific and technological environment is constantly undermined by the leaks spurting out of its foundations—just like the superstitious beliefs that bedevil the hospital staff, so proud of their modern management techniques and yet susceptible to the seances of one of its patients, Drusse (Kirsten Rolffes), who refuses to leave the hospital when she realizes it is haunted by a young girl in an elevator shaft.

Comprises four episodes (of a projected 13) from a Danish TV series.

Like a television soap opera, *The Kingdom,* brims with subplots, romances, angst and alienation. For example, there is Stig Helmer (Ernst Hugo Jaregard), a pompous Swedish surgeon contemptuous of his Danish colleagues (especially of their efforts to run the hospital democratically). Stig comes on like Charles XII of Sweden, exiling himself to the roof of the hospital where he gazes longingly toward Sweden and curses the stupid Danes. Stig is a rationalist and proud of his diagnostic ability, even though it is clear that he has committed malpractice and is desperate to hold on to his position in the hospital. He scorns a brain operation in which a patient is hypnotized rather than put under a conventional anesthetic. Yet so desperate will he become to revenge himself on his Danish colleagues that he resorts to a trip to Haiti, accompanied by a Haitian member of the hospital staff, in order to acquire a voodoo charm to use on his enemies. Stig is one of those characters who thinks he knows the score and yet who is almost completely removed from reality. It is surely a joke to give him the last name of Helmer—that of Nora's fatuous husband in *A Doll's House.*

The Kingdom is a eerie blend of the everyday and the supernatural. The use of handheld cameras and cramped interior shots suggest not only the claustrophobic atmosphere of the hospital but also the television box or frame through which the action is viewed. The huge hospital is a maze of corridors and interiors that mirror the convoluted workings of the human mind. The staff meetings seem reasonable and unremarkable, but they are juxtaposed to Masonic meetings and rituals presided over the by the staff's senior doctors. The building teems with underground life, of the unconscious driven below, because the professional mind has no place for it in daily discourse.

The movie pivots on the conflict between Stig and Drusse. He tries to expose her malingering, rightly pointing out that there is nothing physically wrong with her. But Drusse appeals to the hospital staff because she insists on a realm of knowing that science simply cannot measure. Just because hospital equipment does not detect anything wrong does not mean that nothing is wrong. One almost expects one of the characters to exclaim that something is rotten in the state of Denmark. When Drusse hears the ghost child crying in the elevator shaft, she conducts an extensive investigation, eventually revealing a crime committed many years earlier by one of the doctors. That doctor's evil spirit

CREDITS

Helmer: Ernst Hugo Jaregard
Rigmor: Ghita Norby
Drusse: Kirsten Rolffes
Moesgaard: Holger Juul Hansen
Mogge: Peter Mygind
Bondo: Baard Owe
Krogen: Soren Pilmark
Judith: Birgitte Raabjerg

Origin: Denmark
Released: 1995
Production: Ole Reim for a Zentropa production; released by October Films
Direction: Lars von Trier
Screenplay: Lars von Trier and Niels Vorsel
Cinematography: Eric Kress
Editing: Jacob Thuesen and Molly Marlene
Art direction: Jette Lehmann
Sound design: Per Streit
Music: Joachim Holbek
Running Time: 279 minutes

infects the hospital and finds a way to re-enter human life by impregnating one of the doctors, who resists the idea that she is carrying a devil's baby.

The Kingdom suggests that evil is a force that moderns overlook at their own peril. Drusse is a fine diagnostician; she really listens and observes and pursues her belief in the supernatural in a humble, if tenacious, manner. Unlike Stig, she does not condescend; instead, she opens herself to experience—even if she risks making a fool of herself. Ironically, Stig makes a bigger fool of himself by standing on his dignity and refusing to entertain alternate realities.

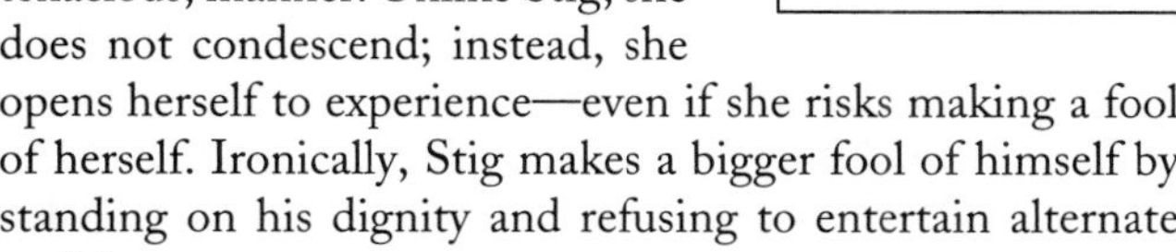

"Danish scum."—Swedish neurosurgeon Stig Helmer on his colleagues from *The Kingdom*

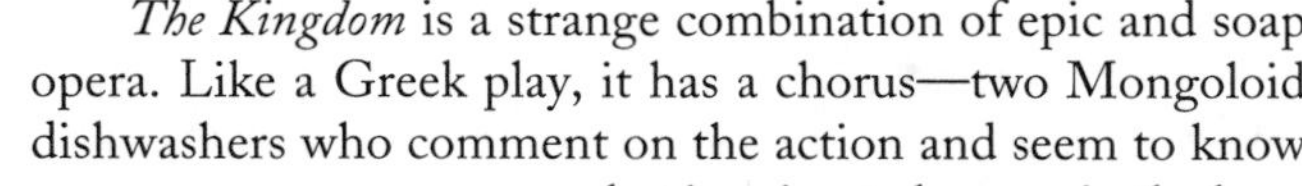

The Kingdom is a strange combination of epic and soap opera. Like a Greek play, it has a chorus—two Mongoloid dishwashers who comment on the action and seem to know what is going to happen in the hospital before the rest of the staff does. They are also like Shakespeare's fools, whose wisdom comes from their simple but clear observations of those in power. Intelligence, as such, certainly cannot save modern man. Indeed, the film could have been prefaced with Hamlet's line to Horatio—that there are more things in heaven and earth than are dreamed of in his philosophy.

—*Carl Rollyson*

Kiss of Death

"The white-knuckle movie of the year! A tightly wound, stylishly photographed thriller...the cast is exceptional."—Stephen Saban, *Details*

"A sleek, muscular thriller played by a terrific ensemble cast."—Janet Maslin, *New York Times*

Box Office Gross: $14,942,422

As a remake of a classic film noir, *Kiss of Death* could afford to take chances, since it belongs to a genre that depends on overstated, psychotic characters and overly complicated plots of Byzantine intrigue punctuated by spasms of violence. *Kiss of Death* lacks a typical femme fatale, but the protagonist, Jimmy Kilmartin, played by David Caruso, is too smart for a typical noir male. In the casting, film noir meets TV's *NYPD Blue*. Jimmy is an ex-convict who has served time, sure enough, but that's in the past. The film picks him up as a family man trying to go straight, until his cousin Ronnie (Michael Rapaport) stops by one night to enlist his aid. Ronnie is short a driver for a shipment of hot cars. Ronnie tells Jimmy that unless he agrees to drive, Ronnie will be dead meat. Ronnie owes his soul to a crimelord named Little Junior (Nicolas Cage), who has a bad temper and no patience for screw-ups. Out of family loyalty and certainly against his better judgment, Jimmy agrees to help Ronnie to save his life.

Things go horribly wrong. Jimmy is driving for a man who turned up drunk and is sleeping in the cab of the truck. Little Junior in a fit of rage pulls the drunk out of the truck and kicks him around. For some unexplained reason (presumably, common decency), Jimmy puts the drunk back into the cab. When his truck is later apprehended by the police, the drunk pulls a gun and starts shooting. Both Jimmy and a Detective Calvin are wounded. Jimmy chooses to serve three years in Sing Sing rather than to rat on Ronnie and Little Junior.

Big Junior (Philip Baker Hall), Little Junior's father, is grateful and orders that Jimmy's wife Bev (Helen Hunt) be paid $400 a week while her husband is serving time; but sleazy Ronnie only offers her $150 a week and pockets the rest, though he tells her she can earn more money by working for him at the illegal chop-shop he runs. Then Ronnie gets her drunk at a strip-joint called "Baby Cakes" that Little Junior owns. Trying to get away from Ronnie, she has a head-on collision with a truck and dies. Jimmy is able to piece together enough information to figure out that Ronnie is to blame and he agrees to do some informing, setting it up so that Little Junior will think Ronnie is the informer. Little Junior takes pleasure in beating Ronnie to death.

An ambitious District Attorney, Frank Zioli (Stanley Tucci), who is determined to be appointed to a Federal Judgeship and Detective Calvin (Samuel L. Jackson), the weeping cop (his right eye was permanently damaged by the truck shoot-out when Jimmy was apprehended) who hates Jimmy, pressure Jimmy into becoming an informer and wearing a wire, and Jimmy cooperates. He does not have much of a choice if he wants to get out of prison, but it is dangerous work, and in his first encounter, Little Junior almost catches him wearing the wire.

After the death of his father, Little Junior turns to Jimmy for sympathy and begins to regard him as a friend. Jimmy is with him when he murders a buyer from Philadelphia named Omar (Ving Rhames), who turns out to have been an undercover federal agent. Because Jimmy was a witness, he gets caught in the middle of a jurisdictional squabble between the Feds and the State authorities. District Attorney Frank Zioli doublecrosses Jimmy when the Feds offer to buy his silence (to protect their cover) by offering him a federal judgeship. As a consequence, Little Junior walks, but by now he knows that Jimmy betrayed him, and he wants revenge, intending to take the life of both Jimmy and his daughter.

Jimmy has rightly concluded that everyone is corrupt, so he takes charge of his life and plans to confront Little Junior on his own turf, with the help of Detective Calvin, who is now about the only friend Jimmy has. Thus the stage is set for the violent conclusion and confrontation between Jimmy and Little Junior. Fortunately, Jimmy is able to hold his own, and with the help of Detective Calvin, sees that justice is done. He has worn a wire while Frank Zioli admitted his willingness to subvert the criminal justice system to achieve his own ambition.

Since David Caruso was determined to jump from a successful television career to cinema, he could not have chosen a better vehicle than *Kiss of Death*, "loosely inspired," the studio confesses, by a 1947 film noir that featured Victor Mature as an ex-convict turned police informer and Richard Widmark as Tommy Udo, an evil psychopath who, in the original film's defining moment, sends a woman in a wheelchair down a flight of stairs. The original was directed by Henry Hathaway from a screenplay written by Ben Hecht and Charles Lederer, based on the novel by Eleazar Lipsky. Screenwriter Richard Price adapted the remake for director Barbet Schroeder, best known for *Reversal of Fortune* (1990), which featured Jeremy Irons as Claus Von Bulow and earned three Academy Award nominations. Richard Price earned an Oscar nomination for *The Color of Money* (1986), written for Martin Scorsese. Price also wrote the screenplay for *Mad Dog and Glory* (1993), in which Caruso played a role before becoming the star of the ABC television series *NYPD Blue*. Caruso's portrayal of detective John Kelly on television earned him a Golden Globe for Best Dramatic Series Actor and made him a national celebrity.

The problem is that some actors may be better on television than in cinema, and Caruso seemed to have burned his bridges when he departed *NYPD Blue*, to be replaced, ironically, by Jimmy Smits, who had himself left a successful television career to try his hand at the movies. Smits is now comfortably at work on the television police beat while Caruso has to prove himself in *Kiss of Death* against Nicolas Cage's psychotic Little Junior Brown and against Samuel L. Jackson's Detective Calvin.

The reviews were mixed. Some reviewers were critical of Caruso, who got top billing, however, and claimed he was not up to the challenge of playing against the flamboyant Nicolas Cage. Some even claimed that Caruso was upstaged by Michael Rapaport's Ronnie, though Ronnie is not so major a character as Calvin, the weeping detective, and Rapaport is surely secondary to Samuel L. Jackson in that role. Rapaport is also outclassed by Anthony Heald, who plays the sleazy mob lawyer Jack Gold with the same level of deviousness that he brought to his role as Dr. Frederick Chilton, the psychiatrist who Dr. Hannibal Lector planned to "have for lunch" at the end of *The Silence of the Lambs* (1991).

Caruso manages to hold his own against Nicolas Cage, whose villainy and brutality is spectacular, but just barely. What saves Caruso is the basic sense of decency that he always brought to his character role on *NYPD Blue*, a man existentially trapped in dirty work that, under other circumstances, he would surely be superior to. The only problem is that in *Kiss of Death* this nobility of character is at odds with Jimmy's background as a punk hood. The actor seems too good for that, and too smart. Those who are not offended by screen violence and gross profanity and are partial to the essential Caruso will get their money's worth here.

Impressed by the commercial success of *Pulp Fiction* in 1994, producers continue to excavate the archives searching

CREDITS

Jimmy Kilmartin: David Caruso
Calvin: Samuel L. Jackson
Little Junior: Nicolas Cage
Bev: Helen Hunt
Rosie: Kathryn Erbe
Frank Zioli: Stanley Tucci
Ronnie: Michael Rappaport
Omar: Ving Rhames
Big Junior: Philip Baker Hall
Jack Gold: Anthony Heald

Origin: USA
Released: 1995
Production: Barbet Schroeder and Susan Hoffman; released by Twentieth Century Fox
Direction: Barbet Schroeder
Screenplay: Richard Price; based on the 1947 motion picture screenplay by Ben Hecht and Charles Lederer
Cinematography: Luciano Tovoli
Editing: Lee Percy
Art direction: Mel Bourne
Music: Trevor Jones
MPAA rating: R
Running Time: 101 minutes

for pulpier fiction and attempting to turn film noir classics into updated neo-noirs without realizing that they cannot step in the same river twice. So we are now seeing faux noirs, remakes made on budgets far out of proportion to their originals, but essentially synthetic. Would anyone accustomed to real café noir settle for instant coffee? Imitation is easier than originality, but each imitated classic needs a gimmick.

Kiss of Death has at least two. The first comes from writer Richard Price, who gives Little Junior an unexpected fascination with acronyms and comes up with one for himself—*Bad*, standing for Balls, Attitude, and Direction. When Little Junior then asks Jimmy to come up with an acronym describing himself, responding to what he surely regards as a stupid request, calls himself *Fab*, which does not quite accurately describe Caruso's cool and surely competent performance as an ex-con forced by circumstances into being a stool pigeon. What this acronym stands for cannot be defined in polite conversation, but it describes Jimmy's feelings about what Fate has done to him ... At Birth. The second gimmick, of course, is the casting of David Caruso, since the producers were surely banking on the speculation that his television fans would follow him back to the movies. The question is not whether there is enough of Caruso's Detective Kelly in his punk stoolie Jimmy, but whether there is too much of it, and whether that is appropriate.

—James M. Welsh

REVIEWS

Entertainment Weekly. No.271, April 21, 1995, pp. 36-38.
The New York Times. April 21, 1995, Cl, C21.
The New Yorker. May 1, 1995, pp. 19-93.
Sight and Sound. Vol.5, No.5 (NS), May 1995, pp.47-48.
The Sun (Baltimore), Maryland Live. April 2l, 1995, p.24.
The Washington Post. April 21, 1995, Dl, D7.
Washington Post Weekend. April 21, 1995, p. 44.
The Washington Times Metropolitan Times. April 21, 1995, C16.
Variety. March 27-April 2, 1995, p.74, p.77.

Land and Freedom

"An absorbing human and political tale."—Caryn James, *New York Times*

In a world where "fighting Fascism" takes on comic book overtones, it is easy to forget that, in the 30s, Mussolini's Fascist government ruled Italy, Hitler was on the rise, and Franco and his dissident generals were trying to overthrow the democratically elected government of Spain. But in 1936 something strange and wonderful happened. From all over the Western world, volunteers flocked to the Spanish front to join the people of Spain in their fight.

In that very year, more than two thousand British volunteers went to fight in the Spanish Civil War. *Land and Freedom* follows one of those men, from his recruitment in Liverpool through his months of hardship and sacrifice fighting trench warfare in Spain, where he and others like him fought to stem the wave of Fascism that was threatening to submerge all of Europe.

Land and Freedom is Director Ken Loach at his best. For the past thirty years, Loach has been making films championing the plight of the working-class man. In *Land and Freedom*, Loach has found the perfect vehicle to introduce a new generation to the socialist struggle of the heroic working-class men and women who sacrificed their lives to safeguard their childrens' freedom. *Land and Freedom* grabs the audience by the heart, making their cause real and meaningful to today's audiences.

In writing *Land and Freedom*, Loach collaborated with Jim Allen, a writer who worked with him on *Raining Stones* (1993). In this tale of the lost revolution, they have created a film that is at once emotionally powerful and idealogically in sync with Mr. Loach's political philosophy. It is a story that is about real people, not the Hemmingways, the Malrauxs, or the Orwells, whose wartime escapades brought world attention to the Spanish Republican struggle. Instead, the film tells the story through the eyes of an out of work Liverpudian, a member of the British Communist Party, who is inspired to put his beliefs into action in Spain.

The film opens in the present. David, now an old man, has a heart attack and his granddaughter rushes him to the hospital in an ambulance. But David dies along the way. Soon after his death, while his granddaughter is sorting through his things, she finds a chest full of old newspaper clippings, letters, and photographs, all from his time in Spain. Among these mementos, she also finds a mysterious red scarf full of earth.

Through his letters home, we follow David's journey to Spain, travelling from Marseilles through the Pyrenees on foot, where he meets members of the *Poum*, the Spanish

Workers' Party, and joins them to fight against the Fascists.

The *Poum* are made up of militia men and women from various trade unions, the Anarchist Party, the Socialist Party, and other foreign volunteers like himself. After Franco's coup against the elected left wing party in '36, 185 out of the 200 generals in the Spanish army defected to the right wing Fascists. Without a trained army, the Spanish government was forced to arm its own people, and men and women throughout Spain formed Republican militias. Their passion and their numbers overcame their inexperience and the people took Madrid, Valencia, Malaga, and Barcelona from Franco.

David, a member of the British Communist Party, had intended fighting with the Communist troops against Franco, but, anxious to get into battle, he joins the *Poum* militia and spends the winter fighting at the front in the trenches.

Their lives are hard but their morale is high, and, in the spring, David's division takes a village from the Fascist army. In this scene Loach successfully captures the frightening chaos of real war, as the militia pursue the Fascist soldiers through the streets of the village. The militia is stymied when a couple of these soldiers take villagers hostage, using them as shields. David, fearful of killing innocent villagers, inadvertantly causes the death of the leader of their squadron, an Irishman named Cougan.

They win the village, but David, suffering from guilt, confesses his part in Cougan's death to the Irishman's girl, Blanca, and they grieve together. In a moving grave-side speech, Blanca tells her comrades that even though they have lost some of their fighters, they are burying them in the earth that they fought to win.

After the funeral, the villagers meet with the militia to discuss their future, and here the film gets bogged down in a debate about collectivizing the land. Everyone speaks, giving the various points of view for and against collectives. But somehow this discussion doesn't ring true. The arguments themselves seem retrospective in content, and the militia seem far too informed about the political situation throughout Europe for a group of people who have been isolated in the trenches for a year. As interesting as this discussion may be, it deflates the emotional energy that the film has, up until then, so masterfully evoked.

More effective is the scene in which the American in their squad decides to join the better armed and professionally trained Communist International Brigade. The scene explains the divisions that are emerging in the ranks, without missing a beat.

Later, in a training accident, a Mauser rifle blows up in David's face, and he is sent to a hsopital in Barcelona. There he meets Blanca again, and their relationship changes from comrades to lovers. But the next day, Blanca discovers that David has joined the Stalin-supported International Brigade. Stalin has been refusing arms to the militias in an attempt to gain control over the war and to entrench the Communists with more power. Blanca tries in vain to explain this to David, and finally leaves him to return to the front.

David fights in the city now, not against the Fascists, but with the Communists against the Republican militia, who are each struggling for autonomy. He is suddenly struck by the madness of his position when a man from Manchester shouts to him from the militia side. They exchange a few friendly words and David finally realizes that he is killing men like himself, who have come to Spain to fight Fascism. He takes out his Communist Party card, tears it up, and deserts the Communists to rejoin the militia and Blanca.

Back at the front, the militia are ordered to take a position in which they are severely outnumbered and are forced to wait for reserves while they are under attack. But for some reason the *Poum* militia is left stranded in the field, and they finally retreat, but with heavy losses.

Soon after they return to their camp, three truck loads of Communist reserves pull up with the American among

CREDITS

Dave Carr: Ian Hart
Blanca: Rosana Pastor
Maite: Iciar Bollain
Lawrence: Tom Gilroy
Vidal: Marc Martinez

Origin: Great Britain, Spain and Germany
Released: 1995
Production: Rebecca O'Brien for a Parallax Pictures, Messidor Films, Road Movies Dritte Producktionen, Television Espanola and British Screen production; released by Alta Films and Gramercy Pictures
Direction: Ken Loach
Screenplay: Jim Allen
Cinematography: Barry Ackroyd
Editing: Jonathan Morris
Art direction: Llorenc Miquel
Costume design:` Ana Alvargonzalez
Sound: Ray Beckett
Special effects: Reyes Abades
Assistant direction: Javier Chinchilla, Neil Grigson and Julian Hearne
Music: George Fenton
Running Time: 106 minutes

AWARDS AND NOMINATIONS

Cesar Awards 1996: Best Foreign Film
British Academy Awards Nominations 1995: Best Film

them. The commmander tells them that the *Poum* is now illegal, accused of collaborating with the Nazis and the Fascists. The militia refuse to put down their weapons, and the Communist commander gives the order to fire against those who won't disarm. As they reluctantly give up their arms, one man refuses, emotionally decrying the injustice of the Communist betrayal and the futility of their hard-won battles.

Blanca runs to the commander trying to make him stop the firing squad, then in a panic, she turns to her disillusioned gun-wielding comrade. As she runs to him, the soldiers fire and Blanca is killed.

Many are arrested and the rest disband. David brings Blanca's body back to the village where her Irish friend is buried, and the villagers bury her in land that is still theirs, but soon to be Franco's. David takes his red scarf and fills it with the red Spanish earth for which they had all fought so hard.

The scene next moves to the present, and we are at David's funeral. His granddaughter unties the red scarf and spills the earth on David's grave, as a couple of old gents raise their fists in salute. To today's generation, who feel that there are no battles left to fight, Loach has dusted off an old cause and made it shiney and new, bringing to the screen an emotionally charged ending that is sure to choke up even the most stolid Tarentino fan.

In writing this film, Loach and Allen wanted to be faithful to the historical facts, so they not only researched various histories and documentaries of the civil war but they also interviewed its veterans. In an interview with *Screen International,* on August 11, 1995, Loach recalled his talks with the civil war veterans. "For old people, it's a memory with a lot of pain, but once they started to talk, they had a lot to say. I got the feeling that it's a subject that isn't at rest."

In the climactic scene where some members of the division are arrested and the rest are disbanded, Loach based the character of the *Poum* captain on a war veteran who visited the set while they were shooting. The scene itself is based on the vet's own experiences as he related them to Loach.

Loach is famous for using actors along with non-actors in his films, adding a dimension of reality that adds to his documentary style. His actors come from all walks of life, from electricians to human rights lawyers, but in *Land and Freedom* they all have two things in commmon: they are all working class and they all hold left wing ideals.

Loach's high standards in all aspects of filming are evident in the quality and power of this film. The ultimate litmus test was its screening in Spain, where it received a standing ovation. *El Pais* wrote, "It is a work of great moral sculpture and brilliance....It contains the most beautiful tribute that cinema has given to the memory of free Spain."

The Spanish weren't the only critics impressed with the film. At Cannes, *Land and Freedom* won the International Critics Prize and the Ecumenical Jury Prize. But Loach is no stranger to Cannes and has won awards for a number of his films, including *Raining Stones* (1993), *Hidden Agenda* (1990), and *Looks and Smiles* (1981).

Land and Freedom is a powerful movie that relights the fires of socialism that have all but been extinguished in recent film history and makes the old arguments suddenly new and pertinent. Loach's working-class heroes are real people, full of the foibles and weaknesses of all of us, but with a courage and loyalty that inspires. David's journey from political naif to hardened soldier unfolds wonderfully, and we are made wiser by his insights and better for his sacrifice.

But *Land and Freedom* is more than the story of one man. It is the story of Stalin's betrayal to the workers and peasants of Spain, of the division of idealogy and consequent fragmentization of the left that ultimately caused the revolution to be lost, and the personal sacrifice of socialist idealists from not only Spain but also the U.S., Britain, Ireland, Germany, France, Italy, and other countries.

"Had we succeeded, we would have changed the world," one of Loach's characters says. Perhaps—just perhaps—he's right.

—Diane Hatch-Avis

REVIEWS

Boxoffice, September 1995.
Entertainment Today, July 21, 1995.
Hollywood Reporter, May 23, 1995, p. 8.
The Independent, July 24, 1994, p. 14.
The Nation, June 26, 1995, p. 936.
New York Times, October 6, 1995.
The Observer (London), October 1, 1995.
Screen International, August 11, 1995.
The Times (London), September 18, 1995.
Variety, April 24, 1995, p. 53.

Last of the Dogmen

"A people lost in time. An adventure they will never forget."—Movie tagline

"A robust movie with a lot of energy and heart."—*Chicago Sun Times*

"An epic adventure...Heart-warming, exciting, romantic!"—Bob Polunsky, *CBS-TV*, San Antonio

"A wonderful romantic adventure!"—Gene Wyatt, *Nashville Tennessean*

"A big, bold energetic outdoor adventure, well-suited for family viewing."—*N.Y. Post*

"Two thumbs up."—*Siskel & Ebert*

"It will touch your heart!"—Dr. Joy Browne, *WOR Radio Network*

Box Office Gross: $7,026,165

For most of Hollywood's cinematic history, Native Americans were called "Indians" or "Injuns," and were depicted as warring savages (e.g., *Fort Apache* [1948]). But of late, Native Americans have been portrayed a bit closer to the truth, most notably in (*Dances with Wolves*, [1990]). *Dances with Wolves* was the most profound example of the depiction of a range of cultural and behavioral differences among a disparate group of people who have been lumped together in the public consciousness for hundreds of years. In addition, *Dances with Wolves* was seen by many as a "politically correct" vision of the world of Native Americans, and its sentimentality was a bit on the sappy side.

And now, a film called *Last of the Dogmen* is here. It is not as successful a film as *Dances with Wolves*, but it certainly rivals it for sappiness. Think of this film as *Lost Horizon* (the 1937 version) plus *The African Queen* (1951) plus *Dances with Wolves*—minus the well-written dialogue of those films. Throw in a little *Brigadoon* (1953) and you get the general idea.

Lewis Gates (Tom Berenger) is a mountain man bounty hunter in the rugged world of Montana's "Big Sky" country, who discovers a strange mystery while on the trail of some homicidal prison escapees. Just as he is about to nab the escapees he hears wailing sounds, sees a cloud of fog and the men are gone—leaving behind only a bit of blood and an arrow. The mystery begins. Gates goes to a library (this is how you know the film takes place in modern times: John Wayne would never have gone into a library) and discovers that over the years there have been 17 similar disappearances. Ever the tracker, he follows the information trail to an anthropologist named L. Sloan, who turns out to be none other than Barbara Hershey. Attractive, sophisticated professor and rough-hewn, man's-man bounty hunter: sounds like a formula for romance, doesn't it?

The romance takes a while to heat up, but it does happen. After all, if you were thrown into the forest searching for the clues to the mystery of several homicidal prison escapees, wouldn't you find it romantic too? Anyway, Gates and Sloan embark on a mysterious journey into the wilds of Montana searching for a possible group of Cheyenne Indians called "dog soldiers" who may have escaped the Sand Creek Massacre of 1864, a true-life encounter in which numerous Cheyenne were slaughtered but several may have escaped. The centerpiece of the film becomes the encounter between Gates, Sloan and the group of Cheyenne who have lived hidden in a valley for 130 years.

Once in the valley, the proceedings become a pastiche of film cliches and ho-hum dramatic moments: a pretty Indian child (Dawn Lavand) befriends Gates' clever dog, Zip; Gates tells Sloan, "this ain't gonna be a picnic, lady...I've seen this country reduce grown men to tears;" Gates tries to

CREDITS

Lewis Gates: Tom Berenger
Prof. Lillian Sloan: Barbara Hershey
Sheriff Deegan: Kurtwood Smith
Yellow Wolf: Steve Reevis
Briggs: Andrew Miller
Sears: Gregory Scott Cummins
Tattoo: Mark Boone Junior
Spotted Elk: Eugene Blackbear
Narrator: Wilfred Brimley

Origin: USA
Released: 1995
Production: Joel B. Michaels for a Carolco Pictures production; released by Savoy Pictures
Direction: Tab Murphy
Screenplay: Tab Murphy
Cinematography: Karl Water Lindenlaub
Editing: Richard Halsey
Production design: Trevor Williams
Art direction: Ricardo Spinace
Casting: Amanda Mackey and Cathy Sandrich
Costume design: Elsa Zamparelli
Sound: David Ronne and David M. Kelson
Music: David Arnold
MPAA rating: PG
Running Time: 117 minutes

save a child by going back to town to get penicillin. You get the idea. Director/writer Tab Murphy, who provided the screenplay for *Gorillas in the Mist* (1988), wrote and directed this film, and may have been so caught up in relating his story that he lost objectivity and allowed a few more cliches than intended.

Sometimes Murphy is able to provide a sense of mystery, such as the early sequence with the prison escapees; at other times, he provides some decent action sequences. He and cinematographer Karl Walter Lindenlaub provide lush and beautiful scenery that display the mystery and wonder which the cliche-ridden plot can only strive for.

"This ain't gonna be a picnic, lady. I've seen this country reduce grown men to tears. It sure ain't no place for a woman."—Lewis Gates from *Last of the Dogmen*

Barbara Hershey delivers a strong performance, fulfilling her duties as a modern version of Katherine Hepburn's character from *The African Queen*. She is intelligent and strong, and delivers an especially fine monologue about the Sand Creek massacre. Berenger is effective as a grizzled mountain-man. Wilford Brimley supplies the voice of a narrator who supposedly heard the story in a saloon (or someplace like that) and is recounting it here. His narration becomes a bit too cute after a while. The Native American characters are played with stoicism and grace by Steve Reevis, Eugene Blackbear, and others.

Audiences can do worse than *Last of the Dogmen*, but they (and writer/director Murphy) can do better. In the future, one can hope Hollywood films which deal with the Native-American experience will have full-blooded Native Americans at the helm of their creative team; such a team might reduce the stream of cliches to a trickle.

—Kirby Tepper

Last Summer in the Hamptons

"Glorious & remarkable, Henry Jaglom's best film by far, this wonderful humane comedy is miles richer than the great majority of what's out there!"—Jay Carr, *Boston Globe*

"Delirious!"—*Buzz*

"Henry Jaglom's best film yet!"—Kevin Thomas, *Los Angeles Times*

"A rare gift!"—Michael Medved, *New York Post*

"A Treat - Two thumbs up!"—*Siskel & Ebert*

Last Summer in the Hamptons is an insider's glance at the personal lives of the actors, directors, and playwrights who bring magic to the stage. Filmmaker Henry Jaglom lets us visit with a family of New York theater people at home and at their most vulnerable. He weaves fictional characters together with their real-life counterparts to form characterizations that are comic, noble, confused, sensitive, and opportunistic, creating potrayals that are almost painfully realistic.

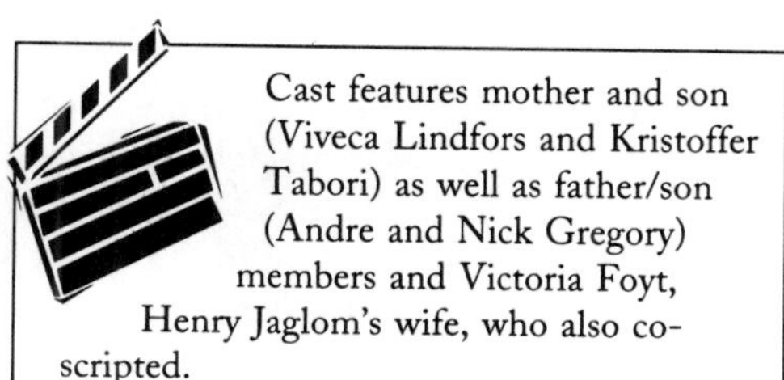

Cast features mother and son (Viveca Lindfors and Kristoffer Tabori) as well as father/son (Andre and Nick Gregory) members and Victoria Foyt, Henry Jaglom's wife, who also co-scripted.

Jaglom has shot the film at what is supposed to be the family's decades old retreat, and is in fact the Jaglom family estate. Actress Viveca Lindfors stars with her real-life son, Kristoffer Tabori; stage director/actor Andre Gregory plays a stage director and his actor son, Nick Gregory, is also among the cast; Jaglom himself has a role in the film, as does his wife, Victoria Holt, who has one of the leading roles. So the production itself is already a family affair in real life, bringing a knell of truth to the interactions of the players in the film.

It opens in the middle of the family's reunion at their summer retreat in the East Hamptons. We are thrown into the gathering, like someone who arrives late to a party, but the fun is in trying to sort out who everyone is and how they all are related. The family of prominent New York theatre people have come together, as they do each year, to put on an end-of-summer backyard play at the house. But this year is different from any other year; this is the last summer they will spend together at the rambling old estate called Proskura.

Helena (Viveca Lindfors), the family's matriarch, bought the house decades before when she was a young Hollywood actress. Now she can no longer keep up the large, run-down estate and has to sell it, so they have all come together for the last time—their last summer in the Hamptons.

The film focuses on this seemingly idyllic creative family, with its ex-film star grandmother (Viveca Lindfors), her successful playwright grandson, and the various other prominent actors and directors in the family. They are bound together by blood and their love of the theatre, but it soon becomes glaringly apparent that this family has some major schisms, and their dramatic way of approaching each little crisis gives the family a dimension that is both funny and very real. These extroverts are passionate about acting, theater, their lost childhoods, their relationships—they are, in fact, passionate about everything.

The film chronicles the sometimes comic, always emotional, scenes among the members of the family, meeting in groups of two's and three's, and sometimes en masse, to hash out their craft and their lives.

But the family are not the only people on the estate. Helena is also a drama coach and she invites her students to spend the summer at the house each year, where they serve as interns, working around the house and on the play. The performance is a very exclusive event and is by invitation only. As the film opens, they are in rehearsal of *The Seagull* by Chekhov. In one of the many ironies of the film, the family rehearses *The Seagull* onstage, as they play out a wacky version of *The Cherry Orchard* offstage.

There are basically two plots in the story. In one, the emotional interconnections among the family members is explored, with all their history and their attempts to resolve old differences. In the other we follow the actors' intrigues as they plot and connive to get into Jake's next play.

When Oona Hart (Victoria Holt) enters into the family dynamics, the two plots intertwine. She is a Hollywood actress, famous for her role as "Mary Marvel," a sort of comic book heroine, who is invited to visit the family at Proskura, and arrives in a limo with her drama coach. But Oona isn't there just for the country air; she has plans. She wants a great deal from this family, and as she wheedles her way into the hearts of the various family members, we watch a deliciously manipulative character exploit her star position to get exactly what she wants. Her laundry list is long: she wants to learn to become a serious actress like her hostess Helena; she wants to be in Jake's next play; she wants the lead; and she wants Jake's famous director father, Ivan (Andre Gregory), to direct it.

In a funny scene, Oona uses her drama exercises to create a persona that will woo the famous stage director Ivan. With the help of her drama coach (Savannah Bouche), who warns her about using The Method toward such devious ends, Oona does her "baby seal" to get into character. As she flops around the floor barking vulnerably, her coach helps her to evoke the more subtle aspects of the seal's character. Later as she flatters and flirts with Ivan, you can almost see the baby seal coming through. But what Oona doesn't know is that Ivan is a bit of a lecher. His wife, Davis (Holland Taylor), offhandedly informs her that Ivan falls in love with all of his leading ladies. Davis says she doesn't mind, that it is part of his creative process. "I embrace that," she tells the surprised Oona, rapturously.

Next, Oona moves on to Jake, Helena's playwright grandson, and the rising star in the family. Again, Jaglom has injected reality into fiction. Jake is played by playwright Jon Robin Baitz, who is fantastic in his film debut. He plays a shy, sensitive man continually approached by family and others who all want a piece of his play. His grandmother, Helena, wants to direct it; his Uncle Eli (Ron Rifkin) wants the lead in it; George (Nick Gregory), one of Helena's interns, wants to sleep his way into a role; and Oona will be anybody to get the lead. He is also beset by his tormented sister, Trish (Melissa Leo), who will do anything, including suicide, to possess her beloved brother. In various scenes, some sympathetically sweet—others rife with human comedy, we watch them all try their luck on the sane but unsuspecting Jake.

Meanwhile, the rest of the family are living out their own dramas. A rebellious teenage daughter, Chloe (Martha Plimpton) acts out whenever and wherever she gets an audience, a drunken Melissa sleeps with George in an attempt at self-destruction, Davis locks horns with her mother Helena about her wretched childhood, Eli worries about his career, Helena reviews her life, and Oona falls in love with Helena's son Nick (Kristoffer Tabori), who wants to whisk her off to the South to do regional theater together. All this occurs against the backdrop of the rehearsals for the upcoming play.

Despite their vanity and self-absorption, this family of thespians retains a certain naivete and charm, especially when contrasted to the ruthlessness of Oona's stratagems. She is the personification of the opportunist, yet actress Vic-

CREDITS

Oona Hart: Victoria Foyt
Helena Mora: Viveca Lindfors
Jake Axelrod: Jon Robin Baitz
Ivan Axelrod: Andre Gregory
Trish Axelrod: Melissa Leo

Origin: USA
Released: 1995
Production: Judith Wolinsky for a Jagtoria Film and Rainbow Film production; released by Rainbow
Direction: Henry Jaglom
Screenplay: Henry Jaglom and Victoria Foyt
Cinematography: Hanania Baer
Editing: Henry Jaglom
Production design: Bruce Postman and Jeff Monte
Music: Ron Baitz
MPAA rating: R
Running Time: 106 minutes

toria Holt somehow makes her character likeable. Jaglom, plays Max, Oona's Hollywood producer, who is as self-interested as she and twice as ruthless. But even though Jaglom plays the Hollywood shark out of water to a tee, their characters are less an attack on Hollywood than a device to reveal the theatrical avant-garde's longings for glamour and all the trappings of the film world, which is, as Jake puts it, their "dirty little secret."

This film is a clever mixture of comedy and pathos, using a chain of vignette's to unveil the family's secrets and frailties. Jaglom has utililized the extraordinary talents of his players on two levels: first as the characters they portray, and second, as their real life characters. Viveca Lindfors, who plays Helena, is in many ways really playing herself. The film is in fact a tribute to the late actress, who passed away in October 1995, while touring in Sweden with "In Search of Strindberg." As Helena nostalgically recalls her years in Hollywood, we watch clips of Viveca Lindfors in old films with Errol Flynn and Ronald Reagan. Jaglom has honored Lindfors and her work in this film, and it is a beautiful tribute to a fine actress.

The film also pokes fun at the theater itself, and Jaglom indulges in a number of insider jokes. Andre Gregory, who plays the stage director Ivan, makes a few humorous allusions to his two and three year rehearsals, parodying his own famous three-year rehearsal for *Uncle Vanya*. There are also jabs at The Method, directors, the theater's avant-garde, and about acting itself, all making this film very New York in its appeal.

Last Summer in the Hamptons is a glorious soap opera of a film, with a humor and personal intensity that touches your heart. Jaglom gives us some comic and yet compassionate portrayals of the narcissism and dramatic passions of his family of actors, yet, by the end of the film, we come to see them as real people, so much so that at times it is almost painful to watch. These characters are really portraying the weaknesses in all of us, expressing our all too human flaws through the outpouring of their souls through their art. In *Last Summer in the Hamptons* Jaglom has captured us at our most vulnerable through the pain of his "clowns." And yet these clowns remain noble, despite their petty human failings, noble in their dedication to their art and the generosity of their souls.

—Diane Hatch-Avis

REVIEWS

Buzz, June/July 1995, p. 62.
The Daily Breeze, November 26, 1995, p. H4.
Drama-Logue, November 23-29, 1995.
Entertainment Today, November 24, 1995.
Hollywood Reporter, September 13, 1995, p. 16.
Los Angeles Times, November 21, 1995, p. F6.
Los Angeles View, November 24-30, 1995.
The New York Times, January 17, 1996, p. C11.
The Reader, November 24, 1995.
Sacramento Bee, December 20, 1995, p. D3.
Variety, September 18, 1995, p. 96.

Leaving Las Vegas

"A masterpiece. Nicolas Cage is extraordinary. Elisabeth Shue's performance is not just the best we will see this year, it is something to put beside the screen's best examples of vulnerable courage in a woman."—David Thomson, *Los Angeles Magazine*

"The most accomplished American movie of the year!"—David Denby, *New York Magazine*

"Passionate and furiously alive."—Janet Maslin, *New York Times*

"For anyone who cares about ravishing filmmaking, superb acting and movies willing to dive into the mystery of unconditional love!"—David Ansen, *Newsweek*

"A uniquely hypnotic and haunting love story sparked by Nicolas Cage and Elisabeth Shue at their career best."—Peter Travers, *Rolling Stone*

Box Office Gross: $2,588,173

In what could be the bleakest film of 1995, Nicolas Cage and Elisabeth Shue turn in sensitive performances in Mike Figgis's stylized *Leaving Las Vegas*, a portrait of a doomed romance between a hard-luck prostitute and an alcoholic determined to drink himself to death. With its haunting visuals and stripped bare narrative, *Leaving Las Vegas* seduces its viewers in much the same way as the alcohol consumes the alcoholic. Unrelenting in his insistence that its realism that makes the viewer uncomfortable, Figgis, in the end, falls victim to romanticizing and very much glorifying despair.

The film begins with a prologue which attempts to give us an overview of the life of Los Angeles alcoholic Ben Sanderson (Nicolas Cage). He merrily jaunts down an aisle at the liquor store, tossing bottle after bottle into his cart. He alienates a film producer (Richard Lewis) by once again borrowing money. And after having drunk himself into near oblivion, Ben hires a prostitute who ends up doing nothing but stealing his wedding ring from his finger. Eventually, Ben is fired from his film production company job. "I'm sorry," he painfully blurts out to his genial boss. "We really liked having you around, Ben," he is told. While the film goes to great lengths to show us what Ben's life is like at this moment in time, no attempt is made at even hinting how or why Ben reached this low point. "I can't remember if my wife left me because I drank or if I started drinking because she left," he casually acknowledges.

CREDITS

Ben Sanderson: Nicolas Cage
Sera: Elisabeth Shue
Yuri: Julian Sands
Peter: Richard Lewis
Terri: Valeria Golino
Sheila: Kim Adams

Origin: Great Britain
Released: 1995
Production: Jean Cazes and Philippe Geoffroy for United Artists and Lumiere Pictures
Direction: Mike Figgis
Screenplay: Mike Figgis; based on the novel by John O'Brien
Cinematography: Declan Quinn
Editing: John Smith
Production design: Waldemar Kalinowski
Art direction: Barry M. Kingston
Set design: Florence Fellman
Costume design: Laura Goldsmith and Vivienne Westwood
Music: Mike Figgis
MPAA rating: R
Running Time: 112 minutes

AWARDS AND NOMINATIONS

Academy Awards 1995: Best Actor (Cage)
Nominations: Best Director (Figgis), Best Actress (Shue), Best Adapted Screenplay (Figgis)
Chicago Film Festival 1995: Best Actor (Cage), Best Actress (Shue)
Golden Globe Awards 1996: Best Actor-Drama (Cage)
Nominations: Best Film-Drama, Best Director (Figgis), Best Actress-Drama (Shue)
Independent Spirit Awards 1996: Best Film, Best Director (Figgis), Best Actress (Shue), Best Cinematography (Quinn)
Nominations: Best Actor (Cage), Best Screenplay (Figgis)
Los Angeles Film Critics Awards 1995: Best Film, Best Director (Figgis), Best Actor (Cage), Best Actress (Shue)
National Board of Review Awards 1995: Best Actor (Cage)
National Society of Film Critics Awards 1995: Best Director (Figgis), Best Actor (Cage), Best Actress (Shue)
Screen Actors Guild 1995: Best Actor (Cage)
Nominations: Best Actress (Shue)
British Academy Awards Nominations 1995: Best Actor (Cage), Best Actress (Shue), Best Adapted Screenplay (Figgis)
Directors Guild Award Nominations 1995: Best Director (Figgis)
Writers Guild Awards Nominations 1995: Best Adapted Screenplay (Figgis)

Ben takes his severance pay, burns or trashes most of his belongings and heads off for Las Vegas, where he intends to drink himself to death. Vegas is the perfect choice, a town where free alcohol is available twenty-four hours a day, where no one would even notice a drunk, much less care, and where time has no meaning. Day is night and night is day and artificiality abounds. Ben checks into a sleazy motel, stocks up on the liquor and hits the Strip. And in the process, he nearly hits, quite literally, a beautiful All-American prostitute named Sera (Elisabeth Shue). Having just escaped from the clutches of her sadistic Russian pimp, Yuri (Julian Sands), Sera is charmed into a mostly non-sexual relationship with Ben, one based on non-judgmental behavior on both their parts. "You must never, ever try to get me to stop drinking," Ben warns her and in return, he must accept Sera's profession.

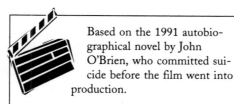

Based on the 1991 autobiographical novel by John O'Brien, who committed suicide before the film went into production.

"You can never, never ask me to stop drinking."—Ben from *Leaving Las Vegas*

Not so much a portrait of an alcoholic as a bleak, desperate romance, *Leaving Las Vegas* relentlessly paints a portrait of two charcters who refuse to be consumed by any self-doubt or self-loathing, people who might be regarded as losers if defined solely by their external circumstances. To his credit, Figgis manages to avoid moral judgment, succeeding instead in presenting a haunting character sketch of a couple desperate for love yet resigned to its fleeting nature. These are two people who are not about to apologize for their lives, nor do they wallow in self-pity. And to his credit, Figgis avoids the kind of bogus happy endings in which love leads to triumph over affliction found in other substance abuse tales such as *When a Man Loves a Woman* (1994) and *Clean and Sober* (1988).

The film is hampered by the hokey device of having Sera talk to her off-screen therapist. Nothing new about her charcter is revealed through this technique and in fact, the film's intensity is dissipated. While Shue, the ingenue in such films as *Adventures in Babysitting* (1987) and *Cocktail* (1988), gives a strong, naked performance, her character is essentially the all-too-familiar hooker with a heart of gold. We know very little about Sera, nor in the end, do we walk away really caring about what happens to her. We just assume she will be fine—after all, she can afford therapy. Sadly, Figgis resorts to employing a brutal rape scene calculated to place Sera in her own personal jeopardy. For a film determined to be more of a character sketch than a narrative, this choice reads as pure plot device.

Actor Nicolas Cage won numerous critical accolades for his portrayal of self-destructive drunk, Ben Sanderson. With his sunken eyes and a ghastly green pallor, Cage embodies the character with a sweet sadness and the determination to leave this life with total and complete conviction. Combining equal parts insouciance and despair, Cage sustains a no-holds-barred approach to his characterization that is both funny and deeply tragic, conveying both pain and pleasure with each slug from the bottle.

Working from a semi-autobiographical novel by John O'Brien, Mike Figgis, whose work includes *Stormy Monday* (1988), *Internal Affairs* (1990) and the disastrous *Mr. Jones* (1993), was determined to make his film without compromising his artistic vision. Funding was difficult to come by and as a result, Figgis ended up, with the help of cinematographer Declan Quinn (*Vanya on 42nd Street,* 1994), shooting the entire film on inexpensive Super 16 film stock, working in a mostly documentary style. Ironically, author O'Brien committed suicide just two weeks after learning that his book was to be made into a film, turning his novel into a kind of suicide note.

Figgis relies heavily on the use of music to set the mood of the film, using his own jazzy musical score, as well as soulful renditions of old standards, such as "It's a Lonesome Old Town." While the music is initially seductive, the repetitive use of Sting's lovesick ballads tends to have a bludgeoning effect. It is as if Figgis did not trust his own ability—or for that matter, his actors' abilities—to convey the emotion without resorting to the obvious. The music tends to sentimentalize these two romantic losers, as well as their fate. If tempted to purchase the soundtrack, be forewarned: it contains annoying snippets of dialogue designed to remind the listener of the film's really "important" lines.

It is very easy to be seduced by *Leaving Las Vegas.* With its haunting visuals, moody musical score and sensitive per-

REVIEWS

Entertainment Weekly. October 27, 1995, p. 66
Los Angeles Times. October 27, 1995, p. F1
Macleans, CVIII, October 30, 1995, p. 57
Newsweek. October 30, 1995, p. 81
The New Yorker. LXXI, November 6, 1995, p. 176
New York Times. October 27, 1995, CXLV, p. B8
Premiere. IX, November 1995, p. 22
Rolling Stone. November 2, 1995, p. 74
Time. CXLVI, November 6, 1995, p. 75
Variety. September 18, 1995, CCCLX, p. 93
Village Voice. October 31, 1995, XL, p. 76
Wall Street Journal. November 3, 1995, p. A12
Washington Post. November 10, 1995, p. 45

formances from its stars, the film is affective, but in the end it reeks of self-indulgence, succumbing to the very thing it sought to avoid: a glossy romance that is merely covered by the sham of suffering. Reviews for the film were slightly mixed, but *Leaving Las Vegas* garnered enough awards to keep the drinks flowing.

—Patricia Kowal

Les Miserables

"Extravagant, energetic, emotion-charged. A spectacular-looking film."—Kevin Thomas, *Newsday*

"One of the year's best films!"—Gene Siskel, *Siskel & Ebert*

"Spectacular. Romantic. Infinitely compelling."—Richard Schickel, *Time*

"Belmondo has one of the best roles of his career."—Mike Clark, *USA Today*

"Magnificent! Jean-Paul Belmondo gives a brilliantly mesmerizing and spectacular portrayal. A must-see movie."—Jules Peimer, *WKDM Radio, New York*

Box Office Gross: $881,630

Les Miserables (1842), Victor Hugo's epic French novel, is the inspiration for this panoramic film. At the heart of the novel is Jean Valjean, an everyman who struggles to prevail over life's vicissitudes and becomes a symbol of the human spirit's triumph. His filmic incarnation is Henri Fortin (Jean-Paul Belmondo), a boxer, a furniture mover, and a fighter in the French resistance during World War II. Fortin is illiterate, a victim of social forces he does not understand, and yet he responds to the ghastly events of this century with a fortitude and decency that remind his contemporaries of Hugo's great survivor.

The film begins with the appalling story of Fortin's father (also played by `Belmondo), a chauffeur who is wrongly convicted of killing his employer. Fortin pere, whose brute strength and determination are awesome, is caught several times trying to escape from a fortress-like prison. Rather than surrender his will or accept his incarceration he dies in the attempt to be free.

Director Lelouch's daughter, Salome, plays the young Ziman daughter while Belmondo's son Paul is seen as the young Fortin.

Fortin pere's son grows up with his mother, who never stops loving her imprisoned husband—even prostituting herself to secure the money that she hopes will win his release. Her son watches his mother's degradation, never forgetting her sacrifices and realizing how the world takes advantage of the compromised, of the persecuted, and of the underclass. But growing up in an inn and waiting on tables while his mother sexually services her customers, his opportunities are limited. Powerfully built like his father, the young Fortin (played by Belmondo's son) becomes a boxer during World War I and afterwards a furniture mover.

Jumping twenty years, the film shows Fortin (Belmondo) moving a Jewish family, the Zimans, fleeing their comfortable Parisian life. As they leave the city, Monsieur Ziman asks Fortin to let them out of the van as they approach checkpoints, so that they can walk through the woods and avoid arrest. Without hesitation, Fortin agrees. His only request is that Monsieur Ziman read to him from Les Miserable, for he has been told many times that he resembles Jean Valjean. Not only does Monsieur Ziman comply, he explains to Fortin that the novel is a summa of human experience, that there are only a few stories to be told about human beings, and those stories happen over and over again. Ziman is, of course, underscoring the film's own idea, suggesting that what Hugo wrote in the nineteenth century is happening to him and to Fortin, has happened before, and is happening now to everyone watching the movie. It is a wonderful moment because art and life meet; the scene of human suffering and endurance is right there—and everywhere.

Fortin not only transports these Jewish refugees, he masquerades as their daughter Salome's father, installing her safely in a convent school, while her parents dare a risky border crossing. They are gunned down, although Madame Ziman (Alessandra Martines) survives in a Nazi camp, and Monsieur Ziman, gravely wounded, is cared for by a farm couple. Fortin is spotted aiding the Jews and is tortured, but he refuses to give up any information.

The heart of the film focuses on Monsieur Ziman's slow recovery hidden on the farm and Fortin's participation in the French resistance. The farmer's wife (Annie Giradot) falls in love with Ziman, but he gently refuses her advances, thinking only of his wife and child. The farmer (Philippe Leotard), jealous of Ziman, begins to make up stories about Nazi victories that seem improbable to Ziman and yet shake the confidence of this man holed up in a cellar and absolutely dependent on saviors, who have also become his captors. His story has become an eerie reenactment of Fortin pere's imprisonment. Although physically weak, Ziman's undaunted humanity is reminiscent of the hardier Fortin's loyalty to his family.

> "Tell me about Jean Valjean. People always say I'm like him."—Henri Fortin, referring to the Victor Hugo character from *Les Miserables*

There is a sentimental and fairy tale-like quality to *Les Miserables*. Writer and director Claude Lelouch has simplified human character, because he is not concerned with psychological verisimilitude but with celebrating the human spirit. He has said that in approaching the age of sixty he wants to make films about hope. This desire to hope, to see human beings who are on the side of the better angels, who will take any amount of suffering without losing their humanity, is a powerful force in this film. Ziman must be reunited with his family; Fortin and the other resistance fighters must reclaim France. And of course, this all happens.

Reviewers have complained that this retelling and updating of Hugo's nineteenth-century classic is forced, but this criticism is beside the point. Les Miserable is not a realistic film, even though it deals with historical events, including a re-enactment of the D-Day landings. Rather, it is a myth about human survival and victory. Fortin is excited to hear Ziman read from the novel, because it inspires him to be like that work of art. His belief in Jean Valjean validates what others have said—that he resembles that fictional character. In other words, the novel's readers, and the book itself, have created Fortin.

Director and writer Claude Lelouch makes Fortin and the other characters credible not on realistic but on sentimental grounds. Lelouch himself had to flee Nazi-occupied France in 1942, a five-year-old traveling with his mother and a handful of falsified papers. As they approached the border of the safe zone, his mother had to bribe an official, who had detected their ruse, with a gold watch. "What a Thenardier he is!" she remarked, comparing him to the greedy innkeeper in Hugo's novel. That night she told her son the story of *Les Miserables*, which he read several times in the ensuing years. It became a metaphor for human experience and later a capstone of Lelouch's own career. As he recently pointed out, "Victor Hugo was 60 years old when he decided to publish *Les Miserables*. I, myself, am going to reach that age soon. It was without a doubt the time to make the film." Part of the film's personal testament is reflected in the fact that Lelouch's daughter plays the part of Salome, the Zimans' precious daughter.

Besides the powerful vision Lelouch brings to the film, there is the extraordinary performance of Jean-Paul Belmondo. American viewers are most likely to remember him from films such as *Breathless* (1959) and *That Man From Rio* (1963), a ruggedly handsome and romantic figure. At sixty-two, he is as charismatic as ever, with a leathery face that shows every line and crevice. He is a commanding presence without any swagger or bravado. Playing Fortin, Fortin pere, and a few scenes as Jean Valjean, he is equally convincing in all roles, suggesting the continuing of the human story. His is a face ruled by history, marked by events. As Jean Valjean he is toughened by imprisonment and almost loses his heart, yet an encounter with a country lad after his release from prison restores his humanity, when he realizes that his mean spirited swiping of the boy's coin has only revealed his own degradation. He cries after the boy—a sequence that inaugurates the film's opening, which centers on Jean Valjean crying across a valley, inconsolable, and ask-

CREDITS

Henri Fortin: Jean-Paul Belmondo
Monsieur Ziman: Michel Boujenah
Madame Ziman: Alessandra Martines
Salome Ziman: Salome
Fantine: Clementine Celarie
Farmer: Philippe Leotard

Origin: France
Released: 1995
Production: Claude Lelouch; released by Warner Brothers
Direction: Claude Lelouch
Screenplay: Claude Lelouch; adapted from the book by Victor Hugo
Cinematography: Claude Lelouch
Editing: Claude Lelouch
Music: Francis Lai, Philippe Sevain, Erik Berchot, Michel Legrand and Didler Barbelivien
MPAA rating: R
Running Time: 174 minutes

AWARDS AND NOMINATIONS

Golden Globe Awards 1996: Best Foreign Film
British Academy Awards Nominations 1995: Best Foreign Film
Cesar Awards 1996: Best Supporting Actress (Girardot)

ing forgiveness. The scene, when it is repeated later, emphasizes that it is not only part of the story of *Les Miserables* but it is part of the human story per se. Jean Valjean and Jean-Paul Belmondo have become archetypes of an agony and an atonement that approach religious intensity.

So close in age to the director, Belmondo is clearly Lelouch's surrogate. Belmondo lives the role, never forcing what otherwise might have been cloying. His lightness of touch has been misconceived by one reviewer as his coasting through the role, as though he were not trying hard enough. But the last thing this earnest film needs is earnest acting. Belmondo has wisely chosen to play against the lesson-like mood of the film.

Lelouch abetted Belmondo's style by withholding the script until shortly before filming each scene. He wanted to guarantee a freshness of approach, as though the character and the actor were arriving at their interpretations on the spot. This spontaneity, which Belmondo welcomed, ensures that the film is never merely an allegory, a replaying of the novel, even though the film's structure is admittedly quite a contrivance, an epic exercise in parallel-making.

Not many contemporary filmmakers would dare to be as open-hearted and optimistic as Claude Lelouch. But the film earns its idealism. The characters who hope the most are also those who suffer the most. Monsieur Ziman, the physically weakest character in the film, drags himself out of his cellar hiding place after days of despair in bed, after his farmers no longer attend him, and he painfully enters the farmhouse, suddenly learning from a newspaper that the Allies have won. His resurrection is the world's, wounded but revived.

—*Carl Rollyson*

Lie Down With Dogs

Box Office Gross: $240,280

Lie Down With Dogs joins *To Wong Foo, Thanks for Everything, Julie Newmar* (1995), *Jeffrey* (1995), and *Priscilla, Queen of the Desert* (1994) in the growing roster of gay-themed films which have some commercial appeal. Granted, this film is not in the artistic league of those mentioned above, but it is good, clean—well, almost clean—fun. In the area of film craftsmanship, it is more in the league of other recent gay-themed films such as *The Incredibly True Adventures of Two Girls in Love* (1995), *Grief* (1994), and *Go Fish* (1994). These films are no less valid because they are less-than-polished in their film craftsmanship. Much of the discrepancy comes from the fact that these films, like *Lie Down With Dogs*, are first-time outings for their directors and writers and have minuscule budgets. They are less commercial than their big-budget counterparts for reasons ranging from quality of the film print to lack of big-name stars, to simple storytelling. But clearly, much is changing in the availability of gay-themed films.

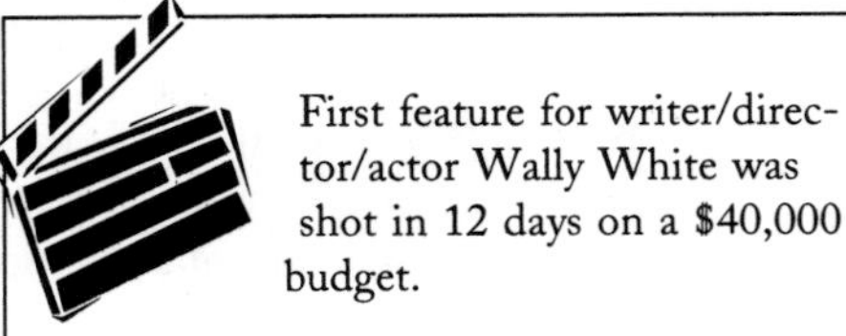

First feature for writer/director/actor Wally White was shot in 12 days on a $40,000 budget.

In the past, it seems that much of what was commercial in the way of gay-themed material was either AIDS-themed, such as *Longtime Companion* (1990) or *Philadelphia* (1993), or a highly dramatic film featuring a big-name star such as *Philadelphia* or *Kiss of the Spider Woman* (1985). It was often the case that the stars of those films spent much publicity time discussing the fact that they themselves are not gay, downplaying the gay themes in order to avoid offending the audience.

While films such as *Philadelphia* are in the best tradition of moviemaking, the lack of "B"-style gay movies with matter-of-fact gay characters has represented the difficulty in finding funding and audiences for such films. Smaller-budget films featuring gay protagonists have simply not been a visible product in the general cinematic marketplace until very recently. It is the continuum of movies, from good to bad, expensive to low-budget, that represents the "coming of age" of a genre or type of film. Only now are gay films showing a wider range of experience and expertise; this influx of films is concurrent with the current cultural trend toward more gay people being "out" in the various media.

With all of the hoopla comes a harmless and charming little film called *Lie Down With Dogs*. The old saying "If you lie down with dogs, you're bound to get fleas" is the basis of the title of this independent film by first-time producer/director/writer/actor Wally White. The saying resonates in the film in that it deals mostly with the lead character's discovery about his own search for relationships. Tommie (Wally White), sick and tired of life in present-day New York City, decides to spend a summer in Provincetown, Rhode Island. "P-Town" is a gay mecca, and Tommie feels like he will have a better time with work and better luck in his relationships if he spends a summer there. Deciding that "for one summer in your life, you do something you haven't done before," he sets out for Provincetown to have an adventure.

Tommie's adventures are engagingly told, though the situations themselves are a bit mundane. He looks for a job, finds a place to live, meets a callous boyfriend also named Tom (Randy Becker), and learns a little bit about himself as the summer progresses. This film is not deep, but it never pretends to be, and its lack of pretense is one of its charms. Several reviews chided White for his less than stellar filmmaking techniques, but who says it has to be sophisticated to be fun? There are some funny clues to the lack of seriousness of the film even before it begins. Prior to the credits, an angry man rants into the camera for a couple of minutes about the lack of political correctness or depth of this film, saying, "Boycott this film! All these guys want is porno!" The credits are a funny, low-budget send-up of those bikini-drenched credits from beach-party movies: all of the credits are printed on Calvin Klein underwear, worn by hunky beach dudes.

Wearing the producer/writer/director/star hats, White seems to have an excellent command of the way in which he wishes to tell his story. He is cognizant and perhaps a little defensive of the film's thin plot and theme, telling the audience "This film isn't *Longtime Companion*....my job is to not be boring." And he succeeds. There are amusing sequences and engaging moments. One of the funniest involves sex on a dining table while cooking a hamburger. White's funny performance and some inventive editing make it more silly than raunchy.

One of White's techniques is to address the camera consistently, making him reminiscent of very early Woody Allen. He is neurotic and a bit self-absorbed, but his screen persona is actually easier to take than Allen's was in his early days. Lying on his bed in the first sequence, White talks to the camera about the film they are about to see, generally defending its shallowness and saying erudite-sounding things like "most people are neither heroes nor fools." His winning smile and easygoing manner are endearing, and it is a smart sequence to include because it allows the audience to bond with Tommie (Wally) before the action gets going. Later, he uses the direct-address technique to tell the audience "If this were a porno film, this is the point where..." and then he does a very funny, PG-rated parody of pornographic films. From speaking to the camera as it chases him around the streets of Provincetown, to telling the audience that he wonders if "alcohol should serve as a metaphor for inner disgust," White maintains a good relationship with his audience. If, as some critics have complained, this is an unsophisticated technique, they are right. But for a novice director and writer, White's use of the technique is assured and clever. There is an age-old adage in writing: it doesn't matter what you do, as long as it works.

White has a good command of dialogue which serves him well. "My idea of horror," he tells the audience about another character "is that he looked like Eric Roberts in *Star 80*." On the phone with his mother, he tells her, "I'm not wasting my life; I'm just postponing things." Later, he states that "everything in life is important and trivial at the same time." These bits of dialogue are good representations of White's engaging style. Sitting on the sofa with a lascivious prospective employer, White turns to the camera and says, "I'm not looking to have sex with the innkeeper." It is typical of White to use "innkeeper" instead of a more ordinary word; his interesting use of words keeps things amusing.

The actors in general are not as likable as White; they have a similar lack of polish (which reads as if they have a lack of acting experience), but don't possess White's charm. The exception is Randy Becker as Tom, the South American cad who steals Tommie's heart. Always bumming a cigarette ("got a cigarette, baby?") and trying to get Tommie to give him money, an apartment, or something else, Becker is sexy and believable as the philandering lover.

The film's production values reflect its small budget. It has the grainy quality of a film blown up to fit projectors larger than its film stock would warrant, and it contains minimal lighting and production design elements. White uses this to his advantage, however, in a couple of sequences which satirize the gay dance-club scene. Tommie and friends dance around against a completely black backdrop

CREDITS

Tommie: Wally White
Eddie: James Sexton
Glen/Herbert: Vann Jones
Guy: Bash Halow
Tom: Randy Becker

Origin: USA
Released: 1995
Production: Carijin Lau, Jennifer Ryan Cohen and Eli Kabillio for a Walrus Production; released by Miramax Films
Direction: Wally White
Screenplay: Wally White
Cinematography: George Mitas
Editing: Hart F. Faber
Production design: Reno Dakota
Assistant director: Jody O'Neill
Music: Jellybean Benitez
MPAA rating: R
Running Time: 84 minutes

and dark lighting as the neon names of dance clubs are superimposed on the screen. It is very funny, both because it is a parody of montage sequences in cheesy B-films, and because it unapologetically points out the dinky budget of this film, thereby making fun of itself and others at the same time.

The ending of the film is a logical conclusion to the action, and represents a fine sense of the arc of a story. Tommie reflects on the events of the summer, and seems to have learned something. The beautiful locales serve as a fine yet melancholy backdrop for the change of seasons.

From some clever new lyrics to "Beautiful Dreamer" (which humorously underscore the action), to several funny montage sequences, White has made the most of his budget and talent. He has a way with a phrase, a charm in front of the camera, and a bunch of playful ideas. Hopefully, these will translate into some other, better-budgeted chances for White to improve upon his talents.

—*Kirby Tepper*

Little Odessa

"A rare, memorable movie debut."—Thelma Adams, *New York Post*

"Exceptionally good, beautifully shot, this film has an extraordinary sense of place and drama."—Caryn James, *New York Times*

Box Office Gross: $1,095,885

Little Odessa is the story of a Russian Jewish family in the Brighton Beach emigre community of "Little Odessa." But don't get the wrong idea, this is no Neil Simon play. *Little Odessa* is about a family so anesthetized by the constant despair and suffering of their lives that they don't even realize they are slowly sliding into tragedy, a tragedy hastened by the return of their son Joshua (Tim Roth), whose dark past pulls the family into deeper despair.

As the film opens, we see a man sitting on a bench waiting for a bus. Joshua walks up and shoots the man in a fast, passionless, and jarringly violent hit-and-run assassination. Joshua is a hit man in the Russian Mafia in America. Years before, he had to leave New York because of a hit on the son of a local kingpin. Now Joshua is ordered to make a hit on an Iranian jeweler in his old neighborhood. His objections are ignored and he reluctantly returns to his hometown.

While planning his hit, Joshua is spotted sitting in his car outside the family's apartment. His younger brother, Reuben (Edward Furlong) hears he's back and finds him. Reuben tells Joshua that their mother is dying of a brain tumor, but when Reuben brings Joshua home to see her, their father (Maximilian Schell) explodes in anger and throws him out of the house. From his father's reaction, it is obvious that the animosity between the two began long before Joshua left the home.

In order to see his mother, Joshua makes a tentative truce between his father and himself. The mother (Vanessa Redgrave) is a strong presence in the family and a focal point to the relationships in the film. She knows what her son is and yet she, unlike his father, loves him in a way that feels

CREDITS

Joshua Shapira: Tim Roth
Reuben Shapira: Edward Furlong
Alla Shustervich: Moira Kelly
Irina Shapira: Vanessa Redgrave
Arkady Shapira: Maximilian Schell
Boris Volkoff: Paul Guilfoyle
Natasha: Natasha Andreichenko
Sasha: David Vadim

Origin: USA
Released: 1995
Production: Paul Webster for a New Line Cinema presentation of a Paul Webster/Addis-Wechsler production; released by Fine Line Features
Direction: James Gray
Screenplay: James Gray
Cinematography: Tom Richmond
Editing: Dorian Harris
Production design: Kevin Thompson
Set decoration: Charles Ford
Costume design: Michael Clancy
Casting: Douglas Abiel
Music: Dana Sono
MPAA rating: R
Running Time: 98 minutes

like no one ever has or ever will. Redgrave's presence on the screen is captivating, too weak to hold a cigarette one day, strong enough to sit up and talk the next, in agony the day after, and just before death—surprised that it has come at last. It reeks of raw reality, and Redgrave gives a performance that is flawless.

"Where you gonna go?" "We're the Jews, we wander. Didn't they teach you that in Hebrew school?"—Reuben to older brother Joshua in *Little Odessa*

It is in these scenes when Joshua is with his mother and brother that we see a man caged inside himself and able to express himself only through his anger. Roth plays a man whose emotional range is limited to vigilance and rage. He is a damaged man with a heart that just can't seem to open, and if it weren't for his fondness for his mother and his little brother, we wouldn't know he had a heart at all.

In a similarly clumsy attempt at sharing emotion, Joshua has an affair with a girl from the old neighborhood, Alla Shustervich (Moira Kelly). Their affair is less tenderness and passion than a fumbling attempt at closeness, but even that attempt comes across stunted and twisted.

When Joshua discovers that his father has beaten Reuben for being truant from school, he decides to get back at him. In a powerful scene, Joshua uses the only way he knows to punish his father. In a symbolic execution, Joshua takes his father out to an empty field and humiliates him, then pointing the gun at him he suddenly stops and walks away. With this final stroke of depravity, his father turns him in to the local Mafia boss, whose son Joshua killed years before. His father's betrayal comes on the heels of his wife's death and puts another nail in the coffin of the Shapiro family. It is ironic that Joshua, the impervious killer, is finally hurt by the only scrap of goodness within him, his love for his brother and mother.

Director/writer James Gray's first attempt is a marvelous first effort. Gray is a New York native, and a recent University of Southern California film school alumni. In his feature debut, Gray, 26, not only has had the opportunity to work with a remarkable cast, but has been recognized for his efforts, receiving the Silver Lion at the Venice Film Festival.

In *Little Odessa* Gray holds a chord of despair and hopelessness throughout the film, punctuated only by shocking murders. That despair is so overwhelming that when someone dies it feels almost like a mercy killing, freeing them from their dreadful lives. Using an overlay of heavy Russian choir music, Gray accents what his characters seem to lack most—a sense of the sacredness of life. Gray gives no excuses for his characters, never succumbing to the temptation to soften their harsh outlines or even to explain their actions.

But this ambiguity also creates a certain lack of clarity. At times the film feels like we missed the first reel. So much family history is assumed that the audience is left to piece together the rest. Gray's use of stark realism doesn't give much reason to care about the characters, and yet he seems to be defying us not to care.

Despite its violence, the film's pacing is slow yet so well-acted that it remains compelling. The real strength of the film lay in the performances of the actors. Roth is thoroughly convincing as the cold-blooded murderer, efficient in the dispatching of lives and tidy in his disposal of bodies. He conveys the uneasy feeling that it's "just a job," and yet he puts his life on the line by going to his mother's funeral. He portrays a man full of contradictions that even he hasn't realized.

As his Americanized younger brother, Edward Furlong brings a vulnerability and warmth to the part, and Moira Kelly is wonderfully understated as the hardened young woman who doesn't expect a whole lot out of life.

The action of the story revolves around these three younger characters, but Schell and Redgrave create a powerful force behind that action. Schell has a dignified power on the screen that is mesmerizing, playing the authoritative father to a tee and Redgrave is the personification of silent suffering.

The filming by cinematographer Tom Richmond perfectly supports the story's theme. His palette is all greys and browns, like the lives of the people in Little Odessa, accented with the occasional reds and whites—of crimson painted sidewalks in the snowy streets and of bloody corpses wrapped in sheets.

Gray uses symbolism effectively in the film. One example of his subtle hand is a scene in which the brothers break into an aquarium after hours to "hang out." Joshua teases the snake in the glass cage and Reuben warns him not to—that it's dangerous. The man who is looking for Joshua has a snake tattooed on his forehead and his hand,

AWARDS AND NOMINATIONS

Independent Spirit Awards Nominations 1996: Best First Feature, Best Actor (Roth), Best Supporting Actress (Redgrave), Best Cinematography (Richmond)

REVIEWS

Boxoffice, April 1995, p. R-32.
Entertainment Today, June 2, 1995, p. 10.
LA Village View, June 2-8, 1995, p. 16.
LA Weekly, June 2-8, 1995, p. 31.
The New Yorker, March 21, 1994, p. 189.
Variety, September 12, 1994, p. 44.
Village Voice, May 23, 1995, p. 28.

and teasing the snake by returning home turns out to be very dangerous.

Although there are far fewer murders in this film than most half hour TV shows, the killings are still shocking, even to the hardened filmgoer. Gray has succeeded in making death real on the screen. It may cause the viewer to wonder whether things like this really happen in the world? That's good filmmaking.

—*Diane Hatch-Avis*

A Little Princess

"Joyous and irresistible! A bright, beautiful, stirringly lovely children's film. This one revels in an exuberant sense of play."—Janet Maslin, *New York Times*

Box Office Gross: $10,019,307

Loosely adapted from the novel by Frances Hodgson Burnett, *A Little Princess* is the third film rendering of the story, following earlier film versions starring Mary Pickford in 1917 and Shirley Temple in 1939. The current remake, directed by Alfonso Cuarón and adapated by Richard LaGravenese and Elizabeth Chandler, follows the success in 1993 of *The Secret Garden*, splendidly directed by Agnieszka Holland from another enchanting story by Frances Hodgson Burnett. *A Little Princess* marks the American feature film debut of Mexican director Alfonso Cuarón. The screenplay was shaped by Richard LaGravanese, who had manipulated fantasy elements so successfully in *The Fisher King*, which earned an Academy Award nomination for best original screenplay in 1991.

A Little Princess succeeds not so much as a literal adaptation of the story but as a transformation of the story's potential for magic, enchantment, and childish wonder. Sara Crewe (Liesel Matthews) has grown up in a wealthy and comfortable setting and has come, in the novel, to regard herself as "a little princess," but she is compassionate, caring, and resourceful, and when Fate reverses her fortune, she is able to draw upon the powers of her imagination to become a survivor. The screenplay intelligently frames the story in Indian mythology.

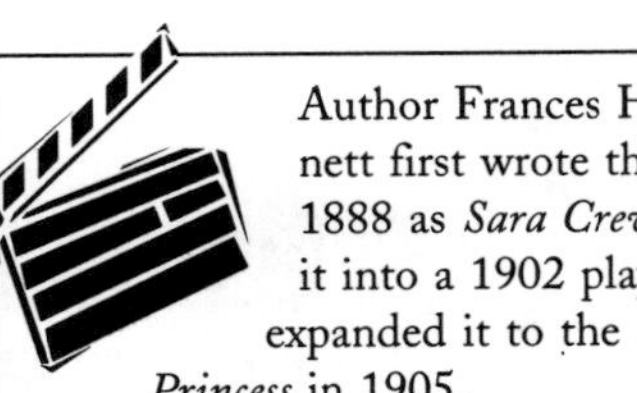

Author Frances Hodgson Burnett first wrote the story in 1888 as *Sara Crewe*, reworked it into a 1902 play, and finally expanded it to the novel *A Little Princess* in 1905.

The novel was first written in 1888 as a children's short story entitled *Sara Crewe, or What Happened at Miss Minchin's*, adapted to the stage under the title *A Little Unfairy Princess* in 1902, and later expanded to novel length and retitled in 1905. The screenplay updates the story in time to the First World War. The film begins in Simla, India, in 1914, in an exotic setting, as Sara listens to Maya, her nanny, tell the story of Prince Rama and Princess Sita, gorgeously visualized and intercut with Sara's adventures. The Princess Sita leaves an enchanted circle Rama has drawn around her to protect her and is captured by the fantastic monster Ravanna, who locks her in a tower, a mythic prefiguring of what will later happen to Sara. Liam Cunningham, who plays Sara's father, Captain Ralph Crewe, also plays Prince Rama, which anchors the mythic Ramayana fantasy to Sara's later adventures. Moreover, the Indian manservant (Errol Sitahal) who later becomes Sara's protector, is named Ram Dass, which translates as the "servant of Rama."

Young Sara Crewe, born in India, is taken to America by her widowed father, an English gentleman of means who is duty-bound to service in World War I and believes Sara will be safer in the Western Hemisphere. He leaves her at Miss Minchin's School for Girls in New York City, the school where her American mother was educated. Immediately the film diverges from the novel, in which the mother was French, not American, and Miss Minchin's Select Seminary for Young Ladies was in London, not New York. In the novel Captain Crewe leaves his daughter in England while he returns to India to seek his fortune working a diamond mine, which seems to be a failure.

In the novel Captain Crewe dies in India of "jungle fever." In the film he is wounded in action in the trenches while attempting to rescue an American soldier named John Randolph (Ken Palmer) and nearly dies after a gas attack, but survives as an amnesiac, leaving hope for an eventual reunion with his beloved daughter. This is a sugarcoated Hollywood fabrication that leaves open the possibility of a happy ending. The plot device is lifted from the earlier Hollywood adaptation, *The Little Princess*, directed by Walter Lang in 1939 as a Shirley Temple vehicle, but at least the earlier film version kept the story in London.

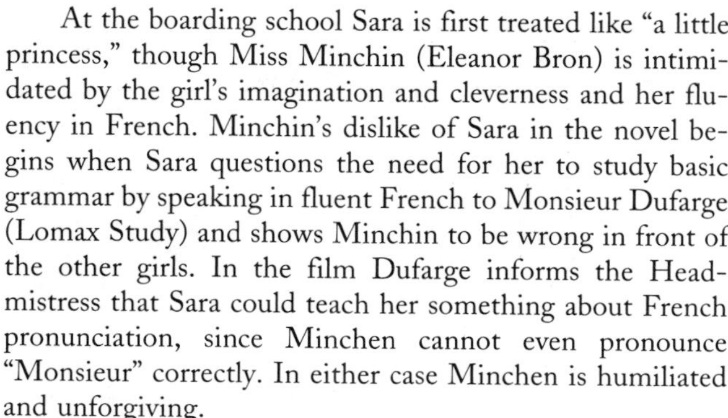

CREDITS

Miss Minchin: Eleanor Bron
Captain Crewe: Liam Cunningham
Prince Rama: Liam Cunningham
Sara Crewe: Liesel Matthews
Amaelia Minchin: Rusty Schwimmer
Charles Randolph: Arthur Malet
Becky: Vanessa Lee Chester
Ram Dass: Errol Sitahal
Ermengarde: Heather DeLoach
Lavinia: Taylor Fry
Jesse: Darcie Bradford
Betsy: Rachael Bella
Gertrude: Alexandra Rea-Baum
Jane: Camilla Belle
Rosemary: Lauren Blumenfeld
Lottie: Kelsey Mulrooney
Ruth: Kaitlin Cullum
Princess Sita: Alison Moir
Frances the Milkman: Time Winters
Monsieur Dufarge: Lomax Study
Mr. Barrow: Vincent Schiavelli
Maya: Pushpa Rawal
Laki: Rahi Azizi
John Randolph: Ken Palmer
Flower Lady: Helen Greenberg
Doctor in Hospital: Norman Merrill
Mabel the Cook: Peggy Miley
Ermengarde's Father: Robert P. Cohen
Rich Boy in Street: William Blomquist
Beggar in Fantasy Forest: David Fresco
Bakery Woman: Judith D. Drake
Policeman: Chris Ellis

Origin: USA
Released: 1995
Production: Alan C. Blomquist and Amy Ephron; A Mark Johnson/Baltimore Pictures Production; released by Warner Bros.
Direction: Alfonso Cuarón
Screenplay: Richard LaGravenese and Elizabeth Chandler; based on the novel by Frances Hodgson Burnett
Cinematography: Emmanuel Lubezki
Editing: Steven Weisberg
Production design: Bo Welch
Art direction: Tom Duffield
Set decoration: Cheryl Carasik
Sound: Richard Beggs
Costume Design: Judianna Makovsky
Music: Patrick Doyle
MPAA rating: G
Running Time: 98 minutes

At the boarding school Sara is first treated like "a little princess," though Miss Minchin (Eleanor Bron) is intimidated by the girl's imagination and cleverness and her fluency in French. Minchin's dislike of Sara in the novel begins when Sara questions the need for her to study basic grammar by speaking in fluent French to Monsieur Dufarge (Lomax Study) and shows Minchin to be wrong in front of the other girls. In the film Dufarge informs the Headmistress that Sara could teach her something about French pronunciation, since Minchen cannot even pronounce "Monsieur" correctly. In either case Minchen is humiliated and unforgiving.

Finding herself in the company of little snobs, some of whom are jealous and spiteful, Sara treats her classmates with loving consideration, winning over all but the most hateful, a spoiled brat named Lavinia Herbert (Taylor Fry). Though Miss Minchin secretly dislikes Sara, who reminds her of everything she is not, she tends to the child's every whim, until, on Sara's eleventh birthday, a solicitor, Mr. Borrow (Vincent Schiavelli), brings news that Captain Crewe was killed in the trenches and left his daughter penniless. (The novel has a rationale for the recovery of Sara's fortune when the diamond mine pays off, but the film does not.) Minchin then takes all of Sara's things, including a locket with pictures of her mother and father, and turns her, Cinderella-fashion, into a badly-treated servant who is forced to sleep in the cold attic in a room next to the scullery maid Becky (Vanessa Le Chester), who was a Dickensian waif in the novel but is a young black girl in the remake.

Brave little Sara accepts her fate stoically and her virtue is eventually rewarded after she has been abused and mistreated by Minchin and the nastier girls. Many of the girls remain loyal to Sara, however, and visit her in the attic to listen to the wonderful stories Sara tells. Her friends steal back the locket Minchin has taken from Sara when all of Sara's nice things were appropriated. When Minchin discovers the locket is missing, she calls the police to have Sara arrested.

By that time, however, Sara has found additional support from Ram Dass, the Indian servant of the next door neighbor, Charles Randolph (Arthur Malet), whose son has also gone to war and has been reported missing in action. Attempting to find his missing son, Randolph locates a wounded soldier who has lost his memory and takes the man home from the hospital. By an absurd and outlandish quirk of fate, this soldier turns out to be none other than Captain Crewe.

AWARDS AND NOMINATIONS

Academy Awards Nominations 1995: Best Art Direction, Best Cinematography (Lubezki)

Sara knows Minchin has called the police to have her arrested. She manages to escape from her attic garret by stretching a board across the window ledge of the adjoining house and walking across the plank, high above the rain-soaked street. Once inside the Randolph house, she locates and recognizes her father, who recovers his memory just as the police are about to take Sara away from him.

"You are and will always be my little princess."—Captain Crewe to his daughter Sara from *A Little Princess*

Reversals of fate and fortune follow hard upon this. Miss Minchin loses her boarding school, which becomes the Randolph School for Girls, and Minchin is forced to earn her keep sweeping chimneys. The novel reached a more sensible conclusion, as did the Shirley Temple movie, in which Sara was reunited with her father in a veteran's hospital.

In the novel Captain Crewe does die, but his partner, the "Indian Gentleman" Mr. Carrisford, who almost died of "brain fever," survives and Sara ends up being heiress to half the profits of a successful diamond mine. In both novel and film Ram Dass is the guardian angel who saves Sara and later Becky, who becomes "the attendant of Missee Sahib." The film adds a goofy subplot involving the elopement of Miss Minchin's sister Amelia (Rusty Schwimmer) with the milkman. In the novel Amelia stays to the bitter end to chastise the heartless Miss Minchin: "The child was a clever child and a good child," she says. "The fact was, she was too clever for you, and you always disliked her for that reason. She used to see through us both."

The kindly "large" Carmichael family is not in the film, and the troubled Mr. Carrisford, the "Indian Gentleman" who feels responsible for Sara and adopts her, is replaced by Mr. Randolph. Of course Ram Dass is in the film with his pet monkey working for another master, but it is not the monkey that draws Sara to the home next door in the film, and Sara is deprived of one of her most endearing lines: "Oh, I do love little animal things."

Regardless of its accuracy as an adaptation, this is a splendid film, expertly crafted, even down to the music composed by Patrick Doyle, his best work, perhaps, since Kenneth Branagh's *Henry V* (1989). Jay Carr of the *Boston Globe* found this "enchanting" film "one of those happy convergences where you sense everything going right." *Variety*'s Todd McCarthy considered it an "astonishing work of studio artifice" in which the "performances could scarcely be improved upon." And if the film is not a faithful adaptation, its distortions are tolerable and serve to protect the story as Frances Hodgson Burnett wrote it. The novel can still be read with pleasure and will fully retain its original charm even after one has seen the picture, which is a wonderful introduction to the spirit of the novel.

—*James M. Welsh*

REVIEWS

The Boston Globe. May 19, 1995, p.64.
Entertainment Weekly. No.276. May 26, 1995, p.65.
The New York Times. May 19, 1995, C13, C17.
The Philadelphia Inquirer, Weekend. May 19, 1995, p.5, p.15.
Premiere. Vol.8, No.10 (June 1995), p.75.
The Sun (Baltimore), Maryland Live. May 19-25, 1995, p.6.
The Washington Post. May 19, 1995, D1.
The Washington Times Metropolitan Times. May 19, 1995, C17.
Variety. May 1-7, 1995, p.35, p.40.

Live Nude Girls

Although the title would make you believe otherwise, there is nothing particularly provocative about this film. In fact, *Live Nude Girls* is best described as a gabfest among a group of five longtime friends who gather for a bachelorette party. Director-writer Julianna Lavin's debut takes a look at life, love, and sex in the nineties from a woman's point of view.

The story centers around Jamie (Kim Catrall), who is about to go to the altar for the third time and her friend Georgina, (Lora Zane), a restauranteur who plays hostess to the evening's get-together. As the night wears on, other personalities are introduced. Jill (Dana Delaney) is a sex-obsessed housewife; Rachel (Laila Robins) is her single, uptight, sister; and Marcy (Cynthia Stevenson) is an accountant with a very jealous, younger lover. Rounding out the group is Chris (Olivia D'Abo) as Georgina's depressed, live-in lesbian lover.

Throughout the course of the evening, sexual fantasies, fears, and petty rivalries are revealed, with none of the issues really carrying much weight. The most serious conflicts consist of Jamie threatening to cancel her wedding because she thinks her betrothed is at a bachelor party with a stripper; Georgina worries because she's having carnal thoughts about her male sous-chef and is no longer certain about her feelings for Chris; and Marcy, who is forced to confront her possessive, blue-collar lover when he shows up at the house. Sisters Jill and Rachel feud endlessly over just about everything. The talk eventually wears thin as the group takes to bickering and pouting, resulting in nothing more than a collective angst session.

The film meanders without ever reaching any solutions. It's particularly difficult to sympathize with any of the character's problems, as their complaining quickly becomes tiresome. The actresses all do an adequate job with their parts, yet they all feel underdeveloped, except for Catrall, who gives a fine performance as the B-movie actress about to hear wedding bells for the umpteenth time. This character-driven vehicle seems better suited for the stage than the big screen.

Although *Live Nude Girls* begins with an interesting subject, the film doesn't lead to any solid conclusion. It could have been more successful with a stronger story line and more fully-developed characters. The women are first introduced as children, but then there is very little background information given to their maturation into adulthood. The film also features some flashback scenes that seem out of place, given the lack of depth of the characters. This ensemble piece certainly tries hard, but chick-flicks have been done better in other settings, such as in this year's *Boys on the Side* and *How to Make an American Quilt* (both of which are reviewed in this volume).

—Beth Fhaner

CREDITS

Jill: Dana Delany
Jamie: Kim Cattrall
Marcy: Cynthia Stevenson
Rachel: Laila Robins
Georgina: Lora Zane
Chris: Olivia D'Abo

Origin: USA
Released: 1995
Production: Cara Tapper for a Spelling Entertainment and Steve White Properties production; released by Republic Pictures
Direction: Julianna Lavin
Screenplay: Julianna Lavin
Cinematography: Christopher Taylor
Editing: Kathryn Himoff
Production design: Jerry Fleming
Costume design: Israel Segal
Sound: Jim Dehr
Music: Anton Sanko
Casting: Gary Zuckerbrod and Marcia Ross
MPAA rating: R
Running Time: 100 minutes

Living in Oblivion

"He only needs two things to get through the day...an espresso and a miracle."—Movie tagline

"Clever and consistently funny! Ingeniously structured. A witty revenge against the dream factory. Starring some of the best actors in the independent world."—Kenneth Turan, *Los Angeles Times*

"Simultaneously hair-raising and hilarious." —Bruce Williamson, *Playboy*

"An irresistible blend of mirth and malice. The cast is comic perfection and DiCillo's lines dazzle. So funny, it hurts. Ditto this gem of a movie."—Peter Travers, *Rolling Stone*

CREDITS

Nick Reve: Steve Buscemi
Nicole: Catherine Keener
Chad Palomino: James Le Gros
Wolf: Dermot Mulroney
Wanda: Danielle von Zerneck
Cora/Nick's mother: Rica Martens
Tito: Peter Drinklage
Gaffer: Robert Wightman
Script: Hilary Gilford
Assistant Camera: Kevin Corrigan
Boom: Matthew Grace
Sound: Michael Griffiths
Clapper: Ryna Bowker
Production Assistant: Francesca DiMauro

Origin: USA
Released: 1995
Production: Michael Griffiths and Marcus Viscidi for A JDI and Lemon Sky Productions; released by Sony Classics
Direction: Tom DiCillo
Screenplay: Tom DiCillo
Cinematography: Frank Prinzi
Editing: Camilla Toniolo
Production design: Therese Deprez
Costume design: Ellen Lutter
Sound: Mathew Price
Music: Jim Farmer
Casting: Marcia Shulman
MPAA rating: R
Running Time: 91 minutes

Tom DiCillo's farcical view of low-budget independent filmmaking in *Living in Oblivion* is partially inspired by his experiences with *Johnny Suede* (1992), his first feature as writer-director. The earlier film, featuring Brad Pitt as a pompadoured would-be Ricky Nelson with limited talent, strives awkwardly to be offbeat. *Living in Oblivion*, in contrast, is a highly accomplished, unpretentious entertainment.

Nick Reve (Steve Buscemi) is directing a very low budget film, also entitled *Living in Oblivion*, in a run-down Manhattan building. The film within the film, having something to do with a young woman's nervousness over her impending wedding, is less important than the technical snafus and emotional entanglements among the crew and actors. DiCillo depicts the filming of three scenes during which almost everything that can go wrong does.

The first, a confrontation between the mother and daughter played by Cora (Rica Martens) and Nicole (Catherine Keener), is afflicted by the boom man lowering his microphone into the shot's frame, the assistant cameraman losing focus, street noise, and an exploding light bulb. Then the actors begin blowing their lines. When Nicole and Cora finally deliver their dialogue brilliantly, the camera is not rolling because Wolf (Dermot Mulroney), the cinematographer, is throwing up because of spoiled milk in his coffee.

The second scene is ruined by the egotism of Chad Palomino (James Le Gros), a minor star doing everyone a favor by deigning to appear in such an unglamourous project. The problem with Chad, in addition to trying to seduce every woman on the set, is that he is overly-creative, never wanting to perform a scene the same way twice. His encounter with Nicole in a hotel room becomes an ordeal for her, Nick, and the crew since Chad changes the staging of the scene for each shot. Because Wolf is wearing an eye patch after Wanda (Danielle von Zerneck), the assistant director, accidentally pokes him, Chad decides his character should wear one as well. Feeling his creativity impeded, Chad finally stalks off, shouting that he agreed to work with Nick only because he had heard that the director was friends with Quentin Tarantino.

The final scene is a dream sequence between Nicole

AWARDS AND NOMINATIONS

Sundance Film Festival 1995: Best Screenplay (DiCillo)
Independent Spirit Awards Nominations 1996: Best Film, Best Supporting Actor (LeGros), Best Screenplay (DiCillo)

and Tito (Peter Dinklage), a dwarf in a pale blue tuxedo. Because no one knows how to operate the smoke machine properly, it produces first too little smoke and then too much. Then Nick's mother (also played by Rica Martens) arrives unexpectedly in her dressing gown, having run away from a nursing home. Then Tito displays a Chad-sized temper tantrum and walks off the set. Just as Nick decides he has had enough and wants to shut down the production, his mother takes over Tito's role in the dream sequence, and everything falls magically into place.

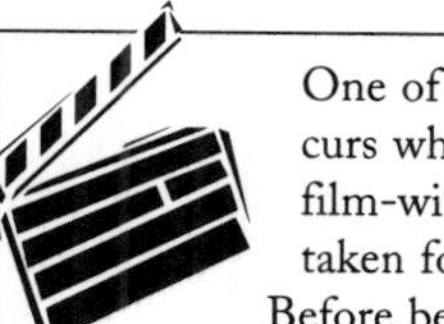

One of the film's in-jokes occurs when the director of the film-within-the-film is mistaken for the cinematographer. Before becoming a writer-director, Tom Dicillo was cinematographer for Jim Jarmusch's first two films, *Permanent Vacation* (1981) and *Stranger than Paradise* (1984).

Living in Oblivion could easily have attempted to say something ponderous about the pain of being an artist or something sentimental about the camaraderie of a group of strangers thrown together with a common goal or something nastily satirical about show business. Instead, DiCillo and his actors settle for what is essentially a slapstick farce. The director must have learned a great deal from making *Johnny Suede*, for while the earlier film is laboriously eccentric, *Living in Oblivion* is always charming and delightful. DiCillo may not attempt to have his audience care deeply for his characters, but he does make them consistently engrossing.

"The only reason I took a part in this movie is because someone said you were tight with Quentin Tarantino!"—Chad Palomino to director Nick in *Living in Oblivion*

Even though DiCillo presents actors as insecure and unpredictable, *Living in Oblivion* is an ode to actors' ability to communicate emotions. (DiCillo himself acted for eight years in Off Off Broadway plays and low-budget films.) This skill can be seen especially in the various changes Keener and Martens ring on their lines during the mother-daughter confrontation as they progress from awkwardness to competence to indifference to truth. Keener shows how Nicole, proud and embarrassed at the same time for her minor fame for being in a shower scene with Richard Gere, manages to find her character's sensitivity within her own confusion and exhaustion. Martens is remarkable in her transformation from the world-weary Cora to Nick's seemingly bewildered mother. Dinklage displays expert poker-faced comic timing as Tito demands to know why his character has to be a dwarf and whether anyone has ever actually dreamed about dwarves. Le Gros has effectively played offbeat characters in films such as *Drugstore Cowboy* (1989) and *My New Gun* (1992), and his portrayal of this not-too-bright lady killer who cannot stand not being the center of attention shows he possesses considerable range. Mulroney and von Zerneck portray talentless people enthralled with posing as artists without reducing these characters to the ridiculous.

Holding it all together on the screen, much as a film director does behind the camera, is Buscemi, who has become one of the most dependable character actors of the 1990's for his appearances in such films as *Reservoir Dogs* (1992) and *In the Soup* (1992), in which he plays a would-be filmmaker. His Nick is not a control freak, but rather he is willing to allow filmmaking to be a creative process, but he wants it to work. He is not aware, however, that the problems may include his insecurities and limited talent. This is no misunderstood genius but just a frazzled ordinary man trying to make a film, and Buscemi is very good at portraying such people caught up in circumstances they cannot control.

Living in Oblivion began as a $38,000 thirty-minute film featuring Keener, the female lead in *Johnny Suede*, and financed in part by Mulroney (Keener's husband) and von Zerneck. Everyone involved loved the short so much that DiCillo expanded his script and raised $750,000, again partly from cast members, to make it as a feature. DiCillo denies that Chad Palomino is based upon his experiences with Brad Pitt, despite the similarity in names, and claims to have offered the role to Pitt, who was unavailable because of other projects.

The film *Living in Oblivion* most resembles is Francois Truffaut's *La Nuit Americaine* (1973; *Day for Night*), rumored to have been partly inspired by his experiences with Julie Christie during the making of *Fahrenheit 451* (1966). Like Truffaut's great comedy, DiCillo's film tries to show how much filmmaking is affected by accident and luck, both good and bad. He demonstrates that the process can be a nightmare by making two of the three segments bad dreams experienced by Nick and Nicole—she in color, he in black

REVIEWS

Entertainment Weekly. July 28, 1995, p. 46.
The Los Angeles Times. July 21, 1995, p. F4.
The Nation. CCLXI, August 14. 1995, p. 180.
The New Republic. CCXIII, August 14, 1995, p. 24.
New York. XXVIII, July 31, 1995, p. 45.
The New York Times. July 14, 1995, p. C8.
People Weekly. XLIV, August 28, 1995, p. 17.
Rolling Stone. July 13, 1995, p. 116.
Variety. January 30, 1995, p. 47.
The Village Voice. XL, July 18, 1995, p. 45.
The Wall Street Journal. July 25, 1995, p. A10.
The Washington Post. August 11, 1995, p. F6.

and white—and the third a planned dream sequence that develops into a nightmare. Nick's last name, Reve, is French for "dream," and the dreams are why Martens is an actress in Nick's dream and his mother when he is awake. A tribute to the craziness of the film industry, *Living in Oblivion* succeeds in making a comic dream out of the horrors of hack filmmaking.

—*Michael Adams*

Lord of Illusions

"Evil waits on the other side."—Movie tagline

"It delivers shocks like some dark messenger from hell!"—Wes Craven

"Clive Barker outdoes himself with masterful visual effects."—Roger Ebert, *Chicago Sun-Times*

"Clive Barker's best and most ambitious movie to date!"—Kevin Thomas, *Los Angeles Times*

"The nail-biter, hair-raiser, teeth-chatterer movie of the season."— Bonnie Churchill, *National News Syndicate*

Box Office Gross: $13,293,081

Harry D'Amour (Scott Bakula) is a New York private eye whose clients never seem to run the normal gamut of cheating spouses or missing persons. Harry's clients, like Harry himself, seem to walk on the edge of the unknown, often looking down into the abyss of Hell. So, when Harry is offered the chance to investigate a case of plain old insurance fraud in sunny California, he gladly takes the job.

While following his quarry, Harry ends up in a fortune teller's parlor (Joseph Latimore) where the soothsayer is being slowly, violently, and graphically tortured to death. Now the case of insurance fraud turns into something much deeper...and much darker.

The fortune teller, Caspar Quaid, was once a part of a cult led by a charismatic leader, Nix (Daniel Von Bargen). But Nix's power went far beyond that of just being able to enrapture people. Nix is an evil messiah who's self-proclaimed mission is to "cleanse the world" through murder. And to achieve his calling, Nix has abilities that go far beyond illusion and magic. "Nix has the power to get into people's heads and make them see things." He has the force of the dark side at his disposal.

Nix only cares about one of his many fanatic disciples, Swann (Kevin J. O'Connor). But Swann is disillusioned with Nix, especially after he kidnaps a young girl, Dorothea, whom he plans on sacrificing. Swann rescues the young girl, and Nix is shot, incapacitated (with an elaborate, metal face mask) and buried so deep in the Mojave Desert that no one will ever find him.

Thirteen years later, Swann has married Dorothea (Famke Janssen) and has a very successful career as a high-paid magician/illusionist, and Harry is on the trail of why a fortune teller was tortured to death. As it turns out, Swann's magic is not an illusion, it is based on the real powers Nix gave him before he died. Swann, however, prefers to make big bucks in Vegas-type extravaganzas rather than murder the world as Nix had wanted to do.

Harry's trail soon leads him to Dorothea since the fortune teller had been with Swann when he rescued Dorthea. The torturer was a man named Butterfield (Barry Del Sherman), one of Nix's loyal, if somewhat viciously deviant, minions. Butterfield wants to know where Nix was buried so he can dig him up. Now that Quaid is dead, Butterfield will try to extract the information from the others who were in on the plot, namely Swann or Dorothea.

Now Harry has been hired by Dorothea and he accompanies her to Swann's last Los Angeles performance where he will be performing a new trick, "The Ten Swords." During this "illusion," ten swords dangle over a prostrate Swann who must release himself from his bonds before the swords are dropped, one by one, through his body. Almost immediately, things begin to go wrong, and Swann is killed while performing the feat.

Harry now turns to the experts in magic to help him figure out what happened to Swann. He attends an intimate

P.I. Harry D'Amour first appeared in Barker's 1985 short story *The Last Illusion*, on which the film is based, and has since appeared in other novels and short stories.

dinner at the Magic Castle in Hollywood where he is warned off by a flamboyant magician named Vinovich (Vincent Schiavelli) and also helped by a young magician named Billy Who (Lorin Stewart). Together, they break into the sacred heart of the Magic Castle, the repository, and there Harry learns the difference between the theatrical magicians' tricks and the reality of the powers of illusions, which are not based on tricks. Once again Harry is staring into the abyss.

"You're drawn to the dark side. It is your destiny. You must accept that."—psychic Caspar Quaid to P.I. Harry D'Amour

And the horrors to come out of that abyss are typical of those created by mastermind of horror, Clive Barker. *Lord of Illusions* is based on one of Barker's 1985 short stories which was written around Barker's recurring character, private investigator Harry D'Amour. However, in Barker's hands, what might have been a Sam Spade mystery turns into a Stephen King nightmare. With films like 1987's *Hellraiser* to his writing and directing credit, and character's like its "Pinhead," one should not be surprised when Barker's vision of a film noir detective film quickly finds itself mired in the supernatural and supersaturated in gore. Throw in a little romance, a bit of action, and a modicum of magic, and *Lord of Illusions* is the end result.

CREDITS

Harry D'Amour: Scott Bakula
Nix: Daniel Von Bargen
Philip Swann: Kevin J. O'Connor
Dorothea Swann: Famke Janssen
Casper Quaid: Joseph Latimore
Jennifer Desiderio: Sheila Tousey
Maureen Pimm: Susan Taylor
Loomis: Wayne Grace

Origin: USA
Released: 1995
Production: JoAnne Sellar and Clive Barker for a Seraphim production; released by United Artists Pictures
Direction: Clive Barker
Screenplay: Clive Barker
Cinematography: Ronn Schmidt
Editing: Alan Baumgarten
Production design: Stephen Hardie
Art direction: Marc Fisichella and Bruce Robert Hill
Set decoration: David A. Koneff
Costume design: Luke Reichle
Sound: Hamilton Sterling
Special Make-up and Visual Effects: Thomas C. Rainone
Music: Carol Sue Baker
MPAA rating: R
Running Time: 109 minutes

Visually, *Lord of Illusions* is permeated with darkness and texture, but they are quickly outstaged by the incredible sadistic violence and abundance of butchery. Instead of relying on a substantial and pliable story, Barker too often substitutes cheap shocks (noises that turn out to be just bumps in the night) and excessive mutilation in place of it. Often the story may leave viewers feeling as if it has unravelled at their feet. Too many plot threads seem to dangle while other threads seem to be picked up out of nowhere by Harry. (Is this the result of bad writing or cut scenes?)

Even basic explanations, such as the source of Nix's power or the reason for his mission, or why Dorothea stays married to Swann whom she does not love, are totally unanswered. Instead we are offered a kind of pseudo-religiosity with Nix's charisma supposedly substituting for any rationale. (It's probably no accident that Nix's compound in the Mojave Dessert looks eerily like David Koresh's in Waco.)

The best thing about the film is Scott Bakula's Harry. Best known for his television series "Quantum Leap" and as Murphy Brown's erstwhile fiance, Bakula is a solid piece of casting. He seems to have no trouble with this off-center role and brings both a sensitivity and a sense of authority to his character. With his rugged good looks and engaging personality, Bakula take what could have been a silly role and gives it strength and depth.

Also of interest is Lorin Stewart whose magician Billy Who is virtually a piece of typecasting. Stewart, a real-life magician and a very likable screen presence, was also a consultant for the film. He worked with O'Connor and saw to it that the illusions presented were remarkable while still being faithful to the facts. It was also Stewart who worked with Barker and designer Stephen Hardie to create a suitably sensational magic show for Swann's farewell performance at the Pantages Theater.

Some of the other actors, however, don't fare as well. Famke Janssen's Dorothea is beautiful, but she seems too aloof to be of romantic interest to Harry and too out of touch with the story to be interesting to viewers. (This is Janssen's first major Hollywood role, but she will also be seen as the female lead opposite Pierce Brosnan's James Bond in *Goldeneye.*) Barry Del Sherman's Butterfield is suitably sadistic and kinky for the story and Daniel Von Bargen's Nix is adequately evil, but perhaps the most jarring character is Kevin O'Connor's Swann. For a man with as much power as he supposedly had, O'Connor's portrayal shows a man who seems more perplex, nervous, and distracted than forceful. He is not a commanding presence. While knowing that Nix is on the way back might be a bit terrifying for him, we never know how Swann knows this will occur. The result is a story that is illogical and a characterization that is not convincing.

Perhaps with a more cohesive story line and a stronger cast of supporting actors, Scott Bakula can pull off a sequel performance as Barker's favorite private eye. But if this film doesn't do well at box offices (and it is being given limited distribution), then it may be a moot point.

—*Beverley Bare Buehrer*

REVIEWS

Chicago Sun Times. August 25, 1995, p. W21
Chicago Tribune. August 25, 1995, Section Friday, p. H
New York Times. August 25, 1995, p. B5
Village Voice. September 5, 1995, p. 74
Variety. August 21-27, 1995, p. 67

Losing Isaiah

"Who decides what makes a good mother?"—Movie tagline

"The movie hits us in the heart."—Michael Wilmington, *The Chicago Tribune*

"As powerful, provocative and moving a drama as you're likely to see this year."—Paul Wunder, *WBAI Radio*

Box Office Gross: $7,603,766

Losing Isaiah is an earnest parable about a child custody battle played out across the great divide of urban America. It pits an inner-city black crack mother (Halle Berry) against a white suburban social worker (Jessica Lange), battling for the right to raise the baby Kyla abandoned.

The film is full of heart, sympathy and common sense, but a little short on plausibility and character development. It has a script that strains to make an agreeable moral point: if parents and the legal system really put first the welfare of the children at stake in such battles, there would be more compromising and less posturing. The point fits into a larger moral theme about how caring about children can unify even the most divided society.

It's a wonderful message, but scripts that start with a message usually end up with rough spots in exposition, and *Losing Isaiah*, unfortunately, has more than its share. Too bad, because there's a lot going for the film, starting with Berry's pull-no-punches performance and an unsparing depiction of what it's like to grow up and live in America's inner-city scrap pile.

Berry's Khaila Richards undergoes a remarkable and implausible transformation. At film's start, she's a South side-Chicago crackhead so desperate for a fix that she leaves her newborn baby inside a box on a garbage heap. She is reformed through a series of vaguely defined self-help groups and discovers that the baby she thought she killed is alive and living in suburban DePaul.

Jessica Lange as social worker Margaret Lewin in *Losing Isaiah*. © 1995 Paramount Pictures. All rights reserved.

Lange's Margaret Lewin finds and fixates on Isaiah as he is struggling for life in the hospital pediatric emergency ward where she works. Margaret falls in love with the baby and, ignoring her own professional common sense, adopts him. Her motivations are unexplained, though there's a vague suggestion that her daughter Hannah's reaching adolescence has left her with an emotional hole to fill, and a later revelation that her marriage to engineer husband

Charles (David Strathairn) is not as happy as it appears to be on the surface.

The script toys with a family tension subplot in an annoyingly predictable scene in which the irritable Isaiah disrupts Hannah's stage review, but that thread goes nowhere. Hannah and the father remain enigmatic characters, and not even Lange's role is ever fully fleshed out.

There are other plot lines that bloom and wither, such as ones involving Khaila and a cornball suitor and Khaila and a nephew who needs her to help him make it through childhood. She must abandon both in her drive to gain the respectability necessary to win back her baby.

Once the battle is joined, the problem is that the title gives away what's going to happen. What should be moving courtroom drama is reduced to a series of pat speeches and exchanges that never would be tolerated in a real courtroom. There's the growing feeling that the whole script is a setup.

The racial arguments that fill the air sound strained and forced. Khaila has a lawyer (Samuel L. Jackson) who is a black activist searching for a cause. Jackson does his usual regal, subtly shaded job, but he is forced to mouth the worst sort of racist claptrap. The Lewins are painted as clueless suburbanites who have completely ignored Isaiah's heritage. Since Margaret is a social worker who deals with deprived minority children for a living, it's hard to believe she's never given a thought to educating her adopted child in black culture.

No matter how reformed Khaila is, it's implausible that a judge would even consider returning a child to a crack addict who threw that child into the garbage. It's demeaning to suggest that even the most ardent black-pride advocates would argue such a case.

We are left to ache with Lange at the injustice of it all, and ache we do. As usual, Lange would have it no other way. Her teary-eyed, jangled, edge-of-hysteria performance is only slightly more subdued than it usually is. She chews on her lip and chews up the scenery. She's an actress whose stock-in-trade—the emotional rollercoaster ride—is definitely a matter of taste.

Balancing the off-kilter argument against returning Isaiah to Khaila are the remarkable performance by Berry and the filmmakers' dogged insistence on an unblinking look at ghetto life. Cutting through the debate about whether America's poor and wretched are victims or agents of their own demise, Berry portrays Khaila as a real human being struggling against overwhelming odds.

Berry refuses to make Khaila a monster (even though she puts Isaiah aside so she can visit a crack den.) She's a woman pulled by two powerful forces—motherhood and her addiction to cocaine. Her horror is palpable, that of a caged animal struggling to break free.

After she is free of her addiction, she is gripped by remorse and a desire to make things right. She is willing to risk everything for her child. Yet Berry makes her no saint: she battles laziness and confusion and remains an addict who nearly succumbs to temptation. But she is determined to let nothing get in the way of her reunion with her son.

Among the obstacles to that reunion is her own background, demeanor and appearance. Ironically, to win a skirmish for black pride, Khaila must straighten her hair and look more "white," presumably to win the judge's sympathy in court.

Berry is astounding. Her performance is authentic, intelligent, wrenching and unsparing. She is an unlikely heroine, one who must overcome the worst influences and impulses. Her humanity is crucial, because it is her selflessness that provides the film's ultimate surprise.

It's too bad Lange's Margaret is so neurotic and ditzy. Casting someone like Susan Sarandon opposite Berry would have made for exactly the sort of titanic clash of righteous mothers the filmmakers seem to be aiming for.

As Margaret's husband, Strathairn is little more than a harried foil. As daughter Hannah, Daisy Eagan is engaging and fresh despite inhabiting a rather stereotyped teenage role. As suitor Eddie Hughes, Cuba Gooding Jr. is too clean-cut to be believable as someone who would attract the tough-as-nails Khaila.

Director Stephen Gyllenhaal sets a sure-handed course through the risky waters of the screenplay by Naomi Foner based on Seth Margolis' novel. This is a film that could have faltered in many ways, but Gyllenhaal keeps it from being too preachy or too predictable.

When Isaiah enters his birth mother's world, the filmmakers switch viewpoints and present the harrowing expe-

CREDITS

Margaret Lewin: Jessica Lange
Khaila Richards: Halle Berry
Charles Lewin: David Strathairn
Kadar Lewis: Samuel L. Jackson

Origin: USA
Released: 1995
Production: Howard W. Koch Jr. and Naomi Foner; released by Paramount
Direction: Stephen Gyllenhaal
Screenplay: Naomi Foner based on the novel by Seth Margolis
Cinematography: Andrezej Bartkowiak
Editing: Harvey Rosenstock
Production design: Jeannine C. Oppewall
Set design: Suzan Wexler
Costume design: Mary Malin
Sound: Thomas Nelson
Music: Marc Isham
MPAA rating: R
Running Time: 106 minutes

rience as seen through his own eyes. This sequence alone is enough to give pause to those who advocate snatching children out of the homes of families that have raised them in order to fulfill some larger agenda.

It's too bad the film couldn't have balanced the scales with a stronger, less racial argument for the birth mother's claim to Isaiah. The film's principal black characters are seen as mercenaries and the principal white characters as ninnies.

Despite its shortcomings, *Losing Isaiah* is a film of deep principle and conviction whose message is inspiring and needed in this age when children too often are pawns in custody battles. But the film's heart is in the right place, and there is plenty of it.

—Michael Betzold

REVIEWS

Entertainment Weekly. March 24, 1995, p. 45.
The Hollywood Reporter. March 17, 1995, p. 12.
Los Angeles Magazine. March 1995, p. 128.
New York Magazine. April 3, 1995, p. 59.
The New York Times. March 17, 1995, p. C9.
People Weekly. March 27, 1995, p. 18.
Variety. March 20, 1995, p. 47.
Los Angeles Times. March 17, 1995, p. F1.

Love and Human Remains

"Welcome to love in the 90's."—Movie tagline

"Chilling, compelling, provocative."—Caryn James, *New York Times*

"A kinky comedy soap opera. A daffy good time. It descends its characters through up-to-the-minute erotic hoops."—Owen Gleiberman, *Entertainment Weekly*

"Brilliant as ever, Arcand retains hip, witty timelessness and adds an edgy sense of danger. Performed to perfection."—Bruce Williamson, *Playboy*

"Heart-stabbingly powerful!"—Barbara and Scott Siegel, *Siegel Entertainment Network*

Box Office Gross: $539,301

Love and Human Remains combines two mutually exclusive genres: the "Generation X" comedy of earnest young adults looking for love and the serial-killer thriller. Like oil and water, the mixture never takes. The film's foreground consists of a dark comedic roundelay of men and women in their twenties—heterosexual, homosexual, and bisexual—all searching for someone to love in a cold, deadening city; its background story follows the spree of a serial killer stalking the city's young women, to which the main characters remain oblivious. In the end, the characters realize that the killer is one of them, and emerge chastened and changed. Although the film's premise—that the failure to love and to connect with others in the modern world helps create killers—is valid enough, the film's structure, which constantly juxtaposes the self-absorbed lovers and the relentless murderer, creates such melodrama that *Love and Human Remains* simply implodes. The film's two stories, rather than complementing each other, remain in pitched battle. One focuses on the characters' awakening to the importance of human connection through their own mistakes; the other, the search for the murderer, becomes an extraneous and increasingly intrusive device to highlight the characters' narcissism. By the end, the whodunit aspect of the story has so overpowered the film that its last third consists purely of plot mechanics, and the more sensitive exploration of character is lost. The discovery of the killer's identity, supposedly tying the two stories together, seems not only arbitrary and poorly foreshadowed, but also irrelevant to the fate of the characters. Nevertheless, the film's main story, which sensitively portrays the tortured, neurotic dating and sexual rituals of people under thirty, is not without charm.

Adapted from Brad Fraser's successful play, *Unidentified Human Remains and the True Nature of Love* (1989) by the author, the film is also the first of French-Canadian director Denys Arcand's eight features shot in English, and the first directed from a script he did not write himself. Arcand's lack of involvement in the script shows: the film's clumsy attempts at witty banter and use of stale devices (television, answering machines) to portray its characters' alienation contrast sharply with the scintillating light dialogue and pointed social observation in Arcand's most recent films, *Le Declin De L'empire Americain*; *The Decline of the Ameri-*

can Empire (1986) and *Jesus De Montreal*; *Jesus of Montreal* (1988). *Love and Human Remains*, Arcand admitted himself in an interview with Maclean's in 1994, is "not very methodically written, and it's not in control. It's this guy's first achieved play, and everything has come out of him at the same time. The writing is messy, but what the hell. I wanted to respect that." Arcand's assessment is both candid and accurate.

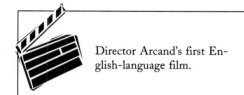

Director Arcand's first English-language film.

Set in a nameless, steely gray Canadian city, the film follows a group of twentysomething Canadians led by the acerbic David (Thomas Gibson), who refuses to believe that romantic love exists. The film opens with David walking with his friend Bernie (Cameron Bancroft). Bernie laments the loss of his close friendship with David, and bemoans his sterile life as a civil servant. He describes his empty life of sex without passion, love, or joy.

David, a once-promising teen star on Canadian television, is now a waiter in a chic restaurant, and tells friends fliply that he finds being a waiter "more artistically satisfying." Once in the closet and pursuing heterosexual relationships, David is now openly gay, and having sex without safety precautions. David takes an acerbic attitude to all this, distancing himself from his friends, his lovers, and his own feelings with a series of cynical poses. His roommmate and ex-lover, Candy (Ruth Marshall), is latently anorexic and socially stunted. She is naive enough to think she can make a living writing freelance book reviews, but complains that all the books she reads are "junk." She is looking for work with "meaning." Candy, too, keeps everyone in her life at arm's length: her main means of accomplishing this is to remain unrequitedly in love with David, with whom she had a relationship before he came out of the closet. In her attempts to meet other people, Candy either scares off potential suitors, or finds herself attracted to people just as inaccessible as she and David. Either way, she retains the illusion that she is in control of her life, when in fact she is keeping real life at bay.

The story follows David's and Candy's relationships with a variety of friends and lovers, and how these relationships subtly change them. David's other female friend, Benita (Mia Kirshner), is a dominatrix who was molested by her father, and performs sado-masochistic acts on clients. David occasionally participates in these rituals, and enjoys humiliating clients. Kane (Matthew Ferguson), an impressionable 17-year-old waiter colleague of David's, idolizes David, to the point where he is willing to have forced, drugged sex with him. Candy either humiliates and rejects potential lovers, or leaps into bed with them to overcome her fear of intimacy: Robert (Rick Roberts), a bartender, briefly becomes her ideal man, until she suspects him without cause of being the serial killer; Jerri (Joanne Vannicola), a sensitive lesbian schoolteacher, falls for Candy but has her heart broken when Candy decides that their sexual relationship is merely an experiment.

The film tries to show how David and Candy derive perverse pleasure, but never love or self-acceptance, from holding back their feelings, remaining in control. David can seemingly only get his kicks from anonymous sex and from sedating and playing with the minds of teenage boys; Candy humiliates Robert and uses Jerri. Contempt, for both of them, is an easy way of keeping the world at a distance. The film's turning point for David comes when he actually has the opportunity to take advantage of Kane and refrains. He realizes he merely wants to teach Kane the lesson that one has choices in life, not actually harm him, and the moment marks the beginning of David's return to humanity. For Candy, the moment of truth comes when both Robert and Jerri appear in the apartment, and she fights with and loses

CREDITS

David: Thomas Gibson
Candy: Ruth Marshall
Bernie: Cameron Bancroft
Benita: Mia Kirshner
Jerri: Joanne Vannicola
Kane: Matthew Ferguson
Robert: Rick Roberts

Origin: Canada
Released: 1995
Production: Roger Frappier for a Max Films and Atlantis Films Ltd. production; released by Sony Classics
Direction: Denys Arcand
Screenplay: Brad Fraser, based on his play, *Unidentified Human Remains and the True Nature of Love*
Cinematography: Paul Sarossy
Editing: Alain Baril
Production design: Francois Seguin
Costume design: Denis Sperdouklis
Casting: Deirdre Bowen and Lynn Kressel
Music: John McCarthy
MPAA rating: R
Running Time: 98 minutes

AWARDS AND NOMINATIONS

Canadian Genie Awards 1994: Best Adapted Screenplay (Fraser)

both of them. Robert, whom she has idealized but never really wanted to know, leaves in disgust, and Jerri, who actually loves her but whom she has never allowed to get close to her, leaves in tears and defiance.

Made aware of their failings, David and Candy suddenly become more aware of the threat of the serial killer, whose signature is ripping his victim's earrings from their earlobes. In the end, they realize the lonely, deadened Bernie is the killer. After attacking Benita and Candy unsuccessfully, Bernie reveals his love for David, and throws himself off the top of David's and Candy's apartment building. Chastened, David and Candy see the importance of love and friendship. David, with Candy and Kane in tow, goes on his first acting audition in years and tells his friends he loves them.

> "It's always the ones who seem to be the most normal who turn out to be ax murderers."—Candy from *Love and Human Remains*

The script for *Love and Human Remains* lacks basic dramatic elements. Neither David nor Candy seems to be at a particular turning point in his or her life, and the situations that befall them seem more slices of life than elements of rising dramatic action. Consequently, the story gives them little framework in which to grow dramatically. The urgency of the serial killer plot seems all the more artificial against the film's meandering storyline.

Against such a formless plot, Arcand's and Fraser's ways of showing anomie or alienation stand out more than they should, and reveal a sophomoric tendency to lean on extraneous details, rather than action, to elucidate character. Witty, bitchy epigrams which mask the characters' spiritual and physical longing abound, but the epigrams are not particularly witty, or revealing. Arcand and Fraser again and again use television to show the banality and despiritualization of modern life—a device that should have been retired twenty years ago—but they do not even do it well: their send-ups of news programs pale next to a typical episode of *The Simpsons*. The hoary device of answering machines to signify the emptiness of modern life pops up here as well; this particular device was dated ten years ago in *Agnes of God* (1985). The filmmakers' ways of showing decadence—panning past go-go dancers, transvestite hookers, characters engaged in meaningless sex—are equally familiar. The details that are inessential to the story pile up while the action fails to build.

All the plot's more human elements are subsumed by this heavy-handed editorializing, which reaches its peak in the final third of the film. The characters' inability to identify their friend Bernie as the killer is supposed to show how distant from their true feelings and instincts they really are. But the writer ineptly fills the film with red herrings: any one of the characters could theoretically be the killer, and so therefore it is not at all obvious, even in retrospect, who the killer is—certainly the characters cannot be blamed for being unable to guess his identity when it is deliberately kept from the audience. The guessing game not only takes over the film, but also destroys it.

This attempt to straddle two genres is a shame, because the film's world of aimless, yearning twentysomethings is at times engaging and artfully drawn. In spite of the ineptitude of the script, the film remains stubbornly charming, primarily because of the appealing performances of Gibson, Marshall, Vannicola, and Ferguson. Gibson's transition from cynical cad to man of conscience and self-esteem is convincing, and Marshall makes Candy appealingly neurotic, never pathetic. Vannicola and Ferguson are exceptionally fresh as young, rather naive people searching for love and commitment. Ferguson gives Kane a puppy-like quality as David's younger alter-ego, whom David finally refuses to allow to be corrupted. Vannicola, as the only character who goes with her instincts, affectingly shows Jerri's vulnerability and resilience in the face of rejection. The cinematography, too, is effective. Arcand has methodically eliminated all vegetation from the film. Shot in Montreal by Paul Sarossy, *Love and Human Remains* shows a cold, nameless, northern city of grey concrete, soulless high-rise apartment buildings, and the underside of freeway ramp, in which its young people's search for love seems almost still-born.

But for all its small pleasures, the film is finally one in which two genres, comedy and thriller, willfully knock each other off balance, then finally butt heads and knock each other out. *Love and Human Remains* finds a veteran director showcasing the work of a young, promising, but undisciplined writer. Alternately dark and frothy, disturbing and silly, serious and sophomoric, annoying and charming, the film is, to paraphrase the film's own director, a mess.

—*Paul Mittelbach*

REVIEWS

The Advocate. May 16, 1995, p.60.
Maclean's. CVII, April 4, 1994, p.58.
The New York Times. CXLIV, June 2, 1995, p.C4(L).
Rolling Stone. June 15, 1995, p.88.
Sight and Sound. IV, August, 1994, p.44.

Mad Love

"O'Donnell and Barrymore soar!"—Kevin Thomas, *Los Angeles Times*

Box Office Gross: $15,453,274

The destruction of idyllic romance by circumstance, fate or parental intervention has been a subject of continuing interest to filmmakers, for instance, *Splendor in the Grass* (1961), *Camelot* (1967), *Romeo and Juliet* (1968), *Love Story* (1970), *Endless Love* (1981). Recently films have tried to find a way to ameliorate the "bad ends" to which the earlier loves have come, arriving at a "it's better that way" ending. One such film is this 1995's *Mad Love*.

The film begins with Matt (Chris O'Donnell) heading off to school after preparing breakfast for his brother and sister, and helping his father locate his misplaced materials. Matt is a responsible person, dependable to the exclusion of his own life. Enter Casey (Drew Barrymore), the new girl in town. She is a free spirit, an iconoclast, a class-cutter. The two fall in love and then escape, when their parents' protestations grow too bothersome. In the course of their travels, the young lovers learn a good bit about reality and about the dangers lurking in the "real world."

Chris O'Donnell's 1995 films have included *Circle of Friends*, in which he plays a heartthrob who falls in love with a plain girl, and *Batman Forever*, in which he plays Robin, the Boy Wonder. Often cast as the straight arrow, the good guy—such as the prep school valet he played to Al Pacino's blind retired army colonel in 1992's *Scent of a Woman*—O'Donnell once again here plays control to Drew Barrymore's experiment. While early in her career she was best known for her role in ET: *The Extra-terrestrial* (1982), Barrymore more recently has played rebellious—even dangerous—women, such as in her recent films, *Poison Ivy* (1993), *Bad Girls* (1994), and *Boys on the Side* (1995). Each feature of the characters emphasizes the differences. Matt's hair is cut so short it is barely visible; Casey's is uncombed, multi-colored. Matt drives the family four-wheel-drive vehicle, while Casey drives a classic (albeit temperamental) Volkswagen Beetle. Matt watches the stars in the heavens; Casey rides a Jet Ski across a moonlit lake, whooping and hollering. Matt cares for his father and siblings, shouldering the guilt of his mother's desertion; Casey causes constant worry for her overbearing father and careful mother. Matt is college bound; Casey is an adventure seeker.

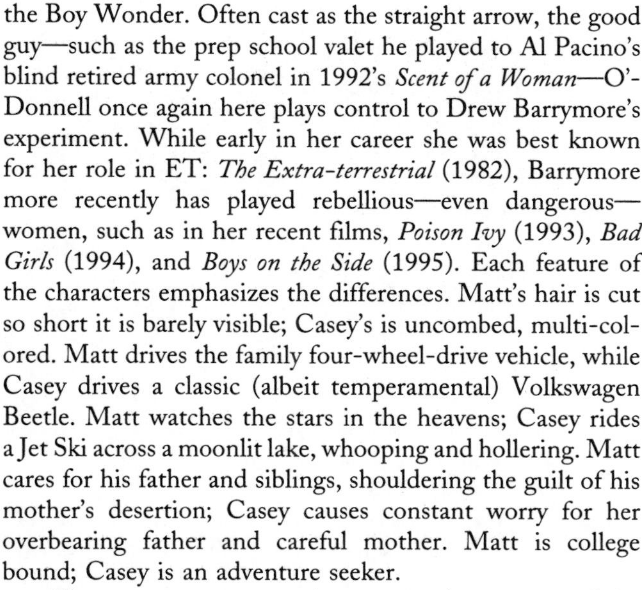

The same contrast can be seen in the settings of the film. The characters live and meet in Seattle, Washington, but once they are alone and on the road, they head to New Mexico. Explains director Antonia Bird in the production notes, "With its coastline, waterways, urban grid and skyscrapers, Seattle provided the characters with a periphery of protection, one that had great contrast to the open, unpredictable and huge landlocked scenery of the hot and arid landscape of New Mexico." The filmmakers have captured most of the refreshing portions of Seattle (e.g., waterfalls, lush greenery), just as they have captured the heat and pressure of New Mexico (e.g., dust, glaring sun, Spanish language). The audience will no doubt pick up on the restfulness of Seattle and will no doubt feel weighed down by the white sands of New Mexico. The distinctions between the two locales also fit the filmmaker's color scheme: "For each film, I have a color palette," said director Bird in the production notes. "For this film, the palette starts with grays,

CREDITS

Matt: Chris O'Donnell
Casey: Drew Barrymore
Eric: Mathew Lillard
Duncan: Richard Chaim

Origin: USA
Released: 1995
Production: David Manson for a TouchStone presentation; released by Buena Vista Pictures
Direction: Antonia Bird
Screenplay: Paula Milne
Cinematography: Fred Tammes
Editing: Jeff Freeman
Production Designer: David Brisbin
Casting: Dianne Crittenden
Music: Andy Roberts
MPAA rating: PG-13
Running Time: Not listed

REVIEWS

Baltimore Sun, May 26, 1995, Features, p. 8
The Boston Globe, May 26, 1995, p. 84
Chicago Sun-Times, May 26, 1995, Weekend Plus, p. 39
Houston Chronicle, May 26, 1995, Weekend Preview, p. 1
Los Angeles Times, May 26, 1995, p. F14
New York Times, May 28, 1995, Section 2, p. 2
Newsday, May 26, 1995, Weekend, p. 5
The Salt Lake Tribune, May 26, 1995, p. E5
The San Francisco Chronicle, May 26, 1995, p. C3
The Washington Post, May 26, 1995, p. FO7

blues, greens and rather muted browns—very watery earth colors and then, when they burst free from their background, suddenly it goes full glorious Technicolor. We have yellows and oranges, browns, sienna colors — real hot earth tones. It's absolutely beautiful."

Also important in the selection of cities was Seattle's claim to fame as the center of "grunge" rock music. For instance, several currently popular bands began in Seattle, including Nirvana, Soundgarden, Hole and Alice in Chains. The filmmakers used a local club, Moe's, for Matt and Casey's first date. Selected because it was aggressive, exciting and full of energy, the club provides the perfect meeting ground for restrained Matt and wild Casey. One Seattle band, 7 Year Bitch, appears in the film. The production notes suggest that the fact that it is an all-girl band appealed particularly to the filmmakers. Unfortunately, watching characters watching bands is rather slim excitement. For what seems an eternity, the audience watches Casey's head bob and shake uncontrollably, while Matt's head lopes along at half-speed. Reminiscent of the creatures who inhabit back car windows and gyrate to the motion, Casey and Matt stand, feet planted, and wiggle. The scene would be humorous if it weren't so visually static. Other films have encountered similar problems, however. In the Seattle-based film *Singles*, several characters also travel to a grunge club and stand amid others in a crowd, wagging their heads. Like swimmers trying to dislodge water from their ears, the actors tilt their heads first this way, then that, shaking violently. Scenes such as these suggest that while film reflects much of life, much of life probably should not be recorded there.

"What happens between Matthew and Casey is something magical and wonderful that hopefully happens to all of us at one point in our lives, and that is they have an absolute electric falling in love—a complete physical and mental attraction for each other. Then the harsh reality starts coming through the relationship, and you realize that person is not the person you're going to be able to live your life with."—Director Antonia Bird explaining her two main characters

While the production notes state clearly that Antonia Bird's work is unerringly reality based, it is important to note that Matt and Casey commit major felonies without repercussions. Additionally, money is never a problem, and, after the bittersweet ending, the lives that seem to have been totally destroyed are now back on track. A quick, and too easy, fix. Perhaps part of the confusion with reality arises from the fact that director Bird is a British filmmaker: "The film is a British director's look at being young in America. . . . So I am standing on the outside and observing. There are things that I chose to show or linger on, like the scenery and the music, that maybe an American would just take for granted, and for that I think it's probably a richer film. It's not a new subject, but it's a new look at it."

Some reviewers labeled the film "realistic" (*Denver Post*); others "state of the art bad" (*Washington Post*). In a scene no doubt intended to show the bond between the lovers and to show how conventional rules can't touch them, Casey covers Matt's eyes as he drives up a curving mountain road. She directs his progress, urges him on. It is clear that the filmmakers see this scene as emblematic of the whimsy of young love. Unfortunately, the scene falls flat, coming out as dangerous stupidity.

Mad Love is just that—madness. Two fine young actors cannot resurrect a leaden script, filled with childish pranks and dime-store-novel romance. Finally, the film is full of sound and fury, but signifies nothing. It is a great disappointment and one best left unseen.

—Roberta F. Green

Magic in the Water

"It's wonderful. It's exciting and absorbing. A fine film in the tradition of a Disney classic. Good for all members of the family."—Colleen Hartry, *Parent Film Review*

"A family adventure for all ages."—James Grant, *Scene Magazine*

"An imaginative modern fable."—Jeff Craig, *Sixty Second Preview*

Memorable movie magic isn't manufactured, it happens. Chemistry between actors, deft photography, a wonderful line of dialogue, an instinctual director—these are some of the many things that can create alchemy on screen. You can't force it, but *Magic in the Water* tries, with disastrous results. It's a ridiculous film dressed up as a profound parable, and not even Houdini could escape from the restraints of its strange, labored plot.

CREDITS

Jack Black: Mark Harmon
Joshua Black: Joshua Jackson
Dr. Wanda Bell: Harley Jane Kozak
Ashley Black: Sarah Wayne
Hiro: Willie Nark-Orn
Uncle Kipper: Frank Sotonoma Salsedo
Mack Miller: Morris Panych
Sheriff Stevenson: Tamsin Kelsey

Origin: USA
Released: 1995
Production: Matthew O'Connor and Rick Stevenson for an Oxford Film Company and Pacific Motion Pictures Production; released by TriStar Pictures
Direction: Rick Stevenson
Screenplay: Rick Stevenson, Icel Dobell Massey and Ninian Dunnett
Cinematography: Thomas Burstyn
Editing: Allan Lee
Production design: Errol Clyde Klotz
Art direction: Eric Norlin
Stunt coordination: Jim Dunn
Special effects coordination: Randy Shymkiw and Rory Cutler
Make-up: Sandy Cooper
Visual Effects Supervision: Gene Warren, Jr.
Music: David Schwartz
MPAA rating: PG
Running Time: 98 minutes

A collaboration between first-time director Rick Stevenson and novice screenwriter Icel Dobell Massey, *Magic in the Water* has all the ingredients of what is becoming a sub-genre of family films: the Pacific Northwest poisoned water-creature movie. How many characters and plot devices does *Magic in the Water* share with the *Free Willy* films? There's a mysterious water denizen with a knack for communicating with children; a kid or two from a broken family looking for love from something with fins; evil cardboard industrialists dumping chemical waste in the creature's habitat; wise old Native Americans who understand the creature's methods of communications; Asian scientists who are trying to study the creature, and a whole lot of blubber.

In *Magic in the Water*, 10-year-old Ashley Black (Sarah Wayne) is on vacation near Glenorky, a remote British Columbia oceanside village. With her are her bored teenage brother Josh (Joshua Jackson) and her addled psychiatrist father Dr. Jack Black (Mark Harmon), whose very name should invoke a guffaw. Jack, divorced from the kids' mom, is a radio talk show host who hasn't spent much time with his kids. He begrudges the vacation time, and rather than play with his children he prefers to work on a book, though he can't get past the title page. The village has concocted a minor tourist trade out of its most famous resident, a legendary sea monster named Orky, who is either a hoax or the spiritual link to our collective ancestral past, depending on whether you believe the natives or the hucksters. To probe the creature for possible mass syndication rights, Japanese scientists are building a submersible that looks like the Beatles' yellow submarine, and they spend most of the movie tightening the bolts on it.

While her cynical brother scoffs, Ashley believes in Orky, and of course the monster responds to the girl's heartfelt innocence. One night under a full moon (the moon has no other phases in this film), Ashley tries to run away back home, and Orky symbolically picks her up along a seaside road. The creature manifests itself as a sparkle on the water in exchange for some Oreo cookies (which substitute throughout the film for the Reese's Pieces in E.T.). When Ashley climbs a ladder to a tree house where she has decided to spend the night, the ladder breaks and she starts to fall. But just then her father spots her, dives into the water, and somehow is transported by Orky to the rocks beneath her, just in time to break her fall.

Jack sustains a concussion and awakes in the living room of the town's resident doctor, who has a home office, is also a shrink and—surprise!—is an attractive and available blond. Dr. Wanda Bell (Harley Jane Kozak) is treating a group of men who all believe they've been possessed by the spirit of Orky, and Jack fits right in. Like the rest, he develops an unexplained rash on his stomach and starts acting like a kid. Instead of ignoring his children, he now outplays them, building an elaborate sand castle, seeing animal shapes in the clouds, and digging a hole to China on the beach. He digs because his father wouldn't help him in the project when Jack was a child; the psychologist is obviously going deep for his lost inner child.

The Asians are around just to be part of a joke. After Jack gets his hole dug about six feet down, a son of one of the scientists, Hiro (Willie Nark-Orn), sees Orky moving offshore and runs along the beach to tell the Blacks, but falls into the hole. Josh comes out from the vacation cottage just in time to see the boy climb out of the hole, and this convinces Josh that his father must have found a passage to China. It's absurd to think this hardboiled teen would conclude that, but the filmmakers like the joke so much they later repeat it.

Stevenson and Massey create those kinds of self-conscious "magical" moments like assembly-line workers build cars. Beware a of a film which markets itself, in its very title, as "magic." In one scene, Jack and the kids lie on the beach and Jack shows them how to orchestrate clouds into fireworks and other formations. This is supposed to test the audience's tolerance for the capacity of imagination to transcend reality, which is part of Orky's message. It's a pleasant little piece of nonsense but you get the impression the filmmakers are really straining to create the magical product they advertised.

Another part of Orky's message is the obligatory environmental one: he's being poisoned. Two one-armed goons who work for the evil Mack Miller (Morris Panych) are dumping barrels of toxic waste into Orky's environment. Miller's business seems to consist solely of manufacturing and dumping hazardous chemicals; in case little ones don't understand, the barrels ooze yellow slime on the ocean floor. Orky sends his message by making the ears of Jack and the other possessed men buzz with an annoying whine whenever Orky hears the hum of the one-armed guys' motorboats. The poisoning apparently accounts for the stomach rash.

To make sure audiences aren't as dimwitted as the earnest, ditzy Dr. Bell in putting all this together, the wise old Indian steps in to explain everything. For most of the film, the camera sneaks shots of this long-haired guy, Uncle Kipper (Frank Sotonoma Salsedo), sitting on his porch near the Black's cottage. He is supposed to look wise and spiritual, though he acts more like a drug-crazed hippie. Kipper (another name to chortle at) gets the Black kids to help him switch medications and sedate his nurse, and then push his wheelchair deep into the woods. Eventually they can't push anymore, so he gets up and walks with his cane. It's not clear whether this is a miracle cure of some sort. Finally, they find a totem with the head of an orca on top, and Kipper explains how in the old days animals could become men and men could become animals and Orky is being poisoned and sending a message through dear old dad. Kipper, like all Native Americans in this genre, knows such things, but why he couldn't have sat on his porch and told the kids is unclear.

The rest of the plot is even more preposterous and pretentious. Eventually the Black kids and Hiro end up getting trapped in a sinking submarine, and Orky arrives in the nick of time to save them. There is a priceless shot of the three children's astonished faces looking through the porthole; it is the film's only high point. The kids and their dad, who falls through his hole on the beach just like Alice going to Wonderland, find Orky's cave just in time to see the monster on his death bed. It's supposed to be a hard lesson in the name of ecology—see what happens when bad capitalists dump chemicals in the water?—but it will seem to young children more like needless punishment.

The plot's ponderous weight drags the film to the bottom, wasting some beautiful cinematography by Thomas Burstyn and some effective naturalistic acting by the young Wayne, an amateur who won the part over 800 others in a Vancouver casting call. Her Ashley is just the right mix of childish wisdom and honest innocence, standing out in a film which is a mix of adult contrivance and patronizing symbolism. Harmon's goofy enough to hold one's attention at moments, but mostly he's insufferable, and the rest of the cast is unremarkable.

My own ten-year-old captured perfectly what's wrong with *Magic in the Water* in terms of its potential marketing appeal to children. "We should have seen Orky much sooner," he said. Having a magical monster just long enough for a funeral doesn't make much sense; it's worse than Puff the Magic Dragon sadly slipping into his cave at the end of the song. The problem is that Orky, who looks suspiciously like an elongated E.T., is more just a mass of green blubber than a special-effects wonder. Given such a flabby star, there's more appeal in portraying him as mysterious ripples in the water than in the awful flesh. Instead of Orky shots, there are boring scenes of group therapy, long stretches of mulling about Jack's mental and physical state, and the repeated attempts to stir up "magic," including too many shots of the water sparkling in the moonlight. Way too much of the film is adult psychobabble about the importance of recapturing one's lost inner child. It's meant to be wondrous, but it's dreadfully contrived.

—Michael Betzold

REVIEWS

Chicago Tribune. Aug. 30, 1995, p. 2.
USA Today. Aug. 30, 1995, p. 6D.
Variety. May 1, 1995, p. 38.

Major Payne

"He's looking for a few good men...or a few guys old enough to shave."—Movie tagline

"Wacky and wild. Pure entertainment. I loved it."—Ron Brewington, *American Urban Radio Networks*

"Damon Wayans delivers a fighting machine of laughs."—Bonnie Churchill, *Group W Radio*

Box Office Gross: $29,412,050

One of the most utilized of plots in film is one where a trained expert is forced to take a group of misfits and whip them into shape. In this plot scenario, the hero learns something about himself, and the formerly disjointed team bonds together, and gains self-esteem where none existed. *The Bad News Bears* (1976), *The Mighty Ducks* (1992), *Slap Shot* (1977), *Renaissance Man* (1994), and many others have trod this well-worn path. One of the early versions of this plot was *The Private War of Major Benson* (1955), which starred Charlton Heston, and was nominated for an Oscar for its screenplay. Now Damon Wayans brings his talents to the remake of that film, and though he does not break any new ground, *Major Payne* proves to be a satisfactory new visit to an old story.

Major Benson Winifred Payne (Damon Wayans) is a model soldier who served in Iraq, Panama, and Kuwait. But, the new world order being what it is, there is little need for a soldier of his type, so Payne is forcibly retired from his beloved Army. The only appropriate job he can find is teaching the R.O.T.C. class at a private school in Maine. The group he inherits are a ragtag assemblage: they are plump, lazy, and undisciplined. Payne's rigid ways do not sit well with the group, nor with the beautiful female school counselor, Dr. Walburn (Karyn Parsons), who feels that young people need encouragement instead of punishment. Audiences will hardly be surprised when the boys, led by rebellious Alex (Steven Martini), try to drive Payne to leave them. Nor will audiences be shocked when the boys bond together, or when Payne and Walburn strike up a romance. Yet, though the road is well-worn, Wayans and company bring their own sense of fun to the proceedings, keeping the film itself from being as stale as its plot.

Damon Wayans's gold-toothed, starchy, sadistic characterization is a fun send-up of the type of gung-ho military man that is the stuff of American myth. Wayans's over-the-top Major Payne can be seen by audiences as very funny, very bizarre, or both. He opens cans with his bare hands, he calls himself a "trained weapon of destruction," he sleeps with his eyes open, and he re-tells the "Little Engine That Could" as "The Little Engine that had a payload of *AK-47*s to Take Across Enemy Lines." When he eats, sound effects of pig noises accompany him. But in the end, Wayans is actually quite affecting, especially in allowing himself to realize how much the boys have come to mean to him.

The rest of the cast delivers good performances, too. In particular, Steven Martini brings enthusiasm to the

Damon Wayans as an emotionally dysfunctional Marine officer faces off with Steve Martini as cadet Stone in *Major Payne*. © 1995 Universal City Studios, Inc. Courtesy of MCA Publishing Rights, a Division of MCA Inc. All rights reserved.

CREDITS

Major Payne: Damon Wayans
Dr. Emily Walburn: Karyn Parsons
Dr. Phillips: William Hickey
Lt. Colonel Stone: Michael Ironside
General Decker: Albert Hall

Origin: USA
Released: 1995
Production: Eric L. Gold and Michael Rachmil
Direction: Nick Castle
Screenplay: Dean Lorey, Damon Wayans, and Gary Rosen' based on a story by Joe Connelly and Bob Mosher and a screenplay by William Roberts and Richard Alan Simmons
Cinematography: Richard Bowen
Editing: Patrick Kennedy
Art direction: David Crank
Music: Craig Safan
MPAA rating: PG-13
Running Time: 97 minutes

cliche role of the street tough who got no love at home, but who responds to the tough love of his new leader. Stephen Wiles and Joda Blare-Hershman provide other able support. Karyn Parsons is beautiful and very sweet as Dr. Walburn. Parsons's biggest accomplishment is in making Wayans's outlandish character appear lovable. Finally, William Hickey rounds out the cast as the truly strange headmaster of the school, whose desk is literally crawling with enormous and grotesque insects. Hickey makes his usual impact with his brief scenes; to have the frail and elderly Hickey chasing butterflies with a net (during a scene with Wayans) is an inspired moment.

Based on the 1955 film *The Private War of Major Benson*, starring Charlton Heston.

Director Nick Castle leads his cast ably, balancing the attempts at making Payne look human, such as a sweet scene with Payne and six-year-old Tiger (Orlando Brown), with the highly technical sequence where the boys compete in military games. Even though the audience knows the boys will win, Castle builds a bit of suspense, blending taut editing and excellent music by Craig Safan. A rap-inspired march at the climax of the games is a highlight visually and musically. And it should be noted that Safan's music throughout is excellent: It is tuneful and appropriate without ever being intrusive.

"There's got to be somebody needs killing."—Payne when told the Marines no longer need his services from *Major Payne*

Major Payne will mostly appeal to kids. Here and there, the film lapses into being gross, such as when the boys replace Payne's cupcake frosting with Pepto-Bismol. Occasionally a remark or a sound effect will remind the audience that this is the age of *Dumb and Dumber* (1995), and that many films nowadays must appeal to kids. But such lapses don't take away the humanity of the performances, the fun of the situations, and the satire of Wayans's central performance.

—*Kirby Tepper*

Mallrats

"They're not there to shop. They're not there to work. They're just there."—Movie tagline

"One of the funniest, crudest, screamingly offensive comedies in years!"—*The Boston Phoenix*

Kevin Smith's debut film, *Clerks* (1994), was one of the genuine discoveries of 1994. Shot at the Quik Stop convenience store in New Jersey where Smith was working, *Clerks* hilariously explored the bizarre netherworld of convenience-store life, combining a dead-on sense of place with over-the-top gags and endless slacker ruminations about the meaning of *Star Wars* (1977) and *The Empire Strikes Back* (1980). The film's minuscule budget ($23,000) and rough-edged look seemed part and parcel of its Generation-X appeal. A jubilation about simply being able to make the film showed through as well.

Mallrats, Smith's second film, has a bigger budget (over $1 million), but not much else. A hodgepodge of bad jokes, incompetently shot slapstick scenes, and pastiches of comic-book style and old TV shows, *Mallrats* has little to recommend it. Even the usually luscious presence of *Beverly Hills 90210*'s (1989-1994) Shannen Doherty is wasted here in a throwaway role. *Mallrats* seems hard evidence of the sophomore filmmaking jinx.

T.S. (Jeremy London) is all set to take his girlfriend Brandi (Claire Forlani) on a long-awaited trip to Florida, where he hopes to propose to her on the Universal Studios Tour, just as "Jaws pops out of the water." Unfortunately, Brandi's friend Julie has just died of an embolism while swimming laps for the swim team, and Brandi must replace Julie in the taping of her father's local television game show pilot. (Exactly how producing local game shows, presumably for public access, keeps Brandi's father so well-heeled remains a mystery.) T.S. sees it all as a plot by Mr. Svenning (Michael Rooker) to keep them apart, and calls her father a "crazy bald man." "You know what's sick?" responds Brandi. "This relationship." Brandi unceremoniously dumps him.

Across town, T.S.'s friend Brodie (Jason Lee), who lives at home with his mother and does nothing but play video games and read comic books, gets a similar heave-ho from his girlfriend Rene (Shannen Doherty). Rene says she is tired of their routine, which involves her knocking on his basement window and sneaking in. Brodie responds that they have a lot going for them. "What?" asks Rene. "That you play videogames and I fall asleep unfulfilled?" Brodie can't believe Rene is dumping him. "Is this because I didn't introduce you to my mother?" he asks.

To drown their sorrows, T.S. and Brodie head to the Eden Prairie Mall, amusingly named considering it is in the middle of New Jersey. But the mall is unfortunately where Brandi and Rene are headed, too, along with their entire social clique. When the guys find out that Mr. Svenning's pilot is to be shot there, they do their best to sabotage it and to win the girls back.

This is what passes for a plot in *Mallrats*, and the rest of the film consists of T.S.'s and Brodie's encounters with various mall denizens as they plot the overthrow of Mr. Svenning. Among the most amusing are Jay (Jason Mewes) and Silent Bob (Smith), repeating their roles from *Clerks* as stoned weirdos with nothing better to do than hang out and pontificate on the merits of songs entitled "Berserker." Here, they have been upgraded to knights-errant, ready and willing to destroy the mall for the sake of their two lonely

CREDITS

T. S. Quint: Jeremy London
Brodie: Jason Lee
Rene: Shannen Doherty
Brandi Svenning: Claire Forlani
Svenning: Michael Rooker
Tricia: Renee Humphrey
Shannon: Ben Affleck
Jay: Jason Mewes
Silent Bob: Kevin Smith
Gwen: Joey Lauren Adams
Ivannah: Pricilla Barnes
Willam: Ethan Suplee
Stan Lee: Himself

Origin: USA
Released: 1995
Production: James Jacks, Sean Daniel and Scott Mosier for Alphaville and View Askew production; released by Gramercy
Direction: Kevin Smith
Screenplay: Kevin Smith
Cinematography: David Klein
Editing: Paul Dixon
Production design: Dina Lipton
Art direction: Sue Savage
Set decoration: Diana Stoughton
Costume design: Dana Allyson
Sound: Jose Araujo
Casting: Don Phillips
Music: Ira Newborn
MPAA rating: R
Running Time: 95 minutes

friends. Also making appearances are Tricia (Renee Humphrey), a 15-year-old writer who has gotten a $20,000 advance to sleep with as many guys as she can for a book on male sexuality called "Bore-gasm"; Willam (Ethan Suplee), who waits in front of a 3-D Magic Eye poster all day, hoping in vain to make out an image; and Ivannah, a topless psychic who surprises T.S. and Brodie not only with her predictions, but also with her third nipple. Comic-book godfather Stan Lee provides the final bit of wisdom that spurs Brodie to win back Rene, and the film's climax is the guys' gleeful destruction of Mr. Svenning's game show, "Truth or Date," through which they win back the girls.

"Hell hath no fury like a woman scorned by Sega."—Brodie after his girlfriend dumps him from *Mallrats*

The dialogue in *Mallrats* is tiresomely "smart" and "witty." Whereas in *Clerks* the characters' intellectual musings on everything from eggs to death to *Star Wars* hilariously accentuated the claustrophobic feeling that these characters were wasting their lives in a convenience store, in *Mallrats* the one-liners have become a tic; the characters no longer sound human. Perhaps that is Smith's intention, since certain scenes seem homages to cartoons, comic books, and even the old *Batman* show (1966-1968). But it seems not at all clear that Smith knows what he is doing. The garishly cheesy sets and color photography draw more attention to themselves than they should, because during most of the film nothing is happening. The action sequences are amateurishly shot and edited, and the action becomes most frenetic usually when there is the least going on and Smith needs something to get himself out of a story jam. London and Lee, a former skateboard star turned actor, are appealingly idiotic, but saddled with too many gross-out jokes and tiresome come-back lines to really make an impression. In short, *Mallrats* has all the characteristics of a film-school project except the school.

Mallrats is disheartening simply because the fresh voice that was so evident in *Clerks* is drowned out by too much noise and slapstick. Presumably the voice will re-emerge; in the meantime, Smith may simply want to chalk up *Mallrats* as a learning experience.

—Paul Mittelbach

REVIEWS

The New York Times. CXLV, October 20, 1995, p.B3(N).
Time. CXLVI, November 6, 1995, p.77.
Variety. CCCLX, October 16, 1995, p.94.

Man of the House

"Laughs...Fun!"—*San Francisco Chronicle*

Box Office Gross: $40,070,995

Man of the House is a bland family comedy in the sunny, sentimental house style of recent Walt Disney films such as *Three Men and a Baby* (1987) and *Mr. Destiny* (1990). Directed by James Orr and co-written by Orr and Jim Cruickshank, the screenwriting team of both *Three Men* and *Mr. Destiny*, *Man of the House* contains the germ of a compelling comedy storyline—a boy who will stop at nothing to prevent his single mother from remarrying—but quickly channels it into a formulaic plot in which the boy and his would-be stepfather bond by foiling a band of inept Mafia hitmen. By turns saccharine and slack in its suspense scenes, the film is further hampered by an unyieldingly wooden performance by Chevy Chase and a glum turn by the ever-photogenic but usually more lively Farrah Fawcett. The popularity of the film's television performers from different generations—Chase, Fawcett, George Wendt of *Cheers* (1982-1994) and Jonathan Taylor Thomas of *Home Improvement* (1992-present)—as well as Orr's and Cruickshank's experience writing Disney Sunday Night Movies for audiences in the two-to-eleven-year-old age group, however, virtually assures *Man of the House* of success in the children's home rental market.

Farrah Fawcett's character Sandy is an assemblage artist. The pieces shown in her home and at her gallery show are by artists Georges Gamache and Micheline La Rose.

Ben Archer (Thomas) is an eleven-year-old only child whose wisecracks conceal his sorrow at his father's having abandoned him and his mother, Sandra (Farrah Fawcett), five years earlier. Ben and Sandra live together comfortably in Sandra's artist's loft in Seattle, and have made a life for themselves without a father figure. Ben, in voice-over narration, claims to have chased off any of his mother's would-be suitors, but Sandra is clearly still looking for both a husband and a father for Ben.

Enter Sandra's new boyfriend, Jack Sturges (Chase), a United States Attorney who has just successfully prosecuted a mob drug kingpin, and whose own wisecracks and corny jokes mask an ineptitude at all things practical and a blissful unawareness of the trials of stepfatherhood. The drug kingpin's son and henchmen threaten Jack in the courtroom as the father is hauled off to jail, but Jack is more concerned with his imminent trial move-in with Sandra and Ben. Little does Jack know that Ben, before even getting to know Jack, is plotting to make life so miserable for him that he will have to leave. Over the course of the film, Jack must overcome his own fear of making a fool of himself in front of the woman he loves in order to overcome Ben's fear of losing his mother.

Jack gamely tries to win Ben over. In an amusing scene that shows off Chase's gift for physical comedy, Jack fixes "eggs Benedict a la Sturges" his first morning in the loft, only to make an unholy mess of the entire kitchen. Sandra sadly informs him that she and Ben already have an established breakfast-making ritual.

Ben foils Jack at every turn, even getting Jack to sleep on the couch by claiming it would be psychologically damaging for him to have Sandra and Jack sharing a bed under the same roof with him. Privately, Ben is convinced that the bumbling Jack is actually a murderer, and consults library volumes entitled "Criminal Psychology: Portraits of Serial Killers." Ben is noticeably disappointed when he does not find Jack among the book's case studies.

Ben thinks he has found the perfect way to get rid of Jack when he befriends a picked-upon boy at school, Norm (Zachary Browne), who suggests Ben join his YMCA Indian Guide troop. Ben figures Indian Guides will be so stupid that Jack will give up in frustration. At their first meeting, headed by Norm's jovial father, Chet (George Wendt), Ben does his best to humiliate Jack by giving him the Indian moniker Squatting Dog. Jack also gets in trouble at the U.S. Attorney's office when he shows up for a hearing in a Native American land-rights case with traces of the war paint Ben has applied to his face with semi-indelible ink.

Ready to give up the ghost, Jack overhears Ben bragging on the telephone to his friend Monroe (Nicholas Garrett) that Jack is "history," and hatches a plot to win Ben over through Indian Guides. Jack hires the Native American lawyer, Leonard Red Crow (Chief Leonard George), who opposed him in court to teach the Indian Guide troop real Native American customs, including tomahawk-throwing, archery, and rain-dancing to rap music.

Just as Ben is warming up to Jack, however, as well as finding a real friend in Norm, the brakes on Jack's car are sabotaged by the Mafia hit-men, and Jack winds up floating in Puget Sound instead of on a rafting trip with Ben and the troop. Unwilling to frighten Sandra and Ben by telling them the real story, Jack allows them to think that he has missed Ben's trip out of carelessness. It then becomes imperative for Jack to accompany Ben on the big Indian Guide overnight camping trip to prove his intentions of stepfatherhood, even if it means ignoring the Mafia threat and putting his own life at risk.

Shadowed into the mountains by the Mafia hitmen, Jack manages to foil their plot to kill him with the help of Ben, Norm, Chet and the other father-son teams and their new knowledge of Native American self-defense techniques. Ben learns of Jack's heroism, bonds with him, and also realizes that he must learn to have faith in people, "even if they disappoint you." The film ends with Ben happily attending his mother's and Jack's wedding.

The very tidiness of *Man of the House*'s plot works against both its characters and its plausibility. The screenplay requires all of the major characters to act, at different times, according to the external logic of the plot, rather than according to their characters' inherent motivations, and this

CREDITS

Jack Sturges: Chevy Chase
Sandra Archer: Farrah Fawcett
Ben Archer: Jonathan Taylor Thomas
Chet Bronski: George Wendt
Lloyd Small: David Shiner
Red Sweeney: Art LaFleur
Joey Renda: Richard Portnow
Leonard Red Crow: Chief Leonard George

Origin: USA
Released: 1995
Production: Bonnie Bruckheimer and Marty Katz for Walt Disney Pictures and All Girls, in association with Orr & Cruickshank Productions; released by Buena Vista Pictures
Direction: James Orr
Screenplay: James Orr and Jim Cruickshank; based on a story by David Peckinpah and Richard Jefferies
Cinematography: Jamie Anderson
Editing: Harry Keramidas
Production design: Lawrence G. Paull
Art direction: David Willson
Set decoration: Rose Marie McSherry
Casting: Amy Lippens
Sound: Rob Young
Costume design: Tom Bronson
Music: Mark Mancina
MPAA rating: PG
Running Time: 96 minutes

creates a strained artificiality in each of the three lead performances. Ben and his friends have either the smart-alecky vocabulary or the wisdom of adults, rarely the vulnerability of real children, especially in the scenes where Ben is plotting to rid himself of Jack. Whether Thomas has an agreeable screen persona or not is obscured by his character's incessantly precocious lines. Chase and Fawcett are required to act far less intelligent than their characters' apparent sensitivity and status would indicate they are. Only very young viewers will not wonder, for example, why Sandra and Jack do not immediately see through Ben's transparent ploys to drive a wedge between them. As well, it seems unlikely that Sandra and Ben would suspect the bumbling but never irresponsible Jack of missing Ben's rafting trip for anything other than a valid reason. More unlikely still is Jack's decision not to tell Ben and Sandra about the threats on his life, which in any universe other than this one would be seen as endangering their lives rather than as a brave choice of family unity over his own skin. Chase, certainly the comedy star with the narrowest acting range in Hollywood, is given even less to work with here than usual. Chase's idea of playing a fuddy-duddy is simply to speak monotonously and to move robotically. Chase has apparently never learned, or been instructed in, the old Hollywood axiom that the key to close-ups is in the eyes: his often dead-eyed, heavy-lidded or squinting expressions serve to make his character cold and oddly distant rather than merely hapless, as if he were walking through the part and silently poking fun at it. Only in two brief scenes, the one in which Jack prepares breakfast and another in the woods when he unexpectedly performs a routine for the boys with a father (David Shiner) who is a circus performer, is Chase allowed to show off his natural gift for physical comedy. (Even Chase's trademark pratfalls are clumsily shot.) Fawcett has the thankless task of spending most of the film scolding Chase for not living up to Ben's standards. Only George Wendt among the film's actors manages to convey a natural warmth as the genial head of the Indian Guide troop, primarily because his character is not required to advance the film's nakedly mechanical plot.

Man of the House unfortunately bears out the recent reputation of Walt Disney Pictures as a factory of "family" films which touch briefly on real family problems, only to lose sight of them in increasingly preposterous and formulaic plot machinations. Less extraneous plot (like Mafia hitmen) and more genuine emotion might make Disney-trademark films like *Man of the House* more than just wan programmers destined for the video-store shelves.

—*Paul Mittelbach*

REVIEWS

The New York Times. March 3, 1995, p.B12(N).
The New York Times. March 5, 1995, p.H22(N).
Variety. CCCLVIII, March 6, 1995, p.63.

The Mangler

Box Office Gross: $1,781,383

The Mangler is based on a Stephen King short story of the same title and contains many familiar Stephen King ingredients. For one thing, there is the small-town policeman who is conscientiously trying to get to the bottom of things. The idea of fantastic happenings in a place where nothing ever happens is not original with King; it probably originated with another New Englander, Nathaniel Hawthorne (e.g., his tale "Young Goodman Brown"), but it is so common in King's stories that it has become a sort of King trademark. In *Needful Things* (1993), based on King's novel of the same title, the devil himself (played by the distinguished Max Von Sydow) opens a curiosity shop in sleepy little Castlerock, Maine with devastating results. King was born and raised in Maine and seems to be conducting a sort of literary vendetta against the citizens of his conservative New England state, although he still lives there and dresses in L.L. Bean jeans and flannel shirts in spite of all the millions his books have earned. It would seem that he declines to move away because the things he dislikes about Maine and Mainers provide the inspiration for many of his stories.

Another familiar Stephen King ingredient is the inanimate object possessed by an evil spirit. In *The Shining* (1980), based on a King novel with the same title, the inanimate object was a hotel. In *Christine* (1983), also based on a novel with the same title, it was a homicidal 1958 Plymouth Fury. In *The Mangler* it is an enormous machine which irons and folds sheets and from time to time irons and folds people who get too close to it. The mangle (called "the mangler" for obvious reasons by the wretches who have to work with it) is the pride and joy of Bill Gartley, owner of the Blue Ribbon Laundry.

This enterprise, which employs some forty or fifty people, is the major industry of Rikers Valley. A roadside sign shows the population as 15,667 and carries the slogan "The Industrial Heart of Maine." The sign was evidently added by the screenwriters to suggest that jobs are very hard to come by in Maine and thereby explains why the poor souls employed by the Blue Ribbon Laundry are willing to put up with ceaseless verbal abuse and nineteenth-century sweatshop conditions. The female employees, who do most of the work, even dress the way female factory workers did at the turn of the century. With their billowing dresses, big aprons, loose blouses and long hair, half-blinded by steam and deafened by noise, they are in constant danger of being caught by the rollers or one of the drive chains. The conscientious small-town policeman in this story drives a modern car and watches television, so there is no doubt that it is taking place in the present time.

Most of the special-effects budget went into the creation of the Hadley-Watson Model 6 Speed Ironer and Folder. This complicated machine is a real horror, even when it isn't running. It is black, greasy, and ugly as sin. It is run by a set of gears and long, unguarded drive-chains that look ready to snatch anyone who passes by. It vaguely resembles the big machine that caught the Little Tramp's co-worker in Charlie Chaplin's *Modern Times* (1936)—except that there is nothing funny about what happens to anyone the mangler catches. In grisly scenes spaced throughout the film, some unfortunate worker is caught and dragged into the bowels of the machine. When this happens there is an enormous quantity of blood and gore spilled all over the machine, the floor, and the clean white laundry. The screams of the victim quickly lead to a chorus of screams by the hysterical female employees who are trying unsuccess-

CREDITS

Bill Gartley: Robert Englund
John Hunton: Ted Levine
Mark Jackson: Daniel Matmor
Pictureman: Jeremy Crutchley
Sherry Ouelette: Vanessa Pike
Stanner: Demetre Phillips
Lin Sue: Lisa Morris
Mrs. Frawley: Vera Blacker
Annette Gillian: Ashley Hayden

Origin: USA
Released: 1995
Production: Anant Singh, in association with Distant Horizon, Filmex (Pty) Ltd. and Allied Film Productions; released by New Line Cinema
Direction: Tobe Hooper
Screenplay: Tobe Hooper, Stephen Brooks, and Peter Welbeck; based on a short story by Stephen King
Cinematography: Amnon Salomon
Editing: David Heitner
Production design: David Barkham
Visual effects supervision: Stephen Brooks
Sound: Richard Sprawson
Makeup effects: Scott Wheeler
"Mangler" creation: William Hooper
Music: Barrington Pheloung
MPAA rating: R
Running Time: 106 minutes

fully to turn the mangler off. The most gruesome scene occurs when a woman is being dragged into the rollers and the maintenance man has to chop her arm off with a fire-axe to save her from certain death.

King's short story "The Mangler" originally appeared in Cavalier in 1972 and was reprinted in a collection of his stories titled *Night Shift* (1976). The screenwriters have made many changes. The most radical is the incarnation of Mr. Gartley, owner of the Blue Ribbon Laundry, who is only referred to in King's original story. Bringing Gartley on camera provides a role for Robert Englund, the venerable horror film star who played Freddy the maniacal slasher in *A Nightmare on Elm Street* (1984), *A Nightmare on Elm Street 2: Freddy's Revenge* (1985), *A Nightmare on Elm Street 3: Dream Warriors* (1987), *A Nightmare on Elm Street 4: The Dream Master* (1988) *A Nightmare on Elm Street 5: The Dream Child* (1989), *Freddy's Dead: the Final Nightmare* (1991), and what appears to be the final, final nightmare only because it did poorly at the box office, *Wes Craven's New Nightmare* (1994).

The elderly Mr. Gartley, who has been mangled by his own machine at some time in the remote past, hobbles around his factory on mechanical legs while supporting himself with aluminum crutches. He has lost one eye and some other body parts but this quintessential nineteenth-century laissez-faire capitalist remains passionately attached to his mangler. The adapters of King's simple story have made the plot more complicated and less logical by specifying that Gartley and some other pillars of the community are well aware that the mangler is possessed by a demon and for many years have been offering it human sacrifices for the sake of profit. Gartley has managed to keep his murderous machine in operation because the local officials are on his secret payroll. Safety inspectors who are called in each time someone is killed or maimed always blame the accident on human error.

Officer Hunton (Ted Levine) does not want to believe the machine is possessed by an evil spirit because he is a realist. Eventually, however, he is forced to admit that too many strange things have been happening at the laundry. It is not until he and his brother-in-law Mark Jackson (Daniel Matmor) try to exorcise the demon with a Bible and holy water that the mangler reveals its true identity. As in King's short story, the machine breaks loose from the bolts holding it to the concrete floor and goes on a rampage. Hunton manages to save sixteen-year-old Sherry Ouelette (Vanessa Pike), whom Gartley and his corrupt young mistress were offering as a human sacrifice. Mark, however, is gobbled up by the now fully ambulatory mangler. Finally Gartley himself, kicking and screaming like Captain Ahab tied to Moby Dick, gets steam-pressed and folded into a compact bundle of gore in a climax which the adapters invented.

Some reviewers have unfairly blamed Stephen King for the confusion in the film's plot. King may have his faults, but he is a competent professional who is never hard to follow. His short story is much simpler than the film version. In King's original, the mangler is just an ordinary machine until it tastes the blood of a virgin for the first time when Sherry cuts her finger and drips blood onto a sheet being sucked into the rollers. Mark, a long-haired sixties hippie who studies the occult, explains to Hunton that virgin's blood is the single most common cause of demonic possession. After adding a fat role for Robert Englund, who was given top billing, the trio of adapters went on to concoct a legend about his character Gartley that piles illogic on what was a fragile concept to begin with. Sherry still cuts her finger and gives the mangler a taste of virgin's blood although this is no longer necessary since the demon took possession of the machine long before she was born.

This sort of confusion often develops when adapters try to stretch the material in a short story into a full-length feature film. A classic example is *The Swimmer* (1968) starring Burt Lancaster in an adaptation of a whimsical story of the same title by John Cheever. In Cheever's story, one of his alcoholic suburbanites gets the harebrained notion of swimming across the county using his neighbors' private pools and regarding the land in between them as "portages." What was a perfectly good little Cheever story became a cinematic disaster when inflated to bursting point. The same grotesquerie can be seen in the many adaptations of short stories by Edgar Allan Poe, including *House of Usher* (1960) and *The Pit and the Pendulum* (1961). Although many successful films have been made from novels, it is difficult to think of a single successful feature film made from a short story.

As critic Godfrey Chehshire correctly predicted in characteristic *Variety*-ese, "That silly contrivance [the mangler], along with lackluster story and thesping, should guarantee the would-be frightfest a short spin and quick fade at the box office." *The Mangler* received unfavorable reviews and disappeared from *Variety's* Domestic Box Office Chart in a matter of weeks. Stephen King's highly marketable name attached to the production, however, will undoubtedly earn it substantial residuals in the videotape market in coming years.

—Bill Delaney

REVIEWS

Daily Variety. March 6, 1995, p. 4.
The New York Times. March 4, 1995, p. 10.
Los Angeles Times. March 6, 1995, p. F7.
The Hollywood Reporter. March 6, 1995, p. 10.

Martha and Ethel

"Ambitious and emotionally deep."—Caryn James, *New York Times*

"Simply beautiful! Deeply moving."—Jeffrey Lyons, *Sneak Previews*

"Exceptional! A vivid portrait."—Mike Clark, *USA Today*

Movies, as the first hundred years of film history point out, have remained primarily a narrative form the world over. The films we enjoy most, it would seem, are films that tell us stories, that weave a web of fiction that is suddenly lifted the moment the lights come back on.

The first films, however, while also enjoyed in the dark, thrilled their audiences with just the opposite effect: showing truth itself. This older tradition survives today on the fringes of film culture. Surprisingly, despite its marginalization, it continues to evolve.

We thus find that, as befitting an older, wiser member of a family, the documentary form makes us question aspects of filmmaking that remain all too conveniently masked when film is used to merely tell a story.

Martha and Ethel, a personal feature-length excursion by Jyll Johnstone, while making clear the command its filmmaker has over her subject, also makes us aware of a far more subtle force at work, the hold her subject has over her, and by extension, on us, watching.

So protected are we customarily from this raw truth that its sudden revelation can even overthrow the structure of meaning the filmmaker would like her film to impart. All it takes, it would seem, is a single scene to turn the director's scheme on its head. That scene occurs in the first few minutes of this loving account of the roles the two eponymous nannies have played in the upbringing, and even in the adult lives, of the filmmaker and her friend, Barbara.

In a bright, sunny kitchen, Martha, in her late eighties, is standing on a ladder, her head out of frame, attempting to retrieve an item stored on a high rack. The filmmaker's voice keeps admonishing her to come down. We can see why. A slight fall at her age could prove serious for her brittle bones. "Martha," the voice of the filmmaker can be heard saying, "You have to get down." When Martha doesn't listen, we see the filmmaker entering the frame, her back to the camera, and begin to hold Martha by the waist, all the while admonishing her to come down, in the tone one would use with a child. When Martha does decide to descend, the roles are promptly reversed, as she slaps the filmmaker playfully and says, right into the face of the camera, "Isn't she awful?" The filmmaker retreats out of frame, but Martha will not let this affront to her age pass so lightly. "You know what a do-do is?" she asks the camera, patting her own skinny bottom clothed in a nightie. "She gets from me!"

Nothing in the film that follows, comprising as it does for the most part of voice-over personal reminiscences interspersed with "talking head" style interviews with family members and the two nannies, comes close to the spontaneous profundity this scene is allowed to impart, by means of filmic truth left to itself. The scene reveals aspects of the film's subject matter that remain concealed beneath the layers of memory and sentiment that suffuse what follows.

While the filmmaker's power over the two nannies is rooted in the present, their power over her, as well as over us, grows out of the past. Clearly, the filmmaker would like the film to be about Martha and Ethel as nannies, and how what they have come to mean to the two families has transgressed that role. However, when Martha and Ethel are allowed to be themselves in front of the camera, the filmmaker's concerns seem to get overshadowed by the fact that both these women are in their late eighties, with each embodying an indomitable stand over the passing of time.

For us, as viewers not close to either of the two families, what emerges as more significant are the film's insights about aging, rendered more harrowing in the context of a society with little respect for age. There thus develops a dichotomy in Martha and Ethel between filmic truth and verbal discourse, which emerges as the filmic correlative of the opposition between what Martha and Ethel mean to the filmmaker and what they mean to us from the few glimpses of their present lives we are allowed to have. This is not to say that the film's ostensible subject matter is not interest-

CREDITS

Narrator: Jyll Johnstone
Narrator: Barbara Ettinger
Martha Kneifel: Martha Kneifel
Ethel Edwards: Ethel Edwards

Origin: USA
Released: 1995
Production: Jyll Johnstone and Barbara Ettinger for Canobie Films; released by Sony Pictures Classics
Direction: Jyll Johnstone
Screenplay: Jyll Johnstone, Barbara Ettinger, Alysha Cohen, Christina Houlihan, Frank Ortega, and Sharon Woods
Cinematography: Joseph Friedman
Editing: Toby Shimin
MPAA rating: G
Running Time: 80 minutes

ing. We learn for example of Martha's strict upbringing in the Germany of the thirties, where "a good licking with a wooden spoon" proved the surest way to instill a sense of what was right, convincing Martha to practice the same in the Johnstone household.

We find Ethel puzzled by the mulatto strain in her South Carolina background, responsible for her straight hair. Unlike Martha, who inspired fear amongst the Johnstone children, Ethel became more of a loving grandparent to the Ettinger family, and continues to look after the mother, now divorced, to this day.

"You don't have to birth a child to love her."—Nanny Ethel Edwards from *Martha and Ethel*

The two approaches to child rearing become starkly juxtaposed in what the two mothers have to say. Martha, according to Mrs. Johnstone, instilled in the children a sense of cleanliness, as well a sense of what was right and wrong: "She was German and she knew what was right and what was wrong." For Mrs. Ettinger, kindness takes precedence over spotlessness: "The children should grow up with love and attention...the kindness and loving attention a nanny gives..."

Whichever side we take in this debate, we cannot help but question the extent to which the lack of the institution of the nanny, so common to the European and eastern middle classes, has deprived the American childhood experience of the full-time parenting, it now seems, only a nanny can provide.

As if to repay that debt, the film then focusses on the lives of the two octogenarians long after they have fulfilled their duties of nannyhood. It is here that the film, itself freed from the shackles of its central concerns, achieves its rare cinematically telling moments.

A top angle shot, looking down a stairwell, shows Martha, at age 87, dutifully trudging up four flights to her apartment in Sunnyside, Queens. On the day she is to leave for a new life in California, we see her bid a painful farewell to the other elderly tenants she has known for years. "We all had a good time all these years," Martha sentimentalizes, her cheer conflicting with a sense of grievous loss visible on the faces of her women friends. "I will never forget you!" When one of them starts to sob, Martha pleads, "Don't...don't," then holding her head with both hands, kisses her on the cheek. When that doesn't work, Martha can only turn away and mutter to herself, "Oh God!" Even so, wanting to remain in emotional control of the situation, Martha looks at those out of frame and quips, "I take her with me."

Despite Martha's front of fortitude, the moment seems to achieve an universality through the intrusion of life itself. In a filmic instant, we become aware of how leave taking amongst the elderly must carry with it a sense of the absolute. We, like Martha's friend, remain unsure of just where Martha is going. It is such moments, like the scene of Martha in the kitchen at the start of the film, that make us wish the filmmaker had found some way to weave her take on the past into the fabric of the present, thereby providing an ironic counterpoint to the reminiscing and, in the process, sparing us the unmitigated nostalgia.

The film goes on to show Martha reluctantly accepting the constraints of life within a community for seniors in Thousand Oaks, California. As a crowning gesture of gratitude, the filmmaker and her husband accompany Martha on a visit to her hometown of Oberkirsh in Germany, where Martha is accorded a proper civic welcome, replete with a marching band.

Similarly, Barbara accompanies Ethel to a tearful family reunion in South Carolina, where Ethel is reunited with her eighty-six year old sister, whom she hasn't seen for several years.

The film closes with an exchange between Ethel and Mrs. Ettinger in which the mother admits to sharing her children with Ethel. "They're our children," the mother affirms. Then, in a close-up that provides the film with its final shot, Ethel adds: "Because I love them. You don't have to birth a child to love it."

Most of the critics writing on the film have been able to identify with its affectionate viewpoint. Louise Gray, in *Sight and Sound,* notes: "Martha and Ethel come across as courageous women, whose attachment to children knows no racial or national divide. But the issue of employee, or even chattel, status never really vanishes." Even so, she finds the film "an honest and touching attempt to represent a series of relationships and commemorate the extraordinary love that characterized them."

The film's social dimension gets foregrounded by Janet Maslin as well in *The New York Times*. She finds the attempt on the part of the film's producers "to study the nannies who raised them while their wealthy mothers were otherwise engaged" resulting in "a seemingly fond film marked by staggering condescension and naivete." She concludes: "*Martha and Ethel* reveals more about mother-daughter friction than about the nannies, pivotal roles in these two families."

—*Vivek Adarkar*

REVIEWS

The New York Times, February 3, 1995.
Los Angeles Times, March 8, 1995.
The Hollywood Reporter, February 3-5, 1995.
Sight and Sound, September 1995.
Variety, January 26, 1994.

Martha and I

"Remarkable! Mr. Piccoli and Miss Sagebrech play two wonderfully rich characters."—Stephen Holden, *New York Times*

"A crowd pleaser!"—J. Hoberman, *The Village Voice*

In his film *Martha and I*, director Jiri Weiss looks back at the lessons he he learned about passion and compassion during his adolescence in pre-World War II Czechoslovakia, and honors the memory of the pure and selfless love shared by his uncle Ernst and a woman named Irmgard in real life and Martha in the film. The quiet beauty of their love is a stark—and instructive— contrast to the roaring tidal wave of brutality and hatred that would soon sweep out across Europe from just over the border in Nazi Germany. Though Ernst and Irmgard were both lost beneath that wave, in Weiss' devoted eyes, and through the preservation of their story on film, the light from that love cannot be extinguished.

The film begins in 1935 Prague, and focuses on Emil (Vaclav Chalupa), a gawky adolescent with raging hormones who represents Weiss at that age. "I was in love, but didn't know with whom," an older Emil (Ondrej Vetchy) recalls in the film's recurring voice-over. "I was a mess." His father slaps him after he dreamily follows a pretty blonde girl around the city, and his mother slaps him when his curiosity about the opposite sex is nearly satisfied by the kitchen maid. Emil is told that he is too young to engage in such pursuits (his mother still calls him "My Kitten"), and it is decided that some distance should be put between the young man and his temptations.

Emil is sent for the summer to his mother's brother Ernst Fuchs (Michel Piccoli), who lives with his tanned, beautiful and much younger wife and their doughy, pudgy maid Martha (Marianne Saegebrecht) in the Sudetenland near the German border. A kindly, highly respected obstetrician, Ernst is referred to by the local townspeople as "the doctor with the golden hands." He adjusts the cost of his services to each patient's ability to pay. He is a robust, earthy free-thinker who provides Emil with an "education" in some of the very things the boy's high-strung, prudish mother wanted kept from him. When Martha tells Emil that he must drink lemonade instead of the wine some adult guests are having, Ernst insists he try the stronger beverage. Emil is also exposed to the racy writings and illustrations of Balzac and de Sade, which he finds as intoxicating as the wine. When

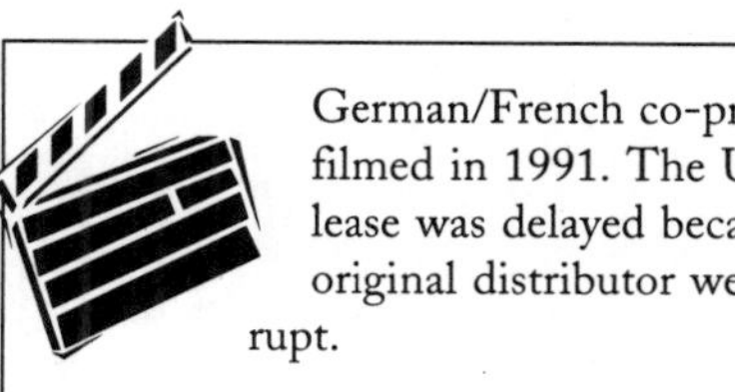

German/French co-production filmed in 1991. The U.S. release was delayed because the original distributor went bankrupt.

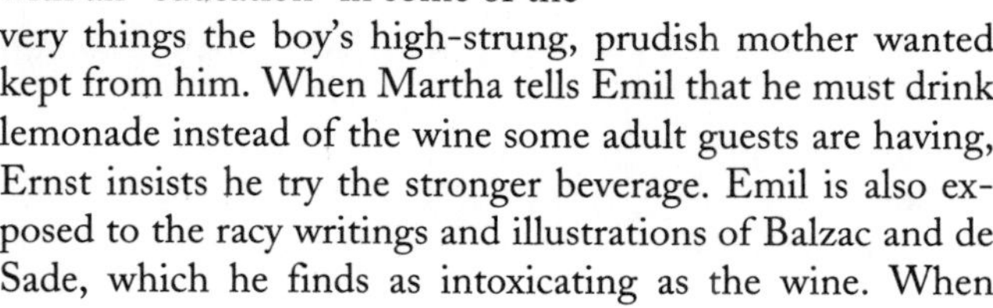

Ernst returns home earlier than expected one evening and catches his wife in bed with another man, Emil gazes with wide-eyed amazement as his uncle throws her naked lover out the front door. Clearly, it is not the pure, bucolic atmosphere and influence Emil's mother had envisioned.

As the film progresses, Weiss' focus shifts from Emil's rights-of-passage to Martha. A scene that plants the seed for this transition is the one in which Ernst allows Emil to shoot sparrows in the backyard so that Martha can make sparrow soup. All but one of the birds are killed instantly, and Martha and Emil are both horrified to see the tiny creature suffer. The sight of the soup on the table that night makes the guilt-ridden young man feel queasy, and he cannot eat it. Through this scene, Weiss not only shows Emil's maturing views on the fragility of life, but also foreshadows the even more striking exhibitions of Martha's good heart that will soon follow.

Martha's dedication and devotion have not gone unnoticed or unappreciated by Ernst, and when he decides that a man of his standing must have a wife, he informs an astonished Martha that they will be married. This is the first of a number of touching, well-acted scenes between Martha and Ernst that are strung out throughout the rest of the film. Chubby, prosaic Martha reacts with a mixture of shock, pleasure and, indeed, gratitude upon hearing this out-of-the-blue proposal from this successful, charismatic man. Ernst plays Pygmalion as he tries to transform her from a frumpy doctor's maid into a proper doctor's wife. He has her undergo a make-over, complete with make-up, expensive clothes, and extensive dental work. One can plainly see that Martha is perplexed by Ernst's efforts, although she is clearly delighted with her new smile. Even with these external changes, Martha has a great deal of trouble changing her maid's mind-set, jumping up to serve instead of waiting to be served, and still calling Ernst "Herr Doktor." On their wedding night, a nervous and painfully shy Martha asks Ernst if the lights can be turned off before they make love. Sensitive to her discomfiture, Ernst replies that, being a doctor, he will have no problems "finding his way" in the dark.

This odd pairing of a Jewish Czech doctor and his gentile former maid, born of mutual, but formally expressed, affection encounters even more imposing and ominous obstacles. Ernst's snobbish, overbearing sisters are not able to hide their horror that their brother has married beneath him, and, worse yet, a non-Jew. None of them attend the wedding or reception, during which

Martha's brother Werner spews forth the Nazi Party line. It is not long before that brother makes a couple of visits to their home—to paint a yellow Star of David and "Jude" on their front gate, and to call his sister the whore of a "filthy Jew."

> "America has been very nice to me. Only here it's not cinema; it's show biz. The producer is king here. In Europe, the director is king."—Director Jiri Weiss

Martha's admiration of, and gratitude for, the wonderful man that has treated her with respect and tenderness she never expected to receive has deepened into love and given her strength, and she will use that newly-gained pluck to protect him. Preservation of Ernst's happiness and well-being is now synonymous with the preservation of her own. So, with Emil's assistance, Martha scrubs off her brother's hateful handiwork, and makes the boy promise not to tell Ernst. Emil must also promise not to tell that, with his help, Martha has stolen the only copy of the New York City telephone book from the central post office, and has set to work writing to every Fuchs in the directory to see if they might sponsor Ernst's emigration to the United States and out of harm's way. Martha states that, even if there were thousands of Fuchs to write to, she would gladly do it for Ernst. When they are forced to sell off a number of possessions, Martha sells her wedding ring so that they can afford to continue having an organ in the house for Ernst to relax while playing.

When Germany takes control of the Sudetenland, Czechs are expelled, and Ernst must move to Prague, while Martha, being German, can stay. With persecution of Jews on the rise, Ernst warns Martha that he does not know what to expect in Prague, and he gently suggests that she should not "take chances because of me." Martha replies with equal feeling that she is his wife, "and I go where you go." Not long after Ernst and Martha move into his sisters' apartment, Ernst loses his job at the Czech clinic, and is reduced

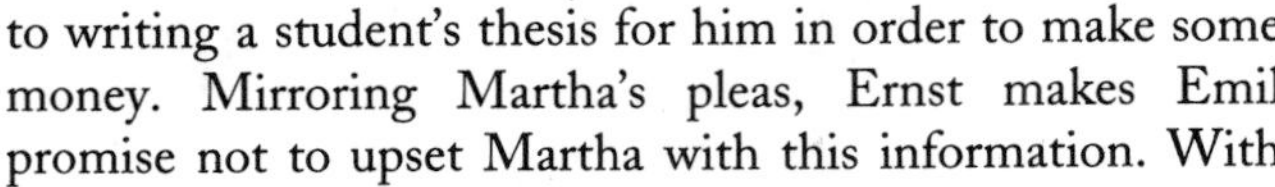

to writing a student's thesis for him in order to make some money. Mirroring Martha's pleas, Ernst makes Emil promise not to upset Martha with this information. With new Nazi laws prohibiting intermarriage, Ernst warns Martha that she may be humiliated in the streets and sent to prison because of him. While he loves and needs her, he could not bear to be the cause of her suffering. Martha states that while she still does not know why he originally wanted to be married to her, her heart cannot now be separated from his without breaking. After painful deliberation, Ernst makes a tremendous sacrifice: in order to save his beloved wife from certain Nazi persecution, he has Martha's Nazi brothers come and forcibly take her away to live with them, and they use their influence within the party to push through a quick and quiet divorce. While Emil is able to flee to England, Ernst and the rest of the family are taken away to concentration camps.

Weiss directs the film's final scene with an especially sure hand. Emil is shown returning from England after the war. Flashbacks are used to show the memories that are darting through his mind as he travels to the village where Martha's family lives. Emil reveals at this point that Ernst and his family have all perished in the camps. As Emil talks with Martha's family, the tension builds to an excruciating level until Emil finally asks where Martha is. The viewer wants to know the answer, and yet, at the same time, is equally afraid to hear it. Emil is told that a disconsolate Martha often stood on a bridge and watched the trains that she hoped would bring Ernst back to her. One day, while a young nephew watched, the smoke from a passing train billowed up from below and obscured Martha from view. When it cleared, Martha was gone. Her body was never found.

While *Martha and I* is the 82-year-old Weiss' first film in over twenty years, it is clear that he has not lost his skills of characterization and attention to telling detail. Weiss began his career in 1934, making a number of prize-winning documentaries. After fleeing Czechoslovakia in 1939, he wrote and directed films in England and was a war correspondent with the U.S. Army Signal Corps. Returning home after the war, Weiss wrote and directed almost twenty films, many of which received awards at various film festivals. Following the Soviet occupation of Prague in 1968, Weiss moved to the United States, became a citizen, and lectured at universities on both coasts. He wrote the screenplay for *Martha and I* in 1989, and filmed it on location in Czechoslovakia in 1990.

Interestingly, the film was actually shot with the actors speaking different languages. Saegebrecht delivered her lines in German, while Piccoli spoke French and the other actors spoke Czech and Slovak. The film was then dubbed so that

CREDITS

Martha: Marianne Saegebrecht
Ernst: Michel Piccoli
Emil as youth: Vaclav Chalupa
Emil as adult: Ondrej Vetchy

Origin: France and Germany
Released: 1991; (1995)
Production: Sabine Tettenborn, Marius Schwartz and Maurice Kanbar; released by Cinema Four
Direction: Jiri Weiss
Screenplay: Jiri Weiss
Cinematography: Viktor Ruzicka
Editing: Gisela Haller
Music: Jiri Stivin
MPAA rating: Not listed
Running Time: 107 minutes

it was completely in German and ready for an audience in that country's theaters. Upon its completion, the German producers of this joint French-German production demanded changes in the final cut that would make it less "anti-German." Weiss refused, and thus the producers never distributed the film for theatrical release in Germany. It was shown in an edited version on German television in 1991 on the anniversary of the 1938 violent anti-Jewish riots known as Kristallnacht, and *Martha and I* garnered the highest ratings of any film ever televised in that country's history. Weiss' work was set to be released in the United States after its success in French theaters, but it would have to wait four additional years when the U.S. distributor went bankrupt.

Upon its release in the United States, critical reaction to *Martha and I* was uniformly and strongly positive, with reviews diverging only on the question of which of the two superb lead performances is more memorable. Clearly, both Piccoli (Godard's *Le Mepris* (1963) and Bunuel's *Belle De Jour* (1967)), and Saegebrecht (Adlon's *Bagdad Cafe* (1987) and *Rosalie Goes Shopping* (1990)) give incandescent interpretations that are richly deserving of high praise. A poignant homage to a human—and humane—bridge that was reduced to rubble long ago, *Martha and I* resonates with a heart-rending beauty. Not a sweeping overview of the ravages of Naziism and the Holocaust, it is the magnification of a single drop in the resulting ocean of tears.

—*David L. Boxerbaum*

REVIEWS

The New York Times. March 24, 1995, p. C14.
The New York Times. March 19, 1995, p. H26.
The New Republic. March 13, 1995, p. 30.
Chicago. October, 1992, p. 22.
The New Yorker. April 3, 1995, p. 95.
The Los Angeles Times. April 21, 1995, p. F2.

Me and the King

A young Elvis Presley impersonator (Lawrence Monoson) in small-town Alabama reflects on his life, in this drama.

CREDITS

No character identified: Lawrence Monoson
Mother: Annie O'Donnell
Uncle: Time Winters

Origin: USA
Released: 1995
Production: Melissa Jenkins for the Directors Guild Mentorship Program
Direction: Melissa Jenkins
Screenplay: Melissa Jenkins; based on a short story by Linda Broggi
MPAA rating: no listing
Running Time: 47 minutes

Miami Rhapsody

"A fresh and wonderfully witty film."—Bill Diehl, *ABC Radio Network*

"It's sophisticated, funny and filled with feeling."—David Sheehan, *KCBS-TV*

"A sunny romantic comedy."—Peter Travers, *Rolling Stone*

Box Office Gross: $5,221,281

Many reviewers noted the similarities between writer/director/producer David Frankel's *Miami Rhapsody* and the comedies of celebrated writer/director/actor Woody Allen. In fact, *Variety* even went so far as to dub the film "Hannah and Her Miami Sisters." Reinforcing this notion is the presence of Mia Farrow, who was a Woody Allen regular player for many years, having starred in thirteen of his films, including *The Purple Rose of Cairo* (1985), *Hannah and her Sisters* (1986), and *Husbands and Wives* (1992). Also in Allen tradition, vintage pop tunes, such as Louis Armstrong's rendition of "Just One of Those Things," grace the sound track. With its offbeat and original script and strong ensemble performances, *Miami Rhapsody* achieves a breezy, whimsical charm.

Sarah Jessica Parker stars, in the Woody Allen role, as a young neurotic professional woman named Gwyn Marcus who appears in virtually every scene and spends the entire film agonizing over her engagement to her boyfriend, Matt (Gil Bellows). Matt may well speak for the audience when he finally says in exasperation that all she ever wants to do is talk and that he does not want to talk anymore.

Miami Rhapsody opens with Gwyn speaking directly into the camera—in effect, to her psychiatrist—about the events of the past year. The film then proceeds in flashback, starting with Matt's marriage proposal and Gwyn's acceptance. Gwyn spends the rest of the film analyzing her relationship with Matt and her own fears concerning commitment. The members of her family fuel her feelings of uncertainty, as one by one they are all revealed to be engaged in adulterous affairs.

During the wedding of Gwyn's younger sister, Leslie (Carla Gugino), their father, Vic (Paul Mazursky), confesses to Gwyn his suspicion that his wife, Nina (Farrow), is having an affair. When Gwyn confronts her mother, Nina is surprised—that Vic is so perceptive. She is indeed having an affair—with Antonio (Antonio Banderas), the hunky nurse of Gwyn's invalid grandmother (Mary Chernoff). Yet Nina counters Vic's accusation with the information that Vic is also having an affair—with his travel agent, Zelda (Kelly Bishop).

Gwyn next discovers that her brother, Jordan (Kevin Pollak), is cheating on his pregnant wife, Terri (Barbara Garrick). When Terri kicks him out of their house, he moves in with his lover, Kaia (Naomi Campbell), a gorgeous fashion model who is the wife of his business partner. The final blow is struck when Gwyn discovers her newlywed sister, Leslie, in bed with an old high school acquaintance.

Needless to say, all these instances of infidelity further provoke Gwyn to question her own upcoming nuptials. She hesitates to set a date and has no interest in planning the ceremony. Gwyn even tries a brief fling with the charming Antonio, who is disconsolate because Nina has broken off their relationship. Unfortunately, Antonio is still very much in love with Nina. With Gwyn unable to commit, Matt

CREDITS

Gwyn: Sarah Jessica Parker
Antonio: Antonio Banderas
Nina: Mia Farrow
Vic: Paul Mazursky
Matt: Gil Bellows
Jordan: Kevin Pollak
Terri: Barbara Garrick
Leslie: Carla Gugino
Jeff: Bo Eason
Kaia: Naomi Campbell
Mitchell: Jeremy Piven
Zelda: Kelly Bishop
Grandma Lil: Mary Chernoff

Origin: USA
Released: 1995
Production: Barry Jossen and David Frankel for Hollywood Pictures; released by Buena Vista Pictures
Direction: David Frankel
Screenplay: David Frankel
Cinematography: Jack Wallner
Editing: Steven Weisberg
Production design: J. Mark Harrington
Set decoration: Bàrbara Peterson
Casting: Renee Rousselot
Sound: Michael Tromer
Costume design: Patricia Field
Music: Mark Isham
MPAA rating: PG-13
Running Time: 97 minutes

eventually decides for her by accepting a position in Africa. They break up.

Perhaps a reflection of the romantic disillusionment of the 1990's, *Miami Rhapsody*, in direct opposition to the traditional romantic comedy, starts with a marriage proposal and a wedding and ends with a breakup and a funeral. Yet, despite the plot synopsis, the film is uplifting. It contains many delightful insights into life and love in the 1990's. Nina an interior designer, expresses a key theme on the subject of love when she states that, at her age, all she wants is someone to hold her hand while she picks out lawn furniture. Thus, one of the last scenes with Nina and Vic shows them doing just that.

"I'm at the age where a lot of people get married—and I see a lot of people getting divorced already, a lot of friends who are not so happy. I wondered why we keep doing it anyway. That's what the movie's about."—Writer/director David Frankel on his idea for the movie

Sarah Jessica Parker is excellent in her leading role as Gwyn. She had previously starred in such films as *Footloose* (1984), *L.A. Story* (1991), and *Hocus Pocus* (1993), but perhaps her best role was opposite Nicholas Cage in the quirky *Honeymoon in Vegas* (1992). In *Miami Rhapsody*, Parker has the opportunity to play a very Woody Allen-esque role, that of comic commentator. Throughout, her Gwyn offers myriad barbed observations and self-absorbed musings. The casting of the lesser known Gil Bellows as Gwyn's good-natured fiance ensures that Gwyn—as played by Parker—remains the focus of the film. Handsome and youthful, Bellows makes a good romantic partner for the equally good-looking Parker.

Paul Mazursky and Mia Farrow are also outstanding as Gwyn's middle-aged parents. Besides being a fine actor, Mazursky is also a highly regarded writer director whose extensive credits include *Moscow on the Hudson* (1984), *Down and out in Beverly Hills* (1986), and *Scenes from a Mall* (1991), which starred Woody Allen. Farrow, a longtime Allen player, would seem to have recovered from the devastating personal problems she suffered with Allen in the early 1990's, resulting in their breakup. Her Nina is a well-developed character and mature woman who realizes that she loves her husband and wants to work out their problems. Both Mazursky and Farrow are strong performers whose extensive experience lends weight to the film.

Antonio Banderas, in his supporting role as the nurse, is put in the enviable position of getting to romance both leading ladies. His Antonio is a gentle but sensual Cuban immigrant who is kind and caring to both women when they feel alone and unloved. Banderas made an impressive English-language film debut when he costarred opposite Armand Assante in *The Mambo Kings* (1992). He then went on to win roles in such films as *Philadelphia* (1993), *Interview with the Vampire* (1994), and *The House of the Spirits* (1994). In a twist on the stereotypical scenario of the young Latin gigolo who woos the wealthy older woman, Antonio is the sensitive, needy one in the relationship, while Nina is the one who uses Antonio and then casts him aside when she no longer needs him.

Miami Rhapsody on the whole is an upbeat film, despite the subject matter. Everyone ends up living happily ever after—at least for the moment. Gwyn's parents get back together. Gwyn's brother realizes the folly of his fling with his partner's fashion-model wife; he sends his wife flowers and makes other attempts at reconciliation. Gwyn and Matt have a final, reconciliatory meeting before Matt leaves the country; they part as friends. Even Gwyn's sister, despite the fact that she and her new husband divorce, finds true happiness in what appears to be a potentially more stable relationship.

Frankel makes his feature-film directorial debut with *Miami Rhapsody*. According to the film's production notes, Frankel "wanted to do a comedy from a woman's perspective ... and deal with contemporary relationships in a way few recent films have." He chose Miami as the film's setting because it is "a place where you feel like you're on vacation, even if you're not." *Miami Rhapsody* was filmed entirely on location and included fifty-four colorful spots throughout the city.

The screenplay is well written. From the first scenes, the viewer realizes that this story will break with convention. When Matt proposes to Gwyn, he presents her with not the traditional diamond ring but a napkin ring. Later, the wedding vows written by Gwyn's sister and her husband include Dr. Seuss-like lines: "Will you love him in the rain, and in the dark, and on a train?" Such whimsical innovations throughout the film keep the tone light and the story fresh.

Further distancing itself from a traditional romantic comedy, *Miami Rhapsody* ends with a funeral, that of Gwyn's much-beloved grandmother, a Holocaust survivor and stroke victim. Grandma Lil is looked up to by both Gwyn and Nina for her inner strength and courage. Yet the funeral is hardly a maudlin affair. In fact, in the midst of the graveside ceremony, Jordan receives a call on his cellular phone, which he brings everywhere. Instead of a business client, however, it is Terri telling him that she has just given birth

REVIEWS

Entertainment Weekly. January 27, 1995, p. 30.
The Hollywood Reporter. January 23, 1995, p. 12.
Los Angeles Times. January 27, 1995, p. F8.
The New York Times. January 27, 1995, p. B10.
Variety. January 23, 1995, p. 12.

to a baby girl. Ecstatic, Jordan rushes to the hospital to be with his wife, and it appears that they will reconcile. Thus the tragedy of the grandmother's death is offset by the joy of her great-granddaughter's birth; the sadness of the past gives way to hope for the future.

—*C. K. Breckenridge*

Mighty Aphrodite

"Mira Sorvino is funny and hugely appealing!"—Jay Carr, *Boston Globe*

"Laugh-out-loud funny! Mira Sorvino is irresistible. It takes a shrewd actress to make ignorance this beguiling."—Owen Gleiberman, *Entertainment Weekly*

Box Office Gross: $5,026,135

For all his immense talent as a screenwriter and director, Woody Allen can never seem to decide exactly what kind of film he wants to make or can get away with making. He has made zany, almost slapstick comedies, sophisticated romantic comedies, and darker explorations of contemporary neuroses, the latter justifiably reviled by critics and audiences. His masterpieces, *Annie Hall* (1977), *Manhattan* (1979), and *Hannah and her Sisters* (1986), have managed to merge the comedic, romantic, and more serious elements, not allowing one component intrude upon any of the others. In more recent films, however, such as *Crimes and Misdemeanors* (1989), *Alice* (1990), *Husbands and Wives* (1992), and *Bullets over Broadway* (1994), his serious side has often gotten in the way of the comedy with Allen almost seeming to wag a disapproving finger at both human foibles and, after the 1992 controversy over his private life, even at himself. The overrated *Bullets over Broadway* ends on a sour note with the artist's self-flagellation over having considered art more important than life. While *Mighty Aphrodite* has its moral concerns, the emphasis is on the ridiculous side of life. While the film is flawed and is not as entertaining as the underrated *Manhattan Murder Mystery* (1993), it is more satisfying than any of Allen's other recent films.

"At my age, if I made love to you, they'd have to put me on a respirator."—Lenny from *Mighty Aphrodite*

The marriage of Lenny (Woody Allen) and Amanda (Helena Bonham Carter) Winerib seems empty to Amanda who wants to adopt a child and does so against Lenny's protestations. As his son grows older and begins displaying an impressive mind, Lenny becomes obsessed with tracking down the boy's biological mother. Another impetus is the new strain on his marriage created by the time Amanda spends on her new art gallery, a strain that leads her into an affair with the seductive Jerry Bender (Peter Weller).

Lenny eventually discovers the mother to be not only a gaudy prostitute and sometime star of pornographic films but a dimwit as well. While he does not tell Linda Ash (Mira Sorvino) he is her son's adoptive father, Lenny learns that she does not know who impregnated her. He becomes protective of this tarnished innocent and tries to lead her into a more respectable life. A sportswriter, Lenny introduces Linda to a naive young boxer, Kevin (Michael Rapaport), who wants to quit the ring and become a farmer. While this relationship ends badly and Lenny and Linda eventually have a brief affair, she does finally find Mr. Right.

Mighty Aphrodite is full of echoes of other Allen films. The sentimental happy ending resembles that of *Hannah and her Sisters.* Linda's tastelessness recalls Mia Farrow's gangster moll in *Broadway Danny Rose* (1984). The most unusual aspect of the film is the Greek chorus that interrupts the film's action to comment on Lenny's predicaments. Lenny's confrontations with the chorus, in an amphitheater in Athens and another in Central Park, and its leader (F. Murray Abraham) have parallels with the Allen character's seeking advice from the spirit of Humphrey Bogart in *Play it Again, Sam* (1972), but Lenny pays little attention to the chrous' warnings.

There is a less-than-subtle mean streak running through Allen's films from sneering at passersby in *Manhattan* to making fun of an overweight woman in *Hannah and her Sisters.* Those not fitting into Allen's insulated Caucasian Manhattan of aesthetics and privilege are often held up to ridicule or treated as grotesque, as in *Stardust Memories* (1980). Linda is initially approached with the same snobbery, but as Lenny gradually overcomes his horror, the film warms to her without sentimentalizing her. Despite her low intelligence and her fondness for blunt profanity and phallic knickknacks, Linda is clearly the film's moral center. (The profanity and casualness about sex are somewhat shocking in an Allen film because, despite his characters' legendary preoccupation with sex, his films are rather prudish compared to the work of his contemporaries.) Although Linda would like to be a hairdresser, she is not demeaned by her current life, and accepts prostitution and performing sexual acts in front of a camera as legitimate work. (The film's working title was *Eros*.) Portraying a woman in such a way, of course, is an open invitation to psychological deconstructions of the filmmaker's attitude toward women.

Linda's matter-of-factness is as much the product of Sorvino's star-making performance as it is of Allen's screenplay. While Sorvino displays some screen presence in *Barcelona* (1994) and *Quiz Show* (1994) and considerably more in the 1995 television miniseries *The Buccaneers*, none of her previous work foreshadows the comic brilliance shining here. While the pixieish smile and squeaky voice (seemingly incongruous on a six-foot-tall woman) together with a stiff-legged walk are the tools of caricature, Sorvino occasionally lets convincing moments of sensitivity shine through Linda's facade. While Sorvino's performance has been compared by some to Jean Arthur and Judy Holiday, it is also reminiscent, because of her obvious delight in creating this seemingly simple yet complex character, with the best work of such actors as Alec Guinness, Peter Sellers, Dustin Hoffman, and Meryl Streep.

Sorvino's interpretation is aided by Linda's wonderfully tacky, predominantly fuzzy and pink outfits designed by Jeffrey Kurland and Santo Loquasto's design of her apartment, glorying in its vulgarity down to the phalluses in the fish tank. Loquasto and cinematographer Carlo Di Palma, who have collaborated on most of Allen's films for the past decade, give Linda's scenes a warm, colorful, lived-in look in stark contrast to the more autumnal, drained look of the rest of the film, with Bender's house on Long Island being particularly sterile.

Allen's other performers do not fare as well as Sorvino. It is good to see Bonham Carter in something other than a period piece, but Amanda is underdeveloped. Bonham Carter delivers her lines in a flat whine that comes close to a parody of Farrow's performances in thirteen Allen films. With Weller, Allen continues his practice, as with William Hurt in *Alice*, of casting a talented performer but giving him little to do. As Amanda's mother, the wonderful Claire Bloom appears fleetingly twice and barely registers. In contrast, Abraham makes his presence known by shouting behind hideous makeup. Of the Greeks, only Jack Warden stands out, playing the blind seer Tiresias like a vaudeville clown.

The Greek chorus sounds like an terrible idea, but Allen makes it work. The chorus' lines shift imperceptively from sounding like a stiff translation of Sophocles to a more modern vernacular. The chorus advises Lenny, "Don't be a schmuck," warns him that children grow up and move away to crazy places such as Cincinnati, and breaks into Cole Porter's "You Do Something to Me." The film has a classical Greek motif beyond the chorus. The presence of Oedipus and Jocasta gives Lenny an unstated reason for wanting Linda to abandon prostitution, and the descent of Linda's

CREDITS

Lenny Winerib: Woody Allen
Linda Ash: Mira Sorvino
Amanda Winerib: Helena Bonham Carter
Kevin: Michael Rapaport
Jerry Bender: Peter Weller
Leader: F. Murray Abraham
Amanda's mother: Claire Bloom
Tiresias: Jack Warden
Jocasta: Olympia Dukakis
Laius: David Ogden Stiers
Ricky: Dan Moran
Released: 1995

Origin: USA
Production: Robert Greenhut for a Jean Doumanian production from Sweetland Films; released by Miramax
Direction: Woody Allen
Screenplay: Woody Allen
Cinematography: Carlo Di Palma
Editing: Susan E. Morse
Production design: Santo Loquasto
Art direction: Tom Warren and Gianni Giovannoni
Set decoration: Susan Bode
Costume design: Jeffrey Kurland
Sound: Gary Alper
Casting: Juliet Taylor
MPAA rating: R
Running Time: 95 minutes

AWARDS AND NOMINATIONS

Academy Awards 1995: Best Supporting Actress (Sorvino)
Nominations: Best Screenplay (Allen)
Golden Globe Awards 1996: Best Supporting Actress (Sorvino)
National Board of Review Awards 1995: Best Supporting Actress (Sorvino)
New York Film Critics Awards 1995: Best Supporting Actress (Sorvino)
British Academy Awards Nominations 1995: Best Supporting Actress (Sorvino)
Screen Actors Guild Awards Nominations 1995: Best Supporting Actress (Sorvino)
Writers Guild Awards Nominations 1995: Best Original Screenplay (Allen)

future husband from the sky in a helicopter is a literal deus ex machina poking fun at the filmmaker's self-conscious borrowings.

Though Allen sometimes resorts, ineffectively, to slapstick, as when Lenny makes a mess of an office while trying to steal adoption records, his verbal humor works much better, as when the Wineribs try to decide what to name their son and Lenny suggests Groucho, Django, Thelonious, Sugar Ray, and Earl the Pearl. Allen's greatest triumph is in letting Lenny grow to see past Linda's surface and care for her as more than just Max's natural mother. Unlike the original Pygmalion who created an ideal woman and fell in love with his creation, Lenny develops a fondness for what Linda is rather than for what he would like her to be.

—Michael Adams

REVIEWS

Entertainment Weekly. November 3, 1995, p. 40.
Maclean's. CVIII, October 30, 1995, p. 57.
New York. XXVIII, October 30, 1995, p. 108.
The New York Times. October 27, 1995, p. C1.
The New Yorker. LXXI, October 30, 1995, p. 112.
People Weekly. XLIV, November 6, 1995, p. 19.
Rolling Stone. November 16, 1995, p. 115.
Time. CXLVI, October 30, 1995, p. 37.
Variety. September 4, 1995, p. 73.
The Wall Street Journal. October 27, 1995, p. A12.

Mighty Morphin Power Rangers: The Movie

"Kids'll love it!"—Owen Gleiberman, *Entertainment Weekly*

In *Mighty Morphin Power Rangers: The Movie*, the parents of Angel Grove have been turned into zombies by the evil Ivan Ooze. After they do his bidding, he orders them to jump into a construction pit. Entranced, they march relentlessly forward, chanting "Leap to our doom. Leap to our doom."

The six Power Rangers, returning from a journey to another planet, have a lot to do in Angel Grove: battle a couple of giant metallic insects, save the town's kids from a monorail derailment, defeat the nefarious Ooze, and bring back their leader, Zordon, from death's door.

Rescuing the parents is at the bottom of the list, they're irrelevant.

That's exactly how parents in the audience must feel, watching *Power Rangers*. You buy the toys, switch the TV set on, pay for the movie tickets, and spring for popcorn. After that, you might as well be on another planet because *Mighty Morphin Power Rangers* inhabits its own universe, and it's not a parent-friendly one.

Adults should not try to make sense out of *Power Rangers*. The TV show which inspired it is pretty lame, but it sells toys. Its heroes are squeaky-clean teens with plenty of kick. The film adds special effects, keeps the corny fights and scripts, and marches forward like a forty million dollar zombie.

To keep adults awake, the film occasionally slips in campy dialogue. That, and its ridiculous plot and cartoonish fight sequences, may remind parents of the old *Batman* TV shows. There's the slimy Ooze rambling on about all the great things he's missed during the 2,500 years he's been buried under Angel Grove: "The black plague. The Spanish inquisition. The Brady Bunch reunion." Too bad there's not more of that.

CREDITS

Billy/Blue Ranger: David Harold Yost
Kimberly/Pink Ranger: Amy Jo Johnson
Tommy/White Ranger: Jason David Frank
Aisha/Yellow Ranger: Karan Ashley Jackson

Origin: USA
Released: 1995
Production: Suzanne Todd, Haim Saban, Shuki Levy for a Rita Enterprises; released by 20th Century Fox
Direction: Bryan Spicer
Screenplay: Arne Olsen and John Camps
Cinematography: Paul Murphy
Editing: Frank Jimenez
Production design: Craig Stearns
Location manager: Peter Lawless
Costume design: Joseph
Casting: Christine King
MPAA rating: PG

Veteran British stage actor Paul Freeman brings a wry wit and a feisty appeal to the purple-faced Ooze. In fact, Ooze has a lot more pizazz than Zordon, the Rangers' pasty-faced intergalactic leader, who resembles a retired circus clown and seems totally inept.

In a spin-off film like this, the marketing points are more important than the plot. The Rangers are cool fighters—in their martials-arts-style fights, they turn their bodies into whirling corkscrews. They have bright, day-glo costumes in primary colors, which helps to tell them apart. And for the showdown, both they and their enemies turn into enormous shiny moving Lego battleships. Color, metal and kung-fu—those are the ingredients of the Rangers' appeal.

For those beyond the marketing curve, however, *Power Rangers* is so stupid it's actually entertaining. You have to laugh when the Rangers speak, because they always raise their fists when they do.

The plot seems cobbled together from dozens of old sci-fi flicks. Construction workers accidentally uncover the grave of Ooze and his minions, buried long ago by Zordon. Ooze sets to work, sapping the strength of Zordon and the Power Rangers and enslaving the parents of Angel Grove. To get a new power source, the Rangers journey to a strange planet, pursued by Zordon's flying poultry-people who remind you of the flying monkeys in *The Wizard of Oz*. They are saved by a warrior-babe in a green string bikini, then must fight through a dangerous jungle to reach a strange monolith that is the source of some universal power. They return to right all wrongs.

Things get fairly dull while the Rangers are off on another planet, but director Bryan Spicer inserts fight scenes at regular intervals. The Rangers are keen with their fists and feet. An estimated forty million dollars was spent on special effects, mostly to create the robotized battle machines.

Slow as we are, we adults are still trying to figure out why "morphing" into clumsy, clanking zords (the Rangers' ever-changing combat vehicles) is so cool, but hey, the movie is bright and shiny, and there's more violence in a typical TV commercial. It could be worse: Expect a sequel where the adults do leap to their doom.

—*Michael Betzold*

REVIEWS

Variety. July 10, p. 35.

Mina Tannenbaum

Mina Tannenbaum can be seen as an illustration of just how far contemporary filmic realism has to stretch so as to accommodate our present-day social realities. As "cyberfibers" bind us ever closer together, the limits of how we interact amongst ourselves begin to elude all definition.

Martine Dugowson's stylish film seems to situate this theme within the context of a bond between two bright, attractive Parisian young women. Their relationship would appear to elude any convenient category, whether institutional or sexual. We could call them friends, but then we would be guilty of the same smugness as the society these two appear pitted against. We are thus forced to see them more as twins, but not of the biological variety; more like two facets of one female personality.

The fact that a woman filmmaker is telling their story further complicates the issue with a possible dimension of self-reflexivity. Even so, the winning carefree ways of these two protagonists, whose innocence endears them to us; as well as the film's framing device of a documentary in progress, which gives its subject matter an equivocal form; combined with the departures into magical spaces, which evoke a refreshing directorial style; all serve to form a kind of filmic triad, that would appear to make clear just where feminist filmmaking ends, and femininity of filmic outlook begins.

Mina Tannenbaum (Romane Bohringer) and Ethel Benegui (Elsa Zylberstein) are born a few hours apart, within the same hospital ward, on the cusp of the fifties. On either side of a partition, their respective fathers cradle them in their arms at the same time. Before the two girls actually meet, it would appear the die has been cast in each case. As five year olds, a skinny bookish Mina is fitted with glassses, only to be mocked as "four eyes," while a chubby Ethel is left sitting by herself during a bar mitzvah dance.

When the two do meet, at the age of ten, just before Mina's first dance class, the occasion is commemorated by their guardian angels, who appear miraculously in the gray sky overhead, as the two mothers hurry the girls onward at the same time. When the two are by themselves in front of the building, Ethel holds the door open for Mina and asks, "You're new?" "Drop dead," Mina answers. That doesn't stop Ethel from joining Mina who is resting on a street bench after class.

A mere circular pan of the camera shows them to have aged six years, and still sharing the same bench as nonplussed teens: Ethel, slimmer but still overweight, Mina, still skinny with long dark hair falling straight down her shoulders.

At a cafe, following a party at which neither has been able to secure a male companion, Ethel bursts forth in accompaniment to a romantic ballad playing on the jukebox. The lyrics speak of a tryst during which a beautiful sky opens up above the lovers' bed. A disbelieving Mina watches, with a half-smile. It is this ballad that brings to light the difference in their personalities that will take them down divergent paths in life.

Soon after, as an art student, Mina is drawn to an equally nonconformist classmate, the long-haired Francois; while Ethel, studying literature, meets the similarly idealistic Didier, a cafe pianist. Neither relationship takes off.

The film then skips eleven years to the opening of an exhibition of Mina's paintings. Mina is now a self-assured woman in her early thirties, having shed her awkward demeanor, along with her glasses. Ethel, though now svelte, has already begun to feel left behind. For the first time, we see Ethel in open admiration of Mina. "You've got talent, brains, beauty," Ethel says. "Will you talk to me when you're famous?" As for the present, it is Ethel, whose personal life, leaves no time for any meaningful exchange, despite Mina's concern for her. Ethel aspires to become an art critic, while having to hide her non-Jewish live-in boyfriend from her orthodox mother. Mina has a fling with a melancholy painter, then realizes that he has stolen her ideas. On the mercenary art scene, Mina resigns herself to being exploited. In desperation, Ethel impersonates Mina so as to obtain an interview with a reclusive painter. While her gumption lands

CREDITS

Released: 1994 (1995)
Mina Tannenbaum: Romane Bohringer
Ethel Benegui: Elsa Zylberstein
La cousine: Florence Thomassin
Francois: Nils Tavernier

Origin: France
Production: George Benayoun; released by New Yorker Films
Direction: Martine Dugowson
Screenplay: Veronique Heuchenne
Cinematography: Donminique Chapuis
Editing: Martine Barraque and Dominique Gallieni
Production design: Philippe Chiffre
Costume design: Marie Lauwers
Sound: Alain Villeval
Casting: Gigi Akoka
MPAA rating: not rated
Running Time: 127 minutes

her the job she has been after, it alienates her from Mina, who becomes reticent when Ethel tells her what she has done.

We can see that what is really troubling Mina is her being exploited in more ways than one. As a distracted Mina is about to cross a street, she is hit by a van. As Ethel comes to visit her in hospital, it is clear the tables have turned. Now it is Ethel who looks successful and confident, dressed in a business suit, her formerly black hair now dyed a shade of blonde. With a bandaged face, Mina confides: "I'm disfigured."

We soon see that a lasting scar down the right of her face has turned Mina into an object of pity. The real toll, however, has been in terms of her personality. As Mina sits by herself in a cafe, we can see that the sophisticated artist we knew has given way to a pensive, despondent figure, alone and bereft.

Mina's plight worsens when the only art dealer to show an interest in her work tells her that her paintings aren't the right size. Nor can Mina confide in Ethel who, in the few moments she can spare for her, can talk only of her job. Things come to a head between them when Ethel, in order to please her dying mother, decides to hold a "casting call" for a Jewish husband, only to settle on Mina's art dealer. "Why have you always wanted what I had?" Mina cries. "You don't love anyone!" Ethel retorts. It becomes clear now, that the two themselves have been unable to grasp the precise nature of the bond between them. "Your influence is over!" Ethel shouts. "You're no model for me anymore!" "Well, you were never a model for me!" Mina shouts back. After exchanging heated abuse, Ethel storms out, vowing never to see Mina again. Mina's current boyfriend, who has overheard the quarrel, looks hurt upon learning of Mina's desire for her art dealer. When Mina refuses to explain, he too walks out of her life, leaving Mina sobbing to herself, coiled into a fetal position on her apartment floor.

The film then alternates again between Mina and Ethel, this time to show how their families are no source of comfort to either. Two years pass, during which Mina compromises her career goals by becoming a copyist, while Ethel, following the death of her mother, marries her non-Jewish boyfriend, with whom she has a daughter she names Mina. As Mina decides to look up Ethel, she waits for her outside her building. Then, as Ethel approaches, pushing a baby carriage down the busy street, Mina pretends to run into her by accident. The two are all smiles, as they plan to meet that weekend. Ethel, as if uncannily sensing this as their last meeting, suddenly turns round to shout back at Mina: "I tried to replace you, but I didn't succeed."

Even so, the pressures of married life cause Ethel to cancel their date. This seems to shatter Mina. As the romantic ballad that Ethel had sung in the cafe comes on the TV, the sentiment proves too overpowering. She straggles towards her medicine cabinet and reaches for a bottle of sleeping pills. We then see her coiled as before, on her apartment floor.

After her suicide, we learn that Mina's paintings are now all the rage, enjoying an esteem that had always eluded her while she was alive.

As we ponder over Mina's tragedy, the only aspect of its filmic rendition that appears problematic is the framing device of the documentary in progress on Mina's life that, like the film's title, does not prepare us for the equal emphasis the film finds necessary to bestow on Ethel.

Critics, for the most part, have seen *Mina Tannenbaum* as a film about friendship. Janet Maslin in *The New York Times* calls it a "sweetly captivating film about girlhood friendship." She notes that "both Mina and Ethel are fully realized characters, drawn with sympathy and self-knowledge. The film creates two precisely shaded women's roles and finds just the right actresses to play them." Rita Kempley in *The Washington Post* finds that Mina and Ethel "both attract and suffer through first love in a series of scenes that women all over the world will identify with." For her, it is only after Mina becomes upset at Ethel having impersonated her that "the story becomes increasingly bleak and needlessly overwrought," so much so that "the ending might be plausible if only it were tagged on to a less insightful film." John Petrakis in *The Chicago Tribune* uncovers "the challenging themes that develop throughout the film, giving the story its texture and strength. There is the understated problem of growing up Jewish (in Ethel's story), while Mina's mother, a concentration camp survivor who can't seem to shed her cloak of despair, transfers this dark and fatalistic side to her daughter." Petrakis doesn't mention the film's political dimension: Mina and Ethel's first meeting is underscored by TV coverage of the student riots of 1968.

Mina Tannenbaum marks the feature film debut of its director-writer, who was awarded the Best Screenplay prize for it at the Cannes Film Festival of 1992.

—Vivek Adarkar

REVIEWS

Chicago Tribune, August 25, 1995.
Los Angeles Times, May 26, 1995.
New York Times, March 3, 1995.
The Hollywood Reporter, March 8, 1995.
Variety, March 29, 1994.
Washington Post, June 23, 1995.

Money Train

"Get on...or get out of the way."—Movie tagline

"Definitely the best and hottest action comedy of the year!"—Daphne Davis, *Movies and Videos*

"Mr. Snipes' impervious cool and Mr. Harrelson's hyperkinetic boyishness mesh perfectly. Once that ride begins, the movie becomes a sustained adrenaline-pumping journey..."—Stephen Holden, *New York Times*

"This has to be the most thrilling and hilarious action film in ages."—Marshall Fine, *Westchester Gannett*

Box Office Gross: $34,461,327

Wesley Snipes and Woody Harrelson star as two foster brothers working as transit cops in *Money Train*. © 1995 Columbia Pictures Industries, Inc. All rights reserved.

Attempting to capitalize on the success of *White Men Can't Jump* (1992), Wesley Snipes and Woody Harrelson have reteamed to make this unfunny action comedy called *Money Train*. It is ostensibly supposed to be a buddy-cop comedy in the tradition of any and all fast-paced action films which use humor to dilute the violence and sociopathy of the protagonists and antagonists. Some films from which it draws its tone include (but are not limited to) *Bad Boys* (1995), *Running Scared* (1986), and the three *Lethal Weapon* movies (1987, 1989, 1992). There are, of course, countless other films of this type.

In the last couple of years police dramas have become increasingly "humorous," with characters making jokes as they murder or maim the film's villains. This all seemed to begin with the witticisms of such tough guys as Arnold Schwarzenegger and Clint Eastwood, whose "Hasta La Vista, Baby" (*Terminator* II, 1992), and "Go ahead, make my day" (*Dirty Harry*, 1971) set the standard for clever aphorisms uttered during the course of murder and mayhem. Perhaps in the turbulent 1990s, filmmakers see this comedy/violence genre as a contemporary extension of the physical comedy of Laurel and Hardy, Abbott and Costello, or even Bing Crosby and Bob Hope. But in the case of *Money Train*, there is very little that is funny.

The scene in the movie where a psycho douses token booths with gasoline and sets the attendant on fire sparked copycat arsons that resulted in the death of a New York City transit worker.

Snipes and Harrelson star as John (Snipes) and Charlie (Harrelson), two tough New York City subway cops, who are always getting into trouble with higher-ups for their unorthodox ways. The fact that they are "the best" (as one character refers to them) seems to make up for the fact that they are unruly and disruptive on the job. Arrogant and clownish, the two cavort around the bowels of New York's vast subway system searching for criminals. In particular they are looking for a fiendish criminal who sprays gasoline into subway toll booths and then throws a match inside just to watch the token booth operator die.

The other wacky aspect of all this hilarity is that John and Charlie, one African-American and one Caucasian, are brothers. The audience is apparently supposed to find this to be the height of wit and humor, with numerous jokes of the "Mom liked you best" variety sprinkled—make that dropped—throughout the first ninety minutes. "You guys don't look alike...." (The story is that apparently Harrelson's character was a poor street kid taken in by Snipes' kindly mother.)

John and Charlie alternate several times between expressing deep brotherly love, and pulling guns on each other. It is quite difficult for the audience to think they love each other when they actually are threatening each other's lives. The filmmakers would have us believe that we are not supposed to take the threats on each other's lives seriously because this is a comedy. When Harrelson says, "when this is all over, remind me to knock you out," we are supposed to know that he doesn't mean it (or we are at least supposed to think it is cute.) But the trouble with this genre is that the real and the ridiculous are juxtaposed too often, and it is difficult to know what to think. If one scene shows a subway token booth operator being doused in gasoline and lit aflame, and the next scene shows the two lead actors threatening each other's lives, what is supposed to make the audience think the good guys are not actually serious? Is it simply because they are the good guys? If so, that is not enough.

One of the reasons these good guys turn on each other is a woman. Grace (Jennifer Lopez) is a tough sexy new cop on their beat who captures the hearts of both men, but only ends up with one of them. In one of the film's only interesting scenes, Lopez and Snipes seduce each other while sparring in a boxing ring. It is a sexy and unique scene, played well by both actors.

In general, both Snipes and Lopez do a credible job with the rather silly material they are given. Lopez fares the best. She is sinuous, intelligent, and sharp-tongued, a perfect tough-girl foil for the two macho guys. Lopez will be remembered for her much gentler role in *My Family, Mi Familia* (1994). It is apparent that she is an actress of enough depth to surpass the inanity of this vehicle.

Snipes continues to bring dignity even to the worst of films. He starred in several less than superlative action films prior to this (*Drop Zone* [1994], *Passenger 57* [1992]), and always managed to bring a sense of intelligence and elegance to his roles. Most recently, Snipes parted with his macho image to star in *To Wong Foo, Thanks for Everything, Julie Newmar* (1995) as a drag queen. The painfully insipid dia-

CREDITS

John: Wesley Snipes
Charlie: Woody Harrelson
Grace Santiago: Jennifer Lopez
Patterson: Robert Blake
Torch: Chris Cooper
Riley: Joe Grifasi

Origin: USA
Released: 1995
Production: Jon Peters and Neil Canton for A Peters Entertainment production; released by Columbia Pictures
Direction: Joseph Ruben
Screenplay: Doug Richardson and David Loughery
Cinematography: John W. Lindley
Editing: George Bowers and Bill Pankow
Production design: Bill Groom
Set decoration: Beth Rubino
Art direction: Dennis Bradford and Sarah Knowles
Costume design: Ruth E. Carter
Special effects: Paul Stewart, Connie Brink, Mark Blatchley, and Albert Griswold
Casting: Francine Maisler
Music: Mark Mancina
MPAA rating: R
Running Time: 110 minutes

logue and the unfunny situations in which he finds himself in *Money Train* are far more treacherous than the high heels he wore in *To Wong Foo*. In one scene, after drawing a gun on his half-brother, and then letting Harrelson's character dangle from a fifty-story ledge just to teach him a lesson, Snipes is required to say "there's no price you can put on a human life." Given the circumstances, the filmmakers will understand if that line sounds a bit hypocritical (not to mention hackneyed). Yet, in spite of the often-trite dialogue and stale action, Snipes seems to rise above it all with great style.

Harrelson does not fare as well. The effortless brilliance Harrelson brought to his character on television's *Cheers* is not evident here. Harrelson certainly has the ability, but instead of being the cute loser, he appears instead to be an addictive sociopath. It is not the type of character that easily gains the audience's sympathy. Early in the film he loses $15,000 to some mafia gamblers, then insists that brother John give him the money to repay his debt. He lies, steals, cheats, and even relieves himself on a parked car—he's not a hero. So, when Charlie gets the idea to steal a "money train" (the train which collects subway token money), he appears more like a criminal than a good-guy who is pushed over the edge. It doesn't help that Harrelson is trying to be hip by adopting street lingo. When he says, without a trace of irony, "I ain't down with that," it is just downright funny. Just as white rap artist Vanilla Ice seemed out of place in the 1980s, trying to be "cool" and be a "brother," so does Harrelson's character seem to be trying too hard to be cool. It would be fine if the character were depicted as being a bit pathetic because of his need to sound like a street kid, but the audience is supposed to think of him as hip, and it doesn't work.

The script, by Doug Richardson and David Loughery (from a story by Richardson) is derivative and rather flat. It lapses occasionally into such cliche dialogue that it's humorous. For example, when the tenacious head cop (Robert Blake) thinks there may be a problem with the trains, he says, "send it through...nothing stops the money train." With heightened music, a close-up, and Blake's overdramatic line reading, this sounds like a parody of bad movies from *Saturday Night Live*. Other choice moments come when Snipes says "I'm the only family Charlie's got," or when he exhorts Charlie to stop his plot to steal the money train: "...and you think by being a thief you're a winner? Charlie, I'm not gonna let you ruin your life!"

Director Joseph Ruben has trouble keeping things moving in the rambling first half of the film. It is as if he is not sure whether the film is a comedy, an action-comedy, or an action vehicle. Then, when the money train is stolen, the pace quickens, and with the help of superlative special effects and editing, Ruben manages to quicken pulses and keep the film from being a complete waste of time. The train wreck sequence is meticulously filmed, reminiscent of the wonderful train wreck sequence in *The Fugitive* (1993). Audiences interested in seeing such special effects are advised to rent the film and fast-forward to this sequence—or better yet, just rent *The Fugitive*.

One footnote to this film is that a gruesome copycat crime occurred in a New York subway one week after the film's opening. (Criminals sent gasoline and flames into a tollbooth). In the current debate about violence and values in the entertainment media, it becomes apparent that filmmakers might consider the effects of the mayhem they are creating onscreen. In the case of *Money Train*, it is fair to say that all the filmmakers were trying to do was make a fun and interesting film, and should not have to censor themselves. The problem is that in making this film, they made not only an unfunny comedy, but they may have made a dangerous one as well. The "values" debate rages, and the *Money Train* rolls on.

—Kirby Tepper

A Month by the Lake

"A charming, wealthy English gentleman. Two beautiful women. If it only takes a moment to fall in love, imagine what can happen in... *A Month By The Lake*."—Movie tagline

A Month by the Lake is one of those films that aspires to be more than it is. It wanted to achieve the respect and adulation which surrounded the Merchant-Ivory films such as *Howard's End* (1992) and *Remains of the Day* (1993); but it achieved only a moderately positive critical response. It wants to create the same captivating charm which made *Enchanted April* (1993) such a wonderful film; what it creates instead is a bucolic simplicity which is neither boring nor interesting, but is, unfortunately, not enchanting. What the film does do, however, is provide its audience with an hour-and-a-half of gentle, untaxing entertainment. If the film is not particularly outstanding as a cinematic achievement, it is at least a harmless and droll story which is competently filmed by director John Irvin. Most importantly, it serves as a serviceable vehicle for its luminous star, Vanessa Redgrave. Her charming performance might be just enough for the numerous audiences members who may see the film with the expectation that it will be as good as *Howard's End*.

Set in 1937, Redgrave plays Miss Bentley, a lonely but optimistic woman who returns every year to the same hotel at Italy's gorgeous Lake Como. It is the same resort she visited every year since childhood, always with her father. Now that he has died, Miss Bentley tries to continue the tradition and spend a month by the lake. At the hotel she meets the stuffy Major Wilshaw (Edward Fox), to whom she is immediately attracted. She tries to get him to play tennis, to coax him into taking day trips with her—anything to get him to show her some interest. Enter the sexy Miss Beaumont (Uma Thurman), an American youth who is working as a nanny for a wealthy Italian family. Major Wilshaw becomes infatuated with her, to the dismay of Miss Bentley. Meanwhile, Miss Bentley is being pursed by the very youthful and handsome Vittorio (Alessandro Gassmann). Miss Bentley's attempts to maintain her British integrity and her feminine propriety while trying to ensnare Major Wilshaw, rebuff Vittorio, and get rid of Miss Beaumont occupy much of the film. Continually hopeful that the Major will show interest, she suffers through a series of broken dates and one-sided conversations as Major Wilshaw himself suffers at the hands of the manipulative and callow Miss Beaumont.

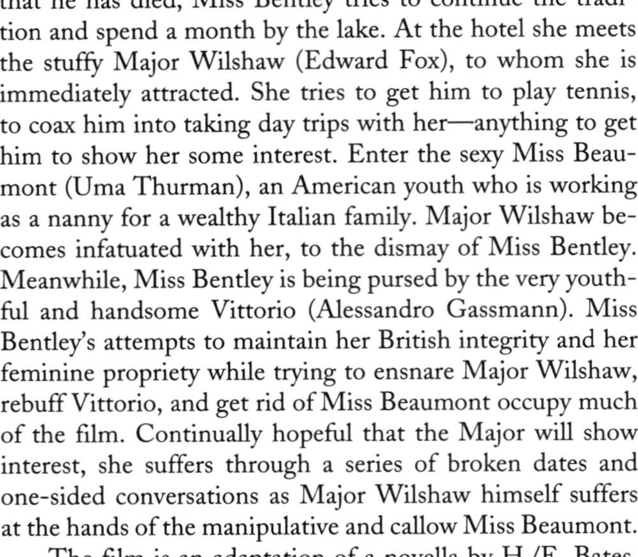

The film is an adaptation of a novella by H./E. Bates, adapted for the screen by Trevor Bentham. Bentham and director Irvin capture the sense of propriety which drives the characters and situations. During their month by the lake, these proper British folks can supposedly "let their hair down" and release some inhibitions, but the most they seem to be able to do is wear less formal clothing and to take a few hikes. Of course, writer Bates and screenwriter Bentham are making a point about the difficulty folks of a certain class have in casting off their proper social straitjackets and following their instincts. The lake might be a symbol for the pool of emotion they can only swim in for a time before being swallowed up. The presence of an American (Thurman's character) provides a contrast to the upper-class formality of Miss Bentley and Major Wilshaw, not to mention her more American ability to manipulate a situation through her sexuality. The character of Vittorio—the handsome, overtly sexual Italian—is a reminder of the joy and simplicity that Miss Bentley and Major Wilshaw have buried somewhere beneath their British manners and their middle-aged fears. The story becomes a dance between four people, ending in a happy coupling. The interplay of youth and middle age, British manners and Italian sensuality, and masculine and

CREDITS

Miss Bentley: Vanessa Redgrave
Major Wilshaw: Edward Fox
Miss Beaumont: Uma Thurman
Signora Fascioli: Alida Valli
Vittorio: Alessandro Gassmann
Signor Bonizzoni: Carlo Cartier

Origin: Great Britain
Released: 1995
Production: Robert Fox; released by Miramax Films
Direction: John Irvin
Screenplay: Trevor Bentham; based on the story by H.E. Bates
Cinematography: Pasqualino de Santis
Editing: Peter Tanner
Production design: Giovanni Giovagnoni
Music: Nicola Piovani
Costume design: Lia Mornadini
MPAA rating: PG
Running Time: 92 minutes

AWARDS AND NOMINATIONS

Golden Globe Awards Nominations 1996: Best Actress-Musical/Comedy (Redgrave)

feminine roles are central to the film's theme, and are nicely played by the four actors.

American filmgoers tend to have high expectations for British films. From Anthony Hopkins to Daniel Day Lewis to Emma Thompson, some of the most vivid performances on American screens of late seem to come from British actors. The Merchant-Ivory films (*Howard's End*, *Remains of the Day*) have quality and intellectual appeal which eludes even the most highbrow of American films. Directors Jim Sheridan (*My Left Foot*, 1989), or Mike Figgis (*Enchanted April*) or Kenneth Branagh (*Henry V*, 1989) are sophisticated artists whose films transcend the typical storylines and predictable visuals on which many commercial American filmmakers rely. (Note that Jim Sheridan is included as a British director even though he is Irish. Americans do not tend to make the distinction: as long as the actors have an accent that comes from somewhere in the British Isles, the film is English.) Fair or not, Americans expect British films to be brilliant. So it is no wonder that *A Month by the Lake* is a bit of a disappointment. It is not a bad film, just not an exciting or brilliant one. It is important to see this film in the context of its expectations. Perhaps it would be a more enjoyable film if it hadn't been born into a cultural climate in which all things British must be brilliant.

"Miss Bentley, I think, has had to teach herself to make the best out of not very much and see the bright side of things. She's very unlike me. I'm not by nature apt to look hard for the bright side of things."—Vanessa Redgrave on her character

John Irvin's direction is a bit formal, making it more difficult to transcend the British stuffiness with which the film concerns itself. An example is the way Irvin will shoot the actors in rather contrived and unspontaneous shots, such as a rather artificial argument on the outdoor stairs of the hotel. Two actors argue in the background, seeming to "hit their marks" before they say a word, which causes the argument to have an unspontaneous, posed quality. Another example is the argument between Redgrave and Thurman after a magic-show sequence: they walk back toward the stage curtain, stop so their bodies are in very specific positions in relation to the stage curtain, and then they begin to argue. A picnic scene involving many of the characters looks staged and stiff. These and other very formal scenes do nothing to underscore the importance of spontaneity and instinct which seems to be central to the film's theme.

The actors acquit themselves nicely in their roles, showing sensitivity to the film's inherently romantic nature. That the film is ultimately not particularly romantic perhaps lies in the aforementioned formality of its direction, for the actors do their best to portray the different levels of comfort and discomfort, artifice and ingenuousness, happiness and sadness inherent in romance. Thurman does a pleasant turn as a girl who knows she is attractive but pretends to be a good girl. She has a good scene with Fox in which she tells him to "kiss me instead of pressing me all over," but then won't let him kiss her. Her callousness does not seem evil, just shallow, allowing Thurman's character to not be hateful. Often Thurman's body language and vocal inflections lapse into an uninspired sense of monotony, and it is hard to tell whether it is the character or the actress who is bored. Unfortunately, it makes for an uneven performance.

Edward Fox is the very model of a stuffy major, and is quite touching in his pathetic attempts to warm the heart of the cold Miss Beaumont. Fox's ramrod-straight posture, his elegant good looks, and his severe nature are perfect for the role. He is all the more charming when he does his magic show, and is quite adept at making the audience sympathetic when Miss Beaumont tampers with his magic tricks.

Redgrave has received some of her best reviews in recent years for her role. She creates a lovely character: coltish and buoyant as she runs all over the village to catch up with the Major, doe-eyed and sad as she realizes he has broken their date to see Miss Beaumont. Redgrave's iconoclastic nature is permanently imprinted in every move she makes. When her character wears a man's bathing suit to swim in the lake, or even when she merely wears a camera around her neck, she appears believable as a woman who is uncomfortable living a conventional life. She is delightful when fending off the advances of Vittorio, particularly in a scene in which he maneuvers her over to his "sister's" apartment. She looks around the room, and with a knowing look, says, "your sister has very masculine taste." The ensuing scene is charming due to Redgrave's ability to play several levels: one can see the wheels turning as she gets the idea to use this young man to make the major jealous, even though it is obvious that she also wishes she didn't have to do so.

The film's individual parts are just lovely: beautiful scenery (shot with care by Irvin and cinematographer Pasqualino de Santis), a sweet story, and fine actors. But something is missing. In a final voice-over, Redgrave's character says that Miss Beaumont brought magic into their lives. And it is then that audiences will realize what is missing. Even by the shores of Lake Como, this film lacks any cinematic magic.

—*Kirby Tepper*

Moonlight and Valentino

"A movie brimming with beautifully conveyed emotions."—Liz Smith, *New York Newsday*

"As deeply poignant as it is extremely funny."—Barbara Siegel, *Siegel Entertainment Syndicate*

"A moving and entertaining film."—Jeff Craig, *Sixty Second Preview*

Box Office Gross: $2,488,858

Elizabeth Perkins delivers a wonderful performance in this otherwise tepid comedy/drama. Based on a stage play by Ellen Simon (written for the screen by her as well), *Moonlight and Valentino* has some vivid dramatic moments and some intelligent dialogue. On the whole, it is an hour and a half of pleasant entertainment that is occasionally moving, and generally enjoyable, though not brilliant.

Like *The Cemetery Club* (1992) or *How to Make an American Quilt* (1995), this is a "women's film" with strong female roles. And in a cinematic climate in which meaty film roles are scarce, this film should be lauded for providing some fine actresses with strong characters to portray. Sadly, women in current American mainstream cinema tend to play roles in which they either support the hero or play the seductress. Roles requiring actresses to take on the challenge of non-stereotypical characterization are rare indeed. The roles in *Moonlight and Valentino* are not meaty and are rather broadly drawn, but the film is exceptional in one aspect: There are more females than males in prominent roles, and the biggest male character is apparently there to serve as a sex object for the women.

The story is about Rebecca Lott (Elizabeth Perkins), a young woman who, in the film's first few minutes, finds out that her husband has unexpectedly and suddenly died. Curiously, she responds with numbness to the devastating news. Returning to their home, she is visited by her best friend Sylvie (Whoopi Goldberg), her sister Lucy (Gwyneth Paltrow), and her former step-mother Alberta (Kathleen Turner), each of whom has arrived to help Rebecca through the ordeal.

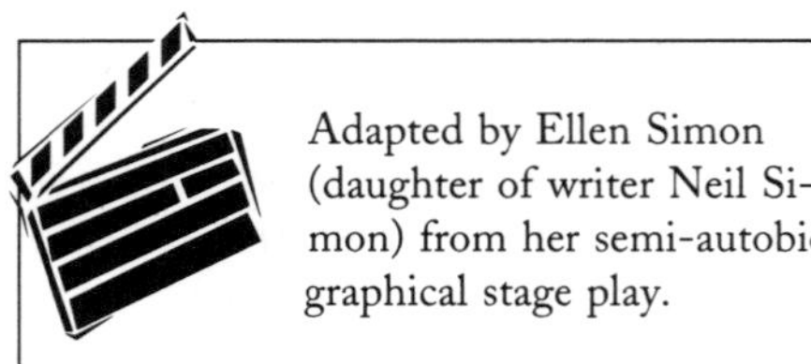

Adapted by Ellen Simon (daughter of writer Neil Simon) from her semi-autobiographical stage play.

Sitting in the hallway on the floor outside her bedroom, Rebecca greets each of the women as if they were coming over to play bridge. They talk about her clothes ("Great jacket!" says Lucy; "Thanks," says Rebecca, "they also had it in a smoky brown.") She doesn't cry, but instead makes clever quips to her friends. When she finally enters the bedroom, she briefly cries, but stops herself saying "I'm not gonna do this." Each of the other characters tries to help her in their own way. Sylvie talks about her marriage, saying that she cried through her dinner last night because she and her husband are not getting along. Alberta, a wealthy businesswoman, makes funeral arrangements and does business from her cellular phone. And Lucy buzzes around her older sister, uncertain about what exactly to do, but offering great sympathy.

Most of the film concerns itself with the characters trying to help Rebecca the best they can. The characters each have a subplot which relates to Rebecca's plight thematically: Sylvie constantly dreams of having a perfect marriage; Alberta tries desperately to win the friendship of young Lucy, who has never forgotten her deceased mother; and Lucy learns about love through a budding relationship with a student in Rebecca's poetry class. Each woman projects their fantasies on to Rebecca, who had a seemingly perfect marriage.

As time passes, Rebecca returns to work as a poetry and literature professor, trying to adjust to life as a widow. At first she is frightened of being a widow saying, "I'm going to be the 'w' word. I'm going to look like Georgia O'Keefe." Curiously, Rebecca does not appear to have any catharsis about the death of her husband, and it is the absence of pain that appears disturbing to the other characters.

Things change when a handsome housepainter (Jon Bon Jovi) and his dog (named Valentino) come to re-paint Rebecca's house. The four women each fantasize about him (the painter, not the dog.) Alberta says, "It is the possibilities of who a man might be that I like." Eventually Rebecca enters into a romantic relationship with the sexy and good-natured painter, which leads to an emotional crisis, and to a resolution which is a fine emotional pay-off for the film. In a beautifully written monologue, the audience comes to understand Rebecca's reasons for holding back her sadness for so long.

Elizabeth Perkins delivers this climactic monologue with the fervor and the momentum one would expect to find in a Broadway play. Throughout the film Perkins is controlled and stoic, but somehow seems to be bubbling just beneath the surface. Perkins is the beautiful and unusual actress best remembered for playing opposite Tom Hanks in *Big* (1988). Perkins has dignity, grace, and an edgy irony in her voice that make her a perfect heroine for a comedy/drama. Her humor comes from pain underneath; Perkins never allows her characters to appear superficial. She has a world-weariness and a sense of irony reminiscent of great screen comediennes such as Paulette Goddard or Claudette Colbert. Perkins is an actress to be treasured, and even in this rather innocuous film she manages to find depth. Her final scenes are positively radiant with energy and emotion.

"I'm becoming one of those people everyone hates to be around."—Newly widowed Rebecca to friend Sylvie

One of the problems of this final emotional pay-off is that it may come too late for many audience members. Writer Simon and director David Anspaugh do not help the rather pedestrian events stay interesting. For much of the film, in spite of Perkins' fine performance, Rebecca is merely a controlled and almost superficial person, and so by the time of her revelatory monologue, the audience's good will may be squandered. (It is Perkins charisma that keeps her likable at all.)

Similarly, the characters played by Whoopi Goldberg and Kathleen Turner are not entirely lovable through much of the film, making it difficult for the audience to fully embrace them. Goldberg's character in particular is rather strident and irritating. All she talks about is how awful her husband is, and when Rebecca appears finally willing to show some sadness, Goldberg's character becomes angry with her, saying that Rebecca is "self-absorbed" and that "from where I sit, you have it pretty good." It seems ludicrous at best (and cruel at second-best) that a woman would be this insensitive to a "best friend" who is grieving the untimely death of her husband.

The contrivance of Goldberg's character is emblematic of some other rather contrived relationships or sequences in the film. Other contrivances appear convenient for the author, such as the fact that Rebecca's grungy sister, rich ex-step-mother and best friend always seem to arrive and leave at the same time; or convenient for the story, such as the housepainter painting at night because he can get some "thinking done" just when Rebecca happens to be home for an evening.

Goldberg acquits herself well in her rather self-absorbed role, and Turner is pleasant, though a bit self-conscious as the motherly but business-like Alberta. The film is, however, "stolen" by Gwyneth Paltrow as gawky Lucy. When she meets Rebecca's handsome pupil (Jeremy Sisto) and asks "are we on a blind date?" or when she expresses her desire to have her older sister look at her naked body and "tell me what you think," she is enchanting. Paltrow is the perfect actress for the part, eager and wide-eyed one moment, cynical and grungy the next—and all of her moments are well-timed, well-played, and just plain delightful.

Like Rudolph Valentino, the housepainter is a silent matinee idol who is a lightning rod for women's fantasies. Rock star Jon Bon Jovi gives a fine debut performance. All those music videos seem to have provided Bon Jovi with a background in acting (either that, or he is a natural.) His big scene with Perkins allows him to display the charm that has won him countless fans. Writer Simon should be commended for keeping his character mysterious, and the casting of Bon Jovi in this role is inspired in that his rock-star status renders him as mysterious and untouchable to the audience as his character is to the women who covet him from afar.

Director David Anspaugh does a credible job with this film. He deserves kudos for his deft direction of Perkins, Paltrow, and Bon Jovi (casting was by Amanda Mackey and Cathy Sandrich). And he has opened up Simon's play enough to make it believable without diluting the intimacy of its relationships. He makes a fine choice in the filming of Rebecca discovering her husband's death: it comes swiftly, unexpectedly, and he jump cuts silent slow-motion reaction shots of Perkins as she goes through the initial reaction, which emphasizes the horror and disbelief accompanying such devastating news. Unfortunately, these fine moments are mixed in with much that appears rather mundane. The film is a mixed bag.

CREDITS

Rebecca Lott: Elizabeth Perkins
Sylvie Morrow: Whoopi Goldberg
Lucy Trager: Gwyneth Paltrow
Alberta Russell: Kathleen Turner
The Painter: Jon Bon Jovi
Steven: Jeremy Sisto
Thomas Trager: Josef Sommer

Origin: USA
Released: 1995
Production: Alison Owen, Eric Fellner and Tim Bevan for a Working Title Film production; released by Gramercy Pictures
Direction: David Anspaugh
Screenplay: Ellen Simon; based on her stage play
Cinematography: Julio Macat
Editing: David Rosenbloom
Production design: Robb Wilson King
Art direction: David Ferguson
Set decoration: Carol Lavoie
Costume design: Denise Cronenberg
Sound: Bruce Carwardine
Casting: Amanda Mackey and Cathy Sandrich
MPAA rating: R
Running Time: 104 minutes

For Perkins' climactic monologue, for Jon Bon Jovi's screen debut, and for what is sure to be seen as a breakthrough performance for Gwyneth Paltrow, audiences might want to see *Moonlight and Valentino*. It is not perfect, but it is a film its creators can certainly be proud of.

—*Kirby Tepper*

Mortal Kombat

"Nothing in this world has prepared you for this."—Movie tagline

"A high-tech fun house!"—Stephen Holden, *New York Times*

"A rock 'em, sock 'em, action flick!"—Rob Salem, *Toronto Star*

"A mix of martial arts and special effects magic!"—Richard Harrington, *The Washington Post*

Box Office Gross: $70,360,285

Literature and film are filled with stories of difficult young people who are nonetheless most treasured and who accomplish phenomenal things. For instance, in *Karate Kid* (1984), an angry young man, cast adrift on the tide of adulthood, destructive and difficult, learns respect for himself and those around him and, in the process, develops self-confidence, all at the hands of a strong yet loving parent figure, Mr. Myagi (Pat Morito). So too, in *The Empire Strikes Back* (1980) (sequel to *Star Wars*, 1977), Yoda, apparently a strict taskmaster, admonishes even as he guides Luke Skywalker (Mark Hamill), teaching him to discover the strength and courage that resides within him. Not unlike the biblical story of the prodigal son, these films focus on proverbial "tough customers," finding the value in the anti-hero, he who eludes connection and fails, only to succeed in even a larger sense. In like manner, Liu Kang (Robin Shou), arguably the centerpiece of *Mortal Kombat*, must leave his home and must abandon what once mattered to him in order to understand and embrace it meaningfully. Said producer Larry Kasanoff, "Our goal is not to preach self-belief, rather it's to make a really entertaining movie, which we've done[.]...But there's a strong underlying story which says 'You can do it if you believe it.' It's done in a really fun, cool way."

An unlikely trio of warriors—Liu Kang (Robin Shou), Johnny Cage (Linden Ashby) and Sonya Blade (Bridgette Wilson)—is assembled and sent to Outworld to battle the forces of darkness (led by Shang Tsung, played by Cary-Hiroyki Tagawa) for dominion over the world. The "good guys" are coached by Lord Rayden (Christopher Lambert) (*Highlander*, 1986; *Greystoke: the Legend of Tarzan, Lord of the Apes*, 1984), a long-haired, lightening-bolt shooting, peripatetic, smirking "Yoda". Also in their corner is 1,000 year old Princess Kitana (Talisa Soto), who is interested in regaining control of her Outworld throne and reestablishing beauty and tranquility. A series of battles ensues, pitting warriors against monsters such as Goro, a four-armed mutant, while the fate of the Earth hangs in the balance.

Along with films such as *Street Fighter*, *Double Dragon*, and *Super Mario Brothers*, *Mortal Kombat* springs from one of the most popular video games of all times, Mortal Kombat, the two versions of which have sold over five million copies ($250 million) and which thereby have outgrossed *Jurassic Park* (1994). Interestingly enough, the game is popular with a wide range of players, i.e., persons aged eight to thirty. Perhaps partly responsible for the popularity of the game generally is the precision of the graphics in the video game. Continuing the high tech appeal onto the large screen are remarkable special effects, whose production was overseen by Alison Savitch (who also supervised visual effects on

CREDITS

Lord Rayden: Christopher Lambert
Johnny Cage: Linden Ashby
Shang Tsung: Cary-Hiroyuki Tagawa
Lui Kang: Robin Shou
Sonya Blade: Bridgette Wilson
Kitana: Talisa Soto
Kano: Trevor Goddard

Origin: USA
Released: 1995
Production: Lawrence Kasanoff; released by New Line Cinema
Direction: Paul Anderson
Screenplay: Kevin Droney; based on the video game
Cinematography: John R. Leonetti
Editing: Martin Hunter
Production design: Jonathan Carlson
Music: George S. Clinton
MPAA rating: PG-13
Running Time: 95 minutes

Terminator 2, 1991). For instance, each fight scene was tweaked slightly to ensure the appearance of contact. Indeed, Savitch reports that the developing technology continues to make better and cheaper morphing effects. "Years ago, when I worked on *T2*, people charged huge numbers for a morph—you could pay $80,000 or $100,000 dollars because almost nobody knew how to do it...Now there's an $89 morph program that 14-year-old kids are using on their home computers. Everything's changing constantly. You can't just do a morph in a movie and get away with it, you have to do something special."

Combining the best of video-game action and mythological-scale testing and reward, *Mortal Kombat* entertains and instructs. Video-game enthusiasts will no doubt be glad for a closer view of this hit game, while the less video-initiated will no doubt enjoy the high-tech visuals. In the classic tradition of *Jason and the Argonauts* (1963), *Mortal Kombat* is must-see kitsch.

—Roberta F. Green

REVIEWS

Chicago Tribune, August 20, 1995, p. 1.
New York Times, August 19, 1995, p. 11.
USA Today, August 21, 1995, p. 3D.
Washington Post, August 19, 1995, p. C3.

Moving the Mountain

In a world where images of unspeakable violence and heart-wrenching courage flit across our TV screens nightly, few of us have the opportunity to investigate the issues behind what we are viewing. In Michael Apted's film *Moving the Mountain*, we have been given that chance. This film is a second look at the event that held the world spellbound during the summer of 1989. Taking us behind the scenes of Tian An Men Square, Apted interviews surviving student leaders who recount the events that led up to the massacre. In so doing, Apted has given us an invaluable insight into why certain decisions were made, what the mindset of the students was, and what has happened to them and their movement since that time.

Michael Apted, a British filmmaker, is known in Hollywood for *Nell* (1994) and *Coal Miner's Daughter* (1980) as well as the British documentary series *7 UP* (1963, 1970, 1977, 1985, 1991). His producer, Trudie Styler, became interested in the project when she met Li Lu, a student leader, in London shortly after the students clashed with the military.

Using archival footage from the world press, Apted is able to bring powerful scenes to the screen. From such unforgettable images as youthful protesters raising the "Goddess of Democracy" in the square or fainting from hunger during their hunger strike, to the famous footage of a lone student standing defenseless before a division of tanks and holding out his bare hands to stop them, the film could stand on its archival footage alone. But more central to the theme of the film is how those events are remembered through the eyes of five students.

The film begins with an interview with Li Lu, one of the democracy movement's student leaders. He tells the story of his youth and gives us a glimpse of life during the Cultural Revolution and how his politics and others of his generation were molded by those experiences.

As Li Lu relates his story, the filmmaker portrays a series of re-enactments that show Li's parents being shipped off to labor camps and his own journey through various foster homes, passing through institutions along the way, until he is finally adopted by a large family. His memories of injustices and personal crisis leave the viewer with the misconception that the film is mainly about Li. It is not.

These dramatized scenes are meant to explain how a generation of Chinese were provoked to rebel against the government. The government's interference in the personal lives of its people and their fruitless efforts to find their voice is far more powerful when seen through the footage of the students who risked their lives for an opportunity simply to talk with the government. Li along with others of his generation went from being a "nobody with no voice," to joining the chorus of 20,000 in Tian An Men Square, whose cries for freedom could be heard around the world.

But Li Lu isn't the only student leader in the film. As he explains, various leaders brought different aspects to the movement. Wang Chaohua was the eldest member of the young student leaders, and she brought an intellectual perspective to the movement. Wu'er Kaixi was a charismatic force. Chai Ling, who was a major force behind the hunger strike, brought a sense of spirituality to the cause. Wang Dan, on China's Most Wanted list because of his involvement in the demonstration, was thc organizer of the revolt.

What few of us in the West realize is that the occupation of the square was a spontaneous event. Hu Yaobang, the Commmunist Party General Secretary, was a supporter of the student movement and an economic and political reformer who had been ousted from his position because of his views. On April 26th, when his death was made public, students came in the thousands to the square to mourn. Li Lu was among their number, coming hundreds of miles to join others at the square. Their sheer numbers emboldened them to meet the following day to elect student leaders. Twenty thousand students gathered there on what was called Liberty Day. Their demands were simple: they wanted a dialogue with the government; the voiceless wanted a voice. On May fourth, the impending visit of Gorbachev brought the world press to Beijing. The press, while waiting for the diplomatic visit, began to follow the story of the students.

In response to negative publicity, the government promised the students a dialogue, but canceled each meeting. With time running out, and the Soviet leader's visit nearing, the students made a courageous and, some feel, fatal move. They decided, though not unanimously, to hold a hunger strike. Chai Ling gave a speech that mobilized the students, and with the backing of their professors, the students marched to the square. Wang Chaohua was one of the leaders who was against the strike, fearing that the government's loss of face would put them at war with the students. Because of these fears, no one initially came to support the hunger strikers in the square. But little by little, young people arrived with blankets and water in a show of support. By May 17th, according to the student leaders' estimates, 2 to 3 million people of all ages and in 150 cities throughout China, demonstrated in support of the students—and overnight the student movement became a national movement.

CREDITS

Wang Dan: Wang Dan
Wang Chaohua: Wang Chaohua
Wu'er Kaixi: Wu'er Kaixi
Chai Ling: Chai Ling
Li Lu: Li Lu
Li Lu, age 10: Zhang Jin-Ming
Li Lu, age 4: Huang Yi-Ming

Origin: England
Released: 1995
Production: Trudie Styler for Xingu Films; released by October Films
Direction: Michael Apted
Screenplay: Michael Apted
Cinematography: Maryse Alberti
Editing: Susanne Rostock
Sound: Scott Briendel
Music: Liu Sola
MPAA rating: not listed
Running Time: 83 minutes

The following day, the government permitted a meeting with student leaders, and directly following the meeting, martial law was declared. In response, citizens of Beijing built barricades to keep the military from entering the city, and people of all ages and walks of life pleaded with the soldiers for compassion and in many cases effectively persuaded the soldiers to leave the square, while in Hong Kong large sums of money was being raised to feed the students in the square.

The negative press and the support that the students received from within and outside of China embarrassed Deng, and he ordered the military to occupy the square. At this juncture, the student leaders warned the twenty thousand protesters of the danger and gave them the option to leave. Only five thousand left the square.

The conclusion of that protest is well known, although the tabulation of the dead varies: Western estimates put it at about one thousand, whereas Chinese students say it is closer to four thousand. The official government count is two hundred dead.

The resulting massacre brought to a close that media event, as the world press moved on to the next heart-wrenching story, and that was the last word on the subject. But *Moving the Mountain* reveals what occurred after the night of bloodshed. With honesty and sympathy, Apted has brought the second act of the Tian An Men Square tragedy to the screen.

Four of the student leaders who were smuggled out of China and into Hong Kong tell of the door-to-door searches, of the thousands who were arrested, of leaving family, and turning to strangers for shelter. They speak of the horrors of flight, hiding in trucks or trains, being recognized over and over again, and how complete strangers,compelled by their cause, help them in their escape to the West. Apted has used re-enactment again as a medium as they relate their stories, this time effectively bringing to life the terror of their escape.

Now scattered across the U.S. and completing their educations—Chai Ling at Princeton, Wang Chaohua at UCLA, Wu'er Kaixi in San Francisco, and Li Lu at Columbia—some are still trying to work for change in China. But when the exiles speak of their homeland, it is with a gut-wrenching homesickness that it is almost too painful to watch.

Another thing they have in common is a deep and unabating remorse for the deaths of June 1989. As Li Lu put it, "We have never really recovered from the fact that so many people died—and yet we are still alive." When they speak of this, their sadness and their sense of overwhelming responsibility turn these articulate leaders into speechless and tortured mourners.

Apted goes even further in his follow-up. He went to China and held secret interviews with Wang Dan, the organizer who was captured after the revolt and imprisoned for three years, and Wei Jingsheng. Wei, the students' hero, just finished a fifteen-year sentence in a Chinese prison for his criticisms of the government. The comments of these two brave men show a fearless and continued commitment to fight for reform from within China. They agree in their view that the exiled student leaders cannot create any change in China from the West.

In his interview with the mature and thoughtful Wei, he gives his insights into how he experienced the revolt from the outside. The activist said that no one was level-headed during the occupation, not the government nor the students. Yet Wei feels that the government bears the burden of responsibility for its outcome.

The danger of Apted's secret interviews can be better understood when we realize that Wei is currently reported missing. But Apted's courage to get this interview is rewarded in that these two interviews are some of the best in the film.

The interviews of the students in exile is also fascinating. When they discuss the occupation, their recollections are spontaneous and sincere, even admitting their disagreements during the incident. But when they speak about freedom and democracy there is a deadness to the polished rhetoric they espouse. Much of it sounds like it is taken directly from their speeches and sounds contrived, hurting the film's freshness.

Another flaw in *Moving the Mountain* is the use of quick cuts, especially in the news footage. There is no need to key up the drama in an already overwhelmingly dramatic event, and it gives the film a manipulative quality.

Liu Sola's musical score is at first exotically interesting and emotionally effective, but is overdone and soon becomes annoying and, worse, distracting.

But the film is a wonderful view behind the scenes of the Tian An Men Square occupation, affording us a look at the decisions that were made and not made. And, perhaps more important, it honors the people who knowingly sacrificed their lives for democracy.

Moving the Mountain is an interesting study of what happens to young people who are given so much power so young, only to be cast out and exiled not only from their homes and family but also the movement that inspired their passion. When the pinnacle of one's power and success is reached so young, what happens to those cut off from it? Power is a cagey tool and sometimes the people who think they are using it are unwittingly the ones being used, whether it be for a good cause or evil.

One thing is certain, the lives of the people involved in the student movement and the lives of all of the survivors of the clash are forever changed. *Moving the Mountain* illustrates that in the hands of these politically naive yet sincere idealists a nation was moved to protest. And as Wei Jingsheng warns, "Next time the people will not wait to talk."

—Diane Hatch-Avis

REVIEWS

The Los Angeles Times, May 19, 1995, p. F.
Daily Variety, September 30, 1994, p. 10.
The Washington Post, p. D1.
The Los Angeles Times, May 29, 1995, p. F.
The Plain Dealer, July 14, 1995, p. 8.

Mr. Holland's Opus

"One of the best pictures of the year!"—Marilyn Beck, *Chicago Tribune Syndicate*

"Wonderful and emotionally overwhelming!"—Michael Medved, *Sneak Previews*

"Don't miss it!"—Paul Wunder, *WBAI Radio*

The time is the 1960s, and Glenn Holland (Richard Dreyfuss) is a young musician—a jazz pianist and composer—who finds himself in the position of relying on the teaching certificate he earned in college as a fall back. He and his wife Iris (Glenne Headly) move to Portland where he begins teaching music at a local high school. Over the years, once he gets used to getting up early and to listening to student music, he finds he has a chance to make a difference in his community, for his students and his family. Of course, in time-honored tradition, he helps underachieving self-doubters turn into successful people who like themselves. He also is tempted by his students, harangued by administrators and scolded by his colleagues, yet it is all part of the life of a teacher.

Perhaps nowhere else do teachers earn more respect than in films. Indeed, in films such as *To Sir with Love* (1967), *Up the Down Staircase* (1967), *The Prime Of Miss Jean Brodie* (1969), *Goodbye, Mr. Chips* (1969), *Fast Times at Ridgemont High* (1982), *Stand and Deliver* (1987), *Kindergarten Cop* (1990), *Dead Poet's Society* (), *The Man Without a Face* (1994) and *Dangerous Minds* (1995), teachers earn their students' respect, even those teachers who are shown to have feet of clay. These films place teachers into schools that are basically foreign to them, focus on their problems getting adjusted to the system, and then explore the extent of their success with their students. For instance, in *To Sir with Love*, Sidney Poitier's character inspires intellectual curiosity in his once-hostile, defeated students and encourages them to see beyond the drudgery and limits around them, beyond their parents' failure and ennui. His interest in them is the warmth of the sun to these otherwise forgotten, struggling students. Soon the students are interested in treating each other and their teacher with respect. Then they are interested in art. Soon they are grown up and ready to set about their lives.

So, too, a large part of *Mr. Holland's Opus* has to do with the self-respect he helps his students gain. For instance, one student, a gangly red-head named Gertrude Lang (Alicia Witt), has the misfortune to be part of a family in which every person excels at something, and Gertrude has worked through a variety of hobbies and school subjects, looking for an area in which to excel as well. When Mr. Holland encounters Gertrude, however, she is in the process of failing miserably at playing the clarinet, just as she has failed at so many other things. She practices endlessly, she has the sheet music memorized, but she cannot play a string of notes so that they are recognizably melodic. Recognizing her plight, Mr. Holland works with Gertrude before and after school, practicing the same piece of music, over and over again. Just as he is preparing to tell Gertrude to give up on playing the clarinet, he comes to the realization that she has given the music all of the intellectual precision she has to offer but none of the heart it requires. While hardly original, the scene in which Gertrude conquers the clarinet is visually interest-

CREDITS

Glenn Holland: Richard Dreyfuss
Iris Holland: Glenne Headly
Principal Jacobs: Olympia Dukakis
Bill Meister: Jay Thomas
Cole (at 15): Joseph Anderson
Cole (at 28): Anthony Natale
Rowena Morgan: Jean Louisa Kelly
Gertrude Lang: Alicia Witt
Adult Gertrude: Joanna Gleason

Origin: USA
Released: 1995
Production: Patrick Sheane Duncan and William Teitler for a Hollywood Pictures, Interscope Communications and Polygram Filmed Entertainment production; released by Buena Vista
Direction: Stephen Herek
Screenplay: Patrick Sheane Duncan
Cinematography: Oliver Wood
Editing: Trudy Ship
Production design: David Nichols
Art direction: Dina Lipton
Set decoration: Jan Bergstrom
Costume design: Aggie Guerard Rodgers
Sound: Tim Chau, Rick Franklin
Music: Christopher Brooks
MPAA rating: PG
Running Time: 121 minutes

AWARDS AND NOMINATIONS

Academy Awards Nominations 1995: Best Actor (Dreyfuss)
Golden Globe Awards Nominations 1996: Best Actor (Dreyfuss), Best Screenplay (Duncan)

ing (Gertrude's red hair and the golden sunlight filtering through the old-style window shades) and thematically rewarding. Until this point in the film, Glenn Holland had found teaching mind-deadening; he lived for the few hours each morning and evening that he could steal to work on his music. The students were a torture to be endured for his art. Yet the Gertrude success seems to energize Mr. Holland, opens his eyes to his students as works in progress as well, and his career is in motion.

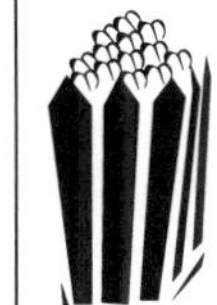

"It's in your head. It's in your fingers. It's in your heart."—Mr. Holland to his pupils from *Mr. Holland's Opus*

One of the problems with a film that chronicles a person's life through episodes is that the episodic structure can become monotonous. Each leap in years is accented by a switch in music, clothing, hair color (the characters age), and background history (i.e., the Vietnam War), and each presents an encapsulated vignette. It becomes a string of pearls, and, while initially interesting, it can become exceedingly boring, especially once the pace is set: problem presented, problem resolved, next problem presented, next problem resolved. So rhythmic is *Mr. Holland's Opus* that audience members will find themselves preparing for the various hairdos and costume changes more than for the plot problem. Equally distracting have been *Mr. and Mrs. Bridge* (1990), *For the Boys* (1991), and *Mr. Saturday Night* (1994), in which the episodes are rigidly paced and endless in number, and the make-up contrived. In all fairness to *Mr. Holland's Opus*, however, the characters age more realistically and with more grace than those in the earlier films.

Interestingly enough, however, *Mr. Holland's Opus* bears a strong resemblance to *It's a Wonderful Life* (1942) in that Glenn Holland and George Bailey go through their lives wishing they were elsewhere, doing something else. Mr. Holland is always the frustrated musician/composer, always fighting for time for himself. He rails against teaching drivers' education; he fails to find the time to learn to sign in order to communicate with his deaf son. George Bailey spends his life trying to escape Bedford Falls, dreaming of traveling the ocean on steamers, taking trains around South America, and escaping from the demands of the "crummy" Bailey Savings and Loan. While the audience does not see Mr. Holland's courtship of Iris, viewers do see George court Mary, fighting the urge to love her because that love (and any subsequent marriage) would distance him from his dream of travel.

In the meantime, both Mr. Holland and George Bailey forget Iris Holland and Mary Bailey, who have created homes for them and borne them children. Mr. Holland considers life in New York with one of his students (Rowena Morgan, played by Jean Louisa Kelly), opting instead to dedicate a piece of music to her. Later in the film, when budget cuts slash through the music education budget, Mr. Holland finds himself lost. George Bailey, on the other hand, considers death. While these men face different problems, in the final analysis, when it appears that all is lost for Glenn and George, it is Iris and Mary that make the difference. Both women find ways to show their husbands that their lives have made a difference to those around them and thereby save the men from despair or death.

Some of the best performances in *Mr. Holland's Opus* are given by persons in minor roles. For instance, Olympia Dukakis plays Principal Jacobs, a stern task mistress who always happens to be around the corner at the least opportune moment, asking the least opportune questions. For instance, it is Principal Jacobs who corrals Mr. Holland into teaching drivers' education. It is Principal Jacobs who corrals Mr. Holland into turning the band into a marching band. It is Principal Jacobs who objects to Mr. Holland's seeing teaching as a fall-back career. And it is Principal Jacobs who has one of the largest impacts on Mr. Holland's career. Olympia Dukakis brings dignity to her role, an iron spine with a loving hand. She is, as always, enjoyable to watch.

Another minor character who makes a difference in this film is Bill Meister (Jay Thomas), the gym teacher and arguably Mr. Holland's best friend. Between the two of them, Mr. Holland and Mr. Meister teach the band to march and teach the football players to sing and dance for the school production of a night of Cole Porter songs. Yet, more importantly, it is Mr. Meister who convinces Mr. Holland to help an athlete who needs passing credits to stay in school, to teach the athlete to play an instrument so that he can earn the music education credits he needs. While today such subjects are difficult and politically charged, in the film Mr. Meister makes the issue into helping a traditional underachiever because you can make a difference in that student's life, because, he admits, he was just that kind of student himself. If someone hadn't taken an interest in him, who knows where he would be now. In many ways, while Mr. Holland no doubt would call himself an artist, those around him supply him with the heart and soul, the vision, he sometimes lacks.

This is not to say that all of the minor characters are artfully drawn, as at least one other minor character is less successful: Vice Principal Wolters (W.H. Macy). Certainly Mr. Wolters is intended to be small minded and simpering. His first observation in the film is that Ralph Nadar has determined that the jazzy car driven by Glenn Holland—a Corvair—is unsafe at any speed. Later in the film, Mr. Wolters opposes the night of Cole Porter songs, at least until it is clearly a money-maker. Finally, when budget cuts become a reality, it is Mr. Wolters who determines that art and music are unnecessary. Prim, prunish and perpetually unkind, the character Mr. Wolters is one of the few one-dimensional features of this film. Even "the bad guy" needs to be convincingly drawn, or the film again becomes predictable, a melodrama.

Mr. Holland's Opus also focuses on the difficult relationship between Glenn Holland and his deaf son Cole. Mr. Holland sees his son's deafness as a curse of sorts, and the film emphasizes this fact. When Iris is pregnant, the filmmaker has used montages of the parents-to-be playing music for the unborn child. When the child is an infant, the filmmaker has shown the family gathered at the piano. And when Mr. Holland is leading his marching band for the first time, proudly, it is then that Cole's deafness is discovered. Sound is Mr. Holland's life, and his son is outside that. The film works through some difficult moments between father and son, and while much of it boils down to scenes similar to those reflecting the stereotypical trouble between parents and children, it adds another dimension to the film and may elicit emotional responses from the audience.

While *Mr. Holland's Opus* covers very little new ground, it effectively and emotionally covers ground of nostalgic interest to many filmgoers. As manipulative as *Terms of Endearment* (1983) or *Steel Magnolias* (1989), this film will make viewers weep, no matter how hard they try to avoid it. With those caveats in place, *Mr. Holland's Opus* is a film with some remarkable performances. Watch at your own risk.

—*Roberta F. Green*

REVIEWS

Entertainment Weekly, January 26, 1996.

Mr. Payback

Touted as the first interactive motion picture, *Mr. Payback* is a combination film/video game, in which audience members help solve mysteries and punish bad guys by voting with a joystick attached to their seat. The title character (Billy Warlock) in the film is a vigilante cyborg, who wreaks vengeance on various villains, with the aid of his pretty assistant, Gwen (Holly Fields).

CREDITS

Mr. Payback: Billy Warlock
Gwen: Holly Fields
Ed Jarvis: Christopher Lloyd
Diane Wyatt: Leslie Easterbrook

Origin: USA
Released: 1995
Production: Jeremiah Samuels; released by Interfilm
Direction: Bob Gale
Screenplay: Bob Gale
Cinematography: Denis Maloney
Editing: Ian Kelly
Special effects: Michael Lantieri, Don Elliott
Music: Michael Tavera
MPAA rating: PG-13
Running Time: 20 minutes

Murder in the First

"One was condemned. One was determined. Two men whose friendship gave them the will to take on the system..."—Movie tagline

"An extraordinary celebration."—Graham Fuller, *Interview*

"Amazing and unforgettable."—Jeff Craig, *Sixty Second Preview*

"Incredibly moving and spellbinding entertainment. Brilliantly conceived and directed."—Paul Wunder, *WBAI Radio*

Box Office Gross: $17,381,942

Murder in the First dramatizes the real-life court case that led to the reform of Alcatraz, the harsh island prison in San Francisco Bay. The film has a very strong script by Dan Gordon. The performances by Kevin Bacon as Henri Young, the Alcatraz prisoner who was kept in solitary confinement for three years, and Christian Slater as James Stamphill, a character composite of many lawyers who worked on Young's case, give the film its humanity and emotion.

The film begins with a dark screen and the sounds of prison guards arresting a group of convicts trying to escape. This foiled escape becomes the reason for Henri Young's punishment in solitary confinement. These early scenes establish the brutality of the dungeons in Alcatraz. Henri is thrown naked into a six-by-nine-foot room where seawater seeps down stone walls. The room is completely dark. The prisoner is fed through a small crack in the door and has no heat, no bed, and no toilet.

Regulations stipulate that the maximum stay for a prisoner in solitary is nineteen days. Henri is confined from March, 1938, until June, 1941, with only thirty minutes of sunlight a year in the prison recreation yard. When he is finally taken out of solitary, he is lectured by the sadistic associate warden, Glenn (Gary Oldman), who ties up Henri and lacerates his ankle with a razor. In the mess hall one day, Henri sees the fellow prisoner who alerted the guards to their escape attempt and wildly rushes at him, killing him with a spoon.

James Stamphill, a public defender, is assigned Henri's case. When he meets with Henri in his holding cell, he cannot at first get his client to talk. Stamphill picks up bits of Henri's life through his research, such as that he was initially arrested for stealing five dollars during the Depression. In their second meeting, Stamphill coyly elicits a response from Henri by mistakenly referring to his theft of $500. Henri corrects him and guardedly begins to talk. He asks Stamphill about Joe DiMaggio and cannot understand his lawyer having the freedom to listen to baseball games and choosing not to. In their third meeting, Henri admits that having a spider in his cell was like having company. He shows off how well he learned the multiplication tables during his stay in the dungeon. Stamphill finally sees that Henri's broken sentences reflect an avoidance of thought, because for three years in solitary all he did was think.

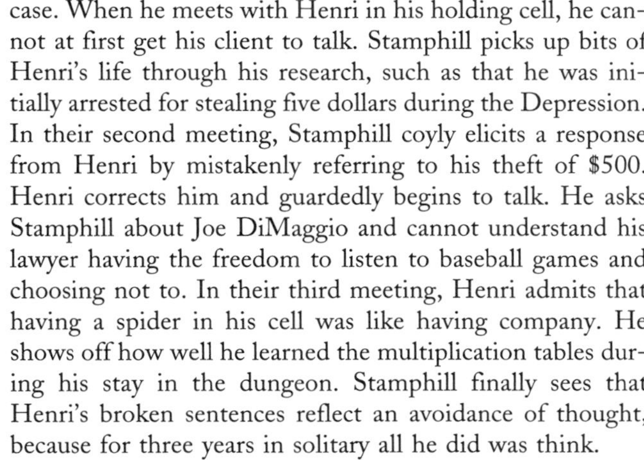

When the trial begins, Stamphill has a surprise prepared. He announces to the judge (R. Lee Ermey) that a coconspirator was also responsible for Henri's murder of the man in the mess hall. The prosecutor jumps to object and obliges Stamphill by reciting the three years of Henri's intense punishment. Alcatraz and this treatment, Stamphill then points out, was the conspirator that made Henri Young into a killer. Stamphill intends to put the prison system itself on trial.

The most compelling scenes in the film are those in which the human element overrides momentarily the plea for reform. A good example occurs when Stamphill finally gains permission to tour the solitary confinement cells. Faced with the squalor of such a dungeon, he realizes for the first time the intensity of Henri's deprivations. Stamphill strikes a match that barely dispels any of the darkness. As the sound track registers the sounds of his shoes on the damp floor, he bends and notices a small outline of a baseball diamond etched in the clay of the cell floor. Now he understands more fully Henri's repeated questions about Joe DiMaggio. These details economically reveal both the personality and passive sufferings of Henri as well as Stamphill's growing moral outrage. The scene in solitary also sharpens the link to subsequent scenes: When Stamphill next approaches convicts to recruit witnesses as to the horrors of the dungeon cells, his motives have been convincingly established.

"I didn't want to make this a Hollywood version of a courtroom or prison drama. I wanted to play the realism, try to be accurate to the time and place. I believe if you do the research and make as many details as real as possible, you can transcend the time period and make it almost timeless in its own way."—Director Marc Rocco on his film

In fact, by choosing justice over profit, Stamphill is doing his job so well that his supervisor, Mr. Henkin (Stephen Tobolowsky), who is alarmed that anyone should question the system, takes him off the case. The news of this demotion finally sinks in as Stamphill watches an Independence Day fireworks celebration and learns that his friend, Mary McCasslin (Embeth Davidtz), another public defender, will try to pick up where Stamphill left off. Henri's confinement, however, has maimed him to the point that he cannot maintain control of himself in the presence of a woman. Henri begs Mary to call him by his first name, then tries to touch her, and finally begins to masturbate in his cell in front of her. When Stamphill returns, Henri immediately scents Mary's perfume on Stamphill's jacket.

As indicated by some reviewers, the moments when the film most clearly advances its thesis for the downtrodden may sacrifice some subtlety. At one point Stamphill sneaks a prostitute, Blanche (Kyra Sedgwick), disguised as a court reporter into Henri's cell. Henri had earlier mentioned to Stamphill that his initial arrest occurred at age seventeen before he had lost his virginity, and he eagerly accepts Blanche as Stamphill's gift. Henri cannot perform, however, and collapses in tears on the shoulder of Blanche, who tenderly mothers him. The larger point that the filmmakers would convey here is perhaps too sharply drawn: The prison system has denied Henri not only his freedom but also his manhood.

The style of other scenes risks belaboring the film's message as well. The early montage of Henri in solitary is occasionally made unduly portentous by repeated shots that show him with his arms extended in a crucifixion posture. In the courtroom scenes, the cell-like witness box is situated by itself in the center of the room away from the judge's bench. When a witness such as Associate Warden Glenn testifies, Stamphill's accusatory questions and the set design combine to show how positions have changed and how for once the sadistic warden must now endure another sort of solitary confinement. In addition, some of the later narration by Stamphill about trying to win and losing sight of the goal of finding justice may be overplayed, as is the irony of Stamphill's dismissal occurring against a backdrop of Fourth of July fireworks.

Director Marc Rocco's visual style utilizes low-key lighting and the moving camera extensively. The courtroom set was darkened by the addition of brown paint and extra railings. The holding cell in which Henri meets his attorneys is featured for almost thirty minutes of the film's running time of 122 minutes. Rocco's sweeping camera moves encircle the cell from every possible perspective and required a special breakaway set and three different types of dollies, two specialized cranes, and an overhead monorail. The results are visually impressive but, after a while, needlessly fussy. As some reviewers indicated, eventually such constant movement of the camera merely distracts from the performances by Kevin Bacon and Christian Slater. According to the film's production notes, production designer Kirk M. Petruccelli commented, "When you think about a set for Marc, you don't design for a few simple shots and you're out.... If it doesn't allow him to put a 28-foot boom in there with a hot-head crane, it's wrong. It's all got to work."

The performances in the film are especially noteworthy. Christian Slater conveys both the energy and the sensitivity required for the role of the crusader for justice who comes to see his client as his friend. Kevin Bacon makes his role of the suffering prisoner deeper and more complex by showing how the three years in solitary have imprisoned Henri emotionally in himself. In the conversations between Henri and Stamphill that conclude the film, Bacon captures well the vulnerability and desperation of a man who is will-

CREDITS

James Stamphill: Christian Slater
Henri Young: Kevin Bacon
Associate Warden Glenn: Gary Oldman
Mary McCasslin: Embeth Davidtz
William McNeil: Bill Macy
Mr. Henkin: Stephen Tobolowsky
Byron Stamphill: Brad Dourif
Judge Clawson: R. Lee Ermey
Rosetta Young (as an adult): Mia Kirshner
Jerry Hoolihan: Ben Slack
Warden James Humson: Stefan Gierasch
Blanche: Kyra Sedgwick

Origin: USA
Released: 1995
Production: Marc Frydman and Mark Wolper for Le Studio Canal Plus, in association with the Wolper Organization; released by Warner Bros.
Direction: Marc Rocco
Screenplay: Dan Gordon
Cinematography: Fred Murphy
Editing: Russell Livingstone
Production design: Kirk M. Petruccelli
Art direction: Michael Rizzo
Set decoration: Greg Grande
Casting: Mary Jo Slater
Sound: Ed White
Costume design: Sylvia Vega Vasques
Music: Christopher Young
MPAA rating: R
Running Time: 122 minutes

AWARDS AND NOMINATIONS

Screen Actors Guild Nominations 1995: Best Supporting Actor (Bacon)

ing to change his plea to guilty and be executed rather than be convicted of manslaughter and return once again to Alcatraz. "I want to stop being afraid," Henri says to Stamphill, a line that seems to organize much of Bacon's performance.

The film concludes with the jury's verdict of involuntary manslaughter and an added comment about the warden being guilty of crimes against humanity. As Stamphill's closing narration relates that Henri was killed in his cell, Henri is led back to solitary in the closing shots of the film.

—*Glenn Hopp*

REVIEWS

Daily Variety. January 16, 1995, p. 2.
Entertainment Weekly. February 3, 1995, p. 37.
The Hollywood Reporter. January 17, 1995, p. 12.
Los Angeles Times. January 20, 1995, p. F8.
The New York Times. January 20, 1995, p. B1.
The New Yorker. February 13, 1995, p. 26.
People Weekly. February 6, 1995, p. 16.
USA Today. February 3, 1995, p. 4D.

Muriel's Wedding

"Uproarious! Enormously funny!"—Kenneth Turan, *Los Angeles Times*

"A fresh fable that's touching and hilarious!"—Rene Rodriguez, *Miami Herald*

"An exuberantly funny Cinderella story! A crowd-pleaser spiced with genuine feeling."—Peter Travers, *Rolling Stone*

Box Office Gross: $15,185,594

This generally misunderstood film from Australia written and directed by P. J. Hogan in 1994 but not released in the United States until 1995, begins with a shot of a falling bridal bouquet being tossed by the bride to her bridesmaids after the wedding. Muriel Heslop (Toni Collette) is an ungainly "big" girl who is obsessed by thoughts of matrimony but cursed by her so-called friends, who reject her because they consider her fat and homely. These other bridesmaids demand that Muriel give the bouquet back because they think it is unfair that such an unlikely candidate for marriage should have this kind of luck. That is how the character of Muriel is established—she is defined through her friends and family.

Muriel is a victim of circumstance, trapped in a dysfunctional family in a miserable resort town in Australia called Porpoise Spit. Her father (Bill Hunter) is a philanderer and a crooked politician; her mother (Jeanie Drynan) is either dimwitted or going senile; her sister Joan and her two brothers are couch potatoes and losers. She goes to her friend's wedding in an outrageous dress she has stolen and she is arrested at the wedding when a woman from the store spots her wearing the stolen goods. Her father "fixes" this problem by bribing the arresting officers.

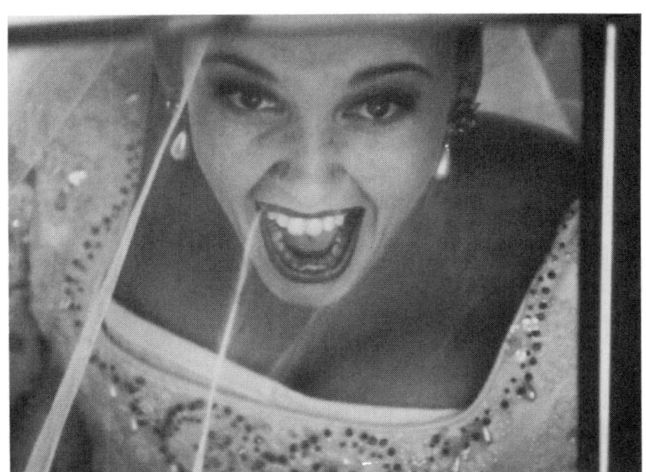

Toni Collette stars in *Muriel's Wedding*. © Miramax Films.

The opening wedding is doomed from the start after Tania, the bride, finds telltale lipstick in unmentionable places on her groom, who has copulated with one of the bridesmaids during the wedding reception. Tania and her friends go on holiday to Hibiscus Island. Muriel is not invited to join them, so she steals $12,000 from the family savings to go on her own. Fortunately, she meets another classmate, Rhonda (Rachel Griffiths), who is more friendly and accepts her. After an expensive vacation, Muriel and Rhonda set off for Sydney, identified by a subtitle as "the city of brides."

This film was misunderstood by many reviewers who considered it a "romantic comedy" that was "raucous" and "zestful" and "downright wacky." More perceptive critics such as Richard Schickel were astonished that the picture was hailed as a "romantic comedy," since it is certainly lacking in true romance and offers very little comedy. David Denby was so alienated by the film that he delayed reviewing it because he found it simply "too embarrassing to write about."

The film is built upon caricatures masquerading as characters, and if it succeeds, it succeeds only as satire, but the purpose of this satire is to ridicule Muriel, her family, her so-called friends, and their values. The satire puts a superficial gloss on a world that is perfectly awful, populated by generally despicable characters. Much of the film is pathetic rather than laughable, even though Muriel is desperately trying to have fun.

When she is first ridiculed and rejected by her friends, she says, desperately, "I can change," but one of them points out, cruelly, "You'd still be you." "I'm not nothing," Muriel protests, weeping. "I'm going to get married," Muriel later tells her mother. "I'm going to be a success. I'll show them. I'll show them all." Fat chance, that, but Muriel does change, though not necessarily for the better, until the end. At least she learns that success is not necessarily defined by matrimony.

In Sydney Muriel gets a job at a video store and even gets a date, but nothing comes of that relationship. Muriel also changes her name to Marial to symbolize her rebirth; but that change, sadly, is superficial. She needs to change from the inside.

Rhonda, who dropped out of high school the year be-

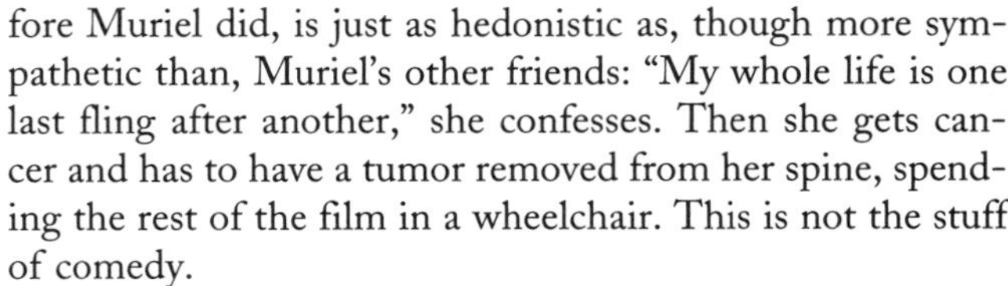

fore Muriel did, is just as hedonistic as, though more sympathetic than, Muriel's other friends: "My whole life is one last fling after another," she confesses. Then she gets cancer and has to have a tumor removed from her spine, spending the rest of the film in a wheelchair. This is not the stuff of comedy.

The film does have its high-spirited moments, however, especially during the first hour, when Muriel meets Rhonda on Hibiscus Island and the two of them, wearing wigs, lip-synch a dance routine to the song "Waterloo," performed by Muriel's favorite (though hopelessly outdated) pop group, ABBA, whose music, Janet Maslin pointed out, Muriel "equates with life's highest pinnacles." In Porpoise Spit Muriel was addicted to listening to ABBA; when she starts playing that music in Sydney, the film seems to suggest that ultimately Muriel cannot run away from herself. Rhonda is now an invalid, and Muriel looks after her and nurses her through therapy, until the film takes a cynical turn.

The third movement of the film is entitled "Muriel's Wedding." After Muriel's father has threatened to return her to Porpoise Spit, Muriel finds a husband by turning to the "personals." Responding to a newspaper ad, she agrees to a marriage of convenience to an Olympic swimmer from South Africa whose manager wants him to compete for Australia. His family is willing to pay her $10,000 for entering into this sham union. This is not the stuff of romantic comedy.

Muriel makes this bad decision about the time Rhonda needs another operation and deserts her friend for a man who clearly does not love her. But he is famous, so her bimbo friends beg Muriel to make them bridesmaids in this celebrity wedding. Muriel walks triumphantly down the aisle not to the music of Mendlessohn but of ABBA, singing "Love me or leave me, make your choice, but believe me." This represents a culmination of pop kitsch and enhances the vulgar superficiality of Muriel and her wedding. Her father comes to the wedding with his mistress Deidre (Gennie Nevinson), and her mother arrives late, after the ceremony has started, and has to sit in the back of the church, unnoticed. Muriel does not even see her mother as she walks out of the church. She is too self-centered to notice.

CREDITS

Muriel Heslop: Toni Collette
Bill Heslop: Bill Hunter
Rhonda: Rachel Griffiths
Betty Heslop: Jeanie Drynan
Deidre: Gennie Nevinson
Brice: Matt Day
David Van Arkle: Daniel Lapaine

Origin: Australia
Released: 1994
Production: Lynda House and Jocelyn Moorhouse for CIBY 2000, in association with Australian Film Finance Corporation; released by Miramax Films
Direction: P. J. Hogan
Screenplay: P. J. Hogan
Cinematography: Martin McGrath
Editing: Jill Bilcock
Production design: Patrick Reardon
Art direction: Hugh Bateup
Set decoration: Jane Murphy and Glen W. Johnson
Casting: Alison Barrett
Sound: David Lee
Costume design: Terry Ryan
Music: Peter Best
MPAA rating: R
Running Time: 105 minutes

AWARDS AND NOMINATIONS

Australian Film Institute Awards 1994: Best Film, Best Actress (Collette), Best Supporting Actress (Griffiths), Best Sound
Nominations: Best Director (Hogan), Best Supporting Actor (Hunter), Best Supporting Actress (Drynan), Best Screenplay (Hogan)
British Academy Awards Nominations 1995: Best Original Screenplay (Hogan)
Golden Globe Awards Nominations 1995: Best Actress-Musical/Comedy (Collette)
Writers Guild Awards Nominations 1995: Best Original Screenplay (Hogan)

Bill Heslop, the father of losers, is a loser himself and a disloyal brute as well. After Muriel's mother gets arrested for shoplifting a pair of slippers (she only put them on because her feet were hurting, but, being dim or preoccupied, she forgot to pay for them), husband Bill tells her that he wants a divorce. Devastated, the mother takes pills and dies. Muriel's wedding, then, is merely a prelude to her mother's funeral. This is not comic, but it does have a sobering effect upon Muriel.

"I know I'm not normal, but I can change."—Muriel from *Muriel's Wedding*

Only then does Muriel's husband show affection and compassion for her, indicating that he wants her to "stay around." Muriel understands that she does not love him, however, and refuses to keep living a lie. Bill is pretty well ruined by then. Deidre the mistress has second thoughts about marrying him if she has to look after his dysfunctional family. Bill's political career is washed up, and he is bankrupt, financially, as well as spiritually: "I'm on the dole," he says. "You reap what you sow," and that's the clichéd truth. Muriel walks away from both her husband and her father and rescues Rhonda from Porpoise Spit by taking her away from her mother and back to Sydney.

Finally, Muriel seems to have grown up. She decides to look after the only true friend she ever had, except, perhaps, for her mother. She has decided to accept herself for what she is. She has moved beyond her wedding fantasies. She makes a good end, and so does the film.

The world of this film is self-centered and hedonistic. Bill Heslop deserves the kind of family he has. Muriel is the best of the lot; though she steals his money, at least she does not suffer from the terminal lethargy that afflicts her brothers and sisters. Her addictive wedding fantasy at least is an active one. Her long-suffering mother, who has a good enough heart, is overwhelmed by her brood of "lay-abouts," whom she serves without complaint, almost to the end, when she sets fire to her middle-class back yard before taking the pills. She is most often seen standing in her kitchen in a state of shock, but she does not give up on life until her husband threatens to desert her. A stronger person might have said "good riddance," but Muriel's mother is no longer young and has lost her spirit, if not her mind. Her happiest moment, sadly, was Muriel's wedding, even though she was totally ignored there. She is pathetic and not appreciated until after her suicide.

Rhonda, Muriel's only true friend, is a hedonist, but she is still capable of being considerate of others. Muriel, the neglected wallflower, indulges her fantasies. She cannot walk past a bridal store without stopping to try on the gowns, then she has her picture taken on the pretense that her invalid "sister" cannot come to the store. When the opportunity comes to have an expensive church wedding and get married to a handsome celebrity athlete, Muriel simply cannot resist, even though this means she will have to leave Rhonda, who depends on her to help pay the bills so they can both live in Sydney. Without Muriel, Rhonda had no option other than return to her mother in Porpoise Spit.

Writer-director P. J. Hogan explained his debut picture by citing Muriel's "victory" as her ability "to find out who she was," after she discovered what she had become, a self-centered idiot who was still trying to impress her chum Tania and the other bridesmaids who had rejected her. The Heslop family is almost grotesque enough to have been imagined by David Lynch. Some viewers may want to escape this domestic freakshow, which moves towards over-the-top perverse melodrama as the story progresses. One wonders if Hogan realized what a monster he had created; the very peevishness of this movie is that the director drops the viewers into a demented freakshow, a domestic zoo, and then expects them to laugh at the pathetic creatures on display.

At the end Muriel has shed her delusions, presumably, and conveniently forgotten about both her beautiful swimmer and her departed mother. That's the context for the superficial liberation as she cheerfully wheels damaged Rhonda off to Sydney and away from Rhonda's domineering but well-meaning mother and Tania and her crew of "suckers." Yes, Muriel has truly found herself and has earned a berth on the *Oprah* circuit as this melodrama is transformed from soap opera to soap *Oprah*. This could be the first motion picture to exploit that kinky audience of confessional television. *Muriel's Wedding*, which some reviewers have compared to *Strictly Ballroom*, is in fact strictly satire, and not the gentle kind. It is etched in acid and relatively heartless as it races towards its mendaciously merry conclusion.

—*James M. Welsh*

REVIEWS

Entertainment Weekly. No.267. March 24, 1995, pp. 43-44. .
New York. Vol. 28, No.14, April 3, 1995, p.58.
The New York Times. March 10, 1995, C-15.
Sight and Sound. Vol.5, No.4, April, 1995, p.49.
Time. Vol.145, No.15, April 10, 1995, p.82.
Washington Times Metropolitan Times. March 17, 1995, c-18.

Mute Witness

"She won't be silenced."—Movie tagline

"A nifty, stylish thriller."—Lisa Schwartzbaum, *Entertainment Weekly*

"Eerie!"—Pia Farrell, *The Hollywood Reporter*

"Riveting!"—Bruce Williamson, *Playboy*

"The most exhilarating frightfest in ages! Sensational!"—Peter Travers, *Rolling Stone*

"In the classic style of Hitchcock! A must see!"—Jeff Craig, *Sixty Second Preview*

Box Office Gross: $1,204,430

A variety of films have focused on a disabled person in peril, perhaps most notably *Rear Window* (1954), in which a wheel-chair-bound Jimmy Stewart battles a murderous Raymond Burr, *Wait until Dark* (1967), in which a blind Audrey Hepburn tries to even the playing field to battle effectively a psychotic Alan Arkin, and *Blink* (1994), in which Madeline Stowe battles her faulty vision to try to identify and thwart her would-be assailant. While some more recent films have addressed the same subject metaphorically, such as *After Hours* (1985), in which a less-than-hip (or normal, depending on the viewer's point of view) Griffen Dunne battles his way through hippest of all hip places (or weirdest of all weird places), Greenwich Village, a stranger in a strange land, hampered mostly by his being a colossal misfit. In key ways, *Mute Witness* combines both literal and metaphoric handicaps, placing a mute person into a strange land in which she knows no one, knows nothing of the language, and fails to understand the powers and pressures of the "new" Russia.

Billy (Marina Sudina) is a young American woman, working as a special effects person with a film crew in Moscow. Along with her sister Karen (Fay Ripley) and the sister's significant other Andy (Evan Richards), Billy is struggling to make a low-budget thriller. After a particularly disappointing day of shooting, complete with a ridiculously (and purposefully) over-played death scene, the three head out to have supper and plan for the next day's shoot. However, as they reach their automobiles, Billy remembers that she has forgotten something and must return to the set. Karen and Andy continue home, Billy returns to the set, and, as cinematic luck would have it, Billy becomes locked inside the building without the key she needs to escape. Bemused by her predicament, Billy soon begins to wander the studio, encountering another shoot in progress, indeed, a pornographic film in the making. While Billy watches, the female character's ecstasy turns to horror as the co-star/lover evolves literally into murderer. In her efforts to remain alive and to ensure that the "bad guys" are caught, Billy must battle with—even while she eludes—the police, the KGB, and the Russian mafia.

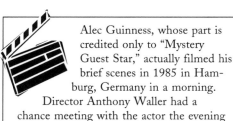

Alec Guinness, whose part is credited only to "Mystery Guest Star," actually filmed his brief scenes in 1985 in Hamburg, Germany in a morning. Director Anthony Waller had a chance meeting with the actor the evening before and persuaded him to take the part.

As much a character in the film as any human are technology generally and special effects specifically. For instance, Billy could call for help, but, as she is mute, the number one technical aid for doing so—the telephone is no help to her. Indeed, her efforts to scratch at the receiver to signal her presence prove fruitless. Later in the film Billy's customized technology for answering the telephone also proves to be cumbersome for calling for help. With her telephone connected to her computer and with software that allows her computer to speak, Billy can achieve a kind of chatty conversation in normal situations, albeit with significant pauses while she types messages and pulls down windows to send them. This system proves less congenial, however, once murderous thugs are trying to knock down the door and the emergency operators do not speak English. Then full-sentence, massive-vocabulary technology becomes a poor substitute for a simple scream.

As in the film *FX* (1986), special effects technology also plays a role in this film. As in *FX*, special effects allow the main character, here Billy, to impose order on chaos by bringing the dangerous action around her into a world known to her by changing the unknown and unfriendly terrain of unknown persons speaking an unknown language in furtherance of an unknown agenda into what Billy knows best—an audience, whose expectations and point of view can be molded through special effects. For instance, if the KGB wants her dead, then what better way to elude them than to oblige them. Suffice it to say, without giving away much of the plot, what the effects lack in originality they more than make up for in timing and style. Unlike films such as *Pacific Heights* (1990), in which the would-be victim learns the predator's game and beats him at it, in *Mute Witness*, the would-be victim draws the predator into her world and defeats him her way: by visual trickery.

If it is worth mentioning that the "bad guys" are tricked by what they see or don't see, then it is also worth mentioning that the audience is tricked as well. For instance, once the police arrive at the film set/murder scene and begin to follow the leads Billy gives them, it is not long before the audience members begin to question what they have seen as well. For instance, the audience members think they watch the killers place bloody pieces of the dead woman's body into trash bags and throw the bags down an abandoned elevator shaft. When the police arrive and search through the trash bags, finding only theater masks dripping in stage blood, the audience begins to question what it has seen, what Billy has seen, and who's telling the truth.

The audience is also manipulated through a roller-coaster of emotions in the cat-and-mouse scenes that prevail throughout. Take, for instance, the scene mentioned above in which Billy attempts to use her computer-assisted telephone to call for help. As discussed earlier, the slowness of the technology, the cumbersome process Billy must follow to send each phrase, torques the audience's frustration and panic inherent in such a scene.

Additionally, Billy's resourcefulness plays a role in this scene. Earlier in the scene, upon her arrival home, Billy disrobes in preparation for her bath. While she undresses, she notices that her cretinous neighbor is watching with great interest. She shuts the draperies more tightly. However, with a thug at the door and the technology inoperable, the peeping neighbor changes from a liability to a possibility. Billy runs to the window, throws open the draperies, disrobes and waves frantically in an attempt to capture his attention. Intensifying the audience's discomfort, the peeping neighbor is oblivious to Billy's call for help.

Once the thug is through the door, the pursuit begins in earnest, with mad dashes around doorways, with people lunging with knives, with more cinematically usual forms of pursuit. Yet the true art here occurs before the man ever enters the apartment, when Billy is alone and vulnerable, locked in an apartment that is both shelter and trap. That is, when she arrives home, Billy locks the door, and it would appear that chaos is locked out. However, with the intruder at the door it becomes clear that Billy is locked in, stuck without exit. This phenomenon is repeated throughout the film, as Billy is placed in the position of a cornered animal, trapped, fleeing, seeking shelter within a shelter that is itself filled with danger. Marina Sudina, who, oddly enough is a Russian actress playing an American filmmaker at risk in Russia, brings the role of Billy to life and is able to capture, without benefit of words, the fear and helplessness that reigns in Billy's life and this film for a considerable time.

For all of its ability to affect the viewers by raising pulse rates across the board, *Mute Witness* is not without its disappointments, such as its cinematic cliches. For example, much of this film has been done before, as noted in the multiple mentions given above, such as *FX* and *Wait until Dark*. While it bears note that much of this has been tried before successfully, this is not to suggest that *Mute Witness* fails to elicit a response from its viewers because it is indeed a very atmospheric film. Further, just as writers are drawn to writing about writing (take, for instance, Ernest Hemingway, James Joyce, William Styron, Joyce Carol Oates), so too filmmakers find it irresistible to make films based on or about film, whether about screenwriters, film students/schools, or the film industry in general. Consider *Sunset Boulevard* (1950), *Day for Night* (1973), *Silent Movie* (1976), *The Big Picture* (1989), *The Freshman* (1990), and *The Player* (1992). The problem with focusing on filmmaking within a film is that it narrows the scope of the film, allows the filmmaker to play it safe by staying within the world he knows, and allows the filmmaker to make in jokes that leave most of the audience behind. It is only fair to state, however, that even with its shortcomings, *Mute Witness* is an effective film.

Mute Witness was shot on location in Moscow, utilizing such interesting sites as the Mosfilm Studio and a notorious cellar used in Stalin's era as a site for mass execu-

CREDITS

Billy: Mary Sudina
Karen: Fay Ripley
Andy: Evan Richards
Larsen: Oleg Jankowskij
Arkadi: Igor Volkow
Lyosha: Sergei Karlenkov
The Reaper: Alec Guinness

Origin: Great Britain
Released: 1995
Production: Alexander Buchman, Norbert Soientgen, and Anthony Waller; released by Sony Pictures Classic
Direction: Anthony Waller
Screenplay: Anthony Waller
Cinematography: Egon Wardin
Editing: Peter Adam
Production design: Matthias Kammermeir
Art direction: Barbara Becker
Executive producer: Richard Claus
Costume design: not listed
Sound: not listed
Music: Wilbert Hirsch
MPAA rating: R
Running Time: 90 minutes

REVIEWS

Daily Variety, February 10, 1995, p. 27.
People, Sept. 25, 1995, p. 22.
The New York Times, September 125, 1995, p. C4.
USA Today, September 15, 1995, p. 4D.

tions. The film received great acclaim at the Sundance Film Festival, where it was screened as a midnight special. *Mute Witness*'s director Anthony Waller, whose background is in advertising, is making his writing and directing debut with this film. Perhaps not exceedingly memorable, *Mute Witness* is nonetheless good fun that Hitchcock fans and film buffs will not want to miss.

—*Roberta F. Green*

My Family; Mi Familia

"Three generations of dreams."—Movie tagline

"*My Family* may be the best film ever on the 20th century Latino experience."—Michael Wilmington, *Chicago Tribune*

"Two thumbs up for the wonderful *My Family*."—*Siskel & Ebert*

"Full of passion!"—Mike Clark, *USA Today*

Box Office Gross: $11,079,373

One of the patriarchs of the Sanchez family, the fictional family whose story is told in this fine film, has a tombstone that reads, "When I was born here, this was Mexico, and where I rest, this is still Mexico." *My Family; Mi Familia* is a dramatic portrait of the struggles of a Mexican-American family in Los Angeles, where the Hispanic population will eventually outnumber other ethnic populations (and where Hispanic children are already the majority in public schools.) By nature, this is a political film, in that it is one of only a handful of films which deal with the Hispanic (specifically Mexican-American) experience in a major commercial release. One other current film, *The Perez Family*, tells the story of a family of Cuban Americans during the Mariel boatlift. Other than that, the most recent large-scale film by and about Hispanic-Americans was *Bound by Honor* (1994), an uneven film about Mexican-American Los Angelenos.

Mexican-Americans have been represented also on film by last year's low-budget *El Mariachi*, and by the director of *My Family; Mi Familia* (Gregory Nava) with *El Norte* (1985). This handful of films appears to be a paltry number of commercial productions, given the vast numbers of Hispanics in the United States—and given their diversity and cultural influence.

This film provides an historical perspective on Central American immigrants to Southern California while telling a sentimental story of one family's struggles with ordinary and extraordinary events. All audiences who see the film will see their own lives mirrored in the Sanchez family: happiness, tragedy, hope and humor are universal.

The story, spanning sixty years and narrated by Edward James Olmos, begins in the 1920's with young Jose Sanchez (Jacob Vargas) migrating north to find a better life. Different than in director Nava's *El Norte*, Jose's travels north are picturesque and relatively free from travail. The cinematography (by Edward Lachman) and the Production design (by Barry Robison) immediately set the tone of the film, as Jose travels beautiful countryside and happens upon cottages looking as if they were designed for *Architectural Digest*, with hanging corn, attractive furnishings and rich colors. Without appearing too unrealistic, Jose's journey to the United States is a signal to the audience that this film is not gritty or hard-edged, but is a big-budget, open-hearted film illustrating the full texture and color of Latino life in America.

Jose marries beautiful Maria (Jennifer Lopez), and life is good. But after she becomes pregnant with their third child, Maria is rounded up by immigration officials and deported deep into Mexico. This happens even though she is a U.S. citizen, and is an historically accurate depiction of a shameful practice of the Immigration Service. Maria gives birth to their son, Chucho, in Mexico, and returns on foot to the United States—but not without a harrowing sequence in which she and the baby cross a rushing river and get swept up in the rapids. The sequence is beautifully filmed by Nava, with heart-pounding camera shots from the point of view of Maria, reminiscent of the river sequence in D.W. Griffith's *Birth of a Nation* (1919). Somehow Maria and Chucho stay alive and arrive to a tearful reunion with their family in Los Angeles.

At this point, the film jumps to the future: the audience is told that it is "1958 or 1959, mas o menos" (more or less). Chucho (Esai Morales) has now grown up to be "one of the baddest pachucos on the east side" and the oldest daughter, Irina (Maria Canals) is getting married. The wedding provides a wonderful chance for the audience to see the family's interactions: Jose (now played by older actor Eduardo Lopez Rojas) tells the gathering that "a good wife is the best thing that can happen to a man." His daughter Toni (Constance Marie) uses the occasion to tell Maria (now played by Jenny Gago) that she is going to be a nun. And Chucho gets involved in a fight with his sworn enemy, Butch (Michael De Lorenzo). Eventually the animosity between Chucho and Butch leads to Chucho's tragic death at the hands of overzealous policemen.

The film jumps forward again; and now youngest brother, Jimmy (Jimmy Smits) has been in trouble with the law like Chucho, having been scarred for life by Chucho's death. Jimmy's redemption comes in the form of a Salvadoran immigrant, Isabel (Elpidia Carrillo), whom he agrees to marry to keep from being deported. After trying to avoid her, Isabel's persistent attempts to develop a relationship with him lead to Jimmy's discovery that he is in love with her. The scene in which Isabel and Jimmy discover their shared family tragedies is well-acted, particularly by Carrillo: Her expressive face, her sensuality, and her earnestness are just what is needed to draw out the emotional side of Jimmy. As an actor, the normally stoic and unemotional Smits appears to be drawn out by Ms. Carrillo, and the result is that he turns in a credible performance as a man whose life is nearly destroyed by tragedy and sorrow. Smits's later scenes with his young son are less successful, but only because the son is played a bit for sentimentality and not for reality.

With the exception of sister Toni's exodus from the church and marriage to a Caucasian priest (Scott Bakula), the other siblings' stories take a back seat to the struggles of Jimmy and his young son. The youngest brother, Memo (Enrique Castillo) becomes a well-to-do attorney, and in one scene he brings the wealthy Caucasian in-laws to meet his family. The scene is unsuccessful in showing the gap between the wealthy "Wasps" and the working-class Mexicans, ironically, because it tries too hard to illustrate the gap. Memo's father-in-law over-pronounces "taquitos"—apparently the actor's attempt to sound like a gringo, and the mother's fake attempts at friendliness are overplayed even while they are an accurate depiction of the cultural divide. Somehow the oversimplification of their lack of understanding of their son-in-law's culture is so badly overacted that it spoils the reality of the situation.

This is one of only a few problems within this excellent film. Another noticeable problem occurs when Toni brings home her new husband (the former priest). She builds him up through a fine scene in which she describes how wonderful he is, and then goes out to the patio to get him once she informs her bewildered parents of her marriage. When she retrieves him, he turns out to be Scott Bakula. Now, Bakula is an excellent actor. But the problem is that his face is so well-known from television (*Quantum Leap*) as a man who inadvertently "pops up" in a wide variety of situations, that he looks as if he has somehow time-traveled once again, landing amidst this contemporary Mexican-American family. The only other minor quibble with the film is that as time progresses, some characters are played by new actors, and some are not. Where Constance Marie continues to play Toni through middle-age, Lupe Ontiveros takes over for Irina, creating a jarring difference in apparent age between her and her sister. Consistency in the change of actors among all the siblings might have created less confusion and maintained credibility.

Director Nava and his co-author, Anna Thomas have created a fine script which tells their tale with humor and strength. From Maria's fascination with telenovelas (the equivalent of American soap opera) to Chucho's attempts to teach the neighborhood boys how to Mambo as they wash his car, to the numerous family deaths, marriages, and holidays, they bring a real sense of the events which make up the life of a family. Nava is interested in the sentimentality and drama of family life in general, and Mexican-American life in particular: For example, he intercuts scenes of Chucho's death with the family's innocent viewing of an *I Love Lucy* episode.

Several times during the film Jose says something about the importance of family, such as, "I'm happy. A good wife

CREDITS

Jimmy Sanchez: Jimmy Smits
Chucho: Esai Morales
Jose Sanchez (older): Eduardo Lopez Rojas
Maria Sanchez (older): Jenny Gago
Paco Sancez: Edward James Olmos
Toni: Constance Marie

Origin: USA
Released: 1995
Production: Anna Thomas for a Majestic Films, American Playhouse Theatrical Films and American zoetrope presentation; released by New Line Cinema
Direction: Gregory Nava
Screenplay: Gregory Nava and Anna Thomas
Cinematography: Edward Lachman
Editing: Nancy Richardson
Production designer: Barry Robison
Costume design: Tracy Tynan
Casting: Janet Hirschenson, Jane Jenkins
Folkloric music score: Pepe Avila
Orchestral music score: Mark McKenzie
MPAA rating: R
Running Time: 125 minutes

AWARDS AND NOMINATIONS

Academy Awards Nominations 1995: Best Makeup
Independent Spirit Awards Nominations 1996: Best Actor (Smits), Best Supporting Actress (Lopez)

is the best thing that can happen to a man." The "family values" inherent in this film come from Jose's desire to do the best for his family, whether teaching his sons how to harvest corn or fretting about what he will say at his daughter's wedding. Contrary to the rather specious "family values" debate started several years ago with Dan Quayle's remonstrations against single motherhood and revived with the beginning of a new presidential campaign, the family depicted in this film doesn't use buzzwords about values—they live them.

Without avoiding the inherent problems of crime and poverty which affect the Latino community of Los Angeles, Nava has portrayed the people in the best way possible—as real people with real struggles. And he has done so with grace and humanity. The beautiful physical production of this film matches the beauty at the heart of its story, and the excellence of its actors matches the excellence of its technical staff. Bravo.

—Kirby Tepper

The Mystery of Rampo

Overwrought, tedious, audacious and fantastic, *The Mystery of Rampo* is not your average 100 minutes at the movies. It's a beautifully crafted, extravagantly costumed and sumptuously photographed psychological muddle from Japan that mixes fantasy and reality in a confusing swirl of contradictory styles and images. Imagine *Altered States* with grand, elegant sets and subtitles. Unfortunately, the visual feast can't make up for a limp and senseless plot. *The Mystery of Rampo* is a mess, but rarely has there been such a wondrous mess.

Based on a story by legendary Japanese mystery writer Edogawa Rampo, the film is a psychological journey into Rampo's tortured mind and soul, where reality can't compete with vivid imaginings. The writer invented Edogawa Rampo as a pen name to invoke Edgar Allen Poe phonetically, and the real Rampo wrote many popular mysteries. This isn't one of them.

The film opens like a layered onion, with several sheddings of expository skin, including newsreels of 1930s Japanese street scenes, an explanation of the importance of hope chests for Japanese brides, a tour through a library filled with psychology books and Poe works, and a wonderfully delicate animated sequence which lays out Rampo's latest story. It's about an ailing husband who hides from his wife in her large trousseau but inadvertently locks himself in. The wife comes home, hears his cries for help, opens the lid and then closes it again, for good.

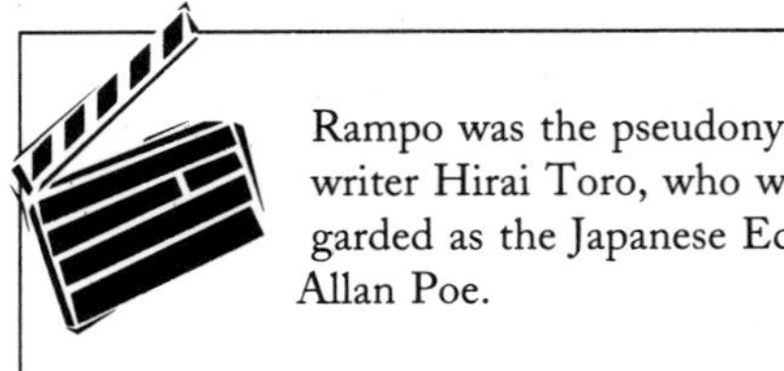

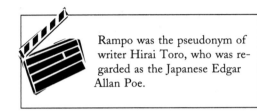

Rampo was the pseudonym of writer Hirai Toro, who was regarded as the Japanese Edgar Allan Poe.

The story is too subversive for the pre-war Japanese government, and we first meet Rampo (Naoto Takenaka) as the censors tell him his work cannot be published. Next he goes to a party for the opening of a popular film based on his more commercial "Phantom with 20 Faces," where he gives a halting, awkward speech. Clearly Rampo is uncomfortable with the social whirl and the bastardizing of his writing into silly, marketable movies. As he leaves the party, he sees visions of a woman beckoning him and silently narrates inexplicable thoughts about being trapped in a "semidarkness." From the start, it's impossible to understand what's bothering Rampo.

His already delicate state of mind is completely disrupted when he is shown a newspaper article about a woman whose husband suffocated to death in a hope chest, just as in his unpublished story. The death is ruled an accident, but many suspect the woman is a murderer. Rampo is told by his literary agent: "The woman you created has taken on the form of a real person." The agent says Rampo is responsible for the woman's fate and must complete her story.

Rampo finds himself entranced with the disarmingly beautiful woman, Shizuko (Michiko Hada), who inexplicably gives him a music box that is her childhood treasure. "I can't write unless I think about you," he confesses to her.

Rampo's psyche spins increasingly out of control. He is beset with visions of Shizuko, troubling premonitions and outrageous hallucinations. He writes a sequel to his story about the woman and the chest. In it, Rampo's dashing young alter ego, Detective Kogoro Akechi (Masahiro Motoki), parachutes onto the estate of the Marquis Ogawara (Mikijiro Hira), who is holding Shizuko as his mistress. The marquis is rich and hideously decadent, dressing up to look like his dead mother and forcing Shizuko to watch pornographic home movies while Akechi peers through an attic window. Akechi wants to rescue Shizuko, but when he does, she turns the tables on him.

When Akechi disobeys the author Rampo's commands, Rampo rushes out into the street and enters his own fantasy world of the marquis' castle. There he finally confronts his own characters, his own story and his feelings for Shizuko. There's a triumphant but murky resolution, but long before that point the film has completely unraveled.

Director Kazuyoshi Okuyama disdains any sort of clarity, always preferring the juxtaposition of troubling, inexplicable images. Actually, there were two directors: Okuyama, the film's producer, took over from Rentaro Mayuzumi and re-shot more than half the film. That's remarkable, because *The Mystery of Rampo* has a distinctive, dizzying style. It's Okuyama's first directorial effort, and it shows promise.

The sets and the actors look like they've stepped out of a 1930s high-class Hollywood mystery. With the men's hair slicked back or hidden under wide-rimmed fedoras and the woman clad in the height of fashion, the performers all have a decidely Western look. The sets, especially at the marquis' castle, are incredibly elegant. The cinematography by Yoshihisa Nakagawa is breathtaking, right down to the smallest detail. Adding to the classic tone of the film is a marvelous waltz score by Akira Senju.

All this richness is a jarring background for Okuyama's bold experimentation. Rampo's hallucinations sometimes appear realistic, sometimes as computer-enhanced animation or special effects, sometimes as stop-action. There is a painterly quality to many scenes, but a distressing incoherence to the whole production.

Dazzling technique is grossly insufficient to carry the film. The acting doesn't help. Takenaka never sheds a hangdog look except for wild, exaggerated expressions of fear and surprise. Hada is beautiful but almost porcelain. Motoki wears a handsome mask that conveys no feeling. The characters are cool and unreachable. They seem overwhelmed by the camera's grandstanding. It is impossible to care about Rampo's dilemma or to understand his feelings for Shizuko; the humans are just more figures on a fantastic cinematic landscape.

Okuyama overuses his visual tricks. The camera's bravado quickly grows wearisome, because it is not used to advance the plot or flesh out the characters. *The Mystery of Rampo* is not a rich story; it is not even a mystery. It is a rather paltry psychological inquiry.

The film attempts to portray a writer whose fictional characters have somehow taken on a life on their own. How or why this happens, or whether it is all a dream of Rampo, is never clear. If it is merely a dream or the hallucinations of a faltering mind, then why should audiences care? And if it is something more, some incredible creative monster that Rampo has unleashed, there is no possible explanation offered. Even Poe, when he stretched the limits of psychic possibilities, grounded his flights of horror in credible reality. That's what makes terror terrifying. Rampo's story is baffling, but worse, it is unmoving and unthreatening.

The Mystery of Rampo at times evokes Ingmar Bergman, at other times Frederico Fellini, and clearly it aspires to the status of Alfred Hitchcock. But merely to suggest with camera tricks the emotional and psychological landscape of those great directors is not to achieve it. Watching *The Mystery of Rampo* is like watching a fireworks display from a great distance away: You can see there is majesty somewhere, but you are never shaken by any explosions. The film is sufficient to intrigue, but it's not enough to inspire awe.

—Michael Betzold

CREDITS

Edogawa Rampo: Naoto Takenaka
Shizuko/Marquis' mistress: Michiko Hada
Kogoro Akechi: Masahiro Motoki
Marquis Ogawara: Mikijiro Hira

Origin: Japan
Released: 1995
Production: Yoshihisa Nakagawa and Yoshinobu Nishioka for a Shochiku and Rampo Project production; released by Samuel Goldwyn
Direction: Kazuyoshi Okuyama
Screenplay: Kazuysohi Okuyama
Cinematography: Yasushi Saskibara
Editing: Akimasa Kawashima
Production design: Kyoko Heya
Music: Akira Senju
MPAA rating: no listing
Running Time: 97 minutes

Nadja

"Visually seductive! Reconfirms the ravishing glamour of the undead."—Kathleen Murphy, *Film Comment*

"A droll, lyrical romance. The movie is oddball, brainy and sensational looking!"—J. Hoberman, *Premiere*

"The lushest film of the year! Shimmering, undulating, exquisite!"—Georgia Brown, *Village Voice*

Nadja is what might have happened if Ingmar Bergman, David Lynch, Dennis Hopper, Roman Polanski, and Quentin Tarantino had all gotten drunk, locked themselves in a room for a couple of weeks and made a vampire movie. Part camp, part pose, part pretentious experimentalism, and part ultra-hip knock-off music video, *Nadja* is a very weird experience. It has some exquisite transcendent moments, hilarious dialogue and an almost feverish disregard for commercial audience expectations.

The director is Michael Almereyda, a cult figure who made the goofy *Twister* (1988) and pioneered the use of the Pixelvision video camera. Here, Almereyda blows up his Pixelvision to 35 millimeters, producing the kind of images that you get when you look through the beveled glass of a shower door. The grainy, cloudy Pixelvision sequences are at first extremely intriguing, and some are remarkable, but Almereyda uses them far too often and they become tiresome. So does his film, but not until it's taken you on a very strange trip.

Lynch is the producer, and *Nadja* shares the look of his early efforts, particularly *Eraserhead* and *The Elephant Man*. It's a dark, brooding tour of a dark, brooding urban landscape with a lot of throbbing, mechanical pulsating music on the soundtrack. Lynch even shows up in a cameo as a morgue security guard.

Almeredya loves jarring juxtapositions of image and word, and with his wacky dialogue, he provides plenty of comic relief, so much so that the whole film seems to be a spoof. At other times, it's so serious that it must be spoofing itself. Either way, it doesn't all add up. Maybe it's not meant to. Certainly it's meant to push the envelope of cinema, and at times it succeeds in doing so in spite of the most hackneyed of all film plots, the vampire story, as its driving force.

Of course, *Nadja* provides plenty of twists on the familiar Transylvanian tale. Its title character, played with laser-like intensity and cool sensuality by Elina Lowensohn, is Dracula's daughter. Nadja is a nineties kind of vampire, jaded, unhappy with her meaningless one-night bloodsucking stands in New York City, and looking for ways both to reconcile with and escape from her family heritage. "I want to simplify my life," she explains drolly.

It's the first of many laugh lines, all spoken in perfect deadpan, that exploit the satiric possibilities of pairing New Age psychobabble with a vampire movie. Nadja, you see, is really just the prototypical lost child of the ultimate dysfunctional family, doomed to acting out old rituals or struggling in vain to escape them. Almeredya gets plenty of mileage from pairing vampirism with this satirical view of the psychology of modern life. When Nadja's brother Edgar (Jared Harris) gets a mental transmission from Nadja, he explains it's like receiving "a psychic fax." When Nadja holds a pet tarantula and its owner says "I tried to teach him French, but he wasn't interested," Nadja replies, "Maybe he has a learning disability."

The neat thing about being a young vampiress in modern America is that you don't need a disguise. Nadja vamps in a traditional black cape with a huge hood, a totally hip costume that blends right in to the scene. Nobody gives her any quizzical glances. In fact, at one point the film suggests that many of the denizens of the modern world are of vampire heritage. Unfortunately, *Nadja* never explores the science-fiction ramifications of that suggestion.

CREDITS

Cassandra: Suzy Amis
Lucy: Galaxy Craze
Jim: Martin Donovan
Dr. Van Helsing: Peter Fonda
Renfield: Karl Geary
Edgar: Jared Harris
Nadja: Elina Lowensohn
Morgue security guard: David Lynch

Origin: USA
Released: 1995
Production: Mary Sweeney and Amy Hobby for a Kino Link production; released by October Films
Direction: Michael Almereyda
Screenplay: Michael Almereyda
Cinematography: Jim Denault
Editing: David Leonard
Production design: Kurt Ossenfort
Casting: Billy Hopkins, Suzanne Smith and Kerry Barden
Costume design: Prudence Moriarty
Sound: William Kozy
Music: Simone Fisher Turner
MPAA rating: R
Running Time: 95 minutes

Nadja's spiritual counterpart is Lucy (Galaxy Craze), an insecure, vaguely troubled young woman. Lucy and her husband Jim love each other but both suffer from anomie and complain a lot about not feeling connected. They are spiritual lost souls in need of awakening. Lucy meets Nadja in a bar and they share their troubled family past. Nadja conceals her identity, but reveals that her father has died. Drunk and mesmerized by Nadja's intensity, Lucy confesses that her parents left her life long ago and that her only brother committed suicide. Nadja reveals that she is looking for her brother, who lives in Brooklyn, hates her and wants to die too.

"He was like Elvis in the end. The magic was gone."—Dr. Van Helsing explains to nephew Jim what Dracula was like before his death

Nadja's father, the notorious fiend, has been killed, apparently for keeps, by Jim's uncle, Dr. Van Helsing (Peter Fonda), a vampire hunter who uses the traditional method: a stake through the heart. He explains that Dracula wasn't all that hard to dispatch because he was worn out by his centuries of evildoing: "He was like Elvis in the end, tired and jaded. The magic was gone." Van Helsing has long, stringy hair and rides a bicycle. Jim and Lucy have always thought of Van Helsing as being off his rocker, but he gradually convinces Jim his words are not the ravings of a maniac but the wisdom of an enlightened student of vampire history.

Fonda makes Van Helsing loony, but not loony enough. A more obvious choice for the part would have been Hopper, Fonda's old road buddy from *Easy Rider*. Hopper would have put Van Helsing over the top, where he belongs. As Fonda plays him, he becomes practically the voice of reason compared to the other lunatics in the story.

When Nadja seduces Lucy and takes over her body, the film is at its most riveting, their lovemaking shot in Pixelvision on Lucy's floor besides a Christmas tree. The next morning, Lucy turns cold to Jim and then malevolent. In the film's most hilarious scene, Lucy mimics Nadja's soliloquy about "the pain of fleeting joy," Jim embraces her, and she throws him along the bar like a cowboy would heave a rustler. Except for Van Helsing, the men in this film are much weaker than women. As Van Helsing explains it to Jim, that's because women menstruate: "Their bodies let them know that nature is one continuous disaster."

This repulsion for the body and aspiration to a higher, less physical plane is one of the subtexts of the film, which flowers fully at the very end. Nadja, confronted with her brother's illness, lectures on how the human body is a clumsy, messy contraption compared to the perfect balance of a plant. It's hard to know whether such messages are meant to be taken seriously in the midst of so much droll satire.

Almereyda's script gradually provides a few more surprises and characters. Van Helsing suggests to Jim that he's really his father, not his uncle. Edgar's nurse, Cassandra (Suzy Amis), turns out to be Van Helsing's daughter and therefore Jim's sister. Renfield (Karl Geary), who at first appears to be Nadja's brother or perhaps her lover, turns out to be her Irish-born slave. But while the family knots get tighter, the plot gets looser and less compelling, turning into a fairly routine quest by Van Helsing and Jim to stop Nadja from taking over Lucy and Cassandra. In the end, the vampire-hunters chase Nadja and Cassandra to her Transylvanian castle, spending way too much time in the basement.

There are two stars to the film: Lowensohn and Almereyda's bold technique. Lowensohn is compelling, ghastly and beautiful all at once, a powerful presence. Almereyda veers between fits of brilliance and boring stretches of self-conscious auteurism. There's too much Pixelvision and not enough drama. And the script revels so much in its own deadpan wit that it becomes cute. Worst of all, *Nadja* occasionally succumbs to commercial temptation (target audience: hip Generation-Xers) and lapses into a feature-length version of a music video (the soundtrack is heavy-metal alternative).

What ends up rendering *Nadja* less than illuminating is that it's actually fairly bloodless, despite all the pretense and the bloodsucking. Except for Lowensohn, it's rarely hot stuff. In fact, it's ice-cold; the experimental style keeps its characters at a long arm's distance from the audience. The film neither frightens nor enlightens, and it only sporadically entertains. But it would be hard to imagine a more bizarre undertaking, and those who relish offbeat filmmaking definitely must see *Nadja.* It takes vampire films, and film in general, into some strange corners.

—Michael Betzold

REVIEWS

Daily Variety, Sept. 19, 1994.
The New York Times. Aug. 28, 1995, p. C5.
The Village Voice. Aug. 29, 1995, p. 51.

National Lampoon's Senior Trip

"Four score and seven beers ago...They came. They saw. They passed out."—Movie tagline

Who says there aren't any old-fashioned movies anymore? *National Lampoon's Senior Trip* is about as retrograde as they come. This lame, moronic film seems to be stuck in a time warp. Except for the inclusion of a few rap songs, it appears to have been made in 1970, stuck in a time capsule, and then released a quarter-century later.

The loose plot concerns a group of dopers and slackers who pass for the senior class at Fairmont High, somewhere in Ohio. When they blame the government and the education system for their own failings, their principal suggests they draft a letter to the President. It's supposed to be punishment, but the President sees the letter as a chance to push his educational reform bill, and a rival Senator, after visiting Fairmont and discovering how loathsome the students are, decides to use their visit as a way to embarrass the President.

This so-called plot is nothing but an excuse to get the gang of teen trash onto a bus and head to Washington. And the trip is nothing more than an excuse to party, though this gang doesn't need much of an excuse.

The anachronisms in this film are astounding. Chief among them is that relic of the 1960s drug culture, Tommy Chong, of the stoned comic duo Cheech & Chong. Chong plays a bandana-wearing bus driver named Red, who inexplicably shows up to drive the school bus to D.C. Red calls his vehicle "the magic bus," puts the principal into a coma by giving him a horse tranquilizer, chugs the tranquilizers himself to no effect, and eventually pulls out a bong the size of a howitzer, passes out, and drives the bus into the woods, pursued by cops. Those in the audience over 40 have seen this all before, in another life.

As in many youth-oriented films circa 1970, *Senior Trip* sees senior citizens as inherently addled and senile. There's a befuddled teacher who strolls the halls in a walker. There's a typing teacher who dies of a heart attack during class, and none of the students notice.

Other targets are familiar and easy ones. At a school assembly, an Up-With-People group attempts to sing "Put A Little Love in Your Heart," a song long past its prime as an object of ridicule. There's a straight-arrow class president, a squeaky-clean, annoyingly perky teacher (Valerie Mahaffey), a fastidious principal (Matt Frewer), and, of course, the brainy class virgin who longs to be part of the "in" crowd.

The "in" crowd is led by a Pauly Shore clone, Dags (Jeremy Renner) and his stoner buddy Reggie (Rob Moore). They are adored by the obligatory Fat Kid, Milosky (Eric Edwards), along with a nerd nicknamed Virus, the open-bloused class slut, and another girl whose hair covers her face. Completing the group and the demographics are an astute, stand-offish black student and a mini-skirted lesbian, each of whom have little to do in the film.

The only inventive touch in the film involves a crazed pursuit of the students by a wacko crossing guard (Kevin McDonald), a "Trekkie" who has an inflatable "Star Trek" officer-doll as a sidekick. This guy commandeers a van driven by a family of Japanese tourists and eventually is torched by an eternal flame in Arlington Cemetery.

Someone forgot to tell director Kelly Makin and screenwriters Roger Kumble and I. Marlene King that teenage drinking and drugs are no longer funny, even to most high school sophomores. Makin, Kumble and King could be pseudonyms; it's hard to believe anyone would use a real name to claim credit for this film. The whole undertaking seems wrapped in an air of profound indifference. There's no regard for logic. The nine students in the ensemble seem to be the only students in Fairmont High. The bus trip takes place mostly on two-lane country roads, as if the interstate

CREDITS

Principal Todd Moss: Matt Frewer
Miss Tracey Milford: Valerie Mahaffey
Sen. John Lerman: Lawrence Dane
Red: Tommy Chong
Dags: Jeremy Renner
Reggie: Rob Moore
Milosky: Eric "Sparky" Edwards
Travis Lindsey: Kevin McDonald

Origin: USA
Released: 1995
Production: Wendy Grean for an Alliance production; released by New Line Cinema
Direction: Kelly Makin
Screenplay: Roger Kumble and I. Marlene King
Cinematography: Francios Protat
Editing: Stephen Lawrence
Production design: Gregory Keen
Art direction: John Dondertman
Casting: Ross Clydesdale
Costume design: Sharon Purdy
Sound: Tom Hidderley
Music: Steve Bartek
MPAA rating: R
Running Time: 91 minutes

freeway system hadn't been built yet. Inexplicably, the President sits on a Senate committee panel and the villainous Senator seems to have the power to fire principals employed by local school systems. Strangest of all is how the kids finally win the day in Washington. They fall on their faces, but the congressmen inappropriately applaud them. It's the lamest of resolutions.

Actually, *Senior Trip* is vastly inferior to most of the counter-culture films of the 1960s it tries to imitate. There is no political consciousness or message in *Senior Trip*, it's just one big party. And it's not even a very creative, psychedelic or interesting party. In fact, there's very little real rock-and-rolling and, aside from the rather stilted and unattractive come-ons of the class slut, there's not even any dangerous lust or forbidden sex. It's just the kind of party where the participants drink a lot and pass out. If you're at the stage in life where passing out is hilarious, then you should definitely see this film. Otherwise, don't bother.

Despite being hampered by the absurd plot, Frewer and Mahaffey do bring some comic life to their characters as the adult foils. Frewer is good at being an object of derision and a physical clown, while Mahaffey is hilariously saccharine. McDonald brings a needed crazed quality to his strange role as the Trekkie, a character whose behavior has no rhyme or reason but adds some diversion.

Senior Trip could have used a lot more craziness. For a film marketed at disaffected youth, it is in fact quite tame. It has its share of the customary jokes involving bodily functions, but it is not nearly as rude or crude as many Z-grade films targeted at teens. That seems to be not from any attempt at respectability, but rather mostly from lack of effort.

The only saving grace of *Senior Trip* is that it has at times a sort of deadpan, low-key silliness. In its customary retrograde way, at its best moments it seems to compare to the kind of gags found in old Mad magazines: the typing-class student who appears to be hard at work but who is writing over and over again: "I hate my life, the world is a joke;" the girl whose face is hidden by her hair; the principal locked in a rest room with an overflowing toilet; the fat kid's strange desire to make love to a blonde-haired Asian woman, who then materializes in a hotel lobby; and the class visit to J. Edgar Hoover's grave, because, as the principal explains, "You kids don't deserve Kennedy."

The filmmakers also don't deserve any encouragement. The National Lampoon imprimatur has seen better days. The drug culture has spawned better movies. Consider this: *Senior Trip* is as laughably out-of-date as a World War II movie would have been in 1970. The halcyon doper days are long gone, folks. Give it a rest.

—Michael Betzold

REVIEWS

Boxoffice. November 1995, p. R-101.
New York Times. Sept. 9, 1995, p. 12.
USA Today. Sept. 11, 1995, p. 4D.
Variety. Sept. 11, 1995, p.105.

The Neon Bible

"Sheer emotional power. Gena Rowlands is superb."—Geoff Andrews, *Time Out*

"Magical...Davies makes rarefied, mysteriously beautiful movies."—Georgia Brown, *The Village Voice*

An overwhelming aura of melancholy and despair enshrouds this haunting tale of a young boy growing up during the 40's in rural Mississippi. Terence Davies, director and writer of *The Neon Bible*, has adapted his screenplay from the novel by Pulitzer Prize winning author John Kennedy Toole.

The film centers around the memories of a 15-year old boy as he travels on a train through the moonlit night. The boy, David (Jacob Tierney), remembers Christmas when he was three, and with that memory David's story slowly, although not necessarily in order of occupance, begins to unfold.

David and his family live in an isolated and claustrophic world where books are burned, otherness is ostracized, and any display of frail humanity is banned. His parents are poor Southerners, and when his father loses his job in the local factory, they become even poorer.

Their hard life is made a little lighter when David's Aunt Mae (Gena Rowlands), an aging nightclub singer, comes to live with them. Mae's last gig in a dive drove her from the stage and into the Bible beating arms of her relatives, who judge her more as a sinner than a commercial failure.

Mae tries to fit into the Bible Belt community, but is shunned for her worldly ways, and she seeks company in little David, becoming his closest companion and making David's world a little less narrow and infinitely less serious because of her influence.

But Aunt Mae is no Auntie Mame, and Rowlands plays a woman who has been around the block one too many times with a subtlety and sympathy that is sheer brilliance. In this desperate and sometimes violent household, Mae manages to retain her unwavering faith in life and in herself, and David's life is made richer because of her.

In a town where ignorance, poverty, and bigotry color their everyday life, it is no wonder that not much light enters the townspeople's lives. The only light that is not forbidden is the light of Jesus and during an evangelist's tent show the townsfolk grab it with both hands.

The only levity in David's life comes while the men are away during the war. The women in the town who work at the local war plant decide to have a dance. There Mae is asked to sing, and for the first time she is loved and respected by her community. That moment of harmony doesn't last long, but it is enough to get Mae back on track with her singing career.

When the war ends, the men return—and inevitably, some come home in coffins. There is a memorable scene in the film where coffins covered with American flags are lined up at the train station as the soundtrack to "Gone With The Wind" plays in the background.

David's father, Frank (Denis Leary), is among the dead. He has died in Italy, where he is buried, and his wife, Sarah (Diana Scarwid), breaks under the pressure of her loss and slowly disintegrates into madness.

Meanwhile Mae is now the sole breadwinner, and she works nights singing with a band at weddings and other events. When David graduates from grade school, he also goes to work in the town drugstore to help support the dwindling family.

One day Mae finally gets her big break, and she leaves on a bus for Nashville to do some radio singing. Mae leaves David to care for Sarah, now hopelessly insane, and tells him that she will send for him in a week or two. But Mae was the magnet that held the family together, and when she leaves, Sarah commits suicide and David goes into a panic.

Unaware that Sarah is dead, the preacher comes to take David's mother to the lunatic asylum, and the distraught boy gets out the shotgun and kills the unsuspecting reverend. To escape the police, and perhaps also his dreary life, David grabs the first train out of town to anywhere, and that's where we find him when the film opens and when it ends.

Toole, the author of the original novel, whose two novels *A Confederacy of Dunces* and *The Neon Bible* were both published posthumously, committed suicide at thirty-one. His mother found the novels and published the former, but *The Neon Bible* went into a legal battle for rights after the huge success of Toole's first book. It wasn't released for publication until after the death of Toole's mother in 1984, when a New Orleans judge forced the various parties into making a settlement.

Although Toole was a New Orleans native, when he was fifteen he had spent a few days visiting a classmate in Mississippi, and by the time he was sixteen he had completed the novel about life there. It is written through the eyes of a fifteen-year-old boy and its autobiographical perspective and frequent use of the song lyrics of the time make it the perfect vehicle for

Adapted from the autobiographical novel of then 16-year-old American southern, John Kennedy Toole, who became posthumously famous for his novel *A Confederacy of Dunces.*

director Terence Davies. But the similarities don't end there. Davies, whose autobiographical films are of that same period, portrayed his own family, whose dynamics closely resembled David's. Both were ruled by a violent father, raised by women, and crushed under the stultifying effects of the church. *The Neon Bible* appears to have been written for Davies.

During the shooting of the film, Davies in an interview with *The Village Voice* (July 26, 1994) said, "I said to the producers what I have said to everyone who has approached me about doing something that was not autobiographical. If I see it visually, then I'll do it, . . . I read it in a single sitting because the opening is so cinematic. And I knew where the camera should be. And I said yes, I'll do it."

Director Davies, best known for his *Distant Voices, Still Lives* (1988), has again relied heavily on the use of music to evoke moods and emotions, and has successfully created a dreamy atmosphere as a backdrop for David's memories. His non-linear storytelling can be wearing, but at the same time it puts forth an interesting perspective on the nature of memory itself. He portrays memory as if it were surfacing in our own minds, with no preface, simply the distillation of experience into an essence—an act of violence, a tender moment, a deep sadness—memories that surface almost of their own will. And as David's mind wanders, we get to understand his life better than if we were restricted to a chronological storyline.

CREDITS

Aunt Mae: Gena Rowlands
David at 15: Jacob Tierney
Sarah: Diana Scarwid
Frank: Denis Leary
David at 10: Drake Bell

Origin: USA and Great Britain
Released: 1995
Production: Elizabeth Karlsen and Olivia Stewart for a Miramax International, Channel Four Films and Scala Films production; released by Miramax
Direction: Terence Davies
Screenplay: Terence Davies; based on the novel by John Kennedy Toole
Cinematography: Mick Coulter
Editing: Charles Rees
Production design: Christopher Hobbs
Art direction: Phil Messina
Costume design: Monica Howe
Sound: Thomas Varga
Casting: Laura Rosenthal
Music: Robert Lockhart
MPAA rating: not listed
Running Time: 92 minutes

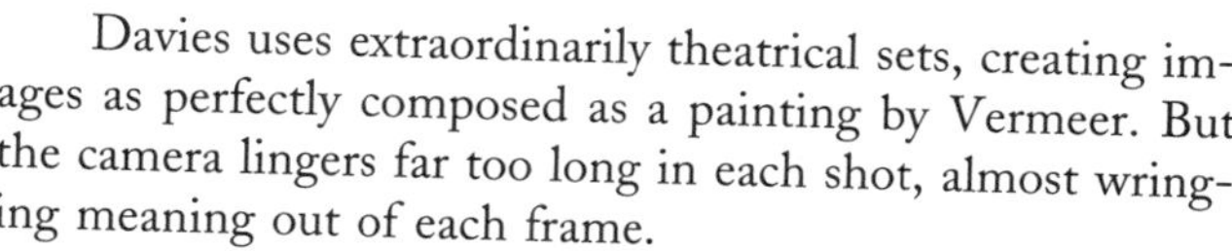

Davies uses extraordinarily theatrical sets, creating images as perfectly composed as a painting by Vermeer. But the camera lingers far too long in each shot, almost wringing meaning out of each frame.

Director of photography Mick Coulter's camera work is exquisite, and whether the scene is moonlit or sunlit, the lighting in this film is phenomenal. One scene has a five-year-old David (Drake Bell) facing the star cluttered night, and we watch as he morphs into a fifteen-year-old. It is pristine and magical and the theatrics add to that magic.

Gena Rowland brings to the film a genuineness and a depth of feeling that is spellbinding. Ms. Rowlands makes excellent use of the lingering camera shots, her face expressing every nuance—looking old and tired in one shot, miraculously vibrant and glamourous in the next.

Diana Scarwid plays David's mother, Sarah. In the film Davies has given the character a far stronger role than she had in the novel, where she was a shadowy presence at best. Sarah's madness is practically Ophelian in the film, escalating from the moment she receives the telegram of her husband's death to a scene where she sings an Irish lullaby while scratching at flies on a screen door, and eventually leading to her suicide.

Davies captures the tenor of this small family's isolated lives wonderfully, but he has included a few scenes that ring false: a KKK lynching, a scene Davies created out of whole cloth, lacks feeling; a scene of a book burning suffers the same emptiness; and the tent meeting scene starts well but evolves into a theatrical contrivance.

The scene begins powerfully with the whole town coming out to go to the religious revival. Davies follows the people walking in their Sunday best toward the tent, their voices raised in hymn. At first there are only a few people, then more and more join them until the street is full, and the holiday atmosphere is practically infectious. But once within the tent, the meeting proceeds like a stilted theatrical device and the moment is lost, its power diminishing into stale artifice.

Davies' film is as sorrowful as its score, which is disappointing, coming from a novel that is so artless and ingenuous. Another problem lies in the pace of the film, which lags at times, minimizing the emotional impact of the film. And despite the beauty of *The Neon Bible* and the excellent performance by Rowlands, there is a lack of emotional connec-

REVIEWS

Daily Variety, May 24, 1995, p. 10.
Hollywood Reporter, May 24, 1995, p. 5.
The Nation, June 26, 1995, p. 936.
The New York Times, October 2, 1995, p. C14.
The Observer (London), October 8, 1995, p.?.
Screen International, June 9, 1995, p.?.
Sight and Sound, October 1995, p.?.
Village Voice, July 26, 1994, p. 54.

tion to David. The boy emotes only twice, so it is difficult to see him as a person; he is more of a wraith passing through the scenes, not touching or being touched by them. With this characterization, the ending seems out of place. It is hard to believe such violence could erupt from a child who has been portrayed throughout the film as a passive poetic figure.

We are left a bit incredulous, which is not a good way to leave a film. Last impressions tend to be lasting, and the final half hour of *The Neon Bible* prejudices the viewer against the film, nullifying the beauty and sensitivity of the hour that proceeded it.

—Diane Hatch-Avis

The Net

"Her driver's license. Her credit cards. Her bank accounts. Her identity...Deleted."—Movie tagline

"An enjoyably creepy thriller...it gives the old story of a wrongly accused innocent a nervewracking 90's twist."—Caryn James, *The New York Times*

"*The Net* is one terrific ride; a skillful blend of edge-of-your-seat suspense, wry humor and a story that looms chillingly real."—Alan Silverman, *Voice of America*

"A high-tech thriller from start to finish."—Bill Diehl, *WBAI Radio*

Box Office Gross: $50,727,965

Sandra Bullock stars as Angela Bennett, a computer systems analyst who becomes caught in a web of intrigue and conspiracy when she accidentally taps into a classified program, in *The Net*. © 1995 Columbia Pictures Industries, Inc. All rights reserved.

Some people will see this computer-oriented thriller as the next logical step in film suspense; some will see it as a film whose technically-inspired storyline is a lukewarm rip-off of several old-style films. *The Net* is actually both, and if audiences are willing to suspend their disbelief enough to realize not all films have to be brilliant to be enjoyable, they will have fun.

Giving a generous nod to some of Alfred Hitchcock's themes, screenwriters John Brancato and Michael Ferris and director Irwin Winkler have fashioned a story about an innocent woman caught up in a dangerous series of events. Angela Bennett (Bullock) is a computer whiz, a "hacker" of the first order who spends all day and evening at her computer, hooked up to the Internet. She has virtually no life outside of her computer, earning a living by evaluating new software systems and troubleshooting viruses through her modem. She almost never leaves the house (even ordering her meals through the net) except to visit her Alzheimer's-stricken mother in a rest home. Angela encounters trouble when she takes her first vacation in several years in Mexico. A friend on the "net" asks if her trip is business or pleasure and she responds, "is there a difference?" But it turns out not to be all pleasure.

Meeting the debonair Jack Devlin (Jeremy Northam), Angela can't believe that she's found someone who is attractive, interested in computers, and sensitive. In fact, he is exactly the combination of traits she wishes for in an earlier discussion on the "net" (she describes her ideal man as "butch, beautiful, and brilliant...Captain America meets Albert Schweizer.") Audiences who have seen more than a couple of films in their day will quickly realize what's happening: Jack works for some sort of shady company that's trying to keep Angela from finding out information that will stop their business. He has taken information about her from the Internet and plans to eliminate her. She unwittingly holds the key—a 3 1/2 inch floppy disk that could keep a group of software terrorists (called the Praetorians) from taking over the United States.

Eventually, Angela's complete identity is erased from any and all computer files—from the DMV to the bank—and, without the aid of anyone, she must recover her identity, unlock the secret of the Praetorians, and save the Internet for posterity. If it sounds a bit like a computer game, it is probably not coincidental. The notion of Angela's identity being erased is played as if it were completely plausible. Bullock's mixture of strength and vulnerability make her an interesting protagonist and a fine heir to other "innocent bystander" stories such as *North by Northwest* (1959) or *The Man Who Knew Too Much* (1956). (Granted, *The Net* is not in the league of those Hitchcock classics, but its story is fun nonetheless.)

It is interesting to note that those Hitchcock films were popular during the days of the cold war, when the fears of a communist takeover were very real in America, causing many Americans to feel that their identity was threatened by the possibility of Communism. In these post-cold war days, when "big government" has become the latest American villain, it is not surprising that the mythology of the Internet has made it to the big screen, since the Internet is often thought of as a monolithic entity with supernatural powers. With many politicians clamoring for new types of censorship, and many people fearing that the Internet was created to "computerize" our private lives, it is inevitable that the Internet itself would become a cinematic villain, just as Communism did in the fifties. This, of course, is not the first time that computers have been integral to a film's story: *2001, A Space Odyssey* (1968), *War Games* (1983), the recent *Disclosure* (1994), and others have had computers at the core of their plots.

Irwin Winkler has more seriously (but less successfully) touched on related territory in *Guilty by Suspicion* (1991), in which Robert De Niro starred as a man whose life is ruined by McCarthyism in the fifties. This time, Winkler has made a film that feeds on cultural paranoia instead of condemning it. Like McCarthyism, this film thrives because of its willingness to only ask the questions that fuel its fears. For example, it seems implausible that Bullock's character would not know anyone at all except her former psychiatrist/lover (played by Dennis Miller). It seems unlikely that someone as beautiful, witty and smart as Angela knows literally no one who can identify her, or that she has no place to go. Doesn't she go to the store, or to the doctor (besides an unscrupulous psychiatrist), or even to the gym?

Of course, Winkler and company are making a thematic point and creating fiction. To take it too literally would be missing the point, and missing out on the fun. The point is, as Angela states, that "computers are a perfect hiding place," and perhaps *The Net* is meant to capitalize on (while acknowledging the dangers of) our increasingly isolated society. It is a simple thriller, and shouldn't be judged as if it were *Hamlet*. But other films, such as *A Clear and Present Danger* (1994), or even the simpler *War Games*, solved the audience's questions in order to make the storyline more believable—and therefore more thrilling.

None of this ruins the film though, or renders it anything less than fast-paced and entertaining. Sometimes reminiscent of *The Fugitive* (1993), it is fun to watch Bullock try to figure out just who is after her and why. One scene in which Angela avoids her stalkers in an AIDS march in San Francisco is reminiscent of Harrison Ford's escape into a St. Patrick's day parade in *The Fugitive*. Some of the suspenseful moments are wonderfully done, particularly a scene in which Jack takes Angela out on a boat, intending to kill her. Scrambling to get away in a lifeboat before Jack catches her, Bullock is excellent and the scene is taut and exciting. Another tense scene where Angela "cracks the code" while her stalkers are unwittingly several feet from her at another office "workstation" is excellent.

Winkler keeps the action moving at a fine pace, utilizing some standard film scenes such as the aforementioned parade, or the climactic scene which takes place in the vast catacombs of a convention center. Many films seem to end with a climactic fight in a warehouse-style setting such as *Terminator II* (1990), and Winkler uses this standard effectively. He handles several scenes at a computer convention in the cavernous George Moscone Convention Center with the same clarity and precision as he does with the more intimate scenes involving Bullock and Northam or Miller.

The dialogue is also effective in creating an atmosphere of authentic high-technology: "just a flex key shift that sent

CREDITS

Angela Bennett: Sandra Bullock
Jack Devlin: Jeremy Northam
Dr. Alan Champion: Dennis Miller
Mrs. Bennett: Diane Baker
Imposter: Wendy Gazelle
Bergstrom: Ken Howard
Dale: Ray McKinnon

Origin: USA
Released: 1995
Production: Irwin Winkler and Rob Cowan; released by Columbia Pictures
Direction: Irwin Winkler
Screenplay: John Brancato and Michael Ferris
Cinematography: Jack N. Green
Editing: Richard Halsey
Production design: Dennis Washington
Art direction: Tom Targownik
Set design: Ann Harris
Costume design: Linda Bass
Sound: Richard Lightstone
Special effects: Dale L. Martin
Computer consultation: Todd Aron Marks
Music: Mark Isham
MPAA rating: PG-13
Running Time: 112 minutes

you a wrong Internet address, that's all," says Bullock to a client. Later, the dialogue helps the audience understand what is going on: "dammit Devlin, it's a virus eating through the mainframe, everything will be destroyed!" Perhaps this will be agonizingly simple for sophisticated computer users, but it helps the uninitiated to understand the accompanying visual images of complicated computer screens and texts.

Sandra Bullock has, with this year's *While You Were Sleeping*, broken through to become a big box-office star. An article in the *Los Angeles Times* on August 8, 1995 describes her as one of six "bankable" female stars. The term "bankable" obviously means that she can "open" a film (i.e., be responsible for getting audiences to buy tickets on the film's opening weekend.) *Speed* (1994) catapulted her to join Barbra Streisand, Demi Moore, and others on the "bankable" list. Bullock's "bankability" seems to be well-earned, for her talent and charisma turn *The Net* into a film worth watching.

Bullock is a consistently engaging heroine throughout. She plays Angela as a gullible and introverted woman who, if she weren't so attractive, might be believable as someone who actually had made no impression on anyone in her lifetime. Bullock played a character with an identity problem in *While You Were Sleeping* (1995) as well; her vulnerability is well-suited to a woman who needs to "find herself." Her relationship to the psychiatrist seems believable (if a bit sad), especially when she says "I forgot he was a shrink; he forgot he was married." Occasionally, Bullock is asked to do things that make Angela almost beg to be a victim: why does she treat the psychiatrist with such tenderness?

As the psychiatrist, Dennis Miller is well-cast in a questionable role. Miller fulfills his role as the quintessential slick character who has a heart of gold. Unfortunately, it is hard to view any psychiatrist who has affairs with his patients, breaks confidentiality, and dispenses medication illegally, as anything but a jerk.

Though it is a difficult story to believe, though all the story holes are not filled, and though there are a few stock characters and situations, the film is successful. It has classy production credits, a wonderful leading lady, and a great villain: that scary Internet.

—*Kirby Tepper*

REVIEWS

Weekly Variety. July 24-30, 1995. p. 69

Never Talk to Strangers

"In a world where love isn't always safe, trust can be deadly."—Movie tagline

"De Mornay's perfect, Miller's funny, Banderas is mysterious and sexy, the suspense is getting tighter and tighter."—Stephen Hunter, *Baltimore Sun*

"*Never Talk to Strangers* emerges as a genuine sleeper, appropriately creepy..."—Joe Baltake, *Sacramento Bee*

Box Office Gross: $6,849,998

When Dr. Sarah Taylor (Rebecca De Mornay) was a little girl, her mother warned her "never talk to strangers," as most mothers do, but the irony is that Sarah was molested as a child not by strangers but by her own father, Henry Taylor (Len Cariou). When her mother found out, she confronted Henry and scuffled with him on an upstairs landing; the mother was knocked down the stairs, and then shot by her little girl, at her father's insistence, to cover up the father's guilt. It's hard to believe that the child would have followed her father's orders, but this screenplay features much that is hard to believe.

This nasty bit of domestic violence became a repressed memory for the disturbed child, who grew up and took advanced degrees in psychiatry, specializing in multiple personalities. All of this psychological background is likewise "repressed" in *Never Talk to Strangers*, as scripted by Lewis Green and Jordan Rush and directed by Peter Hall.

When Henry comes to New York City from Albany to visit his daughter, Sarah remembers enough to be wary. She sends him to a motel rather than inviting him to stay at her flat. To a viewer who does not yet know her case history, this seems odd, unfeeling behavior. She calls her father Henry, not "dad." She seems oddly repressed and unloving.

As a consequence of this blocked memory, Sarah does not get along well with men. One relationship ended when her lover simply disappeared. Her neighbor Cliff Raddison (Dennis Miller) constantly makes passes at her, but these are consistently rejected. Cliff does not seem to be threatening but merely a hedonistic, simpering, sensitive male of the 1990s.

Sarah is an apparent workaholic, serving as a legal consultant for a case involving a serial killer named Max Cheski (Harry Dean Stanton), who clearly does not trust her. She thinks he is a victim of multiple-personality syndrome, her speciality. She is tough in all of her relationships with men.

> "Do I look like the kind of woman who can be bought with a good vintage?"—Psychologist Sarah to Tony from *Never Talk To Strangers*

Her defensive resistance weakens one night, however, as she is shopping at a local market and a dark, handsome stranger, Tony Ramirez (Antonio Banderas), attempts to give her advice. "Do you think you can buy me with a bottle of wine?" she asks, curtly. "No, I think you have to be won," Tony responds winningly.

Certainly, Tony knows how to charm. When Sarah tells him her mother's advice about never talking to strangers, he advises: "If you never talk to strangers, you'll never make any friends." Sarah is a loner and also apparently lonesome. Since she finds him attractive, she gives him her telephone number and later meets him at his loft apartment. He seems to be winning her, but she knows nothing, really, about him.

CREDITS

Dr. Sarah Taylor: Rebecca DeMornay
Tony Ramirez: Antonio Banderas
Cliff Raddison: Dennis Miller
Henry Taylor: Len Cariou
Max Cheski: Harry Dean Stanton
Dudakoff: Eugene Lipinski
Maura: Martha Burns

Origin: USA
Released: 1995
Production: Andras Hamori, Jeffrey R. Neuman and Martin J. Wiley for an Alliance production; released by TriStar Pictures
Direction: Peter Hall
Screenplay: Lewis Green and Jordan Rush
Cinematography: Elemer Ragalyi
Editing: Roberto Silvi
Set decoration: Richard Paris
Costume design: Terry Dresbach
Visual effects: Jon Campfen
Production design: Linda Del Rosario and Richard Paris
Sound effects: Jane Tattersall and David McCallum
Special effects: Frank Carere
Music: Pino Donaggio
MPAA rating: R
Running Time: 102 minutes

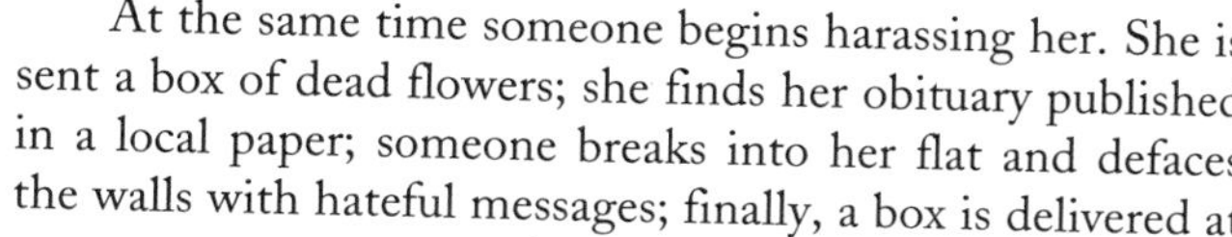

At the same time someone begins harassing her. She is sent a box of dead flowers; she finds her obituary published in a local paper; someone breaks into her flat and defaces the walls with hateful messages; finally, a box is delivered at her door containing her mutilated cat. This latter event really begins to send her around the bend. With Tony's help she begins to practice target-shooting.

Sarah hires a private eye to check up on Tony, about whom she knows nothing, other than that he is Puerto Rican and an expert in security who has to make business trips to Boston from time to time. The private eye follows him on one of these trips and finds that he has gone not to Boston, but to Albany. The investigator also concludes that Tony has a wife and daughter.

Sarah then goes to Tony's apartment and finds documents and clippings from Albany concerning her past. She has reason, apparently, to be worried, but Tony protests that he is not married and loves her, a believable claim for an audience that has witnessed their torrid lovemaking in Tony's loft. Can she trust him? She apparently wants to.

So far the plot has been developed logically enough, but its conclusion involves an unexpected reversal that has been logically prepared for through multiple clues and flashbacks, but that strains credulity beyond reasonable tolerance. As the *Baltimore Sun* headlined its review, the "ending strikes one dumb."

The denouement discloses that Tony is also a private eye hired to investigate the disappearance of Sarah's previous lover. It also discloses that Sarah is quite mad, herself a victim of multiple-personality syndrome occasioned by child abuse and guilty memories concerning the murder of her mother.

The climax comes when Sarah's father comes calling again, unexpectedly. Sarah has a pistol and has learned how to use it, with Tony's help. She pulls the gun on her hated father. Tony appears, armed, and attempts to disarm Sarah. She shoots him, then uses Tony's gun to murder her father. She wipes both guns clean of her fingerprints, and, for all the police can conclude, Henry shot Tony while trying to protect his daughter from an intruder.

The film ends with Sarah back to "normal," being courted now by her neighbor Cliff, who, of course, has no idea of what may be in store for him. The mystery is solved for the audience, but Sarah still seems to be a threatening presence and a killer of men, a purely psychotic femme fatale, and a sort of serial killer. In this respect, *Never Talk to Strangers* belongs to the same trend that produced *Seven* and *Copycat*.

The film operates as an effective psychological thriller with a surprise ending that collapses the plot and makes it absurd. Rebecca De Mornay is as convincing as the absurd

plot will allow her to be, but this performance is not up to her portrayal of the psychotic nanny in *The Hand That Rocks the Cradle* (1992), which operated from a better screenplay. Rebecca De Mornay seems to be trapped in psychotic roles that she admittedly plays so well.

Antonio Banderas gives his most convincing performance of 1995 in *Never Talk to Strangers*. His character is not so cartoonish as the gunfighter he played in *Desperado* and far better defined than the hitman he played in *Assassins*, where his acting was also a triumph of macho style over substance. Though strangely tattooed and menacing, his character is at least likable here. His chemistry helps to drive the plot and give it substance.

Peter Hall's direction advances the plot well, but critics complained that in this instance Hall had chosen an inferior vehicle. At age 29 Peter Hall founded the Royal Shakespeare Company at Stratford-upon-Avon and served as its director from 1960 until 1968. He then became Director of the Royal National Theatre of Great Britain from 1973 until 1988. He directed his first film, *Work Is a Four Letter Word*, in 1967 for Universal Pictures, London and continued making films until 1973, when he became Director of the National Theatre. He returned to filmmaking in 1989 with *She's Been Away*, starring Dame Peggy Ashcroft and Geraldine James, and an adaptation of Tennessee Williams' *Orpheus Descending* (1990) that starred Vanessa Redgrave.

For a man who has directed Shakespeare, Harold Pinter, Peter Shaffer, as well as forty operas, *Never Talk to Strangers* seems a rather cheesy assignment. At times it stretches to be "poetic" in its editing (by Robert Silvi), as when, for example, the film intercuts sequences of Tony and Sarah romping in the snow with shots of them later making love in Tony's loft.

Caryn James complained in *The New York Times* that such a film needs to be "sleek and unpredictable" in order to be effective, but found *Never Talk to Strangers* "slack and unsurprising," though not "aggressively bad." In comparison to the violence of *Seven* it seems utterly restrained. There is rather too much psychobabble in the overly tricky script.

Variety praised the film for its set design and its "innovative use of a steel cage" in the lovemaking scenes that were toned down for domestic consumption. (An uncut version that shows more of Banderas was to be released for foreign markets.) *Variety* also praised Harry Dean Stanton as being "perfect as the smart-but-demented serial killer." *Never Talk to Strangers* is not bad for what it is, a killer-thriller with a deceptive and misleading twist at the end.

—*James M. Welsh*

REVIEWS

The Baltimore Sun. October 21, 1995, D2.
The New York Times. October 21, 1995, p.14.
The Washington Post. October 21, 1995, H3.
Variety. October 23-29, 1995, p.46.

New Jersey Drive

"Two thumbs up!"—*Siskel & Ebert*

Box Office Gross: $3,587,187

In 1992, with a budget under $100,000, twenty-nine-year-old writer/director Nick Gomez won critical acclaim for his debut film, *Laws of Gravity*, a bleak, three-days-in-the-life story of two blue-collar Brooklyn bad-boy gunrunners and their long-suffering women. Gomez' second film, *New Jersey Drive*—supported by executive producer Spike Lee—is equally gritty, but this time the action is across the Hudson River in Newark, the game is carjacking, the young thieves are black, and the real bad boys are the boys in blue.

CREDITS

Jason Petty: Sharron Corley
Midget: Gabriel Casseus
Roscoe: Saul Stein
Rene Petty: Gwen McGee
Ritchie: Andre Moore
Tiny Dime: Donald Adeosun Faison
P-Nut: Conrad Meertins Jr.
Jamal: Devin Eggleston
Ronnie: Koran C. Thomas
Coreen: Michele Morgan
Jackie Petty: Samantha Brown
Prosecutor: Christina Baranski
Lionel Gentry: Robert Jason Jackson
Bo-Kane: Dwight Errington Myers
Jessy: Gary DeWitt Marshall

Origin: USA
Released: 1995
Production: Larry Meistrich and Bob Gosse; a 40 Acres & A Mule Filmworks production in association with the Shooting Gallery; released by Gramercy Pictures
Direction: Nick Gomez
Screenplay: Nick Gomez; based on a story by Nick Gomez and Michel Marriott
Cinematography: Adam Kimmel
Editing: Tracy S. Granger
Production design: Lester Cohen
Set decoration: Lynn-Marie Nigro
Sound: Jeff Pullman
Music: Dawn Soler
MPAA rating: R
Running Time: 100 minutes

Loosely based on a series of articles written by reporter Michel Marriott for *The New York Times* and drawn from actual reports on the local "11 O' Clock News," *New Jersey Drive* takes audiences beyond the headlines and into the passenger seat for a ride with these inner city kids down the road which inevitably leads to their destruction.

We first meet Jason Petty (Sharron Corley) in jail, as his narrative recounts the illegal activities of his crew—Midget (Gabriel Casseus), Tiny (Donald Adeosun Faison), P-Nut (Conrad Meetins Jr.), and Ronnie (Koran C. Thomas)—that landed him there and cost his friends their lives.

Jason begins his story as radio reports fill us in on the mounting tension between police and carjackers in New Jersey, "the car theft capital of the world." As Jason and Ronnie sit, unarmed, in a stolen car, they are fired upon by police lieutenant Roscoe (Saul Stein), a sadistic, vengeful cop from the local precinct's predominantly white police force, who has targeted Jason and his crew since they stole his car. Ronnie is critically wounded and taken to the hospital. Jason, unharmed, spends the night in jail and is released the next morning. Upon returning home, Jason receives a stern warning from his tough, but devoted mother (Gwen McGee). When Jason tells her that the police shot Ronnie for no reason, she replies, "You need a reason to get shot these days?" As Midget earlier observed, "It's open season on a black man out there." Jason is put on two-years probation by a sympathetic black judge and roughed up by Roscoe who warns him to "stay the f*** away from grand juries."

Jason dreams of a life outside "the war going on in his backyard," but continues to jeopardize his future by settling for the temporary escape of joyriding in stolen cars with his friends. Inevitably, Roscoe catches up with Jason—"the one time [he] didn't run." By the time Jason serves his time and testifies against Roscoe before a grand jury, three of his friends have been killed in clashes with the police. Jason returns to the 'hood only to run into new clashes with the crowd his sister runs with, and soon finds himself being chased and fired at by a crazy kid with a gun named Ritchie.

AWARDS AND NOMINATIONS

Independent Spirit Awards Nominations 1996:
Best Debut Performance (Casseus)

With his friends gone, and the threat of local gang violence and police brutality looming all around him, Jason returns to school but feels empty and hopeless: "After school, then what? There's nothin' out there." Yet we see a glimmer of hope for Jason that we did not see in his doomed friends. Jason has a supportive family: a mother, a well-meaning father figure (his mother's boyfriend, whom Jason rejects), and a sister whom Jason protects. And although his sister teases him, as he hides behind an issue of *Car & Driver*, that he supposedly cannot read, we learn not only that Jason can read, but that he realizes education is the key to his survival. As Jason shows his books to a quizzical Midget, he admonishes him, "Think I'm gonna be on the street with you for the rest of my life?" (Interestingly, illiteracy is also hinted at as a contributing factor to crime in *Laws of Gravity.*)

Midget, though fearless in contrast to Jason, is also seen as sensitive: he wants to renew a relationship with a girlfriend, and he takes care of his invalid "grammy," spoon-feeding her as he exchanges profanities with Jason on the phone. We also get the feeling that Midget, upon welcoming Jason home after serving his time, has accepted his own fate. As he leaves Jason to hit the streets for another steal, we feel Midget knows this joyride will be his last. This sense of predestiny was also felt in *Laws of Gravity* through Jon, a ticking time-bomb whose fate was sealed, just as Midget's, Tiny's, and P-Nut's are in *New Jersey Drive.* Flirting with their inevitable destruction, this doomed trio lived for—and off of—the excitement that endangered their already hopeless lives. When you know your days are numbered, "the only thing that matters is the ride," as the film's tagline asserts.

But the film is not all gloom and doom. The joyride sequences are exhilarating and the car chases are exciting and well-filmed. *New Jersey Drive* also has some very humorous moments, most notably the scene in which Midget, Jason, and company steal Roscoe's police car out of his own driveway for a joyride, then order a jeep-load of college boys to pull over, as Midget, in a Barney Fyfe-like cop voice, informs the boys that they "have the right to remain stupid."

The film also has some subtly moving moments, as when the boys, after Tiny's funeral, toast their friend with 40-ounce beers, their figures silhouetted against the dusky Newark sky. In a sad street scene near the end of the film, Jason is shown walking past a spray-painted memorial wall dedicated to Midget and Tiny—a kind of urban tombstone reminding passersby of the violence that is commonplace in such crime-ridden neighborhoods.

Just as *Laws of Gravity* was distinguished by its "mean-streets," Scorsese-like realism, *New Jersey Drive* is driven by its unblinking urban authenticity. Filmed on location in the projects of Queens and Brooklyn with a hand-held camera, the film's sense of realism is conveyed via strong performances by Sharron Corley—a former gang member who lived a life not unlike Jason's—and Gabriel Casseus as Midget. Saul Stein, who also appeared in *Laws of Gravity*, is effective as the dastardly Roscoe, the policeman "who seemed to like his job a little bit too much," but the character is written as a stereotype. This racist caricature ired critics, including Caryn James of *The New York Times*, who described Roscoe as "so bluntly evil he might as well be an old-time villain twirling a moustache." (Audiences may want to check out Spike Lee's *Clockers* for a different, more sensitive portrayal of a white cop [Harvey Keitel] in a black neighborhood.)

While critics praised Corley and Casseus for their naturalistic and believable performances, James again took issue with Gomez' script, noting that "Jason and Midget are written flabbily, as types." James further found Jason's narration to be "trite," a sentiment shared by Pat Dietmeyer, in *Box Office* who commented that "the film doesn't earn its elegiac tone and contains no surprises."

Some critics complained that audiences have seen *New Jersey Drive*'s "familiar, generic story of black men heading for trouble," before, as James asserts, in other movies—most notably John Singleton's *Boyz N the Hood* (1991) and the Hughes brothers' more hopeless, but less sympathetic *Menace II Society* (1993). As Dietmeyer put it, "It's so familiar, both from the news and the films that have gone before, that it's impossible to be shocked at the inevitable."

For those audiences who came to the theater not to be shocked, but to gain some insight into life on the streets the way it really is for countless inner city kids in America today, this urban drama delivers a harsh, but vital message that should not be dismissed.

—Shawn Brennan

Nick of Time

"Ninety minutes. Six bullets. No choice."—Movie tagline

"Powerful and unforgettable!"—Ron Brewington, *American Urban Radio Network*

"A thriller with originality, ingenuity and non-stop suspense."—David Sheehan, *CBS-TV*

"Taut suspense thriller."—Kevin Thomas, *Los Angeles Times*

Box Office Gross: $7,877,270

Gene Watson (Johnny Depp) is an ordinary man leading an ordinary life. But that is all about to change. While returning with his daughter from the funeral of his ex-wife, Gene is randomly singled out in a crowded train station. The man who has chosen Gene is the sinister Mr. Smith (Christopher Walken) who, along with his equally villainous cohort, Ms. Jones (Roma Maffia), has plans for Gene. Pretending to be law officers, Smith and Jones separate Gene from his daughter Lynn (Courtney Chase) and use her as a hostage to blackmail Gene into doing a small job for them—assassinating the governor of California.

It seems that Governor Eleanor Grant (Marsha Mason) was elected on a relatively conservative platform and with a lot of conservative backing. Now that she is in office, however, she has turned into a "flaming liberal," and that has made many people unhappy...and willing to go to any length to get rid of her, including murder. However, these are sophisticated and powerful people, and they cannot afford to be connected with the murder in any way.

Smith tells Gene he has until 1:30 that afternoon, just a little more than an hour, to shoot the governor...or his daughter dies. Now Gene the prosaic certified public accountant must become Gene the assassin. At the nearby Bonaventure Hotel where the governor is having day long appearances, Mr Smith provides Gene with everything he needs to perform his task: a gun, the governor's schedule, and a contributor's pin for access to all events. He also shadows Gene's every move to prevent him from deviating from his assignment. Furthermore, he continually speaks via walkie talkie to Ms. Jones who is waiting in a van outside the hotel with Lynn, and who is ready and more than willing, to "take care" of her young hostage.

Poor Gene, he is not a murderer, but he can't let his daughter die. But he also knows that even if he were to kill the governor, Smith or Jones would probably kill Lynx anyway. What's an everyman to do? Can he come up with any kind of workable plan in just one hour? Will he be able to find someone who can help him without Smith finding out? Perhaps the disabled war veteran (Charles S. Dutton) who shines shoes in the lobby?

This is the basic premise of *Nick of Time*. And if you can buy it, it becomes a compelling, edge-of-the-seat thriller. If you can't, it becomes a groaner. Taking cues from Alfred Hitchcock, director John Badham uses many of that master's touches: skewed and disorienting Dutch angels and especially the plot device of the average John Doe caught up in extraordinary circumstances. One other trick he has borrowed is the way Hitchcock used "real time" in his 1948 film *Rope*, a take on the cold and calculating Leopold and Loeb murders. In "real time" the action within the film takes place at the same time as the audience watches it. So, when Gene has exactly one hour and 14 minutes to kill the governor, the audience lives through it with him in the same amount of time.

One advantage of doing this is that it can increase audience identification with the main character. We desperately try to think of alternative solutions for Gene's situa-

CREDITS

Gene Watson: Johnny Depp
Mr. Smith: Christopher Walken
Huey: Charles S. Dutton
Brendan Grant: Peter Strauss
Ms. Jones: Roma Maffia
Krista Brooks: Gloria Reuben
Gov. Eleanor Grant: Marsha Mason
Lynn Watson: Courtney Chase
Officer Trust: Bill Smitrovich
Mystery Man: G. D. Spradlin

Origin: USA
Released: 1995
Production: John Badham for Paramount Pictures
Direction: John Badham
Screenplay: Partrick Sheane Duncan
Cinematography: Roy H. Wagner
Editing: Frank Morriss
Production design: Philip Harrison
Art direction: Eric Orbom
Set decoration: Julia Badham
Costume design: Mary Vogt
Sound: Willie Burton
Music: Arthur B. Rubinstein
MPAA rating: R
Running Time: 89 minutes

tion at the same time as Gene. We see what he sees, follow all his actions, are privy to all his thoughts. In other words, there are no time-span jumps. Hours or days can't pass in the movie during which Gene can come up with a great plan. He has to think under pressure, and so does the audience.

If one has bought the premise, which can be a large purchase for some people, and if one has caught the tension of the real-time filming, then the next hurdle will be to identify with the main character. Unfortunately, Johnny Depp is sadly miscast as Mr. Everyman. More well known for his quirky roles (*Edward Scissorhands*, *Ed Wood*, *Benny and Joon*), a toothpick chomping Depp does not come across as a timid accountant and doting father.

While Christopher Walken is not miscast as the villainous Mr. Smith, the opposite problem may be in effect here. Walken is becoming too identified with evil malefactors. Just a stare from Walken shows a character on (or usually over) the edge. If there is an interesting turn of acting here, it is the solid performance of Charles S. Dutton as Huey, the hard of hearing, wooden-legged veteran who owns the shoe shine shop where Gene finds his first hint of help.

Nick of Time did not provide good boxoffice returns for its studio, but one might surmise that there is enough of interest here to capture a solid video rental audience.

—*Beverley Bare Buehrer*

REVIEWS

Chicago Tribune. November 22, 1995
Chicago Tribune. November 24, 1995
Entertainment Weekly. December 1, 1995.
New York Times. November 21, 1995
Variety.

Nine Months

"Ready or not."—Movie tagline

"The funniest all-out comedy since *Mrs. Doubtfire*."—John Corcoran, *KCAL-TV*

Box Office Gross: $69,690,778

Director Chris Columbus has made quite a successful career making films that extol the virtues of family. His blockbuster hits *Home Alone* (1990) and *Home Alone 2* (1992) tell of a youngster who fends for himself and fights off criminals after accidentally being separated from his family. *Only the Lonely* (1991) shows the tug-of-war relationship of a "mama's boy" who wants to break his old familial relationships after falling in love and now wants to start a family of his own. And *Mrs. Doubtfire* tells of a father's desperate desire to be with his children after being separated from them by divorce. In all of these films, the value of having and keeping family relationships is celebrated. Now along comes his latest directorial effort, *Nine Months*, and Columbus is praising the importance and value of beginning a family.

Samuel Faulkner's (Hugh Grant) life is just the way he likes it. He has a beautiful girlfriend, Rebecca (Julianne Moore); a steady relationship of five years without marriage; a successful career as a child psychologist; a stunning San Francisco apartment that overlooks the bay; and a cozy, red Porsche that seats only two. As he tells Rebecca, "Why change what's perfect?" So imagine his surprise when Rebecca upsets his "perfect" life by telling him that she's pregnant. Now one of the rooms in the apartment will have to become a nursery, he becomes preoccupied and incompetent at the office where he is constantly bombarded by children warped by and angry at their parents, marriage seems to be rearing its ugly head, and he'll have to trade in the Porsche for a car that fits a baby seat.

Fatherhood was not in Sam's plans, and he is reluctant at best in his support of Rebecca who insists on having this baby. To make matters worse, Sam, despite his best efforts, is constantly coming face-to-face with a set of children and parental role models whom he despises: the Dwyer family. Father Marty (Tom Arnold) is a loud-mouthed, obnoxious and in-your-face car salesman. Mother Gail (Joan Cusack) revels in her fertility and has a life only in relationship to her three ill-behaved and pushy young girls. As the children pillage picnic hampers and feed caviar to their dog, Mom and Pop Dwyer just rapturously beam over their brood.

So, it seems quite understandable that Sam would attempt to avoid the traps of fatherhood and recapture his youth by hanging out with his unmarried artist buddy Sean (Jeff Goldblum). So, Sam gets his ear pierced, attends hip parties, and learns to roller blade, while at night he dreams of being consumed by Rebecca in the form of a praying-mantis.

Then Sam goes too far: he stands Rebecca up for a doctor's appointment. Now she has had enough of his hesitation and selfishness, and she moves out—and into the Dwyer home. It doesn't take long for Sam to miss Rebecca, and after reading a few chapters of the book she has left behind, "What to Expect When You're Expecting," and seeing his son on the ultrasound tape, he becomes misty-eyed and determined to make things up to Rebecca and accept his role as a father. The question is, can he win her back?

"What are we suppose to do, tie the baby to the hood?"—Rebecca explaining to Samuel that his Porsche can't be considered a family car in *Nine Months*

Nine Months was supposed to be the big American breakthrough film for British actor Hugh Grant. After his impressive success in *Four Weddings and a Funeral* (1994), Hollywood thought they might have the next big film star on their hands. Handsome, clever, amusing, ingratiating, and endearing, he reminded some of an updated version of another Brit named Grant whom American's swooned over, Cary Grant. But would Hugh be as perfect for mainstream films as he was for the art films he was known for? Grant has also starred in Roman Polanski's *Bitter Moon* (1994), the Australian *Sirens* (1994), the Merchant-Ivory *Remains of the Day* (1994), and the recent *The Englishman Who Went Up a Hill and Came Down a Mountain* (reviewed in this volume).

A lot was riding on *Nine Months*, and to everyone's surprise, a joker turned up in the film's publicity deck. Just two weeks before *Nine Month's* premier, Grant was arrested and charged with lewd conduct. As news reports led off with the titillating item, everyone wondered if an actor whose appeal seemed to be based on his boyish charm still had a career.

At first Grant isolated himself in his British home with his girlfriend of eight years, model Elizabeth Hurley, but as the movie's premier date loomed, Grant decided to meet rather than run from his many publicity commitments. His first appearance, on *The Tonight Show with Jay Leno*, was so eagerly consumed that it attracted the show's third highest ratings. Obviously, it was the transgression, not the film that viewers wanted to hear discussed, and to his credit, discuss it he did. He nervously admitted that he had done "a bad thing" and apologized to his family and girlfriend. With self-deprecating humor and more of that boyish charm, Grant seemed to redeem himself to the American public and confirm the old idea that "no publicity is bad publicity." Grant followed this success with appearances on cable's *Larry King Live*, NBC's *Today* and ABC's *Regis and Kathie Lee*. And on them all he inveigled upon Americans to forgive him.

Obviously, in light of all this, one cannot view Grant's character in *Nine Months* without thinking of Grant the man behind the acting. Fortunately, however, he seems to be proving to be appealing enough for his offense to be easily overlooked by audiences. His movie is proving successful at the box office—it opened in third place behind the 1995 summer blockbusters *Apollo 13* and *Under Siege 2*—but whether it is from curiosity about Grant, or publicity from the arrest, or because the film is just plain entertaining, is a question that may never be easily answered.

Unfortunately, once one gets past the curiosity and publicity factors, the movie itself can be summed up in one word: predictable. From start to finish, there are no surprises. From Grant's car crash when he hears the news about the pregnancy while driving, to the frantic car chase on the way to the hospital (watch for *Home Alone 7* playing at a theater in the background), we've seen it all before. The audience knows the reason for Sam's reluctance to become a father long before he comes to his own epiphany ("I was scared of losing control and you and my youth.") And we know how he will initially try to run from it, and how he will accept it in the end.

As for the actors, again there are no surprises. Grant endearingly stammers and bumbles his way through his role;

CREDITS

Samuel Faulkner: Hugh Grant
Rebecca Taylor: Julianne Moore
Marty Dwyer: Tom Arnold
Gail Dwyer: Joan Cusack
Sean Fletcher: Jeff Goldblum
Dr. Kosevich: Robin Williams
Truman: Joey Simmrin
Shannon Dwyer: Ashley Johnson
Lili: Mia Cottet
Molly Dwyer: Alexa Vega
Patsy Dwyer: Aislin Roche

Origin: USA
Released: 1995
Production: Anne Francois, Chris Columbus, Mark Radcliffe and Michael Barnathan for a 1492 production; released by 20th Century Fox
Direction: Chris Columbus
Screenplay: Chris Columbus based on the film *Neuf Mois* written by Patrick Braoude
Cinematography: Donald McAlpine
Editing: Raja Gosnell and Stephen Rivkin
Production design: Angelo P. Graham
Art direction: W. Steven Graham
Set decoration: Garrett Lewis
Costume design: Jay Hurley
Music: Hans Zimmer
MPAA rating: PG-13
Running Time: 102 minutes

Moore is a steadfast (but rather boring) straightwoman; Arnold and Cusack lend background humor and slapstick to offset the heart tugging; and Goldblum is suitably confused in his role as advisor. Even Robin Williams, doing just a bit more than a cameo as the couple's emigre Russian doctor delivering his first human baby, is a typically frantic Williams character, but one who is also awfully funny as he malapropos his way through the English language ("I was chief of abstraction...obstruction...obstetrics.") However, when the peripheral characters are more interesting and fun to watch than the main characters, something is cinematically amiss.

Like *Point of No Return* (1993), *Sommersby* (1993), and *Three Men and a Baby* (1987), *Nine Months* was based on a French film (*Neuf Mois*), only this foreign entry was never released in the United States. Consequently, whether or not *Nine Months* owes its shortcomings to the original material or whether it has just been sanitized into innocuousness by Columbus is not known. The American version will, however, find its audience. Even after the curiosity factor fades, there are always those who enjoy their films warm-hearted, their humor slapstick, their plots predictable, and their stories sweetly syrupy.

—Beverley Bare Buehrer

REVIEWS

Chicago Tribune. July 10, 1995, Tempo Section.
Chicago Tribune. July 12, 1995, Arts Plus Section.
Entertainment Weekly. July 14, 1995.
New York Times. July 12, 1995.
Time. July 24, 1995, p. 58-9.
Variety. July 10, 1995, p. 34.

Nixon

"The number one movie of the year!"—Owen Gleiberman, *Entertainment Weekly*

"*Nixon* is gutsy and overpowering!"—Janet Maslin, *The New York Times*

"Brilliant, compelling, powerful!"—David Ansen, *Newsweek*

"Two thumbs up!"—*Siskel & Ebert*

Box Office Gross: $6,973,187

Richard Milhous Nixon (1913-1994) is easily the most controversial American political figure of the twentieth century, and Oliver Stone is the most controversial American film director of the late twentieth century. Stone would seem destined to make a film about Nixon, especially since he has already made so many films exploring political and social events of the 1960's and 1970's: *Salvador* (1986), *Platoon* (1986), *Born on the Fourth of July* (1989), *The Doors* (1991), *JFK* (1991), and *Heaven and Earth* (1993). Stone seems compelled to explain his times to himself and to the public, perhaps.even to exorcise his and the public's demons related to these times. Stone's Nixon also seems possessed by demons and fails because he cannot exorcise them.

Nixon opens with the break-in at the Watergate Hotel in June, 1972, jumps forward eighteen months as Nixon (Anthony Hopkins) and his staff comtemplate the increasing damage caused by the Watergate coverup, and spends the rest of the film going back and forth between the final months of Nixon's presidency and earlier events in his life. These include his childhood in Whittier, California, and his relations with his stern father (Tom Bower), his strict Quaker mother (Mary Steenburgen), and his three brothers. The most significant events during this time are the deaths of his youngest brother, Arthur (Joshua Preston), and his eldest, Harold (Tony Goldwyn), from tuberculosis.

These deaths leave young Nixon not only with a great sense of loss—Harold seems to be the only person he ever truly loves—but with an even greater guilt, especially since he gets to go to law school because Harold dies. The emphasis in *Nixon* is less on politics and history than psychology, and Stone and his co-screenwriters, Stephen J. Rivele and Christopher Wilkinson, make clear that guilt and the need for love are central to their protagonist's character.

Nixon also depicts young Nixon's clumsy attempts to play football at Whittier College, his courtship of Patricia Ryan, his establishing his reputation in Congress during the communist witch hunts by presecuting Alger Hiss, the famous Checkers speech that saves his vice-presidency, his 1960 debate with John F. Kennedy, his losing the presidency to Kennedy, his losing the 1962 California gubernatorial race, his miraculous return to victorious politics in 1968, and the events surrounding Watergate. The Nixon who emerges is surprisingly sympathetic, a flawed but essentially decent human being who simply does not know how to communicate his ideas effectively and how to love and be loved. When

CREDITS

Richard M. Nixon: Anthony Hopkins
Pat Nixon: Joan Allen
H. R. Haldeman: James Woods
John Ehrlichman: J. T. Walsh
Henry Kissinger: Paul Sorvino
John Dean: David Hyde Pierce
Hannah Nixon: Mary Steenburgen
Harold Nixon: Tony Goldwyn
J. Edgar Hoover: Bob Hoskins
Clyde Tolson: Brian Bedford
John Mitchell: E. G. Marshall
Martha Mitchell: Madeleine Kahn
Alexander Haig: Powers Boothe
Ron Ziegler: David Paymer
E. Howard Hunt: Ed Harris
Jack Jones: Larry Hagman
Student protester: Joanna Going
Charles Colson: Kevin Dunn
Nelson Rockefeller: Ed Herrmann
Herb Klein: Saul Rubinek
Mao Tse-tung: Ric Young
Frank Nixon: Tom Bower
Richard Nixon as young man: David Barry Gray
Richard Nixon as boy: Corey Carrier
Arthur Nixon: Joshua Preston
Released: 1995

Origin: USA
Production: Clayton Townsend, Oliver Stone, and Andrew G. Vajna for an Andrew G. Vajna presentation of an Illusion Entertainment Group/Cinergi production and Hollywood Pictures; released by Buena Vista
Direction: Oliver Stone
Screenplay: Stephen J. Rivele, Christopher Wilkinson, and Oliver Stone
Cinematography: Robert Richardson
Editing: Brian Berdan and Hank Corwin
Production design: Victor Kempster
Art direction: Donald Woodruff, Richard F. Mays and Margery Zweizig
Set design: Henry Alberti, Peter J. Kelly and Charlie Vassar
Set decoration: Merideth Boswell
Costume design: Richard Hornung
Sound: David Macmillan
Music: John Williams
Casting: Billy Hopkins, Heidi Levitt and Mary Vernieu
MPAA rating: R
Running Time: 190 minutes

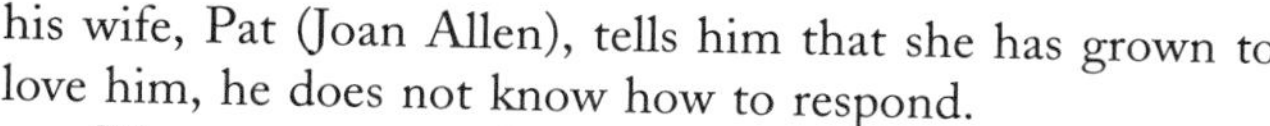

his wife, Pat (Joan Allen), tells him that she has grown to love him, he does not know how to respond.

Nixon was most famous for reinventing himself, for having no stable identity in the public consciousness. As a result, Stone has several Nixons to choose from, and he has surprised both his supporters and detractors by downplaying the easiest Nixon to portray, the drinking, lying, paranoid Nixon, the consummate evader of responsibility, that so readily lends itself to comic or pathetic caricature. Stone's Nixon does listen to Watergate tape-recordings with drink in hand, ending up squirming on the floor, haunted by visions of his disapproving mother, but he is often insightful and self-aware. Making a surprise, unprotected visit to anti-Vietnam War demonstrators at the Lincoln Memorial in the middle of the night, Nixon wants to talk to these idealistic young people about college football, and when that fails, he stumbles miserably, losing a debate over the politics of the war to a nineteen-year-old student (Joanna Going). Afterward, he speaks both admiringly and sadly of her having intuitively grasped political complexities it has taken him twenty-five years to understand.

After the flamboyant style of *JFK* and, especially, *Natural Born Killers* (1994), *Nixon* is surprisingly sedate cinematically. There is, however, the constant jumping about in time, newsreels and photographs altered to have Hopkins appear with real historical figures, the use of black-and-white photography not only in some flashbacks but in some Watergate scenes to emphasize how Nixon is trapped in the past, and the use of time-lapse photography to show storm clouds gathering quickly over the White House. A filmmaker naturally given to cinematic excesses has to give in to them occasionally as Stone does during a summit meeting with Mao Tse-tung (Ric Young) when the Chinese leader says both men are equally evil and their faces overlap.

Stone and his collaborators owe an enormous debt to the greatest political film, Orson Welles' *Citizen Kane* (1941). The flashback structure is patterned after that of

AWARDS AND NOMINATIONS

Chicago Film Festival Awards 1995: Best Director (Stone), Best Supporting Actress (Allen)
Los Angeles Film Critics Awards 1995: Best Supporting Actress (Allen)
National Society of Film Critics Awards 1995: Best Supporting Actress (Allen)
Academy Awards Nominations 1995: Best Actor (Hopkins), Best Supporting Actress (Allen), Best Screenplay (Stone), Best Score (Williams)
British Academy Awards Nominations 1995: Best Supporting Actress (Allen)
Golden Globe Awards Nominations 1996: Best Actor-Drama (Hopkins)
Screen Actors Guild Awards Nominations 1995: Best Actor (Hopkins), Best Actress (Allen), Best Cast

Kane, which Stone acknowledges by ending a newsreel of the highlights of Nixon's career with the sound of the projector winding down just as with the newsreel of Charles Foster Kane at the beginning of Welles' film. An angry dinner confrontation between Nixon and Pat takes place at the opposite ends of a long table, in homage to the famous montage of the decline of the first Kane marriage. After Nixon agrees to resign the presidency, Pat comforts her husband in a shadowy White House vestibule, recalling the puzzle scene between a defeated Kane and his second wife.

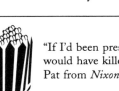

The screenplay for *Nixon* has been published by Hyperion as *Nixon: An Oliver Stone Film.* The book, edited by Eric Hamburg, a former Congressional aide and one of the film's co-producers, includes annotations giving sources of the information in the script; essays by Watergate documents and transcripts of tape-recordings. The bibliography lists 122 sources upon which the screenplay is based.

Stone's achievement is matched by that of his cast. Many of the performers are somewhat younger or older than the people they portray or do not closely resemble them. During Watergate, Nixon's henchmen John Ehrlichman and H. R. Haldeman came across as equally malevolent, though Ehrlichman seemed more smugly evil. In Stone's Watergate, J. T. Walsh's Ehrlichman looks more sympathetic and even tries to act as the voice of reason. James Woods' Haldeman is more obviously up to no good, and Woods, who gives perhaps his greatest performance in Stone's *Salvador*, has a wonderful time with this man who encourages his boss's excesses.

"If I'd been president, they never would have killed me."—Nixon to Pat from *Nixon*

Allen's Pat is one of the film's triumphs since the first lady had little public presence, standing quietly in her husband's shadow. In *Nixon*, she smokes, drinks, worries unselfishly about her husband, and, most of all, is alone, the perfect parallel to this loneliest of presidents. Allen conveys the strength and compassion beneath this woman's despair. Steenburgen nearly dominates the film by displaying Hannah Nixon's inflexible morality and disappointment, walking a fine line between mother as conscience and mother as monster. Corey Carrier as Nixon the boy and David Barry Gray as Nixon the young man capture the protagonist's innocence and need for approval and acceptance.

Holding the film together, even more than Stone, is Hopkins' towering performance. Except for changing his hair and teeth, no effort is made to have Hopkins look like Nixon, and while his accent is inconsistent, sometimes sounding exactly like John Huston, Hopkins becomes Nixon. Hopkins has always, especially early in his career, been the most American of the great British actors, much given to the tics, twitches, and pauses associated with The Method. Ironically, he plays down his mannerisms as this most neurotic of political figures. As he has shown particularly in *The Remains of the Day* (1993), Hopkins is a master of repression, and his Nixon is given more to withdrawal than to outbursts. When Pat tries to discuss love with her husband, Hopkins tries to hide, almost flinches, as he does in a similar scene with Emma Thompson in *The Remains of the Day*. Hopkins is equally effective when Nixon is at his strongest, rejecting the attempt to control him by a cadre of Texas millionaires (led by a sublimely sinister Larry Hagman), and at his weakest, asking Kissinger to get down on his knees and pray with him. Stone acknowledges how much he is indebted to his actors by including a shot of each in the closing credits.

Nixon has been strongly attacked by journalists, historians, and Nixon insiders for taking liberties with history. The filmmaker occasionally distorts time, as when he has Lyndon Johnson announcing he will not seek reelection before the 1968 presidential primaries instead of in the middle of them, and he employs dramatic license several other times, as with a conversation between John Dean and E. Howard Hunt that never took place. Stone defended himself in an *Dateline* NBC interview with Bob Costas by claiming to approach history in the same way as William Shakespeare, choosing, when necessary, drama over fact. His interpretation is obviously more interesting and moving than any docudrama would be.

A more serious problem, shared with *All the President's Men* (1976), Alan J. Pakula's enormously entertaining Watergate drama, is that Stone is making a film for an audience familiar with all these events. Any viewer not aware of the ins and outs of Watergate—which even eluded much of the public at the time—not to mention the McCarthy era, the Bay of Pigs, the opposition to the Vietnam War, etc., may have difficulty understanding what the film is trying to say.

—Michael Adams

REVIEWS

Entertainment Weekly. December 22, 1995, p. 42.
The New York Times. December 20, 1995, p. C11.
Newsweek. CXXVI, December 11, 1995, p. 64.
Time. CXLVI, December 18, 1995, p. 74.
USA Today. December 20, 1995, p. D1.
Variety. December 18, 1995, p. 65.

Now and Then

"A summer when four friends made a promise to return anytime they needed each other. Twenty years later, that time has come."—Movie tagline

"It will touch you like no other movie this year."—Jeffrey Lyons, *Sneak Previews*

"The best coming-of-age movie since *Stand By Me*."—Pat Collins, *WWOR-TV*

Box Office Gross: $26,342,995

Publicity for director Lesli Linka Glatter's first feature film, *Now and Then*, touts it as "an endearing *Stand By Me* for girls," and there are certainly similarities. Both Glatter's film and Rob Reiner's lyrical 1986 success are essentially made up of a flashback bracketed by scenes from the present. The narrator in both films is a successful writer whose memories of his or her twelfth summer are jogged by a major event in an old friend's life. Both films focus on a tightly-knit group of four young friends of decidedly different personalities who go on an odyssey that is prompted by a boy's death. A tree house and the sudden death of a family member are important story elements in both films. Hit songs from the 1950's (*Stand By Me*) and 1970's (*Now and Then*) are used to evoke a more innocent time before that innocence was lost. In short, the script for *Now and Then* derives a striking amount from its admitted cinematic brother. The film also throws elements of Robert Mulligan's classic *To Kill a Mockingbird* (1962) into the mix, visible, for example, in the night scene in which two young people are assisted during a struggle at death's door by a man previously thought to be scary but who had simply been misunderstood. While *Now and Then* borrows many elements in fairly recognizable form from these films, the main thing that is missing here is the presentation of those elements in the form of an interesting, absorbing story.

What gives this surprisingly flat coming-of-age tale what little bounce and verve it is ever able to muster are the four young actresses featured in the flashback which fortunately makes up the bulk of the film. Before they are introduced, however, we are subjected to their more mature, and far less engaging, counterparts. Perhaps because of the relative brevity of this initial "now" scene, the adult characters are presented with broad strokes to speedily render their distinctive personalities. Christina Dewitt (Rita Wilson) the most conservative and unsophisticated of the four, is about to have her first child, and she sends out the S.O.S. that prompts the women's return to their little hometown of Shelby, Indiana. It seems the friends made a pact when they were twelve that they would come running whenever any of them needed a friend. (Hasn't she made any friends in the intervening years? Also, if they have remained such good friends, why have they apparently not seen each other in years?) Christina lives with her husband within the protective confines of the house in which she grew up. Samantha Albertson (Demi Moore) is an author who reluctantly but dutifully heads back to the town she feels she outgrew and transcended. Her cigarette habit, black clothes, glasses, and braided hair wound tightly and pinned to her head act as a big neon sign that flashes "Serious Writer." Throughout the film, Moore's throaty narration imparts Deep Thoughts, many suitable for needlepoint samplers. Tina Tercell (Melanie Griffith) a Hollywood actress, arrives in a limousine and greets her old friends with a jaunty grin and an even jauntier "Hey bitches!" While she has failed numerous times at marriage, Tina has enjoyed greater success in her pursuit of surgical breast augmentation. Roberta Martin (Rosie O'Donnell) is a wisecracking doctor who, like Christina, never left

CREDITS

Young Roberta: Christina Ricci
Young Teeny: Thora Birch
Young Samantha: Gaby Hoffman
Young Chrissy: Asleigh Aston Moore
Samantha: Demi Moore
Roberta: Rosie O'Donnell
Christina: Rita Wilson
Tina: Melanie Griffith

Origin: USA
Released: 1995
Production: Suzanne Todd for A Moving Pictures Productions; released by New Line Cinema
Direction: Lesli Linka Glatter
Screenplay: I. Marlene King
Cinematography: Ueli Steiger
Editing: Jacqueline Cambas
Production design: Gershon Ginsburg and Anne Kuljian
Art director: Gershon Ginsburg
Costume design: Deena Appel
Sound: James Thornton
Music: Cliff Eidelman
MPAA rating: PG-13
Running Time: 102 minutes

Shelby. She is the most entertaining of the four women, relatively speaking.

As the women begin to reminisce near the old tree house in Christina's backyard, *Now and Then* flashes back to the summer of 1970 when the girls were twelve and hoping to pool enough money to buy a tree house. The way the girls are presented, it is striking how they evidently became less interesting and winning with age. Samantha (Gaby Hoffmann), shown to already be a thinker but without the affectations, is dealing with the pain of her parents' divorce and her mother's search for a new boyfriend. She never thought that her parents would break up because they had been battling for quite some time ("There's comfort in consistency," she recalls), and no one in her neighborhood had ever gotten a divorce. Teeny (Thora Birch) is stuffing her bra with pudding-laden balloons, answering sex surveys in Cosmopolitan, and dreamily rehearsing the speech she hopes to give someday upon winning an Oscar. When one of the girls complains that nothing ever happens in Shelby, Chrissy (Ashleigh Aston Moore) characteristically replies "I kinda like it that way." Chrissy's "mommy" (marvelously played by Bonnie Hunt) is making her daughter sit through a euphemistic sex talk which utilizes gardening and botanical references ("All women have a garden, and...need a big hose to water it with.") Roberta (Christina Ricci, possibly the best actress of the eight leading ladies), a confirmed tomboy whose mother has died and who is growing up in a house full of men, is taping down her breasts in a desperate attempt to remain "one of the boys." Her unhappiness about her mother's death is always just below the surface, and she sometimes fakes her own death in an apparent effort to deal with the subject by mocking it. Roberta, along with the other girls, is constantly being tormented by the Wormer brothers, but she is the least willing—or able—to take their abuse without attempted retaliation.

"It's only when you embrace your past that you truly move forward."—the grownup Samantha from *Now and Then*

The weak plotline that ties the 70's scenes together is the girls' dull, uninvolving quest to learn the circumstances surrounding the death of "Dear Johnny," a boy who died in 1945 and is buried in a nearby cemetery. Late one night, Samantha leads a seance to try to contact the boy's spirit. A storm suddenly arises, lightning flashes, and the girls notice that "Dear Johnny's" headstone has been shattered. Sure that they have caused his soul to break through from the Beyond, the girls vow to learn how he actually died. The girls hop on their bikes and merrily sing their way to the library to examine old newspapers for clues. The pages about the youngster's death have been clipped out, but the girls do find an article about the car accident that killed Roberta's mother. Through that article, Roberta is horrified to learn that her mother did not die swiftly and painlessly as she had been told. The four then decide to talk to Samantha's grandmother (Cloris Leachman), but she is unwilling to talk about the tragedy because it is too sad and, furthermore, she will not be made late for bingo. Undaunted, the girls make their way into the attic after she leaves, and learn that "Dear Johnny" and his mother were brutally murdered. This revelation dredges up emotions in the girls, causing Roberta to let loose her grief and anger about her mother's death and Samantha to reveal that her father has left and her parents are divorcing. After this cathartic experience, the girls make their way back to the cemetery, intent upon putting the dead boy's soul to rest. On the way, Samantha almost drowns in a rain drain but is saved by Crazy Pete, an old man the girls had always made fun of because he kept to himself and only came out at night on bike rides to the cemetery. It is then revealed that, lo and behold, Pete is "Dear Johnny's" father, who has blamed himself all these years for his family's demise because he was out at a bar on the night of the killings. Samantha points out that, while he failed to save his family, he did rescue her, and Pete offers newfound wisdom and apparently plans to get out more. When the girls arrive for the seance, they are both disappointed and relieved to learn that a cemetery worker's carelessness had actually caused the destruction of "Dear Johnny's" stone.

By the end of the flashback, the girls have gleefully given the Wormers their comeuppance (they steal the boys' clothes while they are skinny-dipping), and Roberta's attitude towards the eldest boy begins to thaw after they share a first kiss. The girls are able to purchase a tree house, and make their pact to always be there for each other, "whenever we need a friend, no matter what." This scene soon leads to a return to the present, and Roberta's delivery of Christina's baby with Samantha and Tina as birth coaches. (Her husband arrives too late.) In the film's final scene, the four women gather once again in the tree house. The fact that Samantha has found all this reminiscing to be a freeing experience is signalled by the fact that her hair now hangs

REVIEWS

Chicago Tribune. October 20, 1995, p. 7J.
The Detroit Free Press. October 20, 1995, p. 5D.
The Detroit News. October 20, 1995, p. 3F.
Entertainment Weekly. November 3, 1995, p. 48.
Hollywood Reporter. October 17, 1995, p. 10.
Los Angeles Times. October 20, 1995, p. F14.
The New York Times. October 29, 1995, p. H31.
The New York Times. October 20, 1995, p. C12.
Rolling Stone. November 2, 1995, p. 77.
Variety. October 23, 1995, p. 46.
USA Today. October 20, 1995, p. 4D.

down loosely and she no longer has on her serious-looking glasses. All seem moved by this reunion, and the women make a new pact to visit more often.

With the hook of its big-name female stars, *Now and Then* ranked second in domestic box office receipts at the end of its first week in release. By the conclusion of its eighth week, it had made just under $25.5 million. Most reviews of the film included praise for the younger actresses, a decided lack of enthusiasm for the portrayal of the adult characters, and a fair amount of apathy concerning the plot. Wanting to chronicle rites of passage and friendships in the lives of young women is certainly a worthwhile endeavor. In *Now and Then*, it seems that the women producers, director and screenwriter were far more motivated by the conviction to deal with this oft-ignored subject than by a captivating story idea which would serve to illuminate it.

—*David L. Boxerbaum*

Oblivion

A filmmaker has to be pretty confident to name a film *Oblivion*. The title alone invites negative commentary. This lighthearted science-fiction fantasy spoofs a dizzying array of genres. It is best described as a mixture of *Star Trek*, *The Rocky Horror Picture Show* (1975), *My Darling Clementine* (1946), *Blazing Saddles* (1973), and *Plan Nine from Outer Space* (1959) (except it isn't as interesting, funny, or well-executed as any of those films). It does so with a huge dose of sophomoric humor, a dash of wit, a healthy amount of interesting visual images, and a fine musical soundtrack. Though there are good points, only the most ardent fans of fantasy and science fiction will not mind plodding through the torpid ninety minutes of this film.

One frightening aspect of this film is the fact that a sequel was shot at the same time as the first film. That is not mere confidence on the part of the film's creators; it is, to put it discreetly, brazen. *Oblivion* has its moments, but the ratio of truly clever moments to simpleminded ones is sadly lopsided.

Oblivion does have a few funny jokes and a few clever send-ups of traditional genres. (Try 1994's *Wagons East* for a film with absolutely no redeeming qualities, and then *Oblivion* will look like *Citizen Kane* [1941] by comparison.)

The story is meant to parody the western genre. It tells of a town called Oblivion on an unnamed planet where the life forms are predominantly human. The town is reminiscent of the typical wild West. It has a saloon and cathouse named appropriately, "Miss Kitty's." Even more appropriately, Miss Kitty is played by none other than Julie Newmar, who played "Catwoman" in the old *Batman* television series. The town also has a good but drunken doctor named Doc Valentine (George Takei, from the *Star Trek* series) and a conservative, beautiful general store owner, Mattie Chase (Jackie Swanson). Since the film takes place in the future on a distant planet, it is to be expected that there are a host of unexpected characters as well. There is Gaunt (Carel Struycken) the undertaker, an immense man in black, flowing robes, who appears just before someone dies. Another odd creature is actually a conventional one in disguise. It is the villain, which in this film is Redeye (Andrew Divoff), part lizard and part human. Rounding out the strange array of characters is Stell Barr (Meg Foster), a beautiful cyborg deputy marshal.

The plot is set in motion when Redeye returns to Oblivion after having taken hold of a cache of precious metal which seems to give him control over everyone. It is not clear what his plans are, and whether or not this precious metal entitles him to be ruler of the planet or just of the puny town called Oblivion. Either way, Redeye seems very excited about it, and has assembled some other bad guys to kill the marshal, terrorize the town, and generally wreak havoc. He is assisted by his girlfriend, a dominatrix type named Lash (Musetta Vander).

As in all westerns, there is a hero as well, Zack Stone (Richard Joseph Paul), and true to the genre, he even has an Indian sidekick Buteo (Jimmie Skaggs). Zack is lured back to Oblivion by the death of his estranged father, the marshal. It is revealed that Zack left town because he could not condone the violence of humanity. Zack intends to find enough money to get away from this planet for good, until his conscience and certain extenuating circumstances force him to stay and help defend the town of Oblivion against Redeye and his gang. The fact that Zack prevails with the help of Miss Kitty, Doc Valentine, Buteo, and the lovely Mattie Chase should not surprise anyone.

Along the way, Director Sam Irvin and Screenwriter/Co-Producer Peter David concoct a visually vivid but ultimately unsatisfying mixture of comedy and sci-fi. Some of the most interesting moments in the film are visual. For example, one of the first images of Oblivion shows the undertaker Gaunt stepping out of his oddly shaped house onto the town's main street. His two-story house bulges at the center, immediately giving a cartoonish look and feel to the film. The street is a mixture of styles, with the wild West theme predominant, but that motif is peppered with anomalies, such as several strange towers with propellers attached. Additionally, there are numerous other clues that this is not your standard western. For example, the marshals' badges are electronic crime prevention devices, and the foothills surrounding the town are crawling with giant scorpions called "night scorps."

All of these creations are well-designed and/or supervised by Production Designer Milo. The "night scorps" (animated figures reminiscent of Ray Harryhausen's stop-action figures in *Jason and the Argonauts* [1963]) and a funny but lethal toad-like creature were created and animated by David Allen Productions. Michael Roche supplies a fine mixture of costumes which manage to be appropriately bizarre for the film's context, especially for the still-sexy Julie Newmar.

CREDITS

Zack Stone: Richard Joseph Paul
Mattie Chase: Jackie Swanson
Redeye: Andrew Divoff
Stell Barr: Meg Foster
Buteo: Jimmie Skaggs
Mr. Gaunt: Carel Struycken
Lash: Musetta Vander
Doc Valentine: George Takei
Miss Kitty: Julie Newmar
Buster: Isaac Hayes

Origin: USA
Released: 1995
Production: Vlad Paunescu and Oana Paunescu for Full Moon Entertainment; released by R. S. Entertainment
Direction: Sam Irvin
Screenplay: Peter David; based on a story idea by Charles Band, and on a story by John Rheaume, Greg Suddeth, and Mark Goldstein
Cinematography: Adolfo Bartoli
Editing: Margaret-Anne Smith
Production design: Milo
Casting: Robert MacDonald and Perry Bullington
Visual effects: David Allen
Sound: Tiberiu Borcoman
Special makeup effects: Alchemyfx and Michael Deak
Costume design: Michael Roche, Radu Corciova and Oana Paunescu
Music: Pino Donaggio
MPAA rating: no listing
Running Time: 94 minutes

All of these visual elements seem under control by director Irvin. He is to be commended for attempting to make the actor's blocking visually interesting. This is particularly evident in the kinetic scenes with the exotic Lash, whose every move seems choreographed. But not all of these attempts at visual originality are a success.

Although the film is often visually interesting, Irvin's humor does not keep pace with his visual acuity. Some of the visual sight gags simply don't work. In particular, the constant flamenco dance movements of one of the villains are more irritating than interesting or amusing, and the use of some truly violent images, such as Redeye pulling his arm out of its socket, are just plain gross. Further, Irvin allows many of the actors to overact, encouraging their mugging by holding the camera on certain reaction shots. This, in turn, pulls down the pace of the film, and it seems that a parody stuffed with cliches should not sit still long enough for its audience to notice that it is borrowing so many trite elements. To make fun of a genre, you should probably be able to outsmart it.

There is one very funny segment, however, amidst the constant non sequiturs, the asides, and the cliches. Zack's father's funeral takes place inside Gaunt's funeral parlor, where Bingo games are apparently held every Thursday, regardless of whether there is a funeral. The service is occasionally interrupted by the game, to great effect: "Some of you hate me," says Zack to the congregation. "Sometimes I think my father felt the same way." "G-49," intones a voice from above. "I remember when I was seventeen," continues Zack. "I-17," says the voice. And so it goes.

Obviously David is not without talent, and perhaps some of the film's lack of sophistication comes from the actor's performances. Most of them show not a shred of awareness that they have gone over-the-top from "bizarre" to "embarrassing." In particular, Musetta Vander chews the scenery with no mercy. Julie Newmar tries to re-create her famous hissing sounds, and it simply seems weird. Jimmie Skaggs tries so hard to be droll as the philosophical Indian that he becomes exceedingly dull instead. And Jackie Swanson, who played Woody Harrelson's fiancee on *Cheers*, is quite apathetic in her role. The only actor emerging unscathed is Meg Foster as a sympathetic, sexy cyborg.

Special commendation should go to composer Pino Donaggio, whose consistently interesting musical score far exceeds the film itself in sophistication and artistry.

This film won first prize at the Houston Film Festival for Science Fiction and Fantasy. There is an audience out there that will appreciate its irreverence and its visual effects, but for the most part, *Oblivion* will probably only find a home in the great black hole of cult films.

—*Kirby Tepper*

The Old Lady Who Walked in the Sea

Judging by its title, *The Old Lady Who Walked in the Sea* sounds like a thoughtful, literate sketch. Far from it. It's a frothy, foul-mouthed testament to France's unflagging affection for silly sex talk and an embarrassing coda to Jeanne Moreau's long career as a French film goddess.

Released in 1991, *The Old Lady Who Walked in the Sea* didn't cross the Atlantic until 1995. Small wonder. Even with its big-name star, faux-raunchy dialogue and titillating story line, the film doesn't have enough going for it to make even art-house box offices jingle. It's a slight story that relies on the rather mixed pleasures of seeing Moreau turned into a sexagenarian floozy.

The good news is that Moreau is fine. Her character, inexplicably named Milady, is regal in a loony way in outrageous, loud print dresses and huge hats. She looks like a cross between Bette Davis and Sophia Loren. Somehow, Moreau manages not to embarrass herself in these tastelessly revealing outfits; if anything, age has revealed the essence of her beauty. In her mid-sixties, she still retains a coquettish charm and a classic face. But the lines she must recite are such low-brow trash that it's almost a sacrilege. A beautiful woman, aging so gracefully, is turned into a trollop by a no-class script. Her lines are supposed to be the film's main source of humor, but mostly they're sad. How can such a classy woman be such a juvenile boor?

Milady and her partner Pompilius (the redoubtable Michel Serrault) are low-life thieves and con artists in upper-class drag. They rob from the rich and give to themselves; they're masterfully upwardly mobile.

The film's title derives from Milady's efforts to cure her arthritis with occasional walks in the ocean. Milady takes those strolls in her finest dresses. The few sequences of such efforts are not emblematic enough to justify naming the film after them. Milady is certainly not an "old lady" in any customary sense and her walks in the sea are one of the least intriguing things she does.

We first meet Milady primping before a vanity mirror and praying, profanely and selfishly. "Lord, don't you ever tire of me?" she asks, portraying herself as an old biddy "whose ass has been plucked a thousand times." That's the sort of dialogue Moreau recites throughout the film.

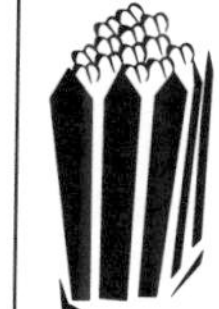

"I stink of age and coming of death."—Elderly Lady M gazing into a mirror in *The Old Lady Who Walked in the Sea*

Milady dresses in flashy costumes with large hats. She walks with a cane but her libido is spry. Her main failing, she concedes to her God, is her "insatiable desire for young flesh." At least her spirit is willing, if her flesh is failing. In fact, the film's main source of jokes is the gap between the still-youthful desires of Milady, and to a lesser extent Pompilius, and their supposedly decrepit bodies. The idea that senior citizens are physically incapable of lovemaking is only one of the many embarassingly backwards attitudes toward sexuality that the film displays.

Pompilius prefers natty cream-colored suits and bow ties. He's meticulous in his dress and speech and occasionally derives pleasure from skewering Milady with his larger vocabulary. She's no match for his intellectual prowess. Often he corrects her grammar. Otherwise he is a thoroughly cuckolded mate, completely at the mercy of his partner's whims. "I only keep you on because of your starched outfits, funny verbs and the way you drink tea," Milady says in one of the film's best lines. She's the boss and he's the lackey, though by film's end it is revealed there are limits to the slights he will endure.

As we meet them in the Antilles, Milady and Pompilius have their criminal routine down pat. They blackmail a wealthy scion and his mistress after Pompilius takes long-distance photographs of their hideaway. They've done this kind of thing so many times that they are elegantly smooth and execute the scam almost effortlessly.

Their relationship is also a finely modulated symphony of mutual insults. Most of the insults are based on sexual incapacity. Among many other epithets, Moreau calls Pompilius "debris of love," "pus-filled raven," "dime-store diplomat," "decrepit drone" and "rotting old ramrod." In one fit of anger, she says: "A starched shirt and creased pants are all that keep you upright." He responds with sometimes angry, sometimes affectionate rejoinders, calling Milady "an old sow," "a tender but tired trollop," and "doctored-up debris." These exchanges are amusing and often outrageous, but sometimes they are just crude and silly. Eventually they become wearisome.

Milady is tired of Pompilius, it seems, mainly because he no longer stokes her sexual fires, but also because he has been too long wrapped around her finger and she is a creature who needs new conquests to make herself feel fresh and youthful. Enter Lambert, a bored young hunk stranded in the islands. Reciting dialogue only the French could appreciate, he rejects another female conquest by explaining how homesick he is for Paris: "I'm sick of blue skies....I want a gray, rainy street."

Milady ensnares Lambert after he deftly steals her ring. He's not only good criminal material, he's also her perfect fantasy boy toy. She offers him a job as her "dauphin," then has to explain to him what that means. He's willing to hook up with her, but one of the major failings of the film is that it's never clear why. He's such an insensitive clod that it seems a stretch to believe he falls for her charms, especially since those charms are so intermittent, but that's what we're supposed to buy. The film's key relationship simply doesn't make sense.

At first, Lambert is overeager in the thievery department. Milady and Pompilius fear he won't respect their elaborate system of honor among thieves. Commissioning him for a big job, she prays: "Let this kid be on the up and up, Lord, and don't let him shaft us." Milady berates him when he blackmails a mark for too princely a sum: "Never hit too hard if you want them to forget you," she lectures. She also warns: "We never pluck the same pigeon twice. It's immoral." Milady and Pompilius have been at their trade so long that they've developed not only their only language but their own idiosyncratic moral code.

The trio, with Pompilius sulking about the new houseboy, moves from the Antilles to a villa on the French Riviera, where the hugely successful Milady and her sidekicks live an ostentatious life of idle luxury that proves that crime does pay. They pull off a forgettable caper that involves stealing a five million dollar diadem from an Arabic sultan who is giving it to his daughter as a birthday present. Milady wants the pricey piece not because she needs the money but because it flatters her vanity, and, besides, it doesn't belong on the plain princess, who in her opinion is a "lumpy sausage" with "a greasy skull." "The thought of that diamond on her head is unbearable," Milady rants.

Milady is a mentor to Lambert not only in crime but in the sensual realm as well. She's like a maternal pimp instructing Lambert in the ways of lust. Lambert has a penchant for quickies, which are ridiculously easy, including one conquest in a library that defies all credulity. Milady approves wholeheartedly of the hit-and-run romp, the shorter the better, but reminds Lambert that he should close his fly afterwards.

Lambert at first agrees to stick to one-hour stands and swear off affairs, but inexplicably becomes enamored of Naomi (Geraldine Danon), a script girl whom Pompilius has picked up at the airport while posing as a limousine driver. It seems the old geezer has his own games he likes to play with young fleshpots. Pompilius tries to flatter Naomi by guessing she's a tennis star. She replies, in the film's peculiarly awful style, "I'm not that good, but I do love tennis. I'd love to be seeded." Such lines sound like they belong in a soft-core porno flick, and indeed they betray a similar attitude. All the women in this film seem to have the same overcharged loins that Milady has. It's just as if feminism never happened and we're back in the mid-sixties. Ah, France, where it's not just the men whose minds are focused on one thing only.

The film's take on sexuality is juvenile and at times almost clinical. There's no romantic sizzle between Lambert and any of his conquests, no customary signs of affection between him and Naomi. Just as in pornographic films, everyone gets right to sex, or at least talking about sex, which robs the proceedings of any real erotic tingle. The height of absurdity comes when Milady videotapes her houseboy and Naomi making love. Milady and Pompilius invite Naomi to lunch, get her drunk, then call in Lambert and roll the film. The youngsters then go at it while the old-timers cluck disapprovingly about their clumsy methods. When Pompilius steps in to show Lambert the right way to do things, *The Old Lady Who Walked in the Sea* goes off the last sand bar and drowns in its own inanity. Heynemann, a respected director, should know better.

What happened to the film between its 1991 debut in France and its 1995 distribution in the states is unclear, but there is some awafully strange editing. Some scenes just pop up and disappear as if they were spliced from another film. Except for some lovely shots of beaches, technically the film is a mess.

While the first half of the film has its amusements, the last half is difficult to endure. Moreau continues gamely to trudge through the awful script. Crowing to Lambert of her previous conquests, she boasts: "Princes would crawl at my feet....I peed in the couscous of an emir." Given how buffoonish such lines make Milady, it is doubly annoying when the film tries to get serious with scenes of betrayal, suicide and the ravages of senility. But just when it appears Milady is turning into a tragic, sinister figure, it all dissolves back into lowbrow mush.

If you think the notion of old people speaking and acting like pre-adolescents in heat is funny, then you should definitely find *The Old Lady Who Walked in the Sea*. If you are a fan of Jeanne Moreau, you'd be better served seeing *Jules and Jim* again. Moreau does not deserve being turned into a clown. The only remarkable thing about *The Old Lady Who Walked in the Sea* is that Moreau somehow manages to retain her dignity and class throughout this hopeless exercise. Perhaps that's the point of the title after all: Moreau can stroll through brine in her finery and still emerge radiant.

—*Michael Betzold*

CREDITS

Milady: Jeanne Moreau
Pompilius: Michèl Serrault
Lambert: Luc Thullier
Naomi: Geraldine Danon

Origin: France
Released: 1991
Direction: Laurent Heynemann

REVIEWS

The New York Times. Sept. 15, 1995, p. C12.

Once Were Warriors

"A family in crisis, a life in chaos...nothing is more powerful than a mother's love."—Movie tagline

"Profoundly compelling!"—Jack Mathews, *New York Newsday*

"Powerful! Lee Tamahori's scorching film is a brutally effective family drama...genuinely poignant with furiously energetic performances."—Janet Maslin, *New York Times*

"Emotionally explosive."—Mike Caccioppoli, *WABC Radio*

"Two thumbs up!"—*Siskel & Ebert*

Two widespread social plagues all but ignored in cinema are domestic violence and the annihilation of native cultures by modern civilization. Rarely does a film touch on either of these shameful subjects. Remarkably, the New Zealand film *Once Were Warriors* takes on both issues, and it does so with unprecedented frankness and astounding verve.

This unflinching film has all the sobering impact of an alcoholic's long look into a mirror the morning after a violent, drunken spree. It is brutally honest in depicting how rapid modernization can obliterate an entire people's dignity, perverting honorable warrior virtues into spasms of self-destructive violence. And few films have been more forthright in chronicling the horrors of an abusive father, a scourge that knows no ethnic or economic boundaries.

How does a modestly budgeted film by virtual unknowns achieve such grand purposes? In the best tradition of cinema, it does so by depicting a few decisive weeks in the life of a family with strong and memorable characters. Set in the lower-class culture of urban New Zealand, dealing with a place and a people unfamiliar to most of the world's film audiences, *Once Were Warriors* gives its principals a universal resonance. That is no small feat.

Based on a novel by Alan Duff, *Once Were Warriors* marks the promising feature-film debut of director Lee Tamahori, widely known in New Zealand for directing TV commercials. Tamahori brings a strong popular presentation to his ambitious film, using rap music and a few MTV-style flourishes to frame his intensely sobering tale.

Once Were Warriors is like a jagged piece of glass that sparkles with tremendous beauty. It is incredible, but it falls short of being a masterpiece. Some scenes are overplayed, the ending is heavyhanded, and the rough edges make for a jarring experience rather than the kind of beguiling entertainment that takes audiences in and then hits them with a moral lesson. But these missteps are those of inexperience, not due to lack of talent or reach, and for the most part Tamahori hits his difficult targets with explosive impact. He has a bright future as an uncompromising director.

The film opens with a panorama of majestic mountains and unspoiled wild land accompanied by a trill of native Maori music. Then the camera rudely pulls back and reveals the landscape to be a billboard on the side of an ugly, busy highway. A woman smoking a cigarette and sporting a tattoo strolls through a barbed-wire-topped walkway. The camera takes us past street rappers, graffiti, abandoned buildings, junkyards and a landscape of urban decay and swaggering, crude hoodlums. This is what has become of New Zealand and its people in a few short decades of violent social change.

The most brutal of the hoods is Jake Heke (Temuera Morrison), who pummels anyone who crosses him. The tattooed woman is his wife Beth (Rena Owen). When they come home to their paperboard house, Jake wants to have sex with Beth on the kitchen table, even though their children are playing just outside. He tells her he's gone on the dole, which is only $17 a month less income than his job. When Beth becomes upset because she wants to stop renting and buy a home some day, Jake erupts in a profane rage.

Beth and Jake have five children, and they obviously started at a young age. The oldest, Nig (Julian Arahanga), who is in his late teens, visits only rarely. Nig is completely disenchanted with his family and is being brutally initiated into a street gang which sports facial tattoos that mimic Maori war paint. Bookie (Taungaroa Emile), who is about 14 or 15, wears dreadlocks and is in trouble for shoplifting and other petty crimes. Grace (Mamaengaroa Kerr-Bell), who is 13, is level-headed, smart and sensitive, and an aspiring writer. She has a friend and confidante, Toot (Shannon Williams), who lives in a hulk of a car beneath a highway underpass and sniffs glue. When we first meet Grace, she is reading the two youngest children, Polly and Huata, a story she's written.

"I got a temper on me, who doesn't?"—Jake from *Once Were Warriors*

Jake is a drunkard who hangs out with a bunch of headknockers and assorted groupies. Frequently and without notice, he brings them home for parties, where they sing drunken love songs and folk anthems while the children lie awake upstairs in bed. Jake is a silky-voiced crooner and he and Beth can sing a beautiful duet. But minutes later, Beth says something wrong after a sudden visit from Nig to ask for money, and Jake pummels her. Upstairs, the children huddle shivering in bed listening to the blows and screams. They've obviously been through these terrifying nights before. Jake finishes his night by raping his bloodied wife.

The next morning, Grace tries to clean up the mess downstairs and get some breakfast for the others. As are so many daughters of alcoholic parents, she's a substitute mother, the one who tries to hold things together. Beth awakens with her assailant's arm across her. The sheets are bloody and her face is beaten to a pulp. She looks so awful that she decides she can't go to Bookie's court hearing; her appearance might convince the judge to send Bookie away. But her absence has the same effect, and Bookie becomes a ward of the state. When a tearful Grace returns home to tell her mother, Jake swaggers in. He berates Beth for looking awful, and says the detention will benefit his son by toughening him up. When Beth argues again, Jake throttles both her and Grace. After he leaves, Grace declares, "I hate him."

This family drama is intensely disturbing and achingly authentic. It's horrible to watch, but it needs watching. Tamahori sugarcoats nothing, but he doesn't make his characters into villains or heroes either. They're real people. When Beth, pushed to the edge by Jake's violence, is wooed back into his good graces, she says, "That's the trouble, Jake, I do love you." After what's happened to her, the statement is repulsive. But it is realistic. Beth fights back, but she is also weak and dependent; she, too, has been corrupted, and she does still love a man who has turned into an animal. Until she breaks free, she is still a slave to her conditioning, as is Jake.

Remarkably, Morrison is popular in New Zealand playing a mild-mannered, gracious doctor on a soap opera. In *Once Were Warriors*, he is unspeakably vicious, but he lets us see the man behind the rage and drunkenness. He is a frightful person who can be charming, as is often the case in a wife-beater. Owen's finely layered performance is similarly remarkable. She never submerges her authenticity behind a movie-star image of either victim or heroine. Her flaws and her dignity are both visible. If either Beth or Jake had been a caricature, *Once Were Warriors* would not have nearly so much impact.

Authentic, too, is the unsparing depiction of ghetto life, New Zealand style. With their leather jackets, motorcycles, and love of popular music, these disenfranchised native peoples are aping and aspiring to the Western modernity which has crushed their culture. They are collaborators in the obliteration of tradition. Everyone smokes, everyone drinks, everyone is promiscuous, everyone is materialistic, though no one has succeeded in escaping slum life. Tamahori's unflinching depiction is itself a biting commentary on societal change. In New Zealand and many other places in the world, a process that took centuries in America and Europe has taken only a generation. Tamahori doesn't cast blame, he simply observes.

The final push over the edge into tragedy starts when Jake, with a fistful of ill-gotten loot, agrees with Beth to rent a car to visit Bookie. Bookie has landed in a sort of Maori-pride boot camp, learning the old warrior chants and rituals from a more dignified but no less demanding father figure. On the ride there, the family is happy, even singing a silly pop song along the way. They stop to picnic near Beth's ancestral home, where her forebearers are buried, and we learn the couple's background: Beth is the daughter of a proud Maori family, just one generation removed from a much simpler, more dignified life. She defied her parents by marrrying Jake, who is the son of a slave. Jake still resents what he considers to be the superior attitude of Beth's clan, and he flees the scene. Next stop is a tavern, where Jake drinks away the family outing. Grace, who was close to her brother, is bitterly disappointed.

As Grace herself is defiled by the violence which engulfs her family, she becomes the martyr who finally moves Beth and her family off dead center. As played with magnificent grace, subtlety and power by Kerr-Bell, Grace becomes the moral center of a film which is about moral decay and the slim hope of redemption.

Tamahori can be forgiven for making the ending of the film a little too obvious and strident, because he has stayed

CREDITS

Beth Heke: Rena Owen
Jake Heke: Temuera Morrison
Grace Heke: Mamaengaroa Kerr-Bell
Nig Heke: Julian (Sonny) Arahanga
Boogie Heke: Taungaroa Emile
Polly Heke: Rachael Morris
Huata Heke: Joseph Kairau
Bully: Clifford Curtis
Toot: Shannon Williams
Dooley: Pete Smith

Origin: New Zealand
Released: 1994
Production: Robin Scholes for Communicado, in association with the New Zealand Film Commission, Avalon Studios, and New Zealand on Air; released by Fine Line Features
Direction: Lee Tamahori
Screenplay: Riwia Brown; based on a novel by Alan Duff
Cinematography: Stuart Dryburgh
Editing: Michael Horton
Production design: Michael Kane
Music: Murray Grindlay and Murray McNabb
MPAA rating: R
Running Time: 108 minutes

so honest throughout. But there is no mistaking the judgments that must be made. *Once Were Warriors* is a searing indictment of much that passes for civilization. Tamahori makes it clear that Jake's violence is not just a personal flaw but a cultural legacy. At the same time, the film makes no excuses for that violence.

Few films have even attempted what *Once Were Warriors* accomplishes in focusing on the effects of societal change on real people in real families. Possibly *The Grapes of Wrath* is the only comparison that would make sense to American audiences. *Once Were Warriors* isn't easy to watch and it's not always executed perfectly, but it does what great art is supposed to do: rip away the curtains that shield us from the truth.

—Michael Betzold

REVIEWS

Commonweal. June 16, 1995, p. 16.
Entertainment Weekly. March 10, 1995, p. 45.
Hollywood Reporter. Jan. 20-22, 1995, p. 10.
Los Angeles Times. March 3, 1995, p. F1.
Maclean's. March 20, 1995, p. 76.
The Nation. March 20, 1995, p. 397.
New Republic. March 27, 1995, p. 28.
New York. March 6, 1995, p. 54.
Newsweek. March 6, 1995, p. 68.
Playboy. April 1995, p. 26.
Variety. March 30, 1004, p. 48.
Vogue. March 1995, p. 256.

Only You

"One of the all-time manic romantic comedies. Tomei proves her Oscar was no fluke. Robert Downey, Jr. has never been this adorable."—*Glamour*

"An old-fashioned romantic comedy that works."—*The New York Daily News*

"A new comedy destined to delight. The witty script is so richly endowed with shocking turnabouts and cute reverses that you'll find yourself admiring the writing just as much as you do the expert performances. Tomei projects an ethereal aura that gives this fairy tale its magical glow. Robert Downey, Jr. should send a dazzled audience home in a pleasant mood of happily ever after."—*The New York Post*

As with *Sleepless in Seattle* (1993) or *When Harry Met Sally* (1992), *Only You* is a sweet romance whose raison d'etre appears to be to emulate the screwball film romances of the thirties and forties while creating a marketable soundtrack. *Only You* is, in a sense, also director Norman Jewison's follow-up to his hugely successful romantic comedy *Moonstruck* (1987). In large part, Jewison and company are successful in creating an atmosphere reminiscent of both the old romantic comedies and the more recent ones. But, while this is by no means a bad film, it is lacking the true wit of *When Harry Met Sally* and the depth of *Moonstruck* (not to mention that its soundtrack is not as wonderful as *Sleepless in Seattle.*) However, a charming story, beautifully shot locations, and the witty performances of the leading characters make this an entertaining film that should not be dismissed.

Faith (Marisa Tomei) is a teacher, a woman whose whole life has been guided by the principle of predetermined destiny. She believes that her destiny is to marry a man named Damon Bradley, and when she discovers that her dull fiancee has a friend named Damon Bradley who is on his way to Venice, she jumps on a plane to find him. Her certainty that she must meet him in order to avoid marrying the wrong man is made believable by lovely Marisa Tomei. Tomei has been given a chance to show a rather broad range of late, having won the Oscar for her role as a tough-talking automobile expert in *My Cousin Vinny* (1992), and having played a Cuban refugee in *The Perez Family* (1995). Here she is a winning comic heroine, possessing a mixture of naivete and strength reminiscent of Claudette Colbert in *It Happened One Night* (1934).

She is accompanied to Venice by her sister-in-law and best friend (Bonnie Hunt), a pretty but insecure woman unhappy in her marriage to Faith's brother (Fisher Stevens). Bonnie Hunt is a revelation in this simple role, playing the part that Eve Arden would have played in the 1930s. When being romanced by the handsome Giovanni (Joaquim de Almeida) she responds to his seductive talk by asking if he wants a cracker. When arriving at the four-star hotel where they think Damon Bradley is staying she says, "We can't afford this, Kathie Lee Crosby stayed here." Hunt's dry delivery and her doe eyes make a perfect best friend/comic foil, and she all but steals the film.

Stealing the film from Robert Downey Jr. is not an easy thing to do. His effortless physical comedy and his goofy but sexy charm are as effective here as they were in *Chaplin* (1993) and *Chances Are* (1993). In fact, his character bears a similarity to his role as a reincarnated soul in *Chances Are* (opposite Cybill Shepherd): Downey used his combination of mischievousness and innocence to great effect in that film, and does so again here. He plays a man so smitten with Faith that he allows her to think he is Damon Bradley, and then continues to help her find Damon Bradley once she learns he is just a shoe salesman from New Jersey named Peter.

While shooting in Italy, the production was headquartered at Rome's famous Cinecitta film studio, which is often referred to as "Hollywood on the Tiber." Cinecitta has been in operation for over 50 years and has hosted some of the world's greatest film personalities.

Norman Jewison knows his way around a romantic comedy, having directed the wonderful *Moonstruck*. He takes the mistaken identities and the beautiful locales and mixes them into a charming paean to those old romantic comedies. From the beauty of Venice by moonlight to the luxury hotels of the seacoast village of Positano, Jewison creates an atmosphere of European romance and beauty similar to films such as *To Catch a Thief* (1953) and *Roman Holiday* (1953). Additionally, Jewison uses the camera in interesting ways, creating shots which artfully use movement as a way to create a flowing pace and maintain visual interest.

After praising the fine performances and the excellent direction, it would seem that this film has no flaws. But it has a few built-in characteristics which keep it from being as fulfilling as many cinematic predecessors. First, Faith's romantic obsession with destiny makes her a seem a bit selfish and a bit silly; second, she travels awfully far (and rather irresponsibly) to follow a man she's never met; third, she dumps her fiance by phone, and the audience does not see it happen; and fourth, Peter seems to be a bit cavalier in his manipulation of Faith's attention. More important, however, is the fact that it seems implausible in the nineties that two people can fall in love at first sight and mean it. But perhaps that's missing the point of a screwball romantic comedy: the characters are just screwball enough to stop being realistic and start being romantic. And there's always that good musical soundtrack.

—*Kirby Tepper*

CREDITS

Faith Corvatch: Marisa Tomei
Peter Wright: Robert Downey, Jr.
Kate: Bonnie Hunt
Giovanni: Joaquim De Almeida
Larry: Fisher Stevens
False Damon Bradley: Billy Zane
Damon Bradley: Adam LeFevre
Dwayne: John Benjamin Hickey
Leslie: Siobhan Fallon
Fortune-teller: Antonia Rey
Faith's mother: Phyllis Newman

Origin: USA
Released: 1994
Production: Norman Jewison, Cary Woods, Robert N. Fried, and Charles Mulvehill for Yorktown Productions Ltd.; released by TriStar Pictures
Direction: Norman Jewison
Screenplay: Diane Drake
Cinematography: Sven Nykvist
Editing: Stephen Rivkin
Production design: Luciana Arrighi
Art direction: Stephano Ortolani, Maria Teresa Barbasso and Gary Kosko
Set decoration: Ian Whittaker, Alessandra Querzola and Diane Stoughton
Casting: Howard Feuer
Sound: Ken Weston
Costume design: Milena Canonero
Music: Rachel Portman
MPAA rating: PG
Running Time: 108 minutes

"My connection to Faith was immediate, because Faith is a true believer...a believer in dreams, in magic and in romance. That's what we have in common: I absolutely believe in destiny, and I believe in risking everything when your soul tells you to find out where you should be and with whom."—Marisa Tomei comments on the bond between actress and character

Operation Dumbo Drop

"A top-secret mission of gigantic proportions!"—Movie tagline

"A lot of laughs!"—Joel Siegel, *ABC-TV*

"A comedy adventure with humor and winning performances—solid laughs and smiles."—Gary Dretzka, *Chicago Tribune*

Box Office Gross: $24,667,779

In many ways, "Tinsel Town" (aka Hollywood) is a land of make believe, where stars are more glamorous than humanly possible in real life, where bravery and romance rise to epic proportions, where a smile and a song make all the difference. Nonetheless, some of the most popular films of all time are drawn from real life: from *The Glen Miller Story* (1954) to *La Bamba* (1987), from *Pride of the Yankees* (1942) to *The Babe* (1992) and *Eight Men out* (1988), from *The Sound of Music* (1965) to *Coal Miner's Daughter* (1980), life itself has grown upon occasion larger than life. *Operation Dumbo Drop* also presents a true story and, in the process, presents another view of not only the Vietnam War, but also of the country of Vietnam and its people.

Captain T. C. Doyle (Ray Liotta) has traveled into the heart of the mountains to take over Captain Sam Cahill's (Danny Glover) command. Upon Captain Doyle's arrival, he quickly demonstrates both his good intentions and his naiveté destroying the village's primary asset: an elephant. In an effort to maintain good relations between the Green Berets and the Montagnard villagers of Dak Nhe, Doyle and Cahill must figure out a way to replace the elephant. *Operation Dumbo Drop* is the story of five soldiers who take an 8,000 pound elephant on a 200 mile trek in order to restore order to the remote village. To the project each soldier brings a special skill-or problem: Harvey 'H.A.' Ashford (Doug E. Doug) is a nervous wreck as he is soon to finish his tour of duty, Lawrence Farley (Corin Nemec) is a farm boy who hates animals, and David Poole (Denis Leary) is a supply "sergeant" (lieutenant, actually) and larcenous facilitator. With the help of the Green Berets, the elephant travels to its new home-by land, by sea, by air, and by parachute.

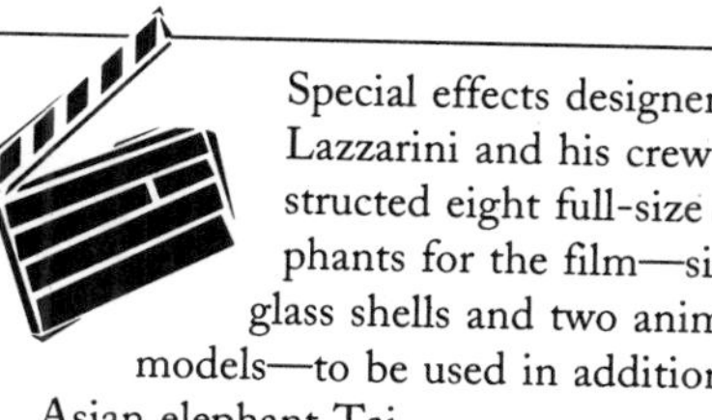

Special effects designer Rick Lazzarini and his crew constructed eight full-size elephants for the film—six fiberglass shells and two animatronic models—to be used in addition to Asian elephant Tai.

Operation Dumbo Drop recounts an actual mission conducted by the 5th Special Forces (Green Berets) in Vietnam on the day of Dr. Martin Luther King's assassination in 1968. Originally covered by Green Beret Information Officer Jim Morris, the story remained virtually hidden until Morris wrote about the series of events as part of a writing assignment at the University of Oklahoma School of Journalism. Then the story disappeared for seventeen years, until it caught the attention of executive producer Robert Cort. Director Simon Wincer (of *Free Willy* fame) was drawn to the project by the opportunity "to make a positive film about a chapter in American history remembered only in negative terms." "There have been so many bad stories to come out of Vietnam," Wincer says [in the press packet]. "It's such a scar on the American psyche. It's good to make a film that actually takes a positive view of a group of characters who make a promise—and keep it."

While overtly trying to distance itself from other stories of war by trying to present a novel view of an unpopular war, *Operation Dumbo Drop* nonetheless draws heavily on other images of war. For instance, the film begins with Ray Liotta's Doyle traveling into the "heart of darkness" to find the illusive but much revered Cahill. Just as in *Apocalypse Now* (1979), Doyle finds Cahill in a native state, dressed like the villagers, speaking the villagers' language, and participating in the villagers' rituals. Where *Apocalypse Now* offers a view of beauty and chaos, *Operation Dumbo Drop* achieves a mise en scene more akin to television's *Mchale's Navy*. Also, as films about Vietnam have become a subgenre within the genre of all war films, it is no surprise that this film has in place the Vietnam icons that have arisen from films such as *Apocalypse Now* (1979), *Platoon* (1986), *Hamburger Hill* (1987), and *Forrest Gump* (1994): rock music, helicopters (both their sight and their sound), and the aura of a vacation in hell (i.e., tropical paradises filled with machinery and fire). Indeed, it is possible that while hardly original, the soundtrack of *Operation Dumbo Drop* may be one of its true drawing cards: "Gimme Some Lovin," "Higher and Higher," "Hang On Sloopy," and Aretha Franklin's "Think."

Beyond its recycling of the typical Vietnam icons, *Operation Dumbo Drop* also fails to present original characters. Take, for instance, Lieutenant David Poole, the facilitator. Blackmailed by Cahill into participation and motivated by the close timing of an upcoming rest-and-relaxation leave in Hawaii, Poole engineers a variety of methods of travel for the unconventional group. For instance, he arranges for a cargo plane and tranquilizers to make the elephant manageable enough to enter the plane. While Poole's characterization is clear, it is not novel. Indeed, Tony Curtis perfected the role of wheeler-dealer con-artist in 1959 in *Operation Petticoat*. Lieutenant Poole is a mere shadow of his predecessor.

Another disappointment with the film is the casting. That is, while the star power of Glover and Liotta could be a bonus, in reality they prove distracting, surrounded by unknowns and minor players. As a result of this casting, coupled with the poor production values and overblown acting, the film seems oddly out of balance, teetering into oblivion. Take, for instance, Ray Liotta's trademark face: broad, pockmarked cheeks, with narrow eyes and mischievous grin/grimace. Best known for his portrayal of Mafiosos and other thugs (*Corrina, Corrina*, 1994, aside), Liotta rose to prominence in such roles as a vicious ex-con in *Something Wild* (1986), a mobster in *Goodfellas* (1990), and a crazed cop in *Unlawful Entry* (1994). Surrounded by Vietnamese villagers and punctuated by West Point crispness, Liotta appears to have dropped from nowhere. He seems as lost as the audience. For instance, in the scene in which Cahill and Doyle meet for the first time, Cahill informs Doyle that he must drink the local wine offered by the leader in order to avoid offending him. Doyle is hesitant but soon complies. As he drinks, Ray Liotta apes, widening his eyes, slackening his jaw. As if caught in a melodrama, Liotta provides larger than life distress and discomfort. Such an overdone portrayal is unlike Liotta and confuses the audience more. Is this the cool mobster? The dangerous thug? Even the dear dad? Or is this a cardboard representation of an otherwise fine actor.

Perhaps director Wincer enlarged and simplified the performers' responses in order to cater to what he believed was his juvenile audience. While perhaps an admirable idea, it fails about as miserably as the string of elephant excrement/intestine jokes that abound in this film. For instance, in order to load Botat onto the cargo plane, the soldiers must administer a sedative available only as an enema. However, as Poole has found the wrong enema, no one is willing to insert it, and the elephant is ill prepared for such a trajectory. The scene results in several unsavory and unnecessary attempts at humor: Liotta cringes from the sight and smell while the other persons attempt to put as much distance as possible between themselves and the elephant. It is oversimplified, unsavory and unkind.

This is not to say, however, that the film is without redeeming features. Take, for instance, Botat (Tai). While the film was made in Thailand, the local elephants could not be used as the trainers work at close range with the elephants, whispering commands. Clearly such direction would interfere with filming. Therefore, Botat is played by Tai, a 26-year-old Asian elephant, weighing eight thousand pounds and standing more than eight-and-a-half feet tall. Elephant consultant Richard Lair auditioned more than five hundred elephants in two months searching for stand-ins for Tai. However, as western elephants are much larger due to better nutrition, the search proved to be quite difficult. Nonetheless, stand-ins were found, as was a baby elephant to play the role of young Botat. Other problems included importing Tai's food and water-200 pounds a day.

While *Operation Dumbo Drop* initially appears to be children's fare, its normalization of war, its acknowledgment of deviousness and its low humor make it a film that is best forgotten and never missed.

—Roberta F. Green

CREDITS

Sam Cahill: Danny Glover
Captain Doyle: Ray Liotta
David Poole: Denis Leary
Harvey Ashford: Doug E. Doug
Lawrence Farley: Corin Nemec
Linh: Dinh Thien Le

Origin: USA
Released: 1995
Production: Diane Nabatoff, David Madden
Direction: Simon Wincer
Screenplay: Gene Quintano, Jim Kouf, based on a story by Jim Morris, U.S. Army (Ret.)
Cinematography: Russell Boyd
Editing: O Nicholas Brown
Production design: Paul Peters
Art direction: Steve Spence
Costume design: Rosanna Norton
Special effects: Brian Cox
Casting: Mike Fenton
Music: David Newman
MPAA rating: PG
Running Time: 102 minutes

REVIEWS

Baltimore Sun, Maryland Live, July 28-August 3, 1995, p. 7
Boston Globe, July 28, 1995, p. 29.
The New York Times, July 28, 1995, p. C12.
USA Today, July 28, 1995, p. 5D
Washington Post, Weekend (capsule review), July 28, 1995, p. 38.

Othello

"Triumphant and thrilling! Fishburne gives a vibrant, dazzling performance!"—Bill Diehl, *ABC Radio Network*

"Passionate and moving...As accessible as *Fatal Attraction*"—Kevin Thomas, *Los Angeles Times*

"One of the most erotically charged productions ever committed to film."—Michael Medved, *New York Post*

"Overflows with passion, life and evil."—Norman Mark, *WAAQ-TV/Chicago*

Box Office Gross: $431,795

To attempt to film a classic Shakespearean tragedy as a debut feature film requires courage and involves considerable risk, especially if the play is *Othello*, which was made into a film with brilliant visual economy by Orson Welles in 1951. In 1965 Stuart Burge directed the flamboyant Laurence Olivier version. Olivier, like Welles, played the Moor in blackface, with a highly talented supporting cast—Maggie Smith as Desdemona, Frank Finlay as a subordinate Iago, and Derek Jacobi as Cassio. Any later attempts to film *Othello* will be measured against the theatrical flamboyance of the Burge-Olivier version and the cinematic brilliance of the recently re-released Welles version.

Kenneth Branagh dared to remake *Henry V* in 1989, knowing full well that his film would be measured against the lavish Olivier version of 1944. But Olivier had shaped his film as patriotic propaganda during World War II and weakened the character of Shakespeare's King by omitting scenes that demonstrated Henry's toughness. Branagh restored these scenes and created a "new" cinematic vehicle that was much closer to the spirit of the play. Though Branagh plays Iago in the recent *Othello*, he did not direct it. Oliver Parker, an actor turned director, understands the theatrical potential of the play but falls short of making his film truly original and cinematic.

The action begins in Venice, circa 1570, with Othello, the Moor (Laurence Fishburne) courting and winning Desdemona (Irene Jacob), the daughter of Brabantio (Pierre Vaneck), a Venetian Senator. Ensign Iago (Kenneth Branagh), Othello's subordinate, is enraged because Othello has promoted Michael Cassio (Nathaniel Parker) over him. When Iago learns that the Moor has secretely courted Desdemona, out of spite and malice in plainspoken and vulgar language he tells her father what has transpired.

Brabantio protests publicly that the Moor has bewitched his daughter, but Othello is highly regarded as a military leader and is sent by the Doge of Venice (Gabriele Ferzetti) to defend Cyprus from the Turkish fleet. Brabantio is forced to give his daughter to Othello but warns him that if Desdemona has deceived her father, she may also deceive her new husband.

After the Turkish fleet is destroyed by a tempest, Othello, now Governor of Cyprus, proclaims a night of revelry to celebrate his marriage and the destruction of the Turkish fleet. Knowing Cassio's weakness for liquor, Iago gets him drunk and coaxes him into a public brawl with Desdemona's embittered suitor Roderigo (Michael Maloney). Unwilling to tolerate such behavior, Othello relieves Cassio of his post and gives "honest" Iago his confidence. Iago suggests that Cassio have Desdemona intercede on his behalf; he intends to enflame the Moor's jealousy by suggesting that Desdemona is having an affair with Cassio.

Othello is unmoved until Iago plants incriminating evidence, a handerkerchief Othello had given Desdemona, taken from her by Iago's wife, her servant Emilia (Anna Patrick). Convinced that his wife has betrayed him, the enraged Othello, advised by scheming Iago, suffocates Desdemona in her bed, then learns from Emilia that Iago had ordered her to steal the handkerchief. Realizing that he has been duped by Iago (who is captured), Othello commits suicide. At the end Othello and Desdemona are buried at sea.

Following the trend of Franco Zeffirelli's *Hamlet* (1990), which set a standard for simplifying Shakespeare, nearly sixty percent of the text has been cut to bring the running time of the film down to just over two hours. The Stuart Burge-Olivier *Othello*, by contrast, was an hour longer. Parker's adaptation vandalizes the text, which is sliced and diced and simplified. Directing *Hamlet* for television in 1990, Kevin Kline noted that with *Hamlet* "every cut bleeds." Likewise *Othello*.

Thus the play is "refashioned," as one critic noted, "into an Elizabethan erotic thriller, told from the villain's viewpoint." The film was made on location in Italy, in Venice and at the Orsini-Odescalchi castle north of Rome. Gondolas ply the canals of Venice. The Mediterranian seems to buffet the battlements of Cyprus.

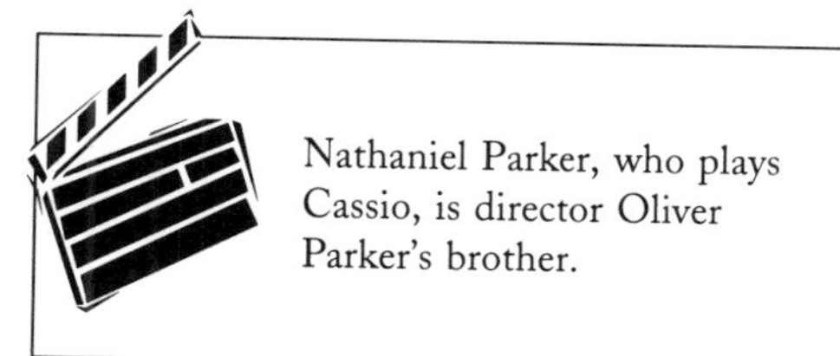

Nathaniel Parker, who plays Cassio, is director Oliver Parker's brother.

The Washington Post editorialized about the film's "uncanny" timing for American audiences, since it coincided with the "Trial of the Century" and the controversy over O.J. Simpson's guilt or innocence: "this tale of interracial marriage, murder and failed cultural assimilation just cuts too near the bone." After all, Shakespeare does tell the story of a "successful black man in a white society" who murders the beautiful white woman to whom he is married. Though the film may be "unremarkable as an interpretation," in the judgment of *Variety*, the tragic denouement could easily disturb viewers currently obsessed with the issues of miscegenation and murder. Of course one could argue that *Othello* is timeless, but during the political events of 1995, it also became potentially timely for Americans.

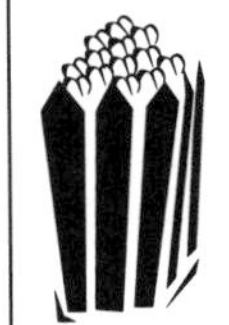

"Instead of it being a massive, four-hour psychological drama, I've gone for a fast-moving, relentless, erotic thriller."— Director Oliver Parker, who cut some 60% of Shakespeare's text for the film.

Reviews were mixed with regard to the casting of Parker's film, though generally favorable. Michael Wilmington of the *Chicago Tribune* found Laurence Fishburne "a sometimes astonishingly moving Othello," for example, even though the actor lacks "classical theatrical training and has never played a Shakespearean role." The danger of producing *Othello* is that the titular character has to hold his own against the play's scene-stealing archvillain. Some critics complained that Fishburne's "quiet" Othello was displaced from center screen by Kenneth Branagh's Iago and the "weirdly heavy Italian accents" of Brabantio and Desdemona, played by the French-Swiss actress showcased so well in Krzyszotof Kieslowski's *Red* (1995). But Todd McCarthy of *Variety* found the "shaven-headed, bearded" Fishburne, ornamented with earrings and tattoos, a "brooding, powerful figure," effective as a smoldering, exotic lover.

It is certainly appropriate to have Othello played by a charismatic black actor, but the inexperienced Fishburne is outclassed by Branagh's more polished and theatrically accomplished Iago. Parker claimed that he wanted to center the play in "the all-consuming love between Othello and Desdemona," but even if Fishburne is able to hold his own, the consensus among critics was that Irene Jacob does not. Desson Howe described her as being "doubly out-of-place—as a 20th-century movie actress doing Shakespeare, and as a French speaker caught in an English-language picture." These two actors, uncomfortable with Shakespeare are also uncomfortable in each other's company, according to Howe, who found their love affair therefore unconvincing.

Iago is a puzzle. Samuel Taylor Coleridge considered Iago's revelation of his motives as "the motive hunting of motiveless malignity." The mystery of his motivation has been analyzed by Stanley Edgar Hyman in his book *Iago: Some Approaches to the Illusion of His Motivation* (Atheneum, 1970). Iago is the most famous and deceptive of all of Shakespeare's villains, and Kenneth Branagh is up to the challenge of playing him with a difference.

Traditionally, Iago has been defined as bitter, jealous, and vituperative. Branagh turns him into a sort of prankster and mischief-maker, gleeful in his villainy to the end. Parker interprets Iago as an ordinary man who initially does not intend to destroy Othello but who gradually becomes "intoxicated by the effectiveness of what he has done and can do," according to Branagh. It is the function of Shakespeare's villains to boast of their evil deeds. When Iago is forced to look on the "tragic loading of this bed" at the end, he regards the bloody consequences of his villainy with, as May Schwartz noted, "the faintest twitch of pleasure." Finally, this ordinary man, transformed into a monster, is beyond remorse.

CREDITS

Othello: Laurence Fishburne
Desdemona: Irene Jacob
Iago: Kenneth Branagh
Cassio: Nathaniel Parker
Roderigo: Michael Maloney
Emilia: Anna Patrick

Origin: USA
Released: 1995
Production: Luc Roeg and David Barron for a Dakota Films/Imminent Films production; released by Sony Pictures Entertainment
Direction: Oliver Parker
Screenplay: Oliver Parker; based on the play *Othello* by William Shakespeare
Cinematography: David Johnson
Editing: Tony Lawson
Production design: Tim Harvey
Art direction: Desmond Crowe and Livia Borgognini
Costume design: Caroline Harris
Sound: Peter Glossop
Assistant direction: Simon Moseley
Casting: Debbie McWilliams
Music: Charlie Mole
MPAA rating: R
Running Time: 124 minutes

AWARDS AND NOMINATIONS

Screen Actors Guild Awards Nominations 1995:
Best Supporting Actor (Branagh)

Geoffrey Macnab was satisfied with the casting of "two magnetic stars" and the clever tailoring of the text but claimed the film lacked "visual flair," objecting to the static framing and the tendency to film characters in medium close-up. One might add that the advantage of such framing is to emphasize the actors and the language. Macnab approved of the way Parker allows Iago "to address the camera directly," but this is hardly a new technique. Tony Richardson used this device effectively in the Nicol Williamson *Hamlet* (1969) and Olivier used it brilliantly in his *Richard III* (1955). Macnab found the strength of Parker's film in its performances. Parker employs a chess metaphor, the shrouded figures of Othello and Desdemona buried at sea at the end recalling the chess figures Iago toys with early on as he plots his villainy, but critics who noticed this visual symbolism found it to be too obvious. On balance the film was judged too theatrical and not sufficiently cinematic.

—*James M. Welsh*

REVIEWS

Boxoffice. December 1995, pp. 10-11.
Boxoffice. February, 1996, p.16.
Chicago Tribune. December 29, 1995, p.4.
Detroit News, December 29, 1995, D3.
Entertainment Weekly. No.306, December 22, 1995, P.48.
Sight and Sound. Vol.6, No.2 (NS), February 1996, pp.51-52.
Time. Vol.147, No.3, 15 January 1996, p.67.
USA Today. December 14, 1995, D8.
Vanity Fair. December 1995, pp. 172-180.
Variety. December 11, 1995, p.83.
Washington Post. December 29, 1995, Fl, F6.
Washington Post. January 28, 1996, G1, G8.
Washington Post. January 24, 1996, A19.
Washington Post Weekend. December 29, 1995, p.32.

Outbreak

"A heart pounding thriller. Movie making at its best."—Bill Diehl, *ABC Radio Network*

"One of the great scare stories of our time. A clever, daunting thriller."—Roger Ebert, *Chicago Sun-Times*

"Killer movie-making. A lot of fun. An incredible cast."—Joel Siegel, *Good Morning America*

Box Office Gross: $67,823,573

In *Outbreak*, producer Arnold Kopelson and director Wolfgang Petersen accomplish the feat of combining one of the most compelling scientific horror stories of modern times, the potential outbreak of a lethal airborne virus among the population of an industrialized country, with one of America's finest actors, Dustin Hoffman, only to create a routine, if proficient, action-adventure potboiler.

Their failure is all the more puzzling given Kopelson's and Petersen's action-film pedigrees. Kopelson's previous film, *The Fugitive* (1993), and Petersen's, *In the Line of Fire* (1993), were among the finest Hollywood thrillers of the last decade—roller-coaster rides which put iconic American actors, Harrison Ford and Clint Eastwood, in the middle of the latest eye-popping stunts and digital effects, and pitted protagonists haunted by their pasts against complex, implacable foes they must understand in order to redeem themselves.

Outbreak's downfall comes in the choice of Kopelson, Petersen and screenwriters Laurence Dworet and Robert Roy Pool to use a different action-film model, that of *Die Hard* (1988), *Die Hard 2* (1990) and *Speed* (1994), in which an Everyman protagonist with little past and more attitude than character becomes the ghost in the machine of a grand conspiracy, the only person who can save the planet. This model unfortunately does a disservice to Hoffman, who has made a career of playing complex characters who elicit sympathy from an audience because they are as full of moxie as they are of confusion—Ben Braddock in *The Graduate* (1967), Ratso Rizzo in *Midnight Cowboy* (1969), Lenny Bruce in *Lenny* (1974), the embattled actor, Michael Dorsey, in *Tootsie* (1982). By having Hoffman play such a generic character and neglecting to tailor the script to his particular genius, Petersen fails to make the most of Hoffman's presence.

As well, if *Outbreak* depersonalizes its protagonist, it also makes the mistake of over-personifying the villains of the piece. The two books on which *Outbreak* is based, Richard Preston's *The Hot Zone* (1994), a non-fiction account of an outbreak of Ebola virus in a suburban Washington, D.C. Army laboratory which threatened to decimate the nation's capital, and Laurie Garrett's more general study of deadly viruses, *The Coming Plague* (1994), are riveting precisely because of the impersonal nature of the viral foes they describe. In *Outbreak*, Dworet and Pool round up the usual suspects—a power-mad general determined to suppress evidence of Army experimentation on humans, a dumb, greedy importer of black-market monkeys, a nasty virus-carrying monkey—and in so doing fail to remind the audience that it is the encroachment of industry and war into tropical ecosystems that is helping to unleash such viruses, an encroachment for which not just evil generals and smugglers are responsible. Dramatically, Dworet's and Pool's emphasis on moustache-twirling bad guys robs the piece of its unique nature—the very impersonality of its villain, and man's responsibility for that villain's having been unleashed.

Outbreak begins with a prologue which effectively shows the chaos produced by the outbreak of a deadly virus in a village in Zaire in 1967. (This fictional prologue is borrowed directly from *And the Band Played On* (1993), the HBO film about the AIDS crisis which began with a scene depicting a real-life outbreak of Ebola fever in Zaire in 1976.) General McClintock (Donald Sutherland), the head of the American rapid-reponse team to the outbreak, orders what appears to be an emergency supply drop. Only at the last moment do the disease-ridden villagers, waving with relief, realize that the drop is in fact a bomb, which exterminates the entire human population of the village. The monkeys which carry the disease, however, return to the jungle.

The film then flashes forward to the present. Colonel Sam Daniels, M.D. (Hoffman) is the sketchily drawn lead doctor at the United States Army Medical Research Institute for Infectious Diseases near Washington. Petersen and his production designer successfully make a great deal of medical information and plot exposition exciting as they show Daniels walking through the increasing levels of security and protection required in the USAMRIID laboratories according to the virulence of the viruses in each room.

USAMRIID's commanding officer, General Billy Ford (Morgan Freeman), dispatches Daniels and a team to Zaire, where the virus thought to have been eradicated in 1967 has re-emerged. Daniels and his team, dressed in spacesuit-like protective garb, discover a horrific scene in the rainforest, a virtually obliterated village in which bodies are stacked like firewood. A local doctor tells Daniels presciently that "the gods were awoken from their sleep when man cut down the trees. This is their punishment."

Daniels returns to Washington, where his team identifies the virus. (Why it took three years to identify the AIDS retrovirus and takes only a few hours to identify this one is not explained.) Daniels convinces his ex-wife, Robbie (Rene Russo), now a doctor with the Centers for Disease Control in Atlanta, that the Zairean virus represents a threat to the U.S. population, but both doctors' superiors, including Ford, inexplicably refuse to put the country on alert. Ford equally mysteriously removes Daniels from the case.

Meanwhile, in Cedar Creek, California, a small town north of San Francisco, a dimwitted young animal smuggler (Patrick Dempsey) sells an African monkey, illegally brought in through San Francisco Harbor, to a pet shop dealer. Boarding a plane to see his girlfriend in Boston, the smuggler is overcome by fever-like symptoms. By the time the Danielses have debriefed the dying smuggler and his girlfriend in Boston and traced the virus to the monkey—which has been let loose in the forest surrounding Cedar Creek—the northern-California hamlet has become the

CREDITS

Dr. Sam Daniels: Dustin Hoffman
Dr. Roberta Keough: Rene Russo
General Billy Ford: Morgan Freeman
General McClintock: Donald Sutherland
Major Salt: Cuba Gooding, Jr.
Jimbo Scott: Patrick Dempsey
Major Casey Schuler: Kevin Spacey

Origin: USA
Released: 1995
Production: Arnold Kopelson, Wolfgang Petersen, and Gail Katz, in association with Punch Productions Inc.; released by Warner Bros.
Direction: Wolfgang Petersen
Screenplay: Laurence Dworet and Robert Roy Pool
Cinematography: Michael Ballhaus
Editing: Neil Travis, Lynzee Klingman and William Hoy
Production design: William Sandell
Special effects supervision: John Frazier
Visual effects: Boss Film Studios
Visual effects supervision: Mark Vargo
Art direction: Nancy Patton and Francis J. Pezza
Set decoration: Rosemary Brandenburg
Set design: Carl J. Stensel, Stella Furner, Thomas Reta and Eric Orbom
Costume design: Erica Phillips
Sound: Richard Lightstone
Music: James Newton Howard
MPAA rating: R
Running Time: 127 minutes

AWARDS AND NOMINATIONS

New York Film Critics Awards 1995: Best Supporting Actor (Spacey)

center of a deadly viral epidemic, and has been isolated by the U.S. military.

Although officially taken off the case, Daniels finagles his way into Cedar Creek and discovers that the military's plan, under the direction of McClintock, is once again to exterminate the population of the town before the disease spreads, thereby covering up evidence that the U.S. military has kept this strain of the virus alive for its biological weapons program. Daniels must then locate the host monkey, isolate the viral antibodies from it, and produce a serum for the disease within the few hours before the military is scheduled to blow up Cedar Creek. With Robbie Daniels's life at stake as well, Sam Daniels ultimately wins a wild helicopter chase against a homicidal McClintock, isolates the antibodies, and enables his medical team to begin "grinding out" the serum "by the liter."

> "I hope that *Outbreak* is like the *Jaws* of the '90s. Both films deal with very realistic scenarios, but *Outbreak* is perhaps even more frightening. With a shark, you simply have to take yourself out of the water to escape the danger. With an airborne virus, it can be anywhere. Wherever you go, whatever place in the world, you can't escape it. You can't see it, you can't feel it, but it could be attacking you all the same."—director Wolfgang Petersen

Outbreak's characters are not strong enough to mask the implausibilities of its plot—that an anti-viral serum could be manufactured from a host within two hours, for example—nor are the action sequences unpredictable enough to mask the sketchiness of the characters. Although director Petersen is said to have hired Hoffman, rather than a typical action star, because of his appearance of physical vulnerability, Hoffman's duties are confined primarily to commandeering helicopters and to relaying the film's medical exposition at his trademark machine-gun pace. Hoffman seems mainly to have been chosen because he is such an effective mouthpiece for the film's admittedly educational content.

The rest of the film's cast is wasted just as egregiously. Russo gets to display none of the sly, sexy humor or professional savvy she did as the Secret Service agent in *In the Line of Fire*, and before coming down with the virus her character is relegated to quibbling with Hoffman about how to split their community property. ("I cannot believe you're turning a deadly virus into a family matter!" he yells.) For Russo, it is an almost demeaning comedown. The mellifluous and often magnificent Morgan Freeman is shunted into a weak role as the General who is just following orders, even though he knows the government's policy—to exterminate the sick before the disease spreads—is designed primarily to cover up its past human experimentation with viruses. Ford's witting collusion with the evil General McClintock—until he realizes the innocent Daniels will be killed because of the government's cover-up—makes Freeman a weak and unsympathetic antagonist for Hoffman. Had Dworet and Pool taken a page from *The Fugitive*, in which Tommy Lee Jones's detective is an implacable foe because he believes, until shown otherwise, that he is right and is bound by law to do his duty, Freeman might have been a more worthy opponent for Hoffman. As Dworet and Pool have stacked the deck, however, Freeman's Ford is merely a gutless shill for the completely evil McClintock. As McClintock, Donald Sutherland merely gives a long-form performance, with an added dash of psychotic brio, of his cameo in JFK (1991) as the shadowy military figure who knows all the government's secrets. The film's action sequences are well-crafted but unsurprising.

Rushed into production to beat another virus-themed project into theaters (the now-defunct *Crisis in the Hot Zone*, which was to have starred Robert Redford and Jodie Foster), *Outbreak* is in the end an odd disappointment both as a vehicle for Hoffman and as an action film. *Outbreak* supplies neither the roller-coaster thrills of *The Fugitive*, *In the Line of Fire* and the *Die Hard* films, nor the thoughtful, sometimes tragic, look at human greed, incompetence and heroism that distinguished HBO's landmark film about the AIDS crisis, *And the Band Played on*. Although it certainly informs a wider public about the dangers to humans of viruses, that *Outbreak's* most memorable scene is a predictable helicopter chase is indicative of the film's underestimation of both the power of its subject matter and the talents of its leading actors.

—*Paul Mittelbach*

REVIEWS

The New Republic. CCXII, April 10, 1995, p.30.
New York. XXVIII, March 20, 1995, p.60.
The New York Times. CXLIV, March 19, 1995, p.H28(N).
Newsweek. CXXV, March 20, 1995, p.65.
Time. CXLV, March 20, 1995, p.71.
The Wall Street Journal. March 16, 1995, p.A18(W), p.A20(E).
The Washington Post. CXVIII, March 14, 1995, p.WN10.

Out of Sync

For an ex-convict rap star, Jason "The Saint" St. Julian (LL Cool J) is a pretty sweet guy. The hero of Debbie Allen's unjustly ignored *Out of Sync* is trying desperately to stay on the straight and narrow despite his past run-ins with the law. He's struggling to pay off gambling debts, stay clean and sober and earn some money working as a deejay at a rave club. And when a salacious groupie comes on to him after a show, he advises her to go home and "come back when you're 21."

The Saint is really no saint. But compared to the gangsters and low-lifes who surround him, he's got his act together. He's trying to navigate without clear direction in a sea of conflicting moral values. Of course, he's betrayed constantly. And he must sort out whom he can trust and whom he can't.

The story is a familiar one, but the setting is different. Actress, dancer and choreography Allen, who became famous on Broadway and in the TV series *Fame,* makes a promising directorial debut at age 45 in *Out of Sync*. This is a film with a black director and mostly black cast which isn't a black exploitation film, a home-boys comedy, or a searing depiction of life in the ghetto. Refreshingly, it's a standard, somewhat formulaic genre film that happens to feature African-Americans in authentic settings. The dialogue is realistic but not in-your-face. Unfortunately, because it doesn't fit into any of the familiar marketing categories for black films, it saw little initial distribution and was almost universally ignored by critics.

Out of Sync is predictable and a bit uneven, but it holds together fairly well, and Allen has coaxed credible performances out of a cast of mostly unknown actors. Her star, LL Cool J, doesn't have tremendous emotional range but he is believable and wonderfully understated. He plays against the rapper image by being soft-spoken, slow to anger and basically decent, and he doesn't overdo "Saintly" righteousness. St. Julian is a reformed alcoholic and trying hard to stay on the wagon, but he is not immune to temptations of the bottle and the flesh. He is too gullible and willing to bend his principles for money. One of the best things about the script by screenwriter Robert E. Dorn is that the hero is flawed, and occasionally his mentor and father substitute, a pool-hall owner named Quincy (Yaphet Kotto), points out his failings. Even his friend Frank (Aries Spears), a bragging deejay-wannabe, can set St. Julian straight when the Saint's gone a little off-kilter.

The plot is basically a no-brainer with a few simple twists and turns. It gets the hero into a corner and then starts closing off exits. St. Julian is being hounded by ruthless bill collectors who threaten his life unless he can pay off his gambling debts. When the nightclub where he's a deejay is busted by narcs, St. Julian meets the quirky Detective Caldwell (Howard Hesseman). Reminding the ex-rap star and record producer of his sordid past—he was jailed for racketeering, tax evasion and bribery for paying radio stations to play his records—Caldwell gives St. Julian a choice. He can either go back to jail on a new drug conviction, or he can help Caldwell finger Danny Simon (Ramy Zada), a cocaine dealer who runs the nightclub. In exchange, Caldwell promises to cool off the thugs who are trying to collect on the Saint's debts.

St. Julian is reluctant to turn informant, but he has little choice. Things get dicey, however, when he can't resist the full-court press of Simon's sexy girlfriend, Monica Collins (Victoria Dillard). Simon warns him not to mess with his woman, but mess they do. To smooth soul ballads that are lame compared to the rest of the film's hip-hop soundtrack, the Saint and Monica make love on a picnic table in a city park. It's choreographed like a balletic dance scene.

When Monica, who is disgruntled with Simon, hatches a scheme to make off with some of his drug money, the Saint gets deeper into trouble. He eventually finds he's been

CREDITS

Jason St. Julian: LL Cool J
Monica Collins: Victoria Dillard
Detective Caldwell: Howard Hesseman
Danny Simon: Ramy Zada
Frank Aries: Spears
Shorty: Don Yesso
Quincy: Yaphet Kotto

Origin: USA
Released: 1995
Production: Tim Reid, Butch Lewis, Earl Edward Saunders and Freddye Chapman for a United Image Entertainment production; released by Bet Films
Direction: Debbie Allen
Screenplay: Robert E. Dorn
Cinematography: Isidore Mankofsky
Editing: David Pincus
Production design: Marek Dobrowolski
Casting: Eileen Mack Knight
Costume design: Winnie D. Brown
Art director: Nicole Koenigsberger
Music: Steve Tyrell
Sound: Dave Hankins
MPAA rating: R
Running Time: 105 minutes

double-crossed and betrayed on more than one front. The ending lacks plausibility, as St. Julian somehow finds a way to get money and independence and preserve his integrity.

If this is a message film of sorts, it's a pretty palatable message that goes down easily. *Out of Sync* doesn't pose moral choices which are too challenging, and it doesn't question the primacy of money in the rap culture. But neither does it glorify materialism to the detriment of all other values. LL Cool J's character is human and incapable of transcending his milieu, but he does prove his worth.

This is a small film with small points to make, but that's OK. It's executed without too much fanfare and very little self-indulgence, a welcome contrast to the Quentin Tarantino style and that of his many clones, which are basically mining the same vein at the edge of the criminal world. In fact, it is noteworthy that both LL Cool J and Andy Garcia in *Things to Do in Denver When You're Dead* share the nickname "Saint" and the mantel of reformed criminals struggling for decency amid compromising circumstances.

Allen's direction is basic and a little uncertain at times. The film is overlong and plodding, with too many scenes at the nightclub. Much of the film is awash in dark pinks, purples and pastels, as if there were no other way of lighting interiors. Thus it has more of a low-budget look than it should, but to no good effect: this is not film noir, and shouldn't pretend to be. There is also some clumsy editing, and Allen has great difficulty with a few transitions. Some scenes abruptly end and the next scene begins on a jarring note.

The supporting cast is uneven. Dillard's performance is a bit wooden; she seems to portray sultriness rather than exude it, and her spoken lines don't carry much emotional range. Spears is excellent in his small sidekick part, and Kotto gives the film a touch of class and dignity in a tiny role. Hesseman is kind of intriguing as a sort of Sean Connery type, an older cop with pretensions to being hip. One wonderful scene has St. Julian returning home to find Caldwell sorting through his albums and raving at his jazz collection. "This is really great music, not like that stuff you play; where did you get these?" Caldwell asks. "They're my father's," St. Julian replies in deadpan. Simon and the other villains, who intriguingly are almost all white men, are stereotypical bad guys.

The filmmakers are to be congratulated for trying to make a movie set in a rap milieu that doesn't insult the intelligence of their viewers. It's too bad that such a reasonable undertaking must fall into a commercial black hole. There should be plenty of room for ordinary, quiet films by black directors and actors that don't have to scream out with violence, music, or lurid subjects. *Out of Sync* has music, and it has a modicum of violence because it's a crimer, but it doesn't call attention to itself with excess. It shouldn't have to.

—*Michael Betzold*

REVIEWS

Entertainment Weekly. October 13, 1995, p. 85.

Panther

"Explosive and dynamic. *Panther* has been long overdue."—Ron Brewington, *American Urban Radio Network*

"A new-jack lesson as provocative as it is entertaining."—Jil Derryberry, *Interview*

Box Office Gross: $6,834,525

Mario Van Peebles garnished a great deal of attention as a director when *New Jack City* was released in 1991. Until that time he was primarily known as an actor, when this $47.6 million box office hit opened nationwide. His intense exposé of the black ghetto drug culture took many people by surprise, and suddenly a new black director had arrived on the scene. This actor/director went on to make *Posse* (1993), which was intended to remind audiences that indeed there were such entities as "black cowboys." The film received generally poor notices and was not a huge commercial success. His interest, however, in the plight of the Afro-American throughout history was not diminished. Van Peebles's next project, *Panther*, has generated strong interest due to its complex and controversial subject matter: the Black Panther party for self-defense. The Panthers were a militant black power group founded by Bobby Seale, now fifty-eight, and the late Huey Newton, in Oakland, California, in 1966. Although nearly thirty years have passed, the volatile issue of racism still permeates this society and threatens its stability. The chaos created by the recent riots in Los Angeles attests to this disturbing reality. Therefore, any film which has this incendiary and sensitive theme at its base deserves to be examined.

The controversy that surrounded the Panther movement continues to haunt the project itself. The film *Panther* was based on a novel written by the director's father, Melvin Van Peebles. It is interesting to note that the elder Van Peebles made a film in 1971 titled *Sweet Sweetback's Baadasssss Song*, which was a favorite of Huey Newton and many other original Panther members. Unfortunately Panther co-founder Bobby Seale denounced the current film as "a bootleg fiction—80-90 percent of what you see on the screen did not happen. I'm going to sue them for falsifying and invading my private character." Seale, who now serves as a community liaison to the African American Studies department at Temple University in Philadelphia, went on to say in *Entertainment Weekly*, "It's got s**t backwards, it's a crying shame." This statement is hardly an endorsement from the man who had been invited by Van Peebles to serve as a consultant on the film.

The film opens with some authentic footage of incidences of civil unrest in the late sixties, interspersed with the action of Van Peebles's film. This technique of intercutting could be taken as a signal from the director to the audience—it was about to see a blend of fact mixed with fiction. Van Peebles had a two-fold responsibility to inform and entertain. In order to achieve this difficult and delicate balance it appears that he found it necessary to employ a great deal of "creative license" in telling this compelling story. There have been many directors who have taken this approach in the past. (One of the best examples recently was Oliver Stone in his embellished *JFK*, 1991.) This is certainly always a risky choice and can incur the wrath of historians. The Van Peebles' collaborative venture was no exception, and it stirred up some negative press because of it. The *L.A. Daily News* called the film "big on idealism and paranoia, lighter on character and historical complexity." Todd McCarthy said that *Panther* is a fictionalized telling of some incidents in the life of the Black Panthers, and represents a gloss on history for the ennobling benefit of its protagonists. This criticism may have been responsible for the film taking in a lukewarm $4 million in its first 12 days of release, according to *Variety*'s May 16th, 1995 film box office report.

The film depicts an incident on a dangerous corner in Oakland as a pivotal event that was responsible for the creation of the Panther Party. A young black boy is run down while riding his bicycle. This results in a large community-led march demanding that a traffic light be installed in order to prevent any further fatalities. This event, according to David Hillard, who joined the Panthers in 1966, "was a factual situation with just a bit of creative license." Van Peebles opted to portray this scene in an extremely slick and theatrical style. The shot of the gang marching down the street in unison seemed overly staged and choreographed. It appeared to be something out of *West Side Story* (1961), rather than a serious depiction of a semi-historical incident. The impact of the film's message was consistently diminished by this slick and glossy approach.

Naturally the protest ends in a brutal beating by the Oakland police, who are all portrayed as hateful, violent Nazi stereotypes. Many of the marchers all land in a jail cell, including a preacher who pronounces "they know not what they do." The scene turns into a quasi-revival meeting, where the solution appears to be self-evident: "all power to the people through weapons." In spite of this scene's glossy veneer and staged theatricality, it did succeed in making its point. It demonstrated the legitimate frustration levels of the people of Oakland at this point in history. It was made clear why they felt that weapons appeared to be the only solution to their problems.

At this point the script revolves around a fictional character named Judge, affectionately played by Kadeem Hardison, formerly of TV's *A Different World.* A Vietnam vet, Judge becomes a pawn and a witness in the alleged battle between the FBI and the Panthers. He becomes an Everyman that summer audiences can root for. This device, although somewhat contrived, is effective because it sets up an objectivity that justifies the slanted position that the Van Peebles take in these events. It's as if the audience views them through the third eye of Judge's character.

Certainly, after the assassination of John F. Kennedy in 1963, the "conspiracy plot theory" gained an ever-increasing momentum. There was an increasing awareness that the federal government and the CIA and the FBI possibly could involve themselves in various covert operations within the boundaries of the United States. This is the track that the Van Peebles take in *Panther*, and it is a valid theory to explore. The substantiation of evidence may be difficult to find, but it does provide an interesting story line. The Van Peebles paint a portrait of the Black Panther party as a well-organized group of fervent youths filled with altruistic motives and high ideals. The police and the FBI are the enemies willing to demolish the party at any cost. Their one aim in life is to maintain control and destroy any "subversive movement" that threatens the status quo. In *Panther* this is accomplished by sending in a redneck FBI agent (Joe Don Baker). His mission, which is authorized by a rather maniacal J. Edgar Hoover, is to investigate and infiltrate the party. It is obvious that it was important to the director to emphasize the benevolent and positive side of the movement. This is done by showing such aspects of the organization as the food distribution programs, the remarkable organization skills and the fervor of its leader. Courtney B. Vance (Bobby Seale) and Marcus Chong (Huey Newton) play the roles with such fierceness that fervor looks more like fever. However, they both managed to convey the necessary passion and conviction of these two legendary characters. The frenetic camera work takes the audience on a lightening-speed ride through the chaotic social climate of the sixties. It was an appropriate decision on the director's part to dodge and weave through these confused events, to demonstrate the energy and complexities of the times. After all, with the assassination of Kennedy, Malcolm X and Martin Luther King, plus the Vietnam war, all hell was literally breaking loose during this era. Van Peebles's fast and furious pacing brought all of this to light. Also, the use of sixties music, dress, jargon all succeed in accurately recreating the era. He utilized all these elements to his advantage. He managed to capture the appropriate emotions that started the Panther Party in its embryonic stage, and offered an interesting insight into the possibility of an alleged FBI-Mafia connection.

However, in order to gain perspective on any controversial subject there needs to be balance. Unfortunately *Panther* chooses to avoid dealing with any issues relating to the responsibility of the leaders themselves for the demise of the organization. The "white establishment" was the sole enemy and demon, which brought down the movement with its hatred and bigotry. It takes an overly biased viewpoint and chooses to rely on cardboard cut-out villains and racial stereotypes. This approach simply weakens the film's impact as it slips into the genre of a propaganda film and veers towards sensationalism. The viewer suddenly finds himself watching just another summer action film, expecting to see Bruce Willis or Arnold Schwarzenegger hanging from a helicopter and single-handedly destroying Oakland. The material is far too relevant to today's continuing racial struggles and deserves better treatment than this.

—Rob Chicatelli

CREDITS

Judge: Kadeem Hardison
Tyrone: Bokeem Woodbine
Bobby Seale: Courtney B. Vance
Huey Newton: Marcus Chong

Origin: USA
Released: 1995
Production: Preston Holmes, Mario Van Peebles and Melvin Van Peebles for Polygram Filmed Entertainment; released by Gramercy Pictures
Direction: Mario Van Peebles
Screenplay: Melvin Van Peebles, based on the novel by Melvin Van Peebles
Cinematography: Eddie Pei
Editing: Earl Watson
Art Direction: Bruce Hill
Sound: Susumu Tokunow
Costume design: Paul A. Simmons
Music: Stanley Clark
MPAA rating: R
Running Time: 124 minutes

Party Girl

"Sassy, savvy, and definitely clued-in!"—Movie tagline
"Smart, sexy, and playfully hip!"—Peter Travers, *Rolling Stone*

Box Office Gross: $472,370

Advertisements for the first film directed and co-written by Daisy von Scherler Mayer state that "Parker Posey is *Party Girl*," and one would be hard-pressed to disagree. Indeed, almost every scene contains, or, to be more precise, is barely able to contain, the actress' highly kinetic performance in the title role of twenty-three-year-old Mary. The film's production notes compare *Party Girl* to *Breakfast at Tiffany's* (1961), referring to Mary as a "Holly Golightly for the '90's." While that comparison raises expectations, viewers expecting a gem like *Tiffany's* will probably be disappointed with this brassy piece of costume jewelry.

Mary has a lot of spunk, but very little cash, and the film begins with the police breaking up her boisterous rent party and carting her off to jail. She calls her godmother, Judy (Sasha von Scherler, the director's mother), the only adult in her life who has the financial resources to bail her out. Judy, a plump woman with a rather formidable manner and gaze, insists that Mary make the commitment to make something of herself and become more responsible. She will not loan Mary more money, but she will get her a job in the library where she works. Mary doubts that she is cut out for such a sedate job—or any job, for that matter. The only skills she recognizes in herself are "partying, flirting, making stuff up." It appears that Mary might be right when her competence on the job leaves much to be desired. For example, when an elderly woman mumbles that she is looking for a copy of Darwin's *The Origin of Species,* Mary directs her to books on oranges and peaches. Judy is chagrined, feeling that Mary is putting the bare minimum of effort and thought into her work. Mary insists that she is making a genuine effort to tighten the reigns on her free spirit. Judy remains skeptical, and who could blame her: Mary is still concentrating on her whirlwind nightlife. When it gets dark is when Mary lights up, throwing on colorful, eye-catching costumes, striking poses and reveling in Manhattan's Lower East Side club scene that runs on the same high frequency that she does.

While on a lunch break from her labors at the library, Mary meets an attractive and likeable Lebanese falafel vendor named Mustafa (Omar Townsend). He is industrious, responsible and levelheaded, the embodiment of the qualities that Mary lacks. It is obvious that he will be the force that will push Mary towards a happy medium. In the meantime, Judy keeps trying to help Mary get on track, but Mary continues to be baffled and bewildered by the Dewey Decimal System. To her, it is an ominous and inscrutable jumble of numbers and letters. As Judy becomes increasingly exasperated and critical, Mary grows more perplexed and hurt. At her wit's end, Mary gets drunk, and instead of showing up for her date with Mustafa she studies the System well into the night. She is desperately determined to prove herself worthy and capable to Judy and Mustafa, but more importantly and significantly to herself. Her epiphany comes in the wee hours of the morning, and she celebrates by dancing deliriously around the library and properly shelving books by call number. Mary has finally found something other than partying that electrifies her, and she now revels similarly in this new-found ability. She reorganizes her friend Leo's (Guillermo Diaz) extensive record collection by

CREDITS

Mary: Parker Posey
Mustafa: Omar Townsend
Mrs. Lindendorf: Sasha von Scherler
Leo: Guillermo Diaz
Derrick: Anthony DeSando
Rene: Donna Mitchell
Nigel: Liev Schreiber
Venus: Nicole Bobbitt

Origin: USA
Released: 1995
Production: Harry Birckmayer and Stephanie Koules for a Party Pictures production; released by First Look Pictures
Direction: Daisy von Scherler Mayer
Screenplay: Daisy von Scherler Mayer and Harry Birckmayer; based on a story by von Scherler Mayer, Birckmayer, and Sheila Gaffney
Cinematography: Michael Slovis
Editing: Cara Silverman
Production design: Kevin Thompson
Set decoration: Jennifer Baime
Costume design: Michael Clancy
Casting: Caroline Sinclair
Sound: Antonio Arroyo
Music: Anton Sanko
MPAA rating: R
Running Time: 94 minutes

the System, complete with a cross-referenced card catalogue. She becomes a zealous protector of the System's integrity, sternly admonishing patrons who reshelve books incorrectly.

Hurt and confused by Mary's breaking of their date, Mustafa refuses to even talk to Mary, let alone give her a second chance. She continues to arrive daily at his stand with her usual lunch order, but Mustafa's cautious nature slows the thawing process. The day arrives, however, when he has a pressing reference question, and Mustafa is surprised and impressed to find a capable Mary behind the library's information desk. She proceeds to give him especially good service, finding the answers to his questions and then making love to him amongst the stacks after closing. Otherwise occupied, Mary forgets to close all the windows, and when Judy arrives the following morning, she is outraged to find that some books have been damaged by an overnight rain. (She is also not thrilled by the used condoms she finds.) Judy decides that Mary will never really change, and she fires her.

The role of Mary's godmother is played by the film director's real-life mother, Sasha von Scherler, who has appeared in more than seventy plays on and off-Broadway.

Mary is crushed. She is forced to sell some of her flashy clothes to pay her rent. She begins to backslide into her old self. After Mary and Mustafa argue bitterly during a party she throws in his warehouse, Mary takes some drugs and is nearly taken advantage of by a brutal former boyfriend (Liev Schreiber). She is at rock bottom. Her plucky spirit will not allow her to remain there for long, however, and she marches into the library and orders Judy to come to her apartment for an important talk that evening. Mary plans to fervently plead for her job back, and reveal that she intends to continue her education in order to make the jump from clerk to librarian. She is horrified when she arrives home to a wild surprise twenty-fourth birthday party, complete with a male stripper who begins his gyrations around the time Judy shows up. It is hardly an atmosphere which will reinforce the sincerity of what Mary wants to say. Afraid that Judy is going to get the wrong idea, Mary explains what is going on and launches into her earnest appeal. Mustafa supports her by informing Judy of how capable Mary was in finding the answers to his reference questions. In the end, Judy realizes that her godchild is finally serious about making something of herself, and she agrees to give Mary her job back. Mary dances elatedly around the room, while Judy appears to size-up the stripper's performance with an approving eye.

Party Girl cost under $1 million dollars to make, and according to *Variety* took in $333,639 at the box office in its first six weeks in limited release. Critical reaction to the film was mixed, although most reviewers agreed that it is an airy concoction, all pep and Posey. Townsend, who came to the United States in 1993 to attend New York University's Stern School of Business and has never acted before, is appealing, and von Scherler is effective, but the other supporting actors labor in forgettably-written, non-essential roles. Von Scherler Mayer clearly thinks that Mary is captivating and delightful, and wants us to be rooting enthusiastically for the character along with her. The problem is that Mary may be too tart and brash for many tastes. Some critics found her "irresistible" (Owen Gleiberman), while others felt she "is good-looking and magnetically energetic, but when she opens her mouth to speak, what comes out tends to be irritating and imperiously bratty" (Stephen Holden). While Audrey Hepburn's Holly Golightly had an attractive, sweet spirit beneath her kooky exterior, Posey's Mary is often more grating than ingratiating. In a film which is driven more by character than plot, that's nothing to party about.

—David L. Boxerbaum

REVIEWS

The Hollywood Reporter. January 24, 1995, p. 11.
The New York Times. June 11, 1995, p. H24.
Entertainment Weekly. June 23, 1995, p. 36.
People. June 19, 1995, p. 21.
The New York Times. June 9, 1995, p. C17.
Variety. January 23, 1995, p. 72.
The Los Angeles Times. June 9, 1995, p. F8.
Rolling Stone. March 23, 1995, p. 128.
The Chicago Tribune Friday. July 7, 1995, p. H.

Paul Bowles—The Complete Outsider

The Complete Outsider takes you inside the world of Paul Bowles, considered by many to be one of the greatest writers of the 20th century. He wrote nearly twenty novels, including *Up Above the World, Let It Come Down, The Spider's House, The Sheltering Sky, The Delicate Prey, A Distant Episode* and many other stories. As an icon to The Beat Generation, his writings and his unique life have influenced everyone from Wm. Burroughs (whose *Naked Lunch* was inspired by Bowles) to David Cronenberg's film of the same name. Also influenced by this brilliant man was Bernardo Bertolucci, whose film adaptation of *The Sheltering Sky*, starring John Malkovich and Debra Winger was a critical and popular hit. Filmed on location in Tangier, Morocco, *Paul Bowles—The Complete Outsider* explores his development as a writer and composer and his unorthodox marriage to fellow author, Jane Bowles. It is an invaluable film to anyone who has ever written or ever read books as it takes the viewer inside the world and the mind of a giant in both music and literature.

The opening shot takes the viewer on an exciting and mysterious journey—the life and adventures of Paul Bowles. The camera travels down the narrow tunnel-like streets of Morocco, inviting the viewer into a new and exotic world underscored by enticing Moroccan music. Once inside, the story begins with shots of what Paul Bowles did best, sitting at his desk, writing. The scenes of him roaming the streets of Morocco seem to suggest that he was an outsider in this foreign land. In many aspects, he felt as an outsider everywhere that he lived. Edouard Rodite, poet and critic, when interviewed about Bowles, said that he had a horror of America and that "he just doesn't like reality." His friend, poet Allen Ginsberg, said that Bowles felt as an outsider from the beginning. He remarked to Ginsberg that, even as a child, he felt "it would be better if he weren't there." So, from the very start, this documentary offers these penetrating insights about the man, causing the viewer to want more information about this enigmatic personality.

Paul Bowles was born in Jamaica, New York in 1910, but went to Paris at an early age. He returned to New York and spent the '30s and '40s writing music. He was a protege of Virgil Thompson and Aaron Copeland, and had a close friendship with Leonard Bernstein. In an amusing anecdote offered by biographer Christopher Sawyer Laucanno, Bernstein was depressed about his career and was going to change his name to Lenny Ambers, only writing pop music. While in New York, Bowles wrote an opera called "Wind Remains." In one of the most moving segments of this film, composer Ned Rorem, while playing an aria from the piece, says "the effect of which I found so contagious that I'm not yet over the delicious illness that it caused me. It was unbearably lonely and sad and voluptuous at the same time—a five-minute aria." It was moments like these that prompted *The Seattle Times* to write, "Like all the best biographical films, *The Complete Outsider* makes you feel you know the person, through his eyes, as well as those closest to him!"

The success of the documentary lies not only with the pictures and the rare archival footage, but the interviews with the author himself. These offer the most personal and intimate look into the man's heart and soul. His off-handed remarks are filled with wisdom that every writer in the audience should store in their memory banks. On writing, he said, "You've got to have trouble when you write. Somebody's got to be in trouble or no one will read it." And still, the film is not just for writers—it is for anyone interested in exploring the possibilities of individuality and the freedom of making your own choices.

In order to paint a complete picture of this complete outsider, the producers delicately invaded the subject's private life. It was not done for sensationalism, but for perspective. Paul Bowles loved men and women, and he made his own rules. His marriage to Jane Bowles (who was also gay) was based on their mutual enjoyment of each other's company. Certainly, their intellectual capacity for exploration also led to their coupling, and they were indeed in love. The biographer, Millicent Dillord, talked about their glamour and compared them to Zelda and F. Scott Fitzgerald. Out of Jane's relationship with Paul came *Two Serious Ladies*. They stimulated each other's creativity, but Jane's alcoholism led to her downfall. Paul, however, was with her up to the end.

So, Paul Bowles was alone, again. He remarked, "Life isn't about other people—it's about one's self against the world." He did not mean this in a hostile way, but to illustrate his philosophy of existence. In the latter part of his life, he was somewhat of a recluse, but viewing this documentary never aroused pity. Once again, he was making his own choices—he was not telling others how to live their lives. There was tremendous care taken by the filmmakers to adhere to a non-judgmental approach in telling Paul Bowles' story. It was this level of integrity that made this piece so remarkable.

Gertrude Stein suggested Morocco to Paul. It seemed like an odd choice to many of his friends, but, once again, Paul made up his own mind. His fearlessness in making his own decisions was never questioned and he lived the remaining years of his life in harsh but beautiful Morocco. Although he lived on the outskirts of accepted moral behavior in this exotic land, he did partake in the richness of its culture. It was here that he became intrigued by the mystery of Moroccan music. His fascination for it prompted him to develop an archive of Moroccan music. His mind, no matter what land he lived in, was constantly churning and creating. Music was not the only thing that he discovered in Morocco—marijuana was the other. Actually, it was "kief," which is Moroccan marijuana. It is to the filmmakers' credit that they chose such honesty in painting their portrait of Paul Bowles. A man is a sum of his parts and this documentary weaves the tapestry of the man with all the different shades and colors. The one aspect of Bowles' personality was that he was never controlled by any one thing. Again, he remained an outsider to his sexuality, his drug use, love and friendship. He was an observer of all these things. Some may criticize him for being detached from reality, but he simply recorded his life experiences and used them for his work. He was not only a true craftsman, but also an artist. In watching his interviews, it was apparent that he did not have many regrets about his life. His work was his legacy and it speaks for itself.

CREDITS

Paul Bowles: Paul Bowles
Brian Woolfenden: Brian Woolfenden
Allen Ginsberg: Allen Ginsberg
Ned Rorem: Ned Rorem
Millicent Dillon: Millicent Dillon

Origin: USA
Released: 1995
Production: Catherine Warnow and Regina Weinreich; released by First Run Features
Direction: Catherine Warnow and Regina Weinreich
Cinematography: Burleigh Wartes
Editing: Jessica Bendiner and Amanda Zinoman
Sound: Samantha Heilweil
Music: Paul Bowles
Running Time: 57 minutes

What makes *Paul Bowles—the Complete Outsider* so "tantalizing" (as it was called by *The Los Angeles Times*) is that it makes the viewer feel that they know the person. Many biographical films make the film the important thing. This piece makes the man the important thing. Once it gets inside his brain, it shows how his thinking developed and how it influenced his work. It had a brilliant balance of music, interviews, photos and narration (Lanie Conklin narrated). There was respect, but never adulation. There was truth, but never voyeurism. The audience, much like the readers of his books, were left to make up their own minds.

In evaluating the worth of a person's life, it is essential to determine his influence on others and the conviction of his beliefs. When a documentary tries to shed light on that life, they must do it in a way that is balanced and offers many perspectives on that person. *The Complete Outsider* manages to expose the viewer to many aspects of Paul Bowles from all angles. It is like watching a puzzle being constructed, piece by piece, to its completion. In this case, however, it illuminates the subject's life, while illuminating the lives of those watching it. The more that is revealed about Paul Bowles, the more that is revealed about oneself. The credit for this achievement must go to the producers Catherine Warnow and Regina Weinreich. Their meticulous research and inspired selectivity is what makes this film such a great achievement. They managed to gather information and present it in such a way that made it hypnotic to watch. The viewer was made to feel that they were on a personal journey of discovery through the eyes of this respected and acclaimed individual. His views may not have been their views, but they were enriched by them, nevertheless. It opened up the possibilities within everyone of living a life without fear of criticism. Paul Bowles was forever true to himself, and *The Complete Outsider* invited everyone in to examine not only his life, but their own as well. Can anyone ask a film to do more?

—*Rob Chicatelli*

The Pebble and the Penguin

"Pure enchantment."—Kevin Thomas, *Los Angeles Times*

Box Office Gross: $3,983,912

While Disney went on a safari to the richly colored lands where regal lions, crazy hyenas and exotic meerkats reside, Don Bluth productions turned to ice-covered Antarctica to do an animated feature about penguins.

The Pebble and the Penguin is surprisingly successful. Part of its charm is the absence of the pretentiousness which has crept into the overproduced Disney films. The Don Bluth company, always considered second-string to the mouse empire, pulls an upset with this simple film about a penguin's quest for the debutante of the rookery.

Wallflower Hubie (voice of Martin Short) pines for the enormously-eyelashed Marina (Annie Golden), but big bad boy Drake (Tim Curry) wants her too. Drake's treachery sweeps Hubie out to sea. Flung far away from Marina, Hubie endures a Homeric odyssey to get back to Antarctica for the full-moon mating ceremony where bachelor penguins present pebbles to their prospective mates.

It's pretty standard cartoon fare until Rocko, an outrageous rockhopper penguin, enters the scene. Given voice by James Belushi, Rocko is an animated comic original on a par with Robin Williams' genie in Disney's *Aladdin* (1993). With his protruding golden brows and aviator scarf, Rocko is funny enough just to look at, but Belushi makes him an uproarious parody of an endangered male species—the blustering, combative, emotion-squashing little guy with a deeply concealed heart of gold.

Belushi's Rocko routine is priceless. Full of bloated pretention, quick to hide behind his prickly exterior, Rocko is sarcastic yet endearing. He is an archly crafted amalgam of festering, ridiculous, marvelous machismo.

Clumsy, dim-witted, sincere Hubie, who wears his heart on his sleeve, is his perfect foil. Hubie gets Rocko to reveal that he too has a dream, an even more improbable dream than Hubie's longing for Marina. Rocko wants to fly. "Our ancestors did it," he explains insistently.

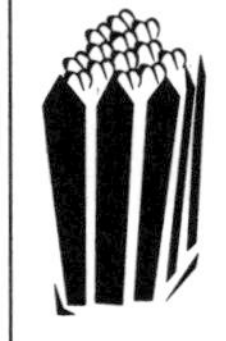

"I just love animation, I love the process of it. When you're recording, the animation hasn't been done yet, so you can do whatever you want. You can just improvise."— Martin Short, voice of penguin-hero Hubie

The two underdogs—or is it underbirds?—make an endearing dynamic duo. Rocko provides enough zest and irreverence to balance Hubie's sappy sentimentality. And Hubie brings out the humanity (or should that be penguinity?) behind Rocko's rough exterior.

The animators provide a startlingly bright and inventive palette, with colorful celestial backdrops to the ice-bound polar tundra. The characters' hues sometimes change with the emotion and the music, which is theatrical Barry Manilow fare.

While much of the animation is good but unremarkable, the production values soar in the sequence where Hubie finds himself captured aboard the "good ship Misery." The ship and the seas are dark and foreboding. A "prisoner" production number, with the captive birds singing about their plight, is outstanding and hilarious.

The film does succumb to some customary cartoon excesses. In the worst Disney tradition, the villainous Drake is outrageously overplayed and oversized—looking more like a bear than a penguin—and his ravenous, gaping cavern appears to be borrowed from the cave of the lamp in the aforementioned *Aladdin.* Marina is a hopelessly fluffy, squeaky paragon of ultra-femininity, the standard sweet damsel in distress. Come to think of it, she's a lot like Minnie Mouse in a penguin get-up.

The story is slight and one-dimensional, but that's fine in a cartoon targeted at children. The ending is cute and satisfying; our heroes get to realize their dreams. What more is needed?

CREDITS

Hubie: Martin Short
Rocko: James Belushi
Drake: Tim Curry
Marina: Annie Golden

Origin: USA
Released: 1995
Production: Russell Boland for Don Bluth Limited; released by Metro-Goldwyn-Mayer Pictures
Screenplay: Rachel Koretsky and Steve Whitestone
Editing: Thomas V. Moss
Art direction: Gerry Shirren
Music: Mark Watters
MPAA rating: G
Running Time: 74 minutes

No one's going to suggest Academy Award consideration for anyone involved in *The Pebble and the Penguin*, although a best supporting actor nomination for Belushi wouldn't be that big of a stretch. This cartoon isn't aiming at anything more than entertainment for children and the adults that invariably escort them to the local cinema, and on that score it succeeds well enough.

After all the highfalutin discussion about political and historical correctness and the grandiose themes involved in some of its contemporary Disney fare, *The Pebble and the Penguin* is somewhat refreshing. It's nothing more than what it is—a cartoon with a simple moral about following your dreams, a standard love story and a win for the underdogs.

—Michael Betzold

REVIEWS

The New York Times. April 12, 1995, p. C21.
Variety. April 10, 1995, p. 45.

Story was inspired by a nature documentary the writers saw on TV about the mating rituals of the Adeli penguins.

The Perez Family

"A family became strangers and strangers became a family."—Movie tagline

"Ultimately irresistible."—Michael Medved, *New York Post*

"Two thumbs up!"—*Siskel & Ebert*

Box Office Gross: $2,832,826

Mira Nair is carving a niche for herself as a film director of rare sensitivity and style, following up the critically acclaimed *Mississippi Masala* (1992) with this enchanting film. Nair's contribution to current cinema lies in her ability to entertain audiences with stories about the cultural stew that is twentieth-century America. *Mississippi Masala* was a unique depiction of the lives of a family that migrates from India to the Mississippi. Much of the plot centered around the difficulties in a relationship between an Indian woman and an African-American man. This time Nair has chosen a story about a group of refugees who migrate from Cuba to Florida, hoping to achieve the American dream. Like *Mississippi Masala*, *The Perez Family* examines the American dream from the point of view of new (third world) immigrants, and shows that no matter what their cultural or economic background, all people need to be loved.

The film opens with a beautiful, surreal dream of Juan Perez (Alfred Molina) and his family in an idyllic beach setting. But the bewitching charm of the dream, with its Fellini-esque images, gives way to the grim loneliness of a Cuban prison: The audience learns that Juan has been a political prisoner for twenty years, and that the dreams of the beautiful young wife are what have kept him alive since his incarceration in the 1960's, when his wife Carmela (Anjelica Huston) and daughter (Trini Alvarado) emigrated to Florida. The film takes place during the Mariel boatlift of 1980, in which thousands of Cuban refugees made their way to Florida to find political asylum in the United States. Juan is released from prison and joins the refugees, planning to reunite with his wife and daughter. Events conspire to cause Carmela and Juan to miss each other upon his arrival, forcing Juan to remain in a refugee camp even though his wife and daughter are U.S. citizens. Simultaneously, Dorinda Perez (Marisa Tomei) is migrating to Florida to find a better life and to fulfill her fantasy of meeting John Wayne. Soon, having replaced the Latina name Dorinda for the more American "Dottie" (and having learned that John Wayne died), she discovers that the most efficient way to be sponsored into American citizenship is to be part of a family. So she corrals Juan and a couple of other refugees named Perez into pretending they are family.

Meanwhile, Carmela has been under the watchful eye of her scheming brother who has virtually imprisoned her in her own home with his over-protectiveness. When her elaborate home security alarm is inadvertently activated, she meets a genteel police detective, Pirelli (Chazz Palmintieri). Eventually she and Pirelli fall in love, as do Juan and Dottie, making Juan and Carmela's eventual reunion a mixed blessing.

It is a seriocomic film, at once highly romantic and highly political. Screenwriter Robin Swicord (basing the screenplay on the novel by Christine Bell) seems to be making a comment on the human need for love and companionship as it is impacted by the individual's place in society. All the characters are imprisoned by their station in society, and are only released from their grim circumstances through love. For example, one-time prostitute Dottie is disappointed by her inability to be fully admitted to the American society which she sees as her salvation. But only when she falls in love with Juan does she find redemption, as symbolized by their brief stay in a monastery. Similarly, aristocratic Juan has been able to endure the dreadful hardship of political prison only through the dreams of reuniting with his loving wife and child. When he is forced to retain the low-class status of "alien" in the inhospitable world of Miami, he too finds salvation when he abandons himself to love.

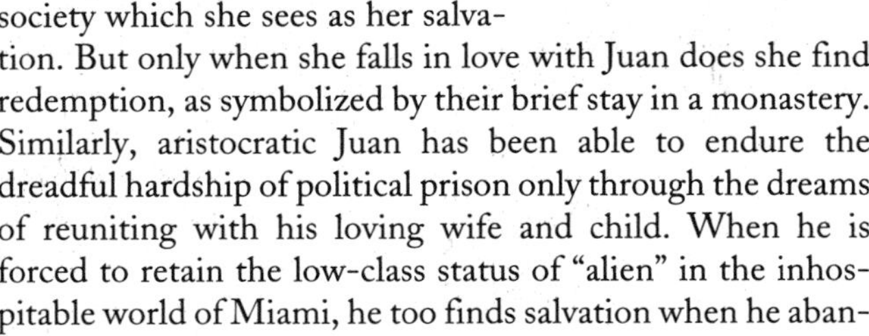

"Who could love such a woman?"—Juan Paul Perez about his pretend wife, the tacky Dottie.

Further, the characters find love only when they accept their current place in the world—rather than postponing happiness for a day that may never arrive. The world is depicted as being inhospitable to those who wish to improve their place in it. Whether they are poor or rich, the characters live in a metaphorical hell which is made palatable by "living for the moment." The filmmakers clearly are committed to the concept of "living for the moment," but they do so in a way that is never cliche. Juan delivers a beautiful speech which illuminates the film's thematic core: "Hell is here on earth. Hell is waiting for the best to happen and it never comes. Hell is waiting for your execution and it never comes. Our only deliverance is to expect nothing; to love desperately without hoping for another."

That is not to say, however, that the film is melodramatic, or that the Miami of 1980 is made to look "hellish." Nair and company maintain a light, comic sense which shines through the characters' painful searches for happiness. For instance, the refugees set up camp in the football stadium where the Miami Dolphins practice. For a while they are allowed to set up a makeshift village there, but are displaced when the Dolphins start practicing, an hilarious image: the irony of the American dream (as exemplified by football) pushing aside those who are trying desperately to achieve that dream is both funny and touching. Similarly, the Little Havana created by Nair and by production designer Mark Friedberg is a colorful beehive of activity with fortune tellers, blaring salsa music, sidewalk food vendors, and an earthy quality that makes hell look quite charming.

Luckily, Nair and her actors straddle the line between tragedy and comedy with delicacy and flair, never allowing the proceedings to be either maudlin or goofy. Marisa Tomei gives a performance most notable for its gusto: she dances on the refugee boat with all the men around her as if she were Dulcinea dancing for the *Man of La Mancha*, and she maneuvers her way around the refugee camp with the conartistry of the Artful Dodger from *Oliver Twist*. Having covered her body in dark makeup, Italian-American Tomei looks convincing as the hot-blooded Cuban refugee. Unfortunately, her accent, while passable, reminds the audience that she is not Cuban. (In fact, the casting of Tomei has caused something of an uproar among Latin-American actors.) But Tomei's full-throttle performance succeeds in bridging the gap between drama and comedy: when she finds out John Wayne is dead, it is as if her life is flashing before her eyes, and it is both funny and touching.

Alfred Molina, the wonderful actor who made such an impression playing Joe Orton's lover in *Prick up Your Ears* (1987), is a perfect choice for Juan. His Bassett-hound eyes and his lanky stature help to win the audience's affection in the early prison scenes. This is not an actor who one would think of as a romantic leading man, yet in a tender scene in which he and Dottie try to say goodbye to each other he is as romantic as Gable.

The other performances are superb. Anjelica Huston and Chazz Palmintieri make a beautiful couple; they are tentative and rather naive, reminiscent of Olympia Dukakis and Vincent Gardenia in *Moonstruck* (1987). Huston (whose casting as a Cuban also caused a bit of a stir, since she is only half Spanish) makes the most of one of the film's weaker scenes—the scene where she and Juan are reunited. Her

CREDITS

Dottie Perez: Marisa Tomei
Juan Raul Perez: Alfred Molina
Carmela Perez: Angelica Huston
Officer Pirelli: Chazz Palmintieri

Origin: USA
Released: 1995
Production: Michael Nozik and Lydia Dean Pilcher for a Samuel Goldwyn Co. production; released by Samuel Goldwyn Co.
Direction: Mira Nair
Screenplay: Robin Swicord, based on a novel by Christine Bell
Cinematography: Stuart Dryburgh
Editing: Robert Estrin
Production design: Mark Friedberg
Makeup: D'Amore and Jay Canistraci
Casting: Ellen Jacoby
Music: Alan Silvestri
MPAA rating: R
Running Time: 112 minutes

gracefulness and elegance allow her to transcend the triteness of lines such as "I didn't feel the courage to let go." A scene in which the couple goes to a Miami nightclub, dancing next to Dottie (without knowing who she is) is a bit contrived: Palmintieri and Huston seem far too elegant to be slumming it at a disco populated with people fifteen years younger than they are. But they manage to transcend the incongruity with their luminous performances.

The joy of this film lies in Nair's eye for the quirkiness of the human condition, especially as exemplified by those struggling to achieve the American dream. One of the film's characters, an old Cuban man who sits on flagpoles, in trees, or on tops of houses, is a perfect example of Nair's ability to make interesting visual statements that exemplify her theme. The aged man, holding out hope that he can rise above his current place in life, looking above the trees for something better, is emblematic of everyone's search for something better.

Beautiful cinematography by Stuart Dryburgh and a rich score by *Forrest Gump*'s (1994) Alan Silvestri (with traditional music by Arturo Sandoval) are essential components of the success of this film. In particular, the delicate yet painfully beautiful melody accompanying some of the serious scenes is one of the film's best assets.

Indian-born Nair, like the old character who sits on flagpoles and traffic lights, proves that she rises above traditional filmmaking to forge an amalgam of whimsy, integrity, color, and depth which transcends American filmmaking even while it helps to point it in a new direction. *The Perez Family* is not a classic; but it is classy.

—*Kirby Tepper*

Persuasion

"Wonderful! Stylish and zestful!"—Jay Carr, *Boston Globe*

"Star-crossed love has rarely been so delicious!"—Elizabeth Pincus, *Harper's Bazaar*

"A wonderful surprise!"—Caryn James, *The New York Times*

"A sharply witty, touching and vital romance! Gorgeously directed, written and acted."—Peter Travers, *Rolling Stone*

Box Office Gross: $3,607,611

Upon first view, Anne Elliot (Amanda Root), the heroine of *Persuasion,* is most unprepossessing. Everything about her—her face, her voice, her stature—is small. Her fortunes seem even less promising. *Persuasion* opens as Anne's father, the vulgar aristocrat Sir Walter Elliot (Corin Redgrave), is forced by his own profligacy to rent out his stately English country manor and move to smaller, less expensive quarters in Bath. He takes with him his favored elder daughter, the equally vulgar and pretentious Elizabeth (Phoebe Nicholls). Anne is handed a less promising assignment: she is to move in with her hypochondriacal, querulous sister, Mary Musgrove (Sophie Thompson), to help care for her nephews and nieces.

The meagerness of Anne's fate is reinforced when we learn that her family home has been rented by Admiral Croft (John Woodvine) and his wife (Fiona Shaw), one of whose brothers is Anne's lost love. Eight years earlier, Anne had fallen in love with Frederick Wentworth (Ciaran Hinds), and he with her. At the time, however, Wentworth's own prospects seemed slim, and Anne allowed herself to be persuaded not to marry him by her surrogate mother, Lady Russell (Susan Fleetwood), who declared Wentworth "A man who had nothing but himself to recommend him." Now returned from the Napoleonic wars a rich naval officer (owing to the wartime practice of claiming captured ships as prizes), Captain Wentworth has everything to recommend him. And he is looking for a wife.

The contrast between Anne Elliot and Captain Wentworth is underscored in the film by their physical differences: as played by the strapping, handsome Ciaran Hinds—a man born to wear the highly decorative and dramatic naval officer's uniform of 1814—Wentworth is the epitome of the dashing romantic hero. Anne, at twenty-seven, with her small, pale face and disheveled hair, seems well on her way to spinsterhood.

Anne's reaction upon seeing Wentworth again is visceral: the camera closes in on a shot of one hand gripping a chair back, as Anne struggles to hang on to her equilibrium. Captain Wentworth, for his part, seems still to be bitter about his previous rejection by Anne, and he enjoys the regard of the giggly Musgrove sisters, Louisa (Emma Roberts) and Henrietta (Victoria Hamilton), who are related to Anne through her sister's marriage. Louisa behaves particularly aggressively towards Captain Wentworth, literally throwing herself at him from the great height of the

Cobb at Lyme when the whole party (including Anne) removes to the seashore. When Louisa is badly injured because of his failure to catch her, the noble Wentworth is obliged to stay and help nurse her back to health.

"A man who had nothing but himself to recommend him."—Lady Russell's opinion of Frederick Wentworth and why she discouraged Anne's accepting him in marriage

Anne retreats to Bath, where she allows herself to be courted by a young bounder and distant relative, William Elliot (Samuel West). Anne's agitated psyche is temporarily soothed by William's solicitude and seeming affection, but she soon hears rumors that William, like her father, has squandered his fortune and now seeks to restore his place in society by marrying her. Furthermore, William seems to be engaged in a dalliance with the common, scheming Mrs. Clay (Felicity Dean), who is ensconced in Bath as Elizabeth's companion, but who really is attached to Sir Walter. About this same time, Captain Wentworth shows up again. Anne, who had assumed he would marry Louisa Musgrove, learns that Louisa has married another, and she begins to suspect—as the audience has for quite some time—that Wentworth is only interested in her.

This is not to say that Anne is in any way dull witted. Indeed, she has gradually, inexorably grown in our esteem, as director Roger Michell—and, of course, her creator, Jane Austen—shows her off to advantage against the self-centeredness of the Musgroves and the venality of Bath's high society. The initial impression she gives of unimpressiveness is gradually transformed into one of self-sufficiency, grace, and a beautiful simplicity. She is helped in this transformation by the few other characters in *Persuasion* who are themselves admirable. Mrs. Croft, who glowingly relates accounts of her life aboard ship with the admiral, provides Anne with a role model, supplanting the misguided Lady Russell. And when she learns that Louisa has married Wentworth's lovelorn friend Captain Benwick (Richard McCabe), who had seemed to give up all hope of happiness, Anne begins to see the possibility of a reconciliation with Captain Wentworth. It is apparent by this point that Anne is the only one worthy of Frederick, and vice versa. For them—and for filmgoers—it is sheer wish fulfillment when the two finally kiss in the streets of Bath.

That improbable (because of the time and place it is bestowed) movie kiss—and much else—has engendered criticism from purists, who find fault with such attempts to modernize, to "improve upon" Jane Austen's nearly faultless novels. But like it or not, Austen is undergoing a renaissance in film, and the change in media inevitably leads to compromises. The most pronounced of these unquestionably occur in *Clueless,* which was released during the summer of 1995. Set in contemporary California, it is, to say the least, very loosely based on Austen's 1816 novel, *Emma.* Another film version of *Emma,* apparently truer at least to the novel's Regency setting, is also in the offing, as is one of Austen's *Pride and Prejudice,* published in 1813. And Taiwanese film director Ang Lee has directed a new movie adaptation of *Sense and Sensibility,* which first appeared in novel form in 1811.

Persuasion was a product of Jane Austen's middle age, begun in 1815, when she was forty and two years away from dying of Addison's disease. It was published posthumously in 1818. Tradition has it that Anne's love story reflects one that occurred in Austen's own life. There is little of substance to support this equation, but there does seem to be some resemblance between the mature, unmarried author and her no longer young heroine—who almost missed her best opportunity for happiness because she had allowed herself to be persuaded by convention. Older and wiser now, Anne comes into her own—and is granted a gratifying second chance.

Amanda Root does a wonderful job of embodying Austen's cautious, but finally confident heroine, conveying Anne's responses to her trying journey towards happiness mostly through use of her expressive brown eyes. Amidst the noisy throng, she is a still point, and her very unobtru-

CREDITS

Anne Elliot: Amanda Root
Cpt. Wentworth: Ciaran Hinds
Lady Russell: Susan Fleetwood
Sir Walter Elliot: Corin Redgrave
Mrs. Croft: Fiona Shaw
Admiral Croft: John Woodvine
Elizabeth Elliot: Phoebe Nicholls

Origin: USA
Released: 1995
Production: Fiona Finlay for a BBC/TV, WGBH/Boston and Millesime and France 2 production; released by Sony Classics
Direction: Roger Mitchell
Screenplay: Nick Dear; based on the novel *Persuasion* by Jane Austen
Cinematography: John Daly
Editing: Kate Evans
Production design: William Dudley
Art direction: Linda Ward
Costume design: Alexandra Byrne
Sound: Terry Elms, Michael Narduzzo
Assistant director: Julie Edward
Music: Jeremy Sams
MPAA rating: PG
Running Time: 102 minutes

siveness—her willingness to play the piano while others dance—makes her stand out. And although she is dutiful and self-abnegating, she also has a backbone—or at least she grows one in the course of the story. When her father insists that she join him at an audience with Lady Dalrymple, Anne refuses, determined to keep a previous engagement with a housebound widow friend. Such turns of events help to advance the plot, of course—Anne's sick friend tells her of William's perfidy—but they also help to reinforce our sense of Anne's uprightness.

Our unobtrusive heroine is, at first, nearly overwhelmed by the crass and boisterous hijinks of those who surround her. And what wonderful, entertaining characters they are. Sir Walter is a loathsome old fool, but Corin Redgrave certainly has a good time—and certainly provides filmgoers with one—playing up his fatuousness. Perhaps the most gloriously abandoned performance is provided by Sophie Thompson as Mary Musgrove, whom she manages to make at once insufferable ("I am so ill," she exclaims just before diving into a plate full of food) and irresistible. And with the empathetic turn Susan Fleetwood lends Lady Russell, one can imagine how the motherless younger Anne was persuaded by her to jilt Frederick Wentworth.

Like the audience, these personages are inclined to take Anne for granted. But when we see those characters who are clearly meant to be admirable—the Crofts, Captain Benwick, and above all, Captain Wentworth—focus on Anne, we cannot help but do the same. And Anne, who had earlier been either struck dumb or rendered otherwise unintelligible in Wentworth's presence, gains a quiet authority that allows her finally to deliver perhaps the most affecting speech in the film: "All the privilege I claim for my own sex is that of loving longest when all hope is gone." Roger Michell may give Sir Walter the last word on his middle daughter ("Marry Anne," he responds to Wentworth's announcement of his intentions, "Whatever for?"), but we in the audience are in on a joke that will forever be beyond his comprehension. It is a delicious experience.

—*Lisa Paddock*

Picture Bride

"A delicate, touching tribute!"—Bruce Williamson, *Playboy*

"Deeply moving and absorbing! Superbly acted and intelligently directed."—Jeffrey Lyons, *Sneak Previews*

Box Office Gross: $940,446

Akira Takayama and Youki Kudoh in *Picture Bride*. © Miramax Films.

Set in Hawaii at the turn of the century, this beautiful and lyrical film is a milestone in that it is the first commercial feature to be directed by an Asian American woman. Kayo Hatta directs a script written by herself and her sister, Mari Hatta, about the arrival of "picture brides" in the early days of Hawaiian colonization. Hatta creates beautiful images and shows great sensitivity with her material and her actors, and provides audiences with an absorbing and poetic story peopled by strong characters.

Picture Bride is the story of Riyo (Youki Kudoh), a seventeen-year-old Japanese girl who, as the film opens, must decide what to do now that her parents have died. Their funeral, filmed in black and white, somberly provides the emotional context in which Riyo's story begins. Anxious to leave her past behind her, she follows the advice of an aunt (Yoko Sugi), who tells her to go to Hawaii, because "no one will know anything about your past." The demure Riyo accepts marriage to a sugarcane worker in Hawaii named Matsuji (Akira Takayama), boarding a boat to Hawaii to marry him, having only seen his picture and corresponded with him.

Upon arrival, she discovers that he sent an old picture of himself, and that now he is not nearly as young and handsome as his picture presented. Angry and frightened, she claims that she will return to Japan, and she attempts to earn the $300 it will take to return home. Earning sixty-five cents a day as a sugarcane worker, she struggles to hold on to her sense of dignity and to the money she earns as she reluctantly stays with Matsuji until she can leave. As time passes, relationships with her husband and the people around her improve, and, perhaps predictably, they all live happily ever after.

This territory has been trod before—at least thematically—in films such as *The Piano* (1993). Indeed, many of the early sequences resemble the themes of *The Piano*: the ocean carries the quiet woman to a remote place, discovers her husband to be gruff and unpolished, and struggles to retain her individuality while adapting to her surroundings. Some reviews have tried to compare the film to *The Joy Luck Club* (1993), which only points out the myopia in commercial filmmaking: both films are about Asian women, but that is the only similarity, especially since *Joy Luck* is about Chinese culture, and this film is about Japanese and Hawaiian culture. Hopefully, the advent of these commercial films will eventually help to truly diversify the cinematic landscape.

Comparisons aside, *Picture Bride* tells its story in its own unusual way, showing its audience something about the evolution of Hawaiian culture while it tells a touching story. Hatta uses the inherent lyricism of Japanese and Hawaiian culture to tell her story. For example, when Riyo arrives on the plantation, she meets a young woman, Kana (Tamlyn Tomita) who tells her that the sound of the wind is actually "just the ghosts welcoming you." A beautifully spoken narration (by pioneering Asian American actress Nobu McCarthy) as a much older Riyo closes the film by saying "sometimes I can still see the moon lighting the cane fields that carry me home...to Hawaii." Hatta beautifully evokes the spirituality of her characters, having Riyo follow the spirit of a beloved friend to the beach after the friend dies.

Hatta also utilizes the songs that the female sugarcane workers used to sing. They are surprisingly ribald, given the stereotypically demure characterizations of Asian women to which American audiences have grown accustomed. One of the songs goes, "Why work all day for sixty-five cents a day, when I can sleep with Chinese men and earn twice the pay?"

The exploration of culture and history are further explored with the use of language: much of the film is spoken in Japanese with subtitles, and much of it is in the pidgin dialect which was an amalgamation of Japanese, Hawaiian, and English. Further, the separation between the different groups working on the plantation is shown by Hatta as having tragic consequences: a bigoted Portugese supervisor has a hand in the tragic death of one of the main characters.

Hatta is beautifully aided in her lyricism by her cinematographer, Claudio Rocha. At times, particularly in the scenes in Riyo and Matsuji's cottage, the lighting is richly varied and quite theatrical, as if it were on stage. Whether or not it was intended, the effect is that the film takes on a magical quality, putting Riyo and Matsuji in their own little world. Their story becomes more poignant as it takes on "storybook" qualities. This does not remove the film from reality, though, and Hatta and Rocha create lush and gorgeous images of the emerald hills and valleys surrounding the plantation, and of the sweeping panorama of the cane fields.

Another wonderful element is the impressionistic, melodic score by Cliff Eidelman. From beautiful majestic music underscoring a series of pictures of real ships and real picture brides to sweet, sensitive music accompanying the burgeoning relationship of Riyo and Matsuji, Eidelman perfectly enhances the action without intruding on it.

—*Kirby Tepper*

CREDITS

Riyo: Youki Kudoh
Matsuji: Akira Takayama
Kana: Tamlyn Tomita
Kanzaki: Cary-Hiroyuki Tagawa
The Benshi: Thoshio Mifune
Aunt Sode: Yoko Sugi

Origin: USA
Released: 1995
Production: Lisa Onodera for Thousand Cranes Filmworks presentation; released by Miramax
Direction: Kayo Hatta
Screenplay: Kayo Hatta and Mari Hatta
Cinematography: Claudio Rocha
Editing: Lynzee Klingman and Mallori Gottleiv
Production design: Paul Guncheon
Costume design: Ada Akaji
Sound: Susan Moore-Chang
Music: Cliff Eidelman
MPAA rating: PG-13
Running Time: 98 minutes

AWARDS AND NOMINATIONS

Sundance Film Festival Awards 1995: Audience Award

Pigalle

"Highly entertaining...plunges us headlong into the raffish world of Paris' Times Square...emotion-charged."—Kevin Thomas, *Los Angeles Times*

"A smartly executed nocturnal narco-trip."—David Rooney, *Variety*

Pigalle tours the red-light drug-infected porno shops, clubs, and boudoirs of Paris. At its center is Vera (Vera Briole), a peep show dancer, and Fifi (Francois Renaud), a pickpocket. Vera and Fifi are small-timers caught in a drug war between The Emperor (Jean-Claude Grenier), a malevolent midget, and Malfait (Philippe Ambrosini), who specializes in drugging and killing his lovers. Vera resists pressures to become a full-time prostitute, and Fifi, coerced by Vera's boss, finds himself involved in a murder plot against Malfait. To complicate matters further, Vera and Fifi are attracted to each other, even though Fifi is in love with Divine (Blanca Li), a transvestite prostitute, who is eventually murdered by The Emperor's gang.

Vera and Fifi survive as best they can in this degraded world. They are surprisingly uncynical and capable of love. Vera is devoted to her manager and lover, Jesus le Gitan, even though he exploits her. When his throat is slashed, she seeks solace from the sensitive Fifi. However, when the two become romantically involved, Fifi brutalizes Vera, sexually assaulting her from the rear as though she is no more than the rough trade he might pick up on the street. Fifi seems appalled by his own behavior but helpless to correct it, and a shocked Vera merely collects her clothes and departs—more in sorrow and disappointment than in anger.

The sexual scenes are the most riveting part of the film—not merely because of their content (in a sense the audience is peeping at these sexual performers as much as their clients are)—but because of their cinema verite quality. The actors do not look like they are acting, and indeed several of them are not professional actors. Rather than plotted actions, such scenes seem reflective of a compulsive, desperate way of life. There is very little dialogue; these characters will not explain themselves, and their personalities will not be rationalized.

If *Pigalle* has a flaw, it is in the pedestrian quality of its story. Another tale about warring drug lords? Except for the grim, arresting details, what is the point? The film has to be savored for its character studies. For example, there is Fernande (Raymond Gil), an aging transvestite cabaret performer who shelters Fifi, bathes and tries to seduce him. Fernande is charming—as amusing and playful offstage as on. Similarly, Mustaf (Younesse Boudache) is a freshly realized acolyte of Fifi's. Even when Fifi abuses him, Mustaf clings to his mentor—not abjectly but proudly, demanding that Fifi accord him attention and respect.

As one reviewer has noted, these characters are treated with great respect. They may be the pawns in a drug war, but they have their dignity. No matter how much they have experienced, there is a core of innocence that can still be shocked. Fifi is paralyzed with fear and revulsion when he is coerced into shooting Malfait. When an old gangster matter-of-factly explains how Fifi must calmly walk up to Malfait and shoot him, and then walk out as if nothing is amiss, Fifi is incredulous. To the gangster the killing is just a job. There is not a flicker of humanity in his words. Such scenes exemplify the film's economical technique. We learn a great deal about Fifi by simply watching his reactions to the stolid gangster.

About all Fifi has are his friends. And when he botches the murder and goes to prison, it is not so surprising to see Vera visiting him and to realize that she has forgiven him for his brutality to her. Is it love? That is a difficult question to answer in a corrupt world that shows precious few signs of redemption. What counts, however, is the solidarity of these struggling denizens.

The film's final shots of Vera and Mustaf on a motor scooter in broad daylight almost hurt the eyes. After being immersed in their night-world, it is disconcerting to see

CREDITS

Vera: Vera Briole
Fifi: Rancois Renaud
Fernande: Raymond Gil
Malfait: Philippe Ambrosini
Divine: Blanca Li
The Emperor: Jean-Claude Grenier

Origin: France and Switzerland
Released: 1994
Production: Romain Bremond and Patrice Haddad for a Premiere Heure LM, UGC, FCC, Delfilm, Canal Plus, Sofinergie 3, Federal Office of Culture of The Federal Dept. of the Interior production; Seventh Art
Direction: Karim Dridi
Screenplay: Karim Dridi
Cinematography: John Mathieson
Editing: Lise Beaulieu
Art direction: Gilles Bontemps
Costume design: Jean Louis Mazabraud
Sound: Jean-Pierre Laforce
Assistant direction: Jean-Jacques Jauffret
Running Time: 93 minutes

them brightly lit. The ending cannot quite be believed. Wouldn't something more shaded be a more appropriate ending? The sunshine verges on the sentimental, and yet it should not be freighted with symbolism. Vera and Mustaf are having their moment of fun, but it does not cancel out Fifi's imprisonment or their dim prospects. There is no hope for them other than the hope they can muster for themselves.

—Carl Rollyson

Pocahontas

"Disney's done it again!"—Joel Siegel, *Good Morning America*

"A gorgeously animated extravaganza!"—*The New York Post*

"Gloriously colorful, cleverly conceived...visually captivating!"—*The New York Times*

Box Office Gross: $141,523,195

After two extraordinarily successful but artistically weak entries in its library of animated films, Disney has returned in bravura style with *Pocahontas*, the studio's most spectacularly realized animated achievement since *Sleeping Beauty* (1959), and its most emotionally satisfying work since *Beauty and the Beast* (1991). Based on the American legend of the seventeenth-century Powhatan maiden who rescued an English settler, John Smith, from execution by her own tribe, the film takes numerous liberties with both the legend and the historical record: it increases the age of its protagonist from 11 or 12 to 17 or 18, and ends the story well before Pocahontas marries another settler and moves to England. But these liberties allow the filmmakers to create a powerful myth for contemporary children: the crux of the story becomes a choice between Pocahontas' love for John Smith and her devotion to her people, and she comes of age by applying the wisdom of her culture to the crisis of this clash with a new one.

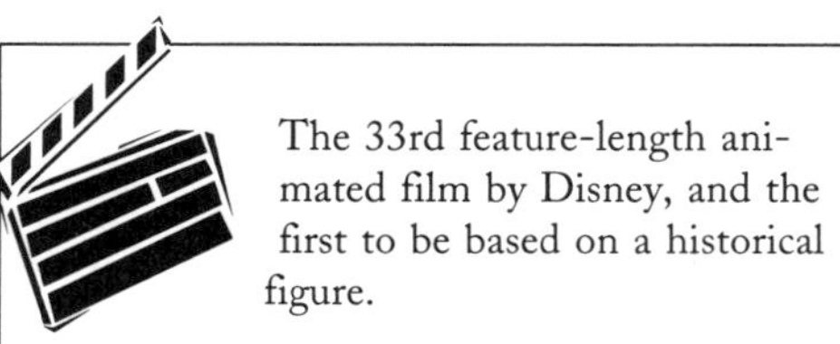

The 33rd feature-length animated film by Disney, and the first to be based on a historical figure.

Pocahontas' magnificent, carefully color-coded animation serves this myth-making with the utmost clarity, evoking at once the oneness of a people with the wondrous majesty of a virgin American continent and the abrupt encroachment of a more technologically advanced European culture. By the end, the film brings the New and Old Worlds to an uneasy visual and thematic unity. If this is a rather optimistic reading of American history, it works perfectly as myth: *Pocahontas*' crisp, coherent storyline and songs and dynamic use of color, movement, and line combine to create a plea for the conservation of both the natural environment and the wisdom of indigenous peoples unprecedented in animated film.

The film begins with an overview map of a teeming London, circa 1607. The map is reminiscent of similar shots in Disney's *Peter Pan* (1953), but here, instead of evoking the magic of flying over a city, it foreshadows English plans for developing the New World. John Smith (Mel Gibson) awaits his departure for America aboard the sailing ship The Susan Constant, but his life of traveling and exploring has left him full of ennui. "I've seen hundreds of new worlds, Thomas," he says in blase tones to his fellow sailor. "What could be so new about this one?" John Smith and Thomas both boast of their capacity to kill red-skinned "savages" in the New World if necessary. On the crossing, however, a storm tests their mettle, and presages the clash of cultures to come. The storm, with its animated spray, foam, clouds, lightning, and wind-whipped sails, is one of Disney's most brilliantly executed action scenes, and rivals, even betters, most action scenes in recent live-action films.

By contrast, on the other side of the Atlantic, the young Powhatan maiden Pocahontas lusts with adolescent fervor for new experience, but her life in the primeval forest remains constant and unchanging. Pocahontas' father, Chief Powhatan (Russell Means) wants her to marry the tribe's bravest warrior, Kocoum (James Apaumut Fall), but Pocahontas is searching for someone or something more exciting. In the exuberant number "Just Around the Riverbend," Pocahontas asks herself, "Should I choose the smoothest course?...Is all my dreaming at an end?" The action during this song, which depicts Pocahontas canoeing down a river and having to choose between two forks, dazzlingly depicts her free spirit as well as the choices she must make between adventure and stability, childhood and maturity, wildness and civilization. Motherless, like so many Disney heroines, and seeking to reconcile these opposing forces, Pocahontas consults with her spirit guide, Grandmother Willow (Linda Hunt), who has become a massive, verdant tree and channels the wisdom of the forest. "Your mother asked the very same questions," responds Grandmother Willow. The blues, greens and aquas of the primeval forest create an animated Eden in which Pocahontas learns the lessons of life and of her culture; the effect is stunning.

Pocahontas gets her wish for adventure in the arrival of John Smith. The Disney animators employ a neat trick: to the Powhatans, the British ship is huge, bigger than the forest; the British, however, find themselves dwarfed by the trees, the river, and the mystery of the new continent. But Smith is in the company of the newly appointed Governor of Virginia, Ratcliffe (David Ogden Stiers), whose greed and hubris are matched only by his girth. Convinced Virginia will yield quantities of gold on par with the Aztec or Inca kingdoms (the songwriters cleverly rhyme "Pissarro" with "tomorrow"), Ratcliffe sets about having the forest cleared. The scene is a brilliant dystopian version of the "Be Our Guest" number from *Beauty and the Beast*: instead of a frenetic welcome from exuberant hosts, "Gold" shows ungrateful guests rampaging through their new home, destroying it as quickly as they can. Trees are chopped down in one blow; whole swaths of land are blown up with explosives. The animators then intercut these brown and black scenes of material exploitation with Smith's journey into the primeval wilderness. The governor's notion of adventure is plunder; for John Smith, it is an inner journey.

John Smith and Pocahontas meet beneath a waterfall, and it is love at first sight, in spite of the growing tensions between the Powhatans and the English. The scenes in which they meet use a pictorial shorthand for the balance between nature and civilization: they are less lush and green than before, more reminiscent of 18th-century landscape paintings which juxtaposed wilderness and civilization. Their love for each other changes how each of them perceives the world, but it is the arrogance of the British thirst for power and gold that awakens Smith from his adventurer's ennui and spurs Pocahontas into maturity. When Smith condescendingly tells Pocahontas that the British will "teach your people how to use this land properly" and calls them "savages," Pocahontas bursts into the film's most moving number, "Colors of the Wind." As visions of elk spirits, cathedral-like stands of trees, and native ancestors fill the sky, Pocahontas scorns the British philosophy of plunder, and plaintively asks whether they, humans, can paint with all the colors of the wind. Smith is stunned by her conviction. The song ends on a somber note, however, with the sound of distant war drums signifying the confrontation to come. Both the Powhatans and the British are massing for war.

Pocahontas at this point borrows liberally from *West Side Story* (1961) in its depiction of the preparations for war between the two rival societies, but its music and color scheme remain entirely original. The musical number, "Savages," in which both sides chant that their opponents are "savages," shows each side demonizing the other; the blues and greens of the Edenic forest, even the purples and golds of the British ship, here yield to the oranges and reds of skin lit by raging fire as both sides gird for battle. In war, the film indicates musically and visually, the Powhatans and the English have become the same. While Pocahontas's animal companions, a native raccoon, Meeko, and hummingbird, Flit, make friends with Ratcliffe's domestic bulldog, Percy, in a parallel story which shows the possibility of accepting otherness, Powhatan gives Pocahontas the grim prognosis: "Nothing is simple anymore." Kocoum is killed, and John Smith is captured and about to be put to death when Pocahontas makes her famous plea for his life. When she does this, she forges an unbreakable link between the two cultures, and

CREDITS

Pocahontas: Irene Bedard and Judy Kuhn
John Smith: Mel Gibson
Powhatan: Russell Means
Grandmother Willow: Linda Hunt
Governor Ratcliffe/Wiggins: David Ogden Stiers
Thomas: Christian Bale
Kocoum: James Apaumut Fall
Nakoma: Michelle St. John

Origin: USA
Released: 1995
Production: James Pentecost; released by Walt Disney Pictures
Direction: Mike Gabriel and Eric Goldberg
Screenplay: Carl Binder, Susannah Grant and Phillip LaZebnik; based on an idea by Mike Gabriel
Editing: H. Lee Peterson
Art director: Michael Giaimo
Visual effects: Don Paul
Casting: Brian Chavanne, Ruth Lambert and Karen Margiotta
Music: Alan Menken and Stephen Schwartz
MPAA rating: G
Running Time: 87 minutes

AWARDS AND NOMINATIONS

Academy Awards 1995: Best Score (Menken), Best Song ("Colors of the Wind")
Golden Globe Awards 1996: Best Score (Menken), Best Song ("Colors of the Wind")

unifies the film visually. Forced to choose between leaving for England with the wounded Smith and remaining with her people, she chooses to remain loyal to the Powhatans and watches Smith's ship sail into the distance.

All the elements of the film work toward this visual and thematic unity. Whereas *The Lion King* (1994) relied on spectacular aerial shots of African wildlife clearly derived from live-action photography, *Pocahontas* uses a brilliant, carefully color-coded palette to evoke the majesty of the unspoiled North American continent and the greed of the civilized Englishmen. Vivid greens, blues, and aquas create a forest of all-enveloping mystery and magic, particularly in scenes where Pocahontas dives beneath the waterfall and visits Grandmother Willow; purples and golds define the velvet-robed British as they dig for gold and find only maize. By the end, however, the film's colors have achieved more of a balance. Judy Kuhn's soaring soprano accentuates Pocahontas' burning desire to find and accept something outside of herself; as the voice of her counterpart, John Smith, Mel Gibson lends a world-weariness to his character which contrasts with his stolid, too-handsome visual aspect. Gibson gives Smith self-doubt, and that is essential to his character's capacity to be truly humbled by the New World and by Pocahontas's strength. The Powhatans are portrayed with appropriate dignity, and if Governor Ratcliffe is a caricatured villain, John Smith and Thomas are revealed to be more accepting. Grandmother Willow is the spirit guide common to all recent Disney animated films, but her character, dispensing the wisdom of the forest and of the Powhatans, is the most intrinsic to the story of any of those in recent Disney films.

"It's not too late, child. Let the spirits of the earth guide you. You know your path child, now follow it."—Grandmother Willow giving Pocahontas advice about John Smith

Pocahontas also marks the welcome return of composer Alan Menken, who collaborated on the songs for *The Little Mermaid* (1989), *Beauty and the Beast*, and *Aladdin* (1992). Following the death of Menken collaborator Howard Ashman, Disney had turned for *The Lion King* to Tim Rice, the lyricist for *Jesus Christ Superstar* (1969) and *Godspell* (1971), and pop superstar Elton John, and produced the weakest song score of all the recent Disney animated films. The songs from *Pocahontas*, though less marketable as singles, are by contrast each integral to, and seamlessly woven into, the story. Menken and Schwartz write songs to tell a story, not merely as showpieces.

Comparisons between *Pocahontas* and *The Lion King* are inevitable and, in every case save the final box-office tally, favorable to *Pocahontas*. Both films feature environmental parables; yet *The Lion King*'s is muddy and tangentially related to the plot, while *Pocahontas*'s is integral to the tale of its protagonist's coming-of-age. *The Lion King* was the first Disney animated film not based on previously published source material, and *Pocahontas* is the first based on a historical figure; yet *The Lion King* blended its various uncredited sources into a bizarre hodgepodge, while *Pocahontas*, though clearly taking liberties with historical events, creates a unified, coherent myth for children. Even the signature Disney shot of its animated protagonist atop a promontory with a vast, majestic landscape below is more effective here than in *The Lion King* because of the clarity of the story: in *The Lion King*, the African plain was Simba's royal domain; in *Pocahontas*, the landscape is tended by Pocahontas' people, and that makes quite a difference. *Pocahontas* also presents a strong, female, non-Anglo role model who makes a choice to defend her people, as opposed to Simba, who must simply reclaim his role as male heir to a crown.

Pocahontas is the most adult of the Disney animated films in that it acknowledges its heroine's loss of youth and innocence, and this perhaps accounts for its not being as successful at the box-office as *The Lion King* or *Aladdin*. It has an ending in which its heroine chooses not romance, but the preservation of her people as her destiny, and observes, as well, the passing of innocence and the onset of maturity not only for Pocahontas, but also for both cultures. If *Pocahontas* does not dwell on the tragic aspects of the decimation of the Native American population, that is because the film is framed not as a tragedy, but as a mythical coming-of-age story, and it succeeds. Neither historical document nor pure fiction, *Pocahontas* scores as myth. In its clarity, in its finely wrought and dazzling animation, and in its treatment of the New World and its indigenous peoples with the respect and awe appropriate to their heritage, *Pocahontas* ranks among the finest of Disney's animated features, and among the finest films of 1995.

—*Paul Mittelbach*

REVIEWS

The New York Times. CXLIV, June 11, 1995, p.19(N).
The New York Times. CXLIV, June 23, 1995, p.H25(N).
Newsweek. CXXV, June 19, 1995, p.77.
Rolling Stone. July 13, 1995, p.115.
Time. CXLV, June 19, 1995, p.59.
Variety. CCCLIX, June 12, 1995, p.59.
The Wall Street Journal. June 16, 1995, p.A9(W).

Postcards from America

"Riveting."—John Andersen, *New York Newsday*
"From hyperrealism to dreamy romanticism...dazzling."—Dennis Demody, *Paper*

When *Rebel Without a Cause* (1955) emerged on the cultural landscape, it spawned a whole genre of films which depicted youth culture, while negatively and implicitly commenting of the pitfalls of everything from smoking to bad parenting. As time went on, the horrors of errant youth have been depicted countless times, from the campy *Hot Rods to Hell* (1967) to the recent *Basketball Diaries* (1995). Many of these films have been fictional exploitations of the drama and sexual energy inherent in "bad kids." Sean Penn played it in *Bad Boys* (1983). James Dean and Sal Mineo played it in *Rebel Without a Cause*. Judd Nelson, Emilio Estevez, and other "Brat-Packers" did a dreadfully watered-down version of it in many films of the eighties, such as *The Breakfast Club* (1985).

CREDITS

Adult David: James Lyons
Teenage David: Michael Tighe
Young David: Olmo Tighe
The Hustler: Michael Imperioli
Father: Michael Ringer
Mother: Maggie Low
Trippy: Les "Linda" Simpson
Porn Theater Drag Queen: Dean "Sissy Fit" Novotny

Origin: USA
Released: 1995
Production: Craig Paull and Christine Vachon for an Islet production in association with Channel Four Films; released by ICA Projects
Direction: Steve McLean
Screenplay: Steve McLean; based on the semi-autobiographies *Close to the Knives* and *Memories That Smell like Gasoline* by David Wojnarowicz
Cinematography: Ellen Kuras
Editing: Elizabeth Gazzara
Production design: Therese Deprez
Art direction: Scott Pask
Makeup: Tim Dark, Barri Scinto and Mandy Lyons
Costume design: Sara Slotnick
Casting: Daniel Haughey and Jakki Fink
Music: Stephen Endelman
MPAA rating: R
Running Time: 93 minutes

Recently, a new form of such films has seemed to emerge. Dubbed "queer cinema" by some, it is a sub-genre, a cross between recent gay-themed films and the old "rebel" films. Often dealing with AIDS, these films tell the grungy stories of troubled, angry, and rebellious gay youth. Gregg Araki's *The Living End* (1992), and Cyril Collard's *Savage Nights* (1993) are emblematic of such films.

Like *Postcards from America*, *Savage Nights* told the story of a young gay man's spiral into degradation and AIDS. But *Postcards from America* is not fiction. It is the real thing, adapted from the writings of David Wojnarowicz, an artist, photographer, and poet who died of AIDS in 1992. (The books from which it is adapted are *Close to the Knives* and *Memories that Smell Like Gasoline.*) It is an uneasy and not particularly likable film, but it is an unmistakably artful and haunting portrait of troubled youth which makes the prettied-up Hollywood versions of troubled youth seem banal by comparison.

Postcards from America is a hard film to judge because while it is emotionally powerful, it misses on several points, mostly in that it is a confusing jumble of vignettes. It tells Wojnarowicz' true life story, portrayed by three different actors at three different stages. (Young David is played by Olmo Tighe, Teenage David by Michael Tighe, and Adult David by James Lyons.) The film does not follow a linear story; the chronology is jumbled around, as if in memory. It is an interesting creative choice, and it is successful in its attempt to capture the essence of David as a little boy, an adolescent, and a young man, but is a bit confusing, as the audience tries to put the pieces together. Additionally, the film occasionally lapses into pretentious visual images, such as a little boy sleeping in a bird's nest, or fast jump cuts which appear to try and keep the viewer on the edge of his/her seat, but instead keep them simply on edge.

The interesting point to be aware of when viewing this film is that the same characteristics which keep it from being a Hollywood version of reality also keep it from being an easy film to watch. Audiences are used to certain conventions in their commercial films, and those characteristics are not present here. Director Steve McLean delivers his series of chronologically indistinct episodes without "prettying it up:" no glossy camerawork, no clever or cliche dialogue, no neatly tied up endings, and no conventional Hollywood storytelling. His creative approach to the material pays homage to the creativity of Wojnarowicz while it eschews Hollywood standards. And it is an appropriate way to tell this story. In so doing, it is truly grungy and gritty where a big-budget film is a stylized version of grungy and gritty.

Why is all this important? Because, when looking at

this film, an audience member might be more inclined to appreciate it if they understand that it seems to aspire to be a hybrid: it is an impressionistic film, but it is also starkly realistic. Within the impressionistic storytelling are highly realistic depictions of Wojnarowicz' harsh life. McLean does not pander to audience expectations. Since it does not follow conventional forms, it is easy to dismiss the film as "too arty" or "out there." That would be a shame, because (while not being a seminal or even an outstanding film) it does present alternative storytelling techniques which should always be welcome in the marketplace of ideas.

Postcards from America tells David's story through images, voice-over monologues, short scenes, and brief episodes. Some of the scenes are quite theatrical, especially the scenes depicting David's childhood with his violent and alcoholic father (Michael Ringer). These scenes are played out on what looks like a stage set of a family living room in the 1950s. David's father and mother (Maggie Low) fight on this stereotypical set which has no walls, but is surrounded by darkness. It is a disturbing impression, seeming to make a point about the darkness that lies just behind the typical American family of the 1950s. Occasionally, the characters directly address the camera. "My husband beat my son," says the mother. "So what if I hit my son?" intones David's father. Later, Adolescent David returns to this scene to ask his mother, "Why did you stay with him, Mom?" The older David returning to the "scene of the crime" is an artful way to show the artist's need to reinvestigate his history, and it is a creative way to tell the story. When Young David turns and talks to the camera during these scenes, it is strange and sad to see a boy so young have an objective view of the horrors of a life he cannot escape.

Other scenes are more realistically filmed. In particular, David's teenage years have more of a conventional cinematic feel. Wojnarowicz lived several of his years as a male hustler on the streets of New York. Accompanied by another young hustler (Michael Imperioli) and drag queen Trippy (Les "Linda" Simpson), several uncompromising but well-played scenes depict Wojnarowicz' life on the streets. A scene where David and his friend, holding concealed meat cleavers, attempt to rob a potential "john" is excellent. They flirt and tease the man, standing in the park, having plotted to rob someone using the meat cleavers. They walk with the nervous man to his apartment, but he realizes they are dangerous at the front door to his building and tries to escape them. They push on the front door; he frantically tries to get inside the door and away from them. There is something quite harrowing about the desperation of both the man as he scrambles for his safety and the youths scrambling to get what they want from him.

Clearly, as a teenager Wojnarowicz lived a brutal, harsh existence. There is a wrenching scene in which Teenage David is raped by a man who picks him up while hitchhiking. At first, the sexual energy between the handsome driver and David is quite strong. But the scene becomes truly frightening as the man turns to violence after pulling over to the side of the road. The rape sequence itself is terrifying. Additionally, McLean seems to echo the physical positions of the rape in other scenes in which David is in a similar physical position with his mother, who is protecting him from the father's violence.

Wojnarowicz' poetry finds its way into the film through voice-over and in some of the dialogue. It is perhaps the most powerful way in which McLean can describe the inner nature of Wojnarowicz. "You can't shut out the sound of a man about to scream that he's about to throw himself in front of the autos....You can't shut out the sights and sounds of death...those images hurl themselves from the images of a fast-paced city," says one passage. Another sequence has adolescent David entering a television into a fake-looking, "perfect" suburban home saying, "In my dreams I crawl across freshly clipped lawns....I enter your house through cracks past [the things] that make you feel safe."

The performances of the three young men who portray David are raw and vulnerable, in particular Michael Tighe as Teenage David. James Lyons is quite effective in his bitter and sad portrayal of a defeated and angry Adult David. Lyons, who appeared in Todd Haynes notorious *Poison* (1991), could make a career out of playing scuzzy cast-offs (that's a compliment).

In the end, Wojnarowicz railed against America's homophobia and lack of attention to the AIDS epidemic, and his anger is made justifiable and palpable in McLean's impressionistic portrait. At the end of the film, McLean shows "negatives" of the film; inside-out images of David's life, while David, in voice-over, says, "America is such a beautiful place, isn't it?" It is a powerful image, undercut a bit by a film that goes on too long and is at times hard to follow. But it is the artist's job to try and make sense of the difficult world we live in. Applaud McLean for trying to make some sense of it.

—*Kirby Tepper*

The Postman (Il Postino)

"An irresistible treat about love, letters, and laughter!"—Movie tagline

"A profound and wondrous film."—John Petrakis, *Chicago Tribune*

"A tender and wistful comedy!"—Kenneth Turan, *Los Angeles Times*

"Sweetly romantic! A warmly affecting film, featuring a wonderful performance by Massimo Troisi. *The Postman* is an eloquent tribute to Mr. Troisi's talents."—Janet Maslin, *The New York Times*

"Unforgettable! *The Postman* does what great films sometimes have to do—simply break our hearts. Fall in love with one of the loveliest movies in a long time."—Peter Stack, *San Francisco Chronicle*

"A rare celebration of poetry and passion."—Gene Siskel, Siskel & Ebert

Box Office Gross: $12,695,407

"When it comes to bed, there's a difference between a poet, a priest or a communist." So says Donna Rosa, a supporting character in this enchanting film. *The Postman* is about that which connects us as humans. It is an intelligent and charming story concerning itself with the deepest essence of poetry—that people need to have connections to each other and to the world around them. It uses poetry as a universal common denominator. It reminds its audience that poetry is not the exclusive property of intellectuals, but that anyone who feels passionate about anything can be a poet.

The film is an international project: it is an Italian film with a main character who is Chilean but is played by a Frenchman (Phillipe Noiret); it is based on a novel, *Ardiente Paciencia*, by a Chilean author who lived in West Germany (Antonio Skarmeta), and it is directed by an English director (Michael Radford).

"I want to give the last piece of my old heart to this movie."—actor Troisi to director Radford on his reason for refusing to postpone filming in order to have a heart transplant. Troisi died of heart failure some 12 hours after completing work on the film.

Il Postino is a fictional story whose foundation is in historical fact. In 1952, the real-life Chilean poet Pablo Neruda traveled to Italy and remained on the island of Capri for a period of several months while there was a warrant for his arrest (on political grounds) in Chile. Neruda later said that Capri's "simple" people were an inspiration to him, and this story is a fictionalized account of Neruda's encounters with these people.

Mario Ruoppolo (Massimo Toisi) sees a newsreel account of the great poet Neruda and is especially taken by the account of how women fling themselves at Neruda, presumably because of his mastery of beautiful words. When the opportunity arises to become the postman whose sole job it is to take mail to Neruda (who has come to Mario's native Capri), Mario jumps at the chance, even though he will only be paid in tips.

But he is paid in many other ways. The barely literate, scraggly Mario befriends the worldly Neruda (Philippe Noiret) and both learn a great deal from each other. When Mario discovers his love for local beauty Beatrice Russo (Maria Grazia Cucinotta), he asks Neruda to help him write words to woo her. He wins over Beatrice though not her skeptical aunt (Linda Moretti) who thinks that "when a man starts to touch you with words, he's not far off with his hands." As time passes, and Neruda returns to Chile, the characters all discover the legacies they have left each other.

Since the film concerns itself with words and ideas, it follows that much of the reason it is artistically successful is its screenplay by Anna Pavignano, Michael Radford, Furio Scarpelli, and Giacome Scarpelli. They have fashioned a story that touches its audience in a similar way to the grandaddy of sentimental Italian films, *Cinema Paradiso* (1990). And in the way that film showed the extraordinary influence of film in the lives of an Italian village, this film shows the influence of the ideas of one man. The writers have focused on the concept that Neruda's influence lies in his ability to unlock Mario's potential for discovering the poetry that surrounds him.

And much of the screenplay is as poetic and filled with metaphor as its main characters. Neruda tells Mario that in order to learn about metaphor, he should "walk along the shore" and "metaphors will come to you." Then when Mario follows Neruda to a quiet beach to talk more of poetry, they engage in a discussion about the lack of water in the village. That this discussion takes place next to the ocean seems to be a metaphor for Mario's inability to see that poetry is all around him, yet he is unable to tap into it. And the metaphor is extended when, in the middle of the discussion, Neruda doffs his outer clothes and confidently wades into the water, showing (symbolically) that he knows how to avail himself of the poetry around him.

The film is filled with exquisite moments when the locals use metaphor as simply and matter-of-factly as Neruda. The difference is that they don't call it metaphor. "It doesn't count", says Mario after being told he created a metaphor, "I didn't mean to." Toward the end of the film though, Mario shows himself and Neruda that he understands how to find poetry in the world around him: He creates a sound poem using the brand new tape recorder left behind by Neruda. In several wondrous scenes, Mario and his friend (Renato Scarpa) record the wind on the cliffs, the "sad nets" of the fishermen, the starry sky over the island, and numerous other "sounds." These are among the simplest and most touching moments a film audience could ask for.

In a bit of tragic, true-to-life poetry, Massimo Troisi died the day after filming was completed. The young (he was 41) Troisi needed a heart transplant, but postponed it until after filming. Troisi was highly popular in Italy where he was a well-known director and actor. The shadow of his death brings a mystical quality to this film.

Troisi's fragility (he was only able to shoot for two hours a day for some of the production schedule) ironically aids his performance. His portrayal of Mario is of a delicate and skittish man who doesn't want to bother anyone, but has a wellspring of curiosity inside him that threatens to overpower himself and the people around him. But Troisi's barely audible delicacy keeps him from even remotely overpowering those around him. His performance is tender and bittersweet. His initial attempts to talk to Neruda are very humorous, particularly when he finally gets an autographed copy of a book only to be vexed that Neruda did not sign it "to Mario." (This, he says, will never help him win over the girls in Naples.) He is also funny in his awkward attempt to meet Beatrice, telling Neruda that he spoke five words to Beatrice Russo. "I said, 'what's your name?'" "What were the other two words?" asks Neruda. "I repeated her name after she told me," he shyly replies. Troisi's simplicity and vulnerability make his transformation later in the film all the more meaningful.

Noiret is a perfect choice for the role of Neruda. He portrays the fame and worldliness of his character with grace, and his imposing stature and wizened features make him a striking figure. This is important, for without this sense of greatness, the influence of Neruda's character on Mario would be lost. Mario's reluctance to approach him seems appropriate considering Noiret's portrayal of Neruda as the sort of man so innately powerful that he does not have to wield his personal power because he naturally exudes it. Noiret's Neruda is kindly, and, like the real-life Neruda, is truly entranced by the simplicity of the people around him. He knows the value of that simplicity, saying (of his poetry) that "even the most sublime idea seems foolish if heard too often." Noiret echoes this idea of understatement in his simple performance. His final scenes, hearing the sound poem created for him by Mario, are beautiful lessons in a wonderful actor's ability to portray a complex helix of emotions without trying. Noiret's droopy eyes and his jowly sweetness are just two features that have made him an international star. And it should be noted that Noiret spoke his lines in French, which were then dubbed into Italian. That he and Troisi could appear to have such a deep relationship even though they are speaking two different languages is a testament to both of these fine actors.

CREDITS

Mario Ruopplo: Massimo Troisi
Pablo Neruda: Philippe Noiret
Beatrice Russo: Maria Grazia Cucinotta
Donna Rosa: Linda Moretti
Telegrapher: Renato Scarpa
Matilde: Anna Buonaiuto
DiCosimo: Mariana Rigillo

Origin: Italy
Released: 1994 (1995)
Production: Mario Cecchi Gori, Vittorio Cecchi Gori and Gaetano Daniele for a Penta Film, Esterno Mediterraneo Film/Blue Dahlia and K2T production; released by Cecchi Gori Group and Miramax Films
Direction: Michael Radford and Massimo Troisi
Screenplay: Anna Pavignano, Michael Radford, Furio Scarpelli, Giacomo Scarpelli and Massimo Troisi; adapted from the novel *Ardiente Paciencia* by Antonio Skarmeta
Cinematography: Franco Di Giacomo
Editing: Roberto Perpignani
Production design: Lorenzo Baraldi
Costume design: Gianna Gissi
Sound: Massimo Loffredi and Alessandra Perpignani
Music: Luis Enrique Bacalov
MPAA rating: not rated
Running Time: 116 minutes

AWARDS AND NOMINATIONS

Academy Awards 1995: Best Original Drama Score (Bacalov)
Nominations: Best Picture, Best Director (Radford), Best Actor (Troisi), Best Adapted Screenplay (Radford/Troisi/Scarpelli)
British Academy Awards 1995: Best Foreign Film, Best Director (Radford), Best Score (Bacalov)
Nominations: Best Actor (Troisi), Best Adapted Screenplay (Radford/Troisi/Scarpelli)
Chicago Film Festival 1995: Best Foreign Film
Directors Guild Award Nomination 1995: Best Director (Radford)
Screen Actors Guild Awards Nominations 1995: Best Actor (Troisi)

It is also a testament to the talents of director and writer Michael Radford who has created a warm and beautiful film. The locales, as perhaps can be expected in a film about the beauty of Italy, are stunning. From the views of the rustic fishermen pulling in their nets to the craggy beach where Troisi speaks his first metaphor, the film is a visual poem. Radford, forced by Troisi's illness to find as many chances for him to sit as possible, is a sensitive actor's director, one who knows enough to allow the camera to discover the feelings of his actors rather than to telegraph what the audience should feel through technique-filled cuts and intercuts.

This film is about the legacies people leave each other if they are willing to reach out to one other and (metaphorically) to the world around them. That some of the film deals with the place of communism in the world seems appropriate since communism's original purpose, like that of poetry, seemed to be to find the commonality between people and to find ways for them to coexist. Watching a film of this level of sensitivity can be a link between peoples—if they are willing to identify its metaphors and to understand its poetry. Like Pablo Neruda, Massimo Troisi has left a wonderful legacy that will be enjoyed by generations of filmgoers.

—Kirby Tepper

REVIEWS

Daily Variety. September 6, 1994. p.16
The New York Times. June 14, 1995 p. C15.
The Village Voice. June 19, 1995. p.43
The Washington Post. June 23, 1995. p. F7

Powder

"*Powder* is absolutely brilliant and unforgettable!"—Ron Brewington, *American Urban Radio Network*

"Thought provoking and compelling!"—Susan Granger, *CRN International*

"A unique and highly entertaining experience!"—Paul Wunder, *WBAI Radio*

Box Office Gross: $29,768,475

Even before his birth, the gods had determined that Jeremy Reed's (Sean Patrick Flanery) life was not to be normal. His mother was struck by lightning as she stood in a rain puddle on her way to the delivery room where she died. His distraught father, upon seeing that his son was born an albino, denies him. Jeremy, called Powder because of his white skin, is cognizant of it all.

Left to be raised by his grandparents who for some reason make him live in the family farmhouse basement, Powder becomes a mysterious phantom to his neighbors. But when his last grandparent dies, Powder is brought into the light by the director of the local boys reformatory, Jessie Caldwell (Mary Steenburgen), and the local Sheriff, Doug Barnum (Lance Henriksen). What Jessie and Doug do not realize is that Powder is not just some teenager suffering from a deficit of social abilities, but rather he has powers at which they can only marvel.

The first of several skills Powder possesses is a photographic memory. But this is not an empty ability because it is reflected in Powder's IQ which tests off the scale. Powder also has psychokinetic expertise and the ability to magnetize metal, an adeptness he uses to try to win the hearts and minds of the bullies at the boys school by making flying silverware into a freeform tower of cutlery in the school's cafeteria. Also on Powder's talent resume is his ability to read thoughts. This gives him extraordinary insight into other people's motives, but also allows him to communicate and connect to those who find it difficult to communicate and connect themselves. And this gives Powder perhaps his greatest ability: his compassion.

So Powder is not only physically different from the other teenagers in town, he is also mentally and spiritually different from everyone. And as often happens when someone is "different," they are suspect. Different from the societal norm, Powder usually finds himself an outcast and the subject of taunts, bullying, and physical harm. His only solace is in Jessie's guidance and in the friendship he creates with science teacher Donald Ripley (Jeff Goldblum) who marvels at Powder's intellect...and his ability to conduct electricity. Powder also finds a degree of acceptance and incipient love in fellow student Lindsey (Missy Crider), but it is cut short by her intolerant father.

Intolerance is the name of the game it would seem in the small town in which Powder finds himself living. And intolerance is just one of the many moral themes preached by this film. In his extreme whiteness, Powder becomes symbolic of racism. In his intense genius, we see America's inherent anti-intellectual bias. In his ability to see the similarities of humanity, we see our powerful sense of individualism threatened.

Powder is the ultimate fish-out-of-water film, but in what pond would Powder swim? He is also the definitive teenage misfit, which allows just about everyone who has ever felt different to identify with him. But as imaginative as the film's premise is, and as captivating as Powder's character is, in the end, the film relies on being sentimentally manipulative instead of intellectually (or even emotionally) challenging.

Too many of the people in Powder's life are extremes. They love him or hate him. Most of us would probably just be incredibly curious. He does no harm, but only good, and indicating that the bulk of the town's population hate him for it is too facile a plot point. While the presumably abused boys at the reformatory would probably hate everyone, wouldn't the "normal" students at Powder's school be more likely to ask him to do tricks for them?

Powder is a well-meaning film that tries to walk into supernatural realms, but even the apparently unmotivated Christ-like martyrdom of the ending leaves one more frustrated and annoyed than edified.

There are, however, a few magical moments in the film. And among them are two scenes which might make the film difficult for younger viewers. When Powder uses his powers to help the Sheriff communicate with his dying, comatose wife and when he "connects" a dying deer to the hunter who just shot it so that he can experience the pain of dying and emptiness of death, one could hear the tissues being pulled out of pockets and purses of viewers.

Undoubtedly, one of the best things about *Powder* is the acting. Henriksen expertly walks the only ambiguous character line in the film, by being humane and yet dutifully providing an authority figure. Steenburgen is suitably sympathetic (although she seems to have little control over the conduct of the boys in her charge), and Goldblum gives yet another amusingly skewed performance as the person who most understands and admires Powder.

But shining above them all is Sean Patrick Flanery's Powder. Best known for his role as the title star in TV series *Young Indiana Jones,* Flanery brings an inner peace and calmness to a character in turmoil which is expressed more through superb use of body language than through dialogue. Flanery communicates Powder's superhuman abilities, while eloquently proclaiming his human need to connect. Because of Flanery's amazing performance, our hearts go out to him and we allow the film to be emotionally exploitive.

Just as *Powder* was being released, controversy erupted when it came to light that the writer and director, Victor Salva, was convicted and served time for molesting the 12-year-old male star of his 1988 feature film *Clownhouse.* With this revelation, some of the scenes in this film became almost embarrassingly awkward. Scenes which might have been puzzling (i.e. why does Powder stop to watch a boy in a shower room when he's on his way out of town?) or innocent (i.e. when Donald senses Powder's loneliness and caresses his bald head) seem a lot less enigmatic or guileless in light of the director's background. Suddenly, uncomfortably, the outsider is not Powder, but Salva.

However, among more innocent and less sophisticated moviegoers, *Powder's* simple and benevolent message geared to teenage audiences and coupled with terrific performances will help it to find a receptive audience.

—Beverley Bare Buehrer

CREDITS

Jessie Caldwell: Mary Steenburgen
Powder: Sean Patrick Flanery
Sheriff Barnum: Lance Henriksen
Donald Ripley: Jeff Goldblum
Duncan: Brandon Smith
John Box: Bradford Tatum
Maxine: Susan Tyrrell
Lindsey: Missy Crider
Stipler: Ray Wise
Mitch: Esteban Louis Powell
Syke: Chad Cox

Origin: USA
Released: 1995
Production: Roger Birnbaum and Daniel Grodnik for Caravan Pictures; released by Hollywood Pictures
Direction: Victor Salva
Screenplay: Victor Salva
Cinematography: Jerzy Zielinski
Editing: Dennis M. Hill
Production design: Waldemar Kalinowski
Art direction: Barry Kingston
Set decoration: Florence Fellman
Costume design: Betsy Cox
Music: Jerry Goldsmith
Visual Effects Supervisor: Stephanie Powell
Special "Powder" Makeup Designer and Creator: Thomas R. Burman and Bari Dreiband-Burman
MPAA rating: PG-13
Running Time: 111 minutes

REVIEWS

Chicago Tribune. October 27, 1995
Entertainment Weekly. November 3, 1995
The New York Times. October 27, 1995
Variety. October 27, 1995

Priest

"One man is about to challenge two thousand years of tradition."—Movie tagline

"An electrifying powerhouse of emotion!"—Rex Reed, *New York Observer*

"Astonishing! Passionate and hypnotic."—Bruce Williamson, *Playboy*

"A triumph! One of the best and most provocative films of the new year! This powerhouse takes hold, shatters your prejudices and stuns you with its wicked humor, passionate romance, and stirring moral force."—Peter Travers, *Rolling Stone*

Box Office Gross: $4,176,932

Unlike the CBC's television movie, *The Boys of St. Vincent* (1994), which took a restrained look at sexual abuse with a Catholic orphanage in Montreal, Antonia Bird's *Priest* is a no-holds-barred indictment of the Catholic religious institution—and the people who are drawn to it by their faith and held there by their ever-elusive religious convictions. The film is a confusing amalgam of venom and good intentions.

When an elderly cleric is forced to retire from the working class parish in Liverpool, Father Greg Pilkington (Linus Roache), a zealous young social conservative priest is sent in as his replacement. It is not long before the boyishly handsome Father Greg butts heads with the senior clergyman with whom he shares a house, Father Matthew Thomas (Tom Wilkinson), a political liberal who goes to no great pains to hide his sexual relationship with the comely parish housekeeper, Maria (Cathy Tyson). Father Greg is morally outraged. "You can't go around changing the rules because they don't suit you. There's just sin." But Father Greg turns out to have his own guilt-provoking secret: he is a practicing homosexual who soon reaches for the leather jacket in the back of his closet and sneaks off to a gay bar where he connects with a stranger, Graham (Robert Carlyle). The two men return to Graham's apartment where they engage in some fairly explicit sex. Afterwards, Father Greg flees with nary a word, cold, detached and obviously tortured. Interwoven with this sexual identity issue is the disturbing subplot of child molestation and the issue of the confidentiality of the confessional. (The latter being a topic explored by previous films, most notably the Alfred Hitchcock 1953 film, *I Confess*, starring Montgomery Clift.)

Father Greg's guilt increases when Graham discovers that Greg is a priest and later visits him at his parish during mass. One of the most compelling scenes in the film occurs when Father Greg cannot bring himself to give his boyfriend communion, startling Father Matthew. Later, when the police bust the couple for engaging in oral sex in a parked car, the scandal breaks in the newspaper and seems to offer Father Greg the "out" that he seemed to be secretly longing for. Instead, his faith in ruins, Greg attempts to end his life by overdosing. He survives, however, and at Father Matthew's insistence, he eventually returns to the parish. Contemptuously reproached by the parishioners, Father Greg attempts to maintain his dignity by serving communion, despite the fact that only one of the Christians seems able to practice the act of forgiveness by queing up to receive the host from him. In a melodramatic climax guaranteed to evoke emotion from even the most repressed viewer, the young molested girl breaks rank to find comfort in the arms of the fallen priest.

Priest telegraphs the direction that its story will take, yet does so in an engaging manner. The two priests are such

CREDITS

Father Greg Pilkington: Linus Roache
Father Matthew Thomas: Tom Wilkinson
Maria Kerrigan: Cathy Tyson
Father Ellerton: James Ellis
Graham: Robert Carlyle

Origin: Great Britain
Released: 1995
Production: George Faber and Josephine Ward for the British Broadcasting Company (BBC); released by Miramax Films
Direction: Antonia Bird
Screenplay: Jimmy McGovern
Cinematography: Fred Tammes
Editing: Susan Spivey
Art direction: Ray Langhorn
Music: Andy Robers
MPAA rating: R
Running Time: 105 minutes

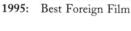

AWARDS AND NOMINATIONS

Australian Film Institute Awards Nominations
1995: Best Foreign Film

extremes that we know they will no doubt end up as friends. And the film's theme is foreshadowed by a puzzling and incongruous juxtaposition of imagery: a painted portrait of Native American Chief Sitting Bull. Father Matthew explains it as representing "nobility even in defeat." One cannot help but wonder why the filmmakers chose this particular hero rather than someone more appropriate to their own culture, such as Mary, Queen of Scots, the last Catholic monarch in Scotland. One may recall that Queen Elizabeth had Mary beheaded because she viewed her as a threat to her claim to the throne.

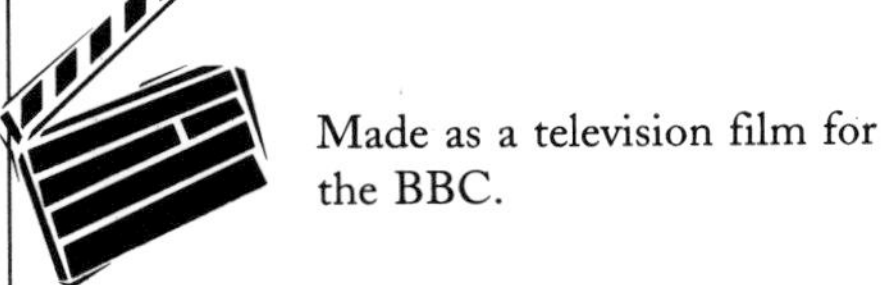

Made as a television film for the BBC.

Originally conceived as a four-part mini-series for BBC television, *Priest*, the second feature film from director Antonia Bird, strives to scrutinize nearly every area of controversy within the Catholic religious institution. The film never escapes its claustrophobic small-screen look and feel, but in some ways this works in its favor, helping to create an atmosphere of oppressive righteousness and moral indignation that tends to characterize the zealous young priest. One of the challenges with this film, however, is that despite all of its best intentions, *Priest* never ceases to feel emotionally manipulative. It is all highly effective and it is difficult to not feel the impact of some intensely charged issues, yet it tends to be handled in a way that feels more like an emotional assault. With a few notable exceptions, scenes have a tendency to come across more as another opportunity for soapbox preaching rather than true dramatic interaction. Replete with the kind of grandstanding speeches that people never seem to have in real-life, the characters appear to be talking *at* you rather than engaging in an exchange with each other. Even the father who sexually abuses his daughter is given a speech that clearly elucidates his position. As Anthony Lake of *The New Yorker* wrote: "(the father is)...not just a molester but a molestation *Expert*, an incest wonk."

"That wasn't a sermon. It was a political broadcast for the Labour Party."—Father Greg disapproving of Father Matthew's left-wing politics.

There rests an inherent danger whenever a filmmaker ventures too far astray from merely telling his/her story and enters the arena of blatant moralizing: the film feels more like a piece of propaganda. And *Priest* leaves the aftertaste of a piece of propaganda—granted, a highly effective piece—but propaganda, nonetheless.

In some ways *Priest* is just as insidious because here is a film that essentially dismisses the very foundations of faith—we never really understand how or why Father Greg became a priest—making a mockery of the Catholic religion, and yet the film incorporates the perplexing sequence in which the priest confronts Jesus in the form of a hanging crucifix, intercut with the mother's discovery of her daughter's sexual molestation by her father. The technique creates a causal effect, making it appear as though the young priest's prayers are being answered. In essence, a miracle, or an epiphany. After the relentless attack on religion, this sequence seems like an afterthought on the part of the filmmakers, especially given its placement within the narrative structure. Perhaps Ms. Bird and Mr. McGovern are as equally at odds with the role of organized religious institutions as they are about the importance of faith and religious belief.

Performances are consistently compelling. Linus Roach, a veteran of British television, portrays the young priest in a believable, inwardly tortured way, exploring the torment of a man torn between his religious vocation and his sexual desires, while Tom Wilkinson provides the comfort and much needed comic relief. Also notable are Robert Carlyle as Father's Greg's lover, Graham, and Cathy Tyson, perhaps best known for her work as the high-priced call girl in Neil Jordan's *Mona Lisa* (1986), as the housekeeper.

Reviews for the film were decidedly mixed. Despite its less-than-subtle approach, *Priest* remains an engaging film. It is successful in evoking both empathy for the young cleric and outrage at many of the antiquated, rigid doctrines of the Catholic Church. It is only afterwards, when the filmic images have disappeared from view and one is left merely with one's own thoughts, that the highly manipulative nature of the film becomes so apparent to the viewer.

—Patricia Kowal

REVIEWS

Entertainment Weekly. March 31, 1995, p. 42.
Los Angeles Times. CXIV, March 24, 1995, p. F10.
The New Yorker. LXXI, March 27, 1995, P. 107.
The New York Times. March 24, 1995.
The Village Voice. March 28, 1995, XL, p. 55.

The Promise (Das Versprechen)

"Powerful and astonishing!"—Barbara Siegel, *Siegel Entertainment Syndicate*

"A great love story set on both sides of the Berlin Wall..."—Casper Citron, *WOR Radio*

Konrad (Anian Zoller and August Zirner)and Sophie (Corinna Harfouch and Meret Becker) are ill-fated lovers in 1961 Berlin whose relationship is severed by the presence of the Berlin Wall. When the two decide to escape to the other side of the Berlin Wall, Konrad is left behind in a mishap and Sophie begins her new life without him. After years of living apart, Konrad and Sophie meet with each other to rekindle their lost love.

CREDITS

Young Harald: Pierre Besson
Sophie Sellman: Corinna Harfouch
Young Sophie: Meret Becker
Konrad Richter: August Zirner
Gerard: Jean-Yves Gaultier
Barbara: Eva Mattes
Young Barbara: Suzanne Uge
Harald: Hans Kremer

Origin: German
Released: 1995
Production: Eberhard Junkersdorf for a Bioskop-Film/Odessa Film/Les Productions JMH production; released by Fine Line Features
Direction: Margarethe von Trotta
Screenplay: Peter Schneider and Margarethe von Trotta
Cinematography: Franz Rath
Editing: Suzanne Baron
Art direction: Benedikt Herforth
Costume design: Petra Kray
Sound: Christian Moldt
Music: Jurgen Knieper
MPAA rating: R
Running Time: 115 minutes

The Prophecy

"Marked by fate, doomed by prophecy...time is running out for mankind!"—Movie tagline

"A must-see!"—*Boston Globe*

"A terrifying supernatural thriller!"—Tony Timpone, *Fangoria*

"Potent and frightening!"—Chris Hewitt, *Knight-Ridder Newspapers*

It should not necessarily be the critic's job to simply say a film has no redeeming qualities and then leave it at that. But *The Prophecy* poses a difficult problem because of its utterly inane premise, its turgid dialogue, and its overly philosophical, complicated plot.

The best thing that can be said about *The Prophecy* is that it is not likely to be remembered long enough to hurt the careers of its lead actors. Nor will it be around long enough to impede the upward movement of its director/writer, Gregory Widen. Widen is the screenwriter responsible for *Backdraft* (1991) and *Highlander* (1986), neither of which would be considered great films, but both of which were quite visible in their initial release. This is

Elias Koteas and Virginia Madsen in *The Prophecy*. © Miramax Films.

Widen's directorial debut, but, with any luck, few people will remember the unfortunate mix of simplistic theology and cheesy horror that he inflicts on his audience, and instead they will recall that there are a few intentional laughs amidst the unintentional ones, not to mention an occasional interesting visual image.

The battle between good and evil (as personified by the devil) is a very standard thematic basis for a film plot, having served *The Exorcist* (1973) and *The Omen* (1976), not to mention countless other films, very well. *The Prophecy*'s inanity comes from the story on which the theme is hung: It is about an apocalyptic battle between good and evil which is won by a good-guy homicide cop who enlists the aid of some Indians and a vixenish elementary school teacher from Arizona. Now doesn't that sound ludicrous? It is. It plays more like a parody of horror films than the real thing, and it is certainly too full of simplistic philosophical declarations to be taken seriously as a piece of sophisticated discourse. From costumes to music, dialogue to plot, the film tries too hard to be interesting and complicated, and it simply falls flat.

> "I draw from the Old Testament, in which there are many descriptions of angels being God's sword carriers, God's 'Wild Bunch,' laying waste to cities, turning people into salt and stealing newborns. No one has ever dealt with that aspect of their personalities before. The idea that angels are complex individuals, and not just 'yes' men, fascinates me."—Writer/director Gregory Widen commenting on his story

The story goes like this: Thomas Daggett (Elias Koteas) is a cop who left the seminary after a spiritual crisis. (The audience witnesses the spiritual crisis in the first few minutes of the film.) Daggett has apparently retained a good deal of knowledge about the Bible, and has a healthy respect for religion, having published a book about it. Into Daggett's spiritually charged world comes Simon (Eric Stoltz), an angel on the run from Gabriel (Christopher Walken) and Lucifer (Viggo Mortenson), who are locked in some sort of epic battle over the souls of mankind. The script calls for one of its characters to explain the battle through bible quotes: "And there were angels who could not accept the elevation of man—and there arose a second war in heaven." But in this film their battle seems more like the Hatfields and the McCoys—no one seems to know just exactly how it got started, but it just keeps going. It appears that the angels have come to earth to do the last battle according to the Biblical prophecy, and they do so with the aid of various low-life characters who they enlist to do their dirty work. (Among them is Amanda Plummer, perfectly cast as a spaced-out whacko whose soul has been sold to Gabriel).

Perhaps it sounds blasphemous to refer to such important subjects with irreverence. But the introduction of other characters in the film almost requires this review not to take this film seriously. For example, Virginia Madsen appears on the scene rather quickly as Katherine, a schoolmarm who is rather trendily and sometimes scantily dressed in midriff-baring outfits and/or Tex-Mex-meets-Hollywood cowgirl togs. She wears all these quasi-hipster outfits while teaching a school full of children in a tiny town in the middle of Arizona. The credibility of the film gets shaken a bit with the introduction of this out-of-place character.

But, of course, credibility had been strained far earlier in the film with the introduction of the battling angels. Simon (Stoltz) and Gabriel (Walken) are unintentionally hilarious in their roles. Stoltz plays Simon as a sort of hip dude; he has the unshaven look of a rock star who has taken too many drugs. With strange contact lenses, weird fingernails, and a penchant for preaching, Simon's welcome wears thin immediately after his arrival on the scene. Stoltz manages to find a shred of sympathy later in the film, when Gabriel pulls out his heart and sets him on fire, but until then he is just irritating.

For his part, Walken seems to be having a great time playing Gabriel as a slithering psychopath. With his dark eyeliner and his jet-black bobbed haircut, he looks like a cross between Rudolph Valentino and Gloria Vanderbilt. Gabriel is all-powerful and all-knowing; Walken plays him with the same kind of scary cruelty he has brought to loftier films, from *The Deer Hunter* (1978) to *Biloxi Blues* (1988) to this year's *Nick of Time* (1995) (reviewed in this edition). In this film, however, Walken is way over the top. Director Widen doesn't rein him in very well; perhaps he doesn't want to. There are a couple of moments which use Walken's extra-

CREDITS

Gabriel: Christopher Walken
Thomas Dagget: Elias Koteas
Katherine: Virginia Madsen
Simon: Eric Stoltz
Mary: Moriah Snyder
Rachel: Amanda Plummer
The Devil: Viggio Mortensen

Origin: USA
Released: 1995
Production: Joel Soisson, W.K. Border and Michael Leary for First Look Pictures and Neo Motion Pictures; released by Dimension Films
Direction: Gregory Widen
Screenplay: Gregory Widen
Cinematography: Bruce Douglas Johnson and Richard Clabaugh
Editing: Sonny Baskin
Production design: Clark Hunter
Costume design: Dana Allyson
Music: David C. Williams
MPAA rating: R
Running Time: 91 minutes

ordinary sense of irony to great advantage. In one scene, Daggett finds him teaching the schoolchildren to play the trumpet. Another example comes when Gabriel is describing all the horrible things that will befall Simon, saying, "you know the routine." These few moments show what the film could have been if it had not taken itself so seriously.

And this film most certainly takes itself seriously. The scene in which Gabriel finally finds Simon (hiding in an abandoned room in the schoolhouse) has some of the most bloated dialogue in recent memory. "You and I, we threw their rebel thrones," says Gabriel. "Oh, Gabriel, when was it that you lost your grace," sighs Simon.

Director-Writer Widen creates a plot that meanders into the realm of Native-American theology, the Korean War, and urban homicide detectives. Widen seems to expect his audience to suspend disbelief just because the film deals with lofty subjects. For example, when Daggett is trying to uncover why the angels have descended on Arizona, he finds an old piece of film about a Korean War veteran who has just died. The next scene shows Daggett with a projector, viewing the super-eight film. How does he know this is important information? Where did he get the projector (since he just arrived in town and knows no one)?

Another suspension of disbelief is required in order to believe Daggett's comfort in going all over town asking questions. He is not from Arizona; does he have jurisdiction over this town? Doesn't he want to inform anyone back home that he is out of town? Why does he hook up with Madsen so quickly? Is it just because she wears such cool clothing? As for Madsen, when a little Native-American girl named Mary (Moriah Snyder) falls ill in the middle of class, Madsen's character simply walks outside and drives the girl home—with no explanation to her class, and no arrangements for someone else to come in. One of the most ludicrous moments comes when Daggett pulls a gun on Gabriel. Everyone knows you can't pull a gun on an angel. Bye-bye credibility.

Besides the occasional clever line, Widen does show a flair for creating arresting visual images. One moment occurs when Simon is being burned up by Gabriel. Another series of good images come when Daggett and Katherine take the Indian girl to a remote mountaintop village to save her from the angels. (Of course, for the cynics in the audience, this provides the best piece of dialogue in the film when one of the tribal elders looks at Daggett and says of the little girl, "we have called the hand trembler to find if she must have a sing.")

By the time that Daggett and Katherine take Mary to the top of the mountain to fight Gabriel and Lucifer, the audience should be rolling in the aisles. Watch for Daggett to (with a straight face) tell a bunch of Native-American tribal elders to go into a straw hut with Katherine and "lock the door" to protect themselves from Lucifer and Gabriel. Lock the door? Of a grass hut? With Lucifer and Gabriel, who can, according to Gabriel, "turn cities into salt"? The best that can be said is that he deserves points for optimism.

Many audiences will enjoy the campy fun, and many audience members will enjoy the biblical references and the well-intended thematic spine of this film. Because of that, it must be acknowledged that Widen tried to do his best on his maiden voyage as a director. He ends his film on an up note, with a voice-over that says, "If faith means never understanding God's plan, maybe that's what being human is after all." Fair enough. But "lock the door" of a grass hut? Come on.

—Kirby Tepper

A Pyromaniac's Love Story

Box Office Gross: $468,240

A Pyromaniac's Love Story contains more than just one blazing love story. In fact, it contains at least three major conflagrations, and several minor brush fires. The first love story involves Mr. and Mrs. Linzer (Joan Plowright and Armin Mueller-Stahl reprising their comfortable and believable relationship from 1990's *Avalon*). He is torn between his love for his business, a debt-ridden bakery, and his wife whom he does not want to drag down into bankruptcy. One night he confesses to his pastry boy Sergio (John Leguizamo) his desire to have his business burned to the ground so he can collect the insurance money and protect his wife.

But Sergio has a confession of his own he needs to make: he has never declared his love to the plucky waitress Hattie (Sadie Frost)—even though just about everyone else in the neighborhood knows about it. Hattie, however, seems oblivious to Sergio's attentions. Why? Because she has her sights set on saving enough money to see the world. Of course Sergio wants to go with her, but there's one problem: he has no money.

If anyone in this story has money to burn, it is Mr. Lumpke. And Mr. Lumpke loves his son, Garet (William Baldwin), who in turn has his own love story. The quirky Garet is enamored of the equally wealthy Stephanie (Erika Eleniak), but their relationship is shaky at best. He is beset by low self-esteem and believes the beautiful Stephanie can never love him. While she, on the other hand, can't understand why Garet doesn't profess his love for her.

After attending a party where Garet seems to snub her, Stephanie walks and walks trying to figure him out, only to find herself in the Linzer's bakery after hours where Sergio is mopping up. They talk and Sergio tells her of his undying and undeclared love for Hattie. Deeply touched by his feelings, Stephanie kisses Sergio...and suddenly decides she is in love with him. The very next night, the Linzer's bakery burns down.

Enter Mr. Lumpke who realizes his son Garet has done the deed, and that a past record of questionable behavior will probably net him a serious sentence. So, he offers Sergio what he needs most to join Hattie on her trip to discover the world—money. If Sergio will take the blame for the fire, Mr. Lumpke will give him $25,000. At first the innocent Sergio refuses, but his desire to be with Hattie wins out, and he turns himself in to the police.

However, Mr. Linzer now feels guilty. He believes Sergio started the fire after their discussion. He confesses this to Mrs. Linzer, and she leaves him. With both of his two loves now lost, Mr. Linzer now goes to the police to free Sergio by confessing that he was the one who set the fire.

When Sergio is released, he soon finds himself in the company of Garet Lumpke who explains that he burned down the bakery because someone who worked there had stolen the heart of his Stephanie. His rationale? "I wanted her to see what her love did to me." "Love turned me into a pyromaniac!" The bakery was Garet's love poem written in flames to Stephanie, giving new meaning to the phrase "carrying a torch."

Sergio tries to explain to Garet that he doesn't love Stephanie because he desperately loves Hattie. This raises Garet's curiosity, and he sets off to meet the woman who could be the catalyst of Sergio's burning love. In the restaurant where she works, Stephanie suddenly finds herself being kissed by Garet, but Garet doesn't know about Hattie's hot temper. She decks him and sends him to the hospital. Incredibly, Garet now believes he is in love with Hattie. After all, it's only fair since Stephanie loves Sergio.

CREDITS

Garet Lumpke: William Baldwin
Sergio Cuccio: John Leguizamo
Hattie: Sadie Frost
Stephanie: Erika Eleniak
Perry: Michael Lerner
Mrs. Linzer: Joan Plowright
Mr. Linzer: Armin Mueller-Stahl
Sergeant Zikowski: Mike Starr
Jerry: Julio Oscar Mechoso
Mr. Lumpke: Richard Crenna
Ass Pincher: Floyd Vivino
Ass Pincher's Wife: Babz Chula

Origin: USA
Released: 1995
Production: Mark Gordon for Buena Vista
Direction: Joshua Brand
Screenplay: Allison Lyon Segan
Cinematography: John Schwartzman
Editing: David Rosenbloom
Production design: Dan Davis
Art direction: Peter Grundy
Set decoration: Jaro Dick
Costume design: Bridget Kelly
Music: Rachel Portman
MPAA rating: PG
Running Time: 94 minutes

Meanwhile, back at the jail, Mr. Linzer's confession has rekindled Mrs. Linzer's love for him. Now it is her turn to falsely confess to the police that she torched the bakery. And, to prove her point, she sets the police sergeant's desk ablaze. Now Mr. Linzer is released and Mrs. Linzer is behind bars.

> "[It] is about how love makes us crazy but we still can't live without it."—Director Joshua Bround on *A Pyromaniac's Love Story*

But this is a fairy tale. We know that because the neighborhood in which Sergio, Hattie and the Linzers live is the perfect setting for a flaming fable. It is picturesque, friendly, clean, and international. (This approved vision of "Anytown USA" was really filmed in various neighborhoods and 37 different set locations throughout Toronto.) And obviously, in a fairy tale, no one who is innocent will pay the price for a guilty person's deed but the culpable culprit.

It is very difficult to ignite a folk tale for today's adults who are more accustomed to sex and violence than amiable and chaste fare at their local theaters. Director Joshua Folsey (better known as the creator of the television shows *Northern Exposure* and *I'll Fly Away*) tackles this difficult feat in his first feature film, and while his efforts may be sincere, he can't seem to start a proper spark on the big screen.

The fault is not with the attractive cast. John Leguizamo (probably known best for his TV show *House of Buggin* and the 1994 film *Super Mario Brothers*) brings an earnest vulnerability to his Sergio that makes his character as sweet as the pastries that surround him in the bakery. Sadie Frost's fiery Hattie is engaging and quite a change of pace from her character of Lucy in Francis Ford Coppola's *Bram Stoker's Dracula*. Erika Eleniak, last seen in 1994's *The Beverly Hillbillies* and televison's *Baywatch*, manages to find just the right note to be likeable even though her Stephanie is self-centered and supercilious.

William Baldwin's Garet is so over the top that he quickly moves from being amusing to annoying. He chews scenery with absolute abandon and gives himself over to a performance that wallows in operatic self-dramatization. His character's low self-esteem is supposedly brought on by his physical limp, but he should take another look at his beard which includes a grubby 5 o'clock shadow and his hair that cries out to be combed and styled. That limp is the least of his problems.

But perhaps the greatest problem with A *Pyromaniac's Love Story* is the plot. For one thing, it doesn't unfold, it untangles—and then tangles again. One doesn't dare pull the strings of this tale's plot lines without finding illogical knots. Why do those who confess to setting the fire never check their stories with each other? How does Mr. Lumpke know Sergio and his problems with Hattie, and what was Jerry doing in the burned out rubble at just the right time to meet him? After Hattie and her father fight, why does he leave the house? And why does an admittedly Puerto Rican character have the Italian name Sergio Cuccio?

One has to wonder if these problems are the result of this being the author's first produced screenplay or if the feature film debuting director was just not up to the task. Whichever the case, it would appear that the story's good intentions just weren't carried out well enough to warrant the price of box office admission.

However, the film is good-natured and refreshingly sweet without being sickeningly so. Finding fault and condemning such an amiable little film seems to be more the work of a curmudgeon than a critic. After all, one shouldn't over-analyze fairy tales, should one?

—Beverley Bare Buehrer

REVIEWS

Chicago Tribune, April 28, 1995.
Entertainment Weekly. May 12, 1995, p. 44
Los Angeles Times, April 28, 1995, p. F6
Variety. 1 May 1995, p. 36

The Quick and the Dead

"The movie is quick-and slick, but it's far from dead."—Michael Wilmington, *Chicago Tribune*

"Great fun! Sharon Stone is terrific. Action-packed and right on target."—Bob Healy, *Satellite News Network*

"A grade-A shoot'em up!"—Jeff Craig, *Sixty Second Preview*

Box Office Gross: $18,636,537

With Edwin S. Porter's *The Great Train Robbery* (1903), two popular American film genres were born-westerns and films about violence. Also with *The Great Train Robbery* began a tradition of using the western to broach new thematic and stylistic territory. As the western showcases the never-ending battle between civilization and wilderness (or chaos), it is an appropriate genre for pushing cinematic frontiers. From *The Great Train Robbery*, with its continuity of editing and its medium close-up of one of the bandits firing at the camera/audience, to *Johnny Guitar* (1954), the first of the gender-bending westerns, to the modernist minimalism of Sergio Leone's "spaghetti westerns" (such as *For a Few Dollars More*, 1965), to *Unforgiven* (1992), with its glamourless view of gunfighting and death, westerns have dared to be different, albeit with varying success.

The Quick and the Dead begins in the desert with an unknown man, digging hole after hole, searching urgently for something. A lone rider approaches, and the man fires his gun. The rider drops to the ground. The man approaches with his weapon drawn, only to be surprised, beaten and chained to his wagon's wheel by Ellen (Sharon Stone).

Sputtering under the hot desert sun, the man vows revenge. Ellen rides off into the horizon, toward the town of Redemption. Upon her arrival, she proceeds to the saloon, where registration has begun for the annual gunfighting contest. Several likely men sign up for the contest, for instance, an ex-convict named Scars (Mark Boone Junior). A few surprise entrants include Kid (Leonardo DiCaprio) and his putative father (who is also the town tyrant), Herod (Gene Hackman). As Ellen appears to be considering signing up, a ruckus arises when a former gunslinger turned missionary named Cort (Russell Crowe) is dragged into the saloon. Herod has arranged for Cort's mission to be burned and, to encourage Cort to fight in the shoot-out, Herod has his neck placed in a noose, has him placed atop a chair, and begins to shoot the legs off the chair one at a time. Both Cort and Ellen enroll in the contest, and over the next four days, gunfighters challenge gunfighters, eventually fighting to the death. Alliances are forged and broken, and only two of the fighters will remain alive by film's end.

Evil John Herod making a suggestive proposition to gunslinger Ellen: "I could give you more money than you could spend." Ellen: "I'd never feel like I'd earned it." John: "Oh yes you would."

Although she first appeared as a lovely, unattainable Woody Allen daydream in *Stardust Memories* (1980) and has appeared in more than twenty films since, Sharon Stone rose to notoriety only recently by portraying a bisexual murderess with an aversion to wearing undergarments (*Basic Instinct*, 1992). Known for her look more than her range, Stone nonetheless has appeared in a series of high-profile films, opposite a series of high-profile actors. Indeed, her co-stars have included Arnold Schwarzenegger (*Total Recall*, 1990), Sylvester Stallone (*The Specialist*, 1994), Michael Douglas (*Basic Instinct*), Richard Gere (*Intersection*, 1994), Billy Baldwin (*Sliver*, 1993), and in this film Academy Award winner Gene Hackman. In *The Quick and the Dead*, Stone adopts the style of acting made famous by Clint Eastwood in the Sergio Leone westerns. She is an enigma; she rides alone. She speaks only rarely, and even then in monosyllables: In response to "You need a man," she says, "You need a bath." She tries to avoid the fights-except for the ones she has come to Redemption to fight. In a Zorro-like fashion, she leaves her mark and disappears. Like in another western *The Outlaw Josey Wales* (1976), her cheracter fights for her dead family. One of the new twists is that the character Ellen has a social conscience and intervenes on behalf of the helpless. For instance, the bartender's young daughter very nearly falls prey to a predatory, unsavory, lascivious drunkard. Ellen steps in and instills in him a recognition of 1990's sensitivities. All of this Stone accomplishes in virtual deadpan, leather britches, and revealing decollete.

Also new is the fact that Ellen battles side-by-side with the men. Unlike the women in traditional westerns (see Grace Kelly and Katy Jurado in *High Noon*, 1952), Ellen is no schoolmarm, no saloon gal; she is a gunslinger. Even when women have had central roles in westerns, they have battled only with other women. For instance, *Johnny Guitar* climaxes with Mercedes McCambridge and Joan Crawford shooting it out, punching it out, cat fighting over a man. In *The Quick and the*

Dead, however, Ellen becomes a modern heroine, fighting to redeem herself and her life. In several recent films, such as *Buffy the Vampire Slayer* (1992), *Pacific Heights* (1990), and *Blue Steel* (1990), women restore order by personally combating men. No more rooting from the sidelines; they are in the fray, and they are winning.

Gene Hackman is once again the "bad guy," apparently having as much fun being bad as he did as Lex Luther in *Superman* (1978). Here, there is also something blackly comedic about his character Herod. While Herod dedicates himself to making sure others are as "bad" as he is, he is actually very needy and tries to reach out to those around him. For instance, he hints that he killed his wife for her unfaithfulness, yet he is dedicated to the idea of love and tries to woo Ellen. He pities himself for being alone, yet he destroys the young man who would call him father. He forces Cort to shoot a priest, and when Cort dedicates himself to God, Herod intervenes and, not unlike a game-show host, forces Cort to play the game or lose. In a town filled with poor people who sell their silver to try to have Herod killed, Herod nonetheless strolls the town in his smoking jacket, enjoying the thought that the gunfight makes his enemies face him rather than sneak up on him. It is an odd kind of logic, but that is part of the charm.

Leonardo DiCaprio's Kid is flamboyant and yet timid, a flashy, deadly gunfighter and an honest businessman. His story is one of the most engaging in the film; his need for recognition signals the difficult boy-man that he is. For example, while the town's folk love him and turn out for all of his fights, it is his father's approval that matters most to him. That he may never feel that he has that approval makes him something of a tragic figure. Yet he is also a picaro, pursuing adventures and women. Says Director Raimi in the production notes, "He's the embodiment of wild youth. The Kid thinks he can't die. All he wants out of life is his father's respect. He'll go to any lengths for that recognition."

The reviews of *The Quick and the Dead* have fallen into one of two general groups. One set wonders at the odd production values, the thundering hooves, the wratcheting weapons, the sqeakiest of doors, the jangliest of spurs. The other set of reviews accepts the givens of this cinematic world and laughs at the quirky accessories. Director Sam Raimi (*Darkman*, 1990) would no doubt endorse the second approach. "This is the Old West of our fantasies. Realism was not our goal. We weren't making a documentary. Admittedly, we owe more to Sergio Leone than to John Ford."

The Quick and the Dead was filmed in Mescal, Arizona, approximately forty miles east of Tucson. Production designer Patrizia von Brandenstein designed the town around the outlaw theme: The only merchants are coffin makers, saloon keeps, and gun sellers. "Nothing lives in the town. Even the cactus is dead, like the spirit of the people. Graves

CREDITS

Ellen: Sharon Stone
Herod: Gene Hackman
Cort: Russell Crowe
Kid: Leonardo DiCaprio
Dog Kelly: Tobin Bell
Doc Wallace: Roberts Blossom
Eugene Dred: Kevin Conway
Sergeant Cantrell: Keith David
Ace Hanlon: Lance Henriksen
Horace the bartender: Pat Hingle
Marshall: Gary Sinise
Charles Moonlight: Woody Strode
Scars: Mark Boone Junior
Katie: Olivia Burnette
Mattie Silk: Fay Masterson
Ratsy: Raynor Scheine
Blind boy: Jerry Swindall
Gold teeth man: Scott Spiegel
Spotted Horse: Jonothon Gill

Origin: USA
Released: 1995
Production: Joshua Donen, Allen Shapiro, and Patrick Markey, in association with Japan Satellite Broadcasting and IndieProd; released by TriStar Pictures
Direction: Sam Raimi
Screenplay: Simon Moore
Cinematography: Dante Spinotti
Editing: Pietro Scalia
Production design: Patrizia von Brandenstein
Art direction: Steve Saklad
Set decoration: Hilton Rosemarin
Casting: Francine Maisler
Sound: Dennis L. Maitland
Costume design: Judianna Makovsky
Gun coach: Thell Reed
Music: Alan Silvestri
MPAA rating: R
Running Time: 103 minutes

REVIEWS

Boston Globe. February 10, 1995, p. 47.
Chicago Sun Times. February 10, 1995, p. 35NC.
Daily Variety. February 2, 1995, p. 2.
Entertainment Weekly. February 17, 1995, p. 40.
The Hollywood Reporter. February 8, 1995, p. 9.
Los Angeles Times. February 10, 1995, p. F1.
The New York Times. February 10, 1995, p. B6.
Rocky Mountain News. February 10, 1995, p. 4D.
San Francisco Chronicle. February 10, 1995, p. C1.
Washington Post. February 10, 1995, p. N37.

and abandoned safes are landscape hallmarks. The grand town clock serves only to define gunfights. The civic monument is Herod's house, dominating the town just as its occupant does. I wanted it to reflect a bloated predator," said von Brandenstein.

To add to the authenticity of the film, the production hired Thell Reed, credited as the world's fastest draw, to serve as gun coach, and the costume designer Judianna Makovsky found a vintage 1870's slicker for Stone to wear in the film.

A self-described "funny movie that incorporated horrific violence," *The Quick and the Dead* is the newest of a tradition of quirky westerns, genre films that keep the genre alive. Not all audience members will appreciate or understand this film, but for those who do, it is an exciting and interesting cinematic adventure.

—Roberta F. Green

Raging Angels

Young couple Chris (Sean Patrick Flanery) and Lila (Monet Mazur) become entangled with a satanic cult led by rock n' roll singer Colin (Michael Pare).

CREDITS

Chris: Sean Patrick Flanery
Lila: Monet Mazur
Colin: Michael Pare
Kate: Diane Ladd

Origin: USA
Released: 1995
Production: Chako Van Leeuwen for a Nu Image Films production; released by Vidmark Entertainment
Direction: Kevin Rock
Screenplay: Terry Plumeri, Chris Bittler and Bryan England
Music: David Markov
MPAA rating: R

Reckless

"Three cheers for a delightfully dysfunctional stocking stuffer."—Laurence Schubert, *Detour*

"A wonderfully demented fable."—Dennis Dermody, *Paper*

Rachel (Mia Farrow) thought she was living the perfect suburban life until one Christmas Eve her husband Tom (Tony Goldwyn) breaks down and tells her he has hired a hitman to kill her. After his confession, he throws her out of the house and she is left to fend for herself. Mysterious couple Lloyd (Scott Glenn) and Pooty (Mary-Louise Parker) takes Rachel in and helps her create a new identity.

CREDITS

Rachel: Mia Farrow
Lloyd: Scott Glenn
Pooty: Mary Louise Parker
Tom: Tony Goldwyn
Sister Margaret: Eileen Brennan
Tom, Jr: Stephen Dorff
Game show Emcee: Giancarlo Esposito
Trish: Deborah Rush

Origin: USA
Released: 1995
Production: Amy J. Kaufman for a Playhouse International Pictures; released by Samuel Goldwyn Co.
Direction: Norman Rene
Screenplay: Craig Lucas; based on the play *Reckless* by Craig Lucas
Cinematography: Frederick Elmes
Editing: Michael Berenbaum
Production design: Andrew Jackness
Costume design: Walker Hicklin
Sound: Michael Barosky
Casting: Billy Hopkins, Suzanne Smith and Kerry Barden
Music: Stephen Endelman
MPAA rating: PG-13
Running Time: 91 minutes

Red Firecracker, Green Firecracker

"Erotic and beautiful."—Henry Cabot Beck, *Interview*

"Exotic, lush and romantic."—Dennis Dermody, *Paper*

"Exquisite, explosive, extraordinary...A firestorm of unleashed passion."—Peter Stack, *San Francisco Chronicle*

Box Office Gross: $272,232

From the novel *Little Master* comes the bittersweet *Red Firecracker, Green Firecracker*, a Chinese film which received moderate critical acceptance and limited release in the United States. It is a film filled with beautiful visual images and interesting symbolism. But it will inevitably be compared to more emotionally and visually lush Chinese films such as *To Live* (1994) or *Farewell, My Concubine* (1993), perhaps diminishing the impact of its story and symbolism.

It is the story of Chun Zhi (Ning Jing), a young woman who has inherited a vast fireworks-producing empire in rural China. The film takes place prior to the Chinese revolution in 1911, and the fireworks serve (for the purposes of the film) as more than just the lifeblood of the local economy: they also foreshadow the enormous political upheaval about to change the Chinese cultural landscape. Fireworks were used in China for ceremonial and entertainment purposes, but also played a role in breaking up ice on the Yellow River during the winter.

Fireworks also represent sensuality here; becoming a symbol of the explosive nature of a young woman's discovery of her sexuality. Chun Zhi, having run her family's business for years, is known as "the Master" to everyone in the town, most of which are under her employ, and she is treated like an Empress. Dressed in men's clothing and wearing her hair pulled under a man's cap, she has quietly held up the duties prescribed by her inheritance, which states that she may only hold on to the fortune as long as she does not marry. (Having been the only female in her family, ownership of the business would naturally fall to her husband, thereby severing her family's centuries-old ownership.)

Chun Zhi is not the only person with a stake in the ownership of the company. Her butler (Gao Yang) and her foreman, Mr. Mann (Zhoa Xiaorui) carefully protect their sinecure, aware that if Chun Zhi were to marry they would lose their enviable positions. The film's conflict arises when a drifter comes into town. The drifter is an artist named Niu Bao (Wu Gang), a handsome loner who is unimpressed by Chun Zhi's wealth and influence. After an initial scrape with town officials for peddling his artistic wares in the street, his talent attracts Chun Zhi's eye, and he is given a position painting doorways in her vast estate.

As time passes, Chun Zhi comes to his studio and admires his paintings, enjoying the company of someone who treats her like a woman. His lack of reverence toward her shifts gradually into admiration and then into love. They enter into a romantic relationship, metaphorically and literally setting off fireworks everywhere. Niu Bao rather inexplicably dares to toss firecrackers into Chun Zhi's inner courtyard, and Mr. Mann nearly kills him. Niu Bao is tied up and hung over fire, with firecrackers tied to his body, when Chun Zhi intervenes. No longer willing to play the role of "the Master," she flaunts her love affair with Niu Bao even after firing him from his job. In flagrant violation of her societal and cultural role, she starts wearing feminine clothing, and visits Niu Bao at night, plotting to marry him.

Simultaneously, Mr. Mann and the old butler plot to protect their positions by trying once agian to kill Niu Bao and securing Mr. Mann as the rightful person to marry Chun Zhi. Finally, a competition for the hand of Chun Zhi culminates in some very exciting fireworks displays, as the suitors show their virtuosity with firecrackers in dangerous but exciting "performances." The film retains its sense of impending doom and its sense of the sorrow of cultural and sexual repression to the end.

Director He Ping captures that sense of sadness even while he maintains an emotional distance from his characters. Perhaps the film might be more involving if there were more scenes of interaction between Chun Zhi and confidantes to whom she could display her feelings. Similarly, Niu Bao's motivations remain an enigma. The depth of the lovers' feeling for each other seems hard to empathize with, given that the audience does not know the individuals very well. He Ping keeps the early scenes between them very tentative, which seems appropriate, but there is a lack of warmth between them. Certainly, in later scenes where the lovers meet in secret, their passion for each other is obvious, but the camera's distance from them, plus He Ping's allegiance to creating arresting visual images at the expense of character development, diminishes the audience's ability to empathize.

Another way in which He Ping diminishes impact is by maintaining a slow pace. For example, Chun Zhi enters Niu Bao's room more than once by walking slowly around the room, looking at his paintings. Other scenes seem to take a little long in getting their point across, such as a scene in which Mr. Mann discovers the lovers in Niu Bao's room. His slow ascent up the stairs has the effect of numbing the audience's attitude toward the scene: they know where he's going, and are probably wishing he would get there already.

At times, He Ping seems to squander the inherent drama of a scene. For instance, there is an early scene in which a fire destroys part of the fireworks production area on Chun Zhi's property. The importance of the scene seems to be to display Chun Zhi's power over her employees, to bring Chun Zhi and Niu Bao together for the first time, and to symbolically provide fireworks as a foreshadow of upcoming events. The initial fireworks blast is effective, but the rest of the scene's impact is diminished when He Ping's use of close-ups replaces coverage of the fire and the chaos among Chun Zhi's employees as they try to put it out. The scene ends abruptly, with the workers becoming immediately silent upon Chun Zhi's entrance. The scene feels incomplete; the audience has incomplete visual experience of the fire, consequently, the metaphorical impact of the fireworks becomes lost.

Other visual images in the film are striking, however; He Ping's strength seems to be in creating a melancholy mood through cinematic pictures. The unusual setting of the film amidst the strange, labyrinthian town by the Yellow River, provides many exotic images, especially unusual to Western audiences. A chase through the town reveals asymmetrical doorways, vast stairways, and huge entrances to enormous grey buildings. The fireworks themselves provide many wonderful images, in particular, the climactic fireworks competition between Chun Zhi's suitors is extraordi-

CREDITS

Cai Chunzhi: Ning Jing
Niu Bao: Wu Gang
Man Dihong: Zhoa Xiaorui
Old Butler: Gao Yang

Origin: China
Released: 1994 (1995)
Production: Chen Chunkeung and Yung Naiming for a Yung and Associates production; released by October Films
Direction: He Ping
Screenplay: Da Ying; based on a story by Feng Jicai
Cinematography: Yang Lun
Editing: Yuan Hong
Art direction: Qian Yunxiu
Costume design: Ma Defan
Sound: Gu Changning
Music: Zhao Jiping
MPAA rating: not rated
Running Time: 116 minutes

nary. A strange but enchanting attempt by the townspeople to exorcise evil spirits from Chun Zhi is also a visual treat, as numerous people parade outside of her home in bizarre ritualistic masks. Finally, He Ping returns often to images of a rowboat making its way along the Yellow River; he makes the most of this forlorn image by eliminating the sound of oars in the water, and by allowing the image to speak for itself. It seems to symbolize Chun Zhi and Niu Bao's fight against the current of their society, at the same time evoking the power of the river and the inexorable movement of time in spite of humanity's best efforts to fight it.

With all of these images, it is a shame that some of the beauty is undercut by subtitles that attempt American colloquial translations but simply don't work. For example, at one point, Niu Bao thanks another man for a favor, by saying, "I owe you one." At another point, a character says, "scholarship...that's just reading old books and studying old crap." Finally, a co-worker warns Niu Bao, to "be careful, or Mr. Mann will slap you one." These pieces of dialogue seem at odds with both the time (early 1900's) and the character of the people who say them. Though a more careful translation would be more formal, it would be more appropriate.

In her central role, Ning Jing is delicate and beautiful, but does not, at first, hint at the sexual repression inherent in the script. If the theme of the film has to do with the pain of being unable to fully express one's passion, then there must logically be the hint of a passion that has no outlet. As played by Chun Zhi, there is no passion until her affair with Niu Bao becomes exposed. At that point, her struggle against her repressive world is quite painful and beautiful, particularly in a scene where she closes her bedroom door and weeps. If the audience knew her better, this scene would be even more moving.

Red Firecracker, Green Firecracker fails to ignite completely, but is nonetheless a visually arresting and intelligent film.

—*Kirby Tepper*

Restoration

"Sensuous and thrilling!"—Michael Medved, *New York Post*

"Amazingly lavish! The sets, locations, and especially the costumes by James Acheson are all magnificent. Thrilling, sensuous and consistently fascinating."—Michael Medved, *New York Post*

"This big, rollicking film has more than enough heart! Robert Downey, Jr. is charming, Sam Neill is delightful, and Hugh Grant is hilarious!"—Janet Maslin, *The New York Times*

"One of the most impressive jobs of historical recreation that I've ever seen."—Roger Ebert, *Siskel & Ebert*

"Wonderful. As good-looking a picture as I've ever seen."—Gene Siskel, *Siskel & Ebert*

"Lively, lavish and inspiring!"—Peter Travers, *Rolling Stone*

Box Office Gross: $3,713,485

The year is 1660, a benchmark in British history marking the re-establishment of the Monarchy in England under King Charles II (Sam Neill) after over a decade of Puritan rule. The title *Restoration* also represents a return to a former natural or unimpaired state or condition, when theatres could be reopened after having been closed for years by the Puritans, a return to uninhibited life, gaiety, sensuousness, and color after the grim social restraints of Oliver Cromwell's government. It's also a time, as an opening title ironically informs us, of plagues, the great fire of London, and abysmal ignorance concerning the sciences and medicine. All of this represents a typically shorthand reduction and simplification of a time of far greater complexity than the screen can easily capture.

Beginning in London in 1663, *Restoration* is mainly the story of Dr. Robert Merivel (Robert Downey, Jr.), a young, skillful physician who is invited to serve at the Court of King Charles II after his training at the Royal College Hospital. During these ribald years Merivel indulges himself in wine, women, and song. This combination of moral depravity and medical skill comes to the attention of King Charles, who brings him to court to cure his spaniel dog. Robert does very well at Court—he even cures the dog—and soon he finds himself in an intrigue of the King's devising: He is to marry Celia Clemence (Polly Walker), the King's mistress, a marriage of convenience that will allow the King to continue his clandestine intrigues with the woman. In return Robert is given a title, a handsome estate in Suffolk, and many playmates, but he is forbidden to consort with his own wife. Of course, Robert promptly falls in love with Lady Celia and is subsequently banned by an angry King from the Court and stripped of his estate and title.

All of this occurs in the first half of the film, but an overall pattern eventually begins to assert itself. The bright extravagance of the Court in contrast to the dismal disasters of the age, notably the Great Plague of 1665 and the Great Fire of London of 1666, pattern the film's formal structure. During the latter half of the film Robert is removed from the light and brilliance of the Court and plunged into the shadows of the plague and fire. After he is taken in by the Whittlesea Quakers, his bright sashes and clothes will be replaced by severe robes and black hats. His indolent gaiety and licentiousness will yield to stark abstinence and self-sacrifice. As Robert labors, the charm and wicked humor of the film is laid upon the rack of its own moral preachments.

"I need a man who is far too enamored of women in general to make the mistake of loving one in particular."—King Charles II proposes that Merivel platonically marry the King's troublesome mistress, Celia

Robert first returns to a Quaker insane asylum to work with his dedicated physician friend John Pearce (David Thewlis), who had never lost faith in Robert's talents as a physician and his merits as a man since their student days together at the Royal College Hospital. And Pearce's confidence is repaid. Gradually discarding his colorful raiment, Robert introduces more enlightened methods for treating the ill. Robert also falls in love with Katherine (Meg Ryan), one of the patients at the asylum, who is not insane but severely depressed and grieving the death of a drowned child. They become lovers, and Katherine later bears Robert a child; but when Robert has to deliver the baby by caesarean section, Katherine dies.

Robert returns with the baby, Margaret, to London, where the Plague is rampant. Working under the pseudonym of his friend John Pearce, a recent Plague victim, Robert battles the Plague and becomes famous for his healing powers. Eventually he is called to Court, where he cures the King's mistress—his own wife!—whom Charles fears is infected by the Plague. Wearing a plague mask, Robert treats her and tells Charles that she will be healed if the King confesses his true affection for her. News of the Great Fire sends Robert to London to save his daughter. Trying to reach her he falls unconscious into a boat that drifts downstream to Suffolk. A grateful King Charles discovers Robert's true identity (from Celia, who recognized him behind the mask) and restores his estate and daughter to him, stating that Robert has become a man at last. Why the King should feel free to offer such judgments, considering that he was the agent of Robert's temptation and downfall, and considering that the King himself is no more guiltless of licentiousness than Robert, is rather mystifying.

Restoration is based on Rose Tremain's novel of the same title, first published in Britain in 1989 and winner of the Angel Literary Prize and the Sunday Express Book Award. It was also short-listed for England's coveted Booker Prize. Director Michael Hoffman was impressed by the novel and optioned the film rights with producer Sarah Black. Hoffman, a native of Idaho who went to Oxford as a Rhodes Scholar, then asked his Oxford colleague Rupert Walters to write the screenplay. According to *Variety,* the film's main liability was "an overly episodic story that loses some steam in the second half."

The film's title is a metaphor and the story a sort of moral allegory that takes its cue from the C.B. DeMille Hollywood costume epics in which flamboyant wickedness reaps its just desserts on the way to redemption. After indulging himself licentiously at Court, Robert finds himself governed by a Puritan ethic as his dedication to medicine and science is "restored." Later, after redeeming himself through good deeds, he is "restored" to his property and standing at Court,

CREDITS

Robert Merivel: Robert Downey Jr.
Charles II: Sam Neill
Pierce: David Thewlis
Celia: Polly Walker
Katherine: Meg Ryan
Finn: Hugh Grant

Origin: Great Britain
Released: 1995
Production: Cary Brokaw, Andy Paterson and Sarah Ryan Black for a Segue, Avenue and Oxford Film Company production; released by Miramax
Direction: Michael Hoffman
Screenplay: Rupert Walters; based on the novel by Rose Tremain
Cinematography: Oliver Stapleton
Editing: Garth Craven
Production design: Eugenio Zanetti
Costume design: James Acheson
Music: James Newton Howard
MPAA rating: R
Running Time: 113 minutes

AWARDS AND NOMINATIONS

Academy Awards 1995: Best Art Direction, Best Costumes

as his service and skill are rewarded. And of course London itself needs to be "restored" after the blight of the plague and fire.

By the time Robert redeems himself, he has become an agent, even an angel; those burning rays at his back as he single-handedly battles the Plague to a standstill and breaks down the walls confining its victims ennoble and sanctify him. Robert also becomes an agent and precursor of the Enlightenment.

Robert Downey, Jr. is quite believable as a rascal and libertine, but rather less convincing as a reformed saint. Nick James was critical of Sam Neill's Charles II, whom he considered "as arbitrary and unpredictable a force as Nigel Hawthorne's George III" in *The Madness of King George* (1994), but James thought Neill's performance was better suited to "a Richard Lester Musketeer film." The problem is that the film opts for melodrama over tragedy, farce over irony. The cast also includes Hugh Grant, who describes his character, Finn, as a "disgustingly ambitious and disgustingly self-obsessed" portrait artist hired by the King to paint Lady Celia, and Ian McKellen as Robert's servant at Bidnold, his Suffolk estate, a "formula factotum," according to Nick James.

Beyond the silliness and contrivances of the plot is the staggering sumptuousness of the production values of Argentinean production designer Eugenio Zanetti and the Academy Award-winning costume designer James Acheson, who worked with Bernardo Bertolucci on *The Last Emperor* (1987) and Stephen Frears on *Dangerous Liaisons* (1988). With reason, *Restoration* won Academy Awards for Art Direction and Costume Design. This costume epic was effectively presented through the cinematography of Oliver Stapleton. The major achievement of this motion picture is the "restoration" of the era in which the action is set.

Restoration wears its heart and its intentions on its lavishly embroidered sleeve. It's like the beating heart of the English peasant in the film's first scene. Due to an accident, his chest cavity has been damaged, leaving the beating organ open to view. Stunned, the medical students gather round to see the miracle. But it's only Downey's character who dares to reach out and touch it. That beating heart exposed for all to see is an apt metaphor for the overt sentiments and emotions of the picture. One can stand aside from it, like the other students, or one can openly embrace it for what it is.

—James M. Welsh and John C. Tibbetts

REVIEWS

The Baltimore Sun, February 2, 1996, E1, E5.
The New York Times, December 29, 1995, C-3.
Sight and Sound. Vol.6, No.4 (NS), April 1966, Pp. 51-52.
Variety. December 18-31, 1995, p.65, p.71.
The Washington Post, February 2, 1996, B1, B6.
Washington Post Weekend, February 2, 1996, p.39, p.41.
Washington Times Metropolitan Times, February 2, 1996, C17.

Rhythm Thief

New York hustler Simon (Jason Andrews) is eking out a living by selling illegal recordings of local bands. His occupation soon gets him into a lot of trouble when one of the bands come after him. His troubles are further stretched when unstable girlfriend Marty (Eddie Daniels) comes for a visit.

AWARDS AND NOMINATIONS

Sundance Film Festival 1995: Special Jury Prize

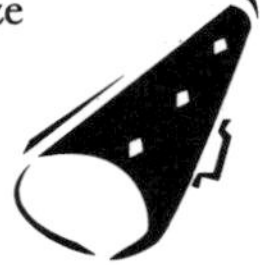

CREDITS

Simon: Jason Andrews
Fuller: Kevin Corrigan
Cyd: Kimberly Flynn
Shayme: Sean Hagerty
Marty: Eddie Daniels

Origin: USA
Released: 1995
Production: Jonathan Starch for a Film Crash production; released by Strand
Direction: Matthew Harrison
Screenplay: Christopher Grimm and Matthew Harrison
Cinematography: Howard Krupa
Editing: Matthew Harrison
Costume design: Nina Canter
Sound: Charles Hunt
Music: Danny Brenner, John L.Horn, Hugh O' Donovan and Kevin Okurland
Running Time: 88 minutes

Richard III

"Power conquers all."—Movie tagline

"*Richard III* is breathtaking! I cheered at the genius of it all!"—Joel Siegel, *Good Morning America*

"Two Thumbs Up! This is a visual feast of a movie."—*Siskel & Ebert*

"Mesmerizing...stunning...absolutely devastating with superb performances by everyone."—Jeffrey Lyons, *Sneak Previews*

"Brilliant! *Richard III* is among this year's small handful of motion picture treasures."—Gene Shalit, *Today Show*

Box Office Gross: $2,081,622

Taking on a major Shakespearian role presents a daunting challenge to any actor. Yet one would never know this watching the stunning performance of Ian McKellan in the eponymous role of *Richard III.* As all artists must do, he stamps his authority in the part, and makes it his own.

In this new version of *Richard III*, McKellan and his co-screenwriter Richard Loncraine, who also directs, set the play in 1930's England. As seductive as that concept is, and it is a winning one, it is the accessibility of the pared down speeches and the wicked Machiavellian plotting by Richard that render the motion picture a captivating experience.

Historically speaking, of course, Richard preceded the Italian Machiavelli, but the Englishman could surely have taught the latter much if they had ever met. In a stunning opening, the present King of England is all but trapped in his bunker. The Yorks are besieging his kingdom and advancing on his headquarters. The rattling of a teleprinter serves as a clever first image establishing the period. Its printout bears ominous news of the enemy's progress. Suddenly, a tank smashes through a wall as the King eats his dinner. Richard is in the vanguard of the attack, and this is the only occasion one sees him in action. With a grimace, he shoots the King in the head.

It is Richard's brother Edward (John Wood), however, an already elderly man, who succeeds the throne. A sumptuous banquet, with a band and guests adorned in the elegant clothing of the period, forms the setting for the play's famous opening speech. A seemingly delighted Richard toasts the turning of the "winter of discontent" into "glorious summer" with the ascension of his older brother. Yet the real feeling within him is unveiled as he continues his speech in the men's art deco bathroom, while urinating and smoking his habitual cigarette. What is clear is that Richard's ambition is naked to his audience, whilst hidden to his contemporaries, and he will not rest until he becomes the "sun of York."

Despite the hunchback and withered left arm, Richard is able to command much charm as a supplement to his outrageous audacity. In the morgue of a mental hospital, he approaches the grieving Lady Anne (Kristin Scott Thomas), the former King's widow, and connives to turn her hatred for him into lustful favor. He even bluffs to the point of giving her a knife to kill him if she so desires. She cannot, and her collapse begins.

With Richard busy behind the scenes, his brother Clarence (Nigel Hawthorne) is sent to the Tower of London. Richard declares that he will help Clarence, but a soliloquy to the camera assures us that Richard's vaulting ambition to attain the throne dictates that all obstacles, whether kin or not, must be removed.

CREDITS

Richard III: Ian McKellen
Queen Elizabeth: Annette Bening
Buckingham: Jim Broadbent
Earl Rivers: Robert Downey, Jr.
Clarence: Nigel Hawthorne
Lady Anne: Kristin Scott Thomas

Origin: Great Britain
Released: 1995
Production: Lisa Katselas Pare and Stephen Bayly for a First Look Pictures, British Screen and United Artists Pictures production; released by MGM/UA
Direction: Richard Loncraine
Screenplay: Ian McKellen and Richard Loncraine; based on the stage production by Robert Eyre of the William Shakespeare play *Richard III*
Cinematography: Peter Biziou
Editing: Paul Green
Production design: Tony Burrough
Costume design: Shuna Harwood
Casting: Irene Lamb
Music: Trevor Jones
MPAA rating: R
Running Time: 105 minutes

Clarence's meditation in prison, through gloomy corridors and into the exercise yard, is one example of the splendid sequences in the film: the poetry of Shakespeare is married to the grimness of the history being told, and the ugly concrete of a prison. And the magnificent interiors and exteriors of Brighton's astonishing Royal Pavilion cannot mask the tensions within the royal court, most notably between Queen Elizabeth (Annette Bening) and Richard.

King Edward is ailing; Richard's power increases. Soon, Richard has recruited Buckingham (Jim Broadbent) to his cause, and together they bring off the grisly yet clever murder of Elizabeth's playboy brother Earl Rivers (Robert Downey Jr.) It is not long before King Edward dies naturally in his bed, and now Richard must engineer matters to rid himself of the King and Queen's two sons, one of whom is set to become the monarch. The boys are sent to the Tower, and despite Elizabeth's entreaties, are never seen again.

Richard stands on the threshold of power, and the fascistic possibilities of Loncraine and McKellan's conceit are exploited. The uniforms turn black in crypto-Nazi manner. Richard and Buckingham have the Prime Minister murdered, and ironically, Richard is begged to become Lord Protector. In a magnificently chilling scene, the smiling villain is acclaimed at a militaristic rally, and at last he is on the throne.

But now his troubles begin, as Richmond of Lancaster (Dominic West), who has been betrothed to Elizabeth's daughter, gathers his military forces in France. Richard takes as his outpost a steam train, after suffering the curses of his mother, the Duchess of York (Maggie Smith), and he launches a verbal assault at Queen Elizabeth to give him her daughter in marriage. She resists, and escapes to Richmond's camp.

Battle is joined, with airplanes whistling and bombing, jeeps and tanks, rocket launches and hand grenades everywhere. Richard's desperate plea for a horse to take him away comes into play when his jeep becomes stuck in the mud, but the game is over. Richmond, the day's victor, stalks his adversary, and the final shot jarringly presents a smirking Richard willingly falling to his death into billowing flames.

Critical reaction to this new version of *Richard III* has been, in general, very positive. Kenneth Turan in the *Los Angeles Times* calls the film a "triumph of modernization and popularization," and he makes a perceptive point when he writes: "It's part of McKellan's gift to make it seem that

AWARDS AND NOMINATIONS

Academy Awards Nominations 1995: Best Art Direction, Best Costumes
Golden Globe Awards Nominations 1996: Best Actor-Drama (McKellen)

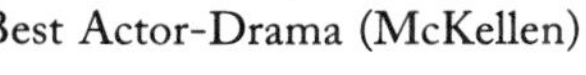

Richard is taking the audience into his confidence via his monologues because his contemporaries are too dense to be appreciative and he has to share his consummate villainy with someone." Terrence Rafferty in *The New Yorker* has a dissenting view. Calling McKellan "charmless," Rafferty calls his Richard "dull, efficient, affectless," and feels that the motion picture is "mis-shapen." But Stephen Holden in *The New York Times* accurately pins down the appeal of the film when he says that it is "a sensationally flashy blend of pageantry and gore, acted to the hilt....Who could resist?"

"I want as many people as possible to be put in touch with Shakespeare, whose characters and stories can be shown to be as relevant to our lives today as they were to an audience who first saw them 400 years ago. I wanted to make a Shakespeare film that could be accessible to as wide as audience as possible..."—Ian McKellen

Ian McKellan has made the point that Shakespeare's audience saw his plays acted in contemporary dress, and he feels, therefore, that twentieth century costuming is the most appropriate choice for us. Of course, in this film, the dress is not contemporary to the nineteen nineties, but neither is it "classical." The conceit of the motion picture requires thirties clothing, and costume designer Shuna Harwood's work is excellent.

McKellan and Loncraine's *Richard III*, in sum, is a small triumph. They ally wonderful visuals of long sinewy corridors, dark alleyways, gorgeous state rooms, functional and vast bureaucratic arenas with rich costuming, a snappy pace, jazz riffs, and an accomplished cast. One example of an inspired use of the modern period is Richard's viewing of his Coronation (very reminiscent of Elizabeth II's in 1953) on film, his cigarette smoke billowing into the light of the projector, and his court surrounding him, including Lady Anne injecting herself with another syringe.

Although a fine cast has been assembled, several actors are given too little to do. Maggie Smith is hardly more than a footnote in a role that in Shakespeare's play is full of its own evil. Robert Downey Jr. is allowed precious few moments to shine. In contrast, the murdered Clarence, as played by Nigel Hawthorne, makes his mark with his stoicism, and Jim Broadbent, who more often plays comic roles, is distinctive as a behind the scenes plotter whom Richard needs in the latter's haul to the throne. Annette Bening does creditable work as the noble Elizabeth, and Kristin Scott Thomas cuts a pathetic figure as the drug-addicted Lady Anne.

So accomplished, and so confident, is McKellan's Richard that one quibble might be that his grasp of power is almost easy. One sees little of his struggle with inner demons. Shakespeare does provide several moments of worried introspection in his play, but in the film, the only crisis of Richard's self-doubt surfaces during the small hours of the morning before battle with Richmond.

Throughout the swift one hundred and five minutes of the film, it is McKellan's Richard who enthralls us. What a villain he is! Yet despite his cruelty, one almost wishes for his success, so cunning and ruthless is his progression. McKellan is masterful in the role, soliloquizing to the audience in a way that underlines his superior intelligence. He is seductive to women when he needs them; he smiles when he triumphs; he is calculating when he needs to fight.

McKellan adopts the customary handicaps attributed to the historical Richard, but does not overplay them; rather, it is his lined face that perhaps causes dogs to bark after him, as he notes early on.

Loncraine's work as director ensures a fluid tale of intrigue and murder. In tandem with Harwood's costuming, and Tony Burrough's evocative production design, Loncraine and McKellan present an all too plausible military state within England. Sweet jazz plays when Richard views gruesome photographs of the princes he has murdered, and the contrast is memorable.

Shakespeare has always been accessible, but people often lack the interest in his history plays that they show for his tragedies and comedies. McKellan and Loncraine do justice to this great writer's cold-blooded, and yet often amusing, delineation of the grasping for power in the House of York, and they make this *Richard III* immensely seductive.

—Paul B. Cohen

The Ride to Wounded Knee

Focusing on the centennial commemoration of the 1890 Wounded Knee massacre of three hundred unarmed Lakota Sioux by the U.S. Army, this documentary combines interviews, photographs, newspaper articles, private journals, and silent-film clips with scenes of a 1990 memorial ride, in which hundreds of Sioux retraced their people's doomed retreat from the Cavalry.

CREDITS

Mark White Bull: Mark White Bull
Jim Swan: Jim Swan
Joe Walker: Joe Walker
Nancy Clapsadle: Nancy Clapsadle
Rick Afraid of Hawk: Rick Afraid of Hawk
Isaac Dog Eagle: Isaac Dog Eagle

Origin: USA
Released: 1992
Production: Carol Wolman for Ghost Dance; released by Panorama Entertainment
Direction: Robert Clapsadle
Screenplay: Robert Clapsadle
Cinematography: Frances Reid
Editing: Greg Bezat
Running Time: 85 minutes

Rob Roy

"He loved one woman. He feared no man. An ordinary man. An extraordinary legend."—Movie tagline

"It's *Robin Hood* meets *The Last of the Mohicans* meets *Death Wish*."—Owen Gleiberman, *Entertainment Weekly*

"A great time at the movies."—Joel Siegel, *Good Morning America*

"One of the best films of the year."—Gene Siskel, *Siskel & Ebert*

Box Office Gross: $31,596,468

Michael Caton-Jones is a Scottish director who has found fame in Hollywood. After first making his mark with the British film *Scandal*, his subsequent motion pictures, including *Doc Hollywood* and *This Boy's Life*, have found him on location in the United States. In *Rob Roy*, Caton-Jones must surely have felt at home on the startling landscape of Scotland's Highlands. Working from a script by fellow countryman Alan Sharp, Caton-Jones' vision of a rugged, heroic Robert Roy MacGregor, based loosely on the historic Rob Roy, is an epic one. Yet in actuality the story's heart is a bloody, if vivid, vendetta between two men, and despite the director's efforts, the execution of the tale falls short of its aspirations to reach epic scope.

On the blustery slopes of verdant hills, a small party of highlanders, led by the handsome and charismatic Rob Roy (Liam Neeson) is tracking the theft of cattle by a renegade band. Caught off guard in the early morning by Rob's more disciplined troupe, the leader of the brigands is given the chance to save his skin after lunging at Rob, but he foolishly lunges once more and is dispatched by the strong and agile MacGregor with a sharp sword.

With this little battle won, and the cattle re-taken, Rob returns with his men to the tiny village he protects, and then decamps to his own turf. Home is the picture of bucolic happiness: a long stone cottage with a roof of turf and thatch stands idly alongside a glistening loch. Rob plunges into the water, and emerges, followed by his happy dog, into the cottage. Two children slumber inside, and Rob finds his lady fair, Mary (Jessica Lange) dozing. He wakes her up to make tender love to her.

With pacing as slow as a long winter's night in the Highlands, a number of subsequent scenes present Rob and Mary as a middle-aged, highly principled, and very much in love couple. On one summery afternoon, Rob waxes lyrical on the subject of honor to his children, and then sends them off to play elsewhere while he and Mary make sport.

Concomitant with this picture of seventeenth century family values is our introduction to the aristocratic Montrose (John Hurt) at the castle of Duke of Argyll (Andrew Keir). In tow with Montrose is the dandy, foppish Archibald Cunningham (Tim Roth), a newly arrived courtier from London. The latter shows unsuspected prowess at fencing and general swordsmanship in a successful contest with Argyll's best fighter, and Montrose cheerily pockets the winnings of a bet placed with Argyll as to the fencing match's outcome.

Englishman Cunningham is swiftly revealed to be a cad—to say the least. He dallies with Betty (Vicky Masson) a maid in the service of Montrose, and entertains, with some scorn at first, the machinations of Killearn (Brian Cox), another employee of Montrose eager to curry favor. As Cunningham is short of cash, he finds himself listening to Killearn's plot to remedy that situation.

"Men have honour." "Do women have honour, Daddy?" "Women are the heart of honour and we cherish and protect it in them. You must never mistreat a woman or malign a man, nor stand by and see another do so."—Rob Roy to his son

Killearn's plot concerns Rob Roy's plan to secure capital to see his village folk through the long winter ahead. In an audience with Montrose, Rob successfully gains a loan of a thousand pounds (certainly a very large sum in those days) from the English peer to purchase some cattle. With the aid of his brother Alasdair (Brian McCardie), and devoted companion Alan McDonald (Eric Stoltz), Rob intends to drive the beasts across country and sell them at a profit in a city market. Although the money loaned was not supposed to be in coinage, it is handed to McDonald after he is forced to wait all day by none other than Killearn. The ambush has begun. While Rob, Mary and his villagers enjoy themselves at an unspecified Scottish get-together replete with Gaelic song and dance, a wary McDonald rides home through the eerie forests until being trapped and killed by the ruthless Cunningham.

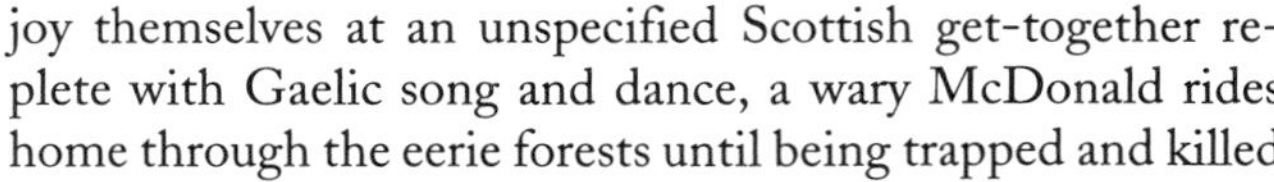

Montrose, who knows nothing of Cunningham and Killearn's plot, expects his loan to be repaid in full; it is a sum Rob cannot meet. Montrose is furious after the Duke of Argyll's accusation that he, Montrose, has been calling Argyll a Jacobite. At a meeting of Montrose and Rob concerning the lost money, with Killearn and Cunningham in attendance, Montrose asks Rob to name Argyll a Jacobite. Rob, honor-bound as he proclaims himself to be, refuses—although he would escape his debt by so doing—and resists Cunningham's attempts to detain him. Suddenly, he is a wanted man.

Rob takes to the hills, while Mary and the children remain in the cottage. One silent morning, Cunningham and a brigade of English soldiers appear out of the mists on the loch, having slipped through the thin net of Rob's watchmen. With pre-meditated relish, Cunningham rapes Mary, and then has the cottage set on fire and the cattle slaughtered. As the Englishmen sail away, Alasdair MacGregor charges on the scene—too late. Discovering the fact of Mary's rape, Mary implores him to promise not to tell Rob of her violation. He reluctantly agrees.

The thought among Rob's men is that McDonald has run off to America with the money, but Rob does not believe that. Unwitting of Mary's rape, but ready to act against Montrose, he orders a campaign of disruption against Montrose's property and rent collections. Cunningham, still unsuspected of McDonald's murder despite his sudden acquisition of money and a new wardrobe, spurns the now pregnant Betty. Desperate, the maid runs to Mary and reveals details of a possible plot between her former lover and Killearn concerning a thousand pound sum. Now matters turn very dark. Betty hangs herself after being offered food and shelter by the sympathetic Mary; Mary is less sympathetic to Killearn, and wounds him in the neck. Alasdair, in the first of a number of rash acts, disposes of Killearn by drowning him, and Rob orders Killearn's body sunk in a lake.

With her husband still a fugitive, Mary makes a plea to Argyll, a man of fairness, and reveals to him Rob's courage

CREDITS

Robert Roy MacGregor: Liam Neeson
Mary MacGregor: Jessica Lange
Marquis of Montrose: John Hurt
Cunningham: Tim Roth
Alan McDonald: Eric Stoltz
Killearn: Brian Cox
Argyll: Andrew Keir
Alasdair: Brian McCardie
Sibbald: David Hayman
Guthrie: Gilbert Martin
Betty: Vicki Masson

Origin: USA
Released: 1995
Production: Peter Broughan and Richard Jackson for Talisman Productions; released by United Artists Pictures
Direction: Michael Caton-Jones
Screenplay: Alan Sharp
Cinematography: Karl Walter Lindenlaub
Editing: Peter Honess
Art direction: Assheton Gorton
Music: Carter Burwell
MPAA rating: R
Running Time: 139 minutes

AWARDS AND NOMINATIONS

British Academy Awards 1995: Best Supporting Actor (Roth)
Academy Awards Nominations 1995: Best Supporting Actor (Roth)
Golden Globe Awards Nominations 1996: Best Supporting Actor (Roth)

in refusing to name Argyll a Jacobite. Meanwhile, Cunningham, enlarged by his grasp of power, sets off in pursuit of Rob, and after Alasdair foolishly takes a shot at Cunningham's men, Rob is captured after seeing his brother killed. Bound and gagged and brought to the now icy Montrose, Rob is ordered to be hung from the bridge. But in a surge of ingenuity and strength, Rob manages to escape after plunging into a roaring river, and at one point, he hides from the pursuing soldiers in the reeking carcass of a dead beast.

Reunited with Mary, Rob is finally told of her rape, but contrary to her expectation, he receives the news calmly. At an audience with Argyll, Rob begs the nobleman's help in arranging a duel with Cunningham. It is arranged.

As one would expect, the duel is bloody and tense, but after Rob sustains several bloody gashes, the hero snatches victory when all seems lost, and a dead Cunningham clatters to the stone floor in Argyll's castle. Rob and Mary reunite to swelling music and luscious scenery.

The look of the picture is in all respects very pleasing. Shot entirely on location in the Scottish Highlands by cinematographer Karl Walter Lindenlaub (a friend of director Caton-Jones from film school days), and presumably in summer, since well-nigh all the daytime shots are resplendent in sunshine, the wide screen cinema experience is one reason to see *Rob Roy* at the movies. Montrose's home base is located at the imposing Castle Drummond; its marvelous, manicured landscaped gardens are a visual pleasure in themselves. And Carter Buswell's swelling music is an additionally evocative element.

Costume Designer Sandy Powell dresses Rob Roy and his merry band in plain white shirts, sashes, kilts and long knee socks; the color of their sashes gives each man individuality. Not surprisingly, the aristocracy display more colorful outfits, especially the villainous Cunningham after he has taken the loot from McDonald. All the aristocrats wear the required long, dropping wigs and cake their faces in wan makeup.

Another strength of the film is its action sequences. Rob Roy's escape from Cunningham into the raging river, Cunningham's rampage at Rob and Mary's cottage, and the climactic duel scene between the antagonists are vivid. For the film's finale, swordsmaster William Hobb must take much credit, as the duel is strenuous, gripping, and ultimately cathartic.

Critical reception for *Rob Roy* has been mixed. Chicago TV pundits Siskel and Ebert over-enthusiastically endorsed the film, but the *Los Angeles Times* was less generous in its praise, identifying the "bucolic interludes" of Mary and Rob as "blandly unconvincing." Yet the *Times*, along with other papers, praised Lange's performance. *Variety* had its reservations about the film, but followed the course of most critical view in praising Tim Roth.

Roth's Cunningham is certainly a man to be detested, and the English actor chomps on his meaty role. He is at his best when hovering between his character's courtly dandiness, and the dark violence exploding within him. John Hurt's Montrose is cunning and pragmatic, with Hurt taking the role in his stride. Eric Stoltz's McDonald is killed off early on, but he shows himself to be a sturdy friend to Rob. As for Liam Neeson, he is unusually reminiscent of Oscar Schindler in the opening sequences of *Rob Roy*. As provider and protector, it is hard not to think of Neeson playing the German businessman. Never very strong with accents other than his own, Neeson generally sounds more Irish than Scottish. Although Neeson's delivery is at times a touch ponderous, he looks dashing and muscular throughout, and appears convincingly as a charismatic and courageous leader.

It is Jessica Lange who takes the acting honors. In a motion picture not endowed with deep characterization, her Mary is the most interesting person; she is the one who has real depth to her. Whereas Neeson's Rob Roy is somewhat earnest and unwavering, Lange's Mary is a woman of resources. Deeply attached to her husband, she is yet independent of spirit. Lange is a fine actress and she is subtle one moment, fiery at another. And her accent is convincing and thorough.

In total, *Rob Roy* demands to be seen on the big screen. Certainly it is too long. Both screenwriter Alan Sharp—who has crafted a colloquial and appealing script—and Michael Caton-Jones share the blame here. By blowing up the scale of Rob Roy MacGregor's conflict with Cunningham, they weaken the tension inherent in the conflict between the two men. But effective action sequences and gorgeous scenery offer enough visual stimulus to tempt the viewer to see this at the cinema.

—Paul B. Cohen

REVIEWS

Entertainment Weekly. April 14, 1995, p.42.

Roommates

"Some people talk. Some people listen. When you're 107 and going strong, you do whatever you want."—Movie tagline

"Strong story, strong performances, strong film."—Gary Franklin, *KCOP-TV*

"Something truly special. Rarely will you be this touched by a movie."—Jeffrey Lyons, *Sneak Previews*

Box Office Gross: $12,096,881

CREDITS

Rocky Holeczek: Peter Falk
Michael Holeczek: D. B. Sweeney
Beth: Julianne Moore
Bolek Krupa: Jan Rubes
Professor Martin: Frankie Faison
Michael (five years old): Noah Fleiss
Barbara: Joyce Reehling
Stash: Ernie Sabella
Michael (fifteen years old): David Tom
Burt Shook: John Cunningham
Judith: Ellen Burstyn

Origin: USA
Released: 1995
Production: Ted Field, Scott Kroopf, and Robert W. Cort for Hollywood Pictures, Interscope Communications, and Polygram Filmed Entertainment, in association with Nomura Babcock & Brown; released by Buena Vista Pictures
Direction: Peter Yates
Screenplay: Max Apple and Stephen Metcalfe; based on a story by Apple
Cinematography: Mike Southon
Editing: John Tintori
Production design: Dan Bishop
Art direction: Jefferson Sage
Set decoration: Dianna Freas
Casting: Linda Lowy
Sound: Douglas Axtell
Special makeup effects: Greg Cannom
Costume design: Linda Donahue
Music: Elmer Bernstein
MPAA rating: PG
Running Time: 113 minutes

Whistling its way past life's darkest moments, *Roommates* is a low-key, low-energy, easily digestible and passably entertaining homily on the most basic of old-fashioned family values: taking care of one's own. It's about a crusty Polish immigrant, baker Rocky Holeczek (Peter Falk), who raises his grandson Michael (D.B. Sweeney) after Michael's parents die before he reaches age five.

The film opens and closes with tragedy and graveside scenes, with Rocky whistling "Roll Out the Barrel" at funerals. But most of what happens in between is light, sweet and folksy. It's a sandwich of hard sourdough around a marshmallow middle, which is also an apt description for Rocky.

Playing Hollywood's umpteenth grumpy old man with a heart of gold, Falk is the centerpiece of the movie. Everything depends on whether audiences will find him believable, funny and poignant, because Sweeney doesn't plumb any great depths in his character and the plot is unremarkable.

Falk is an actor who pours himself into his roles. His Rocky is a rock-solid monument to the simple virtues of hard work and loyalty. Falk plays the grizzled codger much as it's been played dozens of times before, by Jack Lemmon and Walter Matthau and many others, but he adds an extra edge of brusque authenticity. Rocky is brutally honest and sometimes unkind, but his words are overshadowed by his actions, which flow from his unshakeable and dutiful love for his family. What saves him from being cloying is that he's not just prickly, but imperfect. Rocky's character flaws don't get healed or resolved over the course of the film; Michael and the rest of the family just have to put up with him and love him for what he is.

The characters ring true-to-life, almost too much so; they are not remarkable enough to sustain a film. When Rocky and Michael finally confess their mutual pride and admiration on Rocky's deathbed, the scene works because many old-fashioned types never make such professions until the end. They don't need to if they've proven their love in deed. Yet it comes off too pat.

The script has Rocky and Michael rescuing each other several times. When Rocky takes an ill-advised last stand against his Pittsburgh apartment being condemned, Michael

AWARDS AND NOMINATIONS

Academy Awards Nominations 1995: Best Makeup

swoops in from medical school and convinces Rocky to move in with him in Columbus, Ohio. When Michael accepts a residency back in Pittsburgh which will take him away from his lover Beth (Julianne Moore), Rocky tells Michael he'll lose her if they try a long-distance relationship, so Michael marries her. When Rocky is diagnosed with a tumor, Michael convinces him to overcome his fear of cancer and get treatment. And when Michael has to cope with yet another horrible tragedy, Rocky keeps him focused on his family. But neither can deflect life's cruel blows.

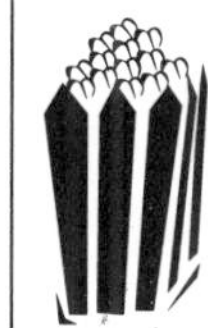

"Am I coming to live with you?" "If you want; that's your decision." "For how long?" "For as long as you need me."—Five-year-old orphaned Michael to his 75-year-old grandfather, Rocky

These are the linchpins of a story based on scriptwriter Max Apple's relationship with his own centenarian grandfather. Still, it's hard to believe *Roommates*' time line. The script has Michael's father killed in Vietnam in 1963, before any but a handful of American troops were there. And Rocky is supposed to age from his mid-70s to about 105 over the course of the film. While Falk and the makeup artists give it a game try, it's impossible to believe the character is as old as the script makes him. Rather, it appears Rocky ages from about 60 to 80.

Setting the film in Columbus and Pittsburgh gives it a solid blue-collar feel. The opening sequences, with Michael narrating his family history, are enchanting. But *Roommates* falls into a painfully slow rhythm. At least 15 minutes could have easily been cut from its 108-minute length. The story has a few dramatic moments and a lot of hokum. The scene of Rocky fighting his eviction is cornball stuff. And once Rocky moves to Columbus with Michael, the generational conflicts that are supposed to be occurring in the 1980s seem like trite material from the 1960s: Michael sleeps on a water bed in a house with five Chinese students. Rocky has never seen a water bed before. He calls the students Communists, then teaches them gin rummy, his favorite game. He discovers a *Playboy* magazine and tosses it out, scolding Michael. And he is aghast that Michael and Beth have premarital sex. When she comes for dinner, Rocky cooks meat, and of course Beth announces she's a vegetarian.

Too much in the film is predictable. When Beth first appears at a patient's bedside as an emotive social worker, you know she'll be the love interest. You know she'll lecture Michael about his lack of sensivity, and that the mandatory initial spat will lead to romance. You know that Beth's stiff upper-crust mom Judith (Ellen Burstyn, wasted in a thinly scripted part) will be scandalized by Rocky.

Moore gives the film some zing even though the script holds few surprises for her character. She has to play sweet and light, but when the script gives her rare opportunities to be seductive, she excels. But she looks too glamorous for Sweeney, who's a rumpled, comfortable sort. Sweeney, in his first major role, is appealing because of this boy-next-door quality, but his blank expressions don't help carry the load. The chemistry between Moore and Sweeney, and for that matter between Falk and Sweeney, rarely sizzles.

Falk makes the best of some rather lame routines. Rocky shows up at a college history class, and when the teacher mentions Samuel Gompers and a 1907 strike, Rocky shouts out his first-hand observations of the man and the event. Then he asks the teacher to get him a job, and he does — as a baker at a natural food store, where Rocky complains about the lack of sugar and white flour. And when Rocky gets older, he has to sit on a park bench and complain to an old buddy about how he wants to work but can't get a job. It's not very original or compelling material.

Director Peter Yates (*Breaking Away*) treats much of this sitcom material in a very understated sitcom style. Yates tends to linger on Falk's comic routines, as if making a film homage. In fact, Yates lingers too long on just about every scene. So pedestrian is much of the film that one almost wishes for a laugh track to liven things up.

The light tone of the film isn't great preparation for the last half-hour, when things turn grim and preachy. Rocky's confrontation with Judith seems contrived. The tension that should be in these final scenes is undermined by the total absence of tension in all that has come before.

Roommates staunchly holds onto its dignity and its story, and while it's commendable that the film is so respectful of its characters and audiences, it's not enough to make it successful entertainment. The acting and screenwriting are too thin and light to make this a serious character study, and the plot is too trifling to make it anything more than a character study. It's not a film to offend anyone, and some will find it precious, but it's not likely to leave most audiences with any lasting impact.

Too obviously, Yates is trying to make us stand up and cheer for good, old-fashioned decency. But to stand up and cheer, you have to be roused. Unfortunately, *Roommates* misses every opportunity to be rousing.

—*Michael Betzold*

REVIEWS

Daily Variety. March 1, 1995, p. 4.
Hollywood Reporter. March 1, 1995, p. 10.
Los Angeles Times. March 3, 1995, p. F6.
The New York Times. March 3, 1995, p. B3.

The Run of the Country

"Marvelous! Well-crafted, entertaining and full of life!"—Marjorie Sweeney, *The Irish Echo*

"A film of great polish and charm. One of the year's most pleasant surprises."—David Kehr, *New York Daily News*

"Fresh and heartfelt. I recommend this film."—Gene Siskel, *Siskel & Ebert*

Danny (Matt Keeslar) is devastated by the death of his mother and is frustrated by his stern and cold father (Albert Finney). He runs away to live with his rebellious young friend Prunty (Anthony Brophy) and falls in love with beautiful Annagh (Victoria Smurfit). Their relationship turns complicated when Annagh becomes pregnant.

Matt Keeslar and Victoria Smurfit star in *The Run of the Country*. © 1995 Castle Rock Entertainment. All rights reserved. Photo by Jonathan Hession.

CREDITS

Father: Albert Finney
Danny: Matt Keeslar
Annagh: Victoria Smurfit
Prunty: Anthony Brophy

Origin: Great Britain and Ireland
Released: 1995
Production: Peter Yates and Ruth Boswell for One Two Nine production and Castle Rock Entertainment presentation; released by Columbia Pictures
Direction: Peter Yates
Screenplay: Shane Connaughton; based on the novel *The Run of the Country* by Shane Connaughton
Cinematography: Michael Southon
Editing: Paul Hodgson
Assistant director: Lisa Mulcahy
Art direction: David Wilson
Set decoration: Mark Geraghty
Sound: Ken Weston
Music: Cynthia Millar
MPAA rating: R
Running Time: 109 minutes

Sabrina

"You are cordially invited to the most surprising merger of the year."—Movie tagline

"Nobody does romance better than the Academy Award-winning Mr. Pollack."—Gene Shalit, *NBC-TV*

"Two very enthusiastic thumbs up!...for the wonderful love story *Sabrina*."—*Siskel & Ebert*

Box Office Gross: $28,841,220

Before saying anything about the 1995 remake of *Sabrina*, it should be noted that it would be impossible to surpass the 1954 original, simply because it starred Audrey Hepburn in one of her best roles. There is more than just the "Hepburn factor" going against this remake: the original film was written and directed by the legendary Billy Wilder, a filmmaker of remarkable sophistication and style. So, in light of the fact that director Sydney Pollack has undertaken the remake of a film that is indelibly etched in the collective memory of many filmgoers, it is nice to report that the film does not fall completely flat. That doesn't sound like much of a recommendation, but given the mystique of the original film, it is a compliment.

There was something about the combination of Audrey Hepburn, William Holden, Humphrey Bogart, and that fizzy Billy Wilder style that made the original film wonderful. Something about the elements of that film made it feel as if it were a classic, even though it isn't generally considered to be one. (Many critics don't feel it is even a particularly good film, citing Humphrey Bogart's dour performance and some two-dimensional characterizations as debits.) So what was it that the first *Sabrina* had that the second one doesn't? One word: magic. Flawed though it may be, the first film was a deft romantic comedy that made its audience sigh and swoon. The 1995 *Sabrina*, though blessed with a fine cast, director, and script, just doesn't have the same effect.

The story (which began as a 1953 Broadway play by Samuel Taylor) is meant to be a light variation on the Cinderella story, set in modern high society. The film takes place in the present day, and, to set the mood, a voice-over tells the audience that "once upon a time, on the north shore of Long Island," there lived a girl named Sabrina Fairchild (Julia Ormond). Sabrina is the daughter of a chauffeur, simply known as Fairchild (John Wood), who works for the ultra-wealthy Larrabee family. The family consists of two brothers, Linus (Harrison Ford) and David (Greg Kinnear), and their mother, Maude (Nancy Marchand). Living on their immense estate in a carriage house all of her life, Sabrina has been in love with handsome, rakish David ever since she can remember.

But David doesn't even know she exists. The story begins as Sabrina is enjoying her last night in the U.S. before going to Paris to study photography. Shy, bespectacled, and a bit gawky, she watches a fabulous party from her favorite spot in a tree overlooking the Larrabee's home. As she has for many years, Sabrina ruefully watches David seduce a beautiful society girl, certain that he will never notice her.

After a couple of years in Paris, she returns to the States a gorgeous and sophisticated woman. Callow David finally notices her and falls head over heels in love. The hitch is that he is now engaged to a wealthy socialite named Elizabeth Tyson (Lauren Holly) whose parents (Richard Crenna and Angie Dickinson) own a company whose interests are essential and valuable to the Larrabee family business. David's workaholic brother Linus (Harrison Ford) has seen to it that David and Elizabeth's union has progressed without incident. Seeing Sabrina's return as dangerous to the merger of the two families, Linus sets out to woo Sabrina to steer her away from David. Eventually he discovers that he has feelings for Sabrina, and she must choose between the two brothers.

In the original film Humphrey Bogart played the older brother Linus, and William Holden played David. Having taken over for Cary Grant at the last minute, Bogart seemed an unlikely match for Hepburn, and that is precisely why it worked. In order for the story to be any fun, it seems important that there be no question that David is more attractive than Linus, since the joy of the story is Sabrina's recognition that true love generally takes people by surprise. William Holden was tall and handsome while Bogart was short and plain. Holden was loose and charming, Bogart stiff and uncomfortable. Those differences were intrinsic to the actors, not just to the roles of David and Linus. In this version, Harrison Ford wears glasses, bow ties, a stuffy grey suit and a Homburg hat, but it is difficult for him to hide his sex appeal. In contrast to the scruffy charm of Greg Kinnear, it seems difficult to believe that Sabrina would have trouble realizing which of the two is more attractive.

Greg Kinnear makes his acting debut in the role of playboy David, a part he was offered after Tom Cruise became unavailable.

Only after having lived a little does Sabrina begin to see David for the one-dimensional playboy that he is. But given the choice between sexy Indiana Jones (Ford) or the cute talk-show host (Kinnear), it seems obvious who she will choose. And it is precisely the lack of suspense that makes this version of the story a bit ho-hum. The audience is waiting from the very beginning for Ford to throw off his glasses and take Sabrina into his arms. The story seems to be just marking time until this happens.

Ford, trying to downplay his heroic image, is serious and introspective. But his seriousness seems to intrude on the fun rather than enhance it. His scenes with Julia Ormond are rather dull, especially the final scenes in which he agonizes over whether to join her in Paris. In contrast to Bogart, who looked ridiculous as he tried to loosen up for the much younger Sabrina, Ford looks more comfortable when not wearing his bow tie and dark suit. Of course, Ford's dyspeptic performance does give rise to some fun moments, such as when he directs his secretary (the wonderful Dana Ivey) to get tickets for a Broadway musical and she tries to make him understand that "occasionally the characters break into song for no apparent reason." Ford provides the requisite stuffiness, but is clearly acting. Of course, Harrison Ford in a weaker performance is still preferable to most other actors.

Greg Kinnear received a huge career boost when Tom Cruise became unavailable to play the role of David. Sydney Pollack made quite a gamble on Kinnear, and Kinnear holds his own quite well with his more seasoned co-stars. Seducing society girls in the greenhouse or wearing tennis clothing under a cashmere overcoat, Kinnear seems every bit the Long Island playboy. "Going to work? On Sunday?," he asks Linus. "It's Wednesday," Linus replies, and Kinnear shrugs and goes inside the house, oblivious to the fact that most people have to work for a living. Kinnear is funny and winsome in the scenes where he is tipsy from pain medication after having sat on champagne glasses. It is a big screen debut, indeed.

Julia Ormond is one of the loveliest actresses on screen today. It is hard to imagine the pressure of filling Audrey Hepburn's shoes, and Ormond does so with grace and dignity. She does not, however, possess the same kind of extraordinary charisma that this story seems to require. Hepburn was truly magical, filling the screen with heartache so romantic that it made you cry just to watch her sit in her rocking chair, daydreaming. Ormond plays the scenes with a sense of reality, providing a fine performance, but missing the storybook lilt that made Hepburn's original performance so indelible. She is appropriately dowdy in the early scenes, contrasting beautifully with her post-Paris scenes. She brings a lovely emotional arc to the role, clearly showing Sabrina's disappointment that her storybook life may never happen. She moves from naivete to confidence to maturity with ease and polish, but is missing that difficult-to-define quality that turns a solid performance into an extraordinary one.

One of the surprises of this version of *Sabrina* is Nancy Marchand's wonderful performance as Maude, the mother of Linus and David. In the 1954 version, Linus and David had both parents, and their blustery father was the more prominent of the two. But here, Maude is a widow who runs the family and the family business with steely strength and dry humor. "Mother, go outside and blow out your candles," Linus tells her at her birthday party. "Can't we send somebody?," she cries. Marchand delivers the best performance in the film. In this scene, Marchand is wearing an absolutely hilarious evening dress with a gargantuan bow tied across

CREDITS

Linus Larrabee: Harrison Ford
Sabrina Fairchild: Julia Ormond
David Larrabee: Greg Kinnear
Fairchild: John Wood
Maude Larrabee: Nancy Marchand
Patrick Tyson: Richard Crenna
Ingrid Tyson: Angie Dickinson
Elizabeth Tyson: Lauren Holly

Origin: USA
Released: 1995
Production: Scott Rudin and Sydney Pollack for a Constellation Films and Mirage/Scott Rudin/Sandollar production
Direction: Sydney Pollack
Screenplay: Barbara Benedek and David Rayfiel; based on the film *Sabrina* (1954) written by Billy Wilder, Samuel Taylor and Ernest Lehman; based on the play by Samuel Taylor
Cinematography: Giusseppe Rotunno
Editing: Frederic Steinkamp
Production design: Brian Morris
Art direction: John Kasarda
Set decoration: George DeTitta, Jr. and Amy Marshall
Costume design: Ann Roth
Sound: Danny Michael
Casting: David Rubin
Music: John Williams, Alan Bergman and Marilyn Bergman
MPAA rating: PG
Running Time: 127 minutes

AWARDS AND NOMINATIONS

Chicago Film Festival Awards 1995: Most Promising Actor (Kinnear)
Academy Awards Nominations 1995: Best Score (Williams), Best Song ("Moonlight")
Golden Globe Awards Nominations 1996: Best Film-Musical/Comedy, Best Actor-Musical/Comedy (Ford), Best Song ("Moonlight")

the back. The dress (clothes were designed by Ann Roth), like most of the other clothes in the film, is perfectly suited to the character.

Sydney Pollack and screenwriters Barbara Benedek and David Rayfiel have reinvented the original Samuel Taylor script for the 90's without losing its romantic essence. And Pollack guides his actors with subtlety and grace. If the film seems uninspired, it is perhaps because in comparison, it lacks the storybook quality of the 1954 film. Pollack and company can be proud that they did a decent job remaking a film that did not cry out to be remade.

—*Kirby Tepper*

Safe

"Elegantly unnerving...beautifully directed...hauntingly effective."—Janet Maslin, *The New York Times*

"Seductive...scarily confident, beautifully acted. It will seize any viewer who dares to surrender to its spell. Feel free to laugh or scream."—Richard Corliss, *Time*

"Brilliant, beautiful and dauntingly ambiguous!"—John Powers, *Vogue*

Box Office Gross: $512,245

Every now and then there emerges a director who tackles his subject matter with such depth that his place among the short list of true risk-takers is insured. Director Todd Haynes is such a director. Audiences may not always like or even approve of his weird films, but his talent is unmistakable. Ever since Haynes' debut with *Superstar*: The Karen Carpenter Story, it has been clear that he likes to make films which provoke thought and cause discussion. He has done it again with *Safe*.

In this film, Haynes takes a contemporary problem and explores it from all angles, creating an ultimately satirical (but tragic) film that takes an uncompromising, severe look at an aspect of society. Much like he did with *Superstar*, Haynes uses an illness which seems to be peculiar to twentieth-century America and makes some disturbing observations. In *Superstar*, the problem was Karen Carpenter's anorexia. He told the story of Karen Carpenter using only Barbie dolls which were posed into different scenes that told the story of Carpenter's life and battle with anorexia. Haynes was able to comment on the superficiality in Carpenter's superstar life, and to wryly comment on the American obsession with beauty and fame through the use of Barbie's plastic perfection.

He explores related territory in this film. This time the illness is "environmental allergy," a new medical problem that seems to be diagnosed more and more frequently. The film's heroine, Carol (Julianne Moore), is a beautiful housewife living in Southern California's San Fernando Valley. She is married to the boring and selfish Greg (Xander Berkeley), and shares a shallow life with him and his stepson. The audience is at first treated to scenes from her everyday life: Carol mechanically goes to the dry cleaner, to lunch with friends, and she limply but dutifully takes care of the decorating chores. The decorating becomes an interesting symbol for Carol's superficiality: when the new sofas are delivered in the wrong color, she is visibly upset.

Slowly, Carol's routine is revealed as being more than dull; it is dangerous. The dry cleaning fluids, the fibers on the sofa (which should have been teal instead of black, according to Carol), the various sprays that her husband uses to groom himself are eventually seen as the cause of Carol's bizarre and alarming physical symptoms. She coughs uncontrollably after visiting the dry cleaner, she wheezes violently at a baby shower, and she becomes increasingly fatigued and depressed following an all-fruit diet suggested by her best friend.

As Carol undergoes her ordeal, Haynes drops clues that he sees this film as more than a depiction of the latest disease. Rather than simulate a television movie that depicts the trials and triumphs of a person's disease, Haynes uses the disease as a metaphor for twentieth-century life in much the same way he did with anorexia and Karen Carpenter. "We don't own our own lives," complains an aerobics classmate of Carol's. Haynes sees dangers in Carol's life that transcend the dangers of biological irritants. For example, the camera lingers (seemingly forever) on images of the interior of Carol and Greg's home, and its stark and unpleasant formality is underscored by Ed Tomney's frightening, otherworldly music. A strange bluish light casts a pall over their living room, which is a foreboding room dominated by chrome, glass, and polyester. The light, the music, and grey austerity of the room is Haynes' evidence of the alienation inherent in Carol's world. Her alienation, he seems to be saying, is both the cause and the symptom of her environmental allergy.

Other clues to Haynes' view about Carol's world are in the baby shower scene, where Carol and her friends all wear floral print dresses made of synthetic fabrics. A bit reminiscent of *The Stepford Wives* (1975), these women live in the controlled environment of the San Fernando Valley: they dress alike, talk alike, and look alike.

Carol's discovery, almost by accident, of the concept of environmental allergy leads her to a New Mexico refuge for people allergic to the environment. Wrenwood, as it is called, is run by the motherly Claire (Kate McGregor Stewart) and the eerie Peter (Peter Friedman), a charming but dangerous man who is clearly on his way to becoming a cult leader. "I've stopped reading papers, watching television....I've heard the media gloom and doom, and I transform that negative stimulus into something that will not hurt me. If I believe life is that dangerous, I'm afraid my immune system will believe it too." As Carol spends more time in Wrenwood, she becomes even more ill, and she finally moves into a "safe-house" on the Wrenwood property, isolating herself even further from her family and friends.

Carol's retreat from the world is seen by Haynes as having begun with her submission to a world in which she is required to be passive simply to fill a traditional "woman's role." In Carol's world, the men seem to hold the power: the first scene in the film is of Carol succumbing to uninteresting sex intended only to please Greg. Other scenes show Carol's lack of power in a male world. For example, when her symptoms become severe, her traditional doctor tells her the illness is in her mind, and gives a psychiatrist's business card to Greg. (Not only does he think it's all in her head, but he only sees the male as the one to be trusted with the "treatment.") When Carol goes to the psychiatrist, she tells him what she does with her days, "I'm a house—....a homemaker," she replies, trying to make herself sound more legitimate for the male psychiatrist.

Moore, who has recently achieved notoriety in *Nine Months* (1995) is outstanding. She plays the character as a detached, modern day *Camille* (1937). Her vacant stare seems to be the outward sign that there is nothing going on inside this person's head. Carol questions little and apologizes a lot. Moore makes her a woman who is not mentally equipped to understand when she is being mistreated by her husband or is being duped by the cult-like people at Wrenwood. She makes the scenes depicting the allergic reactions truly harrowing—particularly the scene in which she tries not to bring attention to herself while being unable to breathe at her friend's baby shower. Her pauses speak volumes, and her transformation from vacant, coiffed housewife to vacant, uncoiffed Wrenwood resident is gradual and frightening.

The other actors fare quite well, particularly Kate McGregor Stewart, who manages to make Claire seem dangerous and truly kind at the same time. Xander Berkeley creates the character of a husband who just wants everything to be perfect. He is particularly (and appropriately) obnoxious when Carol tells him that she cannot have sex again because she is sick: his insensitive and selfish response is beautifully played. James LeGros makes a brief and amiable appearance as an apparently normal Wrenwood resident who looks like he may be able to save Carol from complete alienation. Only Peter Friedman, as Wrenwood's leader, is off the mark. Friedman seems to enjoy playing the bad guy a bit too much; his constant pauses and his exaggerated smarminess don't add the same texture to his role that others bring to theirs.

For many audiences, the ponderous nature of Haynes' camera shots (the camera lingers for endless shots of Carol's home, of the pool, of the car, etc.) and the bizarre soundtrack may make them call the film "too slow." Some of the pauses sound like they come from a Pinter play (Pinter was

CREDITS

Carol White: Julianne Moore
Peter: Peter Friedman
Greg White: Xander Berkeley
Linda: Susan Norman
Claire: Kate McGregor Stewart
Nell: Mary Carver
Dr. Hubbard: Steven Gilborn
Chris: James LeGros

Origin: USA
Released: 1995
Production: Christine Vachon and Lauren Zalaznick for a Chemical Films production in association with Good Machine/Kardana/Channel Four Films; released by Sony Pictures Classics
Direction: Todd Haynes
Screenplay: Todd Haynes
Cinematography: Alex Nepomniaschy
Editing: James Lyons
Production design: David Bomba
Art direction: Anthony Stabley
Sound: Neil Danziger
Costume design: Nancy Steiner
Casting: Jakki Fink
Music: Ed Tomney
MPAA rating: R
Running Time: 121 minutes

AWARDS AND NOMINATIONS

Independent Spirit Awards Nominations 1996: Best Film, Best Director (Haynes), Best Actress (Moore), Best Screenplay (Haynes)

known for writing an excessive number of pauses into his scripts) and add to the weight of the film. But for many people, these characteristics will make the film feel like a *Twilight Zone* episode, and Haynes' themes of the alienation of the individual in today's society will be underscored.

The film is both a dark satire and an allegory for the age of AIDS. In fact, there are several references to AIDS, an example of which is that "Peter is a chemically sensitive person who has AIDS, so he's particularly sensitive to people." Haynes seems to be deriding those that use psychological mumbo-jumbo which is intended to make something positive out of the tragedy of AIDS. He is also perhaps offering a cautionary tale on the dangers of the world: especially since the advent of AIDS and of the Ebola virus, the world may be seen as less and less safe to many people.

Haynes takes the film to an unexpected place when he takes Carol to Wrenwood. Instead of making her get well, he makes Carol retreat more and more into an inner-world that is never really safe. While satirizing the self-help movement ("give up the rage," implores Peter), the film makes the point that a world which is physically "safe" (Wrenwood) is still psychologically "unsafe." Is Haynes saying that the world is dangerous? Is he saying that middle-class values are dangerous? Or is he simply making fun of how people prefer to justify their psychological problems through vague diseases? Only Haynes knows for sure. The film raises these and other questions, and it is fascinating.

—Kirby Tepper

REVIEWS

The Hollywood Reporter. January 30, 1995 p. 6
Daily Variety. January 27, 1995. p. 2
Boxoffice. July 1995. p. 55
The Village Voice. June 27, 1995. p. 49

Samba Traore

Whereas a society's loss of innocence in the face of technological progress is an issue we here in the West tend to see in terms of the past, amongst the poorer nations of the world, it remains a matter of vital concern in the present.

The films of Idrissa Ouedraogo, coming as they do from Burkino Faso, an African nation few have even heard of, inscribe this loss onto an open world with open faces, trustful of age-old moral values, conflicting with an all too recent distrust and amorality, spawned by creeping industrialization.

Undoubtedly then, Ouedraogo's efforts must comprise the rarest of contemporary film genres: cinema about a world of today untouched by cinema. It is as if from our sophisticated vantage points on the film festival circuit, we feel not the slightest qualm about looking at those who lack the means to look back.

The equation of power, though, isn't all in our favor.

When old Yaaba, ostracized as a witch by her village, lies down to die outside her burnt hut, at the end of *Yaaba* (1989), Ouedraogo's second feature, but his first seen here, the tranquil acceptance in her gestures must surely draw envy from those of us dreading the prospect of being rendered helpless by modern medicine's desperate attempts to prolong life.

Samba Traore (1992) has a similar lesson to teach us about crime. After robbing a filling station, in a holdup that turns fatal, the eponymous Samba (Bakary Sangare), the epitome of a newly emergent African manhood, escapes to his village, no one seemingly aware of his guilt but himself.

Shorn of the clutter of materiality, the sparse village setting, surrounded by arid land, becomes the filmic correlative for a moral substratum upon which this parable about the nature of guilt and industrial progress is acted out.

Halfway through the film, we are offered a clue as to how to perceive what is happening to Samba, in the form of a fable that Samba himself narrates to his stepson.

"There once was a stubborn rascal named Moriba," Samba begins, "who went to market to buy trousers on the feast day, but when he got home, he realized the legs were much too long. So he asked his father to shorten them, but his father refused. Then his mother refused, as did all his sisters, because Moriba was such a stubborn rascal. So Moriba went to bed very sad. But without telling anyone, his father got up and shortened the trousers. Then his mother got up and shortened them. Then, one after one, his sisters got up and shortened them, too. The feast day dawned, and Moriba found himself wearing plain old shorts."

The film similarly counterpoints the effect that Samba's dirty money has on the village with the increasing toll that it takes on Samba's personal happiness.

On market day, Samba is able to raise the stakes in a game of "three card molly" run by his old friend, Salif (Abdoulaye Komboudri), a jovial fellow his age. Samba not only wins all of Salif's money, but his cart and donkey as well.

Then, as a gesture of friendship, returns most of the money, but keeps the cart.

From the admiration in the eyes of the villagers, it becomes clear that they see Samba as a hero, deserving of the luck brought on by his money, which, as rumor has it, he earned by working on a plantation.

> "You know that you are beautiful. I love you. That's what I wanted to tell you. Now you must decide."—Samba courting Saratou

Everyone also expects him to court Saratou (Mariam Kaba), a once-married single mother who, like Samba, has returned to the village after living in town, and is now raising a young son.

"Are you married?" Samba asks her boldly, while giving her a lift on his cart. Saratou feigns sleep, and does not answer. That night, while drinking with Salif, Samba admits to being in "serious trouble." We can see the pressure the moral fibre of the village is exerting on Samba when he begins, "I have to tell you the truth," and then stops short. Salif wags a finger as he guesses, "Maybe you took someone's money." It is more of a playful taunt, than an accusation. Salif's rustic awareness will not lead him to even suspect the gravity of Samba's crime. "Do I look like a thief?" Samba asks. As the two forget their woes by getting drunk, it becomes clear that Salif will function as a moral anchor for Samba, the only support Samba will need to live with his conscience.

Encouraged by Salif, Samba dons his best threads and sets off on his bicycle to woo Saratou. With Salif's advice ringing in his ears, Samba keeps his proposal simple but earnest. "You know that you are beautiful," he says to her. "I love you. That's what I wanted to tell you." He then starts to walk away. Behind his back, Saratou smiles knowingly. Her maturity becomes evident as she conveys her decision by silently getting onto the pinion of Samba's bicycle.

CREDITS

Samba Traore: Bakary Sangare
Saratou: Mariam Kaba
Salif: Abdoulaye Komboudri
Binta: Irene Tassembedo

Origin: Burkina Faso, West Africa
Released: 1993
Production: Idrissa Ouedraogo; released by New Yorker Films
Direction: Idrissa Ouedraogo
Screenplay: Idrissa Ouedraogo, Jacques Arhex, and Santiago Amigorena
Cinematography: Pierre Laurent Chenieux and Mathieu Vadepied
Editing: Joelle Dufour
Music: Fanton Cahen and Lamine Konte
Running Time: 85 minutes

Saratou's past, however, catches up with her in the form of Ismael, who arrives from the nearby town, hoping to take Saratou away with him. In a manner most uncharacteristic of tradition, Saratou asserts her independence as she tells him, "I love someone else." "Is this a joke?" Ismael asks, reaching for Saratou. It is then that an enraged Samba knocks Ismael to the ground, who can then only ride away on Samba's bicycle. Samba's sudden burst of violence leaves everyone stunned. When Salif chides him for it, Samba threatens to hit him too. It is as if, in an uncanny way, Samba has seen in Ismael the town, and its system of law enforcement, about to catch up with him, just when he has found happiness.

That night, Samba opens the valise he brought with him from the town, and looks at the gun and the money. We see from his anguished expression that it is all extraneous to the new life he has started. When Samba buys cattle and presents them to his father and other villagers, Salif admits in awe: "You've become a king." Saratou though remains unconvinced about the source of Samba's riches. "Isn't it enough that I love you?" he shouts at her, when she tries to probe into his affairs.

Their wedding day shows a Samba brimming with joy, yet shaking his head, as if half-mocking the ceremony, the entire village in a procession behind him. When they are alone, he says to Saratou, "I'll build you a house bigger than any house here. And Salif and I will open a bar, so the village is more cheerful."

With his money, Samba does become a ruler of sorts, putting the villagers to work, first on his two-story brick house, then on a structure that will house the village bar. In the midst of the feverish construction, Saratou takes her doubts to Salif. "I think he's lying to us," she says, making clear that she holds morality above any marital allegiance.

The bar proves an instant success, allowing Samba to launder his money into legitimate gains. It is only Saratou's difficult pregnancy that upsets this order. Samba is at first hesitant to take her to the nearest town, even though she needs urgent attention. He finally tags along, as Salif, Salif's wife and Saratou's mother carry the prostrate Saratou on a cart. It is only when Salif manages to flag down a truck that Samba feels that fate is about to trap him. He gives the money he has to Saratou's mother, and runs off into the fields.

We see Samba's misgivings proven valid, as bit by bit, like the rascal's trousers in the fable, Samba is shorn of his respectability, and exposed as the criminal he is. First, his father discovers the gun and the stolen loot. Then, when Salif returns from the town, he finds Samba drunk, and his worst suspicions confirmed. As the two vent their anger at each other in a violent scuffle, it is Samba's father who intervenes and confronts Samba with the gun. Mocking the father's morality with a sneer, Samba admits to his guilt.

It is then that the film takes up a truly revolutionary stance. Samba's father, with a flaming torch in each hand, sets fire to the house that Samba has built, and to all of Samba's things. If crime has to be stopped, the film seems to say, then the fruits of crime have to be destroyed at their root by those closest to the criminal. Samba himself begins to look relieved, now that he has nothing to hide.

When the law finally catches up with him, led to him by none other that Ismael, Samba, handcuffed, takes leave of his loving wife, his newborn son and even Salif, with whom he makes up, promising to return to them after having served his time. His punishment, Samba seems to realize, is also his cleansing.

Janet Maslin, writing in *The New York Times,* notes: "Crime is not forgiven or forgotten within this film's moral universe." We can understand Samba's life, she argues, through those closest to him, as well as through his shame, his regret, and his hope for redemption. She concludes: "The wisdom that emerges from this film's primitive-looking setting deserves to be heard in many a more sophisticated-looking place."

Gene Seymour, in *Newsday,* notes "an organic design to the narrative that makes Samba's story resemble a folk tale." For him, the film emerges as being "at once distinctly African and bracingly universal." A conflicting opinion is offered by Dave Kehr of *The New York Daily News,* who finds that the director's approach "remains disturbingly exterior to his material," as if he were "making his films mainly for European audiences." In support, one could cite Saratou's character, seemingly alien to the village setting and, seen from Kehr's viewpoint, possibly created for European audiences to identify with. For Kehr, the film is nothing more than "a simple story meant to underline a number of eternal moral truths while showing off some exotic scenery and native costumes."

Samba Traore, the director's fourth feature, became the first to win him a major international award, the Silver Bear at the Berlin Film Festival of 1993.

—*Vivek Adarkar*

REVIEWS

The New York Times, September 9, 1993.
New York Daily News, September 10, 1993.
The New Republic, October 4, 1993.
Newsday, September 10, 1993.
Variety, March 8, 1993.
The Village Voice, September 21, 1993.

The Scarlet Letter

"Passionate, provocative, superb! Demi Moore and Gary Oldman have real chemistry."—Pat Collins, *WWOR-TV*

Box Office Gross: $10,378,982

The production notes that accompany *The Scarlet Letter* characterize the source novel as "the quintessential American novel. A tale of redemptive love set amidst the fear, hypocrisy and a violent clash of cultures that marked the first settlements in the new world...a rich exploration of the nation's eternal conflict between passion and convention, between the desire for freedom and the need for order[,]...a daring look at the ways in which Americans are drawn to the very vices they denounce." The same notes describe Nathaniel Hawthorne himself as "of a divided mind. Fascinated by unbridled sexual, intellectual and creative explorations, yet shamed by the supposed sinfulness of going beyond proscribed limits." Certainly any viewers who have studied Hawthorne's works in high school or in college will have trouble recognizing these characterizations and may indeed wonder if this was the case, why was American literature class so tame? And why does the Cliffs Notes companion to *The Scarlet Letter* remain one of the best-selling titles year after year, according to Cliff's marketing manager?

The film *The Scarlet Letter* is the story of Hester Prynne (Demi Moore), head-strong hedonist Puritan, and her illicit love for Rev. Dimmesdale (Gary Oldman). Hester's husband, Roger Chillingsworth (Robert Duvall), sends Hester to the New World, intending to follow her shortly. However, as luck would have it, his ship is captured, and he is waylaid for sufficient time for Hester and Rev. Dimmesdale to fall in love, consummate that love, and create Pearl, an illegitimate child. For this, Hester becomes an outcast, although she protects the identify of her lover. In this cinematic version, however, it is the Native Americans that finally are able to save Rev. Dimmesdale from his fate.

To say that critics had a heyday reviewing *The Scarlet Letter* would be an understatement, just as it would be to say that those reviews were unflattering. It's not that filmmakers should stay away from literary masterpieces. For example, several remarkable films have been made from Shakespearean sources, from Franco Zeffirelli's *Romeo and Juliet* (1968) to Kenneth Branaugh's *Henry V*, from Laurence Olivier's *Hamlet* (1948) to Franco Zeffirelli's *Hamlet* (1990), from Fred McLeod Wilcox's *Forbidden Planet* (1956) (a sci-fi version of Shakespeare's *The Tempest*), to Robert Wise's and Jerome Robbins's *West Side Story* (Shakespeare's *Romeo & Juliet*). Indeed, *The Scarlet Letter* has been made into films on several other occasions with more success than the one at hand: Victor Seastrom's version (1926), starring screen legend Lillian Gish, and Wim Wenders' 1979 version, starring international beauty Senta Berger (although it should be noted that the set of Wenders' film appears more like a cliff-side Dodge City than seventeenth-century Massachusetts—but then the icons associated with various eras of American history are confusing even to many Americans).

"Who is to say what is a sin in the eyes of God?"—Pearl, Hester's illegitimate daughter from *The Scarlet Letter*

CREDITS

Hester Prynne: Demi Moore
Authur Dimmesdale: Gary Oldman
Roger Prynne (Chillingsworth): Robert Duvall
Horace Stonehall: Robert Prosky
John Bellingham: Edward Hardwicke
Harriet Hibbons: Joan Plowright
Thomas Cheever: Roy Dotrice

Origin: USA
Released: 1995
Production: Andrew Vajna and Roland Joffé for a Lightmotive/Allied Stars/Cinergi/Moving Pictures production; released by Buena Visa
Direction: Roland Joffé
Screenplay: Douglas Stewart; based on the novel *The Scarlet Letter* by Nathaniel Hawthorne
Cinematography: Alex Thmpson
Editing: Thom Noble
Production design: Roy Walker
Art direction: Tony Wollard
Set design: Gordon White, Richard Harrison and Rocco Matteo
Set decoration: Rosaline Shingleton
Costume design: Gabriella Pescucci
Sound: Doug Ganton
Casting: Elisabeth Leustig
Music: John Barry
MPAA rating: R
Running Time: 135 minutes

However, a version of *The Scarlet Letter* that was reportedly as perplexing and displeasing a cinematic version of Hawthorne's masterpiece as the version at issue here was made in 1934, starring Colleen Moore, erstwhile flapper and star of the silent screen. And a 1979 PBS version starring Meg Foster and John Heard has dropped from view altogether.

It is possible, however, that filmmakers should not try to remain true to the original text except for modernizing a few meaningful details. Indeed, David Ansen, writing in *Newsweek* magazine, has created an epic catalogue of "modern" details disastrously added by the filmmakers: Hester Prynne spies Rev. Dimmesdale skinny-dipping and watches until she glimpses significant portions of flesh; Hester and Rev. Dimmesdale consummate their love atop a pile of grain (a scene which this viewer found largely reminiscent—although a dicier version—of the famous promotional still of Jane Russell in Howard Hughes' *The Outlaw*, 1943); Mituba, Hester's mute black servant girl witnesses the consummation and follows the viewing with her deeply aroused, autoerotic luxuriating in the seventeenth-century version of a hot tub; Hester is nearly raped by a lecherous colonist; Rev. Dimmesdale heroically works to unite the Iroquois and the Puritans; Roger Chillingsworth scalps an innocent man; and the Native Americans rescue Rev. Dimmesdale from the gallows. Todd McCarthy, writing in *Variety*, has labeled the changes "P.C.-era feel-good revisionism"; Tom Gliatto writing in *People* expresses concern that the filmmakers have "gotten it into their heads that Hawthorne based his 1850 book on the 1993 movie *The Piano*." Susan Wloszczyna, *USA Today*, finds it a hybrid of *The Piano* and *Last of the Mohicans*. However, the best term to describe this film may well be "silly" or, less charitably, "insulting", insulting to Nathaniel Hawthorne, who wrote the novel to explore and denounce just the sort of narcissism that led to the making of this film. When filmmaker Roland Joffé states (as he did in *USA Today*) that he is telling the story that Hawthorne wished he could have told in 1850, it becomes questionable whether Mr. Joffé checked his sources regarding Hawthorne's fascination with the Puritan period and regarding one of the main reasons for which Hawthorne wrote: an effort to expiate familial guilt.

Also troubling about the film is the casting of Demi Moore as Hester Prynne. Certainly it is true that Ms. Moore has sufficient name recognition to instantly draw audiences to her films. Yet, along with that name recognition comes the baggage of each of the roles she popularized. For instance, even as Demi Moore is complicating Rev. Dimmesdale's life, audience members will remember how she complicated David Murphy's and John Gage's (Woody Harrelson and Robert Redford) lives in *Indecent Proposal*

(1993). Or audience members will remember the complications Ms. Moore introduced into Michael Douglas' character's life in *Disclosure* (1995). In each of these films, as on two covers of *Vanity Fair*, Ms. Moore has bared significant portions of her unquestionably well-toned physique, but it would not be taking this process too far to say that audiences will recognize more of Ms. Moore's terrain than that of Hawthorne's novel. In a dimly lighted scene, Ms. Moore's Hester bathes provocatively, caressing herself and, no doubt, thinking of Rev. Dimmesdale. The scene is attractive enough but is definitely a scene out of twentieth-century cinema, especially Demi Moore's ouvre of twentieth-century cinema, and once again Hawthorne is left behind. With Ms. Moore's past roles and her upcoming role as a stripper in the film *Striptease* (scheduled for 1996 release), audiences may well question when enough of Demi Moore is enough.

Gary Oldman, however, brings significant depth to his role as Rev. Dimmesdale. Dimmesdale's suffering may remind some viewers of —albeit a lighter version—his role in *Sid & Nancy* (1986). However, what is largely new terrain for Oldman is the light-hearted desire and romantic-lead passion he brings to the portion of this film that precedes the return of Roger Chillingsworth. For instance, while it is largely a set piece, it no doubt will interest viewers to see Oldman's Dimmesdale racing horses across the countryside with Demi Moore's Hester happily at his side. Certainly Hawthorne never envisioned the pair involved in such activities, but the interesting part is that Gary Oldman, who is more likely to play a misfit or an evil character (*Bram Stoker's Dracula*, 1992), is quite believable as a young preacher smitten with love.

The Scarlet Letter, like other well-loved and well-known literary works, continues to fall prey to the urge of writers and other artists to fix it up a bit, to "improve" it. However, even without seeing Joffé's film, many Hawthorne fans no doubt were squirming at the thought of the new enhanced version. After the film's release, it seems clear to at least this viewer that the better part of wisdom is to leave this classic alone. While it is unquestionably filled with epic scale guilt and passion, it is a guilt and passion that is best visualized by each individual reader rather than recreated for twentieth-century sensibilities.

—*Roberta F. Green*

REVIEWS

Detroit Free Press, October 13, 1995, p. 1D.
Detroit News, October 13, 1995, p. 1F.
Entertainment Weekly, October 20, 1995, p. 43.
Newsweek, October 16, 1995, p. 87.
The New Yorker, p. 114.
The New York Times, October 13, 1995, p. C16.
People, October 23, 1995, p. 17.
USA Today, October 13, 1995, p. 1D.
Variety, October 16, 1995, p. 94, 117.

Search and Destroy

Box Office Gross: $389,731

The trendy platitudes that govern the lives of some modern men are blown to bits in *Search and Destroy*, a devastating satire on self-actualization and the "New Age" male. The title conveys the filmmakers' methods. First-time director David Salle and screenwriter Michael Almereyda are like heat-seeking missiles, ferreting out and exploding every hypocritical aspect of the "me-first" mentality that masquerades as soulful sensitivity.

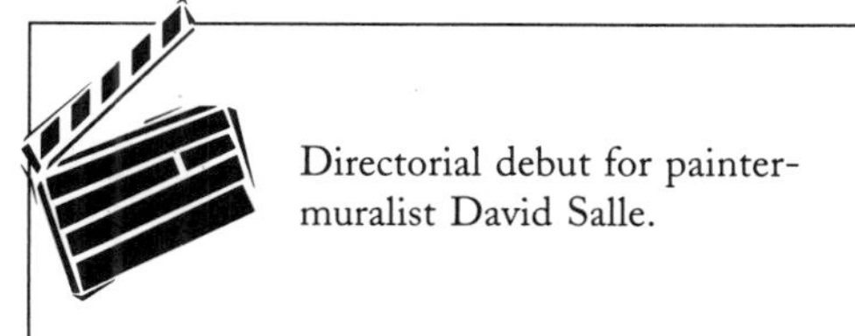

Directorial debut for painter-muralist David Salle.

Based on an off-Broadway black comedy by Howard Korder, *Search and Destroy* is a cinematic theater of the absurd. Collage artist Salle, experimenting with a new medium, is a lot like the hands-on painter who is a bit character in the film. Salle throws a lot of vivid stuff onto the screen. Some of it sticks and some of it doesn't.

With over-the-top performances from Dennis Hopper, John Turturro and Christopher Walken, *Search and Destroy* succeeds only sporadically as audience-pleasing entertainment, but that hardly matters. Much of the fare is hard to digest and some of it absolutely stupefying, but many bits are hilarious and the film, taken as a whole, is worthwhile. Salle achieves his apparent purpose. He skewers everything in sight, takes no hostages and at moments come close to inventing a new kind of filmmaking. It's like watching a mad scientist at work.

After the opening titles flash against the backdrop of a life preserver in a pool, Hopper's voice instructs: "You can only rescue yourself." Hopper is playing Dr. Luthor Waxling, a cable-TV self-help guru pushing a vapid survivalist philosophy cloaked in fashionable nineties psychobabble. Waxling's four rules that govern life are: (1) Strength needs no excuses; (2) The past is pointless; (3) Just because it happened to you doesn't make it interesting; and (4) The things you apologize for are the things you want.

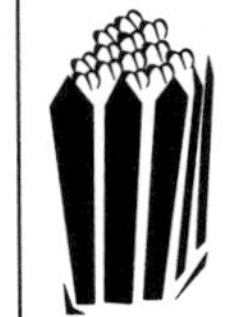

"I am what I say am. If I say I'm a movie producer, I'm a movie producer."—Martin Mirkhein

Waxling's psychological buckshot hits a bullseye with Martin Mirkhein (Griffin Dunne), an unscrupulous, self-centered small-time entrepreneur with big dreams. The character's name evokes the famous 1980s Wall Street insider trader Michael Milken; Mirkhein is a Milken wannabe, though he's in the entertainment business, not the stock market.

When we meet Mirkheim, he is trying to explain to a tax auditor why he owes the state of Florida over $147,000 in back taxes: "Taxes just aren't in my focus," he explains. He is too busy self-actualizing. "I want to leave something lasting of myself," he tells the auditor. "I want to let people know I was here."

When the auditor warns him he must pay up, Mirkhein gets angry and his wife Lauren (Rosanna Arquette) explains, "He doesn't respond well to threats." Lauren doesn't either. After years of cleaning up after Mirkhein's creative messes, Lauren is fed up and demands a separation. Before Martin leaves, she gives a party at which he meets a mysterious guest named Kim Ulander (Walken). Mirkhein has become obsessed with his latest and most ambitious scheme: to buy the rights to Waxling's book, *Daniel Strong*, and make a movie of it. Ulander, also a disciple of Waxling, thinks Mirkhein has a great idea, but the hosts, whispering that Ulander is a drug dealer, escort him from the party before he and Mirkhein can talk turkey.

Daniel Strong is a new-male adventure story/sermon about a young man who goes to the wilderness to get in touch with his inner self. At ripe moments throughout *Search and Destroy* we see snippets of the novel as filmed, presumably, by Mirkhein. These are hilarious satirical bits.

Mirkhein flies to Dallas to pitch his idea to Waxling, but is turned away by Waxling's personal assistant, Roger (Ethan Hawke). He meets Waxling's secretary Marie Davenport (Illeana Douglas), who is fascinated by Mirkhein's film ambitions. It turns out she has written a script of her own. In a great comic scene, the squeaky-clean Marie glowingly tells Martin the details of a sickening *Alien*-type plot which involves a gruesome monster's attack on a chainsaw-wielding heroine. Martin, however, isn't a horror fan: "I'm interested in changing people's lives," he puffs.

Mirkhein takes this New Age man stuff seriously. Marie is delicious and available; Martin confesses his attraction but explains, "I've taken a vow of celibacy." We get a clip from *Daniel Strong*, showing the hero struggling with the temptations of beauty, sculpting a voluptuous naked woman while resisting her advances. Martin and Marie spend a platonic night together, but that's enough to set-off Waxling, who has his claws into Marie. (Explaining to Martin her relationship with Waxling, Marie asks, "Did you ever have the sensation your body's being operated on at a distance by somebody else?")

Roger throttles Mirkhein and ties him to a chair, but despite his awkward position, Martin manages to pitch his idea to Waxling, who is interested at the prospect of more fame and money. But when Waxling realizes Mirkhein has no means of financing the film, he roars, "You're a guy in a suit who wants to sit at the grown-up table?...Get some money!"

This command sets Mirkhein off on a mission. Marie signs on as his assistant and they go to New York. Mirkhein tracks down Ulander who tells him he's not a drug dealer but a Pacific Rim market analyst. Ulander enlists his friend Ron (Turturro), a wired-up wild man, to help raise the funds, and the film shifts into its second segment, titled "Destroy." Taking Waxling's advice seriously, the inept trio sets out to deal drugs, run phony credit card scams, and do whatever plundering they need to raise the money. Somewhere along the way, Martin decides he'll finance Marie's

CREDITS

Martin Mirkhein: Griffin Dunne
Marie DavenPort: Illeana Douglas
Dr. Waxling: Dennis Hopper
Kim Ulander: Christopher Walken

Origin: USA
Released: 1995
Production: Ruth Charny, Elie Cohn, Dan Lupovitz for a New Image production; released by October Films
Direction: David Salle
Screenplay: Michael Almereyda; based on the play by Howard Korder
Cinematography: Bobby Bukowski, Michael Spiller
Editing: Michelle Gorchow
Production design: Robin Standefer
Costume design: Donna Zakowska
Casting: Billy Hopkins
Music: Elmer Bernstein
MPAA rating: R
Running Time: 90 minutes

horror film first, and use that to raise the money for *Daniel Strong*.

The second half of *Search and Destroy* is darker, loonier, more violent and less successful than the first, but it provides the necessary follow-up punch. The would-be filmmakers don't shirk the task they've set for themselves: to carry out Waxling's absurd philosophy to its logical extremes. In so doing, they search out and destroy the post-modern entrepreneurial ethic, the movie business, New Age pseudo-morality and manhood, just to name a few targets.

The actors, especially Walken and Turturro, behave more like performance artists than standard film actors. Walken is fascinatingly off-kilter in slicked-back, patent-leather hair, ghostly white face and blank expression, and he carries off the transformation from a business predator to a gun-toting predator with frightening aplomb. In a black fright wig, Turturro sends up the hyper New York hustler. He never stops talking, wheeling and dealing.

Hopper is perfectly outrageous as the mellow, manic fraud Waxling, yet his performance is almost subdued compared to the others. Dunne is a raging, amoral Everyman, constantly irritating but managing a necessary air of believability.

Douglas is radiant in her role as the innocent, heart-of-gold woman caught up in the nefarious dealings of the scheming men. She is comparable in looks and portrayal to Shelley Duvall in several early Robert Altman films, serving as a reminder that there is some decency left in an amoral business world. Douglas has a great deadpan comic talent and a unique and fetching manner.

Salle doesn't dabble as a debut director, he plunges right in, experimenting with a whole range of artistic techniques. He demonstrates a countless number of genres and styles. It doesn't all fit together, but then Salle is a collage artist, and the overall picture is a crazy-quilt of sharply pointed details. Elmer Bernstein's carnival-like score, which sounds like it should be played on a calliope, helps immensely.

Search and Destroy is a challenging, take-no-prisoners enterprise with an ambitious reach and a fascinating attitude. If true art is about smashing pretentions, *Search and Destroy* is a smashing success. Salle's targets are utterly destroyed, but the timid in the audience probably also will be done in by the film's outrageous leaps of illogic and lapses in execution.

—*Michael Betzold*

REVIEWS

Entertainment Weekly. May 26, 1995, p. 66.
The Hollywood Reporter. January 25, 1995, p. 12.
Maclean's. June 19, 1995, p. 61.
The Nation. May 22, 1995, p. 733.
New Republic. May 8, 1995, p. 26.
New York. May 15, 1995, p. 63.
New York Times. April 28, 1995, p. C16.
Playboy. June 1995, p. 17.
Rolling Stone. May 18, 1995, p. 97.
Variety. January 30, 1995, p. 49.

Sense and Sensibility

"Vivid, immediate and engaging. This is nourishment for the mind and the heart."—Leonard Maltin, *Entertainment Tonight*

"A very cool movie."—Amy Dawes, *Los Angeles Daily News*

"Sheer fun...grandly entertaining. A sparkling, colorful and utterly contemporary comedy of manners."—Janet Maslin, *The New York Times*

"Brilliant. The screen teems with superlative actors, brilliant costumes, gorgeous landscapes."—Jack Kroll, *Newsweek*

"*Sense and Sensibility* is one of those totally satisfying films. It's just wonderful."—Wendy Wasserstein, *Premiere*

"Terrifically entertaining! One of the 10 best pictures of the year!"—Peter Travers, *Rolling Stone*

"The year's most beautiful and satisfying film."—Jeff Craig, *Sixty Second Preview*

"Impeccable. Emma Thompson achieves one of those privileged moments we are always hoping to find at the movies and so rarely do. Mostly you feel terrific, in touch with something authentic inside yourself."—Richard Schickel, *Time*

Box Office Gross: $4,032,165

Emma Thompson and Kate Winslet star as Elinor and Marianne Dashwood in *Sense and Sensibility*.

Sense and Sensibility, Jane Austen's first published novel, appeared in 1811 and grew out of "Elinor and Marianne," a sketch first conceived by the author between 1795 and 1796. During this same period, Romanticism had taken root in England, finding its fullest expression in the poetry of Byron, Shelley, and Keats. In creating Elinor and Marianne Dashwood, the heroines of the piece, Austen, who penned most of her fiction on scraps of paper in her family's parlor, clearly meant to provide a commentary on the turn-of-the-century interplay of the restrained, rational values of the Enlightenment with the extravagant excesses the Romantics displayed in reaction.

The Dashwood sisters are meant to embody these conflicting value systems, with Elinor, the elder, serving as the thoroughly sensible one, and Marianne exhibiting a surfeit of sensibility. In the scheme of things, it is only when each sister modifies her stance, adopting some of the other's characteristics, that their dilemmas can be resolved.

"Underneath the strange customs and costumes, I began to feel a strong and immediate spiritual kinship with my own tradition: in both societies, there is a similar concern for harmony, and achieving a careful balance of opposites."—Taiwan-born director Ang Lee on his first non-Asian film

In the new film version of the novel, first-time screenwriter Emma Thompson—who also plays the part of Elinor Dashwood—remains true to Austen's scheme as well as to the spirit of her work. While Austen purists will doubtless quibble over Thompson's textual alterations, most clearly enhance the viewer's experience of the story. It is, after all, incredibly gratifying to see Elinor, during the film's denouement, utterly lose her composure in front of her beloved Edward Ferrars (Hugh Grant), rather than in another room. And how could Elinor's absorption of some of her sister's "sensibility" (or sensitivity) be more vividly illustrated?

Marianne (Kate Winslet) and Elinor are two members of a household of four women—which also includes their widowed mother (Gemma Jones) and juvenile sister, Margaret (Emilie Francois)—set adrift as the story opens. When Mr. Dashwood dies, he is obliged to leave his considerable estate to his son by his first marriage. Immediately following the credits, we see Henry Dashwood, as he expires, extracting a promise from his son John (James Fleet) to care for his stepmother and half-sisters. This scene, however, is immediately followed by a hilarious series of scenes in which John's pledge to support his father's second family is gradually (but shamefully easily) diminished to token status by the entreaties of his rapacious wife, Fanny (Harriet Walker). Dressed ostentatiously in black, John and Fanny move into the ancestral estate, Norland, which they now own. The other four Dashwood women, who are now so reduced in circumstances that they can only afford to trim their garments with somber ribbon, are elbowed aside. Shortly thereafter, they move out—but not before Elinor has an opportunity to meet and fall in love with Fanny's older brother, Edward. Edward, for his part, seems to exhibit a similar level of attachment to Elinor, albeit tinged with a peculiar reluctance.

The Dashwood women take up the kindly offer of a Devonshire cottage from a distant relative and benefactor, Sir John Middleton (Robert Hardy). Cut off from their old society and financially pinched, Elinor and Marianne are left to contemplate their diminished marital prospects. Edward disappoints, failing to appear for his promised visit. Elinor sadly, but sensibly, retreats into housekeeping. Marianne, on the other hand, is seemingly rescued from her boredom with the English countryside and with her middle-aged suitor, Colonel Brandon (Alan Rickman), by a chance encounter with the wildly romantic John Willoughby (Greg Wise). When Marianne sprains her ankle while out on a country walk, Willoughby appears as if by magic to sweep her up with him on his spirited horse. Marianne is captivated. Throwing all caution and propriety to the winds, she throws herself at Willoughby. He reciprocates until one day, mysteriously, he suddenly departs for London, leaving Marianne in tears.

Mrs. Jennings, Sir John's garrulous and nosey friend, offers the sisters comfort in the form of a visit to her London town house. In London, Elinor meets Lucy Steele (Imogen Stubbs) who reveals, pledging Elinor to silence, that she and Edward Ferrars have been secretly engaged for years, and Elinor suddenly comprehends the reason for Edward's seeming indifference. Marianne, too, meets with disappointment when Willoughby, who has ignored her entreaties that he contact her, publicly snubs her at a ball. Marianne, far from exhibiting Elinor's forbearance, collapses, and the sisters immediately leave London.

Back in Devonshire, distraught with grief, Marianne repeats her earlier ambulatory experience when she ventures out in the rain to gaze at Willoughby's neighboring estate—the occasion for his engagement to an heiress who, unlike Marianne, has money that will allow him to maintain his lavish lifestyle. When Marianne collapses this time, overcome with emotion and an incipient fever, she is rescued by her stalwart admirer, Colonel Brandon. As she recovers, Brandon is always by her side, and gradually she comes to realize the worth of this eminently sensible fellow.

CREDITS

Elinor Dashwood: Emma Thompson
Mrs. Dashwood: Gemma Jones
Edward Ferrars: Hugh Grant
Marianne Dashwood: Kate Winslet
Fanny Dashwood: Harriet Walter
Colonel Brandon: Alan Rickman

Origin: Great Britain
Released: 1995
Production: Lindsay Doran for a Mirage production; released by Columbia Pictures
Direction: Ang Lee
Screenplay: Emma Thompson; adapted from the novel by Jane Austen
Cinematography: Michael Coulter
Editing: Tim Squyers
Production design: Luciana Arrighi
Art direction: Philip Elton
Set decoration: Ian Whittaker
Choreography: Stuart Hopps
Costume design: Jenny Beavan and John Bright
Music: Patrick Doyle, Lawrence Ashmore and Robert Ziegler
MPAA rating: PG
Running Time: 135 minutes

AWARDS AND NOMINATIONS

Academy Awards 1995: Best Adapted Screenplay (Thompson)
Nominations: Best Picture, Best Actress (Thompson), Best Supporting Actress (Winslet), Best Cinematography (Coulter), Best Costumes
Berlin Film Festival 1995: Golden Bear
British Academy Awards 1995: Best Film, Best Actress (Thompson), Best Supporting Actress (Winslet)
Nominations: Best Director (Lee), Best Supporting Actor (Rickman), Best Supporting Actress (Spriggs), Best Adapted Screenplay (Thompson), Best Score (Doyle), Best Cinematography (Coulter)
Golden Globe Awards 1996: Best Film-Drama, Best Screenplay (Thompson)
Nominations: Best Director (Lee), Best Actress-Drama (Thompson), Best Supporting Actress (Winslet), Best Score (Doyle)
Los Angeles Film Critics Awards 1995: Best Screenplay (Thompson)
National Board of Review Awards 1995: Best Film, Best Director (Lee), Best Actress (Thompson)
New York Film Critics Awards 1995: Best Director (Lee)
Screen Actors Guild Awards 1995: Best Supporting Actress (Winslet)
Nominations: Best Cast, Best Actress (Thompson)
Writers Guild Awards 1995: Best Adapted Screenplay (Thompson)
Directors Guild Award Nominations 1995: Best Director (Lee)

Elinor, too, is saved by an reversal of fortune. When Lucy Steele, unable to keep her engagement a secret, reveals it in confidence to Fanny Dashwood, Fanny is outraged and immediately informs her mother that her eldest son is engaged to a common girl with no prospects. Mrs. Ferrars responds by disinheriting Edward. Lucy, keeping to the main chance, now switches her affections to Edward's younger brother, Robert, who stands to inherit the family property. Edward is thus freed from an unwanted engagement he had felt bound to keep both by honor and by financial dependence on his mother. When he is offered the opportunity of making a modest living as a clergyman, he is freed at last to make his feeling known to Elinor.

These are the outlines of Austen's narrative, to which Thompson remains true while at the same time adding some welcome details. By fleshing out young Margaret Dashwood (who leaves virtually no trace in the novel), for example, Thompson is able to add a great deal of entertaining and even plot-enhancing stage business. And director Ang Lee, though such devices as camera angles, also adds a lot to Austen's intricate plotting in *Sense and Sensibility.* Regency society was notable for its social constraints—without which Austen would have had no story—and Lee underscores this sense of restraint by frequently photographing his characters from outside the door frames of the rooms they inhabit.

Director Lee, a native of Taiwan who had never before read Jane Austen and whose fluency in English is sometimes strained, was producer Lindsay Doran's choice. His two best known pictures, *Eat Drink Man Woman* and *The Wedding Banquet,* which concern contemporary Asian and Asian-American society, would not seem to offer the most conspicuous qualifications for interpreting late eighteenth-century British society. But it was in these films that Doran saw what Lee could bring to *Sense and Sensibility*: a delicate but wry comprehension of social niceties and a flare for satire. Together, Lee and Thompson are terrific; instead of having Elinor rush from the room when she learns the truth about Edward, as in the novel, the camera jocularly follows the three other Dashwood women as they struggle to get out of the room and out of the way.

Besides providing a brilliant script, Thompson endows the film with a solid center by giving a glorious performance as Elinor. She is surrounded by a cast of outstanding actors, among whom she more than holds her own, sounding the right note as the reserved central character who nonetheless lets her emotions loose at just the right moments. Kate Winslet, a relative newcomer, was cast in the other lead role, but her youth and relative lack of experience seems thoroughly appropriate. A number of commentators have remarked that Hugh Grant seems uncomfortable in the role of Edward—or at least uncomfortable in Edward's clothes. This seems unfair. For much of the film Edward is trapped in an exceedingly awkward position, one which Grant's demeanor clearly reflects. And Alan Rickman, usually known for is flamboyant portrayals of film villains, transforms himself into the very essence of the brooding, upright, but romantic Brandon. The supporting cast, too, is terrific, extrapolating on the delicate humor of Austen's work. After Willoughby's rejection destroys Marianne's spirit, the irrepressible but resolutely insensitive Mrs. Jennings seeks some means to comfort her. Winking conspiratorially, she asks if Marianne likes olives. Somehow, it is a hilarious moment.

—Lisa Paddock

Seven

"Seven deadly sins. Seven ways to die."—Movie tagline

"Superior to *The Silence of the Lambs.*"—Johnathon Rosenbaum, *Chicago Reader*

"*Seven* gets a ten!"—Joel Siegel, *Good Morning America*

"A grisly masterpiece."—Jim Seavor, *Providence Journal-Bulletin*

"*Seven* is an evocative, nerve-jangling thriller with a gut-wrenching climax!"—Peter Travers, *Rolling Stone*

"*Seven* is flat out great filmmaking."—Amy Taubin, *The Village Voice*

Box Office Gross: $87,034,954

It is homicide detective William Somerset's (Morgan Freeman) last week on the job. He is a savvy, intelligent and learned man, and he's burned out by the "mean streets" of the urban jungle in which he works. Taking his place is the comparatively boorish and definitely cocky David Mills (Brad Pitt) who is as easy to anger as he is to frustrate, and yet also has an eagerness for his job that Somerset has long since lost.

During this transition week, Somerset and Mills find themselves suddenly investigating a series of murders, each more bizarre and grotesque than the last. A grossly obese man is forced to eat spaghetti (and a few pieces of floor linoleum) until he literally bursts internally; a corrupt lawyer has a "pound of flesh" removed from his body and he bleeds to death in his opulent offices; a drug-dealing pedophile is chained to his bed and very slowly starved to death for a year.

It doesn't take Somerset long to discern that this is the work of a serial killer. But what an unusual set of victims (none of them are innocent), and what an unusual set of modus operandi (each victim exemplifies one of the seven deadly sins). "These murders are [the killer's] sermons to us," says Somerset as he connects gluttony to the fat man's murder, greed to the lawyer's, and sloth to the pedophile's. These murders are their atonements for their sins—whether they wanted to do penance or not. But with three sins down, the detectives know there are four more victims just waiting out there. The question is, will they be able to figure out who this murderer with a penchant for religious literature is before he strikes again?

The answer is no. The next victim, a prostitute murdered with a particularly nasty sex toy exemplifies the sin of lust. Somerset now takes to the library (and a particularly unsavory FBI agent) to research the inspirations used by the villain in this morality play. Eventually an illicit lead from the FBI guides them to an apartment just as the killer is returning home. He runs, with Mills in hot pursuit, but he escapes—however, he also mysteriously spares Mills' life. There is no doubt now that the killer is obviously spooked, and this brings on the fifth murder, pride—a beautiful model with her nose cut off (to spite her face?) and a phone glued to one hand (life but ugliness) and a bottle of sleeping pills (death) in the other. In her pride and vanity, she has chosen the pills.

With two sins left, wrath and envy, the filmmakers have an unusual and demented twist awaiting the audience which would be entirely unfair to disclose here, but in the words of the murderer (whom the filmmakers also wish reviewers to keep under wraps), "If you want people to listen, you can't just tap them on the shoulder, you have to hit them with a sledgehammer." And with this sledgehammer, the film shocks the viewer to the core.

Brad Pitt actually broke his hand during a fall while making this film and a cast had to be written into his part.

Audiences may be left feeling the same way the murderer said those who witness his murders would feel: "When it's finished, people will barely be able to comprehend. But they won't be able to deny." While one can't deny that *Seven* is a visually stylistic film that lingers long in the memory, one may also only be barely able to comprehend why one sat through it. The loving detail of each gruesome murder is only obliterated by an occasional oblique camera angle and the unrelenting gloom and rain of this unnamed every-city urban area. But somewhere in the most primal heart of each of us is the person who drives

AWARDS AND NOMINATIONS

Chicago Film Festival Awards 1995: Best Cinematography (Khondji)
National Board of Review Awards 1995: Best Supporting Actor (Spacey)
New York Film Critics Awards 1995: Best Supporting Actor (Spacey)
Academy Awards Nominations 1995: Best Film Editing
British Academy Awards Nominations 1995: Best Original Screenplay (Walker)

slowly past road accidents—not because we are concerned for the safety of those who stop to help, but to see a fate that might have been ours. Watching *Seven* is like gawking at an accident. We may not want to see the wreckage, but we can't seem to turn our heads.

We (and the filmmakers?) try to justify this staring by dressing up these gory contents with the intellectual works of Dante and Chaucer and St. Augustine, but their cerebral depths are constantly being countered by stomach-churning superficialities.

Contributing to this confusing feeling of aversion and attraction is the film's almost mesmerizing style. Although some scenes may be too dark, and the background noise unrelenting, from its scratchy disorienting opening credits to its claustrophobic startling ending (in an incongruously wide open geographical area), we can't stop watching.

This is not to say *Seven* doesn't have its share of plot problems. Mills' wife, Tracy (Gwyneth Paltrow) seems to be a token who is only needed in the film as a ploy for the ending. The killer's background and motives are never explained, which gives a feeling of incompleteness to the story (but the filmmakers would probably say that that's just like life). And the idea of the FBI tracing the killer through his library card leaves even the intellectuals wondering if they should join a militia—until one realizes that the killer probably would have bought his own books and written all through their margins in obsessively small handwriting. Also, with a little Monday-morning quarterbacking, one may also wonder why the killer who has planned these murders for at least a year (see "sloth") managed to come up with the ending he did which involves a character who has only been in town for a week. But perhaps most jarring of all is that after most of the film has taken place over a week's worth of darkness and rain, for the ending we suddenly find a nearby incredibly sunny and dry desert. What are the odds?

However, undoubtedly the most outstanding element of this film is Morgan Freeman's performance—and it can overcome virtually any of the film's problems. He is a marvel to watch in action.

His portrayal of the intelligent yet world-weary Somerset is a subtly shaded and moving performance. While Pitt is filling the screen with obscenities and an almost unfocused energy, Freeman involves the viewer through his underplayed pauses and glances and his softly delivered pearls of wisdom. This may make the two characters balance each other in the film, but it is Freeman's performance we admire and remember....that and the grisly murders. As to which accounts for *Seven*'s overwhelming box office success, well, that's anyone's guess.

—Beverley Bare Buehrer

CREDITS

William Somerset: Morgan Freeman
David Mills: Brad Pitt
Tracy Mills: Gwyneth Paltrow
Police Captain: R. Lee Ermey
California: John C. McGinley
Talbot: Richard Roundtree
Mrs. Gould: Julie Araskog
Greasy FBI Man: Mark Boone Junior
Officer Davis: John Cassini
Dr. Santiago: Reginald E. Cathey
Dr. O'Neill: Peter Crombie
John Doe: Kevin Spacey

Origin: USA
Released: 1995
Production: Arnold Kopelson and Phyllis Carlyle; released by New Line Cinema
Direction: David Fincher
Screenplay: Andrew Kevin Walker
Cinematography: Darius Khondji
Editing: Richard Francis-Bruce
Production design: Arthur Max
Art direction: Gary Wissner
Set decoration: Elizabeth Lapp, Lori Rowbathom and Hugo Santiago
Costume design: Michael Kaplan
Music: Howard Shore
Casting: Billy Hopkins
MPAA rating: R
Running Time: 125 minutes

REVIEWS

Chicago Tribune. September 22, 1995, Section Friday. p. 4
The Detroit Free Press. September 22, 1995, p. 1F+
The Detroit News. September 22, 1995, p. 7F
Entertainment Weekly. September 22, 1995, p. 36+.
The New York Times. September 22, 1995, p. C18.
Premiere. August 1995, p. 31.
Time. September 25, 1995.
USA Today. September 22, 1995, p. 4D
Variety. September 20, 1995.

S.F.W.

"Words to live by..."—Movie tagline

When a film titles itself as a profane variant of "So what?" it risks posing a fatal question. In the case of *S.F.W.*, the answer is a shrug of the shoulders. Not only is this film poorly conceived, horribly made and ugly to look at, it's pointless.

A beery, loud, self-absorbed and listless film aimed at the teenage "slacker" crowd, *S.F.W.* is an obvious and contrived commentary on how the entertainment industry manufacturers instant celebrities. Its reluctant hero, working-class slob Cliff Spab (Stephen Dorff) attains cult status when he goes to a convenience store with his buddy Joe Dice (Jack Noseworthy) to get a six-pack of beer. (The names, like everything in the film, are painfully contrived.) Cliff and Joe and a few others in the store are held hostage for 36 days by camera-wielding terrorists. Their captors, for reasons never-explained, force videos of the hostages to be aired on prime-time television during their siege. Twenty-year-old Cliff, who has a bent sense of humor and an air of reckless defiance, becomes the show's star, along with his requisite romantic interest: 17-year-old Wendy Pfister (Reese Witherspoon).

This mildly interesting premise is the only idea in the film, which is co-written and directed by Jefery Levy. But any tension is completely spoiled by the film's self-defeating structure. In the first few minutes, we learn that the hostages escaped but only Cliff and Wendy survived, emerging from their ordeal to find they have become fodder for the talk-show and magazine-cover circuit. The remainder of the film is spent tracking Cliff's tortured, cliched struggle to come to grips with his celebrity status and his half-hearted efforts to reunite with Wendy.

As Cliff runs from fame, there is plenty of loud grunge rock on the soundtrack, lame encounters with a couple of unappealing friends, and little real action. Filled with remorse over his friend Joe's death, Cliff returns home with a friend and smashes everything in his bedroom, using an arm that a second earlier was in a sling. Then Cliff goes to Joe's sister's house to bed her down in a gruesomely unattractive sex scene accompanied by a song about a "teenage whore." Cliff then hangs for awhile with his friend Morrow Streeter (Jake Busey), a strange guy who beats up an auto parts store worker and later holds a gun to the head of his alcoholic girlfriend. There's a sequence with Morrow's classy older sister, a lawyer who wants a piece of Cliff's fame. Cliff escapes and is taken for a ride by a pair of aging, drug-crazed hippies. Throughout, everyone is high on something, mostly booze and pot, and everyone hails Cliff as a great hero for saying what's been on America's mind, which is apparently nothing more than that things are hopelessly screwed up and who cares anyway.

"Your message is that there is no message," Wendy finally tells him, "that nothing really matters." The script is full of this kind of alarmingly overwrought cliche. Cliff is the ultimate slacker icon surrounded by sycophants. But Levy tries to have it both ways: he wants to satirize Cliff's cult status and his lame-brained followers but he also wants to make his anti-hero into a teenage box office bonanza. Levy undermines his own attempts at irony by making Spab almost a Christ-like figure, and Dorff cooperates by feigning long-suffering expressions. We're supposed to feel sorry when Cliff looks into a glass of beer, or into an admiring crowd of groupies, and experiences a flashback of the hostage days, but all we feel is weary of Levy's lame and obvious techniques.

The terrorists wear white lab garb, just in case the audience doesn't understand that Cliff is the victim of an experiment. Levy also belabors the point that the hostage situation is just like Cliff's real life, hopeless and pointless. In case you miss that message, there's a flashback that has Joe spelling it out. And Cliff and Wendy endlessly lament that life is crazier on the outside than it was in the old hostage days. This is all supposed to be preciously clever commentary, but it's hollow and hackneyed.

CREDITS

Cliff Spab: Stephen Dorff
Wendy Pfister: Reese Witherspoon
Morrow Streeter: Jake Busey
Joe Dice: Jack Noseworthy

Origin: USA
Released: 1995
Production: Dale Pollock for Polygram Filmed Entertainment and A & M Films, in association with Propaganda Films; released by Gramercy Pictures
Direction: Jefery Levy
Screenplay: Danny Rubin and Jefery Levy; based on the novel by Andrew Wellman
Cinematography: Peter Deming
Editing: Lauren Zuckerman
Production design: Eve Cauley
Set decoration: Sandy Struth
Costume design: Debra McGuire
Music: Graeme Revell
MPAA rating: R
Running Time: 92 minutes

S.F.W. might have been a pointed satire on how the youth culture is even more guilty than the mainstream culture of sanctifying empty-headed celebrities as role models, but Levy cops out, presumably for fear of wounding his target audience. So while most of the adults in the film—Cliff's parents, TV talk-show hosts and a straight-laced couple in an elevator—are heavily satire, Cliff and his pals get kid-glove treatment. Cliff finally reconciles his struggle with celebrity by becoming an MTV-style veejay, as if that were any less of a compromise with his integrity.

The talk-show hosts are laughably made-up figures who are supposed to resemble Phil Donahue and Sam Donaldson, but who look more like refugees from a bottom-drawer sci-fi flick. This is merely the worst aspect of some miserable production and technical glitches. Either the filmmakers are rank amateurs or *S.F.W.* takes some kind of pride in looking bad. It's film grunge carried to an annoying extreme.

The self-congratulatory nature of the slacker images in this film, and Dorff's own performance as an arrogant airhead, are completely at odds with his sappy pursuit of Wendy, a squeaky-clean cheerleader type who seems not at all Cliff's type. But, as Levy repeatedly points out, nobody knows or understands the real Cliff or the real Wendy or what they're really going through in their celebrity prison. Their romance is inexplicable nonetheless, and as saccharine as the one in *Love Story*.

The incompatible parts of *S.F.W.*—the obvious, dim-witted satire; the pandering to youth slacker culture; and the ridiculously sentimental romantic line—are forced together like square pegs in round holes. That's bad enough, but then Levy slams on what's supposed to be a preciously clever surprise ending. That's intended to turn the whole film on its head but instead merely provides minor evidence that there are faint signs of intelligent life on the planet *S.F.W.*

Dorff (who was in *Backbeat*) is an annoying star. He doesn't project enough anger to fill the role of a rebel, and he doesn't project enough intelligence to wear the mantle of a victim. He strives so hard to look like a completely uncaring slob that ultimately his performance doesn't matter; he is a cipher. There are a few more flickers of life in Witherspoon's performance, but not enough to make a difference; her character, like everyone in the film, is written as a caricature.

S.F.W. is like a bad college film project executed by a talentless drone who has illusions that he's an auteur of some sort. We get the hand-held, bouncy camera on occasions when the director remembers he wants a documentary feel. When Levy feels a need for introspective commentary, we get a long shot of Cliff walking across a field as Dorff narrates something about his life being "like a circle spinning out of control." The film has all the subtlety of a sledgehammer but none of the impact.

S.F.W.'s release was delayed nearly six months so it wouldn't conflict with Oliver Stone's *Natural Born Killers*, which has similar themes but far superior execution and a lot more depth. But *S.F.W.* didn't need Stone to blow it out of the water; it quickly vanished into obscurity on its own merits. It probably isn't the worst youth film ever made, but it certainly is one of the most pretentiously bad films of its generation.

—*Michael Betzold*

REVIEWS

Entertainment Weekly. Jan. 27, 1995, p. 34.
Los Angeles Times. Jan. 20, 1995, p. F21.
The New York Times. Jan. 21, 1995, p. 11.
People Weekly. Feb. 13, 1995, p. 28.
Variety. Aug. 29, 1994, p. 43.

Shallow Grave

"A stylish, fast-paced, hard-edged roller coaster of a film."—David Gritten, *Los Angeles Times*

"A smart new shocker."—Anthony Lane, *The New Yorker*

"Stylish, clever and devilishly funny."—Joanne Kaufman, *People*

Box Office Gross: $2,881,508

When *Shallow Grave* opened in London in January of 1995, its Glasgow director Danny Boyle was immediately cheered as Britain's answer to Quentin Tarantino, whose *Pulp Fiction* (1994) was then the hottest ticket in town. Reviewing the film for *What's On,* James Cameron-Wilson claimed that Boyle had "the same sick brilliance, dramatic precision and narrative economy as QT does." Before the London opening, Boyle had tested *Shallow Grave* at a film festival in Munich after its premiere at the Edinburgh Film Festival. Back in Britain, Boyle explained his "mission" for making the film: "we've got to keep people interested in British films" by aiming for "a contemporary audience" and dealing with "contemporary values and contemporary youth in an unsentimental way." The challenge was to make a film that would be both new and innovative as a black comedy.

Certainly films such as *Shallow Grave* are few and far between. Wrought with tension and latent greed, the film is a seething and, ultimately, fatal concoction of brutality, violence, and deceit. Closely following the course of the friendship among three flatmates, the film begins with their caustic, yet comic search for a fourth flatmate, and quickly darkens in both tone and humor as the newly chosen flatmate is subsequently found dead. The discovery of a suitcase filled with money further complicates the situation; becoming the catalyst for each character's development and eventual demise. Having decided to keep the money, the three flatmates dispose of not only the corpse, but their humanity and decency as well. What Boyle places before us is an intricate study of human nature, steeped in cold, calculated realism, blatantly exposing the brutality of humanity, the naked greed driving each character, and the cruelty between "friends."

Boyle and his screenplay collaborator John Hodge drew heavily from the genre of the film noir, and the requisite elements of a film noir plot are easily identifiable within *Shallow Grave* . The three friends in question, David (Christopher Eccleston), a strait-laced accountant, Alex (Ewan McGregor), a shrewd journalist, and Juliet (Kerry Fox), a young doctor, are at the fringes of society, bound together by a mutual disregard for social practice and procedure, as is evident in their process of interviewing prospective flatmates. Having utterly and completely humiliated each applicant for their own enjoyment, it is obvious from the onset that these three friends cannot be expected to act according to the accepted ideas of behavior deemed correct and proper by society. It comes as no surprise, then, that Hugo (Keith Allen) is selected as the fourth flatmate. Hugo is a man of few words, and ultimately, remains so, as he is found dead only a few days after he has moved in. It isn't the discovery of their new flatmate's corpse that most disturbs Alex, Juliet, and David, however; it is the discovery of a suitcase full of money hidden beneath Hugo's bed.

In juxtaposition to these early scenes, the viewer is also introduced to some rather shady characters, their menacing nature clearly identified by their superb ability to inflict pain, as we witness the horrific and hellish torture inflicted upon one of Hugo's acquaintances in an effort to locate Hugo. It seems Hugo was not at all what he appeared to be, a recurrent motif throughout the film, and one central to the film noir tradition. As the three flatmates discuss their options following the untimely demise of Hugo, Boyle never lets us forget what is ultimately behind their deliberations, as each shot includes the open suitcase and the stacks of cash in the foreground, and as the focus of the shot. While Alex and Juliet immediately agree to keeping the money for themselves, and disposing of the body, David repeatedly insists upon calling the police; a futile, if not foreshadowing, attempt on his part to retain his own, rather weak, sense of reason. Yet, after a few days, during which Hugo's decomposing body languishes in the fourth bedroom, David relents, and agrees to the plan. This submission is a strong allusion to film noir conventions and the weak nature of the leading man in the face of temptation. The allusion is well-placed, however, as David, an accountant, is characterized by his talent for meticulous and orderly calculation, yet ultimately, by his talent for meticulous and orderly brutality.

The premise of *Shallow Grave*, also borrowed from film noir, is one that both fascinates and frightens the viewer. Boyle uses this duality to heighten and cultivate the horrific nature of the process in which the flatmates dispose of the body, as well as the brutal consequences of their decision to do so. Once Alex, Juliet, and David transport Hugo's body to a remote and secluded forest, the intimation of what is to occur becomes terrifyingly clear. Alex and Juliet, having decided they cannot participate in the rendering of Hugo's body as unidentifiable, leave David with this horrible responsibility. This turn of events, characteristic of film noir, traps David within a situation from which he is unable to escape. He finds himself becoming further and further immersed in all that is occurring, and increasingly less in control of his life. Thus David finds himself responsible for the removal of Hugo's hands and feet, and the obliteration of any and all identifying facial features. In silhouette, one sees David frantically sawing, and, as one hears the chilling sound of a handsaw grinding against bone, the scene becomes overwhelmingly effective without resorting to graphic and sensational violence. This is not to say neither is employed at other points during the film, as both are equally effective during subsequent scenes.

Having returned to the flat, Alex and Juliet set their sights upon the suitcase, descending upon the boutiques and shops in a frenzied spending spree, while David begins his own descent, a descent into madness. Having discovered his friends' lavish spending spree, David reacts by asking if either has considered the cost for all they have done, the cost for all that they have sacrificed. Squirreling the suitcase away in a corner of the attic, David places himself in charge of the care and protection of the money. Initially, David's concern seems wise and well-placed, as it is only a matter of time before the two men torturing Hugo's friend will locate Hugo's new address, and come to retrieve the suitcase.

The two men succeed in "breaking" their victim and then break into the flat swiftly and suddenly, quickly immobilizing Alex and Juliet. Having had his shins beaten by a lead pipe, Alex sends the thugs into the attic after the suitcase, and David. What neither Alex nor the thugs take into consideration, however, is the state into which David has deteriorated. No longer the meek, well-mannered accountant, David has become a brutal killer. Once again, we are unable to see what is occurring, as only the sound of one body, and then another, falling to the floor of the attic is heard. The subsequent shot, of first one body, and then the other, falling through the hatch onto the floor of the entryway, followed by David silently leaping to the floor below, switchblade in hand, is evidence enough of the change in David. Disposing of the bodies in the very same manner in which he was once forced to dispose of Hugo, David is now a frenzied killer, and far more vicious, as we later discover one of the bodies has been skinned. In a departure from the film noir archetype, David's descent into dementia begins to gain in acceleration and paranoia. This deterioration culminates in his drilling holes into the ceiling of each room so that he is able to know the whereabouts of his flatmates at all times, yet this also suggests the hierarchy of the flatmates in relation to their individual cunning and deceit. While David retreats to the attic and surveys them from above, Alex and Juliet scheme to retrieve the money below.

No film noir would be complete without its femme fatale, and Juliet certainly proves herself more than capable of filling that role. Having become involved with David, ultimately to better acquaint herself with the whereabouts of the suitcase, Juliet preys upon the desires of both her flatmates in a well-planned scheme to gain the contents of the suitcase for herself. Nothing is as simple and as clear as it seems, however, in *Shallow Grave*, and the character of Alex is certainly no exception. Remaining pompous and detached throughout the film, Alex is directly confronted with the reality of what has occurred, as well as his own sense of loyalty and self-preservation once the bodies have been discovered, and his own paranoia begins to set in. Having been assigned the story of the discovery of three "shallow graves" in a nearby forest, Alex seems decidedly unnerved, and very close to confessing to the two investigators regularly appearing at the flat in search of information. It is Alex, however, who is ultimately able to outsmart everyone.

The final sequence of *Shallow Grave* is perhaps the most nerve-wracking sequence of events to have been captured on film. In the tradition of film noir, the resolution of all that has occurred is no simple matter; there are sudden, as well as shocking, reversals, revelations, and reverberations. The flat is dark, and eerily quiet as Alex tentatively dials the number of the police investigator, to confess to his flatmates' involvement we suppose, and as David silently saunters toward the front door, suitcase in hand. He is stopped, however, by Juliet, fully clothed, and curious about where he may be going at such an hour. Having noticed the phone cord stretched across the foyer, David calls to Alex, and in-

CREDITS

Juliet Miller: Kerry Fox
David Stephens: Christopher Eccleston
Alex Law: Ewan McGregor
Hugo: Keith Allen
Detective Inspector McCall: Ken Stott
Detective Constable: John Hodge
Cameron: Colin McCredie
Woman visitor: Victoria Nairn
Male visitor: Gary Lewis

Origin: Great Britain
Released: 1994 (1995 U.S.)
Production: Andrew McDonald for Film Four International, in association with the Glasgow Fund and Figment Film; released by Gramercy Pictures
Direction: Danny Boyle
Screenplay: John Hodge
Cinematography: Brian Tufano
Editing: Masahiro Hirakubo
Production design: Kave Quinn
Casting: Sarah Trevis
Sound: Colin Nicholson
Costume Design: Kate Carin
Music: Simon Boswell
MPAA rating: R
Running Time: 91 minutes

sists he come out into the hallway to join them. David accuses Juliet of planning to escape with the money herself, as he has found a plane ticket in her bureau which Alex claims to have purchased. A struggle between David and Juliet quickly ensues, and the suitcase is momentarily in the possession of first David, and then Juliet. Once Alex becomes involved, the brawl moves toward the kitchen, where David quickly grabs a large knife, and plunges it into Alex's shoulder, pinning him to the kitchen floor. Just as he is about to reach for a second knife, Juliet comes from behind, grabs the knife, and quickly dispatches of David by stabbing him through the throat. In a state of shock, or so we suppose, Juliet pulls the knife from David's body, and turns to face Alex. As he breathes a sigh of relief, Juliet plunges the knife into his other shoulder, completely pinning him to the floor. As she removes her shoe to pound the knife further into the floorboard, we are finally offered a glimpse of the true nature of Juliet, a dangerous femme fatale. Escaping with the suitcase, she leaves both her "friends" in an ever widening pool of blood, and heads toward the airport.

In what would seem the perfect ending, however, there is yet another twist in store for us, and this, too, is typical of film noir. Alex, having managed to survive, although remaining pinned to the kitchen floor, is questioned by the investigator, as a smile slowly creeps across his face. As the camera moves down from the handle of the knife toward the floorboard, the shot is intercut with shots of Juliet in her car, about to open the suitcase. The camera moves further down, and we see Juliet again, a rage passing over her face as she finds the suitcase is filled with stacks of bill-sized pieces cut from the newspaper article Alex had written about the bodies found in the forest. The camera moves further down, and we see the end of the knife beneath the floorboard, and Juliet running toward the ticket counter at the airport. The camera moves further down, and we see the drops of blood slowly falling upon stacks and stacks of money, neatly hidden beneath the floorboards.

In the final shot of the film, we see David, laid upon an examining table in the morgue, the very same shot with which the film began. It is the final, and most taunting irony of the film, as we were led to believe from the onset that David survived to provide the voice-over for the story of the three friends. The noir voice-over, as we are now aware, is that of Alex, and there is a sudden shift in our perception. Where the introductory passage, "I think we all need friends... but if you can't trust your friends, well, what then?" once seemed sincere, but it is now sarcastic, and callous; what once seemed certain is now distorted by mistrust, and skepticism. Yet it is this final revelation that reiterates the noir tone of *Shallow Grave*, and that answers the very question posed by Boyle. Having asked, "What's a little murder between friends?" we have been given an engrossing, and extremely honest answer in Boyle's portrait of three friends and all that came between them.

Danny Boyle was excited by the screenplay John Hodge had written because, as he explained in a promotional statement, "unlike most British writing for television or screen, it was very simple, very dramatic and didn't carry a lot of history or moral baggage with it. Although its social milieu is very British, there is something 'American' about its absolute concentration on the drive of the narrative." John Hodge, a doctor by profession, studied medicine at the University of Edinburgh and practiced there until he took time off for writing *Shallow Grave* in 1992. In the film he plays the role of Detective Constable Mitchell. After his acting and writing debut, he now practices medicine in London. He admits to having watched and imitated "a succession of American films" and designing the story to move quickly so there is no time for the characters to examine "the rights and wrongs of their actions."

The film was not received with the same level of enthusiasm in the United States as it was in Britain. Hal Hinson of *The Washington Post* dismissed it as a "passable thriller," and Anthony Lane of *The New Yorker* opined that the film was "too smart, at times, for its own good" and was appalled by the reaction of a "smiling, unshockable, Tarantino-trained audience." Others objected to the lack of character definition and the shallowness of the style. Obvious comparisons were made to Hitchcock and the Coen brothers, however, and Janet Maslin of *The New York Times* concluded, after objecting to the "emptiness" of the characters, that the film was "too visually savvy to ignore."

—Melissa Brabetz and James M. Welsh

REVIEWS

Entertainment Weekly. No.265, March 10, 1995, p.49.
Movieline. March, 1995, p.40
New York. Vol.28, No.9, February 27, 1995, pp.110-111.
The New Yorker. February 13, 1995, pp. 92-94.
The New York Times, February 10, 1995, C-17.
Premiere. Vol.8, No.6. February 1995, p.26.
Sight and Sound. Vol.5, No.5 (NS), January, 1995, pp. 57-58.
The Sun (Baltimore), Maryland Live. March 9, 1995, p.12.
The Sunday Times (London). January 8, 1995, Sec.10, pp.4-5.
The Times (London). January 5, 1995, p. 33.
The Washington Post. February 24, 1995, C-7.
Washington Post Weekend. February 24, 1995, p.36.
What's On (London). January 4, 1995, p. 30, 32.
Variety. May 30-June 6, 1994, p. 46.

Shanghai Triad (Yao A Yao Yao Dao Waipo Qiao)

"Unforgettable! Gong Li steals the movie and our hearts."—Thelma Adams, *New York Post*

"Magnificent! Zhang Yimou movingly affirms the magnitude of his storytelling power."—Janet Maslin, *The New York Times*

"Some of the most stunning screen images ever."—Jack Mathews, *Newsday*

Box Office Gross: $561,032

Zhang Yimou, China's leading director, has been responsible for a string of outstanding films which have opened the world to the vitality of China's film industry. *Red Sorghum* (1987), *Raise the Red Lantern* (1991), *Ju Dou* (1989), and *To Live* (1994), all directed by Zhang and starring the stunning Gong Li, have been responsible for both praise among cineastes in the United States and harsh criticism among Chinese critics and censors. *Ju Dou* was the first Chinese film to be nominated for the American Academy Award (as Best Foreign Language film), and the other films have also garnered wide critical praise, numerous awards, and growing attention from audiences.

Zhang's latest film is *Shanghai Triad*, and while it is not as beautiful as *Raise the Red Lantern* nor as epic as *To Live*, it is yet another in a series of visually magnificent, impeccably directed films. *Shanghai Triad*, taken from the novel called *Gang Law* by Li Xiao, is a period piece (1930's) that tells the story of a young boy named Shuisheng (Wang Xiaoxiao), who goes to work for one of Shanghai's crime families. The Tang family is one of two families controlling organized crime in Shanghai, and Shuisheng's elderly cousin (Li Baotian) is the "Boss" of the family. "Being a Tang will change your life," Shuisheng is told by his Uncle Liu (Li Xuejian), and it does.

Having been born and raised in the country, Shuisheng is mesmerized and frightened by the bustling, glamorous world in which he finds himself. Director Zhang does an excellent job at creating a sense of awe in the audience by immediately focusing on Shuisheng's reactions. The very first camera shot in the film is of Shuisheng's awestruck, openmouthed face, surrounded by the countless faces and sounds of Shanghai. From then on, much of the film is told through the eyes of Shuisheng, who witnesses everything from murder to illicit affairs, all by chance. Youthful actor Wang Xiaxiao's simplicity and naivete become the window through which the audience experiences the story.

Zhang brilliantly uses the juxtaposition of Shuisheng's innocence as a metaphor for the loss of innocence in China during that period. Given the political nature of Zhang's other films, it is fair to say that Zhang might be making a statement about the negative influence of the European and American administration of Shanghai that prevailed in the early part of the century. This is not only a coming-of-age film, but also a film about the lost innocence of a people. To extend the symbolism even further (and, hopefully, with some accuracy), it is possible that the "triad" of the title might be a veiled allusion to Britain, France, and the United States, all of whom exerted influence on Shanghai at that time. Perhaps Shuisheng, a simple country boy, might represent the simple ways of the Chinese peasants that were corrupted by the Westerners' arrival. All of this may be mere speculation, however, since Zhang has stated in various media that in making this film he wanted to avoid the trouble brought about by his last film, *To Live*. (In fact, this film encountered legal problems during its production due to the government's displeasure over *To Live*.) As a result, some critics have said that *Shanghai Triad* is the most conventional film audiences can expect from Zhang Yimou.

The film does not need to be a work of great symbolism, however. It is a good story (adapted for the screen by Bi Feiyu from the novel *Men Gum [Gang Law]* by Li Xiao), and the story is absorbing and touching whether or not it is symbolic of larger themes. Shuisheng goes to work for the Boss' beautiful young mistress, Xiao Jinbao (Gong Li), an arrogant, spoiled, cynical nightclub singer, whose stage name is "Bijou." Having herself come from the country, Bijou does her best to hide her humble roots, treating Shuisheng with disdain and cruelty in order to prove her own superiority. Insisting that he call himself "Shuisheng the bumpkin," and calling him "a moron," Bijou strikes fear into Shuisheng immediately.

But Shuisheng's silence and hard work earn her respect by the second or third day, and Bijou gives him several gold coins to put away for "your future." Shuisheng's Uncle is killed while defending the Boss from an attack by the rival family, and Shuisheng, Bijou, the Boss, and others go to a remote island to ensure their safety. Having been told that his uncle's "open eyes cry out for vengeance," Shuisheng begins to feel more secure with the Boss and Bijou. But complications arise. Bijou's affair with the Boss's right hand man, Mr. Song (Shun Chun), is revealed, and Shuisheng uncovers a plot to murder Bijou and the Boss. While the film is not overly violent, it does have its share of bloodshed: several other murders take place before the film is through. Just like *The Godfather* (1972) and other films about gangster life, the bodies pile up as the various intrigues play out between the rival families.

The film ends with the bleak realization that Shuisheng is doomed, and that Bijou's and Shuisheng's lives have been wasted by the corruption that has taken over Shanghai. Director Zhang's pessimistic ending is in keeping with his past themes of the Chinese people's loss of innocence. The images he creates of the crime bosses excesses are sumptuous and fascinating. Zhang has an extraordinary ability to make achingly beautiful pictures out of simple things: boats on a canal, a half-open door that reveals a lavishly decorated bedroom, a trio of people standing on a crude pier, framed by tall reeds. Some of these simple images are among Zhang's most powerful. But he also works magic in the early scenes in the Tang family nightclub where Bijou performs. Cinematographer Lu Yue Zhang evokes the period through the extensive use of amber light. In the nightclub scenes, he filters his images through a haze of smoke that causes the images to be diffused just enough to be reminiscent of old photographs.

Zhang creates visual motifs which emphasize the difference between Shanghai and the remote island where Shuisheng hides out with the Boss and Bijou. For example, in the Shanghai scenes, virtually none of the indoor lighting is natural: every lamp and every candlestick are lit in the Tang family home and nightclub, and there are virtually no lights at Bijou's house except for the one in her bedroom. Once the characters move to the island, Zhang emphasizes the "culture shock" simply by bringing much of the action out-of-doors and into natural light.

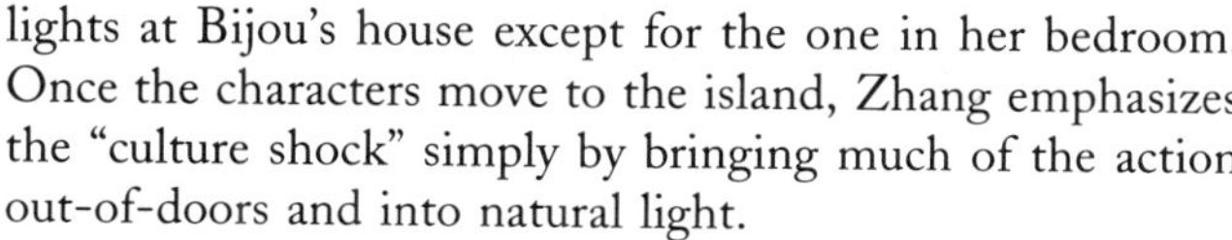

It is the move to the island that leads to the film's tragic ending. Petulant and bored, Bijou decides to walk over to the home of the woman, Cuiha, who lives on the island with her small daughter, Ajiao. Deciding on a whim to borrow some peasant clothes, Bijou discovers a man in Cuiha's bed. Having been followed to Cuiha's house by the Boss' men, this innocent visit ends up costing the lives of several people. It also causes Bijou to re-examine the values that led her to her life with the Boss. Her childlike revelations about having herself been a country girl who was corrupted by city life are painfully wrought by Gong Li.

Gong Li is once again wondrous and touching in portraying a woman whose life has been compromised by both her cultural context and her gender. As in *To Live*, where she played an honest woman who faces constant tragedies in the face of her husband's foibles and in the face of political turmoil, Gong Li plays a woman virtually trapped by her culture and gender. In her early scenes, her imperiousness is almost comical, as she commands everyone around her like an Empress. During her initial scenes with Shuisheng, in which she cruelly orders him about like a slave, it appears that Gong Li's trademark sensitivity may have been set aside in favor of playing a cartoonish vixen. But as the events on the island unfold, she reveals her character as a woman with deep sadness and regret, longing for her lost innocence. A scene in which she sings a nursery rhyme is tender and sad, and the nursery rhyme itself provides an ironic commentary on the tragic loss of innocence that closes the film.

While many followers of Zhang have seen this as his most conventional film, and some have felt that it did not possess the depth of *To Live*, *Shanghai Triad* is no less filled with political symbolism, striking imagery, and sensitivity than any other of Zhang's films. But this time around, he has wrapped his ideas up in an apparently simple story. Looks may be deceiving; there is more here than meets the eye.

—*Kirby Tepper*

CREDITS

Xiao Jinbao(Bijou): Gong Li
Tang, the Triad Boss: Li Baotian
Uncle Liu: Li Xuejian
Song, No.2: Shun Chun Shusheng
Boy: Wang Xiaoxiao Cuihua
Widow: Jiang Baoying

Origin: People's Republic of China and France
Released: 1995
Production: Jean-Louis Piel, Yves Marmion and Wu Yigong for a Shanghai Film Studios/Alpha Films, UGC Images, and LaSept Cinema production; released by Sony Picture Classics
Direction: Zhang Yimou
Screenplay: Bi Feiyu; adapted from the novel *Men Gum (Gang Law)* by Li Xiao
Cinematography: Lu Yue
Editing: Du Yuan
Art direction: Cao Jiuping
Costume design: Tong Huamiao
Sound: Tao Jing
Music: Zhang Guangtian
Running Time: 108 minutes

AWARDS AND NOMINATIONS

Academy Awards Nominations 1995: Best Cinematography (Yue)
Golden Globe Awards Nominations 1996: Best Foreign Film

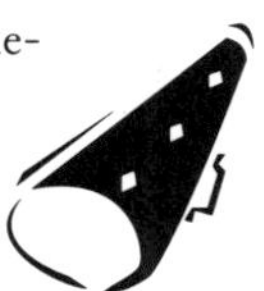

A Short Film About Love

Spying, no doubt a matter of touchy concern in Communist Poland, becomes eroticized in *A Short Film About Love*, much as Hitchcock was to mask its McCarthyesque dimensions in *Rear Window* (1954).

Krzyzstof Kieslowski's film, released belatedly in this country, thus becomes for us as much a tightly wrought, intimate romantic melodrama as a project of deciphering just how much a gifted filmmaker could get past the committees of a state-run film industry. The surprise in store though is how, through a skillful blend of modest filmic form and clever story content, Kieslowski and his scenarist, Krzysztof Piesiewicz, are able to set us thinking about the complex interplay between cinema, technology and desire in our own lives.

Tomek (Olaf Lubaszenko), a 19-year-old postal worker/student, though an orphan, lives in a high-rise apartment through the good graces of a friend's mother. Shy, but also mischievous, Tomek breaks into an electronics store to steal a telescope with which he can spy on Magda (Grazyna Szapolowska), a single, attractive, free-spirited painter who lives in the building opposite his. The film confines itself to charting the eccentric nature of their relationship through four distinct stages.

The first stage makes clear that mere looking is not what Tomek is about. He passes up the 'Miss Poland' pageant on TV so he can watch Magda layer an abstract painting. Linked in a sense by the individualistic nature of their respective endeavors, the two are shown biting into their nightly sandwiches at the same time. Tomek's urges, however, rack him with the guilt imposed by a society in which at one time there was little separation between Church and State. These urges also lead him to phone Magda, but when she answers, he is dumbstruck. He even makes a second call, just to apologize. Similarly, he sends her a false notice of a postal money order, but when she comes to his window, he acts merely bewildered. As Magda entertains a lover, Tomek turns away, allowing her that sanctum of privacy.

It thus becomes one of the film's seductive ploys to get us to think of Tomek as an obsessed voyeur, and then to chide us for our dirty minds. When Tomek takes on the added task of a milkman for his block of buildings, he has to ring Magda's doorbell at dawn to remind her to leave the empties out. The sudden sight of her disheveled self has more of an erotic charge for us, through Kieslowski's tight framing, than it does for young Tomek. In fact, the film's most important moments are all rendered in close shots, making us as an audience feel as if we ourselves are spying on Tomek and Magda, rarely shifting our scopophilic gaze from either. Unlike us, however, poor Tomek seems unable to make sense of what he is watching.

When he sees Magda crying, after her second lover has stormed out, Tomek's incomprehension seems childlike in its innocence. "Why do people cry?" he asks his friend's mother. "When they're hurt," she answers. In the next scene, Tomek opens a large pair of scissors and stabs the spaces between the flared fingers of his downturned palm, quickening his pace, until he draws blood. Again, we are led to infer what Tomek and Magda share, unknowingly. She, disconsolate at the kitchen table, spreads the milk she has spilled, idly with her fingers, while he, observing from his distance, sucks the blood from his. Both, the film seems to say, are nursing a hurt they have brought upon themselves. More important, just as Tomek's action throws light on Magda's situation for us, Magda will eventually come to know herself through Tomek's eyes.

The second stage of their relationship brings Tomek's feelings out into the open, though what those feelings are still remain a mystery. After Tomek slips another false notice of a money order into her mailbox, an enraged Magda complains to the postmaster who, in the manner of an all-powerful Party bureaucrat, accuses her of trying to trick the State. After a helpless Magda runs out of the post office, fighting back her tears, Tomek's guilt becomes too much to bear. He runs after her and admits to everything. Within a single shot, Tomek appears to mature in seconds, as he confesses, "I spy on you!" Magda's initial reaction is to push him away, upset. It soon becomes clear, however, that she sees Tomek's actions as nothing more than repressed sexuality, something with which she is familiar. She then embarks on consciously eroticizing their relationship. Keeping to what she feels are Tomek's terms, she moves her bed to the window. Then, while in the embrace of her second lover, she has one eye on Tomek, and even points him out to her lover, who becomes furious and charges out to confront him. Tomek, not wanting to be called a coward, goes down to meet him. The result is a black eye and a bleeding nose.

As Magda attempts to draw Tomek out, she encounters only adolescent insecurity. "Why do you spy on me?" she asks. "Because I love you." "What do you want?" "I don't know." After leading Tomek into an abortive sexual encounter, Magda finds him overcome with inadequacy, as he shrinks away, sobbing. "Finished?" she asks, coldly. "That's all there is to love. Now go to the bathroom and dry yourself!" The humiliation proves too much for Tomek, who runs back to his room and slashes his wrists.

The third stage of the relationship begins during which it is Magda, now the excluded one, who attempts to become a part of Tomek's life. She first uses a pair of binoculars to spy on him, then learns he is away in hospital, but is not told why. It is only at the post office that she finds out that

Tomek has become a legend for "slashing his wrists out of love." Shocked by the news, she collapses. While we would have expected her to know better, it seems it is Tomek who has changed her, instead of the other way around. When she gets a phone call and the line goes dead, she thinks it is Tomek. "You were right!" she screams into the mouthpiece, but there is only silence. Magda is of course referring to love, though what could have caused such a turnaround remains the film's only problematic aspect. But love, for Kieslowski and his scenarist, is a means, not an end.

The film's final scene encapsulates the fourth stage of the relationship. When Magda visits the sleeping Tomek, back from the hospital, she is not allowed to touch him. As she waits for him to stir awake, she looks through his telescope, still pointed at her apartment window. The instrument of Tomek's mysterious desire now becomes her own. As if cleansed by love, Magda is able to behold a parallel world and her hurt within it. As she sits crying at the kitchen table, a wiser, more mature Tomek approaches her and she reaches to him for comfort. In an extreme close shot, no doubt intended to crystallize the confinement of Party ideology, Magda continues looking through her end of the telescope, then closes her eyes, as the film fades out.

A story about love, the film's title seems to say, is not necessarily a love story. What Tomek feels, and what Magda becomes heir to eventually, emerges more as a purity of sensibility, which finds its correlation in the pure technological space of the stolen telescope that brings the two together. We leave their story, struck by the similarity of that space to that of cinema.

In the end, our view of *A Short Film About Love* has to be the result of a dialectic between the 'unreal' we may have been able to glimpse, like Magda, and what has been said and written about the film. Sandra Brooks, in the British journal *Film*, finds it "a sad film, with little relief from its depressing representation of human love." As she sees it, Magda and Tomek will not resume their relationship at the end of the film. She goes on to remark on the "ugly landscapes and cold weather" and "the photography which is drained, sombre coloured and grainy." For her, what is "wonderful" about the film is that it is "devoid of any moralizing" and "more an observation of human life and those deprived of love and identity." Philip French, in the *London Observer*, notes that "Kieslowski involves us in his anti-hero's voyeurism, making us embarrassed with ourselves..." Kieslowski himself has admitted to his film originating in an impulse to make his audiences perceive afresh the moral firmament under which they lead their daily lives, an idea pervading his Dekalog, a series of ten hour-long films made for television, each based on one of the Ten Commandments. But, Kieslowski emphasizes, "I wanted the audience to ask themselves what the commandment was." *A Short Film About Love* grew out of the sixth film in the series.

—*Vivek Adarkar*

CREDITS

Tomik: Olaf Lubaszenko
Magda: Grazyna Szapolowska

Origin: Poland
Released: 1995
Production: Ryszard Chutkowski
Direction: Krzystztof Kieslowski
Screenplay: Krzystztof Kieslowski
Cinematography: Witold Adamek
Editing: Ewa Smal
Music: Zbigniew Preisner
Running Time: 85 minutes

REVIEWS

Film (Monthly Journal of the BFFS). May/June 1990, pp.6-9.
Observer. 1 April 1990, p. 62.

The Show

"...exudes an infectious, raw energy and allows the performers to speak for themselves."—Susan Wloszczyna, *USA Today*

"A film that bustles with energy...a deft mix of concert footage and offstage interviews."—Richard Harrington, *Washington Post*

Box Office Gross: $2,702,578

A backstage look at hip-hop and rap music with interviews and concert footage of some of the industry's top performers.

"It's like trying to fight fire with fire. You've got to fight fire with water."—Rapper Slick Rick on rappers tough talk

CREDITS

Whodini: Whodini
Craig Mack: Craig Mack
Dr. Dre: Dr. Dre
Naughty by Nature: Naughty by Nature
Run DMC: Run DMC
Snoop Doggy Dogg: Snoop Doggy Dogg
Tha Dogg Pound: Tha Dogg Pound
the Notorious B.I.G.: the Notorious B.I.G.
Warren G.: Warren G.
Slick Rick: Slick Rick
Kurtis Blow: Kurtis Blow
Russell Simmons: Russell Simmons
Kid Capri: Kid Capri

Origin: USA
Released: 1995
Production: Robert A. Johnson, Mike Tollin and Brian Robbins for a Rysher Entertainment; released by Savoy Pictures
Direction: Brian Robbins
Cinematography: Dasal Banks, Larry Banks, Steven Consentino, Ericson Core, John Demps, Todd A Dos Reis, Johnny Simmons (documentary unit) Michael Negrin (concert)
Editing: Michael Schultz
Music: Stanley Clarke
Sound: Abdul Malik Abbot, Swight Brown, Scott Evan, Evan Prettyman, Davis S. McJunkin and Ben Moore
Assistant director: Anton Cropper
MPAA rating: R
Running Time: 93 minutes

Showgirls

"Leave your inhibitions at the door...The show is about to begin."—Movie tagline

"A rich sleazy kitsch-fest!"—Jay Carr, *Boston Globe*

"...An instant camp classic!"—Janet Maslin, *The New York Times*

"...Cult trash...on a spectacular scale!"—*Philadelphia Daily News*

"...It is *All About Eve* in a G-string!"—*Siskel & Ebert*

Box Office Gross: $20,302,961

In 1983 Joe Eszterhas wrote a screenplay about a working girl who had ambitions of becoming a sexy dancer for a film directed by Adrian Lyne called *Flashdance*. Its star, Jennifer Beals, was all but forgotten (she resurfaced in *Devil in a Blue Dress* in 1995), but the idea apparently lingered on in the writer's erotic imagination, and was reworked in *Showgirls*, also about a young woman, Nomi Malone (Elizabeth Berkley), determined to become a sexy dancer in Las Vegas. But Nomi is no working girl; she is a hooker on the make, working her way up through the sleazy strip joints of Vegas to become a showpiece. *Showgirls* might have been entitled "Fleshdance."

Elizabeth Berkley has the same spastic dance moves that Jennifer Beals so artfully introduced in the earlier film, but she has other moves as well, the classic bumps and grinds of burlesque that helped to take *Showgirls* to another rating plateau, the dreaded NC-17 (no children under the age of 17). Since Berkley and scores of other showgirls dance nude in this picture, in earlier times the film would probably have earned an X Rating. The film hardly qualifies as art. It has little more to offer than vulgar dialogue and an almost plotless spectacle of nudity.

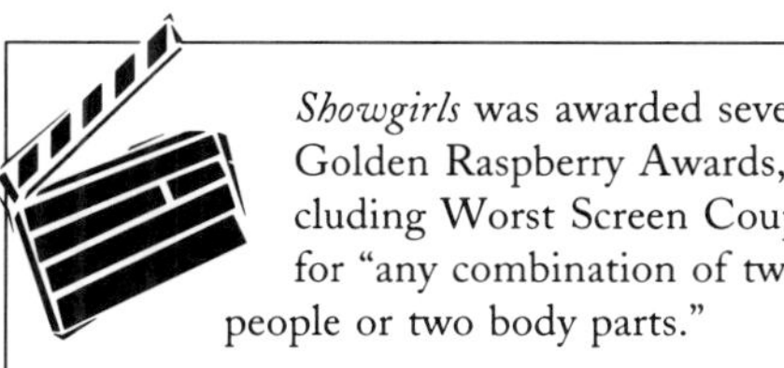

Showgirls was awarded seven Golden Raspberry Awards, including Worst Screen Couple for "any combination of two people or two body parts."

The plot is as scanty as the stripper's G-string, and basically less interesting. It is more about raw ambition than raw sex. The showgirls of the title are stripped down to their bare essentials. The characters are also stripped of any enduring, human qualities; almost without exception they are all flesh and no spirit. "Virtually all the film's human exchanges are sexualized in some debasing manner," Todd McCarthy protested in *Variety*, adding "sex-as-commodity is the overriding theme here."

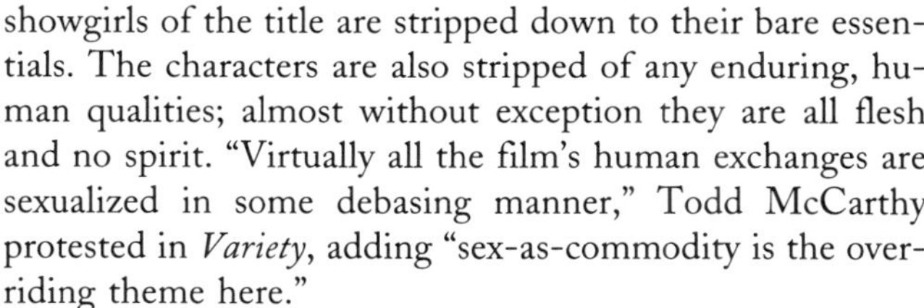

Nomi Malone is determined to make it big in Las Vegas when the film begins with her hitchhiking into town. The driver who brings her to Vegas drives off with her luggage, but the viewer soon learns she is capable of taking care of herself. Even so, she is not a very sympathetic character. Moreover, the actress playing her is not exactly knockout beautiful, making it a moot point whether or not she is clothed. The character is vulgarity personified. Berkley is certainly energetic, but her sweaty, erotic dancing cannot be confused with acting. As one character remarks, her idea of dancing seems to be confused with fornication.

It is rare to see such a high-budget movie with such a no-talent cast, but, then, not much acting talent is required for a nudie spectacle. It is hardly surprising the producers were willing to risk the NC-17 rating. The only selling point of the picture is its continuous nude cavorting. There is one "lap dancing" sequence that is no doubt "stimulating" in what it simulates, but when the same couple later makes love in a kitschy swimming pool, the result is watered down, sex as splashdance. The lap dancing is far more exciting. The problem is that simulated lovemaking requires at least a little acting ability if it is going to seem authentic. Nothing seems authentic here.

"I'm not a whore," brave Nomi keeps asserting, unconvincingly, as she claws her way to the topless top; but she "sleeps" with the director of a dreadful Vegas casino spectacle in order to become the star's understudy. Zack, the director (Kyle MacLachlan), later does a background search and discovers Nomi has indeed turned many a trick. Can this slut turn herself into an honest woman by working the strip joints of Las Vegas? That's what this cretinous screenplay apparently wants us to believe.

Nomi is bad news. She has an attitude that should turn everyone against her (but somehow does not), so why should anyone want this nasty bimbo to succeed? At the height of her success she turns her back on the phony glamour that is Las Vegas, suggesting that she has developed some principles. At the same time, she has only become a star by shoving the reigning beauty, Cristal Connors (Gina Gershon), down a flight of stairs. She even turns her back on Zack when she discovers he is morally corrupt, but who would expect to find a moral paragon in Las Vegas?

In addition to her mendacity and vulgarity, Nomi is handicapped by her stupidity. One imagines the wattage of her I.Q. would not be capable of running a quartz watch. She is uneducated, untrained and foul-tempered, and this ex-hooker is our heroine? None of the characters is especially likable, however, with the possible exception of Nomi's only friend, Molly Abrams (Gina Ravera), a "good" girl who gets raped in one particularly nasty sequence by a performer she admires. Nomi demonstrates her friendship by later kicking the stuffings out of the rapist, also demonstrating unexpected karate skills. It's difficult to take any turn of this absurdly constructed plot seriously.

The Dutch director Paul Verhoeven showed some promise with early features such as *Soldier of Orange* (1979) before he went Hollywood, where he developed a distinctive slam-bam style with such pictures as *Robocop* (1987) and *Total Recall* (1990). Verhoeven and Eszterhas also collaborated on the effectively sleazy thriller *Basic Instinct* (1992). Their combined talents have produced at least one better picture before self-destructing with *Showgirls*.

Eszterhas attempted to defend the film as a morality tale, but this wretched, sad and empty movie cannot be defended as an exposé of how women are exploited in Las Vegas. The women we see (with the exception of Nomi's friend Molly) all appear to be willing victims and are as manipulative as those who would exploit them. Lacking any real talent, Nomi can only advance herself by selling her body. Nor can the film be defended as art. The characters are superficial and lack any endearing or enduring substance. The dialogue is nearly as vulgar as the spectacle.

The reviews were predictably terrible. *The Washington Post* dismissed the picture as "Strip Sleaze," and *The New York Times* headlined its review "$40 million Worth of Voyeurism." Critic Stephen Hunter of the *Baltimore Sun* claimed that *Showgirls* "takes the fun out of nudity," but the silly excess of this picture is risible, if not exactly "fun," and the dialogue is even more laughable. Some religious leaders were outraged, but if they had bothered to see the movie, they would have realized that it is too stupid to be taken seriously, even as soft-core pornography. Noisy protest did little more than to attract attention to a film that, left to its own devices, could not survive long in the movie marketplace on the basis of its achievements. Though the film earned $17 million over its opening weekend, it had little staying power. Like its vulgar star, the picture could only self-destruct in time.

Showgirls is appalling not because of the nude spectacle it promises but because of the cynical calculation it makes about what audiences may be willing to accept. It is not the nature of the spectacle that is truly appalling but the vulgarity of it all. It is clear from the success of confessional television and the proliferation of sleazy talk shows that spectacular vulgarity has become trendy in America, and *Showgirls* represents an attempt to exploit that trend. Purile curiousity made *Showgirls* the top-grossing feature of the

CREDITS

Nomi Malone: Elizabeth Berkley
Zack Carey: Kyle MacLachlan
Cristal Connors: Gina Gershon
James Smith: Glenn Plummer
Al Torres: Robert Davi
Tony Moss: Alan Rachins
Molly Abrams: Gina Ravera
Henrietta Bazoom: Lin Tucci
Phil Newkirk: Greg Tarvis
Mr. Karlman: Al Ruscio
Marty Jacobsen: Patrick Bristow
Andrew Carver: William Shockley
Gay Carpenter: Michelle Johnston
Jeff: Dewey Weber
Penny: Rena Riffel

Origin: USA
Released: 1995
Production: Charles Evan, Alan Marshall, Mario Kassar, Ben Myron and Joe Eszterhas for a Chargeurs and Carolco Pictures production; released by MGM/UA and United Artists
Direction: Paul Verhoeven
Screenplay: Joe Eszterhas
Cinematography: Jost Vacano
Editing: Mark Goldblatt
Production design: Allan Cameron
Art direction: William F. O'Brien
Set design: Stan Tropp
Set decoration: Richard C. Goddard
Costume design: Ellen Mirojnick
Sound: Joseph Geisinger
Choreography: Marguerite Pomerhn-Derricks
Music: David A. Stewart
MPAA rating: NC-17
Running Time: 131 minutes

REVIEWS

The Baltimore Sun. September 22, 1995, E1, E2.
Chicago Tribune. September 22, 1995, p.5.
Detroit Free Press. September 22, 1995, F1, F6.
Entertainment Weekly. No.295, October 6, 1995, pp. 40-42.
The New York Times. September 22, 1995, C1, C16.
The New Yorker. October 9, 1995, pp. 95-97.
Newsweek. September 25, 1995, pp. 88-89.
Rolling Stone. October 19, 1995, p.156.
Variety. Septemper 25-October 1, 1995, p. 91, p. 94.
The Washington Post. September 22, 1995, D7.
Washington Post Weekend. September 22, 1995, p. 43.
The Washington Times Metropolitan Times. September 22, 1995, C16.

weekend it opened, but it would have needed to clear $25 million to cover its costs. There is some comfort in knowing that the film was not exactly a hit with the public and will set no trends and that, apparently, it will be re-edited for an "R" version for video markets. For some it will stick in the memory as perhaps the worst film of 1995, or perhaps of the decade.

—James M. Welsh

Sister, My Sister

"Chillingly effective...powerful...with an erotic edge."—Caryn James, *The New York Times*

Box Office Gross: $217,881

Last year (1994) one of the dominant cinematic achievements of the year was a small-budget, big-performance film called *Heavenly Creatures*. Based on a true story, it was about two young girls in New Zealand who enter into a lesbian relationship. They form what is known as a "shared psychosis," and together they murder one of the girls' mother. The film was nominated for an Oscar and was widely praised by critics for its wonderful directing and astonishing performances.

And now it has happened again. *Sister, My Sister* is virtually the same thing: a small-budget film, based on a true story, about two girls who enter a lesbian relationship that ends in murder. The film has been widely praised and the performances and direction are miraculous. Of course, there are some differences: the girls are British sisters who live in France, instead of British girls who live in New Zealand. The other difference is that they are not really girls, but are old enough that they are more appropriately called women.

Other than that, one could facetiously say that these are the same films. The reason, however, to point out the similarities is that one film about a psychotic lesbian relationship is interesting (and perhaps titillating), appealing to a human fascination for films about crimes of passion; but the presence of two such highly visible and highly praised films might be seen as contributing to a stereotype that lesbian relationships by nature have psychotic, amoral, and tragic ends. Audiences would do well to enjoy this film solely on the merits of its extraordinary gifts, and not interpret that it makes any generalizations about lesbian relationships. For another picture of such relationships, there are films such as *Go Fish* (1994) or *The Incredibly True Adventures of Two Girls in Love* (1995).

Political and social implications aside, this film is truly astonishing. *Sister, My Sister* takes place in France in 1932. Taken from the true story that inspired Genet's classic play *The Maids*, it tells the story of two British sisters, Lea (Jodhi May) and Christine (Joely Richardson), who become maids for the prissy Madame Dansard (Julie Walters) and her frumpy daughter Isabel (Sophie Whitfield). Christine, who has been emotionally scarred by her mother, has worked for Madame Dansard for some time, and has persuaded her to take on sister Lea for a nominal price. "Two girls for the price of one," says the excited Madame Dansard. And they are superior maids, seamstresses and cooks, who live in the same room and maintain a respectful silence around their employers. "Just wait till the Blanchards come to dinner," crows Madame Dansard.

As time passes, their relationship shifts into incest, and they begin spending more time in their room alone. They become a bit more careless in their household duties and stop speaking at all around Madame Dansard and Isabel. Christine becomes jealous of an unspoken friendship between the beautiful Lea and Isabel. Eventually, events progress to a bloody and dramatic conclusion.

In classic tragedy, such as those by Shakespear and Jacob, or in ancient classics such as Aeschylus' *Orestian Trilogy*, the tragedy lies in the faults of the protagonists, their "tragic flaw" makes them powerless to stop themselves from destroying everyone around them. *Othello* is a good example, in that Othello's jealousy causes death and bloodshed that could have been avoided.

The feeling that the tragedy could have been avoided, and that it is brought on not by random events but by the "tragic flaw" of the protagonists makes this film quite classic in its presentation. It also adds to the feeling of suspense. Will the more innocent Lea be saved from her own inner demons and from the more dangerous Christine? The tension between the sisters, and between the sisters and their employers, is so thick that it appears that at some point, someone will snap. And they do.

Credit goes to the taut script by Wendy Kesselman and to Nancy Meckler's direction for maintaining a sense of impending tragedy. Meckler knows how to tell her story through visual images. She presents the simple story creatively, using overlapping scenes and voice overs for an interesting effect. For example, while Madame Dansard is gloating over how wonderful the sisters are, they are seen sewing, ironing, peeling, scrubbing, washing clothes, and polishing silver. Later in the film, a similar voice-over sequence finds the sisters engaged in passionate love-making while Madame Dansard wonders, in voice-over what they are doing in the kitchen.

Meckler never misses a chance to inject a feeling of suspense. When Madame Dansard drops hundreds of tiny beads, Lea, without speaking, slowly tries to pick up the beads with trembling hands. Extreme close-ups of Lea trying to pick up the beads from the floor next to Madame Dansard's foot provide a feeling as suspenseful as awaiting the next appearance of the monster in *Alien* (1979). Occasional shots of a slowly dripping faucet underscore both the characters' escalating carelessness while providing a metaphor: they cannot symbolically "turn the faucet off" of their feelings and behavior. Audiences might subconsciously wonder when the faucet will flow freely.

The visual images are quite striking, from the detailed brocades, satins, and laces of the costumes to the ostentatious interiors of Madame Dansard's home. Nancy Meckler and company have provided a lush picture of upper-middle class France in 1932. Several scenes of Lea and Christine sitting on a bench by the river, dressed in matching hats and coats, watching the ducks play, and framed by lush autumn foliage, are gorgeous. The gruesome images of the final murder sequence are as horrifying as they are fascinating.

A scene where the sisters get their picture taken gives a very real sense of the period, as they are dressed in black dresses with lace collars and period hair-dos so real that one can feel what it must have been like to have a portrait done in those days. Richardson and May are wonderful in this scene as well. Recognizing that these young women would not be used to sitting for pictures like any modern people, they look fearful of and fascinated by the process.

All four of the actresses are nothing short of brilliant. Joely Richardson is tight-lipped and severe as Christine. Her hair tied in a tight bun and her eyes darting back and forth with suspicion and jealousy, she paints a picture of a woman slowly moving toward insanity. Richardson's performance is highly theatrical; she is frightening in the same way as was Judith Anderson in *Rebecca* (1940). Her best moment comes when she finally confronts Madame Dansard, alternately appearing frightened and dangerous.

Jodhi May is sweet and beautiful as the younger Lea. May, like Richardson, relishes the theatricality of her character, being particularly adept at the duality of Lea's nature. Saying, "I slow you down" to her older sister, she is quite fearful of making even the slightest mistake. May's trembling hands and her plaintive pleas that her sister "never leave me" make her a pathetic character who is clearly dominated by her monstrous older sister. The symbiotic relationship established between May and Richardson is as bizarre as (though less cartoonish than) the relationship between Bette Davis and Joan Crawford in *What Ever Happened to Baby Jane?* (1962).

Sophie Thursfield turns in a witty performance as Isabel Dansard, the pampered and petulant daughter of Julie Walters' Madame Dansard. Thursfield looks as if she stepped out of a picture from the 1920's, her chubby frame inappropriately (and humorously) attired in childish outfits that reflect her mother's attempts at infantilizing Isabel. The two actresses play off of each other beautifully and have several choice scenes including one where they play a fast game of solitaire while discussing their bizarre housemaids, and another scene where they dress in absurd hats is hilarious. Walters will be remembered for *Educating Rita* (1983), in which she played a free-spirited working-class woman in present-day England. Walters understands the monstrousness of her own character even while she plays the comedy. She will be hardly recognizable to audiences who remember that film, here playing a stuffy older woman who has nothing better to do than dance around the living room to silly dance music.

Meckler and her actresses have fashioned a psychological thriller of the first order, but it did not receive the same accolades and audiences found by *Heavenly Creatures*. Perhaps because it is more theatrical—the situations are punctuated by melodramatic music, and the characters are very broadly drawn—this film has not enjoyed a long theatrical run in the United States. Audiences who discover it on video will surely appreciate it as a melodrama in the vein of the recent *Dolores Claiborne* (1995) or *Heavenly Creatures*. The saddest part of the lack of American commercial success is that it will take that much longer for these four actresses to be "discovered" by American filmgoers.

—Kirby Tepper

CREDITS

Madame Danzard: Julie Waters
Christine: Joely Richardson
Lea: Jodhi May
Isabelle: Sophie Thursfield

Origin: Great Britain
Released: 1994
Production: Norma Heyman for a Film Four and British Screen production; released by Seventh Art
Direction: Nancy Meckler
Screenplay: Wendy Kesselman; based on the play *The Maids* by Jean Genet
Cinematography: Ashley Ropwe
Editing: David Stiven
Production design: Caroline Amies
Music: Stephen Warbeck
MPAA rating: R
Running Time: 102 minutes

Six Days, Six Nights (A La Folie)

Life with two sisters—the older and competitive Elsa (Beatrice Dalle) and the creative and evasive Alice (Anne Parillaud).

CREDITS

Franck: Patrick Aurignac
Alice: Anne Parillaud
Elsa: Beatrice Dalle
Betty: Marie Guillard
Thomas: Alain Chabat
Raymond: Jean-Claude De Goros

Origin: France
Released: 1995
Production: Alexandre Arcady for a France 3 Cinema and New Light Films production; released by Fine Line Features
Direction: Diane Kurys
Screenplay: Diane Kurys and Antioine Lacomblez
Cinematography: Fabio Conversi
Editing: Luc Barnier
Production design: Tony Egry
Music: Michael Nyman
MPAA rating: R
Running Time: 98 minutes

Smoke

"Where there's smoke...there's laughter!"—Movie tagline
"Two thumbs up!"—*Siskel & Ebert*

Box Office Gross: $8,349,430

The Hong Kong-born, American-educated director Wayne Wang has long expressed his desire to break away from making films only dealing with Asians. Films such as *Chan Is Missing* (1981), *Dim Sum: a Little Bit of Heart* (1985), and *Eat a Bowl of Tea* (1989) are delightful, intimate comedies of manners dealing with Chinese-Americans and Chinese immigrants in urban America. Wang did escape from the art-house ghetto with *The Joy Luck Club* (1993), from Amy Tan's popular novel, a larger scale version of his previous material. The director's only non-Asian-related film prior to *Smoke* is *Slam Dance* (1987), a would-be thriller that completely misfires. *Smoke* represents Wang's typical concerns of family, guilt, responsibility, and desperation transferred to the world of Caucasians and African-Americans in Brooklyn. As with Wang's earlier films, *Smoke* is an affecting blend of drama, comedy, and sentimentality with finely observed insights into the joys and loneliness of contemporary American life.

Wang suggested that Brooklyn-based novelist Paul Auster adapt his "Auggie Wren's Christmas Story," a short story commissioned by *The New York Times* in 1990. Auster expanded this story, which makes up the last few minutes of *Smoke*, into a view of a Brooklyn neighborhood as a microcosm of New York City. The writing of Auster, whose novel *The Music of Chance* was adapted into a 1993 film by Philip Haas, is darker, more sophisticated and dangerous than Wang's cinematic milieu. While Wang honors his collaborator in the film credits by claiming *Smoke* is a film by both the director and his screenwriter, it is much closer to Wang's essential material than to Auster's.

William Hurt and Harvey Keitel star in *Smoke*. © Miramax Films.

Auggie Wren (Harvey Keitel) runs a small tobacco shop on a street corner in Brooklyn where colorful locals with time on their hands hang out. One of Auggie's frequent customers is Paul Benjamin (William Hurt), a novelist who has not written since his pregnant wife was accidentally shot during a robbery. Lost in a daze since her death, Paul is about to walk into traffic when he is saved by Rashid (Harold Perrineau, Jr.), a high school student. Trying to avoid some neighborhood hoodlums who are looking for him, Rashid stays in Paul's apartment for a few days.

Smoke owes a debt to Robert Altman, director of such films as *McCabe and Mrs. Miller* (1971) and *The Player* (1992) who was shown Auster's screenplay by Wang and made suggestions about how to make a collection of fragments more integrated.

Paul, denied parenthood by inexplicable violence, becomes fatherly toward Rashid as he learns more about him, especially after he discovers that Rashid took $5,000 dropped by the criminals trying to track him down. Similar impulses are awakened in Rashid who finds out the father he has not seen in years, since his mother was killed in a traffic accident, is living somewhere north of the city. Even the hard-bitten Auggie is affected by growing family feelings when a former girlfriend, Ruby McNutt (Stockard Channing), arrives from Pittsburgh and the distant past to announce that they have a daughter, Felicity (Ashley Judd), a pregnant crack addict living in a Brooklyn slum.

Like most of Wang's work, *Smoke* has no unified plot, offering instead a series of brief, interrelated character studies. These include Rashid's attempt to get to know his bitter, one-armed father, Cyrus Cole (Forest Whitaker), without revealing his true identity; Paul's return to writing; Auggie and Ruby's confrontation with the angry Felicity; and Auggie's effort to make a profit off illegally imported Cuban cigars only to see them spoiled by a careless Rashid whom Paul has convinced him to hire to work in his shop.

Smoke shows how most of these characters develop not just affection for each other—renewed affection in the case of Auggie and Ruby—but a sense of responsibility for the quality of their friends' lives. *Smoke* triumphs in its most quiet moments as when Auggie shows Paul his life's work, the photographs he has taken across the street from the Brooklyn Cigar Company at Third Street and Seventh Avenue every morning at eight since 1977. When Paul complains that every picture is the same, Auggie challenges him to see how they are different, to open himself up to the variety of everyday life. This scene is a summation of Wang's theory of filmmaking: slow down, pay attention to details, perceive the complexities within the mundane.

In addition to being a master of cinematic mood, Wang consistently elicts effective performances from his actors and continues to do so in *Smoke*, particularly those by Keitel, Channing, and Hurt. In such films as *Thelma and Louise* (1991), *Bugsy* (1991), *Reservoir Dogs* (1992), *Bad Lieutenant* (1992), *The Piano* (1993), and *Pulp Fiction* (1994), Keitel has given more notable performances in the 1990's than any other American actor. His Auggie, who recalls Keitel's tough but kindly police detective in *Thelma and Louise*, gives the actor plenty of opportunity to display his charm, especially when Auggie forgives Rashid for his

CREDITS

Auggie Wren: Harvey Keitel
Paul Benjamin: William Hurt
Thomas (Rashid) Cole: Harold Perrineau, Jr.
Cyrus Cole: Forest Whitaker
Ruby McNutt: Stockard Channing
Felicity: Ashley Judd
Jimmy Rose: Jared Harris
Tommy: Giancarlo Esposito
Jerry: Jose Zuniga
Dennis: Steve Gevedon
Aunt Em: Michelle Hurst
Doreen Cole: Erica Gimpel
April Lee: Mary Ward
Charles Clemm (The Creeper): Malik Yoba
Roger Goodwin: Walter T. Mead
Granny Ethel: Clarice Taylor

Origin: USA
Released: 1995
Production: Greg Johnson, Peter Newman, Hisami Kuroiwa, and Kenzo Horikoshi for a Nippon Film Development, Smokes Production, in association with NDF/Euro Space Productions; released by Miramax
Direction: Wayne Wang
Screenplay: Paul Auster; based on his short story "Auggie Wren's Christmas Story"
Cinematography: Adam Holender
Editing: Maisie Hoy
Production design: Kalina Ivanov
Costume design: Claudia Brown
Sound: Drew Kunin
Music: Rachel Portman
MPAA rating: R
Running Time: 112 minutes

AWARDS AND NOMINATIONS

Independent Spirit Awards Nominations 1996: Best Supporting Actor (Perrineau, Jr.)
Screen Actors Guild Awards Nominations 1995: Best Supporting Actress (Channing)

blunder and when Ruby admits that Auggie may not be Felicity's father.

Keitel's best moment comes near the end of the film when Paul, asked by *The New York Times* to write a Christmas story, wants Auggie to relate such a tale and the shop owner describes his attempt to return a wallet dropped by a would-be thief. (That he is one of the hoodlums after Rashid is one of several such coincidences in the film.) When the young man's blind grandmother mistakes Auggie for her grandson and treats him to Christmas dinner, he repays her kindness by stealing the camera he uses for his daily photographs. Wang's deceptively simple cinematic style is on display here as his camera merely watches the faces of the teller and his listener to register their emotions in the course of the story. Keitel seems to exult in the process of the monologue, and his Auggie breaks into a sly grin at the end when Paul announces he does not believe the story. A coda under the film's closing credits reveals that Auggie's story is true. Wang and Auster observe throughout the film that all the characters have their own ways of interpreting the universe, their individual conceptions of the truth.

"Bullshit is a real talent, Auggie. To make up a good story, a person has to know how to push all the right buttons. I'd say you're up there among the masters."—Paul

Occasionally prone to overacting in her other film and television roles, Channing matches Keitel with her understated performance. Channing displays the complexity beneath Ruby's tawdry surface without condescending to or sentimentalizing the character. Likewise, Hurt avoids similar traps while offering a subtle portrayal of a man struggling to find some reason for living, provided by Rashid's taking Paul outside his self-pity. While the effectiveness of Hurt's performance, his best since *The Doctor* (1991), is slightly undercut by the inconsistency of his Brooklyn accent, he is especially moving when Paul sees his late wife in one of Auggie's photographs.

The melodramatic overtones of some of the material in *Smoke* invite out-of-control acting, and Whitaker and Judd, unfortunately, give in to this impulse. Cyrus is supposed to be angry about his complicity in his wife's death, but Whitaker, a mannered performer at best, makes Cyrus into a pulsating mound of neuroses. Judd, so understated in *Ruby in Paradise* (1993), merely rants in her one scene as Felicity only to sentimentalize the character with a pained expression after Ruby and Auggie leave, one of the few missteps in Wang's direction. In his first film role, Harold Perrineau, Jr., cannot hold his own with Hurt and Keitel.

The success of *Smoke* is not only a result of the collaborative efforts of the actors, director, and screenwriter, but of everyone in the production. Cinematographer Adam Holender, a veteran of such films about New York lowlifes as *Midnight Cowboy* (1969) and *Panic in Needle Park* (1971), helps create a Brooklyn that reflects the characters' view of their environment. Rather than a dark, brooding place, this Brooklyn is full of sunlight since the characters are doing their best to make their way through an often uncaring, hostile world. Fittingly, Tom Waits sings "You're Innocent When You Dream" behind the film's end credits.

—Michael Adams

REVIEWS

Entertainment Weekly. June 23, 1995, p. 36.
Maclean's. CVIII, July 10, 1995, p. 50.
Mademoiselle. CI, July, 1995, p. 69.
The Nation. CCLXI, July 10, 1995, p. 68.
The New Republic. CCXII, June 26, 1995, p. 28.
New York. XXVIII, June 19, 1995, p. 74.
The New York Times. June 9, 1995, p. B10.
People Weekly. XLIII, June 19, 1995, p. 23.
Playboy. XLII, August, 1995, p. 26.
Rolling Stone. June 29, 1995, p. 49.
Variety. CCCLVIII, February 20, 1995, p. 76.
The Village Voice. XL, June 13, 1995, p. 54.

Something to Talk About

"Sensational! Julia Roberts and Dennis Quaid light up the screen."—Bill Diehl, *ABC Radio Network*

"A movie with rich humor, a big heart and a first-rate cast."—Roger Ebert, *Siskel & Ebert*

Box Office Gross: $50,892,190

Director Lasse Hallstrom has shown a knack for exploring American ideals and values through a series of recent films about quirky American families. His *What's Eating Gilbert Grape?* (1993) and *Once Around* (1990) each had a distinctly American feel, showing highly idiosyncratic families with such affection that their oddities seemed perfectly normal. Hallstrom understands love and relationships, and perhaps he brings objectivity to his American subjects because America is not his native country (he is Swedish). Whatever the reason, Hallstrom has once again directed a film about a family in crisis that is humorous, tender, and distinctly American. *Something to Talk About* is nothing fancy—it doesn't have pyrotechnic performances or hugely satisfying scenes of tragedy or comedy—but it does have fine actors, beautiful cinematography, an excellent script by Callie Khouri, and Hallstrom's ability to make the mundane seem almost whimsical.

Callie Khouri wrote the ground-breaking *Thelma and Louise* (1991), for which she won an Academy Award. In *Something to Talk About*, she revisits thematic territory which interested her in *Thelma and Louise*, examining the ways in which women (particularly Southern women) deal with societal expectations. The film is the story of Grace King Bichon (Julia Roberts) and her discovery of her husband Eddie's (Dennis Quaid) extra-marital affair. Grace's reaction (she leaves Eddie immediately) causes problems within the family and within the small, wealthy Southern community in which they live and work.

Wyly King (Robert Duvall), Grace's father, wants her to stay with Eddie because of Eddie's importance in a huge family business deal. Grace's mother Georgia (Gena Rowlands) tells Grace that by leaving Eddie and telling people what he has done, Grace has "gone about this in a way that's gonna make people talk." Georgia asks Grace to "make this a private family affair." But that isn't easy. Grace is angry, and writer Khouri devises several very funny ways in which Grace makes things more and more uncomfortable for both Eddie and her very proper Southern gentry family.

"You marry a guy whose nickname in college was Hound Dog, what did you think was going to happen?"—Emma Rae to sister Grace, who's just discovered husband Eddie's infidelities

One of the funniest moments in the film occurs when Grace attends a meeting of the local ladies' club. Instead of discussing the inclusion of recipes and club socials in an upcoming newsletter, Grace shakes things up by standing up in the middle of the meeting and asking "is there anyone else in here who has [slept with] my husband?" The horrified reactions of the Southern aristocratic woman are hilarious, particularly when Grace gets carried away and tells one woman that her husband has been "keeping all the hookers in town in high heels for years." The women run out of the meeting as if Godzilla were coming to terrorize Tokyo.

Eventually, Grace's outlandish response to her husband's transgression gets her into hot water with her parents. Thinking that her mother already knew, Grace flippantly tells her mother about the affair between Wyly and a local woman. The shock waves resulting from the disclosure cause Georgia to lock Wyly out of the house, and cause the King women to come together, *Thelma and Louise*-style, to define themselves beyond their male-dominated Southern society.

Khouri includes one character who is already quite "liberated" (to use an old cliche). Grace's tough-talking sister, Emma Rae (Kyra Sedgwick), tells it like it is, with her wisecracking responses to her whiny sister and her traditional family: "What did you expect?" she tells Grace, "you married a guy whose nickname in college was 'Hound Dog'!" Sedgwick absolutely steals the show with her sexy, funny performance. This is the part that Eve Arden might have done in earlier years; the unmarried, tart-tongued "sidekick" type. The twist now is that the unmarried Emma Rae, unlike many of her cinematic predecessors, is perfectly well-adjusted to being a single woman.

It is interesting to note that both *Thelma and Louise* and *Something to Talk About* were directed by men. (*Thelma and Louise* was directed by Ridley Scott). That the films appear to be so well-tuned to women's issues is no doubt due to the artistry and sensitivity of the directors, but the credit firmly belongs to Khouri's outstanding screenplays. Without debasing men, she exposes them for the "Hound Dogs" they can be. Wyly and Eddie learn some precious lessons about the value of their marriage and of fidelity, and Georgia and Grace discover their own sense of themselves as they are forced to admit that they have given their power over to the men in their lives.

Hallstrom and Khouri allow the plot to be character-driven; Grace's actions have reactions which set in motion new situations, and so on. Though some of the situations appear a bit cute, they are all in keeping with the idiosyncratic nature of the characters. One scene, in which Grace struggles with her desire to have an affair of her own with a handsome horse trainer, Jamie (Brett Cullen), may be a bit precious: she alternates between jumping on top of Jamie and discussing with him why it is okay that she have this affair. Even if it is a bit cute, the scene works because by this time in the film the audience knows Grace to be anxious and preoccupied. (In the first two or three scenes of the film, Grace forgets to take her young daughter with her when leaving the house.)

Much of the film's success is due to the winning charm of its actors. Julia Roberts delivers arguably her most polished performance yet. Roberts provides a far more well-constructed and thoughtful characterization than she did in *Pretty Woman* (1990). When she discloses the information about her father's affair to her mother, Roberts registers a sadness that shows she realizes the consequences of her behavior. She delivers an excellent monologue about having put away her ambitions to be a veterinarian in order to marry Eddie. This performance is Roberts' demonstration that she is able to grow beyond the "damsel in distress" roles that have made her a huge star.

Perhaps Roberts appears stronger in this film because of her strong co-stars. (Not to take anything away from Roberts, but it is hard to look bad when acting with Gena Rowlands and Robert Duvall.) Rowlands and Duvall both have the ability to boost the quality of any film in which they appear. Duvall plays a variation on the crotchety-but-lovable characters he has done to great acclaim in films like *Tender Mercies* (1983) and *The Great Santini* (1979). As Wyly King, he is the very model of a modern Southern gentleman. Wealthy horse rancher Wyly is forced to reexamine his formerly undisputed role as the head of the household. Duvall is wonderful in an argument with Rowlands, in which she barricades the front door to the house. His bewilderment and frustration are tender and funny, and there is something beautiful in a brief scene when he can be seen pacing outside of his own house, confused and sad that the world is no longer as simple as it used to be. An interesting sidebar is that Duvall, an accomplished horseman, performs his own horse-jumping stunts in this film.

Rowlands is at her best in this film. Rarely have audiences seen this fine actress lately, and it is a treat to see her at first try to quell her daughter's anger, only to cut loose her own anger upon the discovery of her husband's transgression. When she tells Wyly, "you drink too much and you laugh too loud at your own jokes," it is clearly the first time that this proper Southern aristocrat has ever dared to speak her mind. Rowlands brings humor and humanity, and is a pleasure to watch.

Other characterizations are excellent: Dennis Quaid makes a fine repentant rake, and Ann Shropshire is a sly aunt with wicked ideas about revenge.

The actors and the elegant Southern locales are beautifully shot by none other than legendary Sven Nykvist, one of the great cinematographers in film. (Nykvist also served as Cinematographer on *What's Eating Gilbert Grape?*) From the lush photography of the family horse farm to the elegant slow-motion shots of a horse show, Nykvist provides rich colors and exquisite composition.

Jamie tells Grace, "You Southern women are easy to please," to which she replies, "It comes from centuries of being bred to keep our expectations low." Khouri helps her characters to shed some of the expectations of the past, and in so doing they become better people for it. Georgia confronts her husband, and Grace demands more than what her

CREDITS

Grace: Julia Roberts
Eddie: Dennis Quaid
Wyly King: Robert Duvall
Georgia King: Gena Rowlands
Emma Rae: Kyra Sedgwick
Jamie Johnson: Brett Cullen
Caroline: Haley Aull
Hank Corrigan: Muse Watson
Aunt Rae: Anne Shropshire

Origin: USA
Released: 1995
Production: Anthea Sylbert and Paula Weinstein for a Spring Creek production; released by Warner Brothers
Direction: Lasse Hallstrom
Screenplay: Callie Khouri
Cinematography: Sven Nykvist
Editing: Mia Goldman
Production design: Mel Bourne
Set decoration: Robert Holinko
Costume design: Aggie Guerard Rodgers
Sound: Peter F. Kurland
Assistant director: Stephen Dunn
Casting: Marion Dougherty
Music: Hans Zimmer and Graham Preskett
MPAA rating: R
Running Time: 106 minutes

AWARDS AND NOMINATIONS

Golden Globe Awards Nominations 1996: Best Supporting Actress (Sedgwick)

husband can provide. The wonderful symbol of Grace's little daughter riding a challenging horse to victory in a horse show is symbolic of the attempts of these women to reach beyond their narrowly prescribed lives. It is an important message, and the message is wrapped up in a warm, touching, and funny film.

—*Kirby Tepper*

REVIEWS

Daily Variety. July 31, 1995. p. 35
Newsweek. August 7, 1995. p. 60

Species

"Men cannot resist her... Mankind may not survive her."—Movie tagline

"Sexy, horrifying and absolutely gripping."—Patrick Stoner, *Flicks*

"*Species* delivers the grisly goods. The film is riveting."—Michael Medved, *Sneak Previews*

"A sci-fi jolt-athon."—Susan Wloszczyna, *USA Today*

Box Office Gross: $60,054,449

Film monsters have come a long way since *King Kong* (1933), *I Was a Teenage Werewolf* (1957) and even *Predator* (1987). "Sil," the name of the slimy and frightening creature who terrorizes people in *Species* is a creature for the nineties. First of all, she's a female with an attitude. Like her carnivorous cousin, the creature in *Alien* (1979), she goes on a rampage so bloody, it proves that females can be just as lethal as males. Secondly, her killings are related to her procreative urge, perhaps being an allegory for the dangers of sex in the nineties. And finally, she is digitally created for the screen from computer graphics rather than animatronics or from men in rubber monster suits.

Species is an excellent film despite the fact that it does not break any new ground in the area of plot or character development. That is not to say that Dennis Feldman's script is anything but excellent; but it adheres to many of the rules of the genre, which have caused many other films to be less interesting. This is a successful science -fiction thriller mostly due to the terrifying nature of the creature and to the taut suspense created by director Roger Donaldson and his first-rate cast.

Artist H.R. Giger, who designed Sil, also did the creature in *Alien*.

Like most good science-fiction writers, Dennis Feldman has based his story in science fact—namely, the government experiments called SETI (Search for ExtraTerrestrial Intelligence) in the 1970s. The premise here is that the government picks up a message from an apparently friendly alien intelligence who sends instructions for a new way to code DNA. Scientist Xavier Fitch (Ben Kingsley) leads the project which "grows" a new individual with this different DNA. The child, a female, grows at an intensely rapid rate and immediately displays disconcerting and dangerous characteristics which indicate that "terminating" her would be best. Encased in a glass enclosure, the ten-year-old, innocent, and human-looking female starts to be gassed to death but uses her superhuman strength to break through the glass and escape. In a chase scene worthy of *The Fugitive* (1993), she eludes Fitch and the U.S. Army, boards a train, and heads for Los Angeles. in hopes of finding a mate.

Fitch calls in a special force of people to help track down the alien without calling attention to the media. They are biologist Laura Baker (Marg Helgenburger), psychic and "empath" Dan Smithson (Forest Whitaker), psychologist Stephen Arden (Alfred Molina), and soldier-of-fortune Press Farley (Michael Madsen). The ensuing chase, to capture Sil before she mates, takes up the bulk of the film. The numerous characters and the unpredictability of Sil's actions (she "grows" again into the voluptuous Natasha Henstridge who has no problem meeting men) maintain a high level of suspense.

Sil's various mutations are revolting and fascinating. Whenever she is threatened, she emerges from underneath the skin of her human form. Her first mutation is the most frightening: snakes pop out from underneath her human skin in a most frightening manner. Granted, this scene is reminiscent of a similar one in *Poltergeist* (1982), but is no less frightening. In fact, much of the beast's actions have precedent, from the *Alien* films (1979, 1986, 1992) to *The Hidden* (1987).

Richard Edlund, who created special effects for *Star Wars* (1977), and H.R. Giger, who created the beast in *Alien*, have done a wonderful job creating a disgusting and terrifying creature for this film. Giger's creature was actually a puppet controlled by four puppeteers, and when they would move the puppet, electronic sensors would send messages to a computer screen that created the monster seen on screen.

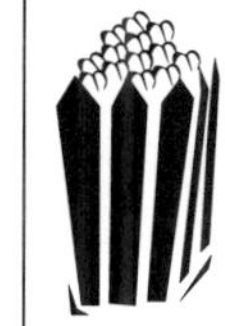

"We decided to make it female so it would be more docile and controllable." "More docile and controllable? I guess you guys don't get out much."—Scientist Fitch and Lennox

As a result, much of the effects had to be added in post-production, and though this may be old hat to many film directors and actors, it is still impressive, considering that the reactions to, and interactions with, the monster were all done by the actors with no monster present during filming. Another film which posed a similar challenge to actors was the semi-animated *Who Framed Roger Rabbit?* (1988), and, as in this film, the actors had to consider angles, sight lines, continuity, and a host of other technical problems in addition to emoting for the screen.

Roger Donaldson has proven himself in other genres as a director who can tell a spirited story and create suspense out of simple situations, having directed *The Getaway* (1994) and *No Way Out* (1987). Here, he chooses to keep the visuals of Sil to a minimum, relying instead on intensely suspenseful quick cuts and long build-ups to the climactic (and violent) sequences. He is particularly good with the final sequence where the remaining members of the special force enter a tunnel in a final face-off with the ever-stronger Sil. Brief images of Sil's tentacles, quick shots of her tongue lashing out (amplified by sharp sounds), and spooky periods of complete silence create an excellent climactic battle.

Donaldson is equally adept at utilizing the mundane to his advantage. When Laura and Press are driving in a car while tracking Sil after she has killed again, their car runs out of gas, creating an even stronger obstacle, doubling the tension. The film's most tense moments come when Laura and Press are trapped in a sealed "safe" room at a laboratory unable to get out because Fitch is afraid that if he opens the door for them the monster they are growing in an incubator might get out. The rapid-fire editing (by Conrad Buff) and the hair-raising screams of Helgenburger (as Laura) coupled with Donaldson's nerve-wracking camera angles make this a wonderful suspense scene.

All of the actors are top-notch; they work together beautifully as a team. They are afforded a chance, by Feldman's script, to be more than two-dimensional characters. Laura and Press' screen romance is unusual in its lack of cliches. Both Madsen, whose past credits include *Reservoir Dogs* (1992), and Helgenburger, best known for her role on TV's *China Beach*, are excellent. These are two actors who have deserved to shine in bigger screen roles, and their chemistry with each other (and with the other actors) proves them to be worthy of leading roles. Madsen is very commanding as a tough-guy, bounty hunter-type. When Fitch tells him that they created Sil as a female because they thought she would be "more docile," he responds, "you guys don't get out much, do you?" Helgenburger is completely believable as a brainy doctor interested in the sexy Farley, quietly crowing "Yes" when he knocks on her hotel door late at night.

Kingsley, Molina, and Whitaker, all quite established actors, are equally well-cast in their roles. Whitaker, known for Clint Eastwood's *Bird* (1988) and Neil Jordan's *The Crying Game* (1992), assumes a spacey character that is at first a bit annoying. Whitaker plays him as if he knows he is annoying, but can do nothing about it. Eventually, his quiet intensity becomes essential to the plot and to the audience's enjoyment of the film. Kingsley, Academy Award winner for *Gandhi* (1982), is terrific as usual in a role that is villainous by default as he plays a scientist and bureaucrat who means well but doesn't understand the implications of his work. Alfred Molina's appearances in everything from *Prick up Your Ears* (1987) to *White Fang II* (1994) prove him to be an actor of great versatility. He is understated and interesting as a raffish intellectual, pathetic in his attempts to impress women.

As the human form of Sil, newcomer Natasha Henstridge has created a stir, mostly because of her mixture of

CREDITS

Xavier Fitch: Ben Kingsley
Press Farley: Michael Madsen
Dr. Stephen Arden: Alfred Molina
Dan Smithson: Forest Whitaker
Dr. Laura Baker: Marg Helgenberger
"Sil": Natasha Henstridge

Origin: USA
Released: 1995
Production: Frank Mancuso, Jr. and Dennis Feldman; released by Metro Goldwyn Mayer
Direction: Roger Donaldson
Screenplay: Dennis Feldman
Cinematography: Andrzej Bartkowiak
Editing: Conrad Buff
Production design: John Muto
Costume design: Joe I. Tompkins
Visual effects: Richard Edlund
"Sil" design: H.R. Giger
MPAA rating: R
Running Time: 115 minutes

va-voom sex appeal and her naivete. An early scene where Sil goes to a wedding boutique to buy clothes is fun. When she plops the wads of cash in front of her to buy an awful wedding gown for streetwear, she is as simple and sweet as alter-ego Sil is exaggerated and horrific. The sequences where she goes to singles bars to pick up men for her mating needs are nineties versions of *Looking for Mr. Goodbar* (1977). The throat-slashing, drowning, and impaling that Sil inflicts on genetically inferior dates could serve as a good safe-sex video for young straight guys entering the dating scene.

With its edge-of-the-seat suspense and excellent performances, *Species* is a perfect popcorn movie. When it is over, it is over. There are no big themes or messages, but what is left after Sil wreaks her havoc is a feeling that you have been to a scary carnival fun house and emerged healthy and safe. Director Donaldson and his team of writers, effects wizards, and actors, should be applauded for making a film that gets the blood racing and the adrenalin pumping.

—*Kirby Tepper*

The Stars Fell on Henrietta

"A raw vision of American enterprise. Duvall burrows deeply into his richly drawn character."—Stephen Holden, *The New York Times*

"Moving, intelligent. A fairytale of earnest hopefulness-pure romance."—Jack Mathews, *Newsday*

Robert Duvall has done it again. In *The Stars Fell on Henrietta,* he creates yet another unforgettable character which elevates a film from the level of "good" to "excellent." Duvall won an Academy Award for working the same magic in *Tender Mercies* (1983). *The Stars Fell on Henrietta,* produced by Clint Eastwood and directed by James Keach, provides Duvall with one of his most colorful roles to date. It is a tender, entertaining, and loving tribute to the Texas oil wildcatters of the 1930s. Sadly, critics did not fully embrace this film in its initial release, causing the film to fade rather quicikly. As a result, fans of Robert Duvall may have missed a wonderful performance, and all other moviegoers may have missed a touching and well-crafted film.

Duvall plays Mr. Cox, whose name is as mysterious as his origins. "What's your first name?" asks one character. "Just 'Mr.'," responds the genial Cox. "Some people are born to be lucky," describes the narrator (Marietta Marich), "Mr. Cox was just lucky to be born." Cox is an oil wildcatter, also known as a "doodlebugger" or a "witcher." ("Doodlebugging" meant to search for oil, and "witching" was a method of holding hand-held metal rods, somewhat like a divining rod, to discover oil.) Looking more like a hobo than a successful oilman, however, it is discovered early in the film that Mr. Cox has been around a lot of successful oilmen, but has never made any money himself. He owns just one threadbare suit, has absolutely no money, and travels with his cat, Matilda.

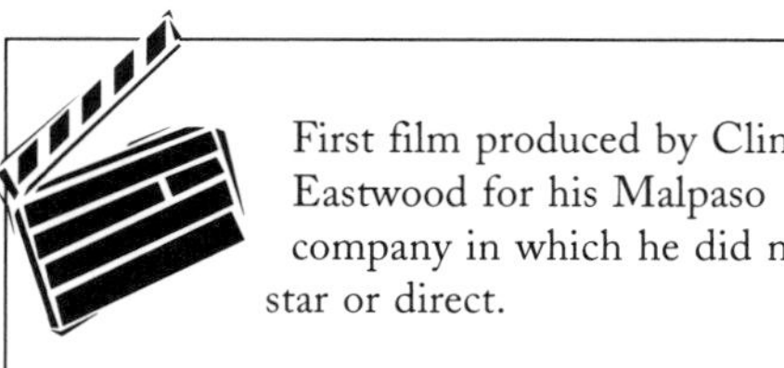

First film produced by Clint Eastwood for his Malpaso company in which he did not star or direct.

Just outside the oil boomtown of Big Stone, Texas, Mr. Cox smells buried treasure: he sniffs at the air, certain that there are rich oil reserves under a patch of land that no one has yet mined. Fate brings him together with Don Day (Aidan Quinn), a penniless farmer about to lose his land to the bank. Having been saved by Don from a tornado, Mr. Cox, certain that the Day farm is on top of those rich oil reserves, offers to help the Days mine it if they invest five thousand dollars. The conservative Cora Day (Frances Fisher) joins her husband in asking Mr. Cox to leave at once, and Cox returns to Big Stone, certain that he will raise the five thousand himself.

Don Day, eager to prove that he can provide for his family, begins to think that maybe there is oil under their land, and uses his wife's savings to buy an oil rig of his own. He risks his marriage, not to mention a local boy's (Landon Peterson) life, in his attempt to discover oil.

But Mr. Cox, working as a dishwasher for an unctuous restaurant owner (Zach Grenier), creates an unsavory plan for raising the money, and returns to the Day's farm with the necessary capital to properly dig for oil. Using money stolen from a wealthy oilman known as Big Dave (Brian Dennehy), Don Day and Mr. Cox triumphantly build an oil well. The outcome of their effort is best left for audiences to discover on their own. Without ruining the story, it can be noted that everyone ends up a better person for following their dream.

From *The Rainmaker* (1956) to *The Music Man* (1962), countless films have used the idea of the stranger who comes into town and brings hope and a little magic to its weary inhabitants. Screewriter Philip Railsback uses the fundamentals of this plot form to good advantage. The story and the character of Mr. Cox are based in part on the grandfathers of both Railsback and director Keach: both shared the experience of having grandfathers who were Texas wildcatters. The utilization of the "drifter who comes into town" story is wise: Railsback and Keach make Mr. Cox an almost mythical character by the end of the story.

In addition, the use of a narrator is a fine concept, helping to create the feeling that this is a fable. The putative narrator is the grown-up voice of Pauline Day (played as a youth by wide-eyed Kaytlyn Knowles), who is the first person to be entranced by the whimsical Mr. Cox when he arrives on the Day farm. Similar to the young boy in *Shane* or the children in *The Music Man* or *The Seven Faces of Dr. Lao* (1964), the magic of believing in something you cannot see is reserved at first for youth. It takes a while for the adults to believe, and once they do, their lives are changed.

Not that this film is didactic in its thematic attempt to show the importance of following a dream. But Railsback, Keach, Duvall and company clearly have an interest in showing the mythical, almost spiritual side of a wildcatter like Mr. Cox and how it may have affected the Depression-weary farmers of the 1930s. One scene in particular emphasizes this quality quite beautifully. One evening when Mr. Cox first comes to the Day farm, he walks one evening out into their vast, dry fields with his cat Matilda. There, in silhouette against a night sky that looks almost like a theatrical stage set, Mr. Cox holds Matilda up to the sky, dancing around his future oil fields as the Day family watches from the farmhouse, enraptured. It is a beautiful scene.

Keach, who started his career as actor (and is the brother of actor Stacy Keach), does a wonderful job with his actors. He wisely knows that reaction shots of his actors will help him to build the character of Mr. Cox. From little Pauline to Don and Cora, the actors stare at Mr. Cox with a combination of disbelife and awe. Keach creates beautiful cinematic pictures, doing a particularly nice job with the climactic oil-well scene involving a lot of actors and special effects.

Duvall plays his role with controlled enthusiasm and characteristic attention to detail. He manages to make the rather larcenous Mr. Cox very sympathetic and lovable. Duvall never missteps in walking the fine line between drama and comedy, instead providing a characterization that is neither comic nor tragic, but simply human. One of the scenes most characteristic of this blend of comedy and drama takes place when Mr. Cox approaches a former wildcatting comrade who has now struck it rich. Mr. Cox, attempting to make himself appear classy, walks up to his old friend in a hotel and immediately pulls out the plans for his oil well, and generally makes a fool of himself as he tries to pretend he is well off in spite of his tattered suit and scruffy hair. "I know there is oil there," says he, "I can smell it, sir." Duvall's subtlety is wondrous after he is rudely brushed off by his old comrade, maintianing his dignity even while he looks emotionally bruised.

Duvall is at his charismatic best when showing young Pauline or her sister Beatrice (Lexi Randall) how to listen to the ground for oil, or when he and Quinn go out in the fields with a witching rod hunting for the exact spot on which they should dig. "Do you feel it here?" he says, slapping Quinn on the stomach. When they both feel it, it is hard not to believe.

Aidan Quinn captures the upstanding and kindly nature of his character, moving from being an overly cautious family man to a risk-taker with complete believability. Don Day's enchantment by the optimistic Mr. Cox is an important (though subtle) part of the story thankfully understood and portrayed by Quinn. And as his wife, Frances Fisher looks as if she was made to play the sterotype of a pioneer woman, but never falls into cliche. Quinn and Fisher are excellent in their scenes of separation and reconciliation.

Much of the film's success in creating an almost "magic realism" might be due to Oscar-winning production designer L. Henry Bumstead. Bumstead designed *Vertigo* (1958), *The Sting* (1973), and Robert Duvall's first film, *To Kill a Mockingbird* (1962). Juxtaposing the dustiness of the depressed farm town with the gaudy hotels and saloons cre-

CREDITS

Mr. Cox: Robert Duvall
Don Day: Aidan Quinn
Cora Day: Frances Fisher
Big Dave: Brian Dennehy
Beatrice Day: Lexi Randall
Pauline Day: Kaytlyn Knowles
Mary Day: Francesca Ruth Eastwood

Origin: USA
Released: 1995
Production: Clint Eastwood and David Valdes for a Malpso production in association with Butcher's Run Productions
Direction: James Keach
Screenplay: Philip Railsback
Cinematography: Bruce Surtees
Editing: Joel Cox
Production design: Henry Bumstead
Art direction: Jack G. Taylor Jr.
Set decoration: Alan Hicks
Costume design: Van Broughton Ramsey
Sound: John Pritchett
Music: David Benoit
MPAA rating: PG
Running Time: 110 minutes

ated for the oilmen, Bumstead is responsible for the highly detailed and almost mythical setting in which the story takes place.

Perhaps one of the reasons this film was not a critical success was because of its sense of innocence. It is a throwback to films of "the olden days" in that it is a character-driven story with no unpredictable plot points and with identifiable and moderately stereotyped characters. But so what; it is an excellent and touching film, masterfully directed by Keach, and beautifully played by its actors. And most of all, it has Robert Duvall. That alone is enough for most everyone.

—Kirby Tepper

Steal Big, Steal Little

"Passion, romance, comedy, drama...*Steal Big, Steal Little* has it all!"—David Sheehan, *CBS-TV*

"Irresistible! Lots of laughs and lots of heart. Andy Garcia is as funny as he is sexy."—Jeanne Wolf, *Jeanne Wolf's Hollywood*

Box Office Gross: $3,150,170

"Capraesque." That is a term that has been coined in recent years to describe a style of filmmaking epitomized by the films of Frank Capra. Capra made *It's a Wonderful Life* (1946), *Mr. Smith Goes to Washington* (1939), and many other cinema classics. His films tended to have an idealistic hero, a gallery of colorful character actors, and clearly identifiable villains. Often the theme had to do with the "common man" being oppressed by wealthy and venal landowners or politicians, such as in *Meet John Doe* (1941). *Steal Big, Steal Little*, directed by Andrew Davis (from a screenplay by Davis, Lee Blessing, Jeanne Blake and Terry Kahn) attempts to duplicate some of these elements from Capra's films, while trying to trade on the Capra style and touch audience's hearts in the same way Capra did. Although there are some sweet moments in this film, it does not succeed in its attempt to be Capraesque. It is as if an earnest and talented costume jeweler tried to duplicate a Cartier bracelet: it may look fine, but it is not the genuine article.

Andy Garcia stars in a dual role as Ruben and Robby, two completely different brothers who get into a struggle over a large parcel of inherited land that becomes an epic battle between good and evil. Ruben is a good samaritan who sees the land as a home for the many immigrant workers who need a place to live, work, and raise their families. Robby is a wealthy and unscrupulous developer who sees the land as the centerpiece of a new resort he plans to develop.

Ruben is aided in his struggle by his wife, Laura (Rachel Ticotin) and their colorful friend Lou Pirelli (Alan Arkin) and a constituency of blue-collar workers. Robby is aided in his attempts to control the land by a retinue of unsavory (and putatitively comic) characters, including a corrupt Judge (David Ogden Stiers), a smarmy attorney (Joe Pantoliano), and a rogue sheriff (Charles Rocket). Both sides are also infiltrated at different times by a goofy loan-shark (Richard Bradford) who, near the beginning of the film, is chasing Arkin's character, but helps him in the end.

Some audiences will simply love this film for its many good points. Arkin's performance, in particular, is the kind of comic gem that made him famous years ago. Although not as funny a role as he played in *The In-laws* (1979), this role provides Arkin with substantial screen time and a broad character (a small-time car-dealer involved with the Mafia who ends up helping Ruben's band of farm workers.) But in scenes where Lou (Arkin), Ruben and Ruben's wife Laura talk to a documentary filmmaker about their fight to save their land, Arkin tempers the broadness of his cartoonish character to create a more textured (and very realistic) portrait of a man who came to California on the lam from the mob but ended up helping people he loved.

There are other positive aspects to this film, such as the lush cinematography by Frank Tidy. Tidy captures the vivid colors of Santa Barbara, California with depth and grace. Each shot looks like a picture postcard, especially the gorgeous vistas taken during a hot-air balloon sequence. Production designer Michael Haller created a great mixture of early-California and modern styles, especially in the wonderful-looking funeral sequence early in the film. In that sequence, the audience gets a glimpse into the family home of Ruben and Robby, and the sprawling Adobe house (decked out for the funeral of their adopted mother) is covered with gorgeous fabrics and sumptuous furnishings. Tidy also creates a spectacularly overdone mansion for the character of Robby, filled with gaudy statues, stuffed animals, mirrors, lots of gold leaf, all of which are (according to Robby) "gifts and acquisitions, gifts of handling trust funds of old ladies." Tidy's ability to make the screenwriter's words come alive is a testament to his talent as a designer.

Other pluses in this film include performances by supporting players. In particular, David Ogden Stiers is in fine form as the evil Judge who gets his comeuppance at the hands of the crafty Lou and Ruben. A sequence where Stiers and the other villains are spending a debauched weekend away from their wives is fun. Stiers (best known for his role in the *M*A*S*H* television series) shifts from pompous to obsequious in a most amusing way. Other character actors are given a chance to play roles which seem to be a departure for them. For example, Holland Taylor, who usually plays very tailored society matrons (*To Die For* [1995]), plays the free-spirited adoptive mother of Ruben and Robby. She wears a long, flowing wig, and portrays a character that is sort of a mixture between Isadora Duncan and Auntie Mame. The fact that Taylor is not quite believable in the role may only be because she has become so identifiable with other types of roles.

Other character actors getting to stretch their talents include Joe Pantoliano, playing a variation on the weasley snitch he perfected in *Midnight Run* (1988) and other films. In this film, Pantoliano is better dressed and less (apparently) low-class than usual. Once his true character is revealed, Pantoliano provides his sneaky character with more goodness and depth than he has been given a chance to do in other films. And finally, Richard Bradford, whose face will be familiar to audiences from many films, lends his dignified stature to the unlikely role of a small-time loan shark. He is quite funny, even though the character's constantly changing allegiances are a bit confusing.

CREDITS

Ruben and Robby: Andy Garcia
Lou Perilli: Alan Arkin
Laura Matinez: Rachel Ticotin
Eddie Agopian: Joe Pantoliano
Mona: Holland Taylor
Judge Winton Myers: David Ogden Stiers

Origin: USA
Released: 1995
Production: Andrew Davis and Fred Causo for a Chicago Pacific Entertainment; released by Savoy Pictures
Direction: Andrew Davis
Screenplay: Andrew Davis, Lee Blessing, Jeanne Blake and Terry Kahn
Cinematography: Frank Tidy
Editing: Don Brochu and Tina Hirsch
Production design: Michael Haller
Music: William Olvis
MPAA rating: PG-13
Running Time: 130 minutes

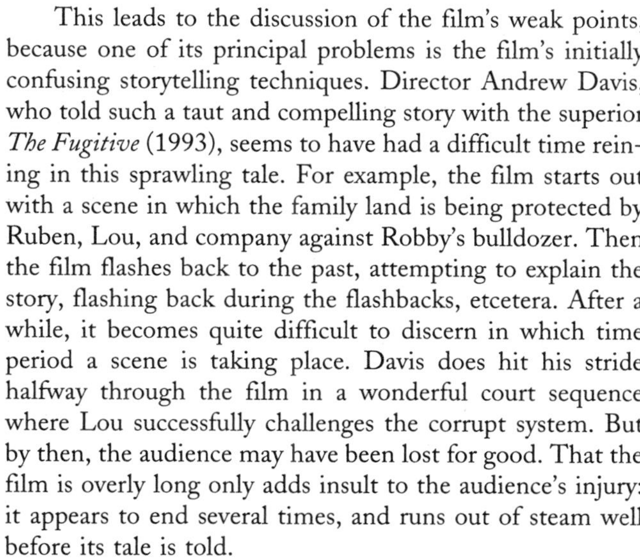

This leads to the discussion of the film's weak points, because one of its principal problems is the film's initially confusing storytelling techniques. Director Andrew Davis, who told such a taut and compelling story with the superior *The Fugitive* (1993), seems to have had a difficult time reining in this sprawling tale. For example, the film starts out with a scene in which the family land is being protected by Ruben, Lou, and company against Robby's bulldozer. Then the film flashes back to the past, attempting to explain the story, flashing back during the flashbacks, etcetera. After a while, it becomes quite difficult to discern in which time period a scene is taking place. Davis does hit his stride halfway through the film in a wonderful court sequence where Lou successfully challenges the corrupt system. But by then, the audience may have been lost for good. That the film is overly long only adds insult to the audience's injury: it appears to end several times, and runs out of steam well before its tale is told.

The filmmakers are so intent on creating the Capraesque atmosphere, they resort to more than a few cliches. On more than one occasion, Ruben talks about "building up our dream," saying the land is "you home, your earth" to the workers. The "dream" talk, combined with William Olvis' occasionally syrupy music make for a one-two punch of sweetness that undermines the sentimentality these filmmakers attempt to achieve. Arkin's character is given other cliches, in the form of his escape from the loan sharks and his telephone relationship with his mother ("Ma, Naomi did not steal your dentures again; look in your purse"). Credibility is undermined throughout the film, such as in the funeral sequence when extras are dressed up from literally every walk of life, as if to show the incredible range of friends of the deceased. But like much else in this film, director Davis and company go too far, having extras wearing cowboy clothes, Gypsy outfits, men in turbans, and characters playing bongo drums. It looks more like a circus than a funeral.

Garcia, while likable, is not able to carry off the Herculean task of salvaging the good parts of this uneven film. His characters are not particularly well-defined, except that Ruben wears some very hip clothes for a working-class person who seems to eschew material things. His elegant shirts and interesting hats make him more polished than he is supposed to be, and the lack of change in gesture and voice between Ruben and Robby keep the distinction from being as vivid as it could be. Especially compared to Jeremy Irons extraordinary portrayal of very different twins in *Dead Ringers* (1988), the usually wonderful Garcia is a disappointment.

Steal Big, Steal Little is ultimately a rather messy combination of several good performances, beautiful photography, good intentions, and a few fun sequences. But its endless length and its super-sweet demeanor simply steal time instead of stealing your heart. At one point in the film, one of the workers says that his house is being auctioned off, reminding audiences of a sequence in *It's a Wonderful Life*. It is at this point that audiences may wish for the real thing; copying Capra is not the same as "paying homage." In fact, it might be considered stealing.

—*Kirby Tepper*

REVIEWS

Chicago Tribune April 29, 1995. p. 2
The Village Voice. September 10, 1995. p. 82
USA Today. September 29, 1995. p. 9B

Stories from the Kronen (Historias Del Kronen)

From the moment Carlos walks into the Kronen, a Madrid bar, we are voyeurs at a wild party that just keeps getting wilder. Tragedy looms from the first frame, and we are impotent to do anything but watch—as impotent as the youthful characters who are swept away by the tidal wave of nilhilism that controls them.

Stories from the Kronen (Historias Del Kronen) is less a compilation of stories than a succession of summer nights. For Carlos and his group of friends, all in their early twenties, the day begins at night, when they either start or end at the bar. In between, they go to clubs to hear bands where they dance to songs that echo their feelings of alienation.

This is an intense film about the empty lives of a group of Generation X'ers, as they search for a reason for their own existence, finding relief from their boredom in those old stand-bys: sex, drugs, and rock'n roll. The film's unrelenting pace pulls the viewer deeper and deeper into their self-destruction.

The anti-hero, Carlos (Juan Diego Botto), is a handsome but self-indulgent young man who shows his apparent disgust for the world of his parents by rising at dinner time, then leaving the family and not returning until the following day.

His character is out of control, always pushing the limit with no thought to the ramifications of his actions. He has a mindless obsession with risking his life, and because of this obsession, he perceives every experience as a macho challenge, whether it be to do more drugs than anyone else (and still survive), to climb on dangerous scaffolding high above the streets of Madrid (and still survive), or to have sex wherever, whenever, and with whoever (and still survive). His self destructive momentum infects the other members of his group to dance to his frenzied rhythms, until they all are spinning out of control.

The first half of the film plays like an advertisement for debauchery, but Carlos's good times start to sour when his grandfather dies. We meet Grandpa in a scene where Carlos has come to visit the shut-in. Grandpa (Andre Falcon) tells Carlos of his concern for the young people of today. They have no enemy to fight, he tells him, no noble cause to offer their lives.

When Grandpa asks Carlos for a cigarette, he unthinkingly gives him one, throwing the dying man into convulsions of coughing. This frightens Carlos, whose own battle with death really is only half-serious; the real thing, until now, is beyond his understanding. When his Aunt accuses Carlos of giving Grandpa a cigarette, he denies it. His grandfather scolds him for lying, saying that if there's no truth, there is nothing. Carlos is visibly impressed and you can see that his grandfather influences him in a way his angry, numbed-out parents never could.

His parents make shallow stabs at motivating Carlos, weakly suggesting that he take summer classes at college, but their own indifference and anger around their son overide any positive influence they might have had over him. The only interaction we see with the family is at dinner, where they quietly eat while the TV news blares out horrific tales of violence and corruption, providing the backdrop of senseless violence and immorality that has become the foreground of Carlos's nightlife.

The media is portrayed as a corrupting influence in itself, as Carlos and his friends watch *Henry: Portait of a Serial Killer* over and over again, finding amusement in scenes of torture and murder. In their discussions after the film, they inevitably begin to talk about getting hold of some snuff films. Grandpa also alludes to the horrors of the media when he tells Carlos that he has seen horrible things "in there," pointing to the TV as if it were an eye into another dimension.

The filmmaker seems to be saying that these young people aren't responsible for their vapid lives, blaming it on the lack of nobility and morality in the models that surround them, as if morality were a infectious virus that you could catch from someone.

Even the most moral character in the film, Roberto (Jordi Molla), is, in the end, divested of his moral stance and seen as a hypocrite whose morality only disguised his own self-interest.

There appears to be only one truly pure character in the film, Pedro (Aitor Merino). From the start he symbolizes the delicate tragic figure. Diabetic, with only one kidney, the frail boy is scapegoated by all. Because Carlos hates anything that is weak, he tries to force Pedro into being more aggressive and defending himself. Carlos feels like Pedro's weakness reflects on himself, and he taunts Pedro throughout the film.

Finally, after a stranger picks a fight with Pedro, Carlos gets him involved in a duel of courage. Pedro and the other fellow hang off a freeway overpass, to see who can hang there the longest without dropping to their death.

The fragile Pedro survives this feat only to be caught by the police. Carlos also gets caught, but Carlos' dad bails them both out, and although angry, he does nothing to curb his son's self-destructive behavior. The reult of his indifference is disaster.

For all his beauty, Carlos isn't a very likeable character. His total lack of morality leads him to break every rule. By the end of the film, you feel like he doesn't even like himself, and he has good reasons. He steals from his mother, getting the maid fired; seduces his friend's girl, even at one point trying to seduce his own sister; and he risks other people's lives for thrills, holding life itself very carelessly. Carlos symbolizes his generation, a generation, according to Armendariz, careening out of control, directionless and doomed.

That's what the film is selling. If you buy the premise, you'll buy the ending. We watch as Carlos and his friends move from adrenaline rush to adrenaline rush through the nighttime streets of Madrid. Scenes of moshing and crowd surfing abound, interspersed with scenes of death-defying drives on city streets, kids getting high until they are either bleeding at the nose or falling down sick, and plenty of impromptu sex. Scattered amid these scenes of their chaotic lives are shots of Madrid. Director of photography Alfredo Mayo's camera pans a skyline full of ugly high rises and an unsightly sprawling metropolis, skillfully adding to the feeling of meaninglessness in the film.

Stories from the Kronen was adapted from the novel by Jose Angel Manas, who co-wrote the screenplay with the director, Montxo Armendariz. Armendariz has effectively captured a realism in the film that has touched moviegoers throughout Spain, who have made it the highest-grossing film of the year.

The final party of the film is at Pedro's house, a celebration of his birthday while his parents are away. They drop acid and film each other on a camcorder, but things start to get out of hand. Armendariz has built up the pace of the film so effectively that at this point you feel like putting on the brakes, only to find they don't work, and Pedro is inadvertantly killed. The camera has caught the murder and the boys finally have their snuff film.

It would be nice to think that Carlos, who wants to show the tape of Pedro's murder to the police, is motivated by his grandfather's admonition from the grave to tell the truth. But it is more likely that going to the police is the ultimate risk. He finally has something to fight for, something to offer his life to.

Roberto for all his preaching about following the rules, is dead against it, and the two fight over the tape. The fight is serious and off camera, and the audience is left wondering its outcome.

Despite the film's realism, Carlos is denied any saving grace, and it makes it almost impossible to connect with his character. As a result, in the final scene, after Roberto has been pulled from his moral pedestal, one neither knows nor cares what happens to either of them. Perhaps that empty feeling is how the director wanted to leave the audience. If so, he succeeded.

—Diane Hatch-Avis

CREDITS

Carlos: Juan Diego Botto
Roberto: Jordi Molla
Amalia: Nuria Prims
Pedro: Aitor Merino
Manolo: Armando del Rio
Silvia: Diana Galvez

Origin: Spain, France and Germany
Released: 1995
Production: Elias Querejeta for a Claudie Ossard, Alert Film GmbH, TVE and Canal Plus Espana productions; released by Alta Films
Direction: Montxo Armendariz
Screenplay: Montxo Armendariz and Jose Angel; based on the novel by Jose Angel
Cinematography: Alfredo Mayo
Editing: Rosario Sainz de Rozas
Art direction: Julio Esteban
Sound: Ivan Marin
Assistant direction: Richard Walker
Casting: Elena Arnao
Running Time: 95 minutes

REVIEWS

Daily Variety, June 19, 1995, p. 16.
Hollywood Reporter, May 24, 1995, p. 10.
The Nation, June 26, 1995, p. 936.

The Story of Xinghau

Set in a bleak village near the Great Wall, *The Story of Xinghau* is a tragic Chinese parable about the clash between corrupt modern values and honorable traditions. Produced by the Youth Film Studio of the Beijing Film Academy, the film bears the promise of novice director Yin Li, but it sorely lacks the authoritative treatment needed to make it memorable. It has dignity and grace and a quiet beauty but not the power and majesty needed to help audiences endure its long dull stretches.

Xinghau (Jiang Wenli) is a hard-working wife in a remote village. She is constantly berated by her domineering husband Wanglai (Zhang Guoli), a wealthy grocer who cheats his customers and sees everything, even sacred relics, as potential profit- makers. Wanglai's biggest gripe with Xinghau is that she has not gotten pregnant. He's sure it's her fault; after all, in his own opinion he's a real man, the biggest man in town. Wanglai buys goods cheaply from the city and sells them for big profits. He even has a crew of men with pick-axes who dislodge rocks from the Great Wall so he can hawk them in the city as souvenirs.

The Story of Xinghau is a film about dismantling traditions. Wanglai, full of modern materialism, has no respect for the Great Wall or its supposedly enchanted watchtower which is rumored to hold a buried treasure. He plunders and exploits whatever and whomever he can, including the plump, teasing wife of a fellow villager. But for all his modernism Wanglai is stuck in the most wretched of traditions: he is a patriarch with an insatiable desire for an heir. Wanglai is a capitalist with a feudal warlord's merciless heart.

Xinghau is no rebel, at least at the film's start. She tries to be a good wife to Wanglai and doesn't complain about her many burdens. She cooks, cleans, runs his grocery and obeys his sexual demands. Yet she is level-headed enough not to be taken in by Wanglai's accusations. She isn't riddled with guilt at not producing a baby, even though Wanglai constantly screams "What's wrong with you?" and occasionally beats her. Xinghau is quiet and compliant yet has an inner dignity which her hellish life cannot erode.

Wanglai's cousin Fulin (Tian Shaojun), a local farmer, is Wanglai's opposite. Wanglai is uneducated, Fulin a college student. Wanglai is brutal, Fulin gentle and kind. Wanglai loves worldly treasures, Fulin loves nature. His sole ambition is to plant trees to beautify the barren landscape of the area.

A triangle develops. For a long time it seems as if Xinghau and Fulin are not strong enough to break the bounds of tradition, but as Xinghau's dissatisfaction grows she becomes more entranced with Fulin. In a beautifully photographed and nicely paced scene, Xinghau and Fulin are weeding a garden one day when a storm hits; they find refuge in a cave and each other's arms. This sexual encounter is as sudden and as cleansing as the thunderstorm.

The film's other plot concerns the watchtower. Wanglai is overcome with lust for gold when an elder tells him there is a treasure buried beneath the sacred tower. Ignoring protests from the more spiritual members of the village, Wanglai gets his crew to dig up the historic site. Wanglai is a defiler with no respect for honor or tradition.

Young director Yin Li handles this simple material in a confusing fashion. When visitors come from a nearby village, it's clear they are rivals of Wanglai's gang, but it is not explained why or what the stakes are. Yin is fond of short scenes that end in fadeouts, which don't work well because the film is already too disjointed.

This kind of film, with so little action and so straightfoward a plot, can work only if it's a fine character study. But both Xinghau and Fulin are underwritten. Xinghau speaks so few lines it's hard to understand her motivations, and when she enters into the affair with Fulin it's a shock. After Wanglai discovers the affair and there is a final confrontation and revelation, Xinghau berates him. It's a shock because she hasn't seemed capable of such an explosion. A quiet character who holds in every emotion may be an accurate portrayal of an isolated villager, but it doesn't work well for a film protagonist. This is supposed to be *The Story of Xinghau*, but audiences must strain too much to read between the sparse lines of Xinghau's undefined personality.

CREDITS

Xinghua: Jiang Wenli
Wanglai: Zhang Guoli
Fulin: Tian Shaojun
Ruifeng: Zhang Haiyan
Wansan: Niu Xingli
Wangni: Zhao Mana

Origin: China
Released: 1995
Production: The Youth Film Studio of the Beijing Film Academy
Direction: Yin Li
Screenplay: Shi Ling
Cinematography: Li Jianguo
Editing: Zhao Yihua
Art direction: Cui Junde
Costume design: Zhao Hui
Music: Liu Wei
Production design: Gao Jingxin, Liu Yue

Jiang does as well as she can given the constraints, and she conveys a sympathetic if somewhat inscrutable integrity.

Fulin is something of a cipher as well—a nice, quiet guy with little spark. As played by Tian, he seems mostly bewildered at the swirl of life around him. Wanglai is nothing more than a caricature of a bullheaded, dim-witted misogynist. He is too much of a buffoon to be the embodiment of evil which the film requires him to be, and when he meets his demise at the end, it evokes only a shrug. Zhang's portrayal doesn't provide the character with any shadings of humanity.

The Story of Xinghau lacks depth and emotion. Of necessity, it must be a story of a woman's awakening from the slumber of a repressed life, but there are so few nuances that it feels almost like a textbook study. Without characters that are developed into complex, real people, audiences will find little to care about.

The film's view of this corner of China is that of a forlorn, dusty, backwards place which seems to have skipped the Communist interlude between feudalism and the new capitalism. The filmmakers seem to honor cultural traditions and relics such as the Great Wall and the sacred watchtower, but even this is done rather listlessly and is devoid of any larger context.

Just as Wanglai's barrenness matches that of the land, Fulin's gift at making things grow is a symbol of his fertility. There is the suggestion that Fulin's ability to plant forests is a way of starting afresh in a civilization that has gone dry and old. But if this is an ecology message, it too is vastly underplayed.

The Story of Xinghau is an earnest film, but it is thoroughly pedestrian. There is little in it to excite a Western audience, and it lacks the sweep and background needed to make it universally appealing.

—*Michael Betzold*

Strange Days

"you know you want it"—Movie tagline

"One of the best films of the year."—Roger Ebert, *Chicago Sun-Times*

"A sexy, kinetic thriller. A sulfur-hot cultural event."—Graham Fuller, *Interview*

"*Strange Days* is visionary...A troubling but undeniably breathless joy ride."—Janet Maslin, *The New York Times*

"Electrifying! A dazzling visionary triumph."—Peter Travers, *Rolling Stone*

"As entertaining as it is visionary, a wild mind-blowing spectacle."—Mike Caccloppell, *WABC Radio*

"Brilliant."—Paul Wunder, *WBAI Radio*

"Four stars. Wow."—Norman Mark, *WMAQ-TV, (NBC) Chicago*

Box Office Gross: $7,918,562

It is December 30, 1999, two days before what some people believe to be the end of the millennium (purists and *Jeopardy* watchers, however, say that the millennium will end on December 31, 2000). But sticklers for accuracy aside, there is no doubt that the turning of the calendar from 1999 to 2000 will probably create one hellacious party. And while the countdown goes on in a Los Angeles four short years in the future, the disintegration of society has kept pace with the disintegration of the century.

While streets team with violence, crime and the constant presence of police, behind the scenes technology has been developed which replaces the awkward audio body wires used by law enforcement. It has been supplanted by *Squid* (Superconducting Quantum Interference Devices), a recording apparatus that turns people into camcorders. Now, experiences can be captured through the wired person's mind and transferred to a small CD called a "clip." But like most technology, it was invented without ever examining its possible bastardization, and it didn't take long for it to find its way onto the black market. Now the addiction of choice is playing back "pieces of other people's lives." More and more people are getting "hooked on fantasy" by trading their own reality for someone else's.

But the reality they are buying are not clips of dream vacations to Tahiti or educational tours of the Louvre, instead, it would appear that the more nefarious the sensation the better. Those who are "jacked in" can experience a heart-pounding crime without leaving the safety and comfort of their easy chairs, or they can have innumerable sexual encounters of any flavor without a pang of guilt—the ultimate pornography. "I can make it happen and you won't even tarnish your wedding ring," says ex-cop and current clip peddler Lenny Nero (Ralph Fiennes). This is not some sophisticated computer-generated virtual reality, this is "the real thing." One can actually experience sex and violence without any of the accountability or risk.

Lenny is the "Santa Claus of the subconscious" as he describes himself, but perhaps Lenny's best customer is himself. Lenny is hooked on his own clips of Faith (Juliette Lewis), a runaway punk singer whom he pulled from the gutter and who then dropped him when a better deal (record promoter Philo Vance [Michael Wincott]) came along.

In order to film the huge party scene, director Bigelow set up a huge party in downtown Los Angeles which drew a crowd of 17,000 who paid a $10 fee.

Lenny's constant playback of his times with Faith create an obsessive nightmare for him which will soon weave itself into an even worse nightmare to come as the 2K date nears. A friend of Faith's, a prostitute named Iris (Brigitte Bako), has a clip for Lenny of the type he refuses to deal in. It is a snuff clip—one which contains experiences of death. This clip is one Iris made which shows a very important and, for her and Lenny, a very dangerous death: that of the extremely popular and controversial rap star Jeriko One (Glenn Plummer) whose lyrics revel in raking the L.A.P.D over the coals. Iris had been wired while she was dating Jeriko One and was with him, but managed to escape, when he was murdered. This clip could set L.A on fire because it shows the killers in action.

Iris knows her life is in danger as long as she knows what she knows and has a clip of it. So she gives the clip to Lenny by slipping it into his office, his Mercedes, which is towed away and impounded before he even realizes the clip exists. The only thing he knows is that Iris has warned him that Faith's life could be in danger, too.

Not long afterward, Lenny receives an anonymous clip and on it, in brutal detail, are the last few minutes of Iris' life. Not only will Lenny experience the unidentified killer as he tortures, rapes and murders Iris, he also sees that the killer has fiendishly "jacked her in" to her own death so she experiences it both as killer and victim.

With Lenny in possession of these two clips his life is in danger from more than one source—those who killed Jeriko One, and whoever wired and murdered Iris. Stepping in like a knight in a black limousine is his friend Lornette "Mace" Mason (Angela Bassett), a tough and sensible chauffeur and bodyguard who is Lenny's unquestioned friend and unrivaled champion. Together the two must solve Iris' murder and bring all the killers to justice...before they, or Faith, become the next victims.

Director Kathryn Bigelow certainly plays with the big boys in this wild, ambitious, and undoubtedly disquieting sci-fi ride. And with *Strange Days* she sends us careening toward the 2K historic mile marker with an intense feeling of apprehension. Bigelow offers us a not-so-distant future that teeters on the brink of Armageddon while looking uncomfortably all too familiar. It's a crazy world where it is no wonder people want to escape into other people's experiences, because it is a world where Libya's Muammar Qaddafi has just won the Nobel Peace Prize.

The result is an intellectually bold film that is as commanding as it is worrisome and as intriguing as it is menacing. From its opening frenetic restaurant robbery, which is shot from the point of view of the robbers, Bigelow and her Cinematographer Matthew Leonetti have developed intriguing, subjective camerawork that helps the viewer "experience clips" as well as the medium allows. They allow us to indulge in our own urge for voyeurism and our own desires for risk-free action and adventure. *Strange Days* is filled with energy and spunk and a luxuriant attention to detail that allows us to be sucked into the action along with Lenny and Mace, and this is the film's strength.

CREDITS

Lenny Nero: Ralph Fiennes
Lornette "Mace" Mason: Angela Bassett
Faith Justin: Juliette Lewis
Max Peltier: Tom Sizemore
Philo Gant: Michael Wincott
Burton Steckler: Vincent D'Onofrio
Jeriko One: Glenn Plummer
Iris: Brigitte Bako
Tick: Richard Edson
Dwayne Engelman: William Fichtner
Palmer Strickland: Josef Sommer
Keith: Joe Urla

Origin: USA
Released: 1995
Production: James Cameron and Steven-Charles Jaffe for a Lightstorm Entertainment Production; released by Twentieth Century Fox.
Direction: Kathryn Bigelow
Screenplay: James Cameron and Jay Cocks
Cinematography: Matthew F. Leonetti
Editing: Howard Smith
Production design: Lilly Kilvert
Art direction: John Warnke
Set decoration: Kara Lindstrom
Costume design: Ellen Mirojnick
Music: Randy Gerston
MPAA rating: R
Running Time: 145 minutes

But when one tries to analyze the story from the cold detachment of a 1995 outside the theater, without the distractions of strong characters, engrossing settings, and great action, one detects a degree of disquieting hypocrisy: Lenny refuses to peddle snuff tapes, but those are exactly what the filmmakers let us experience.

> "I'm the Magic Man, the Santa Claus of the Subconcious. You say it, you even think it, you can have it."—Lenny Nero explaining "clips" to a prospective buyer

Further burdening the film is the fact that Jeriko's murder and Mace's beating seem to be ripped right out of today's headlines instead of being projections of the future. They reverberate with allusions to the Rodney King beating and the 1992 riots. So obvious are the parallels, and so jolting are the contemporary references, that the mesmerizing voyeuristic thrill that the filmmakers were implanting in us from the film's first frame is temporarily shattered.

But these problems aside, *Strange Days* lingers in the memory long after the analysis has stopped. This, in part, is also due to some very strong acting. Lenny Nero may seem like a less than inspiring hero, but as played by Ralph Fiennes, Lenny's fast-talking sleazy exterior often gives way to small comic touches and an interior that hints at gentleness and generousness. He is at the same time resourceful and irresponsible, exploitive and sympathetic. To be able to feel so oppositely about the same character, while still basically liking him, is a true feat of acting.

But perhaps even more appealing is Angela Bassett's Mace. Writer/producer James Cameron is known for his strong female leads (*Aliens* and *Terminator*) who are thrust into danger, and Mace fits the all-too-unfamiliar mold well. It is a delight to find a female character who is courageous and authentic, competent and clever. Bassett imbues Mace with a strong sense of friendship for Lenny, a great deal of physical ability, and yet also acts as the story's moral center. It is a quality performance following her Oscar nominated performance as Tina Turner in *What's Love Got to Do with It*.

Contrasted to Bassett's Mace is Juliette Lewis' Faith. Unfortunately, Lewis throws herself into her lascivious part with such abandon that she is, by comparison, totally unlikable and unsympathetic. We don't really care if she is in danger, and it certainly makes it difficult for us to understand Lenny's obsession with her.

Strange Days is also packed with an outstanding back up cast which includes Tom Sizemore as Lenny's true-blue, easy to trust pal; Michael Wincott as the sinister record promoter we love to hate; and Richard Edson as the underground *Squid*/clip techie who seems too simple to be so smart.

In the end, *Strange Days* easily draws us into the web of this version of a non-computer virtual reality. It makes us want to be voyeurs despite our own best intentions. It poses the fascinating question of what experiences we would want to save and savor, or try without risk. But it also asks us if maybe we shouldn't follow Mace's assessment of clip reality instead: "Memories were meant to fade," she tells Lenny who has been left emotionally crippled by Faith's lack of faithfulness. "They were designed that way for a reason."

—Beverley Bare Buehrer

REVIEWS

Chicago Tribune. October 13, 1995.
Entertainment Weekly. October 6, 1995.
The New York Times. October 6, 1995.
Premiere. November 1995, p. 21.
Variety. September 4, 1995, p. 71.

Strawberry and Chocolate (Fresa Y Chocolate)

"Irresistible! Warm, funny and wise. A triumphant tale."—Kevin Thomas, *Los Angeles Times*

"A stinging comedy of sex and politics."—Peter Travers, *Rolling Stone*

"Amazing! It captures something special."—William Arnold, *Seattle Post-Intelligencer*

In Cuba, where the official response to homosexuality was persecution, a film about the friendship between two men, one gay and the other straight, emerged. Yet *Strawberry and Chocolate* is more than simply a story of friendship. This film by director Tomas Gutierrez Alea takes on much larger issues. It speaks of the loss of personal freedoms under an oppressive government. It speaks of so-called revolutionaries, frozen in their political thought. It also speaks of a bigger world than an exclusively sociopolitical perspective can embrace.

Based on Senel Paz's award-winning short story, "The Wolf, the Forest and the New Man," *Strawberry and Chocolate* is the story of David (Vladimir Cruz) and Diego (Jorge Perugorria), and how, against all odds, they develop a friendship based on honesty, love, and mutual admiration. Diego is an artist. The film never makes quite clear what he does, simply that Diego's life is his art. He is undisguisedly gay and flaunts it like a badge of courage, refusing to be compromised.

Diego meets the lovelorn David, a political-science student at the University of Havana and member of the Communist League, just after David's girlfriend has married another man. On a bet, Diego tries to seduce the naive David, who is slow to understand. Diego tricks David into coming back to his apartment under the pretext that he has some photos of David from when he played in a university production of "A Doll's House." When David gets there, however, he is overwhelmed by his surroundings.

Diego lives in a decaying old building that had once been grand. Now its luxurious rooms, with their high ceilings and ornate balconies, have been broken down into apartments. On the stairway leading up to his place there is an old mural with a quote from Castro in what must have been, at one time, bold colors but now is faded with sections of plaster falling away.

Diego has covered the walls of his flat with art, pictures of favorite writers, and myriad wonderful artifacts to which the unworldly David has never been exposed. He is in the midst of setting up an exhibit for an artist friend of his, German (Jorge Angelino), with the help of a foreign embassy. The exhibit of life-size religious statues dominates the room, their stigmata and thorny crowns dripping with counterrevolutionary meaning.

The stunned David looks like a person suddenly woken out of deep sleep. He allows Diego to serve him black-market Indian tea, as he plays him his Maria Callas records. David even is about to borrow a book by a banned Cuban author, when Diego intentionally spills a drink on him to get him to remove his shirt. David finally comes to his senses, and he leaves in a hurry.

When David complains to his roommate Miguel (Francisco Gatorno), a staunch Communist fellow student, about his narrow escape, Miguel hatches a plot to entrap Diego in his counterrevolutionary deeds. He sends David back to spy on Diego and gather evidence about the "foreign embassy" for the cause.

David, now on a mission, goes to visit Diego, who is delighted at his return. The real Diego whom David comes to know, however, is far from the perverse subversive David thought he was. Diego is charming and alive in a way that David has never before experienced. He delights in life and art, from whatever country, and begins to give David the kind of multicultural education that the university has not been allowed to give him. Besides sharing banned Cuban books and black-market whiskey with him, Diego teaches him to see Havana in its prerevolutionary grandeur, as it crumbles into ruins before their eyes.

The faded elegance of Havana, one of the strongest elements in the film, is unfortunately not seen enough. One wants to see it through Diego's eyes, to see it come back to its former glory through the eyes of an artist. Yet one sees only a smattering of the once magnificent architecture now fallen into neglect and is left wanting more.

David's friendship with Diego evolvs to the point that he stops "spying" on his friend. When David goes to see his lost love, who tells him that she and her husband are moving to Italy, he turns to Diego in his pain. David is devastated, and he languishes at Diego's flat. Diego, although in love with David, conspires with his neighbor and friend, Nancy (Mirta Ibarra), to have her sleep with him. He is hoping not only to cheer David but also, at the same time to relieve him of the burden of his virginity.

Nancy, a lusty forty-year-old former prostitute, is the neighborhood Vigilance officer and also the local black marketeer. Her character adds a lusty boldness to the film that gives it vitality. Although

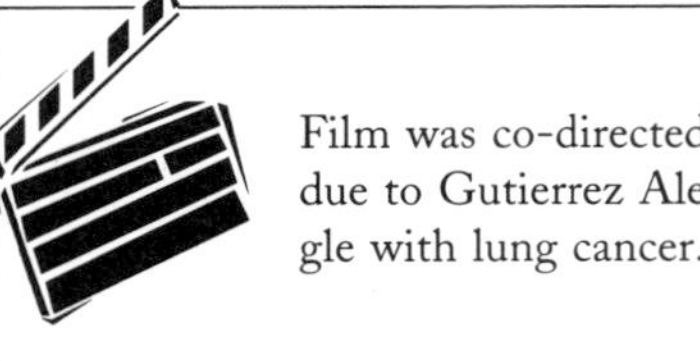

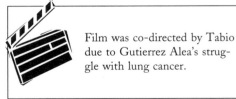

Film was co-directed by Tabio due to Gutierrez Alea's struggle with lung cancer.

she comes across as a survivor, however, she is in fact mentally unstable. David comes to visit Diego one day just as an ambulance is loading Nancy aboard. She has tried to commit suicide. They both go with her to the hospital, and Diego asks David to give blood for her. Diego has given blood the last four times she tried suicide and cannot give any more.

"There was chocolate and he ordered strawberry."—Straight communist David explains to his friend Miguel why he's sure Diego is a homosexual after their meeting at an ice-cream parlor

After this, Nancy and David get to know each other, and Nancy begins to fall for him. Without David's knowledge, she agrees to sleep with him. Diego makes them a dinner, then leaves the two alone on some false pretext. Fortunately, David has fallen in love with Nancy; her prayers to Santa Barbara have finally come true. The two are united, and David's melancholy is finally dissipated.

Meanwhile, the exhibit Diego has planned is banned. Outraged, Diego writes a letter of protest and sends it to the authorities. It is a move that will ultimately send him into exile. First, however, Miguel comes to accuse Diego of corrupting David. After a scene, Miguel leaves, and David confesses to Diego that he and Miguel had plotted to expose him as a counterrevolutionary.

Diego forgives David and tells him that he is not as noble as David thinks he is. Diego then tells David about the bet he made with German that he could seduce David and that he had spread a rumor that he and David were lovers. This revelation, coming at a time when they both know that Diego will soon be leaving the country, acts only to free them both to love each other honestly. In a cozy ending the two embrace.

Strawberry and Chocolate was the result of a collaboration between the Cuban Institute of Art and Film Industry, the Mexican National Film Office, Tabasco Films, Telemadrid (Spain), and S.G.A.E. (Sociedad General de Autores de Espana). It was filmed on location in Cuba, Mexico, and Spain. The film was directed by Tomas Gutierrez Alea, who is best known for his *Memories of Underdevelopment* (1968), and Juan Carlos Tabio, who shot some scenes while Alea was hospitalized for lung cancer.

Strawberry and Chocolate is set in 1976, a time when, according to news reports, persecution of gays was commonplace in Cuba. Yet one does not feel the hand of authority, rather the pressure of peers and neighbors. In the film, Diego's persecution stems more from his outspoken criticism of the government than from his sexual preference. In fact, homosexuality only comes into question with the homophobic Miguel.

One could surmise from the film that, except for the lack of personal freedoms from which all the characters suffer, Diego is not really persecuted for his homosexuality any more than gays in the United States are. This would paint a drastically different picture from that portrayed in Nestor Almendros and Orlando Jimenez Leal's documentary *Improper Conduct* (1983).

Nevertheless, *Strawberry and Chocolate* is a humorous and life-affirming chronicle of the friendship of three oddly matched fringe personalities: David, a loner; Diego, an intellectual ecstatic; and Nancy, a black marketer Vigilance officer. Their bond is their pursuit of love, trust, and friendship. They find all three, and then some.

Jorge Perugorria, who plays Diego, is an entrancing actor. He is handsome, subtle, and a joy to watch on the screen. Although Perugorria falls into some of the more stereotypical mannerisms, his character is still not only credible but fascinating. He makes him whole: from the glint in his eye

CREDITS

Diego: Jorge Perugorria
David: Vladimir Cruz
Nancy: Mirta Ibarra
Miguel: Francisco Gatorno
German: Jorge Angelino

Origin: Cuba
Released: 1994
Production: Miguel Mendoza for the Cuban Institute of Art and Film Industry, the Mexican National Film Office, Tabasco Films, Telemadrid, and S.G.A.E.; released by Miramax Films
Direction: Tomas Gutierrez Alea and Juan Carlos Tabio
Screenplay: Senel Paz; based on his short story "The Wolf, the Forest and the New Man"
Cinematography: Mario Garcia Joya
Editing: Miriam Talavera and Osvaldo Donatien
Production design: Fernando O'Reylly
Production management: Miguel Mendoza
Sound: Germinal Hernandez
Costume design: Miriam Duenas
Music: Jose Maria Vitier
MPAA rating: R
Running Time: 111 minutes

AWARDS AND NOMINATIONS

Academy Awards Nominations 1994: Best Foreign Language Film

when he watches David to the doting way he covers him as he sleeps. He is always entirely convincing as Diego, and it is difficult to envision anyone else playing the part.

Although Perugorria had originally auditioned for the part of David, that part was given to Vladimir Cruz, whose big eyes and sullenness bring a boyish naivete to the part. Cruz makes David's evolution from self-centered despairing boy to a playfully tolerant and confident young man a smooth transition.

The director, Tomas Gutierrez Alea, decided to do this film after reading Senel Paz's short story. He called Paz and asked the writer to do the screenplay. Together, they both agreed that the theme of the film should be "intolerance" within the context of Cuban society.

Asked if intolerance is a prevalent theme in Cuban society, Alea said, "It has to do with living under the rule of a repressive government. It would be the case in any country where the government tries to control its people. I think that this film is coming out at an important time in Cuba's history. As a society we are becoming aware of the mistakes we have made over the years, and it's time for change. *Strawberry and Chocolate* points out a basic problem within Cuban society—our inability to accept others who are different from ourselves."

Strawberry and Chocolate won awards at the Berlin International Film Festival and the Latin American Film Festival in Havana, Cuba. It is also the official Cuban entry for the Academy Award for Best Foreign-Language Film.

In the film, neglected and crumbling Havana becomes a metaphor for the waste of Cuba's cultural gifts. If indeed things are changing in Cuba, it is the hope that that waste finally will come to an end and that the world will see more Cuban films made of this caliber.

—*Diane Hatch-Avis*

REVIEWS

The Hollywood Reporter. September 20, 1994, p. 12.
Los Angeles Times. January 27, 1995, p. F1.
The New Republic. February 6, 1995, p. 24.
The New York Times. Steptember 24, 1994, p. 12.
The New York Times. January 20, 1995, p. B10.
Sight and Sound. December, 1994, p. 48.
Variety. February 14, 1994, p. 10.
Variety. February 21, 1995, p. 48.

Stuart Saves His Family

"You'll laugh because it's not your family. You'll cry because it is."—Movie tagline

"Two thumbs up!"—*Siskel & Ebert*

Lisping and wearing paisley shirts and pastel sweaters, comedian Al Franken has perfected a sharp parody of a 12-step addict. Like millions of Americans, Franken's character, Stuart Smalley, has adopted the unique lingo and life-style of the recovery movement, from the daily affirmations practiced in front of a mirror to the practice of making amends to people he has wronged. Franken created Smalley for television's *Saturday Night Live,* parlayed his success into a book (*I'm Good Enough, I'm Smart Enough, and Doggone It, People Like Me!*) and finally, like so many other SNL alumni, landed a starring movie role for his character.

Like other *Saturday Night Live* movie spinoffs, *Stuart Saves His Family* is more a series of skits than a feature-length film. The story line, written by Franken, is embarrassingly paltry, much less substantial than his previous screenwriting foray, *When a Man Loves a Woman,* a serious treatment of how alcoholism affects a family. Here, Franken simply creates a series of situations for Smalley's schtick, and it quickly becomes repetitive and tiresome.

Al Franken as Stuart Smalley and Vincent D'Onofrio, Lesley Boone, Shirley Knight, and Harris Yulin as his dysfunctional family in *Stuart Saves His Family.*

While Smalley is an accurate personification of a 12-stepper, his comic routine is not nearly enough to carry a film. For one thing, it's not hilarious, only mildly humorous. What's more, Franken doesn't want the parody to get too rough. Like many in the recovery movement, he wants to be loved. He wants audiences to find Smalley funny but not ridiculous. Franken is walking a thin line between satire and sympathy. By the last half-hour of the film, that line disappears as Franken asks viewers to root for Smalley rather than sneer at him. It's tough to start out making a character a fool and end up making him a hero, even a low-key one, and Franken doesn't pull it off.

Stuart Saves His Family is a confusing and inconsistent mix. At first Franken makes Smalley the butt of most of the jokes, but he also tries to make Smalley's alcoholic family funny. Then he wants to treat both alcoholism and the recovery movement seriously, turning on the schmaltz while keeping the laughs coming. It's a mess, and a dull one to boot.

The plot, such as it is, has Smalley as the star of a Chicago public-access cable-TV show. The program opens with him staring into a mirror and affirming "I'm going to do a terrific show today," then confessing he has a problem with perfectionism, and then adding: "That's OK, because I own my perfectionism." He explains that he's wearing a sweater knitted by a viewer who is a sex addict and needed "something to do with her hands." There's also a deftly done scene early on where Smalley, who's also a waiter, tries unsuccessfully to get a belligerent, red-meat-loving customer to order healthier food. That's about as good as it gets in *Stuart Saves His Family.*

The cable station's boss is cancelling Smalley's show. "Holocaust survivors in Skokie said they liked our skinhead hour better than your show," she tells him in one of the film's more outrageous lines. Despondent, Smalley retires to his apartment, where he stays in bed for days and eats cookies. Even a group visit by the sponsors from his various recovery programs doesn't help. Smalley belongs to overeaters anonymous (he's thin, but formerly obese), debtors anonymous ("I have a problem with money," he explains, "mostly, I don't have much of it") and adult children of alcoholics, among other groups.

In the Adult Children of Alcoholics group his sponsor is Julia (Laura San Giacomo), an attractive, sensible woman who is his closest friend. Franken doesn't have a clue what to do with Julia's character, so he does nothing. That's a shame, because San Giacomo, an actress who exudes intrigue, adds some life to the film by her very presence. She could have added a lot more if she had a real role.

The film needs a lot more because so little of interest happens. Stuart must go home because an aunt has died. On the bus, he writes in his journal, "As I am sucked inexorably toward home, I am filled with dread," but he vows to confront his family problems with the slogan "I will trace it, face it, and erase it."

Stuart's family consists of an alcoholic father (Harris Yulin); a co-dependent, overweight mother (Shirley Knight) who covers up her feelings by cooking; a dope-smoking, unemployed brother, Donnie (Vincent D'Onofrio), and Jodie (Lesley Boone), a sister with an eating problem. All four are scripted as obvious stereotypes from the catalogue of dysfunctional families and are given no nuances or depth to make them come alive. They are cardboard characters for Smalley to bounce off, except for Yulin, whose bullheaded belligerence steals most of the scenes he's in.

As directed by Harold Ramis in his customary anecdotal style, *Stuart Saves His Family* moves by fits and starts. A few flashbacks successfully mingle humor with family horror, as when young Stuart loses a TV contest to name a commercial sponsor's white knight and his father ridicules him mercilessly. The best flashback tells the story of how dad, having overslept after a drinking binge, turns a family trip to Hollywood into a final hour of sightseeing terror. He insists on taking a family photo of the children posed in the middle of a busy street. This scene is both horrifying and funny—exactly what Franken is aiming for but fails to achieve in most of the rest of the film.

But in the film's present, dramatic developments are thin and dry, centering around negotiations with a neighbor over an easement affecting the disposal of the dead aunt's property. Not even a documentarian would attempt to make an easement the center of a plot, but Franken does, with predictably dull results.

So weak is the family story line that the plot interrupts itself to resurrect Smalley's TV career. Julia helps him land a spot on a health cable network. This allows Franken to fall back on his familiar skits, which is more comfortable territory. The best thing in this part of the film is an apologetic secretary whose self-esteem is so low that she can't say a sentence without the phrase "I'm sorry."

When Smalley regains his show and his confidence, the film starts cheering him on and falls apart completely. Stu-

CREDITS

Stuart Smalley: Al Franken
Julia: Laura San Giacomo
Donnie: Vincent D'Onofrio
Stuart's Mom: Shirley Knight
Stuart's Dad: Harris Yulin
Jodie: Lesley Boone

Origin: USA
Released: 1995
Production: Lorne Michaels and Trevor Albert for Paramount Pictures in association with Constellation Films
Direction: Harold Ramis
Screenplay: Al Franken; based on his book
Cinematography: Lauro Escorel
Editing: Pembroke Herring
Art direction: Joseph T. Garrity
Music: Marc Shaiman
MPAA rating: PG-13

art really doesn't save his family, but his brother does take a sudden, miraculous vow of abstinence and drugs after dad, in a drunken stupor during a hunting trip, mistakes him for a deer and shoots him. But the family fails to convince the father to change his ways despite the threat of a prison sentence and their withdrawal of affection. After listening to their complaints in a group confrontation session, Dad explodes, "If this is what it's like in rehab, send me to jail!" By this point, audiences might want to make the same choice.

By the end of the film, Franken is playing to all possible feelings. He panders to believers in the recovery movement by making Smalley a hero. He panders to skeptics by keeping dad drunk and defiant. He panders to those who think alcoholics and overeaters are funny by making fun of them. He panders to those who think they are villains by making pitiful victims of Stuart and Julia. He panders to those who think 12-steppers are strange by making Stuart a parody. But most of all he wants audiences to find him adorable. The film ends with hugs all around, especially for Smalley. Small wonder: it's a great marketing coup for Franken to write and star in his own movie which promotes his own book and his own TV role. No lack of self-esteem here; in fact, quite the opposite.

It's too bad there's not a TV Comics Anonymous group for people like Franken and for Hollywood studios and producers who think every successful television skit can be turned into a feature-length film. It must be the ancillary video profits that keep them all in denial.

—Michael Betzold

Sudden Death

"Terror goes into overtime."—Movie tagline

"A superior action thriller loaded with jaw-dropping stunts and special effects."—Kevin Thomas, *Los Angeles Times*

"Action-packed suspense like you won't believe."—Jim Ferguson, *Prevue Channel*

"A pure adrenalin rush."—Jeff Craig, *Sixty Second Preview*

Box Office Gross: $12,260,935

Action star Jean-Claude Van Damme makes another move away from the strict martial-arts emphasis which launched his career with the more traditional action picture *Sudden Death*. He teams with director Peter Hyams, who directed Van Damme's successful *Timecop* (1994), to create this fast-paced thriller about one man's attempt to save his daughter, the U.S. Vice-President, and 17,000 hockey fans from a crazed bomber.

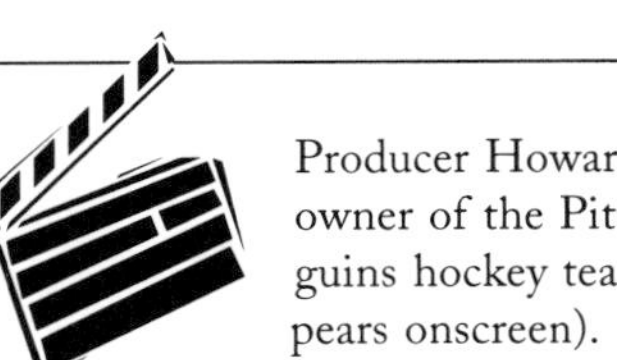

Producer Howard Baldwin is owner of the Pittsburgh Penguins hockey team (who appears onscreen).

This film will never be described as original. It is a mixture of *Die Hard* (1988), where Bruce Willis fought terrorists who held the occupants of a high-rise captive, and *Black Sunday* (1977), where mad terrorists nearly blew up the Super Bowl. In *Sudden Death*, Van Damme plays Darren McCord (which sounds suspiciously like the name of Willis' character in *Die Hard*, John McCain), a former fireman who has left firefighting because of a tragic experience. He is currently a fire inspector at the Pittsburgh arena where the Stanley Cup (hockey) finals are about to be played. Being a loving father, he takes his two children Emily (Whittni Wright) and Tyler (Ross Malinger) to the game.

The Vice-President (Raymond J. Barry) is also attending the game, viewing it from a V.I.P. box. Unbeknownst to McCord, the Vice-President, or the 17,000 screaming hockey fans in the stadium, a crazed former CIA agent named Foss (Powers Boothe) has masterminded a plot to hold the Vice-President hostage in the viewing box until a complicated (and incomprehensibe) plot to electronically transfer billions of dollars to Foss' account, is completed. If the authorities do not cooperate, Foss intends to kill one member of the Vice-President's party at the end of each of the game's four quarters. And at the end of the game, ten bombs placed all around the stadium by Foss' henchmen will kill everyone inside.

But, wouldn't you know, lowly fire inspector (but lightning fast martial-arts expert) McCord discovers the plot, and single-handedly attempts to dismantle the bombs and save the stadium. His attempts are complicated by the fact that through a mishap in the ladies' room, McCord's daughter Emily is abducted by Foss and held hostage with the rest of the V.I.P.'s.

The action moves at a breakneck pace under Hyams' expert direction. At no time is there a moment to consider that the plot is tired and the characters are two-dimensional. It will probably make no difference to audiences that the extraordinary coincidences and the hackneyed plot devices are predictable. Hyams and Van Damme know what this film is about—action. And they deliver. The race against time, the absolute evil of the villain, the heightened stakes for McCord as he tries to save his daughter...it all works.

Hyams has a great handle on the quick cuts and the sense of humor needed to make the martial arts scenes more than a series of juts and thrusts punctuated by thuds and crunches. A sequence in the stadium kitchen is excessively gory, but by Van Damme's standards the sequence is tame. Hyams makes the most out of different ways for Van Damme to dispatch the villains. A lethal Pittsburgh Penguin mascot fights to the death with Van Damme on a giant meat grinder, a huge spice rack, and across an industrial-size grill. Another henchman fights Van Damme on top of a vat of french-fry oil, and dies by being run through the conveyor belt of a giant dishwasher. Pots and pans fly, pepper gets in their eyes, and uncooked chickens are used as weapons. The scene's humor is punctuated by Van Damme's explanation that he killed the mascot because "the penguin had a gun." This sequence manages to seem like a parody of martial arts films even while it serves up admittedly gruesome but expertly filmed action.

Hyams outdoes himself with other fight scenes, including one in which Van Damme battles one of the bad guys on top of the arena's dome. With wonderful aerial photography, Hyams then raises the stakes by having the dome open (it has the capability to be an open-air stadium in good weather). It is a thrilling sequence, worthy of high praise simply for the difficult logistics, not to mention the fine choreography of the fight.

Another exciting piece of action comes when McCord decides to elude the bad guys by donning the uniform of Pittsburgh Penguin Brad Tolliver, who is assumed to have been injured. Emerging from the locker room in full hockey gear, the coach assumes McCord is Tolliver, sends him in to the game, and McCord scores (of course). This is strictly super-hero stuff, and the quick edits (by Steven Kemper), pulsating score (by John Debney), and overblown events make this a real winner for Hyams. It should also be noted that Hyams serves as his own director of photography, which is quite unusual. The taut pace with which this film progresses comes from Hyams' ability to photograph the film exactly as he sees it in his mind's eye.

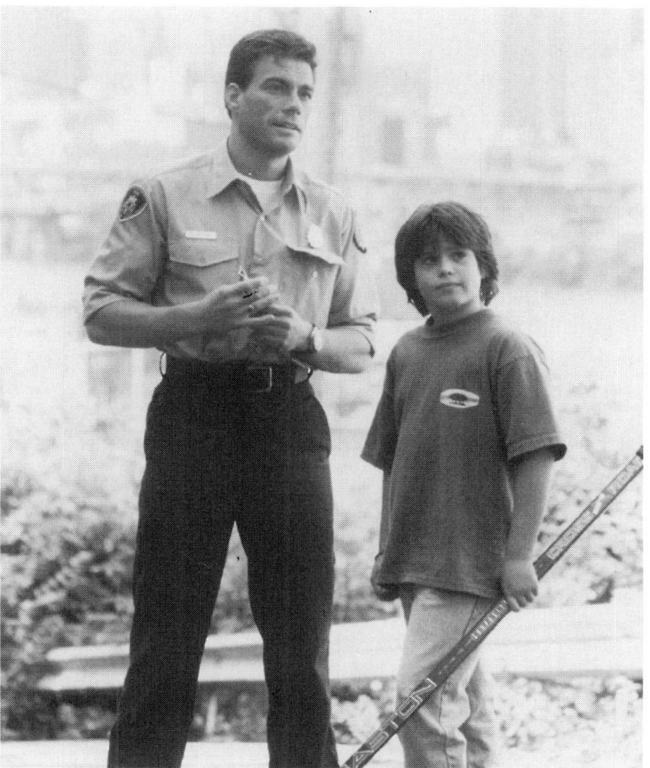

Jean-Claude Van Damme and Ross Malinger in *Sudden Death*.

CREDITS

Darren McCord: Jean-Claude Van Damme
Joshua Foss: Powers Boothe
Vice President: Raymond J. Barry
Emily McCord: Whittni Wright
Tyler McCord: Ross Malinger
Hallmark: Dorian Harewood

Origin: USA
Released: 1995
Production: Moshe Diamant and Howard Baldwin for a Signature and Imperial production; released by Universal
Direction: Peter Hyams
Screenplay: Gene Quintano and Karen Baldwin
Cinematography: Peter Hyams
Editing: Steven Kemper
Production design: Philip Harrrison
Art direction: William Barclay
Costume design: Dan Lester
Sound: Les Lazarowitz, Gary Bourgeois, Brad Sherman and Tom Perry
Visual effects: Gregory L. McMurry
Special effects: Garry Elmendorf
Casting: Penny Perry Davis, Deborah Brown
Music: John Debney
MPAA rating: R
Running Time: 110 minutes

The script, written by Gene Quintano from a story by Karen Baldwin, is laced with some unusually fun dialogue for this sort of film. Occasionally the dialogue goes a little over-the-top, such as when the evil Foss asks little Emily if she wants a glass of wine and a cigarette because "it's customary to offer these minor vices to people before they die." As for the plot, it might just be wishful thinking that there are undiscovered ways in which to make an audience feel dramatic tension other than having a crazed killer, a high-stakes crime, and one lone man who must save everyone through sheer ingenuity. As is often said, there are only six plots that are continually recycled. This one obviously recycles much of what has worked in the past, and since it is absorbing, perhaps no one should complain.

"World peace, an end to bigotry and no more mini malls."—Joshua Foss replies when asked about his ransom demands

But the introduction of the two children seems contrived at best, as was the introduction of a child in Schwarzengger's *Terminator* II: *Judgment Day* (1991) and *Commando* (1985). Admittedly, the introduction of children into the plot raises the stakes for Van Damme's character. It's hard to find fault with that. But it is so clearly contrived to pull at the audience's heartstrings that it runs the risk of being simply foolish. Writer Quintano deserves kudos for knowing the limitations of the genre, going along with them, and then putting a fun twist on the character of Van Damme's young son Tyler. As mentioned, much of the dialogue is comical, such as when Foss sarcastically tells FBI agent Hallmark (Dorian Harewood) that "I want world peace, the end of bigotry, and no more mini-malls," or when he acerbically claims that he wants $500 million dollars "to pay off my American Express."

Van Damme is, like many stars who are strictly known for action roles, rather stiff. It is surprising that Van Damme, who looks more like a standard leading man than Stallone or Schwarzenegger, has not yet been able to cross over into other types of roles. If Schwarzenegger, who has had some success with his rather wooden performances in comedy, could do it, why couldn't Van Damme? Perhaps he might simply need to find the right script, a sharp comedy director, get a few more acting lessons, and let himself be carried by what seems to be a natural sense of humor. Though his line delivery is often stiff, Van Damme does get the humor across in various throwaway lines. For example, after his fights in the kitchen, Hallmark asks him "have you had contact with the terrorists?", and Van Damme replies "I killed two...is that contact?" He delivers this and other lines with just the hint of concern that won't be mistaken for trying to do more than throw his trademark kicks. He is perfectly credible in the scenes with his children, especially where is required to be stern and angry with them. But of course, where Van Damme excels is in the action sequences. For this kind of film, he consistently proves himself to be a strong and likable hero.

Powers Boothe is suave as the caustic villain. Boothe is quite natural at delivering his lines with great sarcasm, and seems to be having fun with the role. One critic called him a "James Bond gone crazy," a perfect description. Boothe is sort of a mixture of James Bond and Bob Hope; his dry wit and icy demeanor make him a believable and formidable foil for Van Damme.

So what if it has a few cliches. So what if some of the lines are a bit corny. And so what if the ending seems far-fetched, even by the over-sized proportions of the rest of the film. *Sudden Death* is as fun and exciting as the Stanley Cup playoffs themselves, but probably not as dangerous either.

—*Kirby Tepper*

The Sum of Us

"Not your typical father and son story."—Movie tagline

"Warm and deeply affecting."—Kevin Thomas, *Los Angeles Times*

"A skillful film that wins big laughs while achieving an emotional impact."—Michael Medved, *New York Post*

"Touching, funny, warm...*The Sum of Us* hits relationships on so many levels it should be seen by everyone."—Bob Healy, *Satellite News Network*

Box Office Gross: $766,464

Many films about gay people are morose and desolate. *The Sum of Us* breaks the mold: It is bright and chirpy and inane.

Based on a stage play by David Stephens, *The Sum of Us* has the look and feel of a 1950's TV sitcom—and it is just as corny. Jeff Mitchell (Russell Crowe) is a young plumber who plays football and is futilely searching for a nice bloke. His dad, Harry (Jack Thompson), is a widower with a heart of gold—a too-good-to-be-true Dad.

Father and son share as much as they can given their different sexual orientations. When Jeff brings home Greg (John Polson), Harry intrudes on their tete-a-tete, invites himself to share a few beers and gets to know the new guy, much like an old-fashioned father would chaperone his daughter's date. Then, with a few broad winks and nudges, he retreats to his room and leaves his son and date to their own devices. This unsettling evening is "too domestic" for Greg, who flees, leaving Jeff sulking and dear old Dad offering sage advice about the number of fish in the sea.

When Harry uses a computer dating service to latch onto Joyce (Deborah Kennedy), a minimal amount of plot tension creeps into the insipid proceedings. Will Dad and Joyce get married? Will Joyce accept Jeff? Will Jeff move out? Will Jeff ever find true love?

That's all the plot *The Sum of Us* offers, except for the most desperate of all conventions. When one of the major characters suddenly falls ill, you know you've got a writer grabbing for any life raft to rescue a sinking story.

While Stephens's play was a success, his screenplay is much less so. Directors Kevin Dowling and Geoff Burton do little except transport rather stodgy theatrical proceedings to the larger screen. Dowling directed *The Sum of Us* as a play; Burton made the jump from veteran cinematographer to co-director.

With little plot to exploit, *The Sum of Us* leans heavily on characterizations. Both the central performances fall far short of being compelling. Thompson (who was much better in *Breaker Morant*, 1980) plays Harry broadly, almost as a vaudeville comic. Crowe is winsome and strives hard to be the most ordinary of ordinary guys, but he is so low-key his performance barely registers emotionally.

Thompson's schtick revolves around Harry's well-meaning attempts to appreciate his son's life-style and help him along on a path to happiness. He so much wants his son to be happy that he helpfully buys some gay porno magazines in case Jeff needs to consult on sexual techniques.

Dowling's strictly theatrical devices do not translate well to the big screen. The film is filled with asides to the

CREDITS

Harry Mitchell: Jack Thompson
Jeff Mitchell: Russell Crowe
Greg: John Polson
Joyce: Deborah Kennedy
Jeff (8 years old): Joss Moroney
Gran: Mitch Mathews
Mary: Julie Herbert
Jenny: Rebekah Elmaloglou

Origin: Australia
Released: 1994
Production: Hal McElroy for Southern Star, in association with the Australian Film Finance Corporation; released by the Samuel Goldwyn Company
Direction: Kevin Dowling and Geoff Burton
Screenplay: David Stevens; based on his play
Cinematography: Geoff Burton
Editing: Frans Vandenburg
Production design: Graham Walker
Casting: Faith Martin
Music: Dave Faulkner
MPAA rating: no listing
Running Time: 99 minutes

AWARDS AND NOMINATIONS

Australian Film Institute Awards 1994: Best Adapted Screenplay (Stevens)
Nominations: Best Film, Best Supporting Actor (Polson), Best Supporting Actress (Kennedy)
Montreal World Film Festival Awards 1994: Best Screenplay (Stevens)

audience which are laughably ill-conceived for a movie. Harry and Jeff often switch from dramatic interaction to talking to the audience in mid-scene. Clearly, these knowing asides are supposed to making the characters more endearing. In fact, they have the opposite effect: the audience is constantly reminded that these are only actors playing roles and are continually prevented from suspending disbelief and developing affection for Jeff and Harry.

American theater director Kevin Dowling, who directed the play on stage, finally managed to get financing for his film debut from the Australian Film Finance Corp. by agreeing to a co-director—veteran Australian cinematographer Geoff Burton.

In the last third of the film, Harry the character is physically unable to speak but Thompson the actor still talks to the camera when Jeff leaves the room—again testing the audience's belief in the story.

Were it played merely for laughs, the film could be tolerated. There are a few good lines, though American audiences may have a great deal of difficulty understanding many of them, given Thompson's Australian accent and staccato delivery.

"I don't want to live in a world that begins and ends with being gay... I like women. Me and the girls in the office get on great. They know and they don't care, we laugh about it. Fancy the same blokes sometimes."—Jeff to dad Harry

Although *The Sum of Us* aspires to a serious commentary on love, tolerance and family. Yet the film continually undermines its own pretentious ambitions with its pedestrian plot, script, directing, and editing.

One suspects *The Sum of Us* would be getting absolutely no attention were Jeff a heterosexual character. The attempt is to create an "Odd Couple" situation and mine it for laughs and pathos. The buzz that this is a "gay-positive" movie gets it a lot of play and sympathy from the get-go—all of it undeserved.

The filmmakers earnestly set out to show that a gay son is no different than any other son, apart from sexual preference. The result is the shallowest sort of liberal fantasy. Harry apparently has arrived at his acceptance of his son without a struggle. Jeff's only struggle is to find true love, just like countless other leading men in films. Jeff and Harry live in a "gee-whiz" world where being gay is like preferring strawberry ice cream to chocolate. If these characters approximated real people living in a real world, one might expect more conflict between Jeff and his father. Harry's father-knows-best attitude is downright insulting. Yet Jeff eats it up.

Churlishly, one is forced to ask what's so positive about an adult man who has a rotten self-image, is desperate for love, is totally dependent on his father's advice and cannot stop his dad from intruding on his dates?

The only effective parts of the film are black-and-white flashbacks depicting a lesbian relationship between Harry's mother and another woman. Almost harrowing are scenes of the family forcing the two elderly women apart, into separate nursing homes. The raw tension of those scenes is totally missing from the rest of the film.

The flashbacks celebrate the pastoral, fragile beauty of the two women's love, and the scenes of their parting illustrate the brutal clash between that love and what society demands. But in modern Sydney, the rest of the film seems to be saying, that clash doesn't exist.

The filmmakers don't have the courage or conviction to include the frank, unsettling observations of the flashbacks in the larger story. Instead, they are determined to gloss over any possible tensions in the father-son relationship, in society or inside the characters' heads.

The message of *The Sum of Us* seems to be that everything would be alright, even if you're gay, if Ward Cleaver, of TV's *Leave it to Beaver,* was dad. It's a reassuring 1950's image that doesn't fit a 1990's reality—nor does it make for a very interesting film.

—*Michael Betzold*

REVIEWS

Entertainment Weekly. April 7, 1995, p. 66.
Denis Seguin, Eye. March 23, 1995, p. 31.
Kevin Thomas, Los Angeles Times. March 8, 1995, p. F8.
Janet Maslin, New York Times. March 8, 1995, p. C19.
People Weekly. March 27, 1995, p. 17.
David Stratton, Variety. May 9-15, 1994, p. 80.
Wall Street Journal. March 9, 1995, p. 16.

Swimming With Sharks

"In Hollywood, no one can hear you scream."—Movie tagline

"Guaranteed to make viewers howl...Audiences haven't seen a movie with this much bite since *Jaws*."—Larry Worth, *New York Post*

"Witty...savvy."—Janet Maslin, *The New York Times*

"Spacey gives a bravura performance that moves with perfect comic timing."—Jeff Salamon, *The Village Voice*

Box Office Gross: $376,928

"This is showbiz...punching below the belt is not only all right, it is rewarded." So states the outgoing assistant (Benicio del Toro) to powerful Hollywood dealmaker Buddy Ackerman (Kevin Spacey). The assistant is briefing his replacement, an eager beaver named Guy (Frank Whaley), whose job with Buddy Ackerman becomes a descent into hell. The assistant's assessment is a perfect description of the back-stabbing world of movie deals. It is also an explanation of this film's own existence, because from *Sunset Boulevard* (1950) to *The Big Picture* (1989), biting the hand that feeds you is a favorite genre of filmmakers.

Writer/director George Huang worked as a studio assistant and intern for six years.

And this film definitely has a bite. The satirical story of the symbiotic relationship between powerful Buddy and the up-and-coming Guy is a harsher portrayal than many films about showbiz. Though this film is not in and of itself an excellent example of filmmaking, it hits its target with poison darts, due mostly to Kevin Spacey's lacerating, tour-de-force performance.

The plot is simple, involving Guy's arrival in Los Angeles, fresh from school and ready to do his best to get ahead so he can make "serious" films. He has already landed the job as Buddy's assistant, a coveted position because of Buddy's highly placed position in the business. He becomes involved with an attractive producer, Dawn Lockard (Michelle Forbes), who is also trying to become a mover and shaker. Both Guy and Dawn need Buddy to get ahead. But the difficulty is that Buddy is sadistic, egomaniacal, cruel, mercurial, and unethical. Eventually, Guy tires of being degraded and humiliated by Buddy, and attacks him one night in his home. In one of the sharpest (and for the audience, one of the most rewarding) revenge fantasies on film, Guy turns on his boss on the same night he is losing his relationship to Dawn. The outcome is tragic.

Using a flashback format reminiscent of (and clearly paying homage to) *Sunset Bolulevard*, writer-director George Huang sets up the film's tone in an excellent opening sequence. Emergency vehicles surround a Hollywood mansion, wheeling out a murder victim not visible to the audience. A voice-over warns, "there are stories of love surviving over success...this is not one of them." Huang has a knack for interesting and very realistic dialogue. Buddy's dialogue is oozing with cynicism: "you're happy; I hate that;" "avoid women directors; they ovulate". With Buddy, Huang has written a character he knows well, having himself been an assistant to a film executive.

Where Huang misses is in his attempt to craft a story that descends into more melodrama than many satires; and in his rather uninspired direction. The scenes in which Guy tortures Buddy (in between flashbacks) become increasingly outlandish, with Guy pouring salt into Guy's wounds, tying him to a chair, and brandishing a gun. (In fact, these scenes are directly reminiscent of the recent *Death and the Maiden*

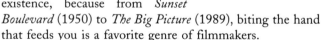

CREDITS

Buddy Ackerman: Kevin Spacey
Guy: Frank Whaley
Dawn Lockard: Michelle Forbes

Origin: USA
Released: 1995
Production: Steve Alexander and Joanne Moore; released by Trimark Pictures
Direction: George Huang
Screenplay: George Huang
Cinematography: Steven Finestone
Editing: Ed Marx
MPAA rating: R
Running Time: 93 minutes

AWARDS AND NOMINATIONS

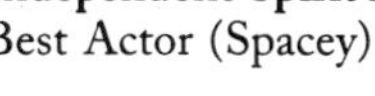

New York Film Critics Awards 1995: Best Supporting Actor (Spacey)
Independent Spirit Awards Nominations 1996: Best Actor (Spacey)

(1994), where Sigourney Weaver ties Ben Kingsley to a chair and tortures him in retaliation for her own torture years before). Huang's attempts to make Buddy sympathetic, and his creation of the implausible love triangle involving both men and Dawn take the film away from its fun central concept: a horrible Hollywood archetype gets his well-deserved comeuppance. The result is that the film becomes more a melodrama than a satire. In addition, Huang's overuse of shadows in the torture scenes, the intrusive musical underscore, Spacey's unsubtle make-up, and under-average sound all remove the sense of reality which makes the satire work in the wonderful early scenes.

"Shut up, listen, and learn."—Studio exec Buddy Ackerman to his flunky Guy in *Swimming With Sharks*

Those early scenes work mostly because of Kevin Spacey's extraordinary performance. Spacey is an actor of astonishing range and power; he snarls better than most anyone on screen today. Though this film is probably an insufficient vehicle for an Oscar nomination, it would not be surprising that Spacey's portrayal of the sociopathic Buddy would be considered at Academy Award time. From screaming about the difference between Sweet 'N Low and Equal, to drooling about a woman in stiletto heels (telling his assistant to "fetch" her for him), to becoming a sniveling wretch at the hands of his former employee, Spacey's performance makes this film worth seeing.

As Guy, Whaley is credible, but it is not clear why the ambitious Dawn falls for him. As Dawn, Michelle Lockard is even less successful in making a strong impression, but perhaps it is because the role is problematic: she starts the film as a nasty social-climber and rather abruptly changes to a girl-next-door.

Though a bit uneven, it is a perfect film for audiences who love a showy central performance—or have been having trouble with their employers lately. Bosses beware.

—*Kirby Tepper*

Tales from the Crypt Presents Demon Knight

"Frightfully engaging...handy with the clever and the cleaver. This is one Crypt worth cracking open again."—Susan Wloszczyna, *USA Today*

The story of *Tales from the Crypt Presents Demon Knight* is a thinly disguised reprise of the horror classic *Night of the Living Dead* (1968), which was remade in color under the same title in 1990. The basic idea is that a group of humans are being besieged by a horde of monsters and are destined to be completely overwhelmed by sheer weight of numbers. The tragic mood is similar to that created by old classics like *The Lost Patrol* (1934) and *Beau Geste* (1939). In *Night of the Living Dead* the monsters were zombies; in *Demon Knight*, the monsters are bug-eyed green imps from hell led by a human-looking but even more demonic villain intent on gaining possession of an artifact which looks like some sort of oversized, crudely crafted ancient altarpiece. According to the hero Brayker (William Sadler), who is the only human who understands what is going on, this chalice originally contained some of the blood shed by the crucified Jesus.

In *Night of the Living Dead*, the zombies were unable to break through the boarded-up doors and windows because they were too weak; in *Demon Knight*, the Collector and his minions are unable to break into the old boarding house where the seven humans are holed up because blood poured from the mysterious chalice creates transparent but impenetrable barriers. The blood of Jesus ran out a long time ago but can be effectively replaced by other human blood now that the vessel has been consecrated. This is one of the many hard-to-understand elements of the story; it would appear that the blood of Jesus can be replaced by the blood of whoever is the present custodian of the chalice if that custodian is wounded or killed in its defense.

Much of the suspense in *Night of the Living Dead* was provided by the fact that more and more zombies kept appearing from all directions, making it seem inevitable that they would break into the house sooner or later. In *Demon Knight* the supply of demons is comparably inexhaustible because their master can keep creating new ones by making an incision in the palm of his hand and pouring his green slime on the ground. The besieged humans can easily kill the demons by shooting them between the eyes (creating spectacular electrical effects), but new demons keep materializing to fill the ranks.

The Collector (Billy Zane) wants this ancient artifact, which is called the "seventh key," for no less a purpose than overwhelming all of humanity with his demons. He already has the other six keys in his possession. Only Brayker can save humanity from universal damnation by preventing the Collector from getting the last key. Brayker is only one of a long line of mortals who have each been entrusted with this sacred task by its previous guardian. Evidently—although this is never made clear—the appellation "Demon Knight" refers to the guardian, who is a sort of Knight warring against demons, and not to the Collector, who is certainly a demon but hardly a Knight.

The artifact in question is a good example of what famous film director Alfred Hitchcock often referred to as a "MacGuffin." A MacGuffin, in Hollywood parlance, is a "bone of contention," something that focuses the conflict in a drama. In *The Maltese Falcon* (1941), for example, the MacGuffin was the black statuette that, to quote Sam Spade (Humphrey Bogart), "all the hell was about." In *Kramer Vs. Kramer* (1979), the MacGuffin was the adorable little boy

CREDITS

The Collector: Billy Zane
Brayker: William Sadler
Jeryline: Jada Pinkett
Cordelia: Brenda Bakke
Irene: CCH Pounder
Uncle Willy: Dick Miller
Roach: Thomas Haden Church
Sheriff Tupper: John Schuck
Deputy Bob Martel: Gary Farmer
Wally Enfield: Charles Fleischer
Crypt Keeper: John Kassir (voice)

Origin: USA
Released: 1995
Production: Gilbert Adler; released by Universal Pictures
Direction: Ernest Dickerson
Screenplay: Ethan Reiff, Cyrus Voris, and Mark Bishop
Cinematography: Rick Bota
Editing: Stephen Lovejoy
Production design: Christiaan Wagener
Art direction: Colin Irwin
Set decoration: George Toomer
Casting: Jaki Brown-Karman
Special effects and animatronics design: Scott Coulter
Visual effects: Available Light Ltd.
Visual effects design and supervision: John T. Van Vlient
Sound: Tim Cooney
Special effects makeup: Todd Masters
Costume design: Warden Neil
Demon effects: Scott Patton
Music: Ed Shearmur
MPAA rating: R
Running Time: 92 minutes

the parents were fighting over. In the Arnold Schwarzenegger science-fiction thriller *The Terminator* (1984), the MacGuffin was the woman destined to give birth to the son destined to lead the future revolt against the machines Throughout *Demon Knight,* the audience is rooting for the humans to retain possession of the numinous MacGuffin, while the demons keep trying new strategies to take it away. Just as in a football game, the key changes hands several times. The audience becomes involved in this game because their own fates, after all, are hanging on the outcome.

The super-demon is cunning, like Satan himself. When he finds that he and his slimy green followers are unable to break into the building by force, he begins playing mind games with the humans trapped inside. He convinces young Roach (Thomas Haden Church) that he will let him escape if he will betray his companions, then turns the cowardly traitor over to the demons to be torn to pieces. Borrowing a scene from *The Shining* (1980), the film shows lecherous, alcoholic Uncle Willy (Dick Miller) being tempted by an hallucination in which the Collector plays a bartender pouring delicious drinks in a luxurious saloon while the dirty old man is stimulated by a bevy of big-busted B-girls.

As in both versions of *Night of the Living Dead*, the monsters finally breach the barriers and begin taking over the building. Brayker is killed in a duel with the Collector but refills the key with blood from his own gaping chest wound and passes it on to young Jeryline (Jada Pinkett) who manages to escape with it. She will now carry on the sacred mission of saving the seventh key from the Collector. She seems thoroughly competent to serve as Brayker's successor. The struggle of good against evil will continue as long as humanity exists, and the sacred chalice will continue to be passed on from hand to hand.

Tales from the Crypt originated as a horror comic magazine in the 1950's. It was killed off by the "Comics Code," which was formulated under heavy pressure from the House Un-American Activities Committee. In 1988 it was resurrected as an HBO cable television series which is now in its sixth season. As with the television series, the film is introduced by the Crypt Keeper (John Kassir's voice), a cackling animated dummy with corpse like features who is so obviously a fake that he cannot frighten anybody. The comic strip motif is highlighted throughout the film by the camera zooming in on a comic strip frame that duplicates a scene taking place on the screen. The intention is evidently to defuse the horror for the benefit of the youngest viewers, to make parents feel the proceedings are pretty innocuous, and to insure the widest possible audience appeal.

This kind of all-in-fun approach to horror has become very common, but along with making the film more marketable as family entertainment, it seems to indicate self-consciousness, guilt and apprehension on the part of filmmakers who have received their share of criticism for contributing to the rising tide of crime and violence and may be wondering how long their bloodbath will be allowed to continue. Another example of horror filmmakers distancing themselves from their own creations is *Wes Craven's New Nightmare* (1994), in which the bloody murders are deliberately revealed to have been simulated by special effects artists and other personnel. By pretending that his story is being created by the characters, Wes Craven, author and director, seems to be implying that violent films do not beget violent social behavior but violent social behavior begets violent films. The actors in many horror films often seem to want to distance themselves as well—and possibly for the same motives. Their way of doing this is by deliberately overacting and camping (i.e., not acting but "acting"). An extreme example of this behavior is Robert Englund's bizarre performance as the maniacal sweatshop proprietor Mr. Gartley in *The Mangler* (1995).

Demon Knight contains many parallels, or "homages," to *Night of the Living Dead.* Some slight effort has been made to disguise them. For instance, in *Night of the Living Dead* a little girl dies and turns into a zombie who kills her own mother with a trowel; in *Demon Knight* it is a little boy who becomes homicidal and has to be killed by the humans who have been sheltering him. In *Night of the Living Dead* the hero was African-American and the heroine was Caucasian; in *Demon Knight* the hero is Caucasian and the heroine is African-American.

There was one notable difference between the stories in the 1968 version of *Night of the Living Dead* and the sequel made in color in 1990. In the original version Barbara (Judith O'Dea) remained catatonic throughout the film and was a complete liability to the hero Ben (Duane Jones), who had enough problems trying to board up all the doors and windows with zombies sticking arms through every opening. In the 1990 version, reflecting the influence of women's liberation in the interim, the new Barbara (Patricia Tallman) shook off her terror and became a passionate zombie-hater dressed and armed like an urban guerilla. The makers of *Demon Knight* have copied the 1990 color version of *Night of the Living Dead* by making their heroine Jeryline the same sort of self-sufficient street fighter who is not the least bit squeamish about shooting demons right between the eyes. In modern action films the audience can no longer count on the hero to come riding in on a white horse to save the heroine. More and more film heroines are proving quite capable of taking care of themselves.

—*Bill Delaney*

REVIEWS

The New York Times. January 13, 1995, p. B8.
Los Angeles Times. January 13, 1995, p. F1.
Daily Variety. January 13, 1995, p. 4.

Tales from the Hood

"Where nightmares and reality meet on the street."—Movie tagline

Box Office Gross: $11,797,927

Rusty Cundieff, who directed and wrote the very funny *Fear of a Black Hat* (1995), proves that he truly understands satire with the trenchant horror send-up, *Tales from the Hood.* This film enjoyed fine reviews which predominantly praised Cundieff's sophisticated re-treads of old horror stories, told this time with an African-American urban perspective. *Tales from the Hood* is funny, violent, and clever, even while it is occasionally torpid and clumsy. It is a mixed bag. But say what you will about this film: it makes sharp observations about such American dilemmas as racism, child abuse, police brutality, and gang violence. By taking an old form, the horror anthology (this film mimics the style of *Twilight Zone—The Movie* [1983]), and mixing it with the true horrors of urban life, Cundieff has made an entertaining and socially resonant film. It is interesting to note that last year's *Candyman* and this year's *Candyman II: Farewell to the Flesh* (reviewed in this edition) (both similarly (though not as amusingly) addressed urban problems through the use of tried and true techniques of horror films past. Clearly, and sadly, the real-life problems of the urban experience are a perfect match for the horror genre.

The film stars Clarence Williams III, a fine actor still best known to audiences from his days on television's *The Mod Squad* in the 1960's, as Mr. Simms, a strange mortician who spins four spooky tales to three street kids (Joe Torry, De'Aundre Bonds, Samuel Monroe Jr.) who come to his funeral home looking for drugs. As they wait impatiently, Mr. Simms tells his tales as he displays some dead "clients," each in a different coffin. Williams is excellent in a fun role.

Each tale is a sort of morality play. The first is about a black community activist (Tom Wright) who is savagely murdered by a group of white racist policemen. The policemen eventually get their comeuppance when Wright's character returns from the dead to get revenge. A variation on *Night of the Living Dead* (1968), this vignette goes very far with its revenge fantasy: at one point, the zombie (Wright) nails one of the evil cops to a cross with flying hypodermic needles. It is quite melodramatic, and the beating of Wright by the cops is truly horrific.

"To me, the supernatural stuff is actually the lighter part of the film—the scariest thing is what people do to each other."—Director Rusty Cundieff

Tale two is more disconcerting than the other vignettes, largely because it deals with the subject of child abuse. In this vignette, a young boy (Brandon Hammond, in a fine performance) and his mother (Paula Jai Parker) are brutally terrorized by the boy's stepfather (David Alan Grier). Grier is realistically frightening as an unrepentant abuser, and the boy's revenge fantasy is scary. Cundieff has given himself a role as a schoolteacher who tries to help the boy. Audiences may find this tale uneven: the child abuse scenes are truly terrifying even while the morality of this story is a bit heavy-handed. Grier does a fine job playing against type.

CREDITS

Mr. Simms: Clarence Williams III
Stack: Joe Torry
Strom: Wings Hauser
Clarence: Anthony Griffith

Origin: USA
Released: 1995
Production: Darin Scott for a 40 Acres and A Mule presentation; released by Savoy Pictures
Direction: Rusty Cundieff
Screenplay: Rusty Cundieff
Cinematography: Anthony Richmond
Editing: Charles Bornstein
Production design: Stuart Blatt
Sound: Oliver Moss
Make-up and special effects: Kenneth Hall and (Screaming Mad) George
Casting: Robi Reed-Humes
MPAA rating: R
Running Time: 97 minutes

Also playing a character quite different than usual is Corbin Bernsen, who is featured in the third parable as an ex Ku-Klux-Klansman who is running for governor in the Deep South. Sound familiar? It is clearly a lampoon of the Louisiana governor's race in which former Klansman David Duke made quite a showing several years ago. Bernsen has fun with his caricature named Duke Metger (a hybrid of David Duke's name and Tom Metger, the white supremacist leader). The political satire will be interesting to followers of politics—Metger's campaign ad looks suspiciously like an ad blasting affirmative action that helped Jesse Helms win a tight race against African-American Harvey Gantt a couple of years back. Cundieff seems to have a good time lampooning deserving targets (he did a fine job with the world of rap music in *Fear of a Black Hat*). Eventually, a bunch of African-American voodoo dolls get gory revenge on Metger.

The fourth tale is a takeoff on *A Clockwork Orange* (1971), in which a vicious gangbanger undergoes "behavior modification" at the hands of Dr. Cushing (Rosalind Cash) who has imprinted on his brain a horrific visual history of death and destruction of African-Americans at the hands of white Americans.

All in all, Cundieff does a credible (though sometimes uneven job) at merging real-life drama with comic book satire and truly gory visual effects. Production credits are excellent. Cundieff is a filmmaker to watch.

—Kirby Tepper

Talk

"A celebration of women's work and friendship."—Julia M. Klein, *Philadelphia Inquirer*
"Witty!"—David Stratton, *Variety*

Explores the lives of two friends Julia (Victoria Longley) and Stephanie (Angie Milliken) as they come together on one particular day to work and talk about men, children and sex.

CREDITS

Julia Strong: Victoria Longley
Stephanie Ness: Angie Milliken
Jack/Harry: Richard Roxburgh
The Girl: Jacqueline McKenzie
Mac: John Jarratt

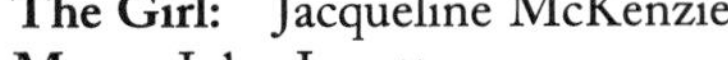

Origin: New Zealand
Released: 1995
Production: Megan McMurchy for a Suitcase Films production; released by Filmopolis Pictures
Direction: Susan Lambert
Screenplay: Jan Cornall
Cinematography: Ron Hagen
Editing: Henry Dangar
Production design: Lissa Coote
Costume design: Clarissa Patterson
Sound: John Dennison, Tony Vaccher
Casting: Liz Mullinar
Music: John Clifford
Running Time: 86 minutes

Tall Tale: The Unbelievable Adventures of Pecos Bill

"Red blooded and entertaining!"—Roger Ebert, *Siskel & Ebert*

Box Office Gross: $8,247,627

The land is the real star of most westerns, the expansive American frontier a metaphor for freedom. Customarily a battle between good guys and bad guys is played out against a backdrop of the limitless land, which remains constant and unaffected by the struggle.

In fact, however, American history is a story of the frontier being pushed relentlessly back by industry and civilization. In *Tall Tale: The Unbelievable Adventures of Pecos Bill*, the good guys are those who defend the land itself and the bad guys are usurpers who would rape and pillage it for profit.

What masquerades as a family film from Disney's Caravan stables is an unlikely place to find such an impassioned creed against the plunder of the West by the robber barons of progress. But *Tall Tale* holds many surprises. It is a rich, remarkable and rewarding film, and one of the most effective pieces of populist propaganda ever made.

Nick Stahl, who wore dreadlocks as the youngest son in *Safe Passage* (1994), here takes great care in crafting the part of Daniel Hackett, a boy pulled in opposite directions at the dawn of the 20th Century. His father, Jonas (Stephen Lang), is rooted in the land, a scroungy family farm in a place called Paradise Valley. Jonas is deeply opposed to selling it to a sinister developer, J.P. Stiles (Scott Glenn). Jonas' farm has his sweat and blood in it as well as that of his father and grandfather, and that's worth more to him than money. Daniel, however, feels beaten down by the hard work of farm life. The boy is so entranced by the modern age that he abandons his plow to chase a horseless carriage into town. He spends hours poring over postcards of nocturnal New York City bathed in street lights.

Daniel also has the dreaded modern disease of skepticism for folk tales. The boy scoffs when his father tells tales of the legendary cowboy Pecos Bill, the giant lumberjack Paul Bunyan, and the ex-slave strongman John Henry.

Folklore is a major casualty of modern life. The march of progress in the 20th Century has destroyed millions of acres of land and countless rich oral traditions that are linked to the land. *Tall Tale* boldly and convincingly draws the connection between loss of land and loss of legend, suggesting that when people are uprooted, so are their best and most heroic attributes, expressed in tall tales of larger-than-life heroes.

Mythical heroes such as Pecos Bill, Paul Bunyan and John Henry are expressions of human strength and courage and heroism in defense of freedom and justice. In *Tall Tale,* these legends have been whittled down and worn out by their losing battle against the onslaught of the mental slavery of the modern era. As people have lost faith in themselves and their own resourcefulness, they have lost the belief in their heroic qualities, and consequently their legends have started to disappear.

Tall Tale humanizes this thesis by putting twelve-year-old Daniel on the brink of manhood and his own moral choices, at the very cusp of change. He rages against his father's old-fashioned beliefs that are rooted in tradition, the land and a fierce individualism; he disparages his old man's heroes. But as in so many coming-of-age movies, Daniel learns that maturity must be based on believing in yourself, and that to believe in yourself is to tap into enormous sources of hidden strength. In the end, Daniel persists even when his father has given up.

The theme of a son discovering and reconnecting to his father's moral compass is reminiscent of *Field of Dreams* (1989). Both films are about redemption and reconciliation and the power of belief in magical and irrational forces. Many reviewers mistakenly considered *Tall Tale* a wan retelling of *The Wizard of Oz* (1939), but though it is about a child's journey home, it is more than that: it is an urgent plea for America to return home to its own forgotten values.

CREDITS

Pecos Bill: Patrick Swayze
Paul Bunyan: Oliver Platt
John Henry: Roger Aaron Brown
Daniel Hackett: Nick Stahl
J.P. Stiles: Scott Glenn
Jonas Hacket: Stephen Lang
Head Thug Pug: Jared Harris
Calamity Jane: Catherine O'Hara

Origin: USA
Released: 1995
Production: Joe Roth and Robert Rodat for Walt Disney Pictures in association with Caravan Pictures; released by Buena Vista Pictures Distribution, Inc.
Direction: Jeremiah Chechik
Screenplay: Steven L. Bloom and Robert Rodat
Cinematography: Janusz Kaminski
Editing: Richard Chew
Art direction: Eugenio Zanetti
Music: Randy Edelman
MPAA rating: PG
Running Time: 96 minutes

All this would be burdensome for a family film if *Tall Tale* did not spin out a rollicking good yarn with raucous, good-natured recklessness. Even the film's legendary trio are not always heroic; they are rough-edged and cantankerous. Their heroism needs to be fed by the wellspring of a boy's belief, and that belief does not come easily.

Tall Tale succeeds wonderfully as family entertainment. It is full of action and tight scrapes, good humor and remarkable characters, and even appealing animals (Pecos Bill's beautiful black horse Widowmaker and Bunyon's famous blue ox, Babe). Though it is a little preachy, it is never cute or cloying. It is rare for such a strong polemic to be so good-humored and gentle.

Patrick Swayze plays Pecos Bill as a big-hearted braggart, dirty and spunky and sometimes foul-tempered, a quintessential cowboy. As John Henry, Roger Aaron Brown manages to be both regal and folksy. Least successful of the legends is Oliver Platt, who looks like a silly hippie in fringed buckskin, and his Paul Bunyan is a bit too much of a misanthrope to be a believable populist hero. But all three characters have a gritty quality that is rare in family-film heroes.

There are occasional strains to link all three legends, which come from every compass point except the East. A cameo by Calamity Jane (Catherine O'Hara) adds nothing to the film except an apparent bow in a feminist direction. Scott Glenn as the slimy capitalist Stiles is genuinely evil.

Achingly beautiful Western landscapes, courtesy of Oscar-winning cinematographer Janusz Kaminski (*Schindler's List*), give soul and substance to the script's too-frequent platitudes about the virtues of the land. Rafting through a pink-walled canyon or frolicking in a meadow exploding with butterflies, Daniel and his heroic legends play second fiddle to the scenery, which is as it should be in a film that issues a passionate cry to defend such wonders. Randy Edelman's memorable score adds an appropriately majestic note to the sprawling landscape.

There is a remarkable moment in the film which turns the world of modern beliefs and values on its head. As Daniel and the three legends talk in a cave, the boy describes how the electric light bulb has turned New York City into a place where midnight is as light as noon. "Then how could anyone see the stars?" Bunyan asks and the heroes agree Daniel is the one telling a tall tale. Rarely does a film provide a viewer with such a new frame of reference, illustrating that modern life can be seen as utterly strange.

Director Jeremiah Chechik, who did *Benny and Joon*, keeps the film whimsical but pointed, a nice balancing act. The script, by Steven Bloom and Robert Rodat, does not indulge in illusions. As he is about to be defeated, the relentless Stiles reminds viewers: "There'll be others just like me, as long as there's a profit to be made. We're coming." Daniel replies, "Not through our land you aren't." So even Daniel's triumph has an air of delaying the inevitable.

Though occasionally heavy-handed and a bit cluttered,

Tall Tale has tremendous reach and fulfills most of its lofty ambitions. In the tradition of authentic stories of the West such as *The Grapes of Wrath* (1940), it is a film rooted in the best American values and virtues. Yet it is also a rollicking good time. That's a lot more than one would expect from what seems to be just another throwaway family film that major distributors just about gave up on (it sat on the shelf six months before being released). Perhaps the meaty message of *Tall Tale* is too tough to swallow, but who says family fare has to be pablum?

—*Michael Betzold*

REVIEWS

People Weekly. April 3, 1995, p. 17.
Variety. April 20, 1995, p. 48.

Tank Girl

"A rip-roaring power surge of a movie!"—Elizabeth Pincus, *L.A. Weekly*

Box Office Gross: $4,064,333

In the year 2033 an ecological disaster has ravaged the land, leaving water a precious and scarce resource. Tank Girl (Lori Petty), a futuristic feminist superheroine, comes to the rescue with her tank to take on the evil Department of Water, headed by the ruthless Kesslee (Malcolm McDowell). Based on the British cult favorite comic book.

CREDITS

Tank Girl: Lori Petty
Jet Girl: Naomi Watts
Kesslee: Malcolm McDowell
T-Saint: Ice-T
Sergeant Small: Don Harvey
DeeTee: Reg E. Cathey
Donner: Scott Coffey
Booga: Jeff Kober
Richard: Brian Wimmer
Rat Face: Iggy Pop
Madam: Ann Magnuson

Origin: USA
Released: 1995
Production: Richard B. Lewis, Pen Densham and John Watson for Trilogy Entertainment Group; released by United Artists Pictures
Direction: Rachel Talalay
Screenplay: Tedi Sarafian; based on the comic strip created by Alan Martin and Jamie Hewlett
Cinematography: Gale Tattersall
Editing: James R. Symons
Production design: Catherine Hardwicke
Music: Graeme Revell
Executive Soundtrack Coordinator: Courtney Love
MPAA rating: R
Running Time: 103 minutes

Theremin: An Electronic Odyssey

"Fascinating."—Janet Maslin, *New York Times*
"Astonishing."—David Ansen, *Newsweek*
"Two thumbs up."—*Siskel & Ebert*

Box Office Gross: $187,923

Truth is stranger than fiction. Anyone who doesn't believe that old adage can go and see *Theremin: An Electronic Odyssey* to find out for themselves. *Theremin* is the fascinating, quirky, and touching documentary which chronicles the life of Leon Theremin, the father of electronic music. It does so with considerable elan, taste, and a healthy dose of good storytelling by its director-writer Steven M. Martin.

The theremin is an instrument that was used in the soundtracks of numerous science-fiction films. It is a wooden box, a little smaller than a television cabinet, which has two antennae thrusting out from it at right angles. The player holds his/her hands near each of the antennae, and the change in magnetic field as the hands move creates different pitches and volume levels. The right hand controls volume, the left hand controls pitch. Through this mixture of magnetic fields and electricity, it creates otherworldly sounds which Baby Boomers will readily identify as the sound they most associate with 1950's science fiction. One might even say that the Theremin sound has entered the American vernacular. People unwittingly imitate the strange sound of the theremin when they want to say they've heard something bizarre: "Ooh—ooh—ooh," they might sing, as if they are introducing an episode of *The Twilight Zone*. The theremin played a significant role in the musical scores to several films, including Hitchcock's *Spellbound* (1945) and Robert Wise's *The Day the Earth Stood Still* (1951). It was also featured onscreen with Jerry Lewis in a classic comedy sequence in *The Delicate Delinquent* (1956), and was used as a background instrument on the Beach Boys huge hit song "Good Vibrations" in the 1960's.

But it turns out that the cheesy sound that Baby Boomers have come to know and love as a signal for campy sci-fi was actually the product of a brilliant and dedicated musical genius. Through the use of interviews and old documentary footage, the film tells Theremin's fantastic story and intersperses delightful footage of some wonderful theremin players. It builds a cast of characters from among Theremin's friends and followers, and weaves their stories together to create a very detailed portrait of the man's character and of the events of his life.

It begins with Clara Rockmore, an elderly New Yorker who is considered the world's greatest theremin player. She is an elegant lady with a thick Russian accent, and with her turban and dyed hair, she cuts quite a figure as she stands before the theremin, seemingly creating music out of thin air. Her soulful "playing" of the instrument is remarkable, one hand trembling back and forth to create pitch, while the other glides up and down to create volume. Rockmore becomes the audience's friend immediately, with her cherubic face and her sweet, intelligent recollections of the early days of electronic music.

Leon Theremin was a handsome young Russian immigrant when Rockmore met him in 1922. In his "laboratory" on 54th street in Manhattan, he created the theremin (and numerous other weird instruments) at a time when electricity itself was still relatively new. The concept that music could be made through electronic means was simply dismissed as a madcap notion, but Theremin persisted. Eventually, his instrument was taken seriously: Clara Rockmore and others performed theremin music with various symphony orchestras. One delightful film sequence shows a series of photos of ten theremin players on the stage of Carnegie Hall. The anomaly of these bizarre instruments taking over Carnegie Hall is one of the more charming moments in this film.

Through interviews with Rockmore, composer Nicolas Slominsky, and others, a picture emerges of Theremin's New York life. He married an African-American modern dancer named Laverne Williams, and "his friends dropped him," according to Beryl Campbell, another dancer and friend of Williams. These interviews range from the informational, such as Beryl Campbell's intelligent memories, to the gently (and unintentionally) comic, such as Slominsky's hilarious discussion of overtones and undertones in one of Theremin's contraptions: Slominsky tries to explain the musical concepts using the piano and then realizes his hands are not quite adept enough for his demonstration.

In the 1940's, Theremin mysteriously vanished, only to have been discovered years later working in an obscure Russian government agency. (By the time of his rediscovery, his wife had died.) It seems that Theremin was abducted late one night by KGB agents and spirited back to Russia to work for Lenin, and later for Stalin. "We did nothing but try to find him...we didn't know whether he was alive or he was dead...nothing," says Rockmore.

But, miraculously, they did find him. It turns out that his musical and electronic genius had been put to work trying to create new ways to improve electronic surveillance and intelligence. One of the glories of this film is when Theremin is rediscovered at 94 years old, his gnarled hands still creating new electronic devices in a tiny Moscow apartment. "I worked on electronic things, and then after that was (sic) aviation things. I was supposed to work on bad things," Theremin tells the documentarians in broken English, saying that he worked in the "Ministry of Inside...Things."

Director-writer Steven M. Martin has done a wonderful job of mixing humor, suspense, nostalgia, and genuine respect for Theremin and his contribution to music in general (and electronic music in particular.) Martin allows the story to unfold slowly, never tipping his hand on the numerous surprises the film has to offer. He also maintains a fine sense of dignity even while creating very funny sequences depicting theremin players (who look absolutely ludicrous as they play the instrument).

Martin takes his audience into some technical territory as well, making certain to emphasize Theremin's extraordinary contribution to electronic music. Interviews with musician Paul Shure and Robert Moog, whose Moog synthesizer was the immediate antecedent to today's dizzying array of electronic instruments, assure the audience that much of what occurs in contemporary music was a result of the experiments of Leon Theremin. Referring to the revolution in electronic music of the 1960's, Moog says, "what came out was nothing like what went in...what went in was Clara Rockmore, and what came out was Brian Wilson." The film then cuts to Beach Boy founder Brian Wilson, trying to describe his use of the theremin, making almost no sense at all, saying that the people who listened to it were "children, children of God...children of 25 and children of...almost 30...they are in their 20's...." Then he stops his own rambling to play the theremin but can't get it to stop when he wants it to. It is as funny as any planned comedy sequence in any fictional film. From this sequence it appears that it might take a healthy dose of quirkiness to be a theremin aficionado.

Some of the best moments are when Rockmore, Slominsky, or others are describing, with great seriousness, some of Theremin's inventions. One invention was a device that would protect a baby from being kidnapped through the use of a magnetic force field around its crib; another invention involved wiring the walls of Sing Sing prison, and another was a platform on which a dancer would dance, with antennae all around, in order to create pitches and volume changes with her whole body. It didn't quite work. The best invention, however, is seen in footage from 1928, when Theremin created a special gift for Rockmore: It is a birthday cake on a turntable, that, when turned, plays "Humoresque" with a theremin-like sound.

Even with all these outlandish gizmos, at no time does filmmaker Martin allow the film to lapse into foolishness. His highly skillful storytelling techniques keep the audience interested, and his reverence for Theremin is evident even in the quirkier segments. As far as film technique, Martin takes a standard documentary approach, alternating chronological sequences with "talking-head" interviews, film footage (some of which is very old), and old photographs. One nice touch is the occasional image of a an old, worn, theremin instrument circling around against a black background. This lovingly gives an up-close view of the instrument while contributing to the science-fiction quality now associated with the theremin.

A reunion in New York (orchestrated by the documentarians) between Rockmore and Theremin is a wondrous moment, full of the beauty and gentle humor that the best of fiction would have to offer, made better because it is all true. Rockmore and Theremin talk about their pasts, and they hobble out to the streets of New York, Theremin seeming to drink in the phenomenal technological advances on display before him. The ending is bittersweet: the cold war (so thinly veiled in the sci-fi movies to which Theremin inadvertently provided sound) deprived him of witnessing the explosion of technology in which he played a small but pivotal role. This film is a charmer.

—*Kirby Tepper*

CREDITS

Leon Theremin: Leon Theremin
Todd Rundgren: Todd Rundgren
Brian Wilson: Brian Wilson
Clara Rockmore: Clara Rockmore
Nicolas Slonimsky: Nicolas Slonimsky

Origin: USA
Released: 1995
Production: Steven M. Martin for a Kaga Bay production
Direction: Steven M. Martin
Screenplay: Steven M. Martin
Cinematography: Robert Stone, Cris Lombardi and Ed Lachman
Editing: David Greenwald
Sound: Andy Green
Music: Hal Wilner
Running Time: 84 minutes

Things to Do in Denver When You're Dead

"Protect. Love. Honor. Avenge."—Movie tagline

"Hip and original!"—Michael Wilmington, *Chicago Tribune*

"A gangster comedy with a hidden romantic heart!"—Kenneth Turan, *Los Angeles Times*

"A knockout!"—Jack Mathews, *Newsday*

"A relentlessly inventive thriller! Andy Garcia gives a dynamite performance, rich in romantic yearning."—Peter Travers, *Rolling Stone*

Box Office Gross: $477,564

Yet another film that asks audiences to fall for gangsters with hearts of gold, *Things to Do in Denver When You're Dead* is a surprisingly sappy film with a hip exterior and a misleading title. The title, derived from a Warren Devon song, suggests some sort of quirky black comedy involving corpses and resurrection, but all you get is the corpses, some wry dialogue and very little comedy.

For this film to make any sense at all, one first has to accept that small-time hoodlums have become the cinematic equivalent of the roles Jimmy Stewart once played. Such is the sorry legacy of Quentin Tarantino. *Denver*'s hero is the angelic Jimmy the Saint (Andy Garcia), who has retired from the gangster trade to run a company called "After Life Advice," which specializes in videotaping homilies, mostly about romance and sex, from dying parents and grandparents to their young progeny, to be delivered post-mortem at the appropriate coming of age.

Jimmy is snatched away from his business, which is having trouble financially, by a call from his former boss, a wheelchair-bound don so revered that his name cannot be spoken. He is simply The Man with The Plan, another in the long line of wacko Christopher Walken villains. Here, Walken, playing a crime lord who is stricken with some unrevealed disease, sucks oxygen from a tube, jokes about his diminished sexual prowess and mumbles in his customary sinister way.

Title comes from a Warren Zevon song.

Calling in an old chit from Jimmy, who thought he had retired from the mob (as David Caruso's character thought in the far better *Kiss of Death*), The Man asks Jimmy to do "an action, not a piece of work," which is, as the film takes pains to explain, a job that is not supposed to entail killing.

The film provides a sort of running mob lingo translator in the person of Jack Warden, who plays an aging gangster know-it-all who sits in a malt shop and dispenses explanations of gangster customs as required. This device is a prime example of how overly serious first-time director Gary Fleder and screenwriter Scott Rosenberg are about their undertaking. They consider their insights into gangster talk so precious that they belabor them. Everything in *Denver* is like that: precious and belabored.

The "action" ordered is for Jimmy to put a scare into the boyfriend of a young woman that The Man's pathetic son Bernard (Michael Nicolosi) used to romance. Seems Bernard lately has been in trouble for fondling schoolyard girls; he's a mess, and The Man's plan is to help his son out by punishing the man she's shacking up with.

To accomplish his mission, Jimmy rounds up his old gang of helpers, a miserable assortment of misfits who are supposed to be nearly as loveable, in their oddball way, as Jimmy. They are Franchise (William Forsythe), a tattooed biker type who's now settled down with a trailer-park wife and kids; Pieces (Christopher Lloyd), an aging porno theater projectionist who is losing toes and other body parts to a mysterious disease; Critical Bill (Treat Williams), a hair-trigger psychotic gunman who claims a jail stint has mellowed him; and Easy Wind (Bill Nunn), a huge but sensitive ex-con who is now an insect exterminator.

Of course, Franchise is reluctant to risk his life now that he's got a family, but the money's too good to turn down. Pieces is eager to join in and get a big payday so he can find a doctor who can diagnose him properly. Bill feigns an air of newfound sanity but really wants to feed his blood lust. Easy Wind is a good soldier who is loyal to Jimmy, and thus doomed. And Jimmy, who seems a little bit too much of a dolt to merit the kind of adulation he gets from all who know him, falls for Bill's charade, places him in a position of key responsibility, and the "action" turns into a sorry piece of work.

It's absurd that The Man's action requires such an elaborate ambush, involving Pieces and Bill posing as cops and the others in various back-up roles. In fact, it's not clear what Jimmy's plan for the action really is. But if Rosenberg didn't have a role for all these quirky characters, then there wouldn't be a plot for the rest of the film.

Even less plausible is the idea that Walken's character orders Jimmy and his sidekicks to leave town, but gives

Jimmy 48 hours to do so. It's a totally contrived and ridiculous plot. The Man orders "buckwheats" for the gang; Warden explains that as the term for rubbing out victims in excruciating ways. To execute his orders, The Man brings to town the cold-hearted killer Mister Shhh (Steve Buscemi), who looks like an insurance salesman.

"Do they still have gangsters? Say 'You dirty rat.'"—Dagney to would-be boyfriend (and gangster) Jimmy the Saint from *Things to do in Denver When You're Dead*

The laborious last half of the film has Jimmy trying to get his assistants to flee town in time to avoid execution. Pieces won't go; he's resigned to die because he's lived a great life as a gangster. Franchise is slow to move on, for no good reason except that the film wants him to get slaughtered too to help evoke sympathy for Jimmy's gang and show the extremes of The Man with the Plan's treachery. Bill intends to make a last stand, and Easy Wind, like most black movie gangsters, is simply going to be slaughtered along with several of his brothers in crime.

Jimmy also lingers inexplicably. Part of the problem seems to be that he can't tear himself away from a budding romance with the incredibly beautiful Dagney (Gabrielle Anwar). But almost every time they're together, Jimmy is thinking of his friends. It's supposed to be some sort of spin on *It's a Wonderful Life:* Jimmy's life is passing before his eyes, but it takes forever for this to happen.

None of it makes much sense. Why are these Bronx-style Mafia types in Denver to begin with? Why don't they flee town? What is the basis for the handsome, beloved Jimmy's inexplicable relationship with a hopelessly stupid and unattractive hooker, Lucinda (Fairuza Balk)? What is someone as elegant as Dagney doing hanging around low-life bars? Why do Jimmy and his friends hang out in a malt shop? And what do the inserted video clips of Jimmy's "After-Life Advice" clients contribute to the film, except to set up a quirky but unsatisfying ending?

The only answer to all these questions is that it's part of *Denver*'s self-conscious attempt to mask its boring plot with all kinds of clever trappings, a la Tarantino. But the conceits are all much too cute and contribute little to any comic effect. Instead, the only salvation of the film is the sizzle between Garcia and Anwar.

Anwar extends her cameo in *Scent of a Woman* to a portrayal that is even more appetizing than her famous dance with Al Pacino. With her liquid eyes and coy manner, Anwar is luscious, though she's given little to do except look inviting.

Garcia plays a guy so sweet that it's impossible to believe he's a gangster of any sort. And that's cheating. If you pull for him, it's not due to the plot but simply because he's unbearably charming. He's an old-fashioned romantic who refuses Dagney's invitation to spend the night after their first date. When Dagney asks, "Do you want to come in?" Jimmy answers, "More than I want the ascot to come back into style, but not tonight."

That line and many others reveal *Things to Do in Denver When You're Dead* as a cornball movie disguised as a hip flick. Jimmy the Saint's saintliness, his gentlemanly wooing of Dagney, his overbearing loyalty, and most especially his plight are all corny. Fleder makes even the minor hoods sappy. For example, Pieces turns down Jimmy's airline tickets and then inexplicably disappears behind a circus poster as if to evoke a Felliniesque exit. Ah, that wonderful gangster life, in the good old days...in Denver!??? It's incongruous, but unlike the incongruity that made for some amusement in *Pulp Fiction* and other early works of this genre, the cuteness here has worn very thin. After viewing *Things to Do in Denver When You're Dead*, you're left with one resounding question: "Who cares?"

—Michael Betzold

CREDITS

Jimmy the Saint: Andy Garcia
Pieces: Christopher Lloyd
Franchise: William Forsythe
Easy Wind: Bill Nunn
Critical Bill Dooley: Treat Williams
Joe Heff: Jack Warden
Mister Shhh: Steve Buscemi
Lucinda: Fairuza Balk
The Man with the Plan: Christopher Walken

Origin: USA
Released: 1995
Production: Cary Woods for a Woods Entertainment production; released by Miramax
Direction: Garey Fleder
Screenplay: Scott Rosenberg
Cinematography: Elliot Davis
Editing: Richard Marks
Production design: Nelson Coates
Art direction: Burton Rencher
Costume design: Abigail Murray
Sound: Jim Stenbe
Casting: Ronnie Yerkel
MPAA rating: R
Running Time: 114 minutes

Three Wishes

"Those who have been longing for a substantive family movie get their wish."—Jeffrey Lyons, *Sneak Previews*

"Moving, magical and utterly charming."—Paul Wunder, *WBAI Radio*

Jack McCloud (Patrick Swayze) is no ordinary drifter. When Jeanne (Mary Elizabeth Mastrantonio) accidentally hits Jack with her car, she takes him into her home to recover from his injuries. Much to the chagrin of her conservative neighbors, Jeanne and her two sons become attached to Jack due to his unconventional philosophies of life.

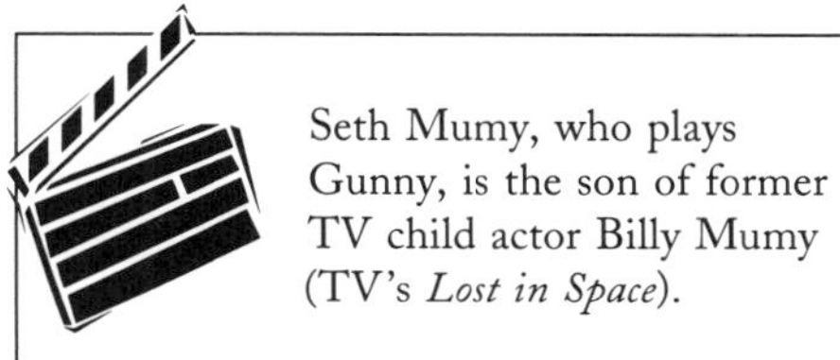

Seth Mumy, who plays Gunny, is the son of former TV child actor Billy Mumy (TV's *Lost in Space*).

CREDITS

Jack McCloud: Patrick Swayze
Jeanne Holman: Mary Elizabeth Mastrantonio
Tom Holman: Joseph Mazzello
Gunny Holman: Seth Mumy
Phil: David Marshall Grant
Joyce: Diana Venora

Origin: USA
Released: 1995
Production: Ellen Green and Gary Lucchesi Clifford for a Rysher Entertainment; released by Savoy Pictures
Direction: Martha Coolidge
Screenplay: Elizabeth Anderson; based on a story by Ellen Green
Cinematography: Johnny E. Jensen
Editing: Stephen Cohen
Production design: John Vallone
Art direction: Gae Buckley
Set decoration: Robert Gould
Set design: Tom Reta
Costume design: Shelly Komarov
Special visual effects: Phil Tippett
Sound: Lee Orloff
Music: Cynthia Millar
MPAA rating: PG
Running Time: 114 minutes

Through the Olive Trees

In this quasi-documentary, a bricklayer (Hossein Rezai) is cast as a newlywed in a film about a Persian village that has been devastated by an earthquake. Ironically, the man is in love, in real life, with the woman (Tahereh Ladania) who has been cast as his wife in the film, but she will have nothing to do with him.

Third film in director Kiarostami's trilogy of Persian village life, following *Where Is My Friend's House* (1989) and *And Life Goes On* (1992).

AWARDS AND NOMINATIONS

Academy Awards Nominations 1995: Best Foreign Language Film

CREDITS

Hossein: Hossein Rezai
Farkhonde: Tahereh Ladania
Director: Mohamad Ali Keshavarz
Director's assistant: Zarifeh Shiva
Brother: Ahmad Ahmadpour
Brother: Babak Ahmadpour
Grandmother: Mahbanou Darabin
No character identified: Farhad Kheradmand
No character identified: Zahra Noruzi
No character identified: Khodabakhsh Defai

Origin: Iran
Released: 1994
Production: Abbas Kiarostami for CIBY 2000; released by Miramax Films
Direction: Abbas Kiarostami
Screenplay: Abbas Kiarostami
Cinematography: Hossein Djafarian and Farhad Saba
Editing: Abbas Kiarostami
Production design: Abbas Kiarostami
Sound: Mahmud Sammakbashi and Changiz Sayyad
Music: Vivaldi
MPAA rating: G
Running Time: 103 minutes

The Tie That Binds

Box Office Gross: $5,772,529

It is probably no coincidence that the producers of *The Tie That Binds* also produced *Hand That Rocks the Cradle*, as in an era of increased domesticity (such as the present), it is logical that horrors should arise from homes and families as well, ensuring the popularity of such films. If the 1950s and early 1960s were a time of nuclear development, space exploration and the Cold War, then it comes as no surprise that horrors came from outer space or nuclear mutations: *Invasion of the Body Snatchers* (1956), *The Blob* (1958), *Dr. Strangelove Or: How I Learned to Stop Worrying and Love the Bomb* (1964). The same is true in an era in which previously unwed, childless people are catching the bug for both marriage and parenthood. Indeed, the screenwriter seems to have developed the idea for the film from several true cases. "It started with news stories about the Baby Jessica case," Michael Auerbach is quoted in the production notes as saying. "Then I read an article in *Atlantic magazine* called 'Problem Adoptions,' which outlined the problems associated with adopting older children—the psychological adjustment that parents and children have to go through. From those two sources, the scenario for this movie evolved."

Russell and Dana Clifton (Vincent Spano and Moira Kelly), an attractive, successful couple, appear to have everything, but, as they are unable to conceive a child, they feel something is missing from their otherwise perfect lives. They decide to adopt a child and visit an agency where a beautiful but odd child, Janie (Julia Devin), practically selects them. As cinematic luck would have it, however, Janie already has biological parents actively interested in her. Criminals caught in a burglary gone wrong, John (Keith Carradine) and Leann (Daryl Hannah) Netherwood are forced to leave their daughter, but they are far from ready to give her up and will stop at nothing to retrieve her.

Michael Auerbach's original script worked its way to David Madden (producer of *Hand That Rocks the Cradle*) and Patrick Markey (producer of *The Quick and the Dead*). It was Madden who brought in Wesley Strick (screenwriter of *Arachnophobia* [1990], *Cape Fear* [1991], and *Wolf* [1994]) to make his directorial debut with this film. Said Strick of his interest in directing this film, "I am interested in the darkness of human behavior as well as redemption. To my mind, there's no hero who isn't in some way villainous or capable of villainy when driven to it. And likewise, there's no villain who doesn't have his reasons. The idea that decency is always tinged with amorality and darkness, and that darkness always has some component of light and the possibility of redemption to it, is fascinating. Even the so-called 'good couple' in the film is forced to descend to a certain level of savagery. They must strike back in the most violent way they can in order to survive."

Directorial debut of Wesley Strick.

Interestingly enough, *The Tie That Binds* has been referred to as a film centering on the universal theme of parental love and devotion and the ideal that loyalty transcends all boundaries. Indeed, Director Strick is quoted in the production notes as stating that he selected *The Tie That Binds* for his directing debut because "the script dealt with issues of loyalty to one's child, and the idea that this loyalty transcends any barrier, which is something I think all parents can identify with." However, working against such a finding is the fact that Janie's biological parents are portrayed as, in the vernacular, "white trash" and murderous, while her adoptive parents are yuppies, completely shielded from life's unpleasantries (except for some medium to heavy financial problems). Early in the film it becomes clear that a showdown will occur, and when it does, it borrows heavily from *Hand That Rocks the Cradle* and all others of the thriller ilk (e.g., the villain who is presumed dead but isn't). It also relies heavily on the bias ingrained in the suppositions behind the film.

Interesting choices have also been made in terms of casting, choices which seem to support the initial bias. The production notes suggest that the filmmakers were looking for actors to play the Netherwoods who could be believable as devoted parents and as murderous psychopaths, rather an amazing combination. Screenwriter Auerbach always had Keith Carradine in mind for the role of John Netherwood, but, while Director Strick was interested enough in Keith Carradine's "all-American face with a glint in his eye that is striking and sinister," he wanted the actor to bulk up, to enhance his threat by having more physical bulk (which Carradine promised to do by eating a lot of protein powder). Auerbach particularly was pleased with Carradine's performance in that he felt Carradine was able "to cultivate some kind of sympathy. . . . It's the responsibility toward his family, whom he loves, that drives him to commit such awful deeds." While it is an interesting idea, it is less clear that director and screenwriter succeed at kindling this sympathy. The Netherwoods break and enter and Polaroid their victims before killing them. They kill a police officer and an adoption agency person in pursuit of their daughter. To say that the Netherwoods become sympathetic characters to the audience is a bit overstated, but to say that it is disappointing and unpleasant to watch this group of adults sink lower and lower into this abyss of violence for the professed sake of "loyalty" and "family" is more accurate. Is it any wonder that Janie, caught, as she is, between two sets of moderately psychotic parents, is cutting her hands with a butcher knife and walking in traffic?

The actors themselves would seem to agree with the pronouncement of their characters as perverse. Keith Carradine has been quoted as saying that he and Daryl Hannah's characters are "obviously a couple of twisted folks. We need some therapy." Ms. Hannah's evaluation of the script would support such a finding because, as chronicled by Director Strick, "When Daryl read the script she immediately jumped at the opportunity to play the kind of role that she's never cast in. Perhaps not since *Blade Runner* has she been asked to embody somebody with a murderous streak and she does it very well."

CREDITS

Leann Netherwood: Daryl Hannah
John Netherwood: Keith Carradine
Dana Clifton: Moira Kelly
Russell Clifton: Vincent Spano
Janie: Julia Devin
Sam Bennett: Ray Reinhardt
Jean Bennett: Barbara Tarbuck
Officer Carrey: Ned Vaughn
Lisa Marie Chandler: Cynda Williams

Origin: USA
Released: 1995
Production: David Madden, Patrick Markey, John Morrissey and Susan Zachary for an Interscope Communications/Polygram Filmed Entertainment production; released by Hollywood Pictures
Direction: Wesley Strick
Screenplay: Michael Auerbach
Cinematography: Bobby Bukowski
Editing: Michael N. Knue
Production design: Marcia Hinds-Johnson
Art direction: Bo Johnson
Set decoration: Don Diers
Costume design: Betsy Heimann
Sound: Steven D. Williams, Jay Nierenberg
Music: Graeme Revell
MPAA rating: R
Running Time: 98 minutes

Interestingly enough, while the filmmakers pronounce their intent to make both sets of parents good parents (in spite of whatever else they may be) and both sets of parents capable of whatever is necessary to maintain the family unit (including violence), the casting guidelines for Cliftons vary significantly from those for the Netherwoods. Indeed, the production notes proclaim that Vincent Spano was cast as "Dana's loving husband Russell" because "he's utterly warm and appealing." Continues Producer Madden, "Vincent has a quality of always being a good guy, no matter how quirky or offbeat his part. And that's what we needed here. He's sort of a macho guy who at the same time has to discover a more parental, more sensitive side to himself. That was a delicate balance he managed beautifully."

On the other hand, Moira Kelly was drawn to the role of Dana Clifton by the chance it gave her to combine her significant interest in motherhood with a thriller. "I liked the idea of being able to play a mother, and I liked the idea of showing a happy, loving couple who wanted to adopt this child, and I especially loved the fact that it was a thriller. I hadn't done a thriller before and I was very excited to experience working on one." In an interview in *Boxoffice*, Ms. Kelly reports that growing up in a small Long Island town she "just wanted to be married and to be happy ever after." Also a strong supporter of families and of the Catholic church, Ms. Kelly saw the role of Dana Clifton as a chance to show Hollywood that she could branch out further than the ingenue's roles she continues to receive. With the release of the film, Ms. Kelly hoped Hollywood would look at her and say, "'Okay, I can see it: Moira Kelly can play a mom.' It's been hard for me to prove to them that I can play a 20-year-old sometimes. They see me as the young college girl, or even back in high school."

Clearly the Netherwoods were cast to be murderous thugs, while the Cliftons were set up to be the warm and fuzzy alternative. The "fix" is in, and any arguments to the sympathy built in for the Netherwoods seem moot.

Rounding out the cast is Julia Devin (who plays Janie), making her feature film debut in *The Tie That Binds*. Director Strick met with fifty children, looking for a little girl who could convey "the wonder and innocence that young children see the world through, but be extremely focused one minute, and in the next, to detach from what's going on around her." In praising her, Director Strick said, "Most kids mug and somehow signal to you what they're doing. Julia intuitively understood the character and knew how to disassociate, and just go blank." Ms. Devin's range was apparent, whether she was walking blankly through traffic or frenziedly running through the forest. Originally "discovered" on a bus by an agent, Ms. Devin has appeared on television in such roles as Scottie in the TNT movie *Zelda* and had a guest starring role opposite Robin Williams on *Homicide (Life on the Street)*.

The production notes report that particular care was given to selecting the locations for the film. "Leann and John Netherwood, the drifters and parents who dwell on the fringes, write their own laws of love and loyalty, and live in rural, desolate areas. Most of their scenes were shot at night and in barren surroundings, such as a bluff-side in Santa Clarita or a diner in the middle of nowhere in Agua Dulce. On the other hand, Russell and Dana Clifton, the nurturing adoptive parents live within the city, and function normally in society. When the Netherwoods return to find Janie and take her back, they are forced to interact in a society foreign to them and it's something that they are unaccustomed to and a bit unsuited for."

The Tie That Binds may successfully reflect the depths to which any person may fall in the name of "loyalty" or "family," but, as for entertainment, it is a disappointment. Unpleasant, unappealing to watch, *The Tie That Binds* is best left on the shelf.

—Roberta F. Green

REVIEWS

USA Today, September 11, 1995, p. 4D.
Variety, September 11, 1995, p. 105.

To Die For

"Outrageously entertaining and provocative...funny, shocking and wickedly paced."—Bill Diehl, *ABC Radio Network*

"The blackest, most wicked comedy in ages. Nicole Kidman is as good as she is beautiful."—Patrick Stoner, *Flicks*

"The most exhilarating American movie since *Pulp Fiction*."—Stephen Farber, *Movieline*

"An irresistible comedy and a wicked delight."—Janet Maslin, *The New York Times*

Box Office Gross: $20,905,881

Nicole Kidman as Suzanne and Matt Dillon as Larry on their honeymoon in *To Die For*.

Gus Van Sant's *To Die For* is a dark, wickedly funny satire on the American obsession with fame. Adapted by Buck Henry from Joyce Maynard's 1992 novel, *To Die For* tells the story of would-be newcaster Suzanne Stone (Nicole Kidman), a pure product of the television age, whose coy sexuality, Dale Carnegie-esque platitudes, and peppy happy-talk mask a personality as manipulative and ice-cold as the idiot box itself. Based loosely on the Pamela Smart murder case, in which a New Hampshire high-school teacher seduced one of her students and then hired him to murder her husband, *To Die For* caustically explores a culture in which fame and celebrity have become the predominant addictions and objects of fantasy.

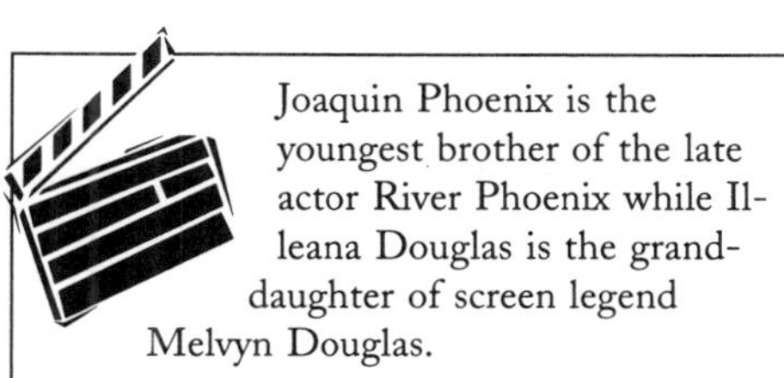

Joaquin Phoenix is the youngest brother of the late actor River Phoenix while Ileana Douglas is the granddaughter of screen legend Melvyn Douglas.

To Die For also represents a happy confluence of talent. The film marks Van Sant's comeback after the disastrous reception of his previous project, *Even Cowgirls Get the Blues* (1994), as well as the return in top form of Henry, not heard from as a screenwriter since the mediocre *Protocol* (1984) and the little-known *I Love N.Y.* (1987). Finally, it contains a breakthrough performance by Nicole Kidman, whose turn as the gorgeous, fame-obsessed sociopath Suzanne is at once sly and cold, funny and monstrous. Although the film underwent a rocky post-production involving extensive cuts, rewrites, and re-shoots, a final version appeared at Cannes in May, 1995, to widespread critical acclaim.

Van Sant begins the film with a slow-motion montage of newspaper and tabloid articles about the Stone-Maretto murder case over a Danny Elfman plucked-violin score. Headlines like "Blonde Temptress" and "I'm 100% Not Guilty" and photos of Stone in short skirts set up the plot, the setting (the amusingly-named town of Little Hope, New Hampshire), and the tabloid nature of the case. Van Sant ends the prologue by zeroing in on the individual pixils of a wire photo.

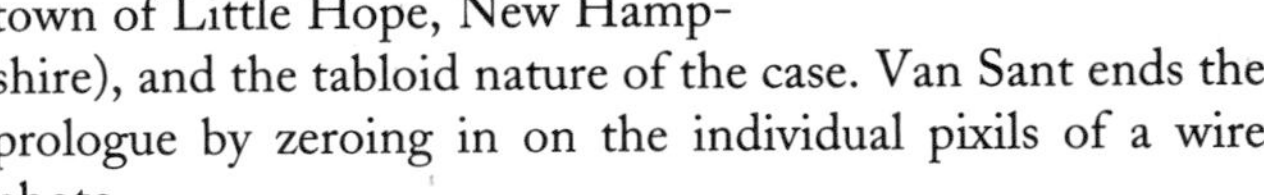

"You aren't really anybody in America if you're not on TV. Because what's the point of doing anything worthwhile if nobody's watching?"—Suzanne's credo of life from *To Die For*

Henry structures the film around Suzanne's obsession with electronic fame and celebrity, and her ability to arouse that obsession in others, usually with a sexual twist. Appropriately, Henry uses electronic media devices to tell the story. Central to *To Die For* is Suzanne's carefully crafted videotape of herself, sent from hiding, in which she mouths phony denials about the murder of her husband as well as unintentionally hilarious platitudes about the TV business in the hopes of getting a lucrative national TV interview. ("Here's what I found out," says Suzanne, discussing the murder of her husband. "All of life is a learning experience.") Clips from this tape are intertwined with interviews with her husband's family as well as the teenagers she has made accomplices to the crime; talk-show appearances by both her husband's family and hers; and scenes showing what actually happened. Van Sant and Henry move back and forth skillfully between scenes on television and scenes in which they show the effects of television on the lives of real people.

CREDITS

Suzanne Stone: Nicole Kidman
Larry Maretto: Matt Dillon
Jimmy Emmett: Joaquin Phoenix
Russell Hines: Casey Affleck
Janice Maretto: Illeana Douglas
Lydia Mertz: Alison Folland
Joe Maretto: Dan Hedaya
Ed Grant: Wayne Knight
Earl Stone: Kurtwood Smith
Angela Maretto: Maria Tucci

Origin: USA
Released: 1995
Production: Laura Ziskin for Rank Film Distributors; released by Columbia Pictures
Direction: Gus Van Sant
Screenplay: Buck Henry; based on the novel *To Die For* by Joyce Maynard
Cinematography: Eric Alan Edwards
Editing: Curtiss Clayton
Production design: Missy Stewart
Art direction: Vlasta Svoboda
Set decoration: Carol A. Lavoie
Wardrobe: Kim W. Chow
Makeup: Patricia Green
Music: Danny Elfman
MPAA rating: R
Running Time: 106 minutes

Larry Maretto (Matt Dillon) is smitten with Suzanne from the moment he eyes her from the stage on which his bar band is playing. His cynical sister, Janice (Illeana Douglas), is suspicious of her from the beginning, but Larry has already succumbed to Suzanne's charms. "I'm tellin' you, Sis," he says to Janice, "she's the golden girl of my dreams." Larry figures he is merely humoring Suzanne when she prattles on, in steely tones, about becoming the next Barbara Walters or Jane Pauley.

Suzanne and the naive Larry are soon married, but Suzanne seems more concerned with the fact that her dress is the "exact same one Maria Shriver wore at her wedding." She cuckolds him on their honeymoon with a famous TV executive (George Segal), and upon their return to Little Hope marches into a local TV station and tells non-plussed station owner Ed Grant (Wayne Knight) that television is the "global messenger," and that "it has always been my dream to be that messenger."

Hired as the station's weather girl, Suzanne barrages Grant with a series of proposals. The one that finally takes is a video documentary called "Teens Speak Out!," important "because," as Suzanne says, pitching her idea to a rapt high-school class, "it's teenagers just like you who are the future of our country." Taken in by Suzanne's bombshell presentation in pumps and a tight mini-skirt, three affable but not-too-bright teenagers, Jimmy (Joaquin Phoenix), Russell (Casey Affleck), and Lydia (Alison Folland), agree to particpate in the after-school project. Suzanne shoots over 250 hours of footage with the three teenagers, over the course of which she becomes Jimmy's "golden girl" as well. "She looks so clean," Jimmy tells Russell. Van Sant and Henry deftly show how the three kids, yearning for some-

AWARDS AND NOMINATIONS

Golden Globe Awards 1996: Best Actress-Musical/Comedy (Kidman)
British Academy Awards Nominations 1995: Best Actress (Kidman)

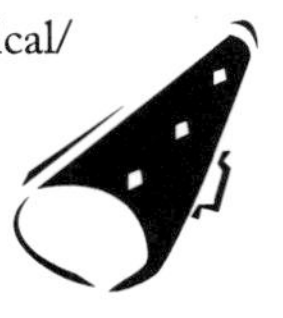

thing beyond their lives in a trailer park, latch on to the fantasies of fame and sex which Suzanne embodies. In one scene, Jimmy masturbates while watching her on television.

Larry's talk of kids and managing his father's Italian restaurant provoke scorn from Suzanne, who tells him that "if you wanted a babysitter, you should have married Mary Poppins." When Larry tells her that her career is unlikely to lead to any network offers, Suzanne's thoughts logically turn to murder. Her final word on Larry's uselessness amounts to a death sentence: "He doesn't know a thing about television."

Suzanne seduces a willing Jimmy, tells him Larry has hurt her, and convinces Jimmy through giving and witholding sex to kill her husband. Jimmy, dumb and smitten beyond his wildest dreams, agrees to do it for a thousand dollars and some CD's. On a wild night, Suzanne, wearing a blue-and-white polka-dot dress and dancing in the rain, becomes Jimmy's every fantasy come true.

In a remarkable scene, Jimmy, fantasizing about his having sex with Suzanne, pulls the trigger on Larry as Larry watches Suzanne give her late-night weather report and wish him a happy first wedding anniversary. Suzanne, to Larry's family's growing horror, gives extensive media interviews, and turns Larry's funeral into her event by playing Eric Carmen's "All By Myself" at the service. Jimmy, Russell, and Lydia, now rejected by Suzanne but still dreaming of moving to California with her to work on an illusory TV talkshow, blow their cover to the authorities, and the net begins closing around Suzanne. In the end, the ice-queen is "iced" by Larry's Mafia-connected family, and Janice, an iceskater, happily glides over the pond where Suzanne is buried —but not without Suzanne getting in the last word through Lydia: "Suzanne used to say you aren't really anybody in America if you're not on TV. 'Cause what's the point of doing anything worthwhile if there's nobody watching?"

To Die For plays to the strengths of all three of its principals. Van Sant, as evidenced in both *Drugstore Cowboy* (1989) and *My Own Private Idaho* (1991), has a talent for keeping enough distance from his down-and-out characters to provide humorous commentary on their fantasies of love and security, yet at the same time never loses sight of their poignant need for substitute families. Van Sant has also shown a willingness to experiment with daring narrative techniques (characters popping off magazine pages, characters speaking in Shakespearean verse). In *To Die For*, with its hapless teenagers reflecting in video interviews how they got involved in a murder plot, Van Sant shows off not only his ability to mix and match narrative devices, but also his knack for evoking feelings for characters who could easily be relegated to caricatures. Van Sant, helped by an extraordinary performance from Joaquin Phoenix, shows how easily these kids, mired in dead-end lives, can be bought simply with promises of sex, California sun, CD's, and TV fame. Henry, too, in his best work since *The Graduate* (1967), writes deadpan social satire yet maintains sympathy for his protagonists. Here, as in *The Graduate*, Henry allows the audience to feel smarter than some of his characters, but never demeans his suburban protagonists as boobs. If the audience is allowed to be wise to Suzanne's tricks, the characters she dupes are all allowed their say—and,in some cases, their revenge. Finally, Kidman's performance is a revelation. She uses her looks and her screen persona's natural pluck and determination to create a feral sociopath in pastels, a delectable piece of poison candy whose soul consists of the pixels of a TV screen.

The mixture of Van Sant's and Henry's sensibilities is rich, as are the contributions of Van Sant's longtime creative team. Costume designer Beatrix Aruna Pasztor chooses solid pastels to accentuate Kidman's poison-candy character. Production designer Missy Stewart captures the surreal quality of Suzanne's apartment, as well as the sadness of the trailer park in which the teenagers live. The film and video sequences are seamlessly woven together to evoke a media-saturated world that has somehow bypassed most of the film's characters, yet continues to attract them. The visual jokes and timing match beat for beat the laugh lines in the script.

Working in a satiric vein rare in recent American movies, Van Sant, Henry, and Kidman have created a hilarious, one-of-a-kind exploration of fame, sex, and celebrity and its corrosive effects on American culture. Only *Network* (1976) rivals *To Die For* as a critique of America's obsession with television.

—*Paul Mittelbach*

REVIEWS

The Christian Science Monitor. LXXXVII, September 26, 1995, p.13.
The New Republic. CCXIII, October 23, 1995, p.28.
The New York Times. CXLV, September 27, 1995, p.B1(N).
The New York Times. CXLV, October 1, 1995, p.H26.
Newsweek. CXXVI, October 2, 1995, p.86.
Rolling Stone. October 19, 1995, p.155.
Sight and Sound. IV, December 1994, p.54.
Vogue. CLXXXV, October, 1995, p.198.
The Wall Street Journal. September 29, 1995, p.A10(W).

To Wong Foo, Thanks for Everything! Julie Newmar

"Attitude is everything."—Movie tagline
"Swayze, Snipes and Leguizamo are absolutely fabulous!"—*Boston Herald*

Box Office Gross: $36,475,691

When reading a child's tale it is wise not to stop and examine the facts of the story line. Somehow the magic is lost when one demands to know if the bears, like those who Goldilocks meets, really sleep in beds, or if wolves can really dress up like grandmothers, or if little boys can prevent their own maturity and fly off to a place called "Never Never Land" without ever booking a flight on United.

And so it is with the film *To Wong Foo, Thanks for Everything! Julie Newmar*. Somehow there is a veil of lighthearted, uplifting magic woven by the three male leads, but it will tear quickly and easily if one examines the plot too closely. Because, you see, after all, this is a fairy tale (literally and figuratively).

Vida Boheme (Patrick Swayze) is the elegant and regal grande dame of drag queendom, and she, along with her protege Noxeema Jackson (Wesley Snipes) have tied to win the Miss New York Drag Queen Contest with its prize of an all-expense paid trip to Hollywood to take part in Drag Queen of America Contest. However, their victory is rained upon by the tears of a young and brash Latino drag queen, Chi Chi Rodriguez (John Leguizamo), who is distraught over having lost.

Miss Vida has a soft spot for anyone in need, and she talks Noxeema into cashing in their airplane tickets and purchasing a car in which all three of them can travel to Hollywood and compete. So, with their good luck omen, a purloined autographed photo of Julie Newmar taken off the wall of the restaurant in which they hatch their plan (and hence the title of the film), they load into their yellow Cadillac and head off across America.

Their road trip runs into its first snag, however, when they are stopped by a police officer (Chris Penn) who not only informs them that they have a tail light out, but also puts the moves on Vida. To protect herself she pushes the officer away, knocking him unconscious, but not before he has discovered that she is a he. The three drag queens now flee into the night, believing they have killed the officer, but like Cinderella at the ball, Vida leaves behind one of her shoes. And the not dead Officer Dollard will be in hot pursuit.

John Leguizamo as Chi Chi, Wesley Snipes as Noxeema, and Patrick Swayze as Vida in *To Wong Foo, Thanks For Everything, Julie Newmar*. © 1995 Universal City Studios, Inc. Courtesy of MCA Publishing Rights, a Division of MCA Inc. All rights reserved.

Title comes from the autographed celebrity portrait of Newmar, hanging in a Chinese restaurant, that Vida swipes as a good-luck charm.

Further complications occur when their car breaks down in the backroads of Nebraska. Unfortunately, the mechanic (Arliss Howard) in the nearby wide spot in the road that passes for a town indicates that the ladies are stuck there over the weekend until he can get a part shipped in on Monday. And, lucky for them, he will rent them a room in his house.

It doesn't take long for the flamboyant drag queens to breath some life and color into the drab little town. Roughnecks are taught how to treat a lady; a woman who hasn't talked for years suddenly finds her voice and a soul mate in Noxeema; a young girl is taught how to woo the boy she has a crush on; and a meek, battered woman (Stockard Channing) finds her backbone. The ultimate conversion happens when the townsfolk become atypically "Red and Wild" during the annual, normally staid Strawberry festival, and their normally isolated ways give way to standing up to Officer Dollard to protect the drag queens they have come to love—even if they don't really know them. While all these changes are less than convincing, they are the details one might be willing to overlook if there is a more compelling element in the fairy tale to overcome it. Thankfully, in *Wong Foo*, there is just that element: the performances of Swayze, Snipes, and especially Leguizamo.

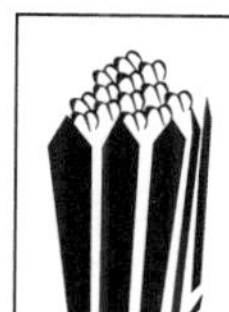

"Ready or not, here comes mama."—Vida from *To Wong Foo, Thanks for Everything! Julie Newmar*

Patrick Swayze, probably best known for his role of the macho dancer in *Dirty Dancing*; Wesley Snipes, normally seen as the action hero of such films as *Passenger 57*; and the relatively unknown John Leguizamo, whose stand-up comedy routines have gotten stand-out reviews (and whom you may have seen on his Fox television show *House of Buggin'* or the film *Super Mario Brothers*) are in a way inspired choices to play drag drag queens. Who would have expected it? All of that red-blooded American heroism trapped under layers of foundation and batting false eyelashes. It is an intriguing concept, and there's no doubt these actors are having great fun with their roles.

Obviously, there are comparisons to make between *Wong Foo* and several other films in which major stars dressed up in drag. Jack Lemmon and Tony Curtis in *Some Like it Hot*, Dustin Hoffman in *Tootsie*, Robin Williams in *Mrs. Doubtfire*, and the recent Australian cult hit *Adventures of Priscilla, Queen of the Desert*, with its bravura performance by Terence Stamp, all come to mind. But while the first three had men dressed as women for ulterior motives, only *To Wong Foo.....*and *Adventures of Priscilla...* are truly about drag queens. Of these two, *Adventures of Priscilla, Queen of the Desert* takes the more outrageously camp path, while *To Wong Foo.....*takes a decidedly more middle America road.

Decked out in fabulous costumes, each drag queen in *Wong Foo* is given her own internal episode and her own miracle or two to work while stuck in Snydersville. What follows is very thinly presented, very Hollywood mainstream, and very predictable. But Swayze, Snipes and Leguizamo put so much gusto into their roles, one can't help but laugh along for the ride. And that is when the film is at its best, when these three macho leads are camping it up; when they are flighty and funny. Unfortunately, too often the film is more concerned with delivering its thin message than in delivering scandalous jokes. (And too often the scenes end in an all-too-abrupt fade to black that leaves a feeling of incompleteness to the narrative.)

But perhaps outrageousness would make these drag drag queens too threatening for American audiences—or at least perhaps that is what the filmmakers thought. For Vida, Noxeema and Chi Chi are decidedly non-threatening (there is virtually no clue as to if they're gay or not, in fact they are decidedly asexual!) These drag queens won't make average American audiences—symbolized by the women of Snydersville—recoil with repugnance or stare in curiosity. In fact, they are taken up by the women of this backwater community as role models. Are the filmmakers saying that only a man in drag can teach a woman how to

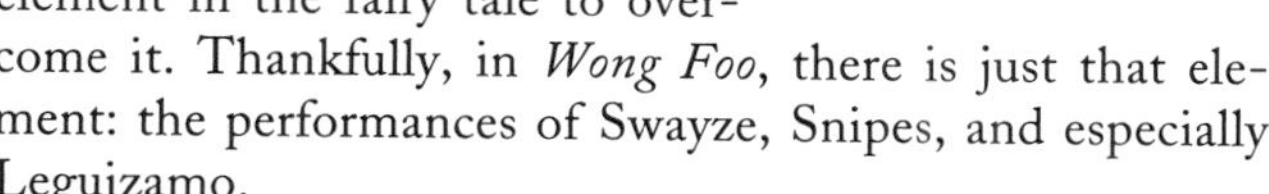

CREDITS

Noxeema Jackson: Wesley Snipes
Vida Boheme: Patrick Swayze
Chi Chi Rodriquez: John Leguizamo
Carol Ann: Stockard Channing
Beatrice: Blythe Danner
Virgil: Arliss Howard
Bobby Ray: Jason London
Sheriff Dollard: Chris Penn
Merna: Melinda Dillon
Loretta: Beth Grant
Clara: Alice Drummond
Rachel Tensions: RuPaul
Julie Newmar: Julie Newmar
Girl: Naomi Campbell

Origin: USA
Released: 1995
Production: G. Mac Brown for an Amblin Entertainment; released by Universal Pictures
Direction: Beeban Kidron
Screenplay: Douglas Carter Beane
Cinematography: Steve Mason
Editing: Andrew Mondshein
Production design: Wynn Thomas
Art direction: Robert Guerra
Set decoration: Ted Glass
Costume design: Marlene Stewart
Music: Rachel Portman
Choreography: Kenny Ortega
MPAA rating: PG-13
Running Time: 108 minutes

AWARDS AND NOMINATIONS

Golden Globe Awards Nominations 1996: Best Actor-Musical/Comedy (Swayze), Best Supporting Actor (Leguizamo)

be a woman in these post feminist days? Or is this too deep a thought for so thin a film? Maybe what they're saying is that sometimes all we need is someone different to shake us up and change our complacent, and often destructive ways? Maybe, as Vida herself says as she views the revived community she and her pals have created, "sometimes it just takes a fairy."

—*Beverley Bare Buehrer*

REVIEWS

Chicago Sun Times. September 8, 1995, p. 15+
Chicago Tribune. September 8, 1995, Section Friday, p. C
Entertainment Weekly. September 8, 1995, p. 49+
New York Times. September 8, 1995, p. B1+
Rolling Stone. September 21, 1995, p. 86
USA Today. September 8, 1995, p. 7D
Variety. September 4-10, 1995, p. 71
Village Voice. September 12, 1995, p. 59

Tom and Huck

"The original bad boys!"—Movie tagline

Mark Twain's two classic novels of the boyhood adventurers Tom Sawyer and Huckleberry Finn have spawned a raftload of Hollywood films. Movies based on Twain's *The Adventures of Tom Sawyer* were made in 1930 (with Jackie Coogan as Tom), 1937 (a David O. Selznick hit), 1939 (with Donald O'Connor as Huck Finn) and 1973 (with Jodie Foster as Becky Thatcher). Films based on the book *Huckleberry Finn* came out in 1931 (with Coogan as Huck), 1939 (with Mickey Rooney as Huck), 1960 (with a cameo by Buster Keaton), 1974 and 1994.

Filming took place in the city of Mooresville, Alabama, which filled in for Hannibal, Missouri.

Walt Disney's *Tom and Huck* is at least the tenth retelling of the Twain tall tales. As the title suggests, the film centers on the fragile bonds of friendship between the two boys, Huck the social outcast and Tom the beloved rebel. The film is a solid if unspectacular effort that is mostly faithful to Twain's conception and thankfully resists too much patronizing updating.

Amazingly in this age of political correctness in Hollywood, the filmmakers keep Twain's Injun Joe (Eric Schweig) as the villain of the piece. If there were any suggestions about changing the character's name or excusing his murderous intent, they were overruled by those wanting to keep the authenticity of the Twain work. Injun Joe in *Tom and Huck* is at least as menacing and beyond moral redemption as Twain wrote him.

Nearly everything in a film about Tom Sawyer and Huck Finn depends on the actors playing the two key parts, and the casting here is excellent. Jonathan Taylor Thomas, a star on television's *Home Improvement* is perfectly pranksterish as Tom, with the facial expressions of a lovable conniver and a nice range of emotional registers. As Huck, Brad Renfro (*The Client*) is noticeably much older and socially more of a misfit. At first glance Renfro looks dangerously close to a slacker mall rat, but he covers up his modern look quite well with a mumbling, careless manner.

The film is careful enough to explore and exploit the tugs and pulls of the tenuous relationship between Tom and Huck. It is clear from the start that Tom thinks the older, wilder Huck is cool and wants to be his friend, but not at the cost of his self-worth. It is also plain that Huck is lonely and needy beneath his uncaring veneer and needs Tom's friendship even more than Tom needs his.

Except for a sappy ending with some too-obvious lines about friendship, the film refrains from psychoanalyzing or wallowing in the Tom-Huck relationship. The strains of trust, betrayal and reciprocity flow from the action of Twain's familiar story, as they should. Director Peter Hewitt and scriptwriters Stephen Sommers and David Loughery are sensible enough to let Twain do the storytelling, and of course his plot carries its subtle, enriching tensions about what is right and wrong behavior.

Tom's dilemma is that he must balance an oath made to Huck not to tell anyone about a murder they see Injun Joe commit with his duty to the truth and to Muff Potter (Michael McShane), the man wrongly accused of the murder. If Tom remains silent, he is safe and can remain Huck's friend, but Muff will be hung for a crime he didn't commit. If Tom testifies to Muff's innocence, he risks losing Huck's friendship and maybe even his life to Injun Joe's vengeful retribution.

It's a harrowing choice, and Hewitt doesn't do much

sugar-coating. In many ways, *Tom and Huck* is a dark and foreboding tale and probably too frightening for most young children. But there is also a nice, meandering quality to the film, as with Twain's story. Tom lives in sunlight and darkness, taking life not very seriously even as his hard moral choices and Injun Joe's threats make his life very serious indeed. Thus the film retains Twain's feel of boyhood as an adventure that careens between safety and innocence and the chasms of fear and danger.

"Mark Twain's characters are smart and complex, and the author was dealing with some interesting and weighty issues, but in the guise of two boys larking around. It's dark and gritty at times, but there is a lot of fun and humor too."—British director Peter Hewitt

Embodying the evil adult world, Schweig succeeds as Injun Joe in creating a menacing, human character. His face is often in closeup and is the more frightening for not being inhumanly monstrous but in fact carrying a strange sort of dignity. Injun Joe is truly wicked but he is truly a man. McShane adds some nice shadings to the one-dimensional Muff Potter role.

CREDITS

Tom Sawyer: Jonathan Taylor-Thomas
Huck Finn: Brad Renfro
Injun Joe: Eric Schweig
Judge Thatcher: Charles Rocket
Aunt Polly: Amy Wright
Muff Potter: Michael McShane

Origin: USA
Released: 1995
Production: Laurence Mark and John Baldecchi for a Walt Disney production; released by Buena Vista
Direction: Peter Hewitt
Screenplay: Stephen Sommers and David Loughery; based on the novel *The Adventures of Tom Sawyer* by Mark Twain
Cinematography: Bobby Bukowski
Editing: David Freeman
Production design: Gemma Jackson
Art direction: Michael Rizzo
Set design: Daniel Bradford
Set decoration: Ellen J. Brill
Costume design: Marie France
Sound: Walter P. Anderson
Music: Stephen Endelman
MPAA rating: PG
Running Time: 92 minutes

Among the major characters the only one miscast is Rachael Leigh Cook as Becky Thatcher. Her face is too patrician and almost porcelain in its beauty; she looks like she has stepped out of the pages of a fashion magazine rather than a scruffy classroom in Hannibal, Missouri. And Cook lacks the range to make the tomboyish side of Becky credible. She doesn't have much soul and it's hard to see why Tom is smitten with her.

What the film lacks is excitement. Extra action is added in a climactic showdown with Injun Joe, but by then it is too late to salvage plot tension. Audiences aren't likely to be carried away. Part of the problem is that Thomas is so clever in his endless mugging that he is almost too easily digested; he leaves behind no residue of continuing pain or unresolved fear from scene to scene. Injun Joe's menace appears suddenly but at times fades completely away. Hewitt wants to be faithful to Twain but at times is almost laconic in his execution. A little tighter editing would add some needed zip to the proceedings.

But those are more paltry failings than most updated renderings of classics these days. It is good news that *Tom and Huck* is a quiet film that depends on Twain's material and doesn't strain for high-tech devices that might make today's jaded audiences sit up and squirm. Neither does Hewitt feel the need to wrap the tale in too much weepy nostalgia. Twain's story holds up at the end of the Twentieth Century about as well as it did in the middle of the Nineteenth Century, since at its heart are piercing questions about duty and loyalty and solid answers to those questions.

In many ways, the complex yet refreshing friendship between the two boys in *Tom and Huck* has its counterparts in many real-life relationships these days between boys with ties to civilization yet urges to be wild and other boys who are outcasts who yearn for more acceptability. Replace the small-town trappings with the urban jungle and the basic issues remain the same, for kids these days see horrible things and must confront awful truths just as Tom Sawyer did. As only he could do so well, Twain still teaches important moral lessons in an unpatronizing yet unapologetic way, and it is nice that a 1990s filmmaker has the sense to get out of the way and let the master storyteller tell it like it was—and still is.

—Michael Betzold

Tommy Boy

"If at first you don't succeed, lower your standards."—Movie tagline

"Sweetly hilarious."—Jack Garner, *Gannett News Service*

"A good belly laugh of a movie."—Kevin Thomas, *Los Angeles Times*

"Keep the jokes coming!"—Mick LaSalle, *San Francisco Chronicle*

Box Office Gross: $32,680,208

Tommy Boy is an affable film notable both for the performance of Chris Farley in the title role, and his match-up with fellow *Saturday Night Live* star David Spade as his reluctant sidekick. These two excellent comedians, backed up by several established screen stars and a fun script, provide a diverting 1 1/2 hours of entertainment mixed with the right amount of poignancy.

Tommy Callahan Jr. (Chris Farley) has just graduated college after a mere seven years with a "D" average. Though he is not the brightest of young men, he is one of the best intentioned, with a huge heart to match his huge stomach. He returns from school to his small hometown in Ohio to discover that his father, Big Tom Callahan (Brian Dennehy) is re-marrying a blonde bombshell named Beverly (Bo Derek). Tommy is also thrilled to discover that Beverly has a "son" (Rob Lowe) who will be his new "brother." But the happiness doesn't last, as Big Tom dies on his wedding day and Beverly turns out to be a goldigger. Meanwhile, the family company, Callahan Auto Parts, is about to be taken over by a rival (Dan Akroyd). Since the takeover means the loss of thousands of jobs to the loyal workers of Callahan Auto Parts, Tommy is forced to go out on the road and save the company—and he takes snippy office manager Richard (David Spade) for assistance.

Written by the writers of *Wayne's World* (1992), Bonnie Turner and Terry Turner, and directed by the director of *Naked Gun 33 1/2: The Final Insult* (1994), Peter Segal, the film mines the comic possibilities of the two opposite characters. Spade and Farley are like a modern Laurel and Hardy. Richard's nasty barbs about Tommy's weight and witlessness are as funny as they are mean: when Tommy says that lots of people took seven years to finish college Richard responds, with fake sweetness, that "they're called doctors." There are some very funny sequences, such as when the two

David Spade as Richard Hayden and Chris Farley as Tommy Callahan in *Tommy Boy*.

CREDITS

Tommy Callahan: Chris Farley
Richard Hayden: David Spade
Paul: Rob Lowe
Beverly: Bo Derek
Big Tom Callahan: Brian Dennehy
Michelle: Julie Warner
Rittenhauer: Sean McCann

Origin: USA
Released: 1995
Production: Lorne Michaels; released by Paramount Pictures
Direction: Peter Segal
Screenplay: Bonnie Turner, Terry Turner, and Fred Wolf
Cinematography: Victor J. Kemper
Editing: William Kerr
Art direction: Stephen J. Lineweaver
Music: David Newman
MPAA rating: PG-13
Running Time: 96 minutes

hit a deer on the road, and thinking they killed it, put it in the back seat only to be surprised when it wakes up. The series of scenes in which they try to sell Callahan Auto Parts products to reluctant company owners are a hoot. In one scene, Tommy plays with the toy cars on one customer's desk, eventually crashing and setting the cars on fire.

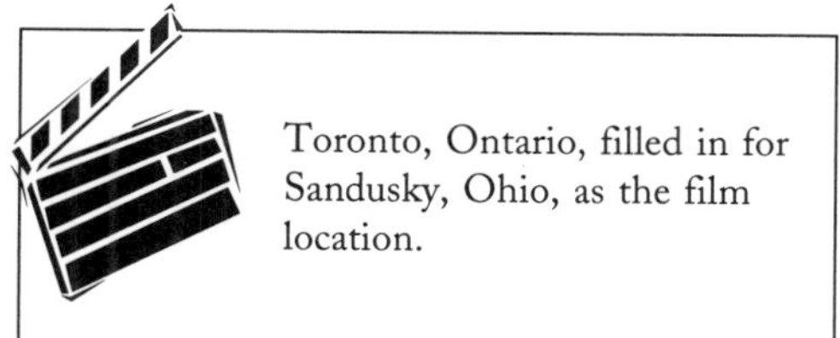

Toronto, Ontario, filled in for Sandusky, Ohio, as the film location.

Richard's nastiness is ceaseless, but the filmmakers wisely have Richard receive his comeuppance along the way, in the form of an equally sarcastic gas station attendant, or by Tommy's discovery of Richard's late-night voyeurism. They also maintain Richard's inner goodness by having him be the one who yells "Call '911'!" when Big Tom dies. This minor moment sows the seeds for Richard's turnaround by showing his love for Big Tom. Eventually and predictably, the two become friends: the poignant moment when Richard admits that he has no friends is well-earned and well-performed.

"I mean, we're two really different people. Chris is a big, loud, obnoxious guy, and I'm a whole lot quieter and more low-key. Actually, that's probably the reason. The contrast is pretty funny. We just work out well."—David Spade explains his and Chris Farley's on-screen chemistry

Farley is a revelation, able to be hilarious and touching. His final scene, talking to his deceased father from a sailboat, is wonderful. Other actors are excellent. Rob Lowe has found a terrific niche in recent years as a villain. Bo Derek looks fantastic as ever, and makes a great villainess. Brian Dennehy appears to be the only person that could play Chris Farley's father. From his size to his charm, Dennehy provides the incentive that could make Tommy want to straighten up and become the man his father would have wanted him to be.

David Newman's music is quite lush and beautiful for a movie that has been dismissed by many as yet another "dumb buddy" movie in the genre of *Dumb and Dumber* (1994), or *Wayne's World*. But composer Newman underscores the gentility of the characters in this film, the humor of the "road" sequences, and the scope of the changes which Tommy is forced to make through the tragedy of his father's death.

The success of this film lies in its ability to create empathy for its characters while relying on the truth of the situations to provide humor. Where *Wayne's World* succeeded because it was just plain silly and goofy, *Tommy Boy* succeeds because it is just plain funny and engaging.

From the terrific title performance, to the restrained direction, to the cinematography by Victor J. Kemper, this is a winner. Audiences shouldn't expect anything brilliant or life-changing from *Tommy Boy*, but it delivers good production values, some hearty laughs, and a big dose of charm.

—*Kirby Tepper*

Top Dog

Office Gross: $5,093,707

Chuck Norris films are aimed squarely at family audiences. His "nice-guy" persona and martial arts skills make him the perfect American action hero. These winning attributes helped make his other films, such as *Sidekick,* a big hit at the box office. It would seem that adding a cute little dog to play opposite Norris would broaden his family appeal even more. The script for *Top Dog* was, by Ron Swanson, based on a story by Aaron Norris and Tom Grayem seemed a perfect formula for an early summer release that would have mass appeal.

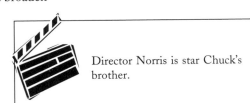

Director Norris is star Chuck's brother.

Suddenly, on April 19, 1995, the horrific bombing of a federal building in Oklahoma City blasted a harsh reality into the minds and consciousness of America. As the images appeared on television, a nation wept in stunned disbelief. The timing of this incident could not have been worse for Norris's film, which opens with a shot of a San Diego housing project being blown to bits by right-wing Nazi terrorists. This rather uncanny similarity to the Oklahoma tragedy certainly must have affected the appeal of this light-weight action comedy, starring, ironically, Oklahoma native, Chuck Norris.

If *Top Dog* were able to be disassociated with Oklahoma and taken on its own merits, the film, directed by Aaron Norris (the star's brother), is a predictable, but amusing film for younger audiences gearing up for summer. Chuck Norris plays Jake Wilder, a maverick cop called in to help solve the murder of his long time friend, Lou Swanson (Carmine Caridi). The catch is that Wilder has to team up with his dead friend's partner, a shaggy dog named Reno. Reno was actually played by a highly intelligent pure-bred herding dog, trained by Boone's Animals for Hollywood. The owner, Boone Narr, is perhaps the best trainer for film animals in the country, and his dog Reno does steal the show.

The premise is that Norris's character likes to work alone, and being teamed up with anyone, much less a dog, is an insult. However, through the course of the movie the two "partners" grow to love and respect one another. As the plot unfolds, it is discovered that an organization, led by Kai Huff, is planning a major attack on a Coalition for Racial Unity rally in San Diego, to be held on April 20, Adolf Hitler's birthday (yet another reminder of the real-life tragedy). Through a series of completely unbelievable events (Norris takes on practically the entire camp of terrorists single-handedly), both Wilder and Reno manage to thwart the plans and ultimately save the day—if not the entire world.

The script for *Top Dog* (putting aside the similarities to the Oklahoma City bombing tragedy), had a difficult mission from the outset: a story line which tires to mesh the threat of a holocaust at the hands of right-wing extremists with a light-hearted "man's best friend" comedy. It's like watching Benji trying to take on Hitler. The film lacks momentum and goes from one scene to the next with no build. The sequences between the explosions and the fight scenes appear like filler, with no merit on their own. When Chuck Norris visits his mother while she is gardening, she just happens to know that the next day is Hitler's birthday. She looks at him and says demurely "It's in all the history books, dear." Reno takes a side trip to a dog show and sneaks up and gets the blue ribbon after posing in various hats and sunglasses. After trying so hard to be cute and silly, the film then cuts to a group of militia giving the "heil Hitler" salute. It's a strange mixture indeed.

Chuck Norris is a likable performer who is skilled at martial arts—no one expects him to be a great actor. Reno the dog is cute—Nazis are not. The combination makes for

CREDITS

Jake Wilder: Chuck Norris
Capt. Cajjahan: Clyde Kusatsu
Savannah Boyette: Michele Lamar Richards
Karl Koller: Peter Savard Moore

Origin: USA
Released: 1995
Production: Andy Howard for Tanglewood Entertainment Group production; released by MGM/UA
Direction: Aaron Norris
Screenplay: Ron Swanson, based on a story by Aaron Norris and Tom Grayem
Cinematography: Joao Fernandes
Editing: Peter Schink
Production Design: Norm Baron
Costumes: Vernika Flower-Crow
Asistant Director: Leo Zisman
Sound: Jim Thornton
MPAA rating: PG-13
Running Time: 85 minutes

a disturbing mixture of elements. Audiences may become confused from one scene to the next and wonder if they should laugh or be outraged. In light of current events, maybe Hollywood should see the danger in trivializing serious issues, and rely less on gimmicks and more on creative pursuit.

—Rob Chicatelli

Total Eclipse

"Touched by genius. Cursed by madness. Blinded by love."—Movie tagline

"Powerful!"—Garrett Glaser, *KNBC*

"Hypnotic! DiCaprio and Thewlis fearlessly delve into the dark lives of poets Rimbaud and Verlaine."—Bruce Kirkland, *Toronto Sun*

Box Office Gross: $339,889

Arthur Rimbaud (1854-1891), symbolist poet and forerunner of surrealism, is still an icon for the modern literary sensibility. His disdain for bourgeois society, his favoring of the imaginative—bordering on the hallucinative and the occult—makes him a perennial hero for the counter culture. His poems distort conventional syntax; his astonishingly short career (he was through as a poet by the age of nineteen), and his subsequent travels to Africa, make his life, like his work, elusive and enigmatic. He remains the epitome of the self-created artist, self-contained and unconfined. Spending his last days as a trader in Africa, and dying before the age of forty, Rimbaud refused to settle down, to explain himself, to concede to any authority outside himself—save for his inexplicable death-bed conversion to Christianity.

It is well to have this background in mind while watching *Total Eclipse*, which provides minimal exposition, beginning with a scene in which Rimbaud's pious sister calls on Verlaine (a physical wreck at fifty), asking him to turn over Rimbaud's manuscripts in her campaign to present a sanitized, religiously acceptable version of her brother's work. The decrepit Verlaine (David Thewlis) appears to accede politely to her request, but as soon as she departs he tears up her card and flashes back to the rebellious youth who was his lover and his poetic inspiration. Verlaine's treatment of Rimbaud's sister is of a piece with his flashbacks, in which he shows himself to be a man constantly capitulating to conventional sentiments and then reneging on them in his sprees with Rimbaud (Leonardo DiCaprio).

The manic Rimbaud comes crashing into the established life of poet Paul Verlaine (1844-1896), safely married to a buxom young wife (Romane Bohringer) who has given him a child and the support of her father's house and income. Verlaine detests playing safe. He knows it is bad for his style, and he is mocked for it by Rimbaud, who belches at the dinner table, urinates on bad poetry, and prances naked on a Parisian rooftop in exuberant good spirits and contempt for the niceties of society.

Leonard DiCaprio plays Rimbaud as a very hard case indeed. He won't tolerate any sort of sentimentality or hypocrisy. He spurns the idea that there is such a thing as love, and when Verlaine tries to get Rimbaud to say he loves him, Rimbaud retaliates by stabbing his fellow poet's hand with a knife. Rimbaud is the intolerant adolescent who will not compromise—not even to get his poetry published. The important thing, he says, is to write. He does not want the encumbrances of what goes along with the literary life, the making of a name for one's self, and the politicking that goes along with a career.

Because very little of Rimbaud's or Verlaine's poetry is recited in the film, their antics seem merely irresponsible. Even reviewers in such progressive periodicals as *The Village Voice* have expressed their contempt for DiCaprio's and Thewlis's renditions of poets who seem oafish and maudlin, although the actors are less at fault (other reviewers concede) than Christopher Hampton's vulgar screenplay, based on a play he wrote when he was eighteen.

> Hampton's screenplay was adapted from a play he originally wrote at age 18.

It is hard to watch Verlaine throw his pregnant wife to the floor because he is in misery over his supposed bad faith as a poet. His actions seem especially vicious because his wife is no bourgeois bauble, but a sensitive, loving wife, genuinely perplexed at her middle-aged husband's silly and self-destructive exploits. Director Agnieszka Holland has been criticized for emphasizing the physical in Verlaine's sexual scenes with his wife and with Rimbaud. But what is a director to do? Verlaine's wife has a beautiful body, and he says he craves it, and the film is narrated from his point of view. Bohringer's ample body is the bourgeois world that Verlaine loves to loll in even as it saps him of his poet's vocation. Of course, he is going to hurl that flesh to the floor and return to Rimbaud's hard, brutal body to satiate quite another kind of lust, one that rejuvenates his poetry because it is not compliant or complacent but is constantly challenging his perceptions.

> "I decided to be a genius. I decided to originate the future."—Arthur Rimbaud from *Total Eclipse*

Rimbaud always scoffs when Verlaine turns sentimental. Yet when Verlaine abandons Rimbaud during their scruffy stay in London, Rimbaud is beside himself with a sense of loss and follows Verlaine right into his wife's hotel bedroom. Just as Rimbaud has stabbed Verlaine in the hand, Verlaine shoots Rimbaud in the hand. The two of them, covered in blood, are inexcusable outlaws. Nothing in the film—not its acting, direction, or writing—makes it easy to sympathize with them. But then that seems to be the point. This is not some Hollywood bio-pic, in which underneath the writer's grime there is a soul of purity. Bourgeois society is not caricatured in order to make it easier for viewers to identify with these poets. These men do ugly things to themselves and to others. Only Verlaine's conviction for sodomy effects his separation from Rimbaud.

Total Eclipse is relentless, working up a fine sense of just how repugnant Verlaine and Rimbaud must have seemed to their contemporaries. An excruciating film to watch, its tensions are relieved only by the cinematography, with scenes of the poets frolicking in the fields, and of Rimbaud's brief return visits to the family farm, where his puzzled mother wonders aloud whether her son's poetry will lead to anything. He does not care to say, vouchsafing only that this is what he does—write poetry. His utter self-confidence is disarming. He really cares for nothing but his own work. In such moments he recalls William Faulkner's reply to his plaintive daughter that nobody remembers Shakespeare's daughter.

Total Eclipse is as ruthless as its poets. It concedes nothing to the audience's desire to find a redeeming value in its literary figures. The beautiful cinematography shows Rimbaud and Verlaine in lighter moments relieving themselves from the intense concentration of work, but there is nothing pastoral in these interludes. The country scenes say nothing about the corruption of society and are not used to enhance our sympathy for the poets. They are not escaping social constraints so much as they are anarchists of the spirit.

Has there ever been a film that showed artists in a less flattering light? DiCaprio and Thewlis do not look any better in nature than they do in society. It is very difficult to make a film in which there is no sympathy for rebellious characters, but *Total Eclipse* achieves that distinction and thus overturns much of the modern mythology of modern literature and film, which has made the outcast the hero, and the criminal the scapegoat—all of whom have been misunderstood and sensitive souls, perverted by society. Artists, in this mythology, have been noble savages, versions of Rousseau's view that left in his natural state man is incorrupt. But it is clear that *Total Eclipse* views its poets as quarrelling with human nature itself. Rimbaud, in particular, is not just angry at society or at poets who form clubs and read to each other, he is upset about the self-deceiving aspect of human nature itself. He begins by acknowledging his own selfishness and detests everyone who does not follow suit. He feels threatened when Verlaine asks him for a declaration of love precisely because he feels love yet knows it is mixed up with his own egotism. He can say he loves, but only with a knife driven into his friend's hand. It is a painful revelation: love can be a stabbing sensation, hurtful as well as helpful.

To say that *Total Eclipse* is not to everyone's taste is an enormous understatement. Seldom has a film provoked so much distaste among reviewers. Even if one concedes its

CREDITS

Arthur Rimbaud: Leonardo DiCaprio
Paul Verlaine: David Thewlis
Isabelle Rimbaud: Domonique Blanc
Mathilde Verlaine: Romane Bohringer

Origin: France
Released: 1995
Production: Jean Paul Ramsey Levi; presented by Fit-Portman-SFP Cinema-K2, Capitol Films, European Co-production Fund, Canal Plus and Le Studio Canal Plus; released by Fine Line
Direction: Agnieszka Holland
Screenplay: Christopher Hampton
Cinematography: Yorgos Arvanitis
Editing: Isabel Lorente
Production design: Dan Weil
Art direction: Nathalie Buck
Set decoration: Francoise Benoit-Fresco
Costume design: Pierre-Yves Gayraud
Sound: Michel Boulen, Laurent Quaglio and Francoise Groult
Casting: Margot Capelier
MPAA rating: R
Running Time: 110 minutes

bold and novel purpose—to attack a modernist view of writers which perhaps has itself become too pious, too sentimental, too self-regarding—and can bear its cruelty, a clearer view of what Verlaine and Rimbaud wrote might have been apposite. What were those words the poets were seeking? How does their poetry correspond to their experience? It is notoriously difficult in a visual medium to make writers' words vivid and to show the writing process itself. Holland wisely avoids those cliched scenes of the writer writhing at his desk, but without finding some fresh equivalent, Holland and screenwriter Christopher Hampton have left themselves exposed to the charge of dwelling solely on the lives and not the work. Reciting poetry would, of course, retard the film's movement, just as literary analysis in biographies arrests the narrative. Yet without taking the risk of becoming uncinematic, *Total Eclipse* falls short of becoming a completely satisfying film.

—*Carl Rollyson*

Toy Story

"A super duper 10! The most fun filled, playful movie of the year!"—Susan Granger, *CRN International*

"Astonishing fun! A magic mix of action and humor!"—Peter Travers, *Rolling Stone*

"Fascinating! Marvelously ingenious and a highly entertaining family film!"—Paul Wunder, *WBAI Radio*

Box Office Gross: $146,198,683

Billed as the first full-length film to be created entirely on computer, Disney's *Toy Story* is more than merely a technological breakthrough. Conceived and directed by Academy Award winner John Lassiter (who used this computer gimmickry before in his 1986 short *Luxo jr.*), these three-dimensional images, which are astonishing in their textured depth, are enhanced by amazing anthropomorphism and a witty and fully developed script. A tale of rivalry and friendship, *Toy Story* offers something for both children and adults: a wild and very smart ride through imagination.

Andy, a six-year-old who's about to have a birthday party, roughhouses in his bedroom with his favorite toy, Woody (Tom Hanks), a floppy, stuffed sheriff with a talking pull-string, a cowboy who rides herd over the other toys the moment the boy leaves the room. The toy community, which contains such notables as the irascible Mr. Potato Head (Don Rickles), the neurotic dinosaur Rex (Wallace Shawn), Slinky Dog (Jim Varney), and the token female with romantic designs on Woody, Little Bo Peep (Annie Potts), comes to life as they anxiously await the unwrapping of Andy's birthday presents, fearing that each will be the next toy to be discarded. Despite his false bravado and pep talks to the troops, Woody is paranoid about losing his revered place atop Andy's bed. A reconnaissance of plastic green army men—in one of the film's many inside jokes, the Sergeant is voiced by R. Lee Ermey, the drill sergeant in Kubrick's *Full Metal Jacket* (1987)—is dispatched to relay via walkie-talkie information about the party back to the toys upstairs. Only Mr. Potato Head is optimistic as he chants, "Mrs. Potato Head, Mrs. Potato Head..."

It almost seems like all are safe from being discarded until Andy opens that last package. Woody's worst fears are realized as Andy receives the year's hottest toy, a boastful space ranger named "Buzz Lightyear" (Tim Allen). Not only is Buzz annoyingly outfitted with the latest gadgets and flashing lights, he is delusional, as well. Buzz refuses to acknowledge that he is a mere action figure; in his egotistical mind, he *is* Buzz Lightyear, defender of the universe who inadvertently crashed into this place when his aircraft malfunctioned while on a special mission to save the world from the evil Emperor Zurg. "You are a toy," Woody condescendingly explains to Buzz, "T-O-Y, toy!" But the other toys are instantly charmed by Buzz's innocence and his unwavering belief in his own superpowers, particularly his ability to fly using his pop-out wings. When Buzz puts on a wild demonstration in which he is catapulted and flung around the room by chance, Woody is appalled at the new toy's arrogance. "That's not flying," he explains, "That's falling with grace." Still, the others are won over and Woody begins to reveal his resentment towards Buzz for having usurped his position as resident top toy.

The character of Woody is named for actor Woody Strode while Buzz is named after astronaut Buzz Aldrin.

When Buzz accidentally falls out the bedroom window, the toys all turn against Woody, suspecting that the cowpoke with the empty holster pushed the flashier spaceman out of "laser envy". In order to redeem himself, Woody must find Buzz and bring him home. In the process the two get stranded at Pizza Planet, a fast food/game emporium that Buzz mistakes for a space station and which thrusts these two contrasting playtoys of different eras into the clutches of Andy's sinister neighbor, the vicious Sid (Erik Von Detten). The duo are held captive by this sadistic punk who mutilates and tortures toys, experimenting with his own version of Frankenstein. Woody and Buzz fear that this surreal collection of mutant toys, led by a one-eyed babydoll head with plucked out hair and grafted on Erector-set spider legs, are cannibals, but in the end, they prove to be poignantly heroic. When Buzz discovers that he is indeed merely an action figure made in Taiwan, he is devastated. "Being a toy is better than being a space ranger," Woody tells him. "What matters is that we're there for Andy when he needs us." It is up to Woody to rally all the toys in order to save Buzz from destruction. By joining forces, our two heroes learn the true meaning of friendship.

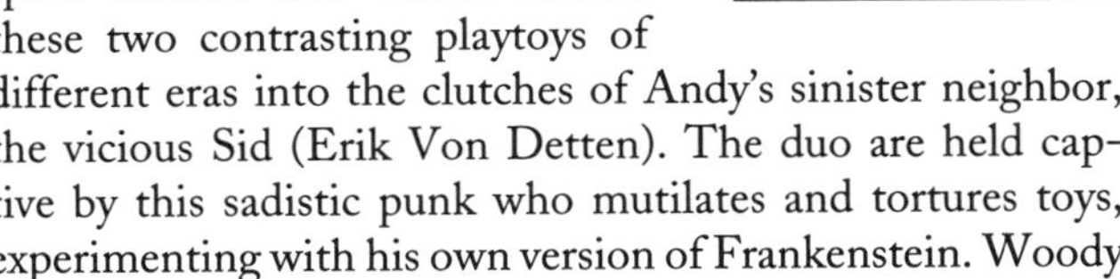

"What do you say I get someone else to watch the sheep tonight?"—Little Bo Peep to Woody from *Toy Story*

The images are captivating and the humor nonstop. The press notes for the film revealed that the filmic influences for *Toy Story* were widespread. One simulated camera move, for instance, is a replica of one Kenneth Branagh used in *Frankenstein* (1995), while another is an homage to Michael Mann's hit television show, *Miami Vice*. Attention was paid to the smallest detail; the hall carpet, for example, in Sid's house is straight out of Stanley Kubrick's *The Shining* (1980). As for the subtle inside jokes, viewers of Tim Allen's television situation comedy, *Home Improvement*, should be amused by the giant tool box that proves problematic for our heroes' escape from Sid; while older viewers may chuckle at Don Rickles' patented put-down, "What are you looking at hockey puck?"—this time, though, it really is a hockey puck. Not all the humor is simplistic by any means, nor is it confined to the medium of film. A particularly amusing piece broadens its references to the art world when Mr. Potato Head rearranges his snap-on facial pieces into a Cubist mass of disarray and proudly proclaims, "Look, I'm Picasso!"

The casting of Tom Hanks as the voice of Woody provides instant likability and bonding with the genially smug cowboy and may be one of Hanks' most compelling performances to date. His chemistry with comedian Tim Allen is obvious and their competitiveness and contrasting performance styles mesh together beautifully. The entire voice cast is wonderful, from the diminutive Wallace Shawn (*Manhattan*, 1979, and *My Dinner with Andre*, 1981) as the actor trapped inside of a dinosaur's body, to Jim Varney (Jed Clampett in *The Beverly Hillbillies*, 1993) as the loyal Slinky

CREDITS

Woody: Tom Hanks (voice)
Buzz Lightyear: Tim Allen (voice)
Mr. Potato Head: Don Rickles (voice)
Slinky Dog: Jim Varney (voice)
Rex: Wallace Shawn (voice)
Hamm: John Ratzenberger (voice)
Bo Peep: Annie Potts (voice)
Andy: John Morris (voice)
Sid: Erik Von Detten (voice)
Mrs. Davis: Laurie Metcalf (voice)
Sergeant: R. Lee Ermey (voice)
Hannah: Sarah Freen (voice)
TV Announcer: Penn Jillette (voice)

Origin: USA
Released: 1995
Production: Ralph J. Guggensheim and Bonnie Arnold; released by Walt Disney Pictures
Direction: John Lasseter
Screenplay: Joss Whedon, Andrew Stanton, Joel Cohen and Alec Sokolow; based on a story by John Lasseter, Pete Docter, Andrew Stanton and Joe Ranft
Editing: Robert Gordon and Lee Unkrich
Art direction: Ralph Eggleston
Supervising Animation: Pete Docter
Sound: Gary Rydstrom
Story Coordination: Susan E. Levin
Visual effects: Mark T. Henne, Oren Jacob, Darwyn Peachy, Mitch Prater and Brian M. Rosen
Character design: Bob Pauley, Bud Luckey, Andrew Stanton, William Cone, Steve Johnson, Dan Haskett, Tom Holloway and Jean Gillmore
Music: Don Davis and Randy Newman
MPAA rating: G
Running Time: 81 minutes

AWARDS AND NOMINATIONS

Chicago Film Festival Awards 1995: Best Score (Newman)
Academy Awards Nominations 1995: Best Screenplay (Whedon/Cohen/Sokolow), Best Score (Newman), Best Song ("You Got a Friend in Me")
Golden Globe Awards Nominations 1996: Best Film-Musical/Comedy, Best Score (Newman)

Dog, to the legendary model of irascibility, comedian Don Rickles (*Casino*, 1995).

The only possible complaint about *Toy Story* might be its decidedly male dominated view of the world in which females are relegated to mere sex objects, as is the case with Little Bo Peep who seems to represent the Hollywood notion of power figures as objects of lust for women, or females as victims, as in the case of Sid's younger sister, Hannah (Sarah Freeman) whose only means of revenge against her brother is to dress up the emotionally distraught Buzz as "Mrs. Nesbitt" at her tea party. The filmmakers expressed their disappointment at the Mattel Toy Company for its refusal to allow the use of the image of that paragon of female body distortion, "Barbie." As a result, in what one could argue is typical Hollywood fashion, the doll is objectified, only her legs appear as part of one of Sid's mutant playthings.

Toy Story is an inspired piece of filmmaking, an impressive technological triumph that is also an entertaining story destined to become another Disney classic. Critics were consistently enthusiastic in their praise of the film's merits. *Toy Story* is above all, good old-fashioned fun.

—*Patricia Kowal*

REVIEWS

Entertainment Weekly. November 24, 1995, p. 74
Los Angeles Times. November 22, 1995, p. F1.
Newsweek. CXXVI, November 27, 1995, p. 89.
The New Yorker. LXXI, November 1995, p. 17
New York Times. November 22, 1995, CXLV, p. C9.
Time. November 27, 1995, CXLVI, p. 96.
Variety. November 20, 1995, CCCLXI, p. 48.
Village Voice. November 28, 1995, XL, p. 64.
Washington Post. November 22, 1995, CXVIII, p. B1.

Traps

A murky but intriguing film, *Traps* is an allegorical tale linking the awakening of a stifled woman to the awakening of a colonized people. It is set in 1950 in French Indochina, where the Viet Minh, the forerunners of the Viet Cong, are beginning what would become a 25-year-long insurrection, first against France and then against the United States. The woman is a British photographer named Louise Duffield (Saskia Reeves), who has come with her Australian journalist husband to concoct a favorable article for a French rubber company.

Traps marks the feature-film debut of Pauline Chan, a Vietnamese director known for her short films. Here, Chan shows an often deft touch for individual scenes but a dismaying lack of control over the whole of the film, leaving a disconnected mess full of unexplained gaps, non sequiturs, and dramatic fits and starts. Chan's attempt to parallel personal and political liberation is clumsy, and the plot and script, at various turns tepid and overheated, are unsatisfying.

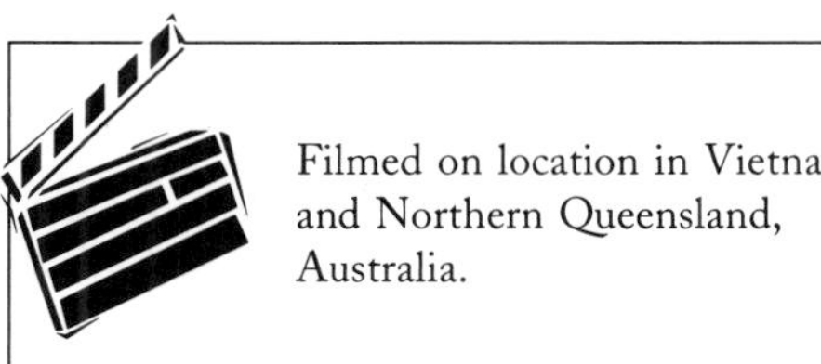
Filmed on location in Vietnam and Northern Queensland, Australia.

The film is brightened by its two female leads, with Reeves displaying an earthy, complex sensuality and a blossoming intelligence. Even more remarkable is that a mesmerizing young actress named Jacqueline McKenzie steals all her scenes in an underwritten role.

Written by Chan and Robert Carter, the screenplay is an ambitious reworking of Kate Grenville's novel, "Dreamhouse," transporting the characters from Italy. The film has an admirably high reach but a severe shortage of character and plot development.

As the title suggests, all the characters are in various political, emotional and psychological traps. Louise is unhappy in her marriage and professional partnership with husband Michael (Robert Reynolds). She's tired of playing second fiddle, with her photos getting not nearly the attention Michael gives his words. And Michael fails to inspire her love. In a telling but typically bizarre stitch of dialogue early in the film, Michael tells Louise he loves her. She replies, "I love me too."

Even that answer is only a half-truth. The film has Louise gradually discovering her own self-confidence, courage and worldly wisdom and shedding a shallow, hot-house sophistication that betrays an underlying naivete. Reeves, who has an odd and distinctive beauty and perpetually wistful eyes, parades about the jungle in prim print dresses that fail to hide her wandering emotions. "You always look as if something is missing," Daniel tells her. Obviously so.

Michael's trap is an ethical one. He wants to succeed as a journalist, but to do so he must ignore half of what he sees to produce a fluff piece for his bosses. The rubber company may give him a job as a publicist in its Paris headquarters if he produces a sufficiently glowing article about what wonderful job opportunities the company's plantations are providing for the peasants. In truth, the company is exploiting its workers and treating them harshly. Michael can choose to report honestly on the situation and go on being a semi-failure, or he can chuck his integrity and become a success. His waffling on the matter only further enrages Louise. Reynolds plays the part with a bland diffidence.

The couple has a strange relationship that, like everything else in the film, is on-again and off-again. There are two steamy sex scenes, one with Louise the initiator and one with Michael the aggressor, and both seem out-of-place and awkward in the middle of the film, as if an intellectual drama had suddenly been invaded by a cheap porno flick. The impression left is that Michael and Louise both are desperate to kindle or rekindle a connection that is slipping away from them.

Also trapped is the couple's host, a doomed plantation boss in a political system that is crumbling. He is a French petty tyrant and petit-bourgeois named Daniel Renouard (Sami Frey). Impeccable in speech and manners, Daniel is corrupt, conniving and sleazy, lusting after Louise and Michael. Daniel is determined to defend his little piece of colonial paradise even after it becomes obvious it's indefensible. Why? Because he's a man who hates routines. Late in the film, Daniel explains that he was in Paris once, had a desk job, and felt trapped. It's a weak explanation and a thankless role, but Frey imbues it with a delicious, understated taste of seductive evil.

Daniel lords it over a strange family group. His daughter is Viola (McKenzie), whose mother left long ago, for unexplained reasons. One scene suggests Daniel and Viola may have, or once have had, an incestuous relationship. Living in a hut on the compound are Tuan (Kiet Lam), Daniel's trusted Vietnamese servant, and his mother Tatie Chi (Hoa To). Daniel bought Tuan's mother when Tuan was young.

Viola is a teenager trapped far from civilization by her rapidly loosening affection for her father. She is insouciant, sarcastic and bullheaded. When she, Tuan and Louise are stranded on a road, Viola enthusiastically climbs aboard a truck full of French soldiers. Viola is desperate to be an adult, to be independent and to discover a direction and meaning in her life. McKenzie portrays her as an angel-faced devil. She has a porcelain, fragile appearance and a quick, lashing tongue. She is half Shirley Temple and half Lolita, and strikingly unique in her appearance and manner. McKenzie is a revelation.

Tuan, who is like a brother to Viola, is torn between his duties to his adoptive father and his increasing awareness of his heritage. When he is revealed as a Communist, it's a development that fails to shock or surprise. Even his mother is trapped, between her mystical, primitive devotions and the rise of a new order.

The developments have Louise and Michael drifting further apart, Louise and Viola thrown together in peril, Tuan rebelling against Daniel and torn apart from Viola, and Michael and Daniel getting increasingly cozy. But most of this seems contrived. When Louise and Viola end up in danger of being executed, Chan has the film's images spin in Louise's head, and she awakens, as if from a fever, a new woman. She gives Michael his marching orders. At the end, there's a storming of the plantation gates, and a muddled sequence of inconsequential showdowns and narrow escapes that lead to an unsatisfying resolution.

Unfortunately, Chan doesn't tie together the loose ends, or even suggest resolutions involving key points and characters. The key relationship between Louise and Viola is confused and confusing. Viola contracts malaria and becomes virtually a non-entity in the last half-hour of the film, dragged about half-conscious like a kewpie doll, a fate McKenzie doesn't deserve and the film doesn't need. Without McKenzie firing things up, the film goes limp. There are other unanswered questions: How are Viola and Louise saved from certain death? Does Michael sell out? What be-

CREDITS

Lousie Duffield: Saskia Reeves
Michael Duffield: Robert Reynolds
Daniel: Sami Frey
Viola: Jacqueline McKenie
Tuan: Keit Lam
Tatie-Chi: Hoa To

Origin: Australia
Released: 1995
Production: Jim McElroy for an Ayer Productions, Australian Film Finance Corp, Austrialian Film Commission, and Film Queensland production; released by Ronin Films and Filmopolis Pictures
Direction: Pauline Chan
Screenplay: Robert Carter and Pauline Chan; based on the characters from the novel *Dreamhouse* by Kate Grenville
Cinematography: Kevin Hayward
Editing: Nicholas Beauman
Production design: Michael Phillips
Costumes: Davie Rowe
Sound: John Sheifelbein
Assistant direction: Chris Short
Casting: Alison Barett
Music: Douglas Stephen Rae
MPAA rating: R
Running Time: 97 minutes

comes of Tuan's mother, who simply disappears from the film?

The holes in *Traps* are discouraging, and on close examination so is the central point. Louise's liberation has little in common with the peasants' struggle, at least nothing that viewers can grab on to. Chan simply juxtaposes the personal and political stories, but the essential emotional glue is missing. The film's director seems even more trapped than her characters, by a ponderous plot and an incomplete script. Still, there is hope that Chan could do virtuoso work given better material. And even more eagerly to be awaited are more performances by McKenzie and Reeves.

—Michael Betzold

REVIEWS

The New York Times. Dec. 1, 1995.
Variety. June 6, 1994, p. 36.

Twelve Monkeys

"Stunning. Pitt is terrific."—James Verniere, *Boston Herald*
"Awesome."—Michael Wilmington, *Chicago Tribune*
"A dizzying spectacle."—Owen Gleiberman, *Entertainment Weekly*
"Intriguing."—Kenneth Turan, *Los Angeles Times*
"A thrilling ride. Exhilarating."—Peter Travers, *Rolling Stone*

Box Office Gross: $56,654,819

In a lecture on Apocalyptic visions, Dr. Kathryn Railly (Madeleine Stowe) talks about the Cassandra Complex: the agony of possessing knowledge of the future coupled with the inability to do anything about it. James Cole (Bruce Willis) is suffering from a mega dose of the Cassandra Complex—but for good reason! He lives in the year 2035, and it is a place where 99% of the population has been wiped out by a rampant viral plague. The resulting toxic air has forced what is left of mankind to abandon the surface of the earth and mine out an existence below ground.

Madeleine Stowe and Bruce Willis in Terry Gilliam's *Twelve Monkeys*.

This lethal plague hit the earth in 1996 and by 2035 the scientists have turned their energies to developing a time machine which will allow them to send someone back into the past to find out what caused the plague, and hopefully prevent it. Because of his superior observational abilities, the "volunteer" they decide to send back is James Cole, a prisoner who may earn parole if he is successful. Unfortunately for James, their machine is less than precise. Instead of landing in 1996, he first lands in 1990. Not realizing it, he is soon in trouble with the police who throw him into a psychiatric facility where he meets two important people, Dr. Railly, and fellow inmate, Jeffrey Goines (Brad Pitt), the raving son of a Nobel prize winning virologist (Christopher Plummer). But no sooner are these contacts made than he is yanked back to 2035, interrogated by the powers that be, then sent back to the past yet again, only to touch down in the French trenches of World War I. Again he is yanked through time and eventually he does land in 1996 where he attempts to get help...by kidnapping Dr. Railly.

James' only clue is a graffiti kind of logo: a circle of red simians indicating the Army of the Twelve Monkeys, an underground animal rights group. It is believed they have something to do with the plague, but it is not known what or how. James must attempt to find out about them, but just as he is convincing Dr. Railly that he really is from the future, James is also beginning to doubt his own sanity. His sense of confusion is heightened not only by the constant shifting time frames and realities, but also by a recurring dream/vision/memory in which a young boy with his parents witness a man's shooting at an airport. Will James be able to hold on long enough to complete his mission or will even time machines be unable to change the past and protect the future?

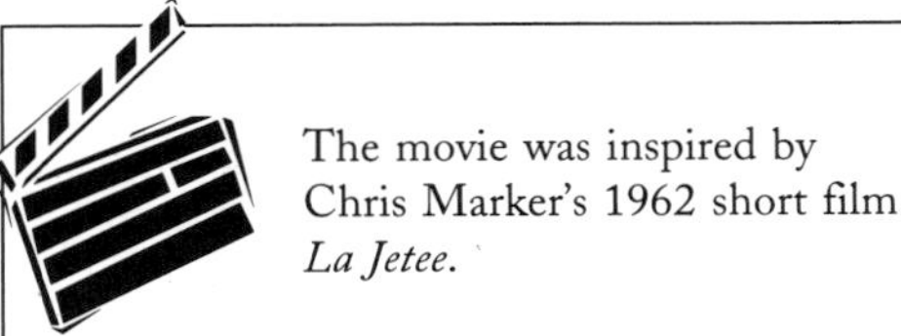

The movie was inspired by Chris Marker's 1962 short film *La Jetee.*

This latest film from director Terry Gilliam (formerly of Monty Python fame) has many similarities to his previous films. His dystopian prediction of a bleak future in which fascist (and virtually unseen) powers control a downtrodden humanity echoes *Brazil*; his fascination with time travel and the uncertain distinction between past and present was treated before in *Time Bandits*; and the fine line between sanity and insanity, genius and madman, fantasy and reality showed up previously in *The Fisher King*. While *Twelve Monkeys* is in the vein of all of the previous, it is a much darker (and in many ways a more provocative) vision. It does, however, prove once again that Gilliam is a unique and intriguing director among the cookie-cutter filmmakers at work today. His stories challenge the imagination as do the images in which he frames them. They may be gloomy or bizarre or disorienting, but they are never dull, because a large part of the appeal of a Terry Gilliam film is to see just what kind of universe he will construct for his story. And the universe of *Twelve Monkeys*, like that of *Brazil*, resembles an exploded and oddly reconstructed junkyard.

If the set designs of a Gilliam film are a star attraction, then it would seem to be difficult for the real flesh-and-blood stars to outshine it. In *Twelve Monkeys*, however, that does not seem to be a problem. Madeleine Stowe not only projects beauty but also compassion. Her portrayal of Dr. Railly shows clearly why she would initially be drawn to hesitantly take up James' cause and eventually come to be his compatriot. But it is her intelligence that must carry her character for she is the rational guide in a film filled with madmen and supposed madmen and with reality and supposed reality.

Also doing an interesting turn in *Twelve Monkeys* is Brad Pitt as the not-quite-connected-to-reality Jeffrey Goines. Known for his James Deanish downplaying, here Pitt offers a decidedly frenzied performance. His bug-eyed, machine-gun fast rantings are punctuated by fitful hand gestures and force a viewer to listen carefully in case something he says makes sense. Pitt's Goines is a character on the edge, and we're never sure on which side he'll fall. Is he a raving lunatic or just a devoted zealot for animal rights? Are his visions those of a radical or a madman? Is he so committed to his cause that he would actually do unspeakable acts? Is he a just a hyperactive activist or is he more dangerous than he seems?

The bravura performance, however, is that given by Bruce Willis. Normally playing the anti-hero who fights

CREDITS

James Cole: Bruce Willis
Dr. Kathryn Railly: Madeleine Stowe
Jeffrey Goines: Brad Pitt
Dr. Goines: Christopher Plummer
Dr. Fletcher: Frank Gorshin
Jose: Jon Seda
Young Cole: Joseph Melito

Origin: USA
Released: 1995
Production: Charles Roven for Atlas Entertainment; distributed by Universal Pictures
Direction: Terry Gilliam
Screenplay: David Peoples and Janet Peoples; inspired by the film *La Jetee* written by Chris Marker.
Cinematography: Roger Pratt
Editing: Mick Audsley
Production design: Jeffrey Beecroft
Art direction: Wm Ladd Skinner
Set decoration: Crispian Sallis
Costume design: Julie Weiss
Music: Paul Buckmaster
Sound: Jay Meagher
Special Effects mechanical and pyrotechnical engineer: Vincent Montefusco
Special Effects Project manager: Shirley Montefusco
MPAA rating: R
Running Time: 130 minutes

AWARDS AND NOMINATIONS

Golden Globe Awards 1996: Best Supporting Actor (Pitt)
Academy Awards Nominations 1995: Best Supporting Actor (Pitt), Best Costumes

against authority, here he plays a beaten almost pitiable victim of the authorities. He hears strange voices, is disorientingly snatched back and forth in time, is tortured by a recurring vision he can't explain, is battered physically by the authorities in the past and mentally by those of the future. And through all the pain, estrangement, and confusion, James must attempt to save the future of the human race while also fighting for his own survival (mental, physical and spiritual). In one poignant scene, he makes Dr. Railly turn on her car radio then we watch as his very soul is touched by rock and roll. They are very moving tears that flow to the music of "Blueberry Hill." The tears show that Willis is capable of portraying more than cynical and sarcastic action anti-heroes.

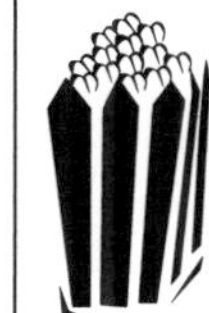

"I'm a mental patient. I'm supposed to act out."—Jeffrey Goines

If there is a weakness to *Twelve Monkeys* it lies in the story. It is supposedly based on Chris Marker's 1962 short film *La Jetee*, but it feels more like *The Terminator*. Only here the post-apocalyptic time-traveller goes back not to prevent a devastating war, but a devastating virus, and Willis' character is not given Schwarzenegger's superhuman powers either.

The story is undoubtedly convoluted and complicated and sometimes all the strands don't seem to tie together neatly—making a second viewing very tempting—but the layered plot and abrupt shifts in time and place help to keep the audience as unsteady and uneasy as James himself. Written by David Peoples, who wrote Clint Eastwood's *Unforgiven* and co-wrote *Blade Runner*, and his wife Janet, the story is both engaging and enigmatic, challenging and relentless, understandable and puzzling. As I said, Terry Gilliam films may be a lot of things, but they are never dull!

—Beverley Bare Buehrer

REVIEWS

Chicago Tribune. January 5, 1996
Entertainment Weekly. January 5, 1996
Time Magazine. January 8, 1996
New York Times. December 27, 1995
Premiere. February 1996, p. 18+
Variety. December 22, 1995

Two Bits

"Al Pacino is pure perfection! He gives a sweet and flamboyant performance. "—Guy Flatley, *Cosmopolitan*

"Thoroughly likable...A nostalgic American answer to *Cinema Paradiso*.—Stephen Holden, *The New York Times*

Al Pacino has provided some of the most memorable characters in contemporary cinema, and continues to deliver with his charming, intricate, and soulful characterization in *Two Bits*. The film as a whole is rather slight, but is enlivened by Pacino's turn as an aging grandfather who dispenses love, advice and some pocket change to his young grandson.

Two Bits is like a short story: there is no intricate plot, but there are interesting characters and a moral. The events of the plot are of secondary importance to the character development. The film is a coming-of-age story; a brief glimpse into a day in the life of a boy and his family during the Depression which yields to the larger theme of the difference between settling for life as it is versus pursuing dreams.

Gennaro Spirito (Jerry Barone) is a 12-year-old boy living in South Philadelphia with his widowed mother (Mary Elizabeth Mastrantonio) and grandfather (Al Pacino). Living on government assistance in the middle of 1933, his mother can afford few luxuries—but Gennaro is desperate to gather "two bits" (25 cents) to go to the new La Paloma movie theater. Having been told "no" by his mother, Gennaro asks his grandpa for the money. Grandpa tells Gennaro that he has two bits, but that he won't give it away until he dies. "If I give you a quarter now, what am I gonna leave you when I die?", he asks his grandson.

Unable to get the money from home, Gennaro sets out to earn the money for himself. His efforts to earn the two bits, combined with life lessons he learns from grandpa, drive the action of the movie. Gennaro first tries to earn money singing on a street corner, just like a poor family he saw singing and dancing for their supper. But that plot is foiled by his Aunt Carmela (Mary Lou Rosato), who discovers him on the corner and makes him stop immediately. (It's all for the best: his singing is appropriately awful, and he made no money.)

Soon, Gennaro's endeavors cause him to become involved in several challenging situations. An innocent attempt to help a doctor (Andy Romano) and his mysterious wife (Donna Mitchell) leads to tragedy. He tries to convince a grocer he should pay Gennaro to help around the store, until a sad episode with a customer leaves Gennaro with the realization that "in the depression, strong people lose their jobs, and the others lose their minds." Finally, Gennaro's most difficult task comes in the form of a favor asked of him by his grandpa: he must go to the home of an old widow, Gwendolina (Joanna Merlin), that grandpa had seduced many years before, and apologize on his grandpa's behalf for his ungentlemanly behavior. This episode becomes yet another life lesson for Gennaro (and is mildly reminiscent of the relationship between Pip and Miss Havisham in Dicken's *Great Expectations.*) There is also an element of sexual awakening in these episodes which adds a darker and more sophisticated feel to the film than audiences might anticipate in its early scenes.

Director James Foley makes the most out of Joseph Stefano's eloquent but simple script. The script is, by nature, episodic. Gennaro returns to his house after each episode, talking to Grandpa, who is permanently ensconced in the yard. Each time he returns to Grandpa there is potential redundancy: How many times can they talk about the value of money as it relates to life and death? But somehow, Foley and company manage to make it work rather sweetly. For example, since Grandpa is old (and apparently on his deathbed), he is quite immobile. The problem, then, is that

CREDITS

Gennaro: Jerry Barone
Luisa: Mary Elizabeth Mastrantonio
Grandpa: Al Pacino
Uncle Joe: Joe Grifasi
Guendolina: Joanna Merlin
Dr. Bruna: Andy Romano
Narrator: Alec Baldwin

Origin: USA
Released: 1995
Production: Arthur Cohn for a Connexion production; released by Miramax
Direction: James Foley
Screenplay: Joseph Stefano
Cinematography: Juan Ruiz-Anchia
Editing: Howard Smith
Production design: Jane Musky
Art direction: Tom Warren
Set decoration: Robert J. Franco
Costume design: Claudia Brown
Sound: Drew Kunin
Music: Carter Burwell
MPAA rating: PG-13
Running Time: 85 minutes

when Gennaro returns to talk to Grandpa, the possibility of redundancy in the visual image is quite high. To reduce the static nature of the image, Foley sets one of these scenes from Gennaro's perspective as he sits in a tree above Grandpa's chair. In doing so, by the way, he makes a visual allusion to *On Borrowed Time* (1939), in which Lionel Barrymore plays a man who, with the help of his grandson, traps "Death" (played by Cedric Hardwicke) in a tree.

Foley also makes the most out of his depiction of Depression-era South Philadelphia. Much like Steven Soderbergh's darker *King of the Hill* (1993), the visual images of the depression as seen through the eyes of a young boy are remarkably accurate, and possess a kind of melancholy beauty. Filmed with the aid of cinematographer Juan Ruiz-Anchia, *Two Bits* is full of rich colors and authentic depression-era scenery. From the neighborhood grocery, where the burlap bags and authentic labels are lit so they look like still-life oil paintings, to the shadowy depths of Gwendolina's dining room, to the sun-dappled yard where Grandpa enjoys his last days of life, the colors are deep and earthy and the settings are a sort of storybook version of the depression. There are moments which are quite vivid and beautiful, such as a wonderful sequence involving a wedding party and a funeral party who discover they have booked the church at the same time. The period costumes, the grimy street, and the beautiful old church make quite a wonderful picture. And of course, the La Paloma movie theater, a sort of Mecca for young Gennaro, is as colorful and cheerful as the street surrounding it is drab and somber.

Cinematographer Ruiz-Anchia deserves much credit for his inventive and lush camera work. Some of the scenes create beauty where there is inherently none, such as the rays of light entering Gennaro's drab kitchen, or the strange shadows lurking in the depths of the doctor's basement. Like the painter Caravaggio, the sources of light come from real sources (such as sunlight filtered through trees, or the light from a single bulb). Often in films, the light sources are too bright or are coming from angles which are physically impossible. Ruiz-Anchia's use of natural light emphasizes the film's naturalistic qualities even while it gives it a fairy-tale beauty.

The performances are first-rate, starting with Al Pacino as Grandpa. This is not the film's starring role, but Pacino's star power and characterization have made it a focal point of the film. He plays Grandpa as a wheezing old man, occasionally cranky but generally loving and docile. The role is unavoidably reminiscent of Marlon Brando's final scenes in *The Godfather* (1972), in which Pacino himself played the young man. He is particularly wonderful in the scene in which he asks Gennaro to go to Gwendolina. Pacino's commitment to his character is so complete that as he tells the story of their one night of passion 50 years before, it is possible to visualize the entire scene.

Pacino is given some choice lines to say, as well. Perhaps in the hands of a lesser actor these words could have been corny, but in Pacino's hands they sound like poetry. One of his best moments comes when he talks with Gennaro about the difference between wanting and needing, saying, "all anyone has to do is hint that something is impossible and people don't want it anymore....promise me one thing, Gennaro...Want." The role is not deep enough or dramatic enough to earn Pacino an Oscar, but it is yet another in a series of wonderful portrayals.

Young Jerry Barone is terrific as Gennaro. He is an actor of apparently no pretension or self-consciousness, and he uses his matter-of-fact style to great advantage. Barone does a fine job in creating the character of a young boy who wants desperately to talk his Grandpa out of two bits, but doesn't want to appear selfish. Barone plays several layers of the character's intention with great intelligence. Additionally, he makes the sometimes syrupy dialogue sound matter-of-fact: "Does it hurt, Grandpa...dying? and "if you don't suffer; can you still go to heaven?" could be treacherous for a young actor intent on sounding precious. Congratulations to Barone for playing against the sweetness of the role.

Finally, Mary Elizabeth Mastrantonio deserves mention for her portrayal of a stalwart and loving mother. She has only one scene of any great depth, but delivers her monologue with warmth. Mastrantonio seems a bit miscast as the hard-living Depression-era mother; her perfect skin and lush beauty make it a little hard to believe she has no time for facials or trips to the beauty parlor. But she is a wonderful actress whose earthiness and grace make her a natural for the role.

Two Bits may never win an Academy Award or may never generate huge box-office revenues. It is a small film. But it is about big things: It is about the ability of an individual to continue to desire to improve his life even when the odds are against him. It is a film worth seeing and a lesson worth learning.

—Kirby Tepper

Ulysses' Gaze (To Vlemma Tou Odyssea)

In *Ulysses' Gaze*, renown filmmaker Theo Angelopoulos has created a film that paradoxically combines surreal fantasy and stark realism, often simultaneously, to explore themes that are both universal and, at times, very personal. The film evokes the experience of traveling through a dream, as we journey through a series of disjointed episodes connected only by the main character's search for three reels of lost film.

Ulysses' Gaze, winner of the Grand Prix at Cannes, is a visually majestic, though sometimes cryptic film that follows a filmmaker named A. on his journey to recover allegedly lost footage shot by the Manakis brothers, pioneers in Balkan cinematography.

In this intensely autobiographical film, Angelopoulos makes a statement about a world where violence and chaos reign, and the role of the filmmaker in that world. Toward that end, director Angelopoulos is ambitious and courageous, mixing theatrical devices with superb cinematography, flying back and forth through time, and even filming through actual sniper fire to tell his tale or—it could be argued—tales, most of which more or less parallel the Homeric epic. In the process, he has strung together a puzzling assortment of scenes that don't necessarily relate to one another, yet are in themselves hauntingly beautiful cinematic poems.

> The film is dedicated to actor Gian Maria Volonte, who died during production. His part was taken over by Erland Josephson.

The hero, A. (Harvey Keitel), is a controversial Greek director who has been working in the U.S. for the past 35 years and returns to his country to attend a screening of his latest film. The ethereal ambiance of *Ulysses' Gaze* is established in the opening scene as the filmmaker walks through the dark rain-drenched streets among a crowd of people, all hidden under a sea of black umbrellas. A.'s film is controversial, and as the umbrella-bearing crowd close ranks, a procession of candle-bearing religious protestors approach from the other end of the street. Riot police silently form a barricade between the two factions, while an oblivious A. calmly explains to his companions his real reason for returning to Greece.

He is looking for three reels of undeveloped film that were perhaps the first ever filmed by the Manakis brothers. A. has been asked by the Athens Film Archive to supervise a documentary about them and hopes that the footage will reveal the reasons and perhaps some solutions to the current Balkan unrest.

The brothers filmed the everyday life-styles and culture of ordinary people at the turn-of-the-century, and *Ulysses' Gaze* is interspersed with short segments of the footage. Some of the opening cuts portray women spinning and carding wool, like Penelopes waiting for their

Odysseus, and it is the possible loss of these "innocent gazes" into the past that keeps A. obsessed with his search.

His path is both difficult and dangerous, and he travels from Greece to Bosnia, passing through Albania, Bulgaria, and Romania on his way to Sarajevo.

To begin his search, A. leaves Greece, hiring a taxi to take him into Albania. When they cross the border, they drive through barren snowy hills where a smattering of drably dressed people stand with their backs to the camera, staring mysteriously off into the distance, evoking an aura of desolation that descends as heavy as the cheerless snow.

They drive on through the snowy mountains to Skoplje, where A. visits a film archive looking for the lost film. The archivist (Maia Morgenstern) tells him that they have much of the Manakis collection, but not the reels he seeks, so he and the archivist get on a train bound for Bucharest to continue the search.

As they cross the border, customs detains them, and the scene slips into fantasy. A. sits blindfolded before an armed guard, reliving one of the brother's own experiences. A. has empathized so much with the Manakis brothers that he has, in a sense, become them; the artist has become his subject.

Finally he is released and continues on his journey to Bucharest. As the train pulls into the Bucharest station, it becomes 1945, and A.'s mother takes us to their home in Constanza, Romania. There follows a theatrical flashback that chronicles five New Year's eves, from 1945-50, in A.'s childhood home.

It is a touching and powerful theatrical piece that exposes the personal tragedies that the rise of Communism wrought. Yet, although the scenes are poignant and symbolically effective, they are diminished by the all too blatant lack of one quality—humor. But after the next scene, we can forgive Angelopoulos almost anything—even his lack of humor.

The scene begins down by the river, at the docks. A gigantic head of Lenin swings precariously from the end of a crane and is loaded onto a barge at the head of the dismembered colossus. The statue is to be shipped up the Danube to Germany. As it pulls away from the dock, A. jumps on board, and we hear his continuing narrative: "One brother went to England . . . , the other went home. . . snuck in past the border patrol." And A. slips unnoticed into the war zone at the foot of this modern-day Trojan horse.

As we watch the barge move slowly up the Danube like the floating bier of a Titan, peasants kneel by the side of the river honoring the dead leader and his dead revolution. It is a magnificent scene, spellbinding in its simplicity.

On the wharf in Belgrade, A. meets an old friend, who introduces him to the retired head of the Belgrade Film Archives. He tells A. to look for the reels in the Sarajevo Film Archive; Evo Levy, its curator, may have the film.

By cover of darkness, a woman (Morgenstern) takes A. to a small boat hidden under a bridge. They sail through beautiful landscapes into a countryside that is devastated by war, and the time period shifts again, making it uncertain which war we are witnessing.

He stays with her at her house by the river for a time, then continues on his quest, taking the boat to Sarajevo, where he is greeted by a scene of utter destruction and chaos. People run through the rubble-strewn streets lined with blackened buildings and burning cars, dodging sniper fire as they lug precious containers of water.

A. finds Evo Levy (Erland Josephson) in an old bombed-out cinema where, in the cellar, Levy has his treasure—the Sarajevo Film Archive. There A. finally tracks down the three reels of undeveloped film along with many other priceless films. A. scolds Levy for his selfishness, locking away these "vanished gazes" in such a precarious shelter.

Evo develops one of the reels, and as they wait for the film to dry, they, together with Evo's daughter, Naomi (Morgenstern), go for a walk in the city. A dense fog has

CREDITS

A: Harvey Keitel
Naomi Levy and the "Wives": Maia Morgenstern
Ivo Levy: Erland Josephson
Taxi Driver: Thanassis Vengos
Nikos: Yorgos Michalokopoulos

Origin: Greece, France and Italy
Released: 1995
Production: Theo Angelopoulos for a Greek Film Center, Paradis Films-La Generale d'Images-La Sept Cinema, Basic Cinematografica-Istituto Luce-RAI, TeleMunchen, Concorde Films and Channel 4 production; released by Paradis Films
Direction: Theo Angelopoulos
Screenplay: Theo Angelopoulos
Cinematography: Yorgos Arvanitis and Andreas Sinanos
Editing: Yannis Tsitsopoulos
Production design: Giorgos Patsas and Miodrack Mile Nicolic
Art direction: Takis Katselis and Panagiotis Portokalakis
Costume design: Giorgos Ziakas
Sound: Thanasis Arvanitis
Special effects: Olivier Zenensky
Music: Eleni Karaindrou
Running Time: 177 minutes

AWARDS AND NOMINATIONS

Cannes Film Festival 1995: Grand Jury Prize

settled over the town, and "in Sarajevo foggy days are celebrations," where nature forces snipers into a ceasefire. As they walk through the streets toward a park, an unseen orchestra plays and people slowly emerge from the earthbound clouds as if stunned by their sudden freedom.

An orchestra of Serbs, Croates, and Muslims have come together to play in the park, while a little further on, actors perform Romeo and Juliet on a park bench. They must perform and we must hear; art must find expression even in these bloody times.

But the mood of celebration evaporates as suddenly as it appears when Evo, his daughter, and their friends are shot as they stroll down by the river. Safely hidden in the fog, only A. survives—he and, of course, his three reels of film.

The scope of *Ulysses' Gaze* is tremendous, and it explores a multitude of questions and themes. Angelopoulos and his co-writer, Italian screenwriter Tonini Guerra, cover so much territory that this review can't do them justice. Some of the major themes are the artist's identification with his subject; the role of the filmmaker to record life; and the need for the artist, even in the midst of chaos and carnage, to aspire to something higher. No matter how diverse the theme, all are infused with a sense of pessimism and loss.

Throughout the film Angelopoulos manages to personalize the various political upheavals in the Balkans, and no where do we experience this better than in Sarajevo, where he's done some of the best work in the film. The Sarajevo sequences were actually filmed in the Bosnian town of Mostar during the Serbian siege, and the stark beauty and honest realism of these scenes makes you hungry for more. That hunger makes it easy to understand how hungry A. is for the vanished gaze of the Manakis brothers—as hungry as future generations will be for footage of Bosnia, especially footage of this quality. Yorgos Arvanitis' cinematography in these scenes and throughout the film is nothing short of genius.

Yet, despite the film's undeniable beauty and its profound effect on the viewer, this unwieldy three-hour-plus epic is far too long and far too slow. In defense Angelopoulos said, "Certain films need to breathe, like plants."

Another flaw is in the dialogue. Harvey Keitel brings to his role an emotional intensity and an intelligence that is mesmerizing, but the dialogue he is given is strained and pretentious. There aren't many English-speaking actors who could get away with lines like: "In my end is my beginning," and still maintain a certain credibility.

Maia Morgenstern, on the other hand, has been saved from expounding any deep truths, and her characters all are fresh and believable. The Romanian actress plays all four of the female roles with a subtlety of nuance and a versatility that is like watching thespian slight of hand.

Ulysses' Gaze is a film that walks the fine line between majesty and pretension, on the whole, falling gracefully on the side of majesty through the extraordinary beauty of its scenes. Angelopoulos has succeeded in creating an epic that, despite its flaws, boldly raises important questions regarding the future of cinema itself.

—Diane Hatch-Avis

REVIEWS

Boxoffice, Deptember 1995.
Daily Variety, May 25, 1995.
Daily Variety, June 9, 1995, p. 52.
Hollywood Reporter, May 30, 1995, p. 5.
The Nation, June 26, 1995, p. 936.
Screen International, February 3, 1995.
Variety, March 27, 1995.
Village Voice, June 13, 1995.

Under Siege II: Dark Territory

"High-speed thrills."—Bob Thomas, *Associated Press*
"*Die Hard* on a train."—Peter Rainer, *Los Angeles Times*

Box Office Gross: $50,024,083

There is a moment in *Under Siege II* when Casey Ryback (Steven Seagal) is dangling by his fingernails from the edge of a cliff. A fleeting look of slight concern crosses his rocky countenance, as if a gnat is buzzing nearby. It is Seagal's only concession to the possibility of acting.

In the rest of *Under Siege II*, Seagal's counter-terrorist Ryback is unflappable. Commandos seize his train? Niece threatened with a hand grenade? Caught in the sights of a sniper? East Coast within seconds of nuclear destruction? No problem. Not a trace of anxiety crosses Seagal's face. In fact, no glimmer of life ever crosses Seagal's face.

Action heroes are supposed to be cool, but encased in ice? Even during the film's most intense fight scenes, Seagal is like a cigar-store Indian. His hands are moving, martial-arts style, but the rest of his body is as rigid as a corpse.

Granted, audiences don't come to Steven Seagal movies to see him act, they come to see him kill. Killing is the only expressive thing Seagal does.

In *Under Siege II*, Seagal kills bad guys by shooting them, choking them, breaking their necks, stomping them, setting them on fire, throwing them off a train, smashing their faces into a cliff, and closing a helicopter door on their fingers. He also maims with knives, karate chops and bone-crushing hand holds.

He does it all without breaking a sweat. Never does a bead of perspiration cross his brow, never is a hair out of place, and never do the bad guys ruffle his composure.

In the best action movies, the heroes are often in bewildering jeopardy. Their resourcefulness is all the more compelling because you can see the pressure they're under when they're pushed to the brink of endurance.

With Seagal, there's none of that kind of tension. He is so invulnerable that he seems inhuman. He speaks every line in the same whispering monotone.

In the original *Under Siege* (1992), Ryback was a cook and Navy SEAL who saved the Hawaiian Islands and the world from nuclear destruction. This sequel merely changes the locale from a ship to a train while keeping the rest of the major plot elements.

As we meet Ryback again, he's retired from the Navy, owns a restaurant and is taking his niece Sarah (Katherine Heigl) on a vacation. But wouldn't you just know it? The train Casey and Sarah take happens to be the one that computer mastermind Travis Dane (Eric Bogosian) picks to turn into a command center for seizing control of a top-secret government satellite super-weapon.

The very smart and very annoying Dane is irked because the military built his space toy and then fired him before putting it into orbit. So Dane and a small army of thugs seize the train, set up his high-tech gizmos, steal "Grazer One" back from the military, and set up shop as a global genocide-for-hire business. Their first customers are the usual unnamed Middle Eastern terrorists who are willing to pay $1 billion for Dane to blow up Washington and the Eastern seaboard.

The satellite can somehow trigger an earthquake, but the film doesn't bother to explain how. Dane demonstrates that his invention works by targeting a Chinese chemical plant and creating an explosion that, as he characterizes it, makes the Bhopal, India chemical disaster "look like a picnic." Since these are only thousands of faceless Asians that die, the incident is shrugged off after the military assures top brass that the United States government has "full deniability" for what appeared to be a natural disaster.

Dane's plan is to target a secret nuclear reactor located under the Pentagon. He broadcasts his intentions to the military high command, who can do nothing about it. They can't figure out where he is because his command center is undetectable if it is moving. That's why he's on the train. Yet, when the train stops while the bad guys try to catch Ryback, the government still can't find Dane. The scriptwriters hope audiences are so fixated on the killing that they don't notice that and a lot of other inconsistencies.

While the mercenaries hold the crew and passengers of the train hostage, Ryback moves with remarkable impunity through the baggage and kitchen cars on the lower levels. He recruits a porter named Bobby (Morris Chestnut) and trains him to be a top counter-terrorist with a few whispered words of advice. He tries to get a fax message out about the train's location but can't defeat a busy signal. He makes explosives that he says he'll use as a bargaining chip but ends up using them merely to roast some bad guys.

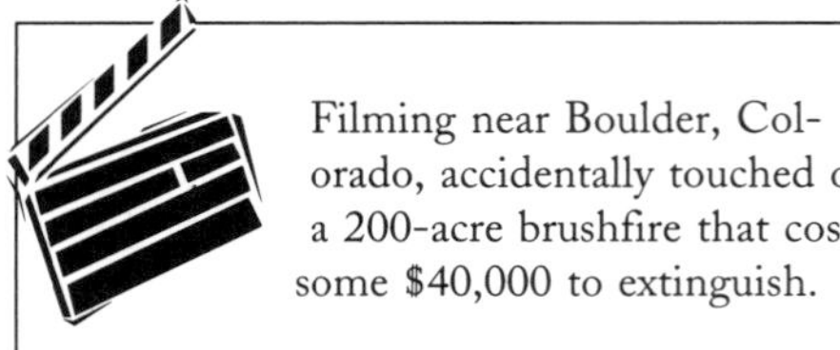

Filming near Boulder, Colorado, accidentally touched off a 200-acre brushfire that cost some $40,000 to extinguish.

Why does it take the mercenaries so long to find Ryback on the train? Don't they know there's a downstairs?

Why does it take Ryback so long to call for help? Doesn't this top counter-terrorist know the phone number of anyone in the chain of command? (Obviously he does because the cook that finally gets the fax places a call to top brass.) And why does it take Ryback and Bobby so long to separate the hostage cars at the rear from the rest of the train, as they finally do at the end?

> "In 15 seconds Arizona could be beachfront property."—Bad guy Dane from *Under Seige II: Dark Territory*

And what's the point of the "Dark Territory" of the title? Late in the chase, the train enters the area, described as a place filled with canyons where communication is impossible. Since communication has been impossible all along, the "dark territory" doesn't make a whit of difference in the plot.

The answer to all these questions is that something must fill time while director Geoff Murphy ploddingly puts all of the plot elements in place for a boffo ending. *Under Siege II* is like a long fireworks show that starts with a lot of duds and finally builds to an explosive grand finale.

Eventually, Ryback gets moving and gets killing, picking off the hapless mercenaries one by one. Bobby learns that being a hero is as easy as Seagal going to the bank to pick up another paycheck. A good thing too since Bobby is scripted and played as a brainless, shucking and jiving black man. Niece Sarah is held hostage, allowing much leering attention to the 16-year-old Heigl's grown-up body. As Dane's henchman Penn, Everett McGill is just like Seagal except he has white hair.

Bogosian sustains some interest during the long, slow stretches. His over-the-top performance is suitably irritating. Out of place among the crew-cut mercenaries, his Dane is the class twit, the unpopular nerd who's grown up to be a power-mad maniac.

There is an anti-intellectual subtext here: Ryback's low-tech killing methods are good and the computer hackers and Pentagon weapon-builders are the bad guys who've created weapons of mass destruction. With his tie, flowered shirt and curly hair, Bogosian is clearly an effete liberal intellectual, and the government is hopelessly incompetent. Just the dark territory needed for a guy like Ryback to become a hero.

The script is as wooden as Seagal's face. Particularly amusing are scenes where Seagal attempts to portray a sensitive uncle. Explaining his lack of contact with niece Sarah, he says, "Time goes by, seems to fly, and before you know it, things happen." That pretty much sums up *Under Siege II*.

Special-effects wizardry helps carry the film and produce a busy, big-bang ending. A climactic train collision is expertly executed with miniatures. But for most of the film, there isn't enough action to sustain a movie that has nothing going for it but action.

Because his fans likes the way he kills, an *Under Siege III* is as sure as another trip to the bank for Seagal. But one wonders if he even shows any emotion when he glimpses at the eight figures on his paychecks.

—*Michael Betzold*

CREDITS

Casey Ryback: Steven Seagal
Travis Dane: Eric Bogosian
Sarah Ryback: Katherine Heigl
Bobby: Morris Chestnut
Penn: Everett McGill

Origin: USA
Released: 1995
Production: Steven Seagal, Arnon Milchan and Steve Perry for a Nasso production; released by Warner Brothers
Direction: Geoff Murphy
Screenplay: Richard Hatem and Matt Reeves
Cinematography: Robbie Greenberg
Editing: Michael Tronick
Production design: Albert Brenner
Visual effects: Richard Yuricich
Costume design: Richard Bruno
Music: Basil Poledouris
MPAA rating: R
Running Time: 98 minutes

REVIEWS

New York Times. July 16, 1995, p. 16.
USA Today. July 17, 1995, p. 6.

The Underneath

"A provocative tale of crime, passion and punishment."—Bruce Williamson, *Playboy*

"A seductively twisted thriller! A hypnotic blend of suspense and eroticism."—Peter Travers, *Rolling Stone*

"Superb! Incredibly entertaining cinema. Brilliantly acted and directed."—Paul Wunder, *WBAI Radio*

Box Office Gross: $536,023

Film noir has been stuck in a neoclassical dead-end for the last fifteen years. Beginning with the success of Lawrence Kasdan's *Body Heat* (1981), film after film in the genre has tried to recapture, usually through slavish imitation, the way the original noir thrillers of the late 1940s and early 1950s visually expressed the alienation and obsession of their protagonists. Most of these neo-noir films—Adrian Lyne's *Fatal Attraction* (1987), Wolfgang Petersen's *Shattered* (1991), and Alan Pakula's *Consenting Adults* (1993)—have relied on flimsy psychology, preposterous plotting, and tenebrous lighting to achieve purely melodramatic effects. A few—David Lynch's *Blue Velvet* (1986) and *Twin Peaks: Fire Walk with me* (1992), John Dahl's *The Last Seduction* (1994), and Steven Soderbergh's *Sex, Lies and Videotape* (1989)—have found contemporary visual equivalents to the old noir grammar, focused on character as well as on plot, and incorporated new elements like eroticism, fantasy, and autobiographical exploration into the old mix. Films like Lynch's, Dahl's, and Soderbergh's have both revived and redefined the noir genre.

The 32 year-old Soderbergh's fourth film, *The Underneath*, promises such a combination of old and new noir styles: *The Underneath* is Soderbergh's remake of an outstanding film from the old noir canon, Robert Siodmak's *Criss Cross* (1949), and Soderbergh indeed infuses it with new blood, blending into the updated script his own obsessions with gambling, lying, and self-help. But Soderbergh ultimately stumbles. Unlike *Sex, Lies and Videotape*—and like most of the recent neo-noir films—*The Underneath* is brought down by one too many plot contrivances. Also, Soderbergh's use of colored filters or lighting to designate a particular character or type of scene—flourescent green for the flash-forwards, red for the scenes with the femme fatale, blue for the scenes which emphasize the pull of the past—comes to seem overly schematic, a kind of self-conscious academic finger-exercise. These flaws are unfortunate because until its final third, *The Underneath* deftly weaves a complex suspense plot that emerges logically from the twisted family psychology at its core.

> Co-screenwriting credit goes to Sam Lowry—actually a pseudonym for director Soderbergh.

The Underneath begins with a cryptic time signature that establishes the theme of the film: the past returning to haunt the present. Michael (Peter Gallagher) sits in the cab of a truck with its driver, Ed (Paul Dooley) in an eerie flourescent-green light. This image, which recurs throughout the film, is in fact a flash-forward to the deadly heist which occurs two-thirds of the way through the film and changes Michael's life irrevocably. These flash-forwards, reminiscent of Resnais's *La Guerre Est Finie* (1966), serve as a reminder that Michael's decisions at each step of the film lead to this fateful moment. The film then flashes back to Michael's face in a taxicab window, then yet again to Michael returning to his hometown, Austin, by bus for the remarriage of his mother (Anjanette Comer) to the genial Ed. As the bus approaches town, Michael meets a nice girl, Susan (Elisabeth Shue), and they seem attracted to one another. But when they exchange numbers, it is in voice-over; Michael is remembering their conversation as his cab pulls up to his mother's house, and clearly has more on his mind than Susan. This complex opening introduces the film's "criss-cross" theme: each bad decision Michael makes based on his unresolved past, about which he thinks constantly, leads inexorably to the intersection of forces depicted in the flash-forwards. As Michael will learn over the course of the film, if one does not come to terms with one's past, one is condemned to repeat it.

Michael's family seems to unsettle him, to haunt his peripheral vision, in scenes shot with wide-angle lenses and in blue light that undulates like the water in a swimming pool. His brother, David (Adam Trese), a local policeman and, Soderbergh hints, a repressed homosexual, reveals he has run a background check on their step-father-to-be: Ed is clean. Yet the very fact that this is normal in Michael's household is bizarre. Gambling, scheming to beat the odds, seem to be the glue that holds the family together, the only way for all the family members to gain control of their lives. Michael's mother is a quick-pick lottery fanatic; Ed's job is driving the armored trucks that collect lottery cash; and even David's role as family investigator and "collector" of

Michael's debts to their mother seems a product of the odd, loveless distance between family members that haunts the household. As for Michael, Soderbergh shows in a series of flashbacks that he has left town because of massive gambling debts to the local mob. When Ed offers Michael a job as a driver, he sets in motion Michael's being caught once again in the family undertow of compulsive gambling.

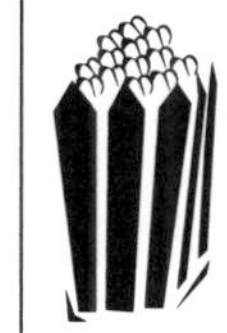

"When I think about being with you again, I have no idea if it's a moment of strength or a moment of weakness."—Rachel to her gambling-addicted ex-hubby Michael from *The Underneath*

These unresolved issues from Michael's past lead him back to his unhealthy relationship with his ex-wife, Rachel (Alison Elliott), both the object of and the spur to his unquenched desire for the big score. Michael left Rachel holding the bag of his debts when he left town, but now, considering himself "squared" with everyone and cured of his gambling addiction, he returns to their former haunt, a rock-and-roll club owned by the violent Tommy Dundee (William Fichtner), only to find Rachel now virtually Tommy's moll. Rachel, scared of Tommy and resentful of Michael, has her own agenda, but Michael is blind to it. Against his better judgment, and despite the presence of the sane and beautiful Susan, Michael finds himself drawn back into his destructive relationship with Rachel, this time under the illusion that he can "save" her from Tommy's clutches. Michael's reading of self-help books with titles like "Saying Hello to Yourself" reassures him that he has reformed, yet Soderbergh makes clear that he is falling off the wagering wagon—Rachel being the worst bet of all. Soderbergh shows the connection between Michael's obsession with Rachel and the lack of affection in his family in the flashback sequences depicting their volatile relationship: Rachel makes subtle demands on Michael for more money and links money with virility; Michael pathologically attempts to gamble his way out of debt to please her. Gambling, it seems, is everywhere: in one flashback, Rachel, a would-be actress, tries out for a job as hostess of the weekly state lottery jackpot drawing on TV. Soderbergh, using the eerie blue light in both the flashbacks and the scenes in the present, evokes the weird, dreamlike slowness of a life lived under the illusion that the next day will finally bring the big jackpot.

The film's turning point occurs, as it did in the original, when Rachel shows Michael the bruises from Tommy's beatings, and Michael vows to get them both out of town and out of Tommy's reach. Tommy, however, reacting to a tip from one of his bar's waitresses, finds out about their relationship, and threatens to kill them both. Thinking quickly, Michael tells Tommy that he is not interested in Rachel, but rather proposing an armored-car heist which the three of them will pull against his employer. Tommy falls for the story, and arranges that the three of them will divvy up half the cut, the other half going to a shadowy Mr. Big known only as "The Broker." Michael is now enmeshed in a web no longer of his own making, a bet with an unlimited downside.

The second meaning of "criss-cross" becomes apparent: the double-crosses begin. Rachel thinks she is controlling the action; so does Tommy. In fact, the robbery goes awry: Susan emerges from the bank just as the heist is about to take place, and Michael and Ed are ambushed. Ed is killed. When Michael wakes up in the hospital, however, he finds himself being lauded as a hero—by everyone but his brother, who suspects that Michael and Rachel were behind the scam. The final plot twists diverge considerably from the original, in which both the male and female lead are killed, but all the characters get their comeuppance. Unfortunately, this is where Soderbergh falters. In trying to mete out fair punishment to all concerned, Soderbergh and his screen-

CREDITS

Michael Chambers: Peter Gallagher
Rachel: Alison Elliott
Tommy Dundee: William Fichtner
Clay Hinkle: Joe Don Baker
Ed Dutton: Paul Dooley
David Chambers: Adam Trese
Mrs. Chambers: Anjanette Comer
Susan: Elisabeth Shue

Origin: USA
Released: 1995
Production: John Hardy for A Populist Pictures Production; released by Gramercy Pictures
Direction: Steven Soderbergh
Screenplay: Sam Lowery, Daniel Fuchs; based on a novel by Don Tracy
Cinematography: Elliot Davis
Editing: Stan Salfas
Production design: Howard Cummings
Costume design: Karyn Wagner
Casting: Ronnie Yeskel
Music: Cliff Martinez
MPAA rating: R
Running Time: 99 minutes

AWARDS AND NOMINATIONS

Independent Spirit Awards Nominations 1996: Best Cinematography (Davis)

writer, Sam Lowery, succeed only in tying the plot up in such a neat bow—none of the characters has ever been in control, and the entire gamble has been fixed from the beginning by a mysterious Mr. Big—that it merely elicits incredulity.

If *The Underneath* is not the breakthrough film that *Sex, Lies and Videotape* was, it is perhaps because, like *Kafka* (1991), another genre exercise, Soderbergh did not write the script himself, and endows the film with less of a personal stamp than the films for which he has written an original or an adapted screenplay—the autobiographical *Sex, Lies and Videotape* or the poignant evocation of writer A.E. Hotchner's Depression childhood, *King of the Hill* (1993). In each of his films, Soderbergh is preoccupied with characters trying to escape the arbitrary nature either of their own compulsions or of their backgrounds: in *Sex, Lies and Videotape*, James's Spader's character must tell the truth through video, as a way to counter his compulsive lying; in *Kafka*, Franz Kafka incessantly re-enacts his tortured family relationships; in *King of the Hill*, the young A.E. Hotchner struggles to survive in the seedy hotel where his parents have abandoned him; and in *The Underneath*, Michael's attempt to put an end to his cycle of risk, debt, and crime without dealing with the underlying family dynamics leads to self-destruction. *The Underneath*, however, with its hoary, if updated, fatalism, femme fatale, goons, gangsters and "Mr. Bigs" borrowed from *Criss Cross*, simply does not offer Soderbergh the freedom that his more personal films do.

The Underneath nevertheless continues Soderbergh's film education, and it remains the most watchable one on the American commercial scene. At 32, Soderbergh has already produced a body of work vastly more varied and entertaining than that of many directors a decade older than him. Unlike Lawrence Kasdan, whose films are often straitjacketed by his slavish imitation of film genres, or the Coen brothers, whose gleeful experiments in the hybridization of genre forms seem to leech their films of any genuine emotion, Soderbergh revisits old genres (Expressionism in *Kafka*, noir in *The Underneath*) in order to re-personalize them, to make them both contemporary and useful to his own personal expression. *The Underneath*, in spite of its flaws, gives another glimpse of the artistic growth of Steven Soderbergh, who, when left to his own devices, is second to none among American directors under the age of 35.

—*Paul Mittelbach*

REVIEWS

The Christian Science Monitor. April 28, 1995, p.12.
The Nation. CCLX, May 22, 1995, p.733.
The New Republic. CCXII, May 8, 1995, p.26.
The New York Times. April 28, 1995, p.B9(N).
Variety. CCCLVIII, March 20, 1995, p.47.
Vogue. CLXXXV, May, 1995, p.156.
The Wall Street Journal. May 11, 1995, p.A14(W).

Unstrung Heroes

"Sometimes you find your heroes in the most unlikely places!"—Movie tagline

"Magical!"—*Associated Press*

"Ravishingly funny."—Polly Frost, *Elle*

"A sweet surprise."—Janet Maslin, *The New York Times*

"Funny!"—*Newsweek*

"Diane Keaton has crafted something rare: a screwball comedy that cuts to the heart."—Peter Travers, *Rolling Stone*

For her feature-film directorial debut, actress Diane Keaton has chosen an off-beat tale of a twelve-year-old boy who must come to grips with his mother's death by embracing his own uniqueness. *Unstrung Heroes* is a story that rejoices in the wholeness of life, of confronting the challenges that come along and finding ways to move forward, rather than wallowing in self-pity. Emotionally moving without being maudlin, *Unstrung Heroes* never succumbs to histrionics, succeeding in evoking tears in the audience while shedding nary a one on-screen. While the quasi-Oriental sound of Thomas Newman's score is often too intrusive for the delicate nature of the story, Ms. Keaton should be applauded for her ability to quickly cut out of scenes before they become too drawn out.

Steven Lidz (newcomer Nathan Watt) clearly adores his mother, Selma (Andie MacDowell). She dances and sings along with Ray Charles while making pancakes, she smiles at her husband Sid's (John Turturro) ingenuity at inventing a myriad of interesting, yet useless items, including a revolving lamp that fills the kitchen with stars—she even looks great in all those cardigan sweaters.

Steven's world comes crashing down when his mother is suddenly taken ill. She collapses and soon finds it difficult to do more than sleep. Sid tries to protect his wife by banning Steven and his younger sister, Sandy (Kendra Krull) from Selma's bedroom, fearing the children will tire out their mother. Unaccustomed to going without his mother's warm embrace and soft touch, Steven reacts to his father's increasing coldness by running to the sanctuary of his two socially maladjusted uncles. Against his parents' better judgement, Steven is allowed to move in with these two social misfits. The uncles encourage the boy to revel in his own uniqueness. "You're the one to watch," they repeatedly tell the boy, renaming him Franz because it is less "ordinary." "A hero," Selma tells Steven, "is anyone who finds his own way through this life." And it is this unlikely pair of eccentric uncles, the unstrung heroes of the title, who eventually help the boy to accept his mother's death not with regret, but rather by rejoicing in her life.

Feature film directorial debut for actress Diane Keaton.

The humor of *Unstrung Heroes*, adapted from autobiographical novel by *Sports Illustrated* writer, Franz Lidz, comes primarily from the eccentricities of the three Lidz brothers (in the book there were four uncles): Sid (John Turturro) is the emotionally aloof father and inventor who attempts to disparage his son from believing in anything but the cold, hard facts of science. "Is dad from another planet?," Steven asks his mother. "No," she replies fondly, "he's just different." Danny (Michael Richards of television's *Seinfeld* fame) is a delusional paranoid who believes that "Idaho is Cherokee for Jew-hater." And Arthur (Maury Chaykin), the sweet romantic who believes in the beauty of other people's junk, teaches the young boy the value of memories. A variation on the *Wizard of Oz* story, the three brothers represent the mind (Sid), the heart (Arthur) and the spirit (Danny) of the story, all of which come together in the young boy through the terminal cancer of Steven's mother, Selma.

Keaton and screenwriter Richard LaGravanese have taken several liberties in their adaptation of Franz Lidz's autobiographical novel. The family has been transplanted from New York's Lower East Side to sunny Southern California, the city of Pasadena (home of the Rose Bowl—and a monthly swap meet that Ms. Keaton visits regularly), a neat and conservative suburb of Los Angeles that critics complained helped to dilute the "Jewish flavour" of the story. And the uncles, the "unstrung heroes," have been reduced in number from four to two, cinematically an intelligent choice since it simplifies the narrative.

For nearly two decades Diane Keaton has been plagued by expectations that she and her on-screen alter ego, Annie Hall from the quintessential relationship comedy, *Annie Hall* (1976), directed by friend and former lover, Woody Allen, are one and the same. That film would secure a position in film history for the actress, but at a definite cost. Smart, driven and extremely talented, Ms. Keaton finally sheds the neurotic insecurity of an actress for a strong directorial vision in *Unstrung Heroes*. The film has a distinct visual feel that Ms. Keaton had previously displayed during directorial bouts on television, in episodes of *Twin Peaks* and *China Beach*, as well as several music videos, most notably for ex-GoGo's lead singer Brenda Carlyle. It was the cable television movie, *Wildflower* (1991), that brought Ms. Keaton to the attention of producers Susan Arnold and Donna Roth, both of whom were convinced that she possessed the insight and emotional depth needed for the telling of *Unstrung Heroes*.

Ms. Keaton's offscreen fondness for searching out treasures at California swap meets reverberates on-screen in the

CREDITS

Selma Lidz: Andie MacDowell
Sid Lidz: John Turturro
Danny Lidz: Michael Richards
Arthur Lidz: Maury Chaykin
Steven/Franz Lidz: Nathan Watt
Sandy Lidz: Kendra Krull

Origin: USA
Released: 1995
Production: Susan Arnold, Donna Roth and Bill Badalato for a Roth/Arnold Production; released by Hollywood Pictures
Direction: Diane Keaton
Screenplay: Richard LaGravenese; based on the book *Unstrung Heroes* by Franz Lidz
Cinematography: Phedon Papamichael
Editing: Lisa Churgin
Production design: Garreth Stover
Art direction: Chris Cornwell
Set decoration: Larry Dias
Costume design: Jill Ohanneson
Sound: Robert J. Anderson
Music: Thomas Newman
MPAA rating: PG
Running Time: 94 minutes

AWARDS AND NOMINATIONS

Academy Awards Nominations 1995: Best Score (Newman)

production design, where artifacts ranging from wedding cake decorations to rubber balls are a reflection of how ordinary objects can embody deeper meaning. The film's set decorations are at once ordinary and extraordinary, each piece carefully and lovingly chosen by a director with a strong and definite vision. Yet these decorations are never intrusive, never overwhelm the story; they remain a subtle reflection of the story's theme of learning to find the specialness in the everyday moments in life. When Uncle Arthur encourages the young boy to hold fast to memories for they are the keys to the future, Steven begins collecting things from his mother's everyday life, her lipstick, a photograph, into a specially dedicated box, a place where his mother will live on forever. The two uncles also encourage Steven to rediscover his Jewish roots, something his father has always frowned upon. "We need our rituals to rise above the patterns of history," Arthur tells the boy.

Credit director Diane Keaton for drawing out one of the finest performances in Andie MacDowell's career. On paper, MacDowell seems an unlikely choice to play the affectionate, high-spirited Jewish mother. Yet the actress, who was pregnant at the time of filming, gives a touching and serenely calm portrayal of a dying young woman. While several critics remarked that the actress looked too pretty to be dying, Ms. Keaton insisted that she wanted Selma to be a reflection of how Steven saw his mother, radiant up until the end. MacDowell, who began her film career amid ridicule for having to have her voice dubbed by Glenn Close in Hugh Hudson's *Greystoke: the Legend of Tarzan, Lord of the Apes* (1984), later received wide acclaim, including the Los Angeles Critics' Best Actress Award and a Golden Globe Award nomination, for her performance as the repressed young wife in Steven Soderbergh's *Sex, Lies and Viedotape* (1989). MacDowell's other films include *Green Card* (1990), *The Object of Beauty* (1991), *Groundhog Day* (1993), Robert Altman's *Short Cuts* (1993), and the surprise hit, *Four Weddings and a Funeral* (1994) with Hugh Grant.

Actor John Turturro also turns in a stellar performance as the emotionally distant father, a man who refuses to acknowledge that there might be something that science cannot fix. Sid Lidz insists to the children that their mother merely has a "very bad cold" rather than face his wife's terminal ovarian cancer and Turturro captures the pain and the fear of a man trying to come to grips with his own inability to save the single most important person in his life. Turturro received enormous acclaim for his role as the disgruntled game show contestant Herbert Stempel in Robert Redford's *Quiz Show* (1994) and won the Best Actor Award at Cannes for his work in *Barton Fink* (1991). His other work includes four Spike Lee films, *Do the Right Thing* (1989), *Mo' Better Blues* (1990), *Jungle Fever* (1991), and *Clockers* (1995). The actor made his film directing debut with *Mac* (1992), which won the Cannes Film Festival's Camera d'Or for Best First Film.

Combining emotional depth with a crazy, yet grounded sense of humor, Diane Keaton succeeds in making *Unstrung Heroes* a moving, yet unsentimental film. Leave it to Diane Keaton to find such life in the midst of death. To paraphrase the film's uncles: Ms. Keaton, you're the one to watch.

—*Patricia Kowal*

REVIEWS

Entertainment Weekly. September 22, 1995, p.57.
Detroit Free Press. September 22, 1995, p. 6F.
Los Angeles Times. September 15, 1995, p. F1.
Newsweek. September 25, 1995, p. 90.
New York Times. September 15, 1995, p.C5.
Rolling Stone. September 21, 1995, p.90.
Variety.

Unzipped

"Stylish, sophisticated and outrageous!"—Susan Granger, *CRN Radio Network*

"Hilarious! A boldly colorful portrait of the fashion world!"—Janet Maslin, *The New York Times*

"The best party movie of the year!"—Peter Travers, *Rolling Stone*

Naomi Campbell, Isaac Mizrahi, and Linda Evangelista in *Unzipped.* © Miramax Films.

Unzipped is an inspired title for Douglas Reeve's documentary about Brooklyn-born fashion designer Isaac Mizrahi. The film opens with Mizrahi breathlessly reading a review of one of his shows. The camera catches him the morning after in a shop where he has just purchased a paper with the fateful criticism of his work. He is devastated at the negative reaction. This is shown by the way he walks out of the shop, head bowed, and almost literally crushed as the critic's words (in a voice over of Mizrahi reading the critic's dismissal) drone on. The grainy, fuzzy black and white images emphasize the early morning hung-over world of a man of fashion with his heart on his sleeve. He is unzipped and violated by this public exposure and censure, and as the film makes abundantly clear, this is the nature of his personality. He is at one with his work, which puts him and his creations constantly on display. An extrovert, he has chosen the most extroverted of all professions, where he daily unzips and shows himself. Yet for all this constant emoting, he is never tiresomely exhibitionistic; on the contrary, his fashion-sense is courageous, moving, and always fun.

Indeed Mizrahi's response to the harsh review is to begin work on another show. The film then performs another kind of unzipping, probing the design process, observing Mizrahi test out ideas, argue with his staff, reminisce with his mother, interact with his models, and hang-out with friends like Sandra Bernhard. His enthusiasm and dedication is infectious. Even when he is hard on his staff—especially in a scene when he is informed that another designer has just publicized the idea Mizrahi has been working on—Mizrahi's own agony preserves our sympathy toward him even as he lashes out at others.

There is plenty of anger and frustration as various items on order are late, as concepts somehow don't work out, and as the pressure mounts to produce a show that will recapture his reputation. But Mizrahi redeems himself with a sense of humor and marvelous stories—like the one about himself at the age of four noticing that his mother had added daisies to a plain pair of mules. Who would have thought Issac was watching the daisies, says Sarah Mizrahi, an obviously proud mother fascinated with her son's work.

"It's '50s cheesecake meets Eskimo fake fur."—Designer Mizrahi from *Unzipped*

Unzipped may be the finest film ever to reveal the gay sensibility. Directed and designed by Douglas Keeve, a fashion photographer and Mizrahi's lover during the time of the filming, *Unzipped* makes no issue of sexual preference or of the gay personality, yet Mizrahi's touching sensitivity and vulnerability, and above all his quest for style, surely make him quintessentially gay. For him, history is fashion plus sensibility; how people dress and carry themselves is not incidental or ancillary. He does not seem to be joking when he says that Mary Tyler Moore and Jackie Onassis are the most important figures of the age, the creators of the culture. This comment is then juxtaposed against a shot of the opening credits from one of Moore's television shows while Mizrahi's sings the theme song. Mizrahi's comments are funny but not frivolous; he understands how such women can move masses of people, and he is unabashed about presenting them as role models.

Part of the gay sensibility, of course, is just plain silliness. There is much ado in the film about fake fur and Mizrahi's efforts to get it to look and feel just right. A very serious fashion critic and Mizrahi confidant makes several appearances to pronounce on the fakes, paradoxically pronouncing them genuine—a wonderful epiphany of what fashion is: always a counterfeit, a putting-on. In the fashion world people are always camping and never at home to reality.

A hilarious visit to Eartha Kitt, the sex kitten, who purrs for Mizrahi and asks him if he is going to make her gowns, rejuvenates him. Of course he will make her gowns Mizrahi says, imitating her voice and manner just as he mimics others, just as fashion, in his hands, always mimics and thus exaggerates the world. The trip to Kitt is a defining moment in the film, for it is summative of the life in search of style. Remembering Kitt and her two poodles, Mizrahi remarks, "It's almost impossible to have style nowadays without the right dogs."

Mizrahi is so charming because he is so knowing about style without becoming cynical. Of course, fashion is manipulative and unreal. One of his favorite movies is *Call of the Wild*, in which Loretta Young, after four days of exposure to the cold, is shown in closeup with her makeup beautifully intact. "If you must freeze on the tundra, this is the way to do it," concludes Mizrahi. Of course women want to flatter themselves and do not want to wear fur pants: "It's about women not wanting to look like cows."

Keeve brings a lover's sensibility to this film, revealing the intimate side of Mizrahi's personality (although not his love life). The film itself mimics Mizrahi's search for style by its assortment of film stocks from black-and-white to color, from 16mm to 35mm, while showing clips from the designer's favorite movies. The ensemble is a kind of melding of biographical and autobiographical forms. Mizrahi is always speaking for himself, but Keeve is always the master of his medium, picking the angles and the focus (from extremely fuzzy to extremely sharp) to suit the mood of his subject and the temper of his documentary.

This is hardly just a personal film, however. There is no cloying, sentimental subtext. Mizrahi's drive is a universal artistic one; his is the energy of the creator. Even a shot of him from a home movie, in which he is like anybody's baby in a playpen, bouncing with excitement to get out, is distinctive because so much of that energy still survives in the man.

If there is a darker side to Mizrahi, if he throws prolonged tantrums or abuses people, it has been edited out of the film, or perhaps was never shown to the camera. There is one moment when Mizrahi is planning to use a transparent scrim for his show, so that the audience will be invited to get a glimple of his models preparing for their performances. An aghast staff members cautions him that the models may not agree to this kind of exposure. "Tough," is Mizrahi's reply—so caught up is he in the concept. In fact, we then see him tentatively proposing the idea to several models, meekly accepting their rebuffs or querulous responses. He knows he's asking a lot of them. Keeve builds suspense around this element. Will the show have a scrim? How will it be possible for some models to agree to this exposure and others not?

But the battle over the scrim is not merely a clever plotting device; it is at the heart of Mizrahi's fashion sense. He knows that people want a good show. They want to watch the models parade down the runway, lights flashing, music pounding. When *Unzipped* culminates in just such a scene, the documentary has given way completely to Mizrahi's world, the world of Hollywood films and glamorous women, flawless makeup and perfect bodies moving against and with fabric—indeed an entirely fabricated world. It is a stunning moment—watching not only the models but the stars watching the models. Roseanne is there; so is Sandra Bernhard, Richard Gere (then married to Cindy Crawford, one of Mizrahi's models). Stars are watching stars and they glitter among each other. What makes this scene work is the scrim, the sense of backstage life. The audience can almost peer through the gauzy fabric that separates the stage and runway from them. They are the privileged voyeurs of the fashion-process. They are getting a purchase not merely on a season's fashions but on the creative moment itself, unzipped, so to speak.

This final scene, in other words, is really a recapitulation of the whole film. There it is: the show itself and the making of a show, the shooting of the film and the film itself. The filmmaker's and his subject's sensibilities fuse in a work of art, a work of love.

There does not seem to be a superfluous shot in this 76 minute movie. It is difficult to imagine it being a second

CREDITS

Isaac Mizrahi: Isaac Mizrahi
Linda Evangelista: Linda Evangelista
Naomi Campbell: Naomi Campbell
Kate Moss: Kate Moss
Cindy Crawford: Cindy Crawford
Polly Allen Mellen: Polly Allen Mellen
Christy Turlington: Christy Turlington
Carla Bruni: Carla Bruni
Sarah Mizrahi: Sarah Mizrahi

Origin: USA
Released: 1995
Production: Michael Alden for a Hachette Filipacchi production; released by Miramax Films
Direction: Douglas Keeve
Cinematography: Ellen Kuras
Editing: Paula Heredia
MPAA rating: R
Running Time: 76 minutes

AWARDS AND NOMINATIONS

Sundance Film Festival 1995: Audience Award

longer or shorter. When Mizrahi reads the rave review the next day, bringing the film full circle, it not only completes the documentary, it describes the fashion cycle, from show to show, from one creative moment to the next. The next one may be a triumph, or it may be a disaster. Either way Mizrahi will be unzipped, having only something like that scrim, the most fragile of shields, to protect him even as it reveals his personality and his art.

—Carl Rollyson

The Usual Suspects

"In a world where nothing is what it seems you've got to look beyond...*The Usual Suspects.*"—Movie tagline

"These suspects are all guilty of being terrific actors, I had a good time."—Joel Siegel, *Good Morning America*

"Christopher McQuarrie's plot sense and vigorous, profane dialogue jolt the film like a high-tension wire."—*Los Angeles Times*

"A whopper of an ending! The tough guys of *The Usual Suspects* radiate confidence in their own movie mythic possibilities."—Janet Maslin, *The New York Times*

"The freshest, funniest and scariest thriller of the year."—Peter Travers, *Rolling Stone*

Box Office Gross: $22,878,463

The Usual Suspects is a highly original blend of film genres. It is a caper film in which the robberies are relatively unimportant. It is a buddy film in which the characters seem to know or care little about each other. It is a Quentin Taratinoesque hip, profane crime comedy-drama that shrinks from violence. It is a film noir in which evil triumphs, though not necessarily over good, which does not seem to exist in the murky world created by screenwriter Christopher McQuarrie and director Bryan Singer.

The film opens with an explosion aboard a ship but then jumps back six weeks to the police rounding up five New York criminals after a truck loaded with gun parts is hijacked in Queens. Following a lineup, the five are locked in a cell where they decide to pull a job together. They are an explosives expert, Todd Hockney (Kevin Pollack), a burglar, Michael McManus (Stephen Baldwin), his partner, Fred Fenster (Benicio Del Toro), a con man, Roger "Verbal" Kint (Kevin Spacey), and a former big-time criminal, Dean Keaton (Gabriel Byrne). Keaton is trying to go straight to please his lawyer-girlfriend, Edie Finneran (Suzy Amis).

After smoothly stealing jewels protected by corrupt policemen, they go to Los Angeles where a fence induces them to stage another robbery ending in violence. They are approached by Kobayashi (Pete Postlethwaite), a lawyer who claims to work for the mysterious master criminal Keyzer Soze. Soze is legendary for his elusiveness and feared for the lengths to which he will go to exact revenge. He even killed his wife and children to prove to the criminal world that he could not be intimidated.

Soze wants the New Yorkers to raid a drug-smuggling ship in the harbor at San Pedro. When they refuse, Fenster is murdered. As the others threaten to kill Kobayashi, the lawyer threatens a relative of each criminal and shows Keaton that Edie is also in danger. Instead of drugs, the thieves find only chaos in San Pedro. Someone blows up the ship, and twenty-seven men are killed. The only survivors are a badly burned Hungarian from the ship and Verbal, uninjured because Keaton told him to keep watch from the shore.

According to screenwriter McQuarrie, Keyser Soze was inspired by John List, a New Jersey accountant who murdered his family and disappeared for 17 years.

The film is narrated by Verbal, so called because of his predilection for talking, as evidenced while being interrogated by U.S. Customs Agent Dave Kujan (Chazz Palminteri). *The Usual Suspects* jumps back and forth between the interrogation and the activities of the title characters with a flashback to Soze's killing his family. Since the explosion and deaths occur at the beginning of the film, the mystery lies in why it happened and what will be the result. Despite Verbal's insistence, Kujan is not convinced that Soze is behind it all or that Soze even exists. He could simply be a myth created by criminals to explain their failures. The film ends with the clever revelation of Soze's identity after a police sketch artist draws the archvillain based on a description by the Hungarian.

Just as Tarantino attempted to reinvigorate the crime film with *Reservoir Dogs* (1992) and *Pulp Fiction* (1994), Singer and McQuarrie breathe new life into it from another angle. Like Tarantino, they delight in deconstructing the genre by toying with linear narrative, but while Tarantino's films seriously explore the depths of their characters and themes such as guilt and responsibility, Singer and McQuarrie settle for celebrating the complexity of mystery plotting.

"Keaton always said 'I don't believe in God, but I'm afraid of him.' Well, I believe in God, and the only thing that scares me is Keyser Soze."—Verbal from *The Usual Suspects*

Even with a straightforward narrative, *The Usual Suspects* would be demanding on its viewers. The film provides complexity for the sheer joy of complexity. The viewer is always suspicious of how these five were thrown together in the first place, why Keaton is a key to it all, why they must go to California, why the robbery there goes so wrong, what exactly is on that ship anyway, and why it has to be blown up. Kobayashi is an enigmatic figure. Is he in control of it all? Is he, in fact, Soze? Does Soze exist? Will Kujan figure out what is going on? All the pieces fall together masterfully at the end when it becomes clear that the audience—and most of the characters—have fallen prey to an elaborate, bloody facade.

In an era when any film or television program with a complicated plot seems doomed to commercial hell, the box-office success of *The Usual Suspects* is a major surprise. The film placed among the top-five moneymakers for several weeks despite being shown on fewer screens than its bigger-budgeted competitors. The film has two gimmicks. One is Keyzer Soze, a secret those who have seen the film can share as with the sexual identity of the hairdresser in *The Crying Game* (1992). The other is the film's unusually engaging complexity that draws viewers into its sticky web despite themselves.

The setting of *The Usual Suspects* may be an homage to *The Big Sleep*, both the 1939 Raymond Chandler novel and the 1946 Howard Hawks film in which a key scene takes place at the docks of San Pedro. Such an allusion would be appropriate since the plot of *The Big Sleep* has a reputation for being difficult to follow. The film's title alludes to Claude Rains' famous line in *Casablanca* (1943): "Round up the usual suspects." The rounding up at the beginning is reminiscent of the opening of Henri-Georges Clouzot's *Le Salaire De La Peur* (1953; *The Wages of Fear*), whose protagonists embark on a similarly doomed existential adventure. It also recalls such caper films as John Huston's *The Asphalt Jungle* (1950) and Stanley Kubrick's *The Killing* (1956). *The Usual Suspects* manages to be heavily allusive without seeming in any way derivative.

CREDITS

Roger "Verbal" Kint: Kevin Spacey
Dean Keaton: Gabriel Byrne
Dave Kujan: Chazz Palminteri
Todd Hockney: Kevin Pollack
Michael McManus: Stephen Baldwin
Kobayashi: Pete Postlethwaite
Fred Fenster: Benicio Del Toro
Edie Finneran: Suzy Amis
Jack Baer: Giancarlo Esposito
Jeff Rabin: Dan Hedaya

Origin: USA
Released: 1995
Production: Bryan Singer and Michael McDonnell for a Blue Parrot/Bad Hat Harry production; released by Gramercy
Direction: Bryan Singer
Screenplay: Christopher McQuarrie
Cinematography: Newton Thomas Sigel
Editing: John Ottman
Production design: Howard Cummings
Art direction: David Lazan
Set decoration: Sara Andrews
Costume design: Louise Mingenbach
Casting: Francine Maisler
Sound: Geoffrey Patterson
Music: John Ottman
Make-up: Michelle Buhler
Special effects: Roy Downey

AWARDS AND NOMINATIONS

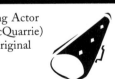

Academy Awards 1995: Best Supporting Actor (Spacey), Best Original Screenplay (McQuarrie)
British Academy Awards 1995: Best Original Screenplay (McQuarrie)
Nominations: Best Film
Chicago Film Festival 1995: Best Supporting Actor (Spacey), Best Screenplay (McQuarrie)
Independent Spirit Awards 1996: Best Supporting Actor (Del Toro), Best Screenplay (McQuarrie)
National Board of Review 1995: Best Supporting Actor (Spacey)
New York Film Critics Awards 1995: Best Supporting Actor (Spacey)
Golden Globe Awards Nominations 1996: Best Supporting Actor (Spacey)
Independent Spirit Awards Nominations 1996: Best Cinematography (Sigel)
Screen Actors Guild Awards Nominations 1995: Best Supporting Actor (Spacey)

McQuarrie and Singer are quite experienced in collaborating together. The Princeton, New Jersey natives worked on two previous projects, *Lion's Den*, a short film, and *Public Access* (1993), a feature shown at the Sundance Film Festival. McQuarrie's script emphasizes structure, plot, and surprises. It might be criticized for not developing the characters fully, but McQuarrie is more concerned with economy, not letting any background details or psychological quirks get in the way of the film's headlong plunge toward its conclusion. He also avoids the cliches of the genre since the five thieves never really become friends and are too afraid of Soze to become suspicious of each other.

As with Tarantino's *Pulp Fiction*, Singer's visual style is subdued. No stylistic pyrotechnics are necessary with a story this complex. Perhaps the most unusual aspect of the film is that Singer realizes that while several characters must die violently, depicting these deaths realistically would detract from the film's essence—and would also turn off a portion of the audience he is trying to attract. As a result, deaths occur in shadows, often in the corner of the frame, or Singer shows other characters responding rather than the violent act itself. That the film was edited and scored, both quite effectively, by the same person, John Ottman, is yet another of its unusual qualities.

The performances are uniformly good. Postlethwaite embodies Kobayashi with a stiff confidence combined with an eccentricity that makes the lawyer seem capable of anything. Byrne presents Keaton as the moral center, such as it is, of the film. He is not convincing as a ruthless killer who murdered fellow inmates while in prison, but the filmmakers may have created this doubt deliberately to suggest that anyone, given the right circumstances, is capable of anything.

The star performance is that of Spacey who has always been either too passive, as with *Glengarry Glen Ross* (1992), or too out of control, as with *The Ref* (1994), in his film roles. His best film work before *The Usual Suspects* is his incestuous, drug-addicted gangster in the 1980's television series *Wiseguy*. Spacey gives Verbal the qualities that allow him to fool Kujan during the interrogation: nervous but in control, weak but attentive to others' weaknesses, able to manipulate without seeming to do so. Verbal seems to be such a mousy character, but Spacey imbues him with a commanding screen presence. Singer's camera keeps calling attention to Verbal's lined face and his goofy haircut with an arrow pointing down his forehead to make him seem harmless and inept. Spacey, McQuarrie, and Singer make Verbal one of the most memorable characters in recent American films.

—Michael Adams

REVIEWS

Entertainment Weekly. August 25, 1995, p. 92.
The New Republic. CCXIII, August 21, 1995, p. 30.
New York. XXVIII, August 28, 1995, p. 118.
The New York Times. August 16, 1995, p. B3.
The New Yorker. LXXI, August 14, 1995, p. 85.
Newsweek. CXXVI, August 28, 1995, p. 58.
People Weekly. September 18, 1995, p. 27.
Rolling Stone. September 7, 1995, p. 75.
Sight and Sound. V, September, 1995, p. 61.
Time. CXLVI, August 28, 1995, p. 69.
Variety. January 30, 1995, p. 46.
The Wall Street Journal. August 18, 1995, p. A8.

Vampire in Brooklyn

"A comic tale of horror and seduction."—Movie tagline

"A ghoulish comedy...with a ton of laughs!"—Ron Brewington, *American Urban Radio Network*

"The most fun vampire movie you have ever seen!"—Bobbie Wygant, *NBC-TV*

Box Office Gross: $19,031,346

Lately, Eddie Murphy has been having a difficult time recapturing the box office throne that he once sat upon in the '80's. It seemed that he could do no wrong with the blockbuster success of his films, such as *Beverly Hills Cop*, *Trading Places*, *48 Hours*, and *Coming to America*. He was the "box office champ" and the star appeared to bask in the glory. However, things seemed to change when *Boomerang*, *Beverly Hills Cop III* and *Harlem Nights* floundered at the box office. Considering these facts, Murphy's latest release, *Vampire in Brooklyn*, could be labeled as a come-back film—a vehicle to restore him to his previous "star status."

With this in mind, the idea of pairing Murphy with shockmeister Wes Craven, (*A Nightmare on Elm Street*) seemed like a winning combination. It would serve to give Murphy the opportunity for a much needed image change. The script for this project, based on an original idea by Eddie himself, was written by Charles Murphy, Michael Lucker, and Christopher Parker. (Charles and Vernon Lynch Murphy, Jr. also get story credit.) It was written to showcase the actor-comedian's considerable talents and put him back on top. It does succeed on some levels, but does not accomplish its goal of redemption.

This comedy-horror genre of film, opens with a narrative over the credit sequence by Murphy, speaking in some sort of a continental Caribbean accent. Meanwhile, an eerie and foreboding ship careens into the misty (lots of mist) docks of Brooklyn, almost killing two blue-collar workers, Julius (Kadeem Harrison) and Silas (John Witherspoon). "Must be a D.U.I." exclaims one of the men. The audience is informed that Murphy's character, Maximillian, has come to find a woman who is half-human and half-vampire. If he can get her to dance with him, he can make her his own. The problem with this device is that it divulges too much information and cuts into the suspense of the plot. Murphy's accent also goes in and out and he intermittently sounds like a cross between the late Bob Marley and Buckwheat (his popular character on *Saturday Night Live*).

Angela Bassett's stunt double, Sonja Davis, was fatally injured during a jump off a 42-foot building.

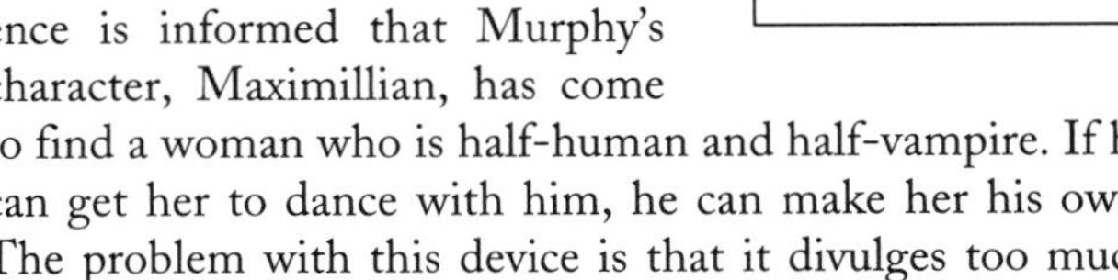

It is discovered, after a thorough investigation by the N.Y.P.D., that everyone on board has been brutally killed by what looks to be some sort of wild animal. Enter Angela Bassett (Rita) and Alan Payne (Justice) as two appropriately horrified detectives assigned to investigate this grisly case. When Rita boards the "ship of death," she comes upon a mysterious coffin in the ship's underbelly. She opens it to discover that it's carrying a body that looks just like her. When she screams for help from her fellow detectives, it suddenly disappears. This opening sequence displays the director's (Wes Craven) talent for creating a sense of the macabre. The special effects that are used in this sequence are well-executed and whets the appetite for what is to come. Mark Irwin, who served as the Director of Photography, and the team of Gary Diamond and Cynthia Charette did a splendid job throughout the film.

Maximillian begins his prowl of the streets of New York to set about seducing Rita—"One dance and she'll be mine." He chooses Julius (by chomping into his neck) to be his chauffeur and assistant. Unfortunately, for Julius, this bite by Max turns him into a ghoul and he starts to decay right before our eyes. This process progresses throughout the film and is one of the weakest and unfunniest sequences in the film. Julius feeds on roaches and steadily rots away, losing a hand, eyeball, and arm. While this is taking place, he is constantly cracking jokes in his best "home boy" style. It appears that the writers thought that reverse black exploitation would be funny. It comes as a surprise, is embarrassing and is in bad taste. Talk about stereotypes—this definitely crosses the line.

As the story unfolds "bite by bite," Maximillian discovers that he has competition for Rita's affections. It seems that Justice, Rita's partner, has had a long-running desire to capture the reluctant Rita's heart. She seems to have a sixth sense that she is different from other people and is leery about getting involved with anyone. She spends her "off-time" painting pictures of a recurring nightmare—a bloody woman impaled on a cross. The two partners continue to flirt with one another, but the relationship has not yet been consummated. Maximillian tries all sorts of devilish and supernatural tricks to come between them. At one point, he picks up Rita's roommate on the streets of New York. Even though it is late and it is New York, the roommate Nikki

(Simbi Khali), astonishingly invites him up for sex. It is difficult to accept that a woman in the 90s could be so reckless, but, then again, it is Eddie Murphy. Lo and behold, she is brutally murdered and impaled on a cross—Rita's prophecy indeed comes true. In another incredulous scene, Max leaves Rita a note in Nikki's handwriting, stating that she has moved out in the middle of the night to move in with Justice. Yeah, right! At this point, the script starts to fall apart as fast as Julius' decaying body. The turn of events becomes so preposterous and farfetched that the film starts to lose all credulity, even for a vampire film. It seems there were just too many writers throwing in their absurd ideas, with no one in control. There were several reviews of the film that pointed this out. For instance, Caryn James in *Film Review Magazine* (Oct. 27th) said "*Vampire in Brooklyn* goes through the motions of a comic-vampire romance with little sense of how to blend its elements. He (Eddie Murphy) might have hired better writers."

There was obviously some agreement by this panel of writers to go back to the origins of Murphy's success, which were the brilliant characters that he created on *Saturday Night Live*. In two short episodes in the middle of the film, Maximillian transforms himself into two completely different characters. First, he becomes Preacher Pauly (an Al Sharpton look-a-like), who preaches that "evil is necessary, evil is good." Then he changes into an Italian street hood named Guido. Not only are the special make-up effects (Kurtzman, Nicotero, Bergen EFX Group) terrific, but Murphy shines. It is at these moments in the film that the film-goer gets to see the reason that he became such a big star in the first place. Sadly, there are just not enough of these moments in *Vampire in Brooklyn* to make it the success for which everyone had hoped.

Back at the crypt, Maximillian is persistent at doing the dance with Rita. At this point, she and Justice are estranged and Rita is extremely vulnerable and open to romance. Late one night, Max suddenly appears at her door-step and invites her over to his place. He sends over the limo, driven by Julius, who now looks like a corpse. She hops in, dressed to the nines, but not before commenting to Justice (who just happens to show up at this precise moment), "Take your ass to Blockbuster. Get a video." Yet another unfunny one-liner.

Angela Bassett (*What's Love Got to Do with It* (1993), *Strange Days* (1995) and *Waiting to Exhale* (1996)) is undeniably a lovely and gifted actress. However, she is limited by a poorly written script that is not funny or scary. She seems to be acting in a different movie than everyone else. Also, the chemistry between her and Murphy falls flat. It never ignites or excites their scenes together.

Finally, Max's persistence pays off and Rita agrees to dance with him. She is intoxicated by the wine, the moon and Max's charm. As they swirl dizzily around the room, Max seizes his opportunity and plants his fangs into lovely Rita's neck, which sends her into a cosmic tailspin. His mission has been accomplished and she now belongs to him, or so we think. At this point, the film lapses into a predictable battle of good versus evil. It utilizes some admirable special effects to wage the war, but winds down to an uninspired ending. *Variety*, in the October 27th issue, says about the ending that it "presents a problem as well, sending the audience out on a relatively flat note."

It is difficult to ascertain how much clout Wes Craven had on the set. When a director is working with a star, who is one of the producers and writers, it must be difficult to have a great deal of creative control. *The Hollywood Reporter* wrote in its October issue, "Directed by shockmeister Wes Craven, the Paramount release is also a washout as a horror film, struggling to build tension and provide the gross-out thrills that are essential to the genre." Perhaps, the fault lies not with the director, but with a star who is wearing too many hats. Omnipotence can sometimes be a liability.

Vampire in Brooklyn was definitely a departure from Eddie Murphy's previous screen outings. *Entertainment Weekly* (Oct. '95) says "What he's really doing is cuing us to see how desperate he is for an image overhaul." If he had been willing to give himself over to a competent director who he

CREDITS

Maximillian/Preacher Pauley/Guido: Eddie Murphy
Rita: Angela Bassett
Justice: Allen Payne
Julius: Kadeem Hardison
Silas: John Witherspoon
Dr. Zeko: Zakes Mokae
Dewey: Joanna Cassidy

Origin: USA
Released: 1995
Production: Eddie Murphy and Mark Lipsky for an Eddie Murphy Production; released by Paramount Pictures
Direction: Wes Craven
Screenplay: Charles Murphy, Christopher Parker, and Michael Lucker; based on a story by Charles Murphy, Eddie Murphy and Vernon Lynch, Jr.
Cinematography: Mark Irwin
Editing: Patrick Lussier
Art direction: Gary Diamond and Cynthia Charette
Set decoration: Robert Kensinger
Costume design: Ha Nguyen
Sound: Jim Stuebe and Paul Clay
Visual effects: Gene Warren
Make-up: Bernadine M. Anderson
Cinematography: Eartha Robinson
Music: J.Peter Robinson
MPAA rating: R
Running Time: 103 minutes

trusted, this may have been the breakthrough role that he had hoped it would be. As it is, it is yet another failed attempt at reviving what appears to be a stalled career.

When Angela Bassett was interviewed in the Dec. 18th issue of the *Los Angeles Times*, she was asked about *Vampire in Brooklyn*. All she said was, "I had fun doing it, but I wish it were done better." So do the people who went to see it, Angela!

—Rob Chicatelli

Village of the Damned

"Beware the children."—Movie tagline

"*Village of the Damned* grabbed me right away...Christopher Reeve gives one of his strongest performances."—Leonard Maltin, *Entertainment Tonight*

"A good-looking, well-wrought film with knockout special effects."—Kevin Thomas, *The Los Angeles Times*

Box Office Gross: $9,417,567

Nine children with supernatural powers wreak havoc on the tiny coastal town of Midwich in *Village of the Damned*. © 1995 Universal City Studios, Inc. Courtesy of MCA Publishing Rights, a Division of MCA Inc. All rights reserved.

In 1960, *The Village of the Damned* was considered a "sleeper hit," with its unearthly depiction of children whose utter lack of humanity overtakes a small town, and possibly the world. The film starred George Sanders and was the film adaptation of a book by John Wyndham titled *The Midwich Cuckoos*. Wyndham was also the author of *The Day of the Triffids*, another science fiction book which became a well-known film. The original *Village of the Damned* is known as a classic in the genre of science-fiction films of the 1960's, most of which were thinly veiled symbolism of the threat of Communism, which was truly seen as a threat to the entire world.

Now, horror and suspense director John Carpenter has re-made *Village of the Damned*, this time starring Christopher Reeve as the doctor in a personal and professional struggle with a group of frightening children. John Carpenter is best known for having directed the original *Halloween* (1978), the remake of *The Thing* (1982) and several other frightening films, many of which paid homage to the science fiction films of the past.

The childrens' white hair was dyed by a bleaching process that took four days and required a special hair stripper.

This story concerns a little town called Midwich, where one strange day the entire town faints simultaneously from an unknown source. Many of the women in town discover, soon after, that they are pregnant. The town doctor, Alan Chafee (Reeve) is joined by a visiting scientist, Dr. Susan Verner (Kirstie Alley) in following the development of the children born to these women. As years pass, the children grow up with the same vacant look, cold eyes, white hair, and supernatural and telepathic powers. Eventually, they try to take over the town before being stopped by Reeve.

This film, unfortunately, lacks some of the intended suspense and fear. Its ability to serve as a cautionary tale for our times is questionable, given that its melodramatic dialogue and story appear more campy than frightening. For the audience member who enjoys a film with some unintentioned humor, this will be fun. It is difficult to report, however, that this film is not as successful as admirers of Carpenter (and of the sci-fi genre) would wish.

Much of the problem rests in the screenplay (by David Himmelstein), which does little to make the original script from the 1960's relevant to the 1990's. While it seems as if Carpenter and Himmelstein may have chosen to retain some of the innocence of the 1960's script and story, it works against the audience's willingness to suspend disbelief. In particular, some of the dialogue appears rather stilted, and, at times, humorous. "Everyone who gives birth gets $3,000.00 per month, plus prenatal and all medical expenses," says Alley. "But I don't want you to see this as pressure." It is hard not to laugh at this line. Furthermore, the word "abortion" is never mentioned, as if not to offend any audience members; but stirring up the audience is just what is needed. Even more ludicrous is Kirstie Alley's shock and surprise that all the women have decided to carry the children to full term, given the extraordinary health coverage and financial rewards offered.

"To me (this film) falls in line with all the other films I've done, although each one is slightly different. It's classic science fiction. It's aliens from outer space. It's also a human drama, told on a very small scale, in a small town. It's a movie about people's feelings."—Director John Carpenter

Some of the lines are unintentionally funny. A serious Mark Hamill as the town Pastor declaims: "You know, the Roberts girl is a virgin." While appropriate to the story, somehow it feels a bit too innocent for a film wishing to shock its audience. And there is more innocence which seems out of character in the sophisticated nineties. Alley melodramatically proclaims that "it is now of interest to national security that we continue to monitor their developing powers." This line sounds like a holdover from the original film, and it doesn't make sense here, given that there are only seven children, and though they have driven several people to suicide, there is no evidence that they are a threat to anything more than the lives of the people in this sleepy town. Though science fiction requires the suspension of disbelief, it is important that the audience feel the situations and the dialogue fit the truth of the situation unfolding in the story. If the audience is not shown that the children are threatening any more than the lives of the townspeople, then the audience will likely not believe there is a threat to "national security."

Still, the film has a host of memorable moments. The night the mothers all give birth is fun; the women are all crying, it takes place in a barn. The melodrama is very campy. Other images and scenes from this film could go into a camp hall of fame: Kirstie Alley wearing what looks like a black party dress for the birth scene; Alley stealing away a stillborn baby and nervously putting it in her car; or the unintentionally funny scene in which the children gather around her and torture her—it is hard not to picture what Alley's Rebecca character from *Cheers* would have said when being tortured by seven six-year-olds who look like extras from the film version of *Hans Brinker and His Silver Skates.*

Perhaps the funniest moment is the first time one of the children displays their nasty temper. Up to this point, they have been adorable babies. Reeve's wife (Karen Kahn) looks nervously at her child while cooking dinner: When the camera turns to the child, she is a cranky-looking infant in a high chair wearing a bright white wig. The juxtaposition of the dark-haired Kahn being terrorized by a child in a high-chair and a bad wig is hard to see as anything but hilarious.

The children become even more humorous as the audience sees them interact with their parents. After a scene in which they are all examined by Kirstie Alley (and they kill an eye doctor) the parents come to pick them up from the clinic. Each parent nervously eyes their child and reaches out their hand to take them away. Here the film unwittingly

CREDITS

Alan Chaffee: Christopher Reeve
Dr. Susan Verner: Kirstie Alley
Jill McGowan: Linda Kozlowski
Frank McGowan: Michael Pare
Melanie Roberts: Meredith Salenger
Reverend George: Mark Hamill
Ben Blum: Peter Jason
Callie Blum: Constance Forslund
Barbara Chaffee: Karen Kahn

Origin: USA
Released: 1995
Production: Michael Preger and Sandy King; an Alphaville production; released by Universal Pictures
Direction: John Carpenter
Screenplay: David Himmelstein; based on the 1960 screenplay by Stirling Silliphant, Wolf Rilla, and George Barclay; and the book *The Midwich Cuckoos*, by John Wyndham
Cinematography: Gary B. Kibbe
Editing: Edward A. Warchilka
Production design: Rodger Maus
Art direction: Christa Munro
Set decoration: Ron De Fina and Rick Brown
Sound: Thomas Causey
Costume design: Robin Michel Bush, Bob Bush, Barbara Hartman-Jenichen and Michael C. Lynn
Visual Effects: Bruce Nicholson
Music: John Carpenter and Dave Davies
MPAA rating: R
Running Time: 98 minutes

becomes a spoof on Baby-Boomers and their perfect parenting of their children: the parents don't know what monsters they've created.

Carpenter does, however, get a chance to display the talents that have made him a well-known director. Several excellent shots of still bodies strewn about the landscape give the audience the eerie feeling clearly intended by Wyndham's story. Then, as all of the people and animals wake simultaneously, eerie music underscoring, the audience will momentarily know the serious intentions of the filmmakers. Reminiscent of the apocalyptic vision in television's recent *The Stand*, the strange quiet fills the screen and is frightening.

The moments where Carpenter generates fear and suspense are excellent. In particular, the scene in which Christopher Reeve's wife is driven to put her hand in a huge pot of boiling water is truly frightening. Actress Karen Kahn generates desperation and fear as she is powerless to stop her own arm from going into the water.

However, the film has a large share of discrepancies and inconsistencies which keep the story from becoming too involving. For example, the birth scene takes place in a barn, where there are numerous beds filled with women in different stages of labor and birth. Rows of these women and volunteer medical staff are shown. Later, though, it appears that only seven children were born. Since much of the story rests on the fact that only one of the children died at childbirth, there is a huge discrepancy between the numbers of people apparently giving birth and the number of children actually born. Another perceived discrepancy is the apparent age difference between some of the children, all of whom are born on the same night. Jill McGowan's (Linda Kozlowski) child (Thomas Dekker) appears to be much younger than Reeve's child. And finally, though the film spans some seven years, no hair styles seem to change, nor do the characters look moderately different as the years pass. This perception of inaccuracy and discrepancy doesn't help the credibility of the film. And in the nineties audiences require much more sophistication, continuity, and credibility than they did in the sixties.

In interviews, the filmmakers have described this film as being about the "banality of violence, of evil." And clearly, there is a message in this story about the growth of children to whom violence is mundane and to whom humanity has no meaning. At one point in the film Mark Hamill asks Reeve to teach the children, because they respect him. "What will I teach them?" says Reeve. "Humanity," says Hamill. The message of the film is clearly stated.

Well-intentioned as it is, it seems, however, that in this remake, something is missing. Perhaps it is that in the nineties, filmmakers such as the talented Carpenter are so interested in paying homage to the sixties that all they can do is mimic the original. The result is that the film is a bit shallow—as thin and gossamer as the cloud that overtakes Midwich. The lack of depth in this film can be seen in its campy dialogue and its discrepancies, causing the film to be an example of the loss of depth and humanity in our culture even as it condemns it.

—Kirby Tepper

Virtuosity

"Justice needs a new program."—Movie tagline

"A must-see that packs a real wallop."—Ron Brewington, *American Urban Radio Network*

"Breathtaking visual and special effects."—Jim Ferguson, *Prevue Channel*

Box Office Gross: $24,047,246

For decades, Hollywood has bounced back and forth between reality and fantasy, from *The Green Berets* (1968) to *2001: A Space Odyssey* (1968), from *The French Connection* (1971) to *Star Wars* (1977), from *Full Metal Jacket* (1987) to *Ghostbusters* (1984). However, with the advent of the 1990s came a terrain offering features of both reality and fantasy: virtual reality. Prefigured by films such as *Tron* (1982) (in which a computer whiz is sucked into a powerful computer, where he must compete in video games) and by more recent films such as *Purple Rose of Cairo* (1985), *Last Action Hero* (1994) (in both of which characters cross from their cinematic domains into the "real world"), and *The Lawnmower Man* (1992) (in which a scientist tries using drugs and computer instruction to turn a mentally slow lawn man into a brilliant, desirable man), *Virtuosity* leaps the barrier between traditional classifications of films.

Parker Barnes (Denzel Washington) is a cop with a past and, as a result, is an incarcerated felon. In response to the deaths of his wife and child, he sought revenge; he hunted down and killed the psychotic responsible. Now he is serving time. As the film begins, Barnes is searching through a surrealistic cityscape for a dangerous criminal. Soon the audience learns that Barnes has volunteered to test a virtual reality training system, intended to teach officers how to deal with violent situations. The pursued "man" is Sid 6.7 (Russell Crowe), the dangerous computer creation of a cold, corrupt scientist Lindenmeyer (Stephen Spinella). As in *Frankenstein* (1931), creator and created have had a falling out and the "monster" is unleashed on the world. Luckily Parker Barnes is available to battle this computer-age villain, as is Madison Carter (Kelly Lynch), his highly educated psychologist partner.

"I slice, I dice, I puree."—Cyber criminal Sid 6.7 as he commits a murder on national TV

As with many cinematic depictions of the future, such as *Soylent Green* (1973), *Escape from New York* (1981), *Blade Runner* (1982), 1984 (1984), and *No Escape* (1994), the world depicted by *Virtuosity* is one run by large corporations, where the profit means everything and citizens mean nothing. For instance, Elizabeth Deane (Louise Fletcher) works to improve a largely privatized police force to ensure that it has a good public image and a positive ledger sheet. However, maintaining a positive image is more important than saving lives. Fletcher had all but disappeared from the screen, and while under used in *Virtuosity* (sounding over and over her one power-and good publicity-mad note), Fletcher happily regains some of the steely edge she brought to perhaps her best-known role, that of Nurse Ratchet in *One Flew over the Cuckoo's Nest* (1975). The voice of authority, the cold stares, the overly calm response to chaos (such as the death of a prisoner whose brain literally "melts down" due to the exertion of the virtual reality chase) reflects Louise Fletcher at the top of her game of playing frighteningly dangerous women.

Denzel Washington also shines in this film which provides a large divergence from his recent roles, such as a newspaper reporter in *The Pelican Brief* (1994) and executive officer on a submarine in *Crimson Tide* (1995), and from his recent hair styles. That is, when the film begins, Washington is a convict-cop who sports dreadlocks (that enhance his appearance much more than the absurd blue leather uniform he is subsequently required to wear) and whose expertise in the virtual reality gun fight endears him to the business persons promoting virtual reality training. While Washington's character sounds largely one note—revenge—he brings a gritty reality and earnestness to his role. For instance, at one point in the film, Parker Barnes is called upon to rescue Madison Carter's daughter. The scene juxtaposes a series of shots of Washington and the frightened child, of Kelly Lynch's frantic psychologist and of Crowe's demonic Sid 6.7. Even with the artificiality created by such a scene (as in the crosscutting scenes at high noon in *High Noon* (1952)), Denzel Washington is able to imbue his character with realistic fear and concern.

Former Elite model Kelly Lynch plays one of her more traditional roles in *Virtuosity*. Prior to this film, she has played a junkie (*Drugstore Cowboy*, 1989) and a lesbian (*Three of Hearts*, 1993). Here, however, she is a single mother and a psychologist, who works to understand Barnes and to guess Sid's moves according to the mass murders who make-up his programming. While Lynch and Washington make a striking couple, their relationship is clearly unromantic. For instance, in *Medicine Man* (1993), two quarreling scientists are secluded in the rain forest and emerge lovers. In *Virtuosity*, two quarreling specialists in criminology are secluded in the world of virtual reality and never feel the pull of attraction. Lynch said in a recent interview published in *Entertainment Weekly*, "You hear about how interracial characters aren't supposed to kiss, but that's not true. There was no romance in the script, and we decided to keep it that way."

Yet, understanding this film as without sexual passion is an oversimplification. Perhaps the most interesting part of the film's world is the characters' lack of interest in each other, their detachment from emotion for and with things in the "real world." For example, Lindenmeyer fears only Sid, his creation. Further, the only physical attraction in the film is one scientist's obsession for a computer-generated, scantily clad, sexually charged whimpering woman. Indeed, it is that scientist's unquenchable lust that unleashes Sid upon the real world. The scientists work around Kelly Lynch's character each and every day, and never seem to see or appreciate her beauty, strength or her wisdom. *Virtuosity* does address and embody emotion, yet the characters love and fear only what they see in the video display terminals before them.

And fear Sid they should, as he has been programmed to have the predilections of 183 mass murderers, such as Hitler and Charles Manson. A cross between Cary Grant and the liquid-metal terminator (*Terminator 2: Judgment Day*, 1991), Russell Crowe's characterization of Sid is particularly malevolent and unpleasant: he is ruthlessly suave and evil. For instance, he tortures Parker Barnes with memories of the death of his wife and child, relying on Barnes' reactions last time to lead him into trouble this time. He abducts Madison Carter's daughter to get her attention. Sid knows everyone's weaknesses and relies upon them to destroy those around him.

In many ways, the film is overly stylized, relying on slick computerized worlds and on slickly and superficially drawn characters. For instance, part of the impersonalization of this world is reflected in the names of the two main characters. Both have only last names-Parker Barnes and Madison Carter-while the villain has only a first name-Sid. Therefore, while we feel we are on a first-name basis with technology, we barely know ourselves and each other. Indeed, *Virtuosity* is part of a continuing genre: fear of change, progress, the unknown. In *The Man Who Shot Liberty Valance* (1962) and *Shane* (1953), the vanishing wilderness, the encroaching civilization, is an enemy to be fought. In *The Fly* (1958, 1986) technology has advanced more quickly than the ability of humans to comprehend it and its implications. Man is morally too immature to treat scientific developments with the care and wisdom they require; chaos ensues. Not unlike the characters in *Forbidden Planet* (1956), *Invasion of the Body Snatchers* (1956), *The Day the Earth Stood Still, Dr. Strangelove Or: How I Learned to Stop Worrying and Love the Bomb* (1964), *Alien* (1979) and *War Games* (1983), the characters in *Virtuosity* must rely on old-fashioned abilities, instincts and values in order to combat the technological danger from beyond or the danger they have encountered due to advanced technology taking them beyond their ken. As basic as Greek drama's emphasis on hubris, these films (among many more) question our ability to address the future before us, questions whether we are as smart as we like to tell ourselves we are, warns us to be humble in the face of what we have yet to understand.

Unfortunately, for all of its interesting themes, *Virtuosity* relies too heavily on visual effects. Once the viewers tire of the amazing technology, not even the rising body count can make a difference. Nonetheless, genre film buffs and technophiles will want to make sure they see this one.

—Roberta F. Green

CREDITS

Parker Barnes: Denzel Washington
Madison Carter: Kelly Lynch
Sid 6.7: Russell Crowe
Lindenmeyer: Stephen Spinella
William Cochran: William Forsythe
Elizabeth Deane: Louise Fletcher
Wallace: William Fichtner
John Donovan: Costas Mandylor
Clyde Reilly: Kevin J. O'Connor

Origin: USA
Released: 1995
Production: Gary Lucchesi; released by Paramount Picture
Direction: Brett Leonard
Screenplay: Eric Bernt
Cinematography: Gale Tattersall
Editing: B.J. Sears and Rob Kobrin
Production design: Nilo Rodis
Art direction: Richard Yanex-Toyon
Set decoration: Jay Hart
Costume design: Francine Jamison-Tanchuck
Sound: Thomas D. Causey
Visual effects: Jon Townley
Casting: Deborah Aquila and Jane Shannon
Music: Christopher Young
MPAA rating: R
Running Time: 105 minutes

REVIEWS

Baltimore Sun, Maryland Live, Aug. 3- Aug. 10, 1995, p. 5.
Chicago Tribune, Tempo, Aug. 4, 1995, p. 5.
New York Times, Aug. 4, 1995, C14.
Washington Post, Weekend, Aug. 4, 1995, p. 42.
USA Today, Aug. 4. 1995, p. 4D.

Waiting to Exhale

"Exhilarating. Heartfelt, funny and funky."—Jay Carr, *Boston Globe*

"Flashy, full-bodied performances."—Stephen Holden, *The New York Times*

"This is one satisfying savvy movie. I wish more films were as intelligent and observant as this one."—Jeffery Lyons, *Sneak Previews*

Something historic happened in 1995. Not the obvious news events like the tentative Bosnia peace accords, nor the O.J. Simpson trial, nor the shutdown of the federal government. The truly historic event is that film distributors may finally have gotten the idea that there is a market for so-called "women's films." *Sense and Sensibility* (1995) and *Persuasion* (1995) were both successful, and both are considered to be "women's films"—no action, no gratuitous sex, just intelligence and wit and well-acted drama.

It is true that several other women's films emerged with less success, such as *Moonlight and Valentino* (1995), *Now and Then* (1995), and *How to Make an American Quilt* (1995). Traditionally in Hollywood, a film about women's relationships with no bona fide movie stars should be box office poison. But a film dealing with the love lives of four African-American women took the 1995 Christmas season by storm, proving the conventional show-business wisdom wrong once again. *Waiting to Exhale*, adapted by Terry McMillan (with Ron Bass) from her novel of the same name, drew excellent audiences without the benefit of car chases, sex, or traditional movie stars. The film stars four African-American women, only one of whom can be considered a bona fide star (Whitney Houston). African-American women are among the most underemployed members of the Screen Actors Guild: there are usually no roles available of any substance, and the roles that are available are usually stereotypes that are secondary to white characters.

Waiting to Exhale is the story of four close friends and their experiences with men. The phrase "waiting to exhale" refers to the feeling that these women are holding their breath, waiting to feel comfortable with a man. Some critics have implied that the film's title, story, and tone, imply that women are all unhappy without a man in their lives. But the strength of the women in this film seems to belie that concept. All four are intelligent, strong women waiting to have their lives enriched by a good relationship. Some discover they can be happy without it; some find happiness with a man. But the film does not support the notion that all women are desperate to find men, nor does it promote the idea, (as other critics have claimed it has done) that all men are bad. This is a good film; funny and touching, well directed by Forrest Whitaker, and well-acted by its powerhouse cast. The story is simple, the characters are human, and its point is clear: These women initially seem to need a man to make them feel whole, but they learn through the course of the film that they can "exhale" without a man around—and that being alone is preferable to being with the wrong man.

Bernadine (Angela Bassett) is a gorgeous, wealthy woman who stopped her own career several years earlier to help her husband promote his business, and to raise their children. At the start of the film she discovers that he is leaving her. Further, he intends to leave her without financial assistance. But the worst indignity of all for Bernadine is that his mistress is a white woman. Bassett's is the showiest role, and it is fitting, since she is the most theatrical of the actresses. Her scene in which she savagely takes all of his belongings, piles them into his car, douses it with kerosene, and then lights it on fire in the driveway is funny and dramatic at the same time. Bassett is an actress of great ferocity, and her ferocity and anger provide much of the sense of resolution in this film as her character fights for what she wants and grows up in the process.

Robin (Lela Rochon) has been the mistress of a man named Russell (Leon) who has been telling her for years that he intends to leave his wife for her. Uncertain that she wants to be of secondary importance any longer, she sets out to meet the right man, someone who understands that "I want to eat out, I want to go away for long weekends, I want children, and I want to be happy." At first, she dates a business associate named Michael (Wendell Pierce): "Michael's not pretty, but he is available," she tells herself. After he undermines her in a business conference, she moves on to drug-addicted Troy (Mykelti Williamson) and then back to Russell. Robin's character represents those people who tend to believe in promises made in the heat of passion. Eventually she learns not to believe the promises, and decides to go it on her own. Rochon is gentle and beautiful and her reversal and self-discovery at the end, though perhaps a bit cliche, is nonetheless touching.

Based on the best-selling novel *Waiting to Exhale* by Terry McMillan.

Savannah (Whitney Houston) is also involved with a married man. A highly successful and attractive television producer, she too believes the promises of her lover, Kenneth (Dennis Haysbert) that he will leave his wife. Savannah is also pushed to rekindle her relationship with him at the insistence of her mother, who feels her daughter's life is wasted without a man. This character shares much in common with Robin: both date various losers before understanding that they are better off alone. These two story lines would be redundant if not for the funny array of scenes depicting the men they date: each of the men are quite different, and show a broad range of the type of people anyone on the dating scene in the 90's might encounter. A particularly funny scene with Houston and a sexy man she meets in a nightclub (Jeffrey Samms) depicts stereotypical male sexual activity with a great dose of humor: after he satisfies himself with a spectacularly loud and primitive climax, Houston's character laments that "now I'm a keeper in the damn zoo." Ironically, even the beautiful and elegant Houston looks almost average compared to her co-stars, and her acting is a bit more self-conscious than the others.

The fourth friend is Gloria (Loretta Devine), a woman who is raising her teenage son (Dohald Adeosun Faison) alone. Gloria is the owner of a beauty salon, and is the catalyst for the friendship between the women, as they all have their hair done at her salon. Where the others are glamorous and beautiful, Gloria is a little less fancy and a lot more earthy. She is heavy, but still sexy and attractive in a different way than her friends, and she lives a more middle-class lifestyle. Having been without male companionship for a long time while raising her son, Gloria's world changes when she meets a handsome new neighbor, Marvin (Gregory Hines). Devine is divine in her role, particularly in her tentative, implicitly sexy scenes with Hines. Her best scene is the scene where they first meet. She sees him from across the street as he is moving in, and comes over to find out just who he is. Devine is so sincere that her character's immediate infatuation with this handsome neighbor is masked by her attempts to welcome him. She casually asks if he wants to come over to join her in some leftovers, and then proceeds to rattle off a list of mouth-watering foods that would feed an army. As she turns to leave, she wonders if he is watching her walk away—and he is— and Devine's reaction to his interest is absolutely delightful.

All of these stories are thinly woven together through the interactions of the four women. Screenwriters MacMillan and Ron Bass opted to make the film rather episodic: each of the stories seem to take turns unfolding. (It should be noted that Ron Bass is the screenwriter responsible for helping Amy Tan with the screenplay of her novel about the lives of several Chinese-American women, *The Joy Luck Club* [1994]). A couple of theatrical devices hold the film together stylistically, and keep it from becoming a choppy series of plot points. One of the devices is voice-over narration by each of the women: they comment on the action during their "segments," and the comments are usually wry and down-to-earth. These comments sound unmistakably like diary entries, and can sometimes be a little corny, such as Robin's comment about Michael's kiss: "he did it right, and it felt like silk." But for the most part, the voice-overs bring the characters closer to the audience.

This film is director Forrest Whitaker's debut. Whitaker is the highly accomplished actor best-known for starring in Clint Eastwood's jazz movie *Bird* (1988). He proves himself to be an earnest and sensitive director here. Whitaker shows his sense of style with subtle moments; for example, when Gloria is assessing Hines' character, the camera moves up and down his body, as if mimicking her eye movements, and it is very funny. Clearly, this film is not intended to be anything but touching and entertaining, and Whitaker never seems to work too hard to prove himself as a director.

Waiting to Exhale has found wide appeal because of its grace, its humor, and its unabashed sentimentality. This is not a classic; just a good, old-fashioned movie with something for everyone.

—*Kirby Tepper*

CREDITS

Savannah Jackson: Whitney Houston
Bernadine Harris: Angela Bassett
Loretta Devine: Gloria Johnson
Robin Stokes: Lela Rochon
Marvin: Gregory Hines
Kenneth: Dennis Haysbert
Troy: Mykelti Williamson

Origin: USA
Released: 1995
Production: Deborah Schindler and Ezra Swerdlow; released by 20th Century Fox
Direction: Forest Whitaker
Screenplay: Ronald Bass and Terry McMillan; based on her novel *Waiting to Exhale*
Cinematography: Toyomichi Kurita
Editing: Richard Chew
Production design: David Gropman
Art direction: Marc Fisichella
Set decoration: Michael W. Foxworthy
Casting: Jaki Brown-Karman
Music: Babyface
Sound: Tim Chau
MPAA rating: R
Running Time: 120 minutes

A Walk in the Clouds

"A man in search. A woman in need. A story of fate."—Movie tagline

"The love story of the year."—Don Stotter, *Entertainment Time-out*

"Rich, romantic and rewarding. A movie you can feel good about."—Rex Reed, *New York Observer*

"I love this movie! I love every single thing about it!"—Roger Ebert, *Siskel & Ebert*

Box Office Gross: $50,012,507

"The Clouds" is the name of a proud estate in the vineyards of Northern California's Napa Valley, owned by the Aragon family, tracing its lineage back for more than 400 years. The film is a visually extravagant romantic fantasy telling the story of Victoria Aragon (Aitana Sanches-Gijon) and a young man she meets by accident on a train. The young man's life is complicated by her problems when he offers to help her through a difficult homecoming. She has gone away to school and become pregnant after an affair with one of her professors. She claims that her father, Alberto Aragon (Giancarlo Giannini) has sworn to kill anyone who brings dishonor on his family. She is clearly a damsel in distress.

Paul Sutton (Keanu Reeves) is the very soul of courage, honor, and decency, a decorated soldier who has just returned from World War II to the wife he hardly knew and left behind. The film opens with his ship arriving. No one is there on the docks to meet him. When he returns to his apartment home, he discovers that his war bride (Debra Messing) never even bothered to read the letters he sent home. She claims she found the details too disturbing.

Paul explained in his unread letters his hopes, plans and ambitions, but his selfish wife wants him to go back to work as a chocolate drummer, which puts him on the train, with a sample case of chocolates, where he first meets Victoria, by accident. They bump into each other on the train and fall down. When he helps her up, she gets sick and vomits on his uniform, the screenplay's idea of a "cute" meeting. Fortunately Paul has a change of clothes in his luggage, but in the confusion his ticket gets exchanged for hers. As a consequence, they eventually find themselves on the same bus, after Paul has had to leave the train before his destination because of the lost ticket.

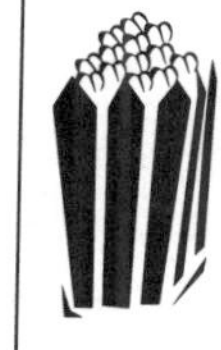

"The most important things in this film are love and family. I was also intrigued by the attachment the characters feel to the earth and the story's depiction of unbending traditional values."—Director Alfonso Arau

Two mashers make a pass at Victoria on the bus and Paul comes to her aid, getting into a fight with the two men. All three are discharged from the bus. Further down the road Paul again finds Victoria, sitting on her luggage, crying. She tells him about her pregnancy and her fear of her father's reaction. Paul then offers to pose as her husband. He will take her home, then abandon her under cover of night, which will put the blame on him and not her.

Alberto the vintner is outraged, of course, to think that his daughter would have married a man who did not have the decency to ask for her hand in marriage. Paul, moreover, is not only an Anglo but also an orphan from Ohio, an alien, an outsider with no lineage and no proper claim to his daughter. The quick-tempered Alberto is also suspicious of the relationship and senses that something is wrong.

On the other hand, Paul is immediately accepted by Victoria's grandfather, paterfamilias Don Pedro Aragon (Anthony Quinn), who takes to the young man and invites him to stay for the harvest, despite Alberto's misgivings. Don Pedro makes this invitation when he sees Paul leaving at night, bags in hand. Don Pedro seems to know that Paul is not what he seems to be, but he senses that the young man has a good heart.

Everyone but Alberto accepts Paul, who is made to feel like one of the family, and the orphan is touched. He also finds himself falling in love with the beautiful Victoria, but he is an honorable man and he finally leaves. When he returns home, however, he finds his wife in bed with another man. He also learns that she has had the marriage annulled. He has discovered that he hardly knew his wife and that they had nothing in common.

Hardly disappointed, Paul heads back to the Napa Valley, where he finds Alberto, sullen, angry, and intoxicated. Alberto throws a lantern at Paul that misses him, but catches the vines on fire. In no time the whole vineyard is destroyed by flames, but Paul goes to the cemetary where Don Pedro has shown him the root of the original Aragon grapevine that started the whole enterprise, and a chagrined but grateful Alberto discovers that the root is still alive. Since Paul is now a free man, he is able to start a new life with Victoria.

Mexican director Alfonso Arau took Hollywood and the critics by surprise in 1993 with *Like Water for Chocolate*, a stunningly visual and intelligent film that earned over twenty-one million in America and prompted many American viewers to seek out the novel upon which the film was based. The critical success of this film cleared the path for *A Walk in the Clouds*, Arau's first American feature film, but several reviewers found this beautifully photographed romantic melodrama overdone.

The film was adapted from Alessandro Blasetti's Italian film *Four Steps in the Clouds* (1942). The Italian original was later remade in France in 1957 as *The Virtuous Bigamist*. The original story, *Quattro Passi Fra Le Nuvole*, by Piero Tellini, Cesare Zavattini, and Vittorio de Benedetti, was adapted for Arau by Robert Mark Kamen, Mark Miller, and Harvey Weitzman. This is an old-fashioned story, given an extravagantly romantic treatment that cynical reviewers tended to reject.

Keanu Reeves has displayed a preference for quirky projects, as far removed from each other as *Speed* (1994) and *Johnny Mnemonic* (1995), on the one hand, and Bernardo Bertolucci's *Little Buddha* (1994), on the other. Reeves and Anthony Quinn are the only talents immediately recognizable to an American mass audience. Aitana Sanches-Gijon is lovely in the role of Victoria and an actress well known in Spain, but *A Walk in the Clouds* marks her American film debut. The Italian actor Giancarlo Giannini would be recognizable to American art-house audiences because of the many films that he made with the director Lina Wertmüller, including *Love and Anarchy*, which earned him the Golden Palm Best Actor Award at the 1973 Cannes Film Festival. Angelica Aragon and Evangelina Elizondo, who play Victoria's mother and grandmother, are among Mexico's best known actresses.

In short, then, the picture is not lacking in talent, and many of the performances are lovely to watch, even Anthony Quinn's overblown and overlovable Don Pedro. Although famous for his role as Zorba the Greek, Quinn was born in Chihuahua, Mexico, in 1915 and still has immense charm at the age of 80. A fifty-year veteran of over 275 films, Quinn still has a commanding presence, and it is still a pleasure to watch him work.

Even so, the film opened to mixed reviews. Stephen Farber of *Movieline* was impressed by Arau's talents as a visual stylist but objected to the "simple-minded narrative." Gary Arnold of *The Washington Times* found the climax absurd. Steven Rea of *The Philadelphia Inquirer* wrote the film off as "dewy, glowy and breathtakingly dumb." Hal Hinson of *The Washington Post* called it "a phenomenally atrocious movie." Joe Brown of *The Washington Post Weekend* was a little more charitable in his evaluation of this "made-to-order Old-Fashioned Romantic Melodrama," but, like the others, objected to Reeve's "politely wooden delivery" and suggested that *A Walk in the Clouds* "should have been a silent film."

Mexican cinematographer Emmanuel Lubezki worked with Alfonso Arau on *Like Water for Chocolate* in 1992 and also did the splendid cinematography for *A Little Princess* in 1995. Without question, *A Walk in the Coulds* is a visual treat. The melodrama is often heavy and hamfisted and the romance overdone, despite moments of great beauty, as when Victoria and Paul don butterfly wings to fan the grapes and keep them warm to protect them from frost. The film is worth seeing for moments like these, which evoke the so-called "magical realism" that distinguished *Like Water for Chocolate*.

Indeed, Stephen Farber wrote that the "ravising look of this movie is almost strong enough to override a lot of other flaws," such as Paul's dedication to the materialistic wife who refused to read the letters he wrote and hardly ever wrote to

CREDITS

Paul Sutton: Keanu Reeves
Victoria Aragon: Aitana Sanchez-Gijon
Don Pedro Aragon: Anthony Quinn
Alberto Aragon: Giancarlo Giannini
Marie Jose Aragon: Angelica Aragon
Guadelupe Aragon: Evangelina Elizondo
Pedro Aragon Jr.: Freddy Rodriguez
Betty Sutton: Debra Messing

Origin: USA
Released: 1995
Production: Gil Netter, David Zucker and Jerry Zucker for a Zucker Brothers production; released by 20th Century Fox
Direction: Alfonso Arau
Screenplay: Robert Mark Kamen, Mark Miller and Harvey Weitzman; based on the film *Quattro Passi Fra Le Nuvole* (*Four Steps in the Clouds*) (1942) written by Piero Tellini, Cesare Zavattini and Vittorio de Benedetti
Cinematography: Emmanuel Lubezki
Editing: Don Zimmerman
Production design: David Gropman
Art direction: Daniel Maltese
Set decoration: Denise Pizzini
Costume design: Judy L. Ruskin
Sound: Jose Antonio Garcia
Special visual effects: Syd Dutton and Bill Taylor
Casting: John Lyons and Christine Sheaks
Music: Maurice Jarre
MPAA rating: PG-13
Running Time: 103 minutes

AWARDS AND NOMINATIONS

Golden Globe Awards 1996: Best Score (Brower)

him while he was in combat. The film's problems are further complicated by its very foreignness (it has the look and feel of a foreign film and a cast dominated by foreigers) and the anachronistic melodrama that may seem flawed to contemporary viewers. If the Keanu Reeves character is a problem, the flaw is more in the screenplay than in the actor's performance. Reeves' alleged "woodenness" is not a major problem here, but even if it were, audiences could still respond to the magic and to the nostalgic romanticism.

—*James M. Welsh*

REVIEWS

The Baltimore Sun. Maryland Live, August 11, 1995, p. 5.
Movieline. Vol.VII, No.1 (September 1995), pp. 36-37.
The New York Times. August 11, 1995, C18.
The Philadelphia Inquirer. August 11, 1995, p. 14.
Time. Vol.146, No.8, August 21, 1995, p.69.
Variety. July 31-August 6, 1995, p.35, p.38
The Washington Post. August 11, 1995, F1, F6.
Washington Post Weekend. August 11, 1995, p.39.

The Walking Dead

Box Office Gross: $6,014,341

As war-is-hell movies go, *The Walking Dead* is fairly conventional in structure and themes. But there are a few delightful surprises in this story of four black Marines on a doomed POW rescue mission in Vietnam. First-time writer-director Preston A. Whitmore II creates compelling characters, though he has trouble concocting original dramatic situations and staging believable action sequences. His debut film shows promise, and the ensemble effort by a group of relatively unknown actors is uniformly good.

The Walking Dead is a strange mix of heavy character drama, ridiculous low-budget action, cartoonish 1960s-era nostalgia and a strong but low-key message about the interaction of racism and warmongering. It avoids the grandiosity of many Vietnam films and keeps its focus firmly fixed on its four central figures, the remains of a platoon which is mostly wiped out after they land in hostile territory.

Taking command of the survivors and keeping them marching on their futile mission to find a POW camp in an abandoned temple is Sergeant Barkley (Joe Morton). The tough-as-nails, philosophical Sarge is a Bible-quoting reverend and career soldier with a shameful secret past. His main nemesis is Private Hoover Branche (Eddie Griffin), a foul-mouthed, dope-smoking, rebellious loose cannon who has a classic bad attitude about the war and being a Marine. Fortunately for Barkley, the other two survivors are good soldiers—Private Cole Evans (Allen Payne), an intellectual with a political, black-pride bent who is a devoted family man, and Private Joe Brooks (Vonte Sweet), a raw young optimist who bravely endures shrapnel in his leg and cheerfully absorbs the Reverend's military and spiritual tutelage.

Filmed on location in Orlando and Chuluota, Florida.

From the moment they touch down, the soldiers are in constant peril of sudden attack. True to the reality of the Vietnam conflict, long stretches of eerie serenity are interrupted suddenly by enemy ambushes. Whitmore spares viewers none of the brutality and carnage of the conflict, though the action sequences are poorly staged. Whitmore stretches credulity in making the four Marines into expert marksmen, picking snipers out of trees with unbelievable precision. Some of the shoot-'em-up scenes are standard over-the-top action-film fare, an unsettling contrast to the quiet dignity of the rest of the film.

Outside of the combat scenes, *The Walking Dead* proceeds like a stage play. The characters, personalities and backgrounds are gradually introduced as the conflicts among the four are revealed, mostly through set speeches that resemble Shakespearean monologues. The dialogue is unsparing and genuine. Not only is Hoover crude, so are the topics of conversation.

Flashbacks that reveal how each man enlisted provide the information needed to understand each character's motivation. Unfortunately, the plot, dialogue and acting in the flashbacks are amateurish. While the Vietnam scenes are authentic, the statewide situations are obviously contrived, with the characters too obviously set up to be victims.

Evans enlists because of housing discrimination back in Los Angeles. He is devoted to his wife, his daughter and his race, and does not want to raise his child in the ghetto he has escaped. When one racist housing manager turns him down, Evans can find no other decent place to live, so he enlists in the Marines because officers get housing. As Hoover observes: "That's a hell of a price to pay for decent housing." And while many blacks did enlist in the Vietnam conflict and do continue to enlist in the armed forces as a means of economic advancement, Evans' situation is played in such a stilted way that it does seem as incredible as Hoover's observation implies.

Hoover's enlistment story bends plausibility even further. Before becoming a Marine, the heartless, fatalistic Hoover is shown as a hard-working, gentle, romantic guy. In a flashback, we see him wooing a girl at a party to which he has brought a ham as an admission token. But it turns out he stole the meat from his employer. In a far-fetched sequence, the meat-packer shows up at the party to fire him, just as naturally as any white employer would track down and dismiss a black employee at an apartment party in the inner city. It's also impossible to believe that getting fired from one job can turn a sweet guy into a hateful cynic and push him into combat.

Joe Brooks' flashback is even sillier. His girlfriend berates him for his lack of ambition, and he can't come up with a plan that will prove to her he's going somewhere. So he announces he's joining the Marines and she throws her arms around him and professes her undying love. This scene plays like a high school production. No less contrived is the eventual flashback revealing the preacher's secret. With these scenes, Whitmore is backing his complex characters with cardboard cut-outs of victims.

The only major white character in the film, Pippins (Roger Floyd), is excessively violent, crazed, bloodthirsty and amoral. Pippin's recruitment story is by far the most entertaining because it's the most outrageous—he escapes to the Marine recruiting office to avoid getting killed by rival gangsters.

Fortunately, the jungle interactions are a lot less stilted than the background material. Whitmore has coaxed outstanding performances from his cast. Morton is compelling and Payne is quite accomplished. It is Griffin as the foul-mouthed, non-stop-talking Hoover who steals the show. Griffin is hilarious, believable and over the top all at the same time; it's hard to put your attention on anything else when he's on the screen. And Whitmore's nicest twist is that he makes the apparently soulless Hoover a hero in the end.

Unfortunately, *The Walking Dead* treads very little new ground in the Vietnam film genre. Whitmore needs better scripts and a firmer grasp of filmmaking technique if he is to overcome the marked amateurish quality that destroys the dignity of his film. But any director who can bring out so many affecting portrayals from such thin material deserves another chance. Whitmore may be a rare actors' director in an era where too many directors are obsessed with special effects and technique. *The Walking Dead* may misfire with its naivete, but it is heartfelt and honest. And it may be remembered as the film which put the very talented Eddie Griffin on the road to stardom.

—*Michael Betzold*

CREDITS

Private first-class Cole Evans: Allen Payne
Private Hoover Branche: Eddie Griffin
Sergeant Barkley: Joe Morton
Private first-class Joe Brooks: Vonte Sweet
Corporal Pippins: Roger Floyd

Origin: USA
Released: 1995
Production: George Jackson, Douglas McHenry, and Frank Price, in association with Rank Film Distributors and Price Entertainment/Jackson-McHenry; released by Savoy Pictures
Direction: Preston A. Whitmore II
Screenplay: Preston A. Whitmore II
Cinematography: John L. Demps, Jr.
Editing: Don Brochu and William C. Carruth
Production design: George Costello
Art direction: Joseph M. Altadonna
Set decoration: Bill Cimino and Craig Anthony
Casting: Jaki Brown-Karman and Kimberly Kardin
Special effects: David H. Watkins
Sound: Adam Joseph
Costume design: Ileane Meltzer
Music: Gary Chang
MPAA rating: R
Running Time: 89 minutes

REVIEWS

Entertainment Weekly. March 10, 1995, p. 50.
The Hollywood Reporter. Feb. 27, 1995, p. 12.
Los Angeles Times. Feb. 25, 1995, p. F9.
New York Times. Feb. 25, 1995, p. 11.
People. March 13, 1995, p. 17.
Variety. Feb. 27, 1995, p. 69.

War of the Buttons

"Funny, tender and wise. A winner."—Kevin Thomas, *Los Angeles Times*

In *War of the Buttons,* two groups of adolescent boys (and as part of one group, girls) square off against one another to do battle—over what, exactly, is never clear. The boys hail from two adjoining villages in County Cork, Ireland: Ballydowse and Carrickdowse. To all appearances, the villages are nearly identical, as are the boys—the most conspicuous difference between them is their clothing: while the Carricks customarily dress in identical school uniforms, the Ballys wear motley. So, after a preliminary exchange of insults, the serious warfare begins when the Ballys disable the Carricks' bully boy by disabling his clothing: they cut off all his buttons.

The film has a screenplay adapted from Louis Pergaud's classic French novel, *La Guerre des Boutons* by Academy award-winning screenwriter Colin Welland.

Director John Roberts' remake of the 1962 French motion picture *La guerre des buttons,* while not surpassing the earlier film, gains much from having been set in Ireland. Roberts' adaptation of the Louis Pergaud novel had been set in Brittany, and when veteran English producer David Puttnam sought to remake the film, Roberts, who still controlled the rights to the story, refused to allow a remake to be set in France or England. Ireland proved a happy compromise. Although the director never expressly makes the point that the Carricks and the Ballys are meant to stand for the Protestant and Catholic countrymen who seek to destroy one another a bit further north, viewers cannot help but make the connection: after the Carricks commence the current round of skirmishes by physically threatening a member of the opposing group, the Ballys retaliate by defacing the Carrickdowse church. Despite some superficial differences, the Protestants and Catholics in Northern Ireland, like the Carricks and the Ballys in southwest Ireland, are brothers beneath their buttons, exaggerating their differences to further some imagined rivalry of obscure origins.

Still, some clear distinctions between the adversaries do surface. When the leader of the Ballys, Fergus (Gregg Fitzgerald), loses his buttons to the Carricks, the consequences are real. Unlike the generosity displayed by the father (Colm Meaney) of Carrick leader Geronimo (John Coffey), Fergus' stepfather (Jim Bartley) reacts to his boy's antics with physical and emotional violence. After beating Fergus, he threatens to send the boy permanently away, thus precipitating the film's only true crisis. Fergus runs away to the cliffs bordering the valley that embraces the two villages, pursued by Geronimo, the adversary he has recently vanquished. Geronimo, however, has come to offer aid and comfort, and when it is his foot that slips on the rocks, Fergus risks bodily injury to save his former enemy.

War of the Buttons is essentially a film made for children, and its tone is predominantly lighthearted. The boys never hurt each other much, and their skirmishes are mostly symbolic. The Ballys—whose point of view we share—are especially inventive in their warfare. In one fray they achieve a total rout simply by charging the Carricks after doffing all their clothes. And in the film's final epic battle, the Ballys storm the Carrick battlements decked out in a wild assortment of improvised pseudo-medieval armor, as Fergus surges forward mounted on a horse.

The high romance of the boys' fantasy is matched by the scenery that surrounds them. County Cork is a particularly romantic corner of the Emerald Isle, and the actual villages that serve as Ballydowse and Carrickdowse are idyl-

CREDITS

Fergus: Gregg Fitzgerald
Big Con: Gerard Kearney
Boffin: Daragh Naughton
Tim: Brendan McNamara
Fishy: Kevin O'Malley
Geronimo: John Coffey
Gorilla: Paul Batt
Mickey Moon: Karl Byrne
Willie: Barry Walsh

Origin: USA
Released: 1995
Production: David Puttam for an Enigma production; released by Warner Brothers
Direction: John Roberts
Screenplay: Colin Welland; based on the novel *La Guerre des Boutons* by Louis Pergaud
Cinematography: Bruno DeKeyzer
Editing: David Freeman
Production design: Jim Clay
Costume design: Louise Frogley
Casting: Ros Hubbard and John Hubbard
Music: Rachel Portman
MPAA rating: PG
Running Time: 94 minutes

lic twin towns separated only by a stretch of tidewater. The bridge that connects them serves, appropriately enough, as the setting for the first confrontation of the film. The beauty of the spot modulates the intensity of the gangs' stand-off, which is engendered, after all, by an exchange of only half-understood verbal abuse. What follows is a war, all right, but only a symbolic one waged over tokens.

When Marie (Eveanna Ryan), who serves as head of the Ballys girls' auxiliary, attempts peace by showering her troops with purchased buttons, they are temporarily distracted by the booty, losing sight of the fact that the Carricks remain unvanquished. The War of the Buttons has some meaning for its participants, but they remain unclear about just what it is—or was, once upon a time. Is it a war over territory, or church, or class, or school pride—or merely buttons? This gentle allegory leaves it to the viewer to decide, while at the same time making the point that reconciliation is only a handclasp away.

—Lisa Paddock

Waterworld

"Beyond the horizon lies the secret to a new beginning."—Movie tagline

"Audiences will be rewarded for their curiosity when they see this watery adventure pic...it is, quite frankly, the most breathtaking action picture to hit the screen in years."—Ed Dodd, *The Herald*

Box Office Gross: $88,246,220

Kevin Costner stars as the Mariner, an enigmatic hero who leads a dying, aquatic civilization on a quest for mythical Dryland, in *Waterworld*.

Waterworld represents the foremost example of Hollywood studio hubris in the Nineties. Not since the disaster of *Cleopatra* (1963) nearly bankrupted 20th Century Fox has so much money been poured into a "star" project with so little to show for it.

Originally written as a low-budget science-fiction film, *Waterworld* began careering out of control once superstar Kevin Costner signed on as both star and producer. In the end, *Waterworld* is estimated to have cost $235 million, including marketing costs, more than any other film in history. Although *Waterworld* grossed only $87 million domestically, its loss to MCA was buried in "studio bookkeeping:" Japanese conglomerate Matsushita agreed to absorb the loss as part of its sale of MCA to the Seagram Company in late 1995.

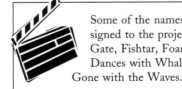

Some of the names critics assigned to the project: Kevin's Gate, Fishtar, Foam Alone, Dances with Whales, and Gone with the Waves.

Peter Rader, a novice B-movie director, wrote the original draft of *Waterworld* in 1986, after a producer suggested to him that he write a low-budget version of *The Road Warrior* (1981). When producer Roger Corman's company rejected the script as too expensive ("Are you out of your mind?" Corman is reported to have said. "This movie would cost us $5 million!"), Rader sold *Waterworld* to Larry Gordon's Largo Entertainment for $350,000. By 1991, the project was in the hands of MCA, with Kevin Reynolds, director of the Kevin Costner epic *Robin Hood, Prince of Thieves* (1991) and a longtime associate of the actor, attached as director. In spite of Reynolds's and Costner's often stormy relationship, Costner was signed to play the film's amphibian protagonist, the Mariner. With Costner, an assured box-office draw, aboard, the film's pre-production budget began to balloon.

As detailed in an August, 1995, *Vanity Fair* article, *Waterworld*'s budget problems began in pre-production. The "Atoll," the artificial island on which the film's first hour takes place, cost $4 million alone to construct in Kawaihae Harbor on the island of Hawaii; the set used all the available steel in the state. The trimarans built for the film cost $1 million each to construct in Hollywood, and were transported by specially equipped 747's to the islands. Rewrites of the script cost at least $700,000.

Once production began, *Waterworld*'s daily costs on its 166-day shoot reached $350,000 per day. Location scouts had failed to report local warnings that Kawaihae Harbor was in fact the windiest place on the island. Since the filmmakers had decided to shoot much of the film on the open sea rather than in studio tanks—meaning shooting floating islands and boats from other floating boats—the wind caused shots not to match from minute to minute, and resulted in costly overruns. The "slave colony," another artificial island set for the film, sank mid-way through production and had to be rebuilt. Often whole days were spent arranging single shots subsequently rendered unusable by shifting currents. Divers and stuntmen on the film reported numerous health and safety violations. Finally, late in post-production and just weeks before the film's scheduled release date—and with expenses already in excess of $170 million—Costner fired Reynolds and shot additional footage himself, at a reported cost of $1 million.

For all the money spent on *Waterworld*, however, its story, theme and characters are paper-thin. *Waterworld*'s first image marks it as the ultimate corporate product: the MCA/Universal logo of the Earth morphs into a water-covered version of the globe. "The future," a voice intones. "The polar ice caps have melted, covering the Earth with water."

To the strains of an insistent, bombastic score by James Newton Howard, the lonely, taciturn Mariner (Kevin Costner) is discovered aboard his specially equipped trimaran detoxifying and drinking his own urine. The Mariner is the sole known member of a new species, Icthyus Sapiens, which has evolved from man by growing gills as a response to his new watery environment. Costner's rusty but powerful boat bears, among other necessities for survival, a small tomato plant growing in precious soil. The plant provokes a ferocious gun battle with another floating drifter intent on stealing it.

The Mariner arrives at the port of an Atoll, an artificial island built of industrial detritus. Among the tribal practices on the island is the burying of the dead in toxic industrial goop. The residents of the crowded island are suspicious of the grim, musclebound Mariner, and become even more so when he tries to sell several kilos of "pure dirt". "What's he got?" residents say, agape and pointing. "Dirt!"

The Mariner meets the beautiful Helen (Jeanne Tripplehorn), who is the proprietor of the understocked atoll general store. But the Mariner is uninterested in her; his credo is pure individualism. All he wants to do is sell his plant for chits and get out.

When the Mariner refuses to mate with another island girl, however, the residents' suspicion turns into outright hostility. They accuse him of being a spy for the Smokers, a band of petroleum-guzzling outlaws who prey on the isolated and vulnerable atolls. When they discover he has gills, they cry, "Mutation! He's a mutant!" and imprison him. His execution in a pit of goop is forestalled, however, by a jet-ski invasion by the Smokers, headed by the bald Deacon (Dennis Hopper). The invasion takes up 15 minutes of screen time, during which the Mariner methodically tries to get out of a cage.

The asocial Mariner is forced to flee the Atoll in his trimaran with Helen and her young adopted daughter, Enola (Tina Majorino), who has been branded a "freak" by the res-

CREDITS

Mariner: Kevin Costner
Deacon: Dennis Hopper
Helen: Jeanne Tripplehorn
Enola: Tina Majorino
Gregor: Michael Jeter

Origin: USA
Released: 1995
Production: Charles Gordon, John Davis, and Kevin Costner for a Gordon Company/Davis Entertainment Company/Licht/Mueller Film Corp. production, released by Universal Pictures
Direction: Kevin Reynolds
Screenplay: Peter Rader and David Twohy
Cinematography: Dean Semler
Editing: Peter Boyle
Production design: Dennis Gassner
Costume design: John Bloomfield
Art direction: David Klassen
Set decoration: Nancy Haigh
Underwater photography: Pete Romano
Stunt coordination: R.A. Rondell
Visual effects: Micheal J. McAlister
Casting: David Rubin
Music: James Newton Howard
MPAA rating: PG-13
Running Time: 120 minutes

AWARDS AND NOMINATIONS

Academy Awards 1995: Best Sound

idents of the Atoll due to the mysterious tattoos on her back. A daffy, elderly scientist, Gregor (Michael Jeter), escapes by balloon. The evil Deacon reveals to the Smokers that the purpose of the invasion was to find the girl with the tattoos.

The Mariner remains unmoved by Helen's and Enola's plight, however, and threatens to abandon them. When Helen offers her body to him to save her daughter, the Mariner buries her beneath a sail and whacks her unconscious with an oar, saying, "You got nothing I need." Later, the Mariner scolds Enola for using his crayons to color his old National Geographics, then slaps her and throws her overboard. Just as his fight with Helen and Enola escalates, however, Smokers attack the trimaran from the air. The Mariner harpoons the Smoker plane and twirls it around the boat until it crashes and explodes. But the Deacon, undeterred and unscathed, swears he will track Enola down.

"Don't just stand there—kill something!"—Deacon to his minions

Ready to trade Helen to drifters for a map that will take him to the long-lost "Dryland," the Mariner thinks the better of it when the drifters try to rape her. Slowly, he softens in his attitude toward Helen and Enola, eventually teaching Enola how to swim and letting her use his crayons. He finds food for the trio by using himself as bait and harpooning a giant sea monster.

But the Smokers strike back, ambushing the trio from an abandoned barter post. Although the Mariner saves Helen by locking her in a kiss, diving, and breathing for both of them underwater—taking her on a tour of the Earth's lost cities now buried by the ocean—the Smokers kidnap Enola and take her to the Deacon's headquarters. Abandoned on a burnt-out, rusty barge and convinced they are going to die, the Mariner and Helen make love. In the morning, they are rescued by Gregor, the balloonist. The Mariner realizes from Enola's drawings that she has seen Dryland, and that the tattoo on her back represents, in fact, a map of how to get there.

The Deacon interrogates Enola back at his fortress, an abandoned supertanker powered by slaves and a dwindling supply of petroleum. (The Deacon's patron saint is Captain Joseph Hazelwood of the Exxon Valdez.) The Deacon must find out how to use Enola's map in order to find Dryland and renew his supply of oil.

In a race to rescue Enola from the Deacon's clutches, the Mariner breaches the security of the fortress and finds her. A battle ensues. The entire supertanker explodes, and the Mariner, Helen, Enola, Gregor and a few other settlers finally reach Dryland, where they find Enola's old home and birthplace. The Mariner, however, like Shane, must leave. An amphibian, he cannot be at home on Dryland; he must continue wandering, having been humanized by his contact with Helen and Enola.

Waterworld fails on a number of levels. Like several of Costner's previous vehicles, it has virtually no subtext; the screenplay merely moves from setpiece to setpiece. Forty-five minutes into *Waterworld*, it is still unclear what is at stake, or what the Mariner, the putative protagonist, wants. Thematically, the film pretends to be a warning about the consequences of the greenhouse effect and the world's current petroleum bender, but this message is undercut by the production's well-publicized waste and profligacy. The film's very conceit, that the world has been covered by water, is only sketchily explained, and undercut by the implausibility of the Mariner's being the sole bearer of knowledge of the Earth's previous state. The implied reference in the Mariner's name—to Coleridge's ancient mariner, bearer of the wisdom of the ages—is merely pretentious.

The direction of the actors is among the most incompetent of any recent studio film. The Mariner character and Costner's performance are unnecessarily grim and tight-lipped; Costner takes himself so seriously that the film's few attempts at humor fall seriously flat. Tripplehorn's talent and beauty are among the most misused in Hollywood, and she is wasted as badly here as she was in *Basic Instinct* (1991) and *The Firm* (1993). Since the film has virtually no supporting characters, actors aside from the principals are reduced to dialogue that is pure exposition. Hopper's Deacon is one-dimensional.

The action scenes and special effects are, as well, remarkably muddy and confused for a film of such unprecedented cost. In the initial battle scene, for example, Helen and Enola dangle from a huge door; not only do the filmmakers refuse to give the audience enough information to care about the characters, but they also shoot the entire scene in extreme long-shot, depriving the audience of any identification with the characters. Often the film's poor sense of space fails to provide simple information as to whether characters are in danger.

Waterworld's sets, too, are a victim of their own gigantism. Although clearly expensive, they appear so under-

REVIEWS

Christian Science Monitor. LXXXVII, July 28, 1995, p.1.
New York Times. CXLIV, July 28, 1995, p.B1(N).
New York Times. CXLIV, August 8, 1996, p.H24(N).
New Yorker. LXXI, August 7, 1995, p.83.
Sight and Sound. V, September, 1995, p.62.
Vanity Fair. August, 1995, p.112.
Variety. CCCLIX, July 24, 1995, p.69.
The Wall Street Journal. July 20, 1995, p.B1.
The Wall Street Journal. July 28, 1995, p.A8(W).

dressed and unlived-in that they come off merely as a set designer's vision of the future. The muck, dirt and industrial waste all seem deliberately and strategically placed. Worst of all, the sets are unpleasant to look at for two hours.

Waterworld's $235 million in the end add up to an epically bad film, on par with big-budget Sixties clunkers like *Krakatoa, East of Java* (1969). Waterlogged by arrogance and poor planning, *Waterworld* is sunk by its most basic flaws: a cliche-ridden script and giantism at the expense of character and performance. The irony that a film decrying the results of overconsumption became a symbol of Hollywood excess seems lost on no one but the filmmakers.

—*Paul Mittelbach*

When Night Is Falling

"Gives rise to a new adult eroticism for the 90s."—Brandon Judell, *Detour*

"Irresistible! A beautiful film! It is near impossible not to find it touching."—Lisa Kennedy, *Village Voice*

Box Office Gross: $912,645

Patricia Rozema's *When Night Is Falling* is a step backwards for the Canadian director who won acclaim in 1987 for *I Heard the Mermaids Singing*. Despite being tenderly photographed and sensitively sympathetic to its two lesbian lovers, *When Night Is Falling* is dragged down by a wooden script, a contrived plot and heavy-handed symbolism.

The film centers on a remarkable transformation in Camille Bak (Pascale Bussieres), a professor of mythology at a conservative Christian college. As it opens, she is lecturing to her class: "Transformations are a staple of mythology, humans changing into gods and gods into humans..." In the next room, Martin (Henry Czerny), a professor who is her lover, is waxing excitedly to his students about the end of relativism and a return to traditional values.

From the get-go, it is clear that Rozema, who wrote and directed the film, is concocting a morality tale about the redemptive power of love, which can transform humans into gods. The contrivance of the plot is obvious throughout. The characters' actions and words all serve Rozema's thesis, and the result is a surprisingly dry, stuffy film about what is supposed to be a heated sexual awakening.

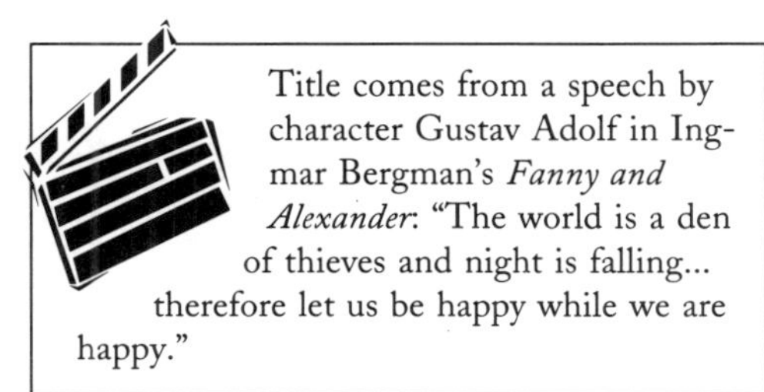

Title comes from a speech by character Gustav Adolf in Ingmar Bergman's *Fanny and Alexander*: "The world is a den of thieves and night is falling... therefore let us be happy while we are happy."

To start things off, Camille's dog dies. Instead of burying him, she puts the carcass in her refrigerator. When at film's end the dog is buried and then resurrected, there is no mistaking Rozema's clumsy intent: the dog represents Camille's soul.

The next scene is in a laundromat where Camille is crying. A woman asks why and Camille explains. The woman, who turns out to be a circus performer named Petra Soft, is sympathetic: "Animals love you in a way people can't," she points out with casual profundity. Camille pours out her feelings about her dead pet to this stranger: "I realized I loved him more than anything or anyone I was supposed to love." Camille adds: "I think everything good just goes eventually." The actresses try to recite these lines as if this were normal laundromat conversation between strangers, but it's an uphill battle.

This encounter somehow shakes Camille to her foundations. It remains a mystery throughout the film exactly why this is so. There is no chemistry between the two in their first meeting, just those ridiculously overwrought words. Camille's motivation in pursuing a romance with Petra is never explained. It appears to be based solely on physical attraction, but there is little sign of lust-at-first-sight in the laundromat scene. But to be fair, many a film about heterosexual romance has been based on even less motivation.

As played rather tentatively by Rachael Crawford, Petra is a dusky, lithe, wild, sweet and audacious lesbian who is unfettered by her usual rejection. She is so uncomplicated, her background and motivation so blank that she is almost a cipher, and that wounds the film immeasurably.

Petra leaves her calling card and switches laundry bags to get Camille to visit her in the warehouse where the circus rehearsals have begun. Conservatively dressed, her hair tied back in a bun, Camille moves through the tattooed, spike-haired circus performers, quite obviously a stranger in a strange land. She first sees Petra in silhouette against a mirror, a dark figure bouncing two balls of light off her body, so seemingly at ease with her freedom that she can juggle it.

Rozema is capable of visual lyricism but, unfortunately, equally capable of hackneyed plot devices. To facilitate Petra's seduction of Camille, the lights in the warehouse suddenly go out. The romance proceeds as in a teenage coming-of-age movie, Petra deliciously seductive and Camille excited and repulsed by her own desires.

The basic conflict of the film is overwrought and predictable. The college's dean, Reverend DeBoer (David Fox), is offering Martin and Camille a joint chaplainship, if they will get married. This puts pressure on Camille to decide how strongly she feels about Martin, a bland conservative type, her career, and her religion.

Like everything else in the film, Camille's conflicts are writ large. Against all logic, she insists on wearing Petra's racy outfit, with a zipper baring a small portion of her torso, to a meeting with the reverend, insisting to Martin in the script's stilted way: "This is the era of the individual." Thus *When Night Is Falling* becomes a tired, recycled 1960s-era film, pitting the dark forces of repression against sexual liberation.

The college regents quiz Camille on her feelings about lesbianism; she founders as Petra peeps in through the window. It's odd that DeBoer and the elders know about and accept Camille and Martin as unmarried lovers as long as they're not leaders of the school but nonetheless consider homosexuality sinful. Theirs is a half-baked orthodoxy.

Petra takes Camille hang-gliding, an obvious reference to the big leap in love that Camille is about to take. Camille hurts her knee; they return to her apartment and Petra rubs it, then starts rubbing other places. On cue, the doorbell rings; it's Reverend DeBoer paying an unannounced visit! This is soap-opera-style plotting, at best; it plays like countless B-movie romances, except that this time the lovers are both women.

The clumsiness of the proceedings is especially apparent against the graceful backdrops cinematographer Douglas Koch provides. When Petra and Camille finally make love, a sensuous but tasteful scene which inexplicably earned the film an NC-17 rating, it is beneath two velvet-clad female trapeze artists. It is always obvious what point Rozema is making—in this case, that their lovemaking is a daring act—but nonetheless she is imaginative in her framing of many scenes. The visual touches, while sometimes trite, are light and occasionally creative. There is a web of visual enchantment woven around the insipid plot.

Bussieres' performance doesn't help. She goes in and out of a Quebecois accent, looks continually blank and confused, and doesn't portray much feeling. She looks almost in a trance throughout the film.

From a feminist point of view, the weakness of the film is that Camille seems absolutely incapable of making decisions on her own. When Martin discovers the truth but then warns her not to speak about it, Camille replies and mutters, "I'm sorry." Rather than make a choice for herself, she falls down drunk in the snow, a helpless victim of love waiting to be rescued by whoever arrives first on the scene. Awakening, she falls into the arms of Petra and there is a too-neat ending.

The illogic of *When Night Is Falling* is that Rozema sets up the story as a showdown between the dark forces of moral repression and the light of freedom, yet the resolution of the struggle is presented as a magical event that doesn't really disturb the balance of power. Camille doesn't take a stand, she is swept away. She joins the circus, where the freaks are, and the ramparts of the college remain unassaulted.

In the end, for all its lyrical poses, *When Night Is Falling* is nothing more than a sappy love story. The fact that it is a love story about two women is not by itself enough to give it any real weight or substance. The film simply floats away, leaving little lasting impression.

—Michael Betzold

CREDITS

Camille Bak: Pascale Bussieres
Petra Soft: Rachael Crawford
Martin: Henry Czerny
Rev. DeBoer: David Fox
Tory: Tracy Wright
Timothy: Don McKellar

Origin: Canada
Released: 1995
Production: Barbara Tranter for a Crucial Pictures and Alliance Communciations in association with Telefilm Canada and the Ontario Film Development Corporation; released by October Films
Direction: Patricia Rozema
Screenplay: Patricia Rozema
Cinematography: Douglas Koch
Editing: Susan Shipton
Production design: John Dondertman
Set decoration: Megan Less and Rob Hepburn
Costume design: Linda Muir
Sound: John Hazen, Alan Geldart
Casting: Deidre Bowen
Music: Leslie Barber
Running Time: 82 minutes

While You Were Sleeping

"Two thumbs up!"—*Siskel & Ebert*
"This year's classic romantic comedy!"—Richard Schickel, *Time*
"A complete winner!"—Pat Collins, *WOR-TV/New York*

Box Office Gross: $81,057,016

Ever since the success of *When Harry Met Sally* (1989), filmmakers have been coming up with inventive ideas for romantic screen comedies which reflect the sensibilities of the 1990's but have the charm and frothiness of screwball romances like *It Happened One Night* (1934), or *The Philadelphia Story* (1940). *Sleepless in Seattle* (1993) confirmed the popularity of the genre among Baby Boomers, with its charming performances and sentimental musical score. Now comes *While You Were Sleeping*, which boasts a star-making turn by Sandra Bullock, and a charming script by Daniel G. Sullivan and Frederic Lebow. Like some of the screwball romances of yore, it is somewhat insubstantial. But only a curmudgeon would resist its sweetness and good humor. This film is proof that when it comes to romance, a film doesn't have to be brilliant to be thoroughly likable.

Hopefully, calling attention to the film's frothiness won't be seen as a slur against it. In fact, this film should wear its simplicity proudly. This isn't a "film" in the artistic sense—it is a "movie," and a darned good one at that.

While You Were Sleeping tells the story of Lucy (Bullock) and the mistaken identities and situations which lead her to fall in love with Jack Callaghan (Pullman). The film takes place in Chicago, where Lucy, who has no family, is a lonely tollbooth operator at a subway station. Every day a man she secretly loves, the dashing and handsome Peter Callaghan (Peter Gallagher), buys a token to ride the train. One day, he is knocked unconscious by thugs and thrown onto the tracks. The rest of the story can be told quickly: Lucy saves him, Peter stays in a coma for several weeks, and the family, led to believe Lucy is Peter's fiancee, takes her into their hearts. Little do they know that Peter doesn't even know Lucy. Problems arise when Lucy realizes that she is in love with his brother Jack, who is far more suitable for her. Eventually Peter wakes up, and more troubles arise for Lucy before everything is resolved happily.

> "You have to tell me what to do." "Pull the plug." "You are sick." "I'm sick—you're cheating on a vegetable."—Lucy asking advice from friend Jerry

Of course, the plot centers around the budding relationship of Lucy and the initially skeptical Jack. The joy of the movie is in watching Lucy agonize over what to do about her feelings for Jack and her discomfort with the mistaken identity. Charismatic Sandra Bullock, who came to wide attention in *Speed* (1994), is radiant. Bill Pullman, who played the jilted, nerdy boyfriend in *Sleepless in Seattle*, is the hero here. It is wonderful to see such an accomplished and engaging actor get a chance to star in a film. Pullman has the laconic charisma and true talent to emerge as a dramatic heir to Henry Fonda or Jimmy Stewart.

Bullock is reminiscent of the classic ingenue/comediennes who were both beautiful and funny, like Jean Arthur or Claudette Colbert. She's a little pretty for the subway job, but this movie doesn't take itself so seriously that she has to make herself look more blue-collar just to fit into the job. Her speech is halting and spontaneous, an accomplishment that appears to be due to the marriage of a talented actress with smart dialogue and good directing. Bullock creates a character that is quite afraid of having gotten herself into this situation, yet is self-possessed enough to put a stop to it when the time comes. She is especially vulnerable and funny when saying lines like, "I have to go. I'm really late 'cause I have to go," with a shyness that only emphasizes her beauty.

One of the film's strengths is its dialogue. Credit goes to authors Daniel G. Sullivan and Frederic LeBow, who, in their first produced screenplay, have set a tone that is halfway between absurd and corny, and is always clever and sweet. "God, you smell good," Lucy says to Peter while he is unconscious on the tracks. She hurriedly tries to pull him off the tracks, saying, "There's a train coming, and it's an express." In the first hospital scene, when she sees Peter lying in a coma, Lucy says, under her breath, "I'm going to be your wife." The nurse who hears this tells Peter's family who she is, and they believe it. Later, Lucy tells the nurse that she was only talking to herself, and the nurse says, "next time you talk to yourself, tell yourself you're single, and end the conversation." When Lucy is invited for the first time to the Callaghan's home, the dinner table dialogue is a fragmented series of several conversations, one trying to top the other: "Argentina had great beef...beef and Nazis" yells one family member, while two others argue about how tall actor Cesar Romero was.

The family, made up of several of the finest character actors around, is like a character unto itself. The family members move in a pack, seemingly bound together for the first several scenes. Ox (Peter Boyle) is Peter and Jacks' father, Elsie (Glynis Johns) is the grandmother, Midge (Micole Mercurio) is the mother, and Saul (Jack Warden) is the next-door neighbor. For Lucy, who longs for a family and for someone she can "laugh with," these colorful characters represent happiness. And, as Saul points out, "they need you just as much as you need them." The brilliance and warmth of the actors and the genuine humor of their dialogue make it perfectly understandable why Lucy would let herself lie to them about her relationship to their son.

As the father, Peter Boyle plays another of the blue-collar, everyman-type of characters which have made him one of the busiest actors in film ever since his debut in *Joe*. "We're in the estate furniture biz," says Ox. "We buy furniture from dead people." His sweet father-son scene with Pullman possesses a heightened sense of truth—it is believable, yet doesn't seem mundane—which is hard to find in film comedy today. It is a shame that this talented and funny actor hasn't had a chance to play meatier roles of late.

All the characters are drawn with an equally idiosyncratic point-of-view. Grandmother Elsie (Johns) says she prefers Mass in Latin "because then you don't have to pay attention to what they're saying." Mercurio is perfect as Midge, the homemaker who dotes on her family. Midge cries every time she looks at her son in the hospital bed, and in her scenes at the home. Mercurio may be known to audiences as Susan Sarandon's mother in *The Client* (1994).

CREDITS

Lucy: Sandra Bullock
Jack: Bill Pullman
Peter: Peter Gallagher
Ox: Peter Boyle
Saul: Jack Warden
Elsie: Glynis Johns

Origin: USA
Released: 1995
Production: Joe Roth and Roger Birnbaum for Hollywood Pictures in association with Caravan Pictures; released by Buena Vista Pictures Distribution, Inc.
Direction: Jon Turtletaub
Screenplay: Daniel G. Sullivan and Frederic Lebow
Cinematography: Phedon Papamichael
Editing: Bruce Green
Art direction: Garreth Stover
Music: Randy Edelman
MPAA rating: PG
Running Time: 103 minutes

Peter Gallagher is just right as the wayward son who Lucy unwittingly brings back to his family. He's quite the peacock, and the filmmakers do an excellent job creating his persona before he wakes up: His phone machine signs off with "ciao;" he carries a picture of himself in his wallet; and his apartment is like a swinging single's "pad"—black and chrome, pictures of himself everywhere.

Director Jon Turtletaub keeps the comedy moving with a farcical flair and a nostalgic touch. In a charming scene in which Jack and Lucy slip and slide their way across the ice, he gently symbolizes that they are falling in love through the uncertainty of their steps, adding a charming visual image to the scene. Turtletaub clearly has a flair with actors, achieving a sense of authenticity even in the face of rather odd situations. He deftly handles a funny scene in which Lucy has to prove she knows Peter by asking his family to see that he is missing a testicle. In the hands of less capable actors and a less elegant director, this scene would merely be crass. But it is extremely funny.

With the help of cinematographer Phedon Papamichael, Turtletaub makes Chicago at Christmas look like a holiday greeting card. Turtletaub, the son of veteran producer Saul Turtletaub, teamed with cinematographer Papamichael in 1993 on the highly successful *Cool Runnings*. These two films share a similar tone in that they offer an undemanding charm and sense of humor that is smart without being intellectual and simple without being silly.

Randy Edelman, Golden Globe nominee for his score for *Last of the Mohicans* (1992), provides the musical score. Edelman underscores the action with a perfect blend of Christmas music and contemporary sound. The producers should be commended for not trying to duplicate the success of the terrific soundtracks to other recent romantic comedies: very few soundtracks can rival the romance of *Sleepless in Seattle* or *When Harry Met Sally*. Their choice to rely on more original material for this film is a smart one.

All in all, the choices throughout this film are well-made. *While You Were Sleeping*, while not a timeless classic, is a delightful film. An even better compliment is that it is a very good movie. A "film" is for all time. A "movie" is for all people.

—*Kirby Tepper*

AWARDS AND NOMINATIONS

Blockbuster Entertainment Awards 1996: Comedy Actress-Theatrical (Bullock), Comedy Actress-Video (Bullock)
Golden Globe Awards Nominations 1996: Best Actress-Musical/Comedy (Bullock)

White Man's Burden

"Nothing stands between these two men - except money and power."—Movie tagline

"Fresh, smart, funny..."—Michael Medved, *Sneak Previews*

"Travolta is an actor you can't take your eyes off!"—Jeannie Williams, *USA Today*

Box Office Gross: $3,760,515

In *White Man's Burden*, a racist character says, "What is inherently wrong is where a people historically and repeatedly burn down their own communities...are these people beyond being helped?" It sounds like the stereotype of an ultra-conservative who has no empathy for the plight of minorities. And that is just who the character is. Only the character is African-American, and the minority he is talking about is Caucasian. This is the world of *White Man's Burden*, in which the dominant culture is African-American, and the "underclass" is predominantly white.

This role-reversal film, starring Harry Belafonte as the ultra-conservative and John Travolta as an angry poor white man is interesting, provocative, well-acted and wonderfully directed and written by Desmond Nakano. The film was not particularly well-received in its initial release, and consequently audiences that might have found it interesting did not get a chance to see it. But the fact that the film was not universally praised nor watched shouldn't reduce its value as an entertaining and important piece of filmmaking.

This was the second film in John Travolta's "comeback" after several years away from the big screen. (The first film was the highly successful *Pulp Fiction*, in 1994.) Producer Lawrence Bender, who produced both *Pulp Fiction* and *White Man's Burden*, asked Travolta to play the role of Louis Pinnock, an uneducated white factory worker who works in a factory that makes chocolate candies. On a routine delivery to the home of Thaddeus Thomas (Belafonte), the factory owner, Pinnock somehow takes a wrong turn on the grounds of the huge mansion, and inadvertently looks up at the house at the same time Thomas' wife, Megan (Margaret Avery) is undressing. Through another window, Thomas notices this, and asks his factory supervisor to send "a different delivery boy" next time.

The factory supervisor (Robert Gossett) is unaware who the "delivery boy" was until Pinnock comes into his office to ask for a promotion. The supervisor praises Pinnock for his years of good work until Pinnock innocently mentions the delivery at Thomas' house. He is immediately fired, with no explanation.

Time passes, and, unable to find a job and pay the rent, Pinnock and his family are unceremoniously evicted in the middle of the night by the county Sheriffs. His wife, Marsha (Kelly Lynch) and children go to stay with her mother (Carrie Snodgress), who will not allow Pinnock to stay with them. Desperate, Pinnock goes to Thomas' house to get him to restore his job. Armed with a gun, he intends only to force Thomas to explain why he was fired, but becomes enraged when Thomas has no recollection of the events that led to his dismissal. He takes Thomas hostage, insisting that he pay him several thousand dollars of overtime owed him, but since Thomas is unable to withdraw that much money through the automatic teller machine, Pinnock decides to hold him hostage until Monday. The rest of the film depicts the fragile understanding that develops between them. Ultimately, though, their understanding is shattered by the wide economic and ideological gulf between them, and the situation leads to tragedy.

Much of the appeal of the film can be found in the interesting depiction of the cultural role-reversal. Nakano makes the switch with accuracy and wit, and no stone seems to be left unturned. For example, all of the story's authority figures, from the factory supervisor, to the policemen to the woman in charge of Pinnock's claim at the Unemployment office, are black. When Pinnock's young son "channel surfs" with the remote control, virtually every face on television is black. At Thomas' house, instead of a fat black maid, there is a fat white one. As Pinnock drives past the elegant homes of Thomas' neighborhood, he sees a ceramic statue of a white jockey in front of one of the homes. Perhaps the funniest, most trenchant of these examples is in a fashion show which is intended to benefit disadvantaged youth. At the end of the show, the lavishly-dressed African-American audiences "oohs" and "aahs" at several adorable poor white children who are trotted out on stage.

> "Your job and your family are your business; the trouble with you is you think the world owes you a living."—Employer Thaddeus Thomas to just-fired Louis

Some of the role-reversal depictions are far less humorous, such as a harrowing scene in which Pinnock is pummeled by black police officers for absolutely no valid reason. Another such scene is when Pinnock and his family are thrown out of their house without warning, having to negotiate to get 15 minutes in order to gather some personal belongings. Given the accuracy of the other scenes, it is far more difficult to shrug off this scene as being an exaggeration of the behavior of many police officers.

Through this and other scenes, Nakano's screenplay presents dialogue that sounds as if it is lifted from real life—but, given the role reversal, the stereotypes are obvious. "You fit the description of a man who committed several robberies," is the excuse given to Pinnock for his being beaten by police. In another scene, Megan Thomas (Avery) says, of the fashion show rehearsal, "there must have been fifty little white kids running around; they were so adorable....of course, some of them were a little undisciplined." The racism of this and other lines sounds outlandish and cartoonish, but it is an unfortunate fact that it accurately represents dialogue from real life.

The polemic and political nature of this film, as depicted by the role reversal and by Pinnock's escalating desperation and criminal activity, have most likely made it too "hot" for audiences to handle. Perhaps some will only see that Nakano went far in stacking the deck against his protagonist. And perhaps critics have a point when they say that Pinnock's descent into crime seems too rapid. But this film is an allegory, and as such, it seems obligatory that Nakano would compress into a short period events that would take years to occur in real life.

CREDITS

Louis Pinnock: John Travolta
Thaddeus Thomas: Harry Belafonte
Marsha Pinnock: Kelly Lynch
Megan Thomas: Margaret Avery
Stanley: Tom Bower
John: Robert Gossett
Josine: Carrie Snodgress
Roberta: Sheryl Lee Ralph

Origin: USA
Released: 1995
Production: Lawrence Bender for UGC and A Band Apart production; released by Savoy
Direction: Desmond Nakano
Screenplay: Desmond Nakano
Cinematography: Willy Kurant
Editing: Nancy Richardson
Production design: Naomi Shohan
Art direction: John Ivo Gilles
Casting: Barbara Cohen and Mary Gail Artz
Costume design: Isis Mussenden
Sound: Ken King
Music: Howard Shore
MPAA rating: R
Running Time: 89 minutes

The performances by Travolta and Belafonte help to keep the film interesting. The screenplay delivers a number of stereotypes, but Travolta and Belafonte work very well to play against those stereotypes. Each delivers a performance that does more than just reverse the color of the skin of some traditional roles.

Travolta plays Pinnock as a man who is a victim of his socioeconomic background, of racism, and of his own desire to take care of his family. He is also a victim of his own temperament and his own masculine pride, but the deck is so stacked against him that it seems impossible for him to take anything but the most drastic of measures. Travolta, who dyed his hair red for this film, does a fine job in portraying a character that could seem too much of a stereotype in lesser hands. Without making Pinnock a saint, Travolta finds his tenderness (especially in scenes with his son), and his nobility ("I used to have pride in the fact that when my son was born there wasn't a night I wasn't home with him"). But at the same time, he doesn't shy away from Pinnock's temper, or from his aggressive side ("How does it feel?," he growls at Thomas, "me having power over you like you have power over me?").

Harry Belafonte, known more for his singing than his acting, makes an impressive return to films as well. Like Travolta, he works against the stereotypical nature of the role. His job seems a bit harder, because his is essentially an unsympathetic character who spouts off lines that sound as if they were uttered by racist politicians. But Belafonte finds the soul underneath the man, providing the glimmer of a conscience and a spark of understanding of Pinnock's plight. A scene in which Pinnock and Thomas take Pinnock's son to a toy store for his birthday is humorous and touching. Belafonte silently watches the tender interaction between father and son, appearing to understand the depth of their relationship, and appearing to get a better feel for why Pinnock has taken him hostage. And then he offers Pinnock money to buy a better toy (Pinnock's son wants to buy the white action figure doll instead of the black one, much to Pinnock's consternation.) Thomas offers the money with a casual lack of understanding of the implications of such a move. Belafonte's subtlety helps to show the man's innocent, stubborn, and misguided understanding of the consequences of his actions. It is a fine performance.

It is inevitable that discussions of this film will be dominated by its controversial premise and its volatile subject matter. People will ponder whether it is too polemical, too stereotyped, and too obvious a piece of rhetoric. But there is another aspect to this film: it is a fine piece of entertainment. Hopefully, that fact won't be lost amidst the controversy.

—Kirby Tepper

Wigstock: the Movie

"The Super Bowl of drag! An unabashedly liberated sign of the times!"—Bruce Williamson, *Playboy*

"Colorful! Imaginative! Entertaining!"—Paul Wunder, *WBAI Radio*

Box Office Gross: $688,512

A person doesn't have to be an aficionado of the often bizarre world of drag to appreciate this good-natured film. *Wigstock: the Movie*, is an affectionate documentary about an annual celebration of drag in New York City. Admittedly, it is not for everyone: Puritanical types might be offended by the outlandish gender-bending and occasional four-letter words. But they would be foolish to miss out on this film's zany humor, earthy wisdom, and underlying sweetness.

Of course, most of these drag queens would rather die than be called "sweet." Many of the people profiled in this brief documentary align themselves with archetypal images of femme fatales and tough-as-nails broads. The stage names say it all: Mistress Formikka, Anita Cocktail, Candis Cayne, and Flotilla DeBarge. Much of the film is taken up with film of live performances from the 1993 and 1994 Wigstock. These performances are lip-synced versions of songs by every dame from Donna Summer to Lauren Bacall, from Ethel Merman to Yma Sumac.

Wigstock is analogous to the original Woodstock, in that it takes place outdoors (on the Hudson River waterfront in New York) with a hand-waving, costume-wearing audience cheering on the performances of favorite stars. It should be noted that also similar to Woodstock, this is a for-profit venture. There is an accompanying festival as well. Police are evident around the perimeter of the astonishingly huge and diverse crowd, and the sound system and stage are highly sophisticated. The film intercuts interviews with drag celebrities with rehearsals, performances, impromptu interviews of "normal" people on the street, and the performances. The film is brief and simple, with good camera coverage of the performers and the audience mingled with simple close-ups. There is no attempt at overly sophisticated camera work, which is to the film's advantage, and the less-than-perfect film stock quality mixes well with the rudimentary cinematography. Anything overly slick would have worked against the grass-roots nature of Wigstock itself. The home-grown quality of the film reflects well the let's-put-on-a-show feel of the performances.

That is not to say that the performers aren't pros, however. Each person who sees this film will find their favorites, and many of the performers are truly gifted. In particular, Lypsinka (who in real life is Jon Epperson) is so talented, funny, and precise that she ultimately delivers a terrific musical comedy performance even while she parodies it. (Epperson describes how Lypsinka has been accepted as a female fashion model, doing runway shows for no less than famed designer Thierry Mugler.) The film's funniest moment is the performance of "The Duelling Bankheads," two Tallulah Bankheads singing "Born to Be Wild." RuPaul, who is pretty much the queen of queens, provides some flashy numbers and some good-natured commentary such as "everyone in the sound of my voice, strut your stuff, honey."

The interviews provide some fundamental insight into why drag has such appeal. But their simplicity ("we're all a family") keeps them from the depth of the interviews in *Paris Is Burning* (1992), a perhaps "deeper" film. Where *Paris Is Burning* explored motivations with some intensity, the interviewees in this film stay away from too much drama: When "pre-operative" transsexual T.J. feels she is getting too far into her story of her transformation, she tells the interviewer, "it's a big messy story, honey, just smile and go on."

Perhaps because of the stunning, Oscar-winning costumes from *Priscilla, Queen of the Desert* (1994), some of the impact of this film's outlandish wigs and costumes might be diminished. Still, from the huge caricature of Julie Christie's hair-do in *Darling* (1965) to the wigs on little children and pets, this film is a visual feast.

The film's co-producer (and Wigstock founder) Lady Bunny provides the tone of the film and of Wigstock. The soft-spoken and polite Bunny (who looks like a cross be-

CREDITS

RuPaul: RuPaul
Deee-lite: Deee-lite
Alexis Arquette: Alexis Arquette
Jackie Beat: Jackie Beat

Origin: USA
Released: 1995
Production: Dean Silver, Marlen Hecht; released by Samuel Goldwyn
Direction: Barry Shils
Cinematography: Wolfgang Held
Editing: Marlen Hecht and Tod Scott Brody
Art director: Linda del Rosario and Richard Paris
Running Time: 85 minutes

tween Dina Merrill and Elly Mae Clampett) brings up the specter of AIDS and how it has decimated much of the community. And later, she suggests that people should "all come together." But mostly, she states that the purpose of Wigstock is to have fun. And when she is seen trying to arrange for a wig for the Statue of Liberty, it is clear what her purpose is. It's big hair and big fun. This film is not a classic, but it is big fun.

—Kirby Tepper

REVIEWS

The Hollywood Reporter. January 27-29, 1994. p. 16
Daily Variety. February 27, 1995. p. 27

Wild Bill

"The name is legendary. The man is real."—Movie tagline

"Jeff Bridges brings *Wild Bill* to life with a smashing performance that blew me away!"—Bill Diehl, *ABC Radio Network*

"*Wild Bill* hits the bullseye!"—Jeffrey Lyons, *Sneak Previews*

Box Office Gross: $2,167,808

Wild Bill is clearly a product of the film industry's perception that moviegoers have recently been interested in revisionist history and in the aging of America (that is, in the reality that the largest portion of the population is middle-aged). From *The Moderns* (1988) to *Jefferson in Paris* (1995), from *Peggy Sue Got Married* (1986) to *Everybody's All-American* (1988), from *Pretty Woman* (1990) to *Regarding Henry* (1991), it would appear that filmmakers are reconsidering who they are, or are encouraging filmgoers to reconsider who they are, or are questioning cultural norms about who we have ever been. Not unlike Gregory Peck in *The Gunfighter* (1950), John Wayne in *The Shootist* (1976), or Val Kilmer in *Tombstone* (1995), Jeff Bridges plays a character, a historic tough guy, Bill Hickok, who has come to the end of his life (actually he was 39 years old) only to question how that life has been spent.

Wild Bill begins and ends at Bill Hickok's grave, with his partner Charley Prince (John Hurt) telling his tale. From the grave, the film moves through montage to Deadwood, S.D., the town in which Bill Hickok died. The rest of his life—largely shootouts, some romance—is viewed in dream-like sequences, shot in monochrome or sepia, although audiences will also get a glimpse of Bill Hickok's stint with Buffalo Bill Cody's Wild West Show. In the film as in history, Bill Hickok is shot in the back by the son of an old lover (who is perhaps his son as well) just as he draws the proverbial dead-man's hand.

Westerns fall into several categories, but perhaps two of the most clear divisions would be those westerns that offer mostly grit, the rough and tumble life on the range, and those westerns that glamorize life on the open road, turning outlaws into mere misfits—handsome, clean, well-dressed and misunderstood. Within the first category are some of the best-known westerns of modern times: John Ford's *The Searchers* (1956), Sergio Leone's *For a Few Dollars More* (1965), Sam Peckinpah's *The Wild Bunch* (1969), Robert Altman's *McCabe and Mrs. Miller* (1971), and Clint Eastwood's *The Outlaw—Josey Wales* (1976) and *Unforgiven* (1992). The protagonists are fallen men, killing for revenge or hate or money. Among these characters are men who will attempt to kill their family members because Native Americans have touched them, men who will kill any and all men who hurt them or their families, and men who will kill for money, period. Many—such as Bill Hickok—remain unrepentant. While the stories of these men work to justify many of their actions, these anti-heroic "cowboys" are part and parcel of the fallen modern and post-modern world. Compare to these grizzly, compromised westerners the movie-star version of the same life, *Butch Cassidy and the Sundance Kid* (1969), filled as it is with happy, glamorous outlaws who are young and in love with beautiful, respectable women, and

James Butler Hickok was killed during a poker game in Deadwood, South Dakota, holding a full house, aces over eights, now known as a "dead man's hand."

Silverado (1985), a Lawrence Kasdan film, a *Big Chill* (1983) western.

Yet Walter Hill has made some effort to conform his film to its historical roots. For instance, Hill has Bridges as Hickok holster his guns butt first (as did the real Hickok). But then again Hill allows Bridges as Hickok to gun down waves of people in virtually endless gunfights, when history reports it is more likely that Bill Hickok shot perhaps seven people in his lifetime.

Traditionally the western genre has showcased significant social change, focusing on the unresolved tension between civilization and wilderness, between change and/or development and the nostalgic, undisturbed past. In *Wild Bill,* Deadwood is a frontier town, complete with prospectors and saloons, and the frontier virtues: a good friend, a good woman, a fast gun. However, *Wild Bill* diverges from the norm in that, apart from its opening sequences, the salient portions of the film are talk and remembrance of things past more than action. Also, even viewers who are unaware of the historical and deadly significance of Deadwood to Bill Hickok have a clear view of the film's narrative path as it begins graveside. Without significant action or narrative twists, *Wild Bill* rattles amiably along the beaten path.

One of the joys of *Wild Bill* is the casting, and while the film earned mixed reviews, none of the reviewers missed the opportunity to comment on the bold casting choices and strong performances. For instance, Bruce Fretts in *Entertainment Weekly* coins Bridges' performance a "masterstroke of squinty-eyed bitterness," while Todd McCarthy, reviewing in *Variety,* lauds Bridges' physical conviction in playing "one ornery, sore-headed s.o.b." Whatever reviewers have said about Bridge's Hickok, however, it far exceeds in depth and import that which has been said about the women characters in the film, such as Calamity Jane (Ellen Barkin) and Susannah Moore (Diane Lane). Certainly the western genre has offered women limited, stereotypical roles: the schoolmarm or the saloon gal, and while *Wild Bill* could be seen as offering women new cinematic role models, i.e., the true love and the passing fling, the reviews of the women's performances are emblematic of the disappointing role women have played in the genre generally. Fretts identifies Barkin's Calamity Jane as "kitten with a whip," while Pat Kramer in *Boxoffice* labels her "men-slugging, whiskey-downing, [and] love-starved." Diane Lane, on the other hand, who plays Hickok's one true love, was described by McCarthy as "one of the dreamiest visions to hit the territories since Claudia Cardinale in *Once Upon a Time in the West.*" Generally intriguing is the casting of Marjoe Gortner (of 1972 *Marjoe* fame) as the preacher and television's *Married With Children's* Christina Applegate as Lurline (the "upstairs girl").

Losing in its fight against the more usual holiday fare, *Wild Bill* enjoyed only limited release and was quickly withdrawn and shelved. Nonetheless it is a film filled with interesting performances, as it also provides a link in the progression of western lore and revisionist history. While this film's true audience may be small, members of that group will want to find a chance to view *Wild Bill.*

—*Roberta F. Green*

CREDITS

Wild Bill Hickok: Jeff Bridges
Calamity Jane: Ellen Barkin
Charley Prince: John Hurt
Susannah Moore: Diane Lane
Jack McCall: David Arquette
Lurline: Christina Applegate
Will Plummer: Bruce Dern
California Joe: James Gammon
Preacher: Marjoe Gortner
Donnie Lonigan: James Remar
Buffalo Bill Cody: Keith Carradine

Origin: USA
Released: 1995
Production: Richard D. Zanuck and Lilli Fini Zanuck; released by United Artists
Direction: Walter Hill
Screenplay: Walter Hill; based on Pete Dexter's novel *Deadwood* and Thomas Babe's play *Fathers and Sons*
Cinematography: Lloyd Ahern
Editing: Freeman Davies
Production design: Joseph Nemec III
Art direction: Daniel Olexiewicz
Costume design: Dan Moore
Sound: Lee Orloff
MPAA rating: R
Running Time: 97 minutes

REVIEWS

Chicago Tribune, December 1, 1995, p. 5.
Entertainment Weekly, December 8, 1995, p. 48.
USA Today, December 1, 1995, p. 13D.
Variety, November 27, 1995, p. 80.

The Wild Bunch

In the late 1960's, the violence that had been implicit and muted in two of the classical genres of American movies—the gangster film and the western—became for the first time graphic and visual. A decade later, it is easy to forget the controversy these films aroused at the time of their release. The mold of the classical gangster film cracked first, with the 1967 Arthur Penn/Warren Beatty production of *Bonnie and Clyde*. Two years later, *The Wild Bunch* not only accomplished for the western what *Bonnie and Clyde* had done for the gangster genre, but it possibly exceeded the earlier film both in its claim to have rewritten the national epic and in the calculated sensationalism of its violence. Writer-director Sam Peckinpah was widely considered to have glorified all that the western had to that time repressed. In the words of *New York Times* critic Vincent Canby, who called the film "the first truly interesting American-made western in years," Peckinpah had "turn(ed) the genre inside out." *The Wild Bunch* contains a theme which Peckinpah developed in his earlier, more traditional work and which is implicit in the genre: that of a way of life coming to an end, and of the Westerner dying with the frontier. Also evident is the director's fascination with the choreographed beauty of violence, which Peckinpah has gone on to develop in many of his subsequent films. The film examines the nature of heroism, which had not been attempted by the western in any significant sense before. Furthermore, it depicts heroism as a quality rendered obsolete by an increasingly corrupt world, and made dangerous by the spread of technology.

The film begins with the Wild Bunch holding up a bank in a desert town while the railroad has its bounty hunters waiting in ambush. The gang spies the trap midway through the robbery, and as the town temperance union coincidentally marches unaware down the street, the bunch makes their break using them as a shield. The trap is sprung anyway. In the slow-motion blood ballet that follows, some gang members are killed and some are abandoned, as the decimated gang takes refuge in Mexico. The bounty hunters follow in pursuit. They are headed by Deke Thornton (Robert Ryan), once the closest friend of Wild Bunch leader Pike Bishop (William Holden), until Pike had abandoned him in the face of oncoming lawmen. Now, in order to win parole, Thornton must bring Pike back.

The gunfight's setting in the town is a harbinger of one of the prevailing themes of *The Wild Bunch*: the frontier is closed. It is, in fact, 1913, and in entering Mexico, the bunch knowingly is entering a three-sided conflict between Pancho Villa's rebels, the Mexican establishment embodied by a corrupt warlord named Mapache (Emilio Fernandez), and the United States government, which is calling out the army to defend the border against Villa's raids.

The gang chooses to work for Mapache. For $10,000, they will steal a shipment of arms from a United States Army supply train. Although Thornton is aboard, the raid is a success. The bunch stands off Mapache's troops who have come to kill them and then claim the arms without making payment. Afterward, they trade the guns for money in a prearranged rendezvous. As a result, Mapache apprehends Angel (Jaime Sanchez), a young Mexican member of the Wild Bunch whose village Mapache has ravaged. Mapache accuses Angel, correctly, of having taken a portion of the shipment to arm the rebels. Meanwhile, still pursued by Thornton, the Bunch must seek refuge in Mapache's village. There, in drunken debauch, Mapache tortures Angel. This action Pike finally cannot abide. The four remaining gang members offer to return their money for Angel. The drunken Mapache produces Angel but slits his throat. Enraged, Pike and Dutch Engstrom (Ernest Borgnine) kill Mapache. In the ensuing climatic gunfight, the gang uses the stolen armaments—a machine gun, grenades, and explosives—to decimate the army and the village before they themselves finally succumb to gunfire. Thornton and the bounty hunters claim the bodies, but Thornton elects to stay and fight with the rebels, who have rescued Sykes (Edmond O'Brien).

Beginning with the freeze-frame credits which open the picture, Peckinpah's visual strategy is to present the bunch in a relentlessly heroic posture. Many of the long-shots are stylized with the characters facing the camera as in formal nineteenth century photographs. Idealized, low-angle close-ups abound. In effect, Peckinpah's first three shots establish a child's point of view. At key moments at the beginning, at the first shootout, and at the gang's first rendezvous, reaction shots of children are intercut. Their hero-worshiping and their objective indifference (they are shown torturing a scorpion at the opening of the film) are both attitudes the audience is induced to share. The limits of this vision are underscored in the dialogue. "You have no eyes," Angel tells the Gorch Brothers (Warren Oates and Ben Johnson), two gang members. "I can't see, but I can ride," says a wounded gang member as he drops from his horse. He turns his face upward; it is covered with blood. He asks Pike to kill him; Pike complies.

The bunch is blinded by blood and Peckinpah's triumph

AWARDS AND NOMINATIONS

Academy Awards Nominations 1969: Best Original Screenplay and Story (Walon Green/Roy N. Sickner/Sam Peckinpah), Best Soundtrack (Jerry Fielding) is to manipulate the audience so that they share this viewpoint; his montage ranks with the classic Russian ones as among the most Manichaean in cinema, as he subtly makes the audience share in the experience of transforming humans into targets. During the first shootout, the camera is placed inside a store window as a gang member riding outside is shot and smashes through the glass, toppling three mannequins. Later, as one abandoned half-wit gang member lies dying inside a bank, he sees three townspeople gawking at him from outside the window. He curses and shoots them. The scene is made to be amusing in a macabre way; it is shot from the same angle as the earlier shot, and the subliminal association provides distance to the action. Similarly, the audience is asked to contemplate with equanimity and even enthusiasm the bodies that are sent flying by the machine gun in the final shootout. In an earlier scene, when the gun is presented to Mapache, his men fire it with no knowledge of how it works. Crockery shatters and people leap for cover. It is a comic scene that paves the way for the establishment of distance at the climax.

The absurdist heroics of *The Wild Bunch* provide settings for good performances. William Holden and Robert Ryan, in particular, played their first good roles in years, and make the most of them. In the area of character acting, the lowlife performances of Warren Oates, Ben Johnson, and Edmond O'Brien are particularly notable. Also significant is the whining depravity of Strother Martin in the role that established him as perhaps the last of the old-style character actors. The film is also distinguished by Lucien Ballard's cinematography and Jerry Fielding's tension-heightening score. The film's hero, however, remains Sam Peckinpah, whose subsequent films have demonstrated that he may possess the most comprehensive command of the resources of cinema of any American director since Orson Welles.

In 1995, *The Wild Bunch* was rereleased in new "director's cut." Ten minutes of film were reinstated, adding depth to the characters. Furthermore, the excellent soundtrack was remixed, and the film was fully restored and color-corrected.

—Harold Meyerson

CREDITS

Pike Bishop: William Holden
Deke Thornton: Robert Ryan
Dutch Engstrom: Ernest Borgnine
Sykes: Edmond O'Brien
Lyle Gorch: Warren Oates
Tector Gorch: Ben Johnson
Angel: Jaime Sanchez
Mapache: Emilio Fernandez
Coffer: Strother Martin
T.C.: L. Q. Jones
Pat Harrigan: Albert Dekker
Crazy Lee: Bo Hopkins
Mayor Wainscoat: Dub Taylor
Ross: Paul Harper
Lieutenant Zamorra: Jorge Russek
Herrera: Alfonso Arau
Don Jose: Chano Urueta
Jess: Bill Hart
Buck: Rayford Barnes
Sergeant McHale: Steve Ferry
Teresa: Sonia Amelio
Aurora: Aurora Clavel
Elsa: Elsa Cardenas
Rocio: Elizabeth Dupeyron
Yolis: Yolanda Ponce
Ignacio: Enrique Lucero

Origin: USA
Released: 1969
Production: Phil Feldman for Minor-Seven Arts; released by Warner Bros.
Direction: Sam Peckinpah
Screenplay: Walon Green and Sam Peckinpah; based on a story by Walon Green and Roy N. Sickner
Cinematography: Lucien Ballard
Editing: Louis Lombardo
Music: Jerry Fielding
Music supervision: Sonny Burke
Sound: Robert J. Miller
Makeup: Al Greenway
Special effects: Bud Hulburd
Production management: William Faralla
Art direction: Edward Carrere
MPAA rating: R
Running Time: 148 minutes

REVIEWS

The Hollywood Reporter. March 2, 1995, p. 14.
Newsweek. July 14, 1969, p. 85.
New York Times. June 26, 1969, p. 45.
Time. June 20, 1969, p. 85.
Variety. June 18, 1969, p. 6.
Variety. February 27-March 5, 1995, p. 70.

Wild Reeds

"Budding sexuality has never been filmed more beautifully."—Stephen Saban, *Details*
"A must see!"—Howard Feinstein, *Out Magazine*
"A stunner...raw, passionate and moving."—Peter Travers, *Rolling Stone*
"One of the year's ten best."—Richard Corliss, *Time*
"Riveting and sensuous."—Brandon Judell, *WBAI-FM*

French filmmakers love coming-of-age stories, but Andre Techine's *Wild Reeds* is no match for the work of Louis Malle, Francois Truffaut or any of the other masters of the genre. *Wild Reeds* is a wonderfully acted and beautifully photographed film with ridiculously stilted dialogue and little or no dramatic tension.

Set in 1962 in a provincial French town, *Wild Reeds* follows the springtime awakening of three boys at a boarding school and a girl who is the daughter of one of their teachers, Madame Alvarez (Michele Moretti). Francois (Gael Morel) is an intellectual but somewhat naive in romantic matters. Serge (Stephane Rideau) is a peasant hunk who is moody and impulsive. Henri (Frederic Gorny), who is a few years older, is a French-born right-winger exiled from Algeria. He is jaded, cynical and bitter. The three represent the intellectual, physical and political aspects of French manhood.

The girl, Maite (Elodie Bouchez), has a deep platonic friendship with Francois. They go to Ingmar Bergman films and talk about anything except how they feel about each other. Henri is attracted to Maite, but it's purely physical, and Maite is holding out for something more. Henri is a late entry in the bidding for Maite's affections, and an underdog. After all, she's a left-wing feminist, but opposites do attract.

Serge makes that clear to Francois, in one of the film's many sequences where the youngsters talk knowingly and with unbelievable profundity about matters of love, sex and politics. Serge suggests to Francois that they could complement each other wonderfully, trading off their strengths in school subjects and combining their different approaches to wooing girls such as Maite. Henri, who is worldly wise, rudely suggests to Francois that Serge could be more than just a friend, and Francois finds himself falling in bed, and then in love with Serge, without knowing how it's happened.

Techine cast novice Morel after receiving numerous fan letters from the young film buff.

As this sexual roundelay unfolds, the Algerian conflict plays in the background. For France, it is the political equivalent of what is happening to the film's young protagonists—the end of innocence and a rude entry into a new, unforgiving world. Serge's older brother is in the Army but wants to desert, but Maite's mother refuses to help him. He ends up being killed in the conflict. Serge is appalled at those who consider his brother's sacrifice heroic, explaining, "When I dropped off my brother at the station, he said, 'Greatness disgusts me.'"

Not only do the adolescents sound like wise adults, they sound like French actors speaking movie lines filled with existential anguish. At a dance, with the Beach Boys playing in the background, Francois suddenly blurts out his confusion about his feelings for Maite and she responds, "I know

CREDITS

Maite: Elodie Bouchez
Francois: Geal Morel
Serge: Stephanie Rideau
Henri: Frederic Gorny
Madame Alvarez: Michele Moretti

Origin: France
Released: 1995
Production: Alain Sarde and Georges Benayoun for a Le Canal Plus, La Sept/Arte, IMA SPF production; released by IMA, Les Films and Strand
Direction: Andre Techine
Screenplay: Andre Techine, Gilles Taurand and Olivier Massart
Cinematography: Jeanne Lapoirie
Editing: Martine Giordano
Set decoration: Pierre Soula
Costume design: Brigette Laleouse
Sound: Francois Groult
Running Time: 110 minutes

AWARDS AND NOMINATIONS

Cesar Awards 1995: Best Film, Best Director (Techine), Best Screenplay (Techine/Taurand/Massart)
Los Angeles Film Critics Awards 1995: Best Foreign Film:
National Society of Film Critics Awards 1995: Best Foreign Film

why I need you, you reassure me." Then he confesses he's had sex with another male, and she responds, "I don't care what you do with others. It's what's between us that matters." Only in French films could one imagine such talk at a sock hop.

> "I slept with a boy." "I don't care what you do with others."—Maite's reply to friend Francois' revelation.

Wild Reeds is dreadfully earnest and dreadfully dull, in both its sexual and political aspects. Henri is always listening to a radio which is always broadcasting the latest reports of the Algerian conflict. He tells Francois while they're watching Serge play football, "I'm scared of real death. Sometimes I want to kill myself to stop thinking about death." Maite's mother is driven mad by Serge's brother's death. Francois looks into a mirror and tells himself disbelievingly: "I'm a faggot." In one of the most hilariously precocious lines of the film, Maite tells Serge, "I hate being young. It's a huge burden." That burden becomes monumental when you're in a French coming-of-age film in which every sentence has to resonate with deep insight.

Techine's attempts to lighten things up are lame. They mostly involve the playing of popular American songs and the schoolchildren's occasional trips to the local swimming hole.

Techine doesn't know how to be gentle with his points. He has to have his characters blurt out revelations that audiences could glean from the events themselves. It's too bad they have to speak such silly lines, because the young performers are uniformly good. The four principals are attractive and interesting, though all except Bouchez look a few years too old for the part. As Francois, Morel captures with great delicacy the confusion of an adolescent whose emerging identity is a mystery. As Serge, Rideau, handsome and direct, adds wonderful emotional shadings to a role which could have been pat. Gorny is excellent at creating an air of intrigue behind Henri's exterior of bravado.

Bouchez's performance is so authentic that it almost sweeps past the idiotic lines she must speak. Rarely has an actress so delicately captured the vivaciousness mixed with caution of a teenager on the verge of womanhood. As the girlish friend of Francois, Maite is dependable and solid, keeping any hint of sensuality from ruining a good friendship. As the object of Serge's lust, she is both teasing, confident and in control. And when she finally makes her choice at the film's end, she is wondrously sexy. Bouchez manages to package all these fascinating features into an intriguing character. She is a delightful, earthy actress.

Wild Reeds is lushly photographed by Jeanne Lapoirie. Techine does know how to use his settings to fullest advantage, but he is masterful at framing small scenes. He can't resist the temptation for grand flourishes, and a ridiculously long pan at the end of the film substitutes intrusive technique for a real climax. At nearly two hours, *Wild Reeds* is more of a burden than a revelation. Just as the school chums wait anxiously for the results of their final exams and their exit into the larger world, so too audiences will wait for *Wild Reeds* to stop its pretentious jabbering. Coming-of-age rarely has been so excruciating.

—*Michael Betzold*

REVIEWS

Los Angeles Times. May 10, 1995, p. 12.
The Nation. July 31, 1995, p. 144.
Playboy. July 1995, p. 20.
Time. June 12, 1995, p. 68.

Window to Paris (Okno V Parizh)

"A winningly rambunctious fairytale."—Jay Carr, *Boston Globe*

"A sharp, no holds-barred satire."—Kenneth Thomas, *Los Angeles Times*

"Broadly funny and provocative!"—Dave Kehr, *New York Daily News*

Box Office Gross: $255,088

Since the breakup of the former Soviet Union, Russia has seen endless economic turmoil and cultural upheaval. As the Cold War becomes an increasingly distant memory, the cultural differences between the West and the (Soviet) East are also becoming less disparate. Rock music, western films and television, even Western-style fast food joints are now a staple of Russian life. Besides cultural changes, the changeover from socialism to capitalism has created vast philosophical and economic divisions in the country, and perestroika and glasnost have shown an unprecedented light on the seemingly insurmountable troubles facing the government and people of Russia and the former U.S.S.R.

Window to Paris, a joint Franco-Russian film, pursues the theme of the effects of Western culture and capitalism on culturally rich but economically bankrupt (and fledgling capitalist) Russians. Essentially an allegorical fable about the clash of prosperous, pompous French, and poor, down-to-earth Russians, *Window to Paris* is itself a dichotomy: Mamin's scattershot editing, clumsy use of musical underscoring, and overly broad direction clash with his charming story and his fine sense of satire. The film is itself emblematic of the disparity in Russian cinema between technological know-how and artistry. On one hand, the film is a visual mess; on the other, it has a richly developed theme and message.

The film takes place in post-Cold War Russia. Nikolai (Serguej Dontsov) is a music teacher at a business high school. Emblematic of the once exalted and now superfluous status of the arts in Russia, Nikolai's job is in jeopardy because the school prepares "businessmen, not musicians." Once a training ground for communist leaders, the school has become an overly efficient school for business leaders, and as Nikolai says, "you used to train communists, now you train capitalists, but both are the same."

Moving into a low-income communal apartment with a group of musicians who work for the "Red October Piano Company," a manufacturer of pianos, Nikolai settles immediately into a raucous life with these hard-drinking peasants. On his first night there, he and the other men in the apartment discover that in his room lies an extraordinary secret: behind the armoire is a window that opens to Paris. In a drunken trek through the window, the men don't at first realize the implications of their discovery. After a night carousing around Paris (initially thinking it to be a section of St. Petersburg that they have never seen), several of the men, including a former Soviet apparatchik and a rock musician, go off in a taxicab, thinking (through a drunken haze) that they will eventually find their way home.

Nikolai and his landlord Gorokhov (Viktor Michailov), however, stumble back to their apartment and realize the importance of their discovery. Gorokhov in particular wants to make use of the window to the west, and he takes his wife (Nina Oussatova), mother-in-law (Kira Kreylis-Petrova), and pregnant daughter (Natalja Ipatova) through the window on numerous attempts to earn some money and sample some of the extraordinary abundance at French markets and stores. His constant theme is that Westerners have so much that they "can afford to throw away" the leftovers. Seeing a bank of television sets at an electronics store, Gorokhov says, "there is more radiation here than Chernobyl." He later marvels at how many churches there are in France, "even though they don't believe in God."

Meanwhile, dedicated musician Nikolai tries to find artistic freedom in the West. This provides some of the best satire in the film, since he discovers that the West has artistic freedom, but no one seems to want to utilize it. For example, he finds a Russian violinist who now works in a fancy French restaurant—wearing liederhosen and doing a novelty act which requires him to play fiddle between his legs. "Nobody here wants art!" he scoffs to Nikolai. Later, Nikolai auditions for a seat in an orchestra. He is perplexed when after the audition he is told that he is hired, but that they must see his legs. Not questioning his new patrons, he does so—and then discovers that the orchestra plays in tux tails only, and is otherwise naked, playing to a naked audience. In one of the film's wittiest lines, Nikolai's friend yells to him that "No one here needs Mozart with pants!"

These scenes are tempered by a lovely speech by that same fiddle-playing friend, who wistfully says, "remember us in a communal apartment at my kitchen table, with a bottle of vodka and one pickle, how we talked about fine arts, the fate of Russia, about God...." This moment is a fine example of Director/Writer Yuri Mamin's (he wrote the screenplay with Arkadi Tigai) sensitivity to his theme that Russian culture may have fared better under the communist regime, and that capitalism does not necessarily ensure intellectual advancement and cultural enrichment.

The clash of cultures and of socioeconomic ideology also comes in the form of a French woman named Nicole (Agnes Soral), a taxidermist, whose studio looks out over the rooftop where the Russians make their constant entrances and exits. At first furious at their boorish intrusions (they enter and exit the building through her studio), she eventually gets a Russian phrase book, and is determined to communicate with them, if only to tell them to leave her alone. Not surprisingly, she and the hapless Nikolai strike up a friendship and a sense of understanding—their own perestroika, if you will—which comes only after she follows them into their apartment and finds herself in the stark and uncompromising world of economically depressed St. Petersburg. Through a series of plot developments, Nikolia saves her from a Petersburg prison, and her gratitude turns to romance.

Through all of this, the three drunken comrades who took a taxi on the first night are seen occasionally, driving around Paris in a taxi, certain that they will find their way home soon. Eventually, they find their way to an archaic communist party haven, where they are treated like heroes, and shown around Paris in a lavish tour bus until they coincidentally encounter Nikolai. The bumbling communists driving aimlessly around an alien world makes for wonderful satire, as do many of the film's numerous symbolic references to the disparity between communism's intentions and its realities, as well as the disparity between communism and capitalism.

All of this action occurs in a short time, as the window to Paris only opens occasionally, and the characters discover that they only have 13 days in which to enjoy Paris before the window closes again. Just before the window closes, Nikolai brings the children from his music class, who have staged a riot at the business school in protest of the dismantling of their arts education. Seeing the West for the first time, and fascinated by Western culture and apparent freedom, the children decide to stay, saying "we'll get jobs...at McDonald's...there are plenty of jobs" in the West, and that "beauty has a value everywhere." This leads to the film's most poignant moment, and to the heart of the film: Nikolai tells the children "you were born at the wrong time, into a miserable, bankrupt country. But it's still your country. Can't you make it a better place? You haven't even tried..."

Clearly, Director Mamin is adept at hitting his satirical targets squarely on the nose, even while managing to infuse his characters with some sympathy and morality. But with all of the beauty, fun, and fantasy of the story, this film is sadly lacking in several areas. As mentioned before, the soundtrack is nothing short of annoying, continually blasting out sounds which, instead of gently promoting the emotional core of the scene, jerk the audience into emotional submission. Additionally, the chronology of the story is not clearly delineated; the characters go back and forth to Paris often enough that the continuity of the scenes is quite unclear.

Mamin also allows his actors (and in particular the children) far too much latitude to be zany and offbeat. Perhaps if the actors were less enamored by the whimsy of the story, it would be a bit more elegantly told. The reduction of some of the overly cute nature of the characterizations might make the characters more likable. As it stands now, Sergej Donstov and Agnes Soral are not bad, but only when their characters are completely battered about by their cultural conflict do they finally let down the pretense of their characterizations long enough to become human.

Still, this is a worthwhile film with a truly wonderful premise. It actually can be an educational film, for to witness its paradoxes, intended and unintended, is to understand the complicated nature of the struggle between communism and capitalism, between East and West, and between human nature and the heavenly aspirations of art.

—Kirby Tepper

CREDITS

Nicole: Agnes Soral
Tchijov: Serguej Dontsov
Gorokhov: Viktor Michailov
Vera: Nina Oussatova
Gorokhov's mother-in-law: Kira Kreylis-Petrova
Gorokhov's daughter: Natalja Ipatova
Kouzmitch: Viktor Gogolev
Maria Olegovna: Tamara Timofeeva
Gouliaiev: Andrej Ourgante
M. Prevost: Jean Rupert

Origin: Russia and France
Released: 1994
Production: Guy Seligmann for Fontaine and Sodaperaga, in association with La Sept Cinema; released by Sony Pictures Classics
Direction: Yuri Mamin
Screenplay: Yuri Mamin and Arkadi Tigai
Cinematography: Sergei Nekrasov and Anatoli Lapchov
Editing: Olga Andrianova and Joele Van Effenterre
Production design: Vera Zelinskaia
Sound: Leonide Gavritchenko
Costume design: Natalya Zamakhina
Music: Yuri Mamin and Aleksei Zalivalov
Running Time: 87 minutes

List of Awards

Academy Awards

Best Picture: *Braveheart*

Direction: Mel Gibson (*Braveheart*)

Actor: Nicolas Cage (*Leaving Las Vegas*)

Actress: Susan Sarandon (*Dead Man Walking*)

Supporting Actor: Kevin Spacey (*The Usual Suspects*)

Supporting Actress: Mira Sorvino (*Mighty Aphrodite*)

Original Screenplay: Christopher McQuarrie (*The Usual Suspects*)

Adapted Screenplay: Emma Thompson (*Sense and Sensibility*)

Cinematography: John Toll (*Braveheart*)

Editing: Mike Hill and Dan Hanley (*Apollo 13*)

Art Direction: Eugenio Zanetti (*Restoration*)

Visual Effects: Scott E. Anderson, Charles Gibson, Neal Scanlan, and John Cox (*Babe*)

Sound Effects Editing: Lon Bender and Per Hallberg (*Braveheart*)

Sound: Rick Dior, Steve Pederson, Scott Millan and David MacMillan (*Apollo 13*)

Makeup: Peter Frampton, Paul Pattison and Loïs Burwell (*Braveheart*)

Costume design: James Acheson (*Restoration*)

Original Music or Comedy Score: Alan Menken (*Pocahontas*)

Original Music or Score, Drama: Luis Enrique Bacalov (*Il Postino, The Postman*)

Original Song: "Colors of the Wind" (*Pocahontas*: music by Alan Menken, lyrics by Stephen Schwartz)

Foreign-Language Film: *Antonia's Line* (Netherlands)

Short Film, Animated: *A Close Shave* (Nick Park)

Short Film, Live Action: *Lieberman in Love* (Christine Lahti and Jana Sue Memel)

Documentary, Feature: *Anne Frank Remembered* (Jon Blair)

Documentary, Short Subject: *One Survivor Remembers* (Kary Antholis)

Honorary Oscar: Kirk Douglas
Chuck Jones

Directors Guild of America Award

Director: Ron Howard (*Apollo 13*)

Writers Guild Awards

Original Screenplay: Randall Wallace (*Braveheart*)

Adapted Screenplay: Emma Thompson (*Sense and Sensibility*)

New York Film Critics Awards

Best Picture: *Leaving Las Vegas*

Direction: Ang Lee (*Sense and Sensibility*)

Actor: Nicolas Cage (*Leaving Las Vegas*)

Actress: Jennifer Jason Leigh (*Georgia*)

Supporting Actor: Kevin Spacey (*Outbreak*, *Seven*, *Swimming With Sharks*, *The Usual Suspects*)

Supporting Actress: Mira Sorvino (*Mighty Aphrodite*)

Los Angeles Film Critics Awards

Best Picture: *Leaving Las Vegas*

Direction: Mike Figgis (*Leaving Las Vegas*)

Actor: Nicolas Cage (*Leaving Las Vegas*)

Actress: Elisabeth Shue (*Leaving Las Vegas*)

Supporting Actor: Don Cheadle (*Devil in a Blue Dress*)

Supporting Actress: Joan Allen (*Nixon*)

Screenplay: Emma Thompson (*Sense and Sensibility*)

Cinematography: Lu Yue (*Shanghai Triad*)

Original Score: Patrick Doyle (*A Little Princess*)

Foreign Film: *Wild Reeds* (France)

Outstanding Documentary: *Crumb* (Lynn O'Donnell and Terry Zwigoff)

National Society of Film Critics Awards

Best Picture: *Babe*

Direction: Mike Figgis (*Leaving Las Vegas*)

Actor: Nicolas Cage (*Leaving Las Vegas*)

Actress: Elisabeth Shue (*Leaving Las Vegas*)

Supporting Actor: Don Cheadle (*Devil in a Blue Dress*)

Supporting Actress: Joan Allen (*Nixon*)
Screenplay: Amy Heckerling (*Clueless*)
Cinematography: Tak Fujimoto (*Devil in a Blue Dress*)
Documentary: *Crumb* (Lynn O'Donnell and Terry Zwigoff)
Foreign Language Film: *Wild Reeds* (France)
Experimental Citation: *Latcho Drom*

National Board of Review Awards
Best English-Language Film: *Sense and Sensibility*
Direction: Ang Lee (*Sense and Sensibility*)
Actor: Nicolas Cage (*Leaving Las Vegas*)
Actress: Emma Thompson (*Carrington*; *Sense and Sensibility*)
Supporting Actor: Kevin Spacey (*Seven*; *The Usual Suspects*)
Supporting Actress: Mira Sorvino (*Mighty Aphrodite*)

Golden Globe Awards
Best Picture, Drama: *Sense and Sensibility*
Best Picture, Comedy: *Babe*
Direction: Mel Gibson (*Braveheart*)
Actor, Drama: Nicolas Cage (*Leaving Las Vegas*)
Actress, Drama: Sharon Stone (*Casino*)
Actor, Comedy or Musical: John Travolta (*Get Shorty*)
Actress, Comedy or Musical: Nicole Kidman (*To Die For*)
Supporting Actor: Brad Pitt (*12 Monkeys*)
Supporting Actress: Mira Sorvino (*Mighty Aphrodite*)
Screenplay: Emma Thompson (*Sense and Sensibility*)
Original Score: Maurice Jarre (*A Walk in the Clouds*)
Original Song: "Colors of the Wind" (*Pocahontas*: music by Alan Menken, lyrics by Stephen Schwartz)
Foreign-Language Film: *Les Miserables*

Life Achievement Award

Clint Eastwood

The 24th annual American Film Institute Life Achievement Award was presented to bona fide Hollywood film icon Clint Eastwood for his contribution to the American film industry. An internationally acclaimed filmmaker on both sides of the camera, this actor/director/producer/film preservationist has remained a top box office attraction for more than 25 years.

The "Man With No Name" was born Clinton Eastwood, Jr. in San Francisco, California on May 31, 1930. A child of the Depression, the young Eastwood wandered from town to town throughout northern California with his younger sister, mother, and father, Clinton Eastwood, Sr., a nomadic accountant. At times the family separated and Clint Jr. lived with his grandmother on a farm near Sunol, California where he learned to ride horses. The family finally settled in Oakland, after Eastwood, Sr. found a job with the Container Corporation of America. The teenaged Eastwood enrolled at Oakland Technical High School, and, at 6' 4", became the school basketball star. While still in high school, Eastwood trained for a career in professional sports, played jazz piano and trumpet in a bar, and worked as a lumberjack and firefighter for the Paradise County Department of Forestry. He was also coaxed into performing in a school play, but was so uncomfortable with the experience that he vowed never to try acting again.

Upon graduation in 1948, Eastwood's parents moved to Seattle, Washington. Eastwood worked for a spell as a lumberjack in Oregon, but later also headed for Seattle where he blasted furnaces at the Bethlehem Steel Company. During the Korean War, Eastwood served as a swimming instructor at Fort Ord, south of San Francisco. Although he was never called for active duty, while at the barracks, Eastwood met three young actors, Martin Milner, David Janssen, and Norman Bartold, who persuaded the reluctant thespian to reconsider acting. An assistant director from Universal-International who was shooting a film at Fort Ord spotted the athletic Eastwood, asked him to read a scene, and invited him to look him up when he was demobilized. However, when Eastwood was discharged in February 1953, he discovered that the director had moved to another studio.

Eastwood studied Business Administration at Los Angeles City College on the GI bill, married model and swimwear designer Maggie Johnson in 1954, and struggled as an aspiring actor while working several jobs. He dropped out of college after he completed a successful screen test and signed a contract for $75 a week with Universal. In the mid-to-late '50s, Eastwood worked almost two years, frequently uncredited or offscreen, in the shadow of studio stars Rock Hudson, John Agar, and George Nader in such B movies as *Revenge of the Creature, Never Say Goodbye, Lady Godiva, Away All Boats, Francis in the Navy* and *Tarantula*—in which Eastwood played the pilot that napalms the giant spider at the end of the film.

Unable to survive on these bit parts, Eastwood wound up digging swimming pools in Beverly Hills to make ends meet until he secured a full-time lead role as cattle driver Rowdy Yates in the TV series *Rawhide.* The one-hour, high-budget series became an instant success, running from 1959-1965. Although Eastwood learned a great deal about acting technique and directing while working on the series, he became frustrated with the John Wayne type of good-guy western hero image he had inherited and wanted to create more complex characters. (The Duke himself considered Eastwood to be "the best cowboy in movies today," and interestingly, was influenced by Eastwood in "tough cop" films such as *McQ* and *Brannigan.*)

It was Italian director Sergio Leone who helped bring about Eastwood's metamorphosis into the quiet, cold, enigmatic loner and mercenary savored by Eastwood fans. For the nameless character in his bravado western, *A Fistful of Dollars* (1964), a remake of Kurosawa's *Yojimbo,* Leone advised Eastwood to scruff up his image, grow his beard, and chomp on a cigarillo—an affectation which the non-smoking actor says helped him overcome his stage fright and transform him into the squinting, surly, laconic character that would become his trademark. This first of the world-famous "spaghetti westerns" launched the careers of Leone and Eastwood, and the actor soon became more famous in Italy than Sophia Loren. The "Dollars" trilogy continued with two other Leone Italian-made westerns: *For a Few Dollars More* (1965), and *The Good, the Bad and the Ugly* (1966), making Eastwood an international star.

Upon his return to the United States, Eastwood set up his own film company, Malpaso, which released the revenge western hit, *Hang 'Em High* (1967), directed by Ted Post, in which Eastwood played lawman, Jed Cooper. However, it was the megahit, *Dirty Harry* (1971), directed by Donald Siegel, in which Clint Eastwood displayed his deadly charisma as rock hard cop Harry Callahan that catapulted Eastwood from stardom to superstardom. The "Dirty Harry" saga continued with *Magnum Force* (1973), directed by Post, *The Enforcer* (1976), *Sudden Impact* (1983) directed by Eastwood, and *The Dead Pool* (1988). Along with immortalizing the lines, "Are you feeling lucky, punk?" (*Dirty Harry*) and "Go ahead, make my day" (*Sudden Impact*), the "Dirty Harry" movies served to reinforce Eastwood's film image as the cynical, action anti-hero.

Although Eastwood became known for his violent roles, he showed his gentler, romantic side in some of his own directorial efforts, including *Bronco Billy* (1980), *Honky Tonk Man* (1983), the suspenseful *Play Misty For Me* (1971, a forerunner to *Fatal Attraction*) and Eastwood's film adaptation of the Robert James Waller best-selling novel, *The Bridges of Madison County* (1995), for which Meryl Streep received a Best Actress Academy Award nomination. Eastwood also revealed a vulnerable side as an aging Secret Service agent in director Wolfgang Petersen's *In the Line of Fire,* one of the highest grossing films of 1993.

As a filmmaker, Eastwood learned from his own best directors, Leone and Siegel, sensing when to add some visual or stylistic flourish to a straightforward scene and how effective a small nuance can be on the big screen. Leone and Siegel's approaches perfectly suited Eastwood's restrained acting style, and he integrated their approach to his filmmaking technique with startling results. Eastwood directed some of his most popular films, including *Play Misty for Me, High Plains Drifter* (1973), and *The Outlaw Josey Wales* (1979), culminating in 1993 with his Best Director Oscar for the myth-defying Old Western *Unforgiven*, in which Eastwood played aging gunman Will Munny.

For Eastwood fans, the actor's offscreen life has held as much intrigue as his films. Eastwood served as mayor of Carmel, California from 1986 to 1988, and attempted to preserve the town and discourage overdevelopment, fighting bureaucracy like a kind of Mayor Harry Callahan. (Eastwood's production company, Malpaso, is named after a creek in Carmel.) After Eastwood left his wife, his leading lady on and offscreen for many years was Sondra Locke. The couple split acrimoniously in the mid-'80s, after Locke brought a widely publicized palimony suit against Eastwood. In March 1996, 65-year-old Eastwood married 30-year-old newscaster Dina Ruiz in Las Vegas.

Eastwood has made over 50 films in his 40-plus years in the business and remains one of the few actors whose name on a movie marquee can guarantee a hit. Clint Eastwood is more than a movie star and living legend. He is a portrait of the American Dream: a wanderer, a worker, a pioneer, a preservationist, a man of the community, a craftsman who became an artist—and these are reasons enough for the American Film Institute to celebrate his accomplishments.

—Shawn Brennan

Obituaries

George Abbott (June 25, 1887-January 31, 1995). Abbott was a playwright, director, screenwriter, and producer who was a Broadway legend, directing numerous hits such as *Twentieth Century, Pal Joey, A Tree Grows in Brooklyn, The Pajama Game, Damn Yankees, Fiorello!,* and *A Funny Thing Happened on the Way to the Forum.* Before he decided to concentrate on the stage, Abbott worked as a director and screenwriter in Hollywood; he also co-directed and co-produced with Stanley Donen the film versions of two of his Broadway successes, *The Pajama Game* (1957) and *Damn Yankees* (1958). Abbott's screen directing credits include *The Imposter* (1918), *Why Bring That Up* (1929), *Half-Way to Heaven* (1929), *Manslaughter* (1930), *The Sea God* (1930), *Stolen Heaven* (1931) *Secrets of a Secretary* (1931), *My Sin* (1931), *The Cheat* (1931), and *Too Many Girls* (1940).

Ted Allan (January 25, 1918-June 29, 1995). Allan was a Canadian writer who wrote biographies and plays as well as screenplays. He is best known for his screenplay of *Lies My Father Told Me* (1975), the autobiographical story of a Jewish boy's coming of age in Montreal in the 1920s, which earned him an Academy Award nomination. His additional film credits include *Out of Nowhere* (1966), *Love Streams* (1986), and *Bethune* (1988).

Maxene Andrews (January 3, 1918-October 21, 1995). Andrews was a member of the Andrews Sisters, popular recording stars of the 1930s and 1940s, with hits such as "Bei Mir Bist Du Schoen" and "Rum And Coca Cola." The trio translated their popularity into numerous film roles, and their screen credits include *Argentine Nights* (1940), *Buck Privates* (1941), *Swingtime Johnny* (1943), *Hollywood Canteen* (1944), and *Road to Rio* (1947).

Danny Arnold (1925-August 19, 1995). Arnold was an actor, screenwriter, and television producer best known for his popular television comedies, including *The Real McCoys, Bewitched, That Girl,* and *Barney Miller.* Prior to moving into television, Arnold worked in film, most notably with the comedy team of Dean Martin and Jerry Lewis. He acted in two Martin and Lewis vehicles, *Sailor Beware* (1952) and *Scared Stiff* (1953), and co-wrote a third, *The Caddy* (1953).

Rick Aviles (1953-March 17, 1995). Aviles was a comic actor who was featured in several film roles, including *Cannonball Run II* (1984), *Street Smart* (1987), *Mystery Train* (1989), *Ghost* (1990), *The Godfather, Part III* (1990), *Carlito's Way* (1993), and *Waterworld* (1995).

David Begelman (1922-August 7, 1995). Begelman was a studio executive and producer who was involved in a financial scandal which led to his resignation as President of Columbia Pictures in 1978. He joined Columbia in 1973, and under his leadership the studio produced such hits as *The Way We Were* (1973), *Tommy* (1975), *Shampoo* (1975), and *Close Encounters of the Third Kind* (1977). But Begelman was accused of embezzling money from the studio, and was forced to resign. In 1980, he became President and CEO of MGM, but his tenure there was unsuccessful and he resigned after a year. He formed an independent production company, which was forced into bankruptcy in 1994. His death was a suicide.

Charles Bennett (August 2, 1899-June 15, 1995). Bennett was a British screenwriter, best known for his collaborations with Alfred Hitchcock, for whom he worked on *The Man Who Knew Too Much* (1934), *The Thirty-Nine Steps* (1935), *Secret Agent* (1936), *Sabotage* (1936), *Young and Innocent* (1937), *Foreign Correspondent* (1940), and Hitchcock's remake of *The Man Who Knew Too Much* (1956). Bennett directed two films himself, *Madness of the Heart* (1949) and *Escape (1953),* but his best work was done as a writer. His additional screenwriting credits include *King Solomon's Mines* (1937), *Joan of Paris* (1942), *Unconquered* (1947), *Kind Lady* (1951), *The Big Circus* (1959), *The Lost World* (1960), *Voyage to the Bottom of the Sea* (1961), and *Five Weeks in a Balloon* (1962).

Vivian Blaine (November 21, 1921- December 9, 1995). Born Vivian Stapleton, Blaine was an actress best known for

Vivian Blaine

her role of Miss Adelaide in the Broadway and film versions of *Guys and Dolls* (1955). She was also featured in the first film version of *State Fair* (1945), and a number of Hollywood musicals and comedies, including *It Happened in Flatbush* (1942), *Girl Trouble* (1942), *Jitterbugs* (1943), *Something for the Boys* (1944), *Skirts Ahoy!* (1952), and *Public Pigeon No. 1* (1957).

Ralph Blane (1914-November 13, 1995). Born Ralph Blane Hunsecker, Blane was a composer who was nominated for two Academy Awards, for "The Trolley Song," from *Meet Me in St. Louis* (1944; with collaborator Hugh Martin), and "Pass That Peace Pipe," from *Good News* (1947; with Martin and Roger Edens). Blane's additional film credits include *Best Foot Forward* (1943), *Summer Holiday* (1948), *One Sunday Afternoon* (1948), *My Dream Is Yours* (1949), *My Blue Heaven* (1950), *Skirts Ahoy!* (1952), and *Athena* (1954).

Julian Blaustein (May 30, 1913-June 20, 1995). Blaustein was a producer who was associated with the Universal, Paramount, Selznick, and Fox studios. His association with Fox began in 1949, and his screen credits include *Broken Arrow* (1950), *The Day the Earth Stood Still* (1951), *Bell Book and Candle* (1958), *Khartoum* (1966), and *Three Into Two Won't Go* (1969).

Robert Bolt (August 15, 1924-February 20, 1995). Bolt was a British playwright and screenwriter. His film career was relatively brief, but he was associated with three of the most memorable films of the 1960s, winning two Academy Awards for *Dr. Zhivago* (1965) and *A Man For All Seasons* (1966), which was based on his own play. Bolt also earned an Academy Award nomination for his screenplay of *Lawrence of Arabia* (1962). His additional film credits include *Ryan's Daughter* (1970), *Lady Caroline Lamb* (1972), which he wrote and directed, *The Bounty* (1984), and *The Mission* (1986).

Jeremy Brett (November 3, 1935-September 12, 1995). Born Jeremy Huggins, Brett was a British actor who was best known for his portrayal of Sherlock Holmes on PBS's *Mystery Theater* from 1984 to 1993. He also acted in films, where his most prominent role was that of Freddy Eynsford-Hill in *My Fair Lady* (1964). His additional film credits include *War and Peace* (1956), *The Wild and the Willing* (1962), *The Very Edge* (1963), and *The Medusa Touch* (1978).

Phyllis Brooks (July 18, 1914-August 1, 1995). Born Phyllis Steiller, Brooks was an actress who was featured in numerous films in the 1930s and 1940s, including Shirley Temple vehicles and the Charlie Chan series. She was once engaged to Cary Grant, but instead retired from acting to marry Robert MacDonald, who later served eleven terms as a Congressman from Massachusetts. Brooks' film credits include *I've Been Around* (1934), *Rebecca of Sunnybrook Farm* (1938), *Little Miss Broadway* (1938), *Charlie Chan in Honolulu* (1938), *Charlie Chan in Reno* (1939), *Lady in the Dark* (1944), and *Dangerous Passage* (1945).

Phyllis Brooks

Alessandro Cicognini (January 25, 1906-November 9, 1995). Cicognini was an Italian composer who began writing scores for films in 1936. He is best known for his work with director Vittorio De Sica, including *The Bicycle Thief* (1948), *Miracle in Milan* (1951), *Umberto D* (1952), and *Indiscretion of an American Wife* (1953). His additional film credits include *Il Corsare nero* (1936), *Four Steps in the Clouds* (1942), *Shoeshine* (1946), *The Gold of Naples* (1954), *Ulysses* (1955), *The Black Orchid* (1958), and *The Pigeon That Took Rome* (1962).

Jack Clayton (1921-February 25, 1995). Clayton was a British director who broke into film doing a variety of jobs for producer Alexander Korda. He began directing wartime documentaries; after the war, his *The Bespoke Overcoat* (1955) won a prize at the Venice Film Festival. His first feature film was the influential working class drama, *Room at the Top* (1958); when the film was released in the United States the following year, it was nominated for four Academy Awards, including Best Picture and Directing; and Simone Signoret and Neil Paterson won Academy Awards for Best Actress and Best Screenplay, respectively. Another of Clayton's actresses, Anne Bancroft, earned an Academy Award nomination for her work in his *The Pumpkin Eater* (1964). Thereafter, Clayton worked only sporadically, with *The Great Gatsby* (1974) being perhaps his most memorable work. His additional directing credits include *Naples Is a Battlefield* (1944), *The Innocents* (1961), *Our Mother's House* (1967), *Something Wicked This Way Comes* (1983), and *The Lonely Passion of Judith Hearne* (1987).

Elisha Cook, Jr. (December 26, 1906-May 18, 1995). Cook was a character actor who specialized in playing weak

Elisha Cook, Jr.

villains and victims. His most memorable role was that of Wilmer, Humphrey Bogart's foil in *The Maltese Falcon* (1941). His additional film credits include *Two in a Crowd* (1936), *Dillinger* (1945), *The Big Sleep* (1946), *The Great Gatsby* (1949), *Shane* (1953), *Baby Face Nelson* (1957), *Platinum High School* (1960), *Rosemary's Baby* (1968), *Electra Glide in Blue* (1973), *The Black Bird* (1975), *Carny* (1980), and *Hammett* (1982).

Peter Cook (November 17, 1937-January 9, 1995). Cook was a British comic actor who worked in a satirical revue called "Beyond the Fringe" in the early 1960s with colleagues Alan Bennett, Jonathan Miller, and Dudley Moore. His best known film role was in *Bedazzled* (1967), which he also co-wrote. His additional film credits include *The Wrong Box* (1966), *A Dandy in Aspic* (1968), *The Bed Sitting Room* (1969), *The Hound of the Baskervilles* (1978), *The Princess Bride* (1987), and *Great Balls of Fire* (1989).

Severn Darden (1931-May 26, 1995). Darden was a comic actor and one of the founders of Chicago's Second City comedy ensemble. He appeared in a number of film roles, including appearances in *Luv* (1967), *The President's Analyst* (1968), *They Shoot Horses, Don't They?* (1969), *Cisco Pike* (1972), *Conquest of the Planet of the Apes* (1972), *Battle for the Planet of the Apes* (1973), *The Day of the Dolphin* (1973), *Mother, Jugs & Speed* (1976), *Hopscotch* (1980), and *Back to School* (1986).

Charles Denner (May 29, 1926-September 10, 1995). Denner was an actor best known for his work with directors Claude Chabrol, Claude Lelouch, and Francois Truffaut. Born in Poland, Denner's family moved to France when he was four. He made his screen debut in *La Meilleure Part* (1956), but his first major role as a leading man was in Chabrol's *Landru* (1963). He was also featured in *The Crook* (1970) for Lelouch, and in *The Man Who Loved Women* (1977) for Truffaut. His additional film credits include *Life Upside Down* (1964; also known as *Inside Out*), *The Thief of Paris* (1967), *The Two of Us* (1967), *Z* (1969), *Such a Gorgeous Kid Like Me* (1972), and *Le Coeur a l'enver* (1980).

Charles Denner

Robert Emhardt (1915-December 26, 1995). Emhardt was a character actor who specialized in overweight characters. He parlayed Broadway success into a film career with *The Iron Mistress* (1952) and *The Big Knife* (1955), and worked extensively in television from the 1950s into the 1980s. His film appearances include two Elvis Presley vehicles, *Kid Galahad* (1962) and *Change of Habit* (1969). His additional film credits include *The Group* (1966), *Alex and the Gypsy* (1976), and *Fraternity Row* (1977).

Cy Endfield (1914-April 16, 1995). Endfield was a screenwriter and director whose career was disrupted in the 1950s when he was accused of being a communist and blacklisted in the United States. He specialized in suspense and adventure films, including *The Underworld Story* (1950) and *The Sound of Fury* (1951; also released as *Try and Get Me*) before his political troubles and *Zulu* (1964) and *Sands of the Kalahari* (1965) after his comeback. He worked in England for several years, often using pseudonyms or working without onscreen credit. He frequently wrote the screenplays for the films he directed. His additional screen credits include *Gentleman Joe Palooka* (1946), *Tarzan's Savage Fury* (1952), *The Master Plan* (1954), *Sea Fury* (1958), *De Sade* (1969), *Universal Soldier* (1971), and *Zulu Dawn* (1979), for which he wrote the screenplay.

Franco Fabrizi (February 15, 1926-October 18, 1995). Fabrizi was an Italian actor who was featured in the films of Italy's most prominent directors. Perhaps his best remembered role was that of the small town Casanova in Federico Fellini's *I Vitelloni* (1953); he also appeared in the director's *Il Bidone* (1955) and *Ginger and Fred* (1985). He was also featured in Michelangelo Antonioni's *The Girlfriends* (1955) and Luchino Visconti's *Death in Venice* (1971). His additional film credits include *Mariti in Citta* (1957), *The Nights of Lucretia Borgia* (1959), *Il Relitto* (1961), *The Birds the Bees and the Italians* (1966), and *The Little Devil* (1988).

Eva Gabor. (February 11, 1921-July 4, 1995). Gabor was a Hungarian born actress best known for her work on the television situation comedy *Green Acres,* which ran from 1965-1971. Her first film appearance was in *Forced Landing* (1941), and she came to prominence in 1950, in Broadway's *The Happy Time.* Gabor and her two sisters, Zsa Zsa and Magda, won notoriety for their frequent marriages and divorces. Her additional screen credits include *A Royal Scandal* (1945), *The Wife*

Eva Gabor

of Monte Cristo (1946), *Artists and Models* (1955), *Don't Go Near the Water* (1957), *Gigi* (1958), *Youngblood Hawke* (1967), *The Aristocats* (1970), *The Rescuers* (1977), and *The Princess Academy* (1987).

Michael V. Gazzo (1923-February 14, 1995). Gazzo was an actor and screenwriter who was best known for his portrayal of mobster Frankie Pentangeli in *The Godfather, Part II* (1974), which earned him an Academy Award nomination in the supporting actor category. He first achieved prominence on Broadway, where his play *A Hatful of Rain* was a critical and commercial success in 1955. Gazzo co-wrote the screenplay for the film version of *A Hatful of Rain* (1957) with Alfred Hayes. He also wrote the script for an early Elvis Presley vehicle, *King Creole* (1958). As an actor, he tended to be cast as a gangster, and his screen credits include *The Gang That Couldn't Shoot Straight* (1971), *Black Sunday* (1977), *King of the Gypsies* (1978), *The Fish That Saved Pittsburgh* (1979), and *Cookie* (1989).

Alfredo Giannetti (1924-July 30, 1995). Giannetti was an Italian screenwriter and director who is best known for his screenplay of *Divorce Italian Style* (1962), which earned him and collaborators Ennio de Concini and Pietro Germi an Academy Award. He worked most often with Germi, a director with whom he made *The Railroad Man* (1956), *The Straw Man* (1957), *The Facts of Murder* (1959), *The Climax* (1967), and *Serafino* (1968). As a director, Giannetti made *Giorno per Giorno Disperatamente* (1961) and *Ragazza in Prestita* (1964). His additional screenwriting credits include *Un Giorno da Leoni* (1961) and *Treasure of San Gennaro* (1966).

Alexander Godunov

Alexander Godunov (November 28, 1949-May 18, 1995). Godunov was a Russian ballet dancer who defected to the United States in 1979 after thirteen years in the Bolshoi Ballet. He appeared in several films, including *Witness* (1985), *The Money Pit* (1986), and *Die Hard* (1988).

Gale Gordon (1905-June 30, 1995). Gordon was a comic actor best known as the foil of Lucille Ball in three of her popular television series, including *The Lucy Show* from 1963-68. He specialized in prissy, blustering authority figures, both in television and in film. His screen credits include *A Woman of Distinction* (1950), *Here Come the Nelsons* (1952), *Our Miss Brooks* (1956), *Rally 'Round the Flag, Boys!* (1958), *Visit to a Small Planet* (1960), and *Speedway* (1968).

Dorothy Granger (1914-January 4, 1995). Granger was an actress best known for her work at the Hal Roach studios, where she was often featured with the comedy stars of the early sound era. She was W.C. Fields' victim in his classic short *The Dentist* (1932). Later in her career, she had small roles in important films such as *Gone With the Wind* (1939) and *It's a Wonderful Life* (1941). She also worked extensively in television in the 1950s. Granger's additional screen credits include *Hog Wild* (1930), *The Laurel-Hardy Murder Case* (1930), *Jitters the Butler* (1932), *Kentucky Kernels* (1934), *Punch Drunk* (1934), *Termites of 1938* (1938), and *The Lady from Cheyenne* (1941).

Eleanore Griffin (1904-July 26, 1995). Griffin was a screenwriter best known for the original story for *Boys Town* (1938), which earned her and co-writer Dore Schary an Academy Award. Griffin's additional screen credits include *St. Louis Blues* (1939), *The Harvey Girls* (1946), *Good Morning Miss Dove* (1955), *A Man Called Peter* (1955), *Imitation of Life* (1959), and *Back Street* (1961).

Harry Guardino (December 23, 1925-July 17, 1995). Guardino was an actor who specialized in playing tough guys in both action films and comedies. He worked extensively on Broadway and in television as well as in film. His screen credits include *Flesh and Fury* (1952), *Houseboat* (1958), *Pork Chop Hill* (1959), *King of Kings* (1961), *Hell Is for Heroes* (1962), *The Pigeon That Took Rome* (1962), *Madigan* (1968), *Dirty Harry* (1971), *Capone* (1975), *Goldengirl* (1979), and *Any Which Way You Can* (1980).

Albert Hackett (February 16, 1900-March 16, 1995). Hackett was a screenwriter who, in collaboration with his wife Frances Goodrich, wrote screenplays for many prominent American films from the 1930s into the 1950s, including the perennial holiday favorite *It's a Wonderful Life* (1946). Their work covered a variety of genres, but they specialized in musicals and comedy, including the Irving Berlin musical *Easter Parade* (1948). They also wrote both the stage and screen versions of *The Diary of Anne Frank* (1959); Goodrich and Hackett won a Pulitzer Prize for their play in 1956. Hackett was the brother of actor Raymond Hackett. Hackett's additional screen credits include *The Thin Man* (1934), *Naughty Marietta* (1935), *Ah! Wilderness* (1935), *Rose Marie* (1936), *Lady in the Dark* (1944), *The Virginian* (1946), *In the Good Old Summertime* (1949), *Father of the Bride* (1950), *Father's Little Dividend* (1951), *The Long Long Trailer* (1954), *Seven Brides for Seven Brothers* (1954), *A Certain Smile* (1958), and *Five Finger Exercise* (1962).

Josef Heifitz (1905-April 24, 1995). Heifitz was a Russian director whose career spanned over half a century. Early in his career, Heifitz collaborated with Alexander Zarkhi for two decades; their two most prominent films, *Baltic Deputy* (1937) and *A Member of the Government* (1940), pioneered the historical realism style adopted by Soviet filmmakers. Zarkhi and Heifitz went their separate ways in 1950; Heifitz's best known work thereafter was *The Lady With the Dog* (1960), a Chekov adaptation that won a prize at the Cannes Film Festival. Heifitz's additional screen credits include *A Song of Steel* (1928), *Noon* (1931), *Red Army Days* (1935), *The Defeat of Japan* (1946), *The Precious Seeds* (1948), *A Big Family* (1954), *My Beloved* (1958), *Horizon* (1962), *The Bad Good Man* (1973), *Asya* (1978), and *First Marriage* (1980).

Jack Hively (1910-December 19, 1995). Hively was a director who specialized in low budget films. He is best known for his contributions to RKO's "The Saint" serials, featuring George Sanders. These included *The Saint's Double Trouble* (1940), *The Saint Takes Over* (1940), and *The Saint in Palm Springs* (1941). He also worked for Paramount and Universal, directing fifteen feature films in all. During the latter portion of his career, he worked primarily in television, directing episodes of *Lassie* and *Death Valley Days.* His additional film credits include *Panama Lady* (1939), *Laddie* (1940), *Four Jacks and a Jill* (1941), *Street of Chance* (1942), and *Are You With It?* (1948).

Sir Michael Hordern (October 3, 1911-May 2, 1995). Hordern was a British actor who specialized in character roles, often playing a harassed bureaucrat. His career prospered in the 1960s, when he appeared in many prominent British and American productions, including *El Cid* (1961), *Cleopatra* (1963), and *A Funny Thing Happened on the Way to the Forum* (1966). His screen credits include *Passport to Pimlico* (1949), *Scrooge* (1951; also released as *A Christmas Carol*), *The Heart of the Matter* (1953), *Sink the Bismarck!* (1960), *The Spy Who Came in From the Cold* (1965), *The Taming of the Shrew* (1967), *How I Won the War* (1967), *Anne of the Thousand Days* (1969), *Barry Lyndon* (1975), *Joseph Andrews* (1977), and *Ghandi* (1982).

Michael Hordern

John Howard (April 14, 1913-February 19, 1995). Born John R. Cox, Howard was an actor who had leading roles in B movie action pictures in the 1930s, and also played second leads in more important films. He starred as the detective in the title role in *Bulldog Drummond Comes Back* (1937) and *Bulldog Drummond's Peril* (1938), but was also featured in *Lost Horizon* (1937) and *The Philadelphia Story* (1940). His additional screen credits include *Annapolis Farewell* (1935), *Border Flight* (1936), *Hold 'Em Navy* (1937), *Touchdown Army* (1938), *Arrest Bulldog Drummond!* (1939), *The Invisible Woman* (1941), *The Fighting Kentuckian* (1949), *The High and the Mighty* (1954), *Destination Inner Space* (1966), and *Buck and the Preacher* (1972).

Burl Ives (June 14, 1909-April 14, 1995). Born Burlce Icle Ivanhoe, Ives was a singer and actor who enjoyed success in both endeavors. Ives was associated with folksingers such as Woody Guthrie, and his recordings of traditional ballads and pop songs sold well in the 1950s and 1960s. As an actor, the burly Ives won an Academy Award as Best Supporting Actor for his work in *The Big Country* (1958), and also had memorable roles in the James Dean vehicle *East of Eden* (1955) and as Big Daddy in *Cat on a Hot Tin Roof.* His additional screen credits include *Smoky* (1946), *So Dear To My Heart* (1948), *Desire Under the Elms* (1958), *Our Man in Havana* (1960), *Ensign Pulver* (1964), *Baker's Hawk* (1972), *Just You and Me Kid* (1979), *White Dog* (1982), and *Two Moon Junction* (1988).

Burl Ives

Dorothy Jeakins (1914-November 21, 1995). Jeakins was a costume designer who won Academy Awards for her work on three films, *Joan of Arc* (1948), *Samson and Delilah* (1950), and *The Night of the Iguana* (1964). Her additional film credits include the following films, each of which earned her an Academy Award nomination: *My Cousin Rachel* (1952), *The Greatest Show on Earth* (1952), *The Ten Commandments* (1956), *The Children's Hour* (1961), *The Music Man* (1962), *The Sound of Music* (1965), *Hawaii* (1966), and *The Way We Were* (1973); as well as *Three Coins in the Fountain* (1954), *Friendly Persuasion* (1956), *South Pacific* (1958), *True Grit* (1969), and *On Golden Pond* (1981).

Nancy Kelly (March 25, 1921-January 2, 1995). Kelly was an actress who came from a show business family. Her mother was actress Nan Kelly Yorke, and her brother was actor Jack Kelly. Kelly began acting in film as a five year old, in *Untamed Lady* (1926), but her most famous role came much later. She earned an Academy Award for her work in *The Bad Seed* (1956), a role

Nancy Kelly

which reprised her Tony Award winning Broadway performance. Kelly's additional screen credits include *Mismates* (1926), *Convention Girl* (1935), *Frontier Marshall* (1939), *Tarzan's Desert Mystery* (1943), *Double Exposure* (1944), *Song of the Sarong* (1945), and *Crowded Paradise* (1956).

Patric Knowles (November 11, 1911-December 23, 1995). Born Reginald Lawrence Knowles, Knowles was a British actor whose career spanned four decades. After appearing in several films in England, Knowles made his Hollywood debut featured alongside of Errol Flynn and Olivia de Haviland in *The Charge of the Light Brigade* (1936). He also worked with Flynn the following year as Will Scarlet in *The Adventures of Robin Hood* (1937). After his career peaked, he moved from playing leads and second leads into character roles. His additional film credits include *Men of Tomorrow* (1932), *Another Thin Man* (1939), *How Green Was My Valley* (1941), *The Wolf Man* (1940), *The Mystery of Marie Roget* (1942), *Frankenstein Meets the Wolf Man* (1943), *Monsieur Beaucaire* (1946), *Tarzan's Savage Fury* (1952), *Khyber Patrol* (1954), *Auntie Mame* (1958), *The Way West* (1967), *Chisum* (1970), and *Terror in the Wax Museum* (1973).

Patric Knowles

Howard Koch (December 12, 1902-August 17, 1995). Koch was a screenwriter best known as the author of the radio script for Orson Welles' *The War of the Worlds* in 1938, and as one of the co-writers of *Casablanca* (1942), for which he won an Academy Award. He was also nominated for an Academy Award for his work on *Sergeant York* (1941). He was an uncredited contributor to the screenplay of *The Best Years of Our Lives* (1946), which won an Academy Award as Best Picture. A victim of the House Un-American Activities Committee inspired blacklist beginning in 1951, Koch wrote the screenplay for *The Intimate Stranger* (1956) using the pseudonym Peter Howard. He resumed writing under his own name in the early 1960s, contributing to screenplays for *The Greengage Summer* (1961) and *The Fox* (1967), for which he was also associate producer. Koch also wrote two books about his career. His additional film credits include *The Sea Hawk* (1940), *Mission to Moscow* (1943), *Letter From an Unknown Woman* (1948), *The War Lover* (1962), and *633 Squadron* (1964).

Priscilla Lane (June 12, 1917-April 4, 1995). Born Priscilla Mullican, Lane was one of the singing Lane Sisters who performed with Fred Waring's Pennsylvanians. She broke into film in *Varsity Show* (1937), a musical featuring Waring's band, and was signed to an acting contract immediately. Her blonde good looks won her feature roles in a number of films, including *Love Honor and Behave* (1938), *Brother Rat* (1938), *The Roaring Twenties* (1939), *Blues in the Night* (1941), *Saboteur* (1942), *Arsenic and Old Lace* (1944), *Fun on a Weekend* (1947), and *Bodyguard* (1948).

Philip H. Lathrop (October 22, 1916-April 12, 1995). Lathrop was a cinematographer who worked on many prominent Hollywood films from the 1960s through the 1980s. He was often associated with director Blake Edwards, with whom he first worked on the television series *Peter Gunn*, and in films such as *The Days of Wine and Roses* (1963) and *The Pink Panther* (1964). He earned Academy Award nominations for his work on *The Americanization of Emily* (1964) and *Earthquake* (1974). His additional film credits include *Experiment in Terror* (1962), *The Cincinnati Kid* (1965), *What Did You Do in the War Daddy?* (1966), *The Happening* (1967), *Point Blank* (1967), *Finian's Rainbow* (1968), *They Shoot Horses Don't They?* (1969), *The Black Bird* (1975), *A Change of Seasons* (1980), and *Deadly Friend* (1986).

Viveca Lindfors (December 29, 1920-October 25, 1995). Lindfors was a Swedish actress who appeared in numerous films, both in Europe and the United States. Her first film was *The Spinning Family* (1940), and she appeared in seven additional films in her own country before moving to the United States in 1948. The next year, she married director Don Siegel, with whom she made *Night Unto Night* (1949) and *No Time for Flowers* (1952); they were divorced in 1953. Some of Lindfors' best work was done on stage, including a starring role in *Anastasia* in 1954 that earned new appreciation for her skills. Thereafter, she appeared in dozens of films, including *Moonfleet* (1955), *King of Kings* (1961), *Coming Apart* (1969), *The Way We Were* (1973), *Welcome to L.A.* (1977), *The Sure Thing* (1985), and *The Exorcist III* (1990).

Viveca Lindfors

Nanni Loy (October 23, 1925-August 21, 1995). Loy was an Italian director who began his career in documentaries before moving on to feature films. His most prominent work, *The Four Days of Naples* (1962), was a realistic recreation of a 1943 uprising against the German occupation of Naples. Loy also worked extensively in Italian television. His additional screen credits include *Parola di Ladro* (1957), *Fiasco in Milan* (1959), *Made in Italy* (1965), *Situation Nor-*

mal All Fouled Up (1970), *Black Is Beautiful* (1973), *Cafe Express* (1980), and *Scugnizzi* (1989).

Arthur Lubin (July 25, 1901-May 13, 1995). Lubin was a director who specialized in light entertainment. He was an actor in the silent era, appearing in *The Woman on the Jury* (1924) and *Afraid to Love* (1927), among others. His first film as director was *A Successful Failure* (1934). After working primarily in the adventure genre in his early years, Lubin teamed up with Abbott and Costello for *Buck Privates* (1941), the film that established the comedy team as stars. This collaboration continued with four more films in rapid order, *In the Navy* (1941), *Hold That Ghost* (1941), *Keep 'Em Flying* (1941), and *Ride 'Em Cowboy* (1942). In the early fifties, Lubin directed the successful low-brow comedy series involving Francis the Talking Mule, in *Francis* (1950), *Francis Goes to the Races* (1951), and four others in the series. He later took the concept of a talking animal to television, where he directed the talking horse, "Mr. Ed." Lubin's additional screen credits include *Mickey the Kid* (1939), *Gangs of Chicago* (1940), *The Phantom of the Opera* (1943), *Ali Baba and the 40 Thieves* (1944), *Francis Goes to West Point* (1952), *Francis in the Navy* (1955), *Star of India* (1956), *The Thief of Baghdad* (1961), and *The Incredible Mr. Limpet* (1964).

Arthur Lubin

Karl Lukas (1919-January 16, 1995). Lukas was an actor who worked extensively on Broadway, in television, and in films. His screen credits include *Don't Give Up the Ship* (1959), *Tall Story* (1960), *Tora! Tora! Tora!* (1970), *Oklahoma Crude* (1973), *Emperor of the North* (1973), *Blazing Saddles* (1974), *Hustle* (1975), and *Reds* (1981).

Ida Lupino (February 4, 1918-August 3, 1995). Lupino was a British born actress who became a director in the 1950s, opening doors for women filmmakers in Hollywood. Lupino came from a show business family; she made her first film, *Her First Affair* (1933) at the age of fifteen. She appeared in five other British films that year and then moved to Hollywood, where she earned progressively better roles. Her breakthrough performance was in *The Light That Failed* (1940), which led to a string of feature roles. Lupino was usually cast as a hard-bitten, cynical woman; she once characterized herself as a "poor man's Bette Davis." Some of her best roles were in *High Sierra* (1941), *The Sea Wolf* (1941), and *The Hard Way* (1943). Lupino had ambitions beyond acting, and in 1949, co-wrote and co-produced her first film, *Not Wanted* (1948), which she also wound up directing when the original director became ill soon after shooting began. She also co-wrote and directed the noir classic *The Hitch-Hiker* (1953). In 1951, she married actor Howard Duff; they starred in the television series "Mr. Adams and Eve" in the late 1950s, which was based on their own experiences in Hollywood. Lupino's additional acting credits include *Money for Speed* (1933), *Search for Beauty* (1934), *Anything Goes* (1936), *Artists and Models* (1937), *They Drive by Night* (1940), *In Our Time* (1944), *Devotion* (1946), *Road House* (1948), *Woman in Hiding* (1950), *Women's Prison* (1955), *The Big Knife* (1955), *Junior Bonner* (1972), and *The Food of the Gods* (1976). She directed and co-produced *Never Fear* (1950), *Outrage* (1950), *Hard Fast and Beautiful* (1951), *The Bigamist* (1953), and *The Trouble with Angels* (1966).

Ida Lupino

Doug McClure (May 11, 1935-February 5, 1995). McClure was an actor whose rugged good looks landed him leading roles in a variety of television series in the 1950s and 1960s, most prominently in *The Virginian.* His film credits include *The Enemy Below* (1957), *Gidget* (1959), *The Unforgiven* (1960), *Shenandoah* (1965), *Beau Geste* (1966), *Backtrack* (1969), *The Land That Time Forgot* (1974), *Humanoids From the Deep* (1980), *Cannonball Run II* (1984), *52 Pick-Up* (1986), *Omega Syndrome* (1987), and *Tapeheads* (1988).

Butterfly McQueen (January 8, 1911-December 22, 1995). Born Thelma McQueen, McQueen was an African-American actress best known for her portrayal of Prissy, the flighty young slave girl in *Gone With the Wind* (1939). She appeared in several other films, usually typecast as an emotional servant. Tiring of these roles, she gave up acting for over twenty years, but took roles in a few films in the 1970s. Her additional film credits include *The Women* (1939), *Cabin in the Sky* (1943), *I Dood It* (1943), *Since You Went Away* (1944), *Mildred Pierce* (1945), *Duel in the Sun* (1947), *Killer Diller* (1948), *The Phynx* (1970), *Amazing Grace* (1974), and *The Mosquito Coast* (1986).

Alan Maley (1930-May 13, 1995). Maley was a British special effects artist who won an Academy Award for his work in helping to create Angela Lansbury's flying bed in *Bedknobs and Broomsticks* (1971). His additional film credits include *Dr. Strangelove Or How I Learned to Stop Worrying and Love the Bomb* (1964).

Louis Malle (October 30, 1932-November 23, 1995). Malle was a French director who made films both in France and the United States. Born into a wealthy family, Malle studied filmmaking and was chosen by Jacques-Yves Cousteau to co-direct the underwater documentary *The Silent World* (1956). Two years later, he made his first feature film, *Frantic* (1958), which starred Jeanne Moreau. His next film *The Lovers* (1958), also starring Moreau, was criticized for its relatively explicit sexuality, but won the Special Jury Prize at the Venice Film Festival. Malle continued to work productively throughout the 1960s, with *Zazie dans le Metro* (1960), *A Very Private Affair* (1962), *The Fire Within* (1963), *Viva Maria* (1965), and *The Thief of Paris* (1967), in a variety of styles. After producing two documentaries about India, Malle returned to feature films with *Murmur of the Heart* (1971) and *Lacombe Lucien* (1973), both critically acclaimed character studies. His first American film was the controversial *Pretty Baby* (1978), which featured Brook Shields as a twelve year old prostitute. *Atlantic City* (1980) marked a triumphal return for Burt Lancaster, and *My Dinner with Andre* (1981) made a film out of a simple conversation between Wallace Shawn and Andre Gregory. After two uninspired films and a television documentary, Malle returned to France to make *Goodbye Children* (1987), a moving study of Catholic and Jewish children during the Nazi occupation of France. Another American film, *Damage* (1992), was again the source of controversy on account of its sexuality, receiving an NC-17 rating. Malle's last film was *Vanya on 42nd Street* (1994). He was married to actress Candice Bergen from 1980 until his death. Malle's additional film credits include *Calcutta* (1969), *Humain trop Humain* (1972), *Black Moon* (1975), *Crackers* (1984), *Alamo Bay* (1985), *God's Country* (1985), and *May Fools* (1989).

Louis Malle

Dean Martin (June 7, 1917-December 25, 1995). Born Dino Paul Crocetti, Martin was a singer and actor whose popularity spanned four decades in a variety of roles. He began his show business career as a lounge singer. It was at such an engagement in 1946 that he met comedian Jerry Lewis. The two hit it off and formed a partnership, with Martin playing the handsome straight man and Lewis playing the clown. Their nightclub routine was so successful that they were offered a film contract. Between 1949 and 1956, the team appeared in sixteen films, including *My Friend Irma* (1949), *That's My Boy* (1951), *Jumping Jacks* (1952), *Scared Stiff* (1953), and *Pardners* (1956). During this time, Martin established himself as a viable recording artist, scoring hits with such songs as "Memories Are Made of This" and "That's Amore" for Capitol Records. Martin tired of playing second fiddle to his frenetic partner, and struck out on his own in 1957. He gave credible dramatic performances in such films as *The Young Lions* (1958) and *Some Came Running* (1959), but it was Howard Hawks' Western, *Rio Bravo* (1959), in which Martin played an alcoholic sheriff and held his own with John Wayne, that made him a solo film star. Thereafter, he was featured in a variety of roles, from the Frank Sinatra-led "Rat Pack" comedies such as *Ocean's Eleven* (1960) and *Robin and the 7 Hoods* (1964) to the James Bond knockoff adventure series based on the exploits of one Matt Helm, in *The Silencers* (1966) and *The Wrecking Crew* (1969). Martin was also an enormously popular television star in the 1960s, and he hosted a series of variety shows on which he honed the persona of the loveable lush. He also prospered as a singer and as a nightclub act in Las Vegas. His last significant film role was in *Airport* (1970). Thereafter, he worked mainly as a singer, until ill health forced him to retire in the early 1990s. Martin's additional film credits include *At War with the Army* (1951), *Sailor Beware* (1952), *The Caddy* (1953), *Living It Up* (1954), *Hollywood or Bust* (1956), *Ten Thousand Bedrooms* (1957), *Bells Are Ringing* (1960), *Sergeants 3* (1962), *Four for Texas* (1963), *Kiss Me Stupid* (1964), *The Sons of Katie Elder* (1965), *Murderers' Row* (1966), *The Ambushers* (1967), *Something Big* (1971), *Cannonball Run* (1981), and *Cannonball Run II* (1984).

Dean Martin

Gunter Meisner (1929-December 5, 1995). Meisner was a German actor who appeared in more than one hundred films. He is perhaps best known to American audiences as the villain, Mr. Slugworth, in *Willie Wonka and the Chocolate Factory* (1971). His additional screen roles include *Babette Goes to War* (1959), *Funeral in Berlin* (1966), *The Quiller Memorandum* (1966), *The Bridge at Remagen* (1969), *The Odessa File* (1974), *The Boys From Brazil* (1978), *Avalanche Express* (1979), *The American Success Company* (1980), and *The Glass Cage* (1989).

Lewis Meltzer (1910-February 23, 1995). Meltzer was a screenwriter who worked extensively in Hollywood from the 1930s into the 1950s. His film credits include *Golden Boy* (1939), *The Lady in Question* (1940), *Once Upon a Time* (1944), *Texas, Brooklyn and Heaven* (1948), *Along the Great Divide* (1951), *The Jazz Singer* (1952), *Man with the Golden Arm* (1955), and *Autumn Leaves* (1956).

Patsy Ruth Miller (June 22, 1905-July 16, 1995). Miller was an actress who was featured in numerous films during the silent era. Her first role was in the Rudolph Valentino version of *Camille* (1921), and she was featured opposite Lon Chaney in *The Hunchback of Notre Dame* (1923). Her acting career waned with the advent of sound, at which point she began writing short stories, radio scripts, and a novel. Her screen credits include *The Sheik* (1921), *Omar the Tentmaker* (1922), *The Breath of Scandal* (1924), *Wolf's Clothing* (1927), *Beautiful But Dumb* (1928), *The Sap* (1929), *Wide Open* (1930), and *Night Beat* (1931).

Eiji Okada (June 13, 1920-September 14, 1995). Okada was a Japanese actor best known to American audiences for his role opposite Marlon Brando in *The Ugly American* (1963). He also starred in Alain Resnais' *Hiroshima Mon Amour* (1959), which enjoyed wide distribution in American art houses. Okada's additional screen credits include *Until the Day We Meet Again* (1950), *Hiroshima* (1953), *The Pirates* (1960), *Woman in the Dunes* (1964), *Stormy Era* (1968), *Zatoichi's Conspiracy* (1973), *Love and Faith of Ogin* (1982), and *The Death of a Tea Master* (1989).

Robert Parrish (January 4, 1916-December 4, 1995). Parrish was an actor, editor, and director who shared an Academy Award with Francis Lyon for his editing work on *Body and Soul* (1947). He broke into film as a child actor, often working for John Ford on films like *Mother Machree* (1928), *Men Without Women* (1930), and *Judge Priest* (1934). Later, he worked for Ford behind the camera, serving as editor both on feature films such as *Young Mr. Lincoln* (1939) and *The Grapes of Wrath* (1940) as well as Ford's World War II documentaries. By the 1950s, he was directing his own films, and he earned plaudits for turning out good work on a limited budget. His early films included *The Purple Plain* (1954) and *The Wonderful Country* (1959). He was one of several directors of the unorthodox treatment of Ian Fleming's *Casino Royale* (1967), and directed Peter Sellers in *The Bobo* (1967). Thereafter, he worked only sporadically, and then on low budget European productions. His best later film was his collaboration with Bertrand Tavernier on the civil rights documentary *Mississippi Blues* (1983). His additional directing credits included *Cry Danger* (1951), *The Wonderful Country* (1959), and *Up from the Beach* (1965).

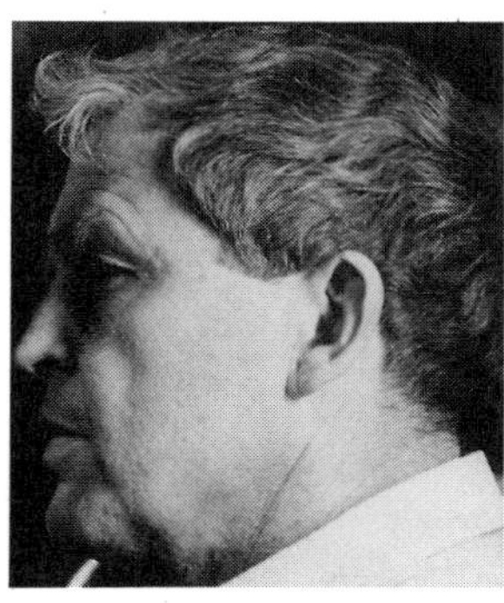

Robert Parrish

Frank Perry (August 21, 1930-August 29, 1995). Perry was a director and producer known for his sensitive studies of human relationships in such films as *David and Lisa* (1962), which was written by his wife and collaborator, Eleanor Perry. Frank Perry earned an Academy Award nomination for his direction of the film, and Eleanor Perry was also nominated for her screenplay. The success of the independently produced *David and Lisa* was widely credited with opening the doors for other independent producers. The Perrys continued their collaboration until their divorce in 1970. His last project was an autobiographical documentary, *On the Bridge* (1992). Perry's additional screen credits include *Ladybug Ladybug* (1963), *The Swimmer* (1968), *Diary of a Mad Housewife* (1970), *Rancho Deluxe* (1975), *Mommie Dearest* (1981), *Compromising Positions* (1985), and *Hello Again* (1987).

Frank Perry

Donald Pleasence (October 5, 1919-February 2, 1995). Pleasence was a British character actor who appeared in scores of films over a screen career that spanned forty years. He specialized in playing villains, most memorably James Bond's nemesis Ernst Stavro Blofeld in *You Only Live Twice* (1967). Pleasence was also featured in the popular horror series *Halloween* (1978) and its sequels. His additional film credits include *The Beachcomber* (1954), *1984* (1956), *A Tale of Two Cities* (1958), *Sons and Lovers* (1960), *Dr. Crippen* (1963), *The Great Escape* (1962), *The Greatest Story Ever Told* (1965), *The Night of the Generals* (1967), *THX 1138* (1971), *Journey Into Fear* (1975), *Telefon* (1977), *Meteor* (1978), *Escape From New York* (1981), *Halloween II* (1981), *Halloween 4: The Return of Michael Myers* (1988), *Halloween 5: The Revenge of Michael Myers* (1989), and *Shadows and Fog* (1992).

Donald Pleasence

Dany Robin (April 14, 1927-May 25, 1995). Robin was a French actress who appeared in many leading roles in European and American films in the quarter century following the end of World War II. Her screen credits include *Lunegarde* (1946), *Man About Town* (1947), *Une Histoire d'Amour* (1951), *Act of Love* (1954), *Frou-Frou* (1955), *Napoleon* (1955), *Maid in Paris* (1956), *Waltz of the Toreadors* (1962), *Les Parisiennes* (1962), *Follow the Boys* (1963), and *Topaz* (1969).

Ginger Rogers (July 16, 1911-April 25, 1995). Born Virginia Katherine McMath, Rogers was an actress and dancer who achieved cinematic immortality in her 1930s films with Fred Astaire. Groomed for a show business career by her mother, Rogers danced on the vaudeville circuit, making her professional debut as a teenager. She reached Broadway in 1929, when she was featured with Ruby Keeler in the musical *Top Speed.* She moved to Hollywood in 1931, where she appeared in such films as *Carnival Boat* (1932), *42nd Street* (1933), and *Gold Diggers of 1933* (1933) before being teamed up with Fred Astaire in *Flying Down to Rio* (1933). The pair were an instant hit, epitomizing the Depression-era glamour and sophistication in films such as *The Gay Divorcee* (1934), *Roberta* (1935), *Top Hat* (1935), and *Swing Time* (1936). The chemistry between Rogers and Astaire was magical, and their ten films continue to please audiences a half a century after their release. Rogers was an actress as well as a dancer, as she proved in her post-Astaire work in the 1940s. She won an Academy Award in the title role of *Kitty Foyle* (1940), and continued to show a flair for comedy in films such as *The Major and the Minor* (1942). She continued appearing in films regularly into the 1950s, but increasingly devoted her efforts to the stage thereafter. She replaced Carol Channing in Broadway's *Hello Dolly* in 1965, and enjoyed a successful run in the London production of *Mame* in 1969. Rogers had a complicated romantic life, among her five husbands were actors Lew Ayres and Jacques Bergerac, and actor-director William Marshall. Rogers additional screen credits include *Hat Check Girl* (1932), *Follow the Fleet* (1936), *Shall We Dance* (1937), *Carefree* (1938), and *The Story of Vernon and Irene Castle* (1939), *Bachelor Mother* (1939), *Tom Dick and Harry* (1941), *Magnificent Doll* (1946), *The Barkleys of Broadway* (1949), *Storm Warning* (1950), *Monkey Business* (1952), *Teenage Rebel* (1956), and *Harlow* (1965).

Ginger Rogers

Jack Rose (November 4, 1911-October 20, 1995). Rose was a screenwriter who worked extensively with Bob Hope, first with Hope's radio series and then in such films as *Road to Rio* (1947), *My Favorite Brunette* (1947), and *The Paleface* (1948). Rose often worked with Melville Shavelson, who directed *The Seven Little Foys* (1955), which Rose wrote and produced. Another collaborator was Melvin Frank, with whom Rose earned an Academy Award nomination for their screenplay for *A Touch of Class* (1973). His additional screen credits include *Sorrowful Jones* (1949), *On Moonlight Bay* (1951), *April in Paris* (1953), *On the Double* (1961), *Papa's Delicate Condition* (1963), *The Incredible Mr. Limpet* (1974), *The Duchess and the Dirtwater Fox* (1976), and *The Great Muppet Caper* (1981).

Ralph Rosenblum (October 13, 1925-September 6, 1995). Rosenblum was a film editor who worked extensively with Woody Allen in films such as *Take the Money and Run* (1969), *Sleeper* (1973), *Love and Death* (1975), *Annie Hall* (1976), and *Interiors* (1978). His additional film credits include *Country Music Holiday* (1958), *Murder, Inc.* (1960), *Long Day's Journey Into Night* (1962), *The Pawnbroker* (1965), *A Thousand Clowns* (1965), *The Group* (1966), *The Producers* (1967), *Goodbye Columbus* (1969), *Bad Company* (1972), and *The Great Bank Hoax* (1978), which he also produced.

Miklos Rozsa (April 18, 1907-July 27, 1995). Rozsa was a Hungarian born composer whose work in film was nominated for sixteen Academy Awards. He won the Award three times, for *Spellbound* (1945), *A Double Life* (1947), and *Ben-Hur* (1959). In the 1940s, he worked most often on psychological dramas, while in the next decade he was in demand for the soundtracks of historical epics. His screen credits include *Knight Without Armour* (1937), *The Four Feathers* (1939), *The Thief of Baghdad* (1940), *Double Indemnity* (1944), *The Lost Weekend* (1945), *The Killers* (1946), *The Naked City* (1948), *Command Decision* (1948), *Adam's Rib* (1949), *The Asphalt Jungle* (1950), *Quo Vadis* (1951), *Julius Caesar* (1953), *Lust for Life* (1956), *El Cid* (1961), *King of Kings* (1961), *The Green Berets* (1968), *The Private Life of Sherlock Holmes* (1970), *Time After Time* (1979), *Eye of the Needle* (1981), and *Dead Men Don't Wear Plaid* (1982).

Miklos Rozsa

John Smith (1931-January 25, 1995). Born Robert Earl Van Orden, Smith was an actor best known for his starring roles in television Western series such as *Laramie* and *Cimarron City* from 1958-1963. His screen acting credits include *Carbine Williams* (1952), *The High and the Mighty* (1954), *We're No Angels* (1955), *The Bold and the Brave* (1956), *Friendly Persuasion* (1956), *The Kettles on Old MacDonald's Farm* (1957), and *Circus World* (1964).

Terry Southern (May 1, 1926-October 29, 1995). Southern was a novelist and screenwriter. He first achieved fame as the pseudonymous co-author (with Mason Hoffenberg) of the comic erotic novel "Candy," in 1958. *Candy* (1968) was made into a movie, as was another of his novels, *The Magic Christian* (1969), for which Southern collaborated on the screenplay. Among his other screenplays, the most notable was that for *Dr. Strangelove or How I Learned to Stop Worrying and Love the Bomb* (1964), which earned him and co-author Stanley Kubrick an Academy Award nomination. His additional screen credits include *The Cincinnati Kid* (1965), *The Loved One* (1965), *Barbarella* (1968), *Easy Rider* (1969), *End of the Road* (1970), and *The Telephone* (1988).

Samuel Douglas Stewart (1919-March 3, 1995). Stewart was a film editor who shared an Academy Award with three collaborators for *The Right Stuff* (1983). His additional film credits include *Games* (1967), *The Great Northfield Minnesota Raid* (1972), *The White Dawn* (1974), *The Shootist* (1976), *The Invasion of the Body Snatchers* (1978), *Rough Cut* (1980), and *Jinxed* (1982).

Woody Strode (1914-December 31, 1995). Strode was an African-American actor who was featured in Hollywood films for four decades. He was a football player at UCLA, and his initial roles were often those of a muscular character actor. John Ford cast him as a soldier on trial for rape and murder in *Sergeant Rutledge* (1960), earning him more challenging roles thereafter. His screen credits include *Sundown* (1941), *The Lion Hunters* (1951), *The Ten Commandments* (1956), *Pork Chop Hill* (1959), *Spartacus* (1960), *The Sins of Rachel Cade* (1961), *The Man Who Shot Liberty Valence* (1962), *The Professionals* (1966), *Black Jesus* (1969), *Once Upon a Time in the West* (1969), *Winter Hawk* (1975), *The Black Stallion Returns* (1983), *The Cotton Club* (1984), *Storyville* (1992), and *Posse* (1993).

Woody Strode

Grady Sutton (April 5, 1908-September 17, 1995). Sutton was a character actor who specialized in playing yokels and hillbillies, most notably as a foil for W.C. Fields in *You Can't Cheat an Honest Man* (1939) and *The Bank Dick* (1940). His additional screen credits include *This Reckless Age* (1932), *College Humor* (1933), *The Man on the Flying Trapeze* (1935), *My Man Godfrey* (1936), *Alexander's Ragtime Band* (1938), *Since You Went Away* (1944), *Anchors Aweigh* (1945), *A Star Is Born* (1954), *White Christmas* (1954), *My Fair Lady* (1964), *Paradise Hawaiian Style* (1966), and *Support Your Local Gunfighter* (1971).

Frank Thring, Jr. (1917-December 29, 1995). Thring was an Australian character actor who appeared in several big budget Hollywood epics, including *Ben-Hur* (1959), *El Cid* (1961), and *King of Kings* (1961). In the early 1960s, he returned to Australia, where he appeared on stage as well as in such popular films as *Mad Max* (1979) and *Mad Max Beyond Thunderdome* (1985). His additional screen credits include *A Question of Adultery* (1958), *The Vikings* (1958), *Age of Consent* (1969), and *Ned Kelly* (1970).

Genevieve Tobin (November 29, 1901-July 31, 1995). Tobin was an actress who split her time between the stage and silent film in her early career. The advent of sound pictures led her to move to Hollywood, where she developed into a leading lady at several studios. She married director William Keighley in 1938; he directed her in several films, including *No Time for Comedy* (1940). Her additional film credits include *No Mother to Guide Her* (1923), *The Gay Diplomat* (1931), *Hollywood Speaks* (1932), *Pleasure Cruise* (1933), *Uncertain Lady* (1934), *The Woman in Red* (1935), *The Petrified Forest* (1936), *Zaza* (1939), and *Queen of Crime* (1941).

Lana Turner (February 8, 1920-June 29, 1995). Born Julia Jean Mildred Frances Turner, Turner was an actress know for her sultry good looks. Legend has it that she was discovered, wearing a revealing tight sweater, at the soda fountain of Schwab's Drugstore on Sunset Boulevard, while playing hooky from Hollywood High. As "The Sweater Girl," Turner became one of Hollywood's top starlets, first with MGM, and then at Warner Bros., where she went as director Mervyn LeRoy's protege. Her first film appearance was a bit part in *A Star Is Born* (1937). She gradually won larger roles, including turns opposite Spencer Tracy in *Dr. Jekyll and Mr. Hyde* (1941) and Clark Gable in *Honky Tonk* (1941). She was most effective in melodramas, playing women of questionable virtue. Her best remembered role is probably that of the frustrated housewife in *The Postman Always Rings Twice* (1946); and she also earned an Academy Award nomination for her work in *Peyton Place* (1957). Turner led a stormy personal life. Bandleader Artie Shaw, to whom she was married and divorced by the age of twenty, was the first of seven husbands. But the affair for which she is best remembered was a romance with reputed mobster Johnny Stompanato. In 1958, Turner's daughter, Cheryl Crane, intervened in an argument between the couple and stabbed Stompanato to death in an incident that was ruled justifiable homicide. The scandal had little effect on Turner's career, as she continued to appear in films regularly for the next decade. She was also featured on the television soap

Lana Turner

opera *Falcon Crest* in the 1970s. Turner's additional screen credits include *Love Finds Andy Hardy* (1938), *Calling Dr. Kildare* (1939), *Ziegfield Girl* (1941), *Johnny Eager* (1942), *Slightly Dangerous* (1943), *Green Dolphin Street* (1947), *Cass Timberlane* (1947), *The Three Musketeers* (1948), *The Bad and the Beautiful* (1952), *Betrayed* (1954), *The Rains of Ranchipur* (1955), *Imitation of Life* (1959), *Portrait in Black* (1960), *Bachelor in Paradise* (1961), *Madame X* (1966), *Bittersweet Love* (1976), and *Witches' Brew* (1979).

Ira Wallach (January 22, 1913-December 2, 1995). Wallach was a playwright, novelist, and screenwriter. He is perhaps best known for his screenplay of *Hot Millions* (1968), which earned him an Academy Award nomination. His additional film credits include *Boy's Night Out* (1962) and *The Wheeler Dealers* (1963).

David Wayne (January 30, 1914-February 9, 1995). Born Wayne McMeekan, Wayne was an actor who was a success both on Broadway and in Hollywood. His best remembered Broadway roles were in *Finian's Rainbow* in 1947, and *Teahouse of the August Moon,* in 1955; he won Tony Awards as supporting actor for his work in these productions. He was also featured in major Hollywood films, including *Portrait of Jennie* (1949), *Adam's Rib* (1949), *How To Marry a Millionaire* (1953), *The Tender Trap* (1955), *The Three Faces of Eve* (1957), *The Sad Sack* (1957), *The Last Angry Man* (1959), *The Andromeda Strain* (1971), and *The Front Page* (1974).

Mary Wickes (1916-October 22, 1995). Born Mary Wickenhauser, Wickes was an actress who specialized in comic character roles. Her career was revived in the Whoopi Goldberg vehicles *Sister Act* (1992) and *Sister Act 2: Back in the Habit* (1993), in which she played Sister Mary Lazarus. Wickes' additional film credits include *The Man Who Came to Dinner* (1942), *Private Buckaroo* (1942), *Now Voyager* (1942), *June Bride* (1948), *Anna Lucasta* (1949), *On Moonlight Bay* (1951), *White Christmas* (1953), *Don't Go Near the Water* (1957), *The Music Man* (1962), *The Trouble With Angels* (1966), *Snowball Express* (1972), and *Postcards from the Edge* (1990).

Calder Willingham (December 23, 1922-February 19, 1995). Willingham was a novelist and screenwriter who contributed screenplays to a number of popular films from the 1950s through the 1970s. He first came to public attention at the age of 24, through his controversial novel "End as a Man," an expose of the sadism at a southern military school. He wrote a stage script for the novel in 1953, and a screenplay four years later, when it was brought to the screen as *The Strange One* (1957). Perhaps his best known screenplay was that for *The Graduate* (1967), for which he and co-writer Buck Henry earned an Academy Award nomination. Willingham's additional screen credits include *Paths of Glory* (1957), *The Vikings* (1960), *One-Eyed Jacks* (1961), *Little Big Man* (1972), and *Thieves Like Us* (1975).

Selected Film Books of 1995

Aldgate, Anthony. *Censorship and the Permissive Society.*
Oxford: Clarendon Press, 1995.

Aldgate examines the changes in the British government's censorship of film and theatre, as the official strictures against the depiction of matters relating to sex were gradually relaxed.

Arrowsmith, William. *Antonioni: The Poet of Images.*
New York: Oxford University Press, 1995.

Editor Ted Perry has organized this posthumous collection of essays by critic Arrowsmith on the work of Italian filmmaker Michelangelo Antonioni.

Bakish, David. *Jimmy Durante: His Show Business Career.*
Jefferson, North Carolina: McFarland, 1995.

Durante was a vaudeville comic who achieved stardom as an actor in film, radio, and television. This is a good survey of his lengthy career.

Bansak, Edmund G. *Fearing the Dark: The Val Lewton Career.*
Jefferson, North Carolina: McFarland, 1995.

Bansak offers a detailed analysis of the work of Val Lewton, the influential producer of atmospheric horror films for RKO in the 1940s.

Barrios, Richard. *A Song in the Dark.*
New York: Oxford University Press, 1995.

Barrios provides a scholarly chronicle of the early years of musical film, from the pre-*The Jazz Singer* experiments with phonographs synchronized with projection systems to the Depression era spectacles that ensured the genre's continued longevity.

Beja, Morris, editor. *Perspectives on Orson Welles.*
New York: G.K. Hall, 1995.

This is a collection of reviews, interviews, and scholarly essays on the work of the seminal American filmmaker.

Bjorkman, Stig. *Woody Allen on Woody Allen.*
New York: Grove Press, 1995.

Bjorkman interviewed Allen at length on the topic of each of his major films; this book is the text of those conversations.

Blake, Richard A. *Woody Allen: Sacred and Profane.*
Lanham, Maryland: Scarecrow Press, 1995.

Analyzing the religious aspects of Woody Allen's films, Blake finds the filmmaker to be representative of the modern school of thought in which religion is little more than a collection of myths to comfort the gullible.

Bogart, Stephen Humphrey. *Bogart: In Search of My Father.*
New York: Dutton, 1995.

Bogart's son was eight when his father died; this biography, written with the advice and encouragement of Lauren Bacall, offers an affectionate insider's point of view on the actor's life.

Brode, Douglas. *Money, Women, and Guns: Crime Movies from Bonnie and Clyde to the Present.*
Secaucus, New Jersey: Citadel, 1995.

Brode surveys fifty films from the past three decades which involve crime and women; each chapter includes a plot synopsis, critical reaction, information on cast and credits, and production stills.

Callow, Simon. *Orson Welles: The Road to Xanadu.*
New York: Viking, 1995.

In this first of a two volume biography of the celebrated actor/director, Callow attempts to view Welles in the context of his time, stripped of the hyperbole that often accompanies discussions of Welles' work.

Carson, Diane, and Lester D. Friedman. *Shared Differences: Multicultural Media and Practical Pedagogy.*
Urbana, Illinois: University of Illinois Press, 1995.

This collection of fourteen scholarly essays on the representation of minorities in film and other media is designed to help teachers use these films in the classroom.

Cendrars, Blaise. *Hollywood: Mecca of the Movies.*
Berkeley, California: University of California Press, 1995.

This is the first English translation of the irreverent commentary of the late French poet on his visit to Hollywood in the 1930s.

Champlin, Charles. *John Frankenheimer: A Conversation with Charles Champlin.*
Burbank, California: Riverwood Press, 1995.

Film critic Champlin engages director Frankenheimer in a series of brief but candid conversations on over thirty of his films.

Champlin, Charles, and Derrick Tseng. *Woody Allen at Work.*
New York: Henry N. Abrams, 1995.

The photographs of Brian Hamill comprise the bulk of this handsome volume, which includes an essay by film critic Champlin and commentary on the photographs by Tseng.

Chandler, Charlotte. *I, Fellini.*
New York: Random House, 1995.

Chandler transcribes fourteen years worth of conversations with the great Italian filmmaker, in which he offers insights on his life, his career, and his colleagues in Italian cinema.

Chunovic, Louis. *Jodie: A Biography.*
Chicago: Contemporary Books, 1995.

This biography of Jodie Foster portrays the Academy Award winner as an actress to whom dignity and control are paramount.

Clark, Danae. *Negotiating Hollywood: The Cultural Politics of Actors' Labor.*
Minneapolis, Minnesota: University of Minnesota Press, 1995.

This is a scholarly study of the labor-management relationships between actors and their studios in the early days of the New Deal.

Cones, John W. *43 Way$ to Finance Your Feature Film: A Comprehensive Analysis of Film Finance.*
Carbondale, Illinois: Southern Illinois University Press, 1995.

Those seeking background information on the economics of feature filmmaking will find much useful information in Cones' account of film financing.

Corey, Melinda, and George Ochoa. *The Dictionary of Film Quotations.*
New York: Crown, 1995.

This reference work collects 6,000 quotes from 1,000 films; the entries are arranged in alphabetical order by film, and there is a brief subject index.

Devereaux, Leslie, and Roger Hillman. *Fields of Vision.*
Berkeley, California: University of California Press, 1995.

The fifteen scholarly essays in this collection apply the insights of anthropology to the subject of visual representation in film and still photography.

Devine, Jeremy M. *Vietnam at 24 Frames a Second.*
Jefferson, North Carolina: McFarland, 1995.

Devine analyzes over 400 films, from 1948 to the present day, following the shifts in emphasis among films dealing with the decades long conflict in Vietnam.

Dixon, Wheeler Winston. *It Looks at You: The Returned Gaze of Cinema.*
Albany, New York: State University of New York Press, 1995.

Dixon offers a scholarly examination of the reciprocity of observation between the film and its audience, ranging from actors looking at or even addressing the audience to more subtle use of images which reinforce the "look back" from the screen.

Doyle, Billy H. *The Ultimate Directory of the Silent Screen Performers.*
Metuchen, New Jersey: Scarecrow, 1995.

Doyle compiles basic biographical information on over 7,500 Silent Era actors, directors, and others associated with the industry. He also provides more extensive biographical essays on fifty obscure figures from the era.

Dunaway, Faye, with Betsy Sharkey. *Looking for Gatsby: My Life.*
New York: Simon & Shuster, 1995.

Dunaway offers a candid assessment of her difficult personal life, as well as insights about the Hollywood personalities she has encountered over the past three decades.

Edwards, Gwynne. *Indecent Exposures: Bunuel, Saura, Erice & Almodovar.*
London: Marion Boyars, 1995.

Edwards examines twelve films by four Spanish directors, noting how they reflect important periods in twentieth century Spain's history and culture.

Edwards, Larry. *Buster: A Legend in Laughter.*
Bradenton, Florida: McGuinn & McGuire, 1995.

This is the authorized biography of the great Silent Era comic actor/director, released to commemorate the centennial of his birth.

Evans, Peter William. *The Films of Luis Bunuel: Subjectivity and Desire.*
Oxford: Clarendon Press, 1995.

This is a scholarly analysis of the work of the Spanish surrealist in the context of contemporary critical theories on the representation of sexuality.

Fehrenbach, Heide. *Cinema in Democratizing Germany.*
Chapel Hill, North Carolina: University of North Carolina Press, 1995.

Fehrenbach examines the role which German cinema played in reconstructing the nation's post-Hitler identity during the years of American military occupation from 1945 to 1962.

Fienup-Riordan, Ann. *Freeze Frame: Alaskan Eskimos in the Movies.*
Seattle, Washington: University of Washington Press, 1995.

This scholarly study surveys films set in the Arctic and finds that Eskimos have typically been misrepresented as simple, igloo-dwelling primitives.

Fishgall, Gary. *Against Type: The Biography of Burt Lancaster.*
New York: Scribner, 1995.

Fishgall offers the most comprehensive study to date of the late actor's life and career.

Foster, Gwendolyn Audrey. *Women Film Directors: An International Bio-Critical Dictionary.*
Westport, Connecticut: Greenwood Press, 1995.

The entries in this useful reference work contain biographical and critical analyses of each individual's work, as well as a selected filmography and short bibliography.

Gehring, Wes. *Populism and the Capra Legacy.*
Westport, Connecticut: Greenwood Press, 1995.

Gehring examines the influence of filmmaker Frank Capra on six contemporary American films. He also includes a chapter on Ron Howard, whom he considers one of Capra's populist heirs.

Goldberg, Lee, Randy Lofficier, Jean-Marc Lofficier, and William Rabkin. *The Dreamweavers.*
Jefferson, North Carolina: McFarland, 1995.

This is a collection of interviews with the actors and directors of nearly two dozen popular fantasy and adventure films released during the 1980s.

Guiles, Fred Lawrence. *Joan Crawford: The Last Word.*
New York: Birch Lane Press, 1995.

This balanced biography shows both Crawford's *Mommie Dearest* dark side as well as the more positive aspects of the actress's life and career.

Halberstam, Judith. *Skin Shows: Gothic Horror and the Technology of Monsters.*
Durham, North Carolina: Duke University Press, 1995.

Halberstam examines issues of sexuality and antisemitism in the horror genre in this scholarly work.

Hamilton, Marybeth. *When I'm Bad, I'm Better.*
New York: HarperCollins, 1995.

Subtitled "Mae West, Sex, and American Entertainment," this book surveys the notorious actress's career and its impact on American culture.

Hayes, Richard K. *Kate Smith.*
Jefferson, North Carolina: McFarland, 1995.

This biography of the popular singer and actress includes a discography, a filmography, and a list of her stage appearances.

Heston, Charlton. *In the Arena: An Autobiography.*
New York: Simon and Schuster, 1995.

Heston surveys his life and times as an actor in this generous and scandal-free memoir.

Heymann, C. David. *Liz: An Intimate Biography of Elizabeth Taylor.*
New York: Birch Lane Press, 1995.

Heymann chronicles the life and times of the actress and celebrity, noting her humanitarian work as well as her difficulties with drugs, food, and romance.

Higson, Andrew. *Waving the Flag: Constructing a National Cinema in Britain.*
Oxford: Clarendon Press, 1995.

Higson studies the evolution of the British national film industry through World War II, as British popular cultural traditions were increasingly influenced by Hollywood.

Holley, Val. *James Dean: The Biography.*
New York: St. Martin's Press, 1995.

A focus on the actor's early life and professional training distinguishes this work from the dozens of earlier Dean biographies.

Hollows, Joanne, and Mark Jancovich, editors. *Approaches to Popular Film.*
Manchester, England: Manchester University Press, 1995.

This is a collection of eight scholarly essays offering different approaches to the critical analysis of popular film.

Juran, Robert. *Old Familiar Faces: The Great Character Actors and Actresses of Hollywood's Golden Era.*
Sarasota, Florida: Movie Memories, 1995.

Juran provides brief biographical sketches of 89 actors and actresses who specialized in character roles during the 1930s and 1940s.

Kagan, Norman. *The Cinema of Oliver Stone.*
New York: Continuum, 1995.

This analysis of the films of the controversial American director, offers extended summaries of Stone's work, from his earliest efforts through *Natural Born Killers.*

Kinnard, Roy. *Horror in Silent Films: A Filmography, 1896-1929.*
Jefferson, North Carolina: McFarland, 1995.

The entries in this international filmography contain information on cast and credits, as well as a brief analysis of each film.

Koseluk, Gregory. *Eddie Cantor: A Life in Show Business.*
Jefferson, North Carolina: McFarland, 1995.

Koseluk offers a detailed analysis of the career of the popular vaudeville comic and singer who made a successful transition to film with the advent of sound.

Langman, Larry, and Daniel Finn. *A Guide to American Crime Films of the Thirties.*
Westport, Connecticut: Greenwood Press, 1995.

This reference work offers plot summaries and information on cast and credits for over 1,100 American crime films released between 1928 and 1939.

Larson, Randall D. *Films Into Books.*
Metuchen, New Jersey: Scarecrow Press, 1995.

This is a compilation of information, including an extensive bibliography and comments by authors, on films and television shows that have been "novelized," or turned into books.

Leaming, Barbara. *Katharine Hepburn.*
New York: Crown, 1995.

Basing her work on Hepburn's correspondence as well as interviews with her subject, Leaming's work stands as the definitive biography of the great American actress.

Lebeau, Vicky. *Lost Angels: Psychoanalysis and Cinema.*
London: Routledge, 1995.

Lebeau offers a feminist critique of Freud and cinema in this scholarly volume.

Leemann, Sergio. *Robert Wise on His Films.*
Los Angeles: Silman-James Press, 1995.

This illustrated survey of Wise's career includes brief comments from the director on each of his films, as well as plot summaries and information on cast and credits.

Leigh, Janet, with Christopher Nicken. *Psycho: Behind the Scenes of the Classic Thriller.*
New York: Harmony Books, 1995.

Actress Leigh offers a breezy account of the making of Alfred Hitchcock's most famous thriller.

Leonard, Sheldon. *And the Show Goes On.*
New York: Limelight, 1995.

Leonard's memoirs cover his career as an actor (he was a memorable screen heavy of the 1940s) and as a director of many popular television series in the 1950s and 1960s.

Lewis, Jon. *Whom God Wishes to Destroy ... Francis Coppola and the New Hollywood.*
Durham, North Carolina: Duke University Press, 1995.

Lewis examines the career of the American filmmaker during and after his failed attempts to turn Zoetrope Studio into a going concern.

Loshitzky, Yosefa. The Radical Faces of Godard and Bertolucci.
Detroit: Wayne State University Press, 1995.

Loshitzky follows the careers of the French and Italian directors as they move from orthodox Marxism to increasingly personal, and even spiritual, filmmaking.

Lumet, Sidney. *Making Movies.*
New York: Knopf, 1995.

Director Lumet, using examples from his own career, analyzes the various aspects of filmmaking, from screenwriting and acting to postproduction politics.

McCarty, John, editor. *The Sleaze Merchants.*
New York: St. Martin's, 1995.

This collection of interviews and essays covers the careers of fifteen directors who have specialized in drive-in exploitation fare.

MacLaine, Shirley. *My Lucky Stars: A Hollywood Memoir.*
New York: Bantam, 1995.

MacLaine takes a break from her exploration of New Age philosophies to chronicle her four decades in show business in this engaging memoir.

Maltby, Richard, and Ian Craven. *Hollywood Cinema: An Introduction.*
Oxford: Blackwell, 1995.

Maltby and Craven offer an introduction to American cinema, from technical production aspects to the politics and economics of Hollywood.

Martin, Joel W., and Conrad E. Ostwalt, Jr. *Screening the Sacred.*
Boulder, Colorado: Westview Press, 1995.

This book contains twelve scholarly essays on the influence of religion on popular American film, and vice versa.

Meade, Marion. *Buster Keaton: Cut to the Chase.*
New York: HarperCollins, 1995.

Meade provides the definitive biography of the actor-director who was one of the acknowledged geniuses of Silent Era comedy.

Millar, Ingrid. *Liam Neeson: The First Biography.*
New York: St. Martin's Press, 1995.

Millar offers a popular account of the acclaimed young Irish actor's career to date.

Miller, Blair. *American Silent Film Comedies.*
Jefferson, North Carolina: McFarland, 1995.

This is an illustrated encyclopedia of American comedies of the Silent Era, with entries on films, individuals, and terminology combined into a single alphabetic sequence.

Miller, Mark A. *Christopher Lee and Peter Cushing and Horror Cinema.*
Jefferson, North Carolina: McFarland, 1995.

Miller offers an extensive analysis of the twenty two horror films in which actors Lee and Cushing appeared together; the book includes illustrations and a filmography.

Myrent, Glenn, and Georges P. Langlois. *Henri Langlois: First Citizen of Cinema.*
New York: Twayne, 1995.

This is a biography of the cofounder and presiding genius of the Cinematheque Francaise, a French film archive which had a significant influence on the development of French cinema.

Neibaur, James I., and Ted Okuda. *The Jerry Lewis Films.*
Jefferson, North Carolina: McFarland, 1995.

Neibaur and Okuda offer extended and appreciative analyses of Lewis's forty six films, including those he made with Dean Martin. The chapters include detailed information on each film's cast and credits.

Neupert, Richard. *The End: Narration and Closure in the Cinema.*
Detroit: Wayne State University Press, 1995.

Neupert analyzes how films end, through close examinations of four films (*The Quiet Man, The 400 Blows, Earth,* and *Weekend*) which represent four major styles of narrative.

Palmer, Bill, Karen Palmer, and Ric Meyers. *The Encyclopedia of Martial Arts Movies.*
Metuchen, New Jersey: Scarecrow Press, 1995.

This reference volume gives plot summaries and information on cast and credits for over 3,000 films, mostly from China, Hong Kong, or Japan, involving Oriental martial arts.

Parish, James Robert. *Pirates and Seafaring Swashbucklers on the Hollywood Screen.*
Jefferson, North Carolina: McFarland, 1995.

Parish compiles plot summaries, critical commentary, and information on cast and credits for 137 films dealing with pirates and nautical buccaneers.

Peucker, Brigitte. *Incorporating Images: Film and the Rival Arts.*
Princeton, New Jersey: Princeton University Press, 1995.

Peucker examines the differing ways various art forms look at the human body, citing the work of a variety of filmmakers, ranging from Lang and through Hitchcock to Fassbinder, Wenders, and Greenaway.

Phillips, Julia. *Driving Under the Affluence.*
New York: HarperCollins, 1995.

Gadfly producer Phillips details her continuing adventures in Hollywood following the publication of her controversial *You'll Never Eat Lunch in This Town Again.*

Phillips, Robert W. *Roy Rogers.*
Jefferson, North Carolina: McFarland, 1995.

This is a biography of the actor-singer who was known as The King of the Cowboys; the work also includes exhaustive lists of Rogers' films, recordings, and various forms of collectible memorabilia.

Pietropaolo, Laura, and Ada Testaferri, editors. *Feminisms in the Cinema.*
Bloomington, Indiana: Indiana University Press, 1995.

This is a collection of twelve scholarly essays, some of which have been previously published, analyzing film from a feminist perspective.

Quinn, Anthony, with Daniel Paisner. *One Man Tango.*
New York: HarperCollins, 1995.

Quinn reflects on his life, his loves, his friendships, and his acting career in this engaging memoir.

Rapf, Joanna E., and Gary L. Green. *Buster Keaton: A Bio-Bibliography.*
Westport, Connecticut: Greenwood Press, 1995.

This bio-bibliography of the Silent Era comic genius contains a compilation of interviews with Keaton in addition to its annotated bibliography and filmography.

Riordan, James. *Stone.*
New York: Hyperion, 1995.

Riordan offers a detailed appreciation of the work of controversial filmmaker Oliver Stone, through 1994's *Natural Born Killers.*

Roberts, Jerry, and Steven Gaydos. *Movie Talk from the Front Lines.*
Jefferson, North Carolina: McFarland, 1995.

Seventeen feature filmmakers discuss one of their films with members of the Los Angeles Film Critics Association in this collection of interviews.

Roberts, Randy, and James S. Olson. *John Wayne: American.*
New York: Free Press, 1995.

Two historians depict Wayne as a non-ideological conservative whose most prominent roles mirrored his private values. They argue that his critical reputation continues to suffer because leftist film critics over the past three decades resent his politics.

Rosenbaum, Jonathan. *Placing Movies: The Practice of Film Criticism.*
Berkeley, California: University of California Press, 1995.

Rosenbaum offers a fascinating blend of film criticism and autobiography in this sequel to his *Moving Places.*

Rowe, Kathleen. *The Unruly Woman: Gender and the Genres of Laughter.*
Austin, Texas: University of Texas Press, 1995.

Rowe offers a feminist analysis of the conventions which govern gender and comedy in American film and television.

Rozgonyi, Jay. *Preston Sturges's Vision of America.*
Jefferson, North Carolina: McFarland, 1995.

Rozgonyi offers essays on fourteen of Sturges's films, stressing the ways in which the director's work emphasizes American values and culture.

Rubin, Stephen Jay. *The Complete James Bond Movie Encyclopedia.*
Chicago: Contemporary Books, 1995.

Rubin compiles an exhaustive list of information, both significant and trivial, on the enduring James Bond series.

Russell, Catherine. *Narrative Mortality: Death, Closure, and New Wave Cinema.*
Minneapolis, Minnesota: University of Minnesota Press, 1995.

This is a scholarly analysis of the role of death and dying in the work of New Wave directors of the 1960s and 1970s, including Godard, Wenders, and Altman.

Salisbury, Mark, editor. *Burton on Burton.*
London: Faber and Faber, 1995.

This is a collection of commentaries by filmmaker Tim Burton on his work, from his early work at Disney through his feature film *Ed Wood* in 1994.

Sampson, Henry T. *Blacks in Black and White: A Source Book on Black Films.*
Metuchen, New Jersey: Scarecrow Press, 1995.

This second edition of Sampson's important reference work on all-Black films prior to 1950 doubles the size of the original 1977 edition, containing chapters on important production companies, biographies of major figures, as well as synopses of the films themselves.

Shattuc, Jane. *Television, Tabloids, and Tears: Fassbinder and Popular Culture.*
Minneapolis, Minnesota: University of Minnesota Press, 1995.

Shattuc offers the story of the making of Rainer Werner Fassbinder's controversial epic, *Berlin Alexanderplatz.*

Sitney, P. Adams. *Vital Crises in Italian Cinema.*
Austin, Texas: University of Texas Press, 1995.

Adams analyzes fifteen films from the important 1945-1963 period in Italian cinema, noting how the tensions between the country's institutions and its artists helped shape the national cinema in the two decades after World War II.

Skal, David J., and Elias Savada. *Dark Carnival: The Secret World of Tod Browning.*
New York: Anchor Books, 1995.

Browning directed the Bela Lugosi version of *Dracula,* as well as the cult film *Freaks* and other early horror films. This book constitutes the first extended analysis of his life and career.

Smith, Murray. *Engaging Characters: Fiction, Emotion, and the Cinema.*
Oxford: Clarendon Press, 1995.

Smith offers this scholarly study of the mechanisms by which film characters engage the emotions of the audience, and the effects of the resulting identification.

Spada, James. *Streisand: Her Life.*
New York: Crown, 1995.

This, Spada's third biography of the singer/actress, is certainly the definitive account to date of her life and career.

Staiger, Janet. *Bad Women: Regulating Sexuality in Early American Cinema.*
Minneapolis: University of Minnesota Press, 1995.

This is a scholarly study of female sexuality in American film from 1907 to 1915, examining the industry's self-regulation through a detailed analysis of *Traffic in Souls*, *A Fool There Was*, and *The Cheat.*

Staiger, Janet, editor. *The Studio System.*
New Brunswick, New Jersey: Rutgers University Press, 1995.

This collection of fourteen scholarly essays make up a case study of the production conventions of the Hollywood studio system of the 1930s and 1940s, and the impact of those conventions on those who worked within the system.

Stapleton, Maureen, and Jane Scovell. *A Hell of a Life.*
New York: Simon and Schuster, 1995.

Stapleton's Broadway and Hollywood career spans decades; she won an Academy Award as Best Supporting Actress for her work in *Reds* in 1981. This is her autobiography.

Stephens, Michael L. *Film Noir.*
Jefferson, North Carolina: McFarland, 1995.

This is an illustrated encyclopedia on the film noir genre, combining entries on films, filmmakers, and terminology into a single alphabetical sequence.

Telotte, J.P. *Replications: A Robotic History of the Science Fiction Film.*
Chicago: University of Illinois Press, 1995.

Telotte analyzes the use of robots, androids, etc., in science fiction films from the Silent Era through contemporary films.

Thompson, Frank. *Robert Wise: A Bio-Bibliography.*
Westport, Connecticut: Greenwood Press, 1995.

Thompson offers a brief biographical sketch of the director, along with a detailed filmography containing reviews, plot synopses, and information on cast and credits for each film.

Vazzana, Eugene Michael. *Silent Film Necrology.*
Jefferson, North Carolina: McFarland, 1995.

This reference work offers biographical information, through 1993, on more than 9,000 actors, directors, producers, and other individuals associated with films from the Silent Era.

Vernon, Kathleen M., and Barbara Morris. *Post-Franco, Postmodern: The Films of Pedro Almodovar.*
Westport, Connecticut: Greenwood Press, 1995.

The editors collect ten scholarly essays on the career of the Spanish filmmaker, as well as a filmography and a bibliography of criticism on his work.

Waller, Gregory A. *Main Street Amusements.*
Washington, D.C.: Smithsonian Institution Press, 1995.

This is a history of moviegoing and popular culture in Lexington, Kentucky, from 1896 to 1930, tracing the impact of film on the life of the city.

Walters, Suzanna Danuta. *Material Girls: Making Sense of Feminist Cultural Theory.*
Berkeley: University of California Press, 1995.

This is a scholarly application of feminist cultural theory to film and television images of women, with its primary focus on recent cinema.

White, Susan M. *The Cinema of Max Ophuls: Magisterial Vision and the Figure of Woman.*
New York: Columbia University Press, 1995.

White offers a scholarly feminist perspective on the work of French filmmaker Max Ophuls.

Williams, J.W. *Hillbillyland.*
Chapel Hill, North Carolina: University of North Carolina Press, 1995.

Williams defines hillbillies broadly to include rural folk generally, in this scholarly analysis of the portrayal of the hillbilly in American film from the Silent Era to modern times.

Williams, Linda, editor. *Viewing Positions: Ways of Seeing Film.*
New Brunswick, New Jersey: Rutgers University Press, 1995.

This is a collection of nine scholarly essays on spectatorship in cinema, focusing both on the apparatus of film and on gender issues.

Winston, Brian. *Claiming the Real: The Griersonian Documentary and Its Legitimations.*
London: British Film Institute, 1995.

This is a scholarly study of the issue of authenticity in documentary film, and the ways in which technology enables filmmakers to shape the reality on the screen.

Zucker, Carole. *Figures of Light.*
New York: Plenum Press, 1995.

Zucker is an authority on film acting; in this book, she interviews twenty one actors and directors on the actor's craft.

Magill's Cinema Annual 1996
Indexes

Title Index

This cumulative index is an alphabetical list of all films covered in the fifteen volumes of the *Magill's Cinema Annual*. Film titles are indexed on a word-by-word basis, including articles and prepositions. English and foreign leading articles are ignored. Films reviewed in this volume are cited in bold with an arabic number indicating the page number on which the review begins; films reviewed in past volumes are cited with a roman numeral indicating the volume number in which the film was originally reviewed (consult the index of the cited volume for the page number on which the film review begins). Film sequels are indicated with a roman numeral following the film title. Original and alternate titles are cross-referenced to the American release title. Titles of retrospective films, as well as those cited in the Life Achievement Award section are followed by the year, in brackets, of their original release. Films cited in the Life Achievement Award section are indexed with the page number of the section in bold.

Directors

Screenwriters

Screenwriters

Screenwriters

Cinematographers

Editors

Art Directors

Music Directors

Performers

Subjects